The Oxford Encyclopedia of the Reformation

The Oxford Encyclopedia
of the
Reformation

HANS J. HILLERBRAND

EDITOR IN CHIEF

Volume 4

New York   Oxford
OXFORD UNIVERSITY PRESS
1996

Oxford University Press

Oxford   New York
Athens   Auckland   Bangkok   Bombay
Calcutta   Cape Town   Dar es Salaam   Delhi
Florence   Hong Kong   Istanbul   Karachi
Kuala Lumpur   Madras   Madrid   Melbourne
Mexico City   Nairobi   Paris   Singapore
Taipei   Tokyo   Toronto

and associated companies in
Berlin   Ibadan

Library of Congress Cataloging-in-Publication Data
The Oxford encyclopedia of the Reformation / Hans J. Hillerbrand, editor in chief
p.   cm.
Includes bibliographical references and index.
ISBN 0-19-506493-3 (set : alk. paper)
1. Reformation—Encyclopedias.   2. Reformation—Biography—Encyclopedias.
3. Theology, Doctrinal—Europe—History—16th century—Encyclopedias.
4. Europe—Church history—16th century—Encyclopedias.
I. Hillerbrand, Hans J.
BR302.8.093   1996   270.6'03—dc20   95-24520   CIP

ISBN 0-19-506493-3 (set)
ISBN 0-19-510365-3 (vol. 4)
ISBN-13: 978-0-19-506493-3

Printing (last digit): 9 8 7 6 5 4 3

Printed in the United States of America
on acid-free paper

S

SCHAPPELER, Christoph (1472?–1551), Swiss Reformation preacher in the imperial free city of Memmingen in southern Swabia. Born in St. Gall, Switzerland, Schappeler became a priest at Saint Martin's in Memmingen in 1513. Previously he had studied theology, as well as both laws, in Switzerland, had been a teacher at a Latin school, and, in 1517, had encountered Andreas Bodenstein von Karlstadt, who dedicated his first publication to him.

His social engagement for the poor appears to have been the catalyst for his subsequent siding with the Reformation; as early as 1516 he had disagreements with the city council. Beginning in 1521 he preached reform sermons, initially with a definite social critique that combined an emphasis on communal Christianity with vehement criticism of the church. In 1523 he traveled twice to Switzerland (in October as one of the presiding officers of the Second Zurich Disputation). At the end of February 1524 he was expelled by the bishop, Christoph von Stadion, but he continued to support the lay movement against the old church. He argued the biblical inappropriateness of the tithe, triggering the Memmingen controversy about the tithe in June and July 1524.

In January 1525 he delineated his notions of reform in seven theses for a disputation. Auricular confession, the invocation of Mary and the saints, the tithe, the sacrificial character of the Mass and the Lord's Supper, and purgatory were rejected. He supported the demand for Communion under both kinds, as well as the notion of the priesthood of all believers. As the basis of authority he accepted only sacred scripture. Through his influence the city council introduced reform measures but opposed radical lay movements. Schappeler, too, rejected the use of force and insurrection. He demanded social conciliation on the basis of the commandment of love.

Despite his convictions, the peasants of the Memmingen area used his teachings to legitimate their insurrection. Whether Schappeler had directly participated in the formulation of the Twelve Articles—the most widely circulated program of the German Peasants' War—is controversial. In all probability the wording is solely that of Sebastian Lotzer. Schappeler, however, endorsed the formulations. In June 1525, after the suppression of the peasant uprising, he fled to St. Gall, where he served as minister until his death on 25 August 1551.

BIBLIOGRAPHY

Brecht, Martin. "Der theologische Hintergrund der Zwölf Artikel der Bauernschaft in Schwaben von 1525." *Zeitschrift für Kirchengeschichte* 85 (1974), 30–58. Places Schappeler in the context of the Lutheran tradition.

Dobel, Friedrich. *Memmingen im Reformationszeitalter.* Vol. 1, *Christoph Schappeler, der erste Reformator von Memmingen, 1513–1525.* 2d ed. Augsburg, 1877. Still the best collection of sources.

Maurer, Justus. *Prediger im Bauernkrieg.* Stuttgart, 1979. See pp. 387–399 and 582–592. Places Schappeler in the context of the Zwinglian tradition.

ADOLF LAUBE
Translated from German by Hans J. Hillerbrand

SCHATZGEYER, Kaspar (1463–1527), Bavarian Franciscan who combined his firm Catholicism with a conciliatory approach to Lutheran theology. Schatzgeyer was educated by observant Franciscans whose order he joined shortly after earning a baccalaureate in philosophy at the University of Ingolstadt. A respected teacher and biblical scholar, he made his mark in the more dynamic areas of clerical strife and religious controversy, first, as spokesman for his order against the Franciscan conventuals, then as champion of Catholic tradition against the Lutheran Reformation.

Named provincial head of his order in 1514, Schatzgeyer gained a working knowledge of conditions in the observant houses and Clarrisan convents that fell under his supervision. While recognizing the need for reforms, he defended monastic life against charges of hypocrisy and proved a source of strength to the monks and nuns, among them Caritas Pirckheimer, who resisted the Reformation's unbridled attack on religious orders.

Schatzgeyer tended to take a conciliatory approach to the new theology and its sympathizers out of a sense that essential reforms and the search for religious truth might be stifled by hasty condemnation. In 1522, hoping to establish an amicable dialogue with Luther, he published a commentary on the disputed teachings giving Luther his due but also pointing out where he was in error on grace and free will, justification, good works, the Mass, Christian freedom, the priesthood, and monastic vows. This presentation of the Catholic case in clear and inoffensive language failed, however, to pacify religious antagonisms. Luther dismissed the work as "a pathetic and foolish attempt to harmonize Holy Scripture and godless scholasticism," and Catholics reproached him for too-ready compliance in seeking common ground with the reformers. Schatzgeyer was highly critical of works righteousness, for example, and acknowledged that the doctrine of transubstantiation had no basis in scripture.

He engaged in more heated polemics with Franciscan defectors like Johann Eberlin von Günzburg, whom he accused of defaming the pious and misrepresenting his arguments commending monastic life. In 1525 Schatzgeyer was drawn into debate with Andreas Osiander over the Mass, prayers for the dead, and other Catholic rituals, as well as Osiander's personal attacks against him.

That same year Schatzgeyer began to compose a larger work in Latin, *Traductio Satanea*, covering all disputed Catholic teachings. Only chapter 20, on predestination, remained unwritten at Schatzgeyer's death; the greater part was published in Latin and in German translation, as were most of the works. While missing their mark, in the sense that Schatzgeyer's conciliatory approach failed to reconcile Luther and the Catholic church, his writings were widely read and helped to affirm the faith of many loyal Catholics.

BIBLIOGRAPHY

Primary Sources

Schatzgeyer, Kasper. *Von der waren Christlichen und Evangelischen freyheit.* Edited by Philipp Schäfer. Münster, 1987.
———. *Schriften zur Verteidigung der Messe.* Edited by E. Iserloh. Münster, 1984.

Secondary Sources

Druffel. "Schatzger, Kaspar." In *Allgemeine Deutsche Biographie,* vol. 31, pp. 783–784. Berlin, 1890.
Iserloh, Erwin. "Schatzgeyer, Kaspar." In *Lexicon für Theologie und Kirche,* vol. 9, p. 372. Freiburg, 1965. Gives most recent references.
Lortz, Joseph. *The Reformation in Germany.* 2 vols. Reprint, London, 1968.
Paulus, Nikolaus. *Kaspar Schatzgeyer, ein Vorkämpfer der Katholischen Kirche gegen Luther in Süddeutschland.* Freiburg, 1898. A major account of Schatzgeyer's life, polemical writings, and theological positions.
Schottenlohr, Karl, ed. *Bibliographie zur deutschen Geschichte im Zeitalter der Glaubensspaltung.* Stuttgart, 1957.

KARIN BRINKMANN BROWN

SCHEGK, Jacob

SCHEGK, Jacob (1511–1587), German Aristotelian polymath. He was born in Schorndorf, Württemberg. His father, Berhard Degen, used the name Schegk, and Jacob adopted this name permanently. Schegk's entire academic career, both as a student and a teacher, was spent at Tübingen University, culminating in the two professorships of medicine and logic. He published more than thirty books: medical and theological treatises, Latin translations of ancient Greek authors (including Theognis and Epictetus), and commentaries on the Aristotelian corpus. His major works were two folio commentaries on the *Organon* of Aristotle, *De demonstratione libri XV* (Basel, 1564), and *Commentaria in organi Aristotelis libros ad artis partem analyticem pertinentes* (Tübingen, 1570). In addition, he engaged in lengthy controversies that involved his application of Aristotelian methodology to contemporary issues. His controversy with the French humanist Petrus Ramus (1515–1572) dealt with Ramus's new methodology and the function of logic. With the Paris theologian Gilbert Genebrard (1537–1597), he debated the doctrine of the Trinity, and with the Heidelberg professor Thomas Lüber (Lat., Erastus, 1524–1583) and the itinerant Simone Simoni (1532–1602), then professor at Geneva, Schegk fought over the philosophical interpretation of the two natures of Christ and the modalities of Christ's human presence. Finally, two medical controversies put Schegk in published disputes with his fellow Tübingen professor and botanist Leonhard Fuchs (1501–1566) on the cause of disease and again with Simoni on the cause of fevers.

When Schegk died in 1587, he left a significant legacy of publication and teaching. Among his loyal students at Tübingen were Nicolaus Taurellus (1547–1606), Germany's first independent Lutheran philosopher; Andreas Planer (1546–1606), Schegk's successor as professor of medicine and logic and teacher and supporter of Johannes Kepler (1571–1630); and Nicodemus Frischlin (1547–1590), the contentious poet and playwright. The French Paracelsian Joseph Duchesne Quercetanus (c.1544–1609) credited Schegk with influencing him, praising him as the "German Aristotle and the foremost philosopher of our time." Schegk shared with other Aristotelians the belief that it is not only possible but necessary to have a method for distinguishing the true from the false in any area of inquiry, a view that supported the further development of scientific methodology in the seventeenth century. Schegk has come to be acknowledged as "the father and pioneer of Protestant scholasticism" (Weber) for his instrumental use of Aristotelian principles on theological topics.

BIBLIOGRAPHY

Emberger-Wandel, Gudrun. "Ein Professorenleben im 16. Jahrhundert: Jacob Schegk gen. Degen aus Schorndorf." *Heimatblätter: Jahrbuch für Schorndorf und Umgebung* 5 (1987), 16–28.
Lohr, Charles H. "Schegkius (Shecius, Schegk, Degen), Jacobus." *Renaissance Quarterly* 33 (1980), 718–720.
Moll, Albert. "Jakob Degen und Oswald Gabelkover." *Medicinisches Correspondenz-Blatt des Württembergischen Ärztlichen Vereins* 26 (1856), 81–85, 89–92, 97–103.
Schmitt, Charles B. "Schegk, Jacob." *Dictionary of Scientific Biography,* vol. 12, pp. 150–151. New York, 1981.
Sigwart, Christoph von. "Jakob Schegk, Professor der Philosophie und Medicin." In *Kleine Schriften,* vol. 1, pp. 256–91. Freiburg im Breisgau, 1889.
Weber, Hans Emil. *Die philosophische Scholastik des deutschen Protestantismus im Zeitalter der Orthodoxie.* Leipzig, 1907.

JAMES A. HINZ

SCHEURL, Christoph

SCHEURL, Christoph (1481–1542), lawyer, professor of law at Wittenberg, humanist, diplomat, and legal adviser from 1512 to 1542 to his native city of Nuremberg. Scheurl was charged with representing the city's interests at various courts, serving on diplomatic missions, and delivering learned legal opinions on problems facing the city government. Scheurl's work apparently satisfied the council, for it continually renewed his five-year contract until his death.

From the onset, Scheurl attached himself to the city's humanist nucleus. A number of these humanists were also members of the council, including Anton Tucher, Albrecht Dürer, Wolfgang Volprecht, Lazarus Spengler, and Willibald Pirckheimer, the last two excommunicated with Luther in 1521. In this group Scheurl served as de facto secretary, and it is from his correspondence that we learn the *sodalitas* changed its name to the *Staupitziana* and, later, *Martinianer*, in honor of visits by Johannes von Staupitz and Luther to Nuremberg in 1517–1518.

Scheurl's religious views may be termed "evangelical catholic." He did not appear to understand the depth of Luther's theology, although he was partial to Staupitz's views and had translated Staupitz's Advent sermons into German in 1517. It was Scheurl who sent Luther's Ninety-five Theses to his lifelong friend Johann Eck immediately after he received a copy from a Wittenberg associate. Furthermore, Scheurl presided at the city's religious colloquy in 1525 that resulted in Nuremberg's acceptance of Lutheranism. Scheurl also served on loan to various smaller Franconian cities—such as Schweinfurt and Weissenburg—that were on their way to becoming Protestant. The lawyer remained active in working for the institutionalization of the Protestant Reformation in Nuremberg.

In spite of it all, Scheurl never broke with the Roman church. In the last seventeen years of his life, his closest friends were such men as Eck, Cajetan, Matthäus Lang, and Albert of Brandenburg, the archbishop of Mainz, and because of these relations Scheurl was viewed with some distrust by younger members of the government who had to deal with the issues of resistance of the emperor. Nevertheless, Scheurl never felt a profound conflict between his own religious views and those of his native city.

BIBLIOGRAPHY

Bebb, Phillip N. "The Lawyers, Dr. Christoph Scheurl, and the Reformation in Nuremberg." In *The Social History of the Reformation*, edited by Lawrence Buck and Jonathan W. Zophy, pp. 52–72. Columbus, Ohio, 1972. Indicates how lawyers, and Scheurl especially, used law to validate religious changes.
————. "Paving the Way for the Reformation in Weissenburg and Schweinfurt." *Archiv für Reformationsgeschichte* 79 (1988), 158–169. Shows how political, constitutional, and economic issues influence confessional alignments. Scheurl served both cities.
Graf, Wilhelm. *Doktor Christoph Scheurl von Nürnberg*. Beiträge zur Kulturgeschichte des Mittelalters und der Renaissance, vol. 43. Reprint, Hildesheim, 1972. Complete, but dated, biography of Scheurl based on published materials.
Grossmann, Maria. "Bibliographie der Werke Christoph Scheurls." *Archiv für Geschichte des Buchwesens* 70 (1968), 658–670. Lists Scheurl's published works.
Soden, Franz von. *Beiträge zur Geschichte der Reformation und der Sitten jener Zeit mit besonderem Hinblick auf Christoph Scheurl II*. Nuremberg, 1855. Written by one who had intimate knowledge of the sources and who was interested in the customs of the time.

PHILLIP N. BEBB

SCHLEIDEN, Johann Phillipson of

SCHLEIDEN, Johann Phillipson of. *See* Sleidanus, Johannes.

SCHLEITHEIM ARTICLES

SCHLEITHEIM ARTICLES. Commonly known as the first Anabaptist confession of faith, the Schleitheim Articles originated at a meeting of Swiss and south German Anabaptists in the small town of Schleitheim in the canton of Schaffhausen on 24 February 1527. The articles were originally entitled *Brüderlich vereynigung etzlicher kinder Gottes, sieben Artickel betrefend* (The Brotherly Union of a Number of Children of God Concerning Seven Articles). This document was widely circulated in manuscript copies among the Anabaptists of the region and soon came to the attention of the Swiss Protestant reformers of Basel, Bern, and Zurich. By late summer of 1527 when Huldrych Zwingli responded to the articles in his *In Catabaptistarum strophas Elenchus* (Refutation of Anabaptist Tricks) he had received four extant copies of the document from as many different sources.

It is generally agreed that the principal author of the Articles was Michael Sattler, a former monk and prior of the Benedictine Monastery of Saint Peter near Freiburg im Breisgau. This tradition goes back to Sebastian Franck, who in 1531 referred to the Schleitheim document as the "articles of Michael Sattler."

By 1527 Sattler had emerged as a major leader within the Swiss Brethren stream of Anabaptism. His departure from monastic life in 1525 was likely related to the general unrest unleashed by the peasant uprising that resulted in the seizure of his monastery by a Black Forest peasant troop in May 1525. Thereafter he appears in the records of the Zurich authorities on several occasions associated in various ways with the circle of radical reformers led by Conrad Grebel and Felix Mantz. After receiving rebaptism himself in 1526, Sattler engaged in Anabaptist missionary activity in the Zurich *Unterland* for several months before moving to Strasbourg.

At Strasbourg Sattler came into contact with Martin Bucer and his colleague Wolfgang Capito. Both of these reformers held Sattler in high respect. Following his trial and execution at Rottenburg on 20 May 1527, they referred to him as "a dear friend of God" and true "martyr of Christ," despite his leadership role "in the baptism order." In a famous farewell letter to Bucer and Capito, Sattler appealed for mercy for certain Anabaptist prisoners in the city. This letter contains twenty theses that enumerate most of the issues later taken up at greater length in the Schleitheim Articles. The close linguistic parallels between the two documents support Sattler's authorship of the latter and may also point to an earlier draft of the basic material adopted at the Schleitheim assembly.

The earliest imprints of the articles included a cover letter that reveals both the pastoral and polemical purposes intended by the statement. The articles are addressed to "the children of light . . . scattered everywhere." They are meant to convey consolation and reassurance to "dear brothers and sisters" who have been confused and misled about several basic doctrines of the faith. At the same time, certain "false brothers" are singled out for condemnation. This term may refer to various spiritualist reformers and Anabaptist fellow travelers such as Hans Denck, Ludwig Hätzer, and Hans Hut. But some scholars have argued that the primary polemical focus of the articles was directed against mainline reformers such as Bucer, Capito, and Zwingli. In either case, the Schleitheim Articles served as a defining moment for the Swiss Brethren stream of Anabaptism. Reprinted along with an account of Sattler's martyrdom, the articles shaped the kind of evangelical Anabaptism that defined itself over against both excessive spiritualism on the left and the "official" Reformation on the right.

Strictly speaking the Schleitheim Articles are not a confession of faith but a manifesto of specific concerns. The seven articles deal with baptism, the ban, the breaking of bread, separation from the world, the role of pastor and congregation, the sword, and the oath.

The article on baptism specifically excludes the practice of infant baptism by requiring voluntary, conscientious commitment as a prerequisite for this rite of initiation. Baptism is to be given only to those who through personal repentance and faith demonstrate evidence of a changed life. Appeal is made to "the writings and the practice of the apostles." The Pauline metaphor of baptism as burial and resurrection with Christ reflects an emphasis prominent in the writings of earlier Swiss Anabaptists such as Mantz, Grebel, and Balthasar Hubmaier.

The article on church discipline, or the ban, comes between those dealing with baptism and the Lord's Supper. It provides a remedy for the congregation to deal with those who have broken the promises made at baptism and have lapsed from their new way of life. The scriptural basis for private and public admonition of offending members is taken from the words of Jesus in *Matthew* 18:15–20. The responsibility of the entire congregation in this process is emphasized, although article 5 also assigns a special role to the pastor as well. The purpose of the ban was remedial, preserving the congregation from the dangers of assimilation without and corruption within. Its aim was to enhance the unity and purity of the baptized community "so that we may all in one spirit and in one love break and eat from one bread and drink from one cup."

The theme of unity within the body of Christ is continued in the third article, on the breaking of bread, which reflects the early Swiss Anabaptist practice of the Lord's Supper. Within the context of the eucharistic controversies of the Reformation, this article clearly supports a memorialist understanding of the Supper. However, the real burden of the article does not focus on the nature of the consecrated elements or the modality of Christ's presence but rather on the character of the community that gathers to break the bread and drink the cup. The purity of the Communion fellowship is again tied to the decisive role of baptism and the ban as safeguards against the intermingling of light and darkness, the table of Christ and the table of devils.

The fourth article, on separation from the world *(absunderung)*, contains the most explicit statement of the sectarian view of the church, which runs throughout the document. The stark dualism of this article clearly differentiates the baptismal community, purified by discipline and united in the common breaking of the bread, from the surrounding culture with its moral corruption: "Now there is nothing else in the world and all creation than good or evil, believing and unbelieving, darkness and light, the world and those who (come) out of the world, God's temple and idols, Christ and Belial, and none will have part with the other. To us, then, the commandment of the Lord is also obvious, whereby He orders us to be and to become separated from the evil one, and thus He will be our God and we shall be His sons and daughters." The children of God are urged to shun various "popish and repopish" (a reference to the essentially unreformed character of the new Protestant churches) customs such as church attendance at the parish assemblies *(Kirchgang)*, and the frequenting of winehouses, as well as "pledges and commitments made in unbelief" ("burgschaften und verpflichten des unglaubens"). This last expression likely refers to the civic guilds and social clubs, which the Anabaptists eschewed because of their worldly associations. This article represents a significant development within the thought of Swiss Anabaptism: the early Anabaptists emerged within the context of the Zwinglian Reformation and only gradually evolved a radically separatist ecclesiology.

Article 5, concerning "shepherds in the church of God," establishes guidelines for the calling of the pastor, outlines the duties associated with this office, and also provides for the discipline and replacement of the pastor. Included in pastoral responsibilities are the reading and teaching of scripture; leadership in worship, including prayer and the breaking of bread; and the administration of the disciplinary process. Pastors are to be called and supported by the congregation over which they preside. They may also be publicly reprimanded for misconduct. The church is portrayed as a small remnant, or little flock, of God's people (*volckle*). The article closes with a word of instruction concerning the immediate ordination of a new shepherd should the present one be driven away or "led to the Lord by the cross," a phrase reflecting the context of persecution in which the Schleitheim Articles were drafted. The urgency of the situation was underscored by the fact that only a few weeks earlier, on 5 January 1527, Mantz had been drowned in the Limmat River by order of the city council of Zurich.

Articles 6 and 7 deal with matters of controversy related to the interaction of Christians with the civil authorities. The article on the sword, the longest of the seven, acknowledges that God has ordained coercive power to be used in the world "outside the perfection of Christ." Within the community of baptized believers, however, the only coercion permitted is the discipline of the ban. The article then takes up three questions related to the Christian's use of the sword. "May a Christian wield the sword against the wicked for the protection of the good?" "May a Christian sit in judgment and pass sentence in worldly disputes and strife about temporal matters?" "May a Christian serve as a magistrate if chosen to such an office?" Each of these questions elicits a negative response that is justified by an appeal to the example of Jesus. Those who wish to be obedient to Christ must abstain from personal participation in the coercive structures of society. "The worldly are armed with steel and iron, but Christians are armed with the armor of God, with truth, with righteousness, peace, faith, salvation, and with the Word of God." Some scholars have related the stance of nonresistance advocated by the Schleitheim assembly to the pacifist strain within Erasmian humanism that influenced even Zwingli in his early career. Sattler's monastic background may also have played a role alongside the strict biblical hermeneutic of the Zurich Anabaptists who had earlier distanced themselves from the violent activities of the peasant uprising. Other Anabaptists such as Hubmaier pursued a different path of reformation, finding a place for a Christian magistracy and a more positive relationship between the community of believers and the temporal order.

The concluding article concerns the swearing of the oath, which is strictly forbidden in keeping with the command of Christ: "Christ taught us similarly when he says your speech shall be yea, yea; and nay, nay; for what is more than that comes of evil. He says, your speech or your word shall be yes and no so that anyone might understand that he had permitted it. Christ is simply yea and nay, and all those who seek Him simply will understand His Word." The New Testament literalism of the Swiss Brethren is evident in their opposing the Old Testament injunction against swearing falsely to Christ's absolute prohibition against swearing at all. Earlier Anabaptists such as George Blaurock had been publicly beaten for refusing to swear an oath. But Schleitheim represents the crystallization of this conviction among the Swiss Anabaptists. The Anabaptists' refusal to take the annual oath required by the cantons of Switzerland and the city republics within the empire further alienated them from the civic expectations and social norms of sixteenth-century European society.

Within the recent historiography of the radical Reformation, the Schleitheim Articles have been the focus of conflicting interpretations concerning the theological nature and origins of the Swiss Anabaptist movement. Traditional Mennonite historiography has stressed the confessional character of the Schleitheim Articles as a normative standard of evangelical Anabaptism. This position assumes a strong connection between the Anabaptism of Schleitheim and that that emerged among the radical Zwinglians in Zurich. A variation of this view has been forcefully set forth by John Howard Yoder, who moves beyond earlier interpretations by emphasizing the decisive role of Sattler as "the most significant of the first-generation leaders of Anabaptism" and the strategic significance of the Schleitheim Articles as a theological landmark and "crystallization point" of the Swiss Brethren movement. Other scholars such as James Stayer and Hans-Jürgen Goertz have interpreted the Schleitheim Articles in the light of the revolutionary impulses of the peasant uprising that swept through southern Germany in the mid-1520s. It is pointed out that the very term "brotherly union" was a common expression of solidarity among the peasants who demanded a congregational egalitarianism with the right to choose their own pastors, to enforce discipline, and to interpret scripture along the lines set forth in the articles. According to this view, the pacifism of Schleitheim was the result of "a hopeless political situation" rather than a pure expression of inspired biblical exegesis. Still another interpretation locates the background of the Schleitheim Articles within the Benedictine monastic order to which Sattler had belonged prior to his conversion to Anabaptism. Arnold Snyder, the most recent biographer of Sattler, points to a number of parallels between the articles and the Rule of Saint Benedict. Thus believer's baptism is seen as an analogue to the monastic vow as a rite of initiation. Both Anabaptism and Benedictine monasticism, especially in its reformed expression, were guided by the ideal of an intentional and disciplined community in which the "perfection of Christ" was sought through a pattern of holy living and separation from the world.

The influence of the Schleitheim Articles is attested by the wide dissemination they received throughout the sixteenth century. In addition to Zwingli's refutation of 1527, John Calvin also published a point-by-point response to the articles in his *Briève instruction pour armer tous bons fidèles* (1541). In addition to the early German imprints there was also a French translation of the articles, which is no longer extant. By 1560 a Dutch translation had appeared. The articles were also incorporated into the formative documents of the Hutterites, who sought to realize the Anabaptist ideals in a communitarian setting in Moravia.

The Schleitheim Articles were drafted as a response to certain pressing concerns and challenges faced by the first generation of Swiss and south German brethren. By no means are they a systematic exposition or balanced testimony of the faith and practice of these early Anabaptists. At the same time, their promulgation at a moment of crisis in the early history of the movement, together with the stirring example of Sattler's subsequent martyrdom, gave the articles a wide influence and normative role for several major streams of Anabaptism in sixteenth-century Europe and beyond.

BIBLIOGRAPHY

Fast, Heinhold, ed. *Quellen zur Geschichte der Täufer in der Schweiz.* Vol. 2. Zurich, 1973.

Friedmann, Robert. "Brüderliche Vereinigung." In *Mennonite Encyclopedia*, vol. 1, p. 448. Scottdale, Pa., 1955.

Goertz, Hans-Jürgen. *Die Täufer: Geschichte und Deutung.* Munich, 1980.

Snyder, Arnold. *The Life and Thought of Michael Sattler.* Scottdale, Pa., 1984.

———. "The Schleitheim Articles in Light of the Revolution of the Common Man: Continuation or Departure?" *Sixteenth Century Journal* 16 (1985), 419–430.

———. "The Influence of the Schleitheim Articles on the Anabaptist Movement: An Historical Evaluation." *Mennonite Quarterly Review* 63 (1989), 323–344.

Stayer, James. *Anabaptists and the Sword.* Lawrence, Kans., 1972.

Williams, George H. *The Radical Reformation.* 3d ed. Kirksville, Mo., 1992.

Winter, Sean F. "Michael Sattler and the Schleitheim Articles." *Baptist Quarterly* 34 (1991), 52–66.

Yoder, John Howard. *The Legacy of Michael Sattler.* Scottdale, Pa., 1973.

TIMOTHY GEORGE

SCHLESWIG-HOLSTEIN. The duchies of Schleswig and Holstein were located between the Elbe, the North and Baltic Seas, and Denmark in the north; the areas of Pinneberg, Hamburg, Lauenburg, the diocese of Ratzeburg as well as the city and diocese of Lübeck in the southeast; and divided by the river Eider. From 1460 they were in a personal union with Denmark, which assured them of indivisibility. Schleswig—Danish-speaking in the north—was a Danish fief and Holstein an imperial one. Ecclesiastically, Schleswig was part of the bishoprics of Schleswig, Ripen, and Odense, and Holstein part of the bishopric of Lübeck. The peasant republic of Dithmarschen in the west, which administratively stood under the Bremen archbishop and ecclesiastically under the Hamburg cathedral provost, had obtained its independence in the Battle of Hemmingstedt

(1500) against King John and his brother, Duke Frederick. Under their common rule the duchies were divided in 1490 into a royal and a ducal part.

Pre-Reformation attempts at reform of the monastic orders had failed because of the resistance of the monasteries. Christian II, successor in 1513 to his father, John, promoted national church and humanist reform efforts and out of a sense of power favored the burghers over the nobility and the clergy. His approval of Luther's *An den christlichen Adel deutscher Nation* and the appointment of Lutheran preachers, such as Andreas Bodenstein von Karlstadt (1521), was hardly based on theological conviction. His efforts at ecclesiastical reform remained ineffective. After he had lost the Swedish crown because of his brutal actions toward the Swedish nobility and had through his restrictive measures angered the Hanseatic cities, he sought with the help of his brother-in-law Charles V to curtail the rights of his co-ruler, Frederick, in the two duchies. In the Bordesholm Compromise (1522), however, he had to recognize the neutrality of the duchies and to surrender the fief over Holstein that he had obtained from the emperor. Thereupon he turned to the emperor's opponent, Francis I. Frederick rose up against the royal nephew, occupied Denmark, and accepted the crown offered by the Jutland estates. On 26 March 1523 he was crowned king, and on 24 April the Schleswig-Holstein estates pledged their allegiance to him as their only duke— which was the end of the division of the land. Exiled in the Netherlands, Christian II planned his return with consideration for his Habsburg hosts and for the development of his homeland as a defender of Catholicism against Lutheranism. In 1531 he landed in Norway, but he was captured and remained in prison until his death (1559).

As a political prize for the victory, Frederick granted the Schleswig-Holstein knights the privilege of estates (1524). This gave them extensive jurisdiction over their manorial subjects and exempted them at the same time from territorial jurisdiction. The legal procedure that went from the duchy of Schleswig to the Danish Privy Council ended; for both duchies the new court of the nobility became the most important instance for the nobility. The nobility assumed all high offices, as well as tax exemption.

The estates had the authority to approve taxes at two annual diets. This was a high point of the power of the estates, with oppressive results for the peasants. In his election agreements of Viborg and at his coronation in Copenhagen in 1524, Frederick guaranteed the nobility and the clergy the privileges of church and prelates, took a stand against Lutheranism, and at the same time took the path toward a princely and national church.

The Reformation here proceeded in the main peacefully and gradually. Frederick's son Christian, from 1523 governor in Schleswig-Holstein, and his steward Johann Rantzau had witnessed Luther's appearance at the Diet of Worms (1521) and had accepted his teachings. Soon thereafter

Luther's ideas took hold in cities and villages of the duchies. In Husum Hermann Tast preached from 1522 to ever larger congregations and to great effect along the whole west coast of Schleswig. Citizens from Lübeck came to hear the preachers in Oldesloe (1524). Others appeared in Rendsburg (1525), Flensburg (1526), and the episcopal city of Schleswig. Although there citizens were generally the supporters of the reform movement, in the north Schleswig county of Hadersleben, where Prince Christian had installed Lutheran clerics in 1525, the Reformation was undertaken by the nobility and immediately encompassed the whole region. Luther's doctrine was established in Tondern and Apenrade in 1526, while its spread in the Elbe marshes—also under Hamburg's influence—had been proceeding since 1522. In addition, the special war tax, with which Frederick in 1524 demanded half of all ecclesiastical income from the duchies, hit the clergy even harder, since both church taxes and offerings decreased at the same time. Moreover, at the Rendsburg Diet of 1525 the knights complained of numerous ecclesiastical deficiencies and faults. Frederick tried to smooth things over, and the diet merely issued admonitions to the bishops, prelates, and priests. The change was completed in 1526, when Frederick's daughter Dorothea was married to Albert of Brandenburg, duke of Prussia. Frederick had given up on the goal of religious unity and tolerated Lutheranism. At the Kiel Diet in 1526 he by another war tax forced the clergy into extensive land sales. This strengthened the basic criticism of ecclesiastical property and encouraged the government, the nobles, and the middle class to usurp it.

A dispute in Hadersleben over fasting gave Duke Christian the oportunity to present his evangelical notions and also to stress his authority in spiritual matters before the Ripen bishop. The Hadersleben Articles (Artickel vor de Kerkheren vp den Dorpern, 1528) are the oldest Protestant church ordinance in the north; they are based on the emergency powers of government in the face of ecclesiastical decay. Their stipulations dealt with the Protestant service, feast days, sermons, priesthood, and sacraments; they combined Luther's teachings with older traditions. Nevertheless, the Reformation in Schleswig-Holstein went slower than in Denmark because the king was more dependent on the Catholic estates. The effective appearance of Melchior Hoffman in Kiel in 1527, which threatened to split the emerging territorial church, brought about a debate under Christian's chairmanship in Flensburg in 1529, in which Hoffman defended his divergent doctrine of the Eucharist against Johannes Bugenhagen. Together with his followers he was exiled.

Frederick's death in 1533 endangered the quiet progress of the Reformation, since Christian, his successor, established himself quickly in Schleswig-Holstein, but in Denmark not until 1534, and afterward had to deal with the Counts' War (1534–1536), for which Lübeck was respon-

sible. On the advice of Philipp of Hesse, Christian III proceeded carefully in the duchies. The diet of 1533 gave free rein to the increasingly Lutheran nobility to criticize the clergy, required substantiation for ecclesiastical tithing, and expressly approved Protestant services in churches and monasteries; for the Schleswig cathedral, limitations on the traditional Mass were agreed upon, and Christian received the right to appoint preachers of his choice anywhere.

In the meantime the Reformation had been established in most of the cities of Schleswig-Holstein; in Hamburg and Lübeck the positions of the cathedral provost and bishop were decisively weakened. In Denmark Christian III rigorously introduced the Reformation against the bishops from 1536, supported by the Schleswig-Holstein theologians. The Danish church ordinance, written by them in accord with the Hadersleben Articles, was revised by Bugenhagen and formally issued together with his coronation of the royal couple in 1537. The ordinance created a pure national church, and it applied nominally also to the duchies. There the old ecclesiastical authorities had lost much of their influence, although the Reformation only slowly expanded from the cities into the country. A legal ordinance was necessary to reform the church uniformly, to prevent through visitations the appointment of improper or radical clerics, and to protect diminishing church property from the greediness of the nobles, peasants, and burghers. But the resistance of the clergy and of the Catholic nobles would not allow such an ordinance. Therefore Christian III convened a synod of clergy and councillors in 1538 from twenty-four evangelical cities, villages, and districts of Schleswig-Holstein to Gottorf. They were pledged to the Danish church ordinance, and four visitators were named for the duchy of Schleswig—a new church authority, which in practice removed the old supervisory institutions. In Holstein this might have caused conflicts with the empire because of the rights of the Lübeck bishop and of the Hamburg chapter. The Diet of Rendsburg in 1540 opposed the Danish church ordinance but confirmed the decisions of the Gottorf synod. This gave the Reformation a free hand in the princely domains. The visitators (now called superintendents) now exercised a church office that was politically legitimized and was supported by territorial officials. In 1541 Christian III also ordered Protestant services for the rural monasteries.

Early in 1541 the Schleswig bishop and leader of the Catholic resistance, Gottschalk von Ahlefeldt, died. Christian's effort to get Bugenhagen as his successor failed, but Tilemann Hesshus proved to be a capable Lutheran theologian. The property of the diocese and of the chapter was guaranteed, but the uses of the income were strictly determined—especially for the schools. The diminished cathedral chapter became the consistory to hear ecclesiastical legal cases in the diocese. With this, the duchies had come step by step for the most part under Lutheran supervision.

On 9 March 1542 the Diet of Rendsburg accepted the

church ordinance, which had been written in Low German and reworked with Bugenhagen's cooperation and which closely followed the Danish church ordinance but also showed Saxon influences. The repeated changes left it badly arranged, but it treated seven main points: doctrine and selection of ministers, schools, ceremonies, diaconate, support of church personnel, the episcopal supervision of the clergy, and the appropriate books for the clergy. While the new church order focused extensively on Schleswig, it had only a short section on Holstein, probably so that the bishop of Lübeck and the Hamburg chapter would not be provoked and in order to allow latitude for the ruler. Thus for Holstein only a provost, not a bishop, was stipulated: in 1542 Johann Anthonii, previously minister in Krempe, was elected. The north Schleswig deaneries of the dioceses of Ripen and Odense were not affected by the church ordinance, which also remained provisional since the new territorial division between Christian and his brothers Johann and Adolf in 1544 created three (after Duke Johann's death in 1581, two) territorial church organizations. The office of provost disappeared immediately, and that of the bishop in 1551, when after Tilemann's death Duke Frederick became the prince-bishop of Schleswig.

The formation of the territorial church became separated from political developments, since the church ordinance remained the common bond of the various church administrations. It solidified the union of the duchies also by language, in that with the exception of north Schleswig areas, German religious service was prescribed, where otherwise Danish was spoken. In the long run, the Reformation accelerated the replacement of the Low German written language by the more strongly unifying High German.

In Dithmarschen the old church itself seemed unshaken when the twenty parishes in 1523 ceremoniously rejected the authority of the Hamburg cathedral chapter because of its extensive demands, extortion, and dubious personnel policy. This did not signify a change in ecclesiastical life. But students from Wittenberg—for example, the Meldorf preacher Nicolaus Boie, who had studied there in 1518 and kept in touch with Luther and Melanchthon—spread Luther's doctrine early. Boie was also host to the former Augustinian monk and evangelical preacher Heinrich von Zutphen from Geldern, who at the end of 1524 through a conspiracy of Meldorf Dominicans, Lunden Franciscans, and rulers was brought to Heide and burned as a heretic. Nevertheless, the new teaching spread until in 1532 a tentative conclusion was reached with the ban on all Catholic services and the dissolution of the monasteries. After the Imperial Cameral Court, to which the Hamburg chapter had appealed, had declared the forty-eight Dithmarschen rulers the legal government of the country in 1532 with responsibility for ecclesiastical affairs, an independent Protestant territorial church developed rapidly, the uniformity of which

was guarded by four superintendents. The church ordinance of 1537 (First Edict), which later was amended and enlarged several times, collided with strong peasant legal habits. It died in 1559 with the end of Dithmarschen independence, when the Dithmarschen territorial church was joined to that of Schleswig-Holstein.

Above all, dynastic reasons caused Holstein-Pinneberg (being part of the county of Schaumburg) to retain the old church system for a long time. Evangelical influences from nearby Hamburg were resisted just as was the 1542 reform attempt of Christian III at the Pinneberg monastery of Uetersen. Count Otto IV (r. 1544–1576, bishop of Hildesheim 1531–1537) kept the old faith for familial reasons: his brother Adolf XIII and Anton I were successively archbishops of Cologne. After Anton's death in 1558 and his own marriage in 1559 to a daughter of Duke Ernst, "the Confessor," of Braunschweig-Lüneburg, the count ordered the introduction of the Reformation in Schaumburg, which was expanded to Pinneberg in 1561.

In the duchy of Lauenburg Luther's teachings found an early entry. As early as the end of 1526 Duke Magnus I (1507–1543) issued a mandate in connection with the recess of the Diet of Speyer that was to assure the continuation of the existing order through a careful acceptance of notions of reform, after the Ratzeburg bishop had refused to reach an agreement. Magnus facilitated the spread of evangelical preaching, while his son Franz I (1543–1571)—also influenced by his uncle, Duke Heinrich the Younger of Braunschweig-Wolfenbüttel—stayed aloof and mainly followed interests of power. His powerful attempt to make his own son bishop of Ratzeburg failed. After the Peace of Augsburg, he used his right of reform with regard to church property. Not until 1557 was there a ecclesiastical inventory, and in 1564, upon the urging of the district, the first general visitation. In 1578 the Mecklenburg church ordinance, which up to then had been used only provisionally, was officially adopted by the regional diet. Not until the reign of Franz II (1581–1619) was the introduction of the Reformation concluded (after a new general visitation in 1581/82) with the church ordinance of 1585. The reasons for the slow progress were the small religious engagement of Magnus I and particularly of Franz I, but also the lack of a strong reform movement in the primarily rural duchy.

BIBLIOGRAPHY

Brandt, Otto. *Geschichte Schleswig-Holsteins: Ein Grundriß.* 8th ed. Corrected and enlarged by Wilhelm Kluver, with a contribution by Herbert Jankuhn. Kiel, 1981.
Göbell, Walter, ed. *Die Schleswig-Holsteinische Kirchenordnung von 1542.* Neumünster, 1986.
Göbell, Walter, et al. *Schleswig-Holsteinische Kirchengeschichte.* Vol. 3, *Reformation.* Neumünster, 1982.
Hoffmann, Erich. *Geschichte Schleswig-Holsteins.* Vol. 4, pt. 2, *Spätmittelalter und Reformationszeit.* Neumünster, 1981.

Opitz, Eckardt. *Schleswig-Holstein. Landesgeschichte in Bildern, Texten, und Dokumenten.* Hamburg, 1988.

RAINER POSTEL
Translated from German by Walter D. Morris

SCHLICK OF PASSAUNI, Joachim Andreas

(Czech, Šlik; 1569–1621), leader of the radical Lutheran movement in Bohemia. An aristocrat from a bilingual German-Czech family of counts, Schlick was educated in Bohemia and in Strasbourg, Geneva, and Jena, where he was elected rector of the university in 1591. In the 1590s Schlick lived at the court of the elector of Saxony in Dresden. From 1593 to 1600 he was a tutor of the princes Christian, Johann Georg, and August. After 1602 he took part in the anti-Habsburg opposition of the Bohemian non-Catholic estates, was a prominent orator, and was elected a defender of the Utraquists (1609). He supported the establishment of the Lutheran church and school of Saint Salvator in Prague. At a crucial moment—the "election" of Ferdinand of Styria as Bohemian king (1617)—Schlick acted in a manner regarded cowardly by the leaders of the Bohemian uprising (1618–1620) and lost their trust. His contacts with the electoral court and clergy of Saxony led Schlick to support an indirect Saxon candidature for the Bohemian throne in 1619, but the majority of aristocrats elected Frederick V of the Palatinate, a radical Calvinist, as king of Bohemia. Schlick was appointed supreme judge of Bohemia and administrator (*Landvogt*) of Upper Lusatia, but not supreme chancellor, as he had wished. After the Battle of White Mountain (8 November 1620) he was imprisoned, sentenced to death, and was the first of the twenty-seven condemned leaders of the uprising to be executed in the Old Town Square of Prague (21 June 1621).

Schlick was influenced by the theology of Saxon Gnesio-Lutherans and belonged to a minority of Protestant noblemen and clergy who attempted to explicate the Bohemian Confession of 1575 and the Letter of Majesty of 1609 in the sense of the Formula of Concord. Thus he increased tensions between the Lutherans, the pro-Calvinist Unity of Brethren (Bohemian Brethren), and some of the Neo-Utraquist priests. Schlick's confessional and political thought was expressed in his publications: an anti-Calvinist polemic (*Gründliche Wiederlegung Calvinischer Lehre*, 1595), an apology for the free election of the Bohemian kings (*Kurtze Information von der Königlichen Erbgerechtigkeit und der Ständewahl in Böhmen*, 1617), the "second apology" for the uprising of Bohemian estates (*Apologie druhá stavův Království českého, tělo Pána našeho Ježíše Krista pod obojí způsobou přijimajicich*, 1618), and an interpretation of the political and religious causes of the Bohemian uprising (*Examen der Recepten und Medicamenten, so etliche Politische Medici vor die Böhmische Kranckheit oder Fieber geordnet*, 1620).

BIBLIOGRAPHY

Janáček, Josef, ed. *Pavel Skála ze Zhoře, Historie česká: Od defenestrace k Bílé hoře* (History of Bohemia: From the Prague Defenestration of 1618 to the Battle of White Mountain). Prague, 1984. Edition of the chronicle by Pavel Skála of Zhoř, with critical evaluation of Schlick's political activity

Lukášek, Josef. *Jáchym Ondřej hrabě Šlik* (Joachim Andreas, Count of Schlick). Prague, 1913. The only biography of Schlick is methodologically old-fashioned but nevertheless useful; it is an apology from the Lutheran point of view.

Petráň, Josef. *Staroměstská exekuce* (The Execution in the Old Town Square of Prague). Prague, 1985. An outline of Schlick's political activity in the network of the Bohemian uprising.

JAROSLAV PÁNEK

SCHMALKALD ARTICLES.

Written by Martin Luther and published in 1538, the document that has come to be known as the Schmalkald Articles—the actual title is "Articles which should have been presented by our side to the council at Mantua (or wherever it might be); regarding what we retain or give up, or not"—presents a summary of the author's mature theological views and his critique of the Catholic church. The articles were adopted into the *Book of Concord* of 1580, and thus this document also officially expresses Lutheranism's basic theological priorities.

Origins. In June 1536 a general council of the church was called by Pope Paul III; it was to have taken place at Mantua, Italy, beginning the following May. (In fact the council would not open until 1545 and would be held at Trent.) The pope's announcement became the occasion for Elector John Frederick of Saxony (1503–1554) to commission Luther to write a document that would serve both as a personal testament of faith, outlining what Luther thought was theologically most important, and as the confessional basis for the Schmalkald League's response to the proposed council. The elector requested this document from Luther in early December 1536, and the reformer had completed the bulk of the text by Christmas (despite an apparent heart attack that forced him to dictate the last twelve articles to secretaries). After revising the articles with a group of seven theologians at Wittenberg (a short section, "On Prayer to Saints," was added), Luther forwarded the document to John Frederick in early January 1537. The elector brought the articles to the February 1537 meeting of the Schmalkald League at Schmalkalden, apparently for possible use as a common confession of faith at Mantua. Because the rulers decided not to attend the general council and Luther himself was unable to participate in any proceedings—at Schmalkalden, he suffered an excruciatingly painful attack of kidney stones—the articles were never brought up for discussion. They did, however, circulate among the theologians present, and the majority indicated their agreement by affixing their personal subscriptions.

Thus, the articles were not officially approved at Schmalkalden. Luther added a formal preface, made a few more changes, and had them published at Wittenberg in June 1538. In the succeeding forty years, the Schmalkald Articles were incorporated into various collections of Lutheran confessional writings (*corpora doctrinae*) until they became part of the *Book of Concord*.

Structure. Luther divided the text of the Schmalkald Articles into three parts. Part 1 outlines ". . . the lofty articles of divine majesty." The four articles of this section form a series of statements or short paragraphs that summarize western catholic theology. This part is brief because "these articles are not matters of dispute or conflict, for both sides confess them."

Part 2, ". . . the articles which pertain to the office and work of Jesus Christ, or to our redemption," also contains four articles, each of which is longer than the longest of part 1. In order, these articles explicate Christ and faith, the Mass, chapters and monasteries, and the papacy.

Part 3 contains fifteen articles, of varying lengths, which Luther was willing to ". . . discuss . . . with learned, reasonable people . . ." The topics dealt with in this section are, in order: sin, law, repentance, the gospel, baptism, Communion, forgiveness, the keys, excommunication, ordination, the marriage of priests, the church, justification and good works, monastic vows, and human regulations.

Finally, there are two important supplements. First, Luther wrote an extended preface while preparing the articles for publication. Second, a list of subscriptions to the articles is attached to the document. These forty-three signatures show the appeal of the Schmalkald Articles to the sixteenth-century German Lutheran theologians.

Content. The preface emphasizes Luther's specific motives in writing and publishing the work. "I wanted to make these articles available . . . in case I should die (as I fully expect and hope) before a council can take place." Larger issues in the surrounding historical context—for example, the long-standing Protestant request for a ". . . truly free council," the recognition of reform-minded people who still "are on the pope's side," parishes that are "empty and deserted"—are also discussed.

Part 1 weaves together quotations from and references to the Nicene, Apostles', and Athanasian Creeds, as well as Luther's own Small Catechism (1529). By doing so, the reformer puts his call for reform of the church in the context of the shared catholic consensus.

Part 2 demonstrates both the constructive and polemical dimensions of Luther's theology. In the opening article Luther presents the core of his proposed reform of the church. This summary (which Luther calls "The First and Chief Article") is a concise constructive statement of Luther's understanding of Christ and faith. In crisp and clear language, the reformer sets forth the main features of evangelical the-

ology: "scripture alone" (*sola scriptura*), "Christ alone" (*sola Christus*), and "faith alone" (*sola fide*). The first of these can be seen in Luther's use of a series of biblical passages, drawn from both the Old and New Testaments, that point to the role of Christ in the redemption of the world. According to Luther, the particularity of Jesus (*sola Christus*) is evident in the scriptures, which bear witness to God's saving act in Jesus Christ. Human beings apprehend this salvation by faith alone; moreover, this faith is a gift from the Holy Spirit. All of this makes sense for Luther when it is placed in the context of humanity's need or "sin." Therefore, the biblical passages Luther uses to summarize his understanding of Christ and faith indicate simultaneously the matrix of human sin into which God comes in Christ.

At the same time, part 2 contains a critical (even polemical) analysis of the sixteenth-century Roman Catholic church, based on Luther's understanding of the scriptures as delineated in article 1. The remaining three articles of part 2 (on the Mass, chapters and monasteries, and the papacy) express Luther's critique of contemporary Roman Catholic church life. This feature of the Schmalkald Articles is distinctive among the early Lutheran confessional writings. Luther articulates quite pointedly what he thinks needs to be reformed in the church, and why he thought the church of his day violated "The First and Chief Article." In a sense the Schmalkald Articles owe their very existence to this thorough evaluation of current Catholic practice in light of Luther's understanding of the gospel. Luther wrote the Schmalkald Articles because he himself had yet to summarize systematically the faith in relation to the Roman Catholic abuses of his day.

The third part of the Schmalkald Articles elucidates the concrete implications of Luther's catholic and evangelical theological emphases as outlined in parts 1 and 2. For Luther, a catholic and evangelical theology leads the church to stress the importance of "the spoken word, in which the forgiveness of sins is preached to the whole world." Second, it leads him to uphold the sacraments (baptism and the Lord's Supper) as means by which forgiveness comes to people. Third, Luther emphasizes "the keys" (confession and absolution), which the reformer defines as "the mutual conversation and consolation of the brothers and sisters."

Reception. The first to accept the articles formally were the seven theologians who had met at Wittenberg to discuss Luther's original draft, each of whom signed the revised document. Luther himself had written: "These are the articles on which I must stand and on which I intend to stand, God willing, until my death. I know of nothing in them that can be changed or conceded." Even Philipp Melanchthon's qualified subscription did not substantively deviate from the theology of the articles, but was instead an expression of Melanchthon's characteristic thoroughness and guardedness: "I . . . regard the above articles as true and Christian.

Regarding the pope, however, I maintain that if he would allow the gospel, we might allow him his superiority over the bishops which he has by human right." Shortly thereafter, Elector John Frederick strongly endorsed the document; writing to Luther in early January 1537, he called the articles "Christian, pure, and clear." Furthermore, the majority of theologians and preachers at Schmalkalden in February 1537 affixed their names to the document. Even before its publication, the Schmalkald Articles were recognized as holding a special rank among Luther's works.

Following their publication in 1538, the articles began in earnest their journey toward confessional status. This journey is best seen in the context of the theological controversies that agitated Lutheranism in the third quarter of the sixteenth century. These confessional debates led Luther's theological heirs to appeal to representative documents from the formative period of Lutheranism (the Augsburg Confession and its Apology, the Schmalkald Articles, the Small Catechism and the Large Catechism, The Wittenberg Concord, etc.) as authoritative sources. Lutherans began to collect these documents into "bodies of doctrine" (*corpora doctrinae*) which would serve as the confessional standard in particular areas. (Between 1560 and 1580, some twenty of these compilations appeared.) These collections tended to reflect the orientation of the compiler(s). The "Philippist" camp (a label used to designate those who were identified more closely with Melanchthon than with Luther) produced works such as the *Corpus doctrinae philippicum* of 1560, edited by Melanchthon himself and containing only the three ecumenical creeds and works by Melanchthon. The "Gnesio-Lutheran" camp, meanwhile, produced works such as the *Corpus Thuringicum* of 1570, which included the Schmalkald Articles and was compiled in conscious opposition to the *philippicum*. In time the Schmalkald Articles were identified as being particularly representative of Luther's own theology, and thus the work became a standard writing in Gnesio-Lutheran *corpora*.

These intra-Lutheran theological conflicts served a number of important functions in establishing a distinctive Lutheran confessional witness. First, these controversies helped form the canon of the Lutheran confessional writings. Not all of the documents contained in the various *corpora* withstood the scrutiny of public debate and were included in the *Book of Concord*; as one of the few that did come to represent confessional Lutheranism, the text of the Schmalkald Articles merits particular attention.

Second, these debates made it plain that, to be acceptable to all Lutherans, a single authoritative body of doctrine must contain works by both Luther and Melanchthon. This happened in the late 1570s when the *Book of Concord* was compiled and published on the fiftieth anniversary of the presentation of the Augsburg Confession to Emperor Charles V. The text of the Schmalkald Articles is one of three documents by Luther included in this authoritative collection of Lutheran confessional texts.

Third, this process produced the Formula of Concord (1577), which furthered the unity of Lutheranism by providing a generally acceptable interpretation of these confessional writings. The formula makes ample use of the Schmalkald Articles, either quoting from the work or referring to it by name nearly a dozen times.

Impact. Despite the fact that they set forth not only Luther's theology but also the official confessional position of Lutheranism, the Schmalkald Articles have received relatively little attention since the time of the Reformation. A possible explanation is that for the most part the early career of Luther has been the focus of scholarly attention; another is that the articles have been overshadowed by such epoch-defining and popular writings as the Augsburg Confession, the Formula of Concord, and the catechisms. Yet the Schmalkald Articles, written under the pressure of Luther's seemingly impending death, may have had a personal significance beyond that of all Luther's other texts. They are best read as Luther's theological testament, as containing the legacy that he wanted to bequeath to posterity.

[*See also* Formula of Concord; Luther, Martin; Lutheranism; *and* Schmalkald League.]

BIBLIOGRAPHY

Bente, F. *Historical Introductions to the Book of Concord.* Saint Louis, 1965. This reprint from Bente's 1929 *Triglotta* is now dated but contains a wealth of useful material.

Daniel, David P., and Charles Arand, eds. *Sixteenth Century Bibliography.* Vol. 28, *A Bibliography of the Lutheran Confessions.* Saint Louis, 1988. The section on the articles is an excellent guide to the literature.

Haile, H. G. *Luther: An Experiment in Biography.* Corr. ed. Princeton, 1983. A lively account that gives specific attention to the articles and to the February 1537 meeting of the Schmalkald League.

Kittelson, James. *Luther the Reformer.* Minneapolis, 1986. Describes the articles in the context of Luther's later life and theology.

Kolb, Robert. "Luther's Smalcald Articles: Agenda for Testimony and Confession." *Concordia Journal* 14 (April 1988), 115–137. Explicates Luther's confessional theology in the articles.

Russell, William R. *Luther's Theological Testament: The Schmalkald Articles.* Minneapolis, 1994. The only book-length explication in English of the history and theology of Luther's articles.

———. "Philip Melanchthon's Subscription to Luther's Schmalkald Articles: Deviance or Conformity?" *Sixteenth Century Journal.* In press.

Schaaf, James. "The Smalcald Articles." In *Interpreting Luther's Legacy,* edited by Fredrick Meuser. Minneapolis, 1969.

Volz, Hans. *Urkunden und Aktenstücke zur Geschichte von Martin Luthers Schmalkaldischen Artikeln, 1536–1547.* Berlin, 1957. A collection of essential primary sources, with extremely helpful annotations.

Zangemeister, Karl. *Die Schmalkaldischen Artikel vom Jahre 1537. Nach D. Martin Luthers Autograph in der Universitätsbibliothek zu Heidelberg.* Heidelberg, 1886. Contains both a facsimile and an edited version of Luther's original manuscript.

WILLIAM R. RUSSELL

SCHMALKALDEN. The iron-mining town of Schmalkalden (Eng., Smalkald or Smalcald), Hesse (Thuringia), hosted and became associated with a number of significant events of the Reformation era. Notable institutions of the town were the collegiate foundation of Saint James's church (the *Kollegiatstift*, disbanded in 1545 and later the site of William IV of Hesse-Kassel's hunting castle called Wilhelmsburg), an observant Augustinian monastery (closed officially in 1564), a hospital, and the church of Saint George's.

Schmalkalden's status as a county seat and its location near the border between Hesse and Saxony (on the eastern slope of a valley to the southwest of the Thuringian forest) made it a relatively convenient spot for meetings of sixteenth-century Protestants. Led by Saxon Elector John Frederick (1503–1554) and Landgrave Philipp of Hesse, the politically most significant convention at Schmalkalden occurred in the winter of 1530/31 when six princes, eleven imperial cities, and two counts formed the Schmalkald League. This alliance was a defensive maneuver in response to the Recess of the Diet of Augsburg (the recess, promulgated in November 1530, demanded Protestant submission to the Roman church) and the January 1531 election of Charles V's brother, Ferdinand of Austria (1503–1564), as "king of the Romans" (thus assuring continued imperial support for Roman Catholicism).

The theologically most significant gathering at Schmalkalden occured in February–March 1537, when the league assembled to reply to Pope Paul III's summons to an ecumenical council of the church. (The council had been scheduled to take place in Mantua, Italy, beginning in May 1537.) This gathering provided impetus for the formulation of two noteworthy statements of Lutheran theology, both of which became confessional writings. First, for this meeting Martin Luther wrote the Schmalkald Articles (published in 1538), a lucid and provocative summary of Luther's and Lutheranism's theological priorities. (As it happened the articles were never brought before the convention, owing both to Luther's falling ill at Schmalkalden and the league's rejection of the council.) Second, during this 1537 assembly Philipp Melanchthon wrote *De potestate et primatu papae tractatus* as an addendum to the Augsburg Confession of 1530 (which, although the theological basis of the league, had contained no article on the papacy).

Schmalkalden itself became a Lutheran stronghold. Indeed, the populace rioted in late 1608 when Landgrave Maurice of Hesse (1572–1632) assigned a pastor to Schmalkalden who sought to introduce Reformed theology and practice into the parish. Soldiers were needed to quell the disturbance and guarantee the landgrave's reforms. As late as 1614, it was reputed that significant numbers of the people in Schmalkalden refused to attend worship.

[*See also* Schmalkald League.]

BIBLIOGRAPHY

Enke, Johann-Friedrich. "Wir Besuchen die Lutherstätten." *Luther: Zeitschrift der Luthergesellschaft* 63 (1992), 85–91. Includes a brief overview of events associated with Schmalkalden.

Haile, H. G. *Luther: An Experiment in Biography.* Corr. ed. Princeton, 1983. Includes a generally accurate account of Luther's stay at Schmalkalden in February of 1537.

Janssen, Johannes. *History of the German People at the Close of the Middle Ages.* 16 vols. Translated by A. M. Christie and M. A. Mitchell. Saint Louis and New York, 1907–1966. Schmalkalden appears in the detailed indexes of this impressive work.

Patze, Hans. "Schmalkalden." In *Handbuch der Historischen Stätten Deutschlands*, vol. 9, *Thüringen*, edited by Hans Patze. Stuttgart, 1968. A densely worded summary of Schmalkalden's history, with a helpful bibliography.

Russell, William R. *Luther's Theological Testament: The Schmalkald Articles.* Minneapolis, 1995. A historical and theological analysis of Luther's articles, with special attention to the 1537 meeting of the Schmalkald League.

Wendehorst, Alfred. "Die Statuten des Stiftes Schmalkalden 1342 und ihre Herkunft." In *Festschrift für Hermann Heimpel*, edited by Mitarbeitern des Max Planck Instituts für Geschichte, vol. 2, pp. 266–276. Göttingen, 1972. Well annotated, this article focuses on pre-Reformation Schmalkalden.

Ziessler, Rudolf. "Die Restaurierung des Reisensaales im Schloss Wilhelmsburg in Schmalkalden." In *Von Farbe und Farben*, edited by Mane Hering-Mitgan, pp. 111–116. Zurich, 1980. Contains a brief history of Schmalkalden, with photographs of the interior of the Wilhelmsburg castle.

WILLIAM R. RUSSELL

SCHMALKALD LEAGUE. A German Protestant military federation (1531–1547), the Schmalkald League was based on an agreement made at Schmalkalden (in Thuringia) in December 1530. The founding treaty was signed there in February 1531. The original members included the two commanders, Elector John of Saxony and Landgrave Philipp of Hesse; the northern princes of Anhalt-Bernburg and Mansfeld-Hinterort; the northern cities of Lübeck, Magdeburg, and Bremen; and the southern cities of Strasbourg, Ulm, Memmingen, Constance, Biberach, Lindau, and Isny.

The Schmalkald League's prehistory reached back to the year 1526, when the evangelical princes of Saxony and Hesse first proposed to expand their League of Gotha-Torgau through an alliance with the major southern cities of Strasbourg, Ulm, Nuremberg, and Augsburg; in the same year, however, the eucharistic dispute between followers of Martin Luther and those of Huldrych Zwingli split the evangelicals into two parties. Important steps toward the alliance were the Pack Affair of 1528, the adoption of a proalliance policy by Jakob Sturm of Strasbourg in the same year, and the common protest (whence the term *Protestants* emerged) against the recess of the Diet of Speyer in 1529, which was accompanied by an agreement to form a military alliance. This progress was throttled, however, during the summer and autumn of 1529 by a widening split in the evangelical camp, which took two forms: Lutheran polemical attacks on the Sacramentarians of the south, especially the Swiss, in which the lead was taken by southern urban Lutherans such as Lazarus Spengler of Nuremberg and Johannes Brenz of Schwäbisch-Hall; and Elector John of Saxony's *post facto* statement of doctrinal agreement, based on the Schwabach Articles, as a condition for alliance. When the elector's attitude changed after the failure of his negotiations with Emperor Charles V at Augsburg in 1530, he still required doctrinal agreement, now based on the new Augsburg Confession, as the price of alliance.

This prehistory influenced the Schmalkald League's character in an important way, for the league's peculiarity, which distinguished it from all the many forerunner federations (*Einungen*), including the Swabian League, was its defined purpose—the defense of religion. It nonetheless mixed this goal with traditional aims: "to the praise of Almighty God, to the spreading and growth of the free, holy gospel, to the awakening and promotion of a united Christian condition and peace in the Holy Roman Empire of the German Nation, also to the common good, welfare, honor, and devotion of our several principalities, cities and lands, but solely for defensive purposes." The league's second peculiarity was that, unlike the Swabian League, it was imperial rather than regional in scope, eventually stretching from Strasbourg to Pomerania and from Constance to Oldenburg. On occasion, it tried to break out of the empire through alliances with foreign rulers, notably with the kings of England and France during the mid-1530s, but the negotiations came to nothing, chiefly because of Henry VIII's unstable and Francis I's hostile religious policies. The league always understood itself to represent in some sense all evangelicals in the empire, including those, such as the city of Nuremberg and Margrave George of Brandenburg-Ansbach, who refused to join it. It began as and remained, however, a federation of rulers—princes and urban regimes—of the traditional German type, and it never intervened to protect fellow evangelicals against their Catholic rulers. The one challenge to this character came in 1543, when the beleaguered evangelicals of Metz petitioned for admission to the league. Their petition was favored by Philipp of Hesse and Strasbourg's Martin Bucer but opposed by the Saxons and Sturm on the grounds that the league could not intervene between rulers and subjects. The evangelical Messins were forced to emigrate.

The Schmalkald League, originally formed for six years, acquired a fixed constitution at Schmalkalden on 23 December 1535, which, because of the great influx of new members, had to be superseded by the revised constitution of October 1536. The new members included the cities of Esslingen, Braunschweig, Goslar, Einbeck, and Göttingen, all of which had joined between 1531 and 1535; the dukes of Pomerania and Württemberg, the count of Pfalz-Zweibrücken, and two princes of Anhalt-Dessau; and the cities of Frankfurt am Main, Kempten, Hamburg, and Hannover.

From 1535 the league was divided into two "circles," a northern, or "Saxon," circle and a southern, or "upper German," one. In the league's original assembly there had been nine votes—two for Saxony, two for Hesse, one for the other northern princes and nobles, and two each for the southern and the northern free cities—and the post-expansion constitution added one new vote each to Württemberg, Pomerania, and the northern and southern cities, bringing the total to thirteen. The cities, which originally possessed four of nine votes and later six of thirteen, never achieved the parity they desired with the princes. There was never any effective cooperation among the cities as a whole, though the southern Schmalkaldic cities continued the practices of routine consultation and coordination of policy, which they had developed in the Swabian League. They regarded, with some justice, the northern evangelical cities to be the least cooperative and most particularist of the league's members.

The league's presidency alternated between the Saxon elector and the Hessian landgrave, who could call the league's assembly, or diet, or the war council. The latter, a separate body, was organized at Coburg in August 1537 and approved at Braunschweig in April 1538, and it issued regulations for the league's forces. Operational command of the league's forces lay with the Saxon elector in northern Germany, with Landgrave Philipp in southern Germany, and with a troika of these two plus Duke Ernest of Braunschweig-Lüneburg in case of a general conflict. To support its army, the league levied taxes according to the principles followed in imperial taxation: an "emergency force" (*eilende Hilfe*) of cash but no troops to aid a threatened individual member; and a "long-term force" (*beharrliche Hilfe*) of troops and guns for a general campaign—both reckoned in a unit called a "month" of support for 2,000 cavalry and 10,000 infantry. This levy—the supplementary tax for other expenses followed the same pattern—was about equally divided between the two circles. The month was reckoned in the beginning at 70,000 Rhenish florins, but it climbed to 105,000 by 1533 and stood at nearly 200,000 in 1546. During the discussions about renewal and reform of the league in 1545–1546, Sturm strongly advocated shifting to a direct tax, called "the common penny" (*der gemeine Pfennig*), which the Imperial Diet had reintroduced at Speyer in 1544 (it dated back to 1495). Although Sturm argued that the direct tax was more equitable, the same argument he had used in the Imperial Diet, the league's assembly refused to introduce it or any of the other reforms Sturm proposed.

The Schmalkald League's operational history shows a very mixed picture. As a statelike formation, it was inferior to the Swabian League in effectiveness, for it possessed no chancellery or court and had no means of dealing with disputes among members, such as the long quarrel between Duke Ulrich of Württemberg and the cities of Esslingen and Ulm. It also had no fixed seat, meeting seven times at Schmalkalden; six times at Frankfurt am Main; three times at Worms; twice each at Schweinfurt, Braunschweig, and Nuremberg; and once each at Ulm (during the Danube campaign of 1546), Naumburg, Arnstadt, and Eisenach. Sturm's proposal of 1545 that the league make its permanent seat at Frankfurt came to nothing.

Though not impressive from the point of view of its institutional development, the league had considerable political success. The league's most effective action led to the suspension of the Imperial Chamber Court (*Reichskammergericht*) from 1543 until its reorganization in 1548. The root of this action lay in the suits for the restoration of ecclesiastical properties and rights by Catholic clergy following the Diet of Augsburg in 1530, relief from which formed a major motive for the small powers, especially cities, to join the league. The emperor suspended suits "on account of religion" (*Religionssachen*) in the Peace of Nuremberg (1532), confirmed at Frankfurt in 1539, but the majority of the court's judges maintained that there was no way to separate religious from nonreligious affairs. This was correct, and some Protestant powers, notably Strasbourg, blatantly sought to gain recognition and thus the league's protection against suits that, as a Hamburg lawyer remarked of one such suit, were "not religious matters." The league's members, therefore, embarked on an action of recusation—refusal to recognize jurisdiction—of the court, first in religious matters alone and eventually in all matters. This action produced the court's suspension in 1543.

On the military side, the Schmalkald League presents a mixed picture. The successful 1534 campaign by Landgrave Philipp, supported by Strasbourg, to restore Duke Ulrich in Württemberg (since 1520 part of Austria) was not an operation of the league, though it surely benefited from the league's existence. In general, the league had little reason to take or support military action in southern Germany after the defeat of the Swiss evangelicals (1531) and the restoration in Württemberg (1534), but the expansion of membership and the fixing of the constitution (1535–1536), plus the achievement of full doctrinal unity through the Wittenberg Concord (1536), permitted the league's commanders to regard the later and slower Reformation movement in northern Germany as a time of opportunity. When the city of Minden was outlawed in the autumn of 1538, some members, notably Elector John Frederick of Saxony (r. 1532–1547), wanted to go to war, his theologians at Wittenberg having declared such a first strike to be "defensive" in the league's understanding of the term. Voices for negotiation, notably Sturm's, prevailed and led to the Peace of Frankfurt (1539). This crisis nonetheless signaled the passage of aggressive leadership in the league from Landgrave Philipp of Hesse, whose bigamous marriage drove him into the emperor's arms and made him cautious, to John Frederick. The elector, however, was both militarily and politically inexpert, and the league passed its best chance when it failed to aid the elector's brother-in-law, Duke William of Cleves-Jülich,

against Charles V in 1543. The same pattern held true in the prince-archbishopric of Cologne, where Elector Hermann von Wied tried to introduce evangelical reforms under the league's implicit protection.

The Schmalkald League's one military success was its invasion in 1542 of the duchy of Braunschweig-Wolfenbüttel, which the league's army successfully held and defended against an attempt in 1545 by its ruler, Duke Henry II, to retake it. This operation, however, was planned and initiated largely for personal reasons by the league's two chiefs, plus Duke Moritz of Saxony, though the league's assembly approved the campaign subsequently, if with some reluctance. The operation brought little permanent gain to the evangelical cause, but its costs became a standing source of grievance in the league, especially on the part of the southern cities, and the bad feeling over Braunschweig contributed notably to the league's disunity on the eve of the Schmalkald War. The logic of striking Braunschweig-Wolfenbüttel, the last Catholic lay territory in northern Germany, was compelling only if the league were strong enough and aggressive enough to topple the shield of ecclesiastical states that separated their own lands from the Habsburg Netherlands. The league, however, had neither the forces nor the ideological cohesion for such an undertaking, a weakness that also made it vulnerable to becoming an instrument of its commanders' personal ambitions.

The beginning of the Schmalkald War in June 1546 found the league in considerable political disarray, though its military organization, at least initially, operated reasonably well. After the two commanders issued the mobilization orders from Ichtershausen, near Erfurt, they began organizing a movement of their combined armies toward the Danube, where the emperor's main army would appear, while the southern cities' contingents attempted a bold but ultimately futile strike toward Füssen to prevent the oncoming papal troops from uniting with him. The strategy of the Danube campaign was relatively simple: the league had to strike the emperor before he united all of his forces against them. It failed, however, either to block the pope's Italian contingents or to hold the Netherlandish cavalry of Maximilian van Egmont, count of Buren, west of the Rhine. The greatest mistake, however, was the commanders' failure to assault Charles V's main forces, which they did not even engage until the end of August at Ingoldstadt. There, after a two-day preparatory bombardment of his entrenched positions, the league's army broke off the fight, retreated westward, and was followed by the emperor's forces. The two armies spent the rest of the campaign season in an indecisive series of skirmishes until settling into camp. In the league's camp near Giengen, the decisive deliberations occurred on 10 November, when Jakob Sturm pleaded for a battle of decision. Instead, the two commanders broke camp for their own lands on 22 November, effectively ending the Schmalkald League.

The league's assembly met at Ulm all through the Danube campaign, and its main task was to oversee the financing of the war. For this task it organized a special treasury unit at Ulm to keep the accounts and to disburse the collected funds. The commanders and the assembly levied six doubled "months," once on the whole league and twice more on the southern circle alone, which in total should have yielded 2.39 million Rhenish florins, nearly 80 percent of it from the southern circle. In fact, the southerners paid about 60 percent of their huge share, and four powers—Württemberg, Strasbourg, Augsburg, and Ulm—paid in full, while the northern circle paid only 18 percent of their much smaller one. It was not enough, but the assembly could not agree on alternatives, such as the proposal of a direct property tax of 1 percent, which Sturm proposed when he came to Ulm in November 1546. The other alternative, borrowing, also yielded little, for the war made money scarce in southern Germany and Switzerland. The commanders, to be sure, thought from the first about sending embassies to France and England to seek alliances and money, but the only fruit of this effort was the large loan organized by Strasbourg's Johann Sturm with the Lyonnais banker Piero Strozzi, and it came too late to save the Danube campaign. On the whole, the league's assembly does not seem to have operated very effectively during this long final session at Ulm. The league's war council, which accompanied the commanders, was, at least by their accounts, more a hindrance than a help in the conduct of the campaign. These institutions, however, had little effect on the campaign's outcome, which was solely determined by the inferiority of the league's commanders on both the strategic and the tactical levels. It was the first and only time that the league went into the field against what was by contemporary standards a modern army rather than mere territorial levies, as in Braunschweig-Wolfenbüttel.

The historical achievement of the Schmalkald League lay not in the field but in politics. For sixteen years it guarded the infant evangelical movement against actions of all kinds by the emperor, the Imperial Diet (which contained a Catholic, though not a militant, majority), and the Imperial Chamber Court. This proved to be enough to allow the movement to become sufficiently strong that, even in military defeat, the Protestants commanded sufficient respect to assure that Charles V's settlement in 1548 respected their liberties and that, after his defeat in 1552, they would secure toleration. For most of its existence, the league's leaders believed that their movement would grow until it captured the imperial monarchy and the entire empire, a goal quite analogous to that of the French Protestant leaders in the next generation. In a military sense, the Schmalkald League was probably inferior to the French Protestant armies, and the fact that their defeat did not lead to the total marginalization of the Protestants, as it did in France, must be explained by the very different political structures and traditions of the

Holy Roman Empire. The Schmalkald League flourished because the empire had no political center, the same reason why it could not take over the empire and why, despite its defeat, Protestantism survived to become a central part of the empire's life.

[*See also* Luther, Martin; Moritz of Saxony; Philipp of Hesse; *and* Schmalkald War.]

BIBLIOGRAPHY

Brady, Thomas A., Jr. "Jacob Sturm and the Lutherans at the Diet of Augsburg, 1530." *Church History* 42 (1973), 183–202.

———. "Princes' Reformation vs. Urban Liberty: Strasbourg and the Restoration of Duke Ulrich in Württemberg, 1534." In *Städtische Gesellschaft und Reformation,* edited by Ingrid Bátori, pp. 265–291. Stuttgart, 1980.

———. "Phases and Strategies of the Schmalkaldic League: A Perspective after 450 Years." *Archive for Reformation History* 74 (1983), 162–182.

———. "A Crisis Averted: Jacob Sturm and the Truce of Frankfurt, 1539." In *Krisenbewußtsein und Krisenbewältigung in der Frühen Neuzeit: Festschrift für Hans-Christoph Rublack,* edited by Monika Hagenmaier and Sabine Holtz. Frankfurt a.M., 1992.

———. *Protestant Politics: Jacob Sturm, 1489–1553, and the German Reformation.* Studies in German History. Atlantic Highlands, N.J., 1994.

Dueck, A. J. "Religion and Politics in the Reformation: Philipp of Hesse and the Consolidation and Expansion of German Protestantism, 1531–1536." Ph.D. diss., Duke University, 1971.

———. "Religion and Temporal Authority in the Reformation: The Controversy among the Protestants prior to the Peace of Nuremberg, 1532." *Sixteenth Century Journal* 13.2 (1982), 55–74.

Fischer-Galati, Stephen A. "Ottoman Imperialism and the Religious Peace of Nürnberg." *Archiv für Reformationsgeschichte* 47 (1956), 160–180.

———. *Ottoman Imperialism and German Protestantism, 1521–1555.* Harvard Historical Monographs, vol. 43. Reprint, New York, 1972.

Fraenkel, Pierre. "Utraquism or Co-existence: Some Notes on the Earliest Negotiations before the Pacification of Nuremberg, 1531–1532." *Studia theologica* 18 (1964), 119–158.

Grimm, Harold J. *Lazarus Spengler: A Lay Leader of the Reformation.* Columbus, Ohio, 1978.

THOMAS A. BRADY, JR.

SCHMALKALD WAR.

Fought between July 1546 and April 1547, the Schmalkald War was a military manifestation of a complex political and religious struggle between Holy Roman Emperor Charles V and the Protestant princes of Germany. The underlying cause of the conflict was Charles's efforts to bring the princes of the Schmalkald League to heel on religious matters. The proximate cause was the unacceptability to the league of the conditions under which Charles convened the Diet of Regensburg, 5 June 1546.

The military threat posed by the Ottoman Turks and Valois France had long constrained Charles in his dealings with the Protestant princes. Then in 1544 and 1546 he negotiated truces with France and the Turks that freed his hands; against this backdrop he called the Diet of Regensburg.

Charles approached the Protestants with a sophisticated mixture of force and diplomacy. He laid the groundwork for his strategy by securing a substantial contribution of troops from the pope and secretly negotiating their free passage through the territories of Duke William of Bavaria. Charles's hole card was Duke Moritz of Saxony, who had left the league in 1542, believing that he could retain religious maneuvering room within the political framework of the Empire. Playing on tensions between Ducal and Electoral Saxony, Charles secured Moritz's support in the struggle to come.

For all his careful preparations, Charles was caught off balance by the league's resort to war. The forces of the league, commanded jointly by John Frederick, Elector of Saxony, and Philipp of Hesse—an arrangement that proved thoroughly unsatisfactory—initially enjoyed major advantages in numbers and position, for Charles was isolated in Regensburg with a small force of Spanish and German regulars while the league enjoyed a surfeit of mercenaries recently released from French service. The league also had the services of a competent field commander in the form of the mercenary captain Sebastian Schertlin von Burtenbach. For his part, Charles was well served by his general, Fernando Álvarez de Toledo, duke of Alba. A master logistician respected by his troops, the duke of Alba was the first commander of his day to grasp the meaning of the revolution in field warfare that had taken place in the Wars of Italy. As the marques del Vasto had demonstrated in disastrous defeat at Ceresole in 1544, the devastating power and limited mobility of the new infantry formations that combined the shock effect of massed pikemen and halberdiers with the missile power of gunpowder shoulder arms made battle a risky business.

The war had four distinct phases. In the first Charles abandoned Regensburg and outmaneuvered the Protestants to effect a junction with the papal reinforcement and a force from the Netherlands under the count of Buren. He was assisted in this by the timorousness of the Protestant princes, who withdrew Schertlin when he was on the verge of blocking the passage of the Italian reinforcement through the Alps and defeating it in detail. The second was a war of maneuver along the upper Danube lasting through October in which Charles and the duke of Alba avoided battle, exhausting Protestant patience and fiscal resources. The third phase was initiated by Moritz with an attack on John Frederick's domains, causing the league's force to disband for the winter and initiating a civil war in which John Frederick more than held his own, overrunning most of Moritz's domains and defeating an imperial relief force under Albert of Culmbach. In the fourth and decisive phase, the duke of Alba and Charles, after reducing the southern Protestants during the winter, joined forces with Moritz to move against John Frederick. The imperial force took the field early, Philipp of Hesse remained quiescent, and John Frederick misjudged the danger to him and moved south. This situation gave Charles and the duke of Alba their chance. Recognizing his error, John Frederick retreated north, interposing the Elbe between himself and the Imperial force, but the duke of Alba discovered a ford and his infantry forced their way across under fire at daybreak on 24 April. They were shortly followed by the rest of the imperial host and found the Protestants strung out in retreat. The result, termed the Battle of Mühlberg, was a slaughter. Although the Protestant infantry fought well, they were all but annihilated and John Frederick was captured.

Protestant resistance collapsed in the wake of Mühlberg. Both John Frederick and Philipp of Hesse were stripped of their domains. Moritz was installed as ruler of all Saxony and Charles restored the appearance of religious conformity with the publication of the Augsburg Interim. Traditionally regarded as an inconclusive affair that reflected credit on no one, the Schmalkald War was in fact a triumph for Charles, albeit a short-lived one, for the Reformation was too far advanced to be contained, a point made by Moritz's subsequent return to the Protestant fold.

[*See also* Augsburg, Peace of; Holy Roman Empire; Moritz of Saxony; Philipp of Hesse; *and* Schmalkald League.]

BIBLIOGRAPHY

Bumgarten, H. "Zur Geschichte des Schmalkaldischen Kriegs." *Historische Zeitschrift* 67(1876), 26–82.

Brandi, Karl. *The Emperor Charles V: The Growth and Destiny of a Man and an Empire.* Translated by C. V. Wedgewood. Reprint, Atlantic Highlands, N.J., 1980.

Maltby, William S. *Alba: A Biography of Fernando Alvares de Toledo, Third Duke of Alba, 1507–1582.* Los Angeles, 1983.

Oman, Charles. *A History of the Art of War in the Sixteenth Century.* Reprint, London, 1987.

JOHN F. GUILMARTIN

SCHNEIDER, Johann. *See* Agricola, Johann.

SCHNEPF, Erhard (1495–1558), Lutheran theologian and churchman. Best known for his work in the reform of Württemberg under Duke Ulrich, Schnepf was active in all phases of the Lutheran Reformation in Germany. He exemplifies those reformers who left an imprint more by virtue of their spirited commitment and personal influence than as primary shapers of doctrine and policy.

Born to an artisan family in Heilbronn, Schnepf was a student of theology at Heidelberg when Luther appeared there to defend his new theology in 1518. Within two years he had joined the ranks of young humanist scholars who took up Luther's cause as evangelical preachers. While a feisty temperament and the uncertain times combined to rob

Schnepf of a settled existence, he held to his vocation and firm Lutheranism, earning wide respect as a theologian, churchman, and teacher.

In the early 1520s Schnepf held successive preaching posts in Weinsberg, Guttenberg/Neckar, and Wimpfen, from where he was expelled in the conservative reaction following the Peasants' War despite his marriage to the mayor's daughter, Margaretha Wurzelmann. In 1525 he affirmed his accord with Luther by signing Johannes Brenz's *Syngramma Suevicum*, which accepted Luther's (while rejecting Zwingli's) teaching on the Lord's Supper. The following year he worked on the reform of Weilburg at the behest of Philipp of Nassau and took part in the Synod of Homberg. In 1527 Schnepf took a post as professor of theology at the University of Marburg, where he also served as theological adviser to Landgrave Philipp of Hesse, whom he accompanied to the Diets of Speyer and Augsburg.

In 1534 Schnepf was called to reform the duchy of Württemberg along with Ambrosius Blarer, a follower of the Strasbourg theologian Martin Bucer. Schnepf and Blarer managed to compromise their differences in establishing a form of Protestantism in Württemberg that followed Brenz's concept of a centralized state church and was strictly Lutheran in theology, while leaning more to the south German Protestants in adopting a simple sermon-centered service and discarding such Catholic vestiges as the use of Latin and the surplice.

In preparation for the Colloquy of Hagenau of 1540 Schnepf drew up a statement of basic doctrinal disagreements between Catholics and Protestants that was published in 1545 under the sponsorship of Philipp Melanchthon. In 1544 Schnepf was named professor of theology at the University of Tübingen, but in 1548 his resolute stand against the Interim forced him into exile. He accepted a chair in Hebrew at the University of Jena, where he also preached and acted as superintendent for pastoral appointments.

In his last years Schnepf was drawn into the controversies that divided Lutherans as Wittenberg's authority was challenged by theologians at other Protestant universities. He sided with the Gnesio-Lutherans against his old friends Melanchthon and Brenz, and died under suspicion of doctrinal laxity.

BIBLIOGRAPHY

Brecher. "Schnepf, Erhard." In *Allgemeine Deutsche Biographie*, pp. 168–172. Berlin, 1891. The most comprehensive of the brief surveys available.

Ehmer, Hermann. "Erhard Schnepf: Ein Lebensbild." *Blätter für Württembergische Kirchengeschichte* 87 (1987).

Hartmann, Julius. *Erhard Schnepff, der Reformator in Schwaben, Nassau, Hessen und Thüringen*. Tübingen. 1870. A substantial but outdated biography.

Rauscher, Julius. *Württembergische Reformationsgeschichte*. Stuttgart, 1934.

Schottenloher, Karl, ed. *Bibliographie zur deutschen Geschichte im Zeitalter der Glaubensspaltung*. Stuttgart, 1957.

Verzeichnis der im deutschen Sprachbereich erschienenen Drucke des XVI. Jahrhunderts. Stuttgart, 1983–. See vol. 18, nos. 3314–3323.

KARIN BRINKMANN BROWN

SCHOLASTICISM. The term *Scholasticism*, along with a group of related terms, owes its origins to the agenda of the later Renaissance. Humanist writers, concerned with undermining the intellectual and cultural credibility of the period now known as the Middle Ages, developed a vocabulary designed to discredit it. The term *Middle Ages* began to emerge in the early sixteenth century in writers such as Joachim Vadian and Beatus Rhenanus, who intended it to be viewed as little more than an interval between the intellectual and cultural glories of classical antiquity and those of the Renaissance. Similarly, within humanist circles by the dawn of the sixteenth century, *scholastici* appears to have become a term of abuse implying a petty or restricted worldview and methodology. This vocabulary of abuse appears to have been designed to reinforce the general Renaissance trend toward marginalizing Scholasticism as an outdated and insignificant movement, that need not be taken seriously in the sixteenth century.

It is therefore important to appreciate that the term *Scholasticism* is laden with ideological baggage. Its continued use in scholarship seems assured given the widespread acceptance it has gained within the secondary literature; for this reason the original negative associations and connotations of the term need to be borne in mind.

There are two major reasons why Reformation historians are concerned with Scholasticism. First, an understanding of Scholasticism is of crucial importance to an appreciation of the intellectual origins of the Reformation. Methodological and theological developments within late medieval Scholasticism are known to have been of major significance in shaping the mind-set of a number of reformers, perhaps most importantly that of Martin Luther. The scholarly community's increasing concern with envisaging the Reformation in its broader intellectual context necessitates an engagement with the forms of Scholasticism current within western Europe, especially at such universities as Erfurt, Heidelberg, Paris, and Tübingen, on the eve of the Reformation.

Second, the early phase of the Reformation often involved a direct polemical engagement with Scholasticism at a number of levels. Of these, the most significant was an attack on the theological method of Scholasticism (especially its alleged overdependence upon Aristotle and its neglect of scripture) and on certain of its leading doctrines. A full understanding of the approaches and intended targets of the polemical literature of the early Reformation thus presupposes at least a degree of acquaintance with Scholasticism.

Defining Scholasticism. Scholasticism is an elusive term resistant to precise definition. The polemical origins of the term are partly to blame for this imprecision; however, the intellectual diversity within the movement is also a contributing cause. Despite these difficulties, there are several general characteristics sufficient to define the various components of the movement.

Scholasticism was concerned with the rational justification of Christian belief and, in particular, with demonstrating the inherent rationality of theology. It is generally thought that this aspect of the movement is seen at its best in the later writings of Thomas Aquinas, especially the *Summa theologiae*. Even William of Ockham, who emphasized the distinction between *ratio* and *fides*, made extensive use of reason in matters of theology.

In its earlier phase the movement made extensive use of Aristotelianism, and this trend can be seen clearly in the writings of Dominican theologians of the late thirteenth century. Aristotelianism, however, was treated in this manner because it was believed to represent a mature and universally valid set of rational assumptions to which any intellectual discipline (*scientia*) should conform. A significant internal debate developed within later Scholasticism about the intellectual credentials of Aristotelianism as growing evidence of intra- and extra-systemic inconsistency emerged, not least on account of the development of the still nascent natural sciences. By the early sixteenth century there was a growing recognition of the shortcomings of Aristotle.

Scholasticism was also concerned with the systematization of Christian theology. Earlier works of theology were often occasional, written in response to controversies or debates and hence limited by the specific shape of the polemical stimulus. The anti-Pelagian writings of Augustine, upon which the Reformation drew with such enthusiasm, are an excellent example of this form of limitation. Scholasticism was concerned with developing a proactive, rather than reactive, approach to theology by anticipating possible questions or objections to existing doctrines.

This systematic approach to theology was encouraged by the publication of Peter Lombard's *Sententiarum libri quattuor*, which offered a comprehensive framework for the discussion of the central questions of theology. These "four books of the sentences" (that is, quotations from the writings of the patristic era, especially from the writings of Augustine) were systematically arranged, thus bringing an order to the material that was generally lacking in their original contexts. The proliferation of commentaries upon these *Sentences*, not to mention the formal importance of such a commentary as a qualification for the advanced teaching of theology, ensured that the scholastic mind-set was characterized by a conviction of the propriety and necessity of such systematization.

Types of Scholasticism. Scholasticism was a heterogeneous movement. Even during the thirteenth century significant divergences became evident within the movement, as may be seen by comparing the writings of Thomas, Bonaventura, and John Duns Scotus, representing, respectively, the characteristic approaches of the early Dominican school, the early Franciscan school, and the later Franciscan school.

By the late medieval period at least nine major schools of thought had developed within the movement, reflecting considerable diversity in both methods and doctrines. Two of these schools were especially important in the Reformation: the *via moderna*, which designates the school deriving from William of Ockham, whose leading late medieval representative was the Tübingen theologian Gabriel Biel; and a loose body of opinion or theological tendency, though not a "school" in the strict sense of the word, that favored more radically Augustinian approaches to the doctrines of justification and predestination. This tendency, sometimes referred to as the *schola Augustiniana moderna*, is associated with such writers as Gregory of Rimini. It occurs, however, in a number of different forms that are not readily susceptible to categorization. The nature and extent of the influence that these two forms of Scholasticism exercised over the theological development of the Reformation—especially in relation to Luther and John Calvin—has continued to be the subject of considerable disagreement.

Four issues were of particular importance in Scholasticism. First, there was the debate between positions that have come to be known as realism and terminism. Writers of the earlier medieval period (including Thomas and Duns Scotus) were committed to realism. This position, clearly influenced by Platonism, acknowledged the existence of universal qualities (such as a universal human nature, which is instantiated in individual human beings). The fourteenth century witnessed the development of a rival position, initially through the influence of William of Ockham, that is generally referred to as terminism or nominalism and entailed the rejection of such universal qualities. According to this position, there is no such thing as a universal human nature; the term *humanity* designates individual humans, not a universal quality that lies behind such individuals. (It should be stressed that the term *nominalism* should be used only to refer to this terminist position. Its use in earlier secondary sources to designate the theological views of such writers as William of Ockham or Gabriel Biel is seriously misleading.) By the time of the Reformation, terminism had gained considerable influence and can be seen echoed in the writings of Luther and others.

Second, there was conflict between logico-critical and historico-critical approaches to theology. In its earlier period Scholasticism tended to assume that theology proceeded by the rational analysis of foundational texts, such as the writings of Augustine. By more precise definition of central terms (such as *gratia*), order could be brought to what at first sight seemed an occasionally inconsistent set of beliefs. In the later medieval period, especially owing to the influence of Ockham, increased use came to be made of the logical tool of the "dialectic between the two powers of God" to clarify such points of interpretation. This approach, however, came to be regarded with suspicion, and some argued that the only appropriate way of dealing with these difficulties was by gaining access to the full text of such writers as Augustine (instead of the isolated extracts of the *Sentences*), and interpreting them within their historical context. This latter consideration was one of the factors that fueled production of critical editions of the works of Augustine and others and may be regarded as having made a major contribution to the origins of the Reformation.

Third, tension existed between the positions of intellectualism and voluntarism. Earlier scholastic writers, such as Thomas and Bonaventura, stressed the priority of the divine intellect over the will. Thus, in the case of human merit, the divine intellect recognizes the morality of a human act and informs the divine will to reward it accordingly. From Duns Scotus onward, the emphasis came to be placed upon the divine will. In the case of merit, the divine will determines the value to be placed upon the human moral action and rewards it accordingly. The intellectualist position is rejected as making God dependent upon created entities. This new emphasis upon the divine will can also be discerned in the increasing sympathy evident for more predestinarian modes of thought, such as those associated with Gregory of Rimini or Hugolino of Orvieto, on the eve of the Reformation. Calvin is an excellent example of a Reformation theologian who appears to have been deeply influenced by this new trend toward voluntarism, evident in his discussion of the grounds of the merit of Christ and his doctrine of predestination.

Finally, there were tensions relating to the doctrine of justification. Perhaps the most important debate within Scholasticism to relate to the Reformation concerned the manner in which human beings find acceptance in the sight of God. Two radically different approaches may be discerned. Writers of the *via moderna*, such as Biel, developed many of the ideas of the later Franciscan school, laying emphasis upon the positive human contribution to justification. Human beings are able to make the foundational response to the divine offer of grace by which they are accepted into the divine favor. This view, which finds its expression in the early writings of Luther, is diametrically opposed to that of such writers as Gregory of Rimini, who stressed the total priority and absolute necessity of grace at every stage in justification.

Luther eventually came to regard the views of the *via moderna* as Pelagian. His 1517 *Disputatio contra scholasticam theologiam* is actually a sustained diatribe against the views of Biel, chiefly as they concern the doctrine of justification. It is not clear, however, whether Luther's new respect for Augustinianism reflects an acquaintance with writings of scholastic authors sympathetic to this viewpoint or whether it emerged from a direct engagement with the anti-Pelagian writings of Augustine, which became readily available at the end of the first decade of the sixteenth century.

The Reformation Attitude toward Scholasticism. The predominant attitude within the early Reformation toward Scholasticism can perhaps best be described as a studied indifference. This attitude, which mirrors that of Renaissance humanism in general, treats the movement as something not worthy of being taken seriously. Reformers sympathetic to the Renaissance outlook—such as Philipp Melanchthon, Huldrych Zwingli, and Vadian—are generally dismissive of the petty views of the *scholastici*. Others, however, including both Luther and Calvin, deemed the movement worth criticizing. It must be stressed that the evidence strongly suggests that Luther's attitudes toward Scholasticism were conditioned by his familiarity with the movement in its late fourteenth- and fifteenth-century forms; he shows little awareness of its thirteenth-century embodiments, including the form associated with Thomas.

Luther's main criticisms are methodological and may be summarized into four general categories. First, the movement fails to do justice to human experience. Its excessively rational character fails to engage with the experiential aspects of the Christian faith. Luther's existential approach to faith contrasts sharply with the more detached and analytic approach of Scholasticism.

Second, Scholasticism places excessive emphasis upon the role of human reason. Luther occasionally suggests a parallel between the scholastic emphasis upon reason and the confidence in human soteriological resources associated with the *via moderna*.

Third, a related criticism concerns the priority given to Aristotelianism. For Luther the Scholastics allowed Aristotle to dominate theology with unbiblical assumptions and outlooks. In part this reflects Luther's deep suspicion of Aristotle's ethics, which he regarded as severely detrimental to a right understanding of the doctrine of justification.

Fourth, Scholasticism fails to do justice to scripture. This criticism is echoed throughout the Reformation and parallels the humanist determination to return *ad fontes*. Luther argues that Scholasticism detaches the Christian faith from its roots in scripture by interposing successive layers of interpretative glosses, hermeneutical devices, and philosophical assumptions between the text and its readers. The task of theology is to return directly to the scriptural text.

In addition to this, Luther engages in sustained polemic against a number of doctrines associated with scholastic writers. Most notable are the notion of *fides informis* and the doctrine of justification associated with Biel.

The Reemergence of Scholasticism within the Late Reformation. Despite the strongly antischolastic mind-set of the early Reformation, the later sixteenth century witnessed a revival of interest in the movement and a new appreciation of its potential role in consolidating and stabilizing the theological achievements of the Reformation. The emergence of Scholasticism, initially within the Reformed and subsequently within Lutheran theological circles, is of considerable interest.

The fundamental motivation for this development appears to have been defensive. Reformed writers such as Théodore de Bèze, were concerned with demonstrating the inherent rationality of the Reformed faith in the light of increasing attacks upon it by both Lutheran and Roman Catholic opponents. The new trend toward systematization, evident within Reformed theology from 1570 onward, reflects a new appreciation of the potential of scholastic approaches in the unstable political conditions of the period. Although full discussion of this development lies beyond the scope of this article, it is interesting to note how a movement initially opposed to Scholasticism eventually resorted to its methods in an attempt to preserve and safeguard the hard-won insights of the first generation of the Reformation.

BIBLIOGRAPHY

Gilson, Étienne. *History of Christian Philosophy in the Middle Ages.* London, 1978.

McGrath, Alister E. "John Calvin and Late Medieval Thought." *Archiv für Reformationsgeschichte* 77 (1986), 58–78.

———. *The Intellectual Origins of the European Reformation.* Oxford, 1987.

Nauert, Charles G. "The Clash of Humanists and Scholastics." *Sixteenth Century Journal* 4.1 (1973), 1–18.

Oberman, Heiko A. *Masters of the Reformation: The Emergence of a New Intellectual Climate.* Cambridge, 1981.

———. *The Harvest of Late Medieval Theology.* 3d ed. Durham, N.C. 1983.

Overfeld, James. "Scholastic Opposition to Humanism in Pre-Reformation Germany." *Viator* 7 (1976), 391–420.

Pieper, Joseph. *Scholasticism: Personalities and Problems of Medieval Philosophy.* London, 1960.

Steinmetz, David C. *Luther and Staupitz: An Essay in the Intellectual Origins of the Protestant Reformation.* Durham, N.C., 1980.

ALISTER E. McGRATH

SCHOOL ORDINANCES. Issued by Protestant governments in Germany, school ordinances (Ger., *Schulordnungen*) were codes of regulations for the organization and operation of schools and part of an effort to reconstruct the religious, moral, and civic order in Protestant realms. The aim of improving education, a salient objective of Lutheran authorities from the 1520s, arose in part from the impact on formal schooling of the widespread acceptance of a scripture-based creed in Protestant cities and territories, as well as from the reforming impulse intrinsic to the Reformation. Amid signs that traditional learning was falling victim to the early Reformation's evangelical thrust, Martin Luther in 1524 appealed *An die Ratsherren aller Städte . . . dass sie christliche Schuler aufrichten und halten sollen* (To the Councillors of All German Cities . . . That They Must Establish and Maintain Christian Schools; WA 15:9–53; LW 45:341–78), charging secular governments with the pro-

motion of institutions of learning as an aspect of their responsibility to the common welfare and inviting them to give newly established or refurbished schools a fresh look by undertaking curricular reform, for "we live in a different world now, and things are not as they were before" (WA 15:46–47). Official responses to this invitation gained urgency from a mass of troubling data concerning actual conditions in church and society, which was obtained in the course of visitations conducted by Protestant governments everywhere in Germany beginning in the mid-1520s. The result of these discoveries and of the decision to rectify the many shortcomings brought to light were *Kirchenordnungen*, comprehensive charters reorganizing the church and religious life in a city or territory. School ordinances were a major component of these charters, a large number of which were published in Protestant Germany in the sixteenth and seventeenth centuries. In their broad scope and their meticulous attention to detail, they are a characteristic expression of the Lutheran way of reform.

School ordinances were intended to achieve several interrelated objectives. First, teaching and learning were to be made methodical; toward that end pedagogical goals and procedures were clearly stated, as were the criteria of competence expected of pupils and teachers. The plan of studies was laid down subject by subject and hour by hour, textbooks were listed, and frequent examinations were set. Second, curriculum and methods were to be made as uniform as possible within the political boundaries of a city or territory. Third, religion, in the form of officially sanctioned Lutheranism, was to be a major subject of study, with the catechism the favored instrument of instruction. Fourth, all learning was to include training in mental and behavioral decorum and discipline (*Zucht*). *Zucht* was in an important sense the defining goal of the educational effort. Fifth, schooling was to advance the cause of liberal studies: throughout the Reformation period the concern of educators was preeminently with the Latin school and its traditional humanist course of studies. Though most government-sponsored school ordinances also provided for "German schools," in which instruction was kept to basic literacy and rote memorization of the catechism, true learning always meant familiarity with the corpus of classical texts, most of which were in Latin. Sixth and overall, schooling at every level was to be closely linked to the purposes of the Christian territorial or urban state; in this way the educational policies of Lutheran governments became part of the process of early modern state building.

For the accomplishment of all these objectives, school ordinances and the bureaucratic organs created to put them into action were effective tools. The earliest codes appeared as chapters in urban and territorial church constitutions (e.g., at Stralsund in 1525, at Hall in 1526, and at Hessen in 1526). Of greatest importance to the subsequent development of schooling in Germany was Philipp Melanchthon's

Unterricht der Visitatoren an die Pfarrherrn im Kurfürstentum Sachsen (Instruction for the Visitors of Parish Pastors in the Electorate of Saxony) of 1528, a blueprint for a reconstituted church. Its concluding section offered a brief plan for a Latin school of three forms (*Haufen* in German; the term *class*, taken from Quintilian, was introduced by Desiderius Erasmus in 1519) to teach, along with religion, the traditional subjects of the humanist Trivium, with strong emphasis on language and with the task of identifying and advancing able pupils as one of the school's chief objects. Many school ordinances followed this model and elaborated it—for instance, at Wittenberg in 1533; at Hanover in 1537; and at Mecklenburg in 1552. The most highly developed ordinance of this kind was the great *Schulordnung* of the duchy of Württemberg, which, following extensive preparatory work undertaken in a series of visitations, was promulgated as part of a long and detailed church constitution in 1559. It clearly defined the chief purpose of schooling, which was to train men capable of serving effectively as preachers, administrators, and heads of households. Only Latin schools could provide the necessary qualifications for these roles. All schools in the land had to follow the uniform teaching program set by the ordinance for local schools of five classes (two classes in villages), with emphasis everywhere on language study, discipline, and the inculcation of the fear of God. The ordinance also provided for "monastery schools"—former regular houses turned into seminaries—for the training of teachers and ministers and set requirements for rigorous testing of their competence and doctrinal reliability. It assured compliance by means of periodic inspections, giving supervision of the entire system to members of the duke's *Kirchenrat*, or consistory, although financing remained in the main a local responsibility. Only in its final section does the ordinance mention "German schools" for the instruction of the broad public, female as well as male, in simple literacy and basic religion. Other comprehensive school ordinances of this type were issued by Pomerania in 1563, Brunswick in 1569, Brandenburg in 1573, electoral Saxony in 1580, and Strasbourg in 1598. (A representative selection of texts is printed in Vormbaum, *Evangelische Schulordnungen*.)

In their pedagogical principles and methods, later ordinances were strongly influenced by the example of one of the most eminent educators of the time, Johannes Sturm, who reorganized the schools of the city of Strasbourg in the 1530s and whose *De literarum ludis recte aperiendi liber* of 1538 and *Classicarum epistolarum libri III* of 1565 helped set the direction of much of the Reformation's educational program, particularly as graduates of his school became teachers and rectors of Latin schools throughout Germany. Sturm also left his imprint on schools in Catholic territories (as Melanchthon had done earlier), where *Schulordnungen* were issued with the same purpose and to the same effect as in Protestant lands. The educational effort represented by school ordinances, however, benefited not just institutions of humanist learning. Though it had not been the intention of the early reformers to do so, vernacular schools proliferated in the course of the sixteenth and seventeenth centuries (up to the Thirty Years' War), as governments—Catholic as well as Protestant—began to see in popular elementary schools (regulated and supervised as parts of a centrally administered educational enterprise) an instrument for the inculcation of desirable and, to the extent possible, uniform mental and behavioral traits in the populace. As reading, at least to the level of Luther's Small Catechism, was taught in every school, literacy must have increased as a result, though the extent to which this actually happened among the German public is virtually impossible to ascertain statistically. What is clear is that both secular and church authorities began in the sixteenth and early seventeenth century to see schools as an important instrument of social policy with which to attempt to mold the lives of their citizens. School ordinances declared the principles of this attempt and set the procedures for implementing them.

[*See also* Catechisms; Education; *and* Literacy.]

BIBLIOGRAPHY

Goebel, Klaus, ed. *Luther in der Schule*. Bochum, 1985.
Hettwer, Hubert. *Herkunft und Zusammenhang der Schulordnungen: Eine vergleichende Studie*. Mainz, 1965.
Mertz, Georg Karl. *Das Schulwesen der deutschen Reformation*. Heidelberg, 1902.
Sohm, Walter. *Die Schule Johann Sturms und die Kirche Straßburgs*. Munich, 1912.
Strauss, Gerald. *Luther's House of Learning: Indoctrination of the Young in the German Reformation*. Baltimore, 1978.
Vormbaum, Reinhold. *Die evangelischen Schulordnungen des 16. Jahrhunderts*. Gütersloh, 1860.

GERALD STRAUS

SCHOOLS AND SCHOOLING, *See* Education; Literacy; Universities.

SCHÜRER, Erasmus. *See* Sarcerius, Erasmus.

SCHWARZERDT, Philip. *See* Melanchthon, Philipp.

SCHWENCKFELD, Kaspar von (also Caspar; 1489–1561), German noble and radical spiritualist reformer. Born on the family estate of Ossig in Lower Silesia, Schwenckfeld studied at Cologne (1505), Frankfurt an der Oder (1507), and other universities, though, like most students, he took no degree. In 1510 he began a career as a courtier in Silesia, but already in 1519, in response to Martin Luther's message, Schwenckfeld had undergone the first of several divine visitations (*Heimsuchung*) that were to determine the course of his life. By 1521 he had assumed leadership of the young Lutheran movement in Silesia, and by 1522 he had won over his then employer Duke Frederick of Legnica. In 1524 the Catholic bishop of Wrocław withdrew into his own principality, and the secular rulers seized control of their local churches. By that time, however, Schwenckfeld's religious views were undergoing a change. Retiring to his country estate at Ossig in 1523 because of increasing hearing loss, he immersed himself in reading and study. He became a representative of the rural nobility and was increasingly concerned with the role that the secular rulers had begun to play in the Protestant movement. He was even more disturbed by what he took to be the moral and religious effects of the Lutheran message. In 1524 he complained that inept preachers had misrepresented Luther's teachings on justification by faith alone, the bondage of the will, and predestination, thereby producing fatalism and antinomianism among nobles and peasants alike. In effect, Schwenckfeld used Luther's theology to criticize the effects of the Lutheran movement.

By 1525 Schwenckfeld had clearly begun to leave the Lutheran fold. Dismayed by the eucharistic controversy that was beginning to divide the reform movement, Schwenckfeld experienced a second *Heimsuchung*, as a result of which he rejected Luther's teaching of the real presence of Christ in the bread and wine. Schwenckfeld's own position, however, differed greatly from those of Andreas Bodenstein von Karlstadt and Huldrych Zwingli, Luther's earliest opponents on the issue. Whereas they had appealed to *John* 6:63 ("the Flesh profits nothing,"), Schwenckfeld proceeded from the diametrically opposite principle (based on *John* 6:35, 6:55, 6:58) that Christ's body and blood were the bread of life that conveyed salvation. Since it was obvious that not all who partook of the bread and wine were saved (the test case was Judas at the Last Supper), Schwenckfeld concluded that there could be no real presence in the material elements of the Eucharist. Schwenckfeld turned to his closest colleague in Legnica, the humanist Valentin Crautwald, for help in interpreting the words of institution (*Mt.* 26:26; *Mk.* 14:22; *Lk.* 22:19), "This is my body." In a vision Crautwald learned that the passage should be understood to mean "My body is this, a food for the soul." Schwenckfeld visited Wittenberg in 1525 to plead their case, but in 1526 Luther condemned it and branded Schwenckfeld and Crautwald as *Schwärmer* ("fanatics") and Sacramentarians. By then, however, they had already begun to follow their own path. Convinced that the bulk of believers were so poorly informed about the Christian faith as to be little more than pagans, the Legnica reformers began a program of popular instruction, for which Crautwald produced the first Protestant catechism. They also announced (1526) the suspension (*Stillstand*) of the Lord's Supper. Schwenckfeld never again partook of the Lord's Supper, and the Sacrament was

reinstated by the Schwenkfelder church only in the nineteenth century. In the years 1525 to 1527 Schwenckfeld's theology became increasingly spiritualistic under the influence of events and the tutelage of Crautwald. These developments produced a third *Heimsuchung* (1527), as a result of which Schwenckfeld openly broke with Luther, accusing him of having become a prisoner of the external word and sacraments. Schwenckfeld now pursued, along with the other Legnica reformers, an avowedly "spiritual" Reformation, but the political situation in Silesia was deteriorating for Schwenckfeld. In 1529, taking advantage of the inopportune publication by Zwingli of one of Schwenckfeld's books, the Catholics and Lutherans were able to force Schwenckfeld's departure. Though not officially exiled, Schwenckfeld was never to return to his homeland.

Schwenckfeld moved to Strasbourg, a place of refuge for many religious dissidents in the 1520s. He was welcomed as a confessor of the faith and lodged with Wolfgang Capito, one of the leaders of the new church there. He found many admirers among the ruling elite of the city. The dissident community attracted him, and he was active among the Anabaptists, who were especially numerous. Nonetheless, he refused to join any of the sects or to openly accept the official church of the city. Despite Schwenckfeld's politic silence, Martin Bucer, Strasbourg's leading cleric, recognized that Schwenckfeld posed a threat to the authority of the new state church in the city. Schwenckfeld's appearance at the Strasbourg Synod (3–14 June 1533), which was designed to convict him of rejecting the new church order, failed to accomplish Bucer's purpose. Even so, in 1534 Schwenckfeld finally left Strasbourg at the unofficial request of the city council in order to pacify the clergy. Since he was not officially banned, Schwenckfeld visited the city occasionally and discreetly. In 1535 Schwenckfeld established his base in Ulm. Bucer and his allies, particularly Martin Frecht, the leading pastor of Ulm, continued to attack Schwenckfeld in public and private. Eventually Frecht was able to force Schwenckfeld to leave Ulm in September 1539. Once again Schwenckfeld was not officially banned; he left in order to alleviate the political pressure on his friends and allies. In March 1540 a conference of theologians meeting at Schmalkald under the presidency of Philipp Melanchthon condemned Schwenckfeld's teachings at the urging of Bucer and Frecht. In 1541 Schwenckfeld took up residence with the noble family von Freyberg at their estate of Justingen some 20 kilometers from Ulm. During his six years there he wrote more than fifty books and five hundred letters. He also traveled constantly, visiting friends, allies, and followers all over southern Germany. This brought him into conflict in 1541–1542 with the Anabaptist leader Pilgram Marpeck, with whom he competed for disciples. Schwenckfeld had to flee Justingen in 1549, when Catholic forces, victorious in the Schmalkald War, seized it. He found refuge for a time in the Franciscan convent in Esslingen under the name

Eliander. The reestablishment of Protestant state churches after the Treaty of Passau (1552) saw Schwenckfeld officially banned in Württemberg (1554) and the Palatinate (1556). His followers were also pressured in Augsburg and Ulm. Schwenckfeld conducted his last major controversy (1553–1559) with Matthias Flacius Illyricus over the role of the Bible and the preached word. He died in Ulm on 10 December 1561.

Schwenckfeld's theology is the product of his experience of God's direct intervention in his life (*Heimsuchungen*) and his disappointment with the moral fruits of Protestantism. Elaborating on his initial insights into the Lord's Supper, Schwenckfeld's eucharistic theology became the template for all his later teachings. Jesus Christ, the incarnated logos and living word, had assumed human flesh in order to renew it. Through his passion, death, resurrection, and glorification, Christ's human flesh was spiritualized and deified. Schwenckfeld's speculations about Christ resulted in a distinctive Christology, that of the *heavenly flesh*, a term used to describe the Christologies of a number of radicals (e.g., Melchior Hoffman, Menno Simons, and Clemens Ziegler). Initially Schwenckfeld taught that the process of glorification had spiritualized the human nature of Christ so that he was no longer a creature. Influenced by Michael Servetus and Sebastian Franck, Schwenckfeld concluded in 1538 that Christ had never been a creature but had always been the Son of God in both his human and divine natures. Fallen humans are saved when a particle of this heavenly flesh is engrafted, a process which brings about a rebirth. The new Christian is in reality two human beings—one new, inner, and spiritual, the other old, outer, and fleshly. The Christian is thus different on both metaphysical and moral planes. The implantation of Christ's heavenly flesh takes place without any external or human mediators. It incorporates the Christian into Christ and, through Christ, into the Godhead. Such externals as the sacraments, the Bible, or the preached word play no role in rebirth. They serve merely to reflect and describe the inner rebirth. The Lord's Supper is a symbolic representation of the prevenient "inner supper." Since water baptism has no meaning without "inner baptism," Schwenckfeld inclined toward believers' baptism. Even so, he rejected Anabaptist rebaptism because he thought it placed too much weight upon the external ritual. Many Schwenckfelders suspended the use of baptism or postponed the baptism of their children as long as possible. Schwenckfeld also carefully distinguished the "inner word" from the "outer." The "inner word," the glorified Christ, works directly in the soul. The "outer word" of scripture and preaching merely points to that "inner word," but does not convey it or augment it. Scripture, the sacraments, and the church as a whole were, for Schwenckfeld, merely aids for the old, outer, fleshly human being in the process of sanctification. Given the direct and unmediated action of Christ in the soul, Schwenckfeld opposed religious coercion,

including all state churches, as senseless. No Christian could advocate coercion without betraying a fundamental misunderstanding of the basic truths of Christianity. In four letters (1533–1534) to Leo Jud of Zurich Schwenckfeld presented the most thorough and visionary argument for religious freedom of the sixteenth century.

Schwenckfeld left behind a numerous following. In Silesia the Schwenckfelders constituted a popular movement embracing whole towns and villages. Lutheran and Catholic persecution slowly reduced their numbers during the sixteenth and seventeenth centuries. In 1734 five hundred emigrated to Pennsylvania, where the Schwenkfelder church has remained. The last Silesian Schwenckfelder died in 1826. Southern Germany also saw a significant Schwenckfelder movement. Urban elites, landed nobility, artisans, and peasants in Strasbourg, Augsburg, Ulm, Württemberg, and elsewhere continued in the movement until the Thirty Years' War. More generally, Schwenckfeld's influence was felt in Holland, in England during the Commonwealth (1649–1660, especially among the Quakers), and in Pietism.

BIBLIOGRAPHY

Primary Sources

Schwenckfeld, Kaspar von. *Von der himmlischen Arzeney.* Allentown, Pa., 1820.
Corpus Schwenckfeldianorum. 19 vols. Leipzig, 1907–1961. The collected works of Schwenckfeld published by the Schwenkfelder church.

Secondary Sources

Erb, Peter C., ed. *Schwenckfeld and Early Schwenkfeldianism.* Papers presented at the Colloquium on Schwenckfeld and the Schwenkfelders, Pennsburg, Pa., September 17–22, 1984. Pennsburg, Pa., 1986. Contains a number of articles about Schwenckfeld and his followers.
Furcha, Edward J. *Schwenckfeld's Concept of the New Man.* Pennsburg, Pa., 1970.
Jones, Rufus M. *Spiritual Reformers in the Sixteenth and Seventeenth Centuries* (1914). Reprint, London 1972.
Loetscher, Frederick William. *Schwenckfeld's Participation in the Eucharistic Controversy of the Sixteenth Century.* Philadelphia, 1906.
Maier, Paul L. *Caspar Schwenckfeld on the Person and Work of Christ: A Study of Schwenckfeldian Theology at Its Core.* Assen, 1959.
McLaughlin, R. Emmet. *Caspar Schwenckfeld: Reluctant Radical.* New Haven and London, 1986. Extensive bibliography.
Schultz, Selina Gerhard. *Caspar Schwenckfeld von Ossig, 1489–1561: Spiritual Interpreter of Christianity, Apostle of the Middle Way, Pioneer of Modern Religious Thought.* 4th ed. Pennsburg, Pa., 1977. A warm appreciation of Schwenckfeld by the editor of the *Corpus Schwenckfeldianorum,* still useful for extensive knowledge of the sources.
Schwenckfeld, Kaspar von. *Passional and Prayer Book.* Translated by John Joseph Stoudt. Pennsburg, Pa., 1961. Schwenckfeld's personal prayer book and meditation on the passion of Christ.
———. *Commentary on the Augsburg Confession.* Translated by Fred A. Grater. Pennsburg, Pa., 1982. Schwenckfeld's point by point criticism of the foundational Protestant confession.
Séguenny, André. *The Christology of Caspar Schwenckfeld.* Lewiston, N.Y., 1987. An attempt to place Schwenckfeld in the Renaissance humanist tradition, but see McLaughin for another view.

Verzeichnis der im deutschen Sprachbereich erschienenen Drucke des XVI. Jahrhunderts. Stuttgart, 1983–. See vol. 18, nos. 4830–5072.

Weigelt, Horst. *The Schwenkfelders in Silesia.* Translated by Peter C. Erb. Pennsburg, Pa., 1985. A remarkable study of the Schwenck-felders in Silesia from the sixteenth to the eighteenth centuries.

Williams, George H. *Spiritual and Anabaptist Writers.* Philadelphia, 1957. Includes a work by Schwenckfeld and an important program-matic statement about the nature of spiritualism in the introduction.

———. *Radical Reformation.* 3d ed. Kirksville, Mo., 1992. Magisterial overview of the entire Radical Reformation.

R. EMMET McLAUGHLIN

SCIENCE. Twenty-six years after Martin Luther's Ninety-five Theses, the Polish canon Nicolaus Copernicus (1473–1543) published an ambitious reform of Ptolemaic astronomy entitled *De revolutionibus orbium coelestium* (On the Revolutions of the Heavenly Spheres; 1543). In it he proposed that the Sun rather than the Earth was the center of the universe. This publication marks the traditional be-ginning of a period of intense intellectual activity known as the scientific revolution. Neither Luther nor Copernicus perceived themselves as radicals when they composed their respective critiques. Rather, they were "reformers" in the initial sense of the word—men dedicated to the purification of institutions that had become corrupted with the passage of time. Just as Luther wished to eliminate religious practices that had diminished the splendor of the Catholic church, Copernicus attempted to restore astronomy to its pristine state by eliminating some of the unwieldy mathematical de-vices used to maintain the Earth as the center of the uni-verse. Arguing for a heliocentric universe was a means of restoring an ancient aesthetic to nature and to mathematical astronomy that had been lost as astronomers had tinkered with small problems rather than addressing the largest is-sues. In this respect Luther and Copernicus had much in common.

There were also many differences. Copernicus never faced the kind of decision that confronted Luther. He died within the fold of the Catholic church, untouched by the furor that his image of a heliocentric universe eventually raised. From this perspective Copernicus should more aptly be compared to the Dutch humanist Desiderius Erasmus (1466–1536), who offered his critique of church practices as a Catholic. Indeed, many scholars have noted the Erasmian tone of *De revolutionibus orbium coelestium,* which attempted to reconcile novelty with tradition. Copernicus dedicated his work to Paul III in the hope that papal patronage would protect it from undue criticism, just as Erasmus dedicated his controversial Latin translation of the New Testament to Leo X in 1517. Copernicus even enlisted the help of a Lu-theran theologian, Andreas Osiander (1496–1552), in the fi-nal preparation of the manuscript for publication, which re-sulted in Osiander's insertion of a preface declaring the entire work to be an interesting hypothesis rather than the literal truth. Osiander hoped to diffuse the controversial message of Copernicus's work, which contradicted the long-standing interpretation of key scriptural passages and almost two thousand years of tradition.

In his own lifetime Copernicus was more successful than Erasmus in finding a middle ground. Explorations of cos-mology indeed touched upon theological issues, but they did not immediately attack the core of Catholic beliefs in the way that the challenges of Erasmus and Protestant reformers did, primarily because they were not initially perceived to threaten the institutional church. Yet despite Copernicus's own orthodoxy and the favor he personally enjoyed under Paul III, by 1616 his name appeared on the Index of Pro-hibited Books, alongside Erasmus, Luther, John Calvin, and other heretical writers. The condemnation of Copernicus's astronomical writings set the stage for the famous trial and condemnation in 1633 of the Florentine mathematician and philosopher Galileo Galilei (1564–1642), who was accused of professing Copernican heresies. While Luther, Erasmus, and Copernicus may have taken dramatically different paths in their own lifetimes, ultimately they were linked together in the pages of the Index, a monument to religious ortho-doxy.

Religious culture provided a particularly important con-text for the emergence of a new scientific culture in the six-teenth century. The Catholic church was not simply an op-positional force for "natural philosophers"—the term most frequently used for early modern scientists—but also a source of patronage and support. In the sixteenth century it was the primary employer of intellectuals outside of the uni-versities. Copernicus was one of many natural philosophers writing from within the institutional church. In fact, the hu-manist culture of the Renaissance church, which sponsored vast translation projects of scientific texts, surely contributed to his abilities to critique Ptolemy's *Almagest.* Giordano Bruno (1548–1600), the first vocal supporter of Copernicus, was a Dominican, as was Tommaso Campanella (1568–1639), the utopian writer who defended Galileo from prison. Diego de Zuñiga (1536–1597), who attempted to reconcile heliocentrism with scripture, was an Augustinian who taught at the University of Salamanca. The university curriculum made the study of natural philosophy a precondition to de-grees in medicine and theology, blurring the distinction be-tween science, medicine, and theology. The German as-tronomer Johannes Kepler (1571–1630) initially intended to take a degree in theology at the University of Tübingen (by then Lutheran), when the offer of a mathematics post in Graz in 1594 interrupted his studies. Copernicus studied medicine as well as canon law in Italy before returning to Poland. The lack of distinction between these different dis-ciplines helps explain not only why so many natural philos-ophers had an interest in theology but also why so many theologians contributed to the investigations of the natural world. Inquiring into the nature of the universe and the place of humans within it was inevitably a process that led to the contemplation of the divine.

Reflecting in 1606 on the scientific developments of the preceding century, Kepler compared the religious Reformation to the contemporaneous renewal of astronomy by Copernicus and the renewal of medicine by the Swiss physician Philippus Aureolus Theophrastus Bombastus von Hohenheim, more commonly known as Paracelsus (1493–1541). Paracelsus was only marginally a member of the medical establishment when he sought its overthrow. Celebrated for his miraculous chemical cures and surgical expertise—he included Erasmus and the Swiss reformer Johannes Oecolampadius (1482–1531) among his patients—Paracelsus offered an alternative to traditional Galenic medicine, in which diagnosis and treatment was conducted according to the balance of the four humors and to the Aristotelian theory of matter that privileged the four elements (earth, water, air, fire). Instead Paracelsus made the "three principles" of salt, sulphur, and mercury the core of his philosophy. Like Kepler, who imagined the Sun as the Father, the sphere of the fixed stars as the Son, and the motive forces of the universe as the Holy Ghost, Paracelsus literally read the Trinity into nature.

In addition to reforming the content of medicine, Paracelsus directly attacked the medical establishment. In a celebrated incident in Basel in 1527, he burned the books of ancient medical authorities, proclaiming them useless for the teaching of medicine. Instead, Paracelsus urged his followers to prepare for their vocation by carefully reading God's two books: nature and scripture. Experience and the word rather than tradition and authority guided the Paracelsian physician. Quickly Paracelsus's name also appeared on the Index.

Paracelsus embodies many of the paradoxes of natural philosophy during the Reformation. Despite his professed orthodoxy, many of his followers—such as the Calvinist Oswald Croll (c.1560–1609), who wrote the *Basilica Chemica* (1609)—were Protestant. The ability to cross confessional boundaries was a signal feature of Reformation science. Paracelsus was one of many natural philosophers whose nonsectarian views outweighed their nominal attachment to particular theologies. In fact, he can be seen as the first of a group of "philosopher-prophets" who argued for a universal, unified church. Others included the French humanist and Cabbalist Guillaume Postel (1510–1581), the Neapolitan heretic Bruno, the English magus John Dee (1527–1606), and Paracelsus's disciple Croll. One study on Bruno suggests that he was a crypto-Protestant who performed the offices of a Catholic priest, particularly during his stay in England (John Bossy, *Giordano Bruno and the Embassy Affair*, New Haven, 1991). Dee alternately conformed to Catholic ritual during his stay at the court of the Holy Roman Emperor Rudolf II in Prague and enjoyed a Protestant benefice under Elizabeth I and James I when he returned to England. Kepler, a Lutheran working for Catholic patrons, was accused of being a Calvinist. Croll's Calvinist beliefs were so highly tinged with hermetic and neo-Platonic imagery that Calvin surely would have despaired had he had occasion to see to what uses his doctrine of the elect could be put in the hands of a chemical philosopher. While many natural philosophers placed their views of nature in the service of various orthodoxies, based on a firm conviction in certain doctrinal beliefs, others perceived nature as an entity with its own theology, superseding the bounds of any institutional religion.

Yet another feature of Reformation science was the keen interest in prophecy. Apocalyptic imagery was an important part of scientific and religious culture, particularly in Lutheran regions, where eschatology played a key role in popular theology. In his own lifetime Paracelsus was as well known for his prophetic writings as for his medical reforms. The former enjoyed immediate publication and widespread readership, while the latter remained largely unread and unpublished until the late sixteenth and seventeenth century. While Paracelsus's interest in prophecy reflected his ongoing inquiry into signs in the universe—a study that began with the human body and moved outward to encompass the world and the heavens—Protestant reformers also engaged in such speculations in order to demonstrate to their congregations that the word and judgment of God was made materially manifest.

Luther and his associate Philipp Melanchthon (1497–1560) were particularly influential in this area. Their 1523 treatise on the pope-ass and monk-calf, two creatures whose monstrosity revealed the "monstrosity" of Catholic abuses, indicates an ability to utilize imagery from the natural world for religious purposes. In 1559 Melanchthon lectured to his students at the University of Wittenberg about the prophetic signs that would be seen in the world during the latter half of the sixteenth century, ushering in the Day of Judgment. Other reformers followed in their wake. Osiander, Copernicus's editor, was better known for his *Conjecturae de ultimis temporibus, ac de fine mundi* (Conjectures on the End of the World; 1544) than for his apologetic preface to *De revolutionibus orbium coelestium*. Discussions of astronomical and astrological events—such as the 1524 conjuncture of the planets, the appearance of a new star in 1572, and the 1531 and 1577 comets—provided common meeting ground for astronomers, mathematicians, and theologians. The development of mathematical studies in the German universities, influenced by the curricular reforms initiated by Melanchthon, served religious as well as scientific purposes. The more accurately one could chart the heavens, the more closely one could predict the coming of the Apocalypse. While scripture contained a historical record of God's communications to mankind, the natural world harbored contemporary and future messages waiting to be revealed.

Just as theologians needed to undergo new forms of training in order to respond better to the needs of their congregation, natural philosophers required new forms of learning in order to read the book of nature more successfully. In Lutheran regions Melanchthon spearheaded these educational reforms. His 1545 reorganization of the faculty of arts at the University of Wittenberg placed greater emphasis on mathematics and botany, two disciplines essential to the proper reading of nature's signs. Despite his initial criticism of Copernicus, Melanchthon soon gathered in his household some of Europe's leading astronomers, including Georg Joachim Rhäticus (1514–1574), who had first publicized Copernicus's ideas in his *Narratio prima* (1540). The "Wittenberg circle" integrated the technical material from Copernicus's work into the university curriculum without adopting his cosmology (Robert Westman, "The Melanchthon Circle, Rheticus, and the Wittenberg Interpretation of the Copernican Theory," *Isis* 66 [1975], pp. 165–193). They offered an Erasmian program of reform that allowed them to reap the benefits of the new science without exposing themselves to any of its theological dangers. Melanchthon expanded this program beyond Wittenberg through his role in the foundation of new universities within Germany and in his writings on the place of science in the new curriculum.

Melanchthon also took a great interest in botany, encouraging medical students to read Dioscorides's *Materia medica* and Pliny's *Natural History*, two ancient Roman texts that had not been part of the traditional university curriculum. A number of prominent sixteenth-century botanists were early converts to Lutheranism (Karl Dannenfeldt, "Wittenberg Botanists During the Sixteenth Century," in *The Social History of the Reformation*, edited by Lawrence P. Buck and Jonathan W. Zophy, Columbus, Ohio, 1972, pp. 223–248). Melanchthon corresponded with Leonhard Fuchs (1501–1566), who taught at the University of Tübingen. Along with Copernicus and Andreas Vesalius (1514–1564)—whose *De humani corporis fabrica* (On the Fabric of the Human Body; 1543) gave new prominence to anatomy—Fuchs is considered one of the principal figures of the scientific revolution. His *De historia stirpium* (On the History of Plants; 1542) made extensive use of detailed empirical descriptions and scientific illustrations, techniques central to the revival of natural history. In Wittenberg Melanchthon's biographer, Joachim Camerarius (1500–1574,) made the study of nature an important part of his theology. His son, Joachim the Younger (1534–1598), continued this tradition by becoming a botanist and was well known for his emblematic studies of the natural world. In this fashion Melanchthon's vision of educational reform as a necessary complement to religious reform led to the introduction of new texts and new ideas into the science curriculum.

Melanchthon was not dramatically different in this respect from Ignatius Loyola (1491–1556), founder of the Society of Jesus in 1540. Both perceived education as a foundation for a successful religion. While Melanchthon reformed a highly traditional institution—the university—Loyola invented a completely novel one: the Jesuit college. By 1600 the Jesuits had established colleges in every corner of Europe, with the Roman College (founded 1551) as their premier institution. With the completion of the *Ratio studiorum* in 1599, the shape of the curriculum was virtually established. Natural philosophy and mathematics played a particularly important role in the teaching at Jesuit colleges. Loyola had urged his followers to study natural philosophy because it "disposed the mind for theology." By the end of the sixteenth century the Roman College boasted one of the strongest and most innovative science curricula in western Europe. The Jesuit commitment to uphold Catholic orthodoxy did not prevent them from exploring such scientific doctrines as Copernicanism and passing on the results of their findings to a wider public. While advising his disciples to stick closely to the tradition of Aristotelian learning, often conflicted with church doctrine itself, Loyola nonetheless recognized that intellectuals were modifying these ancient beliefs. Thus, in the *Ratio studiorum* he allowed room for the introduction of new and unorthodox ideas about the natural world that arose from the consensus of Catholic philosophers. Since the Council of Trent (1545–1563) had offered no concrete pronouncements on any area of natural philosophy, this was a perfectly reasonable stance to take.

At the center of these debates lay the most prominent Jesuit astronomer of the sixteenth century, Christoph Clavius (1537–1612). As professor of mathematics at the Roman College, Clavius increasingly found himself arbitrating the debates among natural philosophers about the actual nature of the universe. He played a central role in the 1582 calendar reform under Gregory XIII, a project on which Copernicus had served as an early consultant, and commented on Euclid's *Elements of Geometry*. His *In sphaeram Ioannis de Sacro Bosco commentarius* (Commentary on the Sphere of Sacrobosco; 1591) became the definitive Jesuit textbook in astronomy. In it Clavius argued for the primacy of mathematics and the importance of astronomical observation in describing the universe. Successive editions incorporated new findings of contemporary astronomers, which Clavius assiduously double-checked with the help of assistants in Rome. In the 1611 edition he included Galileo's telescopic observations of the four satellites of Jupiter as reported in the *Sidereus Nuncius* (Sidereal Messenger; 1610), thereby confirming their "reality" for the Catholic community of philosophers, who looked to the Jesuits to define scientific orthodoxy. While Clavius did not perceive any of the newly observed phenomena as conclusive proof of a heliocentric worldview, he nonetheless allowed that Galileo's "moons of Jupiter" would lead philosophers to rethink the structure of the cosmos. Shortly after his death in 1612, the Society of Jesus adopted the alternative cosmology espoused by the Danish astronomer Tycho Brahe (1546–1601), a Lutheran. Known as the geoheliocentric theory, it placed the Earth at the center of the universe, with the Sun and moon rotating around it, and allowed all other planets (plus Jupiter's four satellites) to orbit the Sun.

Like the Wittenberg reform of astronomy, which utilized Copernican data without accepting its theoretical premise, the Jesuit adoption of the Tychonic view represented a judicious compromise between the old and the new. Even after the condemnation of Galileo, Jesuit astronomers continued to use Copernican and Galilean data, though they no longer openly criticized the geocentric view mandated by the Catholic church. Similarly, Jesuit philosophers publicly condemned alchemy and natural magic only to practice and publish on both under the guise of "orthodox" science. The emphasis on detail in the Jesuit culture of learning, an important pedagogical tool in the training of future missionaries, made their religious order an important source of information about the natural world. While Jesuit astronomers cataloged new stars, Jesuit missionaries made significant contributions to natural history, particularly given their access to regions of the world in which secular philosophers rarely traveled. While the Jesuits themselves might put their training to specific religious uses—as did Matteo Ricci (1552–1610), who studied with Clavius, when he used his mathematical skills to gain access to the imperial court in Ming China—ultimately the information they collected was not in itself denominational.

As the above examples indicate, the first century of the scientific revolution is not a history that divides easily between Protestants and Catholics. Traditional interpretations have made Protestant culture the birthplace of "modern" science, highlighting the burning of Bruno as a heretic in 1600 and the condemnation of Galileo in 1633 as acts that irrevocably closed the doors of the Catholic world to new developments in science until more recent times. In contrast, the absence of such decrees on the part of the Protestants has been viewed implicitly as a sign of their "openness" to new ideas. Yet it should be pointed out that Protestant culture had many reasons to be suspicious of the new scientific learning. Copernican astronomy did not necessarily coordinate well with the scriptural literalism espoused by certain Lutherans, nor did Paracelsian medicine necessarily please Protestant leaders who were attempting to establish their own theological prerogatives. The Protestants did not have the weight of tradition and authority on their side. At times this contributed to their greater openness to new ideas; at other times it made them suspicious of allowing into their midst unorthodox philosophers whose ideas might damage the credibility of their new religion.

Next to Bruno, the other natural philosopher burned for his ideas in the sixteenth century was Michael Servetus (1509/11–1553), condemned to the flames by Calvin for his antitrinitarian ideas. In addition to arguing for a unitarian view of religion, Servetus's *Christianismi restitutio* (Restitution of Christianity; 1553) also included an accurate description of the pulmonary transit of the blood, anticipating the English physician William Harvey's *De motu cordis* (On the Circulation of the Blood; 1628) by more than seventy years. Servetus's religious interest in the Holy Spirit led him to reconceptualize the composition and flow of the vital spirit that coursed throughout the body. Undoubtedly his studies with Vesalius's mentor Johannes Guinter von Andernach (1505–1574) in Paris had sharpened his ability to anatomize the human body. Neither Bruno nor Servetus was burned for scientific ideas. In the case of Bruno, it was his mixture of pagan and religious philosophy and his ideas about the animate and infinite nature of the universe rather than his Copernicanism that disturbed the Catholic authorities. Yet both exemplify the complex interweaving of science and religion in the first century following the Reformation.

[*See also* Copernicus, Nicolaus; Humanism; Medicine and Healing; *and* Paracelsus.]

BIBLIOGRAPHY

Blackwell, Richard J. *Galileo, Bellarmine, and the Bible.* Notre Dame, Ind., 1991.

Boas, Marie. *The Scientific Renaissance, 1450–1630.* Reprint, New York, 1966. A general survey of early modern science.

Céard, Jean. *La Nature et les prodiges: L'insolite au seizième siècle.* Geneva, 1977.

Clulee, Nicholas H. *John Dee's Natural Philosophy: Between Science and Religion.* London, 1988.

Debus, Allen G. *Man and Nature in the Renaissance.* Cambridge, 1978. A general survey oriented to developments in medicine, chemistry, and natural history.

Hallyn, Fernand. *The Poetic Structure of the World: Copernicus and Kepler.* Translated by Donald M. Leslie. New York, 1990. Situates the development of astronomy within the broader cultural context of Renaissance and Mannerist aesthetics.

Hannaway, Owen. *The Chemists and the Word: The Didactic Origins of Chemistry.* Reprint, Ann Arbor, 1990. Focuses on the debates between Oswald Croll and Andreas Libavius about the use of alchemical knowledge; contains a detailed discussion of Croll's natural theology.

Hooykas, R. *Religion and the Rise of Modern Science.* Edinburgh, 1972.

Koyré, Alexandre. *From the Closed World to the Infinite Universe.* Reprint, Baltimore, 1970. Emphasizes the Neo-platonic influence in early modern science.

Kuhn, Thomas S. *The Copernican Revolution: Planetary Astronomy in the Development of Western Thought.* Reprint, Cambridge, Mass., 1985. The classic work on Copernicus's role in the scientific revolution.

———. *The Structure of Scientific Revolutions.* 2d ed. New York, 1986.

Lindberg, David C., and Ronald L. Numbers, eds. *God and Nature: Historical Encounters between Science and Christianity.* Berkeley, 1986. Includes several important essays on science and religion in the early modern period.

Lindberg, David C., and Robert S. Westman, eds. *Reappraisals of the Scientific Revolution.* Cambridge, 1990. Brings together recent work on many specialized subjects in this field.

Olmi, Giuseppe. *Ulisse Aldrovandi: Scienza e natura nel secondo Cinquecento.* Trent, 1976.

O'Malley, Charles D. *Andreas Vesalius of Brussels, 1514–1564.* Berkeley, 1964.

Pagel, Walter. *Paracelsus: An Introduction to Philosophical Medicine in the Era of the Renaissance.* 2d rev. ed. Basel and New York, 1982.

Rossi, Paolo. *Philosophy, Technology and the Arts in the Early Modern Era*. Translated by Salvator Attanasio, edited by Benjamin Nelson. New York, 1970. Focuses on the relationship between scientific and artisanal knowledge.

Webster, Charles. *From Paracelsus to Newton: Magic in the Making of Modern Science*. Cambridge, 1982. Probably the best and most accessible survey of the apocalyptic tradition and the place of "philosopher-prophets" in early modern scientific culture.

Yates, Frances. *Giordano Bruno and the Hermetic Tradition*. Reprint, Chicago, 1991. The classic work on the origins and development of hermetic philosophy in the Renaissance.

PAULA FINDLEN

SCOTLAND. International relations, domestic politics, economic and social problems, as well as religious and ecclesiastical issues shaped the Reformation in Scotland. There was something like a Three Hundred Years' War between Scotland and England (1296–1560)—scarcely a decade without disturbed relations or a generation without serious military operations—but the second half of the fifteenth century, when the English were largely preoccupied with the Wars of the Roses, had given the Scots a taste of some of the advantages of relative peace. The southern parts of the country, naturally the most fertile and productive, were able to recover from the effects of war and to play their appropriate part in the national economy. It was no accident that in 1482 Edinburgh was formally acknowledged the chief town in the kingdom. New burghs were founded and the growing wealth was reflected in lavish expenditure on building, especially the enlargement of churches in burghs and the foundation of collegiate churches in both town and country. The sixteenth century opened with the promise of even better things, for James IV's marriage in 1503 to Margaret Tudor, daughter of Henry VII, was accompanied by a "treaty of perpetual peace." The ultimate result of the marriage was the accession a hundred years later of the great-grandson of James and Margaret to the English throne as James I; but within ten years of the treaty the Scots were at war with England again in a campaign that led to their catastrophic defeat at Flodden (1513).

The long minority of James V (1513–1528) looked superficially like the repetition of a familiar pattern, in which control of the administration was contested by great nobles and their followings. Each magnate had feudal vassals, dependents who had contracted to serve him, tenants accustomed to hereditary service to his house, a vast number of kinsmen and of bearers of his surname who were not related to him by blood, and a host of "servitors," maintained mainly by food and lodgings. Several generations were yet to pass before there was a successful movement without aristocratic leadership. But the rival factions were coming to be divided not only by personal or dynastic interests but also partly by political issues. Some Scots began to feel that the French alliance had been a one-sided affair and that in particular they had been led to Flodden not in a quarrel of their own making but for the sake of France. Precisely at what point one can say plainly that there was a pro-English or Anglophile party competing with a pro-French faction might be difficult to determine. But from the early 1520s the Scots nobles had a marked reluctance to cross that fatal frontier again and risk other disaster, and some thought that the time had come for Scotland's foreign policy to be at least reconsidered. The academic John Major's *History of Greater Britain* (1521) was an oblique but weighty plea for Anglo-Scottish amity. The family that gained control in the last two years of the minority, headed by Archibald Douglas, earl of Angus (who had married Margaret Tudor, James IV's widow and sister of Henry VIII), was committed to an understanding with England.

When James V personally assumed power in 1528 he reacted sharply against the Anglophile Archibald Douglas, who had in effect been keeping him in captivity. His own preference was probably a French alliance, and his tortuous negotiations with the emperor Charles V and his own uncle Henry VIII were probably designed mainly to raise his price in the French market and in the end to prevail on Francis I to permit him to marry the French princess Madeleine. When she died shortly after reaching Scotland in 1537 James almost immediately contracted a second French marriage, with Mary, daughter of Claude, duke of Guise. Scotland was thus more firmly than ever aligned with France.

By this time pro-English opinion had been strengthened by the onset of the Reformation. The Scottish church had undergone many changes over the medieval centuries, some of them successful in maintaining real vitality, and there was a lively devotion to Our Lord's Passion that was not irreconcilable with orthodoxy. Observant Franciscans preserved their zeal, and the many collegiate churches were designed to provide worship with splendor and to facilitate the multiplication of masses. But the parishes were increasingly starved of resources, which were concentrated in bishoprics, cathedrals, abbeys, and colleges.

Lutheran teaching reached Scotland in the 1520s and spread from east-coast ports to the hinterland, leading to iconoclasm and other damage to ecclesiastical properties, refusal to render payments to the church, and a wide circulation of songs and verses, including fierce attacks on the clergy and also some moving expressions of evangelical faith. Some saw the current emphasis on the Passion as devaluing traditional religious exercises and as fitting well with the concept of justification by faith. The focus of much of the criticism, which appeared also in David Lindsay's *Satire of the Three Estates* (1540), was on the corruption of the church, the immorality and ignorance of the parish clergy, the lack of discipline, and the pressure on the poor of "teinds" (tithes) and other exactions. Lower-class poverty could only too easily be contrasted with prelatic wealth, even before the reformers made pointed comparisons between the lifestyle of the apostles and that of bishops and abbots. Bishops were of royal or aristocratic lineage, abbacies increasingly became the perquisites of noble families, and in appointments to lesser benefices kinship was sometimes more important than training or morals. At the same time, as prelates alienated lands, tenants were transformed into proprietors and gained a new assurance.

Thus when Henry VIII threw off papal authority and dissolved the monasteries many Scots thought his example should be followed. Henry tried to persuade James to imitate him, but James, by ingeniously using an implied threat to do so, induced the pope to make unprecedented concessions both in subsidies and in control over ecclesiastical appointments. In short, James was able to get all he wanted out of the church without doctrinal or administrative changes and was quite prepared to remain orthodox—at a price. But his rejection of the English example meant that those of reforming views were more than ever inclined to regard England as an ally and also as a refuge when they were in danger of prosecution in Scotland.

Before the end of James V's reign lines were clearly drawn between a party inclined to reform and favorable to England and a party ecclesiastically conservative and determined to retain the French connection. Therefore, when James finally broke with Henry, it was a deeply divided nation that he tried to lead. His military campaign in 1542 was intended to have something of the character of a crusade on behalf of the papacy against the schismatic English. The consequence was a disastrous defeat at Solway Moss in November 1542, when some Scottish nobles surrendered to the English rather than fight for a king whose expensive tastes had made him "ill-beloved of his subjects" and in whom they had lost confidence.

James died soon after (14 December 1542) in a state of collapse that was perhaps psychological rather than physical. The Scottish Crown had been entailed by statute on descendants in the male line of Robert II (d. 1371), but no such descendants existed; in a remarkable demonstration of indefeasible hereditary succession James was succeeded by the week-old Mary, his daughter by Mary of Guise. During the eighteen years of her minority (1543–1561) both France and England sought, sometimes by war and sometimes by diplomacy, to turn Scotland into a satellite.

The situation changed with almost kaleidoscopic unpredictability, but the main turning points were in 1543, 1547–1548 and 1559–1560. In 1543 control of affairs was assumed by a party that included that old friend to England, Archibald Douglas, now returned from exile, and a number of lords who had been captured at Solway Moss and released on condition of furthering Henry VIII's policy. The party was, if not quite Protestant, at any rate prepared to encourage reforming preachers and come to terms with England.

The infant Mary was pledged by treaty as the prospective bride of Prince Edward, son of Henry, the future Edward

VI. But before the year 1543 was out the Scottish regent (and heir presumptive), James Hamilton, earl of Arran, threw off the influence of the pro-English party, came to terms with the Roman Catholic interest under Cardinal David Beaton, archbishop of Saint Andrews, and in a remarkable volte-face repudiated the treaty with England. Henry's answer was to intensify pro-English propaganda in Scotland, to tamper through bribery with the allegiance of Scottish nobles, and to devastate southern Scotland in a series of invasions known as the Rough Wooing. Cardinal Beaton was murdered in 1546 (to the great satisfaction of England, if not at English instigation).

In 1547, after heavily defeating the Scots at Pinkie, English forces remained in occupation of much Scottish territory and from their bases disseminated propaganda shaped in the now Protestant England of Edward VI. A divided and somewhat irresolute Scotland was incapable of ejecting the invaders by its own resources and had to call in the aid of France. The necessary help was given, but only on condition that the young queen, who had in 1543 been designated as the bride of the heir to the English throne, was sent to France in 1548 for betrothal to the Dauphin, heir to the French throne. James Hamilton became duke of Châtelherault, and France offered material inducements to Scottish nobles to offset English bribery. Hamilton meantime remained regent, however, and Beaton was succeeded as archbishop of Saint Andrews by John Hamilton, the governor's half-brother, who initiated a policy of reforming abuses, giving some countenance to reformed theology and ignoring the papacy, almost along Henrician lines.

But from 1554, when James Hamilton was replaced as regent by the French queen mother, Mary of Guise, Scotland came more and more under French domination. In 1558 Queen Mary married the Dauphin, who the next year became king of France as Francis II. Common Franco-Scottish nationality had been established in 1557, and the prospect for Scotland seemed to be government by descendants of Francis and Mary and ultimately absorption into the dominions of the king of France. Such a prospect was far from pleasing to many Scots, and even those who were favorable to the French alliance and conservative in their religious views were antagonized when they saw a standing army of French soldiers garrisoning Scottish fortresses and Frenchmen thrust into high office in Scotland.

Undisguised attempts to make Scotland a base for aggression against England, to cause a Scottish army to cross the border again, and to levy taxation for fortifications all aroused bitter resentment. National sentiment, which in 1548 had sought help from France to drive out the English, had now become anti-French, and Protestantism was growing all the time. Protestant preachers were active in 1555–1556, and in 1557 a formal bond committed three earls, an earl's son, and an important laird to further the cause of the Reformation.

There was no prospect of help from England, at least on religious grounds, as long as that country was ruled by the Roman Catholic Mary Tudor. But in November 1558 she was succeeded by Elizabeth, who almost at once showed that she would give some countenance to the Protestant cause. Little time elapsed before a rebellion broke out in Scotland. Among the motives, it is hard to disentangle religious fervor from patriotic resentment against the French regent, in whose hands lay the defense of the existing regime, but militancy was first threatened in the "Beggars' Summons," posted at the doors of religious houses around the beginning of 1559 demanding that they should be surrendered to the poor and infirm.

The best known of the reforming preachers at this juncture was John Knox, a native of East Lothian, which had so often been laid waste by English armies. After being associated with the murderers of Beaton and for a time a prisoner in the French galleys, he had next found a home in the England of Edward VI and had married an Englishwoman. During Mary Tudor's reign he had ministered to a congregation of English exiles in Geneva and had become a disciple of Calvin. Such a pro-English and anglicized Scot (who had laid aside his native accent) typified much in the Scottish Reformation. A sermon by him sparked off the rebellion in May 1559, and he advocated an Anglo-Scottish alliance, based on "the preaching of Christ crucified," against France and the papacy. The success of the insurgents against the professional French troops was not ensured until England sent help early in 1560. Mary of Guise died in June, and in July England and France agreed by treaty to withdraw their forces from Scotland.

This withdrawal in effect left the Scots free to settle their own affairs, and this they did in August 1560, when a parliament—significantly attended by scores of "small barons" or lairds whose right to be there was at best debatable—abolished papal authority, forbade the celebration of Mass, and adopted a confession of faith on broadly Calvinist lines. Mary was still in France and it was thought possible that as queen of France, she might not return to a country that had rejected France and what France stood for. A kind of provisional government, mainly of Protestant lords, controlled affairs, and there was some talk of looking for another sovereign to replace Mary. In December 1560 Francis died, however, and Mary, with a poor future in France, decided to return to Scotland, where she arrived in August 1561.

The eighteen-year-old girl, who had been out of Scotland for thirteen years, handled a difficult situation with considerable skill. Although she insisted on having Roman Catholic worship in her own chapel and did not formally consent to the acts passed in 1560, she behaved very much as if those acts were in force. On the one hand, the Reformed church received official recognition and a measure of endowment (partly by means of a division of the ecclesiastical revenues among the existing holders, the Reformed church, and the Crown); on the other hand, many priests were prosecuted for saying Mass in defiance of a royal proclamation issued on two or three occasions. Attempts were made to remedy social injustice by measures in favor of oppressed tenants.

The Reformed church started with only a congregational organization and kirk sessions (composed of lay elders annually elected), which had responsibility for poor relief, but it acquired regional agencies in some bishops who accepted the Reformation and in superintendents, who had the administrative powers of bishops. But a practicing Roman Catholic (whatever she might concede to the reformers) could not be head on earth of a Protestant church or even (like Elizabeth in England) its supreme governor. Consequently, the Scots had to look elsewhere for a central authority. They found it at first (and briefly) in the council of the Protestant lords (which appointed superintendents) and then in a general assembly, which was virtually equivalent to a Protestant parliament, predominantly lay in composition; it comprised the three estates of clergy (superintendents and ministers), burgesses (chosen by town councils), and "barons" (comprising not only nobles who came as individuals but also shire commissioners, locally chosen, who then had no place in the parliament).

All but the most bigoted were satisfied with Mary's compromise, and her charm won the affection of her intimates and the loyalty of the mass of her subjects. But her attitude vacillated. She became less favorable to the Reformed church when, after her marriage to Henry Stewart, Lord Darnley, in 1565, some Protestant lords raised a rebellion against her, and again very favorable when in 1567 she married James Hepburn, earl of Bothwell, by Reformed rites. The reformers certainly gained greater security when Mary was forced to abdicate in 1567 and was replaced by her infant son James, under whom the country was governed by Protestant regents.

In the new political situation the question was raised whether the general assembly was any longer necessary, now that Crown and parliament were Protestant, and there were problems relating to the assimilation of the new Reformed organization to the old ecclesiastical structure (including bishoprics), which had never been abolished. In the rival answers to those questions—one provided by Andrew Melville, who came from Geneva in 1574 with a presbyterian program, and the other, episcopal, model, approved by the regent, James Douglas, earl of Morton and then by King James VI when he reached maturity—lay the history of the Reformed church for the next century. Despite those differences, the predominant consideration in the late sixteenth century was the Protestantism that England and Scotland shared; that, and other influences of the Reformation, not least the introduction of a Bible and service books in English, laid foundations for Anglo-Scottish union.

[*See also* Knox, John; Presbyterianism; *and* Scottish Books of Discipline.]

BIBLIOGRAPHY

Cameron, James K., ed. *The First Book of Discipline*. Edinburgh, 1972. Scholarly edition of key document.

Cameron, Nigel M. de S., et al., eds. *Dictionary of Scottish Church History & Theology*. Downers Grove, Ill., 1993.

Dickinson, W. Croft. *John Knox's History of the Reformation in Scotland*, 2 vols. Reprint, Wilmington, Del., 1979. Many essential documents besides Knox's narrative, with scholarly apparatus and outstanding index.

Dickinson, W. Croft, Gordon Donaldson, and Isabel A. Milne, eds. *A Source Book of Scottish History*. Vol. 2. 2d ed., rev. & enl. Edinburgh, 1958. Convenient collection of documentary material, with commentaries.

Donaldson, Gordon. *The Scottish Reformation*. Reprint, Cambridge, 1979. Described as "indispensable."

———. *Scottish Church History*. Edinburgh, 1985. Contains several relevant articles, many reprinted with heavy revision.

———. *Scotland: James V to James VII*. Rev. ed. Edinburgh History of Scotland, vol 3. Edinburgh, 1987. Best account in print of the general course of events of the period.

———. *The Faith of the Scots*. London, 1990. One of the few attempts to deal with popular beliefs.

Fleming, David H. *The Reformation in Scotland*. London, 1910. A classic, not now easy to obtain; ultra-Protestant in tone, with thorough scholarship.

Kirk, James. *Patterns of Reform: Continuity and Change in the Reformation Kirk*. Edinburgh, 1989. Formidable scholarship on assorted topics, some of it reprinted; critical of Donaldson (above).

McRoberts, David, ed. *Essays on the Scottish Reformation*. Glasgow, 1962. Fifteen papers of high scholarship, mainly by Roman Catholics.

GORDON DONALDSON

SCOTTISH BOOKS OF DISCIPLINE. At the Reformation, Scottish Protesants repudiated the organization of the late medieval church and adopted instead a system of church government modeled on the example of "the best reformed churches" on the continent. Their program took tangible form in the hastily compiled first *Book of Discipline* in 1560 and its successor, the second *Book of Discipline* in 1578.

First Book of Discipline (1560). One of the primary documents of the Scottish Reformation, the first *Book of Discipline*, composed by six Protestant ministers in 1560, was designed as a blueprint for the organization of the Reformed church in the immediate aftermath of the revolution against Rome and France. As early as 29 April 1560 the Protestant provisional government, or "great council of the realm," in Edinburgh had commissioned some ministers to prepare a book containing their judgments on the "reformation of religion." A text was submitted to the government by 20 May and, as the Reformation Parliament met in August, a Latin version of the "Book of Common Reformation" was in preparation for sending to John Calvin, Pierre Viret, and Théodore de Bèze in Geneva and to Peter Martyr Vermigli, Heinrich Bullinger, and others in Zurich. (No copy of this early work is known to have survived, and the contents were not submitted to Parliament for approval.) Parliament, in turn, abrogated papal jurisdiction in Scotland, prohibited the celebration of the Mass, and approved a Reformed confession of faith, but it passed no legislation on ecclesiastical polity. Instead, a fresh commission was issued to six prominent Protestant preachers—John Douglas, John Knox, John Row, John Spottiswoode, John Willock, and John Winram—to compose "in a volume the policy and discipline of the kirk." The contents of the original "Book of Common Reformation" (which were probably confined to a discussion of doctrine, the sacraments, discipline, and administration) then underwent revision and expansion as the *Book of Discipline* took fuller shape. During the autumn and winter fresh material on the ministry, superintendents, endowment, and schools and universities was incorporated into the final text. The work was then submitted for revision to an ecclesiastical gathering—presumably the general assembly of the church that met in Edinburgh in December 1560—before receiving qualified approval from the Privy Council and a convention of nobles and barons in January 1561.

On doctrine the book stressed the need for preaching the word throughout the realm, ministering the two dominical sacraments of baptism and the Lord's Supper, and removing "superstition" and "idolatry." The observance of holy days and feast days, prayers for the dead, the invocation of saints, and the celebration of the Mass were all repudiated, and the religious orders were marked for suppression. Ministers appointed to Reformed congregations were first to be elected with congregational approval and examined by "the best reformed church" in the district. The temporary offices of exhorter and reader were commended until such time as sufficient fully trained and qualified ministers were recruited.

Provision for ministers and their families, for readers and exhorters, for education, and for the deserving poor was recognized as a charge on the church's income. That income, it was envisaged, would be forthcoming from revenues derived from the pre-Reformation church, whose ancient structure of benefices, the book proposed, should be abolished. Benefices were to be dissolved, and teinds, or tithes, were to be separated from other ecclesiastical revenues and assigned to support the Reformed ministry, education, and poor relief. Elders and deacons, elected from each congregation for a term, were to assist in regulating congregational affairs and in maintaining discipline. As financial officers, the deacons were accorded the specific task of collecting and disbursing "the whole revenues" of the church. The book also recommended that manses and glebes be made available for ministers. The existence of a separate ecclesiastical jurisdiction—exercised at the congregational level by the minister, elders, and deacons in the "kirk session"—was duly recognized, and the church's right to excommunicate was explicitly defended. The role of the civil magistrate in supporting the church was also affirmed. The reorganization of the schools and universities commanded exceptionally detailed treatment: emphasis was placed on securing a school in every parish, on Latin grammar schools in towns, and on creating liberal arts colleges in the larger towns. The three universities of St. Andrews, Glasgow, and Aberdeen were to be remodeled to meet the needs of church and commonwealth, and bursaries were to be made available for the able poor. Funding was to be forthcoming from the rents of the bishoprics and collegiate churches.

To promote evangelization throughout the land, appoint ministers where there were none, and supervise the parishes, the authors of the *Book of Discipline* belatedly decided "to make difference betwixt preachers at this time" by recommending the appointment of "ten or twelve" regional superintendents, who were to be based in Kirkwall, Fortrose, Argyll, Old Aberdeen, Brechin, St. Andrews, Edinburgh, Jedburgh, Glasgow, and Dumfries. They were to be active as itinerant preachers and were to be "subject to the censure and correction of ministers and elders" within their jurisdiction. The "provinces" assigned for their labors were distinguished from the old pre-Reformation dioceses.

Such far-reaching ideas might have proved acceptable to the General Assembly, which sought as best it could to give effect to the book's main recommendations, but the radical financial proposals for reorganizing ecclesiastical endowment to enable the Reformed church to inherit much of the patrimony of the pre-Reformation church could not command support from the Crown and nobility, in whose hands much of the church's wealth had come to reside. Thus, the convention of nobles in 1561, which endorsed the book's main findings, took care to ensure that existing clergy willing to support the Reformation should retain their benefices for life, provided they helped sustain ministers. During the personal rule of Mary Stuart (1561–1567), and in the reign of her successor, James VI (1567–1625), the Reformed church increasingly gained a measure of finance through access to the old structure of benefices, but the underlying aims of the first *Book of Discipline* continued to find favor in the General Assembly and received renewed expression in the second *Book of Discipline* of 1578.

Second *Book of Discipline* (1578). As a statement on government, polity, and endowment for the Scottish church, the second *Book of Discipline* was produced in 1578 at the behest of the church's General Assembly in reaction to the Crown's policy which favored "conformity with England" through the introduction of Protestant bishops in 1572. By 1576 the General Assembly had abandoned this short-lived experiment with diocesan episcopacy in favor of entrusting oversight to ministers acting as temporary "visitors" or "commissioners," a move consistent with its earlier claim in 1565 that "every true preacher of Jesus Christ is a Christian bishop." The contents of the book were prepared and revised by a series of regional committees, selected by the General Assembly to meet in Glasgow, Edinburgh, St. Andrews, Montrose, and Aberdeen; participating in the work were over thirty ministers, including two of the surviving authors of the first *Book of Discipline* of 1560. All this serves to correct the common misapprehension that Andrew Melville, the presbyterian principal of Glasgow University, wrote the document. At best he was an active participant, and he served as moderator of the General Assembly in April 1578 as the *Book of Discipline* neared completion.

A more concise and incisive document than the somewhat discursive first book, the second book opened by defining the church as, first, a fellowship of professing Christians; second, the elect; and third, an institution with its ministry and organization. In language reminiscent of the first book's claim that ministers were "promoted to the regiment of the kirk," the church's spiritual jurisdiction and government were upheld as autonomous and distinct from secular authority. Royal supremacy over the church was rejected; the offices of minister and magistrate were recognized as complementary but distinct; and the magistrate's role was understood as defending and upholding the church, not as prescribing rules in doctrine or discipline. Yet, as Knox had earlier appreciated, the minister had a duty to teach the magistrate how to perform his duty in the commonwealth according to the word.

In defining procedures governing admission to the four offices of minister, doctor, elder, and deacon, emphasis was placed on an individual's vocation, his examination by the "eldership," and his public election with congregational consent. Ordination was to be accompanied by the imposition of the hands of the eldership (that is, by the ministers, doctors, and elders of the district). The minister of the word and sacraments was identified with the office of New Testament bishop, or shepherd of the flock, and diocesan episcopacy—"pastors of pastors, pastors of many flocks, and yet without a certain flock"—was condemned as contrary to the word. Visitation was understood to belong to the church, not to an episcopal office; thus, the courts of the church might commission ministers as temporary visitors. The doctor, or teacher, was assigned the task of interpreting scripture. As theology professor first at Glasgow and then at St. Andrews, Melville stressed the importance of studying scripture in the original tongues and of applying the tools of philology to biblical exegesis so that the true meaning of scripture might be grasped. The second *Book of Discipline* recognized the doctor's right to sit on the courts of the church with the ministers and elders. It also proposed that elders, elected from congregations, should be appointed for life in recognition that their vocation was enduring; there was, however, provision for periodic release from their ecclesiastical duties in order to attend to the claims of their everyday occupations. Similarly, deacons were to be elected for life from the congregational membership, but as financial officers, whose duties consisted of collecting the church's revenues and of distributing poor relief, they were not assigned a seat, as were "governors" (ministers, doctors, and elders), on the courts of the church. Unlike ministers and doctors, who were employed on a full-time, salaried basis, elders and deacons received no stipend and were not understood to form part of what might be called a professional ministry.

The courts of the church, defined as elderships or assemblies, were seen to be fourfold: the local eldership of one church or of several adjacent churches in a district (twice mentioned as a "presbytery"); the provincial synod composed of ministers, doctors, and elders in the region; the General Assembly of the nation; and an international assembly of all Reformed churches. In practice, the kirk session continued to be the congregational eldership; the district presbytery came into being as a distinct court, intermediate between session and synod, when the General Assembly recognized in 1579 that the "exercise" for interpreting scripture could function as a "presbytery." The proposal by the authors of the second book to restrict voting membership in the General Assembly to "ecclesiastical persons" (ministers, doctors, and elders) seems to have met with widespread support and possibly weakened the Crown's long-standing claim that the assembly constituted an illegal convocation of the lieges.

As with the first book of 1560, the restoration of the church's proper patrimony lay at the heart of the second book's reforming program, but such a restitution remained anathema to the Crown and nobility, who had profited from the lands and rents of the old church. Far from being suppressed as both books proposed, the ancient structure of benefices remained intact and so frustrated full implementation of the books' proposals. Although the General Assembly registered the second book among its acts in 1581, no parliamentary approval was forthcoming. The Presbyterian constitution approved by Parliament in 1592 was merely a partial concession to some of the second book's proposals. Continuing appeals to the ideals of the second *Book of Discipline* were revived in the Presbyterian revolution of the 1640s and again at the Glorious Revolution of 1689–1690, though on both occasions (when Presbyterianism was reestablished and episcopacy abolished), the program of the second *Book of Discipline* remained imperfectly realized.

[*See also* Knox, John; Melville, Andrew; Presbyterianism; *and* Scotland.]

BIBLIOGRAPHY

Cameron, James K., ed. *The First Book of Discipline.* Edinburgh, 1972.
Kirk, James, ed. *The Second Book of Discipline.* Edinburgh, 1980.
Kirk, James. "The Scottish Reformation and Reign of James VI: A Select Critical Bibliography." *Records of the Scottish Church History Society* 23 (1987), 113–155.
———. *Patterns of Reform: Continuity and Change in the Reformation Kirk.* Edinburgh, 1989.

JAMES KIRK

SCOTTISH CONFESSION. Composed in 1560 as a Protestant statement of doctrine and authorized by the Scottish "Reformation Parliament," the Scottish Confession, or the Scots Confession of Faith, remained the Church of Scotland's official doctrinal standard until superseded by the Westminster Confession of Faith (adopted by the church's General Assembly in 1647). In the aftermath of the Protestant revolution against Rome and France in 1559, and with the reformers' ascendancy in 1560 and as French and English forces withdrew from Scottish soil, the "barons, gentlemen, burgesses and others" professing Protestantism petitioned the nobility and estates of Parliament for action against "such doctrine and idolatry as by God's word are condemned." The sequel was a commission from Parliament to a group of "barons and ministers" to prepare a Reformed Confession of Faith.

Hastily presented within four days of its commission to the Parliament then sitting, the confession was produced by a committee whose members, drawn from various backgrounds, were not always of one mind; hence, the variety of expression and approach. There are signs, too, of repetition and unevenness in preparation. According to John Knox, the authors of the confession were also responsible for producing the first *Book of Discipline*, and are therefore identified as John Knox himself and five colleagues: John Winram, John Spottiswoode, John Willock, John Douglas, and John Row. As a former Augustinian canon regular and subprior of St. Andrews, as a doctor of theology and dean of divinity in the university (where he was esteemed as "wonderfully learned in the New Testament, Old Testament and much more"), and as a participant in the reforming provincial councils of the Catholic church, Winram had stayed long enough in the old church to see the last heretic executed in 1559 but was a welcome enough convert to "the new preaching" to play a prominent part in the reformers' strategies and to attain the rank of superintendent of Fife by 1561. If Winram's previous links had been with Rome and France, those of Spottiswoode show him, for a generation before his appointment as superintendent of Lothian in 1561, to have been a friend of reform and of accommodation with England, whose archbishop of Canterbury, Thomas Cranmer, he had met. Another contributor, John Douglas, humanist scholar and teacher in Paris, was a bachelor of medicine and probably also a doctor of theology who, as provost of St. Mary's college in St. Andrews, had chosen the Protestant path. John Row, by contrast, was freshly recruited from his work as a procurator at the curia Romana by Lord James Stewart and Knox to serve as minister at

Perth. Knox, himself a renegade priest, had an established record of service as minister in the English church and at Geneva, as well as in Scotland.

From such assorted experience the confession took shape. In a preface addressed to the estates and Protestant inhabitants of Scotland and other nations, the authors explained their need for a statement of "the doctrine which we profess," set forth in a "brief and plain Confession," sustained by scriptural warrant, for nourishing the faithful, "our own weaker brethren," and countering the claims of adversaries. The notion of inspired infallibility was disclaimed; and anyone able to detect "in our Confession any chapter or sentence contrary to God's Holy Word" was invited to submit objections in writing so that "we shall alter whatever he can prove to be wrong." The opportunity, therefore, for amending or correcting the contents, in the light of scripture, remained a recognized possibility.

Consisting of twenty-five articles or chapters, the confession opened with a declaration of man's duty to God, in language reminiscent of John Calvin, before proceeding to enumerate God's attributes as one who is "eternal, infinite, immeasurable, incomprehensible, omnipotent, invisible; one in substance and yet distinct in three persons." The central themes of Christian understanding—on man's Creation, Fall, and original sin; the revelation of God's promise in sacred history; the church's preservation; man's election "before the foundation of the world was laid"; the incarnation; Christ's passion, resurrection and ascension; his return for "final judgment"; faith in the Holy Ghost, who is seen to "sanctify and regenerate us, without respect to any merit proceeding from us"; good works "done in faith and at the command of God"; the perfection of the law and the imperfection of man; the universal church containing "the chosen of all ages, of all realms, nations and tongues"; and the immortality of the soul (articles 1–17)—were not the most controversial issues. The place of the law in Christian life was treated in a more positive Calvinist manner than earlier Lutherans were inclined to regard it. In the law were to be found "not only all such works as displease and offend" God "but also those which please him and which he has promised to reward"; but "whoever boasts of the merits of his own works or puts his trust in works of supererogation boasts of what does not exist, and puts his trust in damnable idolatry." An adversarial note is struck in the confession's emphasis on unmerited grace, human helplessness, the sole authority of scripture, the two dominical sacraments, its rejection of Roman transubstantiation, and its definition of the "true Kirk," to be distinguished from "the horrible harlot, the false Kirk."

The central Protestant doctrine of justification by faith alone is professed rather than delineated: "our faith and its assurance do not proceed from flesh and blood, that is to say, from natural powers within us, but are the inspiration of the Holy Ghost . . . who sanctifies us, and brings us into

all truth by his own working . . . without respect to any merit proceeding from us, be it before or be it after our regeneration." Again, predestination, though not ignored, lacks definition and examination. The "eternal and immutable decree of God from which all our salvation springs and depends" was treated sensitively (as Calvin had counseled). Election in Christ, the confession taught, occurred "before the foundation of the world was laid." The righteous or elect were chosen to "inherit that blessed immortality promised them from the beginning," and, by contrast, the "stubborn, disobedient" and unbelieving were "cast into the dungeon of utter darkness where their worm shall not die, nor their fire be quenched." The confession, therefore, pointed to more than God's abandonment of the reprobate; it comprehended their destruction after judgment. God's decree of merciful election, it seems, was accompanied by a retributive decree of damnation. All in all, the confession's teaching suggests a belief in double predestination, but its expression is mild, even indeterminate, compared with later systematic expositions.

In its affirmation of the paramount authority of scripture, the confession repudiated the claims of Catholic apologists for the teaching authority of the church and its tradition, including the early Fathers and ecumenical councils. The Bible did not owe its authority to the church. In responding to Tridentine Romanism, the confession taught (in common with other Protestant confessions) that everything necessary for salvation was contained in scripture, whose authority derived from God and did not "depend on men or angels," and it denounced as blasphemous the claims of "those who say the Scriptures have no other authority save that which they have received from the Kirk." The interpreter of scripture is neither the church nor any individual, however preeminent, but the Holy Spirit alone. Thus, "when controversy arises about right understanding of any passage or sentence of Scripture, or for the reformation of any abuse within the Kirk of God, we ought not so much to ask what men have said or done before us, as what the Holy Ghost uniformly speaks within the body of Scriptures and what Christ Jesus himself did and commanded. For it is agreed by all that the Spirit of God, who is the spirit of unity, cannot contradict himself." The true church, moreover, should be identified not by "antiquity, usurped title, lineal succession, appointed place, nor the numbers of men approving an error," but by true preaching of the word, correct administration of the sacraments of baptism and the Lord's Supper, and by ecclesiastical discipline "uprightly administered." (The elevation of discipline to one of the three "notes" for discerning the true church went further than Calvin's customary acceptance of two notes, though even he could recognize four; it was consistent with the confession of 1556 adopted by the English exiles in Geneva and approved by Calvin and with the Belgic Confession of 1561.) The Scottish Confession also disclaimed the idea that "any policy or order of ceremonies can be appointed for all ages, times, and places; for as ceremonies which men have devised are but temporal, so they may, and ought to be changed, when they foster superstition rather than edify the Kirk."

The church, the confession affirmed, is indispensable to salvation: "out of this Kirk there is neither life nor eternal felicity." From "the beginning there has been, now is, and to the end of the world shall be, one Kirk, that is to say, one company and multitude of men chosen by God, who rightly worship and embrace him by true faith in Christ Jesus, who is the only Head of the Kirk, even as it is the body and spouse of Christ Jesus." It was recognized as catholic, or universal, as it "contains the chosen of all ages, of all realms, nations, and tongues, be they of the Jews or be they of the Gentiles, who have communion and society with God the Father, and with his son, Christ Jesus, through the sanctification of the Holy Spirit." The invisible church, known only to God, was identified as the communion of saints in all ages, the "citizens of the heavenly Jerusalem." This characteristically Protestant emphasis was accompanied by a discussion of the visible church and the need to distinguish the "true Kirk," the "spotless bride of Christ," from "the horrible harlot, the false Kirk." Wherever the notes, or marks, of true doctrine, sacraments, and discipline are observed, "there, beyond any doubt, is the true Kirk of Christ." Besides its universality, the church, the confession observed, is also particular, as was so in "Corinth, Galatia, Ephesus and other places where the ministry was planted by Paul." This apostolic practice was seen to be applicable to Scotland, whose inhabitants "confessing Christ Jesus do claim to have in our cities, townes and reformed districts" churches founded on the doctrines of the Old and New Testaments "in those books which were originally reckoned canonical."

The work of general councils in the past—or, at any rate, "those which deserve the name" and which were "lawfully gathered"—was neither condemned outright nor uncritically accepted: "being human, some of them have manifestly erred, and that in matters of great weight and importance." The proper purpose of councils was neither "to make any permanent law which God had not made before, nor yet to form new activities for our belief, nor to give the Word of God authority," but to refute heresies, give public confession of faith for future generations, and establish good order in the church.

In its sacramental teaching on baptism and the Lord's Supper, "which alone were instituted by the Lord Jesus and commanded to be used," the confession, following Calvin, rejected the idea of the sacraments as "naked and bare signs," for they offered what they signified. They distinguished God's people from those outside his league, exercised "the faith of his children," and sealed "in their hearts the assurance of his promise, and of that most blessed union" of the elect with Christ. In baptism (which "applies as much to the children of the faithful as to those who are of

age and discretion") "we are engrafted in Christ Jesus, to be made partakers of his righteousness by which our sins are covered and remitted." Here the "error" of Anabaptism was explicitly condemned. In the Lord's Supper (available "only for those who are of the household of faith"), the confession affirmed "Christ Jesus is so joined with us that he becomes the very nourishment and food of our souls." Roman transubstantiation was refuted, as was Lutheran "consubstantiation" and the stark symbolism and memorialism associated both with Zwingli and with the "Sacramentarians." Distinguishing "Christ Jesus in his elemental substance and the elements of the sacramental signs," the confession offered a high Calvinist interpretation: this union and conjunction which we have with the body and blood of Christ Jesus in the right use of the sacraments is wrought by means of the Holy Ghost, who by true faith carries us above all things that are visible, carnal, and earthly, and makes us feed upon the body and blood of Christ, once broken and shed for us but now in heaven, and appearing for us in the presence of his Father. Notwithstanding the distance between his glorified body in heaven and mortal men on earth, yet we must assuredly believe that the bread which we break is the communion of Christ's body and the cup which we bless the communion of his blood.

The sacraments required "lawful ministers," appointed to preach the word and called by the congregation. Roman teaching and practice was rejected, not least because its ministers were not recognized as "true ministers (indeed they even allow women, whom the Holy Ghost will not permit to preach in the congregation, to baptize)"; besides, the accretions of past ages had led to such adulteration "that no part of Christ's original act remains in its original purity." The use in baptism of "oil, salt, spittle and such like" was censured as "human additions," and veneration of the host "as the Romanists do" was considered improper: the "sanctified bread and wine" were to be eaten and drunk, not "reserved for worship or honoured as God." The Roman practice of withholding the cup from the people was held to be "sacrilege." The sacrifice of the Mass, offered to God for the sins of the living and the dead, was denounced as blasphemous and derogatory to Christ, the sufficiency of whose "unique sacrifice, once offered on the cross for the cleansing of all who are to be sanctified," was robustly proclaimed.

To the civil magistrate the confession assigned "the conservation and purgation of religion," the maintenance of true religion, and the suppression of idolatry and superstition. Obedience to his rule was enjoined so far—and only so far—as he fulfilled that "which appertains to his charge"; and "those who resist the supreme powers, so long as they are acting in their own spheres, are resisting God's ordinance and cannot be held guiltless." Much emphasis was placed on the condition that "princes and rulers vigilantly fulfil their office"; at the same time, the Christian's duty to "repress tyranny" and to "defend the oppressed" was vigorously defended. The clearly implied limits on obedience in this chapter offended some who argued for the chapter's omission from the confession or at least for some rewording. Such advice, it seems, was not altogether heeded, and Knox maintained that Parliament approved the confession, in the form presented, "without alteration of any sentence."

In broad agreement with other Reformed confessions of the period, the Scottish Confession also exhibited some distinctive characteristics: in form it is shorter than many; it contains few quotations from scripture; much Reformed doctrine is assumed rather than expounded; it lacks full articles on free will, effectual calling, adoption, and sanctification; the terms "justification" and "predestination" do not occur; and there is much on which the confession is simply silent. Not surprisingly, perhaps, one contemporary thought that the confession "should not so soon have come into the light." At the same time, similarities and coincidences of expression in the language employed in the confession indicate a particular indebtedness to Calvin's *Institutes*, Calvin's Catechism, the English exiles' Genevan Confession of 1556, the Gallic Confession, the confession subscribed by students at the Geneva academy, the Forty-two Articles of Religion of 1552, the first Helvetic Confession, the Augsburg Confession, and Jan Łaski's *Summa doctrinae*.

Ratified in 1567 by the first Parliament of James VI's reign and after the deposition of Mary Stuart, the confession remained the official doctrinal statement of the Scottish church until supplemented by the more rigidly predestinarian Aberdeen Confession of 1616 and ultimately superseded (though not wholly displaced) by the Westminster Confession of Faith (adopted by the Scottish church in 1647). To the numerous English editions published in the 1560s, a Latin edition was added in 1572.

BIBLIOGRAPHY

Bulloch, James, ed. and trans. *The Confession of the Faith and Doctrine Believed and Professed by the Protestants of Scotland.* Edinburgh, 1960.
Cheyne, Alex C. "The Scots Confession of 1560." *Theology Today* 17 (1960), 323–338.
Dickinson, William Croft, ed. *John Knox's History of the Reformation in Scotland* (1949). 2 vols. Reprint, Wilmington, Del., 1979.
Hazlett, W. Ian P. "The Scots Confession 1560: Context, Complexion and Critique." *Archiv für Reformationsgeschichte* 78 (1987), 287–320.
Henderson, G. D. *The Burning Bush.* Edinburgh, 1957.
Kirk, James. "The Scottish Reformation and Reign of James VI: A Select Critical Bibliography." *Records of the Scottish Church History Society* 23 (1987), 113–155.
Mitchell, Alexander F. *The Scottish Reformation.* Edinburgh, 1900.
Muir, Thomas. "The Scots Confession of 1560: Its Sources and Distinctive Characteristics." Ph.D. diss., University of Edinburgh, 1926.

JAMES KIRK

SCRIPTURE. In the Reformation of the sixteenth century, the text and teaching, or more precisely, the words (*verba*) and the substance (*res*) of scriptures of the Old and New Testament were the central focus of Protestant demands for the reform and reformulation of doctrine and practice in the church. From this perspective the efforts of Protestants to produce definitive editions of the text of the Bible, their immersion in the linguistic studies and tools of Renaissance humanism, their massive contribution to the method and scope of the biblical commentary, and their focus on the provision of accurate translations into the vernacular must all be viewed as closely correlated with the theological emphases of Protestantism on the authority and inspiration of scripture.

Scripture and Authority in the Sixteenth Century. The Reformation did not invent the view that scripture is the prior norm of doctrine, the source of all necessary doctrines, sufficient in its teachings for salvation. Such was the view of many medieval theologians and commentators. What the Reformation did in a new and forceful manner was to pose scripture against traditions and practices of the church and, at the same time, define scripture as clear and certain in and of itself and therefore "self-interpreting." Where the theologians of the Middle Ages had understood scripture and tradition as largely in agreement, had used tradition as a primary guide to the interpretation of scripture, and had granted tradition and the church to speak, as Jerome had put it, in the silence of scripture, the reformers assumed that no human norm or authority could be set over against or above the text as a rule or guide to interpretation. The only standard for the interpretation of scripture was scripture itself.

The problem of tradition. The problem of tradition can be summarized in the debate between Protestant and Roman Catholic over Augustine's famous statement that he "would not have believed the gospel" had he not been moved by "the authority of the catholic church." Luther's *Antwort auf Sprüche, so man führet, Menschenlehre zu stärken* (Reply to the Texts Cited in Defense of the Doctrines of Men; 1522) and Tyndale's *Answer to Sir Thomas More's Dialogue* (1530) both argued that scripture itself was sufficient to convince believers of its truth and that the "catholic church" referred to by Augustine was the community of believers who, by their authoritative example, led Augustine to examine the scriptures for himself. The same argument appears in Calvin's *Institutes*, Musculus's *Loci communes*, Vermigli's *Loci communes*, and many of the early orthodox theologies. Nonetheless, neither the reformers nor their successors sought to reject the church's tradition. Virtually all of the Protestant confessions of the sixteenth century indicate the normative character, subordinate to scripture, of the ecumenical creeds of the church. As, moreover, Calvin's *Responsio ad Sadoleti epistolam* (Letter to Sadoletto; 1539) indicates, the reformers assumed the identity of their communion with the Holy Catholic church and, consequently, the continuity of their theology with right teaching in the all ages of the church, in particular with the Augustinian tradition. As the sixteenth century progressed, Protestant teachers increasingly stressed the relationship between the reform and the teachings of past ages. On the Lutheran side, Chemnitz's theology is marked by a profound use of the Fathers—while among the Reformed, Lambert Daneau's *Christianae isagoges* (1583) evidenced a respect for such medieval doctors as Lombard, Aquinas, and Durandus. It is clear that the *sola scriptura* did not mean scripture without tradition, but scripture as the prior norm, potentially set in judgment over the tradition albeit not untraditionally interpreted. Continuities in the doctrinal interpretation of scripture often run from the patristic and medieval periods through the Reformation into the era of Protestant orthodoxy.

The solidification of canon. The nature and limitation of the canon was integral to the issue of the authority of scripture in the Reformation. In the early Reformation the notion of canon was somewhat less rigid than in the second half of the sixteenth century. In the first place, the Apocrypha or deuterocanonical books, were still viewed as edifying by Protestants as well as Roman Catholics albeit, following some of the reservations of Jerome concerning books not found in the Hebrew, of lesser authority. In the second place, the Eusebian distinction between homologoumena (books "agreed upon" by all) and antilegomena (books "spoken against") was still observed by such diverse commentators as Luther and Cajetan—with the result that *II Peter, II* and *III John, James,* and *Jude* could be viewed as less authoritative than the other works in the canon of the New Testament. The most extreme comment on such antilegomena was surely Luther's identification of *James* as an "epistle of straw."

The confessional formalization of the mid-sixteenth century included a resolution of the problem of the canon. The Council of Trent dissolved confessionally the distinction between homologoumena and antilegomena in the New Testament and insisted on the doctrinal authority of the Apocrypha. The *Canons of the Council of Trent* make no distinction, in their listing of the books of Bible, between the primary canon and the Apocrypha. The major Protestant confessions of the mid-century, the Gallic Confession, Belgic Confession, Scottish Confession, Thirty-nine Articles, and Second Helvetic Confession, responded to Trent with definitions of the canon that excluded the Apocrypha but, like Trent, abolished the distinction between homologoumena and antilegomena in the New Testament. The effect of this closer definition of the canon was to sharpen the distinction between scripture and tradition and identify the entirety of the canon as normative for Protestant theology in such a way as to press as never before the need to harmonize such problems as the difference between the language of justification and faith in Paul and *James.* Where Luther felt free to dismiss *James* as less than central to the Gospel, Calvin argued the case for the compatibility of their positions.

The Inspiration of Scripture. The inspiration of scripture, unlike the question of its authority, was not a matter of great debate during the Reformation. The reformers and their Roman Catholic opponents agreed both on the inspiration of the text and on its divine authority, and considerable continuity can be identified between medieval views of inspiration and the views of the reformers. Nonetheless, there remains some disagreement among scholars concerning the reformers' precise views of inspiration, particularly in relation to the doctrines of their early orthodox successors. It is certainly true that the pronouncements of the reformers tended to be less dogmatically than kerygmatically governed and that their successors tended to argue the point in a more dogmatic form. There is a proclamatory character in such early Reformation discussions of scripture as Zwingli's *De certitudine et claritate verbi Dei liber* (Clarity and Certainty of the Word; 1524) and Luther's prefaces to the books of the Bible, and even in mid-century works such as Calvin's *Institutio* (1559) and Bullinger's *Decades* (1549–1551) and the Second Helvetic Confession (1566), that is less evident in the systematic writings of early orthodox thinkers such as William Perkins, Amandus Polanus, Leonard Hutter, and Johann Gerhard. The change, however, was gradual and can hardly be identified as an overt alteration of doctrine. It is clear that both the reformers and their successors identified scripture as the word of God without qualification and as given by inspiration of the Holy Spirit. In addition, all held distinctions between the eternal word as second person of the Trinity, the word incarnate, the scriptural word, and the internal word or internal testimony of the Spirit—with the result that scripture as word was recognized as finite, but grounded in the eternal word and wisdom of God. Similarly, both the reformers and their successors assumed a distinction between word as the substance or meaning (*res*) of scripture and the words (*verba*) of the text; the former carried over into translations, the latter did not. The traditional identification of God as principal author (*auctor primarius*) also appears throughout the sixteenth century. Such qualifications as Calvin's statement that the words of the text were dictated "in a certain manner" (*quoddammodo*) ought certainly to be understood as pointing to the analogy between the work of the Spirit inspiring the words of the text and the dictation of a text by one human being to another rather than, as sometimes interpreted, a denial of inspiration as a kind of dictation. This impression is confirmed by Calvin's commentary on *Jeremiah* 36:4–8, where God dictates to Jeremiah a second time the contents of a prophecy that had been lost and Jeremiah then dictates the prophecy to Baruch: both events are described as dictation, but the former is not heard by Baruch. This understanding of the Spirit's work as analogical to dictation is also a major point of continuity between the writers of the Middle Ages and those of the Protestant orthodox era. Protestant theologians differed over the character of the human, secondary authorship of the text, although the majority of writers during both the Reformation and the era of orthodoxy recognized that varieties in style and vocabulary indicated a certain presence of mind in the human authors. It is certainly incorrect to assume that the movement from Reformation to orthodoxy was simply a progressive rigidification of categories. Despite, therefore, the kerygmatic character of early Reformed teaching, there is an underlying continuity of doctrinal intention.

The Divinity of Scripture. The Protestant doctrine of scripture, as it developed in the sixteenth century, argued the authority of scripture in terms of a series of attributes—truth, certainty, infallibility, sufficiency, and perfection. This approach to the doctrine also evidences a continuity between medieval, Reformation, and post-Reformation Protestant teaching. Bullinger's *Decades*, for example, understand scripture as the true word of God that deceives no one and as the sufficient source of truths necessary to salvation, while Musculus's *Loci communes* stress the certainty and truth of God's sayings in scripture. Similarly, the truth of scripture is understood as an infallibility in all matters of faith and Christian life; its sufficiency and perfection are related to the truths necessary for salvation: scripture was not, therefore, viewed by either the reformers or their successors as an infinite guide to all knowledge. Nonetheless, it can be argued that, as early orthodoxy arose in the late sixteenth century, there was an increasingly dogmatic interest in these attributes of scripture and in the divine causality that could and did produce a text with these attributes. The more continuous development of the Protestant doctrine can be identified in such related issues as the internal testimony of the Spirit, the intrinsic and extrinsic evidences of divinity, the foundation and scope of scripture, and accommodation.

The internal testimony of the Spirit. Related to the reformers' claim that scripture is both self-evidencing and self-interpreting is the assumption that the divinity and authority of scripture are known primarily through the internal witness or testimony of the Spirit. As distinct from the Anabaptist or spiritualist assumption of new prophecy or revelation, the reformers' concept of an internal testimony in no way indicated the impartation of information. Rather, as Calvin indicated, the same Spirit who spoke to and through the prophets and apostles also conveys to the reader or hearer of his word a testimony to its truth. This testimony is integral to the reading and hearing of the word and never separate from it: the Spirit enables believers to understand that God is the author of scripture who still "speaks" in it. The concept of an internal testimony of the Spirit is, therefore, virtually identical to the concept of an "internal word" that addresses the believer in and through encounter with the external word read or preached. Both concepts indicate the subjective reception of the word of God and define that

reception as an effective and, therefore, redemptive divine work.

Intrinsic and extrinsic evidences of divinity. Once they had made clear that the inward testimony of the Spirit was necessary to the reception of scripture as divine and authoritative, the reformers and the Protestant orthodox writers of the late sixteenth century insisted that this subjective apprehension of divinity be balanced by a recognition of the objective divinity evidenced by the text. This balance is clearly presented in Calvin's *Institutes* and in Ursinus's *Loci theologici*, and it is reflected as well in the detailed theological systems of early orthodox writers such as Polanus and Gerhard. Virtually all writers declare that the objective marks of divinity are not capable of convincing unbelievers apart from the witness of the Spirit any more than the mere repetition of the words of the gospel apart from God's grace. Rather, the objective evidences are a collateral witness, granting the lively work of the Spirit in and through the text. In addition, it was certainly the conviction of the late sixteenth-century systematizers of Protestantism that theology should recognize a balance of the subjective and the objective—both the inward basis of apprehension and the external reality that is apprehended. Thus scripture is clearly evidenced as intrinsically divine by the majesty of its style, the antiquity of its divine message that gives it priority over all other religions, the consistency of its teaching during many centuries of composition, the truth of its prophecies, and the revelation of saving truths that could not otherwise be known. Even so, people of such humble origins as Hosea and Amos or the twelve apostles could hardly be the inventors or discoverers of such deep truths: the circumstances of the text itself demand recognition of the divine hand at work. Extrinsically, scripture is known to be divine by the providential preservation of its text and by the blood of the martyrs shed for its truths.

The foundation and scope of scripture. Related both to the doctrine of the divinity and overarching consistency of scripture and to the character of scripture as authoritative and self-interpreting is the concept of its foundation (*fundamentum*) and center, or "scope" (*scopus*). Early Reformation documents, such as Luther's preface to the letter of James (1522), the *Acts of the Synod of Bern* (1532), the First Helvetic Confession (1536), and equally so later works like Ursinus's *Loci theologici* and Perkins's *Exposition of the Symbole* (1595), insist on the centrality of Christ to the entire scripture. This centrality does not result merely from the fact that Christ is goal and center of the messianic and covenantal history between the call of Abraham and the eschaton, but also from the ultimate focus of meaning of every text in scripture on the work of God in Christ. Luther could insist that the genuine books of scripture were known by their witness to Christ. Ursinus likewise declared that Christ is taught throughout the whole of scripture as the foundation of doctrine and as the summation and focal point (*summa et scopus*) of the biblical message. On the one hand, this view could lead to a highly christological reading of the Old Testament, particularly of the *Psalms* and the prophets. On the other, granting the relationship between Christ as the word incarnate and scripture as the accommodated form of the eternal word and wisdom of God, it served to reinforce the doctrine of scriptural authority and to maintain a more dynamic view of the text in relation to doctrine throughout the sixteenth century.

Accommodation. Underlying the teaching of the reformers and quite explicitly stated in the theology of the post-Reformation orthodox theologians was a recognition that scripture, albeit identified as the infallible word of God, was not identical either with the second person of the Trinity (the Word) or with the infinite wisdom of God. The character of scripture as both infallible and finite was, therefore, the subject of discussion and definition from the beginning of the Reformation onward. When Luther and Calvin distinguished between the word as God, the word as incarnate mediator, and scripture as word, they not only indicated the integral relationship between the biblical word in the divine wisdom, they also indicated that scripture is accommodated to human need: the wisdom given in scripture is not infinite—rather it is infallibly adapted to the way of human knowing and sufficient in its revelation of saving truth. Luther could characterize scripture as the swaddling clothes around the Christ-child and Calvin could liken the divine word speaking in scripture to a mother lisping or prattling to a child. Calvin in particular used his view of the accommodation interpretively as a way of understanding the limitation of human words, even as used in scripture, to approach the mysteries of God. Thus, in his commentary on *Isaiah* 40:12, he understands the divine measuring of the waters and weighing of the mountains as a way of indicating the indescribable majesty of God that presents the unfathomable in terms suited to the limitations of human understanding. This characteristic of Reformation teaching also carried over into the early orthodox era: in a more formal manner, writers like Franciscus Junius noted that the revelation offered in scripture was neither a knowledge founded on union, such as Christ had, nor a knowledge grounded in direct vision, such as given to angels and to the blessed in heaven, but a knowledge of disclosure suitable to the finite and fallen human condition (*De vera theologia,* 1594). Even so, the doctrines of scripture as sufficient and perfect assumed the limitation of these attributes to the things necessary to salvation.

BIBLIOGRAPHY

Armogathe, Jean-Robert, ed. *Le grand siècle de la Bible: Bible de tous les temps.* Vol. 6. Paris, 1989.

Bedouelle, Guy, and Bernard Roussel, eds. *Le temps des réformes et la Bible: Bible de tous les temps.* Vol. 5. Paris, 1989. A valuable collection of essays on scripture and its interpretation.

Davies, Rupert E. *The Problem of Authority in the Continental Reformers: A Study in Luther, Zwingli, and Calvin.* Reprint, Westport, Conn., 1978. A solid older work that avoids much of the twentieth-century effort to read contemporary theological concerns into the Reformation view of scripture.

Forstman, H. Jackson. *Word and Spirit: Calvin's Doctrine of Biblical Authority.* Stanford, Calif., 1962.

Kropatscheck, Friedrich. *Das Schriftprinzip der lutherischen Kirche: Geschichte und dogmatische Untersuchungen.* Vol. 1., *Die Vorgeschichte: Das Erbe des Mittelalters.* Leipzig, 1904. A fine older work on the background of the Reformation view of scripture.

Lotz, David W. "Sola Scriptura: Luther on Authority." In *Interpretation* 35 (1981), 258–273.

Muller, Richard A. *Post-Reformation Reformed Dogmatics.* Vol. 2, *Holy Scripture: The Cognitive Foundation of Theology.* Grand Rapids, Mich., 1993. A study of the continuities and discontinuities in Protestant doctrine form the Reformation into the era of orthodoxy.

Pelikan, Jaroslav. *Luther the Expositor: Luther's Works Companion Volume.* Saint Louis, 1959. Contains a useful discussion of Luther's understanding of "Word."

———. *The Christian Tradition: A History of the Development of Doctrine.* 5 vols. Chicago and London, 1971–. Volume 4 contains a discussion of the Protestant doctrine of scripture, with reference both to the Reformation and orthodoxy.

Preus, Robert D. *The Theology of Post-Reformation Lutheranism.* 2 vols. Saint Louis, 1970–1972. Volume 1 contains a lengthy presentation of continuities in the Lutheran doctrine of scripture as it developed from Reformation to orthodoxy.

Reventlow, Henning Graf. *The Authority of the Bible and the Rise of the Modern World.* Translated by John Bowden. Philadelphia, 1985. A significant discussion that emphasizes the English scene and the alterations of perspective from the time of the Puritans to the eighteenth century.

RICHARD A. MULLER

ŠCULTÉTY, Severín (also Sculteti; c.1550–1600), pedagogue, Lutheran pastor and senior, and theologian in Upper Hungary (Slovakia). Born in Dolná Lehota near Banská Bystrica in Slovakia, Šcultéty, a Slovak, did not go abroad for his education. In 1565 he enrolled at Bardejov in northeastern Slovakia, where his teachers included the successor of Leonard Stöckel, Thomas Faber (1535–1591). While still a student he became an assistant teacher (1573); upon completion of his studies, he worked at Brezno. He became co-rector of the school in Prešov (1580), where he may have prepared the translation into Slovak of Luther's Small Catechism (Bardejov, 1581). In 1584 he returned to Bardejov, where he became rector and, together with Martin Wagner and Thomas Faber, wrote against the Sacramentarian Gaspar Pilcż (*Examen thesium . . .*). In 1589 he became rector of the Lutheran school in Prešov but returned one year later to Bardejov as pastor after having been ordained in Graz by the orthodox Lutheran superintendent there, Jeremias Homberger.

On his return from Graz he took part in the colloquy at

Csepreg (2 June 1591), called by the Lutheran magnate Francis Nádasdy, at which Gregor Stanšič Horváth de Gradecz and other orthodox Lutherans debated Stephen Böjthe, the Calvinist leader of west Hungary. In 1593 Šcultéty was elected senior of the five royal free cities of northeastern Upper Hungary (Bardejov, Prešov, Košice, Sabinov, and Levoča). As senior he chaired several synods—including those of Prešov, (1593), Bardejov (1594), and Levoča (1597)—during which he urged the acceptance of the Formula of Concord as a doctrinal standard for the Lutherans in eastern Upper Hungary and opposed both Flacian and crypto-Calvinist views. During the synod at Prešov in October 1595 he also had to resolve the question of the *ius patronatus,* or the right of lay magistrates to call or dismiss pastors and teachers without consulting the responsible clerical administrators. Šcultéty died of the plague in June 1600.

BIBLIOGRAPHY

Šcultéty, Severín. *Examen thesium et regularum Zwinglianarum de coena Domini vulgatum per Casparem Pilicum.* Bardejov, 1586. Coauthor with Thomas Faber and Martin Wagner.

———. *Apologia examinis ecclesiae et scholae Bartphensis.* Bardejov, 1590. Coauthor with Martin Wagner, Jacob Wagner, and Thomas Faber.

———. *Historia Colloquii Chepregiensis.* . . . Bardejov, 1591.

———. *Erotemata de communicatione idiomatum, hoc est, proprietatum Divinae et Humanae naturae in una, individua persona Christi.* Bardejov, 1593.

———. *Hypomnima, das ist: Ein kurtze, nothwendige Erinnerung an die fünf löbliche freie Städte in Ober-Ungarn . . . von ihrer Christlichen Glaubensconfession.* Bardejov, 1599.

DAVID P. DANIEL

SEBASTIANO DEL CANO. *See* Cano, Melchior.

SECULAR MAGISTRATE, OFFICE OF.

Given the long history of the complex intermingling of secular and ecclesiastical matters in European society, and given that the papal hierarchy right down to the local bishops and their officials were bitter opponents of the Reformation, the German reformers quickly found that an orderly reformation was not possible without the active participation of friendly secular authorities. But since both their Catholic and their radical critics (for different reasons) denied the legitimacy of this reformation under the aegis of secular rulers, and since they themselves were not disposed to replace the "tyranny" of the pope with the tyranny of the magistrate, the reformers were forced to deal with the question of the nature and the extent of political authority.

The starting point of Martin Luther's analysis of this issue was his *Zwei-Reiche-Lehre* ("Two Kingdoms"), according to which all Christians are simultaneously the citizens or subjects of two divinely established kingdoms or realms

(*Reiche*): the internal, spiritual kingdom of faith and conscience, ruled by Christ himself through his word alone, without external force or compulsion of any kind; and the kingdom of this world (the realm of secular affairs and human reason), in which kings, princes, and other magistrates use force and compulsion ("the sword") to keep peace and to secure the well-being of their subjects. Luther was adamant that human laws or constraints of any kind (whether imposed by a pope, bishop, emperor, prince, or anyone else) were absolutely out of place in God's kingdom; that secular authority extended only to "life and property and external affairs on earth" and not to the government of souls; that secular authority as such was not intrinsically or necessarily Christian; and thus that secular rulers had no routine authority in the church.

Nevertheless, starting in 1520 Luther himself frequently called upon secular authorities (first the emperor and the imperial diet and then, after the emperor and diet had condemned him, the electors of Saxony and other territorial rulers) to intervene in ecclesiastical affairs in the interest of orderly and effective reformation. In some instances he construed such intervention as simply the exercise of routine secular authority to keep peace and order: for example, the restraint of "factious" preaching because of the presumed threat to civic peace, or the regulation of marriage, education, and church property (now regarded as matters of secular rather than ecclesiastical jurisdiction). But when Luther called upon the secular authorities to do things such as summon a church council (1520) or conduct an ecclesiastical visitation (1527–1528), he was asking them to exceed the normal bounds of their jurisdiction as he defined them. He was able to do so because he saw the church faced with an emergency that the established ecclesiastical authorities either would not or could not deal with by themselves and because he believed that in such circumstances Christian rulers, as participants in the priesthood of all believers and as the most powerful members of the Christian community, had a special obligation to serve their fellow Christians as *Notbischöfe* ("emergency bishops"). In theory any Christian could exercise the emergency power to summon a council or inaugurate a visitation, but only the action of the secular authorities was likely to be effective.

The secular rulers themselves took a somewhat less complicated view of their role in "spiritual" matters. Long accustomed to claiming and, in varying degrees, to exercising control over the personnel and property of the church, including oversight of the clergy in the performance of their spiritual office, German territorial rulers—like the *signori* of the Italian communes and the monarchs of England, France, and Spain—were already the heads of what could loosely be called territorial churches. As such, they typically took the view that their political office included responsibility for the establishment and support of true religion as well as the preservation of secular peace and order.

The overwhelming majority of Luther's fellow reformers embraced the same view of the religious obligations of the magistrate and elaborated upon it. Of their reasons for doing so, perhaps the most important was that most of them (e.g., Philipp Melanchthon, Martin Bucer, Johannes Brenz, Huldrych Zwingli, and many others, not to mention Calvin and other non-Germans) had come to the Reformation via that humanism of which Desiderius Erasmus was the oracle. As a consequence, they had absorbed the Erasmian notion, nourished by both classical and Christian sources, that "the commonwealth" (i.e., the state) is itself a moral and religious entity presided over by a Christian prince whose primary obligation is to maintain peace and order by instilling Christian faith and piety in his subjects. So when humanists-turned-reformers turned to the secular authorities for aid in reforming the church, they echoed Luther's appeal to the rulers as baptized Christians to perform a service of love for their fellow Christians, but at the same time (frequently in the same sentence) they also appealed to the rulers as rulers—that is, as the incumbents of a political office established by God for the purpose of establishing and maintaining true doctrine and worship—and they did not limit this role to emergencies. In their care for religion the rulers were to follow the example of the pious kings of the Old Testament (e.g., Hezekiah, Josiah, and Jehu) and of the Christian emperors (e.g., Constantine and Theodosius) who had abolished error and idolatry and established true piety and worship in accordance with God's law.

For the Lutheran reformers, who had to take account of Luther's radical division between the secular and spiritual realms (something that Zwingli and other non-Lutherans pointedly refused to do), justifying the assignment of such a role to secular rulers was a formidable intellectual challenge. When individuals or groups who felt threatened by governmental imposition of uniformity of doctrine and practice charged that the *cura religionis* of the magistrate violated the distinction between spiritual and secular authority, the Lutheran reformers replied with some or all of the following arguments: that the secular and spiritual realms, though distinct, should cooperate in the achievement of God's purposes; that the church on earth straddles both realms (the spiritual realm with respect to preaching the word and administering the sacraments, which is the responsibility of the clergy, and the secular realm with respect to all external means and ceremonies, which are human measures, not binding on conscience, and thus subject to secular authority); that territories divided in religion are ungovernable (an axiom of political thought at the time); that true preaching and worship promote secular peace and order, while false doctrine and worship bring the wrath of God in the concrete form of war, famine, pestilence, and other damage to the secular realm (another political axiom); that individuals may believe as they wish in the privacy of their own hearts and consciences (the spiritual realm) but may

not disturb Christian society (the secular realm) by dissenting from the established ecclesiastical order; and that, in any case, the crucial matter is not the exact boundary between secular and spiritual authority but rather God's clear command to the secular magistrate to serve his kingdom.

It was Melanchthon who in the mid-1530s forged these and other arguments into the more or less definitive theological justification of religious reformation and church government under the authority of the Christian magistrate. In Melanchthon's thought, the magistrate is not simply an individual member of the church who can function from time to time as *Notbischof* but rather "the foremost member" (*praecipuum membrum*) of the church with a routine obligation to care for the church and to see to it that errors are removed and consciences are healed. Moreover, the magistrate is also the leading member of human society, the chief goal of which is that men come to know God, glorify him, and gain eternal life. Thus, secular authority exists "for the sake of the church," and the chief duty of the magistrate is not simply to preserve external peace and order but to establish and preserve discipline, good morals, and true religion. To put it another way, the magistrate is guardian, with respect to external discipline (i.e., only in the secular realm), of both tables of the Decalogue. This means that the magistrate is responsible for the public observance of man's duty to God (the first three commandments) as well as of man's duty to man (the remaining seven commandments). Thus the first three commandments require the magistrate to establish true preaching and worship among his subjects and to abolish false preaching and worship. In Psalm 2:10–12 and in many other texts, God has specifically commanded secular rulers to use their office in this way and has threatened to visit his wrath upon them if they do not. This line of argument had the merit of reconciling church government by the magistrate with the distinction between the secular and spiritual realm that was so important to Lutheran theology. It did so by assigning, on the basis of a formidable array of biblical evidence, a predominantly religious nature and goal to the secular realm. It is thus clear that the establishment of *das landesherrliche Kirchenregiment*, or the state church of the Reformation, was originally conceived as a process of sacralizing the state, not of secularizing the church.

Melanchthon's definition of the office of Christian magistrate rapidly became the official justification for the ecclesiastical polity of the German Protestant territories and was taught to generations of pastors and officials in schools and universities. Moreover, there is abundant evidence of the determining influence of Melanchthon's views on virtually all Lutheran theologians (even Luther himself in the last decade or so of his life) for the balance of the sixteenth century. But there were problems. The assumption of the theologians who justified reformation and church government by the magistrate was that the magistrate would respect the independence of the clergy in the performance of the ministry that Christ had entrusted to them and heed their advice in all matters pertaining to doctrine and worship. But particularly after the Peace of Augsburg (1555)—which formally granted to the Lutheran princes all the jurisdiction in their territories that had once been exercised by the bishops, together with the legal right to determine the religion of their subjects—it was possible for the princes to claim complete jurisdiction in spiritual matters such as doctrine as well as in the external organization of the church. During the sixteenth century and even a bit beyond, the community of interest and outlook between princes and their theologians tended to keep this potential conflict from surfacing. Nevertheless, there were theologians (e.g., Martin Chemnitz) who in the later decades of the sixteenth century felt constrained to remind princes that they were only members and protectors of the church, not its lords and masters, and that in the performance of their ministry the clergy were more obligated to God than to the prince.

In assessing the significance of the territorial church in the history of the Reformation, it must be remembered that the institution had ample precedent, at both the practical and theoretical levels, in developments before the Reformation; that the theological justification for it, cogently argued on the basis of biblical evidence, was extremely persuasive; and that there was no realistic alternative if the Reformation and its message were to survive and endure.

Protestant reformers in France, England, and Scandinavia took essentially the same view of the office of the Christian magistrate as did the German reformers, which is not surprising given that they faced similar problems, were influenced by similar intellectual and political traditions, were well aware of developments in the German Protestant territories, and were thoroughly conversant with the works of their German predecessors and contemporaries. Calvin's view of the religious obligations of secular authority, for example, was much the same as Melanchthon's (see the prefatory letter to Francis I and the chapter on civil government in the *Christianae religionis Institutio*). But Calvin and his followers never succeeded in persuading the kings of France to play the role assigned to them by Protestant theology. In Scandinavia and England, on the other hand, territorial churches analogous to those in the German Protestant territories were established at the national level. Those who effected the Reformation in the Scandinavian kingdoms were directly influenced by the Wittenberg theologians and justified the king's role in church government with arguments borrowed from Melanchthon. Similarly, the doctrine of secular authority advocated by the writers who justified the royal supremacy in England (e.g., John Jewel in part 6 of his *Apology of the Church of England*, 1562) owed much to the influence of Melanchthon, Bucer, Calvin, and other Continental thinkers.

In conclusion, it should be pointed out that Protestant rulers were not the only ones who assumed responsibility for establishing and defending true religion in their dominions. Catholic princes, like the dukes of Bavaria and the kings of France and Spain, were just as zealous in asserting their control over religious life as were Protestant princes and were hardly less successful in doing so, despite the necessity of continuing to acknowledge the authority of Rome and the jurisdiction of the bishops. Moreover, the determination of Catholic monarchs, such as the German emperor and his counterparts in France and Spain, to crush the Protestant movement by force confronted Protestant apologists with the difficult question of the legitimacy of armed resistance to sovereign authority. The answer most commonly given, first by the Lutheran reformers in Germany and then, building on the arguments of the Germans, by the Calvinist reformers in western Europe, was that the individual Christian could take up arms only if summoned to do so by "inferior magistrates" (variously defined) possessing constitutional authority (also variously defined) to resist the tyrannical abuse of authority by a "superior magistrate," that is, a king or an emperor.

[*See also* Magistracy.]

BIBLIOGRAPHY

Cargill Thompson, W. D. J. *The Political Thought of Martin Luther.* Brighton, England, and Totowa, N.J., 1984. Lucid, well-informed, and sensible study. Chap. 8 on "Church and State" includes a useful treatment of Melanchthon, who continues to be unjustly ignored by English-speaking scholars. Unfortunately, Cargill Thompson did not live to supply notes or to revise his manuscript, and the printed text is clearly defective in a number of places. The relevant works by Luther, most of them available in English translation, are listed in the bibliography.

Estes, James M. *Christian Magistrate and State Church: The Reforming Career of Johannes Brenz.* Toronto, 1982. Chap. 2 examines the historical background of the territorial church, of which Brenz was one of the chief organizers, and chap. 3 analyzes Brenz's thought on church and state, which was influenced by Erasmus, Luther, the Nuremberg reformers, and Melanchthon.

Kittelson, James M. *Wolfgang Capito: From Humanist to Reformer.* Leiden, 1975. Chap. 5, "The Campaign for Reform," describes how Capito and the other Strasbourg reformers persuaded the city council that it was their duty as Christian magistrates to support the Reformation and enact it into law.

Manschreck, Clyde L., trans. and ed. *Melanchthon on Christian Doctrine: Loci Communes, 1555.* Reprint, Grand Rapids, Mich., 1982. The section "Of Worldly Authority" contains Melanchthon's summary of his own mature view on the religious duties of the magistrate.

Pauck, Wilhelm, ed. *Melanchthon and Bucer.* Library of Christian Classics, vol. 19. Philadelphia, 1969. Includes an abbreviated translation of Bucer's magisterial work on relations between church and state, *De Regno Christi* (1550), with a useful introduction that briefly summarizes Bucer's earlier thought on the subject.

Walton, Robert Cutler. *Zwingli's Theocracy.* Toronto, 1967. The development of Zwingli's view of the relationship between the secular magistracy and the clergy, emphasizing the influence of Erasmian humanism and of the preexisting relationship between church and state in Zurich.

JAMES M. ESTES

SEILER, Caspar. *See* Hedio, Caspar.

SELNECKER, Nikolaus (1530–1592), German Lutheran theologian and codrafter of the Formula of Concord. Born on 5 December 1530 in Hersbruck, near Nuremberg, where he developed as a prodigy at the organ, Selnecker studied at Wittenberg (1549–1558) as a member of Philipp Melanchthon's inner circle. As a court preacher at Dresden (1558–1565) he attacked hunting practices of the nobility. This may have contributed to his dismissal, perhaps along with some theological disagreements with "crypto-Calvinist" colleagues (although at this time his writings still displayed "Philippist" views on free will and the Lord's Supper).

Selnecker taught at Jena (1565–1568) until ousted by the Gnesio-Lutheran Duke Johann Wilhelm and then at Leipzig (1568–1586), where he also served as pastor of Saint Thomas and superintendent. Frequently sent on ecclesiastical diplomatic missions by Elector August of Saxony, he left Leipzig to assist Martin Chemnitz and Jakob Andreae in the reformation of Braunschweig-Wolfenbüttel (1570–1574). These two drew him away from his Philippist theology to a large extent, and the three formed the nucleus of the team that worked in 1576–1577 under the aegis of Elector August to compose the Formula of Concord and to win support for it. Selnecker played a key role in reorganizing electoral Saxon church life and reversing its earlier "crypto-Calvinist" direction (1574–1586). With Chemnitz and Timotheus Kirchner he composed the *Apologia . . . deß . . . Concordienbuchs* (Apology of the Formula of Concord; 1583). In the second round of "crypto-Calvinist" influence in the electoral Saxon government, Selnecker was dismissed from office and assumed the superintendency of the church of Hildesheim. Recalled to Leipzig in 1591, he died there before assuming office. Selnecker's musical talent produced 120 hymn tunes and numerous hymn texts. His biblical lectures—on *Genesis, Psalms,* and the epistles of the New Testament—contained extensive doctrinal loci. Like his *Institutio religionis christianae* (1573, rev. 1579), they reveal his gradual movement away from distinctive "Philippist" positions in the direction of what was to become the theology of the Formula of Concord.

BIBLIOGRAPHY

Ebel, Jobst. "Die Herkunft des Konzeptes der Konkordienformel." *Zeitschrift für Kirchengeschichte* 91 (1980), 237–282. Summary of Selnecker's involvement in the composition of the Formula of Concord.

Jungkuntz, Theodore R. "Nikolaus Selnecker: The Weather Vane?" In *Formulators of the Formula of Concord: Four Architects of Lutheran Unity*, pp. 89–109. Saint Louis, 1977. Brief biographical overview based on extant published sources and analyses.

ROBERT KOLB

SEMINARIES. With its Seminary Decree of 15 July 1563, the Council of Trent proved epoch making in the training of the Catholic clergy. This topic came on the agenda of the council late in the context of the defense and pastoral legitimation of the sacramental orders against the Reformation (May 1562), a topic that had engaged all three sessions of the council. Friction between papal and episcopal conceptions of the church prevented an ecclesiological reappraisal, so that finally only one set of practical measures "super abusibus circa administrationem sacramenti ordinis" was promulgated. In the seminary, which was supposed to train secular clerics under the direction of the bishop acting as pastor, conciliar reform notions became institutionalized. To this day, the episcopal seminary is the regular location of Catholic training for the priesthood. This historical appraisal of the seminary looks at this new creation primarily in the functional context of the educational institutions of the sixteenth century, and evaluates especially the contribution of the seminary to Catholic reform and Counter-Reformation in the confessionally divided empire.

Only after the Reformation did the widespread call for church reform include, especially in Germany, a reform of the educational structures. In its early phase, the Council of Trent (session V 2) reverted to the Lateran councils of 1179 and 1215 (canons 18 and 11) by requiring lectureships in Bible or at least instruction in grammar at episcopal and collegiate churches as well as in monasteries and convents, in order to achieve an intensification of preaching. The Bible was also to be taught at the universities. Without further heeding German suggestions (Julius Pflug, F. Nausea, C. Jajus, *Formula reformationis* 1548, etc.) to institutionalize recruitment and training of pastoral clergy in endowed episcopal colleges at Catholic universities, the council in its final phase continued to emphasize the cathedral schools. The basis was canon 11 of the Canterbury synod (1555/56) convened by Cardinal Reginald Pole during the brief Catholic restoration in England. Faced with a lack of priests, Pole targeted the new establishment of schools at cathedrals, which already had been set in motion by the Anglican church. These cathedral schools, placed under the bishop and the cathedral chapter, assumed responsibility not only for the care of the teaching staff but also (according to German proposals) for the livelihood of the students, who received spiritual vestment and tonsure in the expectation that they would enter church service. The older students, who were preparing for ordination and in imitation of the Veronese institution of Gian Matteo Giberti, were called acolytes and were promised benefices.

The decree on seminaries, which intended to revive the old cathedral school as a place for training priests, changed ecclesiastical educational policy from the support of elitist university studies for a few to the training of many clergy who generally came from poorer classes. Even if the seminary was by no means the only way to ordination, it was the main route of clerical training apart from the university. Until the coming of the Reformation in the empire, the university had educated a growing number of future clergy, both in Germany and, even more efficiently, in Spain. Italian universities had only marginal theology faculties, a fact that undoubtedly influenced the debates of the Italian-dominated council, for the council seldom cited the contribution of existing institutions toward clerical education. Neither did the council concern itself with the humanist schools that were emerging all over Europe at that time. The decree on seminaries, which required the ability to read and write Latin for admission, focused on the medieval grammar school as a point of departure. This created difficulties in Germany, for these types of schools were being replaced by grammar schools with instruction in German and humanist-style academies with a much longer course of study in classical literature than the medieval Latin grammar school. Few boys at age twelve—the age stipulated for entrance into the seminary—had the necessary Latin skills, but the Council of Trent still felt this young age necessary to keep future priests from worldly temptations.

In addition to grammar, the decree provided for courses in liturgy, ecclesiastical canonical literature, the Bible, and sacramental practice. It was directed not as much toward an educational program—the name *schola* ("school") was completely avoided—as toward the formation of clergy that, alongside classroom instruction, received practical and moral training in the service of the church. This probationary period could be expected to last thirteen years until ordination (subdeacon at 22, deacon at 23, priest at 25 years of age). Despite this, the discussion of the decree *Cum adolescentium aetas*, particularly in the Holy Roman Empire, one-sidedly stressed the instructional elements and ignored the more practical elements of the council's decree.

In addition to such conceptional ambiguities, the establishment of seminaries in the empire was made more difficult by the political situation. As a spiritual imperial prince, the bishop competed with his secular peers, who had seized the *cura religionis* as part of their sovereign task. Surrounded by an aristocratic cathedral chapter, he could act as a pastoral bishop inside or outside the chapter only with difficulty. In that context, the provisions of the decree on seminaries, which intended to functionalize the system of church offices and benefices in the direction of the episcopal *cura animarum*, could not entail a tax for seminaries. Nevertheless, the decree, whose execution was urged by popes, nuncios, and the *Congregatio Germanica*, forced educational-political initiatives, which, according to the precedent set by the Protestant estates, became a lever of humanist school reform, embracing clergy and lay elites alike.

Notwithstanding many misgivings based on canon law, especially on the part of cathedral chapters, the Jesuit order with its broad educational effort became the main body of Catholic educational reform. Prudently, though also expressing episcopal sentiment, the council had not expressed an opinion about the use of members of the monastic order in the episcopal seminaries. It remains an open question how far it heeded the stormy development of the Jesuit colleges, which at first were modeled on the universities, then became independent with their own teaching activities, and finally turned into a school order. With a lilting optimism, the order always saw humanist education and the religious renewal of the Catholic church as a unity, believing that its public school could take the place of a seminary by simply adding a pastoral course. The new order forced open the narrow focus of the seminary program and reconciled education of priests with humanist reform. Indeed, with their own educational program keyed to demanding philosophical and theological studies, the Jesuits opened the perspective of universities, which, in the training of teachers, certainly took into account an urgent need, even though it was at the cost of becoming "monkish." The beginnings of structured training of priests were influenced by the Jesuits and their secondary schools and faculties in Cologne (1544), Trier (1560), and Mainz (1561), even before the seminary decree was promulgated.

The efforts at reform caught on also in secular territories such as Bavaria, where a well-attended classical school was established at Ingolstadt in 1556 and at Munich in 1559, so that the pedagogical principles of the Jesuit order guaranteed a unified intellectual formation of the clergy. With the establishment of the Hieronymus College at Dillingen in 1549/50, the bishop of Augsburg assumed a leading role among the ecclesiastical territories. The college became a theological seminary the Hochstiftsakademie (1551), the leadership of which was taken over by the Jesuits (1563/64). In Germany the conviction generally prevailed that the universities were seminaries for clergy par excellence. In Würzburg this meant the expansion of a Jesuit college to a full university (1575), adjacent to which was a boardinghouse for diocesan priests. The early establishment of a seminary at Eichstätt in 1564, which had close connections with the University of Ingolstadt, where the chancellor was the resident bishop, had to be turned over to the Society of Jesus in 1614 because of a lack of teachers. The same happened in 1611 at the Bamberg seminary, which had been established in 1586. Like Eichstätt, it had from the beginning offered public, generally accessible instruction. At the turn of the century most of the dioceses and cathedral chapters—other than possibly Freising—provided academic-intellectual training for the clergy in Jesuit schools. In addition to the free, public instruction offered by the Jesuits, endowed seminaries came into being for students for the priesthood, the direction of which the society did not assume gladly. For the most part, educational institutions and theological seminaries were established at the episcopal see, as had been stipulated in the conciliar decree. (The exceptions were Breslau, whose seminary functioned for a time in Neisse, and the Braunsberg [Braniewo] academy [1641] of the bishop of Ermland.)

The Roman see recognized this dualism of Jesuit and episcopal schools with the establishment of pontifical seminaries at Jesuit institutions (Vienna, Prague, Graz, Olmütz, Klausenburg, Fulda, and Dillingen between 1574 and 1585). The papal concern for the education and training of priests of the besieged churches in Germany, England, and Ireland was a novelty in church history and made Rome a center of philosophical-theological studies. Central was the founding of the Jesuit Collegium Romanum in 1551, which became, as the Universitas Gregoriana, the pedagogical institution of the worldwide order. Scholarship recipients from foreign colleges studied there; following the precedent of the Collegium Germanicum (1552), it was endowed by Pope Gregory XIII. The cooperation of the Curia Romana and the highly centralized papal order resulted in a trend toward centralization of the church and greater uniformity in ministerial training than had existed before the Reformation.

The seminary decree provided the impetus for church educational policy, but in the empire this did not lead to an entirely separate training program for the clergy. This would not happen until the seventeenth-century church in France developed its own forms of moral and practical training that went beyond matters of formal instruction. Catholic reform and the Counter-Reformation in the empire drew their strength from the school system of the Jesuits.

[*See also* Clergy; Education; *and* Universities.]

BIBLIOGRAPHY

Ammerich, H. "Das Fürstbistum Speyer im Zeichen der tridentinischen Erneuerung." *AmrhKG* 41 (1989), 81ff.

Baker, Derek, ed. *Miscellanea historiae ecclesiasticae III.* Proceedings of an international conference, Cambridge, England, 24–28 September 1968. Louvain, 1970. See pp. 107ff. regarding the recruitment and training of the clergy in the sixteenth century.

Demel, Bernhard. *Das Priesterseminar des Deutschen Ordens zu Mergentheim.* Bonn, 1972.

Hegel, E. "Organisationsformen der diözesanen Priesterbildung in Deutschland: Grundlinien ihrer geschichtlichen Entwicklung." In *Die Kirche und ihre Ämter und Stände: Festgabe J. Kardinal Frings,* edited by W. Corsten et al., pp. 645ff. Cologne, 1960.

Jedin, Hubert. *A History of the Council of Trent.* London, 1961.

———. "Die Bedeutung des Tridentinischen Dekretes über Priesterseminare für das Leben der Kirche." In *Theologie und Glaube* 54 (1964), 181ff.

———. "Domschule und Kolleg: Zum Ursprung der Idee des Trienter Seminars." In *Kirche des Glaubens, Kirche der Geschichte: Ausgewählte Aufsätze und Vorträge,* vol. 2, pp. 348ff. Freiburg, 1966.

Le Bras, Gabriel, and Jean Gaudemet, eds. *Histoire du droit et des institutions de l'Église en occident.* See vol. 14. Paris, 1989.

Merkle, Sebastian. "Das Konzil von Trient und die Universitäten, 1905." In *Ausgewählte Reden und Aufsätze Anlässlich seines 100. Geburtstags in Verbindung mit dem Sebastian-Merkle-Institut der Universität Würzburg,* edited by Th. Freudenberger, pp. 244ff. Würzburg, 1965.

O'Donohoe, James Alphonsus. *Tridentine Seminary Legislation: Its Sources and Its Formation.* Louvain, 1957.

Reiter, Ernst. *Martin von Schaumberg, Fürstbischof von Eichstätt (1560–1590), und die Trienter Reform.* Münster, 1965.

Schieber, H. "Die Vorgeschichte des Bamberger Priesterseminars." In *Seminarium Ernestinum: 400 Jahre Priesterseminar Bamberg,* edited by Michael Hofmann et al. Bamberg, 1986.

Schmidt, Peter. *Das Collegium Germanicum in Rom und die Germaniker: Zur Funktion eines römischen Ausländerseminars, 1552–1914.* Tübingen, 1984.

Seifert, Arno. *Weltlicher Staat und Kirchenreform: Die Seminarpolitik Bayerns im 16. Jahrhundert.* Münster, 1978.

Seminaria Ecclesiae Catholicae. Vatican City, 1963.

Tüchle, H. "Das Seminardekret des Trienter Konzils und Formen seiner geschichtlichen Verwirklichung." *Theologische Quartalschrift* 144 (1964), 12ff.

HARALD DICKERHOF
Translated from German by Susan M. Sisler

SENIOR, Karel. *See* Žerotín, Karl.

SEPARATISTS. Having repudiated the Church of England as unreformed and unbiblical, the Separatists were extreme Protestants who established their own congregations consisting of visible saints alone, that is, only those who lived manifestly godly lives. In addition to the Bible, the Separatists were heavily influenced by John Foxe's *Acts and Monuments* (popularly known as the *Book of Martyrs*), which provided them both with examples of earlier Protestants who had suffered under the repressive, allegedly anti-Christian regime of Mary Tudor and with the arguments they had used to justify withdrawal from a "false" church.

Even before Mary's regime forced Protestants to worship secretly outside the established church, congregations of foreign refugees had been founded in London as early as 1550, providing an example of Reformed congregations independent of episcopal authority. Not until June 1567, however, is there evidence of English Separatists who repudiated the Elizabethan state church. At that time seventeen or eighteen Separatists were imprisoned, but a second wave of arrests nine months later netted seventy-seven Separatists. In June 1568 Edmund Grindal, bishop of London, complained that there were four or five Separatist ministers in the City, with approximately two hundred followers, the majority of whom were women from the lowest social order. They met on ships and in fields and private houses; ordained their own clergy, elders, and deacons; and excommunicated wayward members. Underground congregations continued to worship in London throughout the 1570s.

The earliest Separatist leader of note was Robert Browne, a member of a gentry family from the Midlands, a graduate of the University of Cambridge, and a distant relative of William Cecil, Lord Burghley. In the spring of 1581 Browne and Robert Harrison, another Cambridge man, organized a Separatist congregation in Norwich, Norfolk, whose members, complained the bishop of Norwich, were "the vulgar sort of people." Imprisoned for his efforts, Browne subsequently led his followers into exile at Middelburg in the Netherlands. There he published a number of works setting forth the Separatists' position, including *A Treatise of Reformation Without Tarying for Anie* (1582) and *A Booke Which Sheweth the Life and Manners of All True Christians* (1582). Browne and Harrison soon fell out, and the former, after sampling and rejecting the Church of Scotland, eventually made his peace with the Church of England. Leadership of the movement passed to two former Puritans, Henry Barrow, son of a Norfolk gentleman, and John Greenwood, who had studied at Cambridge before becoming the minister of a church in Norfolk. By the time of their arrest in the fall of 1587, both men had embraced Separatist principles—Barrow possibly as a result of reading one of Browne's books, which he had intended to refute. Both men nevertheless insisted that they were not "Brownists" but had derived their views from scripture. The two men were associated with Separatists in London, and Greenwood in fact was selected as their "doctor" (teacher) in 1592, at which time the congregation elected Francis Johnson as their pastor. Barrow and Greenwood, both of whom had written and distributed Separatist works, were hanged in April 1593 for violating a 1581 statute by allegedly seeking the overthrow of the established church and royal supremacy.

Johnson, son of the mayor of Richmond, Yorkshire, and a Cambridge graduate, had been expelled from his fellowship at Christ's College after refusing to retract his assertion of presbyterian polity. After serving for a time as minister to the congregation of English Merchant Adventurers, a cloth exporting company in Middelburg, he became pastor of the London Separatist church. Despite being imprisoned for more than four years commencing in December 1592, he remained in contact with his flock, some of whom emigrated to Amsterdam. While in jail, he wrote *A True Confession of Faith*, the first published Separatist document of its genre. After Johnson joined his followers in Amsterdam in 1597, the church grew from approximately forty members to some three hundred around 1609, but many members of his congregation died en route to Virginia a decade later.

The Separatists and the radical wing of the Puritans shared many theological convictions. The two groups were not distinguished by ecclesiology but by differences in strategy and timing, notably the willingness of the Separatists to break with the established church rather than seek its further reformation. In most areas the Separatists borrowed heavily from the radical Puritans as they enunciated their desire to recover the spiritual life of the New Testament church. The heart of Separatist piety was deeply existential, and the Separatists' quest for New Testament discipline and polity grew out of their preeminent concern with holy living. Piety, not polity, was the driving force of the movement.

Five additional fundamental principles of the Separatists should be noted. (1) They linked polity to soteriology by asserting that those who did not adhere to the New Testament in ecclesial matters violated the second commandment. Because of their bilateral (conditional) interpretation of the covenant, assurance of salvation required fidelity to New Testament polity. (2) The apocalyptic vision that they shared with radical Puritans depicted history as a stage on which the cosmic war between Christ and Satan was staged. They saw themselves as key players in this drama because they were receptive to fresh revelation from God and were unyielding in their opposition to the Antichrist. (3) Church membership was limited to visible saints; evidence of an inward experience of grace was mandatory. The two marks of saving faith were knowledge of Christian doctrine and obedience to biblical ordinances. (4) Each Separatist congregation was independent and possessed the right to elect its minister and officers, so long as they were spiritually gifted, though some Separatists, such as Browne, advocated a role for synods. (5) Separatists accepted the princes' right to exercise authority over the church as custodians but did not allow them priestly power. Magistrates could compel people to attend church, though acceptance of the gospel had to be voluntary. The Separatists did not advocate the complete separation of church and state.

The significance of the Separatists lies in the fact that they provided the seedbed out of which the Baptists and Congregationalists later emerged. Moreover, they destroyed any hope for a unified Protestant church in England and severely devalued both religious and social traditions by their espousal of strict biblical standards.

BIBLIOGRAPHY

Brachlow, Stephen. *The Communion of Saints: Radical Puritan and Separatist Ecclesiology, 1570–1625.* Oxford, 1988. Definitive account; emphasizes the close relationship of Separatist and radical Puritan principles.

Collinson, Patrick. *The Elizabethan Puritan Movement.* Reprint, Oxford, 1990. Magisterial history of the Puritans that gives considerable attention to the Separatists.

George, Timothy. *John Robinson and the Separatist Tradition.* Macon, Ga., 1982. Best treatment of Robinson.

Greaves, Richard L. *Society and Religion in Elizabethan England.* Minneapolis, 1981. Includes a full account of Separatist social views.

Martin, J. W. *Religious Radicals in Tudor England.* London, 1989. Devoted primarily to unorthodox groups such as the Freewillers and the Family of Love, but useful for the wider context of religious dissidents.

Sprunger, Keith L. *Dutch Puritanism: A History of English and Scottish Churches of the Netherlands in the Sixteenth and Seventeenth Centuries.* Leiden, 1982. Includes a definitive discussion of the Separatists during their sojourn in the Netherlands.

Watts, Michael R. *The Dissenters: From the Reformation to the French Revolution*. Oxford, 1978. First chapter places the Separatists in historical context.

White, B. R. *The English Separatist Tradition: From the Marian Martyrs to the Pilgrim Fathers*. London, 1971. Standard historical account, but on Separatist thought superseded by Brachlow.

RICHARD L. GREAVES

SEPÚLVEDA, Juan Ginés de (1490–1573), opponent of Bartolomé de Las Casas in the Spanish debate on the rationality of Native Americans. Sepúlveda was born in Pozoblanco (Córdoba province, Spain). He studied Greek "from childhood," attended the universities of Alcalá de Henares and Sigüenza, and in 1515 became a fellow of the prestigious Spanish College at the University of Bologna, where he studied Aristotle under the tutelage of Pietro Pomponazzi and by 1523 earned doctorates in both arts and theology.

Already a cleric, he began his career as a writer of Latin prose in 1521 with a description of the Bolognese college and its founder. He translated various works of Aristotle from Greek into Latin (*Parva Naturalia*, 1522; *De ortu et interitu*, 1523; the apocryphal *De mundo*, 1523; and *Meteorum*, 1532). He also produced short works spurred by contemporary religious controversies: *De fato et libero arbitrio* against Luther in 1526; *De ritu nuptiarum* against Henry VIII's divorce proceedings in 1531; and *Antapologia* against Desiderius Erasmus in 1532. He used his rhetorical skill in *Ad Carolum V* (1529) to urge the emperor to fight the Turks and in the dialogue *Democrates* (1535) to defend the concept of a just war based on natural law and compatible with Christianity. Sepúlveda obtained the favor of a series of Italian patrons, notably Pope Clement VII, but in 1536 he returned to Spain as chronicler of Charles V.

By 1545 he turned again to the topic of just war, writing *Democrates secundus* (On the Just Causes of War Against the Indians). When he was denied a license to publish the book in Spain, he defended it in the *Apologia*, published in Rome in 1550. Meanwhile, he published his translation of Aristotle's *Politics* (1548). In *Democrates secundus* Sepúlveda justified Spanish conquest and rule on the grounds that Native Americans were natural slaves (*natura servi*, citing Aristotle) who committed such crimes against natural law as cannibalism, idolatry, and human sacrifice. War against them would prevent these crimes and force them to allow the preaching of the gospel. In 1550–1551 Sepúlveda and the aged Las Casas, self-appointed defender of Native Americans, debated these points before a royal committee of theologians and jurists, who gave no formal decision. In later years Sepúlveda published his Latin letters in seven volumes (1557) and continued his work as royal chronicler. He died in Pozoblanco on 17 November 1573.

BIBLIOGRAPHY

Primary Sources

Sepúlveda, Juan Ginés de. *Opera*. 4 vols. Madrid, 1780. Complete original works in Latin, excluding *Democrates secundus*, and a bio-bibliography.
————. *Tratado sobre las justas causas de la guerra*. Mexico City, 1941.
————. *Epistolario: Selección*. Edited by Angel Losada. Madrid, 1966.
————. *Demócrates segundo*. 2d ed. Translated and edited by Angel Losada. Madrid, 1984. Latin and Spanish edition.

Secondary Sources

Bell, Aubrey F. G. *Juan Ginés de Sepúlveda*. London, 1925. Very short but appreciative biography.
Hanke, Lewis. *All Mankind Is One*. De Kalb, Ill., 1974. Sepúlveda appears in his role as Las Casas's antagonist.
Losada, Angel. *Juan Ginés de Sepúlveda a través de su "epistolario" y nuevos documentos*. Reprint, Madrid, 1973. Lengthy supplement to the Sepúlveda complete works, *Opera*.
Pagden, Anthony. *The Fall of Natural Man: The American Indian and the Origins of Comparative Ethnology*. Cambridge, 1982. Sepúlveda is dismissed as a rhetorician who proved himself to be crass and out of-date by insisting on using the term "natural slave," thus ignoring Francisco de Vitoria's conclusion that Native Americans were childish rather than slavish.
Todorov, Tzvetan. *The Discovery of America: The Question of the Other*. Translated by Richard Howard. New York, 1984. Sepúlveda represents one of several ways of thinking about Native Americans.
Verzeichnis der im deutschen Sprachbereich erschienenen Drucke des XVI. Jahrhunderts. Stuttgart, 1983–. See vol. 19, nos. 5970–5972.

CONSTANCE J. MATHERS

SERIPANDO, Girolamo (1493–1563), Augustinian hermit, theologian, bishop, and cardinal. Born on 6 May 1493 at Troia (Puglia), Seripando came from a Neapolitan family. After his parents' untimely death he lived in Naples, raised by an uncle and a brother. After one year (1507) with the Dominican order, he entered the Convento di San Giovanni of the Augustinians at Carbonara. His education (Greek, arts, philosophy, theology) took place from 1508 to 1513, when he was ordained a priest. In the years that followed, he pursued his studies with the purpose of obtaining academic degrees. During this time he also became one of the closest collaborators of Giles of Viterbo, the superior general of his order and one of the most outstanding theologians of his time, who was active in the reform of the church.

In 1516 Seripando began to teach in the *studium* of the Augustinians in Bologna, first he first a bachelor's degree (1518) and then became master regent (1519–1523). In 1523 he returned to Naples and assumed ever greater responsibilities within his order. He came in contact with humanist circles and became a renowned preacher. In was during these years that he became acquainted with Cardinal Alessandro Farnese, the future Paul III, who was a protector of the Augustinians. In 1539 he was elected superior general of the Augustinian order (reelected in 1543 and 1547). Beginning in 1542 he devoted himself to disciplinary reform of the order, traveling all over Europe. During the first period of the Council of Trent (1545–1547) he played a leading role as a theologian who worked in concert with one of the presiding officers, Cardinal Marcello Cervini (the future Marcellus II). He made a decisive contribution in the formulation of the dogmatic decree on justification.

On the recommendation of Emperor Charles V, he was appointed bishop of Salerno by Julius III in 1554; in his diocese he labored for the reform of discipline. Despite accusations levelled against him alleging that he was less than orthodox, Pius IV entrusted ever greater responsibilities to him, and finally made him a cardinal in 1561 and appointed him to be one the presiders over the work of the third period of the Council of Trent. At Trent Seripando held a high profile, promoting the renewal of Catholicism until his death on 17 March 1563.

BIBLIOGRAPHY

Primary Sources

Seripando, Girolamo. *De iustitia et libertate Christianae.* Edited by A. Forster. Münster, 1970.

———. *In D. Pauli epistolas ad Romanos, et ad Galatos, commentaria.* Naples, 1971.

———. *Girolamo Seripando tra evangelismo e riforma cattolica.* Edited by Abbondanza Rocchina. Naples, 1981.

Secondary Sources

Alberigo, Giuseppe. *I vescovi italiani al concilio di Trento, 1545–1547.* Florence, 1959. Contains discussion of Seripando's activities in the council.

Forster, Anselm. *Gesetz und Evangelium bei Girolamo Seripando.* Paderborn, 1963.

Hudon, William. "Epilogue: Marcellus II, Girolamo Seripando and the Image of the Angelic Pope." In *Prophetic Rome in the High Renaissance,* pp. 373–387. New York, 1992.

Jedin, Hubert. *Papal Legate at the Council of Trent: Cardinal Seripando.* Edited by Frederic Clement Eckhoff. Saint Louis, 1947. Critical bibliography of definitive value.

———. *A History of the Council of Trent.* 4 vols. London, 1957–1961. Fundamental for understanding Seripando's contribution to the Council of Trent.

"Seripando, Jeronimus." *Dictionnaire de la spiritualité.* Edited by David Gutiérrez. Vol. 14. Paris, 1990. See pp. 658–661.

GIUSEPPE ALBERIGO
Translated from Italian by Robert E. Shillenn

SERMONS. *See* Preaching and Sermons.

SERVETUS, Michael (1509/11–1553), radical Spanish antitrinitarian theologian, condemned to death in Catholic Vienne and eventually burned at the stake in Protestant Geneva. Servetus, born in Villanueva de Sijena, was of minor Spanish nobility but his early personal history remains largely a mystery. After leaving Spain in 1528 or 1529, Servetus studied in Toulouse and visited Strasbourg and Basel; from 1533 to 1538 he was in Paris. Using the aliases Michael Villanovanus and Michel de Villeneuve, Servetus studied anatomy and medicine. Thereafter he lived in Charlieu and eventually settled in Lyon and Vienne, where he worked as an editor of scriptural and geographic texts and practiced medicine.

Servetus's diverse accomplishments make him one of the most original thinkers of the sixteenth century. In addition to significant theological works, his innovative exegesis laid an early foundation for higher biblical criticism. He was an avid participant in the debate between Greek and Arabist schools of medicine and is credited with the discovery of the pulmonary circulation of the blood. His publication of *Ptolomaeus Geographicae* (1535) has earned him a place in the history of modern geography. Servetus's uncompromising antitrinitarian theological writings, however, proved controversial and led to his notoriety. His earliest compositions, including *De Trinitatis Erroribus* (1531), the *Dialogorum de Trinitats* (1532), and *De Regno Christi* (1532), attacked trinitarianism as little more than a Christian variant on ancient polytheism. Rather, Servetus believed the Old Testament and the apostles taught a modalistic concept of God, by which the Father expressed himself to mankind through a variety of names, such as El Shaddai, Elohim, Oz, and Ferox (and still others), each of which conveyed a specific divine message. Later, in the New Testament, the names Jesus and the Spirit were added to provide yet other messages. Servetus's gloss on the *Pagninus Bible* (1542) provided an exegetical justification for these unusual views. The *Christianismi Restitutio* (1553), his magnum opus, was a far more mature work, in which Servetus reiterated his earlier views but also presented a coherent, if extremely radical, alternative interpretation of Christian systematics. Servetus's "restitution" of primitive Christianity did not provide satisfaction to his orthodox critics, however, for it was even more radical than his earlier works. Foremost among Servetus's new radical ideas was a very strident sense of neo-Gnostic dualism.

Servetus's radicalism reflected a wide array of sources. He was very knowledgeable in Greek, and his anthropology was indebted to Platonic, middle, and neo-Platonic sources and to Hermes Trismegistus. Servetus's cosmology was influenced by Valentinian and Marcionite Gnosticism, and his overall theology of a progressive divine modalism was indebted to Paul of Samosata, Sabellius, and several ante-Nicene Greek fathers, especially Irenaeus. Servetus also cited over a dozen rabbinic sources, of which the exegesis of Rabbi David Kimchi and the theological concepts of Aramaic Targums of Onkelos and Jonathan were most important. Part of Servetus's genius lay in merging ideas from so many different origins.

Servetus's death in 1553 proved as controversial as his writings. Somehow, perhaps with Calvin's complicity, Catholic authorities in French Vienne became aware of Villanovanus's true identity. Servetus was tried for heresy, his writings were destroyed, and he was condemned to death. Servetus escaped from prison, however, and, perhaps unaware of Calvin's possible role in his prior arrest, attempted to escape to Italy by way of Geneva. Though Servetus remained incognito in that Protestant city, he was discovered, tried for heresy, and burned at the stake for maintaining antitrinitarian views. Calvin's central role in Servetus's prosecution in Geneva was not subject to equivocation, and Sébastien Castellion criticized the Genevan reformer for condemning to death a man who had neither preached nor published heretical opinions in Geneva and who had committed no other crime in that city. Servetus's offense, according to Castellion, consisted of rejecting John Calvin's ideas about the structure of the Godhead.

Though no church bears his name, Servetus's ideas and exegetical method proved influential in the development of subsequent Unitarianism. Along with other itinerant Italians then living in Switzerland, Valentino Gentile and Giorgio Blandrata carried his writings to Poland, Lithuania, and Transylvania, where Unitarianism enjoyed some early successes. Similarly, Francis Dávid and Jacob Paleologus translated large sections of Servetus's writings into Polish and Hungarian and provided a foundation for a more Judaized conception of Unitarinism. Ironically Calvin's own writings, which clearly described Servetus's opinions in order to refute them, also played a major role in disseminating Servetus's views. Statues of Servetus in Geneva and in Villanueva de Sijena commemorate the Spaniard's martyrdom.

BIBLIOGRAPHY

Primary Sources

Servetus, Michael. *De Trinitatis erroribus libri septem*. Frankfurt a.M., 1965.
————. *Christianismi restitutio* (1553). Frankfurt a.M., 1966.
————. *Christianismi restitutio and Other Writings*. Translated by Charles D. O'Malley. Birmingham, Ala., 1989.

Secondary Sources

Bainton, Roland H. *Hunted Heretic: The Life and Death of Michael Servetus (1511–1553)*. Boston, 1953. Best biography of Servetus and the most complete listing and location of his often rare writings.
Barón Fernandez, J. *Miguel Servet: Su vida u su obra*. Madrid, 1970. Author views Servetus from within the context of Spanish intellectual developments.
Friedman, Jerome. *Michael Servetus: A Case Study in Total Heresy*. Geneva, 1978. Work presents the only systematic treatment of Servetus's religious system and places stronger emphasis on Jewish sources than other authors.
Kinder, A. Gordon. *Michael Servetus*. Strasbourg. 1989. Most recent and up-to-date volume on Servetus. Author is excellent on detail but generally summarizes earlier work.
Manzoni, Claudio. *Umanesimo ed eresia: Michele Serveto*. Naples, 1974. Manzoni emphasizes the humanistic element in Servetus's thought and discusses his classical sources.
Wilbur, Earl Morse. *A History of Unitarianism I*. Boston, 1945. Emphasizes the importance of Servetus in the history of early Unitarianism.

JEROME FRIEDMAN

SEXUALITY. Between 1400 and 1700 learned male Europeans systematically investigated human sexuality with unprecedented rigor and intensity. Springing from deep-seated preoccupations with the fundamental ordering of human society—which during this period had profound religious and sexual associations—pious men pondered the proprieties of sexual behavior, excoriating what they deemed offensive to order and approving what they believed was conducive to it. The resultant sexual ethics, which prescribed a certain behavior, was expressed in a variety of media (after 1450 most of it printed matter, such as texts on moral theology, confessors' manuals, sermons, catechisms, and other clerical writings) and is therefore readily available to historical analysis.

These prescribed, learned sexual ethics are well documented, but such cannot be said of the actual sexual behavior of Europeans living at this time. One cannot deduce safely that what was preached was practiced, but one can catch glimpses of the sexual lives of men and women in the past when transgression of prescription occurred. Therefore, court cases hearing sexual offenses are among the best, if not entirely trustworthy, sources for such behavior.

During the period of the Reformation, learned men of whatever confessional persuasion all feared that a providential God would vent his wrath upon his creatures and afflict the commonwealth with plagues and punishments for misbehavior. To preclude God's scourge, all shared a concern about how discipline and order should be constituted, and all agreed that human sexuality was fundamental to thinking about order and disorder. Consequently, whatever their ultimate differences, all focused on the nature of sin, the body, and marriage in their scrutiny of sexuality.

The patristic tradition enshrined as the highest ideal the ascetic sexuality in the monastic lifestyle. Renunciation of things worldly entailed a depreciation and distrust of, or even a revulsion toward, the body and flesh, and learned churchmen through the ages devoted immeasurable energy pondering the paradoxical relations between the earthliness of the body, the purity or even holiness of the soul, and salvation.

Not everyone could be a monk or nun, of course, so the church was also required to formulate an ethic addressing the sexuality of the laity. The pastoral care of late medieval churchmen taught a strict sense of sin, and, although these clerics denounced all kinds of vices and sins—as demonstrated in the extensive literature on confession and penitential practice—they were especially preoccupied with the sexual sins of the laity. They associated sex with impurity and harbored a deep suspicion of sexual pleasure. Such assumptions were rooted in a long Christian intellectual tradition explicitly expressed in the powerfully influential writings of Augustine in the early fifth century. Augustine, whose thought cast a long shadow even across the age of the Reformation and profoundly influenced both Protestant and Catholic reformers in their thinking about sexuality, assumed an antithesis implanted in the human breast since the Fall between irrational physical pleasure and rational self-control. Furthermore, he asserted that the good Christian will harness the former by the latter.

Following Augustine, control of sexuality and its inherent disruptive quality of physical pleasure became a primary task of the church and a constitutive characteristic of its sexual ethics. Although not all late medieval literature on sexuality presents a clear and consistent sexual ethic, it does define legitimate sex as only that which takes place within marriage. It therefore condones sex only between males and females and only for procreation and to render the conjugal debt to avoid adultery, fornication, and sodomy. (By channeling sexual activity to the spouse, the desire for sexual relations with anyone else would supposedly thereby be precluded.) Again following Augustine, this literature steadfastly condemns as sinful any considerations of pleasure as a motivation for sexual relations, even with one's spouse. As an early sixteenth-century French preacher put it, sexual relations are for "procreation of children to honor God, [to] multiply the human race, and [to] renew and refill the celestial mansion."

Since sexual relations within marriage for the purpose of procreation was the only legitimate form of sexual activity, all other forms were deemed illicit and sometimes unnatural and mortally sinful. Thus, fornication and adultery were ferociously condemned, while homosexual or heterosexual sodomy, masturbation, and bestiality were construed as the worst imaginable sexual transgressions. Even contraception was condemned on the same grounds because it circumvented one of the primary purposes of marriage.

To enforce this fundamentally important sexual ethic, the pre-Reformation church made the priest the primary surveyor of sexual morality and instructed him as confessor to inquire closely about his parishioners' sexual activity. The laity was constantly encouraged by confessors to reflect on their own sexuality. Did they deny the conjugal debt? Did they excite desire in their spouse? Did they refrain from sexual activity during sacred times? Did they seek pleasure for its own sake?

The sexual ethics of Protestant reformers beginning in the 1520s illustrate notable continuities with those of the pre-Reformation but also significant departures. Ironically, both the continuities and the divergences spring from the same source—the influence of Augustine. Protestant reformers were deeply committed to the Augustinian notion of original sin, which, though defined as willful disobedience to divine precept in the Old Testament, became in the pen of Augustine inextricably linked to sexual behavior. For Augustine prelapsarian man was a model of willed self-control, and sexual intercourse occurred not by lust but by calm rational volition. In such an idyllic state, "habitual order reigned." The Fall reversed everything; henceforth man became "a slave to lust" and was "not able not to sin."

Whereas the Christian patristic tradition embraced an ascetic sexuality to harness the disorderly sexual appetite, Martin Luther and the first generation of Protestant reformers of the 1520s and 1530s rejected that tradition, if not the concern for channeling sexuality into appropriate institutions. If, however, sexual abstinence was no longer considered to be the estate most pleasing to God, then reformers had to rethink the relationship between sexuality and holiness. The result was a reworking of the monastic ascetic heritage into a Protestant sexual ethic rooted in the patriarchal family.

Consequently, reformers, like their late medieval forebears, thought deeply about the nature of sin, the body, and marriage and like them pondered the difficult problem of finding the place of sexuality, and bodily lust, in holy matrimony. Reformers may have tried to render the heterosexual act indifferent to holiness, thereby separating asceticism from holiness and themselves sharply from the patristic tradition; however, in disciplining and channeling sexuality into the social institution of marriage, where it would no longer be a disruptive force but a pillar of social stability, they were not nearly as far from the sexual ethics of late medieval clerics. Protestant reformers and late medieval clerics were equally convinced that the right ordering of sexual relations was fundamental to marriage, by which they all meant fidelity.

Pre-Reformation and Protestant thought on marriage and sexuality converged in the assumption that marriage orders sexual relations, a convergence that can be traced to shared cultural assumptions about the disorderly capacities of lust. Homosexual lust was deemed unnatural passion, stirred by Satan according to Luther, and since it could not lead to procreation, it was categorically proscribed. Lust for and by women was thought more problematic precisely because of its procreative potential both outside as well as inside the marriage bed. Even Augustine had found cause to tolerate prostitution as a "necessary evil" because it directed male sexual passion away from respectable women. Male lust for women may have been natural, but the inverse was decidedly not the case. The corrective for such "wayward" women (whose unregulated sexual behavior could unsettle the system of patrimonial devolution) was to incorporate them in households, to harness them to the patriarchal family. True, Protestants transferred disciplinary duties from one "father," the priest, to another, the natural one—or, with the new civic moralism in many Protestant cities, to a political one, the Lutheran town council or Calvinist consistory—but the desire to restrain the inherent destructiveness of sexual passion within the patriarchal family was a sentiment shared by Protestant and Catholic alike.

Clearly there were similarities between the pre-Reformation, Protestant, and Catholic views on marriage and sexuality, but one must not lose sight of the fundamental differences as well, not only between Protestant and Catholic beliefs but also among the Protestant sects themselves. The splintering dynamic of the Reformation gave rise to a profusion of views. The antisacramentalist view that marriage was an outlet for fallen human sexual nature may have been a shared premise of Protestants, but the conclusions about sexuality drawn from it were varied in the extreme. While the catechists in Nuremberg, for example, displayed a deep suspicion of sexuality ("chastity until marriage is God's universal rule. Not only must Youth forego all sexual activity; they must also avoid all suggestive talk and suppress all sexual thoughts as well"), Martin Luther vigorously affirmed a naturalistic attitude toward the heterosexual functioning of the body.

Springing equally from the antisacramentalist view of marriage, however, were the views of some radical reformers (including some Anabaptists) who spiritualized heterosexuality. Addressing the same question that all reformers did in trying to find a place for heterosexuality in holy matrimony and salvation, Dreamers (spiritualist Anabaptists from the region around Erlangen), for example, spiritualized intercourse. They rendered the heterosexual act holy by severing its association with the human will altogether and defining it solely as an act of obedience to a divine command.

Even more radical was the thinking of the Thuringian Bloodfriends about marriage, sexuality, the body, and salvation. They defined the heterosexual act as the only sacrament and declared the means of grace to be heterosexual relations with the other members of the sect. They resolved the traditional Christian opposition between the earthly body and the holiness of the soul by spiritualizing the body itself as the gateway to the divine.

Similarly, the Münster Anabaptists' practice of polygamy stemmed from their scrutiny of the relationship between marriage and sexuality. Like the other reformers of their age, they held the belief in the disorderly capacities of female lust, and they were convinced that marriage was its cure. Whereas more mainstream reformers wanted to turn all women into wives within a monogamous patriarchal marriage, the Münsterites, who were just as committed to patriarchy, encouraged more than one wife per husband.

Like other reformers, John Calvin rejected celibacy as a holy state and defined legitimate sexuality as that practiced only within marriage. He is well known for his stern views on sexual license outside of holy matrimony. His views on sexual behavior within marriage, however, were much more positive if less well known. True, he sometimes justified marriage on the Augustinian grounds that it precludes for-

nication, but he also departed from the Augustinian tradition at times, pointing out that sexual reproduction had been divinely instituted and that the sexuality of Adam and Eve had been part of their original perfection. As he put it, "The generation of man. . . is not unclean and viscious in itself, but is so as an accident arising from the Fall." Holy matrimony, for Calvin, was such a positive institution that "Whatever sin or shame is in [heterosexual relations] is so covered by the goodness of marriage that it ceases to be a sin, or at least to be so regarded by God," for "the intercourse of husband and wife is a pure thing, good and holy. . . [within which God] allows husband and wife to give each other delight." From this premise Calvin then deduces a surprising principle: "Therefore he who shall be induced to choose a wife because of the elegance of her shape will not necessarily sin."

Predictably, Henrician reformers in England hewed closer to the pre-Reformation position than did Continental reformers, harboring suspicion of and hostility toward sexuality and stressing the prime importance of "matrimonial chastity," by which was meant moderation of sexual passion. It was not, however, in conflict with the view shared by other Protestants that holy matrimony within the patriarchal family was a source of mutual comfort, as well as a means of satisfying lust and procreating legitimate children. Puritans of the latter half of the sixteenth century echoed the voices of extreme sexual morality on the Continent, revealing a growing concern for sexual sins and stressing the depravity of man and the dangers of unbridled license.

As one might expect, the Catholic view on sin, marriage, the body, and sexuality after the Council of Trent largely affirmed, albeit more systematically and thoroughly, the late medieval pre-Reformation positions. Augustinianism is usually associated with Protestantism, but it was just as influential on Catholic thinking. If the sexual ethics of post-Tridentine Catholicism display continuities with their pre-Reformation counterparts, it is with a deepening and more systematic rigorism.

The sixteenth-century "laxism" of Pedro de Soto (who suggested that limitation of births by refraining from paying the conjugal debt was acceptable if it was determined by the spouses that the ensuing child could not be supported) or Thomas Sanchez (for whom sexual pleasure within marriage was acceptable) was countered and vanquished by a triumphant post-Tridentine rigorism guided by Augustinianism. Here one finds Original Sin identified not primarily with disobedience but with concupiscence and a deepening suspicion of lust joined by an increasing severity toward the flesh. In countering the Protestant position on marriage, the Council of Trent reaffirmed the sanctity of holy matrimony, as well as its sacramental nature, thus maintaining the essential role of the priest in it. Likewise, the reaffirmation of confessionalism (however increasingly privatized and individualized) confirmed the central place of the priest as surveyor and enforcer of the sexual ethic in the parish. The purpose of marriage was procreation and a remedy for fornication, and so rigorous was the thinking of some Catholic moralists that even lust for one's wife could be construed as a form of adultery.

Christian teaching on sexuality during the era of the Reformation was diverse in many important respects. Views on the nature of sin, the sexual body, and marriage, though springing from the same intellectual tradition and largely from Augustine, could lead to extremely diverse conclusions. Even so, the differences between pre-Reformation, Protestant, and Catholic positions on sexuality should not blind us to the similarities. Historians have recently urged an understanding of the Reformation as a series of religious movements emerging from a common culture or as variations on common themes. Regarding sexuality, the common theme was the shared conviction that sexual activity is an inherently destructive force and had to be confined within marriage. Furthermore, since everyone assumed women to be lustful, the ideal marriage was the patriarchal one, whereby women and their sexuality were controlled by men. The patriarchal family, the sole locus of legitimate sex, was in turn the bedrock of moral and civil order and a guard against the howling chaos, not to mention God's wrath, that the undisciplined venting of the sexual passions would invariably unleash. Consequently, learned men agreed that adultery, fornication, homosexuality, bestiality, and masturbation had to be condemned because, occurring outside the marriage bed, they were beyond the sanctioned purposes of matrimony, outside the patriarchal family, and thus in the antisocial world of disorder.

Such were the sexual ethics of learned, mostly clerical men. Just how many men and women throughout society embraced these views on sexuality is much more difficult to determine. Mounting evidence has called into question the assumption that society was "reformed" during the sixteenth and seventeenth centuries, demonstrating that teachings of the reformers, be they Protestant or Catholic, were often passively resisted or eclectically and incompletely appropriated by many men, women, and children. Such an inchoate process of "Reformation" or even "Christianization" should caution us from making the assumption that the sexual ethics of learned men reflected those of the rest of society, half of which comprised women. If, however, prescriptive literature is a largely inadequate source through which to apprehend the sexual behavior and attitudes of most people, what other avenues are available to historical analysis? Pornography, court memoirs, and literature, though produced by literate and therefore elite members of society, take us beyond the world of prescription and draw the outlines of illicit subcultures, both heterosexual and homosexual, in the form of prostitution, pederasty, and even male-to-male marriages. How widespread or numerous

these subcultures were, however, is probably ultimately impossible to determine.

Learned sexual ethics were prescribed in various literary forms, but deviation from them was also proscribed by many laws. That these laws were periodically enforced in ecclesiastical or secular courts has in turn generated historical records in which one can glimpse "deviant" sexual behavior. Trials against incestuous lovers, fornicators, homosexual sodomites, adulterers, adulteresses, male and female prostitutes, and bawds duly appear in these records and are condemned at times in draconian fashion.

Court records, however, reveal more about popular sexual attitudes than that they led to the occasional prosecuted transgression, useful as those may be in determining jurisprudential patterns and practices and sketching the contours of illicit sexual activity. Testimony by men and women from the laboring classes or the middling sort in trials for slander, for instance, often reveals hostility or derision toward such proscribed sexual immorality as fornication, adultery, prostitution, and homosexuality. This testimony illustrates the extreme sensitivity men and women in the popular classes felt toward their image of respectability, in which a certain sexual morality was deeply enmeshed and tied inextricably to a sense of honor and social worth. Men were deeply offended by allegations that they could not control their women—when their wives were alleged to be adulteresses or their daughters to be "whores"—while women were mortally insulted by allegations of wayward sexual behavior that robbed them of a reputation of virginity.

Slanders alleging illicit sexuality—cuckoldry, whoremongering, and "buggery" were exceedingly common—may not reflect the prevalence of the various alleged sexual practices, but they do suggest that such behavior was ostensibly condemned in the culture. Such distinguishing opprobrium therefore functioned to mark off further illicit sexuality and the people who practiced it, lending further credence to the suggestion that illicit sexual subcultures did, in fact, exist. Indeed, the expansion of slander litigation, which has been documented in parts of Europe in the century after the reformations in Protestant and Catholic lands, may indicate increased concern about sexual reputation and hence reflect an increasing austerity in popular attitudes toward illicit sexuality.

This seeming intensification of austerity may be mirrored by a decline, at least in England, where the most extensive and conclusive research in parish registers has been done, in the illegitimacy rate across the seventeenth century, thus perhaps reflecting a decline in premarital sexual activity. Whether these trends toward austerity and licit sexuality were caused by the preaching and teaching of reformers, however, has not been conclusively proved, and the trends themselves may be more illusory than real. An increase in litigation over slander may only reflect that men and women in the popular classes were now bringing to court what they resolved by other means before. Similarly, historians disagree whether contraception was widely practiced; if it was widely practiced in the seventeenth century, then premarital heterosexual activity could actually have increased while illegitimate births declined. The unfortunate conclusion one must draw about sexual behavior and attitudes of the popular classes, unlike the prescriptive attitudes of the learned men of the era, is that, in the current state of research, only tentative generalizations can be drawn.

[*See also* Celibacy and Virginity; Courts, *article on* Marriage Courts; Marriage; Prostitution; Social Discipline; *and* Women.]

BIBLIOGRAPHY

Boswell, John. *Christianity, Social Tolerance, and Homosexuality: Gay People in Western Europe from the Beginning of the Christian Era to the Fourteenth Century.* Chicago, 1980. Best scholarly work on the history of homosexuality.

Bouwsma, William J. *John Calvin: A Sixteenth-Century Portrait.* Oxford, 1988. Best modern biography of Calvin; offers insights seldom seen in other works on the Genevan reformer.

Brown, Judith C. *Immodest Acts: The Life of a Lesbian Nun in Renaissance Italy.* New York, 1986. Despite its misleading title, an excellent analysis of female sexuality in seventeenth-century Italy.

Delumeau, Jean. *Sin and Fear: The Emergence of a Western Guilt Culture, Thirteenth-Eighteenth Centuries.* Translated by Eric Nicholson. New York, 1990. Sweeping interpretation of Western civilization from 1200 to 1800; especially useful for prescriptive learned attitudes, less so for popular practices.

Farr, James R. *Authority and Sexuality in Early Modern Burgundy, 1550–1730.* New York, 1994. Explores the relationships between prescriptive sexual, religious, legal, political, and social attitudes of the learned classes and the sexual attitudes and practices revealed in court cases in Burgundy during the Catholic Reformation.

Flandrin, Jean-Louis. *Families in Former Times: Kinship, Household, and Sexuality.* Translated by Richard Southern. Cambridge, 1979. Classic work by the leading French historian of sexuality.

Foucault, Michel. *The History of Sexuality.* Vol. 1, *An Introduction.* New York, 1980. Offers provocative thesis on the development of modern sexuality from the seventeenth century. A fundamental text in the study of Western sexuality.

Ingram, Martin. *Church Courts, Sex and Marriage in England, 1570–1640.* Cambridge, 1987. Very useful material on sexuality in early modern England.

Muir, Edward, and Guido Ruggiero, eds. *Sex and Gender in Historical Perspective: Selections from Quaderni storici.* Translated by Margaret A. Gallucci with Mary M. Gallucci and Carole C. Gallucci. Baltimore, 1990. Collection of articles reflecting the recent, high-quality scholarship on the history of sexuality.

Roper, Lyndal. *The Holy Household: Women and Morals in Reformation Augsburg.* Oxford, 1989. A superior example of how a local study can illustrate developments of broad significance to the German Reformation, the history of sexuality, and women's history.

———. "Sexual Utopianism in the German Reformation." *Journal of Ecclesiastical History* 42.3 (July 1991), 394–418. An excellent analysis of the sexual ethics of radical Protestant reformers by one of the leading historians of the history of sexuality.

Ruggiero, Guido. *The Boundaries of Eros: Sex Crime and Sexuality in Renaissance Venice.* New York, 1985. Pioneering work exploring the reciprocal influences between sexuality and political culture in fourteenth- and fifteenth-century Venice. A model of its kind.

Stone, Lawrence. *Family, Sex, and Marriage in England, 1500–1800.* Abr. ed. New York, 1979. A pathbreaking book by an acclaimed historian; has been criticized for unsubstantiated generalizations about the popular classes but remains a useful introduction to the subject.

Tentler, Thomas. *Sin and Confession on the Eve of the Reformation.* Princeton, 1977. Remains the best work on pre-Reformation religious thought on sin, confession, and sexuality.

JAMES R. FARR

SEYMOUR, Edward

SEYMOUR, Edward (c.1500–1552), duke of Somerset, lord protector of the realm (1547–49) under Edward VI, and architect of the first phase of the Protestant Reformation in England. Like his father (a Wiltshire knight) and grandfather before him, Seymour was trained for war and service in the Tudor royal household. A matriculant of both Oxford and Cambridge, his extraordinary rise to power and influence at the court of Henry VIII—after 1530 he was one of Henry's most favored guardsmen and gambling companions—is explained by the king's marriage to Seymour's sister, Jane (May 1536). A shower of titles, lands, and offices made him by 1543 one of the king's greatest men and one of England's richest; he became a privy councillor (by 7 April 1536), earl of Hertford (October 1537), knight of the Garter (9 January 1541), and lord great chamberlain (January 1543), acquiring by royal gift so many former monastic estates that in 1540 his income topped £3900. His secret commitment to religious reform probably dates from about this time (1543–1544). Henry's wars in France and Scotland in the 1540s propelled him to supreme authority both in the field (he became commander in chief of all armies overseas in 1546) and at court, where, in alliance with fellow reformists, he was able to use his influence with the declining Henry VIII (who died on 28 January 1547) to ensure the success of his plot to dominate the regency council of Edward VI. The results were confirmed officially in royal commissions appointing him protector and governor of the nine-year-old king (12 March and 24 December 1547).

As protector (and duke of Somerset from 16 February 1547), Seymour assumed *de facto* the powers of the royal supremacy in the Church of England, a church whose doctrines and liturgy were still wholly Catholic at Edward's accession. His early patronage of Protestant propagandists and quick repeal of Henry VIII's laws against heresy signaled his official intentions; an Erastian of Zwinglian persuasion, he would zealously promote "true religion." Three radicals whom he brought into his own household—John Hooper (later bishop of Gloucester), William Turner (his physician), and Thomas Becon, all former victims of Henrician persecution—almost certainly influenced his decisions. Turner's tracts in particular projected reforms that were central to royal policy: the abolition of shrines and processions, a married clergy, Communion in both kinds, and an English rite. The results were to be seen in the government's campaign against images, the dissolution of the chantries, and the Act of Uniformity, which authorized the use in England of the historic first *Book of Common Prayer* (1549).

Recent research has demolished the tradition (based principally on the writings of A. F. Pollard and W. K. Jordan) that Somerset was a liberal inclined to tolerance and clemency. The legend of "the good duke" was an Elizabethan invention. Circumstances and the need to cultivate the favor of Charles V forced Somerset to paint his radical intentions in the colors of moderation. Politically, this was a policy of deliberate deception. He reneged on his promise to channel to charity income from the sale of the chantries, spending it instead on his invasion of Scotland, a military adventure that almost bankrupted England. His repeal of Henry VIII's heresy laws—oft-cited evidence of his love of "liberty"—enabled him to escape the penalties of statutes outlawing his religion; in matters religious his toleration was diplomatic, extending exclusively to the faith of Catholic sovereigns whose armies threatened him. Indeed, the prospect of armed intervention by Charles V on behalf of the "old religion" explains why he represented the prayer book to Charles as something akin to the emperor's Interim (an edict of 1548 permitting Communion in both kinds but retaining transubstantiation and Catholic ceremony). Despite the book's appearance of compromise—the product of Thomas Cranmer's beautifully ambiguous phrasing—it advertised Somerset's radical stance on the real presence. This is clearly evident from the staged "disputation" in the House of Lords over which Somerset presided in December 1548, when he followed from notes provided by Peter Martyr Vermigli a "script" of politically correct questions and answers about the Eucharist. Even so, this prayer book, which was designed to promote domestic tranquillity, helped precipitate in Devon and Cornwall a rebellion against his authority (1549). His policies and high-handed treatment of colleagues led to his downfall; an arrogant, insensitive governor of men, he was overthrown and his protectorate abolished in a coup d'état (October 1549) organized by a scheming former friend, John Dudley (later duke of Northumberland), who eventually rigged Somerset's arrest (11 October 1551), trial (1 December), and execution (22 January 1552) on trumped-up charges of treason.

Somerset's greatest legacy was his assault (1547–1548) on the "superstitious" aspects of popular religious culture. For most contemporaries here was the real Reformation, an uncompromising, sudden, and destructive end to centuries-old traditions. In this sense, Somerset's Reformation was essentially negative; it outlawed familiar images and rituals but failed to convert the nation. Somerset's genuinely attractive qualities—an intellectually rigorous religious idealism (he was revered as a martyr in the French Reformed church) and his patronage of Renaissance music and architecture (Somerset House in the Strand was the first Italianate building in England)—were overshadowed by his acquisitiveness and ambition. Inflexibly proud, he never mastered the duplicity required of those who survived the intrigues of the Tudor court.

BIBLIOGRAPHY

Bush, M. L. *The Government Policy of Protector Somerset.* Montreal, 1975. Demolishes the myth of Somerset's liberality, arguing that circumstances and political ambition, not principles, shaped royal policy.

Hoak, Dale. *The King's Council in the Reign of Edward VI.* Cambridge, 1976. Detailed analysis of the institutional setting, showing how Somerset's financial and administrative methods undermined his authority.

———. "Seymour, Edward, Duke of Somerset." In *Historical Dictionary of Tudor England, 1485–1603,* edited by Ronald H. Fritze, pp. 459–461. New York and London, 1991. Brief sketch of Somerset's official career incorporating previously unpublished research.

Hutton, Ronald. "The Local Impact of the Tudor Reformations." In *The English Reformation Revised,* edited by Christopher Haigh, pp. 114–138. Cambridge and New York, 1987. Making original use of English churchwardens' accounts, reveals the extent of the assault on "superstitious" ceremonies.

Jordan, W. K. *Edward VI: The Young King; The Protectorship of the Duke of Somerset.* London, 1968. Massively detailed and useful for its citation of numerous sources, but must be used with caution, as it frequently advances erroneous, outdated, or unhistorical interpretations.

Parry, G. J. R. "Inventing 'The Good Duke' of Somerset." *Journal of Ecclesiastical History* 40 (1989), 370–380. Traces the source of the myth to elements of Protestant propaganda in the 1587 edition of William Harrison's *Description of Britain.*

Pollard, A. F. *England under Protector Somerset.* Reprint, New York, 1966. Pioneering work of a master historian, most of whose conclusions have been revised by work published since 1975.

DALE HOAK

SEYMOUR, Jane (1509?–1537), third consort of Henry VIII. The eldest daughter of Sir John Seymour of Wolf Hall, Wiltshire, and Margaret Wentworth, Jane was probably born in 1509 at her family's home. She was successively lady-in-waiting to Henry VIII's first two consorts, Catherine of Aragon and Anne Boleyn. In January of 1536, just after Anne miscarried a child at Greenwich, rumors began to circulate that the king was paying marked attention to Jane. Only Eustace Chapuys, the imperial ambassador, reported that in April Henry sent Jane a letter from London, purportedly with an improper request, and a gift, which she was said to have refused. Ambassadorial dispatches provide inadequate and skewed evidence about private royal matters. In this case, it was part of the government's wider diplomatic strategy, in light of the charges to be filed against Queen Anne, to emphasize the chastity of Jane, who, Chapuys also claimed, moved into Thomas Cromwell's apartments at Greenwich with her brother Edward and his wife (the future duke and duchess of Somerset) acting as chaperones.

On 30 May, ten days after Anne's execution, Henry and Jane were married at Whitehall. Her coronation was scheduled for Michaelmas but was deferred, probably because of the Pilgrimage of Grace. Attention has focused on her friendship with Princess Mary, who was permitted to return to court after submitting to her father's demands that she acknowledge her own illegitimacy. Jane's friendship with this future Catholic queen and her plea for monastic reform are the evidence usually cited to prove that she held conservative religious views. Regardless of her beliefs, her greatest contribution to the Reformation was the birth of her son, the future Protestant monarch, Edward VI, on 12 October 1537. She died twelve days later from puerperal fever and was interred in Saint George's Chapel, Windsor, on 12 November. In 1547 the king was buried at her side.

BIBLIOGRAPHY

Ives, E. W. *Anne Boleyn.* Oxford, 1986. Gives the traditional view of court politics in 1536; places more credence on diplomatic evidence.
Seymour, William. *Ordeal by Ambition: An English Family in the Shadow of the Tudors.* London, 1973. Useful for personal details of Jane Seymour's family and life. No recent, scholarly biography of her exists.
Warnicke, Retha M. *The Rise and Fall of Anne Boleyn: Family Politics at the Court of Henry VIII.* Cambridge, 1989. Provides a new interpretation of court politics in 1536 and challenges the validity of diplomatic dispatches.

RETHA M. WARNICKE

SHRINES. *See* Pilgrimages; Saints, *article on* Cult of Saints.

SICKINGEN, Franz von (1481–1523), imperial knight. Sickingen came from a wealthy noble family in southwest Germany whose most important possessions were Landstuhl in the Palatinate, Ebernburg on the Nahe, and Hohenburg in Alsace. His upbringing was influenced by the Heidelberg court, with which his family had a long-standing relationship. Sickingen's own development also took place within the circle of the Prince Elector of the Palatinate. He took part in the Landshut War (1503–1504) and worked as a senior civil servant in Kreuznach and Böckelheim. In 1515 Sickingen left the civil service of the Palatinate. Thereafter he pursued his ambitious political designs as an organizer of military campaigns. His campaigns against Worms (1515–1517), the earldom of Katzenelbogen (1518)—it had been Hessian since 1504—and Frankfurt am Main (1518), earned him political importance in the Middle Rhine region. Through his conflicts against Duke Anthony of Lorraine and the imperial city of Metz (1518) he gained a foothold in the borderlands between Germany and France and thus became a figure in European politics. For a time

Sickingen—because he had been declared an outlaw by the emperor on account of his campaign against Worms—was in the service of the French. In 1518 he reconciled with the emperor, who appointed him field commander. Recruited by the Swabian League, Sickingen took part in expelling Duke Ulrich of Württemberg, and as a reward he was granted Neuenbürg am Enz. In that same year he assumed joint responsibility with Georg von Frundsberg (1473–1528) for the military safeguarding of the election of the emperor. In 1520 Charles V appointed him to a five-year term as counsellor, chamberlain, and captain in his service. However, the very next year Sickingen fell into disfavor because of his unsuccessful campaign against the rebellious vassal Robert II von der Mark (d. 1535). By now Sickingen saw himself as "the Protector of the Reformation" (see Volker Press).

Ulrich von Hutten, with whom he had been on friendly terms since 1519, had acquainted him with Martin Luther and the theological debates. Anticlericalism, church reform, and reform of the nobility were the hallmark of his policies from then on. Sickingen was the first secular follower to declare his support for Luther. In 1520 and 1521 he offered Luther the Ebernburg castle as a refuge, though in each case Luther declined. For a brief while, beginning in 1521, Sickingen's territory became a center of the evangelical movement in the empire. He installed preachers with Reformation leanings (Martin Bucer, Johannes Oecolampadius, Johannes Schwebel) and with them set about restructuring church governance and reordering public worship along evangelical lines. In August 1522 Sickingen assumed the leadership of the Upper Rhine-Alsatian nobility, who formed an alliance that was fueled by Reformation ideas and directed against the clergy. Independent of this alliance, Sickingen soon began a campaign against the archbishop of Trier, Richard von Greiffenklau. Besides wanting to "create an opening for the gospel," he clearly hoped to attain princely status in the secularized archbishopric. After the failure of this undertaking Sickingen retreated to Neinstein near Landstuhl. From here he attempted to mobilize the lower German nobility but without success. In the spring of 1523 the allied princes of Hesse, the Palatinate, and Trier laid siege to his castle. When the relief he counted on did not arrive, Sickingen surrendered (7 May). Having been gravely wounded, he died the same day.

BIBLIOGRAPHY

Meyer, Manfred. "Sickingen, Hutten und die reichsritterschaftlichen Bewegungen in der deutschen frühbürgerlichen Revolution." *Jahrbuch für Geschichte des Feudalismus* 7 (1983), 215–246.
Press, Volker. "Ein Ritter zwischen Rebellion und Reformation, Franz von Sickingen, 1481–1523." *Blätter für pfälzische Kirchengeschichte und religiöse Volkskunde* 50 (1983), 151–177.

ULMAN WEIß
Translated from German by Robert E. Shillenn

SICULO, Giorgio (also Rioli; Sicolo; c.1500–1551), Benedictine monk, radical reformer, and originator of the concept of Nicodemism. Born at San Pietro in Clarenza (near Catania in Sicily), he made his solemn profession of vows in the Benedictine monastery of San Nicolò, l'Arena in Catania on 24 February 1534. Here between 1537 and 1539 he began a friendship with Benedetto da Mantova, author of the *Beneficio de Cristo*. It is likely that through Benedetto he was guided into an awareness of the issues raised by the Reformation: John Calvin's *Institutio Christianae religionis*, the debates over justification by faith, and the divinity of Christ. This reading and the debates that Benedetto led in Sicily must have had an influence on the young monk, who followed him onto the Continent. According to the testimony submitted to the Inquisition in 1570 by Nascimbene Nascimbeni, a man of letters from Ferrara, Benedetto translated the books of Siculo "from Sicilian into good Italian."

On 8 December 1546, from the monastery of San Benedetto Po, near Mantua, Siculo issued the tract *De iustificatione* to Luciano degli Ottoni, who was then at the Council of Trent, to support the thesis, which Ottoni presented at the council, of the impeccability of those regenerated in Christ. Siculo's arguments were taken not only from sacred scripture but also from a revelation made to him personally by Christ himself. The contents of this revelation were set forth by Siculo in a work entitled *Della verità christiana et dotrina appostolica rivellata dal nostro signor Giesù Chrito al servo suo Siculo* (On Christian Truth and the Apostolic Teaching Revealed by Our Lord Jesus Christ to His Servant Siculo), which was disseminated only among his followers, who knew it by the title *Libro grande*. Siculo went to Trent to explain its meaning to the members of the council, but he was unsuccessful. Since he was accused of heresy, he had to leave Riva di Trento and move to Bologna, where in the meantime the pope had transferred the council. Published in 1550 in Bologna were two other writings by Siculo: *Epistola di Georgio Siculo servo fedele di Iesu Christo alli cittadini di Riva di Trento contra il mendatio di Francesco Spiera et falsa dottrina di Protestanti* (The Epistle of Giorgio Siculo Faithful Servant of Jesus Christ to the Citizens of Riva di Trento against the Lies of Francesco Spiera and False Doctrine of the Protestants) and *Espositione di Georgio Siculo . . . nel nono, decimo et undecimo capo della Epistola di San Paolo alli Romani* (Exposition of Giorgio Siculo . . . on the Ninth, Tenth, and Eleventh Chapters of the Epistle of Saint Paul to the Romans). In these works, which were intended to be made public, Siculo uses arguments above suspicion for the inquisitors—that is, polemics against the Calvinist doctrine of predestination—to cover up a series of heretical doctrines: indifference to the question of the true church, mysticism of redemption, and the impeccability of believers. These were teachings intended for all. For those who came to be a part of the sect, there existed a higher level of awareness in which even more radical doctrines were promulgated: any-

one who was a follower of Siculo received the divine spirit, and for such a person neither the sacraments nor even the *Beneficio di Christo* were necessary. They went so far as to deny the divinity of Christ and the immortality of the soul. These doctrines found a hearing among the students of the College of Spain in Bologna and even among professors of the University of Ferrara, theologians and members of the Council of Trent, and ordinary people.

The content of these doctrines was denounced as heretical and "rebellious by both sides, both the Papists and the Evangelicals" (the words of Pier Paolo Vergerio in a printed work directed to the Italian Dominicans in 1550). As a result of this denunciation, Siculo was arrested in September 1550 and jailed by the Inquisition in Ferrara. After his trial he stated that he was ready to recite his abjuration, but once he was before the crowds, he took advantage of the situation to preach his doctrines. On 23 May 1551 he was hanged from a window of the prison of Ferrara. The story of his ideas, however, did not stop there: many still remained in expectation of the fulfillment of his prophecies. Moreover, in 1552 Calvin argued against him in his work *De aeterna Dei praedestinatione* (On the Eternal Predestination of God). In 1568 the Inquisition uncovered a vast network of followers of the "Giorgian heresy," which had meanwhile won over some of the most notable members of the Cassinese congregation of the Benedictine order. As late as 1570 a follower of Siculo, Francesco Severi, a professor of medicine at the University of Ferrara, was put to death by the Inquisition, and at the end of the 1500s Francesco Pucci was still advancing Siculo's ideas.

BIBLIOGRAPHY

Benedetto da Mantova. *Il beneficio di Cristo con le versioni del secolo XVI, documenti e testimonianze.* Edited by Salvatore Caponetto. Corpus Reformatorum Italicorum. Florence and Chicago, 1972.

Cantimori, Delio. *Eretici italiani del Cinquecento: Ricerche storiche.* 3d rev. ed. Edited by Adriano Prosperi. Turin, 1992. Earlier edition available in English translation: *Italian Heretics of the Sixteenth Century*, Cambridge, Mass., 1979.

Collett, Barry. *Italian Benedictine Scholars in the Age of Reformation: The Congregation of Santa Giustina of Padua.* Oxford, 1985.

Ginzburg, Carlo. "Due note sul profetismo cinquecentesco." *Rivista storica italiana* 78 (1966), 184–227.

Prosperi, A. "Opere inedite o sconosciute di Giorgio Siculo." *La Bibliofilia* 87 (1985), 137–158.

———. "Ricerche sul Siculo e i suoi seguaci." In *Studi in onore di Armando Saitta di suoi allievi pisani*, edited by R. Pozzi and A. Prosperi, pp. 35–71. Pisa, 1989.

ADRIANO PROSPERI
Translated from Italian by Robert E. Shillenn

SIDNEY, Philip (1554–1586), Elizabethan courtier, poet, and champion of a European-wide anti-Habsburg policy. He personified the humanist acclamation for the *vita activa*. His life was largely shaped, however, by the conflict that arose between his training and expectations for state service and the caution exercised by Queen Elizabeth I (r. 1558–1603). It was during the early part of the queen's reign that the English church was settled in a broadly Protestant confession and that foreign policy, traditionally one of enmity with France, was reversed.

Sidney was seventeen and completing the grooming sponsored by his uncle Robert Dudley, the earl of Leicester and a favorite of Elizabeth's, when he undertook the journey that became the central informing experience of his life. The signing of the Treaty of Blois (1572) between France and England provided the occasion, and while in Paris he attended the wedding of the Huguenot leader Henry of Navarre (later Henry IV) and the Catholic princess Margaret of Valois. Ostensibly intended to heal the rupture in the French confessional divide, the ceremony signaled instead the beginning of the Saint Bartholomew's Day Massacre (24 August 1572) of French Protestants. Many of Sidney's newly made friends, including the scholar Petrus Ramus, were slaughtered. Henceforth, Sidney was critical of the Valois, opposing in 1579 the marriage negotiations between Elizabeth and François, duke of Anjou, and encountering, in consequence, his queen's great displeasure.

During his first visit to the Continent, Sidney traveled widely and was universally greeted as one destined for high office. Hubert Languet, humanist scholar and servant of Augustus, elector of Saxony, saw in him the makings of the ideal Protestant and learned leader and adopted him as surrogate son and pupil. Sidney became a close friend of another of Languet's notable students, Philippe DuPlessis-Mornay, supposed author of the Huguenot resistance tract *De vindiciae contra tyrannos* (1579). Sidney's interest in resistance theories was later suggested in his pastoral romance *Arcadia*. William of Orange, who repudiated Spanish suzerainty over the Netherlands and was a prime example of the success of resistance, hoped to seal an alliance with England through a marriage between his daughter and Sidney. This was in 1577, when Sidney was completing the first state mission entrusted him by Elizabeth. Subsequently, Elizabeth, who preferred not to provoke the Spaniards, distrusted Sidney's intentions.

Sidney's hopes for state office and honors were mainly thwarted by the queen. He was knighted in 1583 but only to have the qualifications necessary to stand proxy for Count Johann Casimir of the Palatinate, who, selected as a knight of the garter, was unable to attend his own ceremony. The choice of Sidney was by Johann Casimir, who with Sidney attempted in 1577 to establish a Protestant League to counter the Catholic-Habsburg alliance. Sidney's support for the league was founded on his Protestant beliefs, but he was critical of the idea of a church militant. He was Erastian and latitudinarian in matters of church government, an outlook that led him to befriend in 1586 the Flemish humanist Justus Lipsius, who championed the revival of classical Roman morality and promoted the study of the historian Tacitus as a guide for contemporary conduct. Tacitus's critical evaluation of the decline of imperial Rome appealed to Sidney, as did Machiavelli's teachings on political *virtù* and the Livian concept of military virtue.

Sidney encouraged the study of these authors among his circle, but his own political virtues lay untested until late 1585, when the queen finally acceded to the Netherlands' appeal for help after the assassination of William of Orange in 1584. Sidney was granted governorship of the garrison town of Flushing and proved an astute politician and valiant soldier until taking a fatal wound in a skirmish outside Zutphen, succumbing on 17 October 1586. His death was widely lamented, none mourning him more than his friend Fulke Greville, who composed an influential *Life of Sidney* (published in 1652).

Sidney's greatest pride was, he said, to be a Dudley, and he was a Europeanist rather than narrowly English in outlook. The great irony of his life was that, fashioned as he was by so many others, Sidney was not prepared to be the compromising servant demanded by Elizabeth in the post-Reformation context. Disdaining the one role—that of faithful courtier—that might have led to speedy office, he came to symbolize the crisis that overtook humanism in the aftermath of the Reformation and in light of the entrenchment of the "new monarchies" in Europe. Lack of employment often impelled him into seclusion and experimentation with poetics, the outlet for his political frustrations. The irony of his legacy was that he came to be viewed first and foremost as a poet, an image that became widely accepted in England after the kinsman who took up Sidney's legacy, Robert Devereux, earl of Essex, was executed for treason in 1601.

BIBLIOGRAPHY

Primary Sources

Sidney, Philip. *The Poems of Sir Philip Sidney*. Corr. ed. Edited by W. A. Ringler. Oxford, 1971.

———. *The Countess of Pembroke's Arcadia (The Old Arcadia)*. Edited by Jean Robertson. Oxford, 1973.

———. *Miscellaneous Prose of Sir Philip Sidney*. Edited by Katherine Duncan-Jones and Jan van Dorsten. Oxford, 1973. None of Sidney's works were published during his lifetime, although both his prose and verse circulated widely in manuscript. Editions of his work cited represent the most authoritative compilations available.

Secondary Sources

Allen, M. J. B., Dominic Baker-Smith, Arthur F. Kinney, and Margaret M. Sullivan, eds. *Sir Philip Sidney's Achievements*. New York, 1990. Valuable collection of essays examining Sidney from various perspectives: poet, humanist, courtier, and legend.

Buxton, John. *Sir Philip Sidney and the English Renaissance*. 3rd ed. London, 1987. Portrays Sidney as the catalyst for the development of a distinctively English poetics; a seminal study that first appeared in 1954 but which should be contrasted with the interpretations of van Dorsten.

Dorsten, Jan van. *Poets, Patrons, and Professors: Sir Philip Sidney, Daniel Rogers and the Leiden Humanists*. Leiden and London, 1962. Sets

Sidney in the context of an Anglo-Leiden enterprise concerned to establish a Protestant, humanist fellowship dedicated as much to politics as to literature.

Dorsten, Jan van, Dominic Baker-Smith, and Arthur F. Kinney, eds. *Sir Philip Sidney: 1586 and the Creation of a Legend*. Leiden, 1986. Occasionally iconoclastic collection representing the twin concerns of recovering the historical Sidney and separating the man from the myths that surround him.

Duncan-Jones, Katherine. *Sir Philip Sidney: Courtier Poet*. New Haven and London, 1991. The most recent and thorough biography; based on the author's life-long study of Sidney's writings and her keen familiarity with Sidneian scholarship, this work is a tour de force, offering many new insights into Sidney's personality and ambitions.

Greville, Fulke. *The Life of the Renowned Sir Philip Sidney* (1652). Edited by John Gouws. Facsimile repr. Delmar, N.Y., 1984. Greville's biography was a vital factor in posterity's perception of Sidney: his idealistic and rhetorical portrait has only begun to be seriously questioned and reevaluated.

ADRIANA A. N. McCREA

SIGISMUND I OF POLAND (1467–1548), king of Poland (1506–1548) and great duke of Lithuania (1506–1548). The son of Casimir IV and Elizabeth Habsburg, Sigismund was also the brother of Ulászló, king of Bohemia and Hungary. His foreign policy included a rivalry with the emperor Maximilian I (until 1515), the subjugation of the vassal state of the Teutonic Order in Prussia, and numerous wars with Moscow (1507–1508, 1512–1520, and 1534–1537). His domestic policy included the reform of the treasury and military and the codification of laws. He was assisted by the great nobility and criticized by the lesser nobles. Educated by the humanist Philip Buonaccorsi and surrounded by humanists at court, he promoted Renaissance architecture and literature in Poland.

Sigismund's kingdom was multinational (composed of Poles, Ruthenians, Lithuanians, Germans, and Jews, among others) and multiconfessional (Catholic, Orthodox, Jewish, and Protestant). Despite the dominant position of the Catholic church, interconfessional relations were generally pacific. The Lutheran influence began to manifest itself especially in the Pomeranian towns, and religious tensions in Gdańsk (Danzig) provoked the first royal edict against the Reformation (1520). Similar edicts prohibited the import and the reading of Lutheran publications, as well as study at Wittenberg by students from the kingdom. In 1523 the king tried to introduce confessional censorship of publications by the University of Kraków. Religious and social troubles in Gdańsk (1522) caused a royal visit, a trial, and the restitution of the banished municipal authorities (1526). Despite this intervention, the advance of the Lutheran movement was not halted in Gdańsk or in other towns.

Political realities forced a change in the elastic foreign policy of Sigismund when Albert Hohenzollern, previously master of the Teutonic Order, became the secular, hereditary prince in Prussia (1525), and the Lutheran confession was introduced into the new principality without objection from the king. In addition to Lutheranism, Calvinists and even Anabaptists and members of the Bohemian Brethren (Unitas Fratrum) arrived in Poland. The Catholic church and the king, however, seldom seriously sought to combat these movements as long as their activities were not perceived as threats to the kingdom.

The ambivalent confessional policy of Sigismund can be explained by the political tradition of Poland and Lithuania and by his Erasmian attitudes. Although a Catholic, he tolerated among his secretaries Jan Łaski, a future organizer of Protestant communities in Germany, the Netherlands, and England, and Stanislaus Hosius, the future cardinal and leading personality of the Catholic Counter-Reformation in Europe.

BIBLIOGRAPHY

Cieślak, Edmund, ed. *Historia Gdańska*. Vol. 2, *1454–1655*. Gdańsk, 1982.

Jobert, Ambroise. *De Luther à Mohila: La Pologne dans la crise de la chrétienté, 1517–1648*. Paris, 1974.

Tazbir, Janusz. *A State without Stakes*. New York and Warsaw, 1973.

Wojciechowski, Zygmunt. *Zygmunt Stary, 1506–1548*. 2d ed. Warsaw, 1979.

Wyczański, Andrzej, ed. *Polska w epoce Odrodzenia: Państwo, społeczeństwo, kultura*. 2d ed. Warsaw, 1986.

ANDRZEJ WYCZAŃSKI

SIGISMUND III VASA (1566–1632), king of Poland (1587–1632) and king of Sweden (1592–1599). The son of King John III of Sweden and his first wife, Queen Catherine Jagiellon (the sister of King Sigismund II Augustus of Poland), Sigismund was raised as a Roman Catholic according to the provisions of John's marriage contract with Catherine. When the Vatican's hopes of reclaiming Sweden during the reign of the "high church" King John III failed with the clandestine Swedish mission in 1579, hopes were invested in Crown Prince Sigismund, who, by this time, had declared his intention to remain a Roman Catholic.

In 1587 Sigismund won election as king of Poland with the support of the widowed Queen Anne Jagiellon. The Swedish council (*råd*) was convinced of the value of a Swedish-Polish alliance against Russia and urged Sigismund to accept the election. It was an election immediately regretted by everyone: Sigismund, who found the Polish monarchy impotent; John, who regretted losing his son in his old age; Sigismund's Polish subjects, who found him heavy going ("Tria T fecerunt nostro Regi vae: Taciturnitas, Tarditas, Tenacitas," or "Three T's cause our king's woe: taciturnity, tardiness, tenacity"); and the Swedish estates, who began to worry not only about Sigismund's religion but about the constitutional crisis that an absentee ruler would precipitate.

The re-Catholicizing of Sweden was one of the cherished goals of the newly elected Pope Clement VIII, who, on the news of John III's death in 1592, set up a special council of six cardinals for Swedish affairs and appointed Germanico Malaspina as a special envoy to Sigismund. Although no one in Sweden had an inkling of this, the Swedes were genuinely worried about the prospects of the full force of the Counter-Reformation arriving with Sigismund. The council recognized Sigismund's uncle, Duke Charles, as "the leading personage" of the realm and declared him a partner in an interim government until Sigismund should arrive. The first act of the interim government was to convene a national assembly of the church of Sweden, which took steps to unify its faith and practice by adopting as its statement of faith the unaltered Augsburg Confession of 1530 and as its practice the church order of Archbishop Laurentius Petri of 1571. When Sigismund arrived in Sweden for his coronation, the Uppsala Resolutions and the election of the Gnesio-Lutheran Abraham Angermannus as archbishop were put before him. An accession charter with both religious and temporal provisions was also drawn up by the estates as a condition for Sigismund's coronation. This charter guaranteed his subjects' freedom of religion according to the Uppsala Resolutions; allowed no office, spiritual or lay, to be held by any person who was not a member of the Lutheran church; affirmed the Lutheran monopoly on education; and, while tolerating the presence of non-Lutherans in Sweden, denied them liberty of worship.

The coronation was no sooner over than Sigismund was countenancing Roman Catholic services in Stockholm. He paid no attention to the demands of the council that he appoint some kind of regency government in Sweden, in view of his impending return to Poland. He also showed no disposition to make his uncle the regent, and Duke Charles was expressly forbidden to convene the estates. It soon became obvious that Sigismund placed more reliance on his own agents than on officials in Stockholm. When the estates met and confirmed Charles as regent and resolved to carry out the resolutions of the Uppsala Assembly, Sigismund made it clear that he considered this meeting unlawful and their decisions null and void, and offered protection to all loyal subjects who would resist its decisions. This paved the way for civil war. Sigismund invaded Sweden in 1598, but after some skirmishes and a truce suddenly gave up and withdrew to Poland. He was given one more chance to return to Sweden and promise to stay there permanently, in return for the allegiance of the estates. But he never answered this offer, and was finally deposed in 1599. The crown was offered to Duke Charles, who became Charles IX in 1604.

Several councilors loyal to King Sigismund were tried for treason and executed (the Linköping Bloodbath of 1600), which drove members of some leading Swedish families to flee to Poland for safety. A special Swedish chancellory was established at Sigismund's court, and it was hoped to build up a core of Swedish émigrés who could be used against the rigidly Lutheran regimes of Charles IX and later his son Gustavus II Adolphus. Several misbegotten schemes were hatched to re-Catholicize Sweden and Finland by force or by infiltration, but Sigismund proved too vacillating and too diffident of his own judgment for these schemes to succeed. In the end he could accept tranquilly the loss of Sweden and later the loss of Livonia to his cousin, Gustavus Adolphus, as long as he was assured of gaining the kingdom of heaven. After all, history had placed him in an untenable position that would have daunted the ablest monarch.

BIBLIOGRAPHY

Cnattingius, Hans. *Uppsala Möte, 1593*. Uppsala, 1943. A traditional interpretation of the Uppsala Assembly of 1593.

Garstein, Oskar. *Rome and the Counter-Reformation in Scandinavia until the Establishment of the S. Congregatio de Propaganda Fide in 1622*. 2 vols. Oslo, 1963–1980. Volume 2 especially deals in passing with Sigismund's education, the situation in Sweden after the death of John III, the Swedish émigrés in Poland, and several of the schemes for recatholicizing Sweden and Finland or for undermining the positions of Charles IX and Gustavus II Adolphus which involved Sigismund III directly or indirectly.

Pärnänen, J. A. *Le premier séjour de Sigismond Vasa en Suède, 1593–1594*. Helsinki, 1933. A study of Sigismund's journey to Sweden to assume the Swedish crown and deal with the religious and political issues.

Roberts, Michael. *Gustavus Adolphus: A History of Sweden, 1611–1632*. 2 vols. Reprint, London, 1965–1968. Deals with Sigismund III in passing while chronicling Gustavus Adolphus's conquest of Polish Baltic territories in Livonia and Prussia.

———. *The Early Vasas: A History of Sweden, 1523–1611*. Reprint, Cambridge, 1985. Pp. 327–393 provide a detailed history of the revolution, 1592–1600.

Wordsworth, John. *The National Church of Sweden*. London and Milwaukee, 1911. Provides a detailed but idealistic picture of the Uppsala Assembly of 1593; see pp. 247ff.

FRANK C. SENN

SILESIA is a region of central Europe that lies between Bohemia and Poland, bordering the Sudeten mountains in the west and bisected by the river Oder. The principalities upriver, from the source to the city of Brieg, constituted Upper Silesia; those downriver constituted Lower Silesia; Central Silesia lay in between. In Lower and Central Silesia, the German language predominated. In Upper Silesia, Polish prevailed, with Czech enclaves along the Moravian border.

From 999 to 1202, when Roman Catholicism was introduced, the Silesian principalities formed part of the emerging kingdom of Poland. From 1202 to 1335, the Silesian princes of the Piast dynasty maintained their independence, inviting German colonists who founded hundreds of monasteries, towns, and villages in the sparsely populated province. Beginning in 1289 the Piasts became vassals of the king of Bohemia, and in 1459 Silesia, starting with Breslau, broke ranks with the "heretical" Hussite king George Podiebrad;

subsequently they paid homage to King Matthias Corvinus of Hungary (r. 1469–1490), who gave the country its constitution. He reduced the number of enfeoffed princes from about twenty to five, created the *Fürstentag* (a diet of princes, prelates, knights, and delegates of the towns), and strengthened the *Oberamt*, appointing royal stadtholders, usually the bishop of Breslau, who regulated taxation, recruitment, and coinage. When, after the Battle of Mohács (1526), the crowns of both Hungary and Bohemia fell to Ferdinand I of Austria, the centralization of the Silesian administration continued; however, the Silesian princes and magistrates maintained the *ius reformandi* and rights of ecclesiastical patronage, thus enabling the introduction of the Reformation into the region.

Although this pattern was similar to that followed throughout the Holy Roman Empire, Silesia was unique in that the Reformation entered Silesia without iconoclasm or peasant warfare. The gatekeeper of Lutheranism in Silesia was Duke Friedrich II (1499–1547) of Liegnitz, Brieg, Wohlau, and, later (1536), Kreuzburg and Pitschen. Under the influence of Kaspar von Schwenckfeld (1489–1561), Friedrich II in 1524 mandated the holy scriptures as a rule of faith in his territories, and in 1526 began efforts to found the first Protestant university in Liegnitz. By 1525 Schwenckfeld and his associates, notably Valentin Krautwald (1490–1547), had broken with Luther over justification and the Lord's Supper, while King Ferdinand warned Duke Friedrich in 1527 and 1528 against the despisers of the sacrament. Schwenckfeld therefore left Silesia in 1529, and his followers became dissidents. Another casualty of this controversy was the university in Liegnitz, although by 1531 Valentin Trotzendorf (1490–1556) had resurrected it as the "Gymnasium illustre" in Goldberg. By a *Sakramentsordnung* of 1535, Friedrich II tried to reconcile the Lutheran and Schwenckfeldian interpretations of the Lord's Supper; by 1542, however, he commanded all parsons in his principalities to administer the sacraments according to the Augsburg Confession.

The standard for Lutheranism in Silesia was set by the city of Breslau. In October 1523 the city council, whose clerks were reform-minded Christian humanists, appointed Johann Hess (1490–1547) as pastor of one of the city's major churches and justified the action in a public disputation (20–22 April 1524); in 1525, Ambrose Moibanus (1494–1554) was appointed pastor of the second major city church. Hess and Moibanus, both of whom had been educated as humanists, undertook their church and school reforms in close consultation with Luther and Melanchthon.

In the principalities of Oels and Münsterberg, the Wittenberg reformation gained ground only in 1536, after the death of Duke Karl, a grandson of George Podiebrad. Hess had been Karl's court preacher from 1520 to 1523, and in 1515 had tutored Karl's son Joachim, who was to become the first Lutheran bishop of Brandenburg.

The most far-reaching reforming influence was exercised by Margrave George of Brandenburg-Ansbach (1484–1543). This descendant of emperors Sigismund (d. 1437) and Albert of Austria (d. 1439), the kings of Poland and Hungary, the dukes of Bavaria and Saxony, as well as the margraves of Brandenburg, promoted the spread of Lutheranism wherever he went. As guardian of Louis II of Hungary (1516–1526) and his envoy to Breslau (1521), he left the king's mandate against Lutheranism unenforced. He accompanied his brother Albert, grand master of the Teutonic Knights in Prussia, on a trip to Wittenberg to visit Luther (1524), where plans were made to turn Prussia into the first Lutheran territorial state (1525). To regularize this transformation, both Albert and George obtained Prussia as a fief from their uncle, Sigismund I of Poland. After the death of his wife Beatrice (1510), widow of Matthias Corvinus's son John, George married the daughter of Karl I of Oels-Münsterberg, Hedwig (1525). Two of George's sisters were already married to Silesian princes: Sophia to Friedrich II of Liegnitz (1519), and Anna to Casimir II of Teschen (1518). In 1523 George purchased the principality of Jägerndorf and secured as collateral possessions (*Pfandbesitz*) the principalities of Oderberg (1521), Beuthen (1526), and Oppeln-Ratibor (1532) in Upper Silesia. Wherever he enjoyed rights of patronage, George appointed Lutheran preachers and introduced the Brandenburg-Nuremberg church order. As prince of the Empire (*Reichsfürst*), he stood up for freedom of religion at the Protestation of Speyer (1526), and he told Emperor Charles V at the Diet of Augsburg (1530) that he would rather be beheaded than give up the gospel.

Lutheranism and, to a lesser degree, Schwenckfeldianism and Anabaptism penetrated the *Erbfürstentümer*, that is, the principalities of Jauer and Schweidnitz where the Catholic king was also the immediate duke, as well as the principality of Neisse-Grottkau, where the bishop of Breslau figured as duke. Local patrons and magistrates appointed Lutheran preachers, so that by 1570 nine-tenths of Silesia could be considered Protestant. Because of the Catholic overlordship, however, Silesia's diocesan organization—episcopy, cathedral chapters, monastic foundations—remained intact, and this would serve as a base for the Counter-Reformation, which took effect only during and after the Thirty Years' War (1618–1648). During the sixteenth century, the center for resistance and resentment against the Reformation was the Breslau cathedral chapter; meanwhile, the prince-bishops residing in Neisse accommodated themselves, if only for administrative reasons, to their Protestant peers and tolerated, and sometimes even invested, the Lutheran clergy. Thus, until the conclusion of the Council of Trent (1563), the Lutheran city of Breslau recognized its Catholic bishop as *ordinarius loci*, and in the principality of Liegnitz the bishop of Breslau was so recognized as late as 1592. In 1609 Emperor Rudolf II issued a *Majestätsbrief* for both Bohemia and Silesia that established parity between Lutheranism and Catholicism and that allowed Lutherans to organize consistories that assumed the episcopal functions. But this triumph of toleration was soon to be undone by the Thirty Years' War.

Nevertheless, within the Habsburg Crown lands, only Silesia and the more remote Transylvania successfully resisted the Counter-Reformation. Moreover, Silesia's Lutheran humanist school system prepared the soil for a first flourishing of modern high German literature in the seventeenth century. Finally, Silesia's crypto-Calvinist movement during the second half of the sixteenth century supplied much of the personnel for the "Second Reformation" in the Palatinate.

BIBLIOGRAPHY

Benrath, Gustav A., Dietrich Meyer, and Ulrich Hutter-Wolandt, eds. *Quellenbuch zur Geschichte der evangelischen Kirche Schlesiens.* Munich, 1992. Lists both primary and secondary sources.

Buckisch, Gottfried Ferdinand. *Schlesische Religions-Akten 1517 bis 1675.* Cologne, 1982. For an introduction to the archival sources; also lists secondary literature.

Fleischer, Manfred P. "The Reception in Silesia." In *Discord, Dialogue, and Concord: Studies in the Lutheran Reformation's Formula of Concord,* edited by Lewis W. Spitz and Wenzel Lohff, pp. 119–135. Philadelphia, 1977. Discusses the confessional situation during the century of the Reformation.

———. *The Harvest of Humanism in Central Europe: Essays in Honor of Lewis W. Spitz.* Saint Louis, 1992. See Manfred P. Fleischer, "Humanism and Reformation in Silesia: Imprints of Italy—Celtis, Erasmus, Luther and Melanchthon," pp. 27–107; Robert Rosin, "Replanting Eden: The Elizabethanum as God's Garden," pp. 109–137; James Michael Weiss, "The Harvest of German Humanism: Melchior Adam's Collective Biographies as Cultural History," pp. 341–350.

Karzel, Othmar. *Die Reformation in Oberschlesien,* Würzburg, 1979. Presents a reconstruction of the Reformation in Upper Silesia.

MANFRED P. FLEISCHER

SIMONS, Menno. *See* Menno Simons.

SIN. In contrast to scholastic theology, Martin Luther no longer restricted Original Sin in the form of concupiscence to sensual desire, but understood it as the sinful self-seeking desire of the whole person before God. Not merely the inner ordering between sensual desire and spirit was disrupted, but one's relationship to God in one's very being and consciousness. For this reason Luther also called Original Sin *peccatum radicale* and understood it as personal sin. Through the Fall humanity lost the grace-given original divine image and is subjected to the power of the devil, sin, and death, which are powers that one is unable to overcome by one's own strength. Thus human beings are subjected to alien guilt and yet it is human beings themselves who, after the Fall, willfully sin.

Luther described concupiscence as self-seeking desire before God, echoing the words of *1 John* 2:16. "Satan and man are constantly focused on their own longing, so that they are only capable of seeking what is their own." The Original Sin that determines humans in this way remains active even after the reception of the grace of baptism and should not be reduced, as scholastic theology holds, to mere tinder for sin, which itself is no longer sin and still occasionally leads humans astray through temptations to new actual sins.

Since the grace of Christ redeems a person in faith alone and as such is directed to the whole person, it is conversely the remaining Original Sin in the form of the selfseeking desire or unbelief that excludes one from salvation. Thus the reformers were more interested in human sin in terms of person and essence than in the actual sins committed. Actual sins committed after the reception of the grace of baptism are not what turn human residual weakness again into sin; rather this weakness itself permanently retains the character of sin. Nevertheless, through the grace of Christ human beings are forgiven the guilt of Original Sin outside themselves, and at the same time grace as *donum gratiae* begins to sweep sin out. In the power of grace the *peccatum regnans* ("sin that rules") is transformed into *peccatum regnatum* ("sin that is ruled"). Thus grace inasmuch as it is justifying distinguishes the person of a human being from sin and is at the same time internally active, in that grace sweeps out sin and breaks the domination of sin. Accordingly Luther understood the person of man as being *simul iustus et peccator,* just outside himself *apud Deum et in reputatione eius* ("before God and in his reckoning"), but a sinner in himself, yet in such a way that grace does begin to work in him and overcomes the power of sin.

In view of this notion of grace becoming effective within us, Luther could also speak of people being *partim iusti et partim peccatores.* To recognize the Original Sin that permanently determines humanity as a whole was for Luther a matter of faith, even though Luther did not rule out that some consequences of sin are a matter of experience. This insight also includes the notion that, according to *Romans* 3:20, the law leads to the recognition of sin and thus to the recognition of humanity's alienation from God under the power of sin.

Besides the inner evil that followed upon Adam's fall into sin, the *corruptio naturae* or Original Sin, humanity is also subjected to the exterior evil of death and the power of the devil. Death is the enemy of humanity, and here Luther distinguished between an understanding of death as the extinction of an individual life and an understanding of death as the wages of sin (*Rom.* 6:23). Whether death becomes eternal death or life in eschatological fulfillment is decided on the basis of the sin that is the sting of death (*1 Cor.* 15:56).

Both sin and death are the expression of the power of the devil, to which humanity is subjected through the Fall of Adam. The power of the devil is the *potestas peccati* ("power of sin"), from which the power of Christ alone can free. "All that hangs on Christ, tramples the devil." The lordship of Christ and that of the devil stand in contrast to one another. So it is either the devil or God who guides the will of a person, and one cannot effect a change of master from the devil to God by oneself. That happens only through the power of the Holy Spirit or grace. Therefore the innermost being of a person is a *servum arbitrium*. The will is free only in the absolute bonds of faith in God, which fulfills the first commandment, in that it awaits salvation not from human possibilities, but from God alone.

For Philipp Melanchthon too, Original Sin is a power that determines the essence or the person. It is "a distorted emotional state and a distorted movement of the heart against God's law." It is a person's self-love and as such "the first and highest emotional state of man, by which he is led astray to will and to desire only that which appears good, pleasant, sweet, and glorious to his own nature, as well as to hate and fear that which seemingly contradicts his nature, and to resist that which holds him back from what he covets, or that which counsels him to follow and to ask for that which displeases him."

Also for Melanchthon, Original Sin remains intact and the grace that already justifies humanity as a whole increasingly wrenches humanity from the all-pervading power of sin in the power of the Holy Spirit. Consequently, according to Melanchthon's teaching, "thus after Adam's Fall, all men that are born naturally are conceived and born in sin, that is, they all are full of evil desire and inclination from their mother's womb, and by nature are incapable of having any true fear of God or any true faith in God; this selfsame inborn plague and inherited sin is truly sin, and condemns them all under God's eternal wrath, unless they are born anew through baptism and the Holy Spirit."

Zwingli. As for Luther, for Huldrych Zwingli the recognition of Original Sin is a recognition in faith. Following tradition, Zwingli distinguished between *peccatum originale* and *peccata actualia*. Following Augustine, he portrayed *peccatum originale* as *morbus* ("disease") or *prasten* ("ailment"), which means in so many words "incurable break." Ever since Adam our nature has been totally shattered: instead of loving God, we love ourselves. Thus for Zwingli too, the essence of Original Sin is *amor sui* ("self-love") and the turning of man in on himself. The individual death of a person is the consequence and image of eternal death.

Thus Zwingli also held that the power of Original Sin determines a person in his essence, although beginning in 1535 in the dispute with the Anabaptists he distinguished between inherited sin (Original Sin) and inherited guilt. Here Zwingli contested inherited guilt for children, who indeed are subject to the power of Original Sin. The children of one who has fallen into slavery by his own fault (guilt) become slaves without any fault (guilt) of their own. Zwingli would prefer to maintain the innocence of children; for him inherited sin becomes inherited guilt again only when as an inclination to sin (*propensio ad peccandum*) it leads one astray into actual sin and thereby becomes inherited guilt. However, this did not prevent Zwingli from stressing the totality of Original Sin. Nonetheless, children cannot yet sin in the full sense, because they cannot yet be held responsible for their actions. At the Colloquy of Marburg of 1529, Zwingli conceded that in terms of Original Sin even children stand under the punishment of the law, which condemns them. Accordingly in his *Ratio Fidei* of 1530, Zwingli formulated that the disease of Original Sin can also be called sin, following Paul, because "those born in it are enemies and opponents of God." Overall Zwingli was at pains to maintain his understanding of the legally ethical character of sin in order to emphasize that everyone is responsible for being a sinner in his personal deeds. For Zwingli, too, it is definite that human beings can be rescued from the power of sin through the grace of Christ alone.

Calvin. Through Adam's sin humanity lost the divine likeness. God withdrew from humanity the grace-given original righteousness and abandoned humanity to the corruption of human nature. Since Adam sinned on the basis of his free will, John Calvin did not rule out that the Fall did not occur independently from God's foresight. Nonetheless, he maintains that both Adam and humans born after the Fall are responsible for their sin, because they willingly sin. Therefore Original Sin is transmitted to all, because they are born under God's judgment and like Adam are born under the withdrawal of God's gifts in grace.

For Calvin as for Luther, Original Sin is also a power that determines the whole person. Following Augustine, Calvin also portrayed Original Sin as *concupiscentia*, though adding the restriction that "all parts of man, from his understanding to his will, from his soul to his flesh are stained by this concupiscence and completely filled with it." Consequently, as for lost righteousness, the free will is so ensnared by sin that one cannot attain it of oneself. Thus Calvin showed "that man is now deprived of free will and is subjected to wretched servitude" and concluded with Augustine that "the natural gifts in man are corrupted by sin, while the supernatural gifts are utterly eradicated." Among the supernatural gifts, Calvin particularly meant "the light of faith as well as the purity and righteousness that befit heavenly life and everlasting blessedness."

Nevertheless, Calvin asserted that through the Fall man "was deprived not of his will, but of the purity of his will." Therefore he insisted on distinguishing clearly between the will as an anthropological capacity and its function as willing good or willing evil. Thus in terms of salvation, humans are capable only of willing evil, and they need the power of grace in order to will the good. "Simply to will is a matter of man; to will evil is a matter of corrupted nature; to will good is a matter of grace." Though it is humans under the power of sin that will evil, Calvin still maintained that humans themselves will it. "We must observe the following distinction:

man who is corrupted through the Fall sins with his will and not against his will or by force or violence; . . . and yet his nature is so corrupted that it can be moved and driven toward nothing other than evil." Humans can be freed from this willing evil only through Christ, who sets the depraved will aright once more and orients it toward righteousness. The grace of Christ forgives the guilt of sin and gradually heals the will that was subjected to evil. Christ thereby creates a beginning that he himself must make perfect by anchoring a person in perseverance. Until death, the one who is elect must struggle against sin step by step in the knowledge that the sin which comes alive over and over again is obstinate.

Although the will cannot attain salvation of itself (in other words in terms of God's righteousness it is a will in bondage), this does not hold true in terms of the earthly and lowly matters of this life. "When the human spirit concerns itself with something, it does not work so futilely that nothing comes of it." "Among earthly matters I include," Calvin wrote, "all that has nothing to do with God and His kingdom, or with true righteousness and the immortality of the future, but what is connected with this present life and is likewise enclosed within its boundaries. . . . This first grouping encompasses the teaching on secular rule, domestic arts, craftsmanship, philosophy and the so-called liberal arts." Thus Calvin showed that by their nature humans live in community and this community is ruled by laws. "In all men there is a seed of political order, and that is a strong proof that in the conduct of earthly life, no man is without the light of reason." Accordingly Calvin was able to value even the achievements of antiquity and human reason in a humanist manner. Nonetheless all these achievements stand in danger of being misused by human's self-love and used as a basis for self-righteousness before God. Here is where God's judgment on Adam's sin, that is, the withdrawal of his gifts in grace, takes effect.

In contrast to Zwingli, according to Calvin, children are also included in this willfully assumed fate of Original Sin so that their Original Sin at the same time implies their inherited guilt: "for without guilt we would not be condemned." Thus Calvin more closely followed Luther's line of thinking, although he was more strongly interested in the transformation of the human will through grace for the sake of sanctification than was Luther.

The Early Orthodox Dispute over the Essence of Sin. In the so-called synergistic controversy that began around 1555 over the question of the role of free will in the process of justification, a disputation was held in 1560 between the Jena theologian Matthias Flacius Illyricus and his colleague Viktorin Strigel, also from Jena, over the understanding of free will and grace. Strigel defended Melanchthon's idea of synergism and repeated Melanchthon's formulation: "These three factors come together: the Holy Spirit that moves hearts, the voice of God, the will of man that assents

to the divine voice." In opposition to this, Flacius denied any participation of free will in the process of salvation and stressed the radicality of Original Sin; in fact, he stressed that Original Sin adhered to the substance of human nature not in a mere accidental manner, but rather that it is the substance of human nature itself. However, Flacius thereby moved close to a Manichaean position. The disputation between Strigel and Flacius was broken off, and in 1562 Flacius lost his professorship at Jena.

In this debate it became evident how nearly impossible it was to interpret the doctrine of Original Sin with categories of substance and accident. On the one hand, if one thinks of Original Sin in an accidental manner as a vice adhering to the human substance, then one soon becomes a Pelagian or a semi-Pelagian, as the Gnesio-Lutherans under the leadership of Flacius accused Strigel of being. On the other hand, if one thinks of it as a substance, as did Flacius, then there is the danger of a Gnostic dualism or even Manichaeism, whereby Original Sin is a natural principle in humans that is corrupt in itself. The changeover from sin to grace should not, however, be interpreted as a change in properties in a substance that is a neutral given, or else as a mere change in human substance, but rather a change in what rules over the heart and thus over the person of a human, a transfer from the rule of sin and unbelief to the rule of God and faith. This transfer is God's deed alone (or that of grace). In this sense Flacius was right. However, the categories with which he described the relationship of Original Sin and grace were inadequate. Thus both sides ended up with impossible one-sided views. After all, Strigel was neither a Pelagian nor a semi-Pelagian and merely wanted to stress human responsibility for sin. Conversely, Flacius was not a Manichaean, but he was attempting to maintain at all costs the doctrine of justification by grace alone, even at the risk of jeopardizing the full humanity of man.

The Formula of Concord. The Formula of Concord (1577) in its first article takes a position on the question of Original Sin and seeks to hold a middle ground between the extremes of Flacius and Strigel. Thus it sharply formulates the question as to "whether Original Sin is actually and without any distinction man's corrupted nature, substance, and essence, or else the most noble and best part of his essence, as the rational soul itself in its highest degree and powers. Or whether between man's substance, nature, essence, body, and soul there is a distinction even after the Fall and Original Sin so that nature is one thing and Original Sin another which adheres in the corrupted nature and corrupts that nature." In its answer the Formula of Concord starts from the belief in creation and distinguishes clearly between human nature and Original Sin. Even after the Fall, nature as such is God's good creation. The attempt not to distinguish between nature and sin is a violation "against the chief article of our Christian faith concerning the creation, redemption, sanctification, and resurrection of our flesh," because otherwise nature would be degraded into the work of the devil and it would be denied that Christ had assumed our flesh, and because in the end the goal of the redemption, the new creation, would be called into question. Moreover, the *creatio continua*, the ongoing creative work of God, would be denied.

Nonetheless, the Formula of Concord does not fail to stress the radicality of Original Sin, while it observes, as did Luther, that this radicality must be believed on the basis of revelation and cannot be demonstrated through reason. Original Sin adheres to humanity's essence without being identical to this essence. It is a spiritual leprosy, a spiritual disease. Luther's assertions on Original Sin as real sin, as sin in nature or sin of the person, are adopted. Also in accord with Luther, the sinner remains God's creature, who, however, after the Fall stands hopelessly under the rule of sin. Yet the Formula of Concord maintains "that nature and such a corruption of nature can be separated by no one but God alone, and this occurs completely through death in the resurrection, since our nature, which we now bear, shall rise and live forever without Original Sin, having been severed and separated from Original Sin, as it is written, *John* 19."

Correspondingly, the Formula of Concord warns against discussing the concepts of substance and accident in the context of the doctrine of Original Sin in the presence of uneducated people, since only scholars can rightly understand these concepts in this context. As much as the formula is aware of the inadequate categories of medieval substance ontology, it still does not venture forth into a new conceptual manner that would have been more in conformity with the biblical and Reformation thinking about sin. For sin is, for the reformers, not a substance but a power that rules over humanity who remain God's creature. Accordingly the forgiveness of sin is not a change in the properties of human substance, but rather a shift in rule from the power of sin and the devil to the rule of God and Christ. Because the Formula of Concord does not analyze the concepts of substance and accident, however, it merely comes to a mediate position between Flacius and Strigel. It sides with Flacius by stressing that sin must be understood radically as a disease of human nature, and with Strigel in that it distinguishes between human nature and sin. But this did not eliminate the danger of accepting free will as a human capacity or a partial cause in the realization of justification, to whatever degree. Overall the Formula of Concord states: "We believe, teach, and confess . . . that Original Sin is not a slight, but rather such a deep corruption of human nature, that nothing healthy or uncorrupted has remained in the body and soul of man, in his inner and external powers." With this alone the formula emphasizes the radicality of Original Sin, as it became manifest through the revelation of justification from faith.

The Council of Trent. In session 5 (1546/47), the Council of Trent returned to the medieval understanding of Original Sin. Adam through the transgression of God's command lost the *iustitia originalis* in which he had been created and fell under the wrath and disfavor of God and under the rule of death and of the devil, whereby his body and soul were also diminished. The resulting *peccatum originale* is transmitted to the descendants of Adam through reproduction. Original Sin is, however, individual to each person and can be taken away only through the merit of Christ, which is acquired through baptism. Through baptism the guilt of Original Sin is forgiven and all that constitutes the true and actual essence of sin is taken away. Concupiscence is only the material side of Original Sin and remains after the forgiveness of the guilt and the recovery of grace, or *iustitia originalis*, only in the form of a kind of tinder (*fomes*) within us; it is not itself sin, but it can lead the baptized over and over again to actual sins, the forgiveness of which can be obtained each time in the sacrament of penance.

As for the "tinder" that remains after the reception of the grace of baptism and that is not itself sin, but which rather only leads astray again and again into new sin, session 5 of the Council of Trent states: "however, this holy synod confesses and asserts that there remains in the baptized concupiscence or 'tinder' (*fomes*); since it [i.e., concupiscence] has been left behind for the purpose of struggle, it cannot harm those who do not consent to it and who manfully struggle against it through the grace of Christ Jesus. Rather 'he who has justly fought shall be crowned' (*2 Tim.* 2:5). The holy synod declares that the Catholic Church has never understood this concupiscence, which the apostle occasionally calls sin, as being called sin that would be truly and properly sin in those who are reborn, but because it stems from sin and inclines to sin. If anyone thinks the contrary, let him be anathema."

[*See also* Free Will *and* Grace.]

BIBLIOGRAPHY

Primary Sources

Calvin, John. *Opera quae supersunt omnia.* Edited by G. Baum, E. Cunitz, and E. Reuss. 59 vols. Corpus Reformatorum, 29–88. Braunschweig, 1863–1900.

———. *Opera selecta.* Edited by Peter Barth, W. Niesel, and D. Scheuner. 5 vol. Munich, 1926–1952.

Luther, Martin. *Werke.* Berlin, 1905–.

Neuner, Josef. *Der Glaube der Kirche in den Urkunden der Lehrverkündigung.* Regensburg, 1971.

Melanchthon, Philipp. *Werke in Auswahl.* Edited by Robert Stupperich et al. Gütersloh, 1951–.

Zwingli, Huldrych. *Huldreich Zwinglis Sämtliche Werke.* Munich, 1905–.

Secondary Sources

Althaus, Paul. *Die Theologie Martin Luthers.* Gütersloh, 1972.

Braun, Wilhelm. *Die Bedeutung der Concupiscenz in Luthers Leben und Lehre.* Berlin, 1908.

Brecht, Martin, and Reinhard Schwarz, eds. *Studien zum Konkordienbuch.* Stuttgart, 1980.

Geyer, Hans Georg. *Von der Geburt des wahren Menschen: Probleme aus den Anfängen der Theologie Melanchthons.* Neukirchen-Vluyn, Germany, 1965.

Gross, Julius. *Entwicklungsgeschichte des Erbsündendogmas seit der Reformation.* Munich, 1972.

Hermann, Rudolf. *Luthers These: "Gerecht und Sünder zugleich"* (1930). Reprint, Gütersloh, 1960.

Kühn, Ulrich. *Rechtfertigung im Gespräch zwischen Thomas und Luther.* Berlin, 1967.

Ljunggren, Gustaf. *Synd och skuld i Luthers teologi.* Stockholm, 1928.

Locher, Gottfried Wilhelm. "Grundzüge der Theologie Huldrych Zwinglis im Vergleich mit derjenigen Martin Luthers und Johannes Calvins." In *Huldrych Zwingli in neuer Sicht: Zehn Beiträge zur Theologie der Zürchner Reformation,* pp. 173–274. Zurich, 1969.

Maurer, Wilhelm. *Der junge Melanchthon zwischen Humanismus und Reformation.* Göttingen, 1967; Vol. 2, *Der Theologe.* Göttingen, 1968.

Niesel, Wilhelm. *Die Theologie Calvins.* Reprint, Munich, 1957.

Pfister, Rudolf. *Das Problem der Erbsünde bei Zwingli.* Leipzig, 1939.

Schäfer, Rolf. *Christologie und Sittlichkeit in Melanchthons frühen Loci.* Tübingen, 1961.

Schlink, Edmund. *Theologie der lutherischen Bekenntnisschriften.* Reprint, Munich, 1948.

Schmid, Heinrich. *Zwinglis Lehre von der göttlichen und menschlichen Gerechtigkeit.* Zurich, 1959.

Tschackert, Paul. *Die Entstehung der lutherischen und der reformierten Kirchenlehre samt ihren innerprotestantischen Gegensätzen* (1910). Reprint, Göttingen, 1979.

Venneste, A. *Le dogme du péché originel.* Louvain, 1971. See pp. 33–137.

Wendel, François. *Calvin: Ursprung und Entwicklung seiner Theologie.* Neukirchen-Vluyn, Germany, 1968.

zur Mühlen, Karl-Heinz. *Nos extra nos: Luthers Theologie zwischen Mystik und Scholastik.* Tübingen, 1972.

KARL-HEINZ ZUR MÜHLEN
Translated from German by Robert E. Shillenn

SIX ARTICLES. In the last years of Henry VIII's reign, the Act of Six Articles defined in thoroughly orthodox terms the essential doctrine of the Church of England. In the summer of 1539 parliamentary statute decreed that a heretic's death be the automatic punishment for denial of transubstantiation, and that death might also be inflicted on those who denied that God's law required Communion in both kinds, clerical celibacy, vows of chastity, and private masses, or that auricular confession was desirable.

The act became the prototype for England's religious Acts of Uniformity in the reigns of Edward VI and Elizabeth I. It also marked an end to the doctrinal innovations of the 1530s. The Ten Articles (1536) and the Bishops' Book (1537) had been more radical formularies of faith, designed in part to appease the German Protestants at a time when Henry VIII feared a joint invasion by King Francis I of France and the Holy Roman Emperor, Charles V.

It used to be accepted that the passage of the act was a quick, factional triumph for conservatives at court, notably

Thomas Howard, duke of Norfolk, and Stephen Gardiner, bishop of Winchester, who promoted the bill as a means of putting political pressure on the reformist Thomas Cromwell (Baron Cromwell of Wimbledon and later earl of Essex) and the archbishop of Canterbury, Thomas Cranmer. More recently the consensus is that the act reveals not only the extent of the personal involvement of Henry VIII in the formulation of religious policy but also just how much the dynamics of the Henrician Reformation depended on events abroad.

Far from the act being a response to Howard's speech on 16 May in which he outlined the six topics in question, the king had signaled at the beginning of the session his intention to introduce an act of religious conformity. Indeed, the substance of the act had been government policy since the previous year. A royal refusal to concede over the matters of Communion in both kinds, private masses, and priestly marriage had been the principal reason why, in September 1538, talks with representatives of the German Protestants had broken down in London. Moreover, a royal proclamation of November 1538 had demanded the greatest possible reverence for the sacrament of the Eucharist, and John Lambert, a sacramentarian, had been burned after a show-trial presided over by Henry himself.

Henry was edging away from the radical policies of the 1530s for two main reasons. First, in 1538–1539 England genuinely feared an invasion by the Catholic powers of Europe, and the English coast was fortified in preparation. Henry clearly felt that he needed to display his orthodoxy. Second, it seems that the king was concerned by the growth of radical religion in London and especially in his Continental toehold of Calais.

Henry's personal involvement with the passage of the act can be seen in the many emendations he made to drafts of the bill. When Bishop Cuthbert Tunstall of Durham tried privately to persuade the king that auricular confession was more than desirable, Henry even replied in his own hand that he thought "that both the bishops of York, Winchester, and your reasons and texts were so fully answered this other day in our house as to my seeming and supposal the most of the house was satisfied," adding magisterially that Tunstall's latest arguments "make smally or nothing to your intended purpose." The bishop was warned that the king had "more cause to think you obstinate than you me."

The bill was clearly a rebuff for Archbishop Cranmer. Many of his friends were caught by the act, and two bishops resigned on account of it. The act became the legal authority for many searches in London and other parts of the country, including the royal court. On account of its ferocity it soon became known as the "whip with six strings." In 1544 parliamentary pressure led to arrests under the act being made harder; prior indictment by a grand jury was required, along with other safeguards. The act was repealed as a matter of urgency by Edward Seymour, duke of Somerset, in the first year of Edward VI's reign.

[*See also* Parliament.]

BIBLIOGRAPHY

Brigden, Susan. *London and the Reformation.* Oxford, 1991. Discusses the act's effects on London.

Redworth, Glyn. "A Study in the Formulation.of Policy: The Genesis and Evolution of the Act of Six Articles." *Journal of Ecclesiastical History* 37, (1986), 42–67. Reconstructs the parliamentary passage of the bill.

———. "Whatever Happened to the English Reformation?" *History Today* 37 (1987), 29–36. Places the act in the wider context of religious policy in the 1530s.

———. *In Defence of the Church Catholic: The Life of Stephen Gardiner.* Oxford, 1990. Details the act's application to courtiers.

GLYN REDWORTH

SIXTUS V (Ital., Felice Peretti; 1521–1590), pope from 1585 to 1590. He came from a modest but respected family from Montalto in the Marches; Marijan Žugai claims (*Miscellanea Francescana* 86 [1986]) that he was a descendant of Croatian immigrants, but Isodoro Gatti (*Sisto V Papa "Piceno,"* Ripatransone, 1992) refutes this. He began his career in the Franciscan order; he later became inquisitor, first under Paul IV and subsequently under Pius V; in 1570 he was made cardinal. He had been isolated by Gregory XIII, but thanks to the efforts of Cardinal de' Medici he was unanimously elected Gregory's successor.

A scholarly man, interested in the arts, he proved to be above all a strong-willed financial and organizational genius. He promised Philip II of Spain support should the invasion of England succeed, but did not bow to Spanish pressure to depart from a cautious approach to the question of the succession of Henry IV to the throne of France, a policy which was proved correct after his death. His unsuccessful Vulgate edition did not further the momentum of church reform, but the establishment of the Vatican press and particularly the introduction of regular visits of all bishops to Rome (*Visitatio liminum*) did provide impetus for reform. His reorganization of the College of Cardinals was to last four centuries, and reform was also advanced by his creating the Congregations of Cardinals, fifteen specialized "ministries," nine for the church, six for the Papal States. This broke the power of the College of Cardinals and ushered in an age of papal absolutism throughout the territories of the church; for a while even the roaming bands of outlaws were held in check. Through ruthless fiscalism, including the expansion of credit and the increase of the number of venal offices, Sixtus not only financed an ambitious building program in Rome (new road infrastructure, obelisks, water supplies, additions to the Vatican, the Lateran, and the Quirinal palaces, Saint Peter's cupola) but was also able to set aside a reserve fund of 3 million gold and 1.5 million silver scudi.

What the deflationary effect of these measures was is still not clear.

BIBLIOGRAPHY

Feo, Italo de. *Sisto V: Un grande papa tra Rinascimento e Barocco.* Milan, 1987. The only recent biography.

Gamrath, Helge. *Roma Sancta renovata: Studi sull'urbanistica di Roma nella seconda metà del secolo XVI con particolare riferimento al pontificato di Sisto V, 1585–1590.* Rome, 1987. Splendidly illustrated study of the "visualization of the church."

Simoncini, Giorgio. *"Roma restaurata": Rinnovamento urbano al tempo di Sisto V.* Florence, 1990. Discusses the problem of urban planning and provides evidence that there was an ongoing planning concept, especially with respect to the network of streets, but no elaborate master plan.

WOLFGANG REINHARD

SKEPTICISM. The skeptical perspectives of ancient times were revived in the sixteenth century. The classical texts of skeptical argumentation of Sextus Empiricus and of Marcus Tullius Cicero were rediscovered, edited, and used in philosophical and religious discussions during the period of the Reformation and Counter-Reformation.

Ancient skepticism as a philosophical position or point of view was developed in two forms—one, that of the academic skeptics contending that no knowledge was possible and, two, that of Pyrrhonism, which questioned whether there ever was adequate or sufficient evidence to decide if any knowledge claim was true or false. The first view developed in Plato's academy. Cicero was a student at the academy during its skeptical phase and left an account of arguments denying any claim to knowledge. The other type of skepticism is named after Pyrrho of Elis (360–272 BCE), who reportedly suspended judgment on all questions. The Pyrrhonists, by developing arguments to show the unreliability of sensory knowledge and of reasoning, also tried to suspend judgment about the truth or falsity of any knowledge claims (including the academic claim that nothing can be known) and believed that no criterion, standard, or rule for evaluating knowledge claims could be justified. The skeptical schools of antiquity died off as philosophical institutions in the third century.

In the mid-fifteenth century Greek manuscripts of Sextus Empiricus, the sole surviving writer of the Pyrrhonian school, became known in Italy, as did Cicero's *De Academica*. In the early sixteenth century the term *skeptic* began to be employed, first written in Greek characters and then transliterated. Works of Sextus were translated into Latin and published in 1562 and 1569. The Greek text was not published until 1621.

The arguments in Cicero and Sextus were made known through Michel Eyquem de Montaigne's essay "Apologie de Raymond Sebond" and through *Quid nihil scitur*, the skeptical antischolastic work of his cousin, Francisco

Sanches, both written in 1576 and challenging knowledge claims in philosophy, science, and theology. They applied the ancient skeptical questions, put in modern garb, about the reliability of our senses, the acceptability of our reasoning faculties as means of discovering true knowledge, and the possibility of discovering an unquestionable criterion of knowledge. They raised questions about the various types of theories put forth by the different kinds of philosophers, scientists, and theologians over the ages. The impact of their doubting and questioning was such that by the end of the sixteenth century skepticism had become a major intellectual force, challenging the Aristotelian, Platonic, and Stoic philosophies of the time, as well as all sorts of forms of Renaissance naturalism. The new philosophies advanced by Francis Bacon and René Descartes, among others, were attempts to overcome the skeptical crisis in philosophy and to find a new and secure basis for human knowledge.

Skeptical arguments and challenges were applied to the religious controversies of the time and became more important as the Reformation and Counter-Reformation developed. Early in the sixteenth century Gianfrancesco Pico, the nephew of Pico della Mirandola, used Sextus's materials to oppose Aristotelianism and to defend acceptance of the prophetic religious views of Girolamo Savonarola. Desiderius Erasmus used skeptical views to criticize the scholastic world and to oppose Martin Luther in the debate over freedom of will. Erasmus had called the academic skeptics the least surly of the philosophers and told Luther that the question of whether human beings possess free will was too complicated and too difficult to answer, as well as involving too many interminable disputes. Therefore, Erasmus said he would follow the skeptics and suspend judgment on the matter, though *per non sequitur* he would also accept the position of the Catholic church. Luther berated Erasmus for his skepticism and insisted that a Christian must be absolutely certain of the truth of religion. Luther warned Erasmus that "Spiritus sanctus non est scepticus," the Holy Spirit is not a skeptic and has not given us uncertain views.

In the clash between Erasmus and Luther and later between John Calvin and the French Catholic church, a central issue was that of the criterion of religious knowledge—the rule of faith. Erasmus and the French Catholics accepted the church through the decrees of its councils and of the pope as the arbiter of religious knowledge claims. Luther, on the other hand, insisted that religious knowledge had to be based upon scripture and conscience. Each side appealed to a totally different criterion for determining religious truth. How can one tell which of these criteria to accept? This was a question on which one's eternal salvation might depend.

A similar sort of issue came up in the debate between Calvin and Sébastien Castellion about condemning Michael Servetus for his antitrinitarianism. Castellion sought to show that one did not have sufficient knowledge to tell with absolute certainty who was a heretic and who was not. If what was said in scripture was self-evident, then there would be no disagreements. Since there were disagreements, one needed a criterion, or rule, to ascertain who was right. Castellion generalized his questioning in his unpublished *De arte dubitandi*, which suggested a moderate, undogmatic, common sense way of dealing with this fundamental problem.

The ancient skeptics had argued that justifying a criterion of knowledge would involve either an infinite regress of appeals to criteria of criteria or a circular argument, using the criterion to justify itself. The first publication of the ancient skeptical arguments—the Latin translation of Sextus's *Pyrrhoniarum hypotyposeon* (Outlines of Pyrrhonism) in 1562 by the Protestant Geneva printer Henri Étienne—was put forth as a way of curbing the dogmatism and impiety of philosophers. The 1569 publication of the complete works of Sextus in Latin by Gentian Hervet was offered for more polemical purposes. Hervet, an early arguer against the Calvinists, originally translated Sextus, he said, for relaxation. He soon saw that the skeptical arguments were the complete answer to Calvinism. If nothing could be known, then Calvinism could not be known. The skeptical arguments would undermine all the claims of the human sciences and prepare one to accept revelation. Skepticism, Hervet asserted, was a school of humility that would eliminate dogmatism and lead one to accept only the doctrine of Christ.

This rendering of the value of skepticism appeared in Montaigne's presentation as well. After going through the skeptical arguments about the possibilities of knowledge through the senses or reason, Montaigne said that skepticism makes one humble, and renders the mind blank, thus making it ready to receive whatever messages God chooses to give. We are not able to tell by our own means which is the right form of religion and so should accept our religion by faith alone and remain in the religion in which we were born and raised. Montaigne, the skeptical fideist, remained officially a Catholic. His position was put into didactic form by his intellectual heir, Pierre Charron, in *Les Trois Veritez* (1594), and *De la Sagesse* (1601). The first offered a skeptical "defense" of Catholicism; skeptical arguments were used to show there was no adequate evidence that atheism, non-Christian religious claims, or non-Catholic religious claims were true. Those who change religion should have good reasons for doing so. If no such reasons can be offered, then they should stay in their original religion and accept Catholicism on faith alone.

The fideism of Montaigne and Charron, whether sincere or not (and some of their contemporaries questioned whether they were really Catholic believers), and the use of skeptical argumentation against the reformers were made into "a machine of war," especially by early seventeenth-century French Jesuits, such as François Veron, who sought to show that the Protestants had no secure basis for their views and were simply offering their personal, subjective opinions rather than guaranteed religious truths. Veron utilized skeptical points to challenge the Calvinist rule of faith—their criterion that scripture was the basis and source of religious knowledge. Veron asked how does one know what book is scripture. Moreover, if one could answer this, how would one know what it says, what it means, and what to do about it? Calvinist opponents saw that the same sort of skepticism could be raised against Catholics. How could they tell with certainty, for example, what church councils had said or what the Pope had said. This led to the publication of *De Insanabili Romanae Ecclesiae Scepticismo* (The Incurable Skepticism of the Church of Rome), in which it was argued that a Catholic could only have certainty if he or she could determine who was the pope and what he said. Can one rely on questionable sense information or on dubious authorities? Even the man who claims to be the pope may be in error about his status. So, the work concluded, Catholics would be forever in doubt if they relied on their rule of faith.

As reformers and counter-reformers sought to undermine one another's positions by employing ancient skeptical arguments, a compromise position was offered by Castellion, and developed by Hugo Grotius and then by leaders of the Anglican church. One can admit that most of our alleged knowledge is to some degree uncertain, but does this mean that without complete and adequate evidence one is unable to act and to resolve problems? A reasonable person doubts when there really is no way of finding an answer, but in practical affairs the reasonable person does in fact accept less than absolutely certain information and employs hypotheses. One should not ask for more evidence than the case requires. If the same reasonable method is employed in religious questions, one will be able to find some answers, though not necessarily indubitable ones.

The revival of ancient skepticism in the sixteenth century greatly affected philosophy, science, and theology. Perhaps the most important application of the revived skeptical arguments was in the struggle between the reformers and the defenders of Catholicism. A skeptical defense of the traditional religion developed that used skeptical arguments against the reformers and then accepted Catholicism on faith. This Catholic fideism spawned a counterattack by Protestants. In the course of the seventeenth century the skeptical arguments were used against Christianity and Judaism, producing agnosticism about revealed religion and finally, in the eighteenth century, about natural religion as well.

[*See also* Toleration.]

BIBLIOGRAPHY

Burnyeat, Myles, ed. *The Skeptical Tradition.* Berkeley, 1983.
Castellion, Sébastian. *De Arte dubitandi et Confidendi Ignorandi et Sciendi.* Edited by E. Feist Hirsch. Leiden, 1981.
Cicero, M. T. *Academica.* Cambridge, Mass., 1933.
Letocha, Danièle, ed. *Aequitas, Aequalitas, Auctoritas: Theoretical Reason and Legitimation of Authority in XVIth Century Europe.* Paris, 1992.
Montaigne, Michel de. *The Complete Works of Montaigne.* Stanford, Calif., 1958.
Popkin, Richard H. "Skepticism and the Counter-Reformation in France." *Archiv für Reformationsgeschichte* 51 (1960), 58–87.
———. *The History of Skepticism from Erasmus to Spinoza.* Berkeley, 1979.
Popkin, Richard H., and Charles B. Schmitt, eds. *Skepticism from the Renaissance to the Enlightenment.* Wolfenbütteler Forschungen, vol. 35. Wiesbaden, 1987.
Sanches, Francisco. *That Nothing Is Known.* Edited by E. Limbrick and D. Thomson. Cambridge, 1988.
Schmitt, Charles B. *Gianfrancesco Pico della Mirandola, 1469–1533, and his Critique of Aristotle.* The Hague, 1967.
———. *Cicero Scepticus.* The Hague, 1972.
Sextus Empiricus. *Outlines of Pyrrhonism and Adversus Mathematicos.* 4 vols. Cambridge, Mass., 1933–1949.
Van Leeuwen, Henry. *The Problem of Certainty in English Thought, 1630–1680.* The Hague, 1963.

RICHARD H. POPKIN

SLEIDANUS, Johannes (Eng., Sleidan; Ger., Johann Phillipson von Schleiden; 1506–1556), German humanist, diplomat, and historiographer. His history of the Reformation represents a landmark in the development of modern historiography.

Sleidanus witnessed the progress of the new religious movement during its most turbulent phase, first as a student with the Brothers of the Common Life at Liège, subsequently as tutor (1524–1533) in the household of Count Manderscheid. His correspondence shows him very much a part of the excitement, and a warm admirer of Melanchthon. On the foundations of his humanist background, his legal training in France (1533–1536), and his German connections he entered the service of Cardinal Jean du Bellay in Paris. This position placed him close to the political action at the court of King Francis I and proved an invaluable apprenticeship for his diplomatic and historiographic career. During this period Sleidanus's fascination with history manifested itself, specifically in the preface of his Latin paraphrase of Jean Froissart's *Chroniques* (Chronicles). His father's death prompted his return to his native Schleiden in 1542. This decision may have been reinforced by the severe repression of the evangelical movement in France and by Sleidanus's growing skepticism about the motives behind a French policy of rapprochement with the German Protestants.

He maintained close contact with a circle of friends in Strasbourg, including the educational innovator Johannes Sturm, the stettmeister Jakob Sturm, and the reformer Martin Bucer, all deeply involved in the affairs of the city and the Schmalkald League. By 1545 Sleidanus's letters show him settled in Strasbourg, negotiating to become the league's historiographer. He was ready and eager to begin work on *De statu religionis et reipublicae Carolus V Caesare commentarii.* Diplomatic missions as well as difficulties in obtaining archival documents hampered the progress of his work, and the defeat of the Schmalkald League by Emperor Charles V (1547) stalled it altogether.

Meanwhile, as a result of that defeat, Sleidanus represented the city of Strasbourg in negotiations concerning the safety of Protestant theologians, required by the Interim to attend the Council of Trent. The skill and marvelous independence of mind he displayed during this mission—aborted though it was by the Princes' Rebellion in 1552—still awaits due recognition in literature. It led the Strasbourg senate to engage him in its service. The remaining years of his life were taken up with school and church administration, notably in dealing with the French exile congregation formerly headed by Calvin, and with his historiographic project, which he now pursued on his own. As a civil servant, he enjoyed access to the Strasbourg archives, an abundant source due to the city's prominent role in the Schmalkald League and, in particular, to the leadership of Jakob Sturm, who took an active interest in Sleidanus's enterprise. The work was completed and published in 1555.

The impact of his *Commentaries* was immediate and lasting. For the first time, Sleidanus's history-conscious contemporaries obtained an integrated account of the epochal events that had touched everybody in some form but that most could have perceived only in a fragmented way. What this account meant to that society can be gauged by the rousing demand for the book, by both friends and foes of the Reformation. It was extolled and it was maligned; but above all it was read.

The narrative was written during a period when the survival of the evangelical religion was in doubt, and in its painstaking detail it represented a Protestant apology for posterity. Although Sleidanus saw events from a Protestant vantage point, he related them factually. His quest for inclusiveness may be daunting for the reader; but it achieves an unsurpassed immediacy with the complex interrelationships of religious, political, constitutional, and social issues in collision. It is precisely the almost burdensome detail of this history that drives home the fierceness of confrontation between opposing views and interests, and the wily politics and frustrations it engendered.

Sleidanus's account reflects a committed Protestant, yet one who was not a theologian and therefore did not delve into doctrinal minutiae. He emerges as a man deeply stirred by the religious revolution because he could no longer respect the church in its manifestations as a Roman institution. But as a second-generation Lutheran he was not primarily engrossed in the birth of the movement. By the time of his writing Lutheranism had gained a firm spiritual foothold. It was the struggle of Lutheranism for survival against overwhelming political odds that captured Sleidanus's attention.

By his understanding of valid sources and his sense for historical context Sleidanus laid the foundation for Reformation historiography. To students of the sixteenth century his *Commentaries* are of singular value, because they convey the perceptions of an intellectually and personally involved contemporary with a modern grasp of historical process.

BIBLIOGRAPHY

Primary Sources

Baumgarten, Hermann. *Sleidan's Briefwechsel*. Strasbourg, 1881. Virtually the only biographical source material in existence. Leaves considerable chronological gaps.

Sleidan, Johann. *Ioanni Sleidani de statu religionis et reipublicae Carolo V Caesare commentarii*. Strasbourg, 1555.

———. *De quatuor summis imperiis libri tres*. Strasbourg, 1556. Textbook for world history, widely used; the only one of its scope for several generations. Available in microfilm series *English Books Before 1640*. Contains Latin version followed by English translation, *A briefe Chronicle of the four principall Empyres*, translated by Stephen Wythers, London, 1563.

———. *The General History of the Reformation of the Church*. Translated by Edmund Bohun. London, 1689. Available in rare book departments of several libraries, such as Princeton University and Colgate Rochester Divinity School.

———. *Ioanni Sleidani de statu religionis et republicae Carolo V Caesare commentarii*. Annotated by Christian Carl Am Ende. Frankfurt, 1785. The only annotated edition, it also exists in "reproductio phototypica," 3 vols. Osnabrück, Germany, 1968.

Secondary Sources

Dickens, A. G. "Johannes Sleidan and Reformation History." In *Reformation, Conformity and Dissent*, edited by R. Buick Knox, pp. 17–43. London, 1977. Helpful in pointing out the transitional stage of historiography as reflected in the *Commentaries*.

Friedensburg, Walter. "Johannes Sleidanus, der Geschichtsschreiber und die Schicksalsmächte der Reformationszeit." *Schriften des Vereins für Reformationsgeschichte* 52.1 (1935), 157. Most comprehensive treatment available in concise article form. Blend of biography, description, evaluation, and historical background.

Kelley, Donald R. "Johann Sleidan and the Origins of History as a Profession." *Journal of Modern History* 52 (1980), 573–598. Enlightening analysis of the cultural forces by which both Sleidan and historiography came into their own.

Paur, Theodor. *Johann Sleidans Commentare über die Regierungszeit Karls V., historisch-kritisch betrachtet*. Leipzig, 1843. A scholarly investigation of some of Sleidan's sources; resourceful, even if occasionally obsolete.

Verzeichnis der im deutschen Sprachbereich erschienenen Drucke des XVI. Jahrhunderts. Stuttgart, 1983–. See vol. 19, nos. 6644–6726.

Vogelstein, Ingeborg Berlin. *Johann Sleidan's Commentaries, Vantage Point of a Second Generation Lutheran*. Lanham, 1986. Johannes Sleidanus and his work are examined in this volume in the light of their historical context.

INGEBORG BERLIN VOGELSTEIN

ŠLIK OF PASOUN, Sebastian. *See* Schlick of Passauni, Joachim Andreas.

SLOVAKIA. *See* Hungary.

SNECANUS, Gellius (1540–1596?), Frisian Reformed minister. Snecanus was born Jelle Hotzes. He went to the Latin school in Sneek and probably studied in Zwolle and Cologne. He became Roman Catholic parish priest in the Frisian village of Giekerk. Reading Luther led him to leave the Catholic church before 1567. He had to go into exile, and with about fifty other Protestants he went to Emden. He often went back to Friesland to preach in the churches "under the cross." In 1570 he was again in Leeuwarden, but because of the policy of the bishop, Cunerus Petri, he had to leave the capital of Friesland again. After 1578 he gave the first sermon in the Jacobite church in Leeuwarden, but not before the images and paintings were destroyed. In March 1580 the Reformed church became the official church and the situation for Snecanus changed completely. He went to Nijland, a village near Bolsward, lived for a couple of years in Harlingen, and spent probably the rest of his live in Leeuwarden. From 1583 he was appointed by the synod of the Frisian Reformed church to study theology and to write.

Snecanus's career is typical of many other reformed preachers' careers: ordained as a Catholic parish priest, reading books written by Luther, Calvin, and Heinrich Bullinger, breaking with the church, going into exile, and then serving as minister in the privileged Reformed church. Snecanus was one of the founding fathers of the Reformed church in Friesland, in particular in the period when the Reformed were suppressed. He played an important role as well in the organization of the new university in Franeker. The Frisian synod asked Snecanus to publish a book critical of the Anabaptists.

He is the author of a number of other books, as well. In his *Methodica descriptio et fundamentum trium locorum communium sacrae scripturae* (1584) he expressed views on predestination different from Calvin and more like Philipp Melanchthon and Bullinger. The synods and Théodore de Bèze himself considered him unorthodox, but Snecanus did not submit to ecclesiastical discipline. In other works he shows himself to be a disciple of Bullinger, in particular in his views on the convenant. Snecanus was a more tolerant Reformed Protestant, who agreed, for example, with the ideas of Jacobus Acontius, expressed in his *Satanae Stratagemata*. Like Gregory of Nazianzus he declared that he had never returned as a better human being from a synod of the church. Recent research has made clear that the Reformed church had more variety than was previously thought. Snecanus is a good example of this pluriform Calvinism.

BIBLIOGRAPHY

Nijenhuis, W. "Variants within Dutch Calvinism in the Sixteenth Century." In *Low Countries History Yearbook*, pp. 48–65. 1979.
Schilling, Heinz, and Klaus-Dieter Schrieber, eds. *Die Kirchenratsprotokolle der Reformierten Gemeinde Emden, 1557–1620.* Cologne, 1989.

See vol. 1, pp. 335ff. For new information regarding Gellius's time in Eden.

WIEBE BERGSMA

SOCIAL CLASSES. *See* Estates; Nobility; Peasants.

SOCIAL DISCIPLINE. The heuristic term *social discipline* is derived from two well-known concepts in Reformation and early modern historiography: the German sociologist Max Weber's idea of discipline and self-control in the transition to the modern world, and the German historian Gerhard Oestreich's concept of *Sozialdisziplinierung* that describes the transformation of the early modern state and society in central Europe. In his famous essay "The Spirit of Protestantism and the Rise of Capitalism" (1920), Weber locates the origins of rational, disciplined behavior, the defining character of a "modern" attitude and society, in the Reformation, especially in its Calvinist expression. He writes: "We are naturally not concerned with the question of what was theoretically and officially taught in the ethical compendia of the time, however much practical significance this may have had through the influence of church discipline, pastoral work and preaching. We are interested rather in something entirely different: the influence of those psychological sanctions which originating in religious beliefs and the practice of religion, gave a direction to practical conduct and held the individual to it." For Weber, these psychological sanctions consisted of an "inner-worldly asceticism"—the avoidance of one's own sentiments and feelings and a turning instead to the demands, discipline, and the method of living a proper, godly life.

In Oestreich's formulation, *Sozialdisziplinierung* is an abstract concept that connects several developments in early modern Europe—the institution of church discipline after the Reformation with the help of the state, stricter discipline and professionalization of the military, and an ethos of greater self-control. The end result, according to Oestreich was that in the absolutist early modern state "[t]he attitudes and the conduct of even the simple subject were shaped, controlled, and regulated by the process of disciplining. . . . This process of disciplining produced a more or less violent change in the structure of society at all levels." Briefly stated, Oestreich argues that the enforcement of church discipline, the consolidation of confessional identity, and the demand for religious conformity complemented developments in political and philosophical thought.

Since the 1960s the concept of *Sozialdisziplinierung* has become influential in German historical scholarship, and it is often used in conjunction with the concept of "confessionalization" to describe a complex of social, religious, and political developments in central Europe between the sixteenth and eighteenth centuries. In a 1987 essay, the German historian Winfried Schulze analyzes in detail the ideas behind Oestreich's concept and its reception and criticism. He defines *social discipline* as "an idealtype conceptualization that brings together a number of historical events in spiritual and material life, religious-ethical visions as well as socio-economic reality, and gives them an abstract formulation. Social discipline summarizes different well known phenomena and is applied as a common concept for a fundamental unified process, which, although individual phenomena can be observed therein, these are seen as variations of a collective phenomenon." Although social discipline had its roots in church discipline, Schulze argues, its manifestations in early modern Europe extended greatly beyond the confines of religious history. Since the early modern state arrogated to itself the task of enforcing discipline, with the help of the official churches, social discipline came to be synonymous with urbanization, civilization, and the advent of absolutism: it was underpinned by the philosophy of neo-Stoicism and manifested itself in the greater imposition of military discipline in the early modern world. Whereas Schulze, Oestreich, and other historians have emphasized the ubiquity and universalism of the concept, it is helpful to limit its discussion to the specific realm of religious history in general, and the Reformation in particular.

As is evident from the above discussion, it is imperative to distinguish between, on the one hand, the abstract idea of social discipline and, on the other, the historical reality of the promulgation of social control and church discipline both before the Reformation and in the new Protestant territories. The Reformation did not give birth to social control. In pre-Reformation towns, the magisterial impulse to control the behavior of urban residents manifested itself in numerous ordinances regulating vagrancy, festivals, begging, poor relief, and consumption. Firm believers in social hierarchy, the burghers of late medieval towns feared the forces of disorder, often identified with the lower classes. Discipline was thus as much a matter of social control as it was rooted in a theological worldview of sinful human nature. Ideally, the Christian community and the urban commune were synonymous; and disasters that befell cities—fires, plagues, and warfare—were often attributed to the sins of the residents.

In the decades leading up to the Reformation, there were increasing calls for social control and measures to purify the body social of the urban communities. Targets of repression included religious and social minorities, who were held responsible for infecting the Christian community with their moral failings. In Nuremberg, for example, the town magistrates expelled the Jews in 1497, after decades of complaints directed against Jewish moneylenders. Similarly, when an epidemic of venereal disease swept the community during the 1490s, the city fathers closed down all brothels. In addition to Jews and prostitutes, the citizens of Nuremberg resented the clergy as an alien element in their midst,

exempted from civic taxes and guard duty, and competing for the livelihood of residents. In popular culture, reflected in pamphlets, woodcuts, carnival farces, and stories, the clergy were often identified with the other marginal groups: they were represented as whoremongers and not infrequently as customers of Jewish usurers. The Reformation movement drew strength from these resentments. In 1525 the magistrates in Nuremberg closed down the cloisters; and thus the evangelical community was free from Jews, prostitutes, and the Catholic clergy. An increasingly harsh attitude toward vagrancy and begging also became manifest. The increasing number of begging poor was one of the reasons; a long-term shift in civic attitudes toward poverty represented a more significant development. In Nuremberg as in other cities, new and more restrictive poor laws were enacted, often in the wake of the Reformation, in part to centralize and assume the work of charity formerly undertaken by the clergy, but also in part to place a more restrictive regime on public charity by screening and controlling the poor.

The Reformation thus reinforced the burghers' sense of a moral community. In addition to the new regime of poor relief, other institutions were created for the enforcement of social discipline: in cities the creation of church and marriage courts that were staffed by magistrates or by their appointees; and at the level of the larger territorial states, the creation of government-appointed consistories of pastors and officials to enforce religious morality.

A stricter moral regime was the intended consequence of the Reformation; the unforeseen result was the breakdown of morals. Luther's doctrine of justification by faith liberated many consciences from "papal tyranny." During the 1530s Luther came to emphasize discipline instead of "Christian liberty." Reflecting in 1538 on the early days of the evangelical movement, Luther wrote: "But it was a different matter at that time from the present. At that time the world was frightened more than enough. . . . There was no need to drill into or even to teach the law to the oppressed, frightened, pitiable, tearful, tempted conscience. The need was to apply the other side of Christ's message, when he commands that forgiveness in his name be proclaimed. . . . But now, when times are entirely different. . . men have changed. . . . They are becoming and actually are secure and wicked, inconsiderate, thievish, yes Epicurean, and fear neither God nor man." In spite of repeated admonitions from Luther, Martin Bucer, and Johannes Brenz, the stricter enforcement of church discipline remained at the discretion of the secular authorities, who resisted the imposition of an "evangelical papal tyranny." Throughout his tenure as church superintendent at Strasbourg, for example, Bucer never succeeded in establishing the kind of discipline that was to him a sign of the true church.

In the eyes of godly reformers, effective church discipline was established only by Calvin in Geneva. The instrument was the consistory, a committee of the municipal government. The consistory was re-elected every February in the annual elections in which the entire government of Geneva was elected: four syndics, the members of the ruling councils, and members of a number of committees assigned to duties like maintaining the fortifications, maintaining a municipal grain supply, keeping accounts, and the like. One of these committees was the consistory. The presiding officer was one of the four syndics. He was flanked by two benches of consistory members, one of lay elders, the other of pastors. Lay elders were chosen to represent the city councils and neighborhoods; the pastors' bench included all city and village pastors *ex officio*. Calvin dominated the consistory by virtue of his personality and ideas. His supporters in the city were heavily represented among the lay elders, who came mostly from mercantile and professional backgrounds and included many French immigrants. On Calvin's insistence, the Genevan consistory exercised sole authority over excommunication and became the most effective urban institution at maintaining moral discipline. The accused were summoned to the weekly meetings of the consistory to answer charges of blasphemy, adultery, and a catalog of lesser or greater sins. By combining the moral authority of the church and the coercive power of the government, the consistory established a highly successful disciplinary regime in Geneva.

An example of the effectiveness of Calvinist church discipline is found in E. William Monter's study of demography and religious history. Monter has shown that by the late sixteenth century the number of illegitimate births in Geneva had declined sharply, and that most new infants received Old Testament baptismal names, reflecting the self-identification of the godly republic with the biblical chosen people. Between 1560 and 1580, the most successful decades of Calvinist church discipline in Geneva, the rate of illegitimacy was only 0.1375 percent. From 1560 to 1569, of 6,940 infants baptized, only eight were illegitimate. Similarly, prenuptial conceptions averaged 4 percent between 1550 and 1581. To put these figures into perspective: in the Genevan countryside, where church discipline was not as effectively established, the percentage of couples who baptized a child within eight months of their wedding was ten times higher than in Geneva. And in neighboring Lausanne, also a Protestant city, 1.2 percent of baptisms were of illegitimate children and over 10 percent of brides were pregnant. Monter attributes the success of this strict moral regime directly to the teachings of Calvin and to the vigilance of the consistory in enforcing sexual discipline among the urban residents.

Thanks to the convergence of state and church authority, discipline became a mark of the Reformed church. It is important to bear in mind that members of the church voluntarily subjected themselves to a rigorous regime of introspection and congregational supervision, anchored in the soteriology and ecclesiology of Calvin's theology; and that where Calvinism existed as a tolerated confession, as for example in the Rhineland and France, consistorial discipline did not extend beyond the boundary of the Calvinist congregations. Where Calvinism competed with other confessions, as in the Netherlands and Emden, Calvinist consistories and Anabaptist communities both manifested a high degree of voluntary discipline. Where Calvinism became the official religion, however, as in the Palatinate, Nassau, and Cromwellian England, Calvinist pastors readily called upon the state to extend discipline to the ungodly.

In the Lutheran church social discipline came under the joint supervision of government officials and pastors, a partnership in which the clergy usually played the subordinate role. Since the Lutheran clergy owed its appointment to princes and patricians, church affairs also were subject to official control. In many German Lutheran principalities, for example, the church council, a government bureaucracy headed by an official and staffed by lay officials and pastors, enjoyed jurisdiction over the behavior and appointment of pastors. In other Lutheran territories, the consistories, which were colleges of pastors, also reported to counselors of the prince. At the local level, the prince's authority was upheld by both the local pastor and the bailiff: and since many mandates required the subjects to obey both God and prince, the pastor and the official became the twin enforcers of church and social discipline.

The alliance between religion and politics was based on mutual interests: God-fearing Christians made obedient subjects, for Luther and other evangelical reformers admonished Christians to distinguish between the visible and invisible kingdoms of God, and to respect his ordained authority on earth. The suppression of excessive drinking and gambling, for example, served to uphold the Christian household and social order: fathers were enjoined to keep a pious household and not to squander their wealth, lest their wives and children be forced to turn to church and state for charity. In matters of youthful sexuality, meanwhile, the Lutheran church, by attacking the Catholic concept of consensual marriage between young adults, helped to transfer decision-making into the hands of elders and the state. This tighter control over youthful passion served many interests: those of parents and elders, for by withholding marital consent from young people they tightened control over the timing and manner of dividing and passing on family property; those of Lutheran pastors, for permission to marry was coupled with a minimum expectation of catechistic knowledge on the part of the prospective parents, who were admonished to rear their children as God-fearing and pious; and those of the state, for the control of youthful sexuality lessened the volume of marital litigation and helped to suppress illegitimacy. As Thomas Robisheaux has shown, peasant householders of the county of Hohenlohe in southwest Germany welcomed this particular feature of social discipline because it reinforced their authority over young people, even while they were resisting other measures imposed from above by the clergy and officials.

Other institutions to enforce social and church discipline included regular visitations and parish records. Visitations were instituted in the early years of the Reformation to investigate the foundations of the new evangelical faith. The Saxon visitations, carried out under the supervision of Luther and his associates, yielded an overall picture of the new church: the learning and character of local pastors, the physical conditions and finances of local churches, the state of local schools and teachers, the number of parishioners, the degree of their religious knowledge, the practice of magic, and the presence of dissent. Stipulated in the various new evangelical church ordinances, church visitations were institutionalized during the course of the sixteenth century. Organized at the territorial state level, they were carried out at regular intervals. The central church authority—the consistory or the church council—appointed commissioners, usually the higher-ranking members of the pastorate, who then visited the various parishes in person. They would question the local pastor, the schoolmaster, and the parishioners according to questionnaires drawn up by the officials of the state church; the reports, in turn, would be submitted to the central authorities at the end of the visitation. These visitation records, compiled over a matter of decades and centuries, provided indispensable information on their subjects to officials and pastors. Historians have found illuminating details on religious practices in these records: how ordinary people confessed their sins, whether they sent their children to catechism lessons, how often they received Communion, and cases of disobedience to pastoral authority. Discipline and control would have been impossible without abundant records.

Even more detailed information on individual parishioners was compiled in the parish records. From the beginning of the Reformation, registers of birth, baptism, Communion, marriage, and death were kept in parishes, a practice that was to become universal in all Christian churches during the course of the sixteenth century. Pastoral work thus became more systematic, rational, and organized; and parish records enabled greater supervision and administration of souls. The dispensation of sacraments and the performance of rituals created moments when the state church could monitor the behavior, and sometimes the beliefs, of the common people. Absence from sacraments hence marked individuals as nonconformists. The failure to receive Communion at least once a year would become the occasion of pastoral investigation and even official sanctions, as David Sabean has shown from research into visitation records of southwest Germany. Illegitimate births became difficult if not impossible to conceal. And the general tendency was one toward conformity in religious practices, as these measures encouraged a degree of internal discipline among the common people.

These institutions of social and church discipline were not confined to the Protestant churches. Tridentine Catholicism emphasized renewed clerical control over the laity. Visitations and parish records also became institutionalized in the Counter-Reformation. Whereas the focus of Tridentine visitations was on the conduct of the Catholic clergy, parish records provided a means of controlling ritual practices among lay parishioners. The major aim of the Counter-Reformation church, it seems, was to ensure the confessional loyalty of the laity. Stress was placed not so much on enforcing piety and disciplined behavior as on combating religious dissent. It should be pointed out that visitations in Catholic areas were much more effective in controlling the clergy than the laity, especially in comparison to Protestant cases. In Protestant Europe, secular authorities and the clergy jointly enforced social and church discipline: punishments meted out by officials reinforced the sermons of pastors. In Catholic Europe, secular cooperation was often, but not always, present. Social discipline was most effectively enforced when the Catholic state stood behind the clergy, as in Bavaria or Würzburg; in areas where state authority was weak, as in the bishopric of Speyer, the clergy achieved only limited successes in changing the behavior of the laity.

Although the groups targeted for social disciplining varied according to historical circumstances, unmarried women, young men, servants, the poor, and vagrants most often were the objects of social disciplining. In other words, the enforcers of social discipline tended to be socially differentiated from the larger communities targeted for moral supervision. As the Protestant pastorate tended to be recruited from the middling ranks of respectable bourgeois society, the Protestant cleric, at the front line of disciplining the people, often expressed contempt for his social and moral inferiors. The seventeenth-century Hamburg pastor Johann Balthasar Schupp was a self-appointed reformer of popular morals. In his sermons Schupp lashed out at the immoral behavior of the lower classes in the seaport, singling out servants, maids, beggars, soldiers, sailors, and journeymen as targets of censure and discipline.

Unmarried women as well were targeted for disciplinary supervision. In his study of the Calvinist synod's records in the German city of Emden, Heinz Schilling has demonstrated the importance Calvinists placed on controlling sexual behavior. A striking pattern emerges from more than two centuries of cases investigated by the elders and presbyters: whereas in the late sixteenth and seventeenth centuries a variety of sexual offenses were censured—adultery, cohabitation, extramarital sex—during the eighteenth century, unmarried single mothers (who often worked as domestic servants and maids) became the focus of church discipline.

Church discipline, however, was not synonymous with social discipline. The former, at least, was voluntary, in that all church members submitted themselves willingly to the authority of leaders of the church. The Reformed church in Emden was vigilant in maintaining church discipline because it had to compete with the even stricter Anabaptist community. Voluntarism in the enforcement of congregational discipline, however, could easily give way to a call for coercive social discipline wherever Calvinism became the official state church. Such was the case in the Netherlands, in Cromwellian England, in parts of the Rhineland, and in other German territories. Effective social disciplining was achieved by the interpenetration of the religious and political elites. Heinz Schilling has shown that between 1595 and 1825 urban magistrates, academics, and the mercantile elites dominated the Groningen presbytery: about one-third of all magistrates had also served as elders, and although men of lower social status filled the ranks of elders and deacons, they were underrepresented.

Similarly, political domination and religious representation went hand in hand in the rural villages ruled by Calvinist Zurich, as the Swiss historian Markus Schär has shown in his study of suicide in the early modern period. During the mid-seventeenth century, the Zurich city council stipulated that all rural ministers must be citizens of Zurich; the catch, however, was that young men from the villages were not admitted to theological studies. Thus the imposition of church discipline in the countryside—the attack on swearing, herbal medicine, popular beliefs and rituals—represented the increasing suppression of rural culture, with its remnants of magical healing and attachments to rituals, by rational, disciplined, and intolerant urban piety.

Within the family, social discipline reinforced the authority of the father, whose command over his household mirrored the authority of the prince and the pastor. Thus men perceived women and children as objects of discipline, for their very natures were weak. In a theological dissertation of 1618, for example, Jakob Lindinner advanced the thesis that babies had a natural propensity toward evil. Hence, Lindinner argued, the will of children must be broken and tamed early in order to turn their nature from sin to virtue. The father, not the mother, must be the agent of this godly work, this disciplining within the family. Childbearing was the role of mothers, not child rearing, for womanly nature represented a potential source of corruption for children. Writing in 1591, Samuel Hochholtzer, another Calvinist divine, expressed a similar view: "How [women] love to accept strange, false beliefs, and go about with benedictions and witches handwork. When they are not firm in faith and the Devil comes to tempt them. . . they follow him and go about with supernatural fantasies. Daily experience also teaches us that many of them hide in the serious error that they could cure their children with blessings and devilish things, such as the many stories about herbs, which they first empowered with supernatural blessings." To counter the pernicious influence of mothers, therefore, the pastor suggested that fathers must be stern and distant, so that their children would grow up both loving and fearing them.

It is evident that the concept "social discipline" encompasses a broad range of historical issues and that historians are by no means unanimous in their assessments of these developments. Since the articulation of the concept by Gerhard Oestreich in the 1960s, some historians have accepted the concept as reflective of a wide-ranging and effective repression of the common people by church and state. While Oestreich himself stresses both the internalization of discipline through the philosophy of neo-Stoicism and its external imposition by the early modern state, some scholars have focused primarily on external repression. The influence of the French philosopher Michel Foucault was no doubt partly responsible for this interpretive angle. By stressing the repressive nature of early modern society, Foucault and his followers have given "discipline" a negative, distorted meaning, removed from the original intent of the word. Stefan Breuer has shown how Max Weber's notion of voluntaristic, internalized, inner-worldly asceticism has given way to Foucault's notion of the repressive discourse and institutions of the early modern world, where prisons and insane asylums were but extensions of other institutions of social discipline.

Historians who emphasize the coercive nature of social discipline assign the pivotal role to the early modern state. The French historian Robert Muchembled, for example, laments a world in which the spontaneous culture of the common people was displaced by the rigid and repressive culture of the ruling elites. The early modern state, according to Muchembled, played a decisive part in repressing popular revolts and popular culture, a campaign in which the Counter-Reformation church was the handmaiden of the absolutist state. The suppression of Carnival, persecution of witches, and condemnation of popular magic were all elements in the war waged by the elites against the people, in which discipline, symbolized by Lent, would triumph over the people and their culture, symbolized by Carnival. On the basis of extensive reading of police ordinances published by the many territorial states in early modern Germany, the American historian Marc Raeff comes to a conclusion similar to Muchembled's, although he gives a more positive evaluation of the process: the early modern state steadily extended its authority over its subjects through regulation and discipline.

In its exclusive reliance on documents created by the institutions of repression, critics argue, the interpretive approach of Foucault and his followers exaggerates the effectiveness of the early modern state and underestimates the magnitude of popular resistance. Normative sources such as ordinances, proclamations, and regulations cannot be taken as *prima facie* evidence of actual practice: frequent repetition of ordinances for example, might be taken to indicate noncompliance. Another imputed shortcoming is a lack of conceptual distinction between coercive and voluntary discipline. In a significant essay, the German historian Heinz Schilling argues against the identification of Church discipline (*Kirchenzucht*) with social discipline (*Sozialdiszipliniung*). Submission to the former, he argues, was voluntary, as exemplified by Calvinist congregations in Emden, Geneva, and the Netherlands. The fact that church discipline for a congregation expanded into social discipline for an entire urban community, as in Geneva, should not obfuscate the original distinction between the two concepts.

The current interpretive trend has been away from a negative, over-deterministic view of social discipline, and recent research has constructed a more differentiated picture. In Calvinist Zurich, internal discipline coexisted with external discipline, as Markus Schär has shown. A Calvinist elite—the elders and deacons—enforced church and social discipline on society at large while internalizing the same norms. The immense psychological stress, Schär argues, resulted in a substantially higher suicide rate among this elite. Other studies argue that the imposition of social discipline was seriously limited by the actual effectiveness of the early modern state and the official churches. Regarding Lutheran Württemberg, Robert Scribner points to the limited ability of the state to police a substantial migrant population, whose way of life was precisely the target of many church and state ordinances. In Catholic Speyer Tridentine priests failed to suppress popular festivals in the wine-growing parishes of the Palatinate; the growth of a Catholic confessional identity, as Marc Forster argues, was due more to the pressures of conformity exerted by the village communities than to any disciplinary measures of the early modern confessional state.

The moral regime of the early modern state and the official church had clear limitations: social discipline worked where it reinforced the moral community of the villages and towns; it failed when it came into direct competition with a system of autonomous moral regimentation in which the family and neighborhood, not the state, played the key roles. In Calvinist Hesse, where social discipline was imposed from above by a state church, most villagers were reluctant to serve as elders in their local congregations because they would reap resentment from their neighbors as informants and traitors. Wilhelm Zepper, a church superintendent who conducted the 1596 visitation, reported on the difficulties of enforcing social and religious discipline: "Those who should be exercising leading, and administering discipline and church decorum in accordance with their selection and office, however, are anxious that they would be held and labeled as informers and traitors by their neighbors, and would earn much ingratitude, great resentment, and invite hatred and enmity from many upon their own heads." And in regions where church discipline was perceived as merely serving the interests of the state (as in eighteenth-century Württemberg, for example), piety and politics took separate paths. Nonconformists, labeled "separatists" by orthodox

Lutheran pastors, rejected the authority of the state church and accused their ministers of cozying up to the powerful and oppressing the common people. For them, true discipline was voluntaristic, not imposed, and truly moral conduct, a characteristic of the true church of the pious, could not be attained by society at large, which is inherently sinful.

BIBLIOGRAPHY

Blickle, Peter. *Deutsche Untertanen: Ein Widerspruch.* Munich, 1981.

Bossy, John. "Blood and Baptism: Kinship, Community and Christianity in Western Europe from the Fourteenth to the Seventeenth Centuries." In *Sanctity and Secularity*, edited by D. Baker. Oxford, 1973.

Breuer, Stefan. "Sozialdisziplinierung: Probleme und Problemverlagerungen eines Konzepts bei Max Weber, Gerhard Oestreich und Michel Foucault." In *Soziale Sicherheit und soziale Disziplinierung: Beiträge zu einer historischen Theorie der Sozialpolitik*, edited by Christoph Sachsse and Florian Tennstedt. Frankfurt, 1986.

Forster, Marc. *The Counter-Reformation in the Villages: Religion and Reform in the Bishopric of Speyer, 1560–1720.* Ithaca, N.Y., 1992.

Hsia, R. Po-chia. *Social Discipline in the Reformation: Central Europe, 1550–1750.* London, 1989. Synthesis of recent German research on the implementation of confessional conformity and social discipline in Central Europe.

Jütte, Robert. "Poor Relief and Social Discipline in Sixteenth-Century Europe." *European Studies Review* 11 (1981), 25–52.

Kingdon, Robert M. "Calvin and the Establishment of Consistory Discipline in Geneva: The Institution and the Men Who Directed It." *Nederlandsche Archief voor Kerkgeschiedenis* 70 (1990), 158–172.

Monter, E. William. "Historical Demography and Religious History in Sixteenth-Century Geneva." *Journal of Interdisciplinary History* 9.3 (1979), 399–427.

Muchembled, Robert. *Popular Culture and Elite Culture in France, 1400–1750.* Baton Rouge, 1985.

Munch, Paul. "Kirchenzucht und Nachbarschaft: Zur sozialen Problematik des calvinistischen Seniorats um 1600." In *Kirche und Visitation: Beiträge zur Erforschung des frühneuzeitlichen Visitationswesens in Europa*, edited by Ernst Walter Zeeden and Peter Thäddäus Lang, pp. 216–248. Stuttgart, 1984.

Oestreich, Gerhard. *Neostoicism and the Early Modern State.* Cambridge, 1982. Contains several seminal essays on the formation of discipline and social order in early modern Europe.

Raeff, Marc. *The Well-Ordered Police State: Social and Institutional Change through Law in the Germanies and Russia, 1600–1800.* New Haven, 1983.

Robisheaux, Thomas. "Peasants and Pastors: Rural Youth Control and the Reformation in Hohenlohe, 1540–1680." *Social History* 6 (1981), 281–300.

Sabean, David. *Power in the Blood: Popular Culture and Village Discourse in Early Modern Germany.* Cambridge, 1984.

Schär, Markus. *Seelennöte der Untertanen: Selbstmord, Melancholie und Religion im Alten Zürich, 1500–1800.* Zurich, 1985. Original analysis of the relationship between Calvinist theology, confessionalization, and the social history of suicide.

Scharfe, Martin. "The Distance between the Lower Classes and Official Religion: Examples from Eighteenth-Century Württemberg Protestantism." In *Religion and Society in Early Modern Europe, 1500–1800*, edited by Kaspar von Greyerz, pp. 157–174. London, 1984.

Schilling, Heinz. "Reformierte Kirchenzucht als Sozialdisziplinierung? Die Tätigkeit des Emder Presbyteriums in den Jahren 1557–1562." In *Niederlanden und Nordwestdeutschland: Studien zur Regional- und Stadtgeschichte Nordwestkontinentaleuropas im Mittelalter und in der*

Neuzeit, edited by Wilfried Ehrbrecht and Heinz Schilling, pp. 261–327. Cologne, 1983.

——. "Die Bedeutung der Kirchenzucht für die neuzeitliche Sozialdisziplinierung." In *Stände und Gesellschaft im Alten Reich*, edited by Georg Schmidt, pp. 265–302. Wiesbaden, 1989.

——. *Civic Calvinism in Northwestern Germany and the Netherlands: Sixteenth to Nineteenth Centuries*. Kirksville, Mo., 1991. Translations from the German of seminal essays by the leading historian on German Calvinism.

Schulze, Winfried. "Gerhard Oestreichs Begriff 'Sozialdisziplinierung in der frühen Neuzeit.'" In *Zeitschrift für Historische Forschung* 14 (1987), 265–302.

Scribner, Robert W. "Police and the Territorial State in Sixteenth-Century Württemberg." In *Politics and Society in Reformation Europe*, edited by E. I. Kouri and Tom Scott, pp. 103–130. London, 1987.

Spalding, James C. "Discipline as a Mark of the True Church in Its Sixteenth-Century Lutheran Context." In *Piety, Politics, and Ethics*, edited by Carter Lindberg, pp. 119–137. Reformation Studies in Honor of George Wolfgang Forell. Kirksville, Mo., 1984.

Weber, Max. *The Protestant Ethic and the Spirit of Capitalism*. New York, 1974. See also the original essay in his *Gesammelte Aufsätze zur Religionssoziologie*, Tübingen, 1920–1921.

R. PO-CHIA HSIA

SOCIAL ETHICS concerns one's conduct toward others. It defines both what is right or wrong behavior and what is right or wrong motivation for that behavior. For the majority of Europeans social ethics was one dimension of the practice of Christianity: its norms for right behavior derived from examples of Christ's life; its ideals for motivation anchored in one's understanding of Christian faith. For Christians throughout the Middle Ages and Reformation, both clergy and laity, social ethical ideals for all forms of social relations—family, kin, neighborhood, guild, village, town—derived from theological constructs. Social ethics are, moreover, historical, changing over time. As the great German theologian Ernst Troeltsch argued, each age in Christian history was in some way defined by those ideals it applied to the relations of human beings to one another. In the Reformation, one group, evangelicals, shared a certain degree of consensus as to what ideal would be normative in all forms of social relations, distinguishing their understandings of that ideal and its applications from both past and contemporary Catholics.

The biblicism of all reformers—from Martin Luther to the Anabaptists to the peasants of 1525—led them to value the "Second Command," Christ's command to love one's neighbor as oneself (*Mt.* 22:39). In this, they differed from their Catholic predecessors and contemporaries, who considered the other ethical commands in the Bible as well as natural law in their formulation of social ethics. The ideal of Christian "brotherly love" was not a sixteenth-century innovation—it had been invoked throughout the Middle Ages, first by monastic movements and then by confraternities in the fourteenth and fifteenth centuries as the ideal guiding their behavior toward one another and toward other Christians. What distinguished the evangelical reformers was the preeminence they accorded this ideal in their conception of ethics, whether social, political, or economic. This ideal of brotherly love may be said to define evangelical social ethics, even though there was great disagreement about how this should be applied.

While all agreed that Christian brotherly love was to be normative in human action, and all asserted the prior necessity of justification by faith, Protestant theologians differed among themselves as to the precise relation between faith and ethical behavior. For Martin Luther, Christian brotherly love was the probable, but not necessary, expression of faith. For Huldrych Zwingli, Christian brotherly love was the outward sign of the presence of divine grace among a community: it was not possible for one to love one's neighbor, to overcome the essential sin of self-love, without the gift of grace. For the Strasbourg reformer Martin Bucer, faith led directly to the desire to serve one's neighbor and the larger Christian community. For the earlier generation, brotherly love was the ideal against which practice might be judged and policy formulated, from issues of social welfare to the question of usury. The second generation of Protestants spoke less often of brotherly love, but all, from Luther and Zwingli through John Calvin, distinguished their understanding of who constituted one's "brother" from that of Catholics: for Catholics, according to Protestant theologians, "brother" was narrowly conceived as members of a limited gathering of like persons, such as monastic communities or confraternities.

Frequently approximating Zwingli's formulation, especially in the mid-1520s, popular pamphleteers, both lay and clerical, connected love of neighbor directly to faith as its manifestation or expression. Some argued that those who cared for their neighbors numbered among the faithful; those who did not, among the faithless. For many, including some Catholics, an ideal of brotherly love provided a precise norm by which to judge all kinds of commerce and exchange, including tithing. Among them, the Strasbourg scientist and humanist Otto Brunfels held that the clerical use of tithes opposed the command to love one's neighbor. Still other pamphleteers held that Christian brotherly love would bring all men to see the poor as their "brothers"—and hence would lead to a leveling of the social order. The ideal served as a norm by which lay reformers could criticize the practices of the Roman church and its clergy, especially the distance the clergy had built between themselves and the laity. For many, the clergy had failed to extend to all Christians the bonds of neighbor.

The ideal of brotherly love had revolutionary implications. In the Peasants' War of 1525, peasants, artisans, townsfolk, even merchants and a few nobles took up the ideal and applied it as a norm by which they might judge tithing, taxes and other forms of payment demanded of them, as well as the structuring of relations between peasant and lord, artisan and master, and subject and ruler. In their brutal reassertion of dominion, princes, lords, and magistrates defined the limits of brotherly love's application to human relations.

And yet, in the years following 1525, the ideal of brotherly love was not abandoned. It remained in legislation on poor relief in Protestant towns: magistrates consistently offered "brotherly love" as the reason they had taken up the administration of relief, and they admonished citizens to donate to civic chests for the same reason. It was the moral basis of their legislation, that which gave it validity. For magistrates, brotherly love continued to serve, not as an ideal by which society should be reordered, but as that which guided relations within an established order, relations with those less powerful, less wealthy.

By 1540, few Protestant theologians or regimes spoke of the ideal of Christian brotherly love. As the second generation of evangelicals turned to ecclesiology, so, too, regimes in the 1530s and 1540s turned to the specification of moral codes, the definition of moral communities. By mid-century, the ideal of Christian brotherly love was restricted in its application to poor laws, in which the faithful were enjoined to contribute to communal chests out of love of neighbor and God. For Catholics, the restitution of Thomas Aquinas at Trent meant the reassertion of natural law as the basis for social ethics, even as their encounters in the Americas led them to grapple not only with the ethics of empire but with newly discovered limits of natural law in any formulation of social ethics that might comprimise native peoples.

BIBLIOGRAPHY

Althaus, Paul. *The Ethics of Martin Luther.* Translated and with a foreword by Robert C. Schultz. Philadelphia, 1972. An exploration of the implications of justification by faith alone for social and political life.

Bieler, André. *La pensée économique et sociale de Calvin.* Geneva, 1959. Magisterial study of Calvin's social thought and the impact of this thought on social and economic relations.

Blickle, Peter. *The Revolution of 1525: The German Peasants' War from a New Perspective.* Translated by Thomas A. Brady and H. C. Erik Midelfort. Baltimore, 1981.

———. *The Communal Reformation: The Quest for Salvation in Sixteenth-Century Germany.* Translated by Thomas Dunlap. Atlantic Highlands, N.J., 1992.

Forell, George Wolfgang. *Faith Active in Love: An Investigation of the Principles Underlying Luther's Social Ethics.* Minneapolis, 1959.

———. *History of Christian Ethics.* 2 vols. Minneapolis, 1979. A basic introduction to some of the theologians who have shaped Christian ethics.

Kingdon, Robert M. *Church and Society in Reformation Europe.* London, 1985. See especially chapter 8, "The Control of Morals in Calvin's Geneva." Explores the formation and function of the Geneva "morals court."

Roper, Lyndal. *The Holy Household: Women and Morals in Reformation Augsburg.* Oxford, 1989. A major study of formulation of morality in a Reformation city, with particular regard to women.

Troeltsch, Ernst. *The Social Teaching of the Christian Churches.* Translated by Olive Wyon. 2 vols. London, 1931. Magisterial and influential study of the interdependence of theology and ethics in Christian theology.

Wandel, Lee Palmer. *Always Among Us: Images of the Poor in Zwingli's Zurich.* Cambridge, 1990. See especially chapter 2 on Zwingli's social ethics and his particular understanding of "Christian brotherly love," and chapter 4 on the ethical language of legislation on the poor.

LEE PALMER WANDEL

SOCIAL WELFARE. In the 1520s and 1530s, governments that were becoming Protestant mandated the elimination of all begging. In doing so, they took from the poor the gesture that had linked them to Francis of Assisi (d. 1226) and the spiritual connotations medieval Christians associated with the physical condition of poverty. That moment more than any other in the history of the care of the poor marks the change from medieval conceptions of charity to the modern notion of social welfare.

By the sixteenth century, poverty had become a more insistent presence in more people's lives and in more kinds of lives than ever before. As Catharina Lis and Hugo Soly have argued, structural changes in the organization of agricultural and urban labor left many more people vulnerable to the many kinds of disasters—fires, droughts, floods, epidemics—that swept over lives and property with rhythmic force. Freed from serfdom, most agricultural workers became day laborers; in many areas of Europe, close to 50 percent of the rural population belonged to this frequently migrant, nonpropertied group. As Wilhelm Abel has argued, wages did not keep up with the cost of produce or rents; not only day laborers but also tenant peasants lost to dues and rents what wealth they had as well as the food they produced. In towns, guilds monopolized the production of most commodities and food as well as most labor. Masters could command their own fees, but apprentices and journeymen controlled neither their wages nor the prices set for the products they helped to make.

By the end of the fifteenth century, then, many workers, artisanal and agricultural—day laborers, both urban and rural; apprentices and journeymen in most crafts; entire crafts, such as weaving and fishing; household servants; those peasants who rented their land—lived marginally, their wages or products never quite sufficing to feed and shelter them and their families. As much as 25 percent of the population was continually underfed; even more could not be certain of their place of residence. All these people were directly, starkly vulnerable to natural disasters and fluctuations in agrarian and commercial markets. All were perched precariously at the edge of poverty: by the end of the fifteenth century, most would have been "poor" at some point in their lives, and many were "poor" more often than not. As Thomas Fischer said, the poor comprised those who were dependent on others' wills, lived upon their land and in their houses, worked in their shops, and received their wages from them (*Städtische Armut und Armenfürsorge im 15. und 16. Jahrhundert*, Göttingen, 1979). As popular poems and broadsheets proclaimed, all, even the wealthiest, but especially the dependent, could fall to illness, accidental loss of limb, natural disaster, fire—could fall beneath the wheel of fortune.

The poor flowed into the towns, their numbers rising and falling according to those fluctuations, crowding the plazas before churches, sitting on doorsteps, wandering streets, crying out and stretching out their hands to invoke the obligations of charity. Over time, contemporaries came to distinguish types of poverty among the poor, that is, to distinguish among the causes of poverty and the degree to which different poor had contributed to their condition. The oldest category comprised widows, orphans, the maimed, the blind, and the sick—those whose poverty was likely to be permanent. By the sixteenth century, these poor had become the traditional poor, those who had been recognized for centuries as authentically poor and dependent upon others for sustenance and shelter. By then, the traditional poor were distinguished from those whose poverty was contingent—laborers out of work, peasants whose crops had been lost to drought or flood, those whose property had been lost to fire. These poor shared with the traditional poor bad fortune, personal disaster of some kind, but their situation might change with fortune and discipline. The poor, both traditional and temporary, were also divided between those who begged, who went out into the streets, quite possibly lived in the streets, supplicating townspeople and clergy for charity, and those who remained at home, the *Hausarmen*, or domiciled poor. By the sixteenth century, the most important distinction was not between the permanently and the temporarily poor, however, but within the population of the begging poor: between authentic beggars and sturdy or false beggars, who had chosen to beg not out of need but for other, sometimes sinister reasons.

The sturdy beggars frightened townspeople and villagers alike. They had made a career of begging. Most of them were vagrant, moving from town to town, even country to country. Resident nowhere, they did not belong, did not come from local communities, the town, or its surrounding countryside. They could not be located within the extended matrices of familiarity. Unknown locally, they were also strangers in sinister ways: cynically sizing up local residents, they would often "play" them for charity, for their Christian goodwill, manipulating ethical obligations for their personal gain. They might also fake the sores or symptoms of illnesses, such as syphilis, that were devastating but not known to spread easily. Unethical, these beggars were frequently criminal as well: many robbed those who charitably offered them shelter or food, some attacked and harmed their hosts,

and a few murdered them. The sturdy beggars were a deeply disturbing presence. They blended into the begging population, their appearance close to that of other poor, but they manipulated their situation and the responses of the donating population. They were troubling because they might have chosen their poverty—might not have been unwilling victims of chance—and because they were cunning.

These categories or types of poor enabled contemporaries to distinguish among the numbers of poor and to divide them into the "deserving poor," who would and should receive some kind of aid, and the "undeserving," to whom no aid should be offered. The humanist Juan Luis Vives, the Catholic theologian Juan de Medina, Protestant reformers, and the governments of towns, cantons, principalities, duchies, kingdoms, and the Holy Roman Empire would all anchor their discussions of forms of poor relief in the division between the deserving and the undeserving poor. They would differ on the kinds of poor who should receive aid and who should not. All agreed that widows, orphans, the lame, the blind, and the infirm should receive help: shelter, food, schooling for the children, hospital beds for the sick, and alms for all. By the 1530s most Catholics and Protestants agreed that sturdy beggars, those who were physically able and had chosen not to work, should not receive aid. But even on this issue, no clear consensus emerged. In 1544–1545 in Salamanca, two theologians, Juan de Medina and the Dominican Domingo de Soto, debated whether sturdy beggars belonged within the limits of charity. De Soto's position, that all persons, no matter their situation, should be allowed to beg, proved the more popular, and Spanish charitable agencies did not, for the most part, distinguish sturdy beggars from other kinds of poor.

Most poor fell between these two poles, with their clear ethical imperatives. Most found their fates shifting dramatically with the theological and moral debates; and until a single form of relief was designated and instituted in their region, they received aid of varying degrees of sufficiency from a number of different sources—individuals, religious houses, parish and village churches, cathedrals, rulers—the great majority of which were ecclesiastical.

Before the Reformation, the poor sought aid from a plethora of institutions, some providing alms, in food or coin, and some providing shelter as well. Cathedrals and parish churches had tables set up at one of the portals, south, west, or north, from which alms and bread were distributed to the poor. Cloistered orders frequently fed and sometimes housed some of the poor. Secular rulers of various levels of authority might dispense alms on designated days. Guilds and their confraternities would provide support to their own members in times of need, according to their resources; unfortunately, those guilds whose members were likeliest to need aid were also usually among the poorest themselves. In Italy confraternities were frequently founded specifically for charitable purposes. Some established hospitals for the poor; some, hospitals for poor children; some, orphanages. By the end of the fifteenth century, each town had a hospital of some kind, sometimes run by the town council, sometimes run by one of the religious orders. Larger or more devout towns had multiple hospitals to serve the differing needs of the sick: for lepers, for victims of smallpox, for pregnant women, for the old and permanently infirm.

The means by which these institutions collected alms were equally diverse. In theory the tithe that the laity paid to their church and various religious houses served in some part to support the poor. So, too, the laity would designate a portion of their pious donations, made either while living or through wills, for the support of the poor in some way. Churches typically had alms boxes somewhere near the west door where parishioners could drop coins as they departed from the Mass. Mendicant orders, especially the Franciscans, collected alms specifically for the poor. Other orders might draw on their incomes from tithes or rents. Confraternities collected alms from their members through donations, through endowments from wills, and through membership dues. Hospitals received alms both from religious houses and, frequently, directly from the residents of the town and its surrounding countryside; those who had the means sometimes sought to endow a bed in one of the hospitals for themselves or possibly their families in perpetuity.

A variety of these institutions in differing combinations could be found in any town. Frequently they competed for resources, and their responsibilities to the poor overlapped. The poor could and often did seek aid from a number of institutions within the same town or same region. These institutions were increasingly pressed for alms, their resources strained or exhausted by increasing numbers of poor who were demanding aid from multiple sources. By the sixteenth century, a number of the places the poor traditionally looked for aid were turning them away, unable to feed, clothe, or house the poor without jeopardizing their own maintenance, while others were seeking ways to circumscribe the numbers of poor to whom they should give aid.

The reform of poor relief and the Reformation coincided in a number of continental towns and in England. The relation of the two reforms has been much debated. It is now clear that Protestantism did not cause the reform of poor relief. As Brian Tierney argued, twelfth-century canon lawyers made the critical distinction between deserving and undeserving poor. As Maureen Flynn, Linda Martz, and Brian Pullan have demonstrated, Catholic polities also reviewed and reformed their poor relief, some earlier than the advent of evangelicalism. And, as Pullan and Natalie Davis have shown, the impetus for the reform of poor relief in Venice and Lyon was humanist and civic rather than Catholic or Protestant.

The reform of poor relief was more dramatic in Protestant lands, however, because it went hand in hand with the Protestantization of political authority. From imperial cities and German principalities, Swiss cantons and regions of villages, to England and Holland, as governments "became Protestant"— publicly supporting the preaching of evangelical theology, providing protection for evangelical theologians, and in perhaps the greatest revolution, legislating liturgical reforms and the restructuring of Christian practice—they acquired autonomy, some from their Catholic overlords, all from Roman intervention. They also acquired new jurisdictions: over the accumulated wealth, property, lands, incomes, and buildings of monasteries, convents, mendicant houses, churches; and over the practice of religion, its rituals, its rhythms, its physical presence, and its ethic. In Protestant lands, the reform of poor relief was carried out by secular governments, who extended their jurisdiction to encompass the care of the poor and the definition of policy toward them. Because these governments appropriated exclusive control of the administration of relief, that administration was centralized; because the collection of alms and their distribution fell under an increasingly rationalized bureaucracy of government, its mechanisms became more efficient and rational. It does seem clear that, insofar as any sixteenth-century government had the means to enforce its will, the centralization of relief under Protestant regimes gave those programs access to kinds of authority and enforcement not available to Catholic institutions of relief.

Protestant poor laws in Nuremberg (1522), Kitzingen (1523), Regensburg (1523), Ieper (1525), Zurich (1525), and elsewhere gave the relief of the poor a kind of coherence. They distinguished the kinds of care available—hospitals, schools, orphanages, soup kitchens, and shelters—and organized them under one central administration. The many forms of relief no longer overlapped in their respective responsibilities. The legislation also required the administrators of relief to manage the poor, to determine the kind of aid each poor person needed, and to direct that person to the appropriate agency. In each town, moreover, all the various institutions of relief were funded from one "common chest," the replenishment of which was the responsibility not of the individual agencies but of the central administration. Protestant regimes retained the various forms of aid the poor required but placed them all under a single central administration, responsible for the collection and distribution of all forms of care.

The recent work of Flynn and Martz on Habsburg Spain suggests that Catholic monarchs also became increasingly involved in reforming the administration of poor relief, themselves seeking principles by which to rationalize, simplify, and make more effective the care of the poor. The nature of their involvement differed from that of Protestant governments: their role was supervisory and adjudicative, but they did not directly manage programs of poor relief. The administration and management of the care of the poor was left to hospitals, confraternities, bishops, and the various religious orders. Catholic institutions for the care of the poor remained diverse, administered by authorities of differing, sometimes conflicting jurisdictions.

While the extent of their jurisdiction over the care of the poor differed, both Protestant and Catholic governments were increasingly drawn into the problems of caring for the poor. Both sought to articulate principles of justice and charity that accommodated their and their subjects' changing experience of the poor. The poor were becoming a more insistent presence in people's lives. In part, increases in their numbers made them more visible and audible. Contemporaries were struck more, however, by changes in the kinds of poor: widows and orphans seemed less and less visible, while other kinds of poor—the artisan out of work, the day laborer driven from the fields by drought, and the sturdy beggar—became increasingly prominent in broadsheets, popular songs, and more official discussions. One kind of poor dominated discussions more often than any other: the sturdy beggar.

By the Reformation, the sturdy beggar had as fixed a place in the European imagination as Francis of Assisi—and both were identified by their begging. Two hundred years earlier, Francis had made the gesture of begging one of the most powerful of Christian piety. As he, Bernardino of Siena, and other Franciscans had taught, that gesture most fully captured each person's relation to God. In begging, in supplicating for the means to survive, the poor made visible to all an Augustinian anthropology, a vision of humanity impoverished spiritually and entirely dependent upon the gifts of God. In giving them aid, medieval Christians extended to them *caritas*, acknowledging their humble status and offering them gifts of sustenance. The poor demanded—through begging—and the prosperous gave, obligated as Christians to respond with charity to the request. Alms became an essential symbol in a complex web of dependency and reciprocity: donors and poor depended on one another to make visible and articulate a vision of the interrelationship of God and humankind.

By the end of the fifteenth century, that gesture had become polluted, its connotations of Christian humility and dependence clouded by persons of aggression and arrogance. Sturdy beggars had brought to the gesture new connotations: where Francis had been deferential, they were aggressive; where he had been humble, they were assertive; where he had been gentle, they were violent; and where he had been charitable himself, loving of all humankind as his "brothers" and "sisters," they were self-interested, manipulating this extraordinary gesture to "play" the generous for profit. Equally, the laity were increasingly suspicious of the mendicants—Franciscan, Dominican, and Augustinian— who still employed that gesture, but, like the sturdy beggars, no longer lived in accordance with its meaning. The mendicants had become wealthy and powerful; within their local communities, they might be arrogant, harsh landlords, eager for income, aggressively pursuing the rents, dues, and tithes the laity owed them—they no longer enacted the humility and dependency Francis had lived.

Begging had been at the center of the medieval practice of charity: widows and orphans, peasants and artisans had all begged alms from various institutions. Some, the "honorable" and domiciled poor, stayed off the streets, but most had to seek aid, to go to institutions for sustenance and shelter. As begging itself became disturbing, assertive, and abrasive, Protestants and Catholics alike sought to address the problem of begging and to formulate programs of relief that reflected the changes in their positions on begging. For both Catholics and Protestants, their responses to begging were shaped by and grounded in their differing theologies.

For Protestants the issue was simple: all begging was to cease. Martin Luther and Huldrych Zwingli would dismantle the foundation for the begging of the friars. As they both argued, mendicant begging was presumptuous: mendicants were choosing voluntarily a condition, poverty, that was God's to designate—this was human arrogance. Their begging was also false: it presumed the system of works righteousness, wherein human acts held soteriological value. Protestant theology posed a different anthropology. Like Francis, Protestant theologians viewed humanity as spiritually impoverished before God. Unlike Francis, they denied the efficacy of begging: no human acts, no works, no externals, even begging, could earn grace from God—that grace and the ensuant salvation was given freely, without human agency. At the same time, Protestant theology severed the outward condition of each human being from his or her relation to God: all were destitute before God; poverty was in no way indicative of a person's spiritual condition, either good, as Francis posed, or bad, as R. H. Tawney would find for seventeenth-century Puritanism (*Religion and the Rise of Capitalism*, London, 1926). Thus, all begging belonged to those externals Luther, Zwingli, and John Calvin would oppose, and Calvin and Zwingli would actively seek to eliminate.

Protestant governments therefore ordered the elimination of all begging. Neither poor nor mendicants were to beg any longer, anywhere: in the streets, before church doors, in the marketplaces, on the roads. The mendicants were to work with their hands—"honest labor," as Protestant governments named it. Some Protestant governments also mandated that mendicant houses, usually along with all other religious houses, were to be emptied and turned to communal uses. In Zurich those houses were transformed into a soup kitchen for the poor (the Dominican house) and a hospice for the sick poor, especially those with smallpox (the Dominican convent of Oetenbach); the wealth all the mendicant houses had accrued over generations was to be given to the poor—mendicants were to return to the poor what they had received on their behalf.

The Catholics' response to begging was more complex.

Catholic rulers shared for the most part the opposition to sturdy beggars and vagrants. The emperor Charles V, who held the dream of a Catholic Europe until his abdication, mandated the elimination of all public begging within his lands; those who continued to beg were to be sent to the galleys. In Madrid authorities prohibited public begging after 1 February 1582, though with little success. Yet begging remained an essential gesture of Catholic piety. In Florence begging would continue to be one of the means by which the orphans of the Ospedale degli Innocenti supported themselves. In Castile begging was central to the hospital reforms of Miguel Giginta. He requested that the Crown restrict begging exclusively to the inmates of the hospitals he was founding. The poor in his hospitals were then to beg two-by-two, three times a day, invoking loudly Christ's mercy. They were to beg on holy days and to participate in processions for those days and for funerals. The most pathetic were to beg for the others, so that potential donors would be confronted with poverty at its most wretched. For him, and for the Dominican de Soto, begging remained a gesture of powerful resonance, at once providing a visible symbol of dependency and invoking much more powerfully than institutions ever could the demand for charity, for the acknowledgment and amelioration of the wretchedness of that dependency.

Both Catholic and Protestant sought to control begging, the one through regulation, the other through elimination. Both also sought to force sturdy beggars to work, though with little success. In the face of increasing numbers of poor, who were moving about in search of alms, aid, work, some means to survive, both also sought to make the population of poor more stationary. Protestant governments administered sustained aid only to those who could prove their residency within the government's jurisdiction; the transient but still authentic poor, as distinguished from the sturdy beggars, typically received a meal and were then forced to move on. Some governments even required citizenship, a higher level of membership within the polity and one predicated on some level of wealth or property ownership. Catholic authorities, both secular and ecclesiastical, sought to stabilize the poor, to curb the movement of poor from region to region by requiring local residency for the receipt of aid from any of the various local institutions of relief. Catholic institutions found the enforcement of this requirement more difficult, however, since they did not always have the means of verifying residency or of enforcing exclusion.

Both Catholic and Protestant sought to monitor the poor, to locate them spatially and socially, and to make them less fluid. Driven by their fear of sturdy beggars and by real limitations on their resources, both sought to verify the authenticity of each pauper's poverty. The effect of these efforts was to make the poor more visible, as their neighbors, their parish priests, their parish watch, and their governments became more informed about the specifics of their situations. Poverty, if it was to receive aid, could not be entirely private. A few poor, the "honorable poor," were known less widely than other poor. But the great majority of poor who wished to receive aid, who wished to be designated as "deserving," were to be familiar, known to their communities. They were to be visible, for a time in Catholic Spain and permanently in Protestant cities, marked with a metal sign that designated them as "deserving" and also authentically poor.

It is in what that sign designated that Catholic and Protestant regions differed. Following the medieval use of the sign, sixteenth-century Spanish authorities used it to mark those whose poverty had been authenticated; in Spain the sign was a license to beg. In the sixteenth century, as earlier, beggars and donors alike found it arrogant for one human being to judge who ought to beg, as though begging were a "right" and one person able to discern among many others their "authenticity." In sixteenth-century Spain, a traditional Catholic anthropology, held by various theologians, ecclesiastical authorities, and laity, undermined the sign's use.

Protestant theologians called for a different relation between donors and poor. Like begging, individual donations to the poor belonged to the false theology of works righteousness. Like all confraternities, confraternal charity was the expression of a brotherhood defined not by God but by human beings. The practice of charity was to be mediated through the community of true Christians. Protestant legislators framed their reorganization of poor relief in terms of the Christian ethic of brotherly love. The very administration of relief was to be guided by and an enactment of Christian brotherly love—it would receive individual expressions of that love and extend that love to the poor among the community's Christian brothers. For Protestant regimes, the impetus of legislation, therefore, was to define who among the poor were the "brothers" of the community of Christians; the sign was to designate those who were "deserving" not merely of alms, but of membership in the community. It was worn by those resident poor who were moral according to the standards of each Christian community: those who did not blaspheme, gamble, play cards, drink or eat to excess, dress or behave in ways inappropriate to their station; who were neither prostitutes nor pimps; whose demeanor was modest, even humble. The poor were to behave in a way Protestant governments defined as morally Christian. In receiving the sign, the poor received recognition both of the authenticity of their poverty and, much more significantly, of the moral rectitude of their lives and their membership in the community of true Christians. In this way the poor became the new "images" of the Reformed communities, mirroring their morals and making visible their charity.

As their Catholic contemporaries noted, Protestant communities dramatically decreased the numbers of "deserving" poor. In Protestant lands charity was restricted to residential, authentic, and moral poor. The sturdy beggars, the immoral poor—the blasphemous, the prostitutes, the gambling poor, the drunken, the extravagant, and the unseemly—were effectively excluded from aid. And, as the program of relief was centralized, these poor could no longer move from agency to agency, living haphazardly within the jumble of institutions of relief. One central administration determined who was to receive aid and then distributed that aid through the various agencies it managed. The "deserving" poor seem to have benefited from that streamlining, receiving more consistent help and help specific to their needs: orphans were sent to school or apprenticed to a craft; the sick were placed in the hospital best-equipped for their specific illness; poor maids received dowries that might lift them, through matrimony, out of poverty; widows, the lame, and the blind received permanent aid, while those whose circumstances had led them into poverty received aid only as long as necessary.

In Protestant lands, the poor were silenced. If they wished to receive aid, they were not to extend their hand or cry out—they were not to demand but to receive humbly what the community gave them. They were to remain passive, in keeping with the Protestant understanding of unmerited grace. In return, they were visible to their neighbors, not as beggars, but as poor brothers and sisters, members of the community, who had been deprived permanently or temporarily, through God's plan, of their means of subsistence. Their poverty, like the sign that marked it, was temporary on this earth, transient, while their membership in the community of Christians might well be eternal.

Protestant poor relief legislation detailed much more precisely the forms of relief to be administered, the kinds of poor who were to receive relief, and the mechanisms by which that relief would be gathered and distributed. By contrast, the relation of Catholic agencies of relief to the poor precluded this kind of organization. Catholic institutions of relief were predicated on the poor's agency: just as begging actively demanded aid from a donor, so, too, Catholic poor were to seek aid from the various institutions by coming to those institutions, which would then determine the aid they ought to receive. Catholic governments sought to stabilize and regulate the poor, but they could not eliminate begging. Neither Catholic nor Protestant governments had the means to eradicate begging—it persisted throughout Europe during the early modern period—but Catholic governments faced the added resistance of their own subjects, who continued to see in begging a gesture significant within Catholic piety. In Catholic lands the poor remained vocal, crying out for aid, extending their hands in the ancient gesture of request and obligation, a gesture demanding certain responses from the more prosperous. In preserving begging, Catholic countries preserved one relationship between the poor and authorities, both secular and ecclesiastical.

In the second half of the sixteenth century, these two modes of relief were severely tested. During that time the numbers of poor increased dramatically, straining, and sometimes breaking, the systems of relief that governments and churches had established and challenging the principles by which people had chosen which poor to aid. Protestant governments seem simply to have tightened restrictions already in place, seeking to circumscribe more strictly those poor to whom they administered aid. In Spain the numbers of poor confronting the various agencies brought again a review of the efficiency of those agencies and of efforts to centralize them and reform them, but, according to Flynn, the popular understanding and practice of charity undermined any sustained efforts to reorganize and "rationalize" the ways Christians cared for the poor. In Protestant lands, the welfare of the poor depended on the sense of responsibility, of identity of the community; communities such as Zurich that retained a strong sense of communal obligation would seek at midcentury to ensure the resources to care for its own poor. In Catholic lands, the welfare of the poor depended on the individual resources of the different agencies: as they rose or fell with popular pious donations, so, too, would the poor eat better or, perhaps, not at all.

By the sixteenth century, the gesture of begging was no longer the clear and direct expression of human humbleness in the face of divine mercy and love it once had been. Sturdy beggars and mendicants had brought to the extended hand associations of arrogance and aggression, clouding this symbol of medieval charity. Protestant theologians, most troubled by those associations, severed poverty from begging, severed the link between spiritual impoverishment and its outward expression. Even in Catholic Europe, the relation between poverty and begging became more troubled, as the one was distanced from the other. As governments became more involved in the care of the poor, and ecclesiastical institutions came to depend upon them more and more for the regulation and control of the poor, the practice of charity came to be mediated.

In the sixteenth century the practice of *caritas* was reconceived. For Protestants, it was extended to the members of one's own Christian community through the government of that community. For Catholics, it was to be extended personally and through agencies to certain kinds of poor. Both extended *caritas* to poor whose poverty was specified ever more precisely. For the "deserving" poor, that may well have been an improvement. For the "undeserving poor," both Catholic and Protestant, however, *caritas* was to become ever more inaccessible.

[*See also* Begging; Common Man; Medicine and Healing; *and* Social Ethics.]

BIBLIOGRAPHY

Abel, Wilhelm. *Agricultural Fluctuations in Europe from the Thirteenth to the Twentieth Centuries.* Translated by Olive Ordish. New York,

1980. Survey of changes in agrarian economy and its effects upon the rural and urban populations.

Banker, James R. *Death in the Community: Memorialization and Confraternities in an Italian Commune in the Late Middle Ages.* Athens, Ga., and London, 1988. Treats charitable activities of confraternities, including their obligations to the poor.

Biéler, André. *La pensée économique et sociale de Calvin.* Geneva, 1959. Magisterial study of the social and economic implications of Calvin's theology.

Black, Christopher. *Italian Confraternities in the Sixteenth Century.* Cambridge, 1989. A survey of the range of confraternities throughout Italy; discusses directly their attitude toward poverty and the distinctions they made among the poor in their practice of charity.

Chrisman, Miriam Usher. "Urban Poor in the Sixteenth Century: The Case of Strasbourg." In *Social Groups and Religious Ideas in the Sixteenth Century,* edited by Miriam Usher Chrisman, pp. 59–67. Studies in Medieval Culture 13. Kalamazoo, 1978. An account of the reform of poor relief in Strasbourg, focusing on the first administrator of poor relief.

Davis, Natalie Zemon. *Society and Culture in Early Modern France.* London, 1975. See "Poor Relief, Humanism, and Heresy," pp. 17–64; along with Pullan, brought about the reevaluation of the relation of Protestantism to the reform of poor relief.

Flynn, Maureen. *Sacred Charity: Confraternities and Social Welfare in Spain, 1400–1700.* Ithaca, N.Y., 1989. An excellent study of lay conceptions and practice of charity in a Catholic country, locating them in the debates among theologians (Juan de Medina and Domingo de Soto) on begging, the nature of *caritas,* and the obligations of brotherly love.

Gavitt, Philip. "Economy, Charity and Community in Florence, 1350–1450." In *Aspects of Poverty in Early Modern Europe,* edited by Thomas Riis, pp. 79–118. Alphena d. Rijn, Neth., 1981. A suggestive and rich exploration of the practice of charity in a commercial culture.

———. *Charity and Children in Renaissance Florence: The Ospedale degli Inocenti, 1410–1536.* Ann Arbor, 1990. An important study of a foundling hospital and its meaning for civic conceptions of charity.

Grimm, Harold. "Luther's Contributions to Sixteenth-Century Organization of Poor Relief." *Archive for Reformation History* 61 (1970), 222–234.

Jütte, Robert "Poor Relief and Social Discipline in Sixteenth-Century Europe." *European Studies Review* 11 (1981), 25–52. An early and one of the most articulate arguments for social control—the intentional "control" of the poor by governments through legislation, arrest, prosecution, and punishment.

Kingdon, Robert. *Church and Society in Reformation Europe.* London, 1985. Chap. 6, "Social Welfare in Calvin's Geneva," describes the practice of charity in Geneva during Calvin's life, delineating some of the characteristics of Calvinist poor relief; see also chap. 7, "The Deacons of the Reformed Church in Calvin's Geneva."

Lindberg, Carter. " 'There Should Be No Beggars Among Christians': Karlstadt, Luther, and the Origins of Protestant Poor Relief." *Church History* 46 (1977), 313–334.

———. *Beyond Charity: Reformation Initiatives for the Poor.* Minneapolis, 1993. Summary of some Protestant programs.

Lis, Catharina, and Hugo Soly. *Poverty and Capitalism in Pre-Industrial Europe.* Reprint, Brighton, England, 1982. A broad survey of the causes of poverty and the kinds of poverty various structural changes engendered.

Martz, Linda. *Poverty and Welfare in Habsburg Spain: The Example of Toledo.* Cambridge, 1983. Another important study of the practice of charity in Catholic Spain, this one focusing on hospitals and the dynamic between the Crown and the church in reforming the care of the poor in the sixteenth century.

McKee, Elsie Anne. *John Calvin on the Diaconate and Liturgical Almsgiving.* Geneva, 1984. A dazzling study of Calvin's conceptualization of *caritas* and its enactment in the liturgy and in the diaconate.

Midelfort, H. C. Erik. "Protestant Monastery? A Reformation Hospital in Hesse." In *Reformation Principle and Practice: Essays in Honour of A. G. Dickens,* edited by Peter N. Brooks, pp. 73–93. London, 1980.

Mollat, Michel. *The Poor in the Middle Ages.* Translated by Arthur Goldhammer. New Haven, 1987. The major work available in English on attitudes toward the poor in the high and late Middle Ages.

Pullan, Brian. *Rich and Poor in Renaissance Venice: The Social Institutions of a Catholic State to 1620.* Cambridge, Mass., 1971. Seminal study of Catholic practices of charity and their reform in Venice, containing one of the fullest studies of confraternal charity.

———. "Catholics and Poor in Early Modern Europe." *Transactions of the Royal Historical Society,* 5th ser. 26 (1976), 15–34. An excellent overview of Catholic responses to poor and to begging, compared with Protestant.

Tierney, Brian. *Medieval Poor Law: A Sketch of Canonical Theory and Its Application in England.* Berkeley, 1959.

Wandel, Lee Palmer. *Always Among Us: Images of the Poor in Zwingli's Zurich.* Cambridge, 1990. Explores the interplay of Zwingli's theology, changing perceptions of the poor, and the reform of their care in a major Protestant town.

Wright, William J. "A Closer Look at House Poor Relief through the Common Chest and Indigence in Sixteenth-Century Hesse." *Archive for Reformation History* 70 (1979), 225–38.

LEE PALMER WANDEL

SOCINIANISM. The term *Socinianism* refers to a community of antitrinitarian churches that existed in Poland and Lithuania and the groups and the individuals scattered throughout Europe during the seventeenth century who were sympathetic to their cause. The doctrines and organization of these churches developed under the influence of Fausto Sozzini, from whose name the term was derived. After the expulsion of the Socinians from Poland, the term refers too to the centers of this movement in the diaspora. The Socinians themselves protested, however, against this term, which was formed in the circles of Protestant and Catholic polemists. Socinians—also known in Poland as "Arians"—referred to themselves as "brothers" or "Christians" and, by the latter half of the seventeenth century, "Unitarians" or "Polish Brethren."

The History of Socinianism. Seventeenth-century Socinianism was a continuation of the antitrinitarian movement of the sixteenth century, although Fausto Sozzini's reforms were thorough going revisions of antitrinitarian doctrines. The long process of evolution toward Socinianism underwent its final stages in the period surrounding the turn of the seventeenth century.

In 1601 and 1602, at Raków, a small town in Little Poland that for nearly forty years would be the center of the movement, Fausto Sozzini conducted sorts of theological seminars in the presence of leading pastors. Sozzini's pronouncements became guiding principles for further activities of the Socinian church, which departed from the spirit of sectarian exclusivism and which attempted to enter into dialogue with Protestants as well as to attract new followers.

Socinianism was organized as a sort of confederation of local churches. According to some estimates, there eventually were about two hundred such churches across Poland and Lithuania. (During the 1650s, when the movement was severely persecuted, this number quickly dropped.) The churches were governed by general synods, usually convoked once a year. Here basic decisions were made regarding management, financial matters, personnel, and discipline, and special commissions were established to conduct visitations to the various churches and to censor books; it was here also that pastors were ordained. There were provincial synods too and gatherings of the pastors, which prepared the general synod programs and served as theological seminars. Until 1638 general synods were nearly always held in Raków.

Raków was also the home of the leading Socinian secondary school, which opened its doors in 1603. The instruction offered at this five-grade school was of such high quality that it soon attracted youths from Protestant and Catholic circles as well. A separate theological faculty educated future pastors. (The Raków school was closed in 1638; the school reopened at Kisielin, but was never to regain its earlier reputation.) Another important instrument for promoting Socinianism was the Raków printing house, which between 1600 and 1638 published about 250–300 titles, chiefly theological works in Polish, German, Latin, and Dutch. The famous Racovian Catechism was first printed here in Polish in 1605, in German in 1608, and in Latin in 1609.

A distinctive feature of Socinianism in Poland was the participation of many Germans, which in fact greatly facilitated the movement's penetration into German-speaking areas. The first generation of Socinians included, alongside Poles such as the eminent author and activist Hieronim Moskorzowski (c.1560–1625) and the propagandist Andrzej Wojdowski, Germans such as Valentin Schmalz (1572–1622), a prolific theological writer and pillar of the movement; Christoph Ostorodt (d. 1611); and Johann Völkel (d. 1618), a revised version of whose *De vera religione* (On True Religion), a comprehensive doctrinal treatise, was first published in 1630. The leaders of succeeding generations of Socinian activists and writers again were chiefly Poles and Germans: Johann Crell (1590–1633), who was rector of the Raków school as well as a philosopher and theologian; Samuel Przypkowski (1592–1670), a politician and theologian whose works were renowned especially for their defense of tolerance; Johann Ludwig Wolzogen (1599–1661), a mathematician, philosopher, and theologian; Martin Ruar (1589–1657), a philologist and indefatigable propagandist of Socinianism in western Europe; Jonasz Schlichting (1592–1661), the polemist and exegete; Joachim Stegmann the Elder (1592–1633), a mathematician and theologian; and

Stanisław Lubieniecki the Younger (1623–1675), a historian, astronomer, and theologian.

German universities were primary arenas of Socinian missionary activity. This was especially true of the academy in Altdorf, for it was here that Ernst Soner (1572–1612), a popular professor of philosophy, had been won over to Socinianism. The crypto-Socinians of Altdorf maintained vital contacts with Raków and were active from 1605 to 1616, when university officials intervened to put an end to the movement.

All in all, Socinian propagandizing in Germany has not been properly investigated to date, but the fierce polemic that the movement unleashed is well known. The spread of Socinianism into the Dutch Republic is better understood. It began in 1598 with a missionary expedition undertaken by Andrzej Wojdowski and Christoph Ostorodt and ended with their deportation and the burning of the publications they had brought with them from Raków. The Socinians had close ties to the Remonstrants, and orthodox Calvinists often accused the Remonstrants of sympathizing with the "Racovians." The Remonstrants were somewhat less than enthusiastic over Socinian efforts at unification (1632), however, owing to the doctrinal differences concerning soteriological and trinitarian questions. Meanwhile, two prominent Dutch Remonstrants, Johannes Geesteranus (1586–1622) and Dirk Camphuysen (1586–1627), translated works of Sozzini and Schmalz into Dutch and maintained cordial relations with the Raków community. The spread of Socinianism in Remonstrant, Collegiant, and Mennonite circles provoked a series of severe edicts by the States-General in an effort to counteract it, but neither these edicts nor the profusion of polemical treatises by Dutch Calvinist theologians had great effect.

Socinianism likewise reached Britain early on. Although editions of the Racovian Catechism had appeared in London around 1614 and 1623 (both with the false imprint "Racoviae, 1609"), the true expansion of this movement began in the 1630s. As in the Dutch Republic, it attracted much attention. Interest was particularly high among the theologians of the so-called "Tew Circle," two of whom—John Hales (1584–1656) and William Chillingworth (1602–1644)—exerted considerable influence on the development of English religious thought and on John Locke. Locke himself was well versed in Socinian theology, and his library included a large collection of Socinian treatises. John Biddle (1615–1662), sometimes called "the Father of English Unitarianism," translated the works of Przypkowski and Joachim Stegmann; although he did not subscribe to the Socinian view of the Holy Spirit, he too was strongly influenced by Socinianism.

If the first three decades of the seventeenth century were a period of stability and relative peace in the life of the Socinian churches in Poland, the next period brought a number of misfortunes to them. The increasingly powerful camp of the Counter-Reformation considered Socinianism to be its chief and most dangerous adversary. Meanwhile, the weak Polish Protestant movement—internally divided and under attack by Catholics as well—was disinclined to defend a denomination with which it had had differences in the past. Thus isolated, the Socinian movement would become the target of a crippling series of measures: in 1638 a senate resolution closed the school and printing house in Raków; in 1647 Socinians were enjoined from teaching or publishing anywhere in Poland; in 1648 they were excluded from the protection of the Warsaw Confederation of 1573, which had guaranteed religious freedoms to dissidents. The outbreak of the Cossack Wars fundamentally contributed to the decline of Socinianism in Volhynia, which had been an important Socinian center owing to the patronage of nobles there. Finally during the war with Sweden, some Socinian nobles and leaders switched to the side of the invaders; in the wake of this act, which created a wave of anti-Socinian attitudes and which Catholic propaganda magnified, many Socinian churches, especially those in southern Poland, were destroyed.

On 10 July 1658 a Sejm resolution declared that the "Arians" must leave Poland within three years or face death along with the confiscation of property. Followers of Socinianism who declared their desire to convert to Catholicism were exempted. In 1659 the deadline for banishment was shortened to 1660. From that time onward Socinianism was outlawed, although it must be emphasized that, according to dubious estimates, only a few thousand emigrated; the rest remained in Poland, and the phenomenon of crypto-Socinianism endured in Poland until nearly the end of the eighteenth century. These followers, who formally remained Catholic or, occasionally, Calvinist, often provided material assistance for the exiles in the diaspora. Despite the strictness of the 1658 law of banishment, crypto-Socinians who were discovered were not put to death but were expelled from the country, while those who agreed to accept Catholicism had only to pay a small fine for their delayed conversion.

Socinian emigration from Poland began on a large scale in the fall of 1660. Several hundred exiles went to Transylvania, largely because the Unitarian church there had remained in close contact with Polish Socinianism. The Polish exiles were warmly received, although the Unitarian church made efforts to retain its own identity despite Socinianism's clear ideological influence. The Socinians established separate religious communities in Transylvania and worked diligently to maintain their national self-awareness. They remained separate until 1784, when they united with the Transylvanian Unitarian church, the new generation of exiles having come to identify with the Hungarians.

The situation was more difficult for what was probably the largest group of Socinian exiles, those who settled in eastern Prussia and Brandenburg. Although they were constantly attacked by the Lutheran clergy, their church endured until 1811.

Intellectually, the third band of Polish exiles was the most interesting. First, the group went to Silesia, where a number of them remained. Next they sought refuge in northern Germany (Altona, Hamburg, Lübeck, Bremen, and Friedrichstadt). Eventually it became impossible for the Polish Socinians to remain permanently in Germany, however, because from time to time they attempted to proselytize and the Protestant clergy opposed them.

Some of the exiles finally came to settle in the Dutch Republic. The distinguished Socinian theologian, thinker, and activist Andreas Wiszowaty (1608–1678), author of *Religio rationalis,* published posthumously in 1685, played an important role in maintaining the ideology of Socinianism, along with his son Benedykt (d. after 1704 as pastor of a church in eastern Prussia). The monumental eight-volume *Bibliotheca Fratrum Polonorum,* a compendium of writings by Sozzini, Crell, Schlichting, and Wolzogen, was published in Amsterdam (1665–1668) through the efforts of the senior Wiszowaty. New editions of the Racovian Catechism (1665, 1680, 1681, and 1684), Christof Sand's *Bibliotheca antitrinitariorum* (1684), and Stanisław Lubieniecki the Younger's *Historia reformationis Polinicae* (1865) were published.

Members of the Socinian diaspora remained in close contact until the eighteenth century. The leaders Lubieniecki, Przypkowski, and Wiszowaty, who were each in different countries, sought aid from their Dutch and English friends and sympathizers. Synods were regularly held in Transylvania and Prussia that were frequently attended by representatives of other groups as well as by crypto-Socinians still residing in Poland. Throughout nearly the entire seventeenth century the Socinians maintained the fervent hope that the 1658 banishment decree would be repealed, and to that end they employed many strategies and undertook many diplomatic campaigns, all in vain.

Socinian Doctrine. A characteristic feature of Socinianism was opposition to the dogma of the Holy Trinity on the grounds that it is contrary both to scripture and sound reason. On this score Socinian treatises tend to repeat the critical arguments of various (chiefly Italian, Polish, and Transylvanian) antitrinitarians of the seventeenth century. Socinians, however, reflect more deeply on God as the creator of the world, which was formed from matter that had existed from all eternity; the creator, who is of a substance that is limited in space, being located in heaven, acts in time, intervening gradually (*per gradus*) in the created world. He nevertheless remains immutable, because his judgments do not belong to his essence; they are only an accident of it. Christ is merely human (*purus homo*); he was indeed born without sin of the Virgin Mary through the power of the

Holy Spirit but had not preexisted. (According to many Socinian theologians, however—and here they were influenced by the teachings of Fausto Sozzini—Jesus visited heaven before beginning his ministry and was taught by God about his mission.) After his death on the cross, he was raised from the dead and, as the son of God, sat at the right hand of God. The Holy Spirit possesses no separate identity and represents the power of God himself.

Socinians rejected the view that Christ, through his sacrifice on the cross, expiated all human sin, past and future. The significance of Christ's mission consisted in his showing the way to salvation; those who believe that Christ is God's anointed and fulfill his commandments will gain eternal life. Socinians also rejected the dogma of original sin, arguing that human cognitive abilities or moral inclinations are in no way disrupted by that sin because the human being possesses free will. They rejected the concept of divine foreknowledge since, if it were true, any merit before God would be impossible and God would be the originator of human sins.

Socinian eschatology emphasized that Adam was by nature mortal. Immortality was revealed by Christ only—although God reserved it also for those Israelites who followed his commandments—and was a privilege of those who believe in him and his teaching. The traditional doctrine of hell was rejected: godless souls—and this will be their punishment—will simply be annihilated.

Socinian doctrine was permeated with rationalism, present already in the writings of Fausto Sozzini, who taught that true religion must be consistent with reason; at the same time, he argued that one cannot recognize basic truths concerning God by one's own power, because there is no natural religion—there is only revealed religion. This position was questioned by other Socinian theologians who accepted the existence of natural religion and who also examined in great detail the subject of reason in religion. Especially important in this regard were the treatises by Joachim Stegmann the Elder (*Brevis disquisitio . . .* [1633], and *De iudice et norma controversiarum fidei . . .* [1644]), Samuel Przypkowski (*Animadversiones apologeticae in . . . J. A. Comenii libellum* [c.1660]), and Andrzej Wiszowaty (*Religio rationalis* [1685]). Given that human reason is the highest standard of judgment on earth, these thinkers argued, it followed that scripture must be interpreted according to the principles of reason, which also pronounces the truth of the revelation itself. Scripture contains certain truths that are "beyond reason" (*supra rationem*)—that is, not entirely comprehensible—but these truths are not "contrary to reason" (*contra rationem*).

Socinians emphasized the significance of the ethical effort and limited dogmatic settlements to a few points ("the truths necessary to salvation") that were shared by all Christian churches and that were considered to be essential. Belief in Christ and the fulfillment of his promises are a fundamental—and this is the essence of the Socinian irenic principle. The daily practice of the dictates of the gospel is the only benchmark of a person's moral conduct and can secure the person's immortality.

At first the sociopolitical doctrine of Socinianism hewed closely to the teachings of Sozzini. During the seminars held at Raków in 1601 and 1602, Sozzini endorsed private property, serfdom, taking a case to court, and holding office; at the same time, he opposed the death penalty and engagement in war. This position continued to be the Socinian church's official view until the 1640s.

Discussions concerning the state and war began with a treatise by Daniel Brenius (Dutch, van Breen; 1594–1664), a Dutch Collegiant sympathetic to Socinianism. His *De qualitate regni Christi* (1641) was clearly opposed to the state and its institutions. It ushered in a long period of debate that engaged notable Socinian theologians. On the one hand, there were the supporters of Brenius: J. L. Wolzogen, Joachim Stegmann the Younger (c.1618–1678), and Daniel Zwicker (1612–1678). Zwicker even went so far as to advocate the communal sharing of goods, along the lines of the Moravian Anabaptists. On the other hand, Jonasz Schlichting and Samuel Przypkowski vigorously opposed Brenius's position. Especially important were Przypkowski's *Animadversiones in libellum cui titulus est De qualitate . . . regni Christi* (1650), *De iure Christiani magistratus*, and *Apologia prolixior tractatus de iure magistratus*. In these fundamental works Przypkowski presented theoretically grounded reflections on the mutual relations between church and state, asserting that both were absolutely indispensable factors in the life of a society; he stated that the church and state can and should work together harmoniously for the common good, because each has its own sphere of operation and the two do not conflict. Whereas the church has influence only over its own members by virtue of its spiritual authority, to which the members voluntarily subject themselves, the state compels its citizens to obey by force. Przypkowski was also critical of Fausto Sozzini's open aversion to the state. He considered Sozzini's position that Socinians should not take part in political life a relic. It appears that toward the close of the Socinian period these two tendencies, sectarianism, which ties in directly with Anabaptist ideas, and "statism," the notion that calls for a Christian's full participation in politics and society, coexisted with each other, although the editions of the Racovian Catechism seem to prove that sectarian attitudes eventually prevailed among emigrants.

The doctrines of Socinianism awakened great interest, chiefly among theologians and philosophers. During the late seventeenth and the eighteenth century, this attention even led to a sort of mythologizing of the movement, in that Lutheran, Anglican, and Calvinist theologians often presented Socinianism as a sort of ideological plague capable of endangering Christianity and public morality. Conversely, among philosophers Socinianism was usually perceived with a certain degree of sympathy. In keeping with the spirit of the times, particular attention was given to religious rationalism and tolerance as well as to the key role of ethics in Socinian doctrine. At the same time, Socinians were criticized for a kind of partial or haphazard approach to their "rational religion" in that they maintained an undisturbed connection between the Old and New Testaments, between the cruel, erratic Yahweh of the Old Testament and the gracious, kind God of the New Testament. The French philosopher Pierre Bayle (1647–1706), one of his period's greatest experts on Socinianism, went even further in his critique. He considered Socianianism's attempt to make religion compatible with reason a complete failure, since he had already proved that any religion was irrational by its very nature.

[See also Antitrinitarianism.]

BIBLIOGRAPHY

Bock, Friedrich Samuel. Historia Antitrinitariorum, maximo Socinianismi et Socinianorum . . . recensentur (1774–1784). Reprint, Leipzig, 1977. Basic bio-bibliography on the history of Socinianism.

Chmaj, Ludwik. Bracia Polscy: Ludzie, idee, wpływy. Warsaw, 1957. Collection of studies by a distinguished expert on Socinianism.

Chmaj, Ludwik, ed. Studia nad arianizmem. Warsaw, 1959. A series of major articles on antitrinitarian history and doctrine, with the emphasis on Socinianism; many of the articles are in western European languages.

Florida, R. E. Voltaire and the Socinians. Studies on Voltaire and the Eighteenth Century, vol. 122. Banbury, 1974.

Fock, Otto. Der Sozinianismus: Nach seiner Stellung in der Gesamtentwicklung des Christliches Geistes nach seinem historischen Verlauf und nach seinem Lehrbegriff dargestellt (1847). Reprint, Darmstadt, 1970. This work is partially out of date, but it contains much valuable information on Socinian doctrine.

Kot, Stanislas. Socinianism in Poland. Translated by Earl Morse Wilbur. Boston, 1957.

Kühler, W. J. Het socinianisme in Nederland. Leiden, 1912. Focusing on theological problems, it discusses the influence of Socinianism in the Netherlands.

McLachlan, H. John. Socinianism in Seventheenth-Century England. London, 1951.

Ogonowski, Zbigniew. Socynianizm a Oświecenie: Studia nad myśla filozoficzno-religijna arian w Polsce XVII wieku. Warsaw, 1966. Basic work on Socinian philosophical-religious thought.

Ogonowski, Zbigniew, ed. Myśl ariańska w Polsce XVII wieku: Antologia tekstów. Wrocław, 1991. Anthology of Socinian thought in Poland. To be read in conjunction with Williams. Ogonowski's anthology focuses on philosophical problems; Williams's on theological-historical issues.

Slee, J. C. van. De geschiedenis van het socinianisme in de Nederlanden. Haarlem, 1914.

Szczucki, Lech, ed. Socinianism and Its Role in the Culture of the Sixteenth to Eighteenth Centuries. Warsaw, 1983. Collection of articles in English, German, French, and Italian.

Tazbir, Janusz. Bracia Polscy na wygnaniu: Studia z dziejów. Warsaw, 1977. Outlines the history of Polish Socinians who emigrated following the banishment decree.

Wallace, Robert. Antitriniarian Biography. 8 vols. London, 1850. Based for the most part on Bock, but includes much supplementary information, especially concerning English Socinians.

Wilbur, Earl Morse. A History of Unitarianism: Socinianism and Its Antecedents. Cambridge, Mass., 1946. Unexcelled as a guide to Socinian history guide.

———. A History of Unitarianism in Transylvania, England, and America. Boston, 1952.

Williams, George H., ed. and trans. The Polish Brethren: Documentation of the History and Thought of Unitarianism in the Polish-Lithuanian Commonwealth and in the Diaspora, 1601–1685. Harvard Theological Studies, vol. 30. Missoula, Mont., 1980.

Wrzecionko, Paul, ed. Reformation und Frühaufklärung in Polen: Studien über den Sozinianismus und seinen Einfluß auf das westeuropäische Denken im 17. Jahrhundert. Göttingen, 1977. Collection of articles, most of which are devoted to seventeenth-century Socinianism.

LECH SZCZUCKI
Translated from Polish by AnnMarie Mitchell

SOMASCHI. Founded in 1534 by Girolamo Miani (Jerome Emiliani, 1486–1537) with the initial title "Company of the Servants of the Poor," the Somaschi embodied a distinctive desire to exercise charity toward orphans, both male and female. This was the first Catholic foundation to provide not only food and shelter for orphans but also Christian instruction and the teaching of a trade. As the headquarters for his enterprise, Miani selected the northern Italian city of Somasca, near Bergamo in Lombardy, and the members of the association soon came to be called Somaschi. In 1540 Pope Paul III approved their way of life (based on Miani's design for Somaschi life and duties as recalled by his companions). Somaschi efforts to support a number of orphanages and schools in Italy have continued into the twentieth century.

The founder of the Somaschi was born in Venice of patrician parents. After serving as a soldier until 1511, Miani, according to his earliest biographer, was moved by God's inspiration, causing him to withdraw from worldly pursuits. That experience inspired him to undertake the care of orphans and the homeless. After 1525 this new direction was strengthened by membership in the Venetian Oratory of Divine Love, whose benevolent activities included feeding, clothing, and caring for the poor, comforting the sick, and providing burial for bodies abandoned throughout the city. Miani was further encouraged in his mission by contact after 1527 with the Theatine cofounders, Gian Pietro Carafa (later Paul IV) and Gaetano Thiene. During the next seven years he set up a number of independent foundations to care for orphans and in 1534 decided to unite these in a new community of priests and brothers (those who had been participating in this charitable work and were committed primarily to caring for the needs of orphans). After his death in 1537 Miani's fellow Somaschi sought and received papal confirmation of their company.

Miani's legacy included both a practical spirituality and a positive attitude toward work. The lives of members were to be sustained by faith, prayer, humility, and piety. He wrote, "If our Company remains with Christ, the objective will be reached, otherwise all is lost" (letter of 5 July 1535) and also: "Persevere in the ways of God which are love, humility and devotion" (letter of 21 July 1535). His exhortation was reinforced by his own physical labors—working in the fields and accepting the humblest duties within the group.

The community emerged within an environment particular to early sixteenth-century Venice, where Miani had contact with contemporary strains of Catholic reform. Although the Somaschi, unlike other new religious orders of the era, did not have a program either for institutional reform of the Catholic church or of confrontation with Protestants, they did embody a tradition of personal spiritual reform based on the performance of charitable activities aimed specifically at the needy of society. Their personal reform, linked to performing works of mercy, contributed renewed vitality within both the clergy and the Catholic church during the sixteenth century.

[*See also* Religious Orders.]

BIBLIOGRAPHY

Landini, Giuseppe. *San Girolamo Miani dalle testimonianze processuali, dai biografi, dai documenti editi e inediti fino ad oggi.* Rome, 1947. Biography based on original documents includes transcriptions of Girolamo Miani's letters and an extensive bibliography.

Miani, Girolamo. *Le Lettere di San Girolamo Miani.* Fonti per la Storia dei Somaschi no. 3. Rome, 1975. Translated by Cesare Desantis in *Letters of Saint Jerome Emiliani,* Manchester, N.H., 1980. Contains instructions from Girolamo Miani on details of Somaschi life during the initial years of the community.

Pellegrini, Carlo, ed. *Vita del clarissimo Signor Girolamo Miani gentil huomo Venetiano.* Fonti per la storia dei Somaschi no. 1. Rome, 1970. Translated in *Life of Jerome Emiliani, Most Distinguished Venetian Nobleman,* Manchester, N.H., 1973. Earliest extant biography was written by one of Miani's Somaschi companions, probably soon after the founder's death in 1537. Contains eyewitness information.

Somascha: Bollettino di storia dei Padri Somaschi. 1976 and after. No formal, comprehensive history of the Somaschi exists, but this series presents articles on aspects of their history and spirituality.

KENNETH J. JORGENSEN

SOMERSET, DUKE OF. *See* Seymour, Edward.

SONNEGG, Hans Ungnad von. *See* Ungnad, Hans von Sonnegg.

SONNIUS, Franciscus (Dutch, Frans van der Velde; Ital., Francisco del Campo; 1506–1576), Dutch theologian, inquisitor, and first bishop of 's Hertogenbosch and Antwerp. Born at Son, in northeast Brabant, whence he took his Latin surname, Sonnius studied in 's Hertogenbosch, Utrecht, and Louvain, where he won highest honors in 1527. After a brief flirtation with medicine, he studied theology, becoming parish priest at Meerbeck by the early 1530s. In 1535 he returned to Louvain as pastor of Saint Jakob's. He took his doctorate and began teaching at Louvain in 1539. In 1543 he was elected rector of the university and received a prebend the school controlled in the cathedral chapter of Utrecht.

A committed and articulate defender of Catholic orthodoxy, Sonnius attracted favor in government circles. As rector, he first collaborated in a heresy trial at Louvain in 1543. He subsequently appeared in progressively exalted inquisitorial posts. In 1549 Charles V named him inquisitor for Holland, Zeeland, and Friesland; later investigations also included Groningen and Overijssel. He attended the Council of Trent from 1545 to 1547 and 1551 to 1552 and helped write theological reports defending anti-Protestant positions on extreme unction, penance, and the Mass. The Netherlands government also sent him to the Colloquy of Worms in 1557.

Sonnius was an active publicist. His massive *Demonstrationum religionis christianae ex verbo Dei* (1555–1557) attempts a thorough refutation of Protestant theories of faith and justification while grounding orthodox doctrines in God's word. For Sonnius, however, God's word went beyond the biblical text to include a large body of tradition. "The gospel was not initially propagated in scriptures but by a living voice. . . . Not all the mysteries of faith were passed on in writing; some were transmitted by living tradition, to be kept for all generations. . . . What the holy fathers thought worth believing must embody God's word." With this basis, Sonnius offers a rich and sophisticated array of argumentation from scripture, carefully interwoven with patristic interpretations. Though not as widely reprinted as the *Demonstrationum,* three other contemporaneous works provided easily accessible statements of the same doctrines for less erudite readers.

In a lengthy correspondence with Viglius Zuichemius van Aytta, president of the Privy Council, Sonnius played a central role in developing what ultimately became Philip II's program to reorganize the Netherlands church. Between 1558 and 1561, he negotiated papal approval for a scheme that set up fourteen new bishoprics and worked on the commission that implemented the plan. In 1561 he was named bishop of 's Hertogenbosch. The storm of opposition and infighting that Philip's initiative aroused prevented much effective work until 1567. Thereafter Sonnius showed himself an energetic administrator, barely completing his new diocesan organization before being transferred to repeat the task in Antwerp after 1570. In both places his greatest emphasis was on education and instruction, and he produced a variety of books and pamphlets to propagate Catholic doctrine. By the time of his death in 1576, his combination of great learning, pastoral zeal, personal magnetism, and lack of venality had made him widely regarded as an epitome of the Tridentine ideal.

BIBLIOGRAPHY

Clercq, Carlo de. "Kerkelijk Leven." In *Antwerpen in de XVIde Eeuw*, pp. 55–82. Antwerp, 1975. Gives narrative of episcopate in Antwerp; dating of 's Hertogenbosch installation, however, should be corrected by reference to De Schrevel.

De Schrevel, A. C. "Sonnius." In *Biographie Nationale de Belgique*, vol. 23. Brussels, 1921–1924. Still the fullest biographical study, with complete references and citations for Sonnius's publications, and critical evaluations of earlier works.

Goossens, Thomas. *Franciscus Sonnius in de Pamfletten: Bijdragen tot zijne Biografie*. 's Hertogenbosch, 1917. Only book-length work on Sonnius this century, it concentrates on references to him in contemporary anti-Catholic polemics and traces their authorship. Reliable, but limited by the author's inability to work with Belgian sources during World War I.

Laar, L. J. A. van de. "De katholieke restauratie te 's-Hertogenbosch, ca. 1525–1625." *Noordgouw* 19–20 (1979–1983), 171–234. Gives narrative of episcopate in 's Hertogenbosch.

Postma, F. "Nieuw licht op een oude zaak: de oprichting van de nieuwe bisdommen in 1559." *Tijdschrift voor Geschiedenis* 103 (1990), 10–27. Brilliant study of Sonnius's behind-the-scenes work on the new bishoprics, with extensive references to related scholarship.

GUY WELLS

SORBONNE. *See* Faculty of Theology of Paris.

SORCK, Erasmus. *See* Sarcerius, Erasmus.

SOTO, Domingo de (1495–1560), Spanish Dominican theologian, representative of the school of Salamanca. The bane of nominalists, Soto studied philosophy and theology at the Universities of Alcalá and Paris, and obtained a chair in philosophy at Alcalá in 1520. Soto resigned from this post suddenly and headed for the abbey of Montserrat, hoping to join the Benedictines, but he was instead led to the Dominicans, entering their community at San Pablo de Burgos in 1524 and becoming professor of dialectics at their Segovia house of studies in 1525. Appointed to the Dominican chair in theology at Salamanca in 1532, he was promoted to the principal chair in 1552, as successor to Melchior Cano. From his earliest days in the university classroom, Soto undertook an attack on the *via moderna* and pressed for a revival of Aristotle. At Salamanca he collaborated with Francisco de Vitoria and Cano in their methodological reforms and on the development of what came to be known as positive or fundamental theology.

Sent as imperial theologian to the Council of Trent by the emperor Charles V, Soto soon distinguished himself for his learning and piety (1545–1547). Steering the council away from compromise with the Protestants, he served as one of the principal defenders of tradition on such key questions as original sin, predestination, justification, the scriptural canon, and the authority of the Vulgate Bible. In 1547, when the council was interrupted, Soto was appointed confessor and spiritual adviser to Charles V, a post he fulfilled for two years. Immensely pleased by Soto, Charles offered him the bishopric of Segovia. Soto refused the honor and in 1550 returned to teaching at Salamanca. That same year he took part in the celebrated debate held at Valladolid on the treatment of New World natives, joining his Dominican brethren in a thorough condemnation of the idea that the Indians were inferior beings worthy of enslavement.

In addition to producing such influential philosophical and theological works as the *Summulae* (1529), a manual of logic; *De natura et gratia* (1547), a polemic against Protestant soteriology; and his commentaries on Aristotle (1543 and 1545), on Paul's letter to the Romans (1550), and on Peter Lombard's *Sentences* (1557), Soto contributed significantly to the development of political and legal theory, principally through his *De iustitia et iure* (1553). True to the school of Salamanca's predilection for ethical questions and to its conviction that theology should be used to create a Christian moral order based on natural law, Soto also devoted attention to the issue of poverty, producing a landmark study, *Deliberatio in causa pauperum* (1545), and devising ways to feed and lodge the poorer students at Salamanca. Like his fellow Spanish Dominicans Vitoria and Cano, Soto contributed substantially to the reinvigoration of Roman Catholicism in the sixteenth century by strengthening and broadening the theological curriculum, by stressing the need for continuity with the scholastic tradition (especially with Thomism), and by actively seeking social justice.

BIBLIOGRAPHY

Becker, K. J. *Die Rechtfertigungslehre nach Domingo de Soto*. Analecta Gregoriana 156. Rome, 1967.

Beltrán de Heredia, V. *Domingo de Soto, estudio biográfico documentado*. Salamanca, Spain, 1960.

Brufau Prats, Jaime. *El pensamiento político de Domingo de Soto*. Salamanca, Spain, 1960.

———. *La escuela de Salamanca ante el descubrimiento de el Nuevo Mundo*. Salamanca, Spain, 1989.

Carro, V. D. *Domingo de Soto y su doctrina jurídica*. Salamanca, Spain, 1944.

Gutierrez, Constancio. *Españoles en Trento*. Valladolid, Spain, 1951.

Hamilton, B. *Political Thought in Sixteenth-Century Spain*. Oxford, 1963.

Pagden, Anthony. *The Fall of Natural Man: The American Indian and the Origins of Comparative Ethnology*. Cambridge, 1987. Examines the contributions of Soto and his fellow Spanish Dominicans to the debate on the status of the New World natives.

Stegmüller, F. "Zur Gnadenlehre des spanischen Konziltheologen Domingo de Soto." In *Das Weltkonzil von Trient*, edited by Georg Schreiber, pp. 169–230. Freiburg, 1951.

CARLOS M. N. EIRE

SOUTHWELL, Robert (1561–1595), English Jesuit missionary, poet, martyr, and Roman Catholic saint. Born into a prominent East Anglian family, Southwell matriculated in the new English college at Douai in 1576. Torn between the Jesuits and the Carthusians, he finally decided in favor of the former in early 1578. His application, however, was deferred until later that year when he began his noviceship in Rome. After Southwell was ordained, Claudio Acquaviva, the superior-general of the Jesuits, argued that Southwell was too young and too important in his position as prefect of studies at the English college in Rome and refused the Jesuit Robert Parsons's request that Southwell be sent on a dangerous English mission. Acquaviva finally capitulated, and Southwell accompanied Henry Garnet to England in 1586. From his base in London Southwell clandestinely received the recently arrived priests, many of whom he knew from Rome, and arranged for their assignments throughout the kingdom.

Before 1590 Southwell took up residence in the London house of Anne Dacre, countess of Arundel. His *An Epistle of Comfort*, a haunting masterpiece of Elizabethan devotional literature, was a development of the letters that he had sent to Philip Howard, the imprisoned earl of Arundel. This was the only prose work published during Southwell's lifetime, and it appeared secretly. The poems, however, were published anonymously in London by different printers. According to Louis L. Martz, Southwell reformed English poetry by introducing into it the "practice of religious meditation and the conversion of the methods of profane poetry to the service of God" (*The Poetry of Meditation*, New Haven, 1954). *A Humble Supplication to Her Majestie* was posthumously published by English secular clergy opposed to the pro-Spanish policies of the Jesuits to demonstrate that one of their martyred members also disapproved of that policy.

Tracked by one of the cruelest pursuivants, Richard Topcliffe, Southwell was captured in Uxenden, Harrow, in June 1592. Imprisoned and tortured, he was found guilty of being a Catholic priest and was executed on 21 February 1595. Beatified in 1929, Southwell was canonized by Paul VI in 1970.

BIBLIOGRAPHY

Primary Sources

Allison, A. F., and D. M. Rogers. *The Contemporary Printed Literature of the English Counter-Reformation between 1558 and 1640.* Vol. 1, *Languages other than English*; vol. 2, *English.* London, 1889, 1994.
Southwell, Robert. *A Short Rule of Good Life: To Direct the Devout Christian in a Regular and Orderly Course.* N.p., n.d.
———. *The Triumphs over Death* (1595). Edited by John William Trotman. London, 1914.
———. *Spiritual Exercises and Devotions of Blessed Robert Southwell, S.J.* Edited by J. M. De Buck. London, 1931.
———. *An Humble Supplication to Her Majestie.* N.p., 1595. Recent edition edited by R. C. Bald, Cambridge, 1953.
———. *An Epistle of Comfort.* Paris, n.d. Recent edition, edited by Margaret Waugh, Chicago, 1966.
———. *The Poems of Robert Southwell, S.J.* Edited by J. H. McDonald and N. P. Brown. Oxford, 1967.
———. *Two Letters and Short Rules of a Good Life.* Edited by Nancy Pollard Brown. Charlottesville, Va., 1973.
———. *A Poeme Declaring the Real Presence of Christ in the Blessed Sacrament of the Aultar* (1606). Ilkey, England, 1974.

Secondary Sources

Devlin, Christopher. *The Life of Robert Southwell: Poet and Martyr.* Reprint, New York, 1989. In the only true biography, Devlin tries, at times successfully, to move beyond hagiography.
Edwards, Francis, ed. *The Elizabethan Jesuits of Henry More.* London, 1981. A translation and edition of the Elizabethan section of the first history of the English Jesuits (Henry More, *Historia Provinciae Anglicanae Societatis Iesu*, St. Omers, 1660). Treats Southwell with all the consideration due a confessor of the faith.
Janelle, Pierre. *Robert Southwell the Writer.* Reprint, Mamaroneck, N.Y., 1971. Still a valuable study of Southwell as poet and spiritual writer.
McCoog, Thomas M. *Monumenta Angliae.* Rome, 1992. See vol. 2, pp. 483–484, for a full bibliography on Southwell.

THOMAS M. MCCOOG, S.J.

SOZZINI, Fausto and Lelio (1539–1604 and 1525–1562, respectively), founders of sixteenth-century antitrinitarian theology. Born on 25 March 1525 at Siena, Italy, Lelio Sozzini spent his childhood at Padua, where his father was a professor of law. He studied at the University of Padua. Uninterested in his family's tradition of the study of law, he went to Vienna and then in 1547 to the Grisons (Graubünden) in Switzerland. There he was influenced in persistent doubting and in framing questions by Camillo Renato (who was also known as Paul Ricci and as Lisia Phileno). After traveling to France (and possibly to England), he went to Geneva in the winter of 1548/49. In 1549 he composed *De resurrectione*, in which he wrote of a possible death of the soul with the body and of a resurrection of the righteous only.

He lived in Zurich and then traveled via Nuremberg to Wittenberg, where he stayed from July 1550 to June 1551, becoming acquainted with Philipp Melanchthon. In 1551 he went via Prague to Kraków, where he visited Francis Lismanino, an early leader of the Reformation in Poland. He then returned to Zurich. In the spring of 1552 he went to Italy to see his father at Bologna, but, concluding that this would be too dangerous because of the Inquisition, he went to Siena. For two months he then visited Matteo Gribaldi in Padua, learning of Gribaldi's strong interest in the thought of Michael Servetus. Lelio was horrified to learn in 1553 of the burning of Servetus. Now in Switzerland, he was accused of being a Renatian and a Servetian. In early 1554 he traveled to Basel, then to Geneva, and then to Zurich. John Calvin, Heinrich Bullinger, and others, impatient with Lelio's persistent doubts and questions, insisted that he prepare a personal doctrinal confession of faith. Bullinger was convinced by this artful, imprecise document. About February 1555 he wrote *De sacramentis dissertatio*.

When his father died in 1556, the Inquisition took possession of Lelio's part of the estate. Lelio resolved to go to Italy to recover his share, which he thought was rightfully his. In order to be able to travel safely in Italy, he went to Wittenberg to get letters of recommendation from Melanchthon to the king of Poland, the king of Bohemia, and the latter's court preacher. Then he went to Switzerland, where Calvin gave him a letter of recommendation to Prince Nicholas Radziwiłł, a powerful supporter of the Reformation in Poland, and where Bullinger gave him a letter to Jan Łaski, the leader of the Reformation in Poland. After successfully traveling to Poland and Bohemia and securing the desired royal letters of recommendation for safe conduct, Lelio went to Italy, but the Inquisition kept his money. The Sozzini family was even under persecution. In August 1559 he returned to Switzerland, wrote *Brevis explicatio in primum Johannis caput* (Brief Explanation of the First Chapter of John) and died in Zurich on 14 May 1562.

Lelio's remarkable *Brevis explicatio*, written in 1561, not only greatly influenced the thought of Lelio's nephew Fausto but also so impressed Giorgio Biandrata and Francis Dávid that they included it (without giving credit to Lelio) as chapter 11 in *De falsa et vera unius Dei Patris, Filii, et Spiritus Sancti cognitione, libri duo* (Two Books on the False and True Knowledge of the One God the Father, the Son, and Holy Spirit; Gyulafehérvár [Alba Iulia], 1568). Published in this form, Lelio's argument strongly influenced the antitrinitarian movements in both Poland and Transylvania.

Lelio's point of departure in his exposition on the meaning of the prologue to John's gospel begins with the view of Lorenzo Valla and Desiderius Erasmus that *logos*, in John's gospel, means speech (*sermo*), not word (*verbum*). Denying the preexistence of Christ, Lelio asserted that Christ was a man to whom God gave divine qualities. This radical change places the "beginning" in history, as the beginning of the preaching of the gospel, not in cosmology (the latter view would present a preexisting, cosmic Christ). Fausto would take up Lelio's theme.

Fausto Sozzini was born on 5 December 1539 in Siena. His father died when he was two years old, so his education, by his mother and grandmother, was not systematic. His early interests were primarily literary, not in the Sozzini family's tradition of the study of law nor in religious questions. Persecution of the Sozzini family in Siena caused him to leave Italy in 1561. When his respected uncle Lelio died in Zurich in 1562, Fausto went from Lyon to Zurich to claim Lelio's papers. Reading Lelio's manuscripts changed Fausto's life, for he resolved to become a religious reformer, continuing publicly Lelio's secret work. Fausto's first work, inspired by Lelio's *Brevis explicatio* was *Explicatio primae partis primi capitis Evangelistae Johannis* (Explanation of the First Part of the First Chapter of John's Gospel), which basically agreed with Lelio's treatise but differed in certain important

respects. It has been recognized as one of Fausto's most important writings.

Fausto returned to Italy to serve as secretary to Duke Paolo Giordano Orsini, husband of Isabella de' Medici, in the court of Grand Duke Cosimo I, who was Fausto's patron. Fausto remained in Italy from 1563 to 1575. The remarkable feature of this period in his life is that he maintained contacts with heretical friends and comrades in Transylvania, who urged him to permit the publication of his *Explicatio* in Transylvania (in 1567–1568) during the time when Fausto was in Italy.

Upon the death of Grand Duke Cosimo I in 1574, Fausto returned to Switzerland, but the new grand duke, Francisco, protected Fausto's income from the Sozzini family's properties on condition that Fausto not publish under his own name during the life of the grand duke. Fausto first stayed in Basel for three years, studying and acquainting himself with the theological literature of the time. His two years of written controversy with Jacques Couvet (Lat., Covetus), a Reformed minister from France, resulted in Fausto's most important theological work *De Jesu Christo Servatore* (On Jesus Christ, the Saver), which was completed in 1578. It circulated in manuscript form and was finally published in 1594. This book contained an exhaustive refutation of the satisfaction theory of the atonement, an emphasis on Christ's resurrection rather than his death, and a clear statement on the nature of saving faith, which is confidence and trust in Christ and thus in God, who gave Christ supreme power over the church.

Fausto's debate with Francesco Pucci in Switzerland resulted in a third major work. *De statu primi hominis ante lapsum* (On the State of the First Man before the Fall), which was also completed in 1578 and circulated in manuscript form. It was published in 1610. In this work Fausto asserted the natural mortality of humans; eternal life, the goal of all Christians, is possible only through gracious resurrection by God.

Fausto's remarkable theological ability, demonstrated in these three works, George Biandrata, court physician and adviser to Prince Christopher Báthory of Transylvania, to invite Fausto to come to Cluj-Napoca (Kolozsvár), where he was to be lodged at Biandrata's expense in the home of Francis Dávid so that Fausto might persuade Dávid to cease his "innovation"—namely, nonadorantism (opposition to prayer to Christ in religious worship and for aid). Previously, when he was ruler of Transylvania, Stephen Báthory had forbidden innovations—that is, changes in the liturgy or confessions of faith from what they had been under King John Sigismund, the previous (Unitarian) ruler. Fausto spent the winter of 1578/79 in Cluj-Napoca.

Fausto was unable to persuade Dávid to change his views, so he went to Poland. Although here he was not allowed to become a member of the Minor Reformed church of Poland (the Polish Brethren), he soon became a recognized leader of that religious movement, representing it against attacks. In 1580, in response to the inquiries of "a famous person" (probably Andrew Dudith, an important diplomat), Fausto wrote *De sacrae scripturae auctoritate*, which, published in that year under a pseudonym, gained great respect from Roman Catholics and Protestants alike, who did not detect the identity of the author. Debates in 1584 with Christian Francken, a philosophically inclined freethinker, and with Andrew Wolan, a theologically sophisticated Calvinist in Lithuania, are representative of many other occasions on which Fausto represented and defended the Polish Brethren.

During his residence in 1583–1587 at Pawlikowice in the home of Christopher Morsztyn, a noble, Fausto married Morsztyn's daughter Elizabeth. They had a daughter, Agnes. Elizabeth died in 1587.

Upon the death in Italy in 1587 of Fausto's patron, the grand duke Francisco, Fausto's property was seized by the Inquisition. With his income thus cut off, Fausto was destitute and henceforth dependent on the financial aid of friends and supporters.

In 1590 Fausto was asked to respond on behalf of the Polish Brethren to a book by Jacob Wujek on the divinity of Christ and of the Holy Spirit. In his response Fausto stated his view of Christ's pre-Ascension ascension, at which time God instructed Christ in his saving message, which Christ was thereafter to proclaim in his ministry on earth.

Fausto returned to Kraków from Pawlikowice in 1588, but he was attacked by mobs and threatened with death in 1594 and 1598. Thereafter, for safety, he moved to Lucławice, where he lived until his death on 3 March 1604.

His influence and significance to the Reformation were great. More than any other single leader, he unified and virtually dominated the Polish Brethren during his years in Poland, especially from 1590 until his death. He continued to be influential through the *Racovian Catechism*, which his followers prepared, but more specifically through his own writings, which display a rare ability in logical thought and theological sophistication. He was so effective that he was thoroughly hated by conservative religious leaders, Roman Catholic and Protestant alike, for his attacks on the dogmas of the Trinity and Incarnation, which, together with his devastating criticisms of the satisfaction theory of atonement, forced more conservative religious leaders to rethink the grounds for their religious views.

Fausto did, indeed, continue the legacy of his uncle Lelio, and in so doing he developed a form of antitrinitarian theology that is clearly to be distinguished from that of Servetus. There are many aspects to this distinction. Among these one must note that Servetus stressed the preexistence and divinity of Christ, which both Lelio and Fausto rejected in favor of seeing Christ as thoroughly human and historical in nature. Yet Lelio and Fausto are also to be distinguished from each other. Whereas in his (joyous) *Brevis explicatio* Lelio showed the influence of Renato and Bernardino

Ochino in his view that, if one believes in Christ, one already "possesses" eternal life, Fausto reduced any such "illumination" to one's hope of attaining eternal life. Fausto was somewhat more of a rationalist and a moralist than was Lelio. Both men agreed, however, that in the prologue to John's gospel, ἐγένετο meant "was," not "became"—that is, the word was flesh (not the word became flesh)—thus shifting from a cosmological to a historical view of the nature and work of Christ, with enormous consequences for the structure of Christian thought.

BIBLIOGRAPHY

Primary Sources

Marchetti, Valerio, and Giampaolo Zucchini, eds. *Aggiunte all'epistolario di Fausto Sozzini, 1561–1568.* Biblioteka Pisarzy Reformacyjnych, no. 14. Warsaw, 1972. Important letters, in Italian.
Socinus, Fausto. *Fausti Socini Senensis Opera Omnia in Duos Tomos distincta: Bibliotheca Fratrum Polonorum qui Unitarii Appellantur Continens Opera Omnia. Johannis Crellii Francii, Ludovici Wolsogenii, Fausti Socini Senensis & Exegetica Jonae Schlichtingii a Bucowiec.* 2 vols. Irenopoli, 1656. Basic source for Fausto Sozzini's works.
———. *Listy.* 2 vols. Edited by Ludwik Chmaj. Biblioteka Pisary Reformacyjnych, no. 2. Warsaw, 1959. Letters, translated into Polish and arranged chronologically.
Socinus, Lacius. *Opere.* Edited by Antonio Rotondó. Florence, 1986. Critical edition of Lelio's treatises and letters.

Secondary Sources

Chmaj, Ludwik. *Faust Socyn, 1539–1604.* Warsaw, 1963. Thorough biography and theological analysis, in Polish.
Kawecka-Gryczowa, Alodia. *Ariánskie oficyny wydawnicze Rodeckiego i Sternackiego: Dzieje i bibliografia; Les imprimeurs des antitrinitaires polonais Rodecki et Sternacki, Histoire et bibliographie.* Kraków, 1974. Detailed information on original and later publications of Fausto Sozzini's works. Text in Polish and French.
Ogonowski, Zbigniew. "Faustis Socinus, 1539–1604." In *Shapers of Religious Traditions in Germany, Switzerland, and Poland, 1560–1600,* edited by Jill Raitt, pp. 195–209. New Haven, 1981. Brief interpretation of Fausto's life, theology, and role in the church. Ogonowski concludes that Enlightenment thinkers perceived the Socinians as their predecessors.
Szczucki, Lech. "La prima edizione dell' "Explicatio" di Fausto Sozzini." *Rinascimento* 18 (1967), 319–327. Important essay which demonstrates Fausto's contacts with Italian exiles and Transylvanians during the time when he was in Italy.
Wilbur, Earl Morse. *A History of Unitarianism: Socinianism and its Antecedents.* Reprint, Boston, 1977. The standard source for the historical contexts of Lelio and Fausto Sozzini.
Williams, George H. *The Radical Reformation.* 3d ed., rev. & enl. Kirksville, Mo., 1992. Authoritative on the historical contexts and theological interpretation.

JOHN C. GODBEY

SPAIN. From the union of the medieval kingdoms of Aragon and Castile, Spain was created on the eve of the Reformation. Of the two, Castile was by far the larger with a probable population in the fifteenth century of between six and seven million. It included the old kingdom of León and several regions that were Castilian neither in culture nor in language. The most important of these were Galicia, in the far northwest, and Vizcaya, where the Basque language and culture remain vital to this day. Aragon, with perhaps a million people, was equally diverse. Aragon proper was a rugged inland region composed largely of great estates. Its people spoke Castilian but vigorously defended their own legal and historical traditions. The coastal areas of the kingdom were wealthier and more populous than the interior. Catalonia, centered on the great port of Barcelona, had its own language, culture, and legal system, as did the kingdom of Valencia, approximately thirty percent of whose population were Muslims living under Christian rule.

Neither kingdom was especially prosperous. Rainfall in most of the Iberian peninsula has rarely exceeded twenty inches per year, and intensive agriculture is possible only in the well-watered regions along the Cantabrian coast or on irrigated lands, such as the *huerta* of Valencia. Old and New Castile, together with Aragon, were largely devoted to the cultivation of grains and to stock raising. Their major exports were merino wool and hides, though most regions produced wine for local consumption. Andalusia supplied olive oil to the rest of the peninsula and exported its fortified wines to England and the rest of northern Europe.

The merger of the two realms was originally personal. Isabella of Castile married Ferdinand of Aragon in 1469 and claimed the throne in 1474. Five years later Ferdinand inherited the Aragonese crown from his father. In the last eighteen years of his life (1492–1516), Ferdinand would greatly expand his patrimony by gaining control of Sicily and Naples, but if the partnership was at first unequal in material terms, it was nevertheless real. Though marriage fostered the development of common policies, the kingdoms retained separate administrations until the Bourbon reforms of the eighteenth century.

From the beginning, Ferdinand and Isabella pursued a militantly Christian policy. They conquered the Muslim kingdom of Granada in 1492 after a decade of bitter warfare and forcibly converted those inhabitants who were unable to flee, or who chose not to do so. To limit Muslim activities in the western Mediterranean, they established Christian garrisons in the Maghrib and adopted a posture of diplomatic hostility toward the Ottoman empire. Evangelical concerns played a part in their sponsorship of Christopher Columbus, whose voyages ultimately brought Castile a great American empire. The expulsion of the Jews, also in 1492, served notice that *los reyes catolicos*, as they were called, were willing to tolerate religious diversity only in the most unusual circumstances.

The expulsion of the Jews was the final act of a much longer drama. A series of pogroms beginning in 1391 had forced the majority of Spanish Jews to convert or to seek refuge elsewhere. Because many of these conversions were thought to have been false, the monarchs established the Spanish Inquisition as an institutional means of preserving religious purity. Unlike earlier inquisitions, it was a system of courts controlled by the Crown, and its establishment was at first resisted by the papacy. Its authority extended throughout Spain and eventually to the Aragonese possessions in Italy and to America. Between 1480 and 1500 thousands of *Conversos*, or New Christians, were condemned for Judaizing practices and either reconciled to the faith or burned at the stake. The Jews were expelled because it was feared, perhaps wrongly, that they had been assisting false converts to preserve their ancient customs. Though its original purpose was fulfilled in only two decades, the Inquisition continued to evolve, providing a mechanism for the control of religious life that was unique to the Spanish empire.

Like the rest of their generation, Ferdinand and especially Isabella supported the idea of church reform. Their approach to this issue was conservative and essentially regalist in that they intended the reforms to be directed by the Crown. Through hard bargaining with a reluctant papacy, they both gained legal *de facto* control of ecclesiastical patronage, thereby limiting the ability of the clergy to appeal royal decisions affecting the Spanish church. The actual work of reform was entrusted to the cardinal archbishop of Toledo, Francisco Jiménez de Cisneros. When Isabella died in 1504, Cisneros became regent of Castile and, in 1507, inquisitor general. This combination of offices enabled him to reform and reorganize the episcopate, abolishing simony and establishing qualifications for bishops that foreshadowed those of the post-Tridentine era. He imposed new standards on several orders of regular clergy, beginning with his own Franciscans, and made heroic efforts to raise the educational standards of the clergy. In 1508 Cisneros founded the University of Alcalá de Henares to encourage humanist models of biblical scholarship and to permit the teaching of theology by all of the "three ways": Thomist, Scotist, and Ockhamist. One of the university's first products was the Complutensian Polyglot Bible.

By the accession of Charles I in 1517, the Spanish church was for all practical purposes independent of the papacy and cleansed of at least some of the abuses that had inspired anticlericalism in other parts of Europe. Yet the Cisneran reforms, though they addressed popular grievances and improved the quality of the Spanish clergy, set the stage for another form of religious conflict. The cardinal's encouragement of spiritual and theological diversity led to the development of two broadly defined but mutually exclusive schools of thought, both of which fell squarely within the Catholic tradition. The first, derived in part from the cardinal's own observant Franciscan tradition, favored a Christian life based upon apostolic simplicity, moralism, systematic mental prayer, and a kind of scripturalism. It found its natural allies in Erasmian humanism, which was introduced in part by the "Flemish" courtiers of Charles I after 1517, and in Illuminism, a native movement that stressed an "interior" piety verging on the mystical. The second, which emphasized the sacraments, vocal prayer, and the revival of Aristotelian rationalism, has been seen as a reaction to the Cisneran reforms but was in fact a different conception of religious life. Its chief exponents were to be found in the theology faculty at Salamanca.

These "conservatives," many of whom were Dominicans, questioned the orthodoxy of their opponents and enlisted the aid of the Inquisition. That institution, having "solved" the problem of the *Conversos*, now turned its attention to heresy. The foreign contacts of the Erasmians and their criticisms of the church aroused suspicion. The Illuminists, who were not theologically sophisticated, seemed to reject the sacraments in their search for a more direct, personal contact with God, while their exaggerated theocentrism limited human freedom in ways that suggested Protestant influence. Though only a handful of Spaniards appear to have adopted or even understood reformed teachings, it was all too easy to accuse such people of Lutheranism. The first Illuminist communities were destroyed by the Inquisition during the 1520s. Between 1529 and 1535 prominent Erasmians, including the Valdés brothers and Juan de Vergara, were also attacked for their presumed association with the Illuminists and for ideas that seemed to smack of Protestantism. The conviction of Vergara may be said to have killed the Erasmian movement in Spain.

It seemed that orthodoxy was now safe, but between 1556 and 1559, communities of what appeared to be heretics were discovered at Valladolid and Seville. Few of these people were prominent, and most seem to have been influenced by either Illuminist or Erasmian ideas, but there was evidence that they had been in communication with Geneva. The exposure of their activities caused genuine alarm. Two great autos-da-fe were held in 1559 at which the leading figures of the two communities were executed. In a reversal of normal practice, some of those who recanted were burned alive. A new, more restrictive Index of Prohibited Books was published in the same year to replace the first Spanish Index of 1545, and Spanish students were with few exceptions prohibited from studying abroad. With these measures the brief history of Protestantism in Spain ended, and a degree of religious uniformity was imposed that had few parallels in the rest of Europe.

Differing visions of faith could still compete, but only within the strictest limits of orthodoxy. The tradition of "interior" Christianity continued to find striking expression in the lives and writings of Teresa of Ávila, Juan Álvarez, Luis de Granada, and many others. Other, less controversial vestiges of the Cisneran approach to reform could be found in the popular catechism of Bartolomé de Carranza. All of these writers suffered from the attentions of the Inquisition but were generally able to escape its clutches. Their work

exemplifies a major and, perhaps to foreigners, quite familiar strain of Spanish piety.

Similarly, the defeat of the Erasmians did not mark the end of Spanish humanism. A probable majority of Spanish scholars had always found the Erasmian suspicion of formal reason obscurantist and its political ideas naive. They much preferred the humanism imported from the University of Bologna by such figures as Juan Ginés de Sepúlveda because it combined philological and historical criticism with a profound respect for Aristotelian rationalism. The fusion of Bolognese humanism with the neo-Thomism of Salamanca inspired Spain's greatest contributions to sixteenth-century thought—the political theories of Francisco de Vitoria, Francisco Suárez, and Juan de Mariana. It also influenced theology. The revival of Thomism associated with Vitoria's lectures at Salamanca between 1526 and 1546 found authoritative expression in Melchior Cano's *De locis theologicis* (1563). Cano, who believed that theology had no other function than the defense of orthodoxy, was rigidly Thomist in his arguments but employed conventional humanist methods to locate sources of proof that demonstrated the continuity of Catholic doctrine.

The religious history of Spain after the abdication of Charles I in 1556 is one of cautious reform undertaken within a framework of traditional regalism. In this as in many other matters, Charles's son Philip II tried to continue the policies of his ancestors. He was determined to retain all rights of ecclesiastical appointments, to control the publication of papal bulls and briefs in Spain, and to forbid appeals to Rome, especially when they involved the Inquisition. At the same time, Philip needed papal support for his foreign policy and tried to avoid unnecessary confrontations. This concern for the independence of the Spanish church helps to explain Philip's delay in publishing the decrees of the Council of Trent and the careful measures taken by his bishops to improve the catechization of lay people and public morals.

The leading figure in this work was Gaspar de Quiroga, archbishop of Toledo after 1577. Quiroga sought to implement the principles of Tridentine reform primarily on the diocesan level. In 1581 he issued a manual of the sacraments to regulate their administration, and at the Synod of Toledo in the following year the Spanish bishops developed a program to create seminaries, regulate clerical dress, ban absenteeism, and define the minimum qualifications for ordination. Rules were set for the celebration of the Mass, and the church began its long and not always successful campaign to eliminate secular elements from religious festivals. The work of the bishops was supported by the Inquisition, which from the 1570s concentrated its efforts on morals cases and on the elimination of popular errors or "propositions."

Bitter as these struggles could sometimes be, they do not bear comparison to the religious and intellectual convulsions that wracked other parts of Europe in the age of the Reformation. Spain was, and would remain, entirely and often militantly Catholic. As such, it emerged by the 1540s as the political and military champion of the Counter-Reformation.

Spain's international role was determined in large part by the succession of Charles I, the grandson of Isabella and Ferdinand and of the emperor Maximilian I and Mary of Burgundy. Heir to Castile and Aragon, the Aragonese kingdoms of Sicily and Naples, the Low Countries, and the Habsburg lands in central and eastern Europe, his election in 1519 as Charles V, Holy Roman Emperor, made Spain part of a greatly expanded empire.

Charles opposed the Reformation for personal as well as political reasons. In this he was at one with his Spanish subjects, but the enormity of the emperor's responsibilities was such that the Spanish at first feared the absorption of their interests by larger imperial concerns. The revolt of the *Comuneros* in 1520 was an expression of these worries and of Castilian distaste for Charles's counsellors, most of whom were from his native Low Countries. Although they were indeed destined to be absorbed by his empire, what the Castilians could not have foreseen was that their incorporation would not be as a subsidiary kingdom but as its heart and soul.

The gradual evolution of Castilian dominance came about in part because Castile was the only one of Charles's possessions to have evolved a system of perpetual taxation. Taxes, such as the *alcabala*, first imposed in the fourteenth century, generated predictable revenues against which the crown could borrow for military expenses without calling upon a representative body. In time this would be supplemented by silver from Mexico and Peru, but bullion imports from the New World did not reach significant levels until the reign of Philip II. Even so, Castile was, from the beginning, the emperor's greatest source of revenue.

It was also his most important source of manpower. In the course of his wars in Granada and Italy, Ferdinand had built a superb army that would become the core of Charles's own multiethnic force. Spanish troops and Spanish commanders served the emperor well against the French, the Muslims, and the German Protestants. Even Spain's civilian bureaucracy proved indispensable as the burdens of the empire grew. The Spanish system was based upon a series of advisory councils whose work was expedited by royal secretaries. Charles soon found it more useful than the imperial chancery he had inherited from Maximilian I. Inevitably, the emperor became dependent upon those who served him best. By 1545 his chief secretary, his leading military adviser, and even his confessor were Spanish. When he abdicated in 1556, it was to retirement at the remote Spanish monastery of Yuste.

Throughout his reign the Spanish provided vital military and financial support for the policies of the emperor. Span-

ish troops under Fernando Álvarez de Toledo, duke of Alba, formed the core of the army that defeated the Schmalkald League in 1546–1547 and rescued Charles when he was driven across the Alps by Moritz of Saxony in 1552. Politically and theologically, Spanish influence was felt most strongly at the Council of Trent. The Spanish delegates opposed compromise with the Protestants and supported the Thomistic formulations that generally prevailed in the council's restatements of Catholic doctrine. In so doing, they acted against the stated policy of the emperor. Charles claimed to support a more moderate position, though his private feelings may have been very different. The situation was complicated by the fact that several of the most prominent Spanish delegates were Jesuits, an order that, in spite of its nominally Spanish origins, failed to earn full acceptance at court. Both Charles and his son Philip II were suspicious of the Jesuits's declared loyalty to the papacy, and within Spain itself the society never equaled the political or intellectual influence of the Dominicans.

When Charles abdicated in 1556, he left the Spanish and Italian kingdoms to his son Philip II, together with his possessions in the Netherlands. The Habsburg lands in central Europe went to Charles's brother Ferdinand, who was elected emperor in 1558. Philip II was entirely Spanish by birth, sympathies, and education. Austere and devout, he attempted to continue the emperor's policies. An unwanted war against Pope Paul IV and his French allies in 1556–1557 followed by the French defeat at Saint-Quentin in 1559 ended the long struggle with France and left Philip free to pursue the ancient struggle with Islam. His forces expelled the Turks from Malta in 1564, and the Spanish fleet played an important part in the great naval victory at Lepanto in 1571. By this time Philip was enmeshed in the great rebellion that would occupy the remainder of his reign and bring Spain into conflict with England and the French Huguenots.

The Revolt of the Netherlands was caused primarily by the king's efforts to reorganize the government of the seventeen provinces and to reform their church. From Philip's point of view the ecclesiastical organization of the Netherlands was simply inadequate. There were only three dioceses, and major centers of population, including Ghent, Antwerp, and Brugge, remained unserved by bishops. High church offices were often held by the younger sons of great nobles. Few of these men possessed the intellectual and spiritual qualifications demanded by the Council of Trent, and simony was rampant. It was a situation that could only encourage the growth of heresy. In 1559 Philip gained papal approval for the appointment of fourteen new bishops whose incomes were to be partially funded by Spanish dioceses. All were to have been educated in theology or in canon law and to possess acceptable moral and spiritual qualifications for their posts.

The proposal aroused almost universal opposition. It threatened the varied interests of the Protestants, the city councils, and the hereditary nobility. The latter were also opposed to the establishment of a uniform system of royal justice and feared that they would be excluded from a newly reconstituted system of governing councils. Escalating protests led to a serious outbreak of rioting and iconoclasm in 1566. Philip immediately sent the duke of Alba to restore order, but six years of Alba's heavy-handed rule caused a full-scale rebellion to break out in 1572.

The Revolt of the Netherlands forced Philip to maintain an army of occupation there from 1567 onwards, and though his greatest commander, Alessandro Farnese, duke of Parma, restored Spanish control over the ten southern provinces by 1585, the revolt brought Spain into conflict with a variety of other enemies. To prevent the French Huguenots from making common cause with Netherlandish Protestants, Philip supported the Catholic faction headed by the house of Guise and invaded France in 1590 when the triumph of the Protestant Henry IV appeared imminent. These interventions failed, as did Philip's attempted invasion of England in 1588. The Spanish Armada of that year was a reponse to England's support of the Dutch rebels and to English attacks on Cádiz and in the West Indies. It marked the beginning of a naval war that continued sporadically until Philip's death in 1598.

Philip's son, Philip III, secured a twelve years' truce with the Dutch in 1609, but warfare resumed after its expiration, and Spain did not acknowledge the independence of the seven northern provinces until the Peace of Westphalia in 1648. Spanish policy throughout was inspired by dynastic as well as religious considerations, but to Protestants the bitter struggle for the Low Countries and the related attacks on England and France established Spain as the preeminent champion of the Counter-Reformation. The impression was only strengthened by Spain's support for the Austrian Habsburgs and its invasion of the Palatinate during the Thirty Years' War.

It was a role that the Spanish economy could not sustain. To support his policies Philip II had been forced to borrow heavily and to repudiate his debts in 1575 and 1596. Not even the bullion shipments from the New World or Philip's annexation of Portugal and its empire in 1580 could sustain military expenditures that sometimes equaled 140 percent of available revenues. Increased reliance on private military contractors, and the sale of royal properties accomplished little. Castilian taxes remained the crown's primary source of revenue, and by the end of the reign they had multiplied to the point that thousands of peasants were forced from the land. Trade and manufacturing declined while inflation increased. By the final decade of the sixteenth century, the population was declining as well, and it was becoming obvious that Spain could no longer sustain the burdens of empire.

Paradoxically, this age of *desengaño* ("disillusion") produced a flowering of the arts and literature. Writers such as Cervantes, Quevedo, and Calderón and painters such as Velázquez, Murillo, and Zurbarán produced their masterpieces in a society that seemed gripped by irreversible decay. Reformers known as *arbitristas* advanced ingenious and often impractical schemes for improving the economy.

Under Philip III (1598–1621) their ideas were ignored in favor of peace and a policy of benign neglect. Modification of its imperial ambitions might have worked had the Crown been able to control its viceroys. Several of them, trained in an earlier school, unilaterally pursued aggressive policies that led to further expense. Meanwhile, systematic devaluation of the coinage made the economic situation worse.

Gaspar de Guzmán y Pimental, count-duke of Olivares and chief minister of Philip IV from 1621 to 1643, attempted reforms but could not extricate himself from the Thirty Years' War. His efforts to spread the growing burden of finance and recruitment from Castile to the other components of the Spanish empire prompted successful revolts in Portugal and Catalonia in 1640. The defeat of the Spanish armies at Rocroi and the fall of Olivares in 1643 marked the eclipse of Spain as a major European power.

[*See also* Jiménez de Cisneros, Francisco; Philip II of Spain; Valdéz, Alfonso de; Valdéz, Juan de; *and* Vergara, Juan de.]

BIBLIOGRAPHY

Andrés Martín, M. *La teología española en el siglo 16.* 2 vols. Madrid, 1976–1977.
Bataillon, M. *Erasmo y España.* Rev. ed. Madrid, 1979.
Dedieu, Jean-Pierre. " 'Christianisation' en Nouvelle Castile: Catechisme, communion, messe et confirmation dans l'archevèché de Toledo, 1540–1650." *Mélanges de la Casa Velasques* 15 (1979), 261–294.
Elliott, J. H. *Imperial Spain, 1469–1716.* New York, 1963.
———. *The Count-Duke of Olivares: The Statesman in an Age of Decline.* New Haven, 1986.
Fernandez-Armesto, Felipe. *Ferdinand and Isabella.* New York, 1975.
García Oro, J. *Cisneros y la reforma del clero español en tiempo de los reyes Católicos.* Madrid, 1971.
Kamen, Henry. *Inquisition and Society in Spain.* Bloomington, Ind., 1985.
Lynch, John. *Spain under the Habsburgs.* 2d ed. 2 vols. New York, 1981.
Márquez, Antonio. *Los alumbrados: orígines y filosofia.* 2d corr. ed. Madrid, 1980.
Monter, E. William. *Frontiers of Heresy.* Cambridge, 1990.
Parker, Geoffrey. *The Dutch Revolt.* Rev. ed. London, 1988.
Pierson, Peter. *Philip II of Spain.* London, 1975.
Vassberg, David E. *Land and Society in Golden Age Castile.* Cambridge, 1984.

WILLIAM S. MALTBY

SPALATIN, Georg (also Georg Burckhardt; 1484–1545), German humanist involved in the Reformation. The son of the tanner George Burckhardt—from a liaison that the church did not regard as legitimate—Spalatin was born on 14 January 1484 in the small mid-Franconian town of Spalt (southeast of Nuremberg), which at the time formed part of the diocesan territory of Eichstätt. After elementary instruction at the convent school of Saint Nicholas in his home town, he attended the Latin school of Saint Sebaldus in Nuremberg from 1497 onward; it had recently had its curriculum reformed along humanist lines, and here the humanist Heinrich Grüninger from Munich became his teacher. In 1498 he moved to the University of Erfurt, where he earned his bachelor's degree in 1499. There he belonged to the inner circle of students around the Thuringian Nikolaus Marschalk, who was to play a crucial part in introducing humanism in Erfurt.

Once introduced to the *studia humanitatis*, Spalatin never turned back. In the autumn of 1502 he followed his teacher to the newly founded University of Wittenberg in electoral Saxony, where he was given the degree of "Magister artium" on 2 February 1503. He appeared for the first time under his humanist name in the dean's register on that occasion. Subsequently, he studied law, as had his teacher, Marschalk. In the winter term of 1504/05 he returned to Erfurt on his own and accepted a position as tutor in a patrician family, in addition to continuing his legal studies.

In Erfurt he again found his way into the humanist circle, which by that time was headed by the canon Conrad Mutianus Rufus (who lived in Gotha and had been a fellow pupil of Desiderius Erasmus at Deventer). On the recommendation of Mutianus he was given the position of novice teacher—even though he was a layman—at the Cistercian monastery of Georgenthal (south of Gotha at the edge of the Thuringian Forest). At the same time, he was put in charge of the monastery library, for which he bought humanist literature. Together with the monastery's steward, Heinrich Urban, he belonged to the intimate circle about Mutianus. In those days he acquired a Bible and began to study the scriptures in the manner that the northern humanists had made fashionable. He also prepared for an ecclesiastical career, was ordained in 1508, and assumed the parish of Hohenkirchen near Georgenthal, which he left in the care of a vicar. His legal abilities had found recognition in 1507, when he became "notarius publicus." Once again it was owing to the good offices of Mutianus that in 1508 the elector Frederick III ("the Wise") of Saxony called him to Torgau as tutor to his nephew, Duke John Frederick. Two years later the elector entrusted him with the continuation of the Saxon Chronicle, which had been neglected since the death of Adam of Fulda. In 1511 he took up residence in the castle at Wittenberg, where he became the mentor of the dukes Otto and Ernst of Brunswick-Lüneburg, two nephews of Frederick who studied there. In the same function he guided the studies of Sebastian of Jessen, an illegitimate son of Frederick, from 1514 onward. The favor shown him by the elector resulted in his becoming a canon at Saint George's convent in the castle of Altenburg (in eastern Thuringia) in 1511, even though he had to wait four years for the papal dispensation (necessary for a proper exercise of

the rights and duties connected with this position), which his illegitimate birth required. In 1512 he was given charge of the newly established castle library in Wittenberg, which was intended to serve the needs of the university as well. During the time at Wittenberg, the elector had him procure material for Frederick's judgment on the Reuchlin controversy. Through Johannes Lang, whom he knew from his student years in Erfurt, he also sought to establish relations with Martin Luther. This led to an ever closer exchange of ideas and a profound friendship, which found its expression in an extensive correspondence.

Appointed to the elector's chancellery in September 1516, he served Frederick as his private secretary and soon as his spiritual adviser as well (in 1518 he was given special confessional powers by the pope); moreover, from 1522 onward he became the elector's court preacher. His dual function as adviser in worldly and spiritual affairs increased his influence. In the chancellery, his particular responsibilities included church and university matters, and after 1518 he was fully engaged in promoting the university reform demanded by Luther and Philipp Melanchthon.

Following the indulgence controversy he served as intermediary between Luther and the elector, and (in spite of some crises) managed to obtain lasting protection for his Wittenberg friend, cautiously granted by Frederick. Throughout, he sought to restrain Luther while at the same time encouraging the hesitant elector.

This role of intermediary first became obvious during the Diet of Augsburg in 1518, when Luther (cited to Rome) asked for his help in finding some way to avoid that journey and its likely consequences. The elector did, in fact, obtain the concession that Luther merely had to face an examination by the papal legate, Cardinal Cajetan, in Augsburg. At the time of the examination the elector and Spalatin had already returned to electoral Saxony; Luther's reports on events in Augsburg went to Spalatin. He was also engaged in the attempts of the elector's court to interest Erasmus in Luther's cause, having been in correspondence with the Rotterdamer since 1516 (and having kept him informed about, among other things, divergent opinions of Luther's). Most translations by Spalatin of Erasmus's texts, including *Querela pacis*, date back to that period. In his role as interpreter he also was the only other person present when the elector met Erasmus in Cologne in 1520. The fact that Erasmus could not be won over to Luther's side definitively remained a disappointment for Spalatin, the humanist.

In those years he accompanied the elector on all his travels on imperial affairs. At the Diet of Worms in 1521 he advised Luther, who appeared there in obedience to an imperial summons. While Luther stayed at the Wartburg castle, Spalatin became a key figure, as all of Luther's correspondence and manuscripts went out by way of the court and across his desk. Guided by Luther and to a lesser extent by other Wittenberg theologians, Spalatin acquired deep insights into the new doctrine. On his own testimony he severed himself from the papacy in 1523, and this decision affected his work as a preacher at court. His efforts to make Frederick take a direct hand in reordering the church in his own territory turned out to be in vain, however. Although he aimed at being released from his court office, Spalatin allowed himself to be persuaded by Luther to remain at the elector's side.

After Frederick's death he went to Altenburg as a parish pastor, where he preached his inaugural sermon on 6 August 1525. In the same year he married the daughter of an Altenburg burgher, Katharina Heidenreich (Streubel). As this act breached the rule of celibacy, it was followed by a vehement dispute with Saint George's convent. Two daughters, Hanna (born in 1532) and Katharina (born in 1533) issued from the marriage.

Spalatin accompanied the new elector, John ("the Constant"), as a preacher to the first Diet of Speyer in 1526. This elector interpreted the final agreement of the Diet of Speyer rather freely and on that basis took the reorganization of the church in his territory into his own hands, charging Spalatin with great responsibilities in the preparation and conduct of visitations. Thereby the humanist contributed decisively to the establishment of territorial church government, which he had long desired. On 21 December 1528 he became superintendent of the particularly large district of Altenburg; in that role he had to deal to a considerable extent with questions of marriage law.

At the Diet of Augsburg in 1530 he was among the elector's theological advisers, along with Melanchthon, who was in charge of writing the Augsburg Confession. During the committee negotiations he was called in at times as a notary, until the opposition insisted on his being excluded. During this period he twice gave his expert opinion on the issue of the elector's right of resistance against the emperor, changing his mind about it from rejection of the idea to a qualified acceptance after some inner conflict. When in 1532 negotiations regarding a temporary reconciliation over the religious question took place between the adherents of the old church and those who felt akin to the Augsburg Confession, the elector (who, because he was ill, had to send his son John Frederick in his stead) appointed Spalatin to his son's staff of advisers in Schweinfurt and, later, in Nuremberg. In this position Spalatin advocated accepting the truce offered instead of insisting on the inclusion of future adherents to the Augsburg Confession, thereby contributing toward the conclusion of the Peace of Nuremberg.

After the accession of John Frederick (still in 1532) even more was required of him. From March 1533 onward Spalatin was constantly away from home: in visitation matters for more than a year; participating in the negotiations with the papal legate and the emperor's orator about the Council of Weimar; to Kaden (in Bohemia), where the restitution of Württemberg was achieved; with the elector to Vienna on the occasion of his investiture; to Schmalkalden as part of a league meeting; and with the elector on a more private journey to northwest Germany. On the occasion of the new foundation of the University of Wittenberg in 1536, he was confirmed in overall charge of the library. When Duke Henry of Saxony, the brother of Catholic Duke George ("the Bearded"), wanted to introduce the Reformation in the districts of Freiberg and Wolkenstein, Spalatin was delegated by the elector to assist in the visitation. In 1539, after George's death, he belonged to the visitation staff in Albertine Saxony provided by electoral Saxony. In 1542 he was employed to inspect in a particularly difficult area—the town and convent of Wurzen, where the claims of the lines of the house of Wettin clashed—in order to introduce the Reformation there. In 1544 he was asked to take part in the "dedication work," which was to ensure the financial provision of pastors and their staff, but poor health forced him to decline. On 16 January 1545 he died in Altenburg. He was interred in Saint Bartholomew's Church, but his tomb and tombstone do not remain.

Throughout his life Spalatin continued his studies. He was engaged in collecting historical source material, even if only two minor historiographic works were printed in his lifetime: a text on the "dear prince Arminius," which was a result of his journey through the Teutoburg Forest, and a political treatise written at John Frederick's order on the controversy between the houses of Wettin and Welf on the respective ages of their dynasties. His biography of Frederick III was not edited until the nineteenth century by Christian Neudecker and Ludwig Preller (1851). A manuscript of the *Saxon Chronicle* in three volumes, illuminated in the Cranach workshop, is to be found in the art collection of Coburg castle (Mss. 3–5). Most of the manuscripts left by him are in the Thüringisches Hauptstaatsarchiv Weimar. Among his translations that are of interest from a humanist viewpoint is his main work, a translation of Petrarch (Augsburg, 1532), which must be mentioned along with the Erasmus texts indicated above.

As he had never studied theology at a university, he was unencumbered by scholasticism. Under the guidance of Wittenberg theologians—notably the most prominent among them, Luther—he taught himself his theology in private studies. He was successful at spreading the new evangelical theology by translating some of Luther's texts and Melanchthon's *Loci communes* into the vernacular. He gradually worked out for himself Luther's fundamental idea of justification solely through faith. He himself wrote a few minor theological treatises for teaching purposes, the earliest one shortly before the death of Frederick III. (The manuscript is in the Forschungs- und Landesbibiliothek Gotha, Codex Gothensis B26, edited in 1959.) Among those printed in his lifetime were an instruction for the congregation of Schweinfurt in 1534 and a work in 1543 on the sacrament of the Eucharist (which had also particularly interested him in the earlier texts mentioned). He was not given the time for any larger theological works and did not intend to write them in any event. His importance is based primarily on his role as intermediary between Luther and the electoral court in the decisive years of the Reformation, as well as his prominent contribution toward the practical realization of the Reformation and the establishment of a new church order in electoral Saxony.

At the end of 1993, the portrait of the young Spalatin (1509) by Lucas Cranach the Elder (formerly Lipperheide collection), which had been lost since the 1930s, reappeared in a Munich salesroom; it was acquired by the Museum of Fine Arts in Leipzig.

BIBLIOGRAPHY

Primary Source

Spalatin, Georg. *Georg Spalatius Chronik für die Jahre 1513 bis 1520.* Borna-Leipzig, 1919.

Secondary Sources

Holeczek, Heinz. *Erasmus Deutsch, Bd. 1. Die volkssprachliche Rezeption des Erasmus von Rotterdam in der reformatorischen Öffentlichkeit, 1519–1536.* Stuttgart, 1983. This attributes conclusively a number of anonymously published translations of Erasmus's texts to Spalatin.

Höss, Irmgard. "Georg Spalatins Traktat 'De sacramento Venerabile Eucharistiae et de Confessione' vom Jahre 1525." *Archiv für Reformationsgeschichte* 49 (1958), 79–88.

———, "The Lutheran Church of the Reformation: Problems of its Formation and Organization in the Middle and North German Territories." In *The Social History of the Reformation,* edited by Lawrence P. Buck and Jonathan W. Zophy, pp. 317–339. Columbus, Ohio, 1972.

———. *Georg Spalatin, 1484–1545: Ein Leben in der Zeit des Humanismus und der Reformation* (1956). 2d enl. ed. Weimar, 1989. The introduction to the second edition discusses developments in research since 1956.

Kinder, E. "Kommentar zum Traktat Spalatins." *Neue Zeitschrift für systematische Theologie* 1 (1959), 124–137.

Reichert, E. O. "Der Abendmahlstraktat Spalatins von 1525." *Neue Zeitschrift für systematische Theologie* 1 (1959), 110–124.

Spitz, Lewis W. *The Religious Renaissance of the German Humanists.* Cambridge, Mass., 1963. Of importance with respect to Mutianus are pp. 130–154, and to Luther, pp. 236–266.

Verzeichnis der im deutschen Sprachbereich erschienenen Drucke des XVI. Jahrhunderts. Stuttgart, 1983–. See vol. 19, nos. 7401–7446.

Volz, Hans. "Bibliographie der im 16. Jahrhundert erschienenen Schriften Georg Spalatins." *Zeitschrift für Bibliothekswesen und Bibliographie* 5 (1958), 83–119.

IRMGARD HÖẞ
Translated from German by Anna-D. Henning

SPANGENBERG, Cyriakus (1528–1604), German Lutheran theologian. Born on 7 June 1528, he was the son of Johannes Spangenberg, the reformer of Nordhausen and a friend of Luther. Spangenberg began studies at Wittenberg in 1542 and was immediately drawn into Luther's circle. His father had become superintendent of the churches of Mansfeld county in 1546, and Spangenberg was called to teach school in Eisleben in 1547. He returned to Wittenberg to complete his studies in 1550 and then returned to Eisleben as pastor. His sharp attacks on the Augsburg and Leipzig interims earned him temporary exile. In 1553 he was called to Mansfeld as preacher for the town and the castle; in 1559 he assumed the additional duties of general dean of the county's churches and member of the consistory in Eisleben. Assisting the superintendents of Mansfeld county, Erasmus Sarcerius and his successor Hieronymus Menzel, Spangenberg guided Mansfeld policy in a Gnesio-Lutheran direction, combating Georg Major's view of good works beginning in 1552, when Major served briefly as superintendent in Mansfeld. He also criticized Philippist synergism, particularly in his sermons on predestination (1567), which sparked a minor controversy (which lies behind the Formula of Concord article XI). The Mansfeld ministerium published its criticism of Philippist, Calvinist, and other opposing positions in confessions composed at county synods in 1559 and 1564. Spangenberg also traveled to Antwerp in 1566 to help his friend Matthias Flacius Illyricus organize Lutheran church life there, and he played a role in the composition of that church's confession and agenda.

In 1567 Elector August of Saxony, angered at the Mansfeld attacks on his Philippist theologians, began attempts to silence Spangenberg and his colleagues. At the same time differences over the doctrine of original sin held by Flacius split the Gnesio-Lutherans into two camps that became consumed by this dispute. Spangenberg supported Flacius, who taught that Original Sin became the essence, or substance, of the human creature at the Fall and that the sinner is in the image of Satan. He defended Flacius's point of view until the end of his life because he was convinced that Luther had taught that "Original Sin is the corruption of fallen human nature." Attacked first by Flacius's former associates Johann Wigand, Tilemann Hesshus, and Simon Musaeus, who had broken with him over this question and rejected Flacius's use of Aristotelian anthropology and of the terms "substance" and "accident" in explaining Original Sin, Spangenberg in turn was alienated from his Mansfeld colleagues, led by Menzel, who, Spangenberg insisted (to no avail), misinterpreted his and Flacius's intention. The Mansfelders met in several colloquies but could not reconcile their differences. Supported by Count Volrad, who established a printing press in the Mansfeld castle for his use, Spangenberg issued more than a dozen tracts in the ensuing controversy with his former friends inside and outside Mansfeld. In them he defended the teaching of the utter corruption of the human relationship with God and the use of Aristotelian language of "substance" in teaching this doctrine.

Spangenberg was exiled for his defense of his position when, on 7 September 1574, Joachim Friedrich of Brandenburg, administrator of the neighboring archbishopric of Magdeburg, sent armed troops to occupy Mansfeld and to rid it of the Flacians. This occupation was temporary, Spangenberg returned, but he fled again when the troops returned on New Year's day 1575. His pregnant wife was assaulted, and his mother was refused Communion on her deathbed in the ensuing occupation. Volrad supported him in exile in Sangerhausen, where in 1577 he met Jakob Andreae to discuss the Formula of Concord, which Spangenberg opposed because of its rejection of the Flacian position and its use in placing the church under princely control. Frustrated by Andreae's oversimplification and misunderstanding of his position, Spangenberg rejected the Concordianist effort. Driven from Sangerhausen, Spangenberg went to Strasbourg. He served as pastor in Schlitz (Hesse) from 1581 to 1591; thereafter, as a private scholar, he concentrated on preparing material for publication in several areas of learning.

Among the foremost Biblical exegetes of Luther's students, Spangenberg published a series of homiletic commentaries (1557–1564) on seven Pauline epistles—*Romans, 1 and 2 Corinthians, 1 and 2 Thessalonians, 1 Timothy,* and *Titus.* Proceeding from hermeneutic principles laid down in Luther's preface to *Romans,* he reworked for his readers sermons on these epistles that he had preached in Mansfeld. He analyzed the first eighteen books of the Old Testament (*Genesis* to *Job,* in 1563 and 1567, with further material prepared but not published), outlining them in table form; brief comments on the text were incorporated into the elaborate outlining, which was designed to aid readers in understanding its construction. This form, copied from his father and formed by Philipp Melanchthon's instruction in rhetoric and dialectic, anticipated Petrus Ramus's use of tables. Spangenberg's sermons on Christ's passion (1559) and other biblical texts were also widely circulated. The seventy "wedding sermons" in his *Ehespiegel* (1561) reflect Lutheran views of marriage and family. Spangenberg used the "Teufelsbuch" genre to criticize the hunting practices of the nobility and encouraged others to use the genre to attack other sins. His literary creativity produced German translations of several ancient Greek plays and popular religious literature, such as his *Formularbuechlein der alten Adamsprache* (1562). He composed hymns himself and compiled a hymnbook.

His sermons on Luther (1562–1571, reissued in 1589 as *Theander Luther*) analyze the reformer's contributions according to themes, not biographically, but nonetheless they did (along with the works of Johannes Mathesius and Ludwig Rabus) introduce the study of Luther's life and significance. His sermons on Luther's hymns, *Cithara Lutheri* (4 vols., 1569–1570), also present his understanding of Luther's theology.

Although he differed with Melanchthon and the Philippists on many matters of ecclesiastical policy and doctrine, Spangenberg reflected the methods of teaching that he had received from Melanchthon, above all in the assembly of collections of *loci* on several subjects. His *Adelspiegel* (2 vols., 1591 and 1594) collected classical, medieval, and contemporary materials regarding the nobility. A similar work, "Von der Musica und den Meistersaengern," remained unpublished until 1861 but presents a wide-ranging set of materials on music. He pursued historical studies—for example, in his biography of Girolamo Savonarola (1556) and in the composition of historical chronicles in the Melanchthonian style, including those on Mansfeld (1572; revised as the *Saxon Chronicle,* 1585), Henneberg (1598), Querfurt (1590), Holstein (1614), and the bishopric of Verden (1623).

Spangenberg was not only one of Luther's most devoted students but also among the most able and insightful. His involvement in the dispute over Original Sin limited his impact upon the ecclesiastical and theological developments of his day, but his influence through commentaries and other works helped shape Lutheran preaching and teaching in his time.

BIBLIOGRAPHY

Primary Sources

Rembe, Heinrich. *Der Briefwechsel des M. Cyriacus Spangenberg.* 2 vols. Dresden, 1887–1888. Correspondence from 1550 to 1584, vital for any further study of Spangenberg's career.
Spangenberg, Cyriakus. *Mansfeldische Chronica.* Eisleben, 1913.

Secondary Sources

Kawerau, Gustav. "Spangenberg, Cyriakus." In *Realenzyklopädie für protestantische Theologie und Kirche,* 3d ed., vol. 18, pp. 567–572.
Kolb, Robert. "The Flacian Rejection of the Concordia, Prophetic Style and Action in the German Late Reformation." *Archiv für Reformationsgeschichte* 73 (1982), 196–217. Spangenberg opposed the Formula and Book of Concord on grounds of its doctrine of original sin and its failure to confess the faith clearly.
———. "Philipp's Foes, but Followers Nonetheless: Late Humanism among the Gnesio-Lutherans." In *The Harvest of Humanism in Central Europe: Essays in Honor of Lewis W. Spitz,* edited by Manfred P. Fleischer, pp. 167–177. Saint Louis, 1992. Summary of Spangenberg's contributions to the writing of history and to literature.
Midelfort, H. C. Erik. "The German Nobility and Their Crisis of Legitimacy in the Late Sixteenth Century." In *Germania Illustrata: Essays on Early Modern Germany Presented to Gerald Strauss,* edited by Andrew C. Fix and Susan C. Karant-Nunn, pp. 217–242. Kirksville, Mo., 1992. Analysis of the *Adelspiegel* in the context of contemporary discussions of the nobility.
Verzeichnis der im deutschen Sprachbereich erschienenen Drucke des XVI. Jahrhunderts. Stuttgart, 1983–. See vol. 19, nos. 7465–7748.

ROBERT KOLB

SPANISH ARMADA. An ill-fated naval invasion of about 130 ships, the Spanish Armada (1588) was launched by Spanish king Philip II (r. 1556–1598) against England to encourage a Catholic rebellion that would remove Elizabeth I (r. 1558–1603) from the throne. By the mid-1580s events in Europe led Spain to consider seriously this "Enterprise of England," and it hoped to ensure progress of the Counter-Reformation by defeating an insurgent and interfering English navy on the high seas. Elizabeth had openly thrown her support to the Dutch rebels fighting against Spanish overlordship, provided sanctuary for the pretender to the Portuguese throne (Antonio, prior of Crato), given implicit sanction to Sir Francis Drake's attacks on Spanish ports, and, in a peace-shattering act, executed Mary Stuart, a Catholic, who was next in line to the English throne.

The invasion was placed in the hands of Alonso Pérez de Guzmán, duke of Medina-Sidonia, who proved to be a capable organizer and commander. Insurmountable logistical problems, however, doomed from the start the plan for the armada to rendezvous somewhere in the English Channel with the troops of Alessandro Farnese, duke of Parma, coming from the Netherlands. In England Lord Admiral Charles Howard readied about 100 ships at Plymouth, while Pérez de Guzmán, who had led the armada out of Lisbon on 30 May 1588, was forced on 19 June to resupply and make repairs at La Coruña. When the Spanish renewed the invasion four weeks later, the English fleet was caught off guard but now had the wind advantage as it moved out to sea. Skirmishes between the two navies in the channel off the coasts of Portsmouth, Plymouth, and the Isle of Wight between 31 July and 4 August were inconclusive, but the English could not break apart the armada's formidable crescent formation. Worried over the duke of Parma's delay, Pérez de Guzmán laid anchor on 6 August near Calais and dispatched an urgent but hopeless plea to the duke for help. The following day the English sent in eight fire ships, causing the armada to cut its cables and drift apart. Seizing an opportunity, Howard's men attacked with full force the next morning, and the resulting battle, begun off the coast of Gravelines, was the major engagement of the enterprise. English gunners fired broadside on the Spanish galleons and caused significant damage before strong gales forced the armada into the North Sea, whereupon it was decided to return to Spain by sailing north around Scotland and Ireland. The merciless wind and weather did greater harm than the fighting, yet two-thirds of the Spanish fleet survived, and the war continued while Spain rebuilt an even stronger navy.

The moral victory for the British could not be denied, however, even if circumstances had been more of a factor than military skill. Dutch independence was all but assured now, and Protestants in Holland, France, and Germany took heart at this monumental rebuff of Counter-Reformation forces. Soon the truth of the events surrounding the armada's defeat was lost in England, but a new confidence emerged in the late Elizabethan period, and Spain, forced to reevaluate its foreign policy, could no longer depend on the removal of Europe's most powerful Protestant monarch.

BIBLIOGRAPHY

Fernández-Armesto, Felipe. *The Spanish Armada: The Experience of War in 1588.* Oxford, 1988. A major revisionist work that argues Spain's "defeat" was mostly the result of bad weather and only marginally due to superior English tactics.

Martin, Colin, and Geoffrey Parker. *The Spanish Armada.* New York, 1988. This collaboration between an eminent underwater archaeologist and a military historian is the best of the many quadricentennial studies. Using the widest range of evidence it offers a measured correction of traditional views. Beautifully illustrated, too.

Pierson, Peter. *Commander of the Armada: The Seventh Duke of Medina Sidonia.* New Haven, 1989. Portrays a competent leader who was forced, against his own better judgment, to obey a king inept in military matters. Includes excellent maps and descriptions of the naval engagements.

Rodriguez-Salgado, M. J., and Simon Adams, ed. *England, Spain and the Gran Armada, 1585–1604: Essays from the Anglo-Spanish Conferences, London and Madrid, 1988.* Savage, Md., 1991. Collection of papers on themes connected with the armada, including navigation and strategy, medical services, the embargo of 1585, crusade ideology, and the army in Flanders.

Whiting, Roger. *The Enterprise of England. The Spanish Armada.* New York, 1988. Also making use of recent archaeological findings, this captivating retelling of events challenges the view that Philip intended a conquest of England, claiming instead that he wanted simply to eliminate English interference in Spanish affairs.

BEN LOWE

SPENGLER, Lazarus

SPENGLER, Lazarus (1479–1534), German lay leader of the Reformation and municipal secretary for the free imperial city of Nuremberg. Spengler's father had served as municipal secretary for some twenty years, and by the time Lazarus acquired the position (1507–1534), he had also been secretary of the municipal court (appointed 1497) and secretary in charge of municipal records (appointed 1501). Thus no aspect of the city's traditions, rights, obligations, and alliances remained unfamiliar to him. This fact accounted for his appointment as diplomat to numerous imperial, regional, and various other diets to represent Nuremberg's interests.

Spengler studied law at Leipzig before he returned to his native city, where he identified with the humanist elite that, by 1520, functioned as the vanguard for the popularization of Luther's views. This group of about sixteen people referred to itself as the *Sodalitas Celtica*, in honor of the work and visits of Conradus Celtis to the city. After Johannes von Staupitz gave a series of Advent and Lenten sermons there in 1516–1517, the humanists changed the name of the group to *Staupitziana*. Subsequently, when Luther stopped in Nuremberg in 1518 on his way both to and from his meeting with Cardinal Cajetan, the group became the *Martinianer*. Since a substantial number of these humanists were also members of the city government, which decided the religious stance of the city in Luther's favor in 1525—Spengler served as governmental spokesman for the religious changes already made—the humanists paved the way for the Reformation in Nuremberg.

Spengler's emergence as a lay leader of the Reformation stemmed from these contacts with Staupitz, Luther, and, shortly thereafter, Wenceslaus Linck. The secretary had copied a number of Staupitz's discussions on the Fall, predestination, and grace. In 1518 he also wrote *Schützred und christenliche antwurt ainserbarn liebhabers gotlicher warheit der hailigen geschrift* (Defense and Christian Reply of an Honorable Lover of Divine Truth . . .), an apology for Luther that, however, was published and reprinted anonymously. Because Johann Eck, Luther's major opponent, felt himself attacked by the *Schützred*, he caused Spengler and others to be included in the bull excommunicating Luther.

During the last fourteen years of his life, Spengler emerged as a major spokesman for the Lutheran movement, not only in Nuremberg but also throughout Franconia, Bavaria, and Swabia. By such writings as *Die haubtartickel durch welche gemeyne Christenheyt byßhere verfuhret worden ist* (Main Articles through Which Christendom Has Been Misled; 1522), his explanation of why Nuremberg acted as it had in religious affairs (1527), and *Eyn kurtzer außzug auß dem Bebstlichen rechten* (Excerpts from Papal Laws; 1529), Spengler influenced the practical development of the Reformation. These writings testified to his evangelical faith, which was acknowledged by the Nuremburg city government in its continued appointment of the secretary in religious affairs—for example, his work in drawing up the Schwabach Articles of Visitation (1528) and the Brandenburg-Nuremberg church order of 1533.

Perhaps most important was Spengler's advocacy, consistent with Luther's at the time, that Nuremberg had no right to resist the emperor militarily for the sake of religion. His insistence, in spite of repeated attempts to move him to the contrary, led to the city's refusal to join the Schmalkald League. Thus Nuremberg was spared much of the violence that occurred in the late 1540s.

BIBLIOGRAPHY

Engelhardt, Adolf. "Die Reformation in Nürnberg." *Mitteilungen des Vereins für Geschichte der Stadt Nürnberg* 33–34 (1936–1937). Useful for an overview of the city's reformation and for citation of unpublished materials.

Grimm, Harold J. *Lazarus Spengler: A Lay Leader of the Reformation.* Columbus, Ohio, 1978. First full-scale study in English; updates Schubert.

Schornbaum, Karl. *Zur Politik des Markgrafen Georg von Brandenburg vom Beginn seiner selbstständigen Regierung bis zum Nürnberger Anstand, 1528–1532.* Munich, 1906. Older work that draws on unpublished archival materials.

Schubert, Hans von. *Lazarus Spengler und die Reformation in Nürnberg.* Edited by Hajo Holborn. Quellen und Forschungen zur Reformationsgeschichte, vol. 17. Leipzig, 1934. Remains the most extensive work on Spengler although it does not deal with the later years of the secretary's life.

PHILLIP N. BEBB

SPENSER, Edmund (1552?–1599), English Protestant poet.

Spenser's earliest published work, a translation of Jan van der Noot's *Theatre for Worldings* (1569), reflects his Protestant concerns, especially in the four sonnets that epitomize subjects from *Revelation*. His matriculation at Cambridge in the same year put him in contact with such influential proponents of reform as Thomas Cartwright; and his subsequent service as secretary to John Young, bishop of Rochester, made matters of church politics central to his activities. Three eclogues ("Maye," "Julye," and "September") of his first original work, *The Shepheardes Calender* (1579), focus on ecclesiastical issues such as the controversy surrounding Archbishop Edmund Grindal, whom Spenser refers to allegorically under the name "Algrind." The initial installment of *The Faerie Queene* (1590) openly engages the Elizabethan religious question in its first book, "The Legende of the Knight of the Red Crosse, or of Holinesse," which is organized by prominent references to Protestant exegeses of *Revelation*. During Red Crosse's quest he thrice encounters beasts that primarily betoken the church of Rome in its evil enmity toward true religion. He slays the first of these, "Errour," and the third, which has been the object of his quest throughout the book.

Spenser's associations with Robert Dudley, earl of Leicester, and his circle put him in contact with militant Protestants such as Sir Philip Sidney and Robert Devereaux, earl of Essex. The idealism of his early involvement with reform at Cambridge became increasingly political and moderate as he bid for preferment from Elizabeth. Thus, his initial affinity for the inclinations of what became the Elizabethan Puritan movement subsided as the sixteenth century drew to a close. Spenser's lyric poetry, especially *Amoretti* and *Epithalamion* (1595), constitutes a watershed in the Protestant revaluation of married love in the light of both anti-Catholic animus against asceticism and pre-Reformation traditions of Petrachism and Neoplatonism.

BIBLIOGRAPHY

Hamilton, A. C., ed. *The Spenser Encyclopedia.* Toronto, 1990. Contains helpful articles on all facets of Spenser's career.

Hume, Anthea. *Edmund Spenser: Protestant Poet.* Cambridge, 1984. Affiliates Spenser with the Puritans, contra Whitaker, in seeking to trace the evolution of his Protestantism from *The Shepheardes Calender* to *The Faerie Queene.*

Judson, Alexander C. *The Life of Edmund Spenser.* Reprint, Baltimore, 1966. Standard life, which has not been superseded.

King, John N. *Spenser's Poetry and the Reformation Tradition.* Princeton, 1990. Presents Spenser as a Protestant poet especially attuned to the poetics of iconoclasm derived from the Reformation attack against idolatry.

Whitaker, Virgil K. *The Religious Basis of Spenser's Thought.* Stanford, 1950. Sees Spenser as a conservative Anglican hopeful of preserving as much as possible of the Catholic heritage.

LAWRENCE F. RHU

SPERATUS, Paul (1484–1551), German hymnist, theologian, and bishop, as well as a dominant figure in the

formation of the Lutheran church of Prussia. Born in Rötlen near Ellwangen in southwestern Germany, he studied in Freiburg, Paris, Italy, and Vienna and achieved the rank of doctor in philosophy, jurisprudence, and theology. After ordination as a priest in 1506, he was active in Salzburg and Dinkelsbühl until 1519, when he became cathedral preacher in Würzburg. For distinguished service to the church, he was elevated to noble status with the title of count palatine.

While in Würzburg Speratus began to associate with advocates of reform. He spoke out against corruption in the ecclesiastical hierarchy and demonstrated his opposition to celibacy by getting married. When a new bishop less open to church reform was appointed late in 1519, Speratus was forced to flee to Salzburg. In 1522, on his way to a new call in Ofen, Hungary, he preached a sermon in Vienna against monastic vows, prompting the theologians of that city to call for his excommunication. Speratus fled northward to Moravia and settled as city pastor in Jihlova (Iglau). His reform-minded preaching and writing soon came to the attention of the bishop of Olomouc (Olmütz), who cast him into prison. He was condemned to death as a heretic but, after twelve weeks of harsh punishment, received a pardon on condition that he leave Moravia. Speratus took refuge in Wittenberg, where he became acquainted with Martin Luther. From 1523 to 1524 he occupied himself with translating some of Luther's Latin writings into German. An accomplished writer of both Latin and German verse, he also composed three of the eight hymns in the first evangelical hymnbook, which Luther compiled in 1524. Most enduringly significant among these hymns was "Es ist das Heil uns kommen her," which he composed while in prison.

When Albert of Brandenburg, commander of the Teutonic Knights, requested help in introducing religious reforms to east Prussia, Luther recommended the appointment of Speratus as preacher in Königsberg. Albert converted the lands of his religious order into a secular duchy in 1525, and Speratus helped draft the church order that established an evangelical territorial church. He served on the commission that conducted the first church visitation in 1526, participated in the preparation of the first Prussian hymnbook in 1527, and was appointed bishop of Pomesanien in 1530.

From 1530 until his death, he exercised decisive leadership in establishing the theological norms and administrative structures of the Prussian church. His vigorous campaign against spiritualistic tendencies spread by Schwenckfelders and Dutch refugees persuaded Albert to issue a mandate in 1535 that strengthened the Lutheran identity of the territorial church. While he devoted much effort to the defense of Lutheran doctrine and the preservation of a conservative liturgy, he also labored to provide pastoral care for all the different ethnic groups that inhabited Prussia: Germans, Poles, Lithuanians, and immigrants from Bohemia and Hol-

land. Frequent illness gradually diminished his prominence after 1537, but he played a role in the theological controversies that developed after Andreas Osiander arrived in Königsberg in 1549.

BIBLIOGRAPHY

Tschackert, Paul. *Urkundenbuch zur Reformationsgechichte des Herzogthums Preussen* (1890). 3 vols. Reprint, Osnabrück, 1965. Collection of primary sources: letters by Speratus, etc.

———. *Paul Speratus von Rötlen: Evangelishcher Bischof von Pomesanien in Marienwerder.* Halle, 1891. Most extensive biographical study.

Verzeichnis der im deutschen Sprachbereich erschienenen Drucke des XVI. Jahrhunderts. Stuttgart, 1983–. See vol. 19, nos. 8269–8280.

ERIC LUND

SPEYER, PROTESTATION OF. In the recess of the first Diet of Speyer in 1526, it was left to each estate of the empire to proceed regarding the question of religion, that is, the implementation of the 1521 Edict of Worms, as it was deemed justifiable before "God and his imperial majesty." This freedom was limited until the convening of a council. With this formula, the Edict of Worms, which had banned Lutheran teaching, was de facto suspended. Various princes and imperial cities used the recess of 1526 to introduce the Reformation, or at least to promote it.

To inhibit this development, a proposition was presented by the imperial representative Ferdinand at the beginning of the second Diet of Speyer on 15 March 1529 to repeal the article on religion of 1526 on the grounds of its misuse and erroneous interpretation. Thus, at the same time the Edict of Worms was put back into force, again until the time of a council. A large working committee (*Grosser Ausschuss*) of the diet formulated new stipulations for the resolution of the religious question, which were to be incorporated into the recess: estates of the empire that had observed the Edict of Worms should stay with it; estates that had turned toward the Reformation ("where the different teachings had arisen") and that could not reverse the changes without risking rebellion should, where possible ("as is possible and humane"), introduce no further innovations; in territories and cities that had become Protestant, no one should be forbidden to hear the Mass or receive Communion in one kind; other teachings on the Lord's Supper were to be forbidden, as were Anabaptists; and clergy were to refrain from preaching anything that might incite the common people against the authorities, and they were not to discuss controversial questions. Clergy were to interpret the gospel according to the standard authorities approved by the church. Each government should implement book censorship. The confiscation of ecclesiastical or secular property was prohibited. All provisions were to be in force until the decision of a council.

In response to the committee's proposal, a group of evangelical estates coalesced according to their self-understanding: "those who had accepted the word of God." The group consisted of six rulers and fourteen imperial cities: Elector John of Saxony; Margrave George of Brandenburg-Ansbach; the dukes Ernst and Franz of Braunschweig-Lüneburg; Landgrave Philipp of Hesse; Prince Wolfgang of Anhalt; and the cities of Strasbourg, Nuremberg, Ulm, Constance, Lindau, Memmingen, Kempten, Nördlingen, Heilbronn, Reutlingen, Isny, St. Gall, Weissenburg, and Windsheim. Their opposition to the committee draft was dismissed by the overwhelming majority of electors and princes. At the same time, this majority demanded that within a year the emperor should convene a council that would meet no later than eighteen months afterward. If this council did not convene, a national council (a gathering of all estates of the German nation) was to take its place.

On 12 April 1529 the evangelical rulers submitted a written declaration to the diet that constituted an early draft of the subsequent protestation. They rejected the committee's document and announced they would not submit to the decision of the majority on a matter that concerned their consciences. Several imperial cities joined this declaration. On 19 April after the committee's draft had been accepted as a decision of the diet by the majority of the estates, King Ferdinand, and the imperial commissioners, the first protestation followed. It was rejected. Accordingly, the evangelical estates presented a second protestation on 20 April which repeated the previous day's arguments in greater detail.

The evangelical rulers protested against the following stipulations: (1) the binding nature of the Edict of Worms, in that it prevented future acceptance of the Reformation by estates still loyal to the pope; (2) the petrification of the ecclesiastical and liturgical status quo in the evangelical territories, which would have thwarted the still incomplete development of new church structures; (3) the undifferentiated ban of new teachings on Communion, which threatened the south German imperial cities close to Zwinglian theology, and, according to a strict interpretation, even those princes and cities that followed the Lutheran understanding of Communion; (4) the obligation to tolerate the Mass, but without the toleration of Protestant worship in the territories adhering to the Edict of Worms; and (5) the postulate of the binding force of majority decisions in questions of faith.

The protesting estates declared themselves willing to render the emperor and empire all obedience to which they were obligated; in matters concerning the salvation of souls and God's honor, however, God had to be obeyed above all. The reference to the *clausula Petri*, (Acts 5:29) is evident. As far as the Protestants were concerned, there could not be a collective decision in matters of conscience. If they agreed to the formula accepted by the majority, it amounted ultimately to a recognition of the binding nature of the Edict of Worms even in the evangelical territories and to a dis-

criminating relativization of the truth of the reform teachings. Consequently, they declared they would continue to adhere to the decisions of the first Diet of Speyer, and protested explicitly, in case the majority did not make concessions, against the articles on religion in the recess.

The protestation was buttressed both legally and religiously. Legally the Protestants submitted an appeal of rights, the premise of which was their sentiment—legally altogether contestable—that a unanimous decision, as had been the case in Speyer in 1526, could only be unanimously rescinded. Religiously they declared their conscience to be the final authority. But the Protestant estates did not recognize the same right to invoke conscience for their subjects so that, as regards the persecution of the Anabaptists, they were of the same opinion as the majority. Dogmatic statements in the sense of a substantive confession are not found in the protestation.

King Ferdinand did not accept the detailed protestation; thus its wording remained unknown to the majority of estates. Mediation attempts undertaken on behalf of the majority remained unsuccessful. The recess of the diet was drafted on 22 April 1529, including the controversial articles on religion, and no mention was made of the protestation. The potential danger of the religious stipulations was alleviated, however, when both sides promised not to attack the other for religious reasons.

Legally, the notion of a protestation was controversial. Since the diet had no firm standing orders at its disposal, there were also no regulations regarding the principle of majority rule. Usually the minority joined with the majority. Otherwise a majority decision lacked effective moral force.

The protestation received legal status through the appeal that the Protestant princes and imperial cities lodged before two notaries in Speyer on 25 April 1529. This appeal contained a report on the proceedings between majority and minority and all important documents. The text was immediately disseminated in print. The appeal was directed to a general council and to Charles V, who all the same immediately rejected the document presented to him by a delegation of the Protestant estates.

The appeal thwarted the execution of the recess of the diet. It was to be of great significance for the future of the constitution of the empire and the negotiations at future diets that in 1529 the individual conscience was established for the first time as a norm of decisions not to be outvoted in political negotiations. Against the positive law was set the conformity of the evangelical teachings to the scriptures; the legal act of protestation presupposed a religious decision. Clearly, the protesting estates intended no political separation.

The protestation of Speyer provided the Protestant estates with a new corporate identity. For the first time in the history of the Reformation, they came together in a common act of confession. By their unanimous stance, they made evident the existence of a separate religious-theological group in the empire differing from the majority of estates. The dangers associated with this stance triggered the development of this distinctive, religiously oriented group into a political community. Therefore electoral Saxony, Hesse, Nuremberg, Strasbourg, and Ulm agreed, while still in Speyer, on the essentials of an alliance in which they promised each other military aid in case of an attack. This alliance was also to be operative when, for reasons other than religious, military action was threatened; this included the possibility of an imperial ban.

The subsequent negotiations in 1529 to put the Speyer agreement into concrete form failed over the question of doctrine (Schwabach Articles, Colloquy of Marburg). Moreover, the question was raised about the right to resist the emperor, an idea opposed by Luther in a brief of 6 March 1530. A definitive verdict on an *exceptio Caesaris*, the exclusion of the emperor from the stipulations of the alliance, was not rendered, because the invitation to the Diet of Augsburg eased tensions.

The Protestant estates held firmly to their protestation and appeal, which, after Charles V's rejection, remained addressed only to the council, although in the recess of Augsburg in 1530, all appeals against it, as against earlier recesses, were explicitly declared invalid. The separate existence of Protestant estates was reinforced theologically in 1530 by the Augsburg Confession and politically by the Schmalkald League. The Protestation of Speyer lost its legal significance through the recognition of the Protestants (the elector of Saxony and his supporters) in the Peace of Nuremberg of 23 July 1532.

[See also Charles V; Diet; and Empire.]

BIBLIOGRAPHY

Becker, Hans-Jürgen. "Protestatio, Protest: Funktion und Funktionswandel eines rechtlichen Instruments." *Zeitschrift für historische Forschung* 5 (1978), 385–412.

Bornkamm, Heinrich. "Die Geburtsstunde des Protestantismus: Die Protestation von Speyer, 1529." In *Das Jahrhundert der Reformation. Gestalten und Kräfte*, pp. 112–125. 2d ed. Reprint, Frankfurt a.M., 1983.

Conrad, Hermann. "Ein Notariatsinstrument als rechtliche Form des Protestes und der Appellation in Glaubensfragen auf dem zweiten Reichstag zu Speyer, 1529." In *Festschrift für Alexander Knur*, pp. 55–64. Munich, 1972.

Friedensburg, Walter. *Der Reichstag zu Speier, 1526, im Zusammenhang der politischen und Kirchlichen Entwicklung Deutschlands im Reformationszeitalter* (1887). Reprint, Nieuwkoop, 1970.

Kühn, Johannes. *Die Geschichte des Speyrer Reichstags, 1529.* Leipzig, 1929. Detailed history of the diet.

Kühn, Johannes, ed. *Deutsche Reichstagsakten: Jüngere Reihe.* Stuttgart, 1935. Sources of the Diet of Speyer of 1529.

Ney, Julius, ed. *Die Appellation und Protestation der evangelischen Stände auf dem Reichstage zu Speier, 1529* (1906). Reprint, Darmstadt, 1967. Text of the appeal, along with editor's introduction.

Schlaich, Klaus. "Maioritas, protestatio, itio in partes, corpus Evangelicorum: Das Verfahren im Reichstag des Hl. Römischen Reichs

Deutscher Nation nach der Reformation." *Zeitschrift der Savigny-Stiftung für Rechtsgeschichte: Kanonistische Abteilung* 63 (1977), 264–299.

Steglich, Wolfgang. "Die Stellung der evangelischen Reichsstände und Reichsstädte zu Karl V. zwischen Protestation und Konfession, 1529/30." *Archiv für Reformationsgeschichte* 62 (1971), 161–192.

EIKE WOLGAST
Translated from German by Susan M. Sisler

SPIEßHEIMER, Johann. *See* Cuspinian, Johannes.

SPIRITUALISM.

This branch of the radical Reformation was the most thoroughgoing expression in the Reformation era of a religious impulse that has dominated the West since the end of the Middle Ages. All three of its major elements make their appearance in the eleventh and twelfth centuries: an antimaterialist bias, a growing individualism, and an emphasis on subjectivity and interior experience. Popular dualist heresies, such as Catharism, which viewed all matter as evil, were but the most extreme form that the suspicion of the material elements in Christianity took. The sacraments remained a lightning rod among dissenters throughout the later Middle Ages. Even within the church establishment, medieval Scholastic theology acknowledged a distinction between the material sacrament (*sacramentum*) and the spiritual reality (*res*) that it represented.

Accompanying the spiritualist distrust of the material was a new insistence upon the interior and the affective. Mysticism, which first came to prominence in the West during the twelfth century and then reached larger and larger sections of the population in the fourteenth and fifteenth centuries, was the most developed form of this inward-looking emotive piety. More broadly, the emphasis upon "devotion" in the later Middle Ages found expression in art, prayer, and even sacramental life. The church, for example, urged believers to achieve communion with Christ during the Mass by the devout commemoration of his life and death. This spiritual Eucharist provided a real participation in the body and blood of Christ even when the believer did not partake of the bread and wine, or even when that same believer was not physically present at a mass.

The emphasis upon the spiritual, the interior, and the subjective entailed a new religious individualism that also made its first appearance in the twelfth century. In the fourteenth and fifteenth centuries the popularity of books of hours for private meditation and prayer, of private chapels, and of confraternities and mendicant third orders for the laity, which gave individuals the opportunity to break out of the parish system and choose their own religious community, all point to the decay of the communalism of traditional Christianity. As a result, the later Middle Ages saw a profound malaise in liturgy, that most visible, public, and communal expression of Christianity. The trajectory was one that increasingly focused on the individual's direct access to God to the exclusion of the Church or any other mediatory agency. This spiritualization of the Christian experience was especially marked among urban dwellers, the literate, and the religiously earnest, the same groups that formed the initial audience for the Protestant Reformation.

All the leading figures of the era's reform—for example, Luther, Zwingli, Calvin, Erasmus, and Loyola—spiritualized the medieval heritage to a greater or lesser degree, condemning those who were less "spiritual" as fleshly and repudiating those who were more "spiritual" as Sacramentarians or *Schwärmer* ("fanatics"). Because the spiritualistic impulse was so pervasive and because the reformers were primarily concerned with distinguishing themselves from those more radical, the individuals who are now designated as spiritualists were simply lumped together with the Anabaptists and other radicals as *Schwärmer* by their more conservative Protestant opponents. Alfred Hegler (1892) was the first to identify Sebastian Franck as representing a distinctive type of Christian experience. Ernst Troeltsch (1912) expanded upon Hegler's insight and as a general theory posited individualistic spiritualism as a third form of Christian social organization alongside the church and the sect. The Quaker Rufus M. Jones (1914) specified a group of individuals in the sixteenth and seventeenth centuries as "spiritual reformers." Johannes Kühn (1923) recognized spiritualism as one of five primary forms of Protestantism. Nonetheless, it remained difficult to pinpoint exactly who was to be accounted a spiritualist. Alongside those readily recognized as such (Thomas Müntzer, Sebastian Franck, Kaspar von Schwenckfeld, Valentin Crautwald, Hans Bünderlin, Christian Entfelder, Johannes Campanus, Valentin Weigel, Dirk Volkertszoon Coornhert) are others with Anabaptist characteristics (Hans Denck, Ludwig Hätzer, David Joris, Hendrik Niclaes), while still others are difficult to classify in any sense (Michael Servetus, Sébastien Castellion, Andreas Bodenstein von Karlstadt, Theophrastus Paracelsus, Jakob Böhme). George Williams (1957) proposed distinguishing the spiritualists from the Anabaptists on the one hand and from evangelical rationalists (e.g., Unitarians) on the other. Within spiritualism he distinguished revolutionary spiritualism (Karlstadt, Müntzer, the Zwickau Prophets), rational spiritualism (Paracelsus, Weigel, Franck), and evangelical spiritualism (Schwenckfeld).

Part of the problem with defining and categorizing the spiritualists is that they had no Rome, Wittenberg, or Geneva to provide uniformity. Another reason is that, like Luther's theology, spiritualism evolved under the pressure of events and its own internal logic, achieving its classical expression only in the 1530s. Most moved to spiritualism by way of Luther, Zwingli, or Anabaptism. The two forces that drove them were a dissatisfaction with the results of the Protestant Reformation and a dualistic vision of the world that contrasted spirit and flesh, spirit and matter, and inner and outer. Most were convinced that they lived in a new age of the spirit to which the old, fleshly, outward ways would give way. Since for most the Catholic church was beyond the pale, spiritualists defined themselves by criticizing more conservative Protestant reformers on scripture, the sacraments, and the church.

Spiritualists distinguished an inner word, or spirit, from the outer word, or letter of scripture. It was only the inner word, communicated directly by the Holy Spirit, that brought a true living faith and rebirth, which transformed the believer into a new spiritual human being capable of, and required to live, the true Christian life. Only those who had first been illuminated and instructed by the inner word could appreciate and profit from the outer word. Luther's teaching that the Holy Spirit was conveyed through scripture and preaching was resolutely rejected, as was Luther's view of justification as imputed.

There was variation among the spiritualists, however, concerning the nature of the inner word and the fate of the outer. For Müntzer the inner word was a prophetic wind that brought an inner baptism of fire and with it revelations and eyes for the believer to see the real meaning of scripture. For Schwenckfeld the inner word was Christ himself, the substantial Word whom scripture and the sacraments described but did not convey. Franck equated the inner word with reason and seemed to consign scripture, along with the outward sacraments, to an earlier, less perfect, and now surpassed stage of Christian development.

The spiritualists also held a range of views on the nature of the church. Franck advocated a purely individualistic, invisible church of believers. By contrast Müntzer, drawing upon medieval Joachite and Taborite traditions, saw the spirit gathering together the godly into a visible and militant force. While Schwenckfeld awaited a new Pentecost that would reinstitute the spiritual church of the apostles, he encouraged the suspension of the outer sacraments and the formation of small, family-based conventicles for prayer and mutual consolation. For Schwenckfeld, Franck, and most spiritualists (but not Müntzer), their vision of the church made Protestant state churches and religious coercion useless and profoundly un-Christian. As a result, the spiritualists were the most consistent proponents of religious freedom in the sixteenth century.

Because of their emphasis on the spirit and their dualism, spiritualists often produced distinctive Christologies (e.g., "heavenly flesh," a theology that argues that Christ brought his flesh from heaven and did not receive it from his mother, the Virgin Mary) and trinitarian theologies (Unitarianism, Arianism). But it was a vision of the individual, the church, and their relationship to the state and larger society that made them truly significant. It is impossible to establish their numerical strength. Organized groups were found in Silesia and southern Germany (Schwenckfelders) and the Low

Countries (Davidjorists), but spiritualistic principles were pervasive among those called Libertines, Epicureans, and Nicodemites, as well as among countless others who, to all appearances, were solid Lutherans or Calvinists. Spiritualism was particularly popular among urban elites, professionals, and women, all of whom had reason to resent the "new papacy" of the Protestant established churches. Printing helped spread the message (Schwenckfeld was especially prolific), but many people may simply have drawn directly upon the same sources as the spiritualists (scripture, mystical treatises, Luther, Erasmus), because the sociological forces that had undergirded the spiritualist impulse since the twelfth century remained: urbanization, with its atomization and individualism, and rising rates of literacy. To these were added the dissatisfaction caused by the mutually exclusive claims of the competing churches and the disgust with the war and civil strife that those claims caused. In the late sixteenth and early seventeenth centuries, such figures as Valentin Weigel (1533–1588), Dirk Volkertszoon Coornhert (1522–1590), Jakob Böhme (1575–1624), as well as the Dutch Collegians and the sects of the English Civil War (particularly the Quakers), witness to a continuing tradition. They formed a bridge between the spiritualist impulse of the sixteenth century and its many heirs in the post-Reformation world. Late-seventeenth-century Pietism owed much to Anabaptism but betrayed a strong spiritualistic influence reminiscent of Schwenckfeld: the emphasis on the heart over the mind, the use of scripture as a contemplative tool rather than a source of doctrine, and the formation of conventicles within the official church. Franck's rationalistic spiritualism lived on in Enlightenment deism. For example, John Locke's *The Reasonableness of Christianity* (1695) provided a form of Christianity in which religious toleration made sense: the triumph of individual human reason over scripture and tradition, the reduction of Christianity to an inner state of mind and a code of ethics, the characterization of public worship as a human convention of no great value, and the demotion of the church to humanly contrived, voluntary associations. It was the pervasiveness of both these religious mentalities within most denominations in the nineteenth and twentieth centuries (particularly in North America) that alerted Hegler and Troeltsch to the existence of spiritualism and to its significance for both the Reformation and the modern world.

BIBLIOGRAPHY

Bornkamm, Heinrich. *Mystik, Spiritualismus und die Anfänge des Pietismus im Luthertum.* Giessen, 1926. Examination of the ties linking spiritualism to early Lutheran pietism.

Chenu, M. D. *L'Eveil de la conscience dans la civilisation médiéval.* Paris, 1969. Seminal work exploring the medieval origins of the modern concept of "conscience" and its broader implications.

Hegler, Alfred. *Geist und Schrift bei Sebastian Franck: Eine Studie zur Geschichte der Spiritualismus in der Reformationszeit.* Freiburg, 1892. Groundbreaking analysis of the concept of spiritualism.

Jones, Rufus M. *Spiritual Reformers in the 16th and 17th Centuries.* (1914). Reprint, Gloucester, Mass., 1971. First effort to categorize the spiritualists, seen from a Quaker perspective.

Klaassen, Walter. "Spiritualization in the Reformation." *Mennonite Quarterly Review* 37 (1963), 67–77. Study of the process of spiritualization with special regard for the Anabaptists.

Kühn, Johannes. *Toleranz und Offenbarung.* Berlin, 1923. Very influential study of theories of religious toleration that gives special attention the spiritualists.

Morris, Colin. *The Discovery of the Individual, 1050–1200.* Reprint, Toronto, 1987. Very influential study of the origins of modern individualism.

Ozment, Steven E. *Mysticism and Dissent: Religious Ideology and Social Protest in the Sixteenth Century.* New Haven and London, 1973. Study of the influence of medieval mysticism on a number of Reformation dissenters.

Rupp, Gordon. "Word and Spirit in the First Years of the Reformation." *Archive for Reformation History* 49 (1958), 13–26. Examines the dialectic of word and spirit in the early Reformation.

Troeltsch, Ernst. *Social Teachings of the Christian Churches* (1912, in German). 2 vols. Reprint, Louisville, Ky., 1992. Places spiritualism as one of the three main types of Christian social organization.

Williams, George H. *Spiritual and Anabaptist Writers.* Reprint, Philadelphia, 1977. Collection of treatises by spiritualists and Anabaptists in translation with an important programmatic introduction.

———. *Radical Reformation.* 3d ed. Kirksville, Mo., 1992. Magisterial overview of the entire radical Reformation.

R. EMMET MCLAUGHLIN

SPIRITUALITY. *See* Piety.

STANCARUS, Francis (Ital., Francesco Stancaro; c.1501–1574), heterodox Italian reformer. Stancarus was born in Mantua, in central Italy, probably to a Jewish family. He was a scholar and *homo trium linguarum* ("man of three languages"), although he never learned German. He served as a Catholic priest and as a lecturer at the University of Padua. About 1540 he became a Protestant, was imprisoned, and then fled to Switzerland, where he married (his second wife would be a Pole).

In 1544 he applied for a professorship at the University of Vienna, but after two years the Habsburg authorities expelled him for his religious views. After wandering about southern Germany and Hungary, Stancarus arrived in Poland in 1549. He lectured in Hebrew as a professor at the University of Kraków, but soon found himself again in prison. He was released by the Protestant nobility, and in the fall of 1550 he was in Pińczów, the capital of the Minor Poland Reformation. Persecuted in Poland, Stancarus spent the summer of 1551 among the Lutherans in Prussian Königsberg, debating passionately with the adherents of Andreas Osiander on Christ's mediation between God and humanity. Stancarus did agree with some aspects of the moderate Lutheran Reformation, however, and advocated the supremacy of the secular authority over the church. Nevertheless, the thesis of his *De Mediatore*, which asserted that Christ's mediation was solely according to his human nature, was unique among Protestants. An enemy of antitrinitarianism, his christological views indirectly helped its spread in Poland and Hungary. He also showed a strong interest in the Old Testament.

Diligent, quick acting, and erudite, Stancarus prepared over fifty treatises during his life. As early as 1547 he published the monumental *Opera nuova della riformatione . . .*, in which he advised the Venetian seigniory on how to create a Protestant state church in the city. During his stay in Brandenburg in 1552, he published his most famous work, *Canones reformationis ecclesiarum Polonicarum*, in which he advised the king of Poland to follow the example of the archbishop of Cologne and establish a national church.

During his stay in Hungary from 1555 to 1559, Stancarus frequently debated with evangelical ministers. He returned to Minor Poland in 1559. Stancarus carried on a furious battle of words with Jan Łaski at Protestant synods that were held in Pińczów. He managed to gain some followers, including the rector of the Pinczovian school, Gregory Orszak of Oświęcim, the writer Andrew Frycz Modrzewski, and Jerome Ossoliński, the politically active nobleman.

Between 1559 and 1563 it looked as if a Stancarian church might be created, but this chance was missed since Stancarus was an indomitable quarreler. Until 1563 Dubiecko, a little town owned by a Stancarian, Stanislas Mathew Stadnicki, on the Ruś Chervona–Minor Poland border, was his main abode. After Stadnicki's death, Stancarus had to escape to Moldavia because of Catholic opposition, but he soon returned to Stopnica, which was owned by the Zborowscy family, who sympathized with his views. He stayed there until his death on 12 November 1574. Although most of the Stancarians joined the Calvinist church at the meeting held in Sandomierz in April 1570, at the end of that year Stancarus issued an abridged version of the thirty-eight articles of his confession under the title *Summa fidei Christianae. . . .*

According to the Catholic polemicist Stanislas Orzechowski, Stancarus was an eccentric, short-lived, and destructive chimera. He destroyed the unity of the Minor Poland Protestants and contributed to the downfall of the Reformation movement there. His son, Francis Stancarus the Younger, became a superintendent of the Minor Poland Calvinists and entered the Polish nobility.

BIBLIOGRAPHY

Hein, Lorenz. *Italienische Protestanten und ihr Einfluß auf die Reformation in Polen während der beiden Jahrzehnte vor dem Sandomirer Konsens 1570.* Leiden, 1974.
Ossoliński, Józef Maksymilian. "Franciszek Stankar." In *Wiadomości historyczno-krytyczne do dziejów literatury polskiej*, vol. 4. Lvov, 1851.
Ruffini, Francesco. "Francesco Stancaro." In *Studi sui riformatori italiani*. Turin, 1955.
Urban, Wacław. "Die großen Jahre der stancarianischen 'Häresie,' 1559–1563." *Archiv für Reformationsgeschichte* 81 (1990), 309–318.
———. "Canones reformationis ecclesiarum Polonicarum di Francesco Stancaro." In *Zeszyty Naukowe Uniwersytetu Jagiellońskiego.* Prace historyczne, no. 94. Kraków, 1991.
———. *Dwa szkice z dziejar reformacji.* Kielce, 1991.
Wotschke, Theodor. "Francesco Stancaro." *Altpreußische Monatsschrift* 47 (1910).

WACŁAW URBAN

STANŠIČ HORVÁTH DE GRADECZ, Gregor

(also Stansith de Gradec; 1558–1597), founder and professor of the secondary school in Strážky, Slovakia, as well as polemist-defender of Luther's teachings. Born in Körmend, Hungary, he studied at the universities in Padua, and Strasbourg. In 1581 he returned home and in about 1588 he founded a three-year secondary school in Strážky. There Horváth lectured on dialectics, rhetoric, and ethics. He also founded an extensive library and twice a week led public disputations in Latin on theological issues. The school was under the influence of Luther's Reformation, and philosophy and theology were the most important subjects. Horváth brought in a number of professors from Germany, including Albert Grawer (1575–1617) and the Slovak Eliáš Láni.

In 1591 Horváth, together with Severín Šcultéty, defended the teachings of the Lord's Supper in accordance with the Formula of Concord against Stephen Beythe, who preferred the Calvinist position. At Kežmarok castle in December 1595 and January 1596, Horváth, along with Albert Grawer, Eliáš Láni, and others defended their teachings against the crypto-Calvinist Sebastian Lam, who denied Christ's presence in the Lord's Supper. The defence was characterized by two major ideas: insistence on the real presence of Christ's body and blood in the Lord's Supper and opposition to removing altars, sculptures, pictures, and organs from churches and to correcting spiritual songs in the spirit of crypto-Calvinists. Just one year later, in 1597, Horváth died in Strážky.

BIBLIOGRAPHY

Kvačala, Ján. *Dejiny reformácie na Slovensku.* Liptovský Mikuláš, 1935.
Weber, Samuel. *Gradéczi Horváth Stansith Gergely és családja.* Kežmarok, 1896.

ANDREJ HAJDUK

STAPLETON, Thomas

(1535–1598), English theologian and controversialist, called by an Oxford chronicler of the seventeenth century "the most learned Roman Catholic of all his time." Born at Henfield, Sussex, Stapleton was educated at Winchester and New College, Oxford, of which he was elected fellow in 1553. In 1558 he was ordained a priest and awarded a prebend in Chichester Cathedral. The accession of Queen Elizabeth I later that year and the subsequent passage of the acts of Supremacy and Uniformity induced Stapleton to depart England for the Low Countries.

"Fearing the contagion of schism in my tender years," he wrote, "I came a fugitive to the learned benches of Louvain." The appeals of his family brought him back to England in 1563; when presented the oath of supremacy by the bishop of Chichester, however, he refused to take it and returned to the Low Countries, where he resided for the rest of his life.

In 1569 Stapleton participated in the foundation of the English college at Douai. At various times he taught at the university there as well as at Louvain, and in 1590 Philip II appointed him regius professor of scripture at Louvain. During 1585–1586 he tried his vocation as a Jesuit but discovered that he was unsuited by temperament and habit to join the Society of Jesus, for which, however, he maintained a high opinion.

Stapleton's earliest controversial works—*Fortresse of the Faith* and *A Counterblast*—were written in English and deal specifically with the religious situation in England. He also translated into English the Venerable Bede's *Historia ecclesiastica.* After 1570 Stapleton wrote prolifically in Latin, intending, he said, to counter "the poisons of Calvin and Bèze." Most significant among these later treatises are *Principiorum fidei doctrinalium demonstratio* (1578) and *Auctoritatis ecclesiasticae defensio* (1592). In 1588 he published his most famous work, *Tres Thomae*, which includes an early biography of Thomas More. Stapleton's *Omnia opera* were published in four large volumes in Paris in 1620.

BIBLIOGRAPHY

Primary Source

Stapleton, Thomas. *Opera quae extant omnia, nonnulla auctius et emendatius.* . . . Paris, 1620. Microfilm ed., London, 1989.

Secondary Sources

O'Connell, Marvin R. *Thomas Stapleton and the Counter Reformation.* New Haven, 1964.
Schützeichel, Herbert. *Wesen und Gegenstand der kirchlichen Lehrautorität nach Thomas Stapleton.* Trier, Germany, 1966.
Seybold, Michael. *Glaube und Rechtfertigung bei Thomas Stapleton.* Paderborn, 1967.
Verzeichnis der im deutschen Sprachbereich erschienenen Drucke des XVI. Jahrhunderts. Stuttgart, 1983–. See vol. 19, nos. 8610–8621.

MARVIN R. O'CONNELL

STAPULENSIS, Faber. *See* Lefèvre d'Étaples, Jacques.

STARINUS, Michael. *See* Sztárai, Michael.

STARKEY, Thomas (c. 1495–1538), English humanist and political thinker. Starkey has long been accorded a central role in the ideological origins of Anglicanism and considered a major follower of Marsilio of Padua. As an intimate of Reginald Pole, he also enjoyed a brief moment at center stage in the Henrician Reformation.

Starkey was educated at Magdalen College, Oxford (M.A. 1521), Padua (probably 1521–1526 and 1533–1534), and perhaps Paris. He studied subjects from natural science to law, together with the extracurricular topic closest to his heart, current politics (especially the model of Venice). A convinced Aristotelian as a result, Starkey had no need of Marsilio to undergird his famous "Dialogue between Pole and Lupset," written between 1529 and 1532. The work was intended initially as encouragement to Pole to enter royal service and later as a blueprint for the more general aristocratic reform of England.

In 1534 Thomas Cromwell responded to Starkey's request for employment and put him to work, first as an intelligencer for Italy and then as a writer of popular propaganda. *The Exhortation to the People Instructing Them to Unity and Obedience* (1536) is the most tangible result. Although the work remained virtually without influence, it has been considered important because of Starkey's use of *adiaphora,* or things indifferent, to justify the Anglican *via media.* In fact, that aspect of the work arose more from Cromwell's direction than Starkey's own inclination and was consistent with official policy since at least 1533. Although more muted in the *Exhortation* than it was in the "Dialogue," Starkey's greatest intellectual and religious significance lies rather in his conciliarism. In politics his continued friendly relations with both Pole and Henry VIII until near the end of his life made him a good marker of the fluid circumstances of the middle years of the Henrician Reformation.

BIBLIOGRAPHY

Elton, G. R. *Reform and Renewal: Thomas Cromwell and the Common Weal.* Cambridge, 1973. Most informative work on Starkey's reforming efforts in their English context.
Mayer, Thomas F. *Thomas Starkey and the Commonweal: Humanist Politics and Religion in the Reign of Henry VIII.* Cambridge, 1989. Revisionist interpretation of Starkey's thought and life.
Mayer, Thomas F., ed. *Thomas Starkey: A Dialogue between Pole and Lupset.* Royal Historical Society, Camden Fourth Series no. 37. London, 1989. Diplomatic edition of Starkey's best-known work.
Zeeveld, W. Gordon. *Foundations of Tudor Policy.* Cambridge, Mass., 1948. Basic work on Pole's circle.

THOMAS F. MAYER

STAUPITZ, Johann von (1460/69–1525), vicar-general of the observant Augustinians, provincial of the Saxon province of the Hermits of Saint Augustine, abbot of Saint Peter's Benedictine cloister in Salzburg, and ecclesiastical superior and spiritual adviser of the young Martin Luther. Staupitz was educated at Leipzig, Cologne, and Tübingen, served as prior of Augustinian houses in Tübingen and Munich, and was appointed dean of the theological faculty at the newly founded University of Wittenberg by his child-hood friend, the elector Frederick III of Saxony. In 1503 he was elected vicar-general of the Reformed congregation of the Hermits of Saint Augustine, an association of observant Augustinians scattered throughout four provinces of the order: Saxony, Rhenish-Swabia, Cologne, and Bavaria. In 1509 he was elected provincial of Saxony as well. Because the Augustinian generals were opposed to the fragmentation of the order in German-speaking territories, Staupitz was charged with the task of integrating the reformed congregation into the Saxon province. In the end his attempt to merge them failed because of the implacable opposition of large observant houses such as Nuremberg and Erfurt, who appealed to the pope against the leadership of their own order.

Although Staupitz was unsuccessful in reuniting the Augustinian observants and conventuals, he nevertheless prospered as an ecclesiastical administrator and gained a reputation as a preacher and spiritual counselor. In Tübingen he preached a series of sermons on *Job* (1497/98) that were preserved in manuscript and printed in two critical editions in the twentieth century. He was himself not fond of these early sermons and remarked wryly that he feared he had afflicted *Job* with a worse plague than boils. He preached additional series of sermons in Salzburg (1512/13, 1518, 1519, 1520, 1523), Nuremberg (1516, 1517, 1518), and Munich (1517). Many of his later sermons were reworked and published as pamphlets, including an important treatise on predestination.

In no city was Staupitz more popular than in Nuremberg, where a circle of friends formed a sodality around him. This so-called *Sodalitas Staupitziana* numbered in its membership many of the more prominent citizens of Nuremberg, including Lazarus Spengler, the city secretary, Albrecht Dürer, the artist, and Christoph Scheurl, a former colleague from the University of Wittenberg. The sodality provided an important community of support for Staupitz. Scheurl translated his treatise on predestination into German, and an unnamed member of the sodality preserved his "table talk," a collection of edifying extracts from his conversations.

At the heart of Staupitz's theology was his doctrine of election. Whereas some medieval theologians thought that election was nothing more than the response of God to foreseen human behavior, Staupitz thought it was another name for the gracious initiative of God toward sinners, grounded in the mystery of uncreated love, unmotivated by human thought or action, and incapable of reduction to simple rational intelligibility. He was confident that human salvation begins with and rests at every point on such election.

Staupitz's stress on the initiative of God in election led him to redefine the doctrine of justification. The entire medieval tradition had defined justifying grace as the grace that makes men and women pleasing to God. This definition seemed to Staupitz to mirror inadequately the nature of God's act. It was not justification but election that made men and women pleasing to God. The function of the grace given in justification was to make God pleasing to human beings. Staupitz commended this robustly Augustinian theology to his listeners and readers, among them his troubled protégé, Martin Luther.

During his early years in the Augustinian order, Luther had sought out Staupitz as a confessor and spiritual adviser. Staupitz attempted to help, but found it difficult to understand the complexity and depth of the spiritual torment through which Luther was passing. While Luther was clearly suffering from a crisis prompted by an overly scrupulous conscience, he was also depressed by a deeper and darker tangle of anxieties that baffled Staupitz. Nevertheless, in spite of his limited understanding of Luther's problems, Staupitz was able to help him see the positive purpose of God in the temptations that assailed him and to understand and embrace a more Augustinian view of grace and predestination. Luther later confessed that he would be an "ungrateful papistical ass" if he did not acknowledge the enormity of the debt he owed Staupitz.

Part of that debt was practical and mundane. Because Staupitz was busy in his administrative activities as vicar-general and provincial, he had little time to spend as professor at Wittenberg. He therefore encouraged Luther to earn a doctor's degree in theology and assume the chair Staupitz felt he could no longer fill. As Luther later recounted the story, he opposed the suggestion that he become a theologian with a long list of excuses, only to have them all wittily countered by Staupitz, who was not to be thwarted in this matter. In 1512 Luther was inaugurated as professor of Bible at Wittenberg, a position that he kept until his death in 1546.

When the indulgence controversy broke out in Germany in 1517, Staupitz at first stood by Luther, though he urged him to consider the possibility of recantation. Even when Luther was summoned before Cardinal Cajetan, Staupitz joined him in Augsburg and attempted to mediate the dispute. As soon as it became clear to Staupitz that the dispute could not be mediated and that Luther was in danger of arrest, he released Luther from his vows so that he could act with greater freedom.

In 1520 Staupitz resigned as vicar-general of the Augustinian observants in order to accept an invitation from Cardinal Lang to become a preacher and adviser at his court in Salzburg. In 1521 he received permission from Rome to leave the Augustinian order and join the Benedictine monastery in Salzburg, where he was promptly consecrated as abbot. Although in his last letter to Luther in 1524 Staupitz compared his love for Luther to the love David bore for Jonathan, he also made clear he was not completely in sympathy with the direction the Reformation had taken. It seemed to him that the adherents of the new movement had made issues of conscience out of matters that were theologically neutral and had abused the freedom of the gospel by their conduct.

Shortly after composing his reply to Luther, Staupitz died (28 December 1524). His body was buried in the Benedictine monastery in Salzburg. While Staupitz had not broken communion with the Catholic church and had even attempted to put some distance between himself and Luther, his works were nevertheless placed on the Index of Prohibited Books by Pope Paul IV in 1559.

BIBLIOGRAPHY

Primary Sources

Knaake, J. F. K. *Johannis Staupitii, opera quae reperiri poterant omnia: Deutsche Schriften.* Potsdam, 1867. See vol. 1.
Staupitz, Johann von. *Sämtliche Schriften: Abhandlungen, Predigten, Zeugnisse, Lateinische Schriften.* 2 vols. Edited by Lothar Graf zu Dohna and Richard Wetzel. Spätmittelalter und Reformation, Texte und Untersuchungen, vols. 13–14. Reprint, Berlin and New York, 1987.

Secondary Sources

Steinmetz, David C. *Misericordia Dei: The Theology of Johannes von Staupitz in Its Late Medieval Setting.* Studies in Medieval and Reformation Thought 4. Leiden, 1968.
———. *Luther and Staupitz: An Essay in the Intellectual Origins of the Protestant Reformation.* Duke Monographs in Medieval and Renaissance Studies 4. Durham, N.C., 1980.
Wolf, Ernst. *Staupitz und Luther: Ein Beitrag zur Theologie des Johannes von Staupitz und deren Bedeutung für Luthers theologischen Werdegang.* Quellen und Forschungen zur Reformationsgeschichte 9. Leipzig, 1927.
Wriedt, Markus, *Gnade und Erwählung: Eine Untersuchung zu Johann von Staupitz und Martin Luther.* Veröffentlichungen des Instituts für europäische Geschichte Mainz, Abteilung Religionsgeschichte, vol. 141. Mainz, 1991.

DAVID C. STEINMETZ

STEPHEN BÁTHORY

STEPHEN BÁTHORY (Hung., István; 1533–1586), ruler of Transylvania (1571–1576) and king of Poland (1576–1586). Báthory descended from the junior (Somlyói) branch of an ancient aristocratic family in Hungary. As a youth he studied at Padua and also spent time at the court of Ferdinand I. In 1571 after the death of János Zsigmond Zápolya he was elected ruler of Transylvania, and five years later Báthory became king of Poland. His younger brother Kristóf succeeded him in Transylvania, but even as Polish king Báthory played an integral role in the government of his former possession in eastern Hungary. The acquisition of the Polish crown encouraged Báthory to make plans for a united Christian effort to drive the Turks out of Europe. This scheme came to nothing, however, and Báthory achieved his greatest political and military successes in the eastern Baltic against Ivan III Vasilyevich ("the Terrible").

Although Báthory was a devout Catholic, he practiced toleration toward most Protestants. In both Transylvania and Poland he ruled over large, influential, and well-organized Protestant nobilities. Consequently practical politics demanded that Báthory refrain from any aggressive confessional policies. Nevertheless he sought to limit further expansion and radicalization of Protestantism by encouraging Calvinist opposition to Unitarianism. Furthermore Báthory enthusiastically promoted the fortunes of Catholicism through encouraging conversions to the old church and improved education.

His chief weapons for fostering a revival of Catholicism were close diplomatic relations with Rome and extensive use of the Jesuits. As early as 1571 Báthory had attempted to bring the Jesuits to Transylvania, but his effort was foiled by the excessive caution of the Jesuit leadership in Vienna. After he became king of Poland Báthory became a great patron of the Society of Jesus and promoted its efforts vigorously in both Poland and Transylvania. With Báthory's strong political and financial backing the Jesuits quickly established schools at Kolozsvár (Cluj), Nagyvárad (Oradea Mare), and Gyulafehérvár (Alba Iulia) in Transylvania.

An even more expansive effort to strengthen Jesuit influence and Catholic education was undertaken by Báthory in Poland. By the time he died in 1586 the Jesuits had founded twelve colleges along with numerous residences and missions scattered all over the kingdom. In Transylvania the Counter-Reformation collapsed after Báthory's death, but in Poland he succeeded in laying the foundation for the seventeenth-century Catholic revival.

BIBLIOGRAPHY

Makkai, László, et al., eds. *Erdély története* (A History of Transylvania). 3 vols. Budapest, 1987. A thoughtful recent synthesis by members of the Hungarian Institute for Historical Studies.
Pollard, A. F. *The Jesuits in Poland.* New York, 1971. Although he erroneously claims that Báthory converted to Catholicism, Pollard's work was based on Jesuit archives and includes much useful information.
Reddaway, W. F., et al., eds. *The Cambridge History of Poland.* 2 vols. New York, 1971. Vol. 1 contains a good summation of Báthory's reign in Poland.
Veress, Andreas, ed. *Epistolae et Acta Jesuitarum Transylvaniae Temporibus Principium Batory.* Vol. 2. Budapest, 1913.
Veress, Endre, ed. *Báthory István erdélyi fejedelem és lengyel király levelezése* (The Correspondence of of Stephen Báthory, Ruler of Transylvania and King of Poland). 2 vols. Kolozsvár, 1944.

PETER SCHIMERT

STEUCO, Agostino

STEUCO, Agostino (1497–1548), Italian humanist, Old Testament scholar, Neoplatonist, and Counter-Reformation polemicist. Born in the Umbrian town of Gubbio, Steuco joined at the age of sixteen the Augustinian Canons of the Congregation of San Salvatore of Bologna. From this order of learned monks he received a humanist education and a spirituality based on Christian Neoplatonism. Completing his education in 1525, he was sent to Venice, where he began teaching and writing in the congregation's house of Sant Antonio di Castello. Steuco quickly rose within the order and from 1529 to 1536 served as prior of several houses of canons in northern Italy. His writings attracted the attention of Paul III, and in 1536 the pope called him to the papal court. In 1538 the pope made Steuco bishop of Kisamos and appointed him Vatican librarian, and in 1547 he sent Steuco to the Council of Trent to help represent papal interests. When the council was suspended in February 1548, he traveled to Venice, where he became suddenly ill and died in March of the same year.

Steuco's annotations on the Pentateuch (1529) marked a major advance in Old Testament studies. Using Hebrew manuscripts, he corrected numerous errors in Jerome's Vulgate Latin text, which had been poorly translated or corrupted over the centuries. He subjected both the Hebrew and Latin texts to close paleographic and grammatical analysis and offered solid conjectures as to why Jerome had mistranslated a particular word or phrase into Latin. To arrive at a literal, historical understanding of the Old Testament, he used Rashi (Shlomo Yitzhaqi), Ibn Ezra, David Kimchi, and the Aramaic Targums, while shunning Cabbalistic or allegorical interpretations.

In Venice Steuco attacked reform efforts based on Pauline spirituality in his *Pro religione christiana adversus Lutheranos* (1530). He carefully shaded his arguments to demonstrate how the criticisms of Martin Luther, Desiderius Erasmus, and the Italian *Spirituali* posed a serious threat to Venetian political and social institutions that long had been given legitimacy through close association with the sacred. This emphasis on the social and political necessity of Catholic rituals and late medieval forms of piety was characteristic of Steuco's Counter-Reformation thought. His attacks on Erasmus in his annotations and the *Adversus Lutheranos* were instrumental in creating the image of Erasmus as a partisan of Lutheran reform in Italy. These attacks provoked an angry letter from Erasmus in April 1531, to which he responded in August of the same year.

At the papal court he attempted to justify the Renaissance papacy's role as both a temporal and spiritual power. His *Contra Laurentium Vallam de falsa donatione Constantini* (1547) is an excellent example of the sophisticated philological and historical analysis produced in pre-Tridentine Italy to counter the historical and textual arguments advanced by humanist critics of the late medieval church.

Neoplatonic mysticism closely paralleled Pauline spirituality in its emphasis on individual piety and its inherent tendency to reject good works as necessary for salvation. Aware of this danger, Steuco articulated a defense of the doctrines and practices of the church based on his Neoplatonism. Following the thought of Marsilio Ficino, he argued that mankind had been created in God's image and imbued with an innate knowledge of the creator. Weaker souls, he argued, needed rituals and ceremonies to awaken this innate knowledge of God and sustain them in their piety. Steuco's Neoplatonism, evident throughout his polemical works, was given fullest expression in his *De perenni philosophia* (1540).

BIBLIOGRAPHY

Delph, Ronald K. "Polishing the Papal Image in the Counter-Reformation: The Case of Agostino Steuco." *Sixteenth Century Journal* 23.1 (1992), 35–47. Shows the Neoplatonic element in Steuco's Counter-Reformation thought.

———. "From Venetian Visitor to Curial Humanist: The Development of Agostino Steuco's Counter-Reformation Thought." *Renaissance Quarterly* 47 (1994), 102–139. Sets Steuco's Counter-Reformation humanism within the social and civic context of Renaissance Venice and Rome.

Freudenberger, Theobald. *Augustinus Steuchus aus Gubbio, Augustinerchorherr und päpstlicher Bibliothekar (1497–1548)*. Münster, 1935. Provides basic information on the career and works of Steuco, but lacks a fundamental understanding of the role of late medieval religion in the social and civic life of Italy. Hence it neglects a major impetus for Steuco's Counter-Reform activities.

Schmitt, Charles B. "Perrenial [sic] philosophia: From Agostino Steuco to Leibniz." *Journal of the History of Ideas* 27 (1966), 505–532. Examines the philosophical antecedents of Steuco's Neoplatonism.

Verzeichnis der im deutschen Sprachbereich erschienenen Drucke des XVI. Jahrhunderts. Stuttgart, 1983–. See vol. 19, nos. 8933–8935.

RONALD K. DELPH

STEWART, HOUSE OF. *See* Stuart, House of.

STIFEL, Michael (also Styfel; 1486/87–1567), evangelical theologian and preacher, numerologist, and mathematician. After abandoning the Augustinian monastic life (1522), Stifel became an ardent follower and personal friend of Luther, whose recommendations were instrumental in Stifel's appointments to various preaching posts. Stifel also benefited from Luther's intercession when Prince Johann Friedrich threatened imprisonment following Stifel's public prediction and involvement of the community of Lochau in preparations for Judgment Day (19 October 1533, 8:00 A.M.).

Stifel was noted for his persistent use of numerology to interpret the books of *Revelation* and *Daniel* and to decipher phrases and titles related to the papacy in ways that indicated a connection with the Antichrist. Although his numerological methods have never been satisfactorily explained, his use of word calculations based on the Latin alphabet brought him attention if not support from his contemporaries. The one brief period during which he abandoned this interest was after Luther expressed misgivings about the value of such calculations. Stifel's mystical interpretations of *Revelation* and *Daniel* led him to the conviction that Luther was a saint chosen by God to reveal the treachery of the Antichrist.

The literary expressions of his views in poetry and prose reveal skill in the use of German in original efforts or to convey concepts and images from Latin sources. His song "Der X. Psalm" (The Tenth Psalm) was included in a Wittenberg hymnbook (1524) and in many other hymnals.

Stifel's apocalyptic interpretations combined with his admiration for Luther as an avenging angel contributed to his sense of the imminence of the last days and led to an extended satirical, polemical dispute with Thomas Murner (1523). His controversial views and behavior also led him into the dispute between Andreas Osiander and Matthias Flacius Illyricus in support of a friend, Joachim Mörlin, and in opposition to Osiander. In later years, Stifel turned his attention to scholarly applications of mathematics, producing his *Arithmetica integra* (1544) and *Deutsche Arithmetica*, in which he provided a survey of traditional mathematical and algebraic knowledge and original contributions relevant to the discovery of logarithms and the application of binomial coefficients.

BIBLIOGRAPHY

Berger, A. E. *Lied-, Spruch-, und Fabeldichtung im Dienste der Reformation: Deutsche Literatur in Entwicklungsreihen.* Reihe Reformation, col. 4. Leipzig, 1938; reprint, Darmstadt, 1967. Standard collection of sixteenth-century German literary texts.

Clemen, O. *Flugschriften aus den ersten Jahren der Reformation.* 4 vols. Halle, Germany, 1906–1911; reprint, Nieuwkoop, Netherlands, 1967. Most accessible collection of sixteenth-century pamphlet literature.

RICHARD ERNEST WALKER

STÖCKEL, Leonard

STÖCKEL, Leonard (also Leonhard Stoeckel; 1510–1560), pedagogue, theologian, and early leader of Lutheranism in Upper Hungary (Slovakia). A theological and educational leader during the early Reformation in Slovakia, Stöckel well deserves the title *Praeceptor Hungariae.* Born in 1510, he was the son of a successful smith and citizen of Bardejov, one of the royal free cities of Upper Hungary with about 2,500 inhabitants, mainly of German origin but with a strong Slovak minority. Stöckel was educated in Bardejov, Košice (under the English humanist Leonard Cox), Breslau (Wrocław), and finally at the University of Wittenberg (1530–1534) where both Martin Luther and Philipp Melanchthon served as his mentors. He briefly taught in Eisleben (1534–1535) but had difficulties with the antinomianism of Johann Agricola, the town pastor. He returned to Wittenberg and worked as a private tutor in the princely family until he was called by his native city to become the rector of its "humanist" school. Luther and Melanchthon reluctantly agreed to his departure, believing he deserved a more prestigious position.

From 1539 until his death in 1560, except for one year spent in nearby Kežmarok (1555–1556), Stöckel was both the leading educator and Lutheran theologian in Hungary. At the school in Bardejov Stöckel introduced a three–class system of instruction and composed, in 1540, his *Leges scholae Bartphensis,* which in fifteen articles governed the life of the school. Lutheran theology was to be inculcated and, in accordance with the humanist principles of Johannes Sturm and Melanchthon, eloquence and piety were fostered. For the school he prepared a catechism; a play, *History of Suzanna,* the first school play performed in Hungary (1556); annotations of Melanchthon's *Loci communes;* extracts from Marcus Tullius Cicero's work on civic duties; and other theological and pedagogical treatises. Under Stöckel's leadership the school became one of the significant Lutheran educational institutions in Hungary, and among his pupils were the sons of some of the most influential noble families in Hungary, as well as future ecclesiastical and intellectual leaders.

Stöckel also regularly participated in the formative synods of Lutherans in Upper Hungary. In 1546 he attended the synod of the five free cities of eastern Upper Hungary (Bardejov, Prešov, Košice, Levoča, and Sabinov), which accepted the Augsburg Confession and Melanchthon's *Loci communes* as their doctrinal standard. After the Hungarian Diet outlawed Anabaptism and Zwinglianism in 1548, these five cities accepted the *Confessio Pentapolitana* (1549), which had been prepared by Stöckel. The twenty articles were drawn from the Augsburg Confession and were intended to demonstrate that Lutherans were not heretics and were thus entitled to toleration. The confession, therefore, was moderate in expression and did not anathematize the teachings of others.

Even so, Stöckel's theology was not firmly Lutheran. He became involved in several theological disputes: with Matthias Lauterwald, who did not accept Luther's solafidianism; with the antitrinitarian Francis Stancarus; and with the Sacramentarians and Calvinists Gregor Szegedi and Márton Kálmancsehi. He also corresponded regularly with Melanchthon and other reformers, as well as with Hungarian political leaders. Only a few of his works were published, and these were issued posthumously. Stöckel, moreover, cultivated the arts, wrote a tract on music theory, and may have been responsible for collecting the material included in the so-called Bardejov manuscript of Renaissance and early Reformation music preserved in Budapest.

Stöckel died in 1560, shortly after receiving a letter from Melanchthon, who, in the meantime, had also died. He was survived by his wife and six children.

BIBLIOGRAPHY

Hajduk, Andrej. "Philipp Melanchthon und Leonhard Stöckel." *Communio Viatorum* 20 (1977), 171–180.

———. "Leonhard Stöckel." *Zeichen der Zeit* 34 (1980), 229–232.

Škoviera, Daniel. "Epistulae Leonardi Stöckel." *Zborník Filozofickej fakulty UK* 7.8 (1975–1976), 265–359.

ANDREJ HAJDUK

STOCKHOLM BLOODBATH. On 8 November 1520 one of the most debated events in Scandinavian history occurred. From 1397, Denmark, Norway, and Sweden had been united in a common Danish monarchy known as the Kalmar Union. Throughout the fifteenth century Sweden was restless under the union and staged rebellions under Engelbrekt Engelbrektsson, Karl Knutsson, and the two Sten Stures. In 1518 Sten Sture the Younger repulsed the Danish forces of Christian II (r. 1513–1523) at the Battle of Brannkyrka but was himself mortally wounded. Two years later Christian II returned with a huge army and besieged Stockholm, which was heroically defended by a motley Swedish army led by Sture's widow, Kristina Gyllenstierna. But on 7 September Stockholm opened its gates to Christian II, having been given a promise of general amnesty.

By 1 November Christian II was hailed as the hereditary king of Sweden and crowned three days later by the archbishop of Uppsala, Gustav Trolle, who was himself a Dane. The leading Swedish nobility, prelates, and others in high places had gathered in Stockholm for these events and a series of reconciliation banquets. On 7 November Trolle appeared with a list of personal grievances and accused the Swedish leaders of heresy and treason. According to Trolle heresy need not be doctrinal in nature but could also involve detrimental action against the church and schism. Trolle had long been in conflict with the Swedish leaders, who had leveled his castle. Since one did not need to keep one's word to a heretic, the banquet guests were detained. The next day, 8 November, after a hasty trial, the leadership of Sweden was beheaded in the Great Market Square of Stockholm. Estimates of the number beheaded range from seventy to ninety-nine persons. Included were not only the leading nobility of Sweden but two Swedish bishops, Matthias of Strengnas and Vincent of Skara. On his return to Copenhagen, Christian II had many more Swedes executed along the way. Christian II now became known as Christian "the Tyrant." Under the young Gustavus Vasa, Sweden rose in rebellion against Denmark and gained its independence in 1523.

The events leading up to and following immediately upon the Stockholm Bloodbath did not involve the new religious questions spreading across Europe from Wittenberg. Rather the massacre set the stage for the Reformation in Sweden by squandering the spiritual treasure of the Roman church and making the Swedish people and their new sovereign open to the message of the Protestant appeal. Ardent Lutheran advisers such as Laurentius Andreae and Olaus Petri were eager to serve their king in this manner.

Was the Stockholm Bloodbath planned or the result of a moment's insanity? For years Scandinavian graduate classes in history have sharpened their tools of historical criticism by focusing on the event. The sources are few and are open to varying interpretations. Nationalistic, religious, political, economic, and judicial factors were all involved. As one Swedish historian aptly stated: "The Bloodbath was no isolated event nor a tyrannical attack nor a sudden event but rather a climactic catastrophe to a long bitter battle in a torn up, divided Sweden."

BIBLIOGRAPHY

Kolsrud, Oluf. "Blodbadet i Stockholm aar 1520." *Kyrkohistorisk Årsskrift* 40 (1940), 175–237.
Nordstrom, Gerd Z. *Stockholms blodbad: Ett drama fran 1520 i bild ach text.* Gavle, 1979.
Weibull, Lauritz. *Stockholms blodbad och andra kritiska under sokningar.* Stockholm, 1965.

TRYGVE R. SKARSTEN

STOSS, Veit (also Wit Stwosz; c.1438/47–1533), major late Gothic sculptor, engraver, and painter active primarily in Kraków and Nuremberg. Most scholars suggest that Stoss possessed a volatile temperament, but his many commissions and his influence on the next generation of sculptors indicates he probably had a sizable workshop. Although little is known about his early training, stylistic similarities are sometimes noted between his work and the sculptural realism of Nicolaus Gerhaert of Leiden (active 1462–1473/78). Beginning in 1477 Stoss resided in Poland for nineteen years. One of his major works there—the large carved and painted *Cracow Altarpiece* (1489), showing the death and assumption of the Virgin—was created for the Church of the Virgin Mary. Stoss also created several carved tombs, including one for King Casimir IV Jagiellon (1492). In addition to altarpieces and tombs, he is known for his freestanding and relief sculpture focusing on traditional Catholic themes. In Nuremberg's Church of Saint Lawrence, the *Angelic Salutation* (1517–1518) combines the Annunciation with rosary imagery, and the *Wickel Crucifix* (1520) in Saint Sebald emphasizes the emotional pathos of Christ's passion.

After Stoss returned to Nuremberg in 1496, his career overlapped with the Nuremberg printmaker and painter Albrecht Dürer (1471–1528). Stylistic interrelationships, however, are difficult to establish. Stoss continued to receive important commissions even after his conviction for forgery and subsequent pardon by Holy Roman Emperor Maximilian I (1459–1519) in 1506. His last major work, known as the *Bamberg Altarpiece* (1520–1523), was originally carved for the Carmelite convent church in Nuremberg, where his son Andreas (d. 1540) was prior. In 1525, after Nuremberg became Lutheran, the Carmelite convent disbanded, and the need for carved altarpieces disappeared. Bamberg, a

Catholic stronghold, purchased the Carmelite altarpiece for one of its churches. Stoss died in Nuremberg in 1533.

BIBLIOGRAPHY

Isphording, Eduard, ed. *Veit Stoss: Die Vorträge des Nürnberger Symposions.* Munich, 1985. An outstanding, thematically arranged bibliography containing over fifteen hundred entries primarily in German.

Müller, Theodor. *Sculpture in the Netherlands, Germany, France, and Spain: 1400–1500.* Harmondsworth, England, and Baltimore, 1966. Brief biography of Stoss within the context of other contemporary sculptors.

Metropolitan Museum of Art, New York. *Gothic and Renaissance Art in Nuremberg, 1300–1550.* New York, 1986. Exhibition catalog with discussion of seven sculptural images by Stoss.

MARY EM KIRN

STRASBOURG. Located on the west bank of the Rhine River and therefore an entrepôt for east-west and north-south trade, Strasbourg (Ger., Strassburg; ancient Argentoratum or Argentinae), a free imperial city of the Holy Roman Empire, was both the breeding and receiving grounds for nearly every cultural and religious movement of the sixteenth century. At that time its population was about 25,000, and within its walls were late medieval reformers, mystics, humanists, spiritualists of every stripe, Lutherans, Zwinglians, Schwenckfeldians (including Kaspar von Schwenckfeld himself), Anabaptists, French Calvinists, English émigrés, and millenarian revolutionaries. Its location on the Alsatian plane between the Vosges and the Black Forest and its reputation for relative tolerance made it both easily accessible and attractive. By 1600, however, Strasbourg was officially within the camp of Lutheran orthodoxy and then quickly became an important source for Pietism. Strasbourg's economy was based upon regional trade, agriculture, small manufactures (save for its famous cannon), printing, and Alsatian financial arrangements. Unlike Augsburg, for example, with its heavy dependence upon wool and banking, Strasbourg had what would today be called a strongly diversified economy. Consequently, although the city experienced the common, wild price fluctuations—dictated for the most part by the weather—of early modern Germany, it remained relatively stable with little by way of enormous prosperity or wretchedly bad times. These facts may explain why, until the French Revolution, the city underwent no violent uprising from its lower classes.

Ostensibly its government was dominated by the craft guilds, each of which elected representatives to serve on the senate and XXI (the term "XXI" may have originally referred to these guild representatives) on an annually rotating basis. In fact, there were three merchants' guilds, and the sons of the heads of these guilds commonly invaded the lower ones and were elected to represent them as well. As a consequence, a handful of families effectively governed Strasbourg during the sixteenth century, and the truly influential among them constituted what amounted to a plutocracy with far-flung interests that went well beyond the city's walls and even its rural dependencies. Many received much of their income from *rentes* (long-term loans at rates that vastly exceeded what was legal) that they sold in the countryside. Still, the city's bishop was forcibly nonresident, the nobility and patrician classes were on the fringes of real political authority, and the government recognized no one save the emperor as its lord (and at that only minimally).

Save for the poorest parish churches, the ecclesiastical establishment was equally privileged and, as reforming bishops discovered, utterly ungovernable. The monasteries and convents obviously posed their own problems as independent corporations, but the collegiate churches were the most intractable. Of the cathedral chapter, it was remarked that Jesus himself did not have enough quarterings on his coat of arms to qualify for membership, and Saint Thomas was the largest landholder in all of Alsace. The clergy (which also sold *rentes* in the countryside), grouped into their various *collegia*, paid taxes not as individuals but *Schirmgeld* (protection money) as semi-independent corporations; legally they were not even citizens.

These two systems of parallel governance by no means lacked their critics. Among them was Jakob Wimpfeling, who excoriated the clergy not only for their privileges but also on the grounds of their ignorance. The great preacher Geiler von Kaysersberg, for whom the huge stone pulpit in the cathedral was carved, attacked not just the privileges of the clergy but those of the laity as well. Both were moral reformers or social critics in a mold that was common to the late Middle Ages and the Renaissance, but neither had much interest in doctrine as such. Hence, while they tended to create, as well as to mirror, a climate that was generally critical of both church and society, they were "prereformers" only in the loosest sense of the term. Nonetheless, when criticized for his leanings toward the Reformation in the 1520s, Jakob Sturm, the city's most important politician, could reply to Wimpfeling that it was he who put him onto that path.

Conceived in theological terms in the manner of Luther, the Reformation first came to Strasbourg in the person of Matthias Zell, who was *penitentiarius* of the bishop and preached in one of the side chapels of the cathedral. In the latter half of 1521 he announced a series of sermons on Paul's letter to the Romans and immediately began to draw enormous crowds. The bishop demanded that the government silence him and deliver him to the episcopal court, but the politicians engaged in their favorite tactic of delay. Zell was simply too popular.

By mid-1523 Zell was joined by Wolfgang Capito, Martin Bucer, and Caspar Hedio, who knew one another through the circle that had formed around Desiderius Erasmus in

Basel some years earlier. These three each took preaching posts and in addition began a series of theological lectures for both clergy and laity in which they propounded Luther's theology and eventually converted substantial majorities in each group. Their work bore fruit in the autumn of 1524, when the government demanded that all clergy become citizens and pay individual taxes like everyone else, although they would be excused from military duty. Capito, the second most highly placed cleric in the city, seconded the politicians in print, and the deed was done. Monks and nuns who wished to remain cloistered were allowed to do so, but no further recruits were allowed. The reformers and politicians were working hand-in-hand.

Their relationship was by no means always amicable. It became especially strained during a five-year campaign for the abolition of the Mass in the city, in part because the struggle began just before the Peasants' War of 1524–1525. The reformers nonetheless saw success by 1529 and even the establishment of public schools, a welfare system, and a marriage and morals court. The second critical moment came in the mid-1530s, when the government finally agreed to juridical hearings of the Anabaptists and the promulgation of a rudimentary church order. The third critical juncture for this first generation of reformers revolved around Charles V's victory in the Schmalkald War and the Interim, by which the Mass was reintroduced in the cathedral and other Strasbourg churches. The years 1547 and 1548 thus featured not only the exodus, and ultimate return, of some of the city's most prominent politicians (who had the most to lose from the emperor) but also the expulsion of Bucer, who took refuge in England during the reign of Edward VI.

A generational change marked the mid-sixteenth century in Strasbourg both for its leading clergy and its most important politicians. The new group had experienced not only the Interim, which was abolished in 1559, but also the at least tentative end to hostilities with the Saxon theologians on the subject of the Lord's Supper. The Sacramentarian controversy, which raged during the second half of the 1520s, came to a climax at the Diet of Augsburg (1530), where the Strasbourg theologians were not allowed to sign the Augsburg Confession but had to offer (it was never received) their own statement of faith, the Tetrapolitan Confession. It came to an end in 1536, when the city and its confessional allies—under pressure from their politicians—agreed to the Wittenberg Concord, by which they subscribed (at least nominally) to Luther's views. This new generation of both pastors and politicians was thus formally "Lutheran" in the sense that it subscribed to the Augsburg Confession. The fact that the Peace of Augsburg (1555) gave political, as well as confessional, force to this self-identification became an important element in the remaining story of Strasbourg's reformation.

The career of the man who in 1552 became Strasbourg's chief pastor illustrates the transition. He had been educated at Strasbourg, was sent to Wittenberg to study theology in the aftermath of the Wittenberg Concord, and then returned to the city as both pastor and (initially) sometime professor of theology in the academy. In the process he became a "Lutheran" to his very core. He was, in fact, chosen to be, first, Strasbourg's representative in negotiations regarding the second session of the Council of Trent, and then president of the Compagnie des Pasteurs (or *Kirchenkonvent*) precisely because he would "please" the Saxon theologians. The city was looking for both political and confessional allies, and Johannes Marbach was the best fit they could find. He also held a doctorate, and Luther himself had presided over his final disputation.

In addition to being an intentional Lutheran, Marbach was horrified by disorder of any kind. He thought it a public scandal that, as the Reformation unfolded, individual pastors created public worship services—including baptism, marriage, the Lord's Supper, burial, and the like—more or less of their own choosing. At midcentury there was no uniformity to religious services in Strasbourg's various churches. Consequently, Marbach immediately created an "Agenda" (it also touched on the daily conduct of ecclesiastical business), persuaded most of the pastors to endorse it, and received sanction from the civil authorities to conduct a visitation of the urban parishes.

This visitation occurred in 1554 for the first and only time. Marbach pronounced himself pleased with it, and the subsequent reordering of worship and ecclesiastical practices bore him out. But it created an uproar that centered around the pastor of Saint Thomas and his assistant, who insisted with some justification that visitations and standardized practices amounted to innovations and a return to papism. Henceforth, the regular meetings of the Compagnie des Pasteurs effectively substituted for a parish-by-parish visitation in the city; it nonetheless continued for Strasbourg's rural parishes, whose pastors could not come to the company's meetings on a regular basis. Scholars have disagreed about the results of these visitations, but it appears that by the early 1560s all the country parishes had their own pastors, parishioners were attending church regularly, and at least the young were learning the catechism.

Strasbourg's academy, with its fledgling theology faculty, was the main impulse behind these developments, even in the countryside. Ministerial candidates (many of whom enjoyed stipends from one or another fund in the city) were educated in the academy, frequently boarded with the president of the company, and were examined and placed by the company with the approval both of the local parish and the senate and XXI. In addition, the academy trained pastors for other cities and principalities throughout southern Germany.

The academy nonetheless also caused difficulties for Marbach and his colleagues because its rector, the famous humanist educator Johannes Sturm, and those who taught in the other faculties were what may only be called "generic Protestants" with distinct leanings toward Calvin and Reformed beliefs. The first controversy erupted between Marbach and Girolamo Zanchi (a theologian) in the early 1560s on the subjects of the Lord's Supper and predestination. It lasted more than two years and finally required the government to enlist the services of foreigners to render a decision, which fully vindicated Marbach and led eventually to Zanchi's departure.

This "consensus" (1563) did not, however, end the matter. In late 1569 Sturm abruptly announced his intention to resign, basically on the grounds that the company and the theologians (who overlapped) were introducing "barbarism" into the school with their constant disputations on matters of doctrine. This opinion is perfectly understandable from Sturm's point of view, as he was a humanist educator for whom doctrinal confrontations were exceedingly disagreeable, especially when they involved condemning the teachings of his closest associates outside the city, that is, the Reformed.

The government found itself in a very difficult situation. Sturm was a highly respected educator, one whose influence reached as far as England. To dismiss him was unthinkable. Moreover, the Elector Palatine, once again of the Reformed persuasion, remained one of the keystones in the city's system of alliances. Finally, the issues at stake were not nearly so easily explicable as they had been some years earlier in the struggle with Zanchi. Sturm had chosen his ground well; no doctrinal issues were at stake. It was simply a question of which body—the school or the church—had responsibility for and oversight of theological education in the academy. For Marbach it was the theology faculty, who were also members of the Compagnie des Pasteurs. For Sturm it was the faculty of the academy as a whole. Marbach and the pastors lost this round. He was stripped of his post as dean of the faculty of theology and firmly told that he was not "superintendent" (or bishop) of Strasbourg's church. Sturm was authorized to develop a curriculum that would be binding on the theology students, as well as on the academy as a whole.

In 1581 Marbach died a spent man, but he lived long enough to see his eventual successor, Johann Pappus, turn the tables once again. The year 1577 saw the "theologians of the Augsburg Confession," as they called themselves (albeit not including those from Strasbourg), agree on the Formula of Concord, and in 1580 the formula was published along with other confessional statements in *The Book of Concord*, which remains to this day the major repository for distinctively Lutheran confessions. After stating their positive beliefs, they added a section (called the *condemnamus*) in which they condemned what they regarded as contrary teachings. Pappus took advantage of one of Sturm's frequent absences from the city to hold a public disputation on the question of whether it was possible to condemn someone's teachings without condemning the person.

Sturm was furious and, in an attempt to bring the matter back to questions of how the school was to function, he charged Pappus with insubordination on the grounds that he had not received Sturm's approval before holding the disputation. Pappus merely replied that it was a timely subject, Sturm was out of town, and it was impossible to get his approval.

This confrontation became a literary war not just between the principals but also among their allies outside the city. It naturally featured the usual backbiting and allegations about who was slandering whose reputation. But the core of the matter harkened to a much older issue, one that had featured prominently in the debate between Luther and Erasmus on the freedom of the will more than fifty years earlier: were doctrinal assertions crucial to true Christianity, and, if so, who had the right and obligation to make them? To Sturm they belonged to all the educated; to Pappus and his allies they resided with trained theologians.

It would be too much (although perhaps not untrue) to assert that the controversy was decided on its merits. The political situation had changed once more; now the Elector Palatine was again a Lutheran. Moreover, Sturm made the mistake in one of his books against Pappus of speaking disparagingly about yet another purging of the theology faculty at the University of Heidelberg. The Elector complained mightily to the XIII (the city's committee on foreign affairs), as well as to the Senate and XXI. In 1581 Sturm was dismissed as "lifetime" rector of the academy.

The victory of Lutheranism in Strasbourg was, however, by no means complete. In the first place, the position held by Marbach remained vacant until late 1581 while the politicians tried to decide just how they would make a reality of their insistence that they, and only they, were "superintendent" of the city's church. While insisting all along on their superintendency, they nonetheless heaped on Pappus one after another of the responsibilities that had fallen to Marbach—preaching the noon sermon at the cathedral, boarding the theology students, conducting the visitation in the countryside, lecturing in theology at the academy, presiding over the meetings of the company, and representing it to the government. At last, in December, after once more declaring that Pappus was not "superintendent" of the church but president of the Compagnie des Pasteurs, the senate and XXI confirmed him in what had been, functionally, Marbach's office. This structure continued until the French Revolution.

Although the government had been under both internal and external pressure to do so for some time, it had also not yet formally subscribed to the Formula of Concord. As soon as it became available to them, the pastors all subscribed and used the formula within the company to judge the teachings of candidates for the ministry of word and sacrament in the churches of Strasbourg. At last, in late 1597, the authorities asked Pappus and the company to draft a new church order that would include formal adherence to the formula. In doing so they essentially codified procedures that had become common practice during Marbach's tenure and—at the behest of the Senate and XXI—added a lengthy historical introduction in which they argued that this new confession was in agreement with the history of the city's reformation. Again, a combination of confessional conflict (this time with a Calvinist preacher in nearby Bischweiler) and foreign policy considerations (the city had become embroiled in a nasty series of armed conflicts known as the "Bishops' War" in 1592) forced the city at last to decide between the Reformed Electoral Palatinate and Lutheran Württemberg. The politicians officially adopted the order in 1598, and Strasbourg became formally Lutheran, although it had been so in reality ever since the expulsion of Sturm seventeen years earlier.

Strasbourg's reformation thus came to an end at the dawn of the seventeenth century. But religious change continued, for this city was also the breeding ground for German Lutheran Pietism. Johann Arndt's *Four Books on True Christianity* were published there (by the official printer of the theology faculty) and became immensely popular; Philipp Jacob Spener was educated in the very same faculty; and Albert Schweitzer, the city's most notable modern Christian, performed on the Silberman organ in the collegiate church of Saint Thomas. It was not, however, until the seventeenth century that true religion ceased also to be a political reality and the two began to go their separate ways.

[*See also* Augsburg Confession; Bucer, Martin; Capito, Wolfgang; Franck, Sebastian; Marburg, Colloquy of; *and* Zwingli, Huldrych.]

BIBLIOGRAPHY

Abray, Lorna Jane. *The People's Reformation: Magistrates, Clergy, and Commons in Strasbourg, 1500–1598*. Ithaca, N.Y., 1985. Has the virtue of carrying the outline of the story to the end of the century but is theologically poorly informed.

Brady, Thomas A. *Ruling Class, Regime, and Reformation in Strasbourg, 1520–1555*. Leiden, 1978. Detailed prosopographical study of the city's politicians and their reactions to the reform movement, with special attention to the Peasants' War and the Interim.

Chrisman, Miriam Usher. *Lay Culture, Learned Culture: Books and Social Change in Strasbourg, 1480–1599*. New Haven, 1982. Based on a companion volume (*Bibliography of Strasbourg Imprints*) published the same year by the same press, this work examines the development of both popular and elite culture in Strasbourg during the Reformation.

Eells, Hastings. *Martin Bucer*. Reprint, New York, 1971. Dated in terms of its interpretations but basically reliable in its details.

Kittelson, James M. *Wolfgang Capito from Humanist to Reformer*. Leiden, 1975. Only complete biography of one of the city's leading clerical and intellectual figures.

———. "Marbach vs. Zanchi: The Resolution of Controversy in Late Reformation Strasbourg." *Sixteenth-Century Journal* 8.3 (1977), 31–44.

———. "Successes and Failures in the German Reformation: The Report from Strasbourg." *Archive for Reformation History* 73 (1982), 153–175.

———. "Visitations and Popular Religious Culture: Further Reports from Strasbourg." In *Pietas et Societas: New Trends in Reformation Social History*, edited by Philip N. Bebb and Kyle C. Sessions. Kirkwood, Mo., 1985.

———. "Strasbourg, the *Landesherrliche Kirchenregiment*, and the Relative Autonomy of the Churches in Sixteenth-Century Germany." *Locus. An Historical Journal of Regional Perspectives* 2 (1990), 131–143.

Rott, Jean. *Investigationes historicae: Églises et société au 16e siècle*. 2 vols. Strasbourg, 1986. The collected articles of the most learned and prolific student of Strasbourg's reformation in this century.

Schindling, Anton. *Humanistische Hochschule und Freie Reichsstadt: Gymnasium und Akademie in Strassburg, 1538–1621*. Wiesbaden, 1977. Definitive work on the academy, although lacking in theological sophistication.

Weyrauch, Erdmann. *Konfessionelle Krise und Sozial Stabilität: Das Interim in Strassburg, 1548–1562*. Stuttgart, 1978. The standard work, although somewhat obscured by sociological theory.

JAMES M. KITTELSON

STRAUß, Jakob (c.1480–after 1527), Reformed preacher. He was originally from Basel, left the town in 1495, became a Dominican, and preached from about 1506 in unidentified places. In 1515 he studied in Freiburg im Breisgau, and later completed his doctorate in theology. As a Reformed preacher he appeared for the first time in Hall in the Tirol; he preached against the orthodox clergy and the religious orders, particularly criticizing the exploitation of the poor and rejecting the Catholic practice of confession and Mass. Because of his great following among citizens and miners, and in spite of the council's support, the bishop of Brixen, Sebastian Sprenz, pushed through his expulsion at the beginning of May 1522.

Strauß went to Wittenberg and enrolled at the university. In that same year Count Georg von Wertheim accepted him as preacher on Luther's recommendation, but after a few weeks dismissed him because his reforming innovations were too brazen. In January 1523 he was called to be a preacher at Saint Georg in Eisenach in Thuringia. His doctrines were Lutheran, recorded in texts on confession, the veneration of relics, the marriage of priests, baptism, purgatory, the standing of Protestant preachers, and the church ban. But once again he pushed toward swift implementation. On the basis of a biblically founded social ethic with the tenet of love at its core he became the advocate of the poor and the common people, opposed their exploitation through the leveling of the tithe by the old church, but also opposed merchants and usurers. In fifty-one theses he rejected any taking of the interest as usury; to him all wealth was un-Christian.

This stance produced the Eisenach dispute about usury, including the refusal to pay interest by many debtors. Johann, the Saxon baron in charge, the prince elector's brother, had to intervene; Luther and Philipp Melanchthon played a role as assessors and negotiators. The dispute ended in 1524 with a fixing of the interest rate at 5 percent. In spite of mounting opposition against him, Strauß remained in the baron's favor. In January and March of 1525 he acted at the prince's behest as inspector of Eisenach and held several other offices. At the beginning of March 1525 he was the third—after Luther and Melanchthon—whom rebellious peasants of southwestern Germany put on a list of judges to adjudicate the legitimacy of the peasants' demands in accordance with divine right.

When the Peasants' War reached even Thuringia in April Strauß warned against any use of violence. He tried to keep the peasants and citizens from engaging in combat. But in sermons and pamphlets he developed an attitude toward the authorities that held them as responsible as the rebels for the Peasants' War. When he was arrested after the rebellion had been put down he continued to subscribe to these views, but he was spared from prosecution nonetheless.

In September 1525 he left Eisenach and went to Schwäbisch-Hall via Nuremberg, and to Baden-Baden in 1526. He also participated in the dispute about Holy Communion through pamphlets against Huldrych Zwingli and Johann Oecolampadius. After October 1527 nothing else is known of him; in 1532 his death was documented.

BIBLIOGRAPHY

Barge, Hermann. *Jakob Strauß: Ein Kämpfer für das Evangelium in Tirol, Thüringen und Süddeutschland.* Leipzig, 1937. A still-valid source of materials on his life.
Rogge, Joachim. *Der Beitrag des Predigers Jakob Strauß zur frühen Reformationsgeschichte.* Berlin, 1957. Biography with an analysis of Strauß's texts and his theology.

ADOLF LAUBE
Translated from German by Wolfgang Katenz

STREJC, Jiří (also Strejček; Ger., Vetter; 1536–1599), Czech theologian, priest of the Unity of Brethren (Bohemian Brethren), and poet and translator of the Bible. Strejc was educated in Mladá Boleslav (central Bohemia), Königsberg (eastern Prussia), and Tübingen (Württemberg). An excellent orator, he was ordained as a diaconus (1562) and then as a priest of the Bohemian Brethren (1567), became administrator of the community of brethren in Hranice (eastern Moravia) and later in Židlochovice (southern Moravia), and was elected cosenior of the Bohemian Brethren in 1577.

At the Prague diet of 1575 he took part in the commission that compiled the text of the Bohemian Confession. As a partisan of Calvinism he opposed the anti-Calvinist elements in this text and supported the influences of the Second Helvetic Confession, the Heidelberg Catechism, and the brethren's confession. Thus he intensified the ecumenical accents in the Bohemian Confession. (Strejc wrote an

interesting description of the diet of 1575 from the point of view of the Bohemian Brethren.)

Strejc translated Calvin's *Institutio religionis Christianae* into Czech (prepared 1595, published 1612–1614). He took part in the translation of the whole Bible by a group of theologians of the Bohemian Brethren (*Biblí kralická*, published in Kralice, southern Moravia, 1579–1594), and prepared an excellent translation of the *Psalms* (*Žalmy aneb zpěvové sv. Davida*, 1587). Strejc's literary work also included moralizing verses (e.g., *Mravové aneb naučení potřebná*, published 1600) and spiritual poems.

Strejc was a nonconformist clergyman of the Bohemian Brethren. He refused the strict discipline of the church and tried to live as a free man and a creative personality. He fostered closer links between Bohemia and Moravia and west European Calvinist thought and culture by his translations and by his acceptance of French music (melodies of *Psalms*). Strejc's legacy can be found in the ecumenical dimension of the Bohemian Confession.

BIBLIOGRAPHY

Čapek, Jan B. *Záření ducha a slova* (The Flare of the Spirit and the Word). Prague, 1948. An interpretation of Strejc's literary work.
Hrejsa, Ferdinand. *Česká konfesse: její vznik, podstata a dějiny* (The Bohemian Confession: Its Origin, Essence and History). Prague, 1912. The most important monograph to date on the Bohemian Confession; analyzes the theological thought of Strejc.
Hrejsa, F., J. B. Čapek, and J. B. Imek. *Český žalmista Bratr Jiří Strejc* (The Czech Translator of *Psalms* Jiří Strejc). Prague, 1937. A collection of studies of the theological, literary, and musical work of Strejc.
Říčan, Rudolf. *Dějiny Jednoty bratrské* (The History of the Unity of Brethren). Prague, 1957. An evaluation of Strejc's activities in the context of the history of the Bohemian Brethren. An abridged version is available in German, *Die Böhmischen Brüder*, Berlin, 1961.

JAROSLAV PÁNEK

STRIGEL, Viktorin (Lat., Victorinus Strigelius; 1524–1569), German Lutheran theologian and controversialist opposed to Matthias Flacius Illyricus in mid-sixteenth-century Lutheranism's so-called anthropological controversy. Strigel debated with Flacius over the Lutheran doctrines of original sin and justification by grace. Strigel was labeled a "Philippist" and "synergist" because he maintained that the human will played a positive role in one's conversion and salvation.

Strigel's most significant teaching post was at the University of Jena (1548–1562), where he taught views consistent with those of his teacher, Philipp Melanchthon. When Jena was raised to university status (1558), Duke John Frederick II asked the faculty for a normative doctrinal statement. During preparation of the document, Strigel and Flacius (who joined the Jena faculty in 1557) disagreed over the role of the human will in the reception of God's grace. Flacius's position prevailed, and the document, *Confutationes Wider-*

legungen und Verdammung (Weimar Book of Confutation; 1559), became binding.

Strigel refused to submit to what he called the "Areopagitic book" and was imprisoned in the spring of 1559. The duke released Strigel in September and called for a public debate between Strigel and Flacius. The two professors met at the Weimar Disputation, before large crowds, in August 1560. Strigel maintained that the Holy Spirit uses the word of God to initiate conversion (i.e., bring on to faith), and that when the sinful human will is so moved by the Spirit, the will cooperates with God's grace. Flacius disagreed. After thirteen sessions, the duke halted the debate and ordered both parties to stop all public polemics.

Strigel moved to the University of Leipzig in 1563 but was suspended from that post in 1567 because of suspicions that he held Calvinist views of the Lord's Supper. He then moved to the Palatinate, openly confessed a Reformed understanding of the sacrament, and taught at the University of Heidelberg from 1567 until his death.

The importance of Strigel's role in Reformation thought and history is best understood when seen in the context of the confessional strife that agitated German Lutheranism in the third quarter of the sixteenth century. Strigel's notions regarding Original Sin, the human will, and justification were carefully formulated and helped to define the issues at stake for later Lutheranism. Strigel's positions were not all accepted by confessional Lutherans, but his concerns influenced the Formula of Concord (1577) both positively (article 1) and negatively (article 2).

BIBLIOGRAPHY

Bente, F. *Historical Introductions to the Book of Concord.* Reprint, Saint Louis, 1965. Interprets Strigel in relationship to the emerging sixteenth-century Lutheran confessional consensus.

Reimann, Henry W. "Matthias Flacius Illyricus: A Biographical Sketch." *Concordia Theological Monthly* 35 (1964), 69–93. Devotes considerable space to Strigel's conflict with Flacius.

Richard, James. *The Confessional History of the Lutheran Church.* Philadelphia, 1909. Dated and uneven in its interpretation, but presents a wealth of material; see pp. 3–371.

Schultz, Robert C. "Original Sin: Accident or Substance; The Paradoxical Significance of FC I, 53–62 in Historical Context." In *Discord, Dialogue, and Concord,* edited by Lewis W. Spitz and Wenzel Lohff, pp. 38–57. Philadelphia, 1977. A historical and theological interpretation of the issues at stake between Strigel and Flacius and how they influenced the Formula of Concord.

WILLIAM R. RUSSELL

STRIJCKER, Herman. *See* Moded, Hermannus.

STUART, HOUSE OF. The royal house of Stuart derived its name from the position of its twelfth-century ancestors as stewards of the kings of Scotland. It may not seem a very glorious beginning. Certainly the first two kings of the line, Robert II (1371–1390) and Robert III (1390–1406), there because of the failure of the great house of Bruce to produce male heirs of line in the second generation, were dismal creatures. More generally, death was not kind to the Stuart kings; all died young, and minority was as familiar a feature of Scottish royal government between 1406 and 1584 as adult personal rule. Yet throughout that period all save Mary were monarchs of ruthless power, ability, and in some cases genius at self-propaganda. They were respected; they were, on the whole, obeyed; they ran an effective, self-confident kingdom.

But it was at their one period of weakness that the Reformation movement in Scotland flourished. Until his death in 1542, James V (r. 1513–1542) held back pressure for reform. He was succeeded by a week-old girl, Mary, whose long minority and inept and brief personal rule (1561–1567) witnessed the greatest upheaval in Scottish history: the success of the Protestants and the turmoil in foreign policy as Scotland lurched from its traditional alliance with Catholic France to an uncertain but essential new one with its traditional enemy, England. In the absence of the monarch, this "revolution" was presided over by the magnates and greater lairds, giving point and context to George Buchanan's arguments that kings were answerable to their peoples, and peoples could depose kings—as indeed happened to Mary Stuart in 1567. For the leading reformers, clearly in the ascendant from 1559, royal weakness opened the way for a radical view of the separation of the powers of church and state. The normal rules, whereby kings could determine the religious state of their kingdoms—seen most dramatically in the repeated shifts and turns in England from the 1530s to the late seventeenth century—were wholly broken in Scotland. When at last an effective king, James VI, tried to assert control over the Reformed church, from the mid-1580s, he was starting some twenty-five years behind the establishment of a totally non-Erastian church; the old battle of the two swords, between pope and Holy Roman Emperor, was played out again in the 1590s between king and leading presbyterian, Andrew Melville. By the time he succeeded to the English throne in 1603, James had to a considerable extent managed to assert his authority, although he had to settle for the compromise polity of an episcopal and a presbyterian church. He had the skill to maintain that compromise. But absentee kingship brought new problems. His more foolish son Charles I tried instant imposition from London of Anglican Arminianism on the Scottish church, and brought civil war and constitutional revolution down on himself, while in the longer term reviving hostility to bishops that was to ensure, when long-lasting settlement came in 1690, that never again would the Church of Scotland be an episcopal church, and ensure also Presbyterian influence over Scottish society that kings might well have envied.

BIBLIOGRAPHY

Donaldson, Gordon. *Scotland: James V–James VII.* Edinburgh, 1971. Sees the first generation of reformers as anxious to link their fortunes to a godly prince.

Grant, Alexander. *Independence and Nationhood: Scotland, 1306–1469.* Reprint, Edinburgh, 1991.

Kirk, James. "The Polities of the Best Reformed Kirks . . . A Revision Article." *Scottish Historical Review* 59 (1980), 22–53. Provides the best and most convincing discussion of the non-Erastian stance of the church from the beginning.

Nicholson, Ranald. *Scotland: The Later Middle Ages.* 2d ed. Reprint, Edinburgh, 1989.

Wormald, Jenny. *Court, Kirk and Community: Scotland, 1470–1625.* Reprint, Edinburgh, 1991.

JENNY WORMALD

STURE, Sten the Younger (1492/93–1520), regent of Sweden, 1512–1520.

Son of the former regent Svante Nilsson, whom he succeeded, Sture was a capable statesman who proceeded to engage his house in a struggle against the Danish kings of the union to obtain political independence. He sought support especially among the peasantry.

Sture's early political successes did not last. He came into conflict with the archbishop of Uppsala, Gustav Trolle, who belonged to the hostile nobility, obtained papal support, and was consecrated by the pope in Rome in 1515. He then procured permission for an armed escort and fortifications, and Sture, in case he resisted, was threatened with excommunication and the interdict, which indeed was twice proclaimed. The archbishop of Lund excommunicated Sture first, in 1517, because of his hostilities against Trolle, who was deposed by the regent as a traitor. Sture freed himself from the excommunication by cooperating with the papal commissioner Arcimboldi, who in 1518 was won over by Sture and took over the archbishopric. Under the cover of the bull of excommunication, the Danish king Christian II legitimated his renewed attack on Sweden in 1519. During these struggles Sture was hit by a Danish bullet and died of the wound in February 1520.

Sture's acts against the church and the archbishop were revolutionary and portended the actions of Gustavus Vasa. Not to acknowledge an archbishop consecrated by the pope was threatening and showed that the church was losing its influence. Sture even claimed the right of the state to dispose of the secular property of the church, which idea Vasa realized in 1527. The romantic Swedish historians and painters of the nineteenth century depicted Sture as a knight of light. Today he is seen more as a ruthless statesman.

BIBLIOGRAPHY

Bergström, R. *Studier till den stora krisen i Nordens historia, 1517–1523.* Uppsala, 1943.

Carlsson, G. *Hemming Gadh: En statsman och prelat från Sturetiden.* Uppsala, 1915.

———. "Sten Sture d.y.: En karaktärstudie." *Scandia* 2 (1929), 107–133.

Olsson, G. *Stat och kyrka i Sverige vid medeltidens slut.* Uppsala, 1947.

Palme, S. U. *Riksföreståndarvalet 1512. Studier i nordisk politik och svensk statsrätt, 1470–1523.* Uppsala, 1949.

Stensson, R. *Peder Jakobsson Sunnanväder och maktkampen i Sverige, 1504–1527.* Uppsala, 1947.

Wieselgren, Greta. *Sten Sture d.y. och Gustaf Trolle.* Lund, 1949.

INGUN MONTGOMERY

STURM, Jakob (1489–1553), stettmeister ("chief magistrate") of Strasbourg and founder of the Schmalkald League.

Son of a patrician magistrate and great-grandson (through his mother) of the city's leading fifteenth-century political figure, Sturm was originally intended and educated for the church. Under the guidance of Jakob Wimpfeling (1450–1528) of Sélestat, he studied arts at Heidelberg in 1501–1504 and theology at Freiburg in 1504–1508. Following nine years of relative idleness at Strasbourg, during which time he and others of Wimpfeling's circle fell under the influence of Erasmus, Sturm worked as secretary to Count Palatine Henry (1487–1552) from summer 1517 until November 1523, when he converted to evangelical religion and abandoned his clerical career. Sturm's 1522 memorial on the reform of university studies at Heidelberg confirms his support for humanism in the Erasmian sense, and he attributed his religious conversion both to Wimpfeling's influence—"If I am a heretic, you made me one!" (1523)—and to reading the controversial literature of the time.

In January 1524 Sturm entered the Senate & XXI (the large council) and rose very rapidly, becoming in 1526 a *stettmeister* and life member of the privy council of the XIII, which dealt with foreign affairs. Shortly after his conversion he married a daughter of *Stettmeister* Hans Bock von Gerstheim (d. 1542) and Ursula von Fleckenstein; she died (probably) by 1529, and he never remarried.

Sturm's formative political experiences were the Peasants' War of 1525, which he probably experienced at closer hand and in more theaters than did any other politician of his time, and the imperial Diet of Speyer in 1526, where he represented a policy of conciliation. In 1528, however, he came to favor an alliance with the Lutheran princes of central Germany, Landgrave Philipp of Hesse and Elector John of Saxony, over the alternative policy of alliance with Zurich, Basel, and Bern. He signed the protest and the alliance agreement at Speyer in April 1529, worked with Landgrave Philipp against the Lutheran rejection of the "Sacramentarians" of the south, and played an important secondary role at the failed Colloquy of Marburg (September 1529). At the Diet of Augsburg in 1530 he sponsored the separate doctrinal statement (the Tetrapolitan Confession) as preparation for a possible agreement with the Lutherans, and he played a central role in the ensuing negotiations for the Schmalkald League (Schmalkalden, December 1530). Thereafter Sturm became spokesman for the southern free cities in the league, a close collaborator with the landgrave, and the agent of Strasbourg's acceptance of the Augsburg Confession.

At Strasbourg Sturm was a principal architect of the suppression of the sects and the establishment of the state church during and after the synod of 1533. From 1526 until his death he was a member of the school board (*Scholarchen, Schulherren*), and his special love was the Latin school, or gymnasium (established 1538), to which he called Jean Sturm (1509–1581) as rector as well as many other distinguished scholars.

Sturm's differences with the landgrave over the conquered duchy of Braunschweig-Wolfenbüttel disturbed their relations from 1542 onward, and Sturm fought a losing battle in 1545–1546 to reform the Schmalkald League by strengthening its central institutions, sharing power more equally between cities and princes, and introducing direct taxes (the "Common Penny"). Sturm took little direct part in the Schmalkald War until the end of the Danube campaign (November 1546), when he urged the commanders to seek a decisive battle.

After the war Sturm's policy of reconciliation with Charles V was opposed by many guildsmen and some clergy, led by Martin Bucer, who broke with Sturm over the provisional religious policy (the "Interim") after the "Armored Diet," which sat at Augsburg in 1547–1548. Controversy over the Interim brought Strasbourg to the brink of revolution in August 1548, but under Sturm's leadership the settlement was negotiated, sending Bucer into exile. Sturm's last years were marked by a growing provincialization of policy. He died, perhaps of malaria, on 30 October 1553. Johannes Marbach preached his funeral sermon on the following day, and Johann Sturm gave the official eulogy in Latin before the Senate & XXI.

Jakob Sturm was the most remarkable and influential urban politician of his day in the Holy Roman Empire. He provided an unusually skilled level of leadership to Strasbourg, to the southern Protestant cities, and to the Schmalkald League. His religious views were generally Erasmian-Zwinglian, for though he was thoroughly sacramentarian in doctrine, he held that Catholicism was a form of genuine Christianity. In ecclesiastical policy Sturm strongly supported lay control of the church and uniformity of preaching, but he did not believe in the possibility of making society truly Christian—"laws make hypocrites."

BIBLIOGRAPHY

Brady, Thomas A., Jr. *Protestant Politics: Jacob Sturm (1489–1553) and the German Reformation.* Studies in German Histories. Atlantic Highlands, N.J., 1994.
Chrisman, Miriam U. "Jakob Sturm of Strasbourg." In *Contemporaries of Erasmus: A Biographical Register of the Renaissance and Reformation,* edited by Peter G. Bietenholz, vol. 3, pp. 293–294. Toronto, 1987.

THOMAS A. BRADY, JR.

STURM, Johann (1507–1589), educator and diplomat in Strasbourg. Sturm attended the College of Saint Jerome in Liège, the College of Three Languages at Louvain, and the University of Paris. Rector of the first Strasbourg gymnasium (1538) and academy (1566), his forte was pedagogical, not political, but he labored at peacemaking so Protestantism might prosper. A brilliant rhetorician and logician, his patrons included Guillaume Budé, the du Bellay brothers, and Marguerite d'Angoulême. Theologians such as Philipp Melanchthon, Martin Bucer, Calvin, and Théodore de Bèze were also supporters. Queen Elizabeth I, Wolfgang, duke of Zweibrücken (a former pupil), and Henry III of France asked Sturm for advice, and the houses of Navarre, Condé, and Coligny petitioned him for loans.

As a diplomat he failed to arrange a conference involving Melanchthon, Bucer, and Francis I in the early 1530s. As ambassador to France (1545–1547) he failed to get the Schmalkald princes to ally with France. His intervention with Henry II for the Vaudois (1550s) did win them better treatment. At Saverne (1562) Sturm believed the Cardinal Charles de Guise's promise to tolerate Lutheranism in France, but he was unprepared for the massacre of Huguenots at Wassy by François of Lorraine, the duke of Guise. Sturm failed to assess French reluctance to relieve French Huguenots in return for German Protestant support against the emperor. He was unaware of the duke of Anjou's (later Henry III's) complicity in the Saint Bartholomew's Day Massacre (24 August 1572) when he agreed to support his candidacy for Poland's throne. Charles IX and Henry III died owing Sturm money lent to benefit Huguenots.

Sturm was an idealist, believing truth liberated people from "barbarism." At the Collège de France he popularized the logic of Roelof Huysman (Rudolf Agricola) and encouraged students to combine logic with rhetoric to improve their writing style. He wrote many textbooks and treatises and was an innovator in logic.

Because he represented a northern humanism more concerned with piety than was Italian humanism, many commentators have questioned his commitment to teach the classics without Christian bias, but Sturm's program of pure Latinity sheltered the classical heritage from a rigid Lutheran pastorate jealous of boys' time. He hoped *Pietas litterata* ("learned piety") would promote Christian morals. Sturm's liberalism was unacceptable to pastors Johannes Marbach and Nicholas Pappus and forced him (1570s) into doctrinal controversies resulting in his dismissal as rector (1581). His program, however, endured until 1604, the dispute having concerned orthodoxy in the theological faculty more than pedagogy in general.

The impracticality of Sturm's classical curriculum had its critics. Sturm's biographer (revealing a modern bias for science) found it deficient in science and technology, while later nationalists resented his slighting vernacular languages. Sturm integrated scholastic with humanist techniques, dialectic with rhetoric. Although some fault his program as too verbal, others find daily speaking, notebook keeping, and essay writing dynamic learning devices. His language-learning methods resembled the aural-oral (Glastonberry) method developed in the United States during the Sputnik crisis. Sturm saw the need for rapid learning, and one of the hallmarks of his curriculum was that for him formal education in the classroom ended at a certain point with finished students who could now continue on their own. His program shaped schools in Germany, France, England, Poland, Bohemia, Romania, and Hungary, countries whose Strasbourg graduates carried classical knowledge home again. Sturm's method also influenced Jesuit education.

BIBLIOGRAPHY

Primary Source

Sturm, Johann. *Classicae Epistolae; Sive Scholae Argentineses restitutae.* Translated by Jean Rott, with introduction and notes. Paris, 1938.

Secondary Sources

Engel, Charles. *L'école latine et l'ancienne Académie de Strasbourg, 1538–1621.* Paris, 1900.
Faerber, Robert. "La pensée religieuse et théologique de Jean Sturm." In *Strasbourg au coeur religieux du 16e siècle: Hommage à L. Febvre.* Actes du Colloque Internationale, pp. 189–195. Strasbourg, 1975.
Halkin, Léon-E. "Jean Sturm et le Collège Liégeois des Frères de la Vie Commune." In *L'humanisme en Alsace.* Paris, 1939.
Mesnard, Pierre. "La pédagogie de Jean Sturm et son inspiration évangélique, 1507–1589." In *3e Rapport du 12e Congrès Internationale des Sciences Historiques,* pp. 95–100. Vienna, 1965.
Ryan, Lawrence V. *Roger Ascham.* Stanford, Calif., and London, 1963.
Schmidt, Charles. *La vie et les travaux de Jean Sturm* (1855). Reprint, Nieuwkoop, 1970.
Schindling, Anton. *Humanistische Hochschule und freie Reichsstadt; Gymnasium und Akademie in Strassburg, 1538–1621.* Wiesbaden, 1977.
Vasoli, C. "Richerche sulle dialettiche del Cinquecento: III. Sturm, Melantone e il problema del metodo." *Rivista Critica di Storia dela Filosofia* 21 (1966), 123–127.
Verzeichnis der im deutschen Sprachbereich erschienenen Drucke des XVI. Jahrhunderts. Stuttgart, 1983–. See vol. 20, nos. 9898–10,006.
Vos, Alvin, ed. *Letters of Roger Ascham.* Translated by Maurice Hatch and Alvin Vos, with an introduction. New York, 1989.

BARBARA SHER TINSLEY

STYFEL, Michael. *See* Stifel, Michael.

SUÁREZ, Francisco (1548–1617), Jesuit philosopher, theologian, and political theorist. Suárez was born at Granada, Spain; his father, a successful lawyer, early destined him for the priesthood. He entered the Jesuits in 1564. After a weak beginning, he soon became a brilliant student at the University of Salamanca, which was then a center of revived Thomism. Upon completing his Jesuit training, he taught philosophy briefly at Segovia (1571–1574); he then devoted six years to teaching theology at various Jesuit colleges. The lecture notes from these courses became a quarry for his later publications.

In 1580 he was called to teach theology at the prestigious Jesuit Roman College, where he lectured on the *Summa theologiae* of Thomas Aquinas, but because of failing health he returned to Spain and occupied a chair of theology at Alcalá (1585–1593). His last years at Alcalá de Henares were marked by a bitter rivalry with his fellow Jesuit, the more flamboyant Gabriel Vázquez, so Suárez was happy to move to Salamanca, where he taught and wrote until 1597. He spent the last period of his life (1597–1617) at the University of Coimbra, at the behest of Philip II, who wanted to enhance the prestige of the Portuguese university.

Suárez's personal life was that of a pious priest and largely uneventful. His health was never robust, and his teaching duties cut into the time he would have preferred to devote to preparing his manuscripts for publication. Many were left only partially revised at his death and were published posthumously; others, most notably his commentaries on Aristotle, were never published. The 1856 Paris edition of his works ran to twenty-eight volumes.

Suárez's main philosophical works were his treatise on the soul (Lyon, 1621) and especially his *Disputationes metaphysicae* (Salamanca, 1597), which enjoyed great popularity (eighteen editions in the century after its publication) not only in Catholic countries but also in Protestant Germany, where it contributed to the renewed scholastic reshaping of philosophy and theology during the age of Protestant orthodoxy. While working within the regnant Aristotelian tradition, Suárez's philosophical works develop their own order of presentation. Written in humanistic Latin, his works are systematic and clear but often prolix; they draw on a wide reading in philosophers from Plato to his own day. His book on metaphysics is noteworthy for rejecting the Thomistic real distinction between essence and existence.

The most important of Suárez's theological works were his extensive commentaries on the *Summa theologiae* of Thomas Aquinas, especially the tracts *De Deo Uno et Trino* (Lisbon, 1606), *De Angelis* (Lyon, 1620), *De Opere sex Dierum* (Lyon, 1621), and *De Legibus* (Coimbra, 1612). The last of these tracts has been much studied in the twentieth century, and along with the works of Francisco de Vitoria and Hugo Grotius it laid the intellectual foundations of international law. In choosing to write on the *Summa* rather than Peter Lombard's *Sententiae,* Suárez was following the precedent set a half century earlier by Francisco de Vitoria at Salamanca and thereby contributed to making Thomism central to revived scholasticism, even though he often departed from the teachings of Thomas on particular issues.

Suárez's *Opuscula sex* (Madrid, 1599) contain his teaching on grace, human freedom, and God's foreknowledge—a set of questions then under bitter dispute by Jesuits and Dominicans. Suárez does not go so far as his fellow Jesuit Luis de Molina in stressing human freedom in the process of salvation. At the request of the Jesuit general Claudio Acquaviva, Suárez wrote a four-volume study of religious orders, *De virtute et statu religionis* (Coimbra, 1608–1625); much of it was devoted to a defense of the innovations begun by the Jesuits and by other new orders of the Counter-Reformation.

Most of his writings dealt with traditional questions in Scholastic philosophy and theology. His main contribution to anti-Protestant polemics was his long *Defensio Fidei catholicae et Apostolicae adversus Anglicanae sectae errores* (Coimbra, 1613, partial English translation in 1944), which was largely directed against the oath that King James I demanded from his Catholic subjects. James I had it burned at Saint Paul's in London and arranged for refutations. Its statements about papal power also led to its being burned by the Parlement of Paris, and it provided Gallicans with ammunition against the Jesuits.

Suárez was the culmination of the scholastic revival in Counter-Reformation Spain and the greatest and most systematic theologian among the early Jesuits. Few of his works have been translated into English, but a distinctive Suárezian school flourished among Spanish Jesuits into the twentieth century.

BIBLIOGRAPHY

Primary Sources

Suarez, Francisco. *Selections from Three Works of Francisco Suarez, S.J.* Oxford, 1944.
———. *De iuramento fidelitatis.* Madrid, 1978–79.
———. *Francisci Suarez Opera omnia.* LaCrosse, Wis., 1982. 28 vols. on microfiche.

Secondary Sources

Bastit, Michel. *Naissance de La loi moderne: la pensée de loi de saint Thomas à Suárez.* Paris, 1990. His contribution to the philosophy of law in historical perspective.
Fichter, Joseph H. *Man of Spain: Francis Suárez.* New York, 1940. Semipopular biography.
Hughes, Lachlam. *The Suarezian Concept of Episcopal Jurisdiction.* Rome, 1963. Scholarly study of his ecclesiology.
Mullaney, Thomas U. *Suárez on Human Freedom.* Baltimore, 1950. Monograph on an important aspect of his theology.
Polgár, Lászlo. *Bibliographie sur l'histoire de la Compagnie de Jésus, 1901–1980: Les personnes.* Rome, 1990. Detailed bibliography on Suárez and all aspects of his thought; see especially vol. 3, pp. 268–329.
Rommen, Heinrich Albert. *La teoria del estado y de la comunidad en Francisco Suárez.* Madrid, 1951. An eminent scholar explores his political thought.
Scorraille, Raoul de. *François Suarez de la Compagnie de Jesus, d'après*

ses lettres, ses autres écrits inédites et un grand nombre de documents nouveau. 2 Vols. Paris, 1913. Massive study.
Verzeichnis der im deutschen Sprachbereich erschienenen Drucke des XVI. Jahrhunderts. Stuttgart, 1983–. See vol. 20, nos. 10,073–10,075.
Wilenius, Reijo. *The Social and Political Theory of Francisco Suárez.* Helsinki, 1963. Scholarly monograph.

JOHN PATRICK DONNELLY

SÜLEYMAN I. *See* Ottoman Empire.

SUMPTUARY LAWS. *See* Social Discipline.

SUPERSTITION. *See* Magic; Popular Religion, overview article; Prodigies and Portents; Witchcraft.

SWABIAN LEAGUE. In 1488 a peace-keeping federation was formed in southern Germany that lasted until 1534. It began as the Habsburg dynasty's marshaling of smaller powers in Upper Swabia, a deeply fragmented region, against Bavarian expansion. Its original membership consisted of smaller imperial estates—counts, knights, cities, and prelates—though from around 1500 it admitted the leading princes of southern Germany as far northward as Franconia and Hesse.

The league's assembly, which usually met at Ulm, comprised two houses, the nobles and the cities, and later a third house for the princes; the presidency was also tripartite in this sense. The league's court promoted the development of a more widely effective jurisprudence in this fragmented region, became a significant agent of the reception of Roman law, and tried at one point to acquire direct jurisdiction over the members' subjects. The league's taxes, like the empire's, were based on a conventional "month" of pay for fixed numbers of infantry and cavalry, which the members divided according to a matricular list. The growth of princely power in the league reduced both the influence and the tax shares of the other houses, that of the nobles much faster and further than that of the cities. For example, the cities' share of taxes fell from 37 percent in 1488 to 28.6 percent in 1500 and 21 percent in 1530. The cities nonetheless remained the league's most dutiful members, and they developed a custom of routine consultation and cooperation, which supported their ability to act together in the urban diet (*Städtetag*), the imperial diet, and the Schmalkald League.

The Swabian League acted as an imperial viceroy in Swabia, Franconia, and, to a lesser degree, the Upper Rhine. The league successfully blocked Bavaria in 1492, and it supported Emperor Maximilian I in the Swabian War against the Swiss Confederacy in 1499 and the War of the Bavarian

Succession in 1504. In 1519, as Maximilian was dying, Duke William of Bavaria united with the league's cities against Duke Ulrich of Württemberg, his brother-in-law, and led the league's army in the conquest of Württemberg, one of its most successful campaigns. As the league had no institutions that could manage a long-term occupation, it transferred the duchy to Emperor Charles V in 1521 against the promise to pay the members' war costs, and Württemberg remained under Austrian rule until 1534.

The Swabian League took part in suppressing the Knights' Revolt in 1522, when its army razed twenty-five noble castles in Franconia, but its most important military operation came during the Peasants' War of 1525. When the Upper Swabian rebel armies united at Memmingen on 6–7 March, the league's assembly was meeting at Ulm, and its army was away in Württemberg, which was threatened by Duke Ulrich's ten thousand Swiss mercenaries. The league's cities hoped for a negotiated settlement, but when Ulrich's mercenaries deserted him, the league commander, Georg Truchsess von Waldburg, brought the army to the Danube, where in mid-April he broke some of the Upper Swabian armies and made terms with the others (Treaty of Weingarten, 17 April 1525). He then moved through Württemberg into Franconia, defeating rebel armies at Böblingen (12 May), Königshofen (2 June), and Ingolstadt (8 June). After the insurrection, the league moved to punish the rebels and those who had aided them, including nobles, such as the redoubtable Goetz von Berlichingen, who by tradition invented on this occasion the "Swabian greeting" (*Lech mich am Arsch*), and those member cities, such as Heilbronn, that had opened their gates to rebel armies.

The league's remaining nine years were shaped by the rivalry between the houses of Wittelsbach and Habsburg, as the Bavarian dukes became deeply entwined in the movement to prevent King Ferdinand, Charles V's brother, from being elected king of the Romans and successor to the imperial monarchy. This policy led to Bavarian apathy toward the league's renewal in 1533 and 1534 and to Bavarian cooperation with the French-financed and Hessian-led strike to restore Duke Ulrich in 1534. The league's dissolution was also encouraged by the Reformation, though its role in checking the spread of Protestantism was probably less than has been alleged.

The appeal of the Swabian League to the small powers of southern Germany survived its demise, for barely a year later, King Ferdinand organized a new association, the Nine Years' League, at Lauingen on 11 April 1535. This aspect of his policy to revitalize Maximilian's system of clientage in southern Germany extended to the imperial knights during the 1540s. Although the Nine Years' League did not flourish, the desire for such an association with the monarchy remained strong in some southern cities, especially at Nuremberg. As one Nuremberg politician wrote, "the Swabian league was the proper form of the German Nation. It

was feared by many, and in many ways it protected and sustained the public peace and law and order."

[*See also* Charles V; Empire; Schmalkald League; *and* Württemberg.]

BIBLIOGRAPHY

Sea, Thomas F. "Imperial Cities and the Peasants' War in Germany." *Central European History* 12 (1979), 3–37.
———. "The Swabian League and Government in the Holy Roman Empire of the Early Sixteenth Century." In *Aspects of Late Medieval Government and Society: Essays Presented to J. R. Lander*, edited by J. G. Rowe, pp. 249–276. Toronto, 1986.

THOMAS A. BRADY, JR.

SWEDEN. On the eve of the Reformation, there was no widespread movement of reform in the Swedish medieval church. What agitated the minds and hearts of the people was the question of political independence from Denmark. The Kalmar Union was the overriding political reality in Scandinavia at the outset of the sixteenth century. Members of all the Scandinavian royal houses had declined in number in the fourteenth century as a result of infertility, intermarriage, high mortality, and the Black Death of the 1350s. In 1380 the ten-year-old Olaf V began a dynastic union between Denmark and Norway. When he died seven years later, his strong-willed mother (Margaret) assumed control of the monarchy and within six months was also proclaimed ruler of Sweden-Finland as well. In 1397 Queen Margaret summoned a pan-Scandinavian assembly at Kalmar in order to legitimize her reign and make it hereditary. Though failing to achieve the latter goal, the Kalmar Union lasted until 1523. Throughout the fifteenth century, however, Swedish independence movements arose under the leadership of Engelbrekt Engelbrektsson (1434–1436) and three of the Swedish regents, Karl Knutsson and the two Sten Stures (1438–1515). Nationalistic feelings ran high in Sweden in opposition to the Danish rulers, who dominated the Kalmar Union. This century-long turmoil was to have a direct bearing on the course of the Reformation in Sweden.

As the sixteenth century dawned, the winds of reform in the church provided yet another destabilizing element in Sweden. In Scandinavia two diverse principles were operative in the final triumph of Lutheranism. The principle of *cuius regio eius religio* (whoever the king, his religion) was at work in Denmark-Norway while the principle of popular sovereignty best describes what transpired in Sweden-Finland. Under Christian III of Denmark (r. 1536–1559), Lutheranism was promulgated by royal decree, Christian being an ardent Lutheran ever since the Diet of Worms. In Sweden-Finland, however, the principle of popular sovereignty triumphed over the wishes of the various Swedish monarchs, forcing them in the end to opt for Lutheranism as the religion of the realm.

The Kalmar Union was unpopular in Sweden because of its political domination by Denmark. After repeated Swedish attempts to overthrow Danish control during the fifteenth and early sixteenth century, the Danish king Christian II (r. 1513–1523) decided to bring an end to the opposition once and for all. With the seeming assistance of the archbishop of Uppsala, Gustav Trolle, himself a Dane, Christian II invited the leading opposition members of the Swedish nobility and clergy to a reconciliation banquet in November 1520. During the course of the reconciliation banquet, Danish guards took more than eighty of the guests and summarily executed them in what has come to be known as the Stockholm Bloodbath.

Gustavus Vasa, son of one of the executed noblemen, rose up and rallied the Swedish people in a successful rebellion against Christian "the Tyrant." During the three years of conflict (1520–1523), Vasa was aided by the Hanseatic city of Lübeck. This aid came with strings attached that were to plague the Swedish king repeatedly during the first decade of his reign. In 1523, in the city of Strengnäs, Vasa was proclaimed king of Sweden (r. 1523–1560). During the course of his stay at Strengnäs, the newly proclaimed king was introduced by his secretary, Laurentius Andreae, to the preaching of a young evangelical priest by the name of Olaus Petri, who had studied at Wittenberg.

It was Olaus Petri, often called the "Martin Luther of Sweden," who introduced the teachings of Luther to Sweden in 1518. He had begun his studies at Wittenberg in 1516, when Luther was lecturing on *Galatians*. He had experienced firsthand the momentous events surrounding the Ninety-five Theses in October 1517. The next autumn, following the Heidelberg Disputation, Petri returned to his native Sweden filled with a passion to introduce needed evangelical reforms both in doctrine and in practice. The reforms Petri introduced were conservative and reflected the convictions of the early Luther. Philipp Melanchthon had not even arrived on the scene at Wittenberg. The Leipzig Debate with Johann Eck, the Reformation treatises of 1520, and the Diet of Worms were still in the future. There was no thought whatsoever of breaking with Rome when Olaus Petri returned to Sweden. Yet as events unfolded, a gradual ecclesiastical transformation transpired under the leadership of Petri and his younger brother, Laurentius, who had also studied at Wittenberg. Both were convinced that all the church needed was to allow the word of God free reign in preaching and teaching, and reform would come about. No new confessional subscription was envisaged, just the word alone (*sola scriptura*).

During the first decade of Vasa's reign following his coronation, the Swedish monarch was sore pressed to keep the ship of state afloat. Economic pressures to repay the Lübeck debt were ever-present. While many people rejoiced in their newly won political independence from Denmark, they did not understand their rebellion to be against the old faith, even though it was against the archbishop of Uppsala. Others did not like what they saw in Vasa and were not about to exchange a Danish tyrant for another strong, centralized monarch, even if he was Swedish. Rebellion after rebellion arose among the peasants and local nobility of Dalarna and Småland provinces during the early years of Vasa's rule. During the years when Clement VII was pope (1523–1534), Rome offered no positive initiatives to overcome an ever-worsening situation except to insist that Gustav Trolle be reinstated as archbishop of Uppsala. Swedes of all backgrounds were opposed to such a move since they suspected that Trolle was implicated in the Stockholm Bloodbath. Unable to collect taxes to repay the Lübeck debt, with sporadic rebellions throughout the land, dissension among all classes because of a strong, centralized monarchy, and with no help forthcoming from the church, Vasa resigned suddenly in 1527.

Many have contended that this was a shrewd move on the part of Vasa because it galvanized support around him. At a hastily summoned meeting of the *Riksdag* at Västerås, Vasa was persuaded to rescind his resignation. In the light of the pope's failure to offer a satisfactory solution for reform of the church, an agreement was reached at Västerås that severed the church of Sweden from the Roman see. The church's income was to be controlled by the state and used to pay off the Lübeck debt. The Dalarna rebellion was to be dealt with forthrightly. Clergy were to come under the jurisdiction of civil law, and any property bequeathed to the church after 1454 was to be returned to its legal heirs. As a result of the decrees of the Diet of Västerås in 1527, the foundation for an independent, national church and a strong, centralized monarchy that represented the will of all the estates was established. The pure word of God was to be preached and not the "uncertain wonders, human inventions and fables, as has been much the practice hitherto." No complaints against the new faith were to be tolerated so long as the word of God was preached. Though granted a measure of independence, the Swedish church assembly derived its authority from the state.

In the meantime Olaus Petri had been called to the city parish in Stockholm (1524) and was busy spreading the precepts of the Wittenberg reformers. In 1526, the year before he was joined by his brother, Laurentius, Olaus published his Swedish translation of the New Testament as well as a catechetical instruction book. Polemical works against Paul Helie also appeared from his pen at this time. In 1529 Olaus Petri produced the first evangelical manual to assist clergy in their ministry. This work did not insist on uniformity in pastoral practice and worship but represented a middle ground between Rome and Wittenberg. In 1530 Olaf Petri published his Swedish hymnbook and in the following year his Swedish Mass. The transition to vernacular worship and hymn singing accelerated greatly during the 1530s.

When the Reformation commenced in the 1520s, five of

the seven bishoprics in Sweden were vacant. In 1524 the abbot of the Brigittine monastery in Rome, Petrus Magni, was consecrated bishop of Västerås after papal confirmation. Under royal pressure Magni ordained three other bishops in 1528 but without papal approval. In 1531 Laurentius Petri became the first evangelical archbishop of Uppsala when he was ordained by Petrus Magni and the other Swedish bishops. A combination of royal pressure and wishful thinking on the part of the bishops, who thought they saw in Laurentius an Erasmian reforming bishop, seems to be the reason they agreed to participate in ordaining the Wittenberg-trained evangelical. Thus it was that the historic episcopate was maintained by accident in the Lutheran church of Sweden. Not much was made of this fact until the twentieth century, when Anglicans and Swedish Lutherans in the ecumenical movement came to view it as a fortuitous happenstance.

The 1530s were marked by a steady, gradual consolidation of evangelical strength under the leadership of the two Petri brothers. At this point there was no talk of a Lutheran church in Sweden, but only of a reform-minded, evangelical, national catholic church. Early in the 1540s Vasa sought to reign in the growing independence of the evangelical church by appointing George Norman, a German nobleman and tutor to Prince Erik, to be the lay superintendent of the church with power to exercise the king's jurisdiction "over bishops, prelates, and all other clergy and their subordinates, in matters of religion." Olaus Petri and Laurentius Andreae were accused of treason and condemned to death for supposedly undermining obedience to royal authority. The decision was never carried out, but the king had made his point. Nevertheless, the Petris were able to maintain the relative independence of the Swedish church in the face of royal opposition. Fifty years later, this independence was crucial, for as yet no legal confessional subscription bound the Swedish church to either Wittenberg or Rome. Vasa had sought a relationship similar to that delineated in many German church ordinances drawn up by Johannes Bugenhagen, one of which had recently been enacted in Denmark-Norway (1539). In the midst of all these events, the Swedish Bible was published in 1541. This was a great boon to religious education throughout the nation, since every parish was to possess a copy.

During the four decades after Vasa (d. 1560), a series of succession problems and family squabbles plagued the nation. The eldest son of Vasa imprisoned his younger brother and his wife because he suspected them of foul play. Considered by many to be insane, the new king, Erik XIV (r. 1560–1568), issued repeated death sentences to keep the nobility off balance. He quickly undid his father's policy of peaceful coexistence by launching the disastrous Northern Seven Years' War (1563–1570) against Denmark, Poland, and Lübeck. Only in the early years of John III's reign could Sweden extricate itself from the conflict. In the church, the

Lutheran archbishop had intended to introduce a Lutheran church order in 1561. Erik XIV had strong Calvinist sympathies, and so a theological stalemate developed. Laurentius Petri decided to drop the matter of confessional subscription and continue his program of education and nurture by issuing a revised catechism and hymnbook.

In 1568 Erik XIV was overthrown by his younger brother, who assumed the title John III (r. 1568–1592). The legitimacy of this move was to haunt the new king throughout his reign, and he was always careful to avoid alienating his supporters and the general populace. The expansionist policy of turning the Baltic into a Swedish lake nevertheless continued.

The capstone of Laurentius Petri's long tenure as the first Lutheran archbishop of Uppsala came in 1571 with the enactment of the church ordinance. For over a decade, Petri had been frustrated by the Calvinist views of Erik XIV but had wisely bided his time. The new king was open to regularizing and codifying the religious changes that had occurred during the century. The church ordinance did not require any formal Lutheran subscription, as it reflected the generic *sola scriptura* principle with which Petri had become acquainted during the early 1520s when he had studied at Wittenberg.

Three years after Petri's death, John III published his revision of the liturgy commonly known as the Red Book (*Liturgia Suecanae Ecclesiae*, 1576). The king had always fancied himself a liturgical scholar. Soon he was faced with a determined opposition from clergy and laity alike, especially after his high church sympathies and his close ties to a secret Jesuit mission in Stockholm came to light in 1580. Through the influence of the queen's Polish chaplains and the Norwegian Jesuit Laurentius Norvegus, John III had converted to Roman Catholicism and permitted a secret Jesuit theological college to operate in Stockholm for four years. Most Swedes supposed this to be a high church Lutheran theological college sponsored by the king to rival the low church theological faculty at the University of Uppsala. Afraid because of his tenuous claims to the throne and the anticipated reaction of the Swedish people, John III refused to make his conversion public unless the pope would promise to allow Swedish clergy to marry, Mass to be said in the vernacular, and Communion to be given in both kinds. Pope Gregory XIII refused. John III publicly denied he had ever converted to Roman Catholicism and summarily expelled the Jesuits from Sweden, thereby terminating the secret Jesuit mission.

Rome was prepared to bide its time, however, because the next person in line of succession to the Swedish throne was John III's son, who happened to be not only an ardent Roman Catholic, having been raised by his Polish mother, but also the king of Poland, Sigismund III Vasa (r. 1587–1632). Upon John III's death in 1592, the future for the Counter-Reformation in Sweden appeared auspicious. At this point the Swedish clergy and laity under the leadership of John III's younger brother, Charles, hastily convened a church assembly at Uppsala in 1593. Laurentius Petri's church ordinance was reinstated, John III's Red Book was rejected, and for the first time, subscription to the Augsburg Confession was required of all, including anyone who wished to be king of Sweden. All future monarchs of Sweden-Finland would have to be Lutheran. *Cuius regio eius religio* had been turned on its head, with the people dictating the religious allegiance of their monarchs. Though Sigismund III was advised by his Jesuit counselors to subscribe to the Augsburg Confession "with his fingers crossed," he never took possession of his native land. In 1598 he was forced to invade his own kingdom and suffered a disastrous military defeat at Stångebro. His uncle continued to govern Sweden as regent until 1604, when he was crowned in his own right as Charles IX (r. 1604–1611). With the dawn of the seventeenth century, the ecclesiastical transformation of a determined Roman Catholic populace to that of an ardent Lutheran nation was complete.

BIBLIOGRAPHY

Andersson, Ingvar. *History of Sweden.* Reprint, Westport, Conn., 1975.

Bergendoff, Conrad. *Olavus Petri and the Ecclesiastical Transformation in Sweden, 1521–1551.* Philadelphia, 1965.

Butler, C. M. *The Reformation in Sweden.* New York, 1883.

Holmquist, Hjalmar. *Reformationstidevarvet, 1521–1611.* Stockholm, 1933.

Roberts, Michael. *The Early Vasas: A History of Sweden, 1523–1611.* Reprint, Cambridge, 1986.

TRYGVE R. SKARSTEN

SWITZERLAND. Until the mid-eighteenth century, the Swiss called their country *Schwitzerland* and from then on employed the term *Schweiz*, because it was shorter. Both the original name and the shorter one derived from the region of Schwyz, one of the original regions and the eighth smallest of the allies that made up the "oath fellowships" that were called the Swiss Confederation. Switzerland remains today a small country. At the most only about 20 percent of its inhabitants ever lived in the Alps, which cover three-fifths of the Switzerland. Important as the Alps have been in Swiss history, they are often wrongly viewed as its key. Instead, as much as the Alps, water played a decisive role in the development of the Swiss Confederation. For example, without the link that the lake of Lucerne provided to the earliest members of the Confederation, (Schwyz, Uri, Unterwalden, and Lucerne), there might never have been a Swiss Confederation.

Populations, Geography, General Problems. The major rivers flow out from the massif of the Aare and the Saint Gotthard, which together form the geomorphic and hydrographical center of the Alps. The Rhone flows out from the massif to the southwest, and the Rhone Valley splits the heart of the Alps. The Rhine extends the line of the Rhone to the northeast, then turns to the north, flowing into Lake Constance, and finally on to Basel and what was in 1500 the German Empire. The Rhone and the Rhine valleys provided the routes to the Alpine passes that led south toward Italy. In the western part of Switzerland the Simplon pass connected the Champagne fairs in the north with the shortest routes to Venice. The Great Saint Bernard also offered a direct route to the Val d'Aosta or to the Simplon and Lombardy. The route to the Semptimer pass carried the Rhine traffic that came south from Strasbourg to Basel and then to Chur. The construction of the Devil's bridge over the Reuss was the step necessary for the opening of the Saint Gotthard pass in about 1200. It provided a direct north-south link that influenced the economic growth of Lucerne, Zug, and Zurich. The importance of all the passes, in particular the Gotthard, encouraged cooperation among the Alpine communities. The extent of this cooperation is probably best reflected in the Pfaffenbrief (the priests' letter) of 1370. All the Swiss regions that signed the letter agreed among other things to guarantee the security of traffic from the Gotthard pass to Zurich. This naturally encouraged further cooperation among the Confederates. The Gotthard quickly became a center of commercial life and linked Switzerland more closely with the rest of the Holy Roman Empire and northern Italy.

The geography of the Confederation explains the importance of the transit fees that aided the development of a consolidated Swiss economy in the sixteenth century and also encouraged the beginnings of banking in Switzerland. By 1504 Basel had a bank that was partially supported by the city. The geography of valleys, lakes, rivers, and mountains did indeed influence its political and economic development and left the Confederation at the center of Europe's north-south trade.

It is also remarkable that Swiss geography should make a place for four radically different linguistic groups in a country whose population in the sixteenth century was well under a million. Northern and eastern Switzerland spoke a Swiss German dialect derived from old Alemannic and made up more than 70 percent of the Confederation's population. The French-speaking population represented roughly 20 percent of Switzerland's inhabitants and was confined to western Switzerland, that is, to what is now the cantons of Vaud, Neuchatel, a good part of Fribourg, a small part of Bernese territory (which has been recently formed into the canton of Jura), and about half of Wallis. A debased Latin or Romansch is spoken in the valleys of the modern canton of Grisons (Graubünden); in the sixteenth century the use of this language was far more widespread. Today only one in one hundred Swiss speaks Romansch. Italian speakers were found only in the south of Switzerland, and, as the Confederation increased the size of its Italian holdings in the early decades of the sixteenth century, that number grew. Today the Italian speakers in Switzerland make up between 6 and 7 percent of the population.

As the result of its geography, the bulk of Switzerland's population and agriculture lies in a band of hilly country about 50 kilometers broad that stretches about 240 kilometers from Lake Geneva to Lake Constance in the northeast. It was in this "middle land" that the grain production and livestock farming typical of Swiss agriculture developed. A process of more satisfactory specialization in agriculture arose during the sixteenth century. In both the mountainous regions and some part of the middle land, wine and grain production were abandoned in favor of livestock farming, which was more lucrative and soon also found a market beyond the borders of the Confederation. Despite a wet period in the second half of the sixteenth century, which made the cultivation of grain and wine more difficult, the population growth, begun even before the turn of the century, continued, but it is hard to establish reliable statistics for this period. In some areas population growth was sufficient to have a damaging effect upon the wages and living standards of the day laborers, who were also responsible for the cultivation of small plots of marginal land. But this development was not everywhere the case and in some regions the wages of the day laborer rose.

In any case Switzerland had a built-in agricultural problem. Twenty-five percent of its soil was unproductive in comparison with Germany's 6 percent and Austria's 8 percent. The problems caused by the three-field system further limited the agricultural productivity of the middle land. The decline of Swiss agriculture during the wet period of the sixteenth century made matters worse. Northern Switzerland, Zurich, Lucerne, and Basel were able to feed themselves. The Berner middle land and the Aargau were able to export grain. The rest of Switzerland imported grain, rice, and wine and was surrounded by suppliers, happy to profit from the Swiss needs. French salt exports to Switzerland were also of great importance and could be used to put the Confederation under political pressure. The imports cost money, as did the domestic grain and wine required to satisfy the needs of the population. They simply had to have better sources of income.

Switzerland's general poverty can be seen when its towns are compared with those of the rest of Europe, which boasted some twenty-six cities with populations of forty to a hundred thousand inhabitants. The Swiss cities were small and offered no great chances of riches through trade and manufacture. At the beginning of the sixteenth century Zurich had between five and eight thousand inhabitants. Basel and Geneva—the latter not a part of the Confederation—were considered large, with populations of nine or ten thousand. In most instances the urban guilds prevented the development of industrial ventures. Nevertheless, in the long run it was hard to prevent the development of the put-out system that employed the small farmer at home. St. Gall, with a population of four to five thousand residents, was an exception to guild restrictions, and the entire region was involved in linen production. Attempts were made at Zurich and Geneva to use Italian refugees to develop a silk industry, but with very mixed results. All of Bern's attempts to develop a silk industry failed. But the Basel printers successfully employed the put-out system. The important thing for the future was that in Basel, Zurich, and Geneva the put-out system was accepted, though it did not create great wealth in the sixteenth century.

The Swiss did, however, succeed in other ways. It has been argued that the ongoing specialization in agriculture was the result of the cooperation between the urban and rural regions within the Confederation. Each recognized the interests of the other. The internal and external problems that the Confederation faced in the sixteenth century led naturally to its further political articulation. Probably the best proof of the Confederation's political maturity in this period was the surprisingly moderate solution to the problem of the Reformation that the Catholic and Protestant regions finally accepted after the Second Kappel War in 1531. The further growth of political and economic interest groups within the Confederation cannot be considered without a careful look at the development of urban manufacturing and the general dependence of farming interests for profit upon such gatherings as the yearly Lucerne cattle market. Swiss merchants also appeared at the great German fairs at Leipzig and Frankfurt, as well as at Lyon to sell cattle, hard cheese, and wood, but little else.

Despite the two great threats to the future of the Confederation in the sixteenth century—the system of mercenary service with its ubiquitous network of pensions, and the Reformation, which for a while threatened to divide and destroy the Confederation—it reached the full extent of its political and linguistic borders between 1515 and 1569. The year 1536 saw Bernese imperialism on the march westward against the lands and the power of the duke of Savoy. Indeed, Bern's expansion explains in good measure the rather reluctant support for Zurich in the Second Kappel War, which also marked the end of the expansion of the Zwinglian Reformation in German Switzerland. The Bernese, allied with Wallis and Fribourg, conquered Vaud, the basin of Lake Geneva, and the regions of Gex, Gaillard, Ternier, and Chablais south of the basin. The Walliser took the south bank of the lake, as well as the Chablais. In 1564/69 Bern was compelled to return the regions south of the basin to the duke of Savoy, but elsewhere it kept what is now called the Bernese.

The conquest of Vaud provided a shield behind which Calvin's Reformation in Geneva could flourish, not always with the full approval of Bern or Zurich. Geneva was allied with Fribourg since 1519 and with both Bern and Fribourg since 1526. Bern's attempts to bring Geneva into the Confederation failed, and Geneva remained an independent republic until 1798. The king of France joined the alliance to protect Geneva in 1579 and remained a permanent ally, as did Zurich after 1584. Emperor Charles V compelled Constance to leave the Confederation in 1548, and Mülhausen gradually drifted away from its Swiss alliance.

Mercenary Service and the Confederation. Although it is not correct to say that because many Swiss lived marginally, they therefore became mercenaries, for at least some the system of mercenary service was of considerable value and was a source of wealth and prosperity. This was especially true for the so-called *Pensionenherren*, or pensioners, who received pensions from the king of France, the pope, and the emperor to act as recruiting officers and often as military commanders. These military entrepreneurs were also usually part of the oligarchic government of their region, a position that gave them great advantages in defending the status quo. The case of Zurich's mayor, Hans Waldmann, who rose from poverty to wealth and power as a mercenary leader, is not entirely typical, because he was eventually brought down and executed by the Zurich establishment (1489). Not only were there men ready to organize the ire of mercenaries, but there were also young men, often with little military training, who were willing to serve. They belonged to bands of young men who wandered through the countryside seeking adventure and plundering villages. The local authorities were always glad to send them along to a recruiting *Pensionenherr*. It is also hard to deny that there was a surplus of young men who needed employment. As Potter has observed, the abolition of mercenary service, which the Zurich reformer Huldrych Zwingli finally demanded in the interest of protecting Swiss independence from French domination, overlooked the fact that the regions of central Switzerland needed the money brought back from the Italian wars to purchase grain, rice, and wine. Their earnings guaranteed a minimal subsistence in their region. The blockade of grain and other foodstuffs imposed upon the central regions by the Protestants caused the Second Kappel War.

The Swiss were brought into the Italian wars as mercenaries and later became unsuccessful conquerors, in part because the assembly of the Confederation, the *Tagsatzung*, attempted to be a central government in the modern sense. The employment of the Swiss involved them in a long battle between the Habsburgs and Valois for hegemony in Europe (1494–1559). At the time the domination of Europe also meant the control of Italy and the papacy. The weakness of the Swiss was that they were usually employed by both sides in the conflict and refused to fight each other. At Novara in 1500 the Swiss refused to fight each other, but in the process they betrayed Duke Ludovico Sforza and allowed the French to take him prisoner. That the French never released the duke damaged their reputation. The French attempt to capture the kingdom of Naples began to change the Swiss

attitude toward the system of mercenary service. The year 1503/1504 saw the death of thirty thousand Swiss mercenaries in southern Italy, some 6 percent of Switzerland's male population. The meeting of the *Tagsatzung* (diet) in July 1503 attempted to put an end to the business of mercenary service, but the flood of French money that poured into the Confederation caused the attempt to fail by 1508. Each region was left free to do what it wanted, but the anti-French feeling remained. That the *Tagsatzung* could not put an end to French bribes reveals how weak the assembly was, for it was merely a collection of regions that had sworn oaths to cooperate with each other. The Confederation had neither a constitution nor a legal code. Indeed, it was not until the fifteenth century that it had a name and not until the nineteenth century that it adopted an official seal. According to late medieval practice a name and a seal were requisite for political and legal recognition. Neither in dealing with Switzerland's brief period of independent military power in Italy nor in facing the problem of the Reformation was the *Tagsatzung* able to do much.

The result was a deeper involvement in the Italian wars that led to a defensive alliance with Pope Julius II and an agreement with Emperor Maximilian I. After the French had defeated Pope Julius in the battle of Ravenna, the Swiss decided upon an independent anti-French policy and with the support of Venice, captured Pavia, Milan, and in a three-week campaign all of Lombardy (1512). Zwingli, the young chaplain from Glarus, could not conceal his delight at these Swiss victories and the defeat of the French. He was not alone; the pope designated the Confederation as "the defenders of the freedom of the church." The French were determined to turn the Swiss out of Milan, but their first attempt failed in the battle of Novara (1513). The French then began to divide the Confederates. For the payment of a million crowns the Swiss army in the field signed the Treaty of Gallarate, which gave up Genoa and Milan. The troops at Milan and reinforcements from the west of Switzerland held the city, but suffered a bloody defeat at the battle of Marignano (1515). Outraged by these events, Zwingli, who was at Milan, preached on the subject of treason and the division of the Confederation. These developments caused him to reject the mercenary system. It is ironic that Zwingli's later success in combating the promercenary party at Zurich helped to demoralize Zurich's militia, which did not trust the new officers appointed in place of the old pensioners and was unwilling to fight for Zurich in the Second Kappel War. Zwingli paid for this mistake with his life.

Within a year the Confederation had signed a mercenary agreement with France. The treaty was again renewed in 1521, when only Zurich remained true to its papal alliance. After the end of the Second Kappel War Catholic and Protestant alike continued to accept the mercenary system. The service was not of itself as dangerous to the Confederation as Zwingli had believed, but when combined with a determined attempt to spread the Counter-Reformation in the Confederation it could be a menace. This was the case with the Borromeo League of 1585 (Cardinal Carlo Borromeo, archbishop of Milan), which won the seven Catholic regions and encouraged the work of the Capuchins and Jesuits in the Confederation, as well as the policies of Spain and France beyond Switzerland's borders.

The Protestants after Kappel. The Second Kappel War, in which Zwingli died fighting, divided but did not destroy the Swiss Confederation. The military advantages won by the five Catholic regions from the Second Peace of Kappel remained until the Second Villmerger War, which resulted in the defeat of the Catholics and the Fourth Territorial Peace of 1712. From 1712 to the collapse of the old Confederation in 1798 the Protestants, led by Bern and Zurich, had the upper hand. The opposite had occurred in 1656, when the Protestants led by Zurich lost the First Villmerger War. At the behest of the Catholic victors the Third Territorial Peace had characteristically left the solution to religious problems in the hands of individual members of the Confederation.

Long before this decision was made, Josias Simler, theologian at Zurich's theology faculty (Carolinum) and author of the *De Republica Helvestiorum* (1576) had carefully stressed the rights of each individual member of the Confederation. Simler's argument was developed to defend the rights of the Protestant regions in the divided Confederation. Later one of Simler's descendants, Johann Jakob Simler, asserted that "the church of the canton of Zurich, though far away from the hierarchy of the Roman church nevertheless was best in tune with the awakened spirit of republican and Christian freedom." Behind this screen of liberty Heinrich Bullinger and John Calvin were able to develop a theology and confessions of faith for the Protestant world.

[*See also* Basel; Bern; Bullinger, Heinrich; Calvin, John; Consensus Tigurinus; Geneva; Zurich; *and* Zwingli, Huldrych.]

BIBLIOGRAPHY

Bonjour, E., H. S. Offler, and G. R. Potter. *A Short History of Switzerland.* Reprint, Greenwood, Conn., 1989. Still the standard work in English.

Carlen, Louis. *Rechtsgeschichte der Schweiz.* Monographen zur Schweizer Geschichte, vol. 4. 2d, enlarged ed. Bern, 1978. A good introduction to a difficult study.

Dierauer, Johannis. *Geschichte der Schweizerischen Eidgenossenschaft* (1921). 5 vols. Reprint, Bern, 1967. See vols. 3 and 4. A classic study, but cannot be expected to be up-to-date.

Gagliardi, Ernst. *Geschichte der Schweiz von den Anfängen bis zur Gegenwart.* 3 vols. Zürich and Leipzig, 1920–1927. Somewhat outdated, but still gives a good general summary of events in Switzerland.

Haas, Martin. *Huldrych Zwingli und Seine Zeit.* 2d ed. Zurich, 1976. The best account of Zwingli's political career.

Handbuch der Schweizer Geschichte. 2 vols. Zurich, 1972. The standard handbook, though portions of it already need revision.

Im Hof, Ulrich, et al. *Geschichte der Schweiz und der Schweizer.* Basel, 1986. An up-to-date study which uses the *Annales* approach.

Luck, James Murray. *A History of Switzerland: The First Hundred Thousand Years.* Palo Alto, Calif., 1985. Luck was a chemist and not an historian; nevertheless, this book is up-to-date and often used.

Pfister, Rudolf. *Kirchengeschichte der Schweiz.* 3 vols. Zurich, 1974. See vol. 2. A thorough and reliable general church history of Switzerland.

Walton, Robert C. "Heinrich Bullinger: Repräsentant der reichen Bauern und seine Beziehung zur städtische Oligarche." In *Reform, Reformation, Revolution,* edited by Siegfried Hoyer. Leipzig, 1980. Introduces the reader to the economic problems and attitudes toward wealth that were common in the Confederacy in the early decades of the sixteenth century.

ROBERT C. WALTON

SYBRANDSZOON, Taco (d. 1613), Reformed minister and "Libertine" opponent of Calvinism in the Netherlands. Of Frisian origins, Sybrandszoon served in the 1570s as the last Catholic pastor of Nieuwland, a village in Friesland. In 1582 Sybrandszoon joined Herman Elconius as minister to the "Libertine" Jacobskerk congregation in the city of Utrecht. In 1586 Sybrandszoon refused, despite intense pressure, to agree to the union of the Jacobskerk with Utrecht's Calvinist congregation. Sybrandszoon objected particularly to the requirement set by the articles of union that all ministers sign the Belgic Confession (1561). He took special exception to article 16 of the confession, which formulated the doctrine of predestination in an explicitly Calvinist manner. Initially he offered to sign the confession on the condition that he be allowed to follow the Zurich confession of faith concerning predestination. He soon backed away from this compromise position, however, and was dismissed by the Utrecht magistrates.

Sybrandszoon moved to Alkmaar, in northern Holland, where he held no ministry. In 1589 the magistrates of Medemblik appointed him as minister in the Reformed church of their own city, a post Sybrandszoon accepted and filled until his death. The appointment in Medemblik, however, occurred without the approval of either the local consistory or the classis. A conflict immediately ensued, lasting (with one respite, in 1590–1591) until 1598. During this time Sybrandszoon did not attend any classes or synods. He refused to sign the Belgic Confession or the Heidelberg Catechism (1563), though he said he had nothing against either so long as they were understood according to the meaning of scripture. Sybrandszoon also departed from the Calvinist norms of the Dutch Reformed churches in his administration of the sacraments and his use of ecclesiastical discipline. He probably admitted people to Communion whom the Calvinists deemed unworthy and refused to excommunicate anyone; such had been the custom of Utrecht's Jacobskerk. In protest, some Calvinist members of the Medemblik Reformed church refused to attend Sybrandszoon's services, causing a schism.

In 1595 the local conflict between church and state expanded into a provincial one when the States of Holland ordered the north Holland synod not to involve itself in the affair and reserved to itself the right to judge whether Sybrandszoon's beliefs were orthodox. The synod insisted on its right to judge doctrine and to discipline wayward ministers. In 1598 the synod finally declared Sybrandszoon deposed from office. Soon after Sybrandszoon gave up the battle. He agreed to sign the confession and catechism, to conform to accepted practices, and to submit to the authority of classes and synods.

Sybrandszoon left no known writings except for a personal confession of faith. He seems typical of those ministers in the Netherlands in the late sixteenth century who considered themselves Reformed Protestants and yet rejected certain distinctly Calvinist doctrines and practices. Those ministers opposed the rising confessionalism of the Dutch Reformed church. Faced with a Calvinist majority in the church, they relied perforce on the secular authorities for protection. Besides Sybrandszoon, the best known were Caspar Coolhaes, Cornelis Wiggertszoon, Hermannus Herbertszoon, and Hubert Duifhuis.

BIBLIOGRAPHY

Bor, Pieter. *Oorsprongk begin, en vervolgh der Nederlandsche oorlogen, beroerten, en borgerlyke oneenigheden.* 4 vols. Amsterdam, 1679–1684. No article or book has ever taken Sybrandszoon as its primary subject; mentions of him draw chiefly on this primary source and on the North Holland synodal acts. (See Reitsma and Van Veen).

Kaplan, Benjamin J. *Calvinists and Libertines: Confession and Community in Utrecht, 1578–1620.* Oxford, forthcoming.

Reitsma, J., and S. D. Van Veen, eds. *Acta der provinciale en particuliere synoden, gehouden in de noordelijke nederlanden gedurende de jaren, 1572–1620.* Vol. 1, *Noord-Holland, 1572–1608.* Groningen, Netherlands, 1892.

BENJAMIN J. KAPLAN

SYLVANUS, Johannes (d. 1572), Tirolean theologian. He was probably born in the southern part of Tirol near the river Adige, but nothing is known about his childhood and youth. In 1555 he was preacher at the court of the bishop of Würzburg (Franconia). After having become acquainted with the writings of Philipp Melanchthon, he took part in the 1557 Colloquy of Worms. Two years later in Tübingen, he converted to Lutheranism. Beginning in 1560 he was a Lutheran pastor in the town of Calw (Württemberg), but in 1567, after a short stay in Kaiserslautern, he became a Calvinist superintendent in Ladenburg (Baden) in the Palatinate, where he assisted with the preparation of the Heidelberg Bible.

Here he became involved in the religious controversies that then were virulent in this territory. Together with Adam Neuser he opposed the rigorous church discipline introduced by Kaspar Olevianus according to the model of John Calvin's Geneva. Moreover, he rejected the dogma of the Trinity and established contacts with antitrinitarians in Transylvania. Secretly he wrote a confessional treatise about the original faith in the one God and in Jesus the Messiah and "against the Three-Person-Idol and the two-natured false deity of the Anti-Christ." In a letter to the Italian Unitarian Giorgio Biandrata, he expressed his hope to emigrate to Transylvania and to be redeemed from idolatry. This letter was discovered. Despite his readiness to recant and to emigrate, Sylvanus was sentenced to death in line with the theological dogma of Geneva, despite theological advice from Heidelberg and Zurich in favor of an amnesty. On the day before Christmas Eve he was beheaded on the marketplace of Heidelberg in the presence of his wife and children.

BIBLIOGRAPHY

Horn, C. "Johannes Sylvan und die Anfänge des Heidelberger Antitrinitarismus." *Neue Heidelberger Jahrbücher* 17 (1913), 219–310.

Rott, H. "Neue Quellen für eine Aktenrevision des Prozesses gegen Sylvan und seine Genossen." *Neues Archiv für die Geschichte der Stadt Heidelberg* 8 (1910), 184–259; and 9 (1911), 1–70.

Schaab, Meinrad. *Geschichte der Kurpfalz.* Stuttgart, 1992. See vol. 2, p. 45.

KARLHEINZ BLASCHKE

SYLVESTER, János (Hung., Erdősi; 1504?–c.1552), scholar and translator of the New Testament. Born of well-to-do parents in the middle sized market town of Szinérváralja (Seini, Romania), Sylvester attended schools at home and matriculated at Kraków University in 1526. The following year he became the senior of the Hungarian *bursa*, and in 1529 he matriculated at Wittenberg. After that events of Sylvester's life are uncertain until 1534, when he accepted the invitation of Count Tamás Nádasdy to teach at the school he had established at Sárvár. Eight years later he left there and went to the University of Vienna, where he first was a student and then, from 1544, taught Hebrew and later Greek. In 1552 he was mentioned as a professor in history. The latter is the last fact known about Sylvester's life.

In Kraków Sylvester's attention turned to Erasmian cultural ideas, especially to those touching the erudite use of the vernacular. Already while at university he worked on the first texts printed in Hungarian; these were the parts he composed in Hungarian for the trilingual version of Donatus's and Heyden's grammars, published for the first time in 1527 by Hieronymus Vietor in Kraków. In 1539 Sylvester edited, at Sárvár, a Hungarian grammar in Latin for boys in which he set down certain laws of the Hungarian language. The work that made Sylvester one of the outstanding figures of

Hungarian culture was his translation of the New Testament published in 1541. He used, besides the Vulgate, a translation of the full Bible by two Hussites (which had remained in manuscript) and the rendering by Desiderius Erasmus.

Through the New Testament in Hungarian Sylvester sought to place into the hands of the people the gospel in their own language and to show the world that the Hungarians could keep pace with the nations that already had the Bible in their vernacular. As an afterthought, explanatory and summarizing verses in distichs were added to the text because Sylvester came to realize in the course of translating "the great nobility in all of our language."

Count Nádasdy established a printing shop at Sárvár to publish Sylvester's works. This was the first press in the country to print materials in Hungarian. Before this, printed Hungarian had appeared only in Kraków and Vienna.

The religious stance of Sylvester is much debated. It seems certain that he started his career as a Roman Catholic. Whether he accepted or had been influenced by Protestantism by the time he produced the translation of the New Testament or whether he remained Catholic are unresolved questions. The translation, at any rate, was dedicated to King Ferdinand I and his two sons.

Sylvester was a family man, especially fond of his son Teodor, and he worked together with his brother Mihály at Sárvár. His financial situation, however, was generally poor, and Sylvester was not of a pleasant or happy disposition. He came into conflict with those around him, including Count Nádasdy after the translation of the New Testament had been published.

BIBLIOGRAPHY

Primary Sources

Sylvester, János. *Grammatica Hungaro-Latina* (1539). Facsimile ed. Edited by Thomas A. Sebeok. Indiana University Publications Uralic and Altaic Series, vol. 55. Bloomington, Ind., 1968.

————. *Uf Testámentum magyar nyelven, melyet az görög és diák nyelvböl ujonnan fordítánk, az magyar nipnek keresztény hütben való épülisire* (The New Testament in the Hungarian Language, Newly Translated from the Greek and Latin Languages for the Edification in the Christian Faith of the Hungarian People; 1541). Facsimile ed. Edited by Béla Varjas. Bibliotheca Hungarica Antiqua 1. Budapest, 1960.

Secondary Sources

Balázs, János. *Sylvester János és kora* (János Sylvester and His Times). Budapest, 1958.

Payr, Sándor. *Sylvester János sárvári tanitó és magyar bibliafordító* (Janos Sylvester, Teacher of Sárvár and Translator of the Bible). Budapest, 1905.

KATALIN PÉTER

SYNERGIST CONTROVERSY.

Synergism (Gk., *synergos*, "working together") in theological usage denotes the belief that the human will cooperates with divine grace in effecting salvation. The original Reformation message regarding salvation—the message of, for example, Melanchthon's first *Loci communes* (1521) and Luther's *Bondage of the Will* (1525)—reiterated that of Paul and Augustine, asserting that the unregenerate natural will, though capable of conforming to civil laws, was not only incapable of fulfilling divine law but even unable to respond to the gospel. Instead the sinner was justified by God's free grace experienced through faith ("monergism"). To convey their conviction that one's belief was God's choice, the reformers embraced the Pauline/Augustinian language of predestination and employed the deterministic-appearing simile that God acts toward the individual as a sculptor toward a block of wood. Rightly understood, however, this soteriology was not deterministic: faith was an experience of the human, and the reborn soul, while in mortal flesh still bearing the burden of sin, was thus freed in the will to respond in love toward God and fellow humans.

The synergistic controversy erupted in the late 1550s as another of a series of issues dividing the Lutheran movement between Philipp Melanchthon and his adherents, the "Philippists," and the "Gnesio-Lutherans," or "Flacians," who felt they were endangering Luther's message by fatal compromises, here as in the preceding adiaphora and Majorist controversies, to Roman Catholic theology and practices. The Flacians first accused Johann Pfeffinger (1493–1573) and then Viktorin Strigel of teaching that the human will while still in the unregenerate state was a causative factor alongside grace in the initial conversion of the sinner to God. The genesis of their thought was Melanchthon's exploration, beginning in the late 1520s, of the human experience of the Christian life. By then he had become concerned about moral laxity in the Lutheran territories, which he sought to address by discussing the psychological dimensions of God's call and regeneration and by stressing moral responsibility. Recoiling now against the deterministic simile, he believed God acted differently toward humans than toward other creatures, having bestowed reason and choice upon them. His focus was God's public offer of grace to all, the individual's experience of deciding for or against the word of God, and the character of the Christian life. Thus in the two later editions (1535, 1543) of the *Loci* he wrote of three causes of "good actions": "the Word of God, the Holy Spirit, and the human will assenting to and not contending against the Word of God"; elsewhere he described these as the three causes of "conversion." With "good actions" and "conversion" he was describing the life of reborn Christians, not the initial change effected by grace, and sought to impress his readers with the notion that grace had freed their wills so that they were indeed responsible for nurturing faith and moral behavior. While these additions were not in his mind a departure from the original Lutheran message, his colleague Nikolaus von Amsdorf privately criticized the discussion already in 1536 along the lines that he and his fellow Gnesio-Lutherans later took up against Pfeffinger and Strigel.

Protestant defeat in the Schmalkald War (1546–1547) and the largely Catholic religious settlements, the Augsburg and Leipzig Interims (1548), caused the Gnesio-Lutherans to become more sensitive to any shifting of the original Lutheran message in the direction of Catholicism. The Leipzig Interim combined Melanchthonian themes in soteriology, particularly that God did not act with humans as with a block, with a Catholic (synergistic) view of human cooperation. So when Pfeffinger published *Five Questions Concerning the Freedom of the Will* in 1555, they were ready to pounce on any expression that appeared synergistic. Pfeffinger's book replicated the Melanchthonian position on salvation, beginning with a standard Lutheran statement that the human will was unable to approach God without grace. Then, like Melanchthon, Pfeffinger took up the role of the will: "Since the promise of grace is universal, and it is necessary for us to obey the promise, it follows that some difference between the elect and non-elect is to be assumed by our will; we see that in rejecting the promise we are rejected, and to the contrary embracing the promise we are accepted." Pfeffinger attempted to correlate the human experience with God's prior decision (election) for the sake of human responsibility. Since such statements followed those asserting an infirm natural will, he felt, as he later protested, that in context readers should have understood that he was speaking of the regenerated will. But for him that natural will was only infirm, not in active resistance to God's word, and therefore in rejecting the simile of the block he differed fundamentally from Gnesio-Lutheran anthropology and their radical monergism. Amsdorf attacked Pfeffinger in 1558, even attributing falsely to him the statement "Man is able with his own natural powers to assent to the Word" (*Offentliche Bekentnis . . .*). An exchange of treatises between the two was joined by other Gnesio-Lutherans, notably Matthias Flacius Illyricus, who coined the label *synergists* for their enemies.

At this point Amsdorf and Flacius prevailed upon Johann Friedrich of ducal (Ernestine) Saxony to issue a book condemning a variety of errors, including those of the synergists. This *Book of Confutation* was to be subscribed to by all pastors in the territory. Strigel, a leading theologian at the University of Jena, refused to sign, partly because he too rejected the anthropology reflected in the simile of the block. (Melanchthon, who remained out of the limelight in the controversy, wrote to Elector August of Albertine Saxony that the position of the book on free will was destructive to calls for personal virtue, and amounted to a deterministic "Stoic and Manichaean delirium.") Strigel was imprisoned and then kept under house arrest until finally a debate was arranged between him and Flacius at the ducal residence in Weimar (2–8 August 1560). The debate was the high point of the controversy. Against Flacius's use of "conversion" solely as the brief event of repentance and bestowing of faith, Strigel defended the propriety of using the term in the sense of the lifelong process. Yet he sidestepped Flacius's repeated request that he identify that will that was active in conversion as specifically regenerated—had he so agreed, Flacius said, he would drop his objections. Strigel refused, apparently in line with the Melanchthonian concern to emphasize that the natural will has the ability to perform external good, and that thus there is only a quantitative, not qualitative, difference between the will before and after it is acted upon by the Holy Spirit. God's word does not possess "magical powers," changing a block into a believer all by itself, but rather regenerates the human by engaging the mind and moving the will. In refusing to distinguish clearly the unregenerate from regenerate will, Strigel courted danger. He threatened Lutheran soteriology by comparing divine and human roles in salvation to a rich man and poor man paying a bill, the rich one paying the most but the poor contributing his tiny *Heller*, suggesting that the human will does have an independent role in the process. Flacius was provoked to declare that sin is the substance of human nature after the Fall, which even his allies repudiated. By this point Johann Friedrich, who was following the debate intently, had become convinced that Strigel was not the dangerous heretic that Flacius and Amsdorf had made of him, and broke off the debate, allowed him to resume his teaching, and eventually exiled Flacius and his remaining adherents. Strigel refused to become engaged in the issue further, and damaged his position within Lutheranism first by fleeing unauthorized to Leipzig and then later to the Calvinist Palatinate.

The resolution of the problem came in the treatment of free will in article 2 of the Formula of Concord (1580). Informed opinion has always regarded its rejection of synergism as a rejection of the Melanchthonian perspective and the triumph of the Gnesio-Lutheran position. And indeed "conversion" was limited here to the narrow sense of the act, in which situation the will would be only a passive recipient of grace. (For the lifelong process the Formula of Concord used the term *sanctification*.) Therefore such phrases of Melanchthon as the three causes of conversion, the ability to apply oneself to grace, God drawing the person but drawing him or her willingly, and the will not being idle in conversion, were rejected. The simile of the block and other such expressions were approved, as was the notion that the natural will was worse than a block, since it refused God's word until grace converted it. The Gnesio-Lutheran caricature of the opposing camp was perpetuated with the claim that the latter taught that the human "has so much of his natural powers prior to his conversion that he can to some extent prepare himself for grace" (art. 3:3, cf. 77, 86, 90). But such was not the teaching of Melanchthon or Pfeffinger or (for the most part, at least) Strigel, who sought instead to describe the psychological experience of responding to God's call and living the life of Christian responsibility, in which, as the Formula of Conford described in very similar fashion, the individual's will was "not idle in the daily exercise of repentance but cooperates in all the works that the Holy Spirit does through us" (art. 3:88). While their anthropology of the fallen creature was rejected in the Formula of Concord and their words describing the life of "conversion" may sometimes have threatened the Lutheran *sola fide* in their ambiguity, their chief concern was exonerated.

[*See also* Gnesio-Lutherans *and* Philippists.]

BIBLIOGRAPHY

Green, Lowell C. "The Three Causes of Conversion in Philipp Melanchthon, Martin Chemnitz, David Chytraeus, and the 'Formula of Concord.' " *Luther-Jahrbuch* 47 (1980), 89–114. Crucial examination of the use of the terms *conversio* and *causa* in Melanchthon and the Formula of Concord.

Kawerau, G. "Synergismus, Synergistischer Streit." In *Realencyklopädie für protestantische Theologie und Kirche*, 3d. ed., vol. 19, pp. 229–235. Leipzig, 1907. The best short description of the topic, remarkably thorough and balanced.

Kolb, Robert. *Nikolaus von Amsdorf, 1483–1565: Popular Polemics in the Preservation of Luther's Legacy.* Nieuwkoop, 1978. Touches upon Amsdorf's reservations about Melanchthon and explains with admirable balance his controversy with Pfeffinger (although, on p. 196, the author accepts as authentic Amsdorf's false quotation from his rival).

Lohse, Bernhard. "Innerprotestantische Lehrstreitigkeiten." In *Handbuch der Dogmen- und Theologiegeschichte*, vol. 2, pp. 102–129. Göttingen, 1980.

Muehlenberg, Ekkehard. "*Synergia* and Justification by Faith." In *Discord, Dialogue, and Concord: Studies in the Lutheran Reformation's Formula of Concord*, edited by Lewis W. Spitz and Wenzel Lohff, pp. 15–37. Philadelphia, 1977. A study of article 2 of the Formula of Concord that accepts its caricature of Philippist soteriology, but finds the formula's own presentation short-sighted and contradictory.

Preger, Wilhelm. *Matthias Flacius Illyricus und seine Zeit.* 2 vols. Erlangen, 1859–1861. Important for all of Flacius's controversies, and vol. 2 gives a German translation of much of the Latin transcript of his debate in Weimar with Strigel.

Ritschl, Otto. *Dogmengeschichte des Protestantismus.* Leipzig, 1912. See vol. 2 for a thorough study of Melanchthon's concerns about the life of faith (chap. 34) and of the Synergist Controversy (ch. 38), in the latter rather unsympathetic to the Philippist position.

LUTHER D. PETERSON

SYNOD OF _____. *See under latter part of name.*

SYNODS.
[*This entry comprises two articles focusing on the various ecclesiastical assemblies called in efforts to stabilize and standardize the new Protestant confessions and the significance of these assemblies to sixteenth-century life. The first presents a survey of synods in western Europe; the second considers synods in eastern Europe. For discussions of individual synods, see* Dordrecht, Synod of; Emden, Synod of; Homberg, Synod of; La Rochelle, Synod of; *and* Nîmes, Synod of.]

Synods in Western Europe

Meetings of representatives of a group of churches to regulate doctrinal or disciplinary matters in the churches are know as synods. Within the Reformed tradition, synods varied widely in terms of composition, responsibilities, and role in ecclesiastical polity.

The Swiss Cantons. Although synodical polity is generally associated with Calvin and Geneva, the city itself never held any synods. Calvin himself did not develop systematic church structures above the local level, and even Théodore de Bèze, an ardent defender of so-called presbyterial polity later in his career, supported a limited episcopacy as late as 1559, the year that a nonepiscopal synodical system was established in his native France. Geneva thus had only a limited impact on the development of synodical polity.

Zurich's first synod, held in 1528 under Huldrych Zwingli's leadership, was called to examine the lives and morals of the clergy of the city and to address issues raised by the Anabaptists. Although Zwingli intended that such synods be held regularly, they quickly fell into disuse; Heinrich Bullinger thus found it necessary to restore and revitalize the canton's synods in 1532, less than a year after he took over Zwingli's position in the city. The principal purpose of these synods continued to be clerical discipline centered on a time of mutual censure, but the synods also discussed and made recommendations to the city on a wide range of other topics, including discipline within the churches (education, attendance at worship, sumptuary legislation, Christian behavior, etc.) as well as placement of ministers and poor relief. The synods were under the direction and authority of the civil government, however, which could thus accept or reject the ministers' proposals.

The canton of Bern established regular synods as part of its ecclesiastical government. This canton was considerably larger than Zurich, with both German- and French-speaking areas; hence the church polity was of necessity more complex. The churches were under the control of the civil government, which was advised by the leaders of the church in the capital city. In practice most ecclesiastical policy was formulated by the *Convent* (the assembly of pastors and professors of the city) and the *Chorgericht* (Bern's morals court).

To maintain clerical discipline, each linguistic community was to hold a general synod annually. The first German synod was held in 1532; the first French synod met in 1536. In practice, the synods met far less frequently; for example, the French held only three annual synods, and then were denied permission to hold another until 1549. This synod, attended by Pierre Viret, the most prominent pastor in Bern's French-speaking churches, was held not in the French region but in Bern itself, under the watchful eye of the city's magistrates and theologians. The government closed the synod before it had even passed beyond mutual censure, however; the Germans found the behavior of the French ministers unseemly. This was the last general synod of the French churches of the canton. In order to maintain a point of contact with the canton's French churches, Bern replaced the general synod with a "general chapter," a visitation by members of the Bernese civil and ecclesiastical government who examined all civil officials and ministers from the French-speaking region and reported back to the canton's civil government.

In addition to the general synods, the Bernese churches held lower-level synods in each district within the two linguistic communities. These meetings, called "chapters" in the German areas and "classes" in the French, were originally planned to meet weekly, but the size of the districts soon reduced the frequency to quarterly. The meetings were held under the direction of a dean selected from the ministers in the area, and included exposition of scripture, examination of candidates for the ministry, administrative matters and other business raised by Bern, and mutual censure. The dean and his assistants were also responsible for maintaining clerical discipline in their area by conducting regular visitations to the churches.

Strasbourg. Rather than incorporating synods as an element of the ecclesiastical government, Strasbourg held synods on an ad hoc basis to resolve specific issues that arose in the city's churches, following the medieval tradition of diocesan synods. During the period when Martin Bucer was the city's leading theologian, Strasbourg held two synods (1533 and 1539) to deal with doctrinal issues—the nature of the church—and with sacramental and liturgical matters and pastoral activities.

France. The first national synod of the French Reformed churches was held in Paris in 1559. Before this synod, French Protestantism was essentially an unorganized collection of individual churches; this synod established a systematic ecclesiastical organization (outlined in the *Discipline ecclésiastique*, or church order) and a statement of faith (the Gallic Confession) for the French Protestants in an effort to gain legitimacy in the eyes of the monarchy and to present a united front against their Catholic opponents. The *Discipline*, which seems to have been written largely by Antoine de la Roche Chandieu and François Morel, the moderator of the synod, established two clear levels of synods within the church: the provincial and the national. Unlike Zurich and Bern, where the synods were composed exclusively of ministers, the French synods were to include not only pastors but also elders and deacons. The system evolved somewhat over the first few years, but by the middle of the 1560s the composition of the synods was established. Each church

in a province was to send its pastor and either an elder or a deacon to the provincial synod; each provincial synod, in turn, was to send a delegation of one or two pastors and an equal number of elders to the national synod.

The 1559 edition of the *Discipline* included provisions for informal meetings of pastors and elders from neighboring churches to discuss matters of mutual interest. These meetings soon evolved into the colloquy, a term used for both the subdivision of a province and the meetings themselves. The colloquy was formally added to the *Discipline* by the Synod of Nîmes (1572), though acts of prior national synods and earlier editions of the *Discipline* also include references to colloquies.

The most important synod of the French Reformed churches was held at La Rochelle in 1571. This synod was attended by virtually all of the Protestant leaders in the kingdoms of France and Navarre, including Admiral Gaspard II de Coligny, Jeanne of Navarre, and Henry of Navarre (the future Henry IV); Bèze came from Geneva to act as the synod's moderator. The synod established a definitive text for the Gallic Confession (subject to modification by future synods) from among the variant readings, and reorganized and rewrote the *Discipline*. Both the Gallic Confession and the *Discipline* were subsequently associated more prominently with the Synod of La Rochelle than with that of Paris, which first adopted them.

One key principle was built into the French churches' polity: unlike the de facto polity of Bern, all churches and all ministers were fundamentally equal in authority. For example, no church could make decisions for another church; disputes were to be settled among the parties involved with as little outside interference as possible, though appeal to a higher synod was generally permitted. Further, synodical officers had no ongoing functions within the church beyond their usual duties as ministers, elders, or deacons, unlike the Bernese deans and their assistants. The synods thus had no continuing bureaucracy, no hierarchy, and no offices, giving the French Reformed churches a structure distinct from not only earlier ecclesiastical systems but also the French estates and other representative institutions in medieval and early modern Europe. This structure would influence the polity of the other national Reformed churches in western Europe.

The Netherlands. Protestants in the Netherlands were strongly influenced by the French Reformed churches. The Synod of Antwerp (1563) adopted a constitution for the churches of Walloon and Flanders similar to that of the French Reformed churches; another synod held at Antwerp (1566) approved the Belgic Confession (which was itself inspired by the Gallic Confession) as the Walloon and Flemish churches' confession of faith. With the return of the southern provinces to Catholic control by Fernando Álvarez de Toledo, duke of Alba, exiled pastors from the northern provinces met for a synod at Emden (1571). This synod approved the Belgic Confession and drafted a church order influenced again by the French Reformed churches. The Synod of Dordrecht (1574)—the first official synod of the Dutch Reformed churches—approved the Emden Articles but was unable to implement them because of the opposition of William of Orange and the council, who thought that they allowed the churches an unacceptable degree of independence and authority. Subsequent synods held at Dordrecht (1578) and Middelburg (1581) failed to secure an agreement between church and state. The impasse was resolved by eliminating the national synod from the polity, leaving seven independent provincial synods subdivided into classes; each church sent a minister and elder to a classis, and each classis sent representatives to the provincial synod.

A special synod was called at Dordrecht in 1618–1619 to deal with the Arminian controversy. The Arminians, led by Hugo Grotius and Johan van Oldenbarnevelt, had issued a series of remonstrances (hence "Remonstrants," the name of their party) in 1610 against the conservative Calvinist theology of the Dutch churches. They were opposed by a party headed by Franciscus Gomarus and Maurice of Nassau, who took a hard-line stand on the issues under discussion. The synod, which included twenty-eight representatives from foreign churches (England, Scotland, Germany, Geneva, etc.), decided in favor of the Calvinists, condemning the Arminians under five principal points. This synod helped establish "five-point" Calvinism as the dominant theology of the international Reformed community.

Great Britain. A form of synodical polity also took root in Scotland during the 1560s, though it would take some time before it evolved its mature structure. At the request of Parliament, John Knox and a few other ministers drew up a confession of faith (1560) and the *First Book of Discipline* (1561). In 1577, the general assembly (essentially a national synod) adopted the *Second Book of Discipline*, drafted largely by Andrew Melville, which outlined a local church polity much closer to that of Geneva than had the *First Book of Discipline*. Presbyteries (roughly equivalent to the French colloquy or Dutch classis) began developing in the 1580s, though they were first adopted formally as part of the church's polity in 1592. The presbyteries were abolished by James VI in 1612, only to be definitively reestablished as a result of the National Covenant approved by Parliament in 1639.

The Reformation in England, led by a monarchy that ardently supported the authority of bishops, held no synods in the period before the Civil War. During the war, however, Parliament—led largely by Puritan Calvinists—formed an alliance with the Scots called the Solemn League and Covenant (1643) to preserve presbyterianism in Scotland, to reform the English church, to stamp out Catholicism, and to protect each country's political liberties. As part of the agreement, the Westminster Assembly (1643–1649) was called to draft the foundational documents of a Calvinist state church for England. Although circumstances prevented the provisions of the synod from being implemented in England, the Westminster Confession and the Longer and Shorter Catechisms were adopted by the Presbyterian churches.

BIBLIOGRAPHY

Chrisman, Miriam Usher. *Strasbourg and the Reform: A Study in the Process of Change.* New Haven and London, 1967. A general history that includes a brief but useful discussion of the Strasbourg synod of 1533.

Félice, G. de. *Histoire des synods nationaux des églises réformées de France.* Paris, 1864. Although not readily accessible, this remains the best history of the French national synods. Lacks critical apparatus.

Gordon, Bruce. *Clerical Discipline and the Rural Reformation: The Synod in Zurich, 1532–1580.* Bern and New York, 1992. The only study in English of the ongoing role of the synod in clerical discipline in Zurich.

Hammann, Gottfried. *Entre la secte et la cité: Le projet d'église du réformateur Martin Bucer, 1491–1551.* Geneva, 1984. A survey of Bucer's ecclesiology; includes brief discussions of the two Strasbourg synods.

Kirk, James, ed. *The Second Book of Discipline.* Edinburgh, 1980. Includes an extensive introduction detailing the development of the church order in Scotland.

———. *The Records of the Synod of Lothian and Tweeddale, 1589–1596, 1640–1649.* Reprint, Holmes Beach, Fla., 1992. Good examples of the way synods actually functioned in Scotland. Introduction is very helpful.

Lechler, G. V. *Geschichte der Presbyterial- und Synodalverfassung seit der Reformation.* Leiden, 1854. One of the best books on the subject, though somewhat dated and not readily accessible.

Mitchell, Alexander Ferrier. *The Westminster Assembly: Its History and Standards; Being the Baird Lecture for 1882* (1883). Reprint, Edmonton, Canada, 1992. The standard work on the history of the Westminster Assembly.

Moreau, G. "L'organisation synodale des églises réformées des Pays-Bas de 1561 à 1579." In *Les Églises et leurs institutions au XVIème siècle,* pp. 193–199. Montpellier, France, 1978. Emphasizes Dutch dependence on French ecclesiastical models.

Pettegree, Andrew. *Emden and the Dutch Revolt: Exile and the Development of Reformed Protestantism.* Oxford, 1992. A detailed, though more locally focused, history with a fairly extensive discussion of the Synod of Emden (1571).

Quick, John. *Synodicon in Gallia Reformata: Or, The Acts, Decisions, Decrees, and Canons of Those Famous National Synods of the Reformed Churchs in France.* London, 1692. Despite being an English translation, the best edition to date of the acts of the national synods of the French Reformed churches, 1559–1659.

Vuilleumier, Henri. *Histoire de l'église réformée du Pays de Vaud sous le régime bernois.* Vol. 1, *L'Âge de la Réforme.* Lausanne, 1927. Particularly useful for its discussion of the ecclesiastical structure of the Bernese church.

GLENN S. SUNSHINE

Synods in Eastern Europe

During the Reformation era in eastern Europe, synods became an important mechanism of fostering and consolidating the various reform movements in a particular area. They were established on the basis of late medieval clerical fraternities, which were slowly transformed into pastoral conferences of evangelical communities. Laymen sometimes took part in synods, especially in those that established formal organizational structures for various Protestant churches. Although regular meetings of regional pastoral organizations (fraternities, contubernia, or seniorats) were defined as synods and met regularly to discuss doctrinal and disciplinary questions, the most important synods in eastern Europe were the irregularly summoned general assemblies, which were convened to establish or resolve doctrinal issues, establish confessional standards, adopt rules governing the life and activities of the clergy and congregations, and establish the administrative structure of individual churches. These had a constitutive significance for the various religious communities in eastern Europe, especially in the kingdoms of Hungary and Poland.

In the patrimonial lands of the Austrian Habsburgs (Upper and Lower Austria; Inner Austria, including Styria, Carinthia, and Carniola; and the Tirol and the Forelands), general synods did not play a significant constitutive role. Most of the existential questions of ecclesiastical polity and confessional orientation were established by individual noble or urban patrons of the reform movements and the estates of each of the territories. They obtained modest privileges from the sovereign (the religious concession for Upper and Lower Austria of 1571 and the religious pacification of 1572 and 1578 for Inner Austria), including the privilege to establish Protestant, primarily Lutheran, worship services according to a common agenda and order (e.g., Nathan Chytraeus's agenda of 1570/71). Synods with a constitutive significance were also infrequently held in Bohemia. The ecclesiastical order in the kingdom had been defined during the fifteenth century on the basis of the Basel Compacta of 1436. For the established Hussite Utraquist church, governed by a consistory, the confessions prepared by the theologians were given constitutive force through the actions of individual nobles and the estates who also established the general polity of the Hussite churches governed by its own consistory. The clergy of the Bohemian Brethren (Unity of Brethren, or Unitas Fratrum), most numerous in eastern Bohemia and Moravia, regularly met to discuss practical and theological matters, but laymen generally did not take part in these assemblies until the second half of the sixteenth century.

During the sixteenth century, the so-called neo-Utraquists—who sympathized with the Protestant reform movements and did not seek, as did the old Utraquists, an accommodation with the Roman Catholic church—sought in vain during 1567 to obtain their own consistory through the estates. In 1575 a national meeting of representatives of the various Protestant communities (neo-Utraquists, Lutherans, and Bohemian Brethren) sought to establish a common confession (Bohemian Confession of 1575). This attempt to gain recognition was not successful, and it was only in 1609 that the "Letter of Majesty" of Rudolf II extended recognition and religious liberty to the nobles, cities, and even serfs who adhered to the Bohemian Confession. Some Lutheran communities in the Czech lands organized assemblies of local clergy to establish their confessional standards or ecclesiastical polity or had these defined by local nobles (Velké Meziřiči, Jáchymov [Joachimstal], and Jihlava [Iglau]). This occurred also among the Protestants in Silesia (Heidersdorf, 1574), although legal recognition was granted by Rudolf II only in 1609.

In Hungary scores of pastoral conferences or synods were held during the sixteenth century. As the Protestants slowly obtained control of existing pastoral associations, these served, de facto, as regional organizations of the various Protestant communities, even though they legally remained under the jurisdiction of the Roman Catholic hierarchy until the Peace of Vienna (1606) and the Diet of 1608. The convocations accepted doctrinal standards and established rules for pastoral and educational activities. They elected their own seniors, who supervised the affairs of the assembly and ordained new clergy. The first evangelical synod for which some records exist was held in Ardud (Erdöd), Transylvania, in 1545, followed by an assembly in Prešov in 1546. After midcentury regional assemblies, whether synods or colloquies, were held with increasing frequency to discuss theological and practical issues, as Lutherans engaged in controversies with crypto-Calvinists and the Reformed, and the Reformed contended with the antitrinitarians. The most significant constitutive assemblies of Protestants in the kingdom of Hungary, however, were the synods of Žilina (1610) and Spišské Podhradie (1614), which established superintendencies for the Lutherans of Upper Hungary and accepted the Book of Concord as their doctrinal standard; the Reformed synods of Debrecen (1567), Hercegszölös (1576), Galánta (1592), and Komjatice (1621) established doctrinal standards and the organizational structure of the Hungarian Reformed church. Despite their theological differences, the Lutherans, the Reformed, and the antitrinitarians established very similar administrative structures, which elected their own leaders.

In Poland, where there was noble and civic patronage of a wide range of reform views, numerous local and regional convocations, colloquies, and synods were held during the sixteenth century by the Lutherans, the Reformed, the Anabaptists, the Bohemian Brethren, and the antitrinitarians. Especially significant were the several synods held by the Reformed at Pińczów during the 1550s, which tried to establish a national Reformed church; the numerous meetings of the antitrinitarian antipedobaptists during the 1560s and 1570s, which assisted the emergence of organized Socinianism; and the attempt by Jan Łaski in April 1570 to effect a union among the Reformed, the Bohemian Brethren, and the Lutherans at an assembly that adopted the Consensus Sendomiriensis and agreed to establish a compendium of accord between the Augsburg Confession, the

Second Helvetic Confession, and the Bohemian Confession—a resolution that remained as unfulfilled as the hoped-for union. On the basis of this transitory cooperation, however, the Protestants in Great Poland were able to obtain partial legal recognition of their existence and organizations in the Pax Dissidentium, or Peace of the Dissidents, which was wrested from Henry, duke of Anjou, then the king-elect of Poland, through the Warsaw Confederation of 1573.

BIBLIOGRAPHY

Bucsay, Mihály. *Der Protestantismus in Ungarn, 1521–1978: Ungarns Reformationskirchen in Geschichte und Gegenwart.* Vol. 1, *Im Zeitalter der Reformation, Gegenreformation und katholischen Reform.* Vienna, 1977.

Fox, Paul. "The Reformation in Poland." In *The Cambridge History of Poland,* edited by William F. Reddaway et al., vol. 1. Cambridge, 1950.

Hrejsa, Ferdinand. *Česká Konfessie, její vznik, podstata a dějiny.* Prague, 1912. Appeared in an abridged German version as "Die Böhmische Konfession: Ihre Entstehung, ihr Wesen und ihre Geschichte," *Jahrbuch der Gesellschaft für die Geschichte des Protestantismus in Österreich* 35 (1914), 81–123; 37 (1916), 55–80; 38 (1917), 96–174.

Loesche, Georg. *Geschichte des Protestantismus im vormaligen und in neuen Österreich.* Vienna, 1930.

Říčan, Rudolf. *Das Reich Gottes in den böhmischen Ländern.* Stuttgart, 1957.

Szeberinyi, Johannes, ed. *Corpus maxime memorabilium synodorum Evangelicarum Augustanae Confessionis in Hungaria in singulas.* Pest, 1848.

Völker, Karl. *Kirchengeschichte Polens.* Leipzig, 1930.

Williams, George H. *The Radical Reformation.* 3d ed. Kirksville, Mo., 1992.

DAVID P. DANIEL

SZAPOLYAI, János. *See* Zápolya, János.

SZAPOLYAI, János Zsigmond. *See* Zápolya, János Zsigmond.

SZEGEDI KIS, István (Lat., Szegedinus; also Stephen; 1505–1572), bishop and theologian of the Swiss Reformation in Hungary. Born of a burgher family in Szeged, Szegedi Kis first attended school in his native town and then in nearby localities, but he was orphaned early. Therefore, although he was a talented and diligent scholar, he could not go to a university before having earned money by teaching. Szegedi Kis matriculated in 1537 at Kraków University and in 1543 at Wittenberg; in between he was a teacher in the region of Szeged. He therefore was in Hungary when the Turks, after having taken the capital Buda, started to establish their dominion over the country, and Szeged fell under their control in 1542. In the following years a huge part of Hungary was under direct Turkish rule. Szegedi Kis returned from Wittenberg to this occupied territory in 1544 and for the remainder of his life worked in different parishes in territories controlled by the Turks.

Szegedi Kis was among those Protestant ecclesiastics who did not seek ordination from a Catholic bishop; he was ordained in 1544 by the Lutheran bishop Michael Sztárai. In the years before his ordination Szegedi Kis had been persecuted by Catholic authorities and harassed by military activities. Afterward he was forced to move frequently and, for brief periods between 1544 and 1554, was a teacher, preacher, or both at Csanád (Cenade), Gyula, Cegléd, Temesvár (Timişoara), Tur, Békés, and Tolna. He enjoyed some peace for four years at Laskó, but after having moved, at the request of certain commanders of area castles, to Kálmáncsa (near the most important Hungarian fortress, Szigetvár), Szegedi Kis was captured by the Turks in the summer of 1561. He was liberated only one and a half years later, after a ransom had been collected from a wide spectrum of the population. The parish of Kevi—Ráckeve, as it was called later—contributed much to the ransom and was able to persuade Szegedi Kis to accept their call to be their pastor. He moved to Kevi in 1563 and remained there until his death nine years later.

The history of Szegedi Kis's changes in religious persuasion cannot be entirely elucidated. According to his contemporary biography by Máté Skaricza (1544–1591), Szegedi Kis was already evangelical in his views when he went to Kraków. This biography does not mention his turn to the Swiss form of the Reformation. Nevertheless, Szegedi Kis's theological works show that he had clearly been of that persuasion. The dates of his works, however, are uncertain. To Szegedi Kis are also attributed two church ordinances—the first of them, in the 1550s, was only influenced by sacramentarian tenets, while the second, in the 1560s, was wholly sacramentarian. Because of this Szegedi Kis, who was elected bishop in 1554, is regarded as one of the first bishops of the Reformed church in Hungary. Perhaps a result of his levelheaded approaches, his break with Martin Luther did not cause the same hostility that raged in other Protestant areas of Hungary between early adherents of the Swiss Reformation in Hungary and the Lutherans.

Szegedi Kis did not turn against Lutheranism in his writings. Rather, he devoted all of his attention to opposing Catholicism and antitrinitarianism. His works seem to have been very well received by many people. The *Assertio vera de Trinitate,* which he directed against the "foolery" of the followers of Michael Servetus in Hungary, twice appeared in Geneva, and had an introduction by Théodore de Bèze. The *Speculum Romanorum pontificum* was an even greater success. This book, unlike most antipapist works of the time, addressed the intellect rather than seeking to arouse the passions. Two much longer works by Szegedi Kis were *Theo-*

logiae sincerae loci communes and a volume of sermon outlines called *Tabulae analyticae*. The first was introduced by Johann Jacob Grynaeus, who mentioned Huldrych Zwingli as his greatest teacher. The texts, however, were adapted from the works of all Swiss reformers, as well as of Philipp Melanchthon. The *Tabulae* elaborated on *Psalms* and some other books of the Bible in a sense perhaps nearest to Calvin. Szegedi Kis also composed fairly popular hymns. In the late twentieth century one of them was even included in the hymnal of the Hungarian Reformed church.

Szegedi Kis was short of stature and, especially in his later years, exceedingly fat. This contrasted with his engaging personality. He was an able communicator, gifted at teaching and at sermonizing. He had social contacts with magnates, high officials, merchants, and soldiers, and even the Turkish authorities sought his advice and company. Szegedi Kis did not marry the first time until 1548 but nevertheless had eleven children by three wives. A posthumous daughter, a young son, and two grown daughters survived him. The son, of the same name, died early, but not before having prepared an edition of his father's manuscripts.

BIBLIOGRAPHY

Primary Sources

Szegedi, Kis, István. *Assertio vera de Trinitate contra quorundam deliramenta quae ex Serveti aliorumque phanaticorum hominum opinionibus nunc primum in quibusdam Hungaries partibus exorta et publicata sunt.* Geneva, 1573, 1576.

————. *Speculum Romanorum pontificum in quo decreta cum verbo Dei pugnantia, vitae cursus, prodigia horrenda accurata brevitate depinguntur.* Basel, 1584, 1586; n.p., 1592, 1602; Basel, 1586 (in German).

———— *Theologiae sincerae loci communes de Deo et homine perpetuis explicati tabulis et scholasticorum dogmatis illustrati.* Basel, 1585, 1588, 1593, 1608.

———— *Tabulae analyticae: quibus exemplar illud sanorum sermonum de fide, charitate et patientia, quod olim prophetae, evangelistae, apostoli litteris memoriaeque mandarunt fideliter declaratur.* Schaffhouse, 1592; London, 1593; Basel, 1598, 1599, 1610.

Secondary Source

Földvári, László. *Szegedi Kis I. élete és a Tisza-Duna mellékének reformációja.* Budapest, 1894.

KATALIN PÉTER

SZENCI MOLNÁR, Albert (also Szenczi; 1574–1634), Hungarian Reformed religious writer, translator, and teacher. Born in Szenc (Senec), Slovakia, on 30 August 1574, Molnár was one of the five children of a wealthy Calvinist miller and vintner. His education was entrusted to a wandering tutor, and prior to enrolling in the Reformed academy in Debrecen in 1588, he studied in Szenc (1586), Györ (1587), and Göncz, where he served briefly as a printer's apprentice. In 1591 Molnár left Hungary, enrolled at the University of Wittenberg, and joined the Liber Bursae Wittenbergae (Hungarian Coetus). But his stay in Wittenberg was brief, and he traveled on to Heidelberg, Strasbourg, and Herborn, where he remained until 1596, when he visited Geneva and Rome. He then returned to Heidelberg.

His student years set the pattern for the remainder of his life, half of which was spent in numerous towns of Germany. Almost all of his published works were prepared and published abroad. He returned to Hungary only for brief periods of time and did not settle in Hungary until 1626, living briefly in Košice (Kassa, Kaschau) and finally in Cluj (Klausenburg, Kolozsvár), Transylvania, where he died on 18 January 1634. He married a widow, Kunigunda Vietor, with whom he had two sons and four daughters. While in Germany his patron was Mauritz of Hesse-Kassel and Frederick IV of the Palatine, and in Hungary he was assisted by Stephen Tököli and Gabriel Bethlen.

Although his service as a Reformed pastor and scholar in Hungary was brief, during the years he incessantly and almost compulsively wandered throughout Europe, he produced works of considerable importance for the development of the Hungarian language and the Reformed movement in Hungary (including the *Psalterium ungaricum*, 1607). This Hungarian Psalter was based upon the Psalter by Ambrose Lobwasser used in the Palatinate and the Huguenot Psalter of Clément Marot (1529). It subsequently appeared in more than one hundred editions and greatly influenced the development of literary Hungarian. Prior to this he had prepared his two-volume dictionary of the Hungarian language, and after completing the Psalter he produced revisions (1608, 1612) of the Hungarian translation of the Bible, which originally had been issued by Gáspár Károlyi in 1590 at Viszoly. He then turned his attention to producing a grammar for the Hungarian language based on the linguistic theories of Petrus Ramus. Finally, he prepared a translation of John Calvin's *Institutes* into Hungarian—*Az keresztényi religióra és igaz hitre való tanítás*—which was published in Hanau in 1624. In addition to his linguistic tools and translations, Molnár also published a translation of sermons by Abraham Scultetus (Oppenheim, 1617).

BIBLIOGRAPHY

Primary Sources

Szenci Molnár, Albert. *Dictionarium Latinoungaricum . . . Item vice versa Ungaricolatinum.* Nuremberg, 1604.

————. *Kis katechizmus.* Heidelberg, 1607.

————. *Psalterium ungaricum* (Herborn, 1607). Reprint, Budapest, 1984.

————. *Szent Biblia az az Istennec Ó es Uy Testamentomanac prophetac es apastaloc által megiraltott szent könyvei.* 1608.

————. *Novae grammaticae Ungaricae, succincta methodo comprehensae et perspicuis exemplis illustratae libro duo.* Hanau, 1610.

————. *Az palatinatusi catechismussal, egyházi könyörgéseknec és ceremoniaknac formáivol egyetembe, Szenci Molnar Albert által.* Oppenheim, 1612.

Secondary Sources

Dézsi, Lajos. *Szenczi Molnár Albert.* Budapest, 1897.
Incze, Gábor. *Szenczi Molnár Albert.* Budapest, 1939.

Klaniczy, Tibor. *Handbuch der ungarischen Literatur.* Budapest, 1977. See pp. 69–70.

Szenci Molnár Albert és a magyar késő-reneszánsz. Szeged, 1978.

Vásárhely, Judit. *Eszmei áramlatok és politka Szenci Molnár Albert életmüvében.* Budapest, 1985.

DAVID P. DANIEL

SZTÁRAI, Michael (Hung., Mihály; Lat., Starinus; c. 1520–1575), Hungarian reformer, man of letters. Of noble parentage, Sztárai was, according to Catholic and Protestant tradition, a Franciscan friar in his youth. The first known fact about his life is that he was a schoolteacher in 1542 at Siklós, the home of the Perényi family. In the same year he served as tutor to Ferenc Perényi, but only for a short time, because in 1543 Sztárai was already in Padua. Most probably he studied at the university. His wish at that time was to take "the consolation of the Christian faith" to the inhabitants of southern Hungary who in the previous decades had fallen under Turkish occupation. He realized his wish the following year. From 1544 until 1564 Sztárai served in Turkish-occupied territory as Lutheran preacher in different communities. Before 1551 he organized 120 parishes, was the senior of various church districts, and had many conflicts with Turkish officials. Sztárai left the territory occupied by the Turks only in 1564 when he went first to Sárospatak and then to Pápa.

Of lively character and very cultured, Sztárai was a most gifted reformer whose methods pleased many. He evangelized by sermonizing, singing, and making jokes. But Sztárai was a fierce debater and a strict ecclesiastical disciplinarian. His literary activity was part of his struggle to reach individuals. He rendered sixteen psalms into Hungarian and composed hymns. Some of them appeared in several editions of contemporary and later hymnals. The biblical epic songs of Sztárai can be considered as works of fiction. They are of breathtaking tension, especially the *History of King Holofernes and Goodwife Judith.* His most important works, however, were his plays, two or perhaps a whole series of Reformation dramas, as the one drama by Sztárai that has been preserved in its full text seems to imply. The preserved drama deals with the priesthood and defends the doctrine of the priesthood of all believers. Only a fragment of the text of a second play, against celibacy, has been preserved.

Sztárai remained celibate. This way of life and cast of mind made him popular in the eyes of the people. His works not only propagated Reformation tenets but also had a clear, sharp socio-critical character.

BIBLIOGRAPHY

Kardos, Tibor, ed. *Régi Magyar Drámai Emlékek.* Vol. 1. Budapest, 1960. Modern editions of the plays.

Szilády, Áron, ed. *Régi Magyar Költők Tára.* Vol. 5. Budapest, 1886. Modern editions of the epic works.

Sztárai, Michael. *Comoedia lepidissima de sacerdotio.* Óvár, 1559. The text is in Hungarian.

KATALIN PÉTER

T

TAFFIN, Jean (1529?–1602), pioneer of the *Nadere Reformatie* ("Second Reformation"), a seventeenth-century movement in the Netherlands, influenced by English Puritanism, that emphasized heartfelt experience of Reformed doctrine and personal sanctification in all spheres of life. Born into a wealthy family in Tournai (today in Belgium), Taffin was converted to the Reformed faith during the mid-1550s when he was hired for three years by Antoine Perrenot de Granvelle, then bishop of Arras, as librarian/secretary and charged to judge the soundness of various books. After briefly assisting a Reformed church in Antwerp (1557), Taffin spent some months in Strasbourg with Martin Bucer and Wolfgang Capito, and then went to Geneva to study theology under Calvin and Théodore de Bèze (1558–1560). He served as pastor for churches in Aachen (1560–1561), Metz (1561–1566; 1567–1569), Antwerp (1566–1567), and Heidelberg (1570–1573) before his appointment as court chaplain to Prince William of Orange (1574–1583). He again ministered briefly to the Antwerp congregation (1584–1585). From 1585 to 1587 he served the Walloon church at Haarlem, after which he served at Amsterdam until his sudden death from plague in 1602.

Taffin was more of a practical than a systematic theologian. Inwardly experienced piety and sanctification permeated his life and writings. This pervades his two most prominent works: *Traicte de l'amendement de vie* (1594; translated as *The Amendment of Life*, London, 1595), which deals with repentance as a way of life, and *Des Marques des enfans de Dieu et des consolations en leurs afflictions* (1586; translated as *The Marks of the Children of God, and of Their Comforts in Affliction*, London, 1590; reprinted in 1608, 1609, 1615, 1634).

This latter work was written to "comfort God's troubled people" after William of Orange's assassination. Taffin describes the felicity of Christians in three successive stages: first, "peace of conscience and joy in the Holy Ghost"; second, the soul in heaven with Christ; and third, the ultimate state of bliss when soul and body shall be reunited to serve God eternally. He stressed that in order to be prepared for such bliss, one must have a personal knowledge and experience of the marks of saving grace—outward marks (e.g., willingness to hear the word "purely preached," to receive the sacraments "purely administered," and to pray) and inward marks (e.g., "the testimony of the Holy Ghost in our hearts, the peace and quietness of our consciences before God, feeling ourselves justified by faith"). In sum, Christians are spiritual pilgrims who strive to live *unto* God and to die *for* him.

For Taffin life and death are twins; Christians live to die, and die to live. Such a way of life will bring the Christian into spiritual conflict, temptation, and affliction. After discussing six temptations, Taffin devotes the bulk of his treatise to affliction, emphasizing the need for heartfelt "holy affections and desires" as indications of saving faith and the Holy Spirit's indwelling. For Taffin, knowledge is important, but love has the last word. It is better to possess a "learned ignorance" than a "rash knowledge." Happily, Taffin subjected all knowledge, love, feeling, and experience to scripture as the ultimate guide.

Taffin served as delegate to several prominent Dutch synods (e.g., Emden, 1571; Dordrecht, 1574 and 1578; Middelburg, 1581), but remained aloof from the polemical battles of his day, thus displaying his mild, amiable personality. His stress was on preparation for eternity, the resurrection, and the homecoming of the true Christian to glory.

BIBLIOGRAPHY

Boer, C. *Hofpredikers van Prins Willem van Oranje, Jean Taffin en Pierre Loyseleur de Villiers.* The Hague, 1952. An informative Leiden dissertation, but largely superseded by van der Linde's work.

Linde, S. van der. *Jean Taffin: Hofprediker en raadsheer van Willem van Oranje.* Amsterdam, 1982. This two-hundred-page, highly readable and nontechnical monograph is the best source to date on both Taffin's life and theology. The fruit of many years of study by a careful scholar specializing in the *Nadere Reformatie.*

———. "Jean Taffin: Eerste pleiter voor 'Nadere Reformatie' in Nederland." *Theologia Reformata* 25 (1982), 6–29. Argues persuasively that Taffin should be regarded as the earliest representative of the *Nadere Reformatie,* rather than as a precursor of it.

Sepp, Christiaan. *Drie evangeliedienaren uit den tijd der Hervorming.* Leiden, 1879. Oldest significant study of Taffin; first eighty pages devoted to his life and preaching.

Stoeffler, F. Ernest. *The Rise of Evangelical Pietism.* Leiden, 1971. Brief, but only good source in English; focuses on Taffin's theology in *The Marks of the Children of God.* See especially pp. 121–124.

JOEL R. BEEKE

TALLIS, Thomas (1505?–1585), English composer. More than that of any other English composer, the career

of Thomas Tallis spans the years of the Reformation. Probably born in the county of Kent early in the sixteenth century, he was organist of the Benedictine priory of Dover by 1532. In 1538 he moved to Waltham Abbey, a large Augustinian house, where he had a choir of men and boys. When the monastery was dissolved in 1540, Tallis, not a monk himself, was granted a "reward" but did not receive the pension normally paid to the ex-religious.

After several years of service as a lay clerk at Canterbury cathedral, Tallis took up his position as a gentleman of the Chapel Royal. Here he served four monarchs—Henry VIII, Edward VI, Mary Tudor, and Elizabeth I. Although listed as one of the singing men, he probably acted as organist and chief composer throughout the period from 1543 to his death in 1585. Queen Mary granted him the lease of a manor in Kent, and in 1575 Queen Elizabeth gave Tallis and William Byrd jointly a monopoly on the printing and sale of music. About 1552 Tallis married a woman named Joan. He was buried in the parish church of Greenwich, where he owned a house.

In his youth, prior to the introduction of *The Book of Common Prayer*, Tallis wrote a number of Latin motets and votive antiphons. He continued to set Latin texts during the reign of Queen Elizabeth, who enjoyed Latin settings in her private chapel even though only English texts could be used legally in other churches and cathedrals. Tallis did set a number of English texts, however. His English motets, of which the best known is *If Ye Love Me*, are generally in a simple chordal style that contrasts sharply with the polyphonic settings of such Latin texts as *Audivi vocem de coelo* and *In jejunio et fletu*. The simple anthems, as well as the Dorian service, reflect the Anglican desire for straightforward, short settings in which the words could be understood clearly.

Tallis's largest and finest works are his setting of the *Lamentations of Jeremiah* and the motet *Spem in alium*. The Lamentations, based on the lessons for Maundy Thursday, convey a sense of deep spirituality and penitence. Set for a five-part choir of men's voices, they are in two sections, probably not written at the same time. The forty-part motet *Spem in alium* is a unique masterpiece written for eight choirs of five voices each. The circumstances of its composition are unknown, but it may have been written to mark Elizabeth I's fortieth birthday in 1573. Such symbolic art forms were popular at the queen's court, and the Latin text could have been accommodated in her private chapel.

Relatively little of Tallis's instrumental music survives. The *Fitzwilliam Virginal Book* contains two extended keyboard works based on the plainsong intonation "Felix namque." The *Mulliner Book* includes a number of short liturgical pieces, probably intended for organ, as well as the music for a few secular part-songs, including *When Shall My Sorrowful Sighing*.

BIBLIOGRAPHY

Doe, Paul. *Tallis.* 2d ed. London, 1976. The authoritative monograph.
Lafontaine, Henry Cart de. *The King's Musick* (1909). Reprint, New York, 1973. An older study of the Chapel Royal, still valuable.
Le Huray, Peter. *Music and the Reformation in England, 1549–1660.* Reprint, Cambridge, 1978. This book and Stevens set Tallis's work in a larger context.
Stevens, Denis. *Tudor Church Music.* Reprint, New York, 1973.

STANFORD E. LEHMBERG

TAURINUS, Jacobus (Dutch, Jacob van Toor; 1577–1618), Dutch Reformed minister, Remonstrant leader, and author. Son of a Reformed minister, Taurinus studied theology at the University of Leiden. He then entered the ministry, serving in 't Woud (1600) and Delfshaven (1601–1605), both villages in South Holland, and then in Utrecht (1605–1618). Taurinus came to Utrecht as part of a new generation of ministers. In his first years there he worked to rebuild the city's Reformed church, devastated by years of schism, and to move it away from its former libertinism to a moderate Calvinism. He also played an important role in extending Calvinist reforms to the Utrecht countryside. In 1606 Taurinus attended Utrecht's first provincial synod, which put him on a committee to oversee countryside reforms. In 1612 he served as secretary at a second provincial synod. This synod approved a church ordinance that Taurinus had helped to draft. The ordinance was designed both to continue the reform process and to prevent the budding Remonstrant controversy from causing unrest. Remonstrants in Holland soon viewed this ordinance as a model, and in 1614 the States of Holland incorporated some of its provisions into its own "Resolution for the Peace of the Churches."

In the 1610's Taurinus emerged as leader of the Remonstrant party in Utrecht province. He achieved national prominence also through his published writings. His *Brand-Clock*, appearing anonymously in 1611, defended the appointment of Conradus Vorstius as professor of theology at Leiden. Contra-Remonstrants had accused Vorstius, a Remonstrant, of Socinianism. Taurinus's most important work, *Van de onderlinge verdraagsaamheyt*, appeared in two volumes in 1615. It is a plea for mutual tolerance between Remonstrants and Contra-Remonstrants that draws largely on historical arguments; it is also an erudite and thoughtful treatment of religious tolerance generally. In his *Na-Sporingh* (1617) Taurinus examined the religious politics of William of Orange in order to show that the Contra-Remonstrant position on predestination had never formed the basis of the Dutch polity. Of all Taurinus's works the most notorious and politically consequential was his *Weegh-Schael* (1617), published anonymously. In it Taurinus responded to a speech in which Dudley Carleton, the English ambassador to the Netherlands, had attacked the Remonstrants. (Carleton's sovereign, James I, supported the Contra-Remonstrants.) The *Weegh-Schael* so infuriated Carleton that he pressured the Dutch States-General into offering a huge reward of a thousand guilders to anyone who would reveal the author's name.

In the summer of 1618 came Prince Maurice's bloodless coup. In its wake the printer of the *Weegh-Schael* exposed Taurinus as its author. Utrecht's new, Contra-Remonstrant magistracy summarily dismissed Taurinus from office and sought his arrest. Taurinus fled to Antwerp, as did other leading Remonstrants. There he suddenly grew ill and died.

BIBLIOGRAPHY

Nauta, D. et al., eds. *Biografisch Lexicon voor de geschiedenis van het nederlandse protestantisme.* 3 vols. Kampen, Netherlands 1978–. See vol. 2, pp. 416–418.

Rogge, H. C. "Jacobus Taurinus en de Utrechtsche kerk in het begin der 17de eeuw." *Archief voor Nederlandsche Kerkgeschiedenis* 3 (1889), 105–264.

Tidemans, Joannes. *De Remonstrantie en het Remonstrantisme.* Amsterdam, 1851.

BENJAMIN J. KAPLAN

TAUSEN, Hans (1494–1561), Danish reformer and bishop. Possibly from a lower noble family, Tausen was accepted as a monk in the monastery of the Order of Saint John of Jerusalem at Antvorskov. During a period of study at the University of Rostock (from 1516), where he obtained a master's degree, he became acquainted with humanism, and he taught himself Leonardo Bruni's Latin translation of the pseudo-Aristotelian *Oeconomia*. In 1521 he matriculated at the University of Copenhagen, where he came under the influence of the Carmelite provincial Paul Helie, lecturer at the university, who was a reform Catholic of Erasmian persuasion and who strongly urged his students to take a personally critical position on the basis of New Testament studies. Like his mentor Desiderius Erasmus, Tausen wanted no break in the church. In 1522 Tausen studied at the University of Louvain, where he probably received the thorough knowledge of Greek and Hebrew that he later demonstrated. From 1523 to 1524 he studied at Wittenberg University, but at that time, in 1524, the Danish national council clearly distanced itself from the Lutheran movement. Tausen's prior took part in the declaration of loyalty to the Roman Catholic church, and this is certainly the reason that Tausen was called back to the monastery from Wittenberg.

The fact that he was asked to preach and teach shows that the order's leadership still had confidence in him, but after he moved to Viborg (Jutland), his sermons became more and more Lutheran and aggressively critical of Roman Catholic teachings and institutions. He was expelled from the order probably in the spring of 1526. King Frederick I, who mediated between the religious factions, appointed him as a royal preacher, and a year later the Reformation was introduced in Viborg, the most important city in west Denmark, the outgrowth of a strong citizens' movement. Tausen's most important co-worker was Jorgen Jensen Sadolin, who took over the leadership in 1529, when Tausen became a minister at Saint Nikolaj Church in Copenhagen, where he worked effectively toward the Reformation's success. The king's planned religious colloquy with participants from both religious parties (June 1530) did not take place, but the preachers' most important contribution, the *Confessio Hafniensis*, a confession of forty-three articles, has been preserved. Both with regard to this confession and in the numerous written complaints that were exchanged between the parties, Tausen played a leading role. After the king's death in 1533, there was a short-lived Catholic reaction in which the bishops tried to legally establish a national Danish Catholic church independent of Rome and to stamp Tausen as a heretic. After popular pressure, however, they had to be satisfied with banning him from Copenhagen; shortly thereafter he was able to resume his work. During the following civil war (1534–1536) Tausen worked in Copenhagen, and in the summer of 1536, when the war's victor, King Christian III, quickly brought about the official introduction of Lutheranism into the kingdom, Tausen became a leading member of the commission that worked out the proposal for a church ordinance (1536–1537). He now became a lecturer in Hebrew at the reestablished university and a preacher at the Roskilde cathedral, where he was to try to convert the recalcitrant cathedral chapter members to the Lutheran belief. In 1541 Tausen was named bishop of the Ribe diocese in Jutland, where he worked until his death.

Tausen left mainly polemical and practical-theological writings. From the time of the Reformation struggle (1526–1536), his Danish version (1527) of Nikolaus Herman's pamphlet *Eyn Mandat Jhesu Christi an alle seyne getrewen Christen* (A Mandate of Jesus Christ to All His True Christians; 1524) has been saved. In it the author uses the popular literary form of "letters from heaven" and, in a humanist-pedagogical way, appeals to ordinary men and women. Shortly thereafter appeared his *Svar til biskoppen af Odenses sendebrev* (Answer to the Bishop of Odense's Missive), in which Tausen in a rough polemic tone rejected the Catholic Bishop Jens Andersen Beldenak's tract against Lutheranism. During this period Tausen also published a Danish translation of Luther's *Täufbuchlein, En ret christelig fadzon at christne børnene med paa danske*, and probably rituals for confession and for the Holy Sacrament and a ritual for marriage service, but all these writings have been lost. *Aftensang med salmer* (Evensong with Psalms, 1528) has also been lost but exists in a reprinted edition from 1533; it was a liturgical vespers that polemically attacked the Catholic ritual. In the middle of the civil war Tausen published one of his main works, *De fem Mosebøger* (The Pentateuch), translated from Hebrew into Danish (1535). For use in the established reformed church, he published a *Postille* (Book of Sermons) with sermons on all the Epistles and Gospel texts for all times of the year; it became of invaluable significance for the first generation of Lutheran ministers because all the Catholic priests remained in office and were "forcefully converted" in 1536. He also prepared a paraphrase of Veit Dietrich's *Kirkebønner* (Common Prayers), but neither this nor a translation of Luther's *Glosse mod det kejserlige mandat* (Notes Against the Imperial Mandate; 1531) was published in his time. On the other hand, scholarship has been able to show that the *Salmebog* (Hymnbook; 1553), once thought to have been published by Tausen, is not by him, even though it contains some of his hymns. He did translate psalms by Martin Luther, and changed some medieval hymns into evangelical psalms, as well as writing some himself. He used Gregorian melodies and tried generally to transfer the Catholic psalms, which had been created around the liturgy of the Mass, to Danish evangelical use.

There is no complete account of Tausen's theological position. A study of early Danish reformers' theology in their *Confessio Hafniensis* (1530) and in the writings of 1526–1536 shows that they did not belong to the Wittenberg-Lutheran but to the biblical humanist persuasion, whose home was the southern and northern German market towns. Tausen, however, was an exception, for he stood near Luther on important points. He gave Nicolai Hermann's biblical-humanist pedagogical *Himmelbrev* (Letters from Heaven) a clearly Lutheran turn by emphasizing human sinfulness and total dependence upon God's grace, and in the answer to Bishop Jens Andersen (1529) he showed direct knowledge of Luther's writings and agreement with his views on the Bible, his principles of interpretation, and his ideas on the general ministry. *Postille*, moreover, shows both literary and theological dependence upon Luther's sermons.

Tausen's interpretation of the Eucharist has been much discussed, but there can hardly be doubt that he was convinced of the real presence. It must be added, however, that as far as the law and its application were concerned, he came close to Philipp Melanchthon's idea, and this also applied to his idea of the relationship between spiritual and secular authorities, where he expressed Melanchthon's humanistically colored idea of the prince's right to reform the church and his duty to act as *pater patriae* and head of the church. Finally, it is interesting that at the end of his life Tausen strongly emphasized the necessity for strict church discipline. For this purpose he used citations from John Calvin's *Institutio religionis christianae*.

BIBLIOGRAPHY

Primary Sources

Rørdam, Holger Fr., ed. *Smaaskrifter af Hans Tausen*. Copenhagen, 1870.
Tausen, Hans. *Postille*. Facsimile ed. 2 vols. Edited by Bj. Kornerup. Copenhagen, 1934.

Secondary Sources

Andersen, Niels Knud. *Confessio Hafniensis: Den københavnske Bekendelse af 1530*. Copenhagen, 1954. Contains a summary in German.
Bugge, Knud Eyvin, ed. *Tro og Tale: Studier over Hans Tausens postil*. Kirkehistoriske Studier II, no. 19. Copenhagen, 1963.
Christensen, Marie. *Hans Tausen*. Copenhagen, 1942.
Lausten, Martin Schwarz. "Hans Tausen." In *Dansk Biografisk Leksikon*, 3d ed., vol. 14, pp. 378–385. Copenhagen, 1983.

MARTIN SCHWARZ LAUSTEN
Translated from Danish by Walter D. Morris

TEELLINCK, Willem (1579–1629), Dutch minister from Zeeland, one of the first representatives of the *Nadere Reformatie* ("Further Reformation"). From a magistrate family of Zierikzee, Teellinck studied law at Saint Andrews in Scotland (1600), and later in Poitiers, where he earned a doctorate of laws (1603). But it was his contact with Puritan-Pietist circles during a nine-month stay in England (1604) that radically changed his life. English Puritanism would henceforth be his philosophy of life. After studying theology at Leiden, he served as minister to the parishes of Burgh-Haamstede (1606–1613) and Middelburg (1613–1629).

Teellinck is considered the father of the *Nadere Reformatie* in the Netherlands. Op't Hof (*Engelse pietistische geschriften in het Nederlands 1589–1622*, Rotterdam, 1987) dates the birth of this movement from 1608, the year of Teellinck's first publication. The principal motive of his life and work is found in the Puritan devotional ideal: the sanctification of life in all its aspects, fed by a deep personal religious life. Teellinck tried to live up to this *praxis pietatis* both in his family life, with his English wife Martha Greendon, and in his parish work.

Meanwhile he kept up intense contact with England, not only through family ties and several voyages overseas but also through his interest in English churches in the Netherlands. He often conducted services at the English parish of Middelburg and translated three English Puritan writings into Dutch. His pious and ascetic way of life made a deep impression on his contemporaries—albeit provoking criticism here and there—but the influence of his writings was much more important.

In spite of weak health Teellinck showed a remarkable energy; in barely fifty years he wrote 127 works, of which some 60 were published. Here all themes of the Puritan-Pietistic world of thought recur. He insisted strongly on the need for personal religious experiences and the detailed regulation of Christian conduct in life, especially the Sunday observance, fasting, religious education, and prayer, but extending also to detailed rules about clothes, meals, and other duties of daily life. Teellinck had in view nothing less than a total reformation, involving all aspects of life; he did not fear confronting the authorities with their shortcomings and pointing out their specific task to help promote religion.

Two years before he died he synthesized his ideas in one book: *Noodwendig Vertoogh* (1627). Also at the end of his life a mystical inclination, already present in his earlier work, mainfested itself more strongly as in the posthumously published *Soliloquium* and *Het Nieuwe Jeruzalem* (1635).

Teellinck's interest in English Puritanism, his personal contacts, and his work contributed to the Puritan color of the *Nadere Reformatie*. His influence reached further than his own country as several of his writings were translated into English and German.

BIBLIOGRAPHY

Primary Sources

Teellinck, Willem. *De parktijk van het heilig avondmal.* Franeker, 1969.
———. *Het nieuwe Jeruzalem.* Oostburg, 1969.
———. *Buren-kout, of, Samenspraak, omvattend tien stichtelijke gesprekken over Godsdienstige zaken.* Vlaardingen, 1988.

Secondary Sources

Engelberts, W. J. M. *Willem Teellinck* (1898). Reprint, Amsterdam, 1973.
Hof, W. J. op't. *Teellinck in het licht zijner geschriften.* Documentatieblad Nadere Reformatie, 1–13. Rotterdam, 1977–1993. Insightful analysis of Teellinck's work.
———. *Bibliographische lijst van de geschriften van Willem Teellinck.* Rotterdam, 1993.
Hollenbenders-Schmitter, Barbara. *Willem Teellinck: Soliloquium, mystisches Gebet im Zeitalter des Barock. Eine Analyse.* Cologne, 1989.
"Teellinck, Willem." In *Biografisch Lexicon voor de Geschiedenis van het Nederlandse Protestantisme,* vol. 1, pp. 373–375. Kampen, 1988.

CL. ROOZE-STOUTHAMER

TERESA OF ÁVILA

TERESA OF ÁVILA (born Teresa de Ahumada y Cepeda; 1515–1582), Spanish mystic, writer, and monastic reformer. Her family on her father's side were *Conversos*, descendents of converted Jews, who made their living primarily in the cloth trade. They aspired, however, to the social prestige only fully enjoyed by Old Christians in early modern Spain and used their wealth to "buy" noble status. Teresa later identified this obsession with honor and pedigree as totally incompatible with true religious life.

After a secure childhood darkened by the loss of her mother at an early age, the charming and vivacious Doña Teresa decided to embrace the monastic life. Moved more by the "servile fear" of hell than by the love of God, as she later wrote in her autobiography, she entered Ávila's Carmelite convent of the Incarnation in 1535, at the age of twenty. She remained in this house for twenty-seven years.

Teresa soon found that life in the convent essentially reproduced in microcosm the values of Spanish society. The Incarnation housed over one hundred nuns at the time of her entrance, mostly the privileged daughters of the city's "honored and principal men." Nuns frequently left the convent and entertained visitors and family members within its walls. Teresa would later voice particular opposition to the lack of monastic enclosure, but in her youth she, too, participated in this form of "laxity."

The transformation of the pampered Doña Teresa de Ahumada to the humble Teresa of Jesus occurred slowly, over a period of nearly twenty years. Eventually she came to reject the social and religious system by which she had lived for so long at the Incarnation.

Teresa's introduction to a meaningful life of prayer began in 1538, when a pious uncle gave her a copy of Francisco de Osuna's *Tercer abecedario espiritual* (Third Spiritual Alphabet; 1521). A great lover of books from childhood, she now began to devour the abundant devotional literature of her day. Finally, around 1555, when she was some forty years old, Teresa began to have frequent and profound spiritual experiences, seeing visions, hearing voices, and even achieving the coveted state of mystical union with God. She at last found the strength to detach herself from worldly things and commit herself totally to the service of God.

In 1560 the dramatically altered Teresa received a terrifying vision of hell. Her immediate reaction was activist and missionary in nature. She pondered how to save the "Lutherans" (i.e., French Calvinist Huguenots) from the torments of hell and began to feel the "pleasant restlessness" that would characterize the rest of her life.

Her first goal was to found a new convent in Ávila along the lines of the reforms undertaken by Peter of Alcántara among the Franciscans. Teresa established the Discalced Carmelite convent of Saint Joseph's in August 1562. By the time of her death in 1582 she had personally founded fourteen more houses for women, directed another two at a distance, and played a critical role in setting up the first two houses for men. The locations and founding dates for these houses are: Ávila, 1562; Medina del Campo, 1567; Malagón and Valladolid, 1568; Toledo and Pastrana, 1569; Salamanca, 1570; Alba de Tormes, 1571; Segovia, 1574; Beas de Segura and Seville, 1575; Caravaca, 1576; Villanueva de la Jara and Palencia, 1580; Soria, 1581; and Burgos and Granada, 1582.

In contrast to her previous life, Teresa stressed strict poverty and strict enclosure in her monastic houses. Departing from custom, she refused to accept the *rentas*, or fixed incomes, that financially supported most religious institutions.

This ascetic principle also gave her nuns a measure of autonomy from the demands of wealthy benefactors, a common problem in religious houses of the time. She strove to establish a genuinely egalitarian atmosphere in which even sisters from aristocratic families adopted religious names and participated in the manual chores of the convent. A true daughter of Catholic Spain, she urged her nuns to pray unceasingly for the priests and missionaries working among the "heretics" and "heathens." Through this apostolate of prayer, she reminded her sisters, they would be doing God's work "although [they] are very cloistered."

During the last seventeen years of her life Teresa composed four major works, *El libro de su vida, El camino de la perfección, Las moradas o el castillo interior*, and *El libro de su fundaciones* (The Book of Her Life, The Way of Perfection, The Interior Castle, and The Book of Her Foundations), as well as poems, meditations, instructions for monastic administrators, and some five-hundred extant letters. This extraordinary literary output attests to her strong vocation as a writer and to the importance she attached to helping souls through the written word. She is regarded as one of the greatest writers of Spain's Golden Age and as a peerless analyst and teacher of the Christian spiritual life. Teresa of Ávila was beatified in 1614 and canonized in 1622. She remains one of Catholicism's most beloved saints.

BIBLIOGRAPHY

Primary Sources

Teresa of Ávila. *The Collected Works of Saint Teresa of Ávila.* Translated by Kieran Kavanaugh and Otilio Rodríguez. 3 vols. Washington, D.C., 1976–1985. This is a fine translation of Teresa's works, rendered in an accessible American English with excellent introductory essays by Kavanaugh. Does not include her letters.
———. *The Complete Works.* Translated by E. Allison Peers. 3 vols. Reprint, London, 1982. Some prefer the more poetic, if more archaic, style of this pioneering scholar of Spanish mysticism.
———. *The Letters of Saint Teresa of Jesus.* Translated by E. Allison Peers. 2 vols. Reprint, London, 1980.
———. *Obras completas.* Edited by Efrén Montalva and Otger Steggink. Madrid, 1974. A good critical edition of Teresa's complete works (including her letters) in one volume.

Secondary Sources

Bilinkoff, Jodi. *The Ávila of Saint Teresa: Religious Reform in a Sixteenth-Century City.* Reprint, Ithaca, N.Y., 1992. Examines Teresa's reform activities in the social and religious context of her native city.
Clissold, Stephen. *St. Teresa of Ávila.* New York, 1982. This is the best recent biography in English, combining a breezy journalistic style with careful archival research.
Egido, Teófanes. "The Historical Setting of Saint Teresa's Life." *Carmelite Studies* 1 (1980), 122–182. This penetrating article, published in two parts, is the only one by this important Spanish Carmelite historian that has been translated into English.
———. "The Economic Concerns of Madre Teresa." *Carmelite Studies* 4 (1987), 151–172.
Luti, J. Mary. *Teresa of Ávila's Way.* Collegeville, Minn., 1991. Provides a very useful introduction to Teresa's spiritual teachings.
Montalva, Efrén, and Otger Steggink. *Santa Teresa y su tiempo.* 2 vols. Salamanca, 1982–1984. This documentary history by two noted Carmelite scholars offers a wealth of information.
Rossi, Rosa. *Teresa de Ávila: Biografía de una escritora.* Barcelona, 1984. Offers stunning insights from a feminist literary scholar.
Weber, Alison. *Teresa of Ávila and the Rhetoric of Femininity.* Princeton, 1990. A fascinating exploration of the rhetorical strategies utilized by Teresa in her four major works.

JODI BILINKOFF

TETRAPOLITAN CONFESSION. Also known as the *Confessio Tetrapolitana* or *Vierstädtebekenntnis*, this document was presented to Emperor Charles V by the cities of Strasbourg, Constance, Memmingen, and Lindau at the Diet of Augsburg (1530) as their alternative to Philipp Melanchthon's Augsburg Confession. Composed by Wolfgang Capito and Martin Bucer of Strasbourg, it sheds light on both the confessional and political history of the Reformation. These two theologians were hastily called to the diet even as Melanchthon was at work on the Saxon Confession. At the time it was becoming apparent that Strasbourg's political emissaries would not be allowed to subscribe to it by virtue of disagreements over the Lord's Supper. The city thus required both its own confession and its own allies from the princes, cities, and estates of the empire.

In confessional terms this document reveals the deep split in the nominally Protestant forces of Germany in the late 1520s and early 1530s. This division, which centered upon whether the elements of bread and wine actually became Christ's body and blood in the Lord's Supper, was the subject of a pamphlet war that began in 1524 but that had been latent for some years and whose lines were drawn at the Colloquy of Marburg in 1529. The south Germans and Swiss took a spiritual or symbolic view, while Martin Luther and his followers insisted that the body and blood were really (although inexplicably) present in the sacramental use of the elements. In its initial version, probably composed by Capito, the key article in the Tetrapolitan Confession declared that "Christ the Lord is truly in the Supper and gives his true body truly to eat and his blood truly to drink, but especially to the spirit, through faith." This last clause offended Melanchthon and the other Lutherans at the diet, for in it they rightly sensed a diminution of their teaching that communicants physically consumed Christ's body and blood during the Lord's Supper, without respect to their faith. That they correctly sensed the intent of the new wording is evident from a letter that Capito wrote to his colleagues back in Strasbourg after this article was revised. He insisted that, despite the new phraseology, "we in fact distinctly affirm that only the spiritual eating is useful [for salvation]."

The need to revise the article reveals the political character of the confession as a whole. Jakob Sturm and Matthis Pfarrer, Strasbourg's delegates to the diet, insisted on changes that would make it less offensive to others who might have their doubts about Luther's and the Saxon's insistence on the real presence. They hoped thereby to attract at least a few potential allies in a situation that was fraught with political dangers. Charles V had just returned to Germany from successful campaigns in Italy against both Francis I of France and Pope Clement VII, and, as preparation for campaigns against the Ottoman Turks, he was determined to bring about a religious settlement and therefore political unity in Germany. Political isolation in this situation did not appeal to Strasbourg's ruling authorities, so roughly a year later they in essence deserted their confession and subscribed to the Augsburg Confession in order to become part of a pan-German Protestant alliance that was at base Lutheran and led by Lutheran princes. By virtue of the Wittenberg Concord (1536) even the city's theologians agreed.

The Tetrapolitan Confession nonetheless continued to be part of Strasbourg's formal religion into the 1560s and later, when Girolamo Zanchi appealed to it, as did Conrad Hubert, who had been Bucer's secretary. By this time, however, it had become a symbol of a generic Protestantism that would provide a place for the Reformed within the empire. Strasbourg finally repudiated the confession and its various politics with a new church order in 1598.

BIBLIOGRAPHY

Kittelson, James M. *Wolfgang Capito: From Humanist to Reformer.* Leiden, 1975. See pp. 153–157.

Stupperich, Robert, et al., eds. *Martin Bucers Deutsche Schriften.* Gütersloh, 1969. See especially vol. 3, pp. 13–185. The critical edition in both Latin and German.

JAMES M. KITTELSON

TETZEL, Johann (c.1465–1519), German preacher of indulgences who was important in the indulgences controversy with Martin Luther. Born around 1465 in Pirna, Tetzel studied at Leipzig, earning a bachelor of arts degree in 1487. He entered the Dominican order (date and place unknown), becoming prior at Głogów (Poland) after 1497. In 1509 Cajetan named Tetzel inquisitor for Poland and later for Saxony. In 1509 at Frankfurt an der Oder, he received the license for the doctoral degree, which was conferred in 1518. Between 1504 and 1510 Tetzel preached indulgences from Silesia to Alsace. In 1517, serving the archbishop of Mainz, Albert of Brandenburg, Tetzel preached the indulgence for Saint Peter's in Jüterbog and Zerbst (outside of Saxony but near Wittenberg), where he came to Martin Luther's attention.

Following the *Instructio Summaria* (Mainz Instruction), Tetzel preached that indulgences for the dead could be obtained regardless of the contrition of the one seeking the indulgence and could be applied at the seeker's discretion. Tetzel and some other indulgence preachers did not make

clear that indulgences were intended to remit punishment for sin that had been confessed and absolved but not adequately satisfied. The lack of clarity implied that indulgences could both absolve guilt and remit punishment. These points were scholastic opinion, not church doctrine, and were criticized by Cajetan, among others.

Tetzel's activity provoked Luther's Ninety-five Theses for a disputation on indulgences. The theses were not aimed singly at Tetzel nor at indulgences as a whole. Luther objected to pecuniary abuses and the distortion that indulgences were a means of salvation, criticisms that had been raised earlier.

Against Luther, Tetzel defended a series of counter theses (the 106 Frankfurt Theses) written largely by Konrad Wimpina in January 1518. He countered Luther's subsequent "Sermon on Indulgences and Grace" with a "Vorlegung" (Presentation) condemning twenty errors. In 1518 Tetzel composed his own *Positiones,* defending indulgences and papal authority. The counterattack also illustrates the challenge from some orders against Scholasticism, which the Dominicans continued to defend. Often slandered during his life and afterward by confessional polemics, Tetzel died in Leipzig on 4 July 1519, when Luther was defending himself against Johann Eck at the Leipzig Disputation. Tetzel's significance lies largely in his activity as preacher and defender of indulgences, associated with the Reformation through Luther's Ninety-five Theses.

BIBLIOGRAPHY

Primary Source

Fabisch, Peter, and Erwin Iserloh, eds. *Dokumente zur Causa Luther, 1517–1521.* Corpus Catholicorum, vol. 41, pt. 1. Münster, 1988. Contains such critical texts as Tetzel's 106 Theses, the "Vorlegung" on Luther's sermon on indulgences, and the fifty *Positiones.* Also gives historical introduction to Tetzel, and complete bibliographical references.

Secondary Sources

Paulus, Nikolaus. *Johann Tetzel der Ablaßprediger.* Mainz, 1899. The most recent and thorough biography.

Wicks, Jared. "Roman Reactions to Luther: The First Year, 1518." *Catholic Historical Review* 69 (1983), 521–562. Mentions Tetzel and Dominicans in the context of the struggle with humanism and the challenges of other orders during the first year of the Luther affair.

JEFF BACH

THAMER, Theobald (1502–1569), Lutheran theologian and preacher who reconverted to Catholicism over the doctrine of justification. Born in Alsace and raised in the Catholic faith, Thamer was a fervent Lutheran when he received a stipend from Philipp of Hesse in 1534 to study theology at the University of Wittenberg. He became a spirited disputant and star pupil of Luther and Melanchthon, receiving a master's degree in 1539. He held a teaching post in Frankfurt an der Oder until 1543, when Landgrave Philipp called him to Marburg as professor of theology and preacher at the Elizabeth church.

Described as a person of selfless dedication and uncompromising faith, Thamer was greatly troubled by Protestant disunity and took to attacking the Zurich reformers for failing to accept the Augsburg Confession, particularly in the matter of the Lord's Supper. Although a popular preacher, Thamer's extreme orthodoxy drew criticism from less contentious theologians of his own persuasion as well as from the highly offended Swiss.

More serious problems developed for Thamer in 1546, when he served as chaplain to Landgrave Philipp during the Schmalkald War. Disenchanted with soldiers who cursed, gambled, drank, and plundered while excusing themselves on the grounds that Christ had died for their sins, Thamer began to study anew the scriptural basis for Luther's doctrine of justification. By 1548 he had become convinced that it was based on an erroneous interpretation, and he began to preach against the Lutheran belief that man is reconciled to God through faith alone.

Thamer's insistence on the efficacy of good works created a storm of controversy between his adherents and those of his chief antagonist, Johannes Draconites. A planned public disputation was canceled by the authorities in the interests of civic peace, and Thamer's well-reasoned arguments from scripture (he had prepared twenty-eight theses) were never given the hearing he felt they deserved. These were published to little effect as *Confessio fidei* in 1548.

A succession of meetings with eminent Protestant divines, who declared him hopelessly confused, ended with Thamer's dismissal from his teaching and preaching posts in Marburg. His *Apologia* gives a detailed account of his disputes and ultimate reconversion to Catholicism in 1553. He spent the remainder of his turbulent life as professor of theology at the University of Freiburg.

BIBLIOGRAPHY

Primary Sources

Thamer, Theobald. *An et quatenus Christianis in persecutionibus sit fugiendum, tractatus.* Marburg, 1547.
———. *Wahrhaftiger Bericht Th. Th.s von den Injurien und Lästerungen, welche ihm die Lutherischen deshalb falsch und unchristlich zugemessen.* N.p., 1552.
———. *Apologia Th. Thameri de variis calumniis, quas ab anno 1552 usque 1561 tulit a Lutheranis evangelistis.* Moguntia (Mainz), 1561.
———. *In Sacrosanctam D.N. Jesu Christi passionem brevis introductio.* Moguntia (Mainz), 1561.

Secondary Sources

Backus, Irena. "La doctrine des bonnes oeuvres de Theobald Thamer." In *Les dissidents du 16e siècle,* edited by M. Lienhard and A. Séguenny, pp. 205–217. Baden-Baden, 1983.
Bruck, A. "Thamer." In *Lexicon für Theologie und Kirche,* vol. 10, p. 10. Freiburg, 1965.
Hochhuth, K. W. H. "Theobald Thamer und Landgraf Philipp." *Zeitschrift für historische Theologie* n.s. 31 (1861), 165–279. Balanced Protestant view with selected writings of Thamer.
Neander, August. *Theobald Thamer: Der Repräsentant und Vorgänger moderner Geistesrichtung in dem Reformationszeitalter.* Berlin, 1842. Strong Catholic bias.
Räss, Andreas. *Die Convertiten.* Freiburg i.B., 1866. See vol. 1, pp. 236–297. Scholarly Catholic overview, with German version of Thamer's *Apologia.*
Schottenloher, Karl, ed. *Bibliographie zur deutschen Geschichte im Zeitalter der Glaubensspaltung.* Stuttgart, 1957. See vol. 2, p. 326.

KARIN BRINKMANN BROWN

THEATER. *See* Drama.

THEATINES. This community and later order was founded on 14 September 1524 by four members of the Roman Oratory of Divine Love: Gaetano Thiene (canonized in 1671), Gian Pietro Carafa (later Pope Paul IV), Bonifacio de' Colli, and Paolo Consiglieri. That the name was derived from "Theatinus," Carafa's appellation as bishop of Chieti, testifies to his leading role. The founders envisioned a community of priests united by their apostolic life, observance of church law, and charity to the poor and the sick. Their ministry to the so-called *incurabili,* or sufferers from syphilis, became conspicuous, as did their efforts to promote frequent Communion among the people. Theatines were flexible about common prayer, stressed private meditation, and wore no distinctive habit other than clerical garb. Pope Clement VII approved their rule in 1524, and Clement VIII confirmed the definitive version of their constitution in 1604.

The aim of the Theatines was reform of the church through reform of the clergy. Related to this was their concern with reform of the liturgy. Soon after their foundation, their austere spirituality (their Italian name, *Chietini,* came to denote religious puritans) drew reform-minded clerics and laymen to their house in Rome, which became a center of reflection on the Christian life. Dispersed by the sack of the city in 1527, the Theatines found refuge in Venice. Their third house was established in Naples, followed in the later sixteenth century by houses in other Italian cities. In the seventeenth century the Theatines expanded to Germany, Austria, France, Spain, and Portugal and even engaged in overseas missionary work.

Although never a large order, the Theatines were effective in the formation of zealous prelates and successful in their pastoral and charitable activities. Their distinctive spirituality found its best expression in Lorenzo Scupoli's *Combattimento Spirituale* (Spiritual Combat; 1589), a popular and widely translated treatise still in use.

[*See also* Paul IV.]

BIBLIOGRAPHY

Andreu, F. "Chierici regolari Teatini." In *Dizionario degli Istituti di Perfezione,*" vol. 2, pp. 978–999. Rome, 1975. Best short discussion of the Theatines, with good bibliography.

Evenett, H. O. "The New Orders." In *The Reformation, 1520–1559,* edited by G. R. Elton, pp. 313–338. The New Cambridge Modern History, vol. 2. Cambridge, 1990. Good sketch of the background against which the Theatines arose.

Paschini, Pio. *S. Gaetano Tiene, Gian Pietro Carafa e le origini dei Chierici Regolari Teatini.* Rome, 1926. Still very useful on the early period and nature of the order.

Scupoli, Lorenzo. *Spiritual Combat.* London, 1960. Good modern translation of the Theatine spiritual classic.

ELISABETH G. GLEASON

THEOCRACY. *See* Magistracy.

THEOLOGY. *See* Anglicanism; Calvinism; Lutheranism, *article on* Theology; Roman Catholicism.

THIENE, Gaetano da. *See* Cajetan.

THIRTY-NINE ARTICLES. *See* Articles of Religion.

THOMAS, Illyricus (1485–1529), Italian Franciscan theologian and early defender of Catholic rites and doctrine against Martin Luther. Born in the Dalmatian town of Vrana, Thomas as a young man joined the order of observant Franciscans in the province of Ancona. Although he referred to himself as a professor of theology, was fluent in Latin, and was well versed in scripture, nothing is known of his academic background. In 1510 he began a notable career as an itinerant preacher in Italy, Spain, Germany, and particularly southern France, where he became a familiar figure in Bordeaux, Toulouse, and Lyon.

With his ascetic personality, his missionary zeal, and the high standards he set for Christian living, both lay and clerical, Thomas gained a formidable reputation as a penitential preacher. In 1521, after two volumes of his sermons were printed in Toulouse, he began work on two treatises intended to counter Luther's attacks on Catholic dogma and practice. Thomas took a reasoned analytical approach to Luther's assertions and, omitting any reference to papal decretals or the scholastic theology Luther held in contempt, appealed only to scripture and to the Latin and Greek church fathers in forming his arguments.

Because of funding difficulties, Thomas's first polemical work, *Clipeus status papalis . . .* —primarily a response to Luther's 1520 *An den christlichen Adel deutscher Nation* (Address to the Christian Nobility of the German Nation)—was not published until 1523. In contrast to other critics of Luther, Thomas justified the pope's ecclesiastical jurisdiction while denying papal infallibility in questions of faith, giving precedence here to an ecumenical council. Although he defended the church's teaching on penance and absolution, Thomas showed little enthusiasm for indulgences and warned against misleading the gullible with exaggerated claims for their power to absolve sinners or release souls from purgatory. He also warned against abuses connected with the veneration of saints and holy images. Thomas took occasion at the end of this work to condemn political strife, launch an invective against clerical abuses, and demand a general council for the necessary reform of the whole of Christendom.

A larger treatise, *In Lutherianas hereses . . . ,* published in 1524, addressed Luther's *De captivitate Babylonica ecclesiae praeludium* (Prelude Concerning the Babylonian Captivity of the Church) and *Von der Freiheit eines Christenmenschen* (On the Freedom of a Christian). In it he refuted point by point the reformer's teachings on justification; good works; free will; the sacraments of ordination, penance, Holy Communion, and marriage; and the religious value of celibacy and monastic vows.

In 1527 Pope Clement VII named Thomas grand inquisitor against Lutherans and Waldensians in Savoy. He died near Menton widely venerated because of his saintliness.

BIBLIOGRAPHY

Lauchert, Friedrich. *Die italienischen literarischen Gegner Luther.* Reprint, Nieuwkoop, 1972. Gives a thorough analysis of Thomas' major treatises with extensive quotes from the original Latin texts.

Piolanti, Antonio. "Illirico, Tommaso." *Enciclopedia cattolica,* vol. 6, pp. 1628–1629. Rome, 1951. Bibliography.

Schubert, F. "Thomas, Illyricus." In *Lexikon für Theologie und Kirche,* vol. 10, pp. 128–129. Freiburg, 1938.

KARIN BRINKMANN BROWN

THOMAS OF VILLANUEVA. *See* Augustinians.

THOMESEN, Hans. *See* Thomissøn, Hans.

THOMISM. The word *Thomism* refers to a school of thought in Christian theology that seeks to represent, defend, and build on the work of Thomas Aquinas (c.1225–

1274). Through the centuries, representatives of this school have differed widely on what they take to be the fundamental and distinctive teachings of Thomism. The hallmark doctrines of this school have changed from one historical context to the next, and even within a single historical period there has been great debate over precisely which positions are authentically Thomist. Because of this, many historians are now abandoning the older attempts to define Thomism by listing distinctive teachings. These historians simply accept as Thomist all who understand themselves to be such. The further task then is to make qualitative judgments about how well various Thomists represent the actual teaching of Thomas Aquinas. It is in this sense that the word is used here.

The Late Medieval Context. The dominant feature of the theological landscape on the eve of the Reformation was its pluralism. University instruction in theology allowed students to choose courses in the *via antiqua* or *via moderna.* Moreover, within these *viae* many schools of thought rivaled one another for adherents and influence. Thus nominalists, Scotists, Thomists, Augustinians, humanists, Albertists, and others all vied to become the dominant intellectual current of the age. While some of the differences among these schools were trivial, others were deep, reaching to the very core of the Christian self-understanding. And while some of the heat generated by these debates was the result of rivalry between religious orders, some of it came from disagreements over Christian teaching serious enough to elicit charges and countercharges of heterodoxy. There were those who saw this pluralism as a sign of health—a creative blossoming of opinions and perspectives that would ultimately enrich the whole. Others, especially in the Curia Romana, saw it as a dangerous descent toward chaos and called for the imposition of order.

If any school of thought can be said to have had the upper hand in the fifteenth century, it was the nominalists. As for Thomism, the beginning of the century found it in a sad state of health. Besides having no major thinkers in their ranks, the Thomists in 1387 had been expelled *en masse* from the citadel of academe, the University of Paris. Only after being readmitted in 1403 did the school's fortunes take a turn for the better. Now, what is sometimes called a "renaissance" of Thomism got under way.

The most influential leader of this rebirth was the Dominican John Capreolus (c.1380–1444), known to posterity as the "Princeps Thomistarum." Facing head-on the attacks of rival schools, Capreolus wrote a massive *Defensiones Theologiae Divi Thomae Aquinatis*, (edited by C. Paban and T. Pèques, 7 vols., Tours, 1900–1907). In it he offered a comprehensive, well-reasoned, and spirited response to the many critics of Thomas's theology. Several of these attacks, he held, were based on misunderstandings of Thomas, and accordingly he set down some of the important historical-critical principles for the correct interpretation of Thomas.

This defense of Thomas ignited a new interest in his thought with the result that much new talent was attracted to Thomism in the late fifteenth century.

At the same time (and with great consequences for the Reformation) the Thomist school's center of gravity was gradually shifting from Paris to Cologne. The dominant figure in this transition was Henry of Gorkum (c.1378–1431). A secular priest, Henry was professor of theology in Paris before moving to Cologne in 1419. There he wrote several influential works including a popular compendium of the *Summa Theologiae* entitled *Quaestiones in Summam Sancti Thomae*, and a *Conclusiones super IV Libros Sententiarum*, which Luther himself annotated in the monastery library at Erfurt. This "Thomistarum Coloniensum Monarcha," as he came to be known, inspired a long list of German Thomists in the late fifteenth century. The fact that Thomism was a vibrant force in the young Luther's intellectual world was due in no small measure to Henry of Gorkum.

As Luther embarked on his academic career in 1507, professors at all major German universities were offering courses "in via Sancti Thomae." At Erfurt, where Luther studied, there were Thomists on the theology faculty. Even at the fledgling University of Wittenberg, where Luther received his first faculty appointment, Thomism was well represented. Theological libraries, both at Erfurt and Wittenberg, were replete with works by and on Thomas Aquinas. Early friends and fellow-reformers such as Andreas Bodenstein von Karlstadt (1486–1541) had been formally trained as Thomists. Though his own training was in the nominalist school, Luther can hardly have been oblivious to the prominent Thomist current in his intellectual milieu. Indeed, as he said in 1521, ". . . I have studied the best of this sort of literature."

The Thomist Assault on Luther. The first wave in the attack on Luther's "novelties" was led primarily by Thomists. When one looks at the writings against Luther between 1517 and 1525, there are of course prominent exceptions, such as the eclectic Johann Eck (1486–1543), the Franciscan Thomas Murner (1475–1537), and the humanist Desiderius Erasmus (1467?–1536). Nevertheless, in terms of sheer numbers, Thomists predominate. Little wonder then that Luther came to see Thomism as the antithesis of the gospel as he understood it.

Soon after Luther's Ninety-five Theses "On the Power of Indulgences" were posted in mid-November of 1517, the Thomist Konrad Wimpina (1460–1531) wrote a set of counter-theses, and these were publicly defended by another Thomist, Johann Tetzel (c.1465–1519), on 20 January 1518 (printed in *D. Martini Lutheri opera latina varii argumenti ad reformationis historiam imprimis pertinentia*, vol. 1, pp. 296–305, Frankfurt and Erlangen, 1865–1873). In mid-March Luther composed a reply, his "Sermon von Ablass und Gnade," the opening salvo in his counterattack on the Thomists. In the following months Tetzel responded (in *Lutheri opera latina varii argumenti*, vol. 1, pp. 306–312), eliciting yet another rejoinder from Luther in early June, his "Eine Freiheit des Sermons päpstlichen Ablass und Gnade belangend." That same month another more eminent Thomist joined the controversy: Sylvester Mazzolini Prierias (1456–1523) published his *De potestatae papae dialogus* (in *Lutheri opera latina varii argumenti*, vol. 1, pp. 344–377). Luther's response, *Ad dialogum Silvestri Prieratis de potestate papae responsio* appeared in August. Then, in October, Cardinal Cajetan (1469–1534), the weightiest of his Thomist opponents, confronted him personally in Augsburg (see Luther's account of these meetings in his "Acta Augustana," WA 2, 6–26). Thus, already in 1518, Luther confronted a veritable Thomist phalanx. Here was the beginning of what was to be a lifelong struggle with Thomism.

But 1518, it must be emphasized, was only the beginning. In subsequent years large numbers of Thomists produced a massive and for the most part bitter polemical literature. Among Dominican Thomists alone, at least thirty took up the pen against Luther during his lifetime. Names such as Ambrosius Catharinus, Johann Dietenberger, Hieronymus von Dungersheim, Johannes Augustanus Faber (d. 1530), Jakob Hoogstraten, Konrad Köllin, Johannes Mensing, Ambrosius Pelargus, and Michael Vehe head the list. Some wrote one book against Luther, while others produced as many as fifteen. Moreover, the roster of Thomist opponents who were not members of the Dominican order is at least as long. Thus, to a large extent it was Luther's protest that galvanized the sixteenth century Thomist school and gave it a cause for which to fight.

The foremost representative of this school was undoubtedly Cajetan (Tommaso de Vio), first master general of the Dominican order and later cardinal. Even aside from his polemical engagement with Luther, Cajetan's contributions are of the highest significance for the history of Thomism. Between 1507 and 1520 he wrote what was to become perhaps the most influential commentary on the *Summa Theologiae* (printed in *Thomae Aquinae Opera Omnia*, Issu Leonis XIII, vols. 4–12, Rome, 1882). In the 1520s Cajetan turned his attention to scripture commentaries in an attempt to reclaim the scriptures for the Roman church (some printed in *Epistolae Pauli et Aliorum Apostolorum . . . iuxta sensum literalem enarratae*, Paris, 1532). His exegetical efforts surpassed those of any other Thomist up to his time. Finally, toward the end of his life he also wrote a series of *opuscula* attacking the Lutheran "errors" (in *Opuscula Omnia Thomae de vio Cajetani*, Lyon, 1581; partial translation in Jared Wicks, ed., *Cajetan Responds: A Reader in Reformation Controversy*, Washington, D.C., 1978). And in 1531 Cajetan recommended to Pope Clement VII that concessions could be made to the Lutherans; these should include Mass in the vernacular, Communion under both kinds, and marriage for priests. In these and other ways Cajetan belies the conventional stereotype of sixteenth-century Thomists as backward-looking traditionalists.

Representatives of this school attacked the reformers in the name of Thomas Aquinas. It is important to ask, therefore, how adequately they represented the actual teaching of their thirteenth-century mentor. As historical study of this question continues, it becomes increasingly clear that many of them seriously distorted Thomas's thought on a good number of important issues. For example, apart from a few such as Cajetan, these Thomists lost sight of the profoundly biblical orientation of Thomas's theology. Many of them defended the current practice regarding indulgences on grounds that can scarcely be found in Thomas. Most of them advocated an extreme papalist ecclesiology that again has little basis in Thomas himself. And finally, many overlooked or downplayed the genuinely Augustinian features of Thomas's theology of nature and grace. In these and other ways, the reformers' confrontation with Thomism was not a confrontation with Thomas Aquinas.

Among the major reformers, Luther stands alone in having had some firsthand knowledge of Thomas's writings. Zwingli and Calvin seem to have read little or nothing at all of Thomas. On the other hand, other reformers such as Karlstadt and Martin Bucer (1491–1551) must have read at least some of Thomas since they were formally educated as Thomists. Bucer, in fact, cites Thomas, and Thomist notions can be found in Peter Martyr Vermigli, Girolamo Zanchi, and others. Luther, of course, found much to disagree with in Thomas. But it was his Thomist contemporaries who bore the brunt of his polemic. Not only did they sometimes misunderstand Thomas, but they had, he said, elevated Thomas to the level of an infallible teacher, thus transforming his theological opinions into dogma. Moreover, Luther came to believe in the early 1520s that theological pluralism in the Roman Catholic church had come to an end. Thomism had decisively triumphed over the other schools, and Thomas was now the "teacher of all teachers." With the highest ecclesiastical authorities now sanctioning Thomism, the Roman Catholic church itself had become "the Thomist church." And insofar as this Thomist church had abandoned the gospel as Luther understood it, Thomas was "the source and foundation of all heresy, error and obliteration" of the gospel.

Toward Thomist Hegemony. Was Luther correct in his view that Thomism had triumphed over all other theological schools? The history of Thomism in the remainder of the sixteenth century lends some credence to his judgment. In the Spanish universities, for example, the Scotists and the nominalists continued to hold theological chairs, but it was the Thomists who dominated. Here names such as Diego de Deza (c.1443–1523), Francisco de Vitoria (1483/86–1546), Domingo de Soto (1495–1560), Melchior Cano (1509–1560), Bartolomé de Medina (c.1526–1580), and others stood in the vanguard of the theological enterprise.

At the Council of Trent (1545–1563), too, it seems that Thomism was in the ascendancy. Of course Augustinians, Scotists, and nominalists (to name but a few) were represented, and the bishops often tried to sidestep the rivalry between theological schools. Yet now representatives from all schools were appealing to the authority of Thomas. And Thomists themselves—including Domingo de Soto, Ambrogio Catarino Politi (1484–1553), and Melchior Cano—were among the leading theologians at the council. Thus many Tridentine decrees follow closely the teaching, and sometimes even the wording, of Thomas. Moreover, in its disciplinary decrees for reform, Trent called for the establishment of diocesan seminaries. As these gradually came into being, they invariably used theological manuals that were "ad mentem S. Thomae Aquinatis." Then, too, the famous "Roman catechism" mandated by the council was written by Thomists (Marini, Foscarari, and Foreiro). In all these ways Thomas was emerging as the Roman Catholic theologian *par excellence*.

The Counter-Reformation also saw the establishment of new religious orders, many of which declared Thomas to be their official teacher. The most important of these was the Society of Jesus. In the early constitutions (1547–1550), Ignatius Loyola (1491?–1556) declared that in theology, the Bible and Thomas Aquinas were to be the basic texts. While the "Ratio Studiorum" of 1586 allowed for greater flexibility, a new decree in 1593 ordered all Jesuits to return to and abide by the doctrine of Thomas. Accordingly, many of the foremost Thomists of the late sixteenth century came from Jesuit ranks (e.g., Roberto Bellarmino, 1542–1621, and Francisco Suárez, 1548–1617).

The symbol of Thomist supremacy in the Roman Catholic theological world was the declaration of Pope Pius V in 1567 making Thomas a "doctor of the universal church." It was henceforth scarcely possible for theologians to openly attack his teaching. This is best illustrated by the bitter "De auxiliis" controversy of the late sixteenth century over the respective roles of grace and free will in salvation. Dominicans such as Domingo Báñez (1528–1604) insisted on the primacy of grace, while Jesuits such as Luis de Molina (1535–1600) sought to safeguard the role of free will. But both sides appealed to the authority of Thomas to buttress their position. It was no longer a matter of agreeing or disagreeing with Thomas: all claimed to be his followers. With the authority of Thomas now beyond question, the dispute was henceforth over rival interpretations of Thomas. In this sense Thomism had triumphed. The radical pluralism that was the main feature of the late medieval theological landscape was a thing of the past for Roman Catholic theology.

BIBLIOGRAPHY

Bagchi, David V. N. *Luther's Earliest Opponents: Catholic Controversialists, 1518–1525.* Minneapolis, 1991. Includes analysis of Luther's early Thomist opposition.

Donneley, John P. "Calvinist Thomism." *Viator* 7 (1976), 441–455. Documents influence of Thomas on later Calvinists.

Grabmann, Martin. *Mittelalterliches Geistesleben: Abhandlungen zur Geschichte der Scholastik und Mystik.* 3 vols. Reprint, Hildersheim and New York, 1984. Includes important essays on Thomists up to Cajetan.

Hinnebusch, William A. *The History of the Dominican Order.* 2 vols. New York, 1966. Includes a survey of sixteenth-century Dominican Thomists.

Janz, Denis R. *Luther and Late Medieval Thomism: A Study in Theological Anthropology.* Waterloo, Ont., 1983.

———. *Luther on Thomas Aquinas: The Angelic Doctor in the Thought of the Reformer.* Stuttgart, 1989.

Lauchert, Friedrich. *Die italienischen literarischen Gegner Luthers.* Reprint, Nieuwkoop, 1972. Includes analysis of some of Luther's Italian Thomist adversaries.

Löhr, Gabriel M. *Die Kölner Dominikanerschule vom 14. bis zum 16. Jahrhundert, mit einer Übersicht über die Gesamtentwicklung.* Cologne, 1948.

Paulus, Nikolas. *Die Deutsche Dominikaner im Kampf gegen Luther.* Freiburg, 1903.

Pesch, Otto H. "Thomismus." In *Lexikon für Theologie und Kirche,* edited by J. Höfer and K. Rahner, vol. 10, col. 157–167. 3d ed. Freiburg, 1957.

Weisheipl, James A. "Thomism." In *New Catholic Encyclopedia,* edited by William J. McDonald et al., vol. 14, pp. 126–135. New York, 1967.

Werner, Karl. *Der Heilige Thomas von Aquin.* Vol. 3, *Geschichte des Thomismus.* Reprint, New York, 1963. The most recent full-length history of Thomism.

DENIS R. JANZ

THOMISSØN, Hans (also Thomesen; 1532–1573), Danish hymnal compiler. He studied at Copenhagen University and got his master's degree at Wittenberg under Melanchthon. Appointed rector of Ribe Cathedral School, he there trained Reformation clergy and shaped pastoral piety. As chief pastor of Our Lady Church in Copenhagen, he became prominent for hymns and liturgy. The king decreed his church the norm for liturgy.

Thomissøn's *Den danske Psalmebok* (Danish Hymnbook; 1569) was his great Reformation contribution in Denmark and Norway (then in royal union). Several Danish hymnbooks preceded his, mostly as collections for local congregations. The predecessors were small and often included differing versions of the same hymn. These insufficiencies occasioned Thomissøn's hymnal, which far surpassed all earlier efforts.

Thomissøn's was the first systematic Danish hymnal. Using, he said, "only one [musical] version and Danish translation for each hymn," he divided hymn materials according to "our Christian faith's chief articles." Like most Reformation hymnwriters, Thomissøn was motivated by pedagogical purpose: congregational singing became a versified sermon, explaining law and gospel, faith and works. The texts showed the Reformation's continuity and change, including many medieval Latin hymns and an "index to the

Latin hymns, sequences, responses, and antiphons here found in Danish." Latin texts were frequently changed: hints of Mariolatry were shifted to center on Christ. Thomissøn's hymns, like others of the century of the Reformation, are often, as Borup-Jensen says, "more cause than song."

Thomissøn's 268 hymns included the best from earlier Danish hymnals. Of the roughly 150 new additions, about one-third are Thomissøn's translations or his original hymns and show good versifying ability but no great poetic talent. The remainder came from many European sources. His texts display a common problem: getting word rhythm to fit melody. Although the literary quality in Thomissøn's hymnal is only average, the people loved their new hymns and clung to them.

With Thomissøn and others, noticeably many texts were translations from German, and most other hymns from Latin, Greek, or Hebrew came to Denmark via Germany. With most of Luther's hymns already translated, Thomissøn included "A Mighty Fortress," "Christ Jesus Lay in Death's Strong Bands," "From Heaven Above to Earth I Come," and so forth.

Thomissøn's hymnal was the first to bring complete melody apparatus to Denmark and Norway. His 203 melodies represent a wide Reformation sample, and were the foundation for all later Danish hymnody. About 150 melodies, some originally secular, come from foreign sources; others are from earlier Danish traditions.

Thomissøn's hymnal was officially replaced in Denmark and Norway by Thomas Kingo's hymnal of 1699. But habit and love for the old hymns kept Thomissøn's hymnbook in wide use for three more decades. Its music was often used in Sweden and Iceland. Two of his hymns are still sung in America: "How Blest Are They Who Hear God's Word" and "Around You O Lord Jesus" (*Lutheran Book of Worship*).

BIBLIOGRAPHY

Aaberg, J. C. *Hymns and Hymnwriters of Denmark*. Des Moines, Ia., 1945. This work is the most complete source in English on its title subject.

Hansen, Edward A., et al. "Scandinavian Hymnody." In *Hymnal Companion to the Lutheran Book of Worship*, edited by Marilyn Kay Stulken, pp. 34–47. Philadelphia, 1981. Concise source in English on roots, including Thomissøn, of American Lutheran hymnody in Denmark, Iceland, Norway, and Sweden.

Hens, H. A. "Thomesen (Thomissøn), Hans." In *Dansk biografisk leksikon*, 3d ed., edited by Sv. Cedergreen Bech, vol. 14, pp. 468–471. Copenhagen, 1979–. Thorough biographical encyclopedia article on Thomissøn's life and work, with very strong bibliography of Danish sources.

Jensen, Th. Borup. "Danske salmebøgers historie fra reformationstid til nutid." In *Salmen som lovsang og litteratur*, edited by Th. Borup Jensen and K. E. Bugge. Copenhagen, 1972. Complete modern study of Danish hymnody.

Schousboe, Torben. "Protestant Church Music in Scandinavia." In *Protestant Church Music: A History*, edited by Friedrich Blume, pp. 609–636. New York, 1974. Short treatment of Thomissøn against the wider background of Danish and continental music of the period, especially church music.

Smith, C. Howard. *Scandinavian Hymnody from the Reformation to the Present*. Metuchen, N.J., and London, 1987. A popular account of moderate depth.

KENNETH E. CHRISTOPHERSON

THORLÁKSSON, Guðbrandur (also Þorláksson; 1541/42–1627), Icelandic cleric and scholar. He was a student at Copenhagen University from 1560 to 1564 and then schoolmaster of the cathedral school at Skálholt (1564–1567) and of the cathedral school at Hólar (1569–1570). From 1571 to his death, he was bishop of the Hólar diocese in northern Iceland. An active publisher of books, he issued, among others, *Uppfræðslukver* (Catechism; 1576), the Bible in Icelandic translation (1584), *Messubók* (Mass Book; 1594), and *Visnabók til eflingar andlegum söng* (Book of Verse for the Advancement of Spiritual Singing; 1612).

Thorláksson laid the foundation for Lutheran religious culture in Iceland in the wake of the Reformation. There are, however, some indications that his role has been overestimated by scholars because of his pioneering publishing activity, which has made his contribution seem more obvious and prominent than that of his Lutheran predecessors. Research has shown that early attempts to establish the Lutheran church had been more vigorous in both sees than had been assumed in the past. Thorláksson's contribution was important, and he used all the measures of his office, directional and supervisional, to reform the church. He instituted bishops, deans, and visitations; formed the office of the dean in an evangelical spirit; and convened at least six synods in his diocese. At some of these synods secular officials were present. Thorláksson also laid the foundations of a popular educational system in his diocese that rested on catechismal learning at home and regular supervision by ministers.

Thorláksson faced the tremendous task of instituting the Lutheran religion following the chaos and tumult of the Reformation period. The problems facing the Icelandic bishops were in many ways peculiar. In the sixteenth century Iceland was part of Denmark, which was becoming more and more centralized in most areas. Official matters of the state, including church matters, were increasingly directed from Copenhagen. The aim of the king and his counselors was to form religious life in Iceland in the same mold as Danish religious life, which was based on the church ordinance of Christian III from 1537. This ordinance was approved in 1541 in Skálholt diocese and ten years later in Hólar diocese. The church ordinance of Christian III was fit for shaping religious life in a densely populated society, such as Denmark, where rural parishes were small and communications easy. In Iceland the population was different. There were no villages and no urban localities. The people raised sheep on isolated farmsteads. For most people, to go to church meant a long journey. Many important directives of the church ordinance regarding religious observance and supervision proved impossible to follow. The resolutions of the synods and the instructions of the bishop often show that Icelandic church leaders had to adapt the church ordinance to Icelandic conditions. The difficulty of this adaption process probably slowed the consolidation of the Lutheran church.

On the other hand, this adaption offered the leaders the opportunity to shape religious life in Iceland according to their own theological and ecclesiastical premises. The study of the adaptions made by Thorláksson indicates that in many respects he based his work on a Reformation theology different from the one dominating in Denmark.

The cases in which Thorláksson deviated from the church ordinance can be divided into two categories: those concerning practical matters, where such deviation was imperative because of social conditions, and those involving a theological variation. He probably allowed these variations because the church ordinance could not be instituted unaltered in any case. The variations in practical matters were most obvious in his effort to introduce popular religious instruction. He established an educational system based on instruction in the home which was fit for Icelandic conditions. Thorláksson made an attempt to introduce confirmation in his diocese and make it the pillar of supervision in the church. This was a noticeable deviation from the majority of Lutheran church ordinances and also from the one instituted in Denmark. The Danish ordinance made provisions for catechetical instruction but not confirmation. The theological deviations were most obvious in church discipline and observance. In both of these Thorláksson adhered to practices and even theological explanations from Catholic times to a much larger degree than did the church ordinance of Christian III and Danish church leaders.

Thorláksson's effort to organize Lutheran religious practice in Iceland was heavily influenced by a type of humanism in line with the Reformation theologians following Philipp Melanchthon. He should not, however, be considered a true Philippist. On the contrary, his position is much closer to the ideas of the Swedish archbishop Laurentius Petri (1499–1573). On the whole, Thorláksson's theology is marked by evangelical traditionalism and evangelical biblicism. Therefore, the consolidation of the Reformation in Iceland in his time did not bring about confessionalization.

BIBLIOGRAPHY

Hugason, Hjalti. "Evangelisk traditionalism: Guðbrandur Thorláksson konsoliderinssynoder under 1570- och 1590-talen." In *Reformationens konsolidering i de nordiske länderna 1540–1610*, edited by Ingmar Brohed, pp. 96–118. Skrifter utgivan av Nordiskt institut för kyrkohistorisk forskning, 6.

HJALTI HUGASON

THURZO, George (also Juraj; George Thurzo de Bethlenfalva; 1567–1616), patron of Lutheranism and palatine of Hungary. He was a member of one of the leading families in central Europe, whose members included the bishops of Breslau (Wrocław) and Olomouc and a partner in the Fugger-Thurzo Company, which became rich exploiting the mines of central Slovakia. His father was František Thurzo, the former bishop designate of Nitra, who had resigned his bishopric in 1566 and become a Lutheran. His mother was František's second wife, Catharine Zrínyi. He was trained at home and at the court school of Archduke Ernest of Habsburg. After the death of his father in 1574 and his mother in 1585, George Thurzo inherited the family's extensive estates in Orava county in northwestern Upper Hungary (Slovakia), which were enlarged by his marriage to Alžbeta Czobor.

Throughout his brief but significant career, Thurzo manifested a personal loyalty to the Habsburg dynasty and to his Lutheran faith. During the Fifteen Years' War with the Turks, Thurzo served faithfully in the Habsburgs' army and was rewarded with appointment as a royal councillor in 1598 and cupbearer of the king in 1599. While he opposed the attempts by the Habsburg ruler Matthias to add to the decisions of the diet of 1604 an article forbidding the discussion of religious issues by the diet and the confiscation of the property of Stephen Illesházy, also a Lutheran, he did not support the revolt of Calvinist nobleman Stephen Bocskay of Transylvania but sought to mediate between Bocskay and Matthias.

He was equally firm in his support of Lutheranism. He helped to negotiate the Peace of Vienna (1606), which ended Bocskay's revolt and prepared the way for religious toleration in Habsburg Hungary. He also took part in the negotiations of Hungarian, Austrian, Moravian, and Czech Protestants, who mutually pledged to seek religious toleration in June 1608. In the same year he successfully sought the approval by the Diet of Hungary of an article that granted Hungarian Protestants the legal right to establish their own separate ecclesiastical administration.

Elected palatine in 1609, a post that he held until his death in December 1616, he used his position to provide further assistance to the Lutherans. In 1610 he called for a Lutheran synod to meet in Žilina, and Thurzo and his chaplain, Eliáš Láni, took an active part in its deliberations. The synod meeting on 27–29 March adopted the *Book of Concord* as the doctrinal standard for Lutherans of ten counties in Upper Hungary, approved articles governing their churches, and elected three seniors, or bishops—Eliáš Láni, Izák Abrahamides, and Samuel Melík. In addition, two inspectors were elected for German congregations and one for Hungarian-speaking Lutherans in the region. Four years later a similar synod, held in Spišské Podhradie (Kirchdrauf) under the patronage of Christoph Thurzo, enacted almost identical articles to govern the Lutheran congregations of the eastern counties of Upper Hungary. Only then, nearly a century after the Reformation had begun in Wittenberg, were the Lutheran churches in Hungary formally and legally independent of the authority and supervision of the Catholic hierarchy.

While Thurzo sought in vain to establish a Lutheran university in Hungary, he financially aided students from Hungary to attend Wittenberg. His only son, Emerich (d. 1621), matriculated at Wittenberg in July 1616, and Thurzo regularly corresponded with several professors there.

BIBLIOGRAPHY

Bálint, Ila. *Magyar protestáns egyháztörténeti adattár.* Vol. 15, *A Thurzó levéltár protestáns egyháztörténeti iratai.* Budapest, 1934.

Károlyi, Árpád. *Az ellenreformáció kezdetei és Thurzó György nádorrá választása.* Századok, 1919.

Kubínyi, Mikklós. *Bethlenfalvi gróf Thurzó György levelei nejéhez.* 2 vols. Budapest, 1876.

Lombardini, Alexander. "Palatin gróf Ďuro Thurzo z Betlenoviec." In *Sborník československý: Od Šumavy k Tatrám.* Ružomberok, 1898.

Wagner, Carolus. *Analecta Scepusii sacri et profani.* Pt. 6, Bratislava and Košice, 1778.

PAVEL KOLÁROVSKÝ

TIME. Conceptions of time played a prominent role in the reform movements of the early modern period in European history. In traditional, largely peasant cultures, time was often conceived of as something uneven, as opposed to the modern conception of it as divisible into equal quantities. It had a rhythmic, indeed circular, course through the seasons, each with its appropriate tasks, its peaks and troughs, which contrasts starkly with the linear "march of time." Time was also permeated with religious significance: the calendar was replete with saints' feasts, and the time of day was counted out by the tolling of Nones and Vespers, leading Lucien Febvre (1983) to conclude that "everything still seemed to depend on the church, including time." For the sake of discussion, this cyclical, religious, agrarian conception of time could be called "Catholic." Opposed to this way of conceiving time is one that posits a regular, steady, linear, and secular time. It is the time of town hall belfry clocks and watches, sundials and hourglasses, of urban merchants and bankers, but also of Protestant theologians, moralists, and divines and could therefore be labeled "Protestant" time. In reality, of course, many kinds of time, dependent on different social and economic structures, existed simultaneously, either in symbiosis, as agrarian and ecclesiastical time, or in contradiction, as church and merchant time (Le Goff, 1980).

To be sure, traditional Christian thinking about time also contained a strong linear component. In God's plan, time flowed in a straight line from the Creation and Fall to the Incarnation, Sacrifice, and Resurrection. From this, the central event of history, it was to flow on to the Second Coming and Last Judgment. In the sixteenth century Protestant thinking on time was certainly greatly influenced by the widespread contemporary expectation that this Second Coming, marking the end of time, was near. Such a focus may have helped erode traditional cyclical patterns of time, although it did not yet signal a secular conception in the modern sense of the word. With Calvin, however, eschatological longings were rejected in favor of a step-by-step progress toward God's kingdom; we live this journey in time and must make use of every hour. The way was thus opened to the modern secular and historical approach to time and the "watchmaker God."

Other theological issues and principles were involved in the Protestant rejection of traditional Catholic time. Since every man was his own priest standing in direct relationship to God, the intercession of the church, the saints, and the Virgin was eschewed, indeed regarded as thoroughly idolatrous and non-Christian, a pagan corruption introduced into the religion by Rome. Since time is also a gift from God, it must be used properly and not squandered in the feasting associated with the traditional liturgical and agrarian calendars. For these reasons, Protestant divines fought a hard battle against the abuse and misuse of time, abolishing the traditional feasts wherever they could and recommending a linear and divisible approach to spending one's time based on the regime of the clock. It is no accident that Protestants were heavily represented in the early watchmaking industry or that Calvin excepted watches from his general condemnation of jewelry and ornamentation (Landes, 1983).

The Protestant assault on the traditional calendar, the cult of saints, and idleness brought about some dramatic changes in conceptions of time in many places (Moran, 1981; Cressy, 1989), but even in those countries where Protestants exerted their hegemony, the traditional feasts tended to survive in part or were reinstated at popular behest (Abray, 1985), albeit at times in a transformed guise to accommodate a new politico-religious constellation (Cressy). Consistories and divines were to rail for many years against the ungodly waste of time associated with such merrymaking.

In the countries where the Catholic Reformation took root, the theological principle of appealing to the saints and the Virgin for intercession with Jesus was upheld. The strengthening of the cult of the saints and the Virgin by countless confraternities may well have reinforced the traditional conception of time associated with the liturgical calendar. On the other hand, it was also in this period that the church began using hourglasses to time the sermons of priests and that cardinals wore watches mounted on crosses. Through its manifold financial dealings with the major banking houses, the papacy was thoroughly acquainted with the modern monetary economy in which "time is money" (Wendorff, 1980). The Catholic Reformation's repression of the more exuberant elements connected with the celebration of saints' cults also contributed to modernizing tendencies in society in which a more efficient planning of time was promoted.

The battle over the calendar and the control of time extended to Pope Gregory XIII's reform of 1582, which ordered the excision of ten days from the Julian calendar to make astronomical and church calendars coincide more closely. Protestant countries long resisted this "papist" intervention in time, even though it was correct from a "scientific" or "secular" viewpoint. England, for example, refused to switch over to the Gregorian calendar until 1752. In the German territories two calendars were in use in the seventeenth century depending on whether one was in Protestant or Catholic territory.

Without rehearsing the old debate provoked by Max Weber's famous work, *The Protestant Ethic and the Spirit of Capitalism*, it is clear that the general attack on feast days and idle periods of time was propitious to a deeper penetration of capitalist relations of production. The long-run decline in the number of free days and the linear, secular way of organizing time fostered by Protestants, but also by modernizing Catholics, opened the way for an expansion of productive activity and the introduction of the factory system and mass production. The question of conceptions of time in the reform movement of the early modern period must therefore be placed squarely in the context of the long transition—from the thirteenth to the nineteenth century—from preindustrial, precapitalist forms of economy and society to industrial capitalist ones.

This transition involved the breakup of the largely agrarian peasant society of western Europe and its replacement by a form of organizing work in which time itself was of the essence. Agrarian and church time were serious obstacles to the establishment of the steady, regular pattern of work demanded by industrial capitalism and hence ultimately had to be eliminated.

[*See also* Festivals *and* Liturgical Calendar.]

BIBLIOGRAPHY

Abray, Lorna Jane. *The People's Reformation: Magistrates, Clergy, and Commons in Strasbourg, 1500–1598.* Ithaca, N.Y., 1985. See especially chapter nine, "The Impact of the Reformation," for the reinstatement of feast days.

Cressy, David. *Bonfires and Bells: National Memory and the Protestant Calendar in Elizabethan and Stuart England.* Berkeley, 1989. Deals with transforming the calendar to fit new political and religious constellations.

Crouzet, Denis. *Les guerriers de Dieu: La violence au temps des troubles de religion, 1525–1610.* 2 vols. Seyssel, France, 1990. Massive documentation of Catholic eschatological fears in the French Wars of Religion.

Das, T. K. *The Time Dimension: An Interdisciplinary Guide.* New York, 1990. Useful bibliography covering works on "time" in a wide variety of fields.

Davis, Natalie Zemon. "The Sacred and the Body Social in Sixteenth-Century Lyon." *Past and Present* 90 (Feb. 1981), 40–70. On Protestant and Catholic conceptions of the sacred and time.

Febvre, Lucien. *The Problem of Unbelief in the Sixteenth Century: The Religion of Rabelais.* Translated by B. Gottlieb. Cambridge, Mass., 1982. Classic account of the religious preoccupations of the sixteenth century by the cofounder of the *Annales* school. Perhaps overestimates the influence of religion.

Krudy, Elmer S., Bernadine T. Bacon, and Rollo Turner, comps. and eds. *Time: A Bibliography.* London, 1976. Earlier bibliography with entries of interest in a number of disciplines.

Landes, David S. *Revolution in Time: Clocks and the Making of the Modern World.* Cambridge, Mass., and London, 1983. Very good on the history of time measurement and the rise and fall of the watch-making industry.

Le Goff, Jacques. *Time, Work and Culture in the Middle Ages.* Translated by Arthur Goldhammer. Chicago, 1980. Collection of essays. See in particular the seminal article on "church time and merchant time" that first appeared in 1960 in *Annales, Economies, Sociétés, Civilisations* 15 (1960), 417–433. This is the starting point for much later research on this subject.

Macey, Samuel L. *Time: A Bibliographic Guide.* New York, 1991. New bibliography by a literary scholar who has also published monographs on the subject.

Moran, Gerard T. "Conceptions of Time in Early Modern France: An Approach to the History of Collective Mentalities." *Sixteenth Century Journal* 12.4 (1981), 3–19. Based on archival sources, it posits a sharp drop in traditional conceptions of time under the short-term impact of Protestantism.

Thomas, Keith. *Religion and the Decline of Magic: Studies in Popular Beliefs in Sixteenth- and Seventeenth-Century England.* London, 1971. Feasts and calendars in Tudor and Stuart England and influence of Protestant divines in changing conceptions of time.

Weber, Max. *The Protestant Ethic and the Spirit of Capitalism.* Translated by Talcott Parsons. New York, 1958. Provoked an enormous "chicken or egg" debate on the interrelationship of religion and economics.

Wendorff, Rudolf. *Zeit und Kultur: Geschichte des Zeitbewußtseins in Europa.* Wiesbaden, 1980. Tough going in German, but it contains several chapters on the early modern period with worthwhile discussions of, among others, the differences between Luther's and Calvin's conceptions of time.

GERARD G. MORAN

TITELMANS, Pieter (1501–1572), theologian and inquisitor of Flanders. After his theological studies at Louvain, Titelmans carried out the publication of the theological work of his deceased brother, Frans Titelmans, a Franciscan who in his writings had opposed the ideas of Erasmus.

When Charles V in 1545 broadened the extent of the royal Inquisition in the Netherlands by engaging provincial inquisitors, Pieter Titelmans was named as inquisitor of Flanders, Tournai (city and region), and Walloon-Flanders. Initially he kept strictly to his appointed task. As an examiner of doctrine and belief, he acted in the service of the regional court of justice at Ghent, the Council of Flanders, as well as the town and local authorities. However, after 1550 he began to think of himself more and more clearly as a papal inquisitor, and on this basis he claimed full autonomy for his tribunal. This repeatedly led to intense conflicts, especially with the town governments, who believed that their privileges had been usurped. Titelmans also demanded that he have at his disposal an armed guard so that he would no longer be dependent on anyone in case of a violent confrontation; however, the central government never acquiesced in this demand because it too was not pleased with Titelmans's arbitrary and uncompromising attitude. With only a fixed nucleus of a few co-workers, namely an assistant examiner, a prosecutor, and a notary, and with only modest means, Titelmans nevertheless built his Inquisitorial court into a formidable organ of repression against heresy. In a shrewd tactical move, he and his immediate co-workers spread their residences across the entire area of their responsibility: they located in Ieper, Kortrijk, Lille, and Ghent, cities in the center of regions where Protestantism had penetrated most deeply. Titelmans everywhere demanded the unconditional cooperation of the parish priests. Moreover, he recruited, for pay, a small army of informers and spies and in this way built up a network of informants that spread itself out over the whole of Flanders. And indeed Titelmans himself, as appears from his surviving records, was on the road more than three hundred days per year throughout the region between Tournai, Axel, Dunkerque, and Sint-Niklaas.

After being arrested, individuals were examined by Titelmans in an effort to bring them to a confession of their beliefs. If heresy was discovered, Titelmans then used argument and persuasion to bring the individual concerned to an admission of his errors. If this succeeded, a public abjuration followed and a punishment was imposed, although it was never the death penalty. Only in the case of persistent heresy would the accused be turned over to the secular authorities. If he remained obstinate here as well, he was then sentenced to death as a violator of the heresy edicts. In total, Titelmans handled between 1,500 and 1,600 cases of heresy. Of those whom he turned over to the public authorities as obstinate heretics, 127 were in the end executed, of whom 85 were Anabaptists. Titelmans was thus relatively successful in his battle against the Anabaptist communities. However, when Calvinism became a mass movement in Flanders in the 1560s, he stood powerless. From 1564 on Titelmans lost all support in ruling circles, where the conviction was growing that severe repression had nothing to show for itself, and that instead it stirred up the radicalism of the Calvinists. After the iconoclasm of 1566, his Inquisitorial court survived only as a relic. Together with Fernando Álvarez de Toledo, the duke of Alba, Titelmans has entered into literature and the historical record as the embodiment of an unyielding Catholicism, which through the use of repression desired to purge the land of all heresy.

BIBLIOGRAPHY

Decavele, J. *De dageraad van de reformatie in Vlaanderen, 1520–1565.* 2 vols. Brussels, 1975. See vol. 1, pp. 14–31. Sketches a portrait of the personality of Titelmans and outlines the operation of his Inquisitorial court. Based on records discovered by the author.

Verheyden, A. L. E. *Anabaptism in Flanders, 1530–1650.* Scottdale, Pa., 1961. Examines Titelmans's attitude toward and actions against the Anabaptists.

Wiele, Johan van de. "Itinerarium van inquisiteur Pieter Titelmans en zijn medewerkers, 1547–1566." *Bulletin de la Commission royale d'histoire* 151 (1985), 61–152. Systematizes the results of the research of Decavele.

JOHAN DECAVELE
Translated from Dutch by Michael A. Hakkenberg

TITIAN (Ital., Tiziano Vecellio; c.1488–1576), Italian painter. Titian was the dominant painter of the Venetian school and, with Michelangelo, the most renowned artist of the sixteenth century. Succeeding Giovanni Bellini as official painter to the republic of Venice, Titian became a favorite of the various courts of Italy, particularly after his ennoblement by the Holy Roman Emperor Charles V (1533); the patent of nobility declared that henceforth only Titian was to portray the imperial likeness. In Augsburg at the gathering of the imperial diet in 1548, Titian painted an equestrian portrait of Charles V that celebrates the Catholic victory at the battle of Mühlberg (1547). Among other portraits Titian painted later at Augsburg (1550–1551) is that of Johann Friedrich, elector of Saxony, leader of the Protestant forces, who was taken prisoner at Mühlberg. Titian's European reputation rested solidly on such imperial patronage and, in addition, on the royal Catholic patronage of Charles's son, Philip II of Spain; but it rested ultimately on the power of his art.

Following the technical revolution initiated by Giorgione (c.1478–1510), Titian assumed the leading role in developing a modern aesthetic of oil painting on canvas, resulting eventually in an open surface of brushwork that exploits the oil paint to create a physical correlative to the natural substances represented. In religious painting, Titian's radical achievement lay in his ability to make the transcendent accessible to the senses. He transformed the traditional altarpiece, introducing a new monumentality of both size and scale, as in the *Assumption of the Virgin* at Santa Maria dei Frari, Venice (1518); a new dynamic asymmetry, as in the *Madonna of the Pesaro Family* in the same church (1519–1526); and a new grandeur of dramatic action, in landscape as well as figure, as in the *Martyrdom of St. Peter Martyr* in Santi Giovanni e Paolo, Venice (1530). Titian was especially celebrated for his portraits and his representations of the female nude, images that circulated throughout the courts of Europe in original versions as well as in many replicas produced in his busy workshop.

BIBLIOGRAPHY

Crowe, J. A., and G. B. Cavalcaselle. *Titian, His Life and Times.* 2d ed., 2 vols. London, 1881.

Hope, Charles. *Titian.* London, 1980.

Panofsky, Erwin. *Problems in Titian, Mostly Iconographic.* New York, 1969.

Rosand, David. *Titian.* New York, 1978.

Rosand, David, and Michelangelo Muraro. *Titian and the Venetian Woodcut*. Washington, D.C., 1976.

Wethey, Harold E. *The Paintings of Titian*. 3 vols. London, 1969–1975.

DAVID ROSAND

TOLERATION. In the confessional age the problem of toleration naturally manifested itself as a religious problem. The discussion primarily centered on religious toleration while political (civil), social, and cultural toleration were treated as subsidiary issues only, if at all. It cannot be denied, however, that the defense as well as the practice of religious toleration always stood in close connection with the political, social, and cultural conditions of the time.

There is general agreement among modern historians that the systematic debate on toleration and religious liberty began in the period of humanism and the Reformation. It had, however, a preliminary history in the early Christian centuries as well as in the later Middle Ages. From the very beginning the problem had always been recognized to emanate from the two basic questions as to how to deal with heretics and infidels and as to who had the authority to punish them, if they had to be punished at all. Criticism of religious persecution was expressed by a good many medieval authors such as John Quidort of Paris, William of Ockham, and Marsilius of Padua, but their voices remained isolated and generally lacked the persuasive power to form a coherent polemical tradition. Within the context of the conciliar debates of the fourteenth and early fifteenth centuries the issue of individual religious decision was often approached, and references to the individual conscience appeared repeatedly.

Since religious dissent was generally considered a danger not only to the ecclesiastical but also to the secular order, practical coexistence of different religions within one and the same state was very rare in medieval Europe. It existed, however, in Spain, where, in spite of occasional conflicts and persecutions, Christians, Muslims, and Jews often lived peacefully with one another. This situation came to an end when, in the late fifteenth century, the "Catholic Monarchs" Ferdinand and Isabella no longer accepted religious diversity in their united kingdom and finally decreed the expulsion of the Jews (1492) and Muslims (1501/02, Granada). Attempts at establishing religious pluralism were also undertaken in late medieval Bohemia (e.g., in the peace treaty of Kuttenberg between Catholics and Utraquists, 1485).

The Sixteenth-Century Debate on Toleration. In the course of the sixteenth century the debate on religious toleration led to the emergence of regulations and arrangements that made religious pluralism possible in a number of European states. Within the general context of the history of religious toleration the sixteenth century stands out with some remarkable ideas and achievements. But on the whole the period remains a period of beginnings, of collecting arguments, of temporary and provisional compromises, as well as of many setbacks. The confessional age was characterized by the continuous predominance of ecclesiastical institutions both in Protestant and Catholic countries. Practically everywhere church and state were firmly linked together, established religion prevailed, and religious dissent was identified with political dissent and persecuted as such. Wherever a tendency toward religious individualism became visible, it was almost always condemned as heresy. Leaders of religious establishments, both Catholic and Protestant, tended to think of themselves as instruments of divine will. Toleration to them was at best an irrelevant issue.

A word must be said about sixteenth-century usage of concepts. The nouns *toleration, tolérance,* and *tolerantia* appear relatively rarely. More frequent is the usage of the verb *tolerare.* What we now designate as toleration was mostly called *caritas, pax, mansuetudo,* or *concordia.* To the modern reader these terms appear to imply preconditions or consequences of toleration rather than toleration itself. In order to avoid misunderstanding and idealization, the sources of the sixteenth-century toleration controversy must therefore be read with caution. The designation *haereticus* always referred to propagators of dogmatic errors. Adherents of non-Christian monotheistic religions were usually called *infideles* while the word *pagani* was used for heathen. Designations like *Ariani, Pelagiani,* and *Anabaptistae* were often applied to nonconformists quite at random by their adversaries. *Haeresis* in sixteenth-century usage had two meanings. Some orthodox writers (Catholics, Lutherans, and Calvinists alike) held that heresy arose from *superbia* and *pertinacia,* that is, from arrogance and stubbornness. The advocates of such definitions usually believed that the heretic could not be converted by spiritual exhortation and that punishment and coercion were necessary to divert his or her mind from error. The opponents of this view described the heretic as an erring human being who could indeed be induced to change his or her mind. They thought, however, that conversion could not be achieved by coercion but only by appropriate arguments, by patient instruction, and first of all by the living example of a true *imitatio Christi.* This conviction naturally led to tolerant attitudes that were often motivated by the hope for eventual restoration of religious consensus. Many humanists shared this optimistic persuasion.

Surveying the most important sources one can discern three main categories of arguments for toleration in the sixteenth-century debate, namely the theologico-philosophical, the politico-pragmatical, and the economic category. These categories cannot always be strictly separated from each other. They do not follow each other in chronological order. Several authors emphasize more than one category or shift from one to the other.

Of the three categories, the theologico-philosophical appears most frequently. Its most important element was the hope for restoration of religious consensus, or *concordia.*

The most prominent advocate of this ideal was Erasmus of Rotterdam. It can be said that to him the restoration of *concordia* was more important than a *tolerantia* implying the acceptance of discord. His pleas for reconciliation were founded upon three basic concerns: return to the original texts of the Bible and of the early church fathers; avoidance of theological speculation; and limitation of religious faith to a small number of fundamental doctrines. With these ideas Erasmus influenced a number of later humanist advocates of toleration who also represented what can be called a "theology of reduction." His own concept of toleration was not without limits. He disapproved of Anabaptism, and there is no denying that he hated the Jews.

Wherever the demand for toleration was uttered by representatives of Protestant radicalism, the primary aim was not restoration of consensus but the abolishment of persecution. Not surprisingly, such appeals quite often emanated from the conviction (shared also by young Luther in *Von weltlicher Obrigkeit*, 1523) that the secular magistrate had no authority over the subjects' religious opinions and that religious dissent could only be abated with spiritual means. This argumentation can be found in the writings of several early Anabaptists and in those of Sebastian Franck. Franck was an outspoken individualist who after many years of wandering found himself unable to identify with any religious group or movement. His contribution to the toleration debate is of particular interest, because he was the first sixteenth-century author to question the traditional concept of "heretic." In his "Ketzerchronik" (a part of the famous *Geschichtsbibell*, 1531) he stated that God alone knows his true followers and that no one is ever able to determine who among his fellow-creatures should be called a heretic and be treated as such. Out of this relativism there emerged a universalist concept of toleration that also included non-Christians and that stands unique in the first part of the sixteenth century.

The theology of reduction as formulated by Erasmus and Sebastian Franck's relativism in regard to the concept of *heretic* are two important elements of Sébastien Castellion's defence of religious toleration. The Savoyard humanist, who after his breach with Calvin had found refuge in Basel, advanced his ideas from 1551 to 1563, that is, from the first edition of his Latin Bible with the famous preface addressed to Edward VI of England to the composition of the treatise *De arte dubitandi* shortly before his death. His main contribution to the sixteenth-century toleration debate, however, was the book *De haereticis an sint persequendi*, published in March 1554, almost half a year after the execution of Michael Servetus in Geneva. Here Castellion not only stated his own opinions but also presented those of a number of early Christian and other sixteenth-century authors. In his selection of texts Castellion followed Sebastian Franck's "Ketzerchronik" very closely. The anthology made him one of the best-known advocates of religious toleration of his time. His argumentation was essentially biblical, and his aim was still the restoration of consensus on the basis of persuasion. In his interpretation of the relevant scriptural passages he laid much emphasis on common sense and on God-given human reason. His main concern was that human beings should never be killed on account of their religious opinions. The persecution of alleged heretics he considered an anticipation of the Last Judgment. Castellion's influence was particularly strong among Italian evangelical refugees such as Lelio and Fausto Sozzini, among the Polish Socinians, and within the anti-Calvinist humanist circles of the late sixteenth- and early seventeenth-century Netherlands. His writings on toleration were also read by English Nonconformists, by moderate German Lutherans, and by early Rosicrucians.

As the sixteenth-century debate on religious toleration wore on, it quite naturally began to bear upon political ideas and institutions. The notion that the Christian state must be a political as well as a religious unity gradually began to break up. Some princes and magistrates began to perceive that religious pluralism did not create any real danger for the state but that it might even be profitable and therefore necessary for the realization of their political aims. It is understandable that in the course of such developments the theoretical justification of religious toleration had to be based upon new foundations. The debate was conducted by a new group of participants. In the first two-thirds of the sixteenth century the idea of toleration had been propagated mainly by philologically and theologically educated scholars whose positions had in most cases been more or less on the fringes of social and political life and who carried no responsibility for the preservation of existing church orders. Many of them had been refugees with abundant personal experience of persecution, suppression, banishment, and poverty. Now, in the last third of the sixteenth century, while some of these advocates of toleration were still around, others came increasingly to the fore. Among them were representatives of the political establishments, statesmen, officeholders, and jurists who tended to discard the humanist ideal of reconciliation and to adapt their argumentation to the practical requirements of the political situation in which they lived. This phenomenon can be observed very clearly in France at the outset of and during the Wars of Religion, when the necessity of *sauver le royaume* became more and more urgent. Of particular interest are the statements of the chancellor Michel de L'Hôpital. Under the pressure of the heightening religious conflict and especially after the failure of the Colloquy of Poissy (1561), L'Hôpital gave up the humanist ideal of the restoration of religious consensus and became a political pragmatist and a forerunner of the *politiques*. That the preservation of the French nation was more important than the restoration of ecclesiastical unity had for the first time been asserted by the anonymous author of the very influential pamphlet *Exhortation aux Princes et Seigneurs du Conseil privé du Roy* (1561). This book had evidently influenced L'Hôpital, but it had also been studied by Castellion in Basel, who in the fall of 1562 published his *Conseil à la France désolée*. This tract shows very clearly that in view of the political crisis of France, about which Castellion must have been very well informed, the humanist himself adopted the politico-pragmatical argument for religious toleration and warmly recommended the *Exhortation aux Princes* to his readers.

Ecclesiastical pluralism was defended also by many *politiques* who followed the ideas of Michel de L'Hôpital and the *Exhortation aux Princes*. It cannot be doubted that the secularization of political thought that took place in the second half of the sixteenth century had a very great impact upon the changing argumentation in favor of religious toleration. Among the most radical advocates of confessional coexistence was undoubtedly Jean Bodin. His most original and boldest comment is to be found in the *Colloquium heptaplomeres*. It is determined by total resignation in respect to reconciliation, and Bodin therefore defends the principle of toleration as an absolute necessity for the survival not only of the French nation but for the whole world of his time.

Economic arguments do not yet appear very frequently in late sixteenth-century toleration literature. They practically never appear independently, but always in narrow conjunction with theological and political arguments. The main economic argument for religious toleration generally rested upon the perception that certain religious minorities (Jews and Anabaptists, for instance) contributed substantially to the prosperity of a whole country and should therefore not be disturbed in their religious practices.

In looking for written statements of the economic argument for religious toleration, one finds some interesting documentation in Dutch sources. The general debate on toleration and on religious pluralism as it was conducted in the Netherlands shows some similarity with that of France. From the mid-1540s the defenders of toleration had addressed themselves not only to the Catholics but increasingly also to the militant Calvinists. From the beginning of the Revolt of the Netherlands against Spain, William of Orange as well as many prominent Catholic nobles repeatedly declared themselves against the persecution of any religious group because they knew very well that the political liberty of the provinces could be achieved only if the coexistence of the different religious denominations was guaranteed. This insight found its expression in the Pacification of Ghent (1576), in the famous manifesto "Religionsvrede" (1579), and in the Union of Utrecht (1579).

The Practice of Toleration. It seems that the breakup of the conception of the state as a political *and* religious unity marked an important turning point in the political, religious, and social history of early modern European nations. One must, of course, be careful not to exaggerate the conse-

quences of this development. A number of European countries remained absolutely intolerant and continued to suppress the slightest stirrings of religious dissent. This was the case of Spain and of the Italian states. The impact of Spanish and particularly of Italian refugees upon the development of later humanism, Protestant radicalism, and religious toleration has been stressed by many modern historians.

Within confederated political systems the principle of confessional parity seemed to open up possibilities of coexistence of religious parties once the aim of restoring doctrinal unity had been given up. It is a well-known fact that the two Swiss *Landfrieden* treaties of 1529 and 1531 were based upon this principle. Both of them allowed the two religious parties to keep their faith. On both occasions the victors—first the Protestants and then the Catholics—refrained from taking full advantage of their political and military success. Had they behaved otherwise the Swiss Confederation would almost certainly have fallen apart. This risk nobody wanted to take. Thus religious unity was sacrificed in order to save the secular order. This process of setting priorities can be observed in many other parts of Europe during the later sixteenth century.

A comparison with the Peace of Augsburg of 1555 does not seem out of place here. The Peace of Augsburg was also based upon the principle of confessional parity and upon the principle *cuius regio, eius religio*. One would be tempted to say that the Swiss Confederation provided the Holy Roman Empire with a good example here. There is no evidence, however, that the Swiss settlement of 1531 was discussed by contemporary political theorists or consciously imitated by the architects of the Peace of Augsburg. On the contrary: along with the principle of confessional parity, that of *cuius regio, eius religio* had been discussed and defended by the Protestant estates already at the Imperial Diets of Speyer in 1526 and 1529.

The principle of confessional parity as it was applied in Switzerland and Germany could indeed give rise to a very limited kind of religious liberty, but it was a liberty for the rulers only. It avoided the creation of pluralistic orders, it prohibited individual liberty, and it contributed to the gradual petrification of confessional discord. Situations of peaceful and relatively durable religious coexistence developed in only some imperial cities and in a few Swiss cantons such as Glarus and Appenzell.

Neither the Swiss *Landfrieden* treaties nor the Peace of Augsburg had explicitly stipulated the toleration of nonconformist minorities. Such toleration existed in other parts of sixteenth-century Europe, however. It could reach very different levels.

On the lowest level stood the recognition of individual freedom of conscience under the condition that the "heretics" not pronounce their opinions publicly. Above this came the official permission of private nonconformist worship, then the chartered right to have public church services in specific places. These stages of development can be observed in the different religious edicts issued by the French Crown during the second half of the sixteenth century. The survey, incidentally, shows that the Edict of Beaulieu (1576) was much more liberal than the concluding Edict of Nantes (1598). In none of these royal edicts, however, was the principle of parity adopted. They all went further and at the same time not as far as the Swiss *Landfrieden* of 1531 or the Peace of Augsburg. All of them were based upon the principle of toleration of a religious minority within the French monarchy, but this toleration was more or less limited in every case.

Theoretically, the highest level of religious liberty was reached when a government allowed all denominations existing within its territory to practice their religion without any restrictions. This situation did not prevail very often, however. It did occur in Poland under the Warsaw Confederation of 1573, which gave the authority of *cuius regio, eius religio* to the great landlords but practically established general religious liberty. It also occurred, based on several laws, in the principality of Transylvania while it stood under the political supremacy of the Ottoman rulers, down to the end of the sixteenth century. In the Protestant Netherlands of the late sixteenth century such minorities as Roman Catholics, Lutherans, Mennonites, and Jews were generally tolerated, but specific legislation on this issue had never been enacted.

Within the general context of early modern European history, the sixteenth-century beginnings of religious liberty were modest. They certainly deserve to be recognized, but their significance should not be exaggerated. The early seventeenth century again brought a general increase of intolerance and religious persecution. The French Protestants came under mounting pressure, and English separatist Nonconformists had to leave their country. The Counter-Reformation wiped out religious pluralism in Poland, and the Thirty Years' War was in its beginning phase still characterized by confessional strife. Even in the Dutch Republic religious liberty was again severely threatened when the national Synod of Dordrecht in 1618/19 decided that all Remonstrant preachers (i.e., the opponents of orthodox Calvinism) should be removed from their pulpits. Many of them were banished, and only in 1626 were they allowed to return and to serve as ministers of the "Remonstrant Brotherhood."

[*See also* Persecution.]

BIBLIOGRAPHY

Bainton, Roland H. *The Travail of Religious Liberty.* Reprint, Hamden, Conn., 1971.
Cantimori, Delio. *Italian Heretics of the Sixteenth Century.* Translated by Hilary A. Smith. Cambridge, Mass., 1979.
Güldner, Gerhard. *Das Toleranz-Problem in den Niederlanden im Ausgang des 16. Jahrhunderts.* Lübeck, 1968.
Guggisberg, Hans R. "The Defence of Religious Toleration in Early Modern Europe: Arguments, Pressures, and Some Consequences." *History of European Ideas* 4 (1983), 35–50.
———. *Religiöse Toleranz, Dokumente zur Geschichte einer Forderung,* Stuttgart, 1984.
Guggisberg, Hans R., with Frank Lestringant and Jean-Claude Margolin, eds. *La liberté de conscience, XVIe-XVII siècles.* Geneva, 1991.
Jordan, W. K. *The Development of Religious Toleration in England.* 4 vols. Reprint, Gloucester, Mass., 1965.
Kamen, Henry. *The Rise of Toleration.* London, 1967.
Labrousse, Elisabeth. "Religious Toleration." In *Dictionary of the History of Ideas,* vol. 4, pp. 112–121. New York, 1973.
Lecler, Joseph. *Toleration and the Reformation.* 2 vols. New York, 1960. English translation of *Histoire de la tolérance au siècle de la Réforme.* 2 vols. Paris, 1955.
Lutz, Heinrich, ed. *Zur Geschichte der Toleranz und Religionsfreiheit.* Darmstadt, 1977.
Mandrou, Robert, et al. *Histoire des protestants en France.* Toulouse, 1977.
Schreiner, Klaus, and Gerhard Besier. "Toleranz." In *Geschichtliche Grundbegriffe: Historisches Lexikon zur politisch-sozialen Sprache in Deutschland,* edited by O. Brunner, W. Conze, and R. Kosellek, vol. 6, pp. 445–605. Stuttgart, 1990.
Sheils, W. J., ed. *Persecution and Toleration.* Oxford, 1984.
Tazbir, Janusz. *A State without Stakes: Polish Religious Toleration in the Sixteenth and Seventeenth Centuries.* Warsaw, 1973.

HANS RUDOLF GUGGISBERG

TOOR, Jacob van. *See* Taurinus, Jacobus.

TORRENTIUS, Laevinus (Flem., Lieven van der Beke; 1525–1595), humanist and second bishop of Antwerp. After studying law at Louvain and Bologna, Torrentius lived five years in Rome, distinguishing himself in humanist and Counter-Reformation circles. Subsequently he moved to the prince-bishopric of Liège, where as cathedral archdeacon and vicar-general he carried out assorted diplomatic assignments, including negotiations over the establishment of new bishoprics in the southern Netherlands. Along with Giovanni Francisco Bonomi (1536–1587), nuncio to the imperial court, Torrentius labored for the publication and implementation of the decrees of the Council of Trent and for the installation of a nuncio in Cologne.

In 1587 Torrentius was consecrated bishop of Antwerp, a diocese that had been torn by war and only recently retaken from the Calvinists. His administration focused on the firming up of the diocesan hierarchy and episcopal authority, the betterment of secular and regular clergy (both in Liège and Antwerp Torrentius was an outspoken champion of the Jesuits), and the conversion of Protestants where possible. He maintained a tolerant attitude toward Protestants, such that his opinions on the war with the northern Netherlands were surprisingly mild. This gentle approach greatly facilitated the transformation of Antwerp from a Protestant back to a Catholic regime.

Through his friendship with Benito Arias Montano, Torrentius tried to influence the policies of Philip II of Spain, ruler of the southern Netherlands. The Latin correspondence between these two men reveals the concrete difficulties involved in attempts to introduce the decrees of Trent. It also reveals Torrentius's humanist inclinations and contacts. His literary works included commentaries on Suetonius, Horace, and Pliny the Elder, as well as his own successful anthology of poems, *Poemata Sacra*. Finally, Torrentius was instrumental in the return to the southern Netherlands of the printer Christoffel Plantijn and the humanist Justus Lipsius. As a personality Torrentius is especially interesting because he represents both humanism and the Counter-Reformation and because his correspondence allows a personal, detailed glimpse of each movement.

BIBLIOGRAPHY

Primary Source

Torrentius, Laevinus. *Correspondance*. Edited by Marie Delcourt and Jean Hoyoux. Paris, 1950–1954. A summary in French precedes each letter; covers the years 1585–1595.

Secondary Sources

Haeghen, Ferdinand van der. *Bibliotheca Belgica: Bibliographie générale des Pays-Bas*. 6 vols. 2d ed. Brussels, 1979. Gives a description of the works of Torrentius.
Marinus, Marie Juliette. *Laevinus Torrentius als tweede bisschop van Antwerpen, 1587-1595*. Brussels, 1989. Concentrates on his activities as bishop; contains a summary in French.

MARIE JULIETTE MARINUS
Translated from Dutch by Craig Harline

TOSARRIUS, Jan. *See* Sartorius, Jan.

TOURNON, François de (1489–1562), French statesman and cardinal. As the second son of a prominent family of the Viverais, Tournon was intended for a career in the church. At age twelve he joined the Augustinian Canons. In 1517 Francis I named him archbishop of Embrum, and in 1530 Clement VII made him a cardinal. He accumulated benefices throughout his life, including four archbishoprics.

Tournon caught the attention of Francis I early on and soon became a valued member of his government. His diplomatic skills quickly manifested themselves, and his first major mission was negotiating the ransom of the king after his capture at Pavia in 1525. After a tour of duty at Rome, Tournon returned to France to become one of the most powerful royal advisers, especially in financial matters.

When Francis died in 1547, Tournon found himself out of favor with Henry II. After five years in disgrace he was sent to Rome, where he remained until Henry's death in 1559. Returning to France he resumed his role in government for Francis II and Charles IX.

At first Tournon was a patron of humanists, but once Protestantism began to appear in France, he emerged as one of its most ardent opponents. He advocated making peace with Charles V to present a united front against the Protestants and strongly opposed any alliance with the Lutherans. Tournon was one of the instigators of the repression of the Waldensians of Dauphiné in 1545. His absence from France for most of Henry's reign reduced his influence on religious policy, but in 1559, shortly before Henry's death, he wrote to him urging him to enforce the laws against heresy. Upon Tournon's return to France in 1559 he called the Jesuits to the Collège de Tournon and advocated their introduction into the realm. In 1561 he presided over the Colloquy of Poissy, shortly before his death in 1562.

BIBLIOGRAPHY

Baumgartner, Frederic J. *Henry II, King of France, 1547–1559*. Durham, N.C., 1988. Discusses Tournon's life in context of the life of the king during Tournon's later years.
François, Michel. *Le Cardinal François de Tournon*. Paris, 1951. The only full biography of the cardinal.
Knecht, R. J. *Francis I*. Cambridge, 1982. This volume presents a description of Tournon's role during the reign of his principal patron, Francis I.

FREDERIC J. BAUMGARTNER

TOUSSAIN, Daniel (1541–1602), Swiss Reformed pastor and professor of theology. Born in Montbéliard, Daniel was the son of Pierre Toussain, pastor there since 1535. Daniel grew up speaking fluent French and German, and the church of Montbéliard with a liturgy and theology drawn primarily from the Swiss Reformed tradition of Basel where Daniel attended college. Montbéliard was, however, subject to the Lutheran duke of Württemberg, whose superintendent was Jakob Andreae, an ardent advocate of strict Lutheranism.

By the age of twenty, Toussain was pastor of the church at Orléans, where he remained until the repercussions of the third War of Religion dispersed his congregation and forced him into exile. He fled first to Montargis, ruled by Renée of Ferrara, and six months later he returned to Montbéliard, where it was hoped that he would succeed his aged father as pastor.

But in 1571 Jakob Andreae led a theological delegation sent by Duke Ludwig to Montbéliard, where he was to examine the new pastor from France and assure the Lutheran orthodoxy of the clergy there. When he tried to impose a new confession on the clergy, Toussain spoke for all and affirmed the adherence of the Montbéliardais to the terms of the 1562 agreement, including the Augsburg Confession and the Wittenberg Concord. Toussain said that while he had no objection to the teaching of the Augsburg Confession, he could not accept Andreae's doctrine of the ubiquity of the body of Christ. Nor had he any problem with the Wittenberg Concord as long as Bucer's explanations were included. Finally, he could not condemn "Zwinglians and Calvinists." The eucharistic issue turned also on the *manducatio indignorum.* Bucer had maintained that the faithless, as a category distinct from the unworthy, did not receive the body of Christ, while Andreae, declared Toussain, taught that everyone, even those without faith, received the true body of Christ. Andreae exiled Toussain on 21 August 1571. He was recalled to Orléans, where Calvinists could once more worship but were beset by difficulties.

The terror of the Saint Bartholomew's Day Massacre, 24 August 1572, reached Orléans the next day. Toussain fled with his wife and four children to his former refuge of Montargis, where his son Paul was born the next month. By November Toussain had returned to Montbéliard, where he could stay only a few weeks, and then answered a call to be pastor in Basel. Meanwhile Théodore de Bèze had recommended Toussain to Elector Frederick III of the Palatinate, who wanted to reorganize his territory along the lines of the Reformed churches of France. Toussain arrived in Heidelberg in March 1573 and was present when Frederick III died in 1576. Louis VI, who succeeded his father, was an ardent Lutheran and promptly fired the Calvinist ministers, including Toussain, who went to Neustadt to serve Frederick's younger son, the Count Palatine Johann Casimir. When Louis VI died in 1583, Johann Casimir became the regent of the young Frederick IV and moved to Heidelberg, taking Toussain with him. Toussain served as court preacher, school inspector, and after 1586 as professor of theology at the University of Heidelberg. During his nearly twenty years at Heidelberg, Toussain was sought by William of Orange, the academy at Geneva, and in 1595 the churches of France. Toussain resisted these offers and died at Heidelberg on 10 January 1602.

BIBLIOGRAPHY

Bernus, Auguste. "Trois pasteurs échappés aux Massacres de la Saint-Barthélemy." In *Bulletin historique et littéraire de la Société de l'histoire du protestantisme français* 41 (1892), 393–407.

Mabille, Florent. *Histoire succincte de la Réforme du Pays de Montbéliard.* Bachelor's thesis, University of Geneva, 1873.

Pfister, P. *Colloque de Montbéliard 1586: Étude historique.* Geneva, 1873.

Verzeichnis der im deutschen Sprachbereich erschienenen Drucke des XVI. Jahrhunderts. Stuttgart, 1983–. See vol. 20, nos. 1673–1749.

Viénot, John. *Histoire de la Réforme dans le Pays de Montbéliard depuis les origines jusqu'à la Mort de P. Toussain, 1524–1573.* 2 vols. Paris, 1900. Vol. 2, *Pièces justificatives,* contains primary sources for vol. 1.

JILL RAITT

TOUSSAIN, Pierre (1499–1573), pastor of the church of Montbéliard from 1535 to 1573. Toussain was first appointed by Duke Ulrich of Württemberg to continue the reform inaugurated in Montbéliard by Guillaume Farel in 1524. Thirty-six years old, well educated, and a dedicated churchman, Toussain had early made the acquaintance of Johannes Oecolampadius and Farel in Basel and then had traveled in Germany, France, and Switzerland, suffering imprisonment for his beliefs in Paris and Metz.

From 1535 to 1538, neither Ulrich nor his brother George, count of Montbéliard, dared anger Charles V by fully supporting the reform in their territories. Toussain preached, brought in schoolmasters, and did all that he could, including writing scolding letters to the two rulers. In November 1538 George suppressed the Mass in Montbéliard. By 1541 all of George's territory was reformed and supplied with evangelical pastors.

Between 1541 and 1559 Toussain developed schools and the organization of the Montbéliard church, which included the rural parishes. In 1559 Toussain published at Basel *L'Ordre qu'on tient en l'eglise de Montbéliard en instruisant les enfans, et administrant les saints sacremens, avec la forme du Mariage et des prieres.* As Toussain wrote in the preface to the work, his liturgy had been in use in Montbéliard since 1539.

Throughout his life Toussain considered himself to be simply "evangelical," one who is guided by the principle of *sola scriptura.* Like the Swiss, Toussain found no warrant for insisting on the bodily presence of Christ on every altar; he therefore could not follow Luther in the latter's doctrine of a real bodily presence. Toussain preferred the Swiss Reformed doctrine that the communicant received the body of Christ spiritually, by faith, through the power of the Holy Spirit.

When, in 1550, Ulrich made his son Christoph, soon to be known as "the Pious" for his strict Lutheranism, count of Montbéliard, the situation became tense. Toussain wrote to Calvin and Farel for advice. Calvin advised him to stand firm on matters of principle but to yield wherever his conscience would allow.

Toussain was free from Lutheran pressure from 1553 to 1558, when Christoph, now duke of Württemberg, recalled his uncle George as count of Montbéliard. George had persevered in the Reformed tradition as practiced in Montbéliard and until his death in 1558 supported Toussain. But new problems arose when a theological dispute over predestination distanced Toussain and the Montbéliard clergy from their French Swiss allies, Pierre Viret, Farel, and Calvin. Opposed to capital punishment for heretics, the Montbéliard clergy had also sided with Sébastien Castellion against Calvin and Farel over the Michael Servetus affair. Farel broke with Toussain, but Calvin, while disapproving of Toussain's views, continued to respond to his requests for advice on other issues.

The Lutheran dukes of Württemberg tried again and again to determine just how far they could push the county of Montbéliard after the death of George. The situation was exacerbated when the Wars of Religion broke out in France in 1562 and Montbéliard became a place of refuge for French Calvinists. In 1568 Duke Christoph died and was succeeded by his son, Ludwig, who would do all that he could to unite his duchy not only as Lutheran but indeed as the peculiar type of Lutheranism taught by Johannes Brenz and Jakob Andreae. The consequences for Montbéliard were grave.

In the meantime, Toussain's son, Daniel, driven from his ministry in Orléans by the Wars of Religion, arrived in Montbéliard, where the people agreed that he should succeed his aged father as superintendent. But Lutheran demands on the Montbéliard clergy had become more precise. Not only were they to adopt the Württemberg church order, they were also to adopt Württemberg theology in its entirety. When the Montbéliard clergy refused, Pierre Toussain was "retired" and Daniel was sent back to France.

Soon after the Saint Bartholomew's Day Massacre in 1572, refugees from France flowed into Reformed areas in the empire, including Montbéliard. Among the refugees was Daniel Toussain, who had escaped from the devastation at Orléans. But he could not remain under Duke Ludwig's strict Lutheran control and soon left for Basel. Before the end of 1573 and shortly after he was dismissed as pastor by the Lutheran superintendent, Pierre Toussain, aged seventy-five, died.

BIBLIOGRAPHY

Mabille, Florent. *Histoire succincte de la Réforme du Pays de Montbéliard.* Thèse, Bachelier en Théologie. Geneva, 1873.

Pfister, P. *Colloque de Montbéliard, 1586: Étude historique.* Geneva, 1873.

Raitt, Jill. "The Emperor and the Exiles: The Clash of Religion and Politics in the Sixteenth Century." In *Church History* 52 (June 1983), 145–156.

———. *The Colloquy of Montbéliard: Religion and Politics in the Sixteenth Century.* New York, 1993.

Verzeichnis der im deutschen Sprachbereich erschienenen Drucke des XVI. Jahrhunderts. Stuttgart, 1983–. See vol. 20, no. 1751.

Viénot, John. *Histoire de la Réforme dans le Pays de Montbéliard depuis les origines jusqu'à la mort de P. Toussain, 1524–1573.* 2 vols. Paris, 1900. Vol. 2, *Pièces justificatives*, contains primary sources for vol. 1.

JILL RAITT

TRACH, Johannes. *See* Draconites, Johannes.

TRADITION. From the earliest centuries of Christian history, the concept of tradition played a central role in the effort to describe and define the nature of church authority. In the early church, the content of Christian tradition was defined authoritatively through the rule of faith (*regula fidei*), a thoroughly formulated statement that summed up the main elements of Christian belief descending from the apostles and, beyond that, from Christ himself. In the long run, however, this firm and simple normative definition of tradition proved insufficient. Throughout late antiquity and the Middle Ages, the concept of tradition became more complex, and tensions within the concept were exposed. Three lines of development were especially important. First, there was a growing tendency to discuss the question more in terms of the sources of tradition-building than in terms of the content of the tradition. Who was entitled to interpret and define the normative tradition, the councils or the bishop of Rome? During the late Middle Ages there was evidence of tension—and to an extent conflict—between these two poles of authority. Second, the critiques and analyses of scholastic theologians came to play a more important part in the interpretation and definition of Christian tradition. In institutional terms, the views not only of the bishops but also of the universities and their professors had to be taken into account. Finally, within a growing body of church tradition, and in addition to tensions and conflicts regarding how it was to be interpreted and used, the period saw a widening of the fundamental distinction between, on the one hand, the normative concept of tradition, one rooted in the *regula fidei* of the early church, the teaching of the church fathers, and the decisions of the ecumenical councils of the early church, and on the other, the much broader descriptive concept of tradition, comprising the whole range of teaching and ecclesiastical practice accumulated during the history of the church.

The Lutheran Reformation. In the critical discourse of the Lutheran Reformation, tradition was used primarily in a negative sense. According to Luther, the Roman church was burdened with a multitude of human traditions that were defended in the name of God by the pope and his bishops as holy traditions; and according to Luther, nothing was more dangerous for the church than this confusion of human and divine. The final and the worst of all the enemies of the church was precisely the one who came in the guise of God himself, "who opposes and is lifted up against all that is called god or that is worshipped to such an extent that he sits in the temple of God displaying himself just as if he were God" (*2 Thes.* 2:4). Luther understood the church practices and regulations that had no explicit biblical basis as the fulfillment of just such apocalyptic prophecies. The pope could only be the biblical figure of Antichrist, and his strategy was to lead believers away from the word of God by drawing their attention to his own regulations instead. For Luther, the prophecies concerning Antichrist formed the basis of one of the most important themes of scripture; those who understood the true meaning of these prophetic texts must unmask the papacy as the reign of Antichrist and abandon all human traditions imposed by this reign.

This apocalypticism must be kept in mind in order to understand the radical and uncompromising nature of Luther's attack on the *traditiones* of the papacy. Against these false traditions, Luther upheld the word of God as the only normative instance—the true "tradition"—of the church. The Bible bears witness to the word of God. But by its nature, it is a spoken word, God's *promissio* to man. This *promissio* has accompanied the people of God from the beginning, from God's promise to Eve that her descendant (Christ) would crush the head of the serpent (*Gen.* 3:16). It was repeated and renewed throughout the Old Testament until it was fulfilled in Christ. And from Christ, the *promissio* is passed on to the church through the preaching of the gospel. To receive the gospel and the sacraments is to receive the promise of salvation. This promise is the unfailing foundation of the church. It is to be trusted because God himself is to be trusted. It is also open and clear, and nothing can be added to it; there is no need for a tradition beyond the New Testament to clarify and develop the word of God.

On this basis, Luther displayed a pragmatic attitude toward other classical sources of church tradition. Insofar as the ecumenical councils, the church fathers, and the papacy—before it was captured by Antichrist—confirmed and supported the gospel, they could be useful to the church and to believers. But they could also be wrong and were therefore untrustworthy. Luther had been convinced of this during the critical years of the Reformation (1517–1521), when he was obliged to reject their authority in cases where they were in conflict with him and his view of the gospel.

Zwingli and Calvin. Luther's concept of tradition can be regarded as typical of the Reformation, for arguably Zwingli and Calvin thought along similar lines. Both rejected the *traditiones* of the papacy and upheld the Bible as sole and sufficient authority of the church. However, whereas Luther interpreted biblical tradition primarily according to the concept of *promissio*, Calvin focused on the concept of a covenant (*pactum*) between God and his people, connecting the different parts of the Old and the New Testament to one tradition. The relationship between God and man in the church could also be interpreted as a covenant.

Zwingli and Calvin did not share in the apocalypticism of Luther's attack on the papacy and its traditions. Moreover, both were more strongly marked by the humanist mentality than Luther was, and thus they showed comparatively greater interest in the church fathers as a source of their theology. They did not, however, regard the church fathers as authoritative in church matters, and their answers to the question of the relationship between the Bible and the church fathers were much the same as Luther's.

The Social Context of the New Concept of Tradition. During the Reformation, the medieval concept of tradition was radically reduced and concentrated, both in its content and in its formal structure. First and foremost this was the achievement of rational, critical theology, opposing the traditional authority of accumulated ecclesiastical practice. But in order to be effective and successful, critical theology needed an institutional basis strong enough to stand up against episcopal authority in the church. Such a basis was available in the universities. The universities were firmly connected to the church, yet to a considerable degree they were independent of church authority. To Luther, both this close connection and this institutional independence were necessary to the success of his theology; and any such success was furthered by princes taking up the program of church reform and defending it against the traditional political-ecclesiastical structures of the Holy Roman Empire and the papacy. The critical theology of Zwingli and Calvin, meanwhile, was advanced primarily in the public sphere of the relatively independent cities of Zurich and Geneva. This is most evident in the case of Zwingli's Zurich, where the rejection of the Roman ecclesiastical *traditiones* was decided by an act of the city council on the basis of public debate. Here citizens used reason and public debate as their weapons against the weight of traditional church authority.

Protestant Tradition and Confessional Culture. The radical theological concept of tradition propagated by men like Luther, Zwingli, and Calvin was altered during the process of building new confessional churches on the basis of Lutheran and Reformed theology. As early modern states developed in late sixteenth- and early seventeenth-century Europe, religion came to play a central role in the definition of political identity; states were defined as Lutheran, Calvinist, or Catholic. Theological content was then defined through various documents, none of which had been written in order to define a confession, but which now won official status as confessional texts that laid out the essential teachings of the church (in the case of Lutheranism, for example, the Augsburg Confession and the Small Catechism).

In their confessional documents Lutherans and Calvinists continued to speak of the Bible as the only basis of authority and of the *traditiones* as being among the abuses of the Roman church which were to be rejected. The concept of tradition is used unpolemically only once in the Augsburg Confession, in article 26; and there, too, it is used in connection with the concept of ceremonies, which, having been invented by man and not by God, are extraneous to the church. Through the process of confessionalization, however, the confessional texts of Lutheranism and Calvinism inevitably attained the status of normative traditions in addition to the Bible, and Lutheran and Calvinist tradition came to be authoritatively defined by these texts. The Augsburg Confession in particular acquired a binding status equal to that of the Bible. This normative definition of biblical theology through confessional documents was markedly different from Luther's position regarding God's (spoken) *promissio* as the center of biblical tradition.

The Roman Catholic Definition of Tradition at the Council of Trent. The challenge for the Roman Catholic church in these circumstances was to define more precisely the sources of its authority. What was the Roman alternative to Lutheran and Calvinist teaching concerning the Bible as the sole authority? The Roman church responded to the new confessional situation of Christianity by producing its own confessional texts, the *Professio fidei Tridentina* (1565) and the *Catechismus Romanus* (1566). Earlier, however, and more fundamentally, the Roman church had, in the decree *Sacrosancta*, formally defined the basis of its theology. Issued by the Council of Trent on 8 April 1546, the decree contains the most famous statement of the sixteenth century regarding tradition: "Following the example of the orthodox fathers, the council accepts and venerates with a like feeling of piety and reverence all the books of both the Old and the New Testament, since the one God is the author of both, as well as the traditions concerning both faith and conduct, as either directly spoken by Christ or dictated by the Holy Spirit, which have been preserved in unbroken sequence in the Catholic church." In formulating this brief definition, the product of intense discussion and debate, the council affirmed that the Bible and tradition were to be treated as parallel sources of authority. Several important question, however, were left unanswered.

Much discussion at Trent went into clarifying the concept of tradition. The majority of the delegates wished to restrict the debate to the apostolic tradition as passed on from Christ to the disciples and to the church, and to leave aside the question of the *traditiones,* the wide range of uses, habits, and regulations in church life and liturgy. As to what constituted apostolic tradition, several delegates were considerably influenced by the so-called Louvain school of theology, whose most distinguished representative was Johannes Driedo. According to this school of thought, apostolic tradition represented a specific oral transmission of the gospel and, because it was equally rooted in the teaching of Christ himself, had dignity equal to that of written transmission through the New Testament. From this perspective, equal authority should be attributed to scripture and to apostolic tradition, to the written and to the oral transmission of the gospel. The words *pari pietatis affectu ac reverentia* ("like feeling of piety and reverence") can be interpreted as expressing this view. However, a proposal to define the relationship between the two sources of authority by the words *partim . . . partim* ("partly . . . partly") was rejected by a small majority. This construction could imply a division of the sources of authority, and this would have been to go too far in the application of the principles of the Louvain school of theology.

The perspective of the Louvain school was not shared by all the delegates, of course. One delegate spoke of tradition in a manner similar to Luther, maintaining that scripture was a sufficient basis for theology. In his opinion, tradition was to be defined loosely, so that there was no clear distinction between apostolic tradition and church traditions. Others proposed that the content of apostolic tradition be expressed in more concrete terms, that the council enumerate at least some of the themes in which the teaching of the church was defined through apostolic tradition. This proposal was rejected, however, when it became apparent that the distinction between apostolic tradition and other church traditions was a critical point and that it would be difficult to reach agreement.

The *Sacrosancta,* then, had stated that tradition was a source of church authority; but the structure and content of tradition were quite unclear. This was made plain at the conclusion of the session, when the council drew up the agenda of its future proceedings. The original plan had been to continue discussing methodological questions in order to arrive at a more precise definition of tradition in relationship to other elements of authority; this was abandoned in favor of a more pragmatic procedure in which central issues of dogma were attacked directly, without further methodological clarification. Thus the council sidestepped a foreseeable difficulty. Any further attempt to clarify the relationship between the (oral) apostolic tradition and the broader *traditiones* of the church would inevitably have led to more radical questions regarding the source of tradition, regarding which authority was to interpret and decide in cases of conflict. More specifically, it would have involved the council in an undesirable discussion of the relationship between conciliar and papal authority.

A number of authors later addressed the methodological question left open by the Council of Trent. One important contribution came from the Spanish Dominican Melchior Cano, professor at the University of Salamanca, who in *De locis theologicis* (1563) attempted to define tradition as a source of authority in relationship to such other relevant sources as scripture, the councils, the bishop of Rome, the church fathers, and natural reason. For Cano, tradition was oral apostolic tradition, which must be weighed as one element of authority among others. However, Cano's methodology provided no clear answer as to which was to be the decisive authority in cases of conflict.

[*See also* Scripture.]

BIBLIOGRAPHY

Brosse, Olivier de la, et al. *Lateran V et Trente.* Paris, 1975. General history of the councils.

Congar, Yves. *La tradition et les traditions.* Vol. 1, *Essai historique.* Paris, 1960. Important study by influential Roman Catholic theologian; also available in English translation, *Tradition and Traditions,* New York, 1966.

Dittrich, Bernhard. *Das Traditionsverständnis in der Confessio Augustana und in der Confutatio.* Leipzig, 1983.

Evans, Gillian. *Problems of Authority in the Reformation Debates.* Cambridge, 1992.

Jedin, Hubert. *Geschichte des Konzils von Trent.* Vol. 2, *Die erste Trienter Tagungsperiode, 1545–1547.* Freiburg, 1957. Classic and comprehensive treatment of the council; also available in English translation, *History of the Council of Trent,* London, 1961.

Koopmans, Jan. *Das Altkirchliche Dogma in der Reformation.* Beiträge zur evangelischen Theologie, no. 22. Munich, 1955. Both Luther and Calvin are comprehensively discussed.

Lang, A. *Melchior Cano und die Methode des dogmatischen Beweises*. Munich, 1925. Treats Cano as a pioneer of methodological discussion within theology.

Tanner, Norman P., ed. *Decrees of the Ecumenical Councils*. Vol. 2, *Trent to Vatican*. London, 1990. The documents of the councils in parallel Latin and English text, with a good critical apparatus.

Tavard, George H. *Holy Writ or Holy Church: The Crisis of the Protestant Reformation*. Reprint, London, 1959.

"Tradition." In *Geschichtliche Grundbegriffe*, edited by Otto Brunner, Werner Conze, and Reinhart Koselleck, vol. 6, pp. 607–650. Stuttgart, 1992. General treatment of religious and other aspects of the concept.

"Tradition." In *Realenzyclopädie für protestantische Theologie und Kirche*, 3d ed., vol. 20, pp. 8–13. Leipzig, 1908. Quotes several interesting historical sources.

TARALD RASMUSSEN

TŘANOVSKÝ, George (also Juraj Tranowský; Lat., Tranoscius; 1592–1637), Lutheran theologian, pastor, and hymn writer. George Třanovský was born in Těšin, the capital of upper Silesia, the son of Valentin, a relatively prosperous smith and citizen of the city. He attended the local Latin school as well as the school in Guben in nearby Lusatia and the lyceum in Kolberg in Pomerania. At the age of sixteen he matriculated at the University of Wittenberg.

Třanovský began his career as an assistant teacher at Saint Nicholaus in Malá Strana in Prague and for one year was a private tutor in Třebon in Bohemia. He returned briefly to Prague before accepting the position of rector of the Lutheran school in Holešov, Moravia. His stay here was also brief, and in 1615 Třanovský was in Valašske Mezřiči, whose lord was Jetřich of Žerotín. After reaching the canonical age for pastoral ordination (twenty-four), he was ordained in Olešnica and in October 1616 became the town pastor. Three years after the Battle of White Mountain (1620) Ferdinand II ordered the re-Catholicization of the town, if necessary by force. Třanovský was imprisoned briefly and subsequently forced into exile in Silesia (1625). Here he served as the court preacher of Baron John Suneg of Budátin and his wife Anna, the daughter of Palatine George Thurzo of Hungary. In 1627 he and his patrons were forced to flee Silesia and moved to Oráva and Budátin in Upper Hungary (Slovakia). Finally, in 1631, Třanovský became the pastor of Liptovský sväty Mikuláš in north central Slovakia, where he died in 1637.

While in Mezřiči, Třanovský prepared his first two major works, an exposition, in sermon form, of *Revelation* that remained unfinished and a translation into Czech of the Augsburg Confession (1620). His *Prologus in Apocalipsis divi Johannis Apostoli* (Exposition of the Revelation of Saint John) exhibits the particular ecclesiastical and eschatological concerns of late Reformation Lutheranism, while in his introduction to the Augsburg Confession he expresses his belief that, through this confession, God spoke to the world for the last time before the apocalypse.

His most significant works, however, were his two collections of religious hymns and prayers designed to fill the liturgical needs of Slavic Lutherans. In Bielska in Silesia, he prepared his *Odarum sacrarum* (Sacred Songs; 1629) a collection of 150 hymns in Latin, while in Slovakia he completed his most significant works, the *Phiala odoramentorum* (A Sweet Smelling Vial; 1535), a collection of liturgical prayers, and the *Cithara Sanctorum* (Harp of the Saints; 1536), a collection of over 400 hymns in Czech, ninety of which were written by Třanovský.

Třanovský was a popularizer of the theology of Lutheran orthodoxy and the *Book of Concord*. The *Cithara Sanctorum* became not just a hymnbook but an instrument of Christian instruction and manual for private devotion. Třanovský was not a pioneer or innovator in the cause of ecclesiastical reform, but his liturgical works contributed significantly to the domestication and maintenance of Lutheranism among the western Slavs. Since its first edition, this hymnbook, popularly referred to as the *Tranoscius*, has been issued in more than 150 editions.

BIBLIOGRAPHY

Ďurovič, Ján P. *Životopis Juraja Tanovského, 1592–1942: K 350. výročiu jeho narodenia*. Liptovský Mikulá, Hungary, 1942.

Osuský, Samuel. *Tranovského sborník*. Liptovský Mikulá, Hungary, 1936.

Stökl, Walter. "Georg Tranoscius, der grösste lutherische Liederdichter der Slowakei." In *Ein Leben für Kirche und Volk: Zum 90 Geburtstag des Professors der Theologie, Dr. Roland Steinacker*, edited by Desider Alexy, pp. 54–78. Stuttgart, 1960.

DAVID P. DANIEL

TRANSUBSTANTIATION is the doctrine of the sacramental presence of Christ in the Eucharist according to which, at the priestly words of consecration, the elements of bread and wine are miraculously changed into the very body and blood of Christ. The nature of Christ's eucharistic presence was hotly debated in early medieval theology. In 1079 the church of Rome repudiated the views of the grammarian Berengarius of Tours, who denied that the eucharistic bread and wine were "substantially changed" into the body and blood of Jesus. The term *transubstantiatio* appeared for the first time in the middle of the twelfth century and was given dogmatic status by the Fourth Lateran Council in 1215 and again by the Council of Lyon in 1274. With the help of recently recovered Aristotelian philosophy, Thomas Aquinas further refined and clarified the church's teaching about transubstantiation in his classic treatment of the doctrine in *Summa Theologiae III, quaestiones 75–77*. According to this theory, the substance, or inner reality, of the eucharistic elements are converted into the substance of the body and blood of Christ, while the accidents, or material properties, remain unaltered. The doctrine of transubstantiation was challenged by various theologians in the late Middle Ages, most notably by John Wycliffe, whose theories were condemned along with those of Jan Hus, at the Council of Constance in 1415. Other thinkers, such as William of Ockham, questioned the philosophical basis of transubstantiation even while accepting it as a *de' fide* doctrine of the church.

All of the mainline Protestant and radical reformers of the sixteenth century rejected the doctrine of transubstantiation, although in varying degrees and with different results. In his *De captivitate Babylonica ecclesiae praeludium* (Concerning the Babylonian Captivity of the Church; 1520), Martin Luther repudiated transubstantiation as evidence of the "captivity" of the Eucharist to the metaphysical theories of the "Aristotelian quibblers." Luther found the doctrine of transubstantiation to be an unnecessary and unbiblical accretion to the true meaning of the Eucharist, which he interpreted by analogy to Christology: exactly what is true in regard to the incarnate Christ is also true in regard to the Eucharist. Thus, Christ's body and blood are not equated with but are present "in, with, and under" the bread and wine. Though he rejected transubstantiation, Luther held to as robust a doctrine of real presence as did any of his medieval predecessors.

Huldrych Zwingli went much further than Luther in refusing to connect the body and blood of Christ with the creaturely elements of the Eucharist for fear of lapsing into idolatry. Martin Bucer and John Calvin forged a mediating view that advocated a real spiritual presence while eschewing sacramental materialism. Despite their differences, the Protestant reformers were united in their denial of transubstantiation. With Zwingli, Calvin rejects transubstantiation as an idolatrous doctrine that gives divine honors to a material thing; with Luther, he questions the philosophical basis of a theory based more on reason than scripture (*Institutes* 4, 17–18).

The variety of Protestant opinions on the Eucharist stands in marked contrast to the Roman Catholic effort to arrive at a unified position on this controverted theme. The Council of Trent produced three documents on the Eucharist—one on the nature of the Sacrament (1551), one on the reception of Communion (1562), and one on the Mass as a sacrifice (1562). The classic definition of transubstantiation set forth in the first of these decrees was hammered out in deliberate dialectical tension with the Protestant rejection of this dogma. The fourth chapter of the *Decretum de sanctissimo eucharistiae sacramento* of the Council of Trent offers this statement on transubstantiation: "Since Christ our Redeemer declared that to be truly His Body which He offered under the species of bread, this has always been believed in the church of God; and this holy synod now confirms it afresh: through the consecration of bread and wine there

takes place a conversion of the whole substance of the bread into the substance of the body of Christ our Lord and of the whole substance of the wine into the substance of His blood. This change is suitably and properly called transubstantiation by the Holy Catholic Church." In 1565 the doctrine of transubstantiation promulgated by Trent was set forth by Pius IV in the bull *Iniunctum nobis*. The Council of Trent thus gave official ecclesiastical approval to a major expression of the eucharistic theology of medieval Scholasticism. In this way the Roman Catholic church of the sixteenth century defined itself against both contemporary Protestant alternatives and diverse eucharistic theologies of the pre-Reformation era.

[*See also* Consubstantiation *and* Eucharist.]

BIBLIOGRAPHY

Jones, Paul H. *Christ's Eucharistic Presence: A History of the Doctrine.* New York, 1994.

Muller, B. "Transubstantiatio." In *Dictionary of Latin and Greek Theological Terms.* Grand Rapids, Mich., 1985.

Vollert, C. "Transubstantiation." In *New Catholic Encyclopedia.* Washington, D.C., 1967.

TIMOTHY GEORGE

TRANSYLVANIA (Hung., Erdély; Ger., Siebenbürgen) is the southeastern portion of historic Hungary. During the sixteenth century Transylvania gained a large measure of political autonomy, served as a major center for the Protestant Reformation, and became one of the first areas of Europe to practice religious toleration. Transylvania's political autonomy resulted from the occupation of central Hungary by the Turks in 1541. Süleyman I desired to prevent Ferdinand I from gaining possession of Hungary. Consequently the Turks seized the central third of Hungary and recognized a tributary principality centered in Transylvania and encompassing additional parts of eastern Hungary (the Partium). This new political entity recognized János Zsigmond Zápolya as its ruler. During its period of relative political autonomy Transylvania elected its own rulers, who governed with the assistance and cooperation of a diet. Three so-called nations were represented at the Transylvanian diets: the Saxon (Germans concentrated in the towns), the Magyar (the county nobility), and the Székely (who enjoyed extensive liberties and served as border guards).

Transylvania during the sixteenth century was characterized by religious diversity and the gradual establishment of legal toleration for several Christian confessions. The spread of Protestantism in Transylvania was remarkable because, with the exception of the period from 1563 to 1571, when János Zsigmond Zápolya embraced a series of new religious doctrines, it was ruled by Catholics. During the first half of the 1520s Luther's teachings began to circulate among the largely German-speaking urban population and gained further acceptance during the competition for the crown between János Zápolya and Ferdinand I (1526 to 1540). As a result by the time Transylvania achieved a semiautonomous status the Saxon towns had largely fallen under Lutheran influence.

The Reformation in Transylvania proceeded rapidly in three phases: first, the wide acceptance of Lutheranism by the Saxon communities; second, the destruction of the Catholic hierarchy; and third, the appearance of ever more radical Protestant doctrines. Several factors accounted for the spread of Lutheran teachings among the Transylvanian Saxons. They could read and understand Luther in their mother tongue. Furthermore, political conflicts within Hungary discouraged both Ferdinand I and the Zápolya party from alienating the Saxons by forcibly moving against Protestantism. Finally, the Saxon towns were largely self-governing communities. Protestantism in Transylvania appealed to the desire for local control of religious life by the urban congregations and town fathers in much the same way as it attracted the imperial towns of the Holy Roman Empire. In the major Saxon centers such as Braşov (Kronstadt) and Nagyszeben (Sibiu) Lutheran-minded clergy and influential laymen took religious leadership into their own hands. They seized control of the pulpits and ended the Roman Catholic Mass; they established Protestant schools and presses. John Honter of Braşov, a humanistically educated reformer, composed a Lutheran church ordinance for the Saxon communities in Transylvania by 1543, and four years later the wide acceptance of Honter's scheme provided the necessary organizational structure and cohesion for Lutheranism among the Transylvanian Saxons. By the following decade the Saxons had begun to elect their own Lutheran superintendents, thereby formally establishing their separate church in Transylvania.

During the 1550s the effort to reattach Transylvania to Habsburg Hungary was accompanied by a halfhearted attempt to strengthen the Catholic church hierarchy. But both these undertakings came to naught, and most Catholic ecclesiastical properties passed into secular hands. Without leadership or material foundation, Roman Catholicism was reduced to a small minority religion in Transylvania. The Catholic recovery would be long, slow, halting, and never fully completed.

The destruction of the old church in Transylvania, however, did not signal the complete victory of Lutheranism. During the late 1550s, the moment of apparent Lutheran triumph, Protestants rapidly started to disagree among themselves. Once the forces of ecclesiastical reform had been set in motion, they began to accelerate, and the Magyar communities, which had been sympathetic to Protestantism, soon abandoned Luther for Calvin and Bullinger. The new religious direction and the thirst for continued ecclesiastical reform received increasingly strong encouragement and support from the emerging Calvinist center at Debrecen in eastern Hungary. As elsewhere in Christendom the numerous debates over the Lord's Supper and predestination defied consensus and resolution. Consequently by the mid-1560s Protestantism in Transylvania had split into two groups, Lutherans and Calvinists, each with their own ecclesiastical organization. In general the Saxons remained loyal to Luther's teachings, but the Magyar townspeople and nobles flocked to Calvin's side.

The 1560s proved to be decisive for the history of religion in Transylvania. The emerging Calvinist congregations soon confronted even more radical demands for doctrinal change. Antitrinitarian concepts filtered into Transylvania and lodged themselves at the court of the ruler János Zsigmond Zápolya. Under the guidance of his Italian court physician Giorgio Biandrata and Francis Dávid, János Zsigmond's court preacher, Unitarianism gained the ear and allegiance of the ruler as well as the support of his highest officials and closest advisers. By the time of János Zsigmond's death in 1571 Transylvania's three political nations were divided into four religious communities: Catholics, Lutherans, Calvinists, and Unitarians. The Wallachians living in Transylvania remained under the leadership of their Eastern Orthodox clergy.

The last three decades of the sixteenth century brought to an end the rapid religious transformation of Transylvania. Only one new religious group emerged: the Sabbatarians, who rejected the New Testament and practiced a form of gentile Judaism. During this period of Catholic Báthory rule the Lutherans and Calvinists retained their previous gains, but Unitarianism came under concerted pressure. The more radical Unitarian leader, Francis Dávid, ended his days in prison, and popular support for Unitarianism gradually eroded. The Báthory favored Catholicism and made some efforts to reestablish the Roman church by introducing the Jesuits to Transylvania. After a brief flowering during the 1580s the Jesuits were forced by pressure from the Protestant majority to close their schools and depart.

The diffusion of Protestantism in Transylvania and its division into different confessions was accompanied by the establishment of legal toleration. In this part of Europe circumstances forced a heterogenous population gradually to accept the notion that the only way to preserve the delicate social balance was through toleration. Beginning in the late 1540s the diets repeatedly confronted the difficulties arising from the religious divisions. At first the diets only implicitly recognized the right of confessions other than Catholic to exist, but slowly the laws were adjusted to accommodate the reality of an emerging Protestant majority. Religious toleration came to Transylvania not because most people subscribed to a theory of toleration as socially beneficial, but because practical necessity compelled toleration of other religious viewpoints. János Zsigmond Zápolya's attitude and religious progression from Catholicism to Unitarianism during the 1560s greatly contributed to the establishment of legal toleration. The young ruler was avidly interested in religious doctrine and debate, often personally attending and participating in the discussions, and he helped to nourish the spirit of toleration. Just before his death the diet of 1571 formally declared that no one should be harmed on account of one's confession. Although the spirit of religious toleration did not master every subsequent disagreement over religion, the principle survived and safeguarded the continued existence of various Christian confessions in Transylvania.

[*See also* Hungary; Zápolya, János; *and* Zápolya, János Zsigmond.]

BIBLIOGRAPHY

Barta, Gábor. *Az erdélyi fejedelemség születése* (The Birth of the Transylvanian Principality). Budapest, 1979. Good introduction to Transylvanian politics and society during the sixteenth century.

Balázs, Mihály. *Az erdélyi antitrinitarizmus az 1560-as évek végén* (Transylvanian Antitrinitarianism at the End of the 1560s). Budapest, 1988. Best for its discussion of antitrinitarian doctrines in Transylvania.

Bucsay, Mihály. *Der Protestantismus in Ungarn 1521–1978.* Vienna, 1977. A good brief introduction to Protestantism in Hungary for those without any knowledge of the Hungarian language.

Dán, Róbert. *Az erdélyi szombatosok és Péchi Simon* (The Transylvanian Sabbatarians and Simon Péchi). Budapest, 1987. A basic study of this unusual sect and its most politically influential leader.

Evans, Robert J. W. *The Making of the Habsburg Monarchy, 1550–1700.* Oxford, 1991. A thoughtful grand synthesis of the forces that eventually united a diverse and complex empire.

Makkai, László, et al., eds. *Erdély története* (A History of Transylvania). 3 vols. Budapest, 1987. An excellent recent general history by members of the Institute for Historical Studies in Budapest.

Szilágyi, Sándor, ed. *Monumenta Comitialia Regni Transylvaniae.* 21 vols. Budapest, 1876–1898. An indispensable source collection for the history of the deliberations of Transylvania's diets.

Zoványi, Jenó. *A reformácio Magyarországon 1566-ig* (The Reformation in Hungary to 1566). Budapest, 1922. A thoroughly documented Protestant ecclesiastical history that covers all of historic Hungary.

———. *A Magyarországi protestantizmus 1565-tól 1600-ig* (Hungarian Protestantism from to 1565 to 1600). Budapest, 1977.

Zsilinszky, Mihály. *A magyar országgyülések vallásügyi tárgyalásai a reformátiotól kezdve* (The Debates over Religion by the Hungarian Diets since the Time of the Reformation). 4 vols. Budapest, 1880–1897. A useful discussion of the debates over religion that includes the diets in both royal Hungary and Transylvania.

PETER SCHIMERT

TRAVEL. The Reformation, or, more particularly, the animosity it created between states and cities, created serious difficulties for anyone who wished to travel across sixteenth-century Europe. Even in early modern Europe, well before the age of mass tourism, literally tens of thousands of people were on the roads at any given time: merchants, diplomats, soldiers, pilgrims, educational travelers, as well as itinerant workers, all traveled across Europe. In medieval Europe licenses to travel, or passports, had been obligatory for most travelers, yet after the Reformation regulations controlling the movement of people around Europe became noticeably stricter. Europe had not only become more dangerous for travelers, but, as far as civil and religious authorities were concerned, travelers themselves were potentially much more dangerous. Both Catholic and Protestant authorities, trying to stop the infiltration of rival doctrines, imposed rigorous controls over the licensing and movement of travelers across the continent.

Potential travelers in the second half of the sixteenth century would first have noticed the added restrictions generated by the conflicts of the Reformation when they applied for a license to travel. Civil and ecclesiastical authorities endeavored to make certain that the potential travelers were so firmly established in their own faith that they would not succumb to rival faiths abroad. Alternatively, the authorities were keen not to let members of religious minorities escape their jurisdiction. In England anyone with a recent family history of Catholicism was usually refused permission to travel abroad.

Once abroad, travelers entering a country or a city often faced detailed questions from local authorities regarding their religious affiliation. For example, the Roman Inquisition established offices at the main entry points of Italy, where they examined the minds, bodies, and baggage of incoming travelers in an effort to detect Protestants. Protestant authorities were generally as rigorous as the Inquisition. Calvinist magistrates in Geneva carefully examined all travelers entering the city, while English authorities established strict customs controls along the southeast ports in order to detect Catholics entering or leaving the country.

Travelers often shared a group allegiance that transcended religious affiliations. In some instances Protestant travelers aided their fellow Catholic travelers to evade the authorities, and in other instances Catholics similarly assisted their Protestant comrades. Travelers also shared information about the activities of authorities in particularly dangerous regions, the most dangerous of which, for Protestants, was Italy. Protestant travelers in Italy took extra precautions to protect themselves against the curiosity of the Inquisition. They carried no Protestant devotional books, pretended to attend Mass, changed lodgings regularly, and even assumed false identities for added safety. Catholic travelers had to take similar precautions to evade Protestant authorities who might suspect them of being Jesuit missionaries in disguise. In all, the Reformation added significant complications and dangers for both Protestant and Catholic travelers, who already faced great difficulties in traversing Europe freely.

BIBLIOGRAPHY

Clarke, M. L. "British Travellers to Rome in Tudor and Stuart Times." *History Today* 28 (November 1978), 746–751. Gives some idea of the difficulties Protestant travelers faced in Italy.

Lightbrown, R. W. "The Protestant Confessor, or the Tragic History of Mr Molle." In *England and the Continental Renaissance*, edited by Edward Chaney and Peter Mack, pp. 239–256. Woodbridge, U.K., 1990. Demonstrates what could happen to the unwary Protestant traveler in Catholic Italy.

SARA WARNEKE

TREATY OF CATEAU-CAMBRÉSIS. *See* Cateau-Cambrésis, Treaty of.

TRENT, COUNCIL OF.

The nineteenth general council of the Catholic Church was held at Trent in several phases from 1545 to 1563. When the council opened in the northern Italian city of Trent, it was too late for a reconciliation between the various religious factions, although this was the reason there had been calls for a council since the 1520s. As early as 1521, the papal nuncio reported that at the Diet of Worms, which was supposed to deal with the issue of Luther, there was a significant call for a Catholic council. Nonetheless, the council became a reality only when Emperor Charles V began to call directly for its convocation. The long and complex vicissitudes over the idea of resolving the differences between Catholics and Protestants by holding a council consumed the decades between 1520 and 1545. When Paul III finally became convinced of the need for the council, the division of Western Christendom was already an established fact. The generation that had witnessed the initial break was disappearing and everyone had become accustomed to living divided and poised in combat.

The responsibilities for this tragic delay were grave and lay in a large part with the leaders of Europe. However, even greater was the responsibility of the pope and the Curia Romana. They were entrapped in political maneuverings, with the pope fearing that the council would impinge on the powers of the papacy and the Curia fearing that effective reform might reduce the power that had been concentrated in Rome over the previous centuries.

The image of a conciliar gathering guided by a lucid blueprint for a Catholic comeback was historically outdated. Instead, the bishops gathering at Trent were few in number—beginning with thirty-one who were predominantly Italian—and they were bewildered and overwhelmed by the disaster of the breakup of the religious unity of the West. Moreover, they were uncertain as to whether the pope really wanted the council to meet or whether instead he might consider them excessively zealous for having come to Trent. Almost none of them had any firsthand knowledge of the preaching or the writings of the reformers; rather they relied almost exclusively on the theologians present at Trent. In marked contrast was their awareness of pastoral and disciplinary problems, since many of the bishops had personally experienced the serious decadence in which the church found itself. Emperor Charles V would have preferred that the council deal only with disciplinary reform, while the pope insisted that only doctrinal issues be discussed, in order to move quickly to a condemnation of Protestant positions. These two contrasting perspectives stemmed from two different assessments of the problem that had erupted in Germany. According to the emperor, the dissension had essentially been caused by ecclesiastical abuses and the decadence of the clergy. For Rome only theological dissent was significant, and it was viewed as a catalog of so many heresies from the past.

The gathering at Trent found a balanced solution, since it decided to discuss alternately one theological issue and one reform issue. This resulted in a slow and painstaking pace, but this was what was demanded by the difficulties in which the church found itself. The council, with a great sense of moderation, systematically adhered to the criterion of responding to the objections raised by the Protestants on each issue, constantly resisting the temptation to draw up a summary of Catholic theology on each of the subjects it dealt with (the Mass, sacraments, revelation, tradition, etc.).

The First Phase (1545–1547): Doctrine and Discipline. The first period of the Council of Trent ran from 13 December 1545 to 11 March 1547 and was divided into eight sessions. Of these sessions, the most important ones, from a dogmatic standpoint, were the fourth, the fifth, and the sixth. In the fourth session (8 April 1546) two decrees concerning scripture were approved. The first decree, after establishing the canon of the sacred books, reaffirmed the authority of apostolic traditions, distinct from the ecclesiastical traditions, alongside the authority of the Bible. Thus the Protestant principle of *sola scriptura* was rejected, but without calling into question the sufficiency of the Bible, which, on the authority of Vincent de Lérins, had been defended by some of the council fathers. The second decree affirmed the authenticity of the Vulgate, but it did not prohibit either critical editions in the original languages or translations into the vernacular. In the fifth session (17 June 1546) the decree on Original Sin was approved. The decree rejected both Pelagian optimism about human nature and the Lutheran notion of its total corruption. The decree on justification, approved in the sixth session (13 January 1547), could be considered the doctrinal masterpiece of the council. Although it was the outcome of a laborious debate and underwent numerous revisions, it retained the imprint of the outline prepared by Girolamo Seripando, the general of the Augustinian Hermits, who was close to the positions of the reformers. In the debate he had unsuccessfully defended the doctrine of twofold righteousness that had been accepted by Gasparo Contarini at the Colloquy of Regensburg. The decree managed to reconcile the need to safeguard the gratuity of grace with the concern of reaffirming the need of human cooperation. Justification was thus presented as true sanctification resulting from the indwelling of grace, by which regenerated humans could be considered to be capable of performing meritorious works, the need for which did not compromise the sufficiency of the merits of Christ. Indeed, human merits were none other than gifts of God, and therefore a Christian was obligated to place all trust in God and not in himself.

In contrast, the disciplinary reforms of the first period were disappointing. Matters were far from easy for the council. The vacillations of imperial policy and the reckless movements of French and papal policy had repercussions for the gathering at Trent, repeatedly threatening to derail the council. Thus in March 1547 Paul III's wariness of the emperor necessitated the transfer of the council from Trent, a city that politically belonged to the empire, to Bologna, which belonged to the Papal States. This had the effect of paralyzing the council (the Spaniards refused to move from Trent), and the council was formally suspended in 1549. For the Protestants, while a council held in Trent was already cause for concern, the transfer to Bologna confirmed their worst suspicions that Rome wanted to overwhelm the council. Only in 1551, by the decision of Julius III, chairman of the council, was the council reconvened at Trent with some hope for Protestant participation, but the reality of the division had already made this expectation moot. The council was to remain an exclusively "Roman Catholic" council; thus it became increasingly obvious that the goal of restoring the unity of the church, and hense of Christendom itself, was no longer possible.

The religious and political realities that existed in Europe forced the council, suspended once again in 1552 without having achieved appreciable results, to adopt goals that were more limited, but nonetheless serious and urgent. In more and more regions of Europe, Catholicism had been on the defensive for decades; it no longer seemed capable of overcoming the decadence and the disciplinary and doctrinal breakdown that the aggressive criticism of the Protestants had brought to light and relentlessly aggravated. The youthful forces that had manifested themselves, such as the new Society of Jesus, struggled to find a secure place and to overcome the climate of mistrust of every attempt at reform that increasingly marked ecclesiastical circles.

The Second Phase (1551–1552): Failure to Obtain Protestant Participation. The second period of the Council of Trent ran from 1 May 1551 to 28 April 1552 and included six sessions (9–14). Cardinal-legate Crescenzio was appointed to preside, assisted by two bishops who were experts on German affairs, Pighino and Lippomani. It was thought that at this session the problems in Germany would dominate the agenda, on account of the larger attendance of German bishops and the expected presence of Protestant delegations. The rivalry between France and the emperor once more made itself felt: while a few French prelates had

showed up in Bologna, now they were absent because of the express prohibition of their sovereign, Henry II.

At the center of the work of this period was the teaching on the sacraments. In the seventh session of 3 March 1547 the objective efficacy of the sacraments (*ex opere operato*) was reaffirmed. By taking into account the debates that had taken place in Bologna, it was possible to clarify the teaching on the Eucharist (session 13, 11 October 1551), on penance, and on the anointing of the sick (session 14, 25 November 1551). As in the first period, the reform decrees were totally inadequate. Yielding to pressure from the emperor (October 1551 and March 1552), a few delegates sent by Protestant princes and cities arrived at the council. Their presence turned out to be fruitless, however, since they advanced conditions for their participation in the work of the council that were unacceptable to the council fathers, such as the reaffirmation of the decree *Haec sancta* of Constance, obligating the pope to submit to the doctrinal decisions of a general council, and reopening debate on all the decrees already approved at Trent. At the end of March, Elector Moritz of Saxony, who had allied himself with France, resumed the German princes' struggle against Charles V. Shortly thereafter, the council had to be suspended once more.

In 1555 one final development in the orientation of a Counter-Reformation Catholic church took place. Upon the death of Julius III, Marcello Cervini (Marcellus II) ascended the papal throne. Marcellus II was a proponent of reform humanism who, while a legate, had made a superb contribution to the editing of the decree on justification. However Cervini's pontificate lasted only twenty-two days (9–30 April 1555); Gian Pietro Carafa was elected to succeed him and took the name Paul IV. He promoted purely disciplinary reform, marked by vigorous opposition to Protestantism. One action revealing this tendency was that of entrusting the Inquisition not only with fighting against heresy but also with reforming morals. Suspicions were levied even against some members of the College of Cardinals, who were accused of doctrinal deviation and brought to trial. In 1559 the first *Index auctorum et librorum prohibitorum* (Index of Prohibited Books) under papal authority was promulgated. Even Peter Canisius judged the Index to be inapplicable on account of its severity; among other things, translations of the Bible into vernacular languages were forbidden.

Meanwhile Charles V, having lost all hope of restoring the unity of the church, agreed to the Peace of Augsburg (1555) which sanctioned the principle of *cuius regio eius religio* ("whoever the king, his religion") that was initially favorable to the Protestants. Moreover, Calvinism was spreading in France, especially after the death of Henry II (1559).

The Third Phase (1561–1563): The Catholic Reform. When the council was reconvened at Trent in 1561, initiated by Pius IV, this time with the participation of France, it had to deal with renewing a Catholicism that was as hard-pressed by the new Renaissance mentality as it was by Protestantism, which was experiencing a rejuvenation thanks to Calvin. Some two hundred bishops were present from every part of the Catholic world with a Latin culture. The bishops were accompanied by numerous noteworthy theologians. The first issue was the problem of the residence of clergy charged with the care of souls and of bishops in their dioceses. This problem had already stirred up lively debates on account of the request made by numerous bishops, particularly from Spain, in the first period to declare that the obligation of residence was a matter of divine law. Such a declaration would have rendered papal dispensations impossible. Now the proposal was resubmitted by Pedro Guerrero, archbishop of Granada, who won the support of Gonzaga and Seripando. The procurial faction, headed by Simonetta, strongly opposed the proposal, arguing that it weakened papal primacy. Pius IV, after some hesitation, sided with the procurial faction and the legates decided to suspend the discussion. Thus the doctrinal debates resumed and later defined the doctrine of the Eucharist and the sacrifice of the Mass (sessions 21 and 22, 16 July and 17 September 1562).

The problem of residency remained unresolved, the debate became more heated in the fall of 1562, when, on a parallel track with this problem, there was an attempt to define the teaching on the sacrament of Holy Orders. According to the Spaniards, supported by a few Italians and by the French (who arrived under the leadership of Cardinal Charles de Guise), the *ius divinum* had to be reaffirmed not only of the obligation of residence but also of the powers of the bishop. The clash with the procurial faction, the so-called zealots, provoked the most serious crisis of the entire council. Work came to a standstill for ten months; in March 1563 Gonzaga and Seripando, overwhelmed by fatigue and tension, died. Cardinal Giovanni Morone, who was appointed by the pope to replace them, succeeded in working out a compromise; in session 23 on 14 July 1563 the wording limited itself to stating that the episcopacy was divinely instituted, without spelling out the origins of the bishops' powers, while the obligation of residence was declared to be a divine "precept" (a formula that, although it obligated bishops to reside in their dioceses, left the pope with the faculty of granting dispensations). It was at this session that the institution of seminaries for the formation of the clergy was approved. However, Morone's skill was found in the drafting of an overall blueprint for reform that represented a compromise between the requests of the bishops and the resistance of the Curia. After being debated in the summer and fall of 1563, it was approved in the last two sessions of the council: session 24 (11 November 1563), at which the sacramental character of matrimony was defined, and session 25 (3–4 December 1563), at which the teachings on purgatory, indulgences, and the veneration of the saints were defined.

The reform decrees brought forward by Morone set forth strict norms for the appointment of cardinals and bishops. They prescribed that diocesan synods be held every year and provincial councils every three years; they also mandated that the bishop make an annual visitation of his entire diocese. The contents of these decrees represented the essence of the Tridentine reform. The reform fell far short of the reform ideals that had animated the church in the first decades of the sixteenth century; the powers of the bishops remained deprived of a precise doctrinal foundation and thereby exposed to the limitations imposed by curial centralization and the exemption of religious orders. But its great merit was that it outlined the figure of the bishop as pastor, animated by the highest law of the *salus animarum* ("salvation of souls"), which was to be embodied in an exemplary manner by Carlos Borromeo in the great diocese of Milan.

Results of the Council of Trent. The monolithic image of the Council of Trent must leave room for the image of a gathering that, on account of its duration, not only involved generations that differed in their sensibilities, experiences, and cultural horizons, but also faced a whole variety of different situations. Thus, even within the council itself, there was clearly a spirited and at times harsh debate. While the Protestants were absent, various national and theological currents as well as striking differences of opinion gave rise to tensions that were difficult to resolve. The traditional opinion that pictured a gathering faithfully following the inspirations of the Holy Spirit that arrived from Rome, with the instructions of the pope carried by his legates, can be considered no more than a theme for an idealized oil painting. The approximately two hundred bishops who participated in the final period of the council faithfully represented the souls, mentalities, and theologies that existed in European Catholicism at the beginning of the second half of the sixteenth century. One of the discoveries for which we are indebted to Hubert Jedin is that the gathering at Trent was richly multifaceted, in stark contrast to the image of a drab and homogeneous assembly docile and submissive to Rome, which the popes might have preferred.

Two examples serve to illustrate this diversity. When the council was dealing with the complex and difficult issue of restoring the obligation of the bishops to reside in their dioceses, some council fathers wanted to strike at the root of the abuse of papal dispensations from this obligation by proposing that the obligation itself be declared to be a matter of "divine law" and therefore beyond dispensation by anyone. The supporters of the unconditional authority of the pope and the adversaries of reform were in agreement in their opposition to this proposal. The debate over this issue embroiled the council and threatened to derail it, such was the tenacity with which each of the two groups defended its position. In the course of the debate, the Jesuit Diego Laínez, who enjoyed prestige as the first successor to Ignatius Loyola, advanced the scholastic opinion whereby the power of each individual bishop was connected with the *potestas ordinis* ("power of the sacrament of orders"), which he receives through episcopal consecration (i.e., the sacramental realm), and with the *potestas iurisdictionis* (i.e., the realm of ecclesiastical discipline), which is granted to him by the pope. Despite the theological authority this Jesuit scholar enjoyed, however, many qualified participants in the council asserted that they were of a different opinion. These participants maintained that every bishop receives in episcopal consecration not only the power of orders but also a share in the responsibility for the guidance of the universal church. It was a subtle distinction in doctrine, but the fact that the "orders-jurisdiction" pairing did not receive formal sanction was decisive, in that four centuries later the teaching of episcopal collegiality could be proposed at the Second Vatican Council.

The second example related to the powers of the pope and the conception of the church. These were without doubt two burning issues in the debate with the Protestants. However, the council did not judge them to be ripe for definition. Indeed, the decisions of the Council of Trent do not mention the pope and his powers, nor is there any decree on the church. Again in this instance, as in other high-profile arguments, the presence of divergent orientations suggested that the council should limit its conclusions to what could be approved by all, or at least the greater majority.

At the same time, the image of the Council of Trent that long dominated historiography was that of a council that had "refounded" Catholicism at the threshold of the modern age, endowing it with a new "summa," composed of its dogmatic and reform decrees that encompassed all the relevant aspects of the faith and life of Catholics and of the church. Both for its apologists and for its detractors, the Council of Trent had quickly ended up taking on an image larger than life, endowed with a high degree of both organic unity and solidity.

The Struggle over Interpretation. How was this result that dominated Catholic life for centuries achieved? The answer comes from what occurred in the years immediately following the conclusion of the council. Between 1564 and 1580 an intense and decisive battle was waged about the council; the epicenter of this struggle was no longer Trent but Rome. It was initially waged between those who were asking Pope Pius IV to accept the decisions of the council and to promulgate them with every jot and tittle without delay, and those who, under the pretext of prudence, urged the pope to wait and proceed selectively, either omitting conciliar decisions or at least correcting them, particularly the reform decrees. This phase concluded quickly; Pius IV decided to promulgate the conciliar decrees in their entirety and without delay. This placed the papacy at the head of the movement to implement the council, confronting both the reservations of the secular powers and the obtuseness of many ecclesiastical circles. This decision, which was wise if

not prophetic, swept aside the hesitations and reservations in Rome concerning the council, but at the same time it opened a new chapter in the fight for the council. The issue was no longer whether to take a position for or against the council, but grafting it into the reality of Catholicism.

Also, two trends soon emerged. One, which quickly got the upper hand, had its center in Rome in several popes of notable stature and hinged on the centralized and uniform leadership of the Catholic revival emanating from Rome. Another trend, particularly embodied by the archbishop of Milan, Borromeo, put the emphasis on making full use of local churches and their energies in the conviction that the Council of Trent could penetrate the life of Catholicism through a vast, dynamic, and diversified movement for its implementation. These two orientations converged during the years when the young Borromeo, after leaving Rome and his uncle the pope, took up his episcopal ministry in Milan with great zeal, committing himself to the faithful and complete implementation of the decisions of Trent. This determination, while on the one side drawing to his service men who were generous and confident in the renewal of Catholicism, on the other side brought him up against opposition that grew ever harsher, from among ecclesiastics in Milan, from Spanish political authorities in Milan and in Madrid, or from the adversaries of church reform at the head of dioceses in the Milanese province of which Borromeo was the metropolitan.

The Acceptance of the Council and Its Aftermath. Adequate knowledge about the implementation of the decrees of the Council of Trent is still far from being available, but recent research has brought to light a fundamental distinction between the decisions of the Council of Trent and the line that dominated its implementation from the seventeenth to the nineteenth century, which could be called "Tridentinism." Only in light of the behind-the-scenes but decisive struggle about the council, has it been realized that the council has a historical identity all its own, which cannot be equated with the slogans that oriented its implementation in the centuries that followed. Almost imperceptibly, an interpretation of the council asserted itself in Rome that was at odds with the spirit that had animated the council and the views of the council fathers. To respond to the urgent needs of a new era, it seemed necessary to present the council and its decisions as a systematic, complete, and exhaustive response to every problem. In this perspective Rome claimed for itself the interpretation of the conciliar decrees, blocking attempts at watering them down by circles hostile to ecclesiastical reform, while at the same time refusing to recognize the need for local adaptations. This gave rise to the uniformity and passivity that characterized modern Catholicism. Only political power managed to obtain, at the price of harsh confrontation, a few mitigations that were almost always transitional. Moreover, the polemical confrontation with the Protestants on one side and rationalism on the other led to a desire for theological completeness and solidity that Trent itself had repeatedly declined to formulate. It did this not merely out of awareness of its own limitations but also because of an acute awareness of the value of freedom and the sovereignty of the word of God over and above any theological system.

It was Roberto Bellarmino who provided a systematic and full formulation to the new Catholic theology, presenting it as the coherent development, if not the transcription, of the council. Thus post-Tridentine Catholic theology was born, closing in the name of the council a large number of open questions, which at Trent itself were respected as such. This had the effect of reducing theological pluralism and promoted a tendency to confuse faith with doctrinal intransigence. Consequently it became habitual to trace theological positions that were accredited in Rome back to the Council of Trent, while minimizing any reference to the Bible. This complex phenomenon can be termed "Tridentinism" because of its reference to the Council of Trent in a way that was as ambiguous as it was jealous.

[*See also* Catholic Reformation; Papacy; *and* Roman Catholicism.]

BIBLIOGRAPHY

Primary Sources

Concilius Tridentinum: Diariorum, actorum, epistularum, tractatuum nova collectio. 13 vols. in 18. Edited by Societas Goerresiana. Fribourg, 1901–1985. Critical edition of the sources; includes the journals, the minutes, the letters, and the tracts.

Decrees of the Ecumenical Councils. Vol. 2, *Trent to the Vatican.* Original text established by Giuseppe Alberigo et al. English edition by Norman P. Tanner, London and Washington, D.C., 1990. See pp. 655–799. Edition of the texts of the conciliar decisions in the original language with facing English translation.

Gutiérrez, Constancio. *Trento: Un Concilio para la unión, 1550–1552.* 3 vols. Madrid, 1981. An important collection of Spanish sources.

Secondary Sources

Alberigo, Giuseppe. *I vescovi italiani al Concilio di Trento, 1545–1547.* Florence, 1959. Analysis of the most numerous group of members of the council.

———. "L'ecclesiologia del concilio di Trento." *Revista della storia della Chiesa in Italia* 18 (1964), 227–242. Thesis is that the Council of Trent did not formulate a Catholic teaching on the church.

———. "Vues nouvelles sur le Concile de Trente à l'occasion du centenaire." *Concilium* 1 (1965/67), 65–79. On the end of the Tridentine era in Western Christendom.

Bäumer, Remigius, ed. *Concilium Tridentinum.* Darmstadt, 1979. A collection of contributions by the major specialists on the question, with a rich bibliography on pp. 541–552.

Jedin, Hubert. *Krisis und Wendepunkt des Trienter Konzils, 1562–1563.* Würzburg, 1941. Analysis of the decisive crisis in the unfolding of the council.

———. *Das Konzil von Trient: Eine Überblick über die Erforschung seiner Geschichte.* Rome, 1948. Reconstruction of the history of the historiography concerning the Council of Trent.

———. *Geschichte des Konzils von Trient.* 4 vols. Freiburg, 1948–1975. This history, the most recent and best documented, sheds light on the inner workings of the council within its ecclesiastical and political context. Vols. 1 and 2 have been translated into English by E. Graf, Saint Louis, 1957–1960.

Lecler, Joseph, et al. *Latran et Trente.* 2 vols. Paris, 1975–1981. A synthetic presentation, based on Jedin's research.

Sarpi, Paolo. *Historia del concilio Tridentino* (1619). 3 vols. Edited by G. Gambarin. Bari, 1935. A polemical presentation of the council by the famous Venetian Servite.

Pallavicino Sforza, Pietro. *Istoria del Concilio di Trento.* 3 vols. Rome, 1666. Apologetic reply of the Jesuit scholar to Sarpi. (For more on Pallavicino, see Jedin, Hubert, *Der Quellenapparat der Konzilsgeschichte Pallavicinos,* Rome, 1940.)

Walz, Angelus. *I Domenicani al Concilio di Trento.* Rome, 1961. Analysis of the contribution of the bishops, and especially of the Dominican theologians.

GUISEPPE ALBERIGO
Translated from Italian by Robert E. Shillenn

TRIEST, Antoon (1577–1657), reforming Catholic bishop of the Spanish Netherlands. Born of a noble family in Flanders, Triest won a reputation as a model Counter-Reformation bishop through his leadership of the dioceses of Brugge (1616–1620) and Ghent (1621–1657). Guided by the famous dictum of the Council of Trent—"nulla salus extra ecclesiam"—Triest organized a campaign against the few remaining Protestants in his diocese, an effort that was bolstered on the political side by the pious archdukes Albert and Isabella.

Triest displayed especially remarkable energy and zeal as bishop of Ghent. From 1623 to 1654 he visited the roughly 150 parishes of the diocese at least once every two or three years, writing a summary of each visit. This unique document constitutes a veritable and inexhaustible gold mine. It reveals Triest's focus on the pastoral obligations and personal lives of the clergy, his tireless interviewing of secular authorities, his careful inspections of church properties, and his attention to the maintenance of good parish records. Triest also introduced efficient pastoral organization, dividing the diocese into more manageable rural deaneries, appointing diligent deans to lead them, and insisting on annual reports from each dean. Yearly he convened the deans in Ghent for discussion of pastoral care.

Triest was also known as a patron and connoisseur of art and for his liberality to the poor. Of further importance were his strict and unwavering morals and theological opinions, for these led him into the Jansenist camp and resulted in his condemnation by Rome in 1653; after several tense months, the elderly bishop capitulated and was reconciled. In any event, the diocese of Ghent experienced a deep re-Catholicization during his episcopacy, and Triest was the individual most responsible for this renewal.

BIBLIOGRAPHY

Ceyssens, Lucien. "Les dernières années de Triest." *Handelingen van de Maatschappij voor Geschiedenis en Oudheidkunde te Gent* 13 (1959), 35–51.

Cloet, Michel. "Antoon Triest, prototype van een contrareformator-ische bisschop, op bezoek in zijn Gentse diocees, 1622–1657." *Bijdragen en Mededelingen Betreffende de Geschiedenis der Nederlanden* 91 (1976), 395–405.

Cloet, Michel, ed. *Itinerarium Visitationum Antonii Triest Episcopi Gandavensis, 1623–1654.* Louvain, 1976. Over five hundred pages (260,000 words), in Latin, on Triest's view of parishes in his diocese; given the lack of detailed biographical studies of Triest, probably the single most valuable published source to date.

Schrevel, A. de. "Triest, Antoine." In *Biographie Nationale*, vol. 25, cols. 614–624. Brussels, 1930–1932.

MICHEL CLOET

Translated from Dutch by Craig Harline

TRIGLANDUS, Jacobus (Dutch, Trigland; 1583–1654), Dutch Reformed minister and professor of theology. Born in a Catholic family, Triglandus joined the Reformed church in 1603, was ordained minister 1607, and served as minister at Amsterdam from 1610 to 1634 and as professor of theology at Leiden University from 1634 until his death. During Triglandus's ministry in Amsterdam, the Reformed church of this most populous and powerful town in the Dutch Republic, with about eight ministers and a self-conscious consistory, was at the height of its influence. Until about 1620 the Arminian controversy was the center of attention; afterwards the struggle between consistory and town council was in the limelight. In the Arminian controversy the Amsterdam church was the moving spirit in the Contra-Remonstrant resistance against the Remonstrant party and the majority of the *regenten* ("town magistrates") in Holland, who supported the Remonstrants. Triglandus played a leading role in this struggle by writing against the Remonstrants and visiting, with a colleague, the churches in Holland to unite them against the Remonstrants. In 1618–1619 he attended the Synod of Dordrecht. During this period there was close cooperation between consistory and town council.

In 1622 the town council and the board of burgomasters lost their Contra-Remonstrant character. In the twenties the leading artistic circles of the town (in which nonconformist and nondenominational influences dominated), supported by members of the town government, ridiculed the consistory and its most influential members. The famous poet Joost van den Vondel and the dramatist Samuel Coster published epigrams and lampoons. The looks of Triglandus (he had a drinker's nose) made him an easy target of derision. The growing tensions between consistory and town council came to a crisis in 1629 when Triglandus's colleague Adriaan Smout preached several sermons attacking the magistrates for their tolerant attitude toward the Remonstrants. Notwithstanding the prevailing ban on Remonstrant church services, the Remonstrants had arranged them, and the magistrates refused to take measures. Smout's sermons, in which he (not for the first time in his career) launched severe expostulations against the burgomasters, resulted in disturbances. When the burgomasters banned Smout from the city, Triglandus and three colleagues made a public protest against this alleged interference in the rights of the church. However, the protest was dismissed.

Triglandus's attitude as a minister is characteristic of his stand. He was convinced of the necessity of maintaining the Reformed character of the Dutch Republic, in which the church ought to be qualified to admonish the magistrates for exceeding their authority. However, the course of events shows that soon after 1620 the church lost its grip on the higher levels of society and the magistrates.

It is not surprising that as a minister and a professor Triglandus orally and in writing attacked Catholic, Remonstrant, and Cartesian positions with the usual arguments. His work as a professor was not of outstanding importance. Of lasting value is his extensive work on the history of the Reformation in the Netherlands, the *Kerckelycke Geschiedenissen* (1650). Triglandus opposed the view taken by the Remonstrant Johannes Wtenbogaert in his *Kerckelicke Historie* (1646–1647), namely that the Remonstrant positions represented original, typical Dutch religious convictions over against Calvinism, a foreign element. Triglandus's emphasis on "Reformed religion" as the core of the Dutch Reformation movement is a legitimate correction.

BIBLIOGRAPHY

Evenhuis, R. B. *Ook dat was Amsterdam.* Vols. 1 and 2. Amsterdam, 1965 and 1967. An extensive history of the Amsterdam Reformed church until 1650.

Itterzon, Gerrit P. van. "Triglandus, Jacobus." In *Biografisch Lexicon voor de geschiedenis van het Nederlandse protestantisme*, vol. 3, pp. 355–358. Kampen, Netherlands, 1988. Excellent biographical dictionary, giving full bibliographical details.

CORNELIS AUGUSTIJN

TRITHEMIUS, Johann (1462–1516), German Benedictine humanist, historian, and monastic reformer. He was born to a family named Zeller in the town of Trittenheim (near Trier), from which he later took his Latin name according to contemporary humanist practice. Intellectually stifled at home, he fled to Trier at the age of seventeen and then to Heidelberg, where he pursued a course of humanist studies, including Greek and Hebrew, and formed friendships with distinguished German humanists, such as Rudolf Agricola and Conradus Celtis. On the way to a proper academic career, he turned to theology and, at the age of twenty, entered the Benedictine monastery at Sponheim to prepare for the priesthood.

Finding the moral and intellectual standards at the abbey in a deplorable state, the young novice set about to initiate a general reform. His devotion to learning and the monastic ideal, as well as his personal probity and all around competence, led to Trithemius's election as abbot of his house in 1483, one year after he had taken his final vows. An insatiable bibliophile, he established a library of two thousand printed books and handwritten manuscripts, transforming the abbey into a center of humanist learning. Trithemius at this time produced three works of literary history and a number of edifying tracts aimed at restoring discipline and monastic erudition to his troubled order.

Trithemius also dabbled in occult sciences, writing a cryptographic work titled *Steganographie*, which brought him under suspicion of witchcraft and was placed on the Index of Prohibited Books in 1609. The scholarly abbot was nonetheless held in high esteem in humanist circles and admired by both Emperor Maximilian I and Elector Joachim I of Brandenburg, who invited Trithemius to Berlin in 1505. During his absence the monks at Sponheim, never reconciled to the idea of strenuous learning and moral renewal, erupted in protest against their reforming abbot, and Trithemius resigned his post. In 1506 he accepted an invitation from the prince-bishop of Würzburg, Lorenz von Bibra, to head the Scottish monastery there.

Free to pursue his scholarly endeavors in tranquillity, Trithemius produced a number of historical works of dubious value. Although they reveal wide-ranging knowledge and scholarly diligence, they also betray a less than critical approach to source materials, which Trithemius was not above falsifying or even inventing to enhance the moral force of his text, as in his *Annales Hirsaugienses* (Chronicle of the Cloister of Hirsau).

BIBLIOGRAPHY

Primary Sources

Trithemius, Johann. *Opera pia et spiritualia.* Moguntia (Mainz), 1900.
———. *Steganographia.* Darmstadt, 1900.

Secondary Sources

Arnold, Klaus. *Johannes Trithemius.* Reprint, Würzburg, 1971. A well-regarded modern biography.
Avernheimer, Richard, and Frank Baron, eds. *Johannes Trithemius: Humanismus und Magie im vorreformatorischen Deutschland.* Munich, 1991.
Brann, Noel L. *The Abbot Trithemius, 1462–1516: The Renaissance of Monastic Humanism.* Leiden, 1981. A useful scholarly examination of Trithemius' life and his writings on monastic erudition and piety, with an extensive bibliography.
Gerwalin, Hans, ed. *500 Jahrfeier Johannes Trithemius.* Trittenheim a.d. Mosel, Germany, 1962.
Volk, P. "Trithemius." In *Lexicon für Theologie und Kirche*, vol. 10, pp. 366–367. Freiburg, 1965.

KARIN BRINKMANN BROWN

TROTZENDORF, Valentin (born Valentin Friedland; Lat., Trocedorfius; 1490–1556), German humanist

and Lutheran educator. Born in Troitschendorf, near Görlitz, Valentin Friedland followed humanist convention, adopting his new name when he started university studies. Trotzendorf began his education at the cloister school in Görlitz, but family finances forced him to return home, where the parish pastor tutored him until he returned to Görlitz in 1508.

After both parents died, Trotzendorf sold his modest inheritance and matriculated in 1514 at Leipzig. After receiving his B.A. in 1516, he taught Greek in Görlitz. Luther's row with Johann Tetzel drew Trotzendorf to Wittenberg in 1518. For five years he attended the lectures of Luther and Melanchthon and learned Hebrew from the Spaniard Mattheus Adrianus, a convert from Judaism. Trotzendorf lectured privately on Cicero and on the epistles of Paul.

In 1523 Trotzendorf went to teach at Zlotoryja (Goldberg), and two years later he moved to nearby Liegnitz, where, with Conrad Cordatus and the Hebraist Bernhard Ziegler he planned to establish an academy championing Lutheran theology to counter radical Schwenckfelders. The trio's plans caused Schwenckfeld's group to leave, but the academy never opened. Although Trotzendorf preferred education, more than once he found himself refereeing theological disputes because of his training and his Wittenberg connections. Unhappy with that role and the lack of progress on the Liegnitz school, Trotzendorf went to Wittenberg in 1529, where he stayed until returning to Zlotoryja in 1531. He remained its schoolmaster and rector until his death.

Trotzendorf attracted students from throughout the Holy Roman Empire, Poland, Hungary, Siebenbürgen (modern Transylvania in Romania), and the Austrian lands. The school's objectives were typical—build trust in God, lay a foundation in the liberal arts, and instill those virtues needed by responsible members of society. Trotzendorf was highly respected, and contemporaries routinely numbered him with such influential educators as Johann Sturm in Strasbourg, Michael Neander in Ilefeld, Hieronymus Wolf in Augsburg, and Georg Fabricius in Meissen.

Trotzendorf put his mark on the academic program. Grammar laid the groundwork. Terence, Plautus, Cicero, Virgil, and Ovid were read for form, though substance could hardly be overlooked. Trotzendorf included Desiderus Erasmus's colloquies and Mosellanus's exercises. In Greek instruction he used Paul's epistles and Isocrates for texts. Students studied dialectic, rhetoric, arithmetic, geometry, and music, but Trotzendorf included no Hebrew and little history. Religious instruction weighed heavily in the mix. Echoing a common pattern, beginning pupils learned Luther's Small Catechism in German, the middle group in Latin, and advanced students examined its theology. Luther formed the core, but for variety Trotzendorf supplemented the catechism with materials such as biblical pericopes. He routinely spent an hour reviewing all the previous day's lessons. Each week students wrote two compositions in prose and in verse, and they regularly argued theses in disputation, synthesizing their learning while Trotzendorf examined their progress.

Trotzendorf organized the school as a miniature republic. He put students into six organizational units, further divided into "tribes," each with a *quaestor* (investigator and disciplinarian), *ephor* (public manager), and *oeconom* (house manager). The *quaestor* made sure students did their lessons, admonished the lazy, and chose Latin authors for oral mealtime reading. The *ephor* maintained order at meals. The *oeconom* saw that all observed the bedtime schedule and kept their quarters neat.

Trotzendorf had older students teach the younger, believing one had not mastered material until one could teach others. Trotzendorf supervised instruction at the lower levels and instructed the highest himself. Students governed themselves with a consul, twelve senators, and two censors. A student court handled problems, with judges changed monthly. Behind all stood Trotzendorf as "perpetual dictator," making the system work by modeling high expectations with his own life.

In 1554 fire destroyed the city, claiming everything, including Trotzendorf's belongings and books. Trotzendorf moved the school temporarily to Liegnitz, where on 20 April 1556, while teaching on Psalm 23:4, he suffered a stroke, and died six days later.

BIBLIOGRAPHY

Primary Source

Trotzendorf, Valentin. *Rosarium scholae Trocedorffii, contextum ex rosis decerptis ex Paradiso Domini*. Wittenberg, 1565. Printed with Trotzendorf's "rose garden" of fifty Bible verses and comments done in German, Latin, Greek, and Hebrew is "Oratio de Valentino Fridlando Trocedorfio instauratore et rectore scholae Goltbergensis," a funeral oration for Trotzendorf delivered by former student Balthasar Rhau, providing much of the biography repeated through the centuries.

Secondary Sources

Bauch, Gustav. *Valentin Trotzendorf und die Goldberger Schule*. Berlin, 1921.
Hirzel, Karl. "Trotzendorf." In *Encyklopädie des gesammten Erziehungs- und Unterrichtswesens*, edited by Karl Adolf Schmid, vol. 9, pp. 491–502. Gotha, 1873. Concise, detailed summary of Trotzendorf's life and educational approach.
Mertz, Georg. *Das Schulwesen der deutschen Reformation im 16. Jahrhundert*. Heidelberg, 1902. Mertz weaves Trotzendorf into topical chapters comparing types of schools, subjects taught, materials used, methods, and teachers. Trotzendorf's bibliography appears on pp. 152–153.
Schmid, Karl Adolf, ed. *Geschichte der Erziehung vom Anfang an bis auf unsere Zeit* (1859). Reprint, Aalen, 1970. See vol. 2, pt. 2, for Georg Schmidt's discussion of Trotzendorf, Sturm, Neander, and Wolf.
Vormbaum, Reinhold. *Die evangelischen Schulordnung*. Gütersloh, 1860. See vol. 1, pp. 53ff., regarding Trotzendorf's efforts at the Goldberg school.

ROBERT ROSIN

TRUBER, Primus (1508–1586), reformer among South Slavs and humanist author. Born in Rascica, near Laibach (Ljubljana, Slovenia), he was a son of the miller Michael Truber. He attended Latin schools in Salzburg and Trieste and learned German, Italian, and some Croatian. Through Bishop Peter Bonomo in Trieste he became acquainted with the ideas of Desiderius Erasmus of Rotterdam. After his training for the priesthood he went to Laibach as a Slovenian preacher at the cathedral, but, because of the reform content of his sermons, he had to flee to Trieste. There he read texts by Heinrich Bullinger and John Calvin. When Bonomo sent him to Laibach again to be dean of the cathedral, he became involved in a circle of reformers. After 1547 he was persecuted and sought refuge with Veit Dietrich in Nuremberg. He was given a position preaching at an early service in Rothenburg ob der Tauber. There he conceived the idea of proclaiming the Protestant message in printed Slovenian. "The great love and worship that I harbor for you (my countrymen), and the grace given to me by God, my priesthood, this calling and God's commandment force and urge me to do this," Truber later wrote.

The first book he issued in Slovenian was *Catechismus in der Windischenn Sprach* (Catechism in the Windisch Language), with Bible verses, prayers, a litany, hymns, and a sermon, "On the Faith," by Matthias Flacius Illyricus. Truber thus established a basis for Protestant services in the Slovenian language. He became a reformer and creator of the written language of the Slovenian people. His work was well received, and he was urged to translate the entire Bible into Slovenian and Croatian. Jakob Andreae and even Duke Christoph of Württemberg showed an interest in Truber's translations. With the financial help of the province of Carniola (Krain), the nine-hundred-page work, *First Part of the New Testament* (1557), was completed.

His friends in Laibach appointed him superintendent to help establish the nascent Protestant church there. He traveled back and forth between Laibach and Urach, where, with the help of Hans Ungnad von Sonnegg, a Bible institute had been founded to supervise the printing of Slovenian, Croatian, and Serbian translations. He added a preface in German to most of these translations to enlist interest and support from German towns and princes. As a result of his various occupations—superintendent, teacher, pastor, preacher, author, and translator—Truber required twenty years to finish the entire New Testament. He translated the Psalter, wrote Slovenian hymns, and prepared a collection of rules governing church life, several catechisms, and more than twenty prefaces containing valuable information on the situation in southeastern Europe under the threat of a Turkish attack.

Truber was enthusiastic about his mission of bringing the Protestant message to the peoples of Slovenia and Croatia and was convinced that the Croatian texts would help convert even the Byzantine Turks to the gospel. He has held a position of honor in the history of the European Reformation because his Protestant mission linked, at least temporarily, the peoples of Slovenia and Croatia to European intellectual history. He died on 28 June 1586 in Derendingen, near Tübingen.

BIBLIOGRAPHY

Mirko, Rupel. *Primus Truber*. Revised and translated into German by Balduin Saria. Munich, 1965.
Truber, Primus. *Primus Trubers Briefe, mit den dazu gehörigen Schriftstücken*. Edited by Theodor Elze. Tübingen, 1897.

OSKAR SAKRAUSKY
Translated from German by Wolfgang Katenz

TRUCHSESS, Georg von Waldburg

TRUCHSESS, Georg von Waldburg (also Jörg; Bauernjörg; 1488–1531), German military commander and administrator. Truchsess is best known for his role as commander of the army of the Swabian League that defeated the various peasant armies during the Peasants' War of 1525. Born into an old Swabian noble family, Truchsess had a long and successful career as a military officer and administrator. Between 1499 and 1531 he served in succession (and sometimes simultaneously) the dukes of Württemberg, the dukes of Bavaria, the Swabian League, and the emperor. He participated in the Swabian League's defeat of Duke Ulrich of Württemberg (1519), commanded the league's troops against the Franconian knights (1523) and against Duke Ulrich again in 1524, and fought the Turks in Hungary (1530).

During the Peasants' War Truchsess successfully followed a strategy of divide and conquer. Early in 1525 he cautiously moved his relatively small force against the various peasant armies. Badly outnumbered in upper Swabia, Truchsess concluded the Treaty of Weingarten in April, giving the largest and best-equipped peasant army favorable terms in exchange for disbanding. Freed of this threat, Truchsess's troops defeated one peasant army at Böblingen in Württemberg (12 May), and several other groups in Franconia in June. Despite a reputation as a lenient landlord and administrator, Truchsess and his army brutally suppressed the rebel peasants, executing the leaders, massacring the fleeing peasants after the so-called battles, and on several occasions burning villages and towns. Despite these severe measures, the league criticized him several times for being overly lenient.

Between 1525 and 1529 Truchsess served the emperor as governor (*Statthalter*) of Württemberg, where he focused his efforts on pacifying the peasants and defending the duchy against Ulrich's further attempts to recapture it. There is little indication of his personal religious views, but as the emperor's representative at the imperial diet of 1530,

he appealed for a religious compromise between Catholics and Protestants.

Truchsess was one of the most successful aristocratic freelance warriors and administrators of early sixteenth-century Germany. Truchsess adroitly profited from his activities, especially in imperial service, and greatly enhanced his family's wealth and position in Swabia by bringing several important estates and titles into the family's possession.

BIBLIOGRAPHY

Blickle, Peter. *The Revolution of 1525: The German Peasants' War from a New Perspective*. Translated by Thomas A. Brady, Jr., and H. C. Erik Midelfort. Reprint, Baltimore, 1985. See especially pp. xiii–xxiii. Clear survey of the events of the Peasants' War of 1525.
Franz, Günther. *Der deutsche Bauernkrieg*. 12th ed. Darmstadt, 1984. See especially pp. 132–135 and 279–283.

MARC R. FORSTER

TSCHERNEMBL, George Erasmus von

TSCHERNEMBL, George Erasmus von (1567–1626), Austrian Calvinist nobleman. He was born on 26 January 1567 in Upper Austria where his grandfather, originally from Carniola (Krain), had settled and where his father, Hans, had acquired the castle and estates of Schwertberg. In November 1580, after initial schooling at home, he entered the academy at Altdorf, where his teachers included Calvinist professors. His allegiance to Calvinist views was furthered strengthened by Paul Melissus (Schede), who accompanied Tschernembl on his knightly grand tour, which included stays in London, Paris, and Geneva. By 1588 he was in northern Italy, where he studied law, and in 1591 he was in Speyer. During the 1590s Tschernembl opposed the use of force by peasant farmers in Upper Austria during their revolts (1595, 1597), but he also called for resolving their grievances.

At the same time, together with his fellow Calvinist Gotthard Starhemberg, he attempted to resist the Counter-Reformation activities of Rudolf II, Matthias, and Melchior Khlesl when Hans Jacob Löbl, the royal commander, was ordered to implement edicts restoring Protestant churches to the Catholic clergy. In 1600 Tschernembl was in Prague with a delegation of the nobility to plead with the emperor for recognition of their rights as nobles to freedom of worship. Largely owing to his efforts, evangelical services were again introduced. In February 1601 a Protestant service was even held in the house of the estates in Linz. The court in Prague and Archduke Matthias, however, viewed this as a revolutionary act and responded with a sharp decree condemning it. In August Rudolf issued a decree against the Protestants, while eight members of the estates, including Tschernembl, were ordered to Vienna by Matthias to explain their actions. They were held there as virtual captives until they agreed to implement the royal edicts.

Upon returning home and after the Bocskay revolt (1604–1606) had obtained religious freedom for Protestants in Hungary, Tschernembl and Bernard of Puchheim resumed efforts to obtain recognition for the Protestants in Upper and Lower Austria and supported the efforts of the League of Horn. They sought support from the Moravian noble Karl Žerotin, the Czech Václav Budovec of Budov, and the Hungarian George Thurzo, as well as Christian of Anhalt. As a result of their concerted action and also because of their support of Matthias in his struggle with his brother Rudolf, the Lower Austrian estates recognized their privileges in October 1608. On 19 March 1609 Matthias issued a "Capitulation," which granted Protestant nobles the privilege of sponsoring Protestant worship services. One year later, on 3 March, Matthias extended this privilege to the cities, but, with the Defenestration of Prague and the outbreak of the Thirty Years' War, political and religious differences among the Protestant nobles ultimately led to the decline of Protestantism in Austria above and below the Enns River. Tschernembl, who had consistently sought to maintain the unity of the Reformation movement in the Austrian lands and who helped establish a confederation of the Bohemian and Upper Austrian estates, left Austria and spent his final years in Geneva, where he died on 18 November 1626.

BIBLIOGRAPHY

Sturmberger, Hans. *Georg Erasmus Tschernembl.* Graz, 1953.

DAVID P. DANIEL

wives were Anne Boleyn (executed 1536), Jane Seymour (d. 1537), Anne of Cleves (divorced 1540), Catherine Howard (executed 1542), and Catherine Parr (d. 1548).

On Henry VIII's death the throne passed to his only son, born to Jane Seymour in 1537, who became Edward VI. Protestant reforms were introduced rapidly during Edward's short reign. Following his death in 1553 an attempt was made to crown Lady Jane Grey, a distant relative, but it failed, and Mary Tudor, the daughter of Henry VIII and Catherine of Aragon, became queen. Mary wed Philip II of Spain but had no descendants; her attempt to restore Catholicism died with her in 1558. Anne Boleyn's daughter Elizabeth was the last of the Tudors. She was in part responsible for the moderate Elizabethan Settlement. Elizabeth never married, and the Tudor line ended at her death in 1603. She was succeeded by James VI of Scotland, the founder of the Stuart dynasty in England (1603–1714), whose ancestry could be traced to the marriage between Henry VII's daughter Margaret and James IV of Scotland.

BIBLIOGRAPHY

Cannon, John, and Ralph Griffiths. *The Oxford Illustrated History of the British Monarchy.* Oxford, 1988. Includes genealogical tables and portraits.
Elton, G. R. *England under the Tudors.* 3d ed. London, 1991.
Guy, John. *Tudor England.* Oxford, 1988. Tudor titles listed provide standard accounts of the period.
Williams, Penry. *The Tudor Regime.* Oxford, 1979.

STANFORD E. LEHMBERG

TUDOR, HOUSE OF. The Tudor dynasty ruled England from 1485 to 1603. The first Tudor monarch, Henry VII (1485–1509), acquired the crown when he defeated Richard III in the Battle of Bosworth Field on 22 August 1485. This engagement, in which Richard was killed, ended the Wars of the Roses, a dynastic conflict between two rival branches of the royal family, the Lancastrians and Yorkists. Richard was the last of the Yorkist kings, while Henry claimed descent from the Lancastrians: his grandmother, the French princess Katherine, had been the wife of Henry V before marrying Owen Tudor, and his mother, Lady Margaret Beaufort, was a descendant of John of Gaunt, the duke of Lancaster. The Tudors themselves traced their ancestry to Welsh gentry.

Henry VII married Elizabeth of York, the niece of Richard III, thus symbolically uniting the red rose of Lancaster and the white rose of York. Henry's older son, Prince Arthur, died in 1502 shortly after his marriage to the Spanish princess Catherine of Aragon, so the throne passed to Henry VIII (r. 1509–1547). Henry then married Catherine; their divorce (1533) precipitated England's break with the papacy and the beginning of the English Reformation. Henry's later

TUNSTALL, Cuthbert (1474–1559), Henrician and Marian bishop and religious moderate. Educated at Oxford and Cambridge, Tunstall studied law at Padua from 1499 to 1505. His career began by 1509 as chancellor to William Warham, archbishop of Canterbury, and quickly Tunstall also became a diplomat (first mission, 1515). Rewarded with the mastership of the rolls, Tunstall held that office until 1522, when he became bishop of London. His mathematical treatise, *De arte supputandi*, appeared in the same year. In 1523 he was made lord privy seal and opened Parliament with a classic oration on law and the body politic. During his tenure in London Tunstall was heavily involved in the first efforts to deal with heresy, including the campaign to buy up all copies of William Tyndale's works. Appointed a counsellor to Catherine of Aragon in 1529, Tunstall staunchly opposed both Henry VIII's divorce and royal supremacy over the church.

In 1530 Tunstall was transferred to Durham, probably to get him away from the center of power; he continued to spearhead opposition until 1535. For most of the rest of Henry's reign Tunstall was lord president of the council in the north, despite having played an equivocal role during the Pilgrimage of Grace (1536). Although Tunstall originally belonged to King Edward VI's inner circle, in 1552 he was deprived of this position by John Dudley, duke of Northumberland. A year later Mary Tudor restored Tunstall to Durham, where he once more played a moderating role in a new campaign against heresy. Tunstall died in Matthew Parker's custody shortly after Elizabeth I's accession.

Once regarded as the archetype of a Henrician "trimmer," Tunstall has come to be seen as a humanist politician who put loyalty to prince above other considerations. In theology Tunstall was a moderate, arguing in favor of the real presence, while maintaining that it was pointless to dispute its mechanism. Tunstall's library—a remarkably catholic collection—confirms the judgment that he put a high premium on both learning and intellectual and religious modesty.

BIBLIOGRAPHY

Primary Source

Tunstall, Cuthbert. *Certain Godly and Devout Prayers.* London, 1925.

Secondary Sources

Bartlett, Kenneth R., and Wyman Herendeen. "The Library of Cuthbert Tunstall, Bishop of Durham. BL Add. 40,676." *Proceedings of the Bibliographical Society of America* 85 (1991), 235–296.

Sturge, Charles. *Cuthbert Tunstall: Churchman, Scholar, Statesman, Administrator.* London, 1938. Standard, if cut-and-dried, life.

Thomas, Morley. "Tunstall: Trimmer or Martyr?" *Journal of Ecclesiastical History* 24 (1973), 337–355. Revisionist essay, which may over-emphasize Tunstall's claims to sanctity.

THOMAS F. MAYER

TURKS. *See* Ottoman Empire.

TURMAIR, Johann. *See* Aventinus, Johannes.

TWELVE ARTICLES. The Twelve Articles first appeared as a pamphlet under the title *Dye Grundtlichen vnd rechten haupt Artickel, aller Bauerschafft vnnd Hyndersessen der Gaistlichen vnd Weltlichen oberkayten, von wölchen sy sich beschwert vermainen* (The Principal Basic and Just Articles of All the Peasants, about the Difficulties with the Ecclesiastical and the Secular Authorities by Whom They See Themselves Burdened) at the market in Ulm in March 1525. They take their name from the number of articles (11 and a concluding article) and were so designated by contemporaries. At times, however, they were also called the "Swabian" or "Black Forest" articles, which indicate their origin in south Germany.

The Twelve Articles must be considered the manifesto of the Peasants' War of 1525. In just two months the pamphlet underwent twenty-eight printings. It served—with the exception of the Tirol and Salzburg—in almost all revolutionary areas (Württemberg, Alsace, the Black Forest, the upper Rhein, the diocese of Speyer, the archbishopric of Mainz, Franconia and Thuringia, and partially also Switzerland) as the basis of the peasant demands. At times the Twelve Articles were slightly rewritten; often they were supplemented with regional demands. In Franconia they were presented as the so-called Amorbach Declaration in the form of a mandate by which the nobility and the ecclesiastical princes had to agree, as far as they could be forced to do so by the rebels, to join the movement. Their acceptance by the regent of the archbishopric and the electorate of Mainz, the most important territory in the empire, in the so-called Miltenberg Treaty was sensational.

The Twelve Articles were closely connected to the Reformation. Several theologians gave their opinions of them. Above all, Martin Luther's rejection of them caused lively reactions among his contemporaries. To the extent that negotiations were carried out after the defeat of the peasants, the Twelve Articles also served often as a basis for negotiation (e.g., the Treaty of Ortenau and the treaty with the peasants of the Markgräfler area); even the imperial Diet of Speyer dealt with them in 1526.

The sweeping effect of the articles can be explained by the fact that on the one hand they presented the demands of the peasants in a comparatively abstract but rhetorically rigorous fashion so that they were understood everywhere—notwithstanding their regional origin—while on the other hand they offered, with the gospel as legitimation, a new legal basis for the formation of the relationship between peasant and lord. The Twelve Articles consisted of the following demands. (1) The community must have the right to elect and dismiss clergy, because only in this way can the proclamation of the word of God necessary for salvation be assured. (2) The small tithe (from fruits, vegetables, etc.) is to be abolished; the large tithe (essentially grains) is to be administered by the community for the maintenance of the clergy, for the poor, and for taxes for defense. Insofar as the owners of the tithes can document that they have purchased them legally from the community, they are to be compensated accordingly; if not, the tithe is to be rescinded without compensation for the good of the community. (3) Serfdom is to be abolished, even though the lord's authority is expressly not to be eliminated. (4) Free hunting and fishing are demanded, particularly with concern for the enormous damage done by game. The owners of fishing rights, as far as they can document the acquisition—much like the provision for the large tithe—will be compensated; otherwise, the community will take over the fishing rights. (5) Forests and woodlands will be returned—again, analogous to the provisions of the large tithe and the fishing rights—to the communities and administered by communal forest officials, so that the peasants are properly supplied with free wood for burning and for construction. (6) Services to the lords must be reduced to a tolerable level according to past custom. (7) The determinations of the bills of enfeoffment with regard to labor must be strictly adhered to so that the peasants can properly manage their property and earn a reasonable return. Services for the lords will be performed for compensation when farm duties permit. (8) Since farms can no longer provide tax levys, they must be reevaluated by honorable people according to their productivity. (9) The penalities for punishable crimes must not be increased and arbitrarily passed, but set according to the traditional, written statutes. (10) Communal fields and arable lands will be claimed by the communities in accordance with the provision for tithes, fisheries, and forests. (11) "Death tax" on inheritance must be abolished since it is an unjust burden on the heirs.

The explosiveness of the Twelve Articles found particular expression in the last article: The peasants stated they were ready to submit all the articles to a test of compatibility with scripture. Thus, the gospel became the norm for all the articles. Appropriately, the opinions of theologians were sought, and a list, headed by Luther and followed by all other prominent reformers, was compiled. But the revolutionary demand lay in the insistence on the biblical principle: if the scriptures justified further demands, the peasants retained the right to assert them later.

The revolutionary explosiveness of the Twelve Articles and the entire Peasants' War lay in the change of legitimization from the "old law" and "tradition" to the "gospel" and the so-called divine law. The gospel became the legal norm and appropriately repudiated older legal norms: although it was customary that peasants could not hunt, this custom was not in accordance with "God's word"; to be sure, labor should be measured as was customary earlier, but only insofar as this was in agreement with "God's word"; although the death tax was customary, it was "against God." Finally, it is obvious that the most radical demands (for the election of ministers by the community and the abolition of serfdom) could not have been made without a new principle of legitimization. The election of ministers was necessary to assure the salvation of souls; serfdom had to be abolished because Christ had freed everyone by his redeeming death on the cross.

The Twelve Articles appeared anonymously. This gave rise to much speculation among contemporaries and started lively controversies among scholars. As a result of subsequent research, the following may be said. The Twelve Articles were possibly discussed with the *Bundesordnung* of the Christian assembly in Memmingen in Upper Swabia. The deliberations were probably completed on 6 or 7 March 1525 and (perhaps a week later) ratified and sent to Augsburg for printing. The specific demands are closely related to south German, especially Upper Swabian, conditions. It is striking that the peasants of the villages belonging to the imperial city of Memmingen had presented virtually the same complaints to the Memmingen city council only a few days earlier. But some clues also point to the Upper Rhein region, and it is impossible to completely rule out the possibility that the draft of the Twelve Articles and of the *Bundesordnung* were composed there. The most certain conclusion about the authorship seems to be, although definite proof is lacking, that the preacher at Saint Martin's in Memmingen, Christoph Schappeler, who was close to Zwingli, and the scribe of the peasants of Baltringen, Sebastian Lotzer, who worked as a journeyman furrier in Memmingen, contributed to the theological-evangelical basis of the articles.

[*See also* Müntzer, Thomas; *and* Peasants' War.]

BIBLIOGRAPHY

Blickle, Peter. *Die Revolution von 1525.* Munich, 1975.
———. "Nochmals zur Entstehung der Zwölf Artikel im Bauernkrieg." In *Bauer, Reich und Reformation: Festschrift für Günther Franz*, edited by Peter Blickle, pp. 286–308. Stuttgart, 1982.
———. "Memmingen: Ein Zentrum der Reformation." In *Memmingen: Geschichte der Stadt*, pp. 9–73. Memmingen, 1995.
Franz, Günther. *Der deutsche Bauernkrieg.* Munich, 1933.
———. "Die Entstehung der 'Zwölf Artikel' der deutschen Bauernschaft." *Archiv für Reformationsgeschichte* 36 (1939), 195–213.

PETER BLICKLE
Translated from German by Walter D. Morris

TWO KINGDOMS. According to the medieval teaching of the two kingdoms, or swords, exemplified by Pope Boniface in the bull *Unam Sanctum* of 1302, both the spiritual and secular kingdoms are in the hands of the pope, who has turned the secular jurisdiction over to secular authority. By contrast, in his tract *An den christlichen Adel deutscher Nation von des christlichen Standes Besserung* (To the Christian Nobility of the German Nation concerning the Improvement of the Christian Estate; 1520), Luther emphasized, as did already Marsilius of Padua in his *Defensor pacis* (1324) and William of Ockham in his tract *De imperatorum et pontificum potestate* (Concerning the Power of Emperor and Pope; 1347), the freedom of secular authority from ecclesiastical authority. At the same time Luther appropriated secular authority for the necessary reform of the church. This appropriation could not be claimed by secular authority as such, but only insofar as the holders of secular authority were baptized Christians and acted in lieu of the bishops who failed to undertake the reform of the church.

Luther specifically reflected on the function and distinction of both secular and spiritual authority in his sermons of October 1522 and in his tract *Von weltlicher Obrigkeit, wie weit man ihr Gehorsam schuldig sei* (Concerning Secular Government, How It Is to Be Obeyed; 1523). The immediate cause of this tract was a mandate of the Bavarian dukes, Elector Joachim I of Brandenburg and Duke Georg of Saxony, which prohibited the distribution of Luther's translation of the New Testament of 1522. That prohibition prompted Luther to ask about the function of the two regiments and, at the same time, to reflect on their distinction. In his tract on secular government of 1523, Luther based the secular law, that is, the power of the sword, on *Romans* 13:1–2 and *1 Peter* 2:13–14. Secular government and its responsibility to look after public peace and security and to uphold justice was a theologically legitimate office, instituted by God. The function of government is to punish evildoers and to protect the pious. In carrying out this function government serves God in this world, or rather through government God exercises his rule to maintain order in the world. While secular government is concerned about the maintenance of peace and the punishment of the evildoers with the sword, it is the task of the spiritual government to enhance faith through the preaching of the gospel, to establish the rule of God in the hearts and consciences of people, and to proclaim the eschatological salvation of all people. In view of this distinction of the two regiments of God, secular government has its limitation in God's spiritual rule over the souls and consciences of men and women. Even heresy must be fought spiritually with the word of God and not with external force. Luther later allowed that heresy might be suppressed with political force, but only when such heresy threatened the peace of a city or a territory.

Luther's distinction of the two kingdoms depended on Augustine, but Luther understood, against the background of the Corpus Christianum, the secular realm positively as legitimized by God's ordinance. As did Augustine, Luther distinguished the two kingdoms in terms of their members. Christians belong to both kingdoms, unbelievers only to the kingdom of this world. It is not appropriate to understand Luther's teaching of the two kingdoms as a functional distinction of the two rules, or regiments, of God. In describing the relationship of the secular and the Christian community, Luther used alternately the terms "rule" (*regnum*) and "regiment" (*regimen*) to describe the togetherness of realm and manner of rule. Insofar as he included in the notion of the kingdom of God "all true believers in Christ and under Christ," the biblical concept of the kingdom of God was expressed, which meant God's eschatological rule over Christendom that can be recognized only in faith. Accordingly, even the kingdom of this world will be recognized only in its divinely ordained limitation by faith through the preaching of the gospel. Secular government constantly threatens to transgress this limitation by striving for totalitarian control. For that reason it can be perverted to the kingdom of the devil (*regnum diaboli*).

The proclamation of the gospel must do away with the constant confusion of the two regiments and must express their divinely ordained relationship. If the two regiments are properly distinguished on the basis of the gospel, God is seen to rule through both regiments, externally and inwardly, in a secular and a spiritual manner. While the unbelievers belong only to the kingdom of this world, Christians belong to both kingdoms. They are subject to both secular law (*Rom.* 13:1–2) and the will of Christ as expressed in the Sermon on the Mount (*Mt.* 5:39). This tension between secular law and the law of Christ in the Sermon on the Mount must not be resolved, however, as in the medieval ethic that confined the secular law to the laity and the Sermon on the Mount as evangelical counsel only for those who wished to be perfect (monks). Neither must the tension be resolved along the lines of the radical reformers who cited the Sermon on the Mount in order to reject governmental offices. According to Luther a Christian has the freedom in the kingdom of Christ to renounce the use of force and yet at the same time the mandate to exercise governmental authority in order to preserve law and peace of the neighbor.

The final section of Luther's tract on government offered a series of counsels for rulers, in which the Christian's special duty to exercise governmental offices was affirmed, for only a Christian will do so trusting in God, independently and unselfishly, in the interest of the neighbor. At the same time the Christian manifests equity (*aequitas*) and points to the relativity of all law in relationship to reason and love. Accordingly, the Christian subsumes his or her understanding of secular government in the judgment of love and natural law that is fulfilled in love. The Christian who exercises secular authority according to reason will recognize the dependence of the written law on reason. A Christian is subject to secular authority, which one is to obey even though obedience has limits in God's commandment whenever government acts unjustly. The individual Christian may not resist authority with force but only verbally by naming the specific injustice.

In the 1530s Luther was prepared to supplement this notion of passive resistance with a notion of a right of resistance of the hereditary authority of the territorial rulers against the elected emperor if the latter (as in the religious controversy) oversteps his authority. Luther's teaching of the two regiments or kingdoms is connected with the concept of the three estates, *ecclesia*, *oeconomia*, and *politia*. Luther derived this concept from the medieval catechetical tradition and from late medieval Aristotelian moral philosophy. The historical spheres of human endeavor are determined by the three estates of "priest, marriage, and secular government." *Ecclesia* and *oeconomia* were instituted in creation as divine ordination; after the Fall *politia* emerged from *oeconomia* as a divine order necessary for the curtailment of evil.

Much like Luther, Philipp Melanchthon distinguished two kingdoms or regiments of God in his *Loci communes* of 1521 in the section "De magistratibus" (Concerning the Magistracy) and in his *Loci praecipui theologici* of 1559, in the section "De magistratibus civilibus et dignitate rerum politicarum" (Concerning the Civil Authorities and the Dignity of Politics). In contrast to Luther, Melanchthon established the legitimacy of God's secular regiment from natural law. In article 28 of the Augsburg Confession, Melanchthon distinguished the two regiments of God: "Therefore, the two regiments, the spiritual and the secular, must not be mixed and thrown together. For the spiritual authority has the mandate to preach the gospel and to distribute the sacrament. It is not to pursue alien works. It must not crown kings or remove them, must not suspend or violate secular law and obedience to government. . . . Therefore, the episcopal office must according to divine law, preach the gospel, forgive sins, judge all teaching and reject all teachings contrary to the gospel, and remove the godless, whose godless doing is manifest, from the Christian community but without human power solely through the word of God."

Zwingli. The formulation of Zwingli's teaching concerning the two kingdoms begins with the reality that Zwingli developed his political ethics in what was a formerly free imperial city and a city republic. The city council in Zurich, consisting of the Large and the Small Councils, was responsible for civic affairs. This included jurisdiction over the introduction of the Reformation in Zurich and responsibility for the external religious tranquility in the city. The civic and the Christian community are so closely connected that the Holy Spirit, which focuses on the ethical standards of Christians, is relevant also for political ethics. The renewal of the church leads automatically to a renewal of the civic community, noted by Zwingli in his *Eine göttliche Vermahnung* (A Divine Admonition), *Von göttlicher und menschlicher Gerechtigkeit* (Concerning Divine and Human Righteousness), *Eine treue und ernstliche Vermahnung an die Eidgenossen* (A Faithful and Serious Admonition to the Swiss), as well as his *Wer Ursach gebe zu Aufruhr* (Whoever Causes Insurrection). The boundaries between the civic and the Christian community are fluid. From an ethical perspective, the Christian city is a Christian congregation.

At the same time Zwingli did not simply mix the realms of state and church. When during the second Zurich Disputation of 1523 the Zurich radicals—that is, the subsequent Anabaptists—demanded the keeping of the Sermon on the Mount and the abolition of the tithe even in the body politic, Zwingli preached his sermon "Über die göttliche und menschliche Gerechtigkeit" (Concerning Divine and Human Righteousness), where he distinguished, as did Luther, the realms of church and state. Human righteousness emanates from the will of God, who ordained government in order to maintain this righteousness. Measured by the righteousness of God that is revealed in Christ, however, human righteousness is "a poor and miserable righteousness"; it is only a shadow of divine righteousness. Human righteousness is based on the natural moral law, the Decalogue, and at best gives to each one's own (*suum cuique*). By contrast, divine righteousness freely gives what humans cannot earn

on their own. Soteriologically, human righteousness is, therefore, of lower rank compared with the righteousness of faith. Ethically and morally, however, it has the task to resist evil and to further, as much as possible, human community. God prevents chaos through his moral law and human government. Zwingli knew of a right of resistance of those responsible in state and church, but he developed it in a careful delineation of authority. His struggle with the opponents of the Reformation in Zurich (choirmasters and Anabaptists) strengthened the church-state character of the Zurich church. After 1526 one can discern in Zwingli, according to Farner, the development of the concept of a "prophetic theocracy." The religious community and the city-state became increasingly a single unity. In 1527 a synod convened in Zurich composed of city council members and clergy to monitor proper teaching and morality in the city.

Calvin. As in the city republic of Zurich, the city council of the city republic of Geneva claimed authority for the external religious peace in the city. By the same token, Calvin was even more strongly concerned than Zwingli to see church discipline as a task of the congregation. Civic government and the church are essentially not in tension but complement one another. According to Calvin, a dual regiment of God prevails among humans, namely, the *regimen spirituale* and the *regimen civile*. Calvin did not take over the Augustinian dualism of two kingdoms. Rather, he spoke of two regiments that rule over humans spiritually and politically. Accordingly, Calvin placed alongside the *regnum Christi* ("reign of Christ") or the *regnum coeleste* ("reign of heaven"), the *ordinatio civilis* ("civic ordination") or the *politiae ratio* ("political manner") and distinguished the rule of Jesus Christ, on the one hand, and the civic political order, on the other. Each has different tasks. Christ's spiritual regiment is concerned to instruct consciences in piety and in the adoration of God, while the task of civic government is to demand the fulfillment of civic duties. According to Calvin, both regiments must be considered *sui generis*. The spiritual regiment does not dissolve the civic order, even as conversely the civic law must not rule over consciences. "Both regiments in no way contradict one another." According to *Romans* 13:1, government has a function legitimized by God, namely, to care for peace and law and to "cultivate external worship, protect it, and to defend the wholesome teaching of piety and the good estate of the church." Such care for external piety included, according to valid heresy laws, also the persecution of antitrinitarians and Anabaptists. The trial against the antitrinitarian Michael Servetus was not only prompted by Calvin but was also the application of heresy law in a city republic with a medieval constitution. In case the state transgressed its proper competencies, Calvin argued for a right of resistance against tyrants. However, this right of resistance is legally regulated and does not apply to individuals, who only have a passive right of resistance and are to implore God for help. The so-called lower authorities—specifically the "lower authorities" in France—have an active right of resistance and are entitled to resist royal injustice. Collectively, church and state form the *externa media vel adminicula* ("fundamental supports") "with which God in Christ invites us to live in community and retains us in it."

The Radical Reformation. While Luther, Zwingli, and Calvin emphasized, despite individual differences, a functional juxtaposition of the two regiments, some representatives of the radical wing of the Reformation held to extremist positions that mixed the two regiments, as in the case of Thomas Müntzer or the radical Anabaptist rule in Münster in 1535, or separated them, as was the case among some groupings of the peaceful Anabaptists. By taking the Sermon on the Mount literally, they rejected all claims of governmental authority. Müntzer's mystical theology of the spirit initially exhibited a preference for a biblicistic lay piety in contrast to the clerical rule of the established church. In Bohemia, Müntzer evidently encountered the traditions of the Taborites, which he connected with his mystical conception of a Spirit-filled chiliastic church of the truly elect of God.

The destruction of a chapel near Mallerbach outside Allstedt in March 1524 by supporters of Müntzer expressed a more pointed politicization of Müntzer's theology. He established a secret "league" whose members vowed to obey the gospel, not to pay monks and nuns the tithe, and, in fact, to force them to move away. Müntzer wrote Duke John of Saxony, who had sought to hold Müntzer responsible for the destruction of the Mallerbach chapel: "We know through the testimony of the holy apostle Paul (*Rom.* 13:4) that Your Grace has received the sword in order to revenge the evildoers and godless and to the honor and protection of the pious" (Müntzer, p. 405). Müntzer's Allstedt league soon had some five hundred members. When electoral Prince John Frederick had Müntzer preach in the castle of Allstedt on 13 July 1525, Müntzer challenged the Saxon elector in his "Fürstenpredigt" (Sermon before the Princes) to establish a church of the elect with the sword. "Therefore, you precious rulers of Saxony, boldly step onto the cornerstone" (Müntzer, p. 259). "If you are true rulers you must pull out the rule at its roots as Christ has commanded. Separate his enemies from the elect, for you are the mediator for that purpose" (Müntzer, p. 259). The challenge of the Wittenberg theologians to accommodate the weak in faith must not be heeded. If the rulers do not pursue the godless by force, God will take their futile sword from them. In his sermon Müntzer hinted to whom he might also appeal, namely, to the poor laity and the peasants: they see the approaching avalanche far more clearly than do the princes. Müntzer left Allstedt on 8 August 1524, moved first to Mülhausen and then proceeded to South Germany, where he joined the uprising of the peasants. In March 1525 he returned to Mülhausen and joined the insurrection in Thuringia. He understood himself as God's servant against the godless, smiting them with the sword of Gideon. In the peasant agitation he saw God at work in establishing the rule of his elect.

On 15 May 1525 disaster struck at Frankenhausen. Müntzer fled and was beheaded on 27 May 1525. In his *Sendbrief* (Missive concerning the Harsh Pamphlet against the Peasants) of 1525, Luther condemned Müntzer's apocalyptic chiliasm as a confusion of the two kingdoms.

The Anabaptist movement, which had its origin in 1525, was characterized by a far-reaching spectrum ranging from the refusal to participate in government, to the reception of Lutheran notions, to the violent chiliastic apocalyptic theories of the Anabaptists at Münster in 1535. In Zurich the anticlericalism of the radical Anabaptists encountered the decisive resistance of the city council, and the Anabaptists were eliminated from active participation in the introduction of the Reformation in the city. This triggered dissent from government and a fundamental re-evaluation of the governmental office.

While Balthasar Hubmaier maintained the basic notions of Luther's two-kingdom theory, the Swiss Brethren agreed in Schleitheim in 1527 on the principle that "the sword is an order of God outside the perfection of Christ" (Fast, p. 66). According to Hans-Jürgen Goertz the following resolutions were reached in Schleitheim: government is ordained by God to punish the evildoers and to protect the pious; even though the existence of government is based on a divine mandate, it is outside the community in which the believers obediently follow their Lord Jesus Christ and strive for perfection; and the church needs no government. A clear boundary was established between government and church, and a fundamental dualism was posited between the kingdom of darkness and the kingdom of light. "The regiment of government is according to the flesh, that of the Christian according to the spirit" (Fast, p. 67). This dualism led the Anabaptists to refuse to exercise governmental offices, to reject the oath in keeping with the Sermon on the Mount, and to refuse the payment of taxes when this came into conflict with the obedience owed to God.

Melchior Hoffman represented an apocalyptic revolutionary understanding of government. He demanded that priests be eliminated in Strasbourg and other imperial cities and that the elect arm themselves for the struggle against the emperor—the dragon of the Book of Revelation. Hoffman envisioned that the New Jerusalem would appear in Strasbourg. He conceptualized a theocracy for the time between a war of revenge against the godless and the return of Christ. He himself did not challenge the believers to the use of the sword, but in effect prepared the way for the Anabaptist rule in Münster.

The Münster Anabaptists, under John of Leiden, advanced charismatic and ethical claims that prompted them to resist the episcopal ruler. Hoffman's reservation that only the rulers were to fight against the godless disappeared. This meant the rule of twelve elders in Münster and the establishment of a monarchical, chiliastic, apocalyptic kingdom of God according to Old Testament precedent. Menno Simons stood close to the Melchiorite tradition no matter how much he distanced himself from the militancy of the Anabaptist rule in Münster. He, too, challenged the authorities to act against the dangers that threatened Christendom from priests and clerics. At the same time he advocated peacefulness and subjected himself to pious government. Consequently his followers sought the protection of rulers and magistracies in order to live their faith silently and quietly.

The Beginnings of Territorial Church Government. The Diet of Augsburg of 1555 and its stipulation *cuius regio, eius religio* ("the one who has the rule also determines the religion") entailed in Protestant areas the establishment of a territorial church government. While Luther had involved territorial rulers as "emergency bishops" for the reform of the church, this did not conform to the intention of his notion of the two kingdoms, which demanded a differentiation if not separation of secular government and spiritual regiment in the church. In reality, however, there was no way to reorder the church in individual territories and imperial cities without the authority of the territorial ruler or of city councilors. This meant that after 1555 the place of the territorial ruler was enhanced and a special *potestas ecclesiastica* ("power in ecclesiastical matters"), which described the territorial ruler's rights in ecclesiastical affairs, was juxtaposed to his secular rule. Following Pareus (1548–1622), a distinction was made between internal ecclesiastical authority and the *potestas ecclesiastica externa* ("power in external ecclesiastical matters"). The former, the spiritual mandate expressed in sermon, sacrament, and pastoral care, remained with the spiritual office, while the *potestas circa sacra* ("power outside the sacred"), the power regarding externals, was vested in the territorial ruler. The new territorial church government argued the suspension of the episcopal jurisdiction that had occurred in imperial law. From that they reasoned a transfer of the external power of the bishops to the rulers or the territorial power of the rulers. Theologically this included the law to reform as well as the care for religion. This confirmed the path to territorial church government that existed in Germany until 1918.

[*See also* Law, *article on* Theological Understanding of Law; *and* Magistracy.]

BIBLIOGRAPHY

Primary Sources

Calvin, John. *Opera quae supersunt omnia.* Edited by G. Baum, E. Cunitz, and E. Reuss. Corpus Reformatorum 29–87. Braunschweig, 1863–1900.

Die Bekenntnisschriften der evangelisch-Lutherischen Kirche. Göttingen, 1963.

Fast, Heinold, ed. *Der linke Flügel der Reformation.* Bremen, 1962.

Luther, Martin. *Werke: Kritische Gesamtausgabe.* Weimar, 1883.

Melanchthon, Philipp. *Werke Opera quae supersunt omnia.* Corpus Reformatorum 1–28. Berlin, 1834.

———. *Melanchthons Werke in Auswahl.* Edited by R. Stupperich. Gütersloh, 1951–1975.

Müntzer, Thomas. *Schriften und Briefe.* Edited by Paul Kirn and Günther Franz. Gütersloh, 1968.

Quellen zur Geschichte der Täufer. Leipzig, 1930.

Zwingli, Huldrych. *Werke.* Edited by M. Schuler and J. Schulthess. 8 vols. 1828–1842.

———. *Selected Works.* Reprint, Philadelphia, 1972.

Secondary Sources

Baur, Jürgen. *Gott, Recht und weltliches Regiment im Werk Calvins.* Bonn, 1965.

Bohatec, Josef. *Calvin und das Recht* (1934). Reprint, Feudingen, 1971.

Bornkamm, Heinrich. *Luthers Lehre von den zwei Reichen im Zusammenhang seiner Theologie.* 3 vols. Gütersloh, 1958–1969.

Deppermann, Klaus. *Melchior Hoffmann: Soziale Unruhen und apokalyptische Visionen im Zeitalter der Reformation.* Göttingen, 1979.

Dörries, Hermann. "Luther und das Widerstandsrecht." In *Wort und Stunde,* pp. 195–270. Göttingen, 1970.

Duchrow, Ulrich. *Christenheit und Weltverantwortung: Traditionsgeschichte und systematischer Struktur der Zweireichelehre.* Reprint, Stuttgart, 1983.

Elliger, Walter. *Thomas Müntzer: Leben und Werk.* Göttingen, 1976.

Farner, Alfred. *Die Lehre von Kirche und Staat bei Zwingli.* Tübingen, 1930.

Gänssler, Hans-Joachim. *Evangelium und weltliches Schwert: Hintergrund, Entstehungsgeschichte und Anlaß von Luthers Scheidung zweier Reiche oder Regimente.* Wiesbaden, 1983.

Goertz, Hans-Jürgen. *Die Täufer: Geschichte und Deutung.* Munich, 1980.

Heckel, Johannes. *Lex Charitatis: Eine juristische Untersuchung über das Recht in der Theologie Martin Luthers.* Munich, 1973.

Hillerbrand, Hans J. *Die politische Ethik des oberdeutschen Täufertums.* Leiden, 1962.

Hillerdal, Gunnar. *Gehorsam gegen Gott und Menschen.* Göttingen, 1954.

Hinrichs, Carl. *Luther und Müntzer: Ihre Auseinandersetzung über Obrigkeit und Widerstandsrecht.* Berlin, 1962.

Köhler, Walther. *Zürcher Ehegericht und Genfer Konsistorium.* Vol. 1. Leipzig, 1938.

Lau, Franz. *Luthers Lehre von den beiden Reichen.* Berlin, 1953.

Locher, Gottfried W. *Huldrych Zwingli in neuer Sicht.* Zurich, 1969.

Maurer, Wilhelm. *Luthers Lehre von den drei Hierarchien und ihr mittelalterlicher Hintergrund.* Munich, 1970.

Niesel, Wilhelm. *Die Theologie Calvins.* Munich, 1957.

Schellong, Dieter. *Das evangelische Gesetz in der Auslegung Calvins.* Munich, 1968.

Schmid, Heinrich. *Zwinglis Lehre von der göttlichen und menschlichen Gerechtigkeit.* Zurich, 1959.

Staedtke, Joachim. "Die Lehre von der Königsherrschaft Christi und den zwei Reichen bei Calvin." In *Reformation und Zeugnis der Kirche,* pp. 101–113. Zurich, 1978.

Stayer, James M. *Anabaptists and the Sword.* Lawrence, Kans., 1976.

Törnvall, Gustaf. *Geistliches und weltliches Regiment bei Luther.* Munich, 1947.

Williams, George H. *The Radical Reformation.* 3d ed. Kirksville, Mo., 1992.

KARL-HEINZ ZUR MÜHLEN
Translated from German by Hans J. Hillerbrand

TYNDALE, William (also Hychyns; 1494?–1536), English reformer and Bible translator. Most of what can be known of Tyndale's life is drawn from John Foxe's *Acts and Monuments*, which presents the reformer as serious in purpose, patient in tribulation, and, of course, faithful in death. Tyndale was born into yeoman farmer stock near the Welsh border. His native Gloucestershire in the early sixteenth century could be described as both religiously pious and ecclesiastically corrupt, but it also harbored considerable Lollard sentiment.

Foxe refers to Tyndale as growing up in the University of Oxford, so he was probably quite young when he started at Magdalen Hall before continuing at Magdalen College. The register of the university shows Tyndale received a B.A. on 4 July 1512, and an M.A. on 2 July 1515. This entry provides the first firm dates on which to construct Tyndale's story. Some writers have assumed that such Renaissance figures as Erasmus and John Colet directly influenced Tyndale during his years in Oxford, but such associations are fanciful. Magdalen College was experiencing some educational reform, but its leadership, like most of the university, was traditional in piety and content to dispute the Schoolmen. Tyndale himself consistently refers to his Oxford experience in negative terms, but Foxe describes him as finding satisfaction by meeting with some students privately and reading to them "some parcel of divinity, instructing them in the knowledge and truth of the scriptures."

Almost nothing is known about the next seven years of Tyndale's life, but one can assume that the young Oxford graduate was busy preaching. Thomas More testifies that Tyndale had a considerable reputation as an effective and fervent preacher. It is also possible that during this time Tyndale studied at Cambridge. This university was more advanced in Renaissance values in general and in Greek studies in particular. Almost all the early English reformers were drawn to the reformed cause during their time at Cambridge, but there is no evidence that Tyndale was part of the "Little Germany" discussion group that met at the White Horse Inn to explore Luther's theology.

For about a year (1522–1523) Tyndale served as a tutor and perhaps private chaplain for a knight of Henry VIII, Sir John Walsh, at Little Sodbury Manor in Gloucestershire, but his straightforward speech and his evangelical zeal brought conflict with local religious leaders who frequented the Walsh table. In response to his master's uncertainties, Tyndale translated the *Enchiridion* of Erasmus into English. In this work, Erasmus used the New Testament extensively and called for the practical piety of an internalized spiritual life. It apparently solidified the support of John Walsh, but the continued hostilities of the hierarchy brought Tyndale to the conclusion that England had only one hope for spiritual awakening: the Bible in the language of the people, in the hands of the people, and in the hearts of the people.

The English prelates had rigidly opposed any translation of the Bible because the vernacular text was associated with the heretical followers of John Wycliffe. But with the encouragement of Walsh, Tyndale went to London to request episcopal approval for translating the Bible into English. Perhaps acting on Erasmus's recommendation, Tyndale sought out Cuthbert Tunstall, bishop of London, but he firmly denied Tyndale's request. If a humanist bishop like Tunstall would not sanction the New Testament in English, Tyndale concluded the he would have to do the work abroad. Still in London, Tyndale made the acquaintance of some cloth merchants who were sympathetic to the young man's goals. They agreed to underwrite the translation as well as Tyndale's travels to the Continent. (At least one, Humphrey Monmouth, was later forced to recant publicly his support for the reformer.)

Tyndale slipped away from England and went first to Luther's Wittenberg, where he enrolled in the university. By 1525 Tyndale had translated the New Testament from Greek and started it through the press of Peter Quentel in Cologne, but the project was betrayed to the authorities and the printing was aborted. The translator fled from the city with some of the completed sheets. After securing a new printer in Worms, Tyndale published the first New Testament translated from Greek and printed in English. Both the complete New Testament and the "Cologne fragment" found eager readers when they were smuggled into England. By contrast the ecclesiastical authorities reacted with great hostility. The translation, they claimed, was filled with errors and was very dangerous. They concluded that it should be burned.

Tyndale sought safety within the English cloth-merchant community in Antwerp and almost immediately started producing theological and polemical works to promote the reformed cause. In spite of the instability of his clandestine existence, Tyndale managed to publish much during the next ten years. *The Parable of the Wicked Mammon* (1528) considers justification by faith and has its origins in a sermon by Luther, but Tyndale changed the material by adding and deleting so much that only about fifteen percent of *Mammon* is from the German reformer. *Mammon* was soon followed by *The Obedience of a Christian Man* (1528), which sets forth two more fundamentals of English Protestantism: the ultimate authority of scripture and the necessity of obedience to secular rulers. One often-repeated story quotes Henry VIII as declaring, "This book is for me and all kings to read," but the king apparently did not read the work thoroughly, for it presents an unflattering description of the kings of England being manipulated by traitorous ecclesiastics. Tyndale further developed this theme in *The Practice of Prelates* (1530), which he wrote in response to the attacks of Thomas More but directed against Thomas Wolsey, whom Tyndale satirizes as "Wolfsee." He followed this work by *An Answer unto Sir Thomas More* (1531) and numerous commentaries on various biblical books and passages. In addition, considerable evidence suggests that Tyndale put several Lollard tracts into print. After Tyndale's death, a commentary on the will of a deceased Gloucestershire friend, William Tracy, was found among his possessions and was published posthumously. Tracy, who had Lollard associations, clearly rejected traditional piety and testified to justification by faith alone. Although efforts were made to persuade Tyndale to return to England and place his literary skill in the service of Henry VIII, he remained on the Continent to continue his task.

Tyndale revised his New Testament at least twice and started the publication of his translation of the Old Testament. He managed to finish *Genesis* to *Deuteronomy* and published them individually. He also produced the book of Jonah before he was betrayed and placed in the prison at Vilvoorde near Brussels. He remained there more than a year preparing his defense and continuing his translation of the Old Testament historical books. The theologians of the University of Louvain who had made Erasmus feel uncomfortable and who had been quick to condemn Luther worked against Tyndale's cause. After Tyndale was found guilty, he was executed near Brussels in 1536.

As a writer, Tyndale employed Anglo-Saxon vocabulary in a simple prose style that spoke to his readers directly. He appealed for reform by scripture, common sense, wit (especially sarcasm and satire), shared experience, clear illustrations, and proverbial wisdom. He is credited with coining numerous words and contributing much to the establishment of English form. Tyndale's language is reflected in such seventeenth-century authors as John Milton and John Bunyan.

As a translator, Tyndale demonstrated a level of competency in the original languages that was rare anywhere in sixteenth-century Europe. For example, Miles Coverdale, who produced the first complete Bible in English, knew little Greek and no Hebrew, so he used all of Tyndale's work and translated the remainder from German. The translators appointed by King James (1611) retained at least ninety percent of Tyndale's words and syntax in the New Testament. Thus one can credit Tyndale with establishing the "Bible English" that dominated the English-speaking world until the mid-twentieth century, when the use of contemporary translations began to replace the sixteenth-century model.

Although Tyndale was certainly influenced by his contact with Luther's thought and defended Luther against the attacks of Thomas More, the Englishman disagreed with the German reformer on a number of significant issues. Deliberately distancing himself from Luther's understanding of the Lord's Supper, Tyndale described the sacrament as a memorial of Christ's death that should preach or retell the story of Christ's passion. Whereas the young Luther accepted a certain value of oral confession, Tyndale rejected it completely. Furthermore, Tyndale did not follow Luther's negative opinion of the letter of James.

Considerable evidence suggests that the language, values, concerns, and criticisms of John Wycliffe and his followers also influenced Tyndale. In several passages Tyndale appealed directly to Wycliffe and described the earlier reformer as God's spokesman to call England to repentance. The rejection of the prophet from God, Tyndale said, resulted in civil war, regicide, and the decay of towns and cities.

Regardless of the possible influence of other theologians, Tyndale was primarily concerned with expressing what he believed to be the biblical message to his generation. He argued that the Bible had been hidden in Latin, negated by canon law, perverted by the Schoolmen, and clouded by the glosses meant to explain the passage. He contended that the message of the Bible was so clear that it could be understood even by a plowboy if the book were translated in English, freed from interpretive comments, and understood with common-sense literalism. For Tyndale, the Bible was not a book to argue over (as the theologians of revived Scholasticism were doing) or to admire for its language (as the humanists were doing); it was a book to show one how to lead a godly life. The final intent of all scripture, according to Tyndale, was to bring one into fellowship with Christ and with those who believe in him.

Tyndale held a basic understanding of divine election without giving it much elaboration or a central place in his theology. He affirmed justification by faith alone but consistently held that true faith was contingent on works. Tyndale saw no dichotomy between the Old Testament and the New nor between law and grace. Love, Tyndale repeated, springs from faith and is a natural expression of one's spiritual condition. From such love spring good works. True faith—"feeling faith" as Tyndale called it—touched one's inner motives and expressed itself actively in service. The Christian must love God's law and believe his promises. Tyndale described the relationship between God and human beings as a covenant. This covenant, made at baptism, binds a person to faith in God's promises and obedience to God's law. Even the king had an obligation to search God's law and to obey it.

Tyndale angered Thomas More by using the word *congregation* instead of *church* in his translation of the New Testament. Both men understood the implications of Tyndale's choice. The former term described a gathering or assembly, while the latter suggested a structure or organization. Tyndale saw the church of scripture as a committed minority (a "little flock") gathered around the preaching of scripture with the authority in lay hands. His ideal of the church was constantly and sharply contrasted with the actual practice of the sixteenth-century English church. Tyndale was particularly critical of the popular piety that encouraged the people to pray to statues ("stocks and stones" he called them) or to the saints. He rejected the idea that one place was more holy than another and therefore objected to elaborate buildings or the necessity of pilgrimages. Nonetheless, such structures or practices could be permitted and would be useful if they served worshipers rather than demanding service from them. Tyndale was particularly offended by the sexual sins and the monetary misconduct of the established clergy. Such immorality demonstrated that the pope's church could not really be the congregation of God. The reformer asked his readers to judge for themselves, to decide if the actions of the prelates reflected Christ or Antichrist. Although Tyndale recognized the value of baptism and the Lord's Supper, he envisioned meetings that maximized exposition of scripture and minimized rituals and music. Tyndale's criticism of the traditional practices reveals clearly the parallels between his opinions and the views of the Lollards. Some of the verbal similarities between Tyndale's words and Lollard texts are striking.

Although Tyndale was not primarily a political philosopher, his theological views provided a theoretical foundation for social and political reform. He saw the king as the key to the reformation of the church. The king, not the pope, ruled as God's vicar. If the church did not conform to the biblical pattern, the king had the responsibility to bring about the needed changes. The king was bound by God to maintain order in the realm, and all persons in the kingdom should be required to obey the king. Tyndale rejected the claim that the clergy were exempt from the king's law because they were governed by the people. He objected to a kingdom that had two sets of laws and two sets of courts. Exempt from royal authority, clergy created a situation in which English priests and confessors gave allegiance to a foreign power. The presence of those who were exempt from the authority of the king constituted a constant danger. They were—and always had been—manipulating English kings for their own advantage. They knew people's secrets and owned much of the land. They involved English rulers in European wars to weaken royal power and to consolidate their own influence. In Tyndale's view, the king must act quickly to save his kingdom. (This understanding of Tyndale's political philosophy explains his dying prayer that God would open the king of England's eyes.)

Although the king was the head of the temporal regime as God's appointee, the human ruler must be subject to God's law. Tyndale did not refrain from outlining royal duties, and he described the limits of kingly authority. While hiding in exile, the translator reminded Henry VIII that he was but a servant to execute God's law and should not rule according to his own imagination. Tyndale even opposed Henry's divorce from Catherine of Aragon. Some of Tyndale's political and legal concerns (e.g., rule of law, basic equality before the law, protection against self-incrimination, and freedom of religion) have parallels in the American Constitution and Bill of Rights.

A life of constant danger denied Tyndale the opportunity to systematize his theology or even to organize his arguments. Some of his texts appear to have gone to the printer without careful editing. His contributions, like his life, came to an abrupt end. He did not live to see the Reformation established in England, but he laid the two-fold foundation on which others would build the authority of God's law over human law and the authority of the king over the pope. Tyndale did not found a church or start an organization, yet his significance still abounds. His phrases and expressions have passed into everyday speech. His theology still has relevance, and his biblical translation provided the standard for more than three hundred years.

BIBLIOGRAPHY

Primary Sources

Tyndale, William. *The Work of William Tyndale*. London, 1938.
———— *The Answer to Sir Thomas More's Dialogue*. Cambridge, 1983.

Secondary Sources

Anderson, Marvin W. "William Tyndale (d. 1536): A Martyr for All Seasons." *Sixteenth Century Journal* 17 (1986), 331–351.
Clebsch, William A. *England's Earliest Protestants, 1520–1535*. Reprint, Westport, Conn., 1980. Sets England's first reformers in the context of religious change.
Edwards, Brian. *God's Outlaw*. Wheaton, Ill., 1976. Understandable biography for the general reader.
McGiffert, Michael. "William Tyndale's Conception of Covenant." *Journal of Ecclesiastical History* 32 (1981), 167–184. Provided focus on Tyndale's understanding of salvation.
Mozley, J. F. *William Tyndale*. Reprint, Westport, Conn., 1971. The authoritative biography of Tyndale, although dated.
Pineas, Rainer. "William Tyndale's Use of History as a Weapon of Religious Controversy." *Harvard Theological Review* 55 (1962), 121–141. One of several studies by this author on Tyndale's polemics.
Smeeton, Donald Dean. *Lollard Themes in the Reformation Theology of William Tyndale*. Sixteenth Century Essays and Studies, no. 6. Kirksville, Mo., 1986. Attempts to understand Tyndale in the context of Wycliffite dissent.
Williams, C. H. *William Tyndale*. Leaders of Religion Series, edited by C. W. Dugmore. London, 1969. Readable but serious presentation of the issues surrounding Tyndale.

DONALD DEAN SMEETON

U

ULHART, Philipp (also Ulhard; died c.1568), Augsburg printer and supporter of the Reformation. The first information in Augsburg concerning Ulhart states that he lived in Saint Katharinengasse, later in Kirchgasse bei Saint Ulrich in a house belonging to the printer Sigmund Grimm. It is likely that he first worked for Grimm in the printing shop. On 7 March 1523 the book publishers in Augsburg were called upon to take a solemn oath before the city council that they would no longer publish any work without the name of the author and that of the printer. Among those summoned before the council was Ulhart. It seems that beginning in mid-1522 he started his own printing business, after taking over Grimm's type. It had become an idiosyncracy of Ulhart's to obtain type and title page ornamentation from other local publishers. In addition to Grimm's type, Ulhart also used type from Hans Schönsperger, Silvan Otmar, and Erhard Oeglin.

This use has caused confusion in scholarship over the identification of publications from Ulhart's printshop, especially since Ulhart ignored the city council's directive not to publish anonymous works without the printer's name and the place of publication. Still, 223 publications up to 1529 have been attributed to Ulhart. Since he continued to publish after 1529, including reprinting earlier works, the total number of published works may be much higher. The works printed by Ulhart were marked by the Reformation. Although Augsburg officially remained Catholic, works critical of the Catholic church were tolerated.

At first Ulhart printed works by Augsburg authors; later he also printed works by Johannes Brenz, Andreas Althamer, Theobald Billicanus, Johann Diepolt, and Hans Staygmayer. These indicate Ulhart's connections with the Swabian cities of Hall, Gmünd, Nördlingen, Ulm, and Reutlingen. One set of publications documents the confrontation between the University of Ingolstadt and the young university teacher Arsatius Seehofer, who had declared his allegiance to the Lutheran Reformation. In addition to Luther himself, the noblewoman Argula von Grumbach (Stauff) became involved in this controversy.

Finally Ulhart made his printing press available to Andreas Bodenstein von Karlstadt and Huldrych Zwingli in the context of the controversy over the Lord's Supper. Thus, for example, Karlstadt's writings from Rothenburg ob der Tauber and a defense by Valentin Ickelshamer were first published by Ulhart in 1525. The bookseller Kunz Kern from Rothenburg had arranged the printing by Ulhart. But a connection to Karlstadt must have existed beforehand, since Karlstadt's important work of April 1523, *Was gesagt ist: Sich gelassen,* written in Wittenberg, was printed by Ulhart in Augsburg.

Another group of authors whose works were printed by Ulhart beginning in 1526 were Anabaptists and their sympathizers from the Augsburg brotherhood. Among these were Eitelhans Langenmantel, Johann Landtsperger, Hans Hut, Jörg Haug, Johannes Presta (pseudonym), Hans Denck, and Jakob Dachser. The last is most likely the author of the tract *Offenbarung von den wahrhaftigen Wiedertäufern* and was probably a friend of Ulhart. Ulhart came to be suspected of having printed the forbidden writing and was arrested on 18 August 1528. He was released after swearing to his recantation two days later. In the early 1530s Ulhart published two more anonymous Anabaptist dialogues and reprinted several earlier Anabaptist tracts.

In the decade prior to his death, he no longer identified himself with printing writings of a particular religious orientation. Among other titles he published works by contemporary historians and Latin plays. In 1533 he published a piece by Wolfgang Musculus against the Anabaptists' refusal to swear oaths. But this publication probably did not reflect his true sentiment. Ulhart's attitude throughout his life remained one of opposition to government.

BIBLIOGRAPHY

Benzing, Josef. *Die Buchdrucker des 16. und 17. Jahrhunderts im deutschen Sprachgebiet.* 2d ed. Wiesbaden, 1982. See vol. 1, p. 17. Contains bibliography.

Schottenloher, Karl. *Philipp Ulhart: Ein Augsburger Winkeldrucker und Helfershelfer der "Schwärmer" und "Wiedertäufer," 1523–1529* (1921). Historische Forschungen und Quellen 4. Reprint, Nieuwkoop. 1967. Extensive list of the works printed by Ulhart up to 1529.

SIGRID LOOß
Translated from German by Robert E. Shillenn

ULM. The story of the Reformation in this free imperial city in southern Germany demonstrates the extreme degree, even by sixteenth-century standards, to which politics and religion could be enmeshed. Reform preaching was evident in the city as early as 1521, as Franciscans Johann Eberlin von Günzburg and Heinrich von Kettenbach openly criticized the Church and its abuses. In 1524 the city council appointed native son Konrad Sam city pastor; his preaching, too, contained a constant theme of reform and reliance on scripture. Later that year, the city council further suggested Lutheran sympathies in its refusal to enforce the Edict of Worms on the grounds that it went against God's commandments. A crucial moment for the Ulm reform movement came in 1529, when the city subscribed to the Protestation of Speyer. The other Protestant estates, however, remained wary of Ulm, for the city was increasingly associated not with Lutheran, but Zwinglian, tendencies. After Speyer, therefore, Ulm found itself in an uncomfortable position: now openly Protestant, the city was nonetheless unable to form protective alliances with Lutheran states, leaving it defenseless in the apparent likelihood of retribution at the hands of the Catholic emperor Charles V.

No such retribution came to pass. Following the 1530 Diet of Augsburg, Ulm was again forced to state its religious position. Polling of the leading citizens and guilds indicated strong Protestant loyalties. At this point the city council determined that the Reformation in Ulm be made official. The year 1531 is regarded as Ulm's "Reformation year," as it witnessed the full implementation of Protestantism. Realizing that Ulm lacked a galvanizing spiritual leader, much less anyone with experience in drafting a church order, the city fathers brought in three prominent reformers to assist the city in its efforts: Martin Bucer from Strasbourg, Johannes Oecolampadius from Basel, and Ambrosius Blarer from Constance.

The three reformers arrived in May 1531. Wishing to avoid the appearance of strangers imposing their ecclesiastical viewpoints on an unwilling populace, the reformers spent their first few days in Ulm delivering informational sermons outlining their charge from the city fathers. In early June they met with local and territorial churchmen to assess their enthusiasm for reform. At the same time the visiting theologians presented the clergy with the Eighteen Articles, a concise doctrinal statement, already approved by the city council, which would serve as a basis for the Ulm church order. Among those points affirmed in this document were the sinful nature of man, the efficacy of divine grace, Christ as redeemer, the Bible as sole authority, infant baptism, the Communion ceremony as purely a memorial, and the use of German in worship services. That the articles deliberately avoided the word *justification* and adamantly denied Christ's real presence in the Sacrament strongly suggested Zwinglian, rather than Lutheran, tendencies. The reformers encountered strong opposition from a majority of the Ulm clergy—only five of the city's thirty-five ministers approved of the articles; but the city council was determined to effect reform and thus ignored the protests. Indeed, the council was so concerned about the overwhelming dissent that it

deemed counterproductive a public disputation, an effective means in other cities for crystallizing support for reform.

Reform thereafter progressed quickly. The Mass was abolished in the city on 16 June; three days later new baptismal and matrimonial ceremonies were instituted. The city council decreed the removal of all images and altars from the churches. Surprisingly, and fortunately for civic order, unbridled iconoclasm did not erupt at this time, as had happened in other cities in the initial stages of reform. Instead, the city arranged for the orderly removal of most paraphernalia by donating families—at night for added security. Only the exquisite, carved-wood choir stalls of the Münster, still on view today, were allowed to remain.

Their work essentially completed, Oecolampadius and Bucer left Ulm in late June; Blarer remained another three weeks before departing for neighboring Geislingen. Before leaving Ulm, Blarer witnessed, on 16 July, the city's first reformed Communion service. On 6 August 1531 the city council decreed the church order of Bucer, Blarer, and Oecolampadius "proclaimed, published, and publicly read before the entire community." The Reformation in Ulm was now officially accomplished.

Religious controversy, however, continued in the city and territory of Ulm. By October 1531 the Franciscans and Dominicans had abandoned the city; to those churchmen remaining the council made clear that it would not brook open criticism to the new church order. The year 1533 witnessed a relentless struggle between local minister Martin Frecht and Sebastian Franck, a wandering soapmaker and pamphleteer. A former Lutheran minister himself, Franck placed greater emphasis on inner divine guidance than on biblical revelation and church organization; moreover, he advocated religious toleration. Such ideas Frecht found offensive, and he battled to discredit publicly Franck, who had won the ear of former mayor Bernhard Besserer, a driving force behind the city's Reformation and arguably the most powerful person in Ulm. Concurrently, Frecht inveighed against another Besserer favorite, Kaspar von Schwenckfeld, whose antisacramental and somewhat mystical teachings Frecht found more dangerous than Franck's. In time Frecht succeeded in obtaining the banishment of both Franck and Schwenckfeld from the city; but, it is believed, Schwenckfeld returned secretly several times and was buried in a prominent citizen's cellar.

Following the issuance of the Augsburg Interim and the arrival of Emperor Charles V in Ulm, the city council was compelled to dismantle its Protestant church in 1548. The Mass was reinstituted, and city pastors were imprisoned until they agreed to comply. Local popular support for the reintroduction of Catholicism was minimal at best. Amid the erosion of the Interim, Ulm once again asserted its Protestantism in 1522. The city, however, continued to feel the tensions among Catholic, Zwinglian, and Lutheran forces for another quarter century. Ultimately, in 1577, the local ministers, encouraged by the city council, subscribed formally to the Augsburg Confession. Ulm then took its place among the preeminent south German Lutheran cities.

BIBLIOGRAPHY

Brecht, Martin. "Ulm, 1530–1547: Entstehung, Ordnung, Leben und Probleme einer Reformationskirche." In *Die Einführung der Reformation in Ulm*, edited by Hans Eugen Specker and Gebhard Weig. Ulm, 1981. A useful survey of the initial stages of reform.

Endriss, Julius. *Das Ulmer Reformationsjahr 1531 in seinen entscheidenden Vorgängen*. Ulm, 1931. A thorough narrative of the decisive year in Ulm's reformation.

Fritz, F. *Ulmische Kirchengeschichte: Vom Interim bis zum dreissigjährigen Krieg, 1548–1612*. Stuttgart, 1934. Details the later events in Ulm's reformation history.

Sehling, Emil. *Die evangelischen Kirchenordnungen des XVI. Jahrhunderts*. Tübingen, 1963. See vol. 12, pt. 1. Primary documents relating to the Ulm reformation, plus a brief summary of events.

EILEEN T. DUGAN

ULRICH OF WÜRTTEMBERG (1487–1550), German territorial ruler who introduced Protestantism in the Duchy of Württemberg. Duke Ulrich's life is a study of the tangled connections between religion and politics in the age of the Reformation. His stormy reign left permanent marks on both the sacred and secular orders of his realm.

A vain, capricious, and free-spending adventurer, Ulrich tried the patience of his subjects to the point of open rebellion in 1514. In the wake of a peasant uprising known as "Poor Conrad," he was forced by his estates (*Ehrbarkeit*) to grant a constitution limiting his powers to tax and to make war. In defiance of these restraints, he unleashed a new wave of military aggression ending in the loss of his territory to the custody of Emperor Charles V in 1519.

In the subsequent struggle to regain his land and title, Ulrich successfully exploited both the Protestant Reformation and the German princes' jealousy of Habsburg power. He found an ally in Philipp of Hesse, who, in the hope of winning Württemberg for the Lutheran faith, championed Ulrich's cause. With an army largely subsidized by the French, Philipp invaded Württemburg in 1534 and restored Ulrich as lawful ruler. The chastened and grateful duke proceeded without delay to the conversion of his territory.

Ulrich took a keen personal interest in his reformation, reserving to himself all decisions on doctrine, service, church organization and education, as well as disposal of the old church's legal prerogatives and vast land holdings. Three theologians were engaged to submit proposals and institute the reforms: Erhard Schnepf, Ambrosius Blarer, and Johannes Brenz. Schnepf and Blarer devised a compromise formula on the Lord's Supper (Stuttgart Concord), and Brenz wrote a catechism that placed the new church in accord with the Augsburg Confession.

Ulrich's last years were overshadowed by Württemberg's forced reversion to Catholicism under the Interim imposed by Charles V in 1547. In granting asylum to prominent Lutherans in defiance of imperial law, Ulrich gave evidence of his loyalty to the Lutheran cause. The Württemberg reform was reinstated and carried to completion under his son, Duke Christoph (1515–1568).

BIBLIOGRAPHY

Bühler, Johannes. *Deutsche Geschichte*. Vol. 3. Berlin, 1938.

Estes, James Martin. *Christian Magistrate and State Church: The Reforming Career of Johannes Brenz*. Toronto, 1982. Contains a few pages on Ulrich's involvement in the theological and ecclesiastical reform in Württemberg.

Heyd, Ludwig. *Ulrich, Herzog zu Württemburg*. 3 vols. Tübingen, 1841–1844. Still the best biography.

Maurer, Hans Martin, and Kuno Ulshöfer. *Johannes Brenz und die Reformation in Württemberg*. Stuttgart, 1974. Most detailed modern work; one chapter on Ulrich; illustrated.

Press, Volker. "Ein Epochenjahr der Würrtemburgische Geschichte. Restitution und Reformation." *Blätter für Würrtemhuergische Kirchengeschichte* 47 (1988), 203–234.

Schottenloher, Karl, ed. *Bibliographie zur deutschen Geschichte im Zeitalter der Glaubensspaltung, 1517–1585*. Vol. 3., 2d ed. Stuttgart, 1956. Contains an extensive, though not up-to-date, bibliography of primary and secondary sources.

KARIN BRINKMANN BROWN

ULTRAMONTANISM. This term is applied to movements within Roman Catholicism that emphasized the authority of the papacy in matters of doctrine and ecclesiastical government. The term itself is from the Latin *ultra* ("beyond") and *montes* ("mountains"), the mountains in this case being the Alps, so that for most of Europe the term ultramontane designated someone from Italy. The Italians, of course, had a different perspective and, for example, considered a German pope to be an ultramontane. The term eventually came to connote supporters of the pope, at first in a pejorative sense, as it did during the investiture controversy in the eleventh century between the Holy Roman Emperor Henry IV and Pope Gregory VII. Ultramontane principles are evident in the struggles between the papacy and the conciliar movement in the fifteenth century. Henry VIII's Act of Supremacy (1534) and the maxim of *cuius regio, eius religio* established by the Peace of Augsburg (1555) are antithetical to ultramontanism.

The first ultramontanes in the modern sense of the term were those Catholics in France who opposed the Gallican policies of Louis XIV, in particular the Four Articles of 1682. Even so, the actual modern use of the term itself apparently dates from the eighteenth century. It had increasing currency during the nineteenth century, especially in France and Germany, when the acrimonious disputes between the ultramontanes and their opponents led to the victory of the former at the First Vatican Council and to the definition of papal infallibility in 1870. The use of the term ultramontanism to describe developments in the sixteenth century is thus anachronistic and inappropriate. Most scholars do not use it when referring to the Reformation or the Counter-Reformation, and those who do merely add to the confusion. B. J. Kidd, for example, uses the term ultramontane in his book *The Counter-Reformation* (London, 1963) in the Italian sense by so labeling the non-Italian prelates at the Council of Trent.

[*See also* Papacy.]

BIBLIOGRAPHY

Urquhart, F. F. "Ultramontanism." In *Encyclopaedia of Religion and Ethics*, edited by James Hastings, vol. 12, pp. 505–508. Edinburgh, 1926. Free of the usual polemic that is a feature of much of the writing on the topic; assumes a fair amount of knowledge on the part of the reader. Aside from other encylopedia articles, the literature on ultramontanism concentrates on particular aspects of the topic from the seventeenth to the nineteenth century.

A. LYNN MARTIN

UNGNAD, Hans von Sonnegg (1493–1564), baron and noble patron of the Reformation and printing. Born of noble parents in Sonnegg (Carinthia), he was raised at the court of Maximilian I. Open to the "new faith," he witnessed the presentation of the Augsburg Confession to Charles V (1530). In 1522 he served under King Ferdinand I in the battle against the Turks and in 1526 was assigned the captainship of Cilli (Slov., Celje). Four years later he became head of the government of Styria. His duties included the defense of the borders of the Slovenian, Croatian, and Carinthian lands. In 1540 he was appointed general captain of the governments of the five Lower Austrian, Windisch, and Croatian lands, as well as commander in chief of the royal troops of Hungary. Through these functions he came to know the peoples and countries of southeastern Europe. As a Christian he disapproved of theological disputes and desired that the word of God be proclaimed in its purity and sincerity in the Habsburg lands. He believed that the disaster inflicted by the Turks occurred because the word of God was not being proclaimed.

After the Peace of Augsburg (1555), when the Habsburgs sought to force the Catholic faith upon their subjects, Ungnad resigned his service to Ferdinand. Otherwise he would have been required to implement royal mandates against his convictions. In 1555 he left Styria. His plan to deliver the gospel to the Slovenians, Croatians, and Serbs became a reality when he became familiar with the translations by the fugitive Slovenian canon Primus Trubar. The latter had introduced his countrymen to the basic Protestant principles through a catechism in Slovenian (1550). With the support of Duke Christoph of Württemberg (1518–1568), Ungnad established himself at the guesthouse Amandenhof in Urach

(near Tübingen) and set up a printing shop (1561). He planned to print Protestant texts in Slovenian, Croatian, and Serbian in order to comfort the people living under the Turks with the testimony of Jesus Christ. It was his hope that "thereby the pure message of the Word of God may also be carried to Turkey . . . as if by this means the merciful God wanted to strike the Turks with the sword of his almighty strength, in the same way as, through the blessed Martin Luther, he disclosed and struck down the entire papacy."

When his funds were exhausted, Ungnad wrote to the princes and towns of the empire to request help for his southeastern European mission. He received ample support. He obtained two preachers from Istria—Stephan Consul and Anton Dalmata—to prepare translations. In his house he employed nine people for printing. By 1565 thirty-seven printed works of translated excerpts from the Bible had appeared as well as some thirty-one Reformation pamphlets. Of the printed works four were in Slovenian, thirteen in Croatian, and six in Italian. The printing shop came to its end when Ungnad died on 27 December 1564 in Winteritz (Bohemia). He was buried in Tübingen.

BIBLIOGRAPHY

Sakrausky, Oskar. *Primus Truber: Deutsche Vorreden zum slowenischen und kroatischen Reformationswerk*. Vienna, 1989. See p. 139.

OSKAR SAKRAUSKY
Translated from German by Wolfgang Katenz

UNITARIANS. *See* Antitrinitarians; Radical Reformation; Socinianism.

UNITAS FRATRUM. *See* Bohemian Brethren.

UNIVERSITIES played vital roles in the intellectual life of Europe and the Reformation. They were the locale of most scholarly research in all fields, and they educated practically every important religious and intellectual figure of the Reformation and Counter-Reformation. Indeed, many religious leaders were university professors.

The earliest universities of Bologna, Paris, and Oxford developed spontaneously when students gathered at the feet of famous teachers. Princes and municipal governments then added more professors and created an institutional framework. A university existed when three conditions were met: the pope or emperor issued a charter authorizing the university to award degrees recognized throughout Christendom, an organization was in place, and teaching began. By the early sixteenth century Europe had over fifty active universities. The foundation dates given below indicate when all three conditions were fulfilled. But because the evidence is often ambiguous, some of the dates are uncertain or approximate.

Italy had eleven universities—Bologna (began c. 1190), Padua (1222), Naples (1224), Siena (c. 1240), Rome (1303), Perugia (1308), Pisa (1343), Florence (1348, but merged with a revivified Pisa in 1473), Pavia (1361), Ferrara (1391 and brought back to life in 1442), Turin (1411), and Catania (1445). The University of Paris began about 1208 and was followed by Montpellier (1220–1230), Toulouse (1229), Angers (1229), Orléans (c.1235), Avignon (1303), Cahors (1332), the very weak university at Orange (1365), Aix en Provence (1409), the weak university of Dôle (1422), Poitiers (1432), Caen (1439), Bordeaux (1441), Valence (1452), Nantes (1461), Bourges (1464), Rheims (1548), and Besançon (1565). Louvain (1426) was the university of the Low Countries, Copenhagen (1475) was the university of Denmark, and Uppsala (1477) was that of Sweden.

England had Oxford (c.1208) and Cambridge (c.1231). Scottish universities were Saint Andrews (c.1411), Glasgow (1451), and Aberdeen (c.1500). Spanish universities were Salamanca (c.1243), Valladolid (c.1250), Lérida (1300), Huesca (1354, revived in 1464), Perpignan (1379), Barcelona (1450), Palma in Majorca (1483), Sigüenza (1489), Valencia (1500), Alcalá de Henares (1508), and Saragossa (1583). The sole Portuguese university was founded in Lisbon in 1290; it then moved back and forth between Lisbon and Coimbra until permanently established in Coimbra in 1537.

Central Europe began to found universities at a later date but then saw the establishment of fifteen universities. They were Prague (founded in 1348), Vienna (1365, brought back to life in the 1380s), Erfurt (1379), Heidelberg (1385), Cologne (1388), Leipzig (1409), Rostock (1419), Greifswald (1456), Freiburg im Breisgau (1456), Basel (1460), Ingolstadt (1472), Mainz (1476), Tübingen (1477), Wittenberg (1502), and Frankfurt an der Oder (1506). In every case a prince or city government founded central European universities. The civil power largely controlled the university and paid the salaries of many of the professors. Other teachers, especially in the faculty of arts, lived off student fees. Kraków (1364, brought back to life in 1400) in Poland drew students from throughout eastern Europe.

Characteristics of Universities. All universities had statutes stipulating the number of years of study required for each degree. These varied from one to three years for a bachelor's degree in the arts to five to seven years for doctorates in law and medicine. The doctorate of theology required twelve and more years of studying and teaching beyond the master of arts degree, although the time was sometimes shortened. Martin Luther, for example, received his doctorate after seven years. Statutes indicated which texts were to be studied in the various disciplines. Professors might follow a statutory text closely or use it as a point of departure. Lectures, academic disputations, and examinations (always oral) were conducted in Latin everywhere.

Universities taught theology, canon law, civil law, medicine, and arts. Arts included some or all of the following subjects—grammar, rhetoric, dialectic, natural philosophy, metaphysics, mathematics, astronomy, astrology, and, later, humanities based on the classics of ancient Greece and Rome. But the importance of the various subjects and the level of instruction differed greatly in southern and northern European universities.

Bologna and all other Italian universities emphasized the teaching of law and medicine at the doctoral level. Italian universities were filled with advanced students, aged eighteen to twenty-five and older, who studied for doctoral degrees in law, medicine, and arts. Italian universities almost never awarded the bachelor's degree, while the master's degree with a license to teach was automatically included with the doctorate. Many professors at Italian universities were active researchers who published numerous works in law and medicine.

By contrast, Italian universities taught little theology. Instead, students seeking theological instruction attended the advanced schools of the medieval mendicant orders, especially Dominican, Franciscan, and Augustinian schools. Monastic schools of theology were often located in university towns but were not part of the university. Some Italian universities had only a single professor of theology in the fifteenth century, while Bologna had none. After the middle of the sixteenth century, the majority of Italian universities had two theologians—for Thomist and Scotist theology, respectively—and a professor of scripture.

The prototypical northern universities of Paris and Oxford were decentralized institutions whose most important element was the college, a residence shared by masters and students. A donor typically provided funds for the establishment of a residence in which secular boys and young future clergymen resided. The majority of colleges had a preponderance of young students fourteen to eighteen years of age studying for the bachelor's degree, some candidates for master's degrees, and few, if any, doctoral students. Because teenage males needed to be supervised and instructed, older clergymen with degrees lived in the colleges. Colleges engendered a strong sense of communal life lacking in noncollegiate universities.

Colleges at Paris and Oxford began as residences offering safe havens for boys and young men far from home. They then became teaching centers by the late fifteenth century. After earning a master's degree, the former student was required to spend two to five years teaching in the college. This system provided instruction at low cost and eliminated the need to hire numerous university-wide professors.

Hence, most instruction in the universities of Paris and Oxford occurred within the colleges in the sixteenth century. But these college teachers were seldom professional scholars or researchers. Paris and Oxford focused on the subjects appropriate to their students—arts at the bachelor's level and theology at an advanced level. Law and medicine were little cultivated.

All other universities fitted somewhere between the Italian and the Paris-Oxford models. Spanish universities and French universities outside Paris concentrated on the teaching of law. This was partly because Pope Honorius III in 1219 prohibited Paris from teaching civil law. Stepping into the vacuum, Orléans became famous for legal studies. These universities initially lacked theology because the papacy refused to charter theology faculties in order to protect Paris's monopoly. But in the fifteenth century, when the Faculty of Theology of Paris developed Gallican and conciliarist views undermining papal authority, the papacy willingly authorized other universities to teach and award degrees in theology. Spanish institutions and French universities outside Paris were not known for the arts, and, except for Montpellier, French universities taught little medicine.

Universities in German-speaking lands lacked strong residential and teaching colleges but resembled Paris and Oxford in other ways. They had relatively large faculties of arts, where numerous masters of arts taught young students pursuing bachelor's degrees. But the higher faculties of law, medicine, and theology were small and not highly developed. Cologne, strong in law and theology, was an exception. A German university might have ten or twelve professors of arts, six to eight professors of law, and four to six professors of theology. The medical faculty was small to nonexistent; indeed, some German universities relied on local physicians to teach medicine as part-time instructors. In the fifteenth century most German universities awarded an average of a single doctorate in law and another in theology annually and very few medical doctorates. Thousands of German students with sufficient financial resources went to Italy to study medicine and law.

The number of professors in universities varied greatly from place to place. Paris, probably the largest university, had sixty-three professors of canon law, theology, and medicine combined and more than 400 professors of arts in 1362. The smallest universities had only eight to twenty professors. On the other hand, candidates for higher degrees lacking the title of professor did much teaching in the arts and theology in northern universities.

The size of the student body could be as high as several thousand at Paris and seven thousand at Salamanca in the sixteenth century or as low as one hundred to two hundred students in universities located in provincial towns. The vast majority of European universities were relatively small—three hundred to eight hundred students taught by thirty to forty professors. Paris, Bologna, and Padua attracted an international student body. So to a lesser extent did a few other Italian and French universities, but most universities, especially in central Europe, drew their students from the surrounding territory. Enrollment fluctuated greatly from decade to decade, as war, disease, and the presence or absence of a famous professor caused students to move from one university to another. Students frequently began at one university and took a degree at a second or third.

Curricular and Other Changes. Although universities of the fifteenth and sixteenth centuries are sometimes thought to have been bastions of conservatism and strongly opposed to change, the opposite was the truth. A great deal of innovative research and teaching in all fields of study occurred in universities.

The adoption of humanistic studies in the teaching and research of the arts was the most significant curricular change. The shift from dialectical learning based on medieval logic and grammar texts to humanistic studies based on ancient Latin and Greek works of rhetoric, poetry, and history took place across Europe but at different times. Humanistic studies, including Greek, found a place in Italian universities in the second quarter of the fifteenth century and were important from 1450 onward.

Humanistic studies began to influence research and teaching of other university subjects in the sixteenth century. Humanistically trained medical professors applied philological and critical historical methods to the ancient and medieval medical texts. They uncovered new texts in the original languages (often Greek), edited them, and produced better Latin translations for classroom use. Soon humanist medical scholars went beyond the received curricular texts. They added anatomy based on extensive dissection of human bodies, botany (the study of plants primarily for use as medicines), and clinical medicine to the curriculum. Medical humanists, especially at the University of Padua, produced a revolution in medical research and teaching by 1550. Other universities followed the lead of Padua.

Humanistically trained philosophers in Italian universities modified teaching and research in philosophy through the introduction of Aristotle in the original language, greater use of ancient commentaries, and the jettisoning of medieval commentaries. Although Aristotle continued to dominate the teaching of philosophy, the universities of Ferrara and Rome also taught Plato in the sixteenth century. Galileo's study of ancient Greek mathematics texts led directly to his pioneering work in astronomy and physics. Humanistic jurisprudence influenced the study of law in northern, especially French, universities, but it had little impact in Italian universities.

Universities outside Italy embraced humanistic studies in the early sixteenth century. German universities accepted humanism between 1515 and 1535. They introduced new humanistic Latin grammars and dialectic texts, as well as works by Cicero, Quintilian, Terence, and other ancient literary and rhetorical authors. Universities taught Aristotle based on the original Greek text or in better Latin translations; they added lectureships in Greek and Hebrew. Oxford and Cambridge made the same changes but took most of the sixteenth century to do so. The Protestant Reformation did not spark the humanistic curricular revolution in northern Europe because universities that remained Catholic also embraced humanism at the same time, although Paris was a notable exception. But humanistic studies probably advanced more quickly in Protestant universities in northern Europe because the reformers saw humanistic studies as a necessary part of the reform of belief. Martin Luther introduced humanistic studies at Wittenberg as preparation for his theological curriculum, which required knowledge of Greek and Hebrew.

A distinguishing intellectual mark of German universities in the fifteenth century was the conflict between realism (the *via antiqua*) and nominalism (the *via moderna*) in the research and teaching of philosophy and theology. Luther studied at the University of Erfurt, a stronghold of nominalism, and his early theology developed out of and as a reaction to nominalism. The struggle between nominalism and realism mattered less in French universities and did not exist in English and Italian universities, where realism dominated.

Political and social changes left their mark as well. Kings, princes, and city councils exercised greater control over universities than before. An increasing number of students were wealthy, upper-class laymen rather than penurious clergymen. Those aspiring to governmental posts increasingly felt the need to study at a university. These changes were already under way before 1517, but the Reformation probably accelerated them.

The Impact of the Reformation. The Lutheran Reformation began as a university movement. Luther was a popular professor of theology at Wittenberg and remained so for all of his life. The faculty and students of his home university were Luther's strongest and most loyal supporters throughout. Johann Eck and other faculty members at the University of Ingolstadt took the lead in opposing the Reformation. The Reformation, however, soon burst out of the lecture hall to become a broad religious and political revolution that affected universities in various, sometimes deleterious, ways.

The initial impact of the Reformation and the wars of the first half of the sixteenth century was devastating. Both Catholic and Protestant universities in Germany suffered precipitous declines in enrollment between 1520 and 1540. The abolition of monastic orders in Protestant lands meant the disappearance from universities of monks and friars as students and teachers. A great number left their orders, some transferred to Catholic universities, and others ceased to study. The Habsburg-Valois wars fought on Italian soil

forced several Italian universities to close their doors for long periods of time; among these were Padua (closed 1509–1517), Rome (closed 1527–1539), Pavia (several closures between 1512 and 1541), and Turin (closed 1536–1538 and 1546–1558).

Universities under Protestant rule felt the impact of the Reformation in the classroom. Protestant authorities eliminated "popish" parts of the curriculum by abolishing the teaching of canon law and excluding the *Sentences* of Peter Lombard, the standard theological textbook used for centuries. A little Scholasticism, however, crept back into Protestant university curricula later in the century. In a curious parallel action, some Catholic universities also discarded Peter Lombard in the sixteenth century, but in favor of the works of Thomas Aquinas.

A few new universities were founded as a consequence of the Reformation and Counter-Reformation. The University of Marburg (1527) was the first university to be established by a Lutheran prince. Other new Lutheran universities were Königsberg (founded 1544), Jena (1558), and Helmstedt (1575). The University of Würzburg (established between 1561 and 1582) became a Catholic stronghold.

The new Society of Jesus began to play a significant role in Catholic higher education. The Collegio Romano, founded by the Jesuits in 1551, evolved into a university-level institution teaching the humanities, philosophy, and theology to Catholic seminarians and clergymen from every part of Europe. The Jesuits established residence and teaching colleges in university towns in order to bring a stronger Catholic presence to university communities. Some northern European universities, especially Vienna, appointed Jesuits to teach philosophy, theology, and arts. But Paris and universities in Catholic Italy would not accept Jesuits into their faculties.

Calvinists established a number of important schools in the sixteenth century. These schools, however, could not claim university status, and not until after 1648 would an emperor grant them charters empowering them to award degrees universally recognized. But the existing University of Heidelberg became a Calvinist institution in the 1560s; other German universities later turned Calvinist.

After the division of Europe into Protestant and Catholic camps in the middle of the sixteenth century, civil authorities imposed religious conformity on university personnel. Professors and students in Protestant lands typically had to swear adherence to a confessional statement embodying the prevailing religious orthodoxy. The state used its coercive power to enforce compliance and to punish disobedience.

Confessions of faith may have been most rigorously enforced in England. Some university personnel and students were executed for holding Lutheran beliefs under Henry VIII. Then Thomas Cranmer, Hugh Latimer, and Nicholas Ridley, three prominent leaders of the Protestant Church of England, were burned at Oxford in 1555 and 1556 during the reign of the Catholic Mary Tudor. Even though all three had been students and teachers at Cambridge earlier in the century, they perished for their leadership of the breakaway English church rather than for their university activities. Nevertheless, their execution in Oxford itself must have chilled religious dissent in English universities. Subsequently Elizabeth I punished Catholics for their beliefs during her reign (1558–1603); two priests and two laymen were arrested and executed in Oxford for treason—that is, refusing to abjure Catholic beliefs. Matriculation into the universities and promotion to degrees became conditional upon subscribing to the Elizabethan Articles of Religion and to the act of royal supremacy in the 1580s. Elizabeth also forced out heads of colleges and masters suspected of holding Catholic or Puritan beliefs.

The religious division of Europe had less impact on Italian universities than elsewhere because foreign Protestant students, especially Germans, continued to study in Italy without being molested. The papal nuncio to Venice in September 1566 lamented that there were two hundred German students, most of them Protestants, at the University of Padua. Venice would not bar them entry, he reported, because this would offend German princes. Moreover, wealthy German students spent the immense sum of twenty-five to thirty thousand ducats annually in Padua, and the Venetians believed that the prestige of the university depended on a large foreign enrollment.

In order to impose religious conformity, Pope Pius IV in 1564 ordered all professors in Catholic lands to swear an oath of allegiance to Catholicism. Students had to swear the same oath before receiving degrees. The requirement produced an immediate decline in the number of non-Italian recipients of degrees in Italian universities, but then the number of foreigners receiving degrees rose again. Protestant students found an ingenious way to circumvent the oath.

In the Middle Ages emperors and popes created counts palatine, officials authorized to act for them in certain legal matters, including the odd combination of awarding university degrees and legitimizing bastards. Once conferred, the office of count palatine was inherited indefinitely by legitimate male descendants. In addition, emperors and popes created numerous new counts palatine in the fifteenth and sixteenth centuries; indeed, professors avidly sought the honor. Hence, by the sixteenth century every Italian university and many elsewhere had one or more counts palatine on their faculties.

The counts palatine enabled Protestant students to receive degrees from Catholic universities. After a student passed his examination, a count palatine conferred the degree without demanding the religious oath. For example, in the early seventeenth century the University of Padua had a professor of law who had inherited the office of count palatine from an ancestor invested in 1434. This law professor in 1602 conferred a doctorate in arts and medicine on William Harvey, an English Protestant and future discoverer of the circulation of the blood. (Some Italian scholars argue that he simply wrote down what he had learned from his Paduan professors, a typical dispute over the priority of a scientific discovery.) Whether Catholics also studied and received degrees from Protestant universities without swearing allegiance to a confessional statement is unknown.

With the division of Europe into Protestant and Catholic camps and the development of press censorship on both sides, scholarly communication and free movement of students and professors from one university to another became much more difficult. But it never completely ceased.

[See also Cambridge, University of; Education; Faculty of Theology of Paris; Heidelberg, University of; Oxford, University of; Seminaries; and Wittenberg, University of.]

BIBLIOGRAPHY

Bylebyl, Jerome J. "The School of Padua: Humanistic Medicine in the Sixteenth Century." In *Health, Medicine and Mortality in the Sixteenth Century*, edited by Charles Webster, pp. 335–370. Cambridge, 1979. Excellent discussion of how humanism transformed medical research and teaching.

Cobban, Alan B. *The Medieval Universities: Their Development and Organization*. London, 1975. Describes universal characteristics of European universities with special attention to Bologna and Paris.

———. *The Medieval English Universities: Oxford and Cambridge to c.1500*. Aldershot, England, 1988. Covers the ground admirably.

Curtis, Mark H. *Oxford and Cambridge in Transition, 1558–1642: An Essay on Changing Relations between the English Universities and English Society*. Oxford, 1959.

De Ridder-Symoens, Hilde, ed. *A History of the University in Europe.* Vol. 1, *Universities in the Middle Ages*. Cambridge, 1992. Comprehensive topical survey of universities to 1500. Chapters are written by specialists. Particularly good on northern European developments.

Farge, James K. *Orthodoxy and Reform in Early Reformation France: The Faculty of Theology of Paris, 1500–1543*. Leiden, 1985. A detailed study of the personnel and activities of the major Catholic theological faculty.

Gabriel, Astrik L. "Universities." In *Dictionary of the Middle Ages*, edited by Joseph K. Strayer, vol. 12, pp. 282–300. New York, 1988. Good summary of origins and organization of universities to 1500.

Heath, Terrence. "Logical Grammar, Grammatical Logic, and Humanism in Three German Universities." *Studies in the Renaissance* 18 (1971), 9–64. Describes change from medieval to humanistic forms of grammar and logic at universities of Freiburg, Ingolstadt, and Tübingen.

History of Universities. Avebury, England, 1981–. Annual volume founded by late Charles B. Schmitt. Has many articles on pre-1700 universities, bibliographical surveys of recent research, and reviews. Excellent and useful.

McConica, James K., ed. *The History of the University of Oxford*. Vol. 3, *The Collegiate University*. Oxford, 1986. Excellent comprehensive study of every aspect of Oxford between 1485 and 1603.

Nauert, Charles G., Jr. "Humanist Infiltration into the Academic World: Some Studies of Northern Universities." In *Renaissance Quarterly* 43 (1990), 799–812, 818–824. Good survey of recent works with sound comments.

O'Malley, C. D. *Andreas Vesalius of Brussels, 1514–1564*. Berkeley, 1964. Standard biography of pioneering anatomist.

Overfield, James H. *Humanism and Scholasticism in Late Medieval Germany*. Princeton, 1984. Excellent study with much information on German universities. Argues that the conflict between Scholasticism and humanism was less sharp than supposed.

Rashdall, Hastings. *The Universities of Europe in the Middle Ages*. Edited by F. M. Powicke and A. B. Emden. 3 vols. Oxford, 1936. Revised edition of a work first published in 1895. Covers all of Europe to c.1500. Particularly good on structure and legal aspects of universities.

Schmitt, Charles B. *Aristotle and the Renaissance*. Cambridge, Mass., and London, 1983. Demonstrates the continuing importance of Aristotle for philosophy and other subjects in university curricula of the sixteenth century.

Spitz, Lewis W. "The Importance of the Reformation for the Universities: Culture and Confessions in the Critical Years." In *Rebirth, Reform and Resilience: Universities in Transition, 1300–1700*, edited by James M. Kittelson and Pamela Transue, pp. 42–67. Columbus, Ohio, 1984. Good survey of Protestant universities.

Thorndike, Lynn. *University Records and Life in the Middle Ages*. New York, 1944. A very informative collection of university documents, c.1150 to c.1650, in English translation.

Wear, A., R. K. French, and I. M. Lonie, eds. *The Medical Renaissance of the Sixteenth Century*. Cambridge, 1985. Discusses anatomy, surgery, and other aspects of the medical revolution of the sixteenth century in a European-wide context.

PAUL F. GRENDLER

UPPSALA, DIET OF.

UPPSALA, DIET OF. The historic archbishopric of Sweden was founded in 1164 on the site of an old Viking pagan temple and burial grounds. The boundaries of the archbishopric included that of Old Uppsala and the five sees of Linköping, Skara, Strengnäs, Västerås, Växjö, and Åbo in Finland. In 1477 the University of Uppsala was founded, from whose theology faculty clergy were trained to serve in the church of Sweden. During the medieval and Reformation eras, the archdiocese of Lund (now located in Sweden) and its university were part of Denmark and did not contribute directly to the Swedish Reformation as did Uppsala.

In 1520 the incumbent archbishop of Uppsala was Gustav Trolle, a Dane. He became suspect in connection with the infamous Stockholm Bloodbath of November 1520. As a result he was cast out of office by the irate Swedish people and their new leader, Gustavus Vasa, whom they proclaimed king in 1523. After several abortive requests for reform directed to the pope, the Diet of Västerås in 1527 set up a national church in Sweden and confiscated the church's surplus wealth and property. All the pope proposed was the reinstatement of the much-hated Danish archbishop, Trolle. Thus a golden opportunity for reform of the church of Sweden was squandered and the possibility of retaining Sweden in the Roman fold was lost. From 1520 to 1531, when Laurentius Petri was installed, no one occupied the chair of the archbishop of Uppsala. Though Johannes Magnus had been offered the archbishopric in 1523 by Vasa, it was never actualized by papal confirmation. Four years later Magnus went into exile, first to Poland and eventually to Italy, where he and his brother, Olaus, were to be remembered for their histories of the Swedish kings and the Nordic people of Scandinavia.

In 1531 Laurentius Petri was consecrated as the first Lutheran archbishop of Uppsala. The historic episcopate was preserved as a result of Petri's consecration by Petrus Magni, the Roman Catholic bishop of Västerås, who had full papal credentials and confirmation. Scholars like Sven Kjöllerström have debated whether apostolic succession was preserved during the 1540s when Vasa embarked on his presbyterizing church policy with George Norman as the lay overseer of the Church of Sweden. But it has been maintained that the historic episcopate was preserved in Sweden through the bishop of Åbo.

Petri had a forty-two-year tenure as the first Lutheran archbishop of Uppsala. He did not make anything of his apostolic succession, being most concerned about the succession of the apostolic message found in the scripture, which he was anxious to see handed down to succeeding generations.

During the 1540s, when Vasa was seeking to reduce the independence of the church of Sweden and place it under the central government, the archbishop worked to maintain the autonomy of the church assembly (*Kirkemöte*). Though not entirely successful in this endeavor, he did make it possible for the church to assert itself during the succession crisis of 1593. The Swedish population, which had grown increasingly Lutheran in its confessional loyalty during the sixteenth century, became alarmed in 1593 at the possibility of a Roman Catholic king. There had never been any law binding the Swedish church or society to a Lutheran confessional subscription. All that had ever been said was that the preaching should conform to the plain, simple teaching of scripture. During the 1560s, the confessional scale seemed to be tipping toward Calvinism when Erik XIV was king. But in 1593 the next in line to succeed to the Swedish throne was Sigismund III Vasa, who was already king of Poland. The son of John III and his Polish mother, Catherine Jagiellon, Sigismund had been raised an ardent Catholic. He used the forces of the Counter-Reformation and especially the Jesuits to roll back the Protestant Reformation in his mother's native land. In 1593 the prospects of a Roman Catholic dual monarchy of Poland-Sweden loomed on the horizon as a strong possibility.

The oral tradition handed down in Protestant Europe about "Bloody Mary's" reign in England, John Foxe's *Book of Martyrs*, the Wars of Religion in France and the Netherlands, and the horrors of the Saint Bartholomew's Day Massacre (1572) brought together the leaders of the Lutheran church in Sweden and the Calvinist duke of Finland, uncle of Sigismund and younger brother of John III. A hasty call of 9 January 1593 to the clergy of Sweden to assemble at Uppsala the next month was issued. Members of the council of state were allowed to take part as well. Three hundred and six clergy from all over the nation responded in the dead of winter. Proceedings got underway on 1 March, and on 10 March 1593 it was decreed, in spite of the duke's Calvinist leanings, that all future monarchs of Sweden-Finland must be Lutheran. The church assembly adopted the Augsburg Confession as the legal, binding confession for the entire church, its subjects, and its rulers. The regal principle of *cuius regio eius religio* (whoever the king, his religion) was turned inside out and the Swedish people, who had become thoroughly Lutheran over the course of the sixteenth century, determined the confessional subscription of their rulers. The Diet of Uppsala of 1593 has been important over the years in that it has given to the church of Sweden a degree of autonomy from the state that is unprecedented in Scandinavian circles.

Advised by his Jesuit counselors, Sigismund III subscribed to the Augsburg Confession late in 1593. Everyone knew he did it with tongue in cheek and did not have the slightest intention of becoming a Lutheran. Duke Charles of Finland became the regent of Sweden-Finland in 1593. When Sigismund III tried to invade Sweden and take his own kingdom by force in 1598, he was disastrously defeated at Stångebro by the Swedish army under his uncle. In 1604 the charade came to an end with Duke Charles becoming Charles IX (r. 1604–1611) which set the stage for his more illustrious son, Gustavus Adolphus (r. 1611–1632) the "Lion of the North."

BIBLIOGRAPHY

Cnattingius, Hans. *Uppsala möte 1593*. Stockholm, 1943.
Kjöllerström, Sven. *Kräkla och mitra*. Lund, 1965.
Skarsten, Trygve R. "The Reception of the Augsburg Confession in Scandinavia." *Sixteenth Century Journal* 11.3 (1980), 87–98.
Westman, K. B. *Uppsala möte och deres betydelse*. Stockholm, 1943.

TRYGVE R. SKARSTEN

URSINUS, Zacharias (Ger., Zacharias Baer; 1534–1583), German theologian and reformer of the Palatinate. Ursinus was born in Breslau, Silesia (now Wrocław, Poland), where friends and students of Melanchthon had already begun the Lutheran Reformation. He studied at Wittenberg (1550–1558) when Melanchthon and his Wittenberg colleagues were attacked by Matthias Flacius Illyricus and others over the adiaphora and Majorism, by Andreas Osiander over justification, and by the ubiquitarians over the real presence of Christ's body in the Eucharist. He began teaching Latin and Melanchthon's *Examen Ordinandorum* (1552) in Breslau after a study trip during the fall and winter of 1557/58 on which he visited the cities along the Rhine as well as Zurich, Geneva, and Paris. He met with many of the important scholars in those cities and studied Hebrew in Paris. Breslau was then divided over the elimi-

nation of Roman Catholic ceremonies and over the doctrine of the real presence.

To avoid personal involvement Ursinus took a leave of absence in 1560 to pursue his studies. He went to Zurich, where he studied Hebrew with Peter Martyr Vermigli. From there, on the recommendation of Hubert Languet, the diplomat and close friend of Melanchthon, and Caspar Peucer, Melanchthon's son-in-law, he was called to Heidelberg, where Elector Frederick III moved the Reformation in a Calvinist direction. As professor of theological commonplaces (until 1568) and rector of the seminary, Ursinus played a leading role in establishing the theology of these reforms. As the sole, or at least principal, author of the anonymous Heidelberg Catechism, he wrote its official defense (*Vera doctrina*, 1564) against attacks by the Gnesio-Lutherans, whose doctrine of ubiquity he rejected.

Although the Heidelberg Catechism is Calvinist, Ursinus's personal letters show that he did not include himself among the "sacramentarians," as Calvinists were then often called, but that he was a "cryto-Philippist." In the struggle over the establishment of a strict code of discipline he stayed on the sidelines; he was convinced that the secular government was a "principal part" of the church and thus should be represented in any disciplinary body. After the discovery of antitrinitarians in Heidelberg and renewed attacks on the Palatinate theology by the Gnesio-Lutheran Jakob Andreae, Ursinus wrote a defense (*Confessio de uno vero Deo, . . . ,* 1574) of the Palatinate doctrine of the Trinity. Frederick's son and successor, the Lutheran Ludwig VI, removed the Calvinists in 1576. In Neustadt, at the school established by Duke Johann Casimir, Ursinus wrote his last major attack on ubiquity, the *Admonitio Christiana de libro Concordiae* (1581). Ursinus's *Vera doctrina*, his *Confessio* on the Trinity, and the *Admonitio* became, together with the Heidelberg Catechism, the official confessional books of the Palatinate Church. At the Synod of Dordrecht (1618) the Heidelberg Catechism was established as one of the handbooks of Calvinist theology. Ursinus's greatest influence was undoubtedly exercised as rector of the seminary, where he prepared students for posts in church and school. His lectures on the Heidelberg Catechism were collected and edited by his student and successor, David Pareus. They became the basis for the teaching of Reformed theology for several centuries.

BIBLIOGRAPHY

Primary Sources

Ursinus, Zacharias. *Der Heidelberger Katechismus und vier verwandte Katechismen*. Leipzig, 1907.
———. *The Summe of Christian Religion*. London, 1983.

Secondary Sources

Burchill, Christopher. "On the Consolation of a Christian Scholar." *Journal of Ecclesiastical History* 37 (1986), 565–583. Concentrates on Ursinus's Heidelberg years.

Kolb, Robert A. "Luther, Augsburg and the Late Reformation Concept of Confession." In *Controversy and Conciliation: The Reformation and the Palatinate,* edited by Derk Visser, pp. 33–50. Allyson Park, Pa., 1986. Useful study of the differences between Gnesio-Lutherans and Reformed in Germany.

Sturm, Erdmann K. *Der junge Zacharias Ursin: Sein Weg vom Philipismus zum Calvinismus, 1534–1561.* Neukirchen, Germany, 1972. Places great importance on the theological development of Melanchthon in the intra-Lutheran polemics after Luther's death and the Augsburg Interim and argues that Ursinus's Calvinism followed almost naturally out of this development.

Visser, Derk. *Zacharias Ursinus: The Reluctant Reformer.* New York, 1983. Significantly revised for the Dutch translation (*Zacharias Ursinus,* Kampen, Netherlands, 1991). Differs with Sturm on Melanchthon's moving toward Calvinism and consequently seeks the Calvinism of Ursinus's doctrinal writings in the Heidelberg context after 1561.

DERK VISSER

URSULINES. The Company of Saint Ursula formally came into existence on 25 November 1535 in Brescia when twenty-eight young female followers of Angela Merici acknowledged their acceptance of a life as consecrated virgins living in the world and devoted to piety, charity, and Christian education, and signed their names in a register. The history of the Ursulines in the sixteenth century divides easily into four periods. The first period (1535–1540) is related to Angela's spiritual life and the influence of religious renewal in Italy such as the Company of Divine Love and the Franciscan tertiaries and confraternities. The primordial rule (1536), notable for its simplicity and flexibility, emphasized virginity, fasting, both vocal and mental prayer, frequent confession and attendance at Mass, obedience, and simple dress. Each woman lived a life of prayer and contemplation at home and practiced the apostolate within her family and community. The simple governance of the company was in the hands of four mature women to supervise the younger ones, four matron-widows to offer mature guidance, and four "men of experience and tried virtue" to act as spiritual guides and business managers. In 1537 the foundress was elected to fill the newly created position of mother-general. By 1540, with over seventy women in the company, Angela created another group of supervisors called *colonelle* who were assigned to districts in the city to oversee the daily work of the sisters.

Internal strife marked the period 1540–1559. With the loss of the foundress's charismatic leadership, strong personalities both inside the company and among local clergy struggled for control. The spirit of Trent influenced both clergy and parents to bring the company in line with more traditional religious orders by adopting a distinctive costume, restructuring the governance, and instituting rituals for acceptance. Disputed elections of mother-generals testify to the division.

The years 1559–1584 saw reconciliation of the disputes under the powerful influence of a new confessor and spiritual director, Francesco Cabrini, founder of the Congregation of Fathers; the election of a powerful advocate of local reform, Domenico Bollani, to the long-vacant bishopric of Brescia; and the election of Carlo Borromeo to the bishopric of Milan. The latter revised the rule for his diocese by reducing the sections that emphasized personal piety and enlarging the sections on obedience and governance, placing the company under clerical leadership, and sponsoring a rule "for those Ursulines who wish to live in community." The Ursulines also became formally allied with the Schools of Christian Doctrine. In Brescia, in 1580, Borromeo sponsored a modification of the rule along the lines of the Milanese revisions. Stricter qualifications for mother-general were imposed and her powers restricted in favor of expanded authority of the bishop.

The expansion of the movement after 1584 in northern Italian cities—the fourth period—can be attributed both to the popularity of the ideal of an active apostolate for women, Borromeo's sponsorship, and published papal approval. Although the rule varied from place to place, in general it was based on the Brescian or Milanese modifications regarding virgins living with their families. Gradually, as pressure was applied for solemn vows and claustration, the Ursulines established schools within the cloister walls.

The Ursulines were created in the spirit of early sixteenth-century lay piety; by the late sixteenth century, in the spirit of Trent, such piety was regarded with suspicion. Thus, the ideal of an active teaching apostolate for women succumbed to the Tridentine decrees regarding claustration and lay and clerical fears about uncloistered women.

[*See also* Nuns *and* Religious Orders.]

BIBLIOGRAPHY

Ledóchowska, Teresa. *Angela Merici and the Company of St. Ursula According to the Historical Documents.* Translated by Mary Teresa Neylan. 2 vols. Milan, 1969. This volume is the only scholarly study available in English; contains many documents in translation from the Italian archives although the author did not always make critical use of them.

Liebowitz, Ruth P. "Virgins in the Service of Christ: The Dispute over the Active Apostolate for Women during the Counter-Reformation." In *Women of Spirit: Female Leadership in the Jewish and Christian Traditions,* edited by Rosemary Ruether and Eleanor McLaughlin, pp. 132–152. New York, 1979. Valuable interpretative essay that sets the Ursulines in the context of other contemporary female religious orders.

Mariani, Luciana, Elisa Tarolli, and Maria Seynaeve. *Angela Merici: Contributo per una biografia.* Introduction by Christopher Cairns. Milan, 1986. Best modern study of the life of Angela Merici and the history of the company through the sixteenth century. Contains most of the important documents located in Italian archives, including earliest known version of the rule.

Monica, Sister Mary. *Angela Merici and Her Teaching Ideal.* New York, 1927. Thoughtful discussion marred by the author's failure to cite sources carefully.

CHARMARIE J. BLAISDELL

USINGEN, Bartholomäus Arnoldi von

USINGEN, Bartholomäus Arnoldi von (c.1464–1532), Augustinian hermit and polemical theologian. Arnoldi, born in the village of Usingen in the district of Taunus, registered as a student at the University of Erfurt in the autumn of 1484. There he received a bachelor of arts in 1486 and a master of arts in 1491. Subsequently he wrote several systematic textbooks on philosophy, including *Parvulus philosophiae naturalis* (Leipzig, 1499) and *Compendium totius loyce* (Leipzig, 1500), which were also published in other university cities (Kraków, Vienna, Basel, Cologne) and remained in use for a long time. Along with Jodokus Trutfetter (d. 1519), he imposed Ockhamistic nominalism as the required school of thought at the University of Erfurt.

In 1512 Usingen entered the Erfurt cloister of the Augustinian hermits and two years later received a doctorate in theology. Inspired by humanism in the years that followed, his preference for the scholastic theologians gave way to an interest in the church fathers. In April 1518 he accompanied Martin Luther, also an Augustinian hermit, to the Heidelberg Disputation.

Even at this early date his disapproving attitude toward reform became apparent. It was in this spirit that he served, though with little success, first as prior of the Augustinian hermits' cloister (1519) and later as the dean of the theology faculty (1521). From 1522 onward he held the office of preacher at the collegiate church Beatae Mariae Virginis. He preached before large audiences but was the only major adherent of the old faith in Erfurt.

Usingen and the Reformation preachers conducted a lively polemical exchange through pamphlets over the course of several years. (While his opponents published in German, Usingen wrote in Latin.) Having received no support from the city council, Usingen left Erfurt in May 1525 and went to the Augustinian hermits' monastery in Würzburg. In the years that followed he pursued his debate with Reformation teaching in various writings and defended the positions of the Catholic church (grace, good works, purgatory, veneration of the saints). He devoted particular attention to the Anabaptists. In his sermons, but even more in his Latin publications, Usingen supported reform conducted completely within the church and implemented by the ecclesiastical authorities. He saw various manifestations of the time as the consequence of evangelical preaching (such as decline in university studies, the Peasants' War, the Anabaptist movement). Usingen was one of the participants in the Imperial Diet of Augsburg in 1530. He was a member of the theological commission and one of the authors of the *Catholica responsio* and the *Confutatio*. To the *Apologia* of Philipp Melanchthon he devoted his exhaustive *Responsio contra Apologiam*.

While Usingen's polemical theological writings met with little response in the empire, they became very influential in Poland. One of the foremost theologians of his time, Usingen combined his defense of the Catholic church with proposals for reform that would later be discussed at the Council of Trent.

BIBLIOGRAPHY

Bäumer, Remigius. "Bartholomäus von Usingen OESA, c.1464–1532." In *Katholische Theologen der Reformationszeit,* edited by Remigius Bäumer, pp. 27–37. Münster, 1986.

Estreicher, Karol. *Bibliografia Polska.* Krakow, 1938. See vol. 32, pp. 80–81.

Hoar, George A. "Early Evidences of Catholic Reform in the Thought and Actions of Bartholomaeus Arnoldi von Usingen." *Archiv für Reformationsgeschichte* 56 (1965), 155–165.

Kleineidam, Erich. *Universitas Studii Erffordensis: Überblick über die Geschichte der Universität Erfurt.* Pt. 2, *Spätscholastik und Reformation, 1461–1521.* 2d ed. Leipzig, 1992. See pp. 298–301.

Verzeichnis der im deutschen Sprachbereich erschienenen Drucke des XVI. Jahrhunderts. Stuttgart, 1983–. Vol. 16, nos. 3691–3755.

ULMAN WEIß
Translated from German by Robert E. Shillenn

USURY

USURY was the most important issue in medieval moral theology concerning economics. The epitome of oppressive greed, the usurer—often identified with the Jew in anti-usury polemics—was a stock character in didactic art. By the seventeenth century, however, the matter had been relegated to the status of a theological scruple in a world that accepted lending at interest as an economic necessity.

Usury, as understood in medieval theology, was lending anything for a guaranteed return over and above the principal without risk to the lender. Forbidden by canon law and by many secular law codes, usury was defined as sin in a series of biblical verses, culminating in *Luke* 6:35, "Lend freely, hoping for nothing in return." To do otherwise was to commit theft and murder, damning one's soul.

Thomas Aquinas explained that usury was an unnatural act, making a profit without taking a risk. The mere act of contracting for usury was evil and became punishable as a deadly sin in the church courts. Accordingly, all lenders at interest were sinners; all borrowers were victims.

By the sixteenth century the Thomist definition of usury was under attack from two directions. One critique, associated with Jean Gerson, nominalists such as Conrad Summenhardt, and Johann Eck, argued that usury occurred only when the lender intended to oppress the borrower. This line of reasoning was generally adopted by Protestant reformers, who made the Golden Rule the standard against which lending was measured. If the borrower and lender were in charity with one another there was no usury. Thus Luther, Calvin, and Bucer agreed widows, orphans, students, ministers, and other needy people could lend at interest to support themselves. Charles du Moulin created a highly influential argument that said one should give to the poor, lend without interest to the working people, and lend with interest to those who used money to make money.

Another critique of the mechanical measurement of usury had to do with the definition of risk. If risk included an estimation of the chances of repayment, interest could be charged, since there was no loan without risk. This line of reasoning was developed by Juan Medina (d. 1516) and adopted by the Jesuit theologians Luis de Molina and Leonard Lessius in the late sixteenth century.

The result of these theological attacks meant that the medieval legal tradition was slowly replaced in Protestant regions by a toleration of lending for interest as long as that interest did not offend the law of God in conscience. In Catholic regions a similar change was occurring in regard to risk, though this did not permit the personal aggrandizement encouraged by hiding usury within the unknowable individual conscience.

By about 1600 all European states and their church courts were espousing more liberal definitions of usury. In 1500 any lending at interest with a guaranteed return was sinful; by 1600 the definitions had been stretched until the sin only occurred when there was a break in charity between the borrower and lender, or when the lender charged more for the assumption of risk than was legitimate.

Changes in theology had precipitated changes in law that helped spur the emergence of a capitalist economy, but there were other definitions of usury distinct from the legal ones. The usurer had long been the object of preachers' opprobrium and the name *usurer* had a broad moral content. Usurers became stock literary characters, personifying in their greed, their social climbing, and their callous disregard for suffering many of the social trends disturbing Reformation society. Representing all those who put mammon before God, they were seen as destroying their own societies. Jews were often identified with usurers because, as non-Christians, they could legally lend money. Thus the moneylender was not only damned for his sin against humanity; he was also connected with a group known to be "enemies of Christ." By the early seventeenth century Christian usurers began to disappear in literature, leaving Jews with the opprobrium.

Our understanding of usury has been shaped by two kinds of scholars, the students of the history of ideas and the students of capitalism. The best intellectual histories of usury are John Noonan's superb *The Scholastic Analysis of Usury* (Cambridge, Mass., 1957) and Thomas Divine's *Interest* (Milwaukee, 1959). They trace the history of usury from its origins through the early modern period.

Students of capitalism are influenced by the arguments of Max Weber and Karl Marx. For them usury has great significance as an indicator of the penetration of capitalist ethics. Unfortunately, by becoming linked to debate over the tie between religion and the rise of capitalism, the economics of lending have been ignored. Weberian sociologists such as Benjamin Nelson, who assumed that the decline of usury as a sin was proof that religion gave rise to capitalism, generally ignore the actual operation of the money market in their defense of Weber. Economic historians, following the Marxist model that denigrated theology as a "mere" product of a changing economy, have failed to dissect the operations of the credit market in order to see what evidence there was for the generation of new theology by economic change. They seem to take the market for money as a given, even though the very debate over usury proves it was not. R. H. Tawney is an exception to this criticism. He did try to find the links between theology and practice in England.

More recently legal historians have become interested in the practice of usury as formed by law, attempting to separate polemical myth from economic theory and practice. For instance, R. H. Helmholtz has studied usury in English church courts. Norman Jones has studied the relations between theology, law, and lending by studying English courts.

These recent studies confirm that the Reformation era saw the redefinition of usury. Once a damnable sin, it became nothing more than charging excessive interest. This redefinition, the product of theology and practice, laid one foundation for the emergence of capitalist economies.

[*See also* Antisemitism; Capitalism; *and* Weber Thesis.]

BIBLIOGRAPHY

Divine, Thomas F. *Interest: An Historical and Analytical Study of Economics and Modern Ethics.* Milwaukee, 1959. A good treatment of the concept.

Gordon, Barry. *Economic Analysis before Adam Smith: Hessiod to Lessius.* London, 1975. Especially good on the early history of the controversy.

Grammp, William D. "The Controversy over Usury in the Seventeenth Century." *Journal of European Economic History* 10 (1981), 671–695. Describes usury from an economist's point of view.

Helmholtz, R. H. "Usury and the Medieval English Church Courts." *Speculum* 61 (1986), 364–380. Carries the study into the mid-sixteenth century.

Jones, Norman. *God and the Moneylenders: Usury and the Law in Early Modern England.* Oxford, 1989. Looks at the interplay between law, theology, and economic practice c.1545–1630.

Le Goff, Jacques. *Your Money or Your Life: Economy and Religion in the Middle Ages.* New York, 1988. A brief introduction to usury in theology, pastoral practice, and popular conception.

Nelson, Benjamin. *The Idea of Usury: From Universal Brotherhood to Universal Otherhood.* Chicago, 1969. A Weberian argument that tries to demonstrate the link between changing ideas of usury and Reformation theology.

Stevenson, Laura Caroline. *Praise and Paradox: Merchants and Craftsmen in Elizabethan Popular Literature.* Cambridge, 1984. Includes a fine survey of the usurer in English literature.

Tawney, R. H. *Religion and the Rise of Capitalism.* Harmondsworth, 1984. A classic text stating the larger links between the two.

Tawney, R. H., ed. *A Discourse Upon Usury by Way of Dialogue and Orations by Thomas Wilson.* London, 1925. The long introduction to this classical debate on usury is an attempt to show how money lending was done. Jones supersedes some, but not all, of what Tawney has to say.

NORMAN JONES

UTENHOVE, Jan

UTENHOVE, Jan (1516–1566), elder of the Dutch refugee (stranger) church in London and author. Scion of an ancient line of patricians of Ghent, Utenhove studied under Joris Cassander in the city of his birth. After allowing a heretical rhetorical play to be performed at his country house in 1543, he was pressured to leave the city and fled to Germany. In 1545 he settled in Strasbourg and formed friendships with the leaders of the Alsatian reformation—Martin Bucer, Peter Martyr Vermigli, and Paul Fagius.

With the implementation of the Augsburg Interim in 1548, Utenhove followed Vermigli across the channel to England. At Canterbury he was the guest of Thomas Cranmer, together with the Polish reformer Jan Łaski. He founded there the first refugee congregation, which consisted mostly of French-speaking Protestants. In the spring of 1549 he moved back to the Continent. At Zurich he made a good impression on Heinrich Bullinger with his conception of the Lord's Supper. He possibly spoke with Calvin in Geneva on this same topic in the course of negotiations for the Consensus Tigurinus. After returning to England, he stayed with John Hooper, along with Maarten Micron, also from Ghent. Through the efforts of Łaski, the Dutch refugee congregation received use of the church nave of the Augustinian friars on 29 June 1550. Utenhove was one of the four elders chosen on 5 October 1550 to assist the ministers in leading the Dutch-speaking church. For the benefit of the congregation, he provided at his own cost for the Dutch translation of writings by Łaski. At the same time, Utenhove published his first metrical settings of the *Psalms*, a task that he took very much to heart for the rest of his life.

After the accession of the Catholic Mary Tudor, Utenhove left England on 17 September 1557, together with 175 church members. He later described the unfortunate sea voyage and the eventual reception at Emden in his *Simplex et fidelis narratio* (1560). Utenhove's Dutch translation of the Bible in verse appeared in 1556. Its sales proved to be a financial fiasco. Utenhove spent 1556–1559 in Poland, laboring with Łaski to build up the Reformation. There he worked anew on his *Psalms* translations and wrote his *Rationes quaedam* (1560), a collection of proofs against the Lutheran doctrine of the Lord's Supper.

In the summer of 1559 he was back in London, where the immigrant church was reconstituted. Although he held simply the office of elder, he remained the undisputed leader of the congregation until his death. He came before the royal court and other leaders in defense of the material needs of the church members and espoused the cause of founding the Flemish congregations at Sandwich, Norwich, and Colchester. In 1564 he played an important role in the transfer of the English wool trade from Antwerp to Emden. He had great authority in resolving dogmatic disputes within the London congregation. Against Adriaan Corneliszoon van Haemstede—who, under suspicion of Anabaptist leanings, was suspended as pastor and excommunicated in 1560—Utenhove took an unreconciling posture. He put much energy into the Dutch setting of the *Psalms* according to Clément Marot and Théodore de Bèze. Utenhove's complete rhymed setting, *De Psalmen Davids*, appeared in 1566 but was quickly replaced by the psalms of Petrus Dathenus, which appeared in the same year.

Utenhove was of exceptional significance for the founding and development of the Dutch refugee church in England, both in the realm of organization and discipline and in his theological and liturgical writings. Together with Micron and Łaski, he drew on the church of Zurich much more than on the Calvinist model.

BIBLIOGRAPHY

Itterzon, G. P. van. "Utenhove, Jan." In *Biografisch Lexicon voor de Geschiedenis van het Nederlandse Protestantisme*, vol. 2, cols. 427–430. Kampen, 1983.

Lenselink, S. J. *De Nederlandse Psalmberijmingen van de Souterliedekens tot Datheen*. Cor. ed. Dordrecht, 1983. Considers his translations of *Psalms*.

Pettegree, Andrew. *Foreign Protestant Communities in Sixteenth-Century London*. Oxford, 1986. Considers his significance as elder of the Dutch refugee church and his role in the controversy with Adriaan Corneliszoon van Haemstede.

Pijper, Frederik. *Jan Utenhove: Zijn leven en zijne Werke*. Leiden, 1883.

Slenk, Howard. "Jan Utenhove's Psalms in the Low Countries." *Nederlands Archief voor Kerkgeschiedenis* 49 (1968–1969), 155–168.

JOHAN DECAVELE
Translated from Dutch by Jeff Bach

UTRAQUISTS

UTRAQUISTS. This group formed the majority church of the first Reformation in Bohemia and Moravia. They emerged from the Hussite revolution and represented its moderate wing in contrast to the radical Taborites. Since the Hussites demanded the celebration of the Eucharist in accordance with the Bible, the chalice became their symbol, and they are often called Calixtines. They characterized themselves as the ones "who receive the body and blood of Christ in both forms (*sub utraque specie*)," which led to their designation as "Utraquists." The Communion of the laity in both kinds was not merely a liturgical difference. It was considered necessary for salvation since Christ had ordered it. Therefore, the elements were also given to little children. The biblicism implied in this differentiated the Utraquists funadmentally from the Roman church. They rejected papal authority and tradition, as well as Roman jurisdiction, and alongside the Bible accepted only the teachings of the ancient church fathers. Charles University in Prague was their intellectual center.

Except for the rejection of indulgences and monastic orders, however, the Utraquist church remained essentially Catholic in doctrine. They accepted the seven sacraments and utilized the Roman liturgy of the Mass, which was, however, conducted in Czech. They held to apostolic succession and thus for the ordination of their priests turned to sympathetic Catholic bishops, often those in Italy.

The legal basis for the existence of the Utraquist church was formed by the Basel Compacts and the Religious Peace of Kuttenberg (Kutná Hora) of 1485. The kings had to affirm their allegiance to the principles of these documents by an oath made during their coronation. Until 1471 the church was led by the elected but never confirmed archbishop Jan Rokycana (1390/92–1471). Later appointments to clerical offices and ecclesiastical jurisdiction were in the hands of a consistory in Prague, which consisted of twelve members with an administrator at the head. The deans exercised direct supervision of the lower clergy as in the Catholic church.

Theological issues were decided by synods, but the highest decision-making body was the assembly of the Utraquist estates, which included the nobility and representatives of the cities. They prejudged the decisions to be taken by synods and chose the administrator and the consistory. To represent church interests before the king and the Catholics, they appointed a committee of noble "defenders" (Defensores) whose functions were also supervised by the Prague councillors.

Under the administration of Václav Koranda during the years 1471 to 1479, the Utraquists began to splinter in two directions. The conservatives sought to reestablish their connections with Rome and before 1525 were negotiating a resolution. They were satisfied with the Catholic wording of the Basel Compacts and wished only to retain Communion in both kinds and children's Communion, as well as the secularization of church goods. The radical, leftist Utraquists, on the other hand, sought reform of the church according to their interpretation of the Bible. They reached back to the traditions of the Taborites and appropriated the theology of the Bohemian Brethren, thereby differentiating themselves more clearly from the Roman church. These New-Utraquists—as they are designated in historiography—rejected the compacts as early as 1520 because they considered them to be Catholic chains. They had contacts with Martin Luther after 1519, called Thomas Müntzer to Prague in 1521, and in 1524 adopted a reform program at a synod under the administrator Gallus (Havel) Cahera that included theological elements from both Luther and the Bohemian Brethren. A conservative overthrow among the Prague councillors, however, prevented implementation of the program. Ferdinand I, King of Bohemia (r. 1526–1664), also favored the conservative faction and forbade all new teachings.

As a result of contacts by Prague University professors with Wittenberg and because of the support of the Prague Council, the influence of reform-minded New-Utraquists increased around 1540. At their head stood Václav Mitmá-

nek (c.1510–1553), a disciple of Philipp Melanchthon and a former member of the Bohemian Brethren, and the administrator Jan Mystopol (d. 1568). At a synod in 1543 they tried to abolish the sacrifice of the Mass and to establish the Lutheran doctrine of justification and make possible a common reformed church with the Bohemian Brethren. But because of the meager support of the nobility, the king was able to intervene against them, ban Mitmánek, and establish a conservative church leadership.

Despite the defeat of a rebellion of the non-Catholic estates (1547) and royal pressure on the now compliant consistory to achieve an understanding with the Catholic church, the Utraquist estates opposed re-Catholicization. To be sure, from 1554 King Ferdinand was able to decide the election of the consistory and defenders more to his liking. On the other hand, the Utraquist university professors, clergy, and estates, under the leadership of Baron Bohuslaus Felix Hassenstein von Lobkowitz (1517–1583), moved closer and closer to the growing number of Lutherans, above all in the direction of Melanchthon, who maintained contacts with Charles University. The conservative consistory lost more and more of its authority among the Utraquist clergy. After the clergy and the estates had concluded in 1562 a confession that reached back to older, more radical Hussite notions, they had the Basel Compacts officially annulled in 1567. With this they legally cut any connection to the Catholic church. The Utraquist church was now visibly split into two wings, with reformers supported by the estates and the conservatives by the consistory. The New-Utraquists, with the Lutherans and the Bohemian Brethren, adopted the Bohemian Confession of 1575 as a common doctrinal statement of Bohemian non-Catholics. The text includes much from the Augsburg Confession but contains some Hussite articles and adaptations. Emperor Maximilian II (1564–1576) orally asserted his recognition of this confession of the Bohemian Protestants but rejected their proposed common church order and only tolerated the election of the defenders by the estates.

The conservative Old-Utraquists of the consistory came more and more under the influence of the Catholic hierarchy and Habsburg religious policy. They finally subordinated themselves in 1591 to the Roman church, from which they differentiated themselves by continuing the liturgical practice of Communion of the laity in both kinds. The unified confessional opposition of the evangelical Utraquists, Lutherans, and Bohemian Brethren, led by the noble defenders, continued to demand their legalization and their own church organization. This they achieved in 1609 with the Letter of Majesty of Emperor Rudolf II (r. 1576–1612), which allowed the election of defenders and of the consistory by the estates and a Protestant administration of the university. The church leadership was composed of a mixture of Utraquists, Lutherans, and Bohemian Brethren. After the defeat of the Protestant estates at the Battle of White Mountain in 1620, however, Emperor Ferdinand II (r. 1619–1637) annulled the charter. First the Bohemian Brethren, then the Utraquists, and finally the Lutherans were forced to convert to Catholicism or to emigrate.

BIBLIOGRAPHY

Dillon, Kenneth J. *King and Estates in the Bohemian Lands, 1526–1564.* Brussels, 1976. Contains a chapter on the religious developments.

Eberhard, Winfried. *Konfessionsbildung und Stände in Böhmen, 1478–1530.* Munich, 1981. Stresses above all the differentiation of Utraquism in connection with social and political contrasts.

———. "Bohemia, Moravia and Austria." In *The Early Reformation in Europe,* edited by Andrew Pettegree, pp 23–48. Cambridge, 1992. Studies the period 1520–1550.

Heymann, Frederick G. "The Hussite-Utraquist Church in the Fifteenth and Sixteenth Centuries." *Archiv für Reformationsgeschichte* 52 (1961), 1–26. Primarily covers the end of the fifteenth and the beginning of the sixteenth century.

———. "The Impact of Martin Luther upon Bohemia." *Central European History* 1 (1968), 107–130. On the first half of the sixteenth century.

Hoensch, Jörg K. *Geschichte Böhmens.* 2d enl. ed. Munich, 1992. Contains short but informative surveys of confessional development.

Machilek, Franz. "Böhmen." In *Die Territorien des Reichs im Zeitalter der Reformation und Konfessionalisierung, Land und Konfession, 1500–1650,* edited by Anton Schindling and Walter Ziegler, vol. 1, pp. 134–152. Münster, 1989. A concentrated survey of confessional development from the fifteenth to the seventeenth centuries.

Říčan, Rudolf. *Das Reich Gottes in den böhmischen Ländern, Geschichte des tschechischen Protestantismus.* Stuttgart, 1957.

Richter, Karl. "Die böhmischen Länder von 1471–1740." In *Handbuch der Geschichte der Böhmischen Länder,* edited by Karl Bosl, vol. 2, pp. 97–412. Stuttgart, 1974. With many references to sources and literature.

WINFRIED EBERHARD
Translated from German by Walter D. Morris

UTRECHT. Founded in 690 by Saint Willibrord, Utrecht is a city in the central Netherlands, an (archi)episcopal seat, and the capital of Utrecht province. In the Middle Ages Utrecht was the seat of a large bishopric that encompassed the entire northern Netherlands and the capital of an ecclesiastical principality that included the present provinces of Utrecht and Overijssel. The city had over twenty monastic houses and a large clerical population. Its five collegiate churches, with their immunities, dominated the city both spatially and socially; together they controlled the first estate in Utrecht's provincial estates and owned roughly a quarter of the land in Utrecht province. In 1528 temporal sovereignty over the province (known thereafter as the *Sticht*) passed from the bishop to Emperor Charles V. In 1559, under the "new bishoprics scheme" of Philip II of Spain, Utrecht was elevated to archiepiscopal status.

Protestantism made quick but limited headway in Utrecht. In 1522 Hinne Rode was dismissed as rector of Utrecht's Brethren of the Common Life. An associate of Cornelis Hoen, Rode traveled to Germany and Switzerland to bring Hoen's symbolic interpretation of the Eucharist to the attention of leading reformers, including Zwingli, whom it may have influenced. In 1524, Utrecht's magistrates felt compelled to promulgate an edict forbidding conventicles. Persecution of Protestants grew more severe after the transfer of sovereignty in 1528. Still, the *Sticht* saw far fewer executions for heresy than the neighboring province of Holland: one historian has counted thirty-one in the *Sticht* prior to the summer of 1566. Most of the cases involved Anabaptists, groups of whom were executed in 1535, 1539, and 1541–1545. Utrecht's clergy, as well as its magistrates, did not cooperate with the imperial inquisitors, whom they resented for encroaching upon their jurisdictions.

At least a few Protestant conventicles were held in Utrecht in the late 1550s. A few years later some Utrechters were traveling outside the *Sticht* (e.g., to nearby IJsselstein) to attend Reformed services. An organized Reformed congregation seems not to have existed in Utrecht prior to 1566. Hedge sermons (called such because held outside the gates of cities) began in mid-August of that year, and soon afterward iconoclasts damaged eight churches, four substantially. The city magistrates briefly conceded to the Reformed the use of one parish church, but all concessions ended in February 1567. The Council of Troubles, created by Fernando Álvarez de Toledo, duke of Alba, subsequently condemned over 280 persons from the *Sticht,* including about 230 from Utrecht itself; the condemnations included 65 death sentences, mostly *in absentia.* Utrecht's collegiate churches finally submitted in 1568 with great reluctance to the decrees of the Council of Trent. Even under Alba's harsh regime, however, reform of the Catholic church made scant progress.

Protestant religious life began to revive almost immediately after the Pacification of Ghent (November 1576), by which the *Sticht* joined the Dutch Revolt against Spain. Between 1577 and 1579 Calvinists in Utrecht organized a congregation, modeling it on the Calvinist congregations formed in Holland and Zeeland since 1572. At the same time, however, Hubert Duifhuis, copastor of the Jacobskerk parish, set about reforming his own flock. Two separate Reformed churches thus emerged in Utrecht—one Calvinist, or "consistorial," and the other called "Libertine" by the Calvinists because it had no consistory or ecclesiastical discipline. Duifhuis admitted everyone to Communion in his church, irrespective of morals or beliefs; he also granted secular authorities far more power over religious affairs than did Dutch Calvinists. The Jacobskerk drew the support of Utrecht's patriciate and native poor; master craftsmen and immigrants predominated in the Calvinist congregation. Political pressures and popular agitation (including several waves of iconoclasm) forced Utrecht's rulers to assist the two Reformed congregations in 1578, to issue a religious peace granting them equality with the Catholics in 1579, and finally to outlaw Catholic worship in 1580. In 1582, the central government of the now independent United Provinces (established 1579) secularized the five collegiate chapters. Selected members of the chapters continued to form the first estate in the provincial Estates.

Conflict between Calvinists and "Libertines" (that is, supporters of the Jacobskerk) dominated the course of the Reformation in Utrecht from the late 1570s into the early 17th century. At first the Libertines had the upper hand. Then in 1586 Robert Dudley, earl of Leicester, became governor-general of the Netherlands. Leicester chose Utrecht as his base. An alliance between him and Utrecht's Calvinists led to a series of purges that brought a Calvinist theocratic regime to power in the city. The new regime effectively dissolved the Jacobskerk by forcing it to merge with Utrecht's Calvinist church; it also set about suppressing the remnants of Catholicism and began to Calvinize urban culture. With the collapse of Leicester's power in 1588, the Calvinist regime fell and a Libertine reaction followed. The new magistrates dismissed all of Utrecht's Reformed ministers in 1589; in 1590 they issued a new church ordinance for the city, one based on Libertine principles but retaining a powerless consistory. Utrecht's Calvinists refused to accept the new situation, forming conventicles and traveling outside the city to attend Calvinist services. Finally, in 1605 Utrecht's magistrates relented, and in the next four years Utrecht's Reformed church adopted a moderate Calvinism. In 1606 a provincial synod met for the first time. The old schism finally ended.

No sooner had it done so, however, than a new one arose. In 1610 the Remonstrant controversy came to Utrecht. A large-scale urban uprising that same year complicated matters. All of Utrecht's Reformed ministers were Remonstrants, and by censuring the rebels they helped to drive the latter into the Contra-Remonstrant camp. Once again some Utrechters began to attend church outside the city. In 1612 another provincial synod met. It adopted a new, provincial church ordinance designed to contain the Remonstrant controversy, which it did, at least among the clergy. Remonstrants in Holland soon viewed the ordinance as a model for their own province. Finally, in 1618, with the Netherlands tottering on the brink of civil war, Prince Maurice of Naussau executed a bloodless coup. In Utrecht he purged and restructured both the city government and the provincial Estates, which then approved the holding of a national synod. The Synod of Dordrecht (1618–1619), followed by a provincial synod, brought the complete triumph of the Contra-Remonstrants. In Utrecht, ecclesiastical discipline grew stricter, catechism instruction was promoted more actively, and regional classes finally began to function, making possible for the first time the extension of Calvinist influence to large parts of the *Stichtse* countryside. Utrecht remained, however, a tolerant, multiconfessional urban society. Several Mennonite congregations existed there, as did a Lutheran one. Catholics had never suffered a break in pastoral care, and after a period of recovery and reorganization, they came to constitute a third to a half of the city's population.

[*See also* Duifhuis, Hubert; *and* Sybrandszoon, Taco.]

BIBLIOGRAPHY

Boom, H. Ten, ed. *Utrechters entre-deux: Stad en Sticht in de eeuw van de reformatie, 1520–1620.* Delft, 1992. Valuable miscellaneous articles

Hulzen, A. van. *Utrecht in 1566 en 1567.* Groningen, 1932.

Kaplan, Benjamin J. *Calvinists and Libertines: The Reformation in Utrecht, 1578–1618.* Oxford, forthcoming.

Royaards, Herm. Joh. *Geschiedenis der Hervorming in de stad Utrecht.* Leiden, 1847. Outdated in its methodology and interpretations, but well researched. Covers from 1565 to 1590.

Struick, J. E. A. L. *Utrecht door de eeuwen heen.* Utrecht, 1971. Overview of the city's history.

Vliet, Jan van. *Ketters rond de Dom: De reformatie in Utrecht, 1520–1580.* Utrecht, 1987. Short, semi-popularizing.

BENJAMIN J. KAPLAN

UYTENBOGAERT, Johannes. *See* Wtenbogaert, Johannes.

V

VADIAN, Joachim (also Vadianus; Joachim von Watt; 1484–1551), Swiss humanist, physician, and reformer of St. Gall. Born at St. Gall, he studied in the arts faculty at the University of Vienna beginning in 1501 and received an M.A. in 1508. He then taught at the university, becoming professor of rhetoric in 1516 and rector the same year. During his years in Vienna, he wrote and published poetry and orations, as well as a work in geography, in which field he became an expert for his day. In 1514 he was crowned poet laureate by the emperor. Also in 1514 he began to study medicine and received a doctorate in 1517. Then, in June 1518, he resigned his positions at the university and returned to St. Gall.

Vadian met Conrad Grebel in 1515, when Grebel came from Zurich to study with him at the university. The two became close friends. Grebel accompanied Vadian on one of his geographic adventures. In what has been called the first scientific mountain ascent, the two men, along with Oswald Myconius, climbed to the top of Mount Pilatus in August 1518. They became brothers-in-law when Vadian married Martha Grebel in August 1519.

In September 1518 the city council of St. Gall appointed Vadian to the position of city physician. He became a member of the small council at the death of his father in 1521. In 1526 he became mayor (*Bürgermeister*). For the next twenty-five years, he alternated between the three highest civic offices—mayor, ex-mayor, and imperial officer (*Reichsvogt*).

On his return to St. Gall Vadian also became interested in the biblical humanism of Desiderius Erasmus. Then, from a study of the New Testament and reading the church fathers, he soon turned to the writings of Martin Luther and Philipp Melanchthon. He founded a small study group of clergy and teachers to whom he lectured on the creeds and the *Acts of the Apostles* in the early 1520s. He had begun correspondence with Huldrych Zwingli in 1511, and he attended the second Zurich Disputation in October 1523. He presided as one of the three presidents of the disputation and made the final address, in which he asserted that the results must be judged by scripture alone.

In 1524 the first stirrings of reform in St. Gall were accompanied by a debate about infant baptism, and before long a sizable Anabaptists conventicle existed. At first the council allowed the Anabaptists freedom to preach and to baptize. Grebel, who had become the leader of the Anabaptist movement in Zurich, came to St. Gall at Easter 1525 and baptized a large throng of people. In late April the council decided, under the influence of Vadian, to suppress the movement. Grebel attempted to convince Vadian of the truth of the Anabaptist teaching, but Zwingli succeeded in influencing him against the Anabaptists. Late in 1526, after Vadian became mayor, St. Gall became a reformed city. The council ordered the removal of images, the abolition of the Mass, and Communion in both kinds.

In 1528 Vadian attended the Bern Disputation, where he was moderator. The Reformed victory at Bern made possible the enforcement of the Reformation in the territory subject to the abbey of St. Gall. The abbey itself was secularized in 1529, but it was restored to Roman Catholicism after the Catholic victory in the Battle of Kappel in 1531.

In the last twenty years of his life, Vadian continued his studies and writing. He wrote some works in defense of the Swiss Reformed faith. Hoping for a reconciliation between Luther and the Swiss, he sent Luther a copy of his book on the Eucharist in 1535. In 1540 he wrote against Kaspar von Schwenckfeld's view on Christology. His most important writings were, however, historical. His three-volume history of the abbey of St. Gall was published twenty-five years after his death. But most of his historical writings remained only in manuscript form, including a history of Christianity and a history of monasticism.

BIBLIOGRAPHY

Arbenz, Emil, and Hermann Wartmann, eds. *Die Vadianische Briefsammlung der Stadtbibliothek St. Gallen.* 7 vols. St. Gall, Switzerland, 1890–1913. The letters of Vadian extant in the archives at St. Gall.

Bonorand, Conradin. "Joachim Vadian und die Täufer." *Schweizer Beiträge zur Allgemeinen Geschichte* 11 (1953), 43–72. Covers the activities of the Anabaptists in St. Gall and environs during the time of Vadian, as well as Vadian's relationship with Grebel and his views on how to deal with heretics.

Kessler, Johannes. *Johannes Kesslers Sabbata mit kleineren Schriften und Briefen.* Edited by the Historischen Verein des Kantons St. Gallen. St. Gall, Switzerland, 1902. A contemporary account of the Reformation in St. Gall.

Näf, Werner. *Vadian und seine Stadt St. Gallen.* 2 vols. St. Gall, Switzerland, 1944–1957. The standard biography.

Rupp, E. Gordon. *Patterns of Reformation.* Philadelphia, 1969. Treats Vadian in a short chapter.

Schieß, Traugott. "Bullingers Briefwechsel mit Vadian." *Jahrbuch für schweizerische Geschichte* 31 (1906), 23–68. A study of the contents of the more than two hundred letters exchanged by Bullinger and

Vadian between 1532 and 1551, a large number of which are not printed in Arbenz and Wartmann.

J. WAYNE BAKER

VALADIO, Agostino. *See* Valier, Agostino.

VALDÉS, Alfonso de (c.1500–1533), Spanish humanist. Valdés was born in the Castilian province of Cuenca. He and his younger brother Juan are the most famous children of the *regidor* of Cuenca, Fernando. Little is known of Alfonso's early years. His earliest personal records are three letters he wrote to Pietro Martire d'Anghiera between 1520 and 1521. These letters show his personal impressions on the beginnings of Lutheranism, the imperial election, and the Diet of Worms. Valdés was attached to the secretarial staff of Charles V under the guidance of Maximilianus Transylvanus (d. 1538). In 1522 he returned to Spain with the court. He edited the official reports of the battle of Pavia (24 February 1525) against Francis I. By February 1526 he was made secretary for Latin correspondence and was known as "Imperial Secretary." By October 1526 he became secretary to Mercurino Arborio di Gattinara. In the mid-1520s Valdés made his first known contact with Desiderius Erasmus and became the most enthusiastic supporter of Erasmus at the imperial court. On 23 November 1527 he advised Erasmus to proceed cautiously with regard to the religious orders.

On 6 May 1527 imperial troops began the Sack of Rome, and by July or August 1527 Valdés had written his first major work, *Diálogo de las cosas ocurridas en Roma,* as an apology for the emperor's policy against Clement VII. This writing involved him in bitter conflict with Baldassare Castiglione. Valdés attended the emperor's coronation by the pope at Bologna. On 5 June 1530 Gattinara died, and Valdés took over the former's role of mediator between Catholics and Protestants at the Diet of Augsburg. There Valdés met Melanchthon. Valdés translated into Spanish the Augsburg Confession. His other major work, *Diálogo de Mercurio y Carón,* began to circulate in manuscript in 1528. The Inquisition always looked on Valdés with suspicion. When he died of the plague in Vienna (1533), the moderate forces of reform in Spain lost a prominent ally.

BIBLIOGRAPHY

Allen, P. S., ed. *Opus epistolarum Desiderii Erasmi Roterodami denuo recognitum et auctum.* 12 vols. Oxford, 1906–1958. Contains correspondence of Valdés with Erasmus.

Bagnatori, Giuseppe. "Cartas inéditas de Alfonso de Valdés sobre la Dieta de Augsburgo." *Bulletin Hispanique* 57 (1955), 353–374.

Bataillon, Marcel. "Alonso de Valdés, auteur du *Diálogo de Mercurio y Carón*." In *Homenaje ofrecido a Menéndez Pidal,* vol. 1, pp. 403–415. Madrid, 1925.

———. *Erasme et l'Espagne.* 2d enl. ed., 3 vols. Geneva, 1991.

Boehmer, Edward. *Bibliotheca Wiffeniana.* Vol. 1, *Spanish Reformers of Two Centuries,* pp. 65–115. Strasbourg and London, 1874–1904; reprint, 1962.

Boehmer Edward, ed. "Alfonsi Valdesii litteras XL ineditas." In *Homenaje a Menéndez Pelayo,* edited by Edward Boehmer, vol 1, pp. 385–412. Librería General de Victorianas Suárez. Madrid, 1899.

Briesemeister, Dietrich. "Las repercusiones de Alfonso de Valdés en Alemania." In *El erasmismo en España,* edited by Manuel Revuelta Sañudo, pp. 441–456. Santander, Spain, 1986. There are other articles.

Caballero, Fermin. *Noticias biográficas y literarias de Alonso y Juan de Valdés.* Madrid, 1875. With documentary appendix.

Donald, Dorothy, and Elena Lázaro. *Alfonso de Valdés y su época.* Cuenca, Spain, 1983.

Menéndez Pelayo, Marcelino. *Historia de los heterodoxos españoles.* 2d ed., 7 vols. Madrid, 1911–1932.

Monteserin, Miguel Jiménez, ed. *Los Valdés. Pensamiento y literatura.* Cuenca, Spain, forthcoming.

Morreale, Margherita. "Comentario a una página de Alfonso de Valdés sobre la veneración de los santos." In *Doce consideraciones sobre el mundo hispano-italiano en tiempos de Alfonso y Juan de Valdés,* pp. 265–280. Rome, 1979.

———. "Alfonso de Valdés y la Reforma en Alemania." In *Les Cultures Ibériques en devenir. Essais publiées en hommage à la mémoire de Marcel Bataillon.* Paris, 1979.

Nieto, José C. *Juan de Valdés and the Origins of the Spanish and Italian Reformation.* Geneva, 1970. Mexico City and Madrid, 1979.

———. "Alfonso de Valdés of Cuenca." In *Contemporaries of Erasmus.* Edited by Peter G. Bietenholz, vol. 3, pp. 366–368. Toronto, 1987.

Valdés, Alfonso de. *Diálogo de las cosas ocurridas en Roma.* Edited with introduction and notes by José F. Montesinos. Madrid, 1928. English translation with introduction and notes by John E. Longhurst in *Alfonso de Valdés and the Sack of Rome.* Alburquerque, N. M., 1952.

———. *Diálogo de Mercurio y Carón.* Edited with introduction and notes by José F. Montesinos. Madrid, 1929. English translation with introduction and notes by Joseph V. Ricapito, *Alfonso de Valdés, Dialogue of Mercury and Charon,* Bloomington, Ind., 1986.

JOSÉ C. NIETO

VALDÉS, Juan de (1500/10–1541), Spanish theologian and founder of the Valdesian circle in Naples. Of *Converso* descent on both sides, Juan de Valdés was born in Cuenca, Spain; his father was the *regidor* of Cuenca. He had several brothers and was close to an elder one, Alfonso, who became Latin secretary to Charles V and wrote two strongly Erasmian dialogues, which for a long time were wrongly attributed to Juan. Some part of Valdés's education was received from Peter Martyr de Anghiera, and he may have been a page at the imperial court.

In 1523 Valdés went to Escalona, where he entered the service of Diego López Pacheco, the Marquis of Villena, an Erasmian who encouraged the *Alumbrado* movement. During his time there Pacheco's lay-chaplain was Pedro Ruiz de Alcaraz, an *Alumbrado* later condemned by the Inquisition. Although Alcaraz had little formal education, he knew various devotional works, including the *Imitatio Christi,* and had memorized large portions of the Bible. It is likely that it was in this atmosphere that Valdés began to read not only

Erasmus and the Bible but also Luther and other reformers. Alcaraz was arrested in 1524; at his trial the defense asked in vain for Valdés to be called as a witness. Valdés left Escalona toward the end of that year, apparently to rejoin Alfonso at court.

His movements during the next year or two are not certain, but by December 1527 he had enrolled as a student at the humanist university of Alcalá de Henares, where, judging by his proficiency in Latin, Greek, and Hebrew, he apparently studied humanities. There is no record of his graduation, but with his family connections he may not have needed a degree to obtain employment. Valdés got to know many of the great Erasmians of Spain at the university and subsequently remained in contact with them. It was here that he published anonymously (although its authorship seems not to have been in doubt) his *Diálogo de doctrina christiana* (1529), of which a single copy survives. Initially it passed scrutiny, but it is significant that its printer and every one of the censors were later examined by the Inquisition. Present-day scholars are still debating the nature of this work: claimed as Erasmian, as a product of the unalloyed native reform movement, and plausibly shown to have verbal parallels with works of Luther and others. It sees the Bible in terms of "salvation history." The work was used by Constantino Ponçe de la Fuente to compose his *Summa de doctrina* (which was republished by Zumárraga in Mexico), and also employed in several dioceses in Spain until it was put on the Index of Prohibited Books. Valdés left Alcalá to rejoin his brother, but by 1531 the Inquisition had become hostile; trials of others indicate that proceedings were initiated against both brothers.

Valdés prudently removed himself to Rome, where, with an introduction to Juan Ginés de Sepúlveda, he obtained a semiofficial position as imperial agent, with the title of papal chamberlain, at Clement VII's court. He collaborated politically with Cardinal Ercole Gonzaga and got to know the papal protonotary Pietro Carnesecchi. Valdés was with the imperial court in Mantua in 1532 and got to know Giulia Gonzaga, who was to have a marked influence on his literary output. After a few months in Naples, he returned to the court at Bologna at the time of the meeting between Charles V and Clement VII. At the university he met Peter Martyr Vermigli and others. Clement VII's death in 1534 was a severe blow.

He returned to live in Naples at Chiaggia, apparently supported by income from various benefices. He enjoyed the favor of the viceroy, Pedro de Toledo, who in 1537 appointed him inspector of fortifications. Thus far his life had been that of a courtier with decidedly Erasmian sympathies.

Charles V's court was in Naples in 1535–1536, and during this period Valdés underwent a deep religious experience, conceivably occasioned by a lenten sermon of Bernardino Ochino, which produced a marked change in him. His correspondence begins to reveal a much more spiritual attitude.

In any case, the two men began a cooperation, with reciprocal benefit. Valdés moved from covert to overt evangelical belief, and Ochino passed into the camp of justification by faith. This interaction gave rise to the so-called Valdesian circle of Naples, in which many well-known people participated for varying periods. For six and a half years, Valdés created around himself a private sphere of influence in which his own deepening spirituality was all-pervasive. Giulia Gonzaga went to the city in 1535, making Valdés her spiritual adviser. Several of his writings are dedicated to her. The first concrete result of the discussions of this group was the *Alphabeto christiano* (probably published in 1536), which provides clear evidence of the change in Valdés. Most of his activity, however, became apparent only after his death, when some of his writings were printed and as others publicized his teaching.

Other members of the group included Vermigli and Carnesecchi, who confessed to the Inquisition to reading Protestant writers in Naples. Bernardo de Mantova, the author of the *Beneficio di Cristo*, may have been there as well; it is claimed that this work gives expression to the ideas of the Neapolitan circle.

Valdés's writings bear no date of composition; several were rediscovered and published only in the nineteenth century. Extant besides *Alphabeto* are a translation of *Psalms* and a commentary on the first forty-one; commentaries on his own translations of *Matthew*, *Romans*, and *1 Corinthians*; *Ciento y diez consideraciones* (although in fact 123 considerations are known); a children's catechism; and several short works. A number of commentaries and many shorter pieces have been lost.

Days before his death in Naples in August 1541, he stated that he died in the same faith in which he had lived; neither then nor in his will does he mention papal authority, invoke any saints, or express the usual pious formularies. Since he criticized the reformers for breaking the church's unity but also exalted the doctrine of justification by faith and played down, or condemned, ceremonies of the Roman Catholic church, we are left with an enigmatic figure.

The subsequent careers of his known followers vary so widely, from submission to Tridentine Rome to outright antitrinitarianism, that they provide no basis for firm conclusions about Valdés's doctrinal position. Assessment must therefore be made from his not inconsiderable surviving writings. The early influences of *Alumbrado* belief, Erasmus and the Spanish Erasmians, and some of the northern reformers remained with him all his life, widening as time went on to include an interest in Anabaptist writings and the ideas of Italian evangelism, yet all these strands of religious reform were processed by his own spirituality and experience to produce a form of essential Christianity that laid greater stress on its practical expression in the life of the believer than on its dogmatic formulation. His approach is intensely biblical and Christ-centered, avoiding speculative theology to concentrate on the effects of justification by faith on the individual believer. Bearing in mind that what is left unsaid may be as eloquent as what is expressed, one may note that he avoids mention of hierarchy, priesthood, ceremonies other than the Lord's Supper (but ignoring transubstantiation), devotion to the Virgin or the saints, and most of the externals of religion. It seems impossible to make exclusive claims to Valdés as a Protestant or a Catholic, although it is significant that his works appeared early on the *Index of Prohibited Books* and that the Inquisition used his name in accusation.

Apart from his influence on currents of Italian reform, Valdés's writings were used by the short-lived Spanish Protestant movement. Two of his commentaries in Spanish and the *Le cento e dieci divine Considerationi* in Italian were published in Switzerland in mid-century; of the latter, three editions in French and two in English were issued before 1650. His children's catechism was published in German and Latin in Germany, as well as in Polish translation; these betoken a wider European interest. Valdesianism is not to be confused with the Waldensians.

BIBLIOGRAPHY

Primary Sources

Valdés, Juan de. *Dialogo de doctina cristiana* (1529). Buenos Aires, 1946.
———. *El evangelio segun san Mateo*. Barcelona, 1986.
———. *Alfabeto cristiana*. Rome, 1988.
———. *Il dialogo della dottrina cristiana*. Turin, 1991.

Secondary Sources

Bataillon, Marcel. *Erasmo y España: Estudios sobre la historia espiritual del siglo 16*. Mexico City, 1966.
Gilly, Carols. "Juan de Valdés: Übersetzer und Bearbeiter von Luthers Schriften in seinem *Diálogo de Doctrina*." *Archiv für Reformationsgeschichte* 74 (1983), 257–306.
Kinder, A. Gordon. "Juan de Valdés." In *Bibliotheca Dissidentium*, edited by André Séguenny, vol. 9, pp. 111–195. Baden-Baden, 1986. Contains extensive additional bibliography.
Longhurst, John E. *Erasmus and the Spanish Inquisition: The Case of Juan de Valdés*. Albuquerque, N. Mex., 1950.
Nieto, José C. *Juan de Valdés and the Origins of the Spanish and Italian Reformation*. Geneva, 1970.
———. *Valdés's Two Catechisms: The Dialogue on Christian Doctrine and the Christian Instruction for Children*. Translated by William B. and Carol D. Jones. Lawrence, Kans., 1981.

A. GORDON KINDER

VALERA, Cipriano de (c.1532–1603?), converted Spanish monk, university teacher of theology, and polemical author. A product of the evangelical movement in Seville, Valera fled from the monastery of San Isidro del Campo with others in 1558 and traveled west to Geneva. Soon afterward he moved to London, where before long he obtained a fellowship at Magdalen College, Cambridge, to teach divinity. After eight years there he went to live in London.

No details are available for the next twenty years, except that he attended the Italian Protestant church. In 1588, the year of the Armada, he became useful to the English government in the war with Spain by writing works in Spanish clearly intended to combat the enemy on the religious front. His *Dos tratados* (1588, revised 1599) was a popularization of his erudition, attacking with great verve the Mass and the papacy as the twin pillars of the Roman system. Appearing in 1594 was his consolatory epistle *Tratado para confirmar los pobres cativos de Berueria,* which was possibly a coded reference to the Spanish Protestant victims of the Inquisition. In 1596 he produced a second edition of the Spanish version of Calvin's catechism (originally published in Geneva in 1559) and a revision of Casiodoro de Reina's New Testament. He translated Calvin's *Institutes* (1597), emending it to make it more applicable to the Spanish situation, and adding a long doctrinal preface. He also produced the Spanish version of a French pamphlet, *Aviso . . . sobre la indicción del Jubileo* (1600).

At the age of seventy, Valera traveled to Holland to supervise the production of his revision of Reina's whole Bible (Amsterdam, 1602), financed by Christian I of Anhalt-Bernberg. The revisions are slight, the most striking being the rearrangement of the Old Testament. His name subsequently overshadowed Reina's for more than two centuries, and his version, with other revisions, has remained standard among Spanish-speaking Protestants.

There is no reliable evidence of when he died. From the time that he and other foreigners were brought to Cambridge to strengthen Protestant influence in the universities, he enjoyed the patronage of powerful people and remained a convinced Calvinist, employing his erudition in the service of the land of his adoption and in making available evangelical literature for his countrymen at home and in exile.

BIBLIOGRAPHY

Primary Sources

Valera, Cipriano de. *Tratado para confirmar los pobres cautivo*. Madrid, 1872.
———. *Los dos tradatos del Papa y de la misa*. Barcelona, 1982.

Secondary Sources

Boehmer, Eduard. *Bibliotheca Wiffeniana: Spanish Reformers of Two Centuries*. 3 vols. London, 1904. See pp. 147–174.
Kinder, A. Gordon. "Cipriano de Valera, Spanish Reformer, 1532?–1602?." *Bulletin of Hispanic Studies* 46 (1969), 109–119.
———. "Religious Literature as an Offensive Weapon: Cipriano de Valera's Part in England's War with Spain." *Sixteenth Century Journal* 19 (1988), 223–235.

A. GORDON KINDER

VALIER, Agostino (also Valerio; 1531–1606), bishop of Verona and cardinal, pastor, and writer, best known for his treatise on sermon rhetoric. A Venetian noble, he succeeded his uncle Cardinal Bernardo Navagero as bishop. As first implementer of the decrees of the Council of Trent in the diocese of Verona, Valier made a point of treading in the footsteps of its renowned pre-Tridentine reforming bishop Gian Matteo Giberti; for this reason he republished and glossed the latter's diocesan constitutions rather than producing his own. Although his diocese was not in the ecclesiastical province of Milan, Valier was one of the bishops most closely associated with Carlo Borromeo, the great reforming archbishop of Milan, and was one of the major propagators of the Borromean legend, notwithstanding private criticism of Borromeo's extreme rigor and confrontations with the secular power. In 1580–1581 as papal agent (apostolic visitor) he inspected the Dalmatian dioceses and in 1581 (together with Lorenzo Campeggio) that of Venice; the Campeggio-Valier *Decreta et Hortationes* (1581) for the patriarchate of Venice (decrees prefaced by a hortatory admonition to the clergy) is his most significant official reform document. He maintained a network of relations with other members of the intelligentsia of the college of cardinals.

Relatively little of Valier's large literary output was published before the eighteenth century. Indeed, in a species of autobiography significantly entitled *De cautione adhibenda in edendis libris* (On Caution in Publishing Books; 1719), he censured the mania for publication. Apart from early philosophical treatises composed while still a layman, Valier's main publications in his lifetime were *De acolytorum disciplina* (1570), containing advice to the young seminarians of Verona on studies appropriate to candidates for the priesthood; *De Rhetorica ecclesiastica* (1574); a collection of mirrors for prelates comprising *Episcopus* (1575), proposing a model of the bishop based on the exemplars of Christ and Paul and the latter's precepts, *Cardinalis* (1586), holding up an ideal of contemplative spirituality, and *Vita Caroli Borromei* (1586), extolling Borromeo as an example of asceticism and pastoral virtues and highlighting concrete features of his diocesan activity; and advice on the Christian life to various categories of women—nuns, *dimesse* (unprofessed female celibates devoted to pious and charitable works), widows, and married women—published together as *Istituto di ogni stato lodevole delle donne cristiane* (1565). A collection of over one hundred model homilies written at Borromeo's request for clergy of the Milan diocese, a rare if not unique example of the genre in sixteenth-century Italy that might appear to exemplify Catholic reformers' demands for simple sermons adapted to the comprehension of the multitude, was never published. *De Rhetorica ecclesiastica*, which had twelve Italian editions as well as French, Belgian, and German ones, again written at Borromeo's request, proposes more elaborate and cultivated rhetorical models than Valier really desired, the work being revised in the light of criticisms by Borromeo and the Jesuit rhetorician Francesco Adorno; originally intended for "ordinands and the odd priest of little letters," it was in its final form designed more for an elite of prelates. It is noteworthy for its ideal of emotive oratory, this being connected to a positive valorization of the emotions; the latter is coupled with a critique of the Stoic ideal of "apathy" found elsewhere in Valier's writings.

Major leitmotifs of his work, found not least in his many epistles and treatises written for churchmen and lay noble friends, are *fuga saeculi* ("shunning the world"), the exaltation of contemplation, and the censure of ambition on the part of lay noblemen and the corresponding vice among women, vanity. Valier was among the most significant Counter-Reformation writers on the office of the bishop, and none perhaps said more on the cultural apparatus appropriate to prelates and pastors.

BIBLIOGRAPHY

Bayley, Peter. *French Pulpit Oratory, 1598–1660*. Cambridge, 1980. Useful on the influence of the *De Rhetorica ecclesiastica*.

Logan, Oliver. "The Ideal of the Bishop and the Venetian Patriciate, c.1430–c.1630." *Journal of Ecclesiastical History* 29 (1978), 415–450. For Valier's ideas on pastorality.

———. *The Venetian Upper Clergy in the Sixteenth and Early Seventeenth Centuries: A Study in Religious Culture*. Salzburg, 1995. Contains a detailed study of Valier's writings and a full bibliography.

OLIVER LOGAN

VALLADOLID. It might well be argued that the north-central Castilian city of Valladolid was the birthplace of modern Spain, for it was here on 18 October 1469 that Ferdinand and Isabel were secretly married, thus definitively joining the crowns of Castile and Aragon. Located in the high plains of Castile in an area noted for wheat production, the site of the city has been inhabited continuously since the third century B.C., convenient to arable land and transport on the Pisuerga River. Valladolid itself was founded permanently in A.D. 1035. In the sixteenth century, Valladolid's economy rested firmly on its role as the administrative capital of Castile; although the royal court and the councils of government remained peripatetic, the lesser secretaries slowly established residence in the city. One reflection of the city's status was the establishment of the royal documentary depository at the nearby village of Simancas in the 1540s. As with most of Castile through the period of the Reformation, Valladolid enjoyed great prosperity in the first half of the sixteenth century (when its population surpassed seven thousand households), but experienced a decline in the second half of the sixteenth and early seventeenth century, especially after the removal of the court to Madrid in the 1560s. (By 1644 Valladolid's population fell to some four thousand households). The Chancilleria (high court) remained, as did the great nobles, in particular the admirals of Castile, the Enríquez. Before the enormous population loss of the last decade of the sixteenth century, Valladolid had become a bishopric separate from Palencia.

The religious history of Valladolid in the sixteenth century reflects the general patterns of faith in all of post-Reconquest Castile. There is much evidence to suggest that the Spanish church (and here the term *Spanish* can be used since it existed as a unified institution throughout the kingdoms on the peninsula with the exception of Portugal) had reformed itself before Luther. Cardinal Francisco Jiménez de Cisneros and the University of Alcalá placed the Spanish church squarely in the Erasmian trend toward reforming Catholicism. Valladolid was the site of the March 1527 debate conducted by the Inquisition on the nature of Erasmianism; its suspension without a definitive decision was seen by many in Spain (in particular the most famous of the Spanish supporters of Desiderius Erasmus, Juan Luis Vives) as a vindication of the new Christian humanism. Valladolid also sheltered a small group of *Alumbrados* under the leadership of the *beata* Francisca Hernández; she and a follower were arrested in 1529 by the Inquisition in a precursor to the Lutheran panic of the late 1550s. Beginning a formal investigation in 1558 spurred by the retired emperor Charles V, the Inquisition did find in Valladolid a cell of Protestants led by the Italian Carlos de Seso and given legitimacy by the adherence of Augustín Cazalla, a former chaplain to Charles V and adviser to Philip II. Fifty-five people eventually joined the group. The Inquisition's investigation led to the arrest of the entire congregation, and in two spectacular autos-da-fe twenty-six people were executed. Along with the Inquisition's persecutions in Seville, the 1550s witnessed the virtual elimination of native Spanish Protestantism.

Valladolid both benefited and suffered from its doctrinal purity. Because of its role in the removal of both religious and political threats (as Protestants were seen by Charles V, Philip II, and most Spaniards), the Inquisition gained extraordinary power. As throughout Spain, Valladolid was officially closed off from northern Europe intellectually; no student could attend any university outside Catholic countries and a new and more rigorous Spanish Index appeared in 1584. Religious orthodoxy, however, meant social peace as well; Valladolid suffered none of the violence and social disorder common to its neighbors north of the Pyrenees. One should be cautious in judging the value of this exchange. Several historians have remarked on the tone of the *Lazarillo de Tormes* as an example of the price to Spain: the rollicking good nature of the work, its critical view of the clergy and of poverty, and, indeed, its critical view of all authority contrasts remarkably with the post-Tridentine internal and cautious theological spirit of Teresa of Ávila (so focused on good works), as well as with the inclusive interference of the church into Valladolid's social structure, from private ceremony to public performance. It was a price that all of Spain paid in the sixteenth century.

BIBLIOGRAPHY

Bennassar, Bartolomé. *Valladolid au siècle d'or.* Paris, 1967. A definitive Annales School compendium of structural and conjunctural information with interesting though dated views on *mentalité*; also in a Spanish edition by Francisca Aramburu Riera.

Cruz, Anne J., and Mary Elizabeth Perry, eds. *Culture and Control in Counter-Reformation Spain.* Minneapolis, 1992. Gives insight into behaviors and restrictions (cultural, political, and theological) of the period, though not specifically with respect to Valladolid.

Kamen, Henry. *Inquisition and Society in Spain in the Sixteenth and Seventeenth Centuries.* Bloomington, Ind., 1985. The single best work on the subject although it betrays a subtle anti-Catholic bias.

Rucquoi, Adeline. *Valladolid en la Edad Media.* Valladolid, Spain, 1987. A brilliant economic and social history by the best contemporary historian of the city.

PAUL HILTPOLD

VALOIS, François de (1555–1584), duke of Alençon and Anjou, prince of the blood, and heir to the French throne. He was the fourth and youngest son of Henry II and Catherine de Médicis and thus the brother of the French kings Francis II, Charles IX, and Henry III during the French Wars of Religion. Unlike his father and three older brothers, however, the last Valois heir was never a publicly committed and consistent opponent of Protestantism. As a result, throughout much of his short life he found himself courted and approached by various Protestant leaders both at home and abroad. Created duke of Alençon in 1566 and duke of Anjou in May 1576, the youngest Valois prince was fully expected to succeed his brothers as king of France, as contemporaries were already acknowledging in the late 1570s that Henry III was unable to father an heir. Thus, despite his utter lack of talents and abilities of leadership the duke's career and fortunes mattered greatly to those who supported the Protestant cause.

Largely because of his public support in September 1575 of a policy of religious coexistence, the last Valois heir found himself the object of attention from Protestants both at home and abroad. Although he was clearly trying to further his own personal ambitions rather than lending support to the Protestant cause, he made a public declaration affirming his willingness to tolerate the new religion. The Huguenot leaders—principally Henry, king of Navarre (later Henry IV), and Louis I Condé—were wary of trusting this Valois prince, but they recognized the advantage of having a royal prince of the blood on their side in their struggle for recognition from the Crown. The result was the Peace of Monsieur in May 1576, so called because the duke (the king's eldest brother was traditionally referred to as Monsieur) was used as a go-between in negotiating the peace settlement.

This settlement provided the Huguenots with their most sweeping privileges since the beginning of the religious wars—above all the "free public and general exercise of religion" anywhere in France except within two leagues of Paris and the court. Moreover, the famous *chambres mi-parties* were created in the sovereign courts to guarantee that the parlements would be able to enforce this settlement, a severe problem in all the earlier peace agreements (1563, 1568, 1570, and 1573). Although the duke's role in the fifth civil war was obviously significant, his commitment to his own personal career rather than the Protestant cause became clear only a few months later. During the meeting of the Estates-General at Blois (December 1576–February 1577) François abandoned his former allies and advocated the renewal of war against the Huguenots. This destroyed what little credit he had with the French Protestant leaders and did much to diminish his reputation abroad as well.

Despite the fact that he sold out his support of the Huguenots (for the title of duke of Anjou and the wealthy income that went along with it) the duke's association with the Protestant cause was far from over. Queen Elizabeth I and William of Orange continued to seek his support for the Revolt of the Netherlands against Philip II of Spain, urging him to begin planning a military campaign to the Netherlands to support the Dutch rebels. Fearing a Spanish reprisal against France, both Henry III and Catherine de Médicis refused to support him and did their best to thwart his plans. François nevertheless took up the challenge and organized an army that made a brief foray into the Netherlands in 1578 on behalf of the Dutch rebels. When William managed to get the Dutch rebel provinces to offer the duke their sovereignty in September 1580 (they formally renounced their sovereignty to Philip II the next year) and Elizabeth seemed to offer him her hand in marriage in November 1582, it appeared that François might one day inherit the three crowns of France, England, and the Netherlands.

All these plans collapsed suddenly however when François died of tuberculosis in June 1584. Although he had managed to alienate himself from French, English, and Dutch Protestants because of a lack of personal commitment to their cause, his second military campaign in the Netherlands (1582–1583), as well as his previous negotiating, had done much to shore up the Dutch rebels in a period when they were desperate for foreign support. In France he was as significant in death as in life as his demise set off the longest and bloodiest of the French civil wars and made the Protestant Henry of Navarre heir to the throne.

BIBLIOGRAPHY

Boucher, Jacqueline. *La cour de Henri III*. Rennes, 1986. Contains useful material on the duke of Anjou's role at court.
Holt, Mack P. "Patterns of Clientèle and Economic Opportunity at Court during the Wars of Religion: The Household of François, Duke of Anjou." *French Historical Studies* 13 (1984), 305–322. Analyzes the clients in the duke's household and how this patronage network operated at court.
———. *The Duke of Anjou and the Politique Struggle during the Wars of Religion*. Cambridge, 1986. Fullest and most complete study.
MacCaffrey, Wallace T. *Queen Elizabeth and the Making of Policy, 1572–1588*. Princeton, 1981. Most complete discussion to date of the marriage negotiations between Anjou and Elizabeth. (See also Holt, *The Duke of Anjou*.)
Muller, P. L., and Alphonse Diegerick, eds. *Documents concernant les relations entre le duc d'Anjou et les Pays-Bas, 1576–1584*. 5 vols. Amsterdam and The Hague, 1889–99. All of the primary materials necessary collected from archives in France, Belgium, and the Netherlands, for a study of Anjou's campaigns in the Dutch Revolt.
Yates, Frances A. *The Valois Tapestries*. 2d rev. ed. London, 1975. Fascinating detective story showing what a set of tapestries presented to the Dutch rebels reveals about Anjou's policies in the Netherlands.

MACK P. HOLT

VALOIS, HOUSE OF. A cadet branch of the Capetian dynasty of France, the House of Valois gained the royal dignity with the accession of Philip of Valois, who became king when his cousin Charles IV died without a son. Philip VI (r. 1328–1350) ascended the throne despite the rival claim of his cousin Edward III of England. The result was the Hundred Years' War, during which the Valois kings John II (r. 1350–1364), Charles V (r. 1364–1380), Charles VI (r. 1380–1422), and Charles VII (r. 1422–1461) several times came close to losing the throne.

When the English were driven from France in 1453, the attention of the Valois kings turned to their rivals, the Burgundian dukes. Louis XI (r. 1461–1483) succeeded in turning the Swiss against the duke of Burgundy, Charles the Bold, whom they killed in the Battle of Nancy in 1477. Charles's heiress, Mary, seeking to maintain her inheritance, married Maximilian of Habsburg. Their son Philip wedded Joanna of Spain, passing on to their son, Holy Roman Emperor Charles V, a vast range of lands and the hatred of the Valois that marked relations between the French monarchy and the Habsburgs for the duration of the Valois dynasty.

The attention of Charles VIII (r. 1483–1498) was focused on the French claim to the kingdom of Naples. In 1494 he led a French army into Italy to Naples. This expedition, the First French Invasion of Italy, began a long period of French involvement in Italy that concluded in 1559. Charles died young without an heir, and his cousin took the throne as Louis XII (r. 1498–1515). Louis also claimed Milan by inheritance and led several expeditions into Italy to win those lands. Pope Julius II bitterly opposed Louis's pretensions in Italy and organized the Holy League in 1509 to drive the French out. Louis responded by calling the Council of Pisa to depose Julius. For two years Louis was in schism. By the time of his death in 1515, the Holy League had succeeded in driving his forces out of Italy.

Louis's successor, Francis I (r. 1515–1547), in many respects opened a new era in French history, although he still was occupied with the French claims in Italy. He led a French army across the Alps and crushed the Swiss, who had established a protectorate over Milan, at the Battle of Marignano (1515). It resulted in a treaty with the Swiss by which the French had access to Swiss mercenaries. Worried by Francis's victory, Pope Leo X agreed to the Concordat of Bologna for the French church, which gave the king the right to fill the major benefices in France, with papal oversight. The French hierarchy became largely filled with men whose services the king wanted to reward.

During his stay in Italy Francis became captivated by the Renaissance and brought Italian artists and humanists back to France. He began several major building projects incorporating Italianate design and decor and organized the Collège de France to teach classical languages. He was tolerant of the moderate program of church reform the humanists advocated, although he made no effort to implement it.

More important to Francis was his rivalry with Charles V, with whom he contested the imperial election in 1519 and the rule of Milan. His efforts resulted in his capture at the Battle of Pavia (1525). It was not until 1530 that a ransom was agreed upon that freed his two sons who were serving as hostages for him in Spain. It gave Charles 2 million crowns and renunciation of French claims to Naples, Milan, and Flanders. It was the first in a series of treaties that never lasted for long, because neither prince truly wanted peace. With the emergence of the Lutheran party in Germany, Francis was quick to make a tacit alliance with it against Charles. The Habsburg-Valois wars had a major role in the survival of Lutheranism in Germany by preventing Charles from using his military power against it. Francis regarded Protestantism as a German problem useful for sapping Charles's power, and he refused to support the convocation of the Council of Trent because he had no interest in solving the religious disputes in the empire. He also believed that the French church did not need reform.

French Protestants did appear, although they were few in number until after 1550. The monarchy's campaign of repression was sporadic, but there were a number of executions. When in 1534 placards appeared denouncing the Catholic Mass in Paris, the upsurge in repression persuaded many Frenchmen, including John Calvin, to flee into exile. With Calvin's organizational skills and the publication in 1541 of his *Institutes* in French, Calvinism began to dominate French Protestantism after 1550.

By then, Henry II (r. 1547–1559) was king. Taking seriously his coronation oath to protect the church and eradicate heresy, he created a new chamber in the Parlement of Paris for heresy prosecution. Called the *Chambre ardente* for its zealous pursuit of heresy, it was undermined by the clergy's opposition to placing heresy under the jurisdiction of the parlementaires. Henry shut down the *Chambre ardente* after

two years. The Edict of Châteaubriand (1551) largely returned jurisdiction over heresy to the bishops but demanded much more active involvement on their part. Henry's efforts at eradicating Protestantism were badly weakened by his belief that heresy was a manifestation of lower class sedition, leading him to ignore cases from the elite classes, and by his need for support and mercenaries from Lutheran princes in his wars against the Habsburgs.

Continuing the rivalry with Charles V, Henry made an alliance with the Lutheran princes in 1551, which allowed him to occupy the three bishoprics of Lorraine. He sent an army to Italy in 1557 to reassert the claims to Italian lands. In response Philip II attacked northern France and badly defeated the French at Saint-Quentin (1557). When Philip failed to move on Paris, Henry used the army he had collected for its defense to take Calais in 1558. With Protestantism becoming a serious problem in both kings' lands, they agreed to the Peace of Cateau-Cambrésis (1559).

During a celebration of the treaty, Henry was mortally wounded while jousting. He left to his fifteen-year-old son Francis II a realm deep in debt and bitterly divided by religion and political factionalism. One faction, the Guises, had the upper hand because they were the uncles of the queen, Mary Stuart. The excluded Bourbons and other nobles resented Guisard domination, and this led to the Conspiracy of Amboise (1560) on the part of a group of Huguenot (Protestant) nobles. The conspiracy was betrayed, and several Huguenots were executed. Before the event had much impact, Francis died, and his younger brother, Charles IX, became king at age nine with his mother, Catherine de Médicis, serving as regent. Determined to maintain the power of the monarchy for her son and convinced that the religious divisions were threatening it, she worked for a compromise by convoking the Colloquy of Poissy (1561). It only served to show how far apart the two religions were by then.

The Massacre of Wassy (1563), perpetrated by Francis of Guise, touched off the first of the French Wars of Religion. The monarchy reluctantly supported the ardent Catholics, but the queen mother worked for peace. She persuaded both sides to accept an edict of pacification (1563) that gave the Huguenots limited toleration. Passions were too strong, however, to allow the peace to hold. Over the next seven years, two more episodes of civil war were followed by slightly broader edicts of pacification. In the second War of Religion in 1570 it was agreed that Admiral Gaspard II de Coligny, leader of the Huguenots, would come to the court as a royal adviser and the young Protestant prince, Henry of Navarre (later Henry IV), would marry the king's sister Marguerite. In August 1572, as the marriage was about to take place, Catherine, fearing that Coligny's influence over her son would take France into war with Spain, hired an assassin to kill him. This touched off a series of events leading to the Saint Bartholomew's Day Massacre in Paris and other towns, perhaps the worst blemish on the

Valois dynasty. Stricken with guilt over his role in it, Charles IX died in 1574.

Charles's younger brother Henry III (r.1574–1589) gained the throne. Although he had been active in the anti-Huguenot forces as a prince, he sought a compromise settlement once he was king. The Peace of Monsieur (1576) gave extensive concessions to the Protestants, and angry conservative Catholics organized the Catholic League under the leadership of Henry of Guise to oppose it. When Henry's younger brother died in 1584, the Catholic League committed itself to preventing the succession of Henry of Navarre. In the War of the Three Henrys (1585–1587), Henry III did not openly support the Catholic League, and the leaguers forced him out of Paris during the Day of the Barricades (1588). Henry III responded by assassinating the Duke of Guise and his brother, a cardinal, for which the league exacted revenge by assassinating him in 1589. Henry's death marked the end of the Valois dynasty as the throne passed to Henry of Navarre, who was able to reestablish peace and a strong monarchy.

[*See also* Charles IX of France; Francis I of France; Francis II of France; Henry II of France; Henry III of France; Henry IV of France; Mary Stuart; Medici, House of; Placards, Affaire des; *and* Wars of Religion.]

BIBLIOGRAPHY

Baumgartner, Frederic J. *Henry II, King of France, 1547–1559.* Durham, N.C., 1988.
Bridge, John S. *A History of France from the Death of Louis XI.* 5 vols. Reprint, New York, 1978. Highly detailed history of the reigns of Louis XI, Charles VIII, and Louis XII. Especially strong on diplomacy and war.
Cameron, Keith. *Henri III: A Maligned or Malignant King?* Exeter, England, 1978.
Cameron, Keith, ed. *From Valois to Bourbon: Dynasty, State and Society in Early Modern France.* Exeter, England, 1989. Several essays deal with the government of the last Valois kings.
Cloulas, Ivan. *Catherine de Médicis.* Paris, 1979.
Denieul-Cormier, Anne. *Wise and Foolish Kings: The First House of Valois, 1328–1498.* Garden City, N.Y., 1980. Interesting popular account of the early Valois kings.
Kendall, Paul Murray. *Louis XI: The Universal Spider.* Reprint, New York, 1986.
Knecht R. J. *Francis I.* Cambridge, 1982.
Labande-Mailfert, Yvonne. *Charles VIII et son milieu.* Paris, 1975.
Quilliet, Bernard. *Louis XII: Père du peuple.* Paris, 1986.
Sumption, Jonathan. *The Hundred Years War: Trial by Battle.* Philadelphia, 1991. Recent study of the war that emphasizes the role of the French kings.
Vale, M. G. A. *Charles VII.* Berkeley, 1974.

FREDERIC J. BAUMGARTNER

VAN DER BURCH, Henri-François (1567–1644),

reforming Catholic bishop of the Spanish Netherlands. Like many Netherlandish bishops of the second and third generations after Trent, Van der Burch hailed from a great noble family; but there was no question of his abilities during studies at Utrecht, Douai, and Louvain, where he earned the "licentiaat" in civil and canon law (1590), nor of his devotion when he chose the priesthood (1592). He displayed the same virtues in carrying out his earliest assignments as secretary to the bishop of Arras (1592), dean of the cathedral chapter of Mechelen, or Malines (1593), and vicar-general of the archdiocese of Mechelen (1596), in which function he played a major role at the foundation-laying provincial council of 1607.

The elderly Archbishop Mathias Hovius of Mechelen intended to make Van der Burch his coadjutor and successor, but these plans were preempted when the archdukes appointed the young canon to the see of his native Ghent in 1613. Soon after taking possession, Van der Burch began the classic activities of reform: diocesan synod, pastoral visitations, annual meetings with the rural deans, and, perhaps most notably, religious education for all. Complaints flooded in from his flock when, after only three years, Van der Burch was elevated to the archbishopric of Cambrai, where over the next twenty-eight years he continued his activities and made his greatest mark. Above all, Van der Burch was a superb administrator, both as manager and as shepherd; the three huge journals he kept record countless sermons and visitations (220,000 confirmations), a catechism for children, and munificence (such as Saint Agnes, a school for the poor). He also became briefly involved in the early debate over Jansenism, taking sides with the Jesuits. But his greatest legacy was in pastoral administration; fittingly, he died while on visitation in Mons, and just after composing a circular letter that scolded his priests for their indifference toward preaching and catechizing and caring for the poor.

BIBLIOGRAPHY

Jadin, L. "Procès d'information pour la nomination des évêques et abbés des Pays-Bas, de Liège et de Franche-Comté d'après les archives de la congrégation consistoriale, 1564–1637." *Bulletin de l'institut historique belge de Rome* (1928), 5–263.
Marinus, M. J. "Hendrik Frans van der Burch, 1613–1616." In *Het bisdom Gent: Vier eeuwen geschiedenis,* edited by Michel Cloet, pp. 60–62. Ghent, 1991. Contains a brief but useful summary of Van der Burch's background and years in Ghent.
Pierrard, Pierre, ed. *Les diocèses de Cambrai et de Lille.* Histoire des diocèses de France, vol. 8. Paris, 1978. Perhaps the best overview of all of his days in Cambrai.
Possoz, A. *Vie de monseigneur Van der Burch, archévêque, duc de Cambrai, prince du Saint-Empire, comte de Cambrésis.* Cambrai, 1861. The only full-scale study of Van der Burch, and in need of a successor.

CRAIG HARLINE

VANNIUS, Valentin (1495–1567),

German Lutheran theologian, preacher, and administrator associated primarily with the Reformation in Württemberg. Born in Beilstein in Württemberg to prosperous peasants, Vannius lived long enough to participate in the early and later phases of the German Reformation. Neither an innovator nor a commanding presence, he stands largely unremarked with the second rank of Lutheran notables of his time.

Vannius entered the Cistercian monastary in Maulbronn as a young man and first encountered the new theology during a study year in Heidelberg in 1518. He spent some years pondering Luther's challenge to the Roman church before leaving his monastery and his order during the Peasants' War of 1525. Vannius was not a case of instantaneous conversion, and he sought for some years to combine a reformed sensibility with older practices such as clerical celibacy and private Communion for the sick and dying. His final break with Catholicism came with his marriage and appointment to a diaconate in Brandenburg-Ansbach in 1532.

Although he earned no academic degrees, Vannius came to demonstrate thorough proficiency in dialectic and rhetoric as well as a mastery of Latin and knowledge of Greek and Hebrew. He became a widely respected biblical scholar and church historian while serving in a variety of administrative, pastoral, and pedagogical offices.

Vannius's most productive years as a reformer began with his return to Württemberg in 1535 to assist in the conversion of the duchy after the restoration of Duke Ulrich. He joined forces with Johannes Brenz and Erhard Schnepf to mold a well-ordered Christian community out of a population that years of political instability had accustomed to religious diversity, including the presence of Anabaptists and followers of the spiritualist Kaspar von Schwenckfeld, as well as large numbers who held to the Catholic Mass. With his posting to Stuttgart in 1537, Vannius emerged a champion of orthodox Lutheranism and of the close alliance of church and state. From the pulpit and in direct correspondence with Schwenckfeld, Vannius rejected the latter's assertion that the word of God need not be bound to outward forms; Vannius held to its inseparability from the preaching office and from the Christian community it served.

Vannius's major contributions to the Reformation were a series of pre-Communion sermons published as a handbook for preachers (*Die Exhortationes*) and his scholarly reflections on the history and nature of the Mass seeking to prove its disagreement with Christ's institution of the Holy Supper as specified in scripture. The most widely distributed of these writings was the *Grundtliche Hystoria von der Mess* (Basic History of the Mass) written in 1557 to refute Johann Fabri's defense of the Catholic Mass based on its unbroken preservation through the apostolic succession. Vannius laid no claim to originality, freely acknowledging his theological and scholarly debts to Luther, Brenz, Melanchthon, and others. The value of his work was in his meticulous use of ancient and modern sources and in his systematic presentation of the arguments against the Catholic Mass. In 1563 Duke Christoph, in his self-appointed role as religious

peacemaker, had Vannius's *Hystoria* reprinted in Latin and sent to Catherine de Médicis. In 1590 it was placed on the Index in Rome.

The high regard in which Duke Christoph and fellow churchmen held Vannius is also evident in his appointments to positions of trust and authority in the established church of Württemberg. In 1544 he succeeded Schnepf as superintendent, adding visitations and general supervisory functions to his pastoral duties. In 1552 he joined the Württemberg delegation to the Council of Trent. In 1557 he became the first evangelical abbot of Maulbronn, responsible for the administration of both the monastary and its preparatory school for future clergymen. He remained in this post until his death.

BIBLIOGRAPHY

Ehmer, Hermann. *Valentin Vannius und die Reformation in Württemberg.* Stuttgart, 1976. A comprehensive, scrupulously documented, analytical study of Vannius as theologian.

Tschackert, Paul. "Valentin Vannius." In *Allgemeine Deutsche Biographie*, vol. 39, pp. 483–484. Berlin, 1895.

KARIN BRINKMANN BROWN

VASA, Gustavus (1496–1560), Swedish king from 1523 to 1560. The importance of Vasa in the church history of Sweden must be understood in the light of general historical developments. In 1397 a political union had been forged between Sweden-Finland and Denmark-Norway. This union created a feeling of solidarity between the countries. But because the kings of the union engaged officials from countries outside the union, it created several tensions among different interests of the several countries and the kings. In these tensions leading bishops, such as the archbishop of Uppsala, played an important role. In the early sixteenth century an archbishop was appointed in Uppsala who promoted the union, while the Swedish regent, Sten Sture, wished to install an archbishop devoted to the national Swedish interest. The archbishop was removed, which gave the Danish king, Christian II, reason to interfere with arms not only to consolidate his interests but also to protect the law of the church. This happened in the Stockholm Bloodbath of 1520. Gustavus Vasa, a nobleman who had lost his parents in the struggle with the union, soon emerged as the Swedish head of the resistance to the union. He was a typical late medieval nobleman who saw the international structure of the church as a threat to national independence. Therefore the power of the church had to be broken. At that time the landholdings of the Swedish church were considerable: by 1520 they included over one-fifth of all land in the country. Like many noblemen of his time, Vasa took no deep interest in theology or piety.

In the spring of 1521 Vasa was elected chief of the province of Dalecarlia. Later he became regent of Sweden. He organized an insurrection against the union that gained great support. The church was not involved at the beginning, but when the leading bishop joined the insurrection, he demanded and received a promise from Vasa to protect the privileges of the church. The archiepiscopal see and other bishoprics were vacant, and in the chapters some prelates were inclined toward reform and were also involved in the national struggle. Laurentius Andreae and Olaus Petri in Strängnäs were the leaders of that party. The new thinking in church matters had reached Sweden but had not yet attracted much attention. Vasa's role in the Reformation in Sweden can be divided into three periods: 1523–1527, 1528–1543, and 1544–1560.

In the summer of 1523 Vasa was elected Swedish king. When he took possession of the capital, Stockholm, the struggle for the union was over. Vasa's great problem was how to pay the mercenaries and regulate relations with Lübeck, which had a monopoly on Swedish foreign trade. The king was obliged to borrow from the bishops, churches, and monasteries to settle the crisis. To borrow from the church during crises had not been unusual in the late Middle Ages. When the crisis worsened and Vasa again had to apply to the monasteries, he wrote to Vadstena, the richest monastery in Sweden. In this letter he used words that show that a new view of the church was emerging; the church does not consist of priests but is the "communion of believers." That expression implied that the means of the church belong to the people. He declared this to be the doctrine of scripture, not a new innovation. The opinions of Luther were to be examined with scripture in order to bring this truth to light. It is evident that Lutheran-influenced priests advising the king gave him arguments to support his economic policy in relation to the church.

No action that could be considered a breach in the order of the church was made in these years by Vasa. The newly elected bishops applied for confirmation in Rome, but since they attached certain conditions the elections were not approved. Relations with the pope gradually ceased without formal rupture. The ideas of reform were preached by Laurentius Andreae and Olaus Petri, who received important offices in the capital through the king. One of the elder bishops tried in vain to suppress the Lutheran preachers.

As usual, religious unrest was to be resolved by a public disputation. But that was not enough because political and religious unrest were combined—the king had to intervene against politically active prelates. An agreement was necessary, and this came at the Diet of Västerås in 1527. The Swedish church was freed from canon law through its decision and became a national church with the king as supreme head. But no confession and no order of worship were approved. The king proceeded cautiously. The decisions used typical reform expressions: the word of God was to be preached purely and clearly. The diet decided that the "superfluous means" of the church were to be taken over by the state. The position of the church became tenuous because the king could decide what was "superfluous." As a result of the Diet of Västerås in 1527 a national church without a confession was erected in Sweden, and the church became completely dependent on the king.

After the Diet of Västerås the theologians were charged with providing an order of worship. But the king was not unfamiliar with the authorization given by tradition. Wishing to appear a true Christian king, he was crowned in 1528. To stress the continuity with the Catholic tradition, a Lutheran archbishop was elected in 1531 by bishops and pastors. By authorizing bishops and pastors, the king stressed that he himself did not decide matters of worship; the decision in 1536 to say Mass only in Swedish was made by a synod without the formal participation of the king. In 1536 celibacy was abolished.

The difference between the spiritual and the secular order was stressed by the king during the the 1530s, and by the early 1540s the bishops looked for protection in that distinction. Vasa refused proposals to preserve the Catholic faith, referring to the decisions of Västerås in 1527. Their vague wordings were the foundation of his church policy.

In time Vasa became suspicious of his one-time collaborators. They fell into disgrace, and some were prosecuted. The king feared that the liberty of the church could be grounds for insurrection. For this reason he decided to shape a national church controlled totally by the state. With the assistance of foreign advisers, especially Georg Norman from Pomerania, in 1539 he established a new church government that eliminated the position of bishop, although he did not do away with them altogether. Visitations were carried out in various parts of the country to confiscate superfluous property in the churches. At the same time the bishops supervised religious life.

In 1542 a dangerous rebellion in southern Sweden threatened Vasa. The rebellion proved that too much state authority aroused opposition. The more cautious line followed by Vasa and the first reformers had been abandoned, and the true evangelical religion had become an instrument to maintain the absolute power of the king and the unity of the kingdom. When the rebellion had been crushed the king returned to a more cautious church policy. The German-inspired church government was given up. Again the bishops held a position of leadership of the dioceses. The king concentrated more and more on Sweden. Since he was not a member of the Schmalkald League, he tried to secure his position through an alliance with his old opponent, Christian III, king of Denmark.

At a diet in Västerås in 1544 Sweden was proclaimed an evangelical kingdom. But because the church had no confession, all had to maintain the faith "which is now arisen." Because of the very vagueness of the stipulation, it was an order on which all could agree. Moreover, Sweden was declared a hereditary kingdom by the diet. The king made a simple statement on Holy Communion: Holy Communion is given by Christ as a sign of forgiveness for our sins, in commemoration of his death and through it we are released from death. Although this assertation is decidedly anti-Catholic and pro-evangelical, it says nothing about the various theological opinions concerning Communion. The opposition to Catholic practices could now be harsher since the rebellion had been crushed and the cautious Swedish line ruled church policy.

But now, as earlier, church policy was guided by financial interests. All the socially and economically important guilds were dissolved; the king confiscated their property. The means by which the parish churches paid the clergy were taken away. The bishops were no longer called bishops, but superintendents, and their number was increased. As supervisors of the church they were part of the administration of the state. Vasa continued to refuse to promulgate a church order detailing the relations between church and state; his personal rule of the church did not allow clearly defined limits. Even during the 1550s Vasa feared a Catholic conspiracy and he intervened when he suspected pastors of practicing Catholic customs. But he did not punish lay-people on account of their faith unless they manifestly were involved in a political conspiracy.

Vasa presents the picture of a prince conscious of power. He saw his duty as that of creating a united nation. The church with its means could give him the instrument for that, and the reformers gave him an argument for his church policy. But he showed no deep interest in theology, nor was he interested in learned culture. He exercised a practical church policy that arranged religion for the service of the state and encouraged an obedient people with respect for God and king. Vasa had an unsophisticated faith in God and no interest in liturgical forms. He introduced innovations to religious services carefully in order to avoid misunderstanding. Preaching first, then change, was the motto of the king in church matters. In him a late medieval prince was changed into an evangelical king without a confession, but freed from the papacy.

BIBLIOGRAPHY

Holmquist, Hjalmar, ed. *Svenska kyrkans historia.* Vol. 3, *Reformationstidevarvet, 1521–1611.* Stockholm, 1933.

Svalenius, Ivar. *Gustav Wasa.* Stockholm, 1950.

Westman, K. B. *Reformationens genombrottsår i Sverige.* Stockholm, 1918.

HARRY LENHAMMAR

VASSY, MASSACRE OF. *See* Wassy, Massacre of.

VÄSTERÅS, DIET OF. Many historians see this major Swedish diet, held on 16 June 1527, as the breakthrough of the Reformation in Sweden. In 1526/27 the political situation in Sweden was confused. King Gustavus Vasa and his secretary, Laurentius Andreae, together with the reformer Olaus Petri, were supporting reform ideas. From the spring of 1526 Melchior Hoffman, a notorious agitator, had been preaching among the Germans in Stockholm. The followers of the new faith had been radicalized to iconoclasm. This situation was most inconvenient for the king, who promptly expelled Hoffman.

Alarmed by this radicalization among the Lutherans, and still more by the synodical conference that the king was preparing, the Catholics decided to act. The bishops of Linköping and Skara in central Sweden conspired with the chancellor Ture Jönsson, who owned estates in this area, to dethrone the king. At the same time monks and priests were wandering northward from Västerås to incite peasants in the province of Darlecarlia and promulgate rumors about the new heresy.

The king and Andreae acted quickly and ruthlessly by executing two prelates and encouraging the monks to leave their monasteries. The decisive factors were the revolt of the Darlecarlian junker, an impostor pretending to be of the Sture family; the risk of war with Russia; and the ultimatum presented by the council of Lübeck concerning war debts. Sweden's existence was at stake. A resolution was ultimately found in a parliamentary session, and a diet was convened. Its two most important issues were the king's desire to abdicate and "to establish unity in the discordance of dogmas." In May the location of the diet was changed from Söderköping, in the vicinity of the opposing groups in central Sweden, to Västerås because of the disturbances in Darlecarlia. Because of the possible election of a new king the Estates were already convened.

The diet opened at the appointed time, 16 June, with a wider representation than any earlier diet. The king was accompanied by his secretary, Andreae. Soldiers were stationed in the castle. The proceedings took place in the monastery of the friars and began with the reading of the king's proposals regarding the Darlecarlian rebellion. They were probably written by the king himself in cooperation with Andreae and Olaus Petri. The tenor of the proposals made them the most important document of the Reformation in Sweden.

The king did not propose any ecclesiastical changes but restricted himself to exposing the miserable political and financial situation of the realm. He declared himself prepared to organize a disputation to dismiss rumors of a new religion. As circumstances made his rule impossible, he threatened to renounce the crown. The Estates were thus left to find a counteroffer to convince him to remain. Here one may find the fundamental Swedish principle of cooperation between royal authority and representatives of the nation in governing the realm. The Estates decided without hesitation to support the king against the revolt in Darlecarlia.

The reformers sought to obtain permission from the king for a disputation on religion in order to reach an understanding of the main theological issues. The answer of the bishops was conveyed by Hans Brask, bishop of Linköping, who totally rejected the idea of "a heretical disputation" and invoked the Holy See, without whose "agreement, permission, and goodwill" no changes in ecclesiastical matters could be made. By his masterly oration Brask secured the sympathy of the nobility for the church. When asked, their spokesman, Ture Jönsson, confirmed that the nobility supported the bishop. The king left the proceedings in anger, forcing the parliament to make its most important decision.

The stormy debate of the first day was dominated by chancellor Ture Jönsson. The reformers did not give in, however, and by negotiating with the estates separately succeeded in taking the lead. Hinting at the promised advantages for the nobility and burghers that the king had touched upon in his proposition, they gradually convinced them to offer the king what he required to remain on the throne. The peasants followed the burghers but wanted to retain the old religion. The clergy was paralyzed when the reform bishop of Strägnäs pleaded for concession in political and financial matters.

When the king returned to the proceedings, the most important request of the reformers was accepted, namely, a disputation on religion to force the assembly to form an opinion on the evangelical message and its legal basis. It was organized with several debaters on each side and was held in Swedish. Olaus Petri was unable, as in his sermon for the Estates, to influence those who were still uncertain and thus make it easier for the peasants to accept the resolution.

In a plenary session the diet agreed to make their commitments binding in a letter of obligation, which was drawn up on Midsummer Day and signed by the council and the Estates, except the clergy. This obligation was related to the four deficiencies emphasized in the proposition. Help was promised against the rebellion in Darlecarlia and elsewhere. A reduction of ecclesiastical property was permitted; that is, the king was allowed to secularize the extensive property of the church. The nobility were to be given back the freeholders' estate given to the church after 1454. The Estates certified that the disputation had manifested that the reformers had good intentions and preached nothing but the word of God, "hence they all pledged that the Word of God should be preached purely everywhere in the kingdom." This was the same reform phrasing that had been used in the German diets, and the Obligation of Västerås thus merely proclaimed freedom of religion for Protestants and Catholics alike as long as they based their beliefs on the pure and simple word of God. But this positive recognition of the evangelical doctrine made the resolution of the diet a revolution in religion as well as in church politics. The latter aspect was enforced through the Statute of Västerås that Vasa had written and promulgated through the council. It was meant to complete the obligation but contained many new prescriptions limiting the traditional privileges of the church and increasing the power of the king. The old organization was upheld with bishops, chapters, deans, and ministers. The autonomy of the parishes and the bishop's freedom to settle ecclesiastical matters in his diocese were retained. The pope and Rome were not mentioned.

These two documents of Västerås were the basis for the Swedish church becoming an episcopal national church coincident with the monarchy and with the king as head. No rupture with Catholicism was proclaimed, but in retrospect the decisions of Västerås had laid the foundation for Sweden's transformation into a Protestant state.

BIBLIOGRAPHY

Carlsson, G. "Preußischer Einfluß auf die Reformation Schwedens." In *Festschrift für Otto Scheel*, edited by Harald Thuran, pp. 36–48. Schleswig, 1952.

Hjärne, H. *Reformationsriksdagen i Västerås*. 2d ed. Stockholm, 1912.

Holmquist, Hjalmar. *Die schwedische Reformation, 1523–1531*. Leipzig, 1925.

———. *Svenska kyrkans historia*. Vol. 3. *Reformationstidevarvet, 1521–1611*. Stockholm, 1933.

Kjöllerström, Sven. "Riksdagen i Västerås 1527 och 'goda gamla kristliga sedvänjor.'" *Historisk tidskrift* 80 (1960), 385–412.

———. "Västerås ordinantia." *Scandia* 26 (1960), 41–98.

Sjödin, L. "Västerås möte 1527." *Historisk tidskrift* 47.1 (1927), 101–174; 48.2 (1928), 221–321.

Tunberg, Sven. *Västerås riksdag 1527: Några kritiska anmärkningar*. Uppsala Universitets Årsskrift 1915. Uppsala, 1913.

Weibull, L. "Vesterås riksdag 1527." *Scandia* 10 (1927), 76–128.

Westman, K. B. *Reformationens genombrottsår i Sverige*. Stockholm, 1918.

INGUN MONTGOMERY

VEGETIUS. *See* Krafft, Adam.

VELDE, Frans van der. *See* Sonnius, Franciscus.

VELUANUS, Ioannes Anastasius (Dutch, Jan Gerritszoon Versteghe; c.1520–?), Dutch Reformed theologian. Veluanus was born in Stroe, in the Veluwe of Gelderland. There is a tradition that "Versteghe" may refer to the farmstead "De Steeg" near Stroe. As the Roman Catholic priest in Garderen from 1544 to 1550, he engaged in Reformation preaching. He was arrested on 1 January 1550 and taken to jail in Arnhem. Under intense pressure from his inquisitors, Francisus Sonnius and N. Gruwel, on 27 January he recanted his Protestantism. A week later he was sentenced to perpetual imprisonment in the dilapidated castle of Hattem, near Zwolle, living three days a week on only bread and water.

Sonnius and Gruwel brought him a Bible, some patristic writings, paper, pen, and ink, promising to release him if he would write a treatise in defense of the pope. He delayed; it did not appear. He was transferred to house arrest, however, from December 1551 to 22 May 1553, after which he was released on bond posted by family members and ordered to report in fourteen days to study theology at Louvain. On the way, he opened letters he was carrying from Sonnius that warned the Louvain authorities to keep him under watch.

He resolved to leave the Catholics but faced a dilemma of conscience, knowing that his guarantors would forfeit four hundred guilders bail. Nevertheless, he fled to Strasbourg, where he wrote an apology for his recantation and a confession of his Protestant faith. Dated 12 April 1554, his book, *Der Leken Wechwijser* (The Layman's Guide), was written, as he said, for the untutored Gelderlanders in their vernacular Gelders tongue. Published in Harderwijk, it had such a wide reception that a Dutch edition appeared the next year. It was the first book on Reformed theology to appear in the Netherlands.

He addressed his book to the nobility and towns of Gelderland and the county of Zutphen, but "especially to all true lovers of godly truth." After recounting the course of his persecution, recantation, and return to the Reformation, he begged his readers to forgive him for his inconstancy. In amendment he offered them this "short report" (some 250 modern pages!) as instruction in the faith he now confessed.

He affirmed a Trinitarian doctrine of God and doctrines on Creation, the Fall, repentance, and faith. He attacked Roman Catholicism broadly—on the sacrifice of the Mass, transubstantiation, adoration of the Host, auricular confession, purgatory, and works of supererogation. He opposed Latin in worship and condemned images, preferring paintings of biblical pictures and texts. He complained about ignorant priests and favored allowing them to marry (as he himself did, twice). He defended infant baptism against the "Anabaptists" and followed Huldrych Zwingli and Cornelis Henricxzoen Hoen on the Lord's Supper. He rejected those who tried to coerce faith, especially "popish monks and bishops," but also Protestants who were cruel to Anabaptists.

On predestination and free will he appealed to the early Greek and Latin church against the reformers themselves. He denied any distinction between the hidden and revealed will of God. When Christ says "repent," he offers salvation to all. While the human will must not be esteemed too highly, predestination applies to those who use the means of grace, believe, and continue in obedience.

Pastors should be called by the magistrates and installed by bishops. On church polity and on predestination, the Arminians would later point to Veluanus as proof that Calvinist presbyterianism was an innovation in Dutch Protestantism. He wrote against the Lutherans on the Lord's Supper (1557) and against the Jesuits on the body of Christ (1561). He was the first preacher at Steeg near Bacharach and, in 1561, superintendent at Bacharach. His last years are unknown.

BIBLIOGRAPHY

Primary Sources

Bakhuizen van den Brink, J. N., et al., eds. *Documenta Reformatoria.* Kampen, 1960. See vol. 2, pp. 111–123.

Veluanus, Anastasius. "Der Leken Wechwyser," "Vom Nachtmal Christi," and "Von Dem waren leib Christi." In *Bibliotheca Reformatoria Neerlandica,* edited by F. Pijper, vol. 4. The Hague, 1906.

Secondary Sources

Brandt, Gerard. *The History of the Reformation and Other Ecclesiastical Transactions in and about the Low Countries . . . (1720–1721).* Reprint, New York, 1979. See vol. 1, pp. 96–99.

Itterzon, G. P. van. "Versteghe, Jan Gerrits (Joannes Anastasius Veluanus)." In *Biographisch Lexicon voor de Geschiedenis van het Nederlandse Protestantism,* vol. 2, pp. 436–437. Kampen, 1983.

Knappert, L. *Het Onstaan en de Vestiging van het Protestantisme in de Nederlanden.* Utrecht, 1924. See esp. pp. 242–248.

Oorthuys, G. *Anastasius' "Wechwyser", Bullingers "Huysboeck" en Calvyns "Institutie" Vergeleken in hun Leer van God en Mensch.* Leiden, 1919.

CARL BANGS

VENATOR, Adolphus Tectander (also de Jager; 1569?–1618), minister in the Netherlands who, though not reckoned among the Remonstrants, served as a catalyst in the Arminian controversy. After completing theological studies in Herborn, Germany (1597), Venator came to Nijmegen, the Netherlands, where his brother Johannes (1565–1598) served as pastor. While there he accepted a pastoral call from Alkmaar, and soon became a colleague of Cornelis Hillenius and Pieter Cornelis.

He became embroiled in a lengthy controversy with Hillenius, triggered by Venator's refusal to visit a sick person during an outbreak of bubonic plague (1599) and by Hillenius's criticism of his sermons. The contrast between the two men was great: Hillenius was a straightforward Calvinist who knew no Greek, whereas Venator was a humanist who was conversant with the Greek New Testament and quoted frequently from Dirk Volkertszoon Coornhert and Desiderius Erasmus. In 1603 Venator directed the play *Andria* by Terence, performed by his Latin students, which resulted in his confession of guilt before the Synod of Enkhuizen and the dismissal of his students. Several months later he composed two controversial publications: *Reden-vreucht der wijsen in haer wel-lust ende belachen der dwasen quel-lust* (Alkmaar, 1603), which contained heterodox views and an attack upon Hillenius; and *Nieuw-Jaers-Dicht: Op de wijse van den 23. Psalm* (Alkmaar, 1604), which contained several scandalous passages. In defense, Venator distributed his theological views in the form of 209 questions and answers to all classes. Both Classis Alkmaar and the Synod of Edam demanded a confession of guilt for this—which he refused. This resulted in his suspension from office, which was ultimately reversed when the three ministers of Alkmaar were reconciled in 1604.

The next controversy revolved around Venator's preaching on the Heidelberg Catechism. Hillenius obtained the approval of the classis that all ministers must endorse the Heidelberg Catechism and the Belgic Confession. Venator refused since he believed that the authority of the church rested only upon the scriptures and not upon councils or doctrinal standards. Consequently, he was again suspended on 3 December 1608, but the town council gave him license to continue.

In the spring of 1609 Venator was accused of adultery with the wife of a council member. At a classis meeting on 21 July 1609, he was declared innocent. The next month Venator participated in the conference between Francisus Gomarus and Jacobus Arminius, during which his controversial suspension by Classis Alkmaar was discussed extensively.

The battle between Venator and Hillenius also entered the political realm. The city council decided at last to dismiss both ministers. Venator returned in 1611 when Hillenius's successor could not handle the congregation by himself.

In 1617 Venator published his *Theologia vera et mera ofte een Schrijver; klaar algemein fundamentboek* (Alkmaar). The liberal sentiments expressed in this work, particularly on the deity of Christ, were opposed by Eewoud Teellinck, condemned by the Leiden faculty, and were even unacceptable to Simon Episcopius. The book was banned by the government; Venator was exiled to 's-Gravenzande, but was permitted to return to Alkmaar in 1618. He died in France on 28 November 1618.

BIBLIOGRAPHY

Brandt, John. *The History of the Reformation and other Ecclesiastical Transactions in and about the Low Countries* (1672). Translated by Chamberlayne. 4 vols. London, 1720–1723. Best summary of Venator's life and theology in English; see especially vol. 2, pp. 53–68 and 315–320.

Bruinvis, C. W. *Het Alkmaarsche kerkgeschil op 't ergst.* Alkmaar, Netherlands, 1894. Focuses on Venator's conflicts in Alkmaar.

De Vries, J. "Adolphus Tectander Venator." *Oud-Holland* 40 (1922), 124–160.

Rombach, J. H. "Venator, Adolphus Tectander." In *Biografisch Lexicon voor de Geschiedenis van het Nederlandse Protestantisme*, edited by D. Nauta et al., vol. 2, pp. 433–35. Kampen, Netherlands, 1983. Updated overview of Venator's life and theology.

Roos, M. "Godsdienststrijd in het zeventiende eeuwse Alkmaar." Doctoral diss., Rijksuniversiteit Leiden, 1964. Includes in-depth study of the Venator-Hillenius debate.

JOEL R. BEEKE

VENICE. From the earliest days of the Reformation Protestant ideas and books entered Venice and the large Venetian mainland state, which covered the northeastern quarter of the Italian peninsula. In September 1520 a German monk reported that he had carried some of Martin Luther's works to Venice and had sold them immediately. It is likely that these included the three famous treatises of the summer of 1520. Luther's fiery attacks on papal corruption and his calls for reform may have appealed more than his doctrines at this early stage. At about the same time, the vicar of the patriarch of Venice appeared before the Venetian government to present a papal brief (possibly *Exsurge Domine* of 15 June 1520) condemning Luther's books. He asked the government to move against a German merchant who was selling Lutheran titles at his house. A few months later a friar preached Lutheran doctrines to a large crowd in the center of the city. Indeed, itinerant preachers played a major role in spreading Protestant doctrines in Venice and in the countryside. The influx into Venice of Protestant, mostly Lutheran, books continued during the 1520s and 1530s. Since Venice was the largest publishing center of Europe, this commerce is not surprising.

Books that guilefully propagated disguised Protestant views were published in Venice through the 1530s and 1540s. Antonio Brucioli (c.1490–1566), a Florentine exile who lived for many years in Venice, became a Protestant. Between 1533 and 1546 he published in Venice a number of his own vernacular commentaries on scripture which were simply translations and paraphrases of Martin Bucer's Latin commentaries.

This proselytizing through sermons and books bore fruit. A significant number of Protestants inhabited Venice and the Venetian state in the 1540s and 1550s. The largest group of Italian Protestants were those who accepted in greater or lesser degree the main doctrines of Luther and John Calvin. At a minimum they embraced justification by faith (understood in a Protestant sense) and rejected papal leadership of the Christian church. Some went considerably further in their acceptance of magisterial Protestantism.

Pier Paolo Vergerio (1498–1565) attracted the most attention. Born in Capodistria (Koper) on the Dalmatian coast, the eastern fringe of the Venetian mainland state, Vergerio was a papal diplomat and bishop in his native town. At some point he became Protestant; falling under suspicion, he fled to Switzerland in 1549. From there he wrote numerous Italian anti-Catholic and anti-papal pamphlets that were widely read. Fiery antipapalism and mockery of Catholic practices rather than a developed Protestant position marked his pamphlets.

Protestants who remained in Venice and its state were more cautious. They met in conventicles—small clandestine groups of like-minded believers under the guidance of a committed leader. By the 1540s such conventicles were well established. They continued through the 1550s and early 1560s, embracing a cross section of the Venetian populace. Humanist schoolmasters who taught the children of the patriciate, as well as a few lawyers and physicians who had studied at the nearby University of Padua, participated in the conventicles. Merchants from Venice and abroad joined them. Artisans, including petty shopkeepers (such as a goldsmith, a druggist, and a shoe salesman), may have provided the most participants in the conventicles. It is impossible to estimate the total number involved because almost all the information comes from later Inquisition trials. Those accused of heresy naturally revealed as little as possible.

Teofilo Panarelli, a physician with a degree from the University of Padua, was the leader of one such conventicle. He had first imbibed heretical views in Padua from an Italian friar and schoolteacher in 1550 and 1551. Panarelli, in turn, became a conventicle leader in the late 1550s and 1560s. His group met in a bookstore or pharmacy and then retired to a garden or island in the Venetian lagoon. After listening to music, Panarelli read and interpreted the New Testament, works of Bernardino Ochino (an Italian Protestant exile), and Calvin's catechism. These middle-class Venetian Protestants professed faith alone and the sole authority of scripture while denying purgatory, the efficacy of works, and the intercession of saints. The members of the group agonized over whether they should flee to Geneva. A handful left, but the majority remained to be eventually denounced. Some then fled while others, remaining in Venice, were arrested and released without punishment. Panarelli continued to teach Protestant views until arrested in 1567. Refusing to recant, he was eventually hanged in Rome in 1572.

Andrea di Antonio Da Ponte (1509–1585), a nobleman and younger brother of a future doge of Venice, led another conventicle that included several young patricians. Da Ponte fled to Geneva in or about 1560 but persuaded only one other noble to accompany him. Both Venetian noble and commoner heretics found it extremely difficult to leave behind family, friends, and fortune. It is also possible that their Protestant beliefs were not strong enough to cause them to leave. When a spontaneous confession revealed the existence of this conventicle to the Venetian Inquisition in February 1565, fifteen nobles, almost all young men in their twenties and early thirties, were accused of heresy. Eight abjured their beliefs between 1565 and 1569. They admitted having held Lutheran and Calvinist beliefs and were given light penalties, typically one to four years' imprisonment plus penances.

Italian Anabaptists constituted a smaller body of Protestants, second in importance to the followers of Luther and Calvin but particularly strong and numerous in the Venetian mainland state. Anabaptists from the nearby mountains and valleys of Switzerland may have introduced Anabaptism into the Venetian state. Compared with northern European Anabaptists, Venetian Anabaptists developed beliefs marked by greater rationalism and more frequent denial of the divinity of Christ, but they rejected social radicalism. By midcentury Anabaptists were found throughout the Venetian state, with Vicenza and Padua particularly lively centers.

Anabaptist leaders were educated men, but their followers were often artisans.

Approximately sixty Anabaptist leaders gathered in Venice in September 1550 to resolve their differences on the divinity of Christ and other doctrines. They agreed that Jesus Christ was not God but was "filled with the virtues of God." Hell did not exist. At the death of the body, the souls of the elect slept in the Lord until the Last Judgment, when they were united with him—a belief called psychopannychism. But the souls of the unjust perished at the death of the body. Justification came from the mercy and charity of God rather than from Christ's death; nevertheless, Jesus had died to demonstrate the justice of God. Venetian Anabaptists departed from traditional Catholicism much more than did Venetian Protestants following Luther and Calvin.

One of the participants at the 1550 meeting underwent a crisis of conscience and in October 1551 spontaneously confessed everything to the Inquisition of Bologna. He named dozens of Anabaptists, as well as many Lutherans and Calvinists, across Italy. Relayed to Venice, this information led to arrests that netted only about twenty Anabaptists in the Venetian state. Nevertheless, the Venetian authorities broke up Anabaptist conventicles over the next several years. Although a few individuals in rural areas probably held onto Anabaptist, anti-Trinitarian, and materialist beliefs, Anabaptism as a movement disappeared in the Venetian state.

By the last third of the century, organized conventicles of Italian Protestants of any kind ceased to exist in the Venetian state. Venetian Protestantism was slight, clandestine, and limited to a few individuals. But Protestant beliefs lived on among foreigners permitted to live in the Republic of Venice. In the last quarter of the sixteenth century, some two hundred German students, many of them Protestants, in addition to a few Protestant students from other lands, studied at the University of Padua in any given year. The Venetian government tacitly shielded them from arrest. Another two hundred German merchants and their servants lived and traded in the Fondaco dei Tedeschi, the combination warehouse and living quarters for German merchants in the center of Venice. Within the walls of the Fondaco, the Germans were unofficially allowed to hold Protestant religious services. Another five hundred German artisans, especially bakers, tailors, and watchmakers, lived in the city of Venice. They were obliged to conform outwardly to Catholic practices but often returned to Germany in order to celebrate Easter and Christmas according to Protestant rites.

A blend of commercial ideology and political pragmatism formed Venetian policy toward Protestantism until midcentury. The Venetians proclaimed that they were merchants willing to trade with anyone in the world, whatever his beliefs. Their long experience with the infidel Turk had confirmed the wisdom of this policy. Moreover, they did not wish to offend Protestant princes by persecuting German merchants or denying them entry because of their religious views. Hence, the Republic of Venice tolerated foreign Protestants living under its rule throughout the sixteenth and seventeenth centuries so long as they did not openly declare their beliefs or proselytize.

The Venetian government also closed one eye and ignored local Protestants until midcentury, in part for political reasons but also because they posed no threat. But the Venetians were staunch Catholics, despite their many political and jurisdictional disputes with Rome. Upon discovering that Protestantism had made significant inroads into the indigenous population of Venice and its state, the Venetian authorities cracked down. Then the Inquisition, with the full support of the government, carefully but firmly stamped out Protestantism. Fourteen heretics are known to have been executed in Venice, always by drowning, plus an unknown number in the mainland state. Although the Inquisitorial tribunals of Venice and its state were quite mild by contemporary standards of civil and ecclesiastical justice, they were effective enough. The Protestant Reformation never had a realistic chance of success in Venice.

BIBLIOGRAPHY

Ginzburg, Carlo. *I costituti di Don Pietro Manelfi*. Florence and Chicago, 1970. Critical edition of the confession of 1551 which led to arrests of Anabaptists.

——. *The Cheese and the Worms: The Cosmos of a Sixteenth-Century Miller*. Translated by John and Anne Tedeschi. Harmondsworth, England, 1982. Fascinating account of the materialist views of a miller from Friuli.

Grendler, Paul F. *The Roman Inquisition and the Venetian Press, 1540–1605*. Princeton, 1977. Standard account of prosecution of heresy and heretical books.

Lane, Frederic C. *Venice: A Maritime Republic*. Baltimore and London, 1973. The best one-volume history of medieval and Renaissance Venice in any language. Important for background although it does not discuss Protestantism.

Martin, John Jeffries. *Venice's Hidden Enemies: Italian Heretics in a Renaissance City*. Berkeley and London, 1993. Comprehensive overview of Venetian heretics based on study of Inquisition records. Excellent bibliographical essay.

Olivieri, Achille. "Il *Catechismo* e la *Fidei et doctrinae . . . ratio* di Bartolomeo Fonzio, eretico veneziano del Cinquecento." *Studi veneziani* 9 (1967), 339–452. Key Venetian Protestant executed in 1562. Fonzio taught Panarelli and others.

Santosuosso, Antonio. "Religious Orthodoxy, Dissent and Suppression in Venice in the 1540s." *Church History* 42 (1973), 476–485. Good brief account with statistics on number of Inquisition heresy trials.

——. "The Moderate Inquisitor: Giovanni Della Casa's Venetian Nunciature, 1544–1549." *Studi veneziani* n.s. 2 (1978), 119–210. Excellent account of prosecution of heresy.

Schutte, Anne Jacobson. *Pier Paolo Vergerio: The Making of an Italian Reformer*. Geneva, 1977. Life and beliefs of Vergerio until he left Italy in 1549.

Spini, Giorgio. *Tra rinascimento e riforma: Antonio Brucioli*. Florence, 1940. Biography of the man sometimes called Italy's first Protestant.

Stella, Aldo. *Chiesa e stato nelle relazioni dei nunzi pontifici a Venezia: Ricerche sue giurisdizionalismo veneziano dal XVI al XVIII secolo*. Vatican City, 1964. Text of long report about extent of heresy in Venice and Venetian policies toward Protestants written by former nuncio in 1581, plus good introduction.

——. "Utopie e velleità insurrezionali dei filoprotestanti italiani, 1545–1547. *Bibliothèque d'humanisme et Renaissance* 27 (1965), 133–182. Account of Venetian diplomacy with the Protestant Schmalkald League at a crucial point.

——. *Dall'anabattismo al socianesimo nel Cinquecento veneto: Ricerche storiche*. Padua, 1967. Good study of Anabaptism in the Venetian state.

——. *Anabattismo e antitrinitarismo in Italia nel XVI secolo: Nuove ricerche storiche*. Padua, 1969. On Anabaptism in the Venetian state and other regions of Italy.

PAUL F. GRENDLER

VERGARA, Juan de

VERGARA, Juan de (1492–1557), Spanish theologian and humanist. A New Christian, or *Converso*, of Jewish lineage, Vergara studied at the University of Alcalá, where he imbibed humanist ideals and earned a doctorate in theology. At Alcalá Vergara translated Aristotle and also worked on the Complutensian Polyglot Bible, assuming responsibility for the wisdom books of the Septuagint text. In 1516–1517 he served as secretary to Cardinal Francisco Jiménez de Cisneros, archbishop of Toledo and founder of the University of Alcalá. Vergara also served as secretary to Jiménez's successor, Archbishop Guillaume de Croy, accompanying him and Emperor Charles V to the Low Countries and Germany in 1520–1522. In Brugge Vergara met with Desiderius Erasmus and began the difficult task of mediating with the Spanish anti-Erasmians at Alcalá. Vergara was present at the Diet of Worms, where he witnessed Luther's defiance, and became intensely opposed to Lutheranism. Having served as chaplain for Charles V during this voyage, Vergara reluctantly accepted yet another appointment as secretary to the next archbishop of Toledo, Alonso de Fonseca (1523).

Vergara kept writing to Erasmus and acted as his chief informant concerning the debate against the anti-Erasmians held at Valladolid in 1527. Owing as much to his brother's involvement with a *beata* who was suspected of heresy as to Vergara's Erasmianism, the Inquisition began gathering denunciations against him in 1530. Three years later Vergara was arrested and accused of harboring Lutheran, Erasmian, and Alumbrado sympathies and of having defied the Inquisition's order not to correspond with his imprisoned brother. Vergara denied the charges of heresy successfully but admitted writing letters to his brother in invisible ink with orange and lemon juice. In 1535 he was absolved but fined 1,500 ducats and sentenced to one year's confinement in a Toledan monastery, a light punishment by the standards of the day. Freed in 1537, Vergara lived the next twenty years of his life in relative peace. In addition to collaborating for a time on a biography of his former patron, Cardinal Jiménez, he wrote a scriptural study, *Tratado de las ocho ques-*

tiones del Templo (1522), which influenced Melchior Cano's thinking on the relation between history and theology. His brush with the Inquisition is a graphic reminder of the silencing of the Spanish Erasmians in the 1530s.

BIBLIOGRAPHY

Abellán, José Luis. *El erasmismo español.* Reprint, Madrid, 1982. Hardly mentions Vergara, but is useful as background reading.

Aldea Vaquero, Quintin, et al., eds. *Diccionario de la historia de la Iglesia en España.* Madrid, 1975. The article on Vergara, by José Goñi Gaztambide (vol. 4, pp. 2737–2742), contains a lengthy bibliography, as does the article "Erasmismo en España" by the same author, supplement, pp. 272–281.

Allen, P. S., ed. *Opus Epistolarum D. Erasmi Roterodami.* Reprint, Oxford, 1992. Contains the correspondence between Erasmus and Vergara: letters 1277, 1312, 1684, 1814, 1875, 2004, 2133, 2253, 2563, and 2879.

Bataillon, Marcel. *Erasme et l'Espagne.* 3d ed. Geneva, 1991. See vol. 1, especially pp. 106–109, 127–134, 472–509. The definitive survey of Spanish Erasmianism; sets Vergara in context.

Garcia-Villoslada, Ricardo, ed. *Historia de la Iglesia en España.* Madrid, 1980. Contains a summary of Spanish Erasmianism written by José Luis González Novalín (vol. 3.2, pp. 160–174).

La Pinta Llorente, M. de. *El erasmismo del doctor Juan de Vergara y otras interpretaciones.* Madrid, 1945.

Menéndez Pelayo, Marcelino. *Historia de los heterodoxos españoles.* 4th ed. Madrid, 1986–1987. A polemical but magisterial study of religious dissent in Spain, with a lengthy section on Erasmianism; see vol. 1, pp. 653–737.

CARLOS M. N. EIRE

VERGERIO, Pier Paolo (1498–1565), papal diplomat, bishop of Capodistria (Koper), religious exile, and Protestant propagandist. Vergerio was born in Capodistria, a few miles south of Trieste on the Istrian peninsula, which was subject to the republic of Venice. Son of a local notable and descendant of the renowned humanist Pier Paolo Vergerio the Elder (1370–1444), he obtained a solid education in his hometown before enrolling at the University of Padua, where he earned a degree in civil law in 1524. While studying and then practicing law, he cultivated humanist pursuits in the circle of Pietro Bembo. His earliest published works—two orations and a dialogue in Latin—provide evidence of his literary talent.

Sponsored by his brother Aurelio, Vergerio entered papal service in 1532. Clement VII immediately put him to work as a diplomat, sending him first to Venice to promote a league against the Turks and then to central Europe as nuncio to Emperor Charles V's brother Ferdinand. Here Vergerio received his first exposure to current political and religious problems. His initial reaction to "heresy" was visceral repugnance and alarm about the imminent threat of this penetrating Italy.

Early in 1535, Paul III summoned Vergerio to Rome and gave him a new mandate: to assess support in central Europe for the convocation of an ecumenical council, on which Charles V was insisting. Vergerio crisscrossed the empire, visiting numerous Catholic and some Protestant principalities and cities. Most of those on whom he called, among them Luther (encountered unexpectedly at Wittenberg in November 1535), professed enthusiasm about the proposed council. Firmly committed to the conciliar initiative, the nuncio gradually realized that for his papal master the project was merely a political ploy.

Vergerio returned to Italy in 1536, disillusioned but confident that he would be rewarded appropriately for his services. His nomination to the bishopric of Capodistria, a see with meager revenues further eroded by a pension payable to a papal favorite, disappointed him. Seeking a protector who could get the pension lifted, he accepted hospitality from various Italian princes and prelates, visited the courts of Francis I and Marguerite d'Angoulême, and attended the Worms-Regensburg colloquy (1540–1541). During his travels he encountered and endorsed the platform of the *spirituali*, proponents of renewal within the church inspired by the concept of justification by faith alone through grace.

In the summer of 1541, Vergerio was finally able to settle in Capodistria, take holy orders, and begin to implement his new convictions about reform. His vigorous, often tactless efforts to root out abuses in religious houses and to instruct his flock aroused opposition from friars and others linked to Cardinal Alessandro Farnese, Paul III's grandson. Heresy proceedings against Vergerio began in 1545. Through legal maneuvers and appeals to people in high places, including the prelates assembled at Trent, the accused struggled vainly to establish his innocence. He came eventually to despair of attaining a just resolution of his case. Taking pen in hand, he presented his case to the Italian public in the first of what would become a flood of books and pamphlets. On 1 May 1549, like such *spirituali* as Bernardino Ochino and Peter Martyr Vermigli before him, he left Italy and the church.

Vergerio's "apostasy," the first by a bishop, evoked great excitement on both sides of the Alps. Settling first in the Grisons, a haven for Italian exiles, he became pastor at Vicosoprano and stepped up his production of works aimed at persuading compatriots to follow his example. Italian and Swiss ministers who had welcomed him were soon alienated by his maneuvering to gain control of the Italian Protestant movement. In 1552 he accepted the post of legal adviser to Duke Christoph of Württemberg, for whom he performed several diplomatic missions in eastern Europe. Most of his time and energy, however, went into the writing and publication of Protestant propaganda directed mainly toward his homeland.

Although Vergerio concluded his career in a Lutheran land (he died in Tübingen in 1565), his theological stance remained generically Protestant, not specifically Lutheran. His works, which evince little expertise or interest in doctrinal subtleties, convey a simple, urgent message. First, Italians must recognize that the church is a morass of abuses and unscriptural "human inventions" aimed at exploiting the people. Then, individually and collectively, they must reject the seductive but soul-destroying Nicodemite option and liberate their bodies as well as their hearts from the "tyranny of Antichrist."

Given the sociopolitical configuration of Italian states, Vergerio's campaign to win polities for the Protestant cause was doomed to failure. Frequent mentions of his name and his writings in Inquisition trials until the late 1580s nonetheless attest to his considerable, persistent influence on individual Italians.

BIBLIOGRAPHY

Cantimori, Delio. *Eretici italiani del Cinquecento*. Edited by Adriano Prosperi. Turin, 1992. Obligatory point of departure for Italian Reformation studies, emphasizing theological radicals.

Church, Frederic Corss. *The Italian Reformers, 1534–1564*. New York, 1932. The only general work in English on the Italian Reformation, superseded in large part by more recent scholarship.

Hubert, Friedrich H. V. E. *Vergerios publizistische Thätigkeit nebst einer biblographischen Übersicht*. Göttingen, 1893. Bibliography of Vergerio's numerous works; still valuable but needs updating.

McNair, Philip. *Peter Martyr in Italy: An Anatomy of Apostasy*. Oxford, 1967. A study of another religious exile, Vermigli, useful for comparative purposes.

Nuntiaturberichte aus Deutschland, 1533–1559, nebst ergänzenden Actenstücken. Vol. 1, *Nuntiaturen des Vergerios, 1533–1536*. Edited by Walter Friedensburg. Gotha, 1892. These dispatches, the only generally accessible writings by Vergerio, provide a taste of his style and insight into the formation of his ideas on ecclesiastical politics.

Paschini, Pio. *Pier Paolo Vergerio il giovane e la sua apostasia: Un episodio delle lotte religiose nel Cinquecento*. Rome, 1925. Solid study by a noted Catholic historian unsympathetic to Vergerio.

Schutte, Anne Jacobson. *Pier Paolo Vergerio: The Making of an Italian Reformer*. Geneva, 1977. Covers the Italian phase of Vergerio's career; updated bibliography in the Italian edition, *Pier Paolo Vergerio e la Riforma a Venezia, 1498–1549*, Rome, 1988.

Sixt, Christian Heinrich. *Petrus Paulus Vergerius, päpstlicher Nuntius, katholischer Bischof und Vorkämpfer des Evangeliums*. Braunschweig, 1855. Strongly Protestant interpretation, focusing on post-exilic career.

Tomizza, Fulvio. *Il male viene dal Nord: Il romanzo del vescovo Vergerio*. Milan, 1984. Historically sound, psychologically penetrating biographical study.

ANNE JACOBSON SCHUTTE

VERMIGLI, Peter Martyr (also Pietro Martire; 1499–1562), Florentine humanist, Augustinian monk, and Reformed theologian. He was born to Stefano di Antonio Vermigli, a prosperous shoemaker, and Maria Fumantino in Florence on 8 September 1499. After early schooling in 1514, Pietro entered the monastery of San Bartholomeo at Fiesole. Four years later, having joined the Lateran Congregation of Canons regular of Saint Augustine, he assumed the name of Saint Peter of Verona, martyred in 1252.

In 1518 he entered the University of Padua to study Aristotle. There he met Reginald Pole (1500–1558), cousin of England's King Henry VIII. Vermigli took his doctorate after careful scholastic training in Thomistic method and in the rigorous Augustinianism of Gregory of Rimini (d. 1358). He was ordained a priest in 1525. In 1526 he was promoted to public preacher, and from 1526 to 1530 he taught philosophy and scripture in the houses of the Lateran Congregation of the Canons Regular (Augustinian), lecturing on Homer in Vercelli. As vicar at San Giovanni in Monte at Bologna, Vermigli learned Hebrew well from a Jewish doctor named Isaac. In 1533 he became abbot of Spoleto for three years. While residing in Rome between May 1536 and April 1537, he may have assisted in the remarkable reform proposals that Gasparo Contarini (1483–1542) and others presented to Pope Paul III in 1537. From 1537 to 1540 Vermigli served as abbot of San Pietro ad Aram in Naples. During that time he preached to an audience which also attended the reform salon of Juan de Valdés (1500/10–1541), the Spanish reformer, who became a close friend. It is plausible that Vermigli influenced Valdés, especially on the matter of predestination. His 1540 public lectures on *1 Corinthians* reached only chapter 3, verses 9–17, when he was suspended from preaching for his denial of purgatory. Powerful friends in Rome overturned the local prohibition.

Vermigli was elected prior of San Frediano at Lucca in 1541, a most influential post. A brilliant team of humanists assisted local instruction in Latin, Greek, and Hebrew. One of his canons, Girolamo Zanchi (1516–1590), and the Hebraist Emanueli Tremelli would join him in exile. Vermigli lectured on the Pauline epistles and *Psalms*. The great event was the September 1541 summit conversations in Lucca between Pope Paul III and Emperor Charles V. Josiah Simler, Vermigli's contemporary biographer, records that Contarini and Vermigli engaged in daily religious conversations.

The summer of 1542 led to a crisis of conscience when the Inquisition was established in Italy on 21 July. Vermigli fled Lucca in August by way of Pisa to Florence. He paused to copy a manuscript of John Chrysostom, to entrust his library to a patrician friend, and to pen a letter to his Lucca canons that concluded with the words, "I am free from hypocrisy through the grace of Christ." Bernardino Ochino (?–1564), valued preacher of the Capuchin order, joined Vermigli in flight across the Alps on 25 August.

After some days in Zurich, Vermigli spent a month in Basel, where Bonifacius Amerbach assisted him with books and money. On 5 October he left for Strasbourg at Martin Bucer's invitation. During his five years there he lectured on the Old Testament, succeeding to Wolfgang Capito's chair of divinity, and later also lectured again on *Romans*, publishing comments on the Apostles' Creed in 1544 that clearly deny Roman teaching on the papacy and the Eucharist as well as display his biblical theology and humanism.

Archbishop Thomas Cranmer invited Vermigli to England in 1547. In the spring of 1548 he took up residence in Christ Church, Oxford, as regius professor. Vermigli gave private lectures in his house and public ones at the divinity school. His controversial residence at Christ Church with his wife, Catherine Dampmartin, was the first such clerical marriage. In the midst of his 1549 lectures on *1 Corinthians*, Vermigli held an Oxford disputation on the Eucharist. He delivered lectures on *Romans*, served on the Reform Commission for Ecclesiastical Laws, and contributed to the 1552 *Book of Common Prayer*. The British Library contains a copy of the Oxford *Disputatio* (1549) with marginal notes in King Edward VI's own hand. After Edward VI died, Vermigli returned to Strasbourg late in 1553. There he lectured on *Judges* to the Marian exiles and was pressed by the Lutheran Johannes Marbach to conform to doctrinal constraints on baptism and the Eucharist. He left in 1556 for Zurich.

While in Zurich Vermigli was often invited by John Calvin to pastor the Genevan Italian congregation and to lecture for him. In 1559 he published his massive *Defensio adversum Gardinerum* (Defense Against Gardiner), which was written at Cranmer's personal request. While in Zurich, he prepared his biblical lectures for a European audience. Vermigli dedicated his published 1558 lectures on *Romans* to Queen Elizabeth. At Zurich he lectured on *Samuel*, which Théodore de Bèze and Heinrich Bullinger used in manuscript, and on *Kings*. Vermigli sent letters in 1556 and 1560 to the Polish nobility counteracting the christological views of his countryman Francis Stancarus. In 1561, to answer the Lutheran Johannes Brenz, he published his *Dialogus de utraque in Christo natura*, whose preface, written to Bishop John Jewel, was full of classical references and gratitude for their friendship since their Oxford days. In September 1561 he attended with Bèze the Colloquy of Poissy. Vermigli corresponded with various Elizabethan bishops, including Jewel at Salisbury, Richard Cox at Ely, and Edwin Sandys at Worcester. He contributed a preface to Jewel's influential *Apologia ecclesiae anglicanae* (1562).

Vermigli's presence in northern Europe can be documented from his extant correspondence and publications. One such work is his *Preces sacrae ex psalmis davidis*, a collection of prayers with which he concluded his Strasbourg lectures of the 1540s. Johannes Sudlicius's Czech translation was printed in 1620 in the Old Town Square of Prague, where executions of chief Protestant nobles took place on 21 June 1621. *Modlitby Svaté z u Žalmuv Davida Proroka Božiho . . .* translates Vermigli's prayers given during the Schmalkald War. Whether in the French version of 1571 or the Czech of 1620, such language of consolation links Vermigli with French Protestants of the 1570s and the Czech disaster of the Thirty Years' War.

A second link between the 1542 flight from Italy and the 1621 Czech migration into Poland is his letter *De fuga in persecutione*, included in the *Loci Communes* (1580) and subsequent editions to 1656. In its 1574 French edition, as well as the 1627 Czech version, this document stitches together the hopes and fears of sixteenth-century believers with the

seventeenth-century followers of the Bohemian Bishop John Amos Comenius, whose magnificent library of Protestant authors accompanied them into exile. From Lucca in Italy to Leizno in Poland, Vermigli's phrases consoled these refugees.

His major works instructed the international Reformed community, seen from their presence in personal libraries in England (eighty-five copies in Cambridge alone) and their reprints in Heidelberg (eight) and Geneva (four). His fellow exile Pietro Perna at Basel published the *Romans* in 1558 and again in 1560, 1568, and 1570, along with the three-volume *Loci Communes* of 1580–1582, as part of a cultural agenda. Vermigli's Latin writings were excerpted and published in a Latin *Loci Communes* (1576). This was expanded in 1580 and translated into English in 1583. The *Loci* went through thirteen Latin editions by 1656, while the commentaries are extant in thirty-two editions from the *Corinthians* (1551) to *Lamentations* (1629). Vermigli left a considerable literary corpus.

Vermigli died in his Zurich house on 12 November 1562 in the presence of his wife, Catarina (née Merenda), and such friends as Conrad Gessner, Bullinger, and others. He was indeed the equal of Calvin or Bullinger in his primary task as a Florentine humanist and Reformed Christian scholar.

BIBLIOGRAPHY

Anderson, Marvin. "Royal Idolatry: Peter Martyr and the Reformed Tradition." *Archiv für Reformationsgeschichte* 69 (1978), 157–201. Complete account of Vermigli's political thought as found in the full range of his writings. Omits legal sources handled by Robert Kingdon, "The Function of Law in the Political Thought of Peter Martyr Vermigli," in *Reformatio Perrennis: Essays on Calvin and the Reformation in Honor of Ford Lewis Battles*, edited by B. A. Gerrish, pp. 159–172, Pittsburgh, 1981.

———. "Rhetoric and Reality: Peter Martyr and the English Reformation." *Sixteenth Century Journal* 19 (1988), 451–469. Assesses Vermigli's impact on Archbishop Cranmer's eucharistic views in the two Prayerbooks and the exchange with Stephen Gardiner. Concludes that Vermigli's view of real presence based on patristic evidence was decisive for Cranmer.

Anderson, Marvin Walter. *Peter Martyr Vermigli: A Reformer in Exile, 1542–1562; A Chronology of Biblical Writings in England and Europe.* Nieuwkoop, 1975. Modern account of Vermigli's Protestant career in northern Europe. At points lacks focus. Valuable for its attention to manuscript letters and printed editions of his biblical commentaries. List of letters superseded by revised *Register* in Donnelly and Kingdon, *Bibliography*. Contains one Latin letter to Musculus and translation of seven Lambuth Palace letters to Elizabethan bishops.

Corda, Salvatore. *Veritas Sacramenti: A Study in Vermigli's Doctrine of the Lord's Supper.* Zurich, 1975. Most satisfactory account of Vermigli's eucharistic thought as analogical rather than sacramental.

Donnelly, John Patrick. *Calvinism and Scholasticism in Vermigli's Doctrine of Man and Grace.* Leiden, 1976. Best study of Vermigli's scholastic method. Chapter 4 on his view of humankind in an Aristotelian world is of great value.

Donnelly, John Patrick, and Robert M. Kingdon, eds. *A Bibliography of the Works of Peter Martyr Vermigli.* Kirksville, Mo., 1990. The standard bibliography with reproductions of title pages and description of editions. Gives extensive list of locations of copies of major and minor works as well as a list of partial works. Register of letters is helpful, as is the list of contemporary and modern published accounts about Vermigli.

Kingdon, Robert M. *The Political Thought of Peter Martyr Vermigli: Selected Texts and Commentary.* Geneva, 1980. Useful photographic reproduction of relevant Latin texts and typed English translations from the *Common Places* (1583) as well as *Judges* (1564) and *Romans* (1568). Valuable introduction on the sources of Vermigli's political thought.

McLelland, Joseph C. *The Visible Words of God: An Exposition of the Sacramental Theology of Peter Martyr Vermigli, A.D. 1500–1562.* Reprint, Grand Rapids, Mich., 1957. Pioneering study that helped to launch the renaissance in Vermigli scholarship. Chapters 4–6 are the most valuable for their description of Vermigli's patristic understanding of the Pauline "union with Christ."

McLelland, Joseph C., ed. *Peter Martyr Vermigli and Italian Reform.* Waterloo, Ont., 1980. Publishes lectures given at Montreal in September 1977. Contains five articles on Vermigli and several on Italy. This is the work to read after McNair's account.

McLelland, J. E., and G. E. Duffield. *The Life, Early Letters and Eucharistic Writings of Peter Martyr.* Abingdon, England, 1989. Contains Josiah Simler's *Oratio* (1563), biographical account by Vermigli's Zurich contemporary, as well as relevant eucharistic treatises (Oxford, 1549), letters, and *miscellanea*.

McNair, Philip. *Peter Martyr in Italy: An Anatomy of Apostasy.* Oxford, 1967. First and only modern account of Vermigli's Italian phase (1499–1542). Enriched by archival references. Opening chapter now dated as research continues on the *spirituali* and *intransigenti* of the early Catholic Reformation. Account of Martyr in Lucca (1541–1542) is brilliant (pp. 206–238). Noted for clarity of writing and depth of research. Also available in Italian.

MARVIN W. ANDERSON

VERONESE, Paolo

VERONESE, Paolo (born Paolo Caliari; 1528–1588), Italian painter. Born and trained in Verona, the city in northern Italy from which he took his name, Veronese moved to Venice by 1553 and there established himself as one of the city's three leading painters, along with Titian and Tintoretto (Jacopo Robusti). His style is best known for its visual opulence and pageantry; typically his compositions are large and scenographic and feature splendidly costumed figures in magnificent architectural settings. Veronese's art had an important influence not only on his contemporaries but on generations of Baroque painters, from Annibale Carracci to Giovanni Battista Tiepolo.

On at least one occasion Veronese's propensity to delight the eye and entertain the senses regardless of his subject matter earned him the censure of the Catholic church. In 1573 he was called before the Inquisition to defend his huge canvas, apparently meant to represent the Last Supper, painted for the refectory of the convent of Saints Giovanni e Paolo. His treatment of the subject was judged to lack decorum; in particular he was reproached for including scores of extraneous figures—among them dwarfs, soldiers, buffoons, and dogs—and for depicting the apostles engaged in various unseemly activities. Although this kind of criticism was not new, it is indicative of the post-Tridentine church's heightened sensitivity to issues of artistic decorum that Veronese was actually put on trial. His plea of artistic license fell on deaf ears, but in the end he was able to sidestep the tribunal's demand that he rework the painting by instead simply renaming it the *Feast in the House of Levi* (Venice, Accademia).

BIBLIOGRAPHY

Holt, Elizabeth, ed. *A Documentary History of Art.* New York, 1958. Vol. 2 contains an English translation of the minutes of Veronese's trial.

Pignatti, Teresio. *Veronese: L'opera completa.* 2 vols. Venice, 1976. The essential monograph on the artist.

Pignatti, Teresio, and Filippo Pedrocco. *Veronese: Catalogo completo dei dipinti.* Florence, 1991.

LOUISE RICE

VERSTEGHE, Jan Gerritszoon. *See* Veluanus, Ioannes Anastasius.

VESTIARIAN CONTROVERSY. "Vestiarian" relates to the priestly vestments worn by the officiating clergy at the Christian mysteries, and especially to the eucharistic cope and chasuble. More broadly, the Elizabethan Vestiarian Controversy concerned various items of clerical attire, including the white linen surplice required for "all ministrations," and the square cap (more recently known as a "mortar board") that the clergy were required to wear outdoors. Since the Elizabethan bishops in practice ceased to be insistent on the general use of eucharistic vestments, the Vestiarian Controversy is, strictly speaking, a misnomer. The central issue was the surplice, universally acknowledged to be of itself a matter of indifference.

Ideologically, the principle of "things indifferent" (Greek, *adiaphora*), matters not of the substance of faith, was fundamental. The church and its supreme governor demanded obedience in all things indifferent. Nonconformists (and it was in this context that the word *nonconformist* first entered the English religious vocabulary) complained that to enforce the use of these things on reluctant consciences was to deprive them of their indifference. The doctrine of "Christian liberty," which came to the fore in these circumstances, was arguably the taproot of that species of Christian conviction known ever since as Puritanism. It was not equivalent to individualistic license, but rather to a conviction that the edification of the church, composed of "lively stones," required the emancipation of conscience from all human ordinances and its total subjection to the word of God, whether in its literal sense or general tenor.

The nonconformists found scriptural authority for their position in *I Corinthians* 8, where Paul discusses the indifferent matter of meats offered to pagan idols. Since the idols were not really gods, the meat was only meat. But Paul ruled that while such things were lawful, they were not necessarily expedient. Rather than offend the consciences of the weaker brothers and sisters, he would never eat meat again. Elizabethan nonconformists who refused the surplice favored not so much their own consciences as those of such weaker believers, lay "gospellers," for whom it was symbolic of "popery." In the perception of authority, this was either to pander to "popularity" or a feeble excuse.

The vestiarian issue first arose in the reign of Edward VI, when the "Anglo-Zuricher" John Hooper, appointed bishop of Gloucester, found himself in the Fleet Prison rather than the diocese where he was so much needed, having refused to dress himself in a manner appropriate for his consecration. Controversy broke out on a wider scale in the early Elizabethan church, thanks to a clause of the Act of Uniformity and a related rubric of the 1559 *Book of Common Prayer* that required the use of the traditional "ornaments." The careless drafting of these statements would occasion confusion in the post-Tractarian, Victorian Church of England, and, for the lawyers, no small profit. But in its origins, the rubric was no doubt a concession to conservative feelings, the queen's included. It was with respect to this sufficiently trivial issue that the line between conformity and nonconformity was first drawn, a line proleptic of much of the subsequent history of both establishment and dissent.

In 1566 Archbishop Matthew Parker, in consultation with his suffragans and prompted by the queen, published some "Advertisements," a call to strict conformity. The title thinly disguised the fact that these orders lacked the full authority of the royal supremacy. The resultant crisis rocked both the universities of Oxford and Cambridge and came to its head in London, toward Easter 1566. Thirty-seven ministers, much of the preaching ministry in London, at first refused to conform and were suspended; of these a few, the hardest of the hard core, were eventually deprived of their livings. On the one hand, there was a revival of popular religious voluntarism, rediscovering its roots in the Marian persecution. On the other, the international Protestant community was drawn in by appeals to its arbitration from both sides. The controversy was frozen in print by a manifesto speaking for the hard-line nonconformists and published by the printer-preacher Robert Crowley, who put together *A briefe discourse against the outwarde apparell,* in which it was alleged that those pressing (presumably including Archbishop Parker) for conformity were not sincere Protestants. *A brief examination . . . of a certaine declaration* (to which Crowley promptly replied) was perhaps written by Parker himself.

Although most of the original nonconformists soon came to heel, the Vestiarian Controversy introduced a lasting fault line into the Elizabethan church. The more drastic presbyterianism of the 1570s might never have come about if it had

not been for the episcopal "persecution" of those who cast off the surplice in the 1560s.

[*See also* Grindal, Edmund; *and* Puritans.]

BIBLIOGRAPHY

Collinson, Patrick. *The Elizabethan Puritan Movement.* Reprint, Oxford, 1990.

Coolidge, John S. *The Pauline Renaissance in England: Puritanism and the Bible.* Oxford, 1970. The best account of the ideological and biblical roots of the Nonconformist position.

Dent, C. M. *Protestant Reformers in Elizabethan Oxford.* Oxford, 1983.

Knappen, M. M. *Tudor Puritanism: A Chapter in the History of Idealism.* Reprint, Chicago, 1965. Subtitle indicates Knappen's approach. Knappen and Collinson together provide the best account.

Porter, H. C. *Reformation and Reaction in Tudor Cambridge.* Cambridge, 1958.

Primus, John H. *The Vestments Controversy: An Historical Study of the Earliest Tensions within the Church of England in the Reigns of Edward VI and Elizabeth.* Kampen, 1960. A definitive account of the controversies.

Verkamp, Bernard J. *The Indifferent Mean: Adiaphorism in the English Reformation to 1554.* Athens, Ohio, 1977.

PATRICK COLLINSON

VESTMENTS. *See* Clerical Vestments; Vestiarian Controversy.

VETTER, Jiří. *See* Strejc, Jiří.

VICEGERENT IN SPIRITUALS. In 1534 the English Parliament gave legal status to Henry VIII's claim to be supreme head of the church in England, a title that had been accepted by the Convocation of the Clergy of Canterbury in 1531. As his agent in exercising the royal supremacy, Henry named his chief minister, Thomas Cromwell, to be his vicar-general and vicegerent in spirituals. The appointment probably dates from January 1535.

As vicegerent Cromwell, although a layman, enjoyed vast authority over the church. The normal ecclesiastical jurisdiction of the bishops was inhibited for nearly a year in order to demonstrate that the bishops received their powers from the king, not from the pope or by the law of God, and the vicegerent assumed many of their duties. During the period of the inhibition Cromwell was empowered to conduct visitations of churches and religious houses; the great visitation of the monasteries prior to their dissolution was undertaken by his commissioners. His agents operated ecclesiastical courts, collected revenues from the church, and undertook a revision of canon law. Cromwell himself presided over convocation in 1536, when the king's marriage to Anne Boleyn was annulled, and by a statute of 1539 he acquired a place in the House of Lords above that of the archbishop of Canterbury. He also issued injunctions dealing with Bible reading, preaching, and idolatry. His jurisdiction was in some ways analogous to that enjoyed by Thomas Wolsey as papal legate, although it derived from the king, not the pope.

Cromwell fell from power and was executed in 1540. No other vicegerent was ever named. The position, though temporary, was important in establishing royal supremacy and taking away the bishops' claim to independent jurisdiction in the church.

[*See also* Cromwell, Thomas.]

BIBLIOGRAPHY

Lehmberg, Stanford. "Supremacy and Vicegerency: A Reexamination." *English Historical Review* 81 (1966), 225–235.

STANFORD E. LEHMBERG

VIENNA. Despite the disorders of the fifteenth century that had adversely affected the political and economic position of the city, Vienna entered the sixteenth century as one the few large cities of the Holy Roman Empire—its population was nearly 25,000—and as a center of some political significance, both as an imperial capital and as a seat of the Habsburg court. During the reign of Matthias Corvinus (d. 1490), but especially under Maximilian I, Vienna became more significant culturally as well. German humanism quickly took hold in Vienna thanks not so much to the university (which had been founded in the latter part of the fourteenth century) as to the presence of other associations such as the Danube Society. (Conradus Celtis was the leading scholar.) The calls for church reform that emerged were also promoted by individual clerics, including Bishop Georg Slatkonia. (Of the holders of the small episcopal see that had been founded in 1469, Slatkonia was the first actually to reside in Vienna.) Another reform-minded cleric was Johann Vaesel, the beneficiary at Saint Stephen's, who was disciplined for heresy in 1524.

Although Vienna was not a hub of long-distance trade, the new reformist ideas quickly reached the city and to some extent were favorably received, as was shown by the fact that the Viennese printer Hans Singriener was soon reprinting—anonymously, to be sure—early Reformation writings. In 1520 the University of Vienna took a position against the emerging reform movement. Later, when the reformer Paul Speratus was passing through Vienna on his way to Budapest, Bishop Slatkonia provided him a forum in which to answer attacks that had been made against his theology and his marriage. Thus on 12 January 1522 Speratus delivered a sermon in the cathedral church on the text of *Romans* 12—that Sunday's epistle—wherein he sharply criticed traditional forms of religious life. Speratus was promptly arrested. (Furthermore he had killed his chances of finding employment at the court of the queen of Hungary.)

Whereas Speratus's sermon had been a sensational but altogether isolated incident, the case of Kaspar Tauber suggested that the city indeed harbored partisans of reform. Convicted of heresy after a lengthy trial during which he refused to recant his beliefs, Tauber was executed on 24 July 1525. Tauber's confession, although not entirely in conformity with later Lutheranism, showed that he was neither a radical nor an Anabaptist. Perhaps as early as 1526, however, there was a small Anabaptist community in Vienna, and under the leadership of Oswald Glaidt a congregation was formed. Persecution quickly followed: Balthasar Hubmaier was burned on 10 March 1528, and in the years to come there would be other arrests and executions of Anabaptists in and around the city.

It is unclear whether the trend toward reform was accelerated by the fact that some Viennese (including Martin Siebenbürger) were involved in the troubles at the beginning of the reign of Charles V and of his brother Ferdinand. Indeed the precise cause of the unmistakable growth of Protestant sentiment cannot be ascertained. Besides ordinary burghers, members of the university and various nobles who maintained residences in the city appear to have been involved. Under Maximilian I, whose court stimulated a general burst of intellectual activity that affected both city and university, Protestant notions took definite form. Among the most prominent in this regard may have been such figures as Carolus Clusius, Johann Crato von Krafftheim, Hugo Blotius (as *Aulae familiares*), Kaspar Pirbach and Cornelius Grünwald (as rectors of the university), and Caspar Nidbruck. (Reichart Strein of Schwarzenau was the link between this group and the provincial nobility.) In 1554 Ferdinand I introduced reforms that were intended to preserve the Catholic character of the university. Although the court tried to conceal the fact, it would become obvious—from the changes in the text of the doctoral oath, from the indifference shown to the confessional status of several professorial appointees, from the results of elections to university offices—that the reforms had failed.

During this time the Lutheran tendencies of the families of the city councillors became more pronounced. In 1576 Christoph Huetstocker, an ardent Protestant, became mayor. There was a Protestant majority in the council, including members of the Henckel von Donnersmarck and Pramer families. According to the available evidence, by around 1570 approximately half the burghers (and half the total population) of Vienna may have been Protestant.

In 1568 the nobility of the region below the Enns had gained the right to exercise in their possessions a limited *ius reformandi*. For the Vienna houses (*Freihäuser*) of the nobility the corresponding provisions were less clear. Protestant services may have been held from time to time in the Franciscan church, possibly owing to the dissolution of the monastery there. Not until 1571, however, did a religious mandate (*Religionsassekuration*) make preaching possible in country houses. Thus the demand of the estates for open services had not been honored; still, services could be held for the privileged nobility in which burghers were permitted to participate.

In 1574 the estates called Josus Opitz to be pastor, and provided at least two deacons to administer his office. A library was founded in conjunction with this appointment; a school of distinctly Protestant character had already been reestablished by the estates in 1573.

Meanwhile, Archduke Ernest had made sporadic attempts to halt any obvious demonstrations of Protestant sentiment, and in 1573 measures to strengthen the Catholic character of the university had been introduced. Finally, with the death of Maximilian II in 1576, the forces of the Counter-Reformation swung into action.

The city council was replaced by one that contained a Catholic majority. In 1578 Protestant preachers and schoolmasters were expelled and available supplies of books (Bibles, psalters, orders of worship) were confiscated. A formally Protestant church was no longer to be tolerated in the city. Protestants rioted on Corpus Christi day 1579 (the "Milk War"), and on 19 July of that year they submitted the "Prostration of the Five Thousand," a petition demanding that the Augsburg Confession be recognized. The administration responded by dismissing the Protestant officials (1 December) and expelling the putative ringleaders of the action, which was labeled a rebellion.

The leader of the Counter-Reformation effort was Melchior Khlesl (d. 1630), son of a Viennese burgher, who simultaneously occupied several municipal offices. Successor to an older generation of the likes of the imperial privy councillor Georg Eder, who had been seen as a sensitive advocate of the Catholic cause, Khlesl skillfully and gradually engineered the restoration of Catholic life: Cornelius Grünwald, who had been reelected as rector of the university, was forced to resign in 1579; the safeguarding of assets was deemed to be a prerequisite to the reestablishment of Catholic institutions; the presence in the city of Jesuits and of a papal nuncio (the latter only temporarily because of the transfer of the seat of government to Prague under Rudolf II) proved to be a boon to the Catholic church; education passed entirely into the hands of Catholics (including Peter Canisius); under the new regime bishops became increasingly effective. (Despite the high quality of such previous bishops as Johann Fabri, Anton Brus von Müglitz, Friedrich Nausea, and Johann C. Neubeck, the effectiveness of the office had hitherto been rather limited. Khlesl became Bishop of Vienna in 1580.)

The burghers, however, were not yet Catholic. Some moved to nearby villages—Hernals, Inzersdorf, Vösendorf—that still allowed Protestant church services. From there, preachers guided the shrinking Viennese congregation. Sermons (by, among others, Elias Ursinus and David Hochschildt) show that Flacianism had been overcome and that the goal was conformity to early Lutheran orthodoxy;

clearly the emphasis was on the pastoral-consoling character of preaching. There were also religious legacies and foundations in the outlying Protestant villages. Printed copies of sermons may have served as devotional materials for those who were unable to get to the village churches. Many nobles came to the city and strengthened the confessional consciousness.

The displacement of Protestantism from Viennese public life was unmistakable. Still, as of 1601 eight councillors were Protestant; as of 1619 there were only three. Vienna sent no Protestant citizens as representatives to the hereditary homages (*Erbhuldigungen*) of 1609 and 1619.

The years between 1618 and 1627 witnessed the disappearance of organized Protestant church life in the region below the river Enns. Faced with the suspension of Protestant rights of patronage, the expulsion of preachers, the Catholicization of the foundations, and a deteriorating economic situation owing to the outbreak of the Thirty Years' War, citizens and artisans moved to the nearby Hungarian cities of Preßburg and Ödenburg or to cities in south Germany. (Although scarcely a hundred emigrated—accompanied by an unknown number of household and family members—economically this exodus was not insignificant.)

By 1630 virtually all burghers and residents of the city had become Catholic. Since 1612, however, Vienna had been the seat of several imperial offices and court agencies, so that envoys, imperial privy councillors, agents, and officers from Protestant territories had their businesses in the city. Their presence was tolerated even if they were viewed with mistrust and were unable to conduct religious services. Only after 1652 were these privileged Protestants gradually able to expand their rights. Eventually they were permitted to celebrate religious services in the chapels of foreign embassies. Finally, in the wake of the Edict of Toleration of 1781, two Protestant congregations were formed in Vienna.

BIBLIOGRAPHY

Czeike, Felix. *Wien und seine Bürgermeister*. Vienna, 1974.

Loidl, Franz, and Martin Krexner. *Wiens Bischöfe und Erzbischöfe*. Vienna, 1983.

Mais, Adolf. "Gefängnis und Tod der in Wien hingerichteten Wiedertäufer in ihren Briefen und Liedern." *Jahrbuch des Vereins für Geschichte der Stadt Wien* 19/20 (1963–1964), 87ff.

Matt, Richard. "Die Wiener protestantischen Bürgertestamente von 1578 bis 1627: Eine reformationsgeschichtliche Studie." *Mitteilungen des Vereins für Geschichte der Stadt Wien* 17 (1938), 133ff.

Mayr, Josef Karl. "Wiener Protestantengeschichte im 16. und 17. Jahrhundert." *Jahrbuch zur Geschichte des Protestantismus in Österreich* 70 (1954), 63ff.

Mecenseffy, Grete. "Wien im Zeitalter der Reformation des 16. Jahrhunderts." In *Wien an der Schwelle der Neuzeit*, edited by Franz Baltzarek et al., pp. 54ff. Vienna, 1974.

Mühlberger, Kurt. "Bildung und Wissenschaft: Kaiser Maximilian II. und die Universität Wien." In *Kaiser Maximilian II: Kultur und Politik im 16. Jahrhundert*, edited by Friedrich Edelmayer and Alfred Kohler, pp. 302ff. Wiener Beiträge zur Geschichte der Neuzeit, vol. 19. Vienna, 1992.

Reingrabner, Gustav. "Zur Geschichte der protestantischen Land-schaftsschule in Wien." *Wiener Geschichtsblätter* 27 (1972), 314ff.

———. *Adel und Reformation*. Forschung zur Landeskunde Niederös-terreichs 21. Vienna, 1976.

Wolf, Gerhard Philipp. "Friedrich Nausea, 1496–1552: Prediger, Kon-troverstheologe und Bischof." *Zeitschrift für bayerischen Kirchenge-schichte* 61 (1992), 59ff.

Zink, Fritz. "Hernals, Du Gottessaal." *Alte und moderne Kunst* 4 (1959), 6ff.

GUSTAV REINGRABNER
Translated from German by Susan M. Sisler

VIENNA, Peace of.

This treaty, signed on 23 June 1606, ended the insurrection of Stephen Bocskay against Habsburg rule in Hungary. Besides guaranteeing Bocskay's position as prince of Transylvania and confirming the full autonomy of the kingdom in judicial, administrative, and military matters, the settlement contained religious provi-sions of great importance. Full tolerance was accorded to Protestant lords, citizens of the free towns, and soldiers of the frontier fortresses, while certain restraints were placed on Catholic activity, especially on the Jesuits.

Implementation of the peace proved a complex process. Formally an agreement between the intransigent emperor Rudolf II (in his capacity as King Rudolf I) and the tough Calvinist Bocskay, it was in fact secured by negotiation be-tween Rudolf's brother, Archduke Matthias, and the coun-try's Lutheran-led estates. Moreover, it depended on a par-allel settlement of the gruelling war against the Turks, which had inflamed political passions in Hungary. Though this set-tlement was reached in November 1606, at Zsitvatorok, Ru-dolf refused to accept it, and Bocskay died soon afterward. Formal ratification awaited the diet of 1608, by which time Rudolf and Matthias were in open conflict with one another.

The Peace of Vienna formed the cornerstone of future liberties for Protestants in Hungary, but it failed to spare them the pressures of the Counter-Reformation. The major loophole in it was a clause, inserted at Habsburg insistence, that the agreement had to operate "without prejudice to the Catholic religion." Its effectiveness depended on patterns of political power and social dominance, within Hungary and beyond. Thus renewed consolidation of Habsburg authority and the defection of many magnates to the Catholic camp soon placed Protestants under renewed threat. But Boc-skay's successors as rulers of Transylvania were able to de-fend the religious settlement by force of arms between the 1620s and 1640s, and the Peace of Linz (1645/47) even ex-tended its provisions, on paper at least, to the peasantry at large.

[*See also* Bocskay, Stephen; *and* Hungary.]

BIBLIOGRAPHY

Károlyi, Árpád. *Bocskay és a bécsi béke*. Budapest, 1907. Still the stan-dard account.

Marczali, Henrik, ed. *Enchiridion Fontium Historiae Hungarorum*. Bu-dapest, 1901. Includes the Latin text of the agreement.

R. J. W. EVANS

VIGLIUS, Joachim van Aytta van Zuychem

(1506–1577), humanist, jurist, and government official in the Habsburg Netherlands. Viglius studied at both the Col-legium Trilingue in Louvain and at the University of Dôle in the French-Compte, establishing a reputation as both a humanist and a legal scholar. Between 1534 and 1542 he served in various positions in Germany. He was emissary for the bishop of Münster during the Anabaptist revolt, jurist for the Reichskammergericht (imperial high court), and law professor and rector at the Bavarian University of Ingol-stadt. He soon became disillusioned with the religious divi-sions of the empire, however, and it remained his goal to serve in the Netherlands. While rector at Ingolstadt Viglius was noticed by Cardinal Antoine Perrenot de Granvelle, one of Emperor Charles V's chief ministers, who recommended Viglius to Mary of Hungary, Charles's sister and regent in the Netherlands. In 1542 Mary appointed Viglius to her "Secret Council," first employing him in numerous diplo-matic missions back to Germany and in 1548 promoting him to president of the council.

Viglius's writings from this period clearly express his opinions concerning the major issues facing the Nether-lands. First and foremost was his loyalty to the dynasty. Al-though he might voice disagreement to regent and prince, once a decision was made he felt duty bound to carry out that decision to the best of his ability. In the 1540s, when many pressed for the independence of the Netherlands from the Empire, Viglius produced a legal brief demonstrating that the provinces had long been part of the empire and reminding the Netherlanders of the fealty owed the emperor and the Habsburgs. This work became the basis for his ne-gotiations at Augsburg in 1548, when the ties between the empire and the Netherlands were codified.

Viglius's writings show him to have been a religious mod-erate. He argued that the government could not enforce pri-vate religious opinion, but that no public heresy was to be tolerated. In this Viglius was in full agreement with his hu-manist education. Scholars might hold varying opinions and debate church reform, but heretical preaching, which led the people away from the church, was not to be tolerated. These sentiments were echoed in his 1555 admonition to his nephew, Aggaeus van Albada, whose education he spon-sored. He was dismayed by rumors of his protégé's interests in the reformers, warned him against such folly, and re-minded him of their family's good fortune in service to the Habsburgs. Viglius was a political opportunist and prag-matist, and in his analysis the family's success was tied to service to their prince.

Under Philip II and his regent, Margaret of Parma, Viglius

remained in his post as president of the "Secret Council"; along with Cardinal Granvelle, president of the Council of State, and the senior councilor Berlaymont, he effectively formed the government of the Netherlands. In the 1560s, when this triumvirate attempted to implement the centralizing administrative novelties of Philip II designed to strengthen the enforcement of antiheresy laws, these senior councilors soon ran into difficulties with the Netherlanders' defense of traditional freedoms. In addition, their monopoly of power produced a reaction from Netherlandish nobles, who had grown accustomed to a greater voice in the government. The situation deteriorated throughout the 1560s. Viglius worked for compromise and warned Philip that his attempts at autocratic rule and heavy-handed attack on heresy would fail, but Philip and his northern subjects were on a collision course, and Viglius was caught in the middle. On the one hand, he well understood the position of the people and the nobles of the Netherlands, but he also felt duty bound to serve his prince.

When protests crippled the government of Margaret of Parma, Fernando Philip sent Fernando Álvarez de Toledo in 1567 to restore order, unleashing a reign of terror. The duke of Alba established a special tribunal to deal with heresy and treason known as the Council of Troubles. The duke's tribunal and his autocratic manner soon completed the alienation of the Netherlanders from their Habsburg prince. Viglius continued to serve, however, and his experience and knowledge of the Netherlands were invaluable to the duke. The humanist and religious moderate had become an accomplice in persecution, overshadowing his contributions as councilor, diplomat, and scholar. He continued to serve Philip II until he was captured and imprisoned by the rebellious Netherlanders in 1576. He died in disgrace in 1577. As a result of his fealty to the Habsburgs he would go down in history as a tool of the dynasty, willingly aiding foreign oppression.

BIBLIOGRAPHY

Bergsma, Wiebe. *Aggaeus van Albada, c.1525–1587: Schwenckfeldiaan, Staatsman en Strijder voor Verdraagzaamheid*. Meppel, 1983. A biography of Viglius's nephew that clearly establishes on a family level the division of the Netherlands between those remaining loyal to the Habsburgs and those choosing to join the revolt.

Geyl, Pieter. *The Revolt of the Netherlands, 1555–1609*. London, 1932. Although sparing in its references to Viglius, it does establish both his position relative to the larger events of the revolt and his overwhelming negative reputation in the eyes of scholars of the period.

Parker, Geoffrey. *The Dutch Revolt*. Ithaca, N.Y., 1977. The best and most recent overview of the revolt, although for those interested in Viglius it shares the shortcomings of Geyl's work.

Postma, Folkert. *Viglius van Aytta als humanist en diplomaat, 1507–1549*. Zutphen, 1983. The only work to focus on Viglius; unfortunately, Postma concludes his biography in 1549, before themost controversial and most important period of Viglius's career for Reformation scholars.

DANIEL DOYLE

VILLANOVANUS, Michael. *See* Servetus, Michael.

VIO, Tommaso Gaetano de. *See* Cajetan.

VIRET, Pierre (1511–1571), Swiss Protestant minister, popular preacher, and early leader of the Reformation in French-speaking Switzerland and France. One of three sons of the local tailor, Viret was born in 1511 in Orbe, not far from Lausanne, in the Pays de Vaud of western Switzerland. His teachers introduced him to both humanism and Reformation doctrines at an early age, and he enrolled in the Collège Montaigu at the University of Paris to study theology in 1528 (approximately the same time John Calvin and Ignatius Loyola were students there). It was in Paris that he experienced a conversion to Christ in the evangelical sense and decided to embrace Protestantism.

Returning to Orbe in 1530, Viret met Guillaume Farel, who urged him to become a minister of the gospel. He preached first at Orbe, and then at Payerne and Neuchâtal, meeting with both great success and stiff opposition, including an assassination attempt by stabbing. He then rejoined Farel, this time in Geneva in January 1534. Supported by the Bernese government, Viret had been requested to assist Farel in establishing the Reformation there.

Viret joined Farel in undertaking reform, celebrated the first Genevan baptism according to evangelical forms, survived a second attempt on his life, and took part with Farel in a public disputation with Guy Furbity, a learned Dominican friar and chief local defender of the Roman Catholic cause. The debate, held in late January and early February 1534, ended in a riot but added sizable numbers to the Protestant contingent in Geneva. In an increasingly tense religious and political situation, the previously exiled bishop of Geneva, acting in concert with the duke of Savoy, raised troops to attack the city and laid it under siege. His action advanced the Protestant cause by allowing Farel and Viret to link Protestantism with Geneva's struggle for independence. In June 1535 the two Protestant leaders easily prevailed over Roman Catholic representatives in another public disputation, and on 31 May 1536 their work was completed by a vote of the General Assembly of the citizens of Geneva to become evangelicals. During his stay in Geneva, Viret won the affection of its citizenry and became an intimate, lifelong friend of both Farel and Calvin, the latter of whom joined in the work of the Reformation in that city in July 1536.

Also in 1536 Viret moved to nearby Lausanne, where in a public disputation in October, along with Farel and Calvin, he helped establish the Reformation in that city. Eventually becoming chief pastor of the church of Lausanne, he served in that capacity from 1536 to 1559, with several interludes in Geneva to help with various crises there, including the period of Calvin's homecoming in 1541–1542. While at Lausanne Viret also established, supervised, and taught in the academy of Lausanne before finding himself at loggerheads with the Bernese authorities who controlled the area politically and who objected to his attempts to establish a Geneva-style discipline in the Lausanne church.

Exiled, Viret joined his old friend Calvin from 1559 to 1561 as a minister of the church of Geneva and as a professor in the city's academy, which he helped establish. In 1561, for reasons of health, he moved to southern France, where he served as a pastor, evangelist, church administrator, adviser to the queen of Navarre, and, because of his irenic spirit, peace negotiator between Catholics and Protestants. In particular, Viret helped introduce the Reformation in Lyon and presided over a Reformed national synod there in 1563. He died at Pau on 4 April 1571.

Viret's reputation and influence rested largely on his preaching and writing. An eloquent and moving preacher, he often addressed throngs numbering in the thousands, as in 1561 at Nîmes, where he regularly preached to 8,000 people. More than fifty of Viret's works appeared in at least seven languages, with many of his books going through numerous printings.

Viret considered himself to be a part of the Reformed community of faith, and, generally speaking, his theology was similar to that of Calvin. Yet, in terms of the Lord's Supper, Viret originally was closer to Huldrych Zwingli than was Calvin, and Viret's view eventually was reflected in the Consensus Tigurinus (the Zurich Agreement) of 1549. Viret also favored more lay participation in church government than did most of his Reformed compatriots, including Calvin and Théodore de Bèze. Viret's main contributions to early Calvinist thought, however, lay in the political realm, where he advocated religious tolerance and a church independent of the state. He also provided the earliest known exposition of a Calvinist resistance theory when, in 1547, he wrote that believers, if led by legitimately constituted inferior magistrates, had the right actively to oppose the state for reasons of both religious and political tyranny.

BIBLIOGRAPHY

Primary Sources

Viret, Pierre. *Instruction chrestienne*. 2 vols. Geneva, 1564. Viret's major work, containing a mature expression of many of his theological and political ideas.
———. *Quelques lettres inedites de Pierre Viret*. Saint-Amas, 1911.

Secondary Sources

Barnaud, Jean. *Pierre viret, sa vie et son oeuvre* (1911). Reprint, Nieuwkoop, 1973. Best, most complete biography of Viret available.
Linder, Robert D. *The Political Ideas of Pierre Viret*. Geneva, 1964. Contains the most recent assessment of Viret's importance and the most complete bibliography of works by and on Viret.
———. "Pierre Viret and the Sixteenth-Century French Protestant Revolutionary Tradition." *Journal of Modern History* 38 (1966), 125–
137. Demonstrates that Viret was the first of the Calvinist leaders to allow resistance to established authority under certain circumstances.
———. "Pierre Viret's Concept of a Just War." *Andrews University Seminary Studies* 22 (1984), 213–230. Study of Viret's ideas on war and peace indicating how he argued for peace based on a modified just war theory.
———. "John Calvin, Pierre Viret and the State." In *Calvin and the State*, edited by Peter De Klerk, pp. 99–123. Grand Rapids, Mich., 1993. Points out the similarities and differences between Calvin and Viret concerning the authority of the state; shows Viret to be more qualified in his acceptance of state authority and to be more articulate in stating a justification for resistance to state tyranny.
Vuilleumier, Henri. *Histoire de l'Église Réformée du Pays de Vaud sous le régime Bernois*. 4 vols. Lausanne, 1927–1933. Comprehesive and scholarly assessment of the Protestant Reformation in the Pays de Vaud, Switzerland, in the sixteenth century.

ROBERT D. LINDER

VIRGINITY. *See* Celibacy and Virginity.

VIRUÉS, Alonso Ruiz de (c.1480–1545), Spanish Benedictine, humanist, theologian, and bishop. Proficient in Latin, Greek, and Hebrew, Virués taught scripture at his monastery of San Juan in Burgos, then at San Benito in Valladolid, and finally at San Vicente in Salamanca. He was elected prior of San Vicente in 1520 and abbot of San Zoilo de Carrión in 1532.

Virués became a great admirer and defender of Desiderius Erasmus and corresponded with him. His renown as a preacher eventually brought him to the court of Charles V, and he so pleased the emperor that it was rumored that Charles would attend church only when Virués was in the pulpit. Virués traveled with the emperor to Germany as the Lutheran Reformation was getting under way, and his experiences there led him to engage in scripturally based polemics against the Protestants. Virués translated some of Erasmus's *Colloquies* into Castilian Spanish, and in 1525 wrote an apologia for Erasmus (*Septem Collationes*, now lost) in which he simultaneously defended and critiqued him, asking for greater caution on his part. Erasmus chose not to heed Virués's advice, but the Spanish Benedictine continued to champion his cause, especially at the 1527 debate against the anti-Erasmians convened at Valladolid.

Virués paid dearly for his friendship with Erasmus: in 1534 he was denounced to the Inquisition for leaning toward heresy and imprisoned in Valladolid. Absolved *ad cautelam* in 1538 and penanced with two years' seclusion in a monastery, Virués succeeded in having this sentence nullified at Rome. Within a year Virués was appointed bishop of the remote Canary Islands, a post he held quietly for the remaining six years of his life. Like many other Erasmians in Spain, Virués realized in the 1530s, perhaps with regret, that he could best dodge suspicion by fleeing from the shadow of Erasmus.

BIBLIOGRAPHY

Abellán, José Luis. *El erasmismo español.* Reprint, Madrid, 1982. A concise overview of Spanish Erasmianism.

Allen, P. S., ed. *Opus Epistolarum D. Erasmi Roterodami.* Reprint, Oxford, 1992. The letters between Virués and Erasmus are numbers 1786, 1838, 1968, 2523, 2641.

Bataillon, Marcel. *Erasme et l'Espagne.* 3d ed. Geneva, 1991. The definitive study on Spanish Erasmianism; see especially vol. 1, pp. 236–240; 263–266; 319–334.

Colombás, G. M. *Corrientes espirituales en la España del siglo XVI.* Barcelona, 1963.

Menéndez Pelayo, Marcelino. *Historia de los Heterodoxos Españoles.* 4th ed. Polemical but seminal study of Spanish Erasmianism; sets Virués in context. See vol. 1, pp. 655–737.

Perez Goyena, A. "La literatura teológica entre los benedictinos Españoles." *Razón y fé* 49 (1917), 167–174.

CARLOS M. N. EIRE

VISITATIONS. Derived from Latin *visitatio/visitare*, visitation denominates the action, by authorized officials, of going to a place to observe, inspect, examine, judge, and, if necessary, correct. Known in this sense since the fifth century, the term became current in the ninth, both in Carolingian governance and in the administration of the church. Visitations occurred sporadically throughout the Middle Ages. Only in the era of the Reformation and Counter-Reformation were they methodically developed as an instrument for the organization of religious systems, their integration in society, and their coordination with the objectives of the state.

In medieval times, visitations were among the chief duties of the bishop, which he was expected to perform personally in the fraternal spirit of Paul's "Come, let us return and visit the believers in every city where we proclaimed the word of the Lord and see how they are doing" (*Acts* 15:36). By the ninth and tenth centuries they had largely come into the hands of subordinate officials and were employed as a judicial and administrative device for effectuating the episcopal court's jurisdictions over clergy and laity by probing all aspects of the affairs of local congregations. The model for such investigations was provided by the tenth-century abbot Regino of Prüm, whose handbook for parish visitors, written about 906 at the behest of the archbishop of Trier, touched nearly all the items of inquiry later systematized in early modern visitation formulas. Its centerpiece was a questionnaire of ninety-six points of interrogation concerning the condition of the parish, the quality and comportment of its priest, and his ministration to the faithful. Along with delegation of responsibility for visitations came the need for permanent records; these begin to appear, spottily, in the eleventh and twelfth centuries.

In the later Middle Ages visitations tended to lapse into disuse. But they remained an important device for advancing monastic and secular reform and were often urged upon the church as the most effective way of putting its whole house in order. Early in the fifteenth century Jean Gerson, a French theologian passionately committed to rectifying all that was wrong with the church in his day, proposed in *De visitatione praelatorum et de cura curatorum*, a scheme for submitting ecclesiastical institutions, personnel, and functions to examination with a view to improving performance. Thus, while sixteenth-century reformers claimed in their pronouncements to have revived a long-defunct ancient practice, they could, in fact, build their own visitation procedures on tried and established recent precedent.

The crucial difference in the conduct of visitations in the age of the Reformation was the involvement of the state from the very beginning. Events in electoral Saxony proved paradigmatic in this respect.

First approaches toward an investigation of the Saxon church came from within the evangelically minded clergy. Martin Luther himself repeatedly called upon his sovereign to authorize a general visitation of churches and schools in his lands. Deeply worried about the derelict condition of Saxon churches ("no one gives, no one pays; tithes have disappeared or are too little; the common man respects neither preacher nor pastor"), he urged Elector Johann to consider himself God's "faithful instrument" in using the power of the state to bring stability and order to religious affairs. If people want to have evangelical pastors, Luther told the elector, "it's Your Grace's office to see to it that they pay them for their labors." This was an invitation the elector was not reluctant to accept. Initiative passed quickly to the temporal authority. In 1527 Johann issued an *Instruction und Befehl, darauf die Visitatores abgefertigt sein* (Instruction and Order for the Dispatching of Visitors), a long catalog of items on which four appointed visitors were to gather information. The whole process culminated in the publication in 1528 of a sweeping directive, entitled *Unterricht der Visitatoren an die Pfarrherrn im Kurfürstentum zu Sachsen* (Instruction of the Visitors to the Pastors in the Electorate of Saxony), a basic but comprehensive guide to the evangelical faith and to the duties of its ministers. Written largely by Philipp Melanchthon, it carried a strong prefatory endorsement by Luther. Visiting parishes and congregations, Luther wrote, is a godly and salutary work, the neglect of which by the Roman church was in large part responsible for the fall of religion to its present sad state. The resumption of this ancient practice by Elector Johann, "out of Christian love . . . and for the benefit and welfare of all the wretched Christians in his lands," offers great hope for the future.

A general, territory-wide visitation actually got under way in electoral Saxony in the autumn of 1528 (several partial ones having preceded it) and continued, with interruptions, to 1531, the territory being divided into a number of "circles" for the purpose, each covered by a team of visitors composed of lay as well as clerical officials armed with a set of articles containing the elector's special instructions to, respectively, pastors, town councilors, nobles, and peasants. A second general visitation was undertaken in 1533/34, a third in 1555. Others followed at more or less regular intervals.

Beyond encouraging this course of events, Luther had undergirded it with a persuasive theological justification. His famous tract *An den christlichen Adel deutscher Nation* (To the Christian Nobility of the German Nation; 1520) had assured temporal rulers and magistrates that, as Christians of no lesser spiritual quality than priests or bishops, they had the right to inaugurate, on their own authority, ecclesiastical reform in their domains. A legal basis for claiming this right was found in the 1526 recess of the imperial Diet of Speyer that in effect conceded to secular rulers, as sovereign bodies within the empire's constitutional structure, the power to organize and control religion within their respective realms. To Luther such recourse to the state's power to remake the church was no more than a provisional measure warranted, for the moment, by the desperate condition of the faith. To his sovereign, on the other hand, imbued though the Saxon duke—like most of his fellow rulers—was with a sense of obligation as a Christian prince, it was a welcome opportunity to extend the sway of temporal authority over a segment of society hitherto resistant to it. This was a process long underway everywhere in Europe. The Reformation gave it a powerful boost.

From the start, therefore, visitations served two related aims. One was to take periodic stock of the material and human assets of the church within a domain. The other was to bring about a permanent amelioration—judged by the Protestant standard—in the institutions and practices of religion by subjecting them to direction and supervision. Visitations introduced evangelical teachings to pastors in need of instruction and to populations largely ignorant of the faith they had to profess. They measured the pace at which these teachings were taking root. They superintended ministers and other members of the clerical establishment and ascertained that pastoral procedures were orthodox and uniform throughout the territory, the dangers of freewheeling preaching and uncontrolled religious expression having become evident during the uprisings of 1525.

Just as importantly, visitations tried, at first against stiff opposition, to ensure adequate local financing for churches and schools, helping out with funds—often from confiscated monastic properties—where indigenous resources proved inadequate. More successfully, they took steps to integrate parishes in a centralized territorial church organization demanded by the disappearance of Catholic episcopal authority. In the scope of their interrogation and surveillance, therefore, in the prominent role visitation commissions continued to play in ecclesiastical administration, and in the huge mass of revealing data they collected and made available to church and state bureaucrats, visitations were important steps toward the eventual creation of the *landesherrliche Kirchenregiment*, the territorial state church characteristic of Protestant principalities in the early modern period.

Events elsewhere in Germany soon followed the Saxon pattern. In Hesse in 1531 Landgrave Philipp created the office of superintendent with the obligation of visiting annually all the parishes in his district and "as much as possible investigate and . . . improve and correct the life and preaching of the pastor and other servants of the church, also the conduct of the parishioners, [finding out] how inclined they are to the word of God and the hearing of it, and what their lives are like." In Württemberg, Lutheran since 1534, an agenda for parish visitations was worked out by Johannes Brenz in 1535. Visitations began the following year, were interrupted by the Interim, recommenced in 1551, and were then put on a permanent footing with the creation of a standing agency charged with the systematic conduct and evaluation of visitations. In 1559 this body, the *Visitationsrat*, grew into a much more resourceful *Kirchenrat* with far-reaching supervisory competence over all church matters in the duchy. In Pomerania, Johannes Bugenhagen, who had earlier headed a visitation commission in Saxony, planned and for a time led a visitation in his native country in 1535. He also drafted a *Kirchenordnung* (church ordinance or constitution) that made visitations a permanent responsibility of the Pomeranian church.

In Brandenburg a general visitation of the entire margraviate introduced Elector Joachim II's new church ordinance in 1540/41; more visitations followed in the 1550s, 1570s, and 1580s. Where a Catholic principality was taken over by a Protestant power, the conquest was usually completed by a visitation of the defeated territory; thus the Schmalkald League, having subdued the duchy of Wolfenbüttel, ordered territory-wide visitations there in 1542 and 1544, the latter to monitor the introduction of a new church ordinance. When a land passed, by inheritance or otherwise, into the hands of a new ruler, visitations were employed to establish his authority and that of the faith he professed. For example, inheriting the duchy of Kalenberg-Göttingen in 1585, Duke Julius of Braunschweig-Wolfenbüttel carried out a "church and school visitation" in his newly acquired land in 1588, summoning all pastors to the central town of each district and subjecting them to interrogation on the basis of a thirty-six-point questionnaire. The object, in this instance, was to ferret out surviving Catholic and intruding Calvinistic trends, and to tie the Kalenberg church firmly to Julius's own ecclesiastical constitution, which he had issued for Wolfenbüttel in 1569. Where abrupt confessional changes left the church in disarray and the populace disoriented, as happened in the Rhine Palatinate throughout the late sixteenth century, visitations were used to test the reception of frequent shifts in the official religion—in this case from Catholicism to Lutheranism, and then, back and forth several times, between Lutheranism and Calvinism.

For Catholic authorities, the impetus to the resumption of regular visitations in the sixteenth century came from the alarming spread of Protestantism in their domains. As among Lutherans, visitations undertaken in regions loyal to the old faith served a dual purpose: to assess existing conditions, and to launch improvements. The Council of Trent, in its twenty-fourth session in 1563, reiterated the episcopal obligation to visit—personally if possible, by proxy if not—all congregations within a diocese, "the principal object of all these visitations" being "to lead to sound and orthodox doctrine . . . ; to maintain good morals . . . ; to animate the people by exhortations and admonitions to religion, peacefulness, and innocence." A number of Catholic visitations had been planned earlier, often in response to governmental pressure. But most came in consequence of Trent. Thus, the bishopric of Eichstätt began visiting in 1565, Trier in 1569, Würzburg in 1575.

In staunchly Catholic Bavaria visitations of the entire duchy were inaugurated by Albrecht V in 1558 and continued, with massive effort resulting in equally massive documentation, throughout the reigns of this ruler and his successors. As in Protestant territories, but also in continuation of the medieval tradition, Catholic visitors collected their data on the basis of meticulously prepared printed questionnaires. Points of inquiry, sometimes running into the hundreds, touched—among other things—the parish priest and his clerical and lay colleagues (qualifications, doctrinal reliability, books owned and read, performance in office, personal life, and habits), the congregation (number of communicants, reception of sacraments, attendance and behavior during service, willingness to meet their *onera*—their obligations, attitude toward their priest), parish income in money and *naturalia* (payments in the form of natural products), state of repair of buildings and properties, legal status vis à vis patron and secular jurisdictions. Uniform questionnaires permitted orderly investigative procedures that, in turn, made it possible to put the utilization of the information collected on a rational orderly foundation.

Visitations in the territories and cities of Germany were, broadly speaking, of three types. A "general visitation," always ordered by the territorial sovereign, encompassed his entire domain, or at least the largest part of it, and concerned itself with matters of fundamental doctrinal and administrative importance. A "special visitation" was usually launched by a superintendent to address some acute difficulty in his district or in a parish of it, or it concentrated on a singular territory-wide problem, usually a doctrinal one, in which case it was most often initiated by the central authority. Finally, "local visitations" were carried out by superintendents, in theory every year, throughout their districts; they were also called "particular visitations," especially when visitors thought it necessary to interrogate every individual pastor, sexton, schoolmaster, and other members of the parish staff on their activities, state of learning, moral probity, and walk of life. General, special, and local visitations were not administratively discrete. In practice they interacted, notably when general visitations ran into trouble owing to the vagaries of climate, geography, local resistance, or lack of funds. To these three types, common among Protestants and Catholics, must be added the *visitatio domestica*, instituted in Calvinist regions wherever the Geneva Confession was established, in which a pastor and a *senior* (elder) jointly called upon individual families at regular intervals in order to examine the religious life of all in the household.

A general visitation was always a formal occasion, magisterial in origin, highly structured in execution, and binding in its authority. It was set in motion by a proclamation published under the name of a ruler or governing magistrate. Among Protestants this was a territorial prince or municipal council; among Catholics it was a bishop or sovereign. Explicit, detailed, often very lengthy instructions briefed the visitors on what they were expected to accomplish. A printed *Fragstück*, or questionnaire, listed the—usually many—points of interrogation to be put to the local officeholders examined in the parishes visited.

Bearing these credentials, the visitation party arrived in a parish, normally a centrally located town or market to which people from outlying places had been summoned. Announced by the ringing of bells, the group was ceremoniously received at the church door by the local clergy and other dignitaries. Following a showing of the Host and, perhaps, a display of a relic, the chief visitor addressed the assemblage in a sermon (the text of which was, in some visitation instructions, prescribed verbatim) announcing the reason and purpose of the visitation, assuring everyone of its necessity and benefits, and cautioning clergy and laity to speak freely and to come forward with any information they might want the visitors to hear. Care was taken in official instructions—which tried to leave as little as possible to chance—to encourage relaxed and cordial relations between visitors and parishioners. But there is no way of gauging from the documents the tone in which the former put to the latter a series of questions that must have seemed probing, often intrusive, sometimes hostile. Interrogation proceeded in orderly fashion: clergy first, followed by lay officials, then the people, for whom questions were mostly on the catechism, children before adults. Visitors were instructed to be critical toward what they heard, and if possible to verify information by weighing it against the evidence of other respondents. The questioning session completed, one of the visitors preached a closing sermon in which all present were admonished to mind the cautions and advice bestowed on them. This done, the party moved on to the next place.

Other European countries had their own traditions to preserve or to reconstitute as they invigorated the practice of parish visiting under the pressure of the Reformation. In France, the Gallican church had revived diocesan visitations well before Trent. Throughout the fifteenth century, archdeacons or their deputies, authorized by their bishops, visited parishes more or less annually for the purpose of reform. Interrupted by the Wars of Religion, visiting occurred only intermittently in the sixteenth century. But from the early seventeenth century onward, visitations became regular in the French church and developed essentially the same procedures and forms of record keeping as in Germany. The objective, in accordance with the Tridentine decree, was to promote Catholic doctrine, expose and eliminate heresy, deepen the religious sensibilities of ordinary people, and improve public morals. To this end, French visitors in the late seventeenth and early eighteenth century tended to shift the burden of their inquisitions from matters relating to the material state of the church to the religious practice of parishioners. As in Germany, the written record of these inquiries reveals a persistent and often bitter friction between laity and clergy, much frustration among the latter, and a good deal of religious indifference on the part of the former. But it also shows that, however haltingly, reform was beginning to take hold, and the condition of the church in society was improving.

In England visitations of monasteries had been steady events since the thirteenth century, and of the secular clergy and laity since the fifteenth. Bishops normally visited their diocese in the year of their consecration, and every third or fourth year thereafter. The great change brought by the Reformation came in 1535, when a royal writ suspended all episcopal inspections in favor of an announced royal visitation. Monasteries were visited that same year, and in 1536 bishops were authorized to resume visiting their dioceses. The chief object of English visitations, particularly in the reign of Edward VI from 1547, was the introduction of new legislation on such matters as ritual, clerical garb, training the clergy, maintaining church property, holidays, and the use of images and relics. The accession of Mary Tudor to the throne in 1553 interrupted this activity as the Catholic queen organized her own visitations beginning in 1556—a notable example being the visitation of Kentish parishes by Archdeacon Nicholas Harpsfield in 1557, the returns of which offer a detailed inventory of what the Reformation had accomplished and what Catholicism had to repair.

But with Elizabeth I, in 1558, Protestantism was restored and the conduct of visitations now regulated with a strictness and energy that reflected the political will moving both Crown and church. Standardized visitation procedures were prescribed for the whole country. "Articles to be inquired of" vicars and curates were centrally laid down and made more rigorous to express the high expectations newly placed on the ministry. A locality's refusal to submit to visitation—a common occurrence in Germany and France—was treated as treason. Parsons were required to preach, at least four times a year, not only "against the usurped power, pretended authority, and jurisdiction of the bishop of Rome," but also to affirm that the English monarch's "power, authority, and preeminence . . . is the highest under God." Annual visitations, rarely cancelled, monitored the observance of these regulations.

In Italy visitations, though not uncommon in the later Middle Ages, were invigorated in the spirit of Trent in the 1560s, largely through the efforts of Carlo Borromeo, archbishop of Milan. The scheme he drafted for the conduct of visitations, which he carried out in person annually, and for documenting their findings was widely used by other Catholic authorities. As a *visitatio rerum* this scheme provided for an inventory of a parish's resources; as a *visitatio hominum* it set articles for investigating and recording salient facts about priests' performance in office and about the lives of the faithful in their charge. Borromeo's example as reformer and administrator was instrumental in persuading many other Catholic prelates to follow in his steps: Ludovico Madruzzo in Trent, 1579–1581; Alessandro de' Medici in Florence, 1589; Alessandro Musotti in Imola, 1599, among others.

Among the foremost accomplishments of Reformation visitations must be counted the huge mass of documentary records they produced. The modern historian, sampling this body of sources, can sense in them the extent to which sixteenth- and seventeenth-century governments were coming to rely in their deliberations on data gathered firsthand by experienced examiners and with more or less uniform investigative techniques. Types of documents varied somewhat from region to region and from time to time. But they are alike enough to be briefly described in the following example of the paperwork produced by a full-dress general visitation in a German territory in the late sixteenth or seventeenth century.

To begin the operation, an instruction (*Instruction*, or *Befehl*) was issued by a political or ecclesiastical body having the authority to do so. At some length, it stated the reasons for the visitation about to commence, declared its objectives, named the visitors entrusted with its implementation, and laid down a number—usually a large number—of specific articles for their guidance and for the instruction of the clerical and lay officeholders to be interrogated locally. The latter were informed when and where to assemble, what questions to expect, what books and records to bring to the meeting for official scrutiny, and so on. Printed copies of this instruction were distributed territory-wide. They were also read from pulpits to prepare the lay congregations.

Printed at the same time was an official questionnaire with numbered questions to be put to several categories of respondents in every parish. In later years, questionnaires were usually printed on large folio sheets with blank spaces left for writing down brief answers. Earlier, scribes traveling with the team of visitors jotted answers on scraps of paper from which, once the visitation was concluded, they compiled comprehensive registers containing the responses obtained from all the visited places, every parish or similar unit treated separately, and each piece of information numbered to correspond to the queries in the questionnaire.

To a clean copy of such a register, gathered in a volume, there was often added a prefatory synopsis, headed *Generalia*, summarizing the defects and faults discovered in all or most of the visited parishes and noting other particulars common to them. Bound with or attached to the finished volume, now called protocol, were documents submitted by local respondents: inventories, book lists, financial computations, rosters of communicants and delinquents, repair estimates, a schoolmaster's lesson plan, grievances and complaints, and so on. Copies of the resulting bulky tome were sent to the chancellery of the secular or ecclesiastical authority that had called the visitation whence, on the basis of this document, a recess (*Abschied*) was issued reflecting and commenting on the general conditions brought to light. Additional copies went to consistories and other concerned administrative bodies.

The recess concluded the visitation. But the work of utilizing the information obtained by it was only beginning. This part of the process, too, may to some extent be observed in the documents. In copying the formal protocols, and the less unwieldy digests abstracted from them, called relations, scribes wrote only on the right side of each folio page, leaving the left side blank. Into these spaces were inserted comments and directives for remedial action issued by members of responsible administrative bodies during the discussion of visitation results. Such remarks reveal a good deal about the reactions of responsible officials to the information reaching them from the field. Interesting also are surviving documents illustrating the internal workings of visitations, such as accounts rendered by visitors for travel, lodging, and other per diem costs, logs of journeys from place to place with indications of length of stay in each, notes on hospitality offered, and so on. These documents afford some rare behind-the-scenes glimpses of early modern administrators at work.

Nothing about visitation records from the age of the Reformation has given rise to as much controversy as the question of their reliability. Because inquiries into people's religion and morals yielded largely disheartening intelligence, and continued to do so throughout much of the early modern period, it has been suspected that the methods of data collection may have been flawed. They may have favored negative results, and the impression conveyed by the protocols should not therefore be taken at face value. No one disputes the importance of visitation records as sources for local history, for knowledge of changing economic conditions, of material constraints on clerical life and work, of the development of schools, of the existence of charitable institutions, or of the functioning of village government. But what recent scholars have found most fascinating in these records is the abundance of clues they seem to hold for an understanding of the religious mentalities of ordinary people at a time when these people were experiencing a major onslaught on their lives through the attempt by reformers—Catholic as well as Protestant—to "improve" and "discipline" them.

Many reasons for caution have been given when it comes to interpreting visitation records on this point. The visitors' own perspective was clearly one of "reform." When they sounded out a congregation and its leaders they looked for, and were alert to, the presence of faults. Hence the negative was apt to dominate their observations and their reports. Moreover, recorded statements about local conditions tend to be formulaic: identical phrases describe circumstances in widely different locations. Some scribes took down answers verbatim, but others merely paraphrased or resorted to short-cuts (whole columns of "ditto," for example). Such practices are bound to have distorted the actual state of affairs. Again, different copies of the final protocol of a visitation do not always agree; thus, it seems clear that officials sometimes doctored the records, making conditions seem a little better or a little worse depending on who in the echelon above them was to receive the report. Even taken for what they are, therefore, the records are far from transparent.

More importantly, how open and how candid were local respondents, clerical and lay? Obviously, people did not tell everything. They may have been resentful of snooping outsiders, or they may have welcomed their arrival as an occasion for venting discontent. On the one hand, pastors and priests had ample cause in their depositions to exaggerate dissatisfaction with their parishioners. Clerical complaints about the indifference, if not outright hostility, of lay folk are legion in all visitation records. And visitors may have further inflated the negative so as to convince their superiors of the pressing need to take corrective action. On the other hand, locals, and visitors too, must at times have glossed over unpleasant facts. As the visitation teams nearly always included lay as well as clerical members, the former often men with legal training, one might reasonably think that their reports would have given an honest and by-and-large accurate account of what they heard and saw. But one cannot know this for certain.

There is some hope that these and other doubts and questions about the verisimilitude of visitation records may eventually be dispelled. Recent scholarship has made great strides toward the systematic study of these rich sources, of which the overwhelming mass remains unprinted and widely scattered in state, church, and regional archives. French historians have developed an elaborate analytical scheme for gaining access to the information contained in the protocols and for launching the methodical exploration of them. The *Répertoire des visites pastorales de la France* (the first four volumes of which analyze the records of diocesan visitations in late medieval and early modern times) enables researchers to tell at a glance what documents are extant and what they promise to reveal. Italian scholars have been at work on a scheme for codifying the data contained in regional visitation documents. In Germany a *Repertorium der Kirchenvisitationsakten aus dem 16. und 17. Jahrhundert in Archiven der Bundesrepublik Deutschland* is now in process of publication. A simplified adaptation of the French model, it uses a handy analytical key to make accessible for study the contents of the prodigious number of visitation materials housed in German archives.

BIBLIOGRAPHY

Burkhardt, C. A. H. *Geschichte der sächsischen Kirchen- und Schulvisitationen von 1524 bis 1545.* Leipzig, 1879.

Frere, W. H., ed. *Visitation Articles and Injunctions of the Period of the Reformation.* London, 1910.

Froeschlé-Chopard, Marie-Hélène, and Michel Froeschlé-Chopard. *Atlas de la réforme pastorale en France de 1550 à 1790.* Paris, 1986.

Landersdorfer, Anton, ed. *Das Bistum Freising in der bayerischen Visitation des Jahres 1560.* Münchener theologische Studien I, Historische Abteilung, vol. 26. St. Ottilien, Germany, 1986.

Nubola, Cecilia, and Angelo Turchini, eds. *Visite pastorali ed elaborazione dei dati: Esperienze e metodi.* Annali dell'Istituto storico italo-germanico, quaderno 34. Bologna, 1993.

Sauzet, Robert. *Les visites pastorales dans le diocèse de Chartres pendant la première moitié du XVIIe siècle.* Rome, 1975.

Sensibilité religieuse et discipline ecclésiastique: Les visites pastorales en territoires protestants. Société savante d'Alsace et des régions de l'Est. Recherche et documents, vol. 21. Strasbourg, 1975.

Zeeden, Ernst Walter, and Peter Thaddäus Lang, eds. *Kirche und Visitation: Beiträge zur Erforschung des frühneuzeitlichen Visitationswesens in Europa.* Spätmittelalter und frühe Neuzeit, vol. 14. Stuttgart, 1984.

Zeeden, Ernst Walter, and Hansgeorg Molitor, eds. *Die Visitation im Dienst der kirchlichen Reform.* 2d ed. Münster, 1977.

GERALD STRAUSS

VITERBO, Antonini da. *See* Gileo of Viterbo.

VITORIA, Francisco de (1483/86–1546), Dominican theologian at Salamanca, known for his innovative ethical-juridical applications of theology to new concepts of international law and to the problems of imperialism in the New World. Born in Burgos of a father who had assumed the name of his native city and of a mother descended from converted Jews, the young Vitoria arrived in Paris in 1507 to study at the Dominican studium of Saint-Jacques. There the Flemish nominalist-turned-Thomist Pierre Crockaert was effecting the revival of Thomistic Scholasticism and entrusted Vitoria in 1512 with editing the *Secunda secundae* of Thomas Aquinas's *Summa theologiae.* Vitoria edited other works of moral and spiritual theology in Paris, where he

received a doctorate in the Faculty of Theology in 1522 and taught in 1522/23. Assigned to teach at the Dominican *studium* in Valladolid in 1523, he was elected in 1526 by the students of the University of Salamanca to the "prima" chair in theology, which he held until his death on 12 August 1546.

In his third year at Salamanca, Vitoria abandoned the centuries-long tradition of teaching from the *Sentences* of Peter Lombard and began to comment instead on the works of Thomas. This innovation was widely imitated in Spain and elsewhere and had important consequences for the future teaching of theology in Catholic faculties and for the theological approaches of the Council of Trent. Among his many pupils were Domingo de Soto, Melchior Cano, Bartolomé de Medina, Tomás de Chaves, and Domingo Bañez. Vitoria's political thought strongly influenced the work of Roberto Bellarmino and Francisco Suárez.

Although Vitoria published nothing during his tenure at Salamanca, his students undertook this work after his death. A manual of sacramental theology based on his notes was reprinted over eighty times before 1612. His *Relectiones theologicae* appeared posthumously in 1557 in Lyon and were reprinted eight times in the sixteenth and seventeenth centuries in Spain, Italy, Germany, and the Low Countries.

The *Relección* was an annual formal lecture to the whole university in which Vitoria summed up his lectures given the previous year. He treated such questions as civil and ecclesiastical authority, homicide, charity, marriage, magic, usury, and the authority of popes and general councils. In 1539 and 1540 he turned his attention to the moral and legal problems posed by the Spanish conquests in the New World. His treatises *De Indis recenter inventis* and *De iure belli Hispanorum in barbaros* influenced subsequent imperial legislation, especially the "New Law for the Indies" in 1542, which sought to reduce the brutality of exploitation of the American native peoples.

In *De Indis* Vitoria upheld the natural rights of the aborigines as legal possessors of their property and governors of their lands. But he allowed that a more enlightened state, especially a Christian one like Spain, might assume government of a backward people—as the "Indians" appeared to be—provided this government was for the welfare of the latter and not merely for the profit of the former. The rights of missionaries to preach the gospel were to take precedence, and the emperor's duties to protect converts was paramount. Thus, while Vitoria's teaching broke new ground in the matter of native rights, it failed to block possible avenues of abuse. His doctrine is thus more ambivalent than that of his fellow Dominican Bartolomé de Las Casas, who is the more thoroughgoing champion of the aborigines.

Vitoria's use of Thomas Aquinas, who had drawn on the political thought of Aristotle, presumed the natural rights of the state. Although God is its ultimate cause, the state enjoys full power and authority over the things necessary to its continuance and to the well-being of its citizens, who alone may determine the mode of power and its delegation to individuals. The same natural law likewise governs international relations: the world as a whole (*totus orbis*) is analogous to a single state and can thus create a supranational authority to determine laws appropriate to and binding on all nations. In the twentieth century these theories have earned Vitoria the title "Father of International Law" and have made him the patron of several national and international associations.

Vitoria maintained a correspondence with several humanists. Juan Luis Vives assured Erasmus of Vitoria's admiration. During the inquisition into Erasmus's works held at Valladolid (1527), however, Vitoria took a middle position, opposing a general censure of Erasmus but holding that some of his positions were dangerous and even heretical.

BIBLIOGRAPHY

Primary Sources

Nys, Ernest, ed. *"De Indis et de jure belli relectiones," being parts of Relectiones theologicae XII.* Translated by J. P. Bate and H. F. Wright. Washington, D.C., 1917; reprint 1964.

Truyol Serra, Antonio, ed. *The Principles of Political and International Law in the Work of Francisco de Vitoria.* Madrid, 1946. Short excerpts from a number of Vitoria's *Relectiones*.

Secondary Sources

Beltrán de Heredia, Op Vicente. *Francisco de Vitoria.* Barcelona, 1939. The standard monograph by the modern editor of Vitoria's works.

Farge, James K. *Biographical Register of Paris Doctors of Theology, 1500–1536.* Subsidia mediaevalia 10. Toronto, 1980. Extended *cursus* of Vitoria's career and complete bibliography of his works. See pp. 424–431.

Fernández-Santamaria, J. A. *The State, War and Peace: Spanish Political Thought in the Renaissance, 1516–1559.* London and New York, 1977. Compares Vitoria's positions with those of several contemporaries; contains excerpts of his works. See pp. 58–119.

Garcia Villoslada, Ricardo. *La Universidad de Paris durante los estudios de Francisco de Vitoria, O.P., 1507–1522.* Rome, 1938.

Hamilton, Bernice. *Political Thought in Sixteenth-century Spain.* Oxford, 1963.

Noreña, Carlos G. *Studies in Spanish Renaissance Thought.* The Hague, 1975. See pp. 36–140.

Truyol Serra, Antonio, et al. *Actualité de la pensée juridique de Francisco de Vitoria.* Brussels, 1988. Reflections, pro and con, of six jurists and teachers about traditional views of Vitoria.

JAMES K. FARGE, C.S.B.

VIVES, Juan Luis (1492?–1540), Spanish humanist and educator who lived in the Low Countries most of his life. Vives was born to Jewish parents in Valencia (Spain), where he was baptized as an infant. The Inquisition later victimized both of his parents: his father was sentenced to the stake, his mother's remains were exhumed from a Catholic cemetery, and the family property was confiscated. From 1509 to 1514 Vives lived in Paris, where he attended the university at Montaigu College for three years and received a traditional education. In Paris, however, Vives opened up to the ideals of the Renaissance and turned his back on medieval education, particularly the excesses of terministic logic (*Adversus Pseudodialecticos*, 1519). Instead of going back to Spain, which he never visited again, Vives moved to Brugge, where he joined the Erasmian circle of reform-minded humanists and married the daughter of Jewish merchants. Under Erasmus's guidance he published in 1522 a widely used commentary to Augustine's *City of God*, which unwittingly, perhaps, helped to spread through Europe some of the central tenets of the Reformation. Vives's close association with Erasmus in the 1520s made him suspect to some Counter-Reformation leaders, and the Jesuits managed to have his books included in the Index of Prohibited Books.

In his mature years, and after frequent visits to England, where he taught at Oxford and befriended Thomas More, Vives became progressively indifferent to theological controversy and turned his attention to educational, social, and legal reform. He was an illustrious Latinist, and his popular dialogues (*Exercitatio linguae Latinae*, 1538) were much used for instruction throughout western Europe. He proposed a radical reform of educational institutions at all levels (*De Tradendis disciplinis*, 1531), offered a pioneer plan to secularize assistance to the poor (*De subventione pauperum*, 1526), enlarged the scope of women's education as wives and mothers (*De institutione feminae Christianae*, 1523), and ridiculed the abuse of jargon in legislation (*Aedes legum*, 1519). Vives was one of the earliest champions of a unified Europe and also one of the more convincing pacifists of his age (although he reluctantly warned Europe against the Turkish threat). In one of his later works (*De anima et vita*, 1538), he explored human emotions and linked individual passional control to international order and peace. In the later years of his life he wrote an apology of Christianity that managed to avoid denominational issues (*De veritate fidei*, posthumously published in 1543).

His devotional books were read by Catholics and Protestants alike. The reformers viewed as Pelagian Vives's profound belief in the power of education to improve individual life and to reform society, an attitude completely incompatible with Luther's emphasis on the corruption of nature by sin and human dependence on God's grace. But to characterize Vives as a champion of the Counter-Reformation, as some Spanish historians have done, is to ignore the eclectic, mildly skeptical, highly pragmatic, and nondenominational temper of his intellectual life and his ecumenical religious beliefs.

BIBLIOGRAPHY

Primary Sources

Vives, Juan Luis. *Concerning the Relief of the Poor.* Translated by Margaret M. Sherwood. New York, 1917. Detailed plan of poor relief as financed by lay authorities.

———. *De Tradendis Disciplinis.* Translated by Foster Watson. Totowa, N.J., 1971. Plan for curricular reform at the university level.

———. *Against the Pseudodialecticians.* Edited and translated by Rita Guerlac. Dordrecht, London, and Boston, 1979. Diatribe against the excess of logical instruction at the University of Paris.

Secondary Sources

González y González, Enrique. *Joan Luís Vives. De la escolástica al humanismo.* Valencia, 1987. Corrects traditional chronology of the life of Vives and emphasizes the Parisian background of his conversion to the Renaissance.

Ijsewijn, Joseph, and Angel Losada. *Erasmus in Hispania; Vives in Belgio; Colloquia Europalia.* Louvain, 1986. Contributions of several scholars during the Bruges colloquium of 1985.

Noreña, Carlos G. *Juan Luís Vives.* The Hague, 1970. Complete biography.

CARLOS G. NOREÑA

VLAČIĆ, Matije. *See* Flacius Illyricus, Matthias.

VOCATION. Before the Reformation vocation was understood and experienced in two ways: being assigned to a specific station in the medieval hierarchy, such as feudal lord or serf, in accordance with what was understood as the biblical injunction to remain in the state to which one was called (1 Cor. 7:20); and being called away from the world into a religious and higher order—be it priestly or monastic—that attains a life that is closer to the perfection God has promised, a view made popular by the medieval church.

Martin Luther modified these views and redefined vocation as a call to serve the neighbor in the world rather than withdrawing from the world. In his sermons, collected in the *Kirchenpostille* (Church Postil; 1522), Luther used the German word for vocation (*Beruf*) for the first time to describe a wide range of callings.

On the basis of the biblical injunction of *1 Corinthians* 7:20, Luther labeled the medieval hierarchical stations a series of vocations established, through love and law, for the purpose of keeping order in the world. On the one hand are the basic vocations of family, temporal government, and church, which embody what Luther called "three hierarchies" of "natural law" (in his treatise *Von den Consiliis und Kirchen*, 1539). On the other hand are the various secondary vocations linked to work, such as trade, manufacturing, and providing services for the community. All vocations are subject to sin and abuse, but they become sanctified through baptism and are then sufficiently powerful to evade total chaos.

In his struggle against the church over the stewardship of funds and the proper exercise of authority, Luther became convinced that church vocations had been abused more than any other vocations. To him, the church hierarchy was the devil's victim, making priests, bishops, and popes look like thieves, usurers, and prostitutes. In an extensive treatise (*De votis monasticis Martini Lutheri iudicium*, 1521), Luther tried to show why monastic vows had become the worst evil in the church: such vows are not commanded by the word of God; they conflict with faith; they violate Christian freedom and the Decalogue; and they are contrary to common sense. He based his judgment on his doctrine of justification by faith, a fundamental insight he had gained from Paul (*Romans* 1–5). According to Luther, Paul had contended that it is Christ's death and resurrection that reconciles fallen creatures with God, not their own efforts to please God by doing good works.

Luther concluded that vocations are not good works to appease God but rather witness to faith in Christ. As he put it in the Small Catechism of 1529: "The Holy Spirit has called me through the Gospel." All earthly work is grounded in the gospel's promise that sins are forgiven. In this sense, then, vocations foreshadow God's full reconciliation with his fallen world. That reconciliation will usher in God's eternal rule in Christ. In the meantime, vocations avoid chaos between Christ's first and second coming, and exercise love of neighbor by representing Christ to someone in need of help.

Luther refuted not only the Roman Catholic notion of vocation but also the disregard for vocation on the part of radical reformers, left-wing idealists, or, as Luther dubbed them, enthusiastic "swarmers" (*Schwarmer*). Some of them, such as Thomas Müntzer, advocated an egalitarian society to be ruled only by the Holy Spirit. Others, such as the Anabaptists, called for withdrawal from service in the world so as to remain pure in commitment to Christ. Luther suspected they were all antinomians and charged them with having a total disregard for law and order in the name of utopian ideals.

Luther has been justly criticized for his refusal to condone changes in vocations, such as freeing peasants from slavery and granting them civil rights. According to Luther, believers have no right to move from one station in life to another, even though they are all equal before God through their baptism. He declared that a proper distinction should be made between the realm of faith and the realm of politics, and he viewed faith as an inward spiritual force not to be used to make radical changes in the existing social order. That is why seventeenth-century "orthodox" theologians spoke of vocation in terms of salvation rather than of changes in the existing social order, no matter how unjust.

Whereas Luther tended to see vocation as a station in life, John Calvin saw vocation as a means of change. One can change the world through vocations. According to Calvin, the divine mandates summarized in the Decalogue not only show what one cannot do (Luther's view of the divine laws' basic function) but also what one can do. He is not so much concerned about the question of how one is justified before God as about how God elects someone in earthly life to witness to the divine glory. Calvin's view of vocation is anchored in the doctrine of election or predestination. Confidence about divine election is established, Calvin declared, when "our election is connected with our calling" (*Christiane religionis institutio*, 1558). Believers know that God has elected them to be saved when there are "posterior signs" of divine election linked to a specific calling. According to Calvin, all of Christian life must attest to the majesty and glory of God.

While only hinted at in Calvin himself, who spoke of such external signs as only "little helps for our weak men," later Calvinists and Puritans saw this link between divine glory, election, and vocation as pushing Christians into intensive activity in order to find some assurance of God's love. The German sociologist Max Weber and the English historian R. H. Tawney have in differing ways related Calvinism to the spirit of capitalism, especially among the English Puritans, Calvin's descendants. According to Weber and Tawney, Calvinism created an ascetic self-discipline so as to witness to the glory of God by improving one's social and economic life. This witness can be expressed through an enterprising individualism marked by economic frugality and profit invested in programs for a Christian society, for a theocracy, or for an ecclesiocracy. Calvin's Geneva was the model for others. Calvinism could produce pastoral tyrants who exercised their power in dictating and supervising public morals. English Puritanism became a model for both tyrannical and capitalistic lifestyles.

In the end, so Weber contended, a Protestant ethic for the middle class was created that reflected the typical Protestant morality of later generations: creative individualism, concern for labor and duty, and a strong sense of calling expressed in economic terms. But the Weber thesis has been justly criticized as an overstatement. Capitalism did not result just from religious ideals but also from a non-religious business sense developed in Europe, especially in Italy, before the Protestant Reformation. Enterprising businessmen in Italy hoarded goods from the New World and sold them for high prices in Europe. Moreover, middle-class virtues such as frugality and concern for labor were already extolled in ancient Rome. Nonreligious economic factors were consequently intertwined with Calvinistic ideals.

Doctrines and experiences of vocation among radical or left-wing reformers differed distinctly from Lutheran, Calvinist-Reformed, and other mainline (e.g., Anglican) views. Swiss and German Anabaptists refused to take any vows on the grounds that faithful commitment to the mandate of Christ forbade them. The Anabaptists known as Mennonites and Hutterites considered all vocations to be witnesses to Christ, who, in their judgment, forbids any involvement in secular occupations serving a politicized Christendom. Menno Simons advocated excommunication, later known as "shunning," as a means of protecting a pure church from worldliness. Jacob Hutter created farming communities, called "brethren farms" (*Bruderhöfe*), that prohibited possession of private property. He insisted that the community

as a whole was the steward of all profit from labor, since private ownership violated the concept of the church as a "provisional paradise" in which there is no "mine and thine." Anabaptists established a short-lived theocracy in Münster, Westphalia, in 1534/35, where the leadership insisted that all vocations serve their ideal of reinstituting true apostolicity based on biblical models.

Calvin's view of vocation prevailed both in the sixteenth century and later. It helped shape the community in Geneva during his lifetime, and it created what later became known as "the Protestant work ethic," with its emphasis on laboring for the glory of God and the common good.

[*See also* Monasticism; Ordination; *and* Vows and Oaths.]

BIBLIOGRAPHY

Althaus, Paul. *The Ethics of Martin Luther*. Translated by Robert C. Schultz. Philadelphia, 1972. See chap. 3, "Stations and Vocations (The Orders)." A brief summary with general references to Luther and secondary literature.

Billing, Einar. *Our Calling* (1909). Translated by Conrad Bergendoff. Social Ethics Series, 1. Philadelphia, 1964. Focuses on Luther's views and their contemporary significance.

Calvin, John. *Institutes of the Christian Religion* (1558). 2 vols. Translated by Henry Beveridge. London, 1957. See chap. 24 on "election" and "calling."

Holl, Karl. "Die Geschichte des Wortes Beruf." In *Gesammelte Aufsätze zur Kirchengeschichte*, vol. 3, pp. 189–219. Tübingen, 1928. The only concise history of the term *vocation*, including Reformation views.

Luther, Martin. "The Judgment on Monastic Vows" (1521). In *Luther's Works*, edited by Jaroslav Pelikan and Helmut T. Lehmann, vol. 44, pp. 244–400. Philadelphia and Saint Louis, 1966. Shows how the rejection of religious vows becomes the foundation for Luther's redefinition of "vocation."

Poggi, Gianfranco. *Calvinism and the Capitalist Spirit: Max Weber's Protestant Ethic*. Amherst, Mass., 1983. Turns the Weber thesis around by showing how the capitalistic, not the Calvinistic, spirit shaped the middle class.

Schmid, Heinrich. *The Doctrinal Theology of the Evangelical Lutheran Church*. Translated by Charles A. Hay and Henry E. Jacobs. 2d rev. ed. Philadelphia, 1889. See chap. 3, paragraph 44. Shows how the meaning of vocation shifted from secular work to a divine call for ministry.

Tappert, Theodore G., ed. and trans. *The Book of Concord* (1580). Philadelphia, 1959. See p. 245. Contains Luther's catechisms.

Tawney, R. H. *Religion and the Rise of Capitalism*. New York, 1926. See chap. 2. Links Lutheran and Calvinistic views of vocation to economics, with a modified defense of the Weber thesis.

Troeltsch, Ernst. *The Social Teaching of the Christian Churches* (1922). 2 vols. Translated by Oliver Wyon. New York, 1931. See chap. 3, sections 2 and 3, on Lutheran and Calvinistic ways of life.

Weber, Max. *The Protestant Ethic and the Spirit of Capitalism* (1922). Translated by Talcott Parsons. New York, 1930. Links the Calvinist view of vocation with the rise of capitalism, a thesis that has been debated but is partially justified.

Williams, George H. *The Radical Reformation*. Kirksville, Mo., 1992. See chaps. 14 and 18 on Mennonites and Hutterites.

Wingren, Gustaf. *Luther on Vocation* (1942). Translated by Carl C. Rasmussen. Philadelphia, 1957. A convincing analysis of Luther's views in the context of his theology.

ERIC W. GRITSCH

VONDEL, Joost van den (1587–1679), prolific Dutch poet and dramatist. Vondel was born to Mennonite parents who resided in Cologne after fleeing from religious persecution in their native Antwerp. After a brief period in the Holy Roman Empire, the family returned to the Netherlands and in 1597 settled in Amsterdam. Vondel's father established a hosiery there, a profitable business that Joost took over from his widowed mother in 1613. The shop flourished, and its success enabled him to pursue independent literary studies and to associate with the leading writers of the day, such as Pieter Corneliszoon Hooft, Gerbrand Adriaenszoon Bredero, and Hugo Grotius.

Vondel's early poems and dramas were written for the Rederijkers, a group of middle-class and patrician men, usually from the same city or province, who met regularly in their chambers (*kamers*) to recite Dutch poetry and sponsored public festivals featuring parades and dramatic spectacles. He later participated in the revival of interest in Greco-Roman literature by seventeenth-century Dutch humanists and modeled most of his later works on the prescriptive norms of neoclassical Renaissance poetics.

Vondel's poetic output was staggering, even by prolix contemporary standards: domestic occasional poetry; religious lyric; poetic satires, chiefly against intolerant Calvinists (Contra-Remonstrants); political panegyrics and funerary lyrics; didactic epic poems; numerous verses for emblem books; and translations of Sophocles, Euripides, Horace, Virgil, Ovid, and Seneca. He was the foremost religious tragedian of northern Europe and the author of seventeen biblical and hagiographical plays, mostly on Old Testament figures: Adam and Eve, Noah, Moses, Joseph, Samson, Jephthah, David, and Solomon. His most famous drama, *Lucifer* (1654), is believed to have inspired scenes in Milton's *Paradise Lost*. Vondel also produced dramas with classical and oriental locales and a comedy, but he is most esteemed for his tragedy on the medieval siege of Amsterdam, *Gysbreght van Aemstel* (1637). His few prose writings consist of dedicatory letters to his works in which he formulated his poetic ideas and an essay on the development of a neoclassical Dutch style.

Before the mid-1630s, Vondel's involvement in contemporary religious and political life was conditioned by his Mennonite upbringing. He belonged to the most liberal Anabaptist community in Amsterdam, the Waterlanders, whose membership tolerated his literary activities even after electing him a deacon. For the most part, Vondel was a typical Mennonite: he belonged to the artisan/shopkeeper class; he was a zealous student of scripture, though he lacked training and interest in theological issues; and he had experienced exile and religious persecution. But there were also marked differences: Vondel's voracious appetite for learning brought him in contact with many scholars outside the Anabaptist community, especially university-educated humanists, and his enthusiastic support of the House of Orange in the Revolt of the Netherlands coexisted, paradoxically, with his Mennonite pacifism.

Despite his status as a religious outsider in Reformed Holland, Vondel was involved in the debate between the liberal Calvinists, or Remonstrants, and their conservative opponents, the Contra-Remonstrants. He apparently had little understanding of the complex political motives and religious arguments at the basis of the controversy, but he was appalled at the intolerance of the Contra-Remonstrants and the maniacal ravings of conservative Amsterdam preachers toward their fellow Christians. Many of Vondel's humanist friends were Remonstrants who were forced into exile or imprisoned after the Synod of Dordrecht (1618–1619) for their refusal to accept the Contra-Remonstrant position and for their support of Johan van Oldenbarnevelt, the grand pensionary of Holland who was executed for his Remonstrant sympathies in 1619. After the death of the stadtholder Maurits van Nassau, Vondel published *Palamedes* (1625), a tragedy in classical garb that depicted Maurits's seduction by the Contra-Remonstrants and his subsequent condemnation of the innocent Oldenbarnevelt. Numerous poetic invectives against specific Contra-Remonstrant preachers followed, in which Vondel did not hesitate to satirize and even misrepresent the conservatives because of their narrow-mindedness.

In the 1630s Vondel's disenchantment with the continued oppression of the Remonstrants expanded into a pessimism about the ceaseless warfare among Christian nations. Although he once greeted the stadtholders Maurits and Frederick Henry as the liberators of the Netherlands from Spanish tyranny, he now yearned for a cessation of hostilities between Catholics and Protestants throughout Europe. Sickened by the divisiveness among Protestant churches and sects, and by the commingling of political and religious ambitions, Vondel, like his exiled friend Hugo Grotius, embraced the Erasmian ideal of Christian harmony and peace under the aegis of the Roman church. In the late 1630s he converted to Roman Catholicism, but with the exception of a few hagiographical poems and dramas, including a tragedy on Mary Stuart, and his didactic epics on the sacraments and Catholic church history, Vondel's later writings express an ecumenical Christian ideal virtually free from militant sectarianism.

BIBLIOGRAPHY

Aercke, Kristiaan P. G., trans. *Gijsbrecht van Amstel*. Ottawa, 1991. Modern translation of Vondel's major historical tragedy with a useful historical introduction.

Barnouw, Adriaan. *Vondel*. New York and London, 1925. Sole English-language biography; provides a superficial overview.

Brom, Gerard. *Vondels geloof*. Amsterdam, 1935. Useful, but at times overly subjective, account of the different stages in Vondel's religious development.

Langvik Johannessen, Kåre. *Zwischen Himmel und Erde: Eine Studie über Joost van den Vondels biblische Tragödie in gattungsgeschichtlicher Per-

spektive. Oslo, 1963. Accomplished literary-historical survey of all the sacred plays, occasionally marred by repeated attempts to define Vondel's greatness.

Leendertz, P. *Het leven van Vondel.* Amsterdam, 1910. Detailed biography of Vondel's life with many references to his participation in contemporary religious debates.

Parente, James A., Jr. *Religious Drama and the Humanist Tradition: Christian Theater in Germany and the Netherlands, 1500–1680.* Leiden, 1987. Literary-historical account of Vondel's religious tragedies.

Smit, W. A. P. *Van Pascha tot Noah.* 3 vols. Zwolle, 1956–1970. Major study of all the plays of Vondel from a literary-historical perspective.

Spies, Marijke. "Vondel in veelvoud: Het Vondel onderzoek sinds de jaren viftig." *Tijdschrift voor Nederlandse taal- en letterkunde* 103 (1987), 235–269. Review of Vondel criticism since the 1950s.

JAMES A. PARENTE, JR.

VORMORDSEN, Frans

VORMORDSEN, Frans (1491–1551), Danish reformer and bishop. Born in Amsterdam, Vormordsen became a Carmelite friar and went to Denmark, probably to the friary of Elsinore. In 1519 he was elected a member of the newly erected Carmelite college in Copenhagen. Its master was Paul Helie, whom Vormordsen probably knew from Elsinore. Both were adherents of a reformist, biblical theology. When in 1522 Helie had to leave Copenhagen, Vormordsen may have succeeded him as master of the college. In 1527 he is listed among the teachers of the university as *lector.*

Like other Helie disciples, he may have passed gradually from a moderate to a radical, anti-Catholic biblical humanism. In 1528 he published a Danish translation of the *Psalms,* accompanied by a treatise by Helie, who was now back in Copenhagen. In the preface Vormordsen thanked Helie for having helped him improve his Danish, at the same time protesting against the outcry against Helie as an enemy of the gospel. This is generally taken as a sign that their views were still concurrent and that Vormordsen was not yet an actual reformer. Kristen Valkner has, however, attached crucial importance to the translation (*Paulus Helie og Christiern II. Karmeliterkollegiets oppløning;* Oslo, 1963). In his opinion their cooperation took place earlier, and in publishing his *Psalms* Vormordsen was unaware of the size of the gap that had opened between him and Helie. Both were now attacked by the Copenhagen canons, who were opposed to Bible translations in the vernacular, and when the humanistic Carmelites came to their rescue, it appeared that Helie agreed with neither party. In disappointment the Carmelites left the college, which was dissolved. On about New Year's Day 1529 Vormordsen was involved in a serious conflict with the canons, and in February he went to Malmö to become one of the leaders of the Reformation movement there.

At Malmö he secured permission to preach from the arch-bishop-elect of Lund, Aage Sparre. It is possible that he was considered more moderate than the other Malmö reformers. In June 1529 he became the leader of a newly erected municipal preachers' school. In August he edited Oluf Chrysostomus's *Lamentatio ecclesiae,* for which he wrote a postscript bitterly attacking monasticism, especially that of the friars. In about 1530 he married. He was present at the diet of 1530 in which the reformers drew up the Confession of Copenhagen.

When Frederick I died, the archbishop-elect, Torben Bille, outlawed the Malmö preachers, which led to the outbreak of the Counts' War (1534–1536) and eventually to the victory of Christian III and the Reformation. In 1537 Vormordsen was a member of the commission that prepared the "church ordinance." On 2 September he was ordained superintendent (bishop) of Lund. He became an energetic diocesan who, in spite of the opposition of the canons and the closefistedness of the laity, worked hard to put the church ordinance into effect and had the king's support in this. Vormordsen was also a writer who published Reformation pamphlets, devotional books, and handbooks for clergymen. He was a prominent representative of the biblical, humanistic Danish reformers.

BIBLIOGRAPHY

Andersen, Niels Knud. "Vormordsen, Frans." In *Dansk Biografisk Leksikon,* vol. 16, pp. 54–56. Copenhagen, 1984.

Gierow, Krister, and Kjell Barnekow. "Vormordsen, Frans." In *Lunds stifts herdaminne,* edited by Gunnar Carlquist, 2nd ser., vol. 1, pp. 17–33. Lund, 1980.

Johannesson, Gösta. *Den skånska kyrkan och reformationen.* Lund, 1947. See pp. 314–319.

THORKILD C. LYBY

VORSTIUS, Conradus

VORSTIUS, Conradus (Dutch, Vorst; 1569–1622), Dutch theologian with Socinian tendencies. Though of Dutch parentage, Vorstius was born and died in Germany. After undergraduate work in Cologne (where a bachelor's degree was withheld when he refused to subscribe to the decrees of the Council of Trent) and a brief business education, Vorstius studied theology in Herborn (1589) under Johannes Piscator. In Heidelberg (1594) he graduated as doctor of theology, with David Pareus as his promoter.

Upon visiting Basel and Geneva in 1595, where he participated in disputations on the sacraments and the causes of salvation, Vorstius's stature as a Reformed theologian was such that Théodore de Bèze offered him a position as lecturer in theology in Geneva. Vorstius accepted a theological professorship at Steinfurt (1596) instead. During this tenure evidence began to surface (especially in his 1597 writings, *De praedestinatione; De sancta Trinitate; De persona et officio Christi*) that Vorstius sympathized with the views of Fausto

Sozzini. In 1598 he concurred with Sozzini's rejection of the orthodox doctrine of atonement based on satisfaction of divine justice. In 1599, however, Vorstius apologized for several aberrations and successfully defended his theology before the Heidelberg theology faculty.

Johannes Wtenbogaert's recommendation that Vorstius be called to Leiden to fill the vacancy created by Arminius's death met strong opposition from Franciscus Gomarus, Sibrandus Lubbertus, Pareus, and others. Pareus condemned Vorstius's *Tractatus theologicus de Deo sive de natura et atrributis Deo* (1610) for its Socinian errors relative to the nature of God's being, the divinity of Christ, predestination, and atonement. Moreover, some of Vorstius's former students reprinted Sozzini's *De officio hominis Christiani*, while Vorstius himself reprinted and prefaced Sozzini's *De auctoritate sanctae scripturae*. Nevertheless, after having been examined by six Arminian and six Contra-Remonstrant ministers, and having presented himself to the provincial authorities, Vorstius was installed by the senate of the University of Leiden (1611).

The fears of the orthodox Reformed concerning Vorstius's incipient Socinianism prompted the ministers of Leeuwarden, led by Johannes Bogermannus, to publish a warning to all the Reformed churches. Vorstius responded prolifically in defense of his views, particularly in *Protestatio epistolica contra theologorum Heidelbergensium* (1610).

Vorstius was never permitted to teach at Leiden. His appointment became a symbolic issue in the strife between Remonstrants and Contra-Remonstrants in both church and state. His ultimate defeat came about through the influence of England's King James I. The king used diplomatic channels to exert pressure on the Dutch government to exile Vorstius and ordered his works to be burned publicly in London, Oxford, and Cambridge.

When this controversy threatened political relations between Holland and England, Dutch authorities ordered Vorstius to move to Gouda for eighteen months—which, however, became a period of seven years. The Synod of Dordrecht eventually deposed him on 4 May 1619. The provincial government ratified this decision and the national government made it effective throughout the nation.

After living in hiding in Utrecht, Vorstius moved to Tönningen in 1622, where he died on 29 September. His influence lingered on through his sons and friends. His friends published his commentary on the Pauline epistles posthumously (1631) and a son edited his *Doodsteek der calvinistische praedestinatie* (1653). Some of Vorstius's descendants continued as ministers in Remonstrant churches into the eighteenth century. Though he wrote over forty books and was a man of extraordinary gifts, Vorstius himself apparently did not realize how much his views departed from the doctrines of the Reformed church, for he continued to demand recognition as an orthodox theologian.

BIBLIOGRAPHY

Glasius, B. "Vorstius, Conradus." In *Godgeleerd Nederland: Biographisch Woordenboek van Nederlandsche Godgeleerden,* vol. 3. pp. 550–557. 's Hertogenbosch, 1856. Good overview of Vorstius's life and theology; detailed bibliography of his numerous books.

Harrison, Archibald Walter. *The Beginnings of Arminianism.* London, 1926. Accounts for James I's harsh opposition to Vorstius.

McLachlan, Herbert John. *Socinianism in Seventeenth-Century England.* London, 1951. Shows how Holland became the gateway for the entrance of Socinianism into England through the influence of Vorstius and others; see especially pp. 20–40.

Platt, John. *Reformed Thought and Scholasticism.* Leiden, 1982. Focuses on Vorstius's arguments for the existence of God, showing how he influenced Arminius and was in turn influenced by Socinus; see especially pp. 149–156, 210–214.

Schweizer, Alexander. "Conradus Vorstius: Vermittlung der reformierten Centraldogmen mit den socinianischen Einwendungen." *Theologische Jahrbücher* 15 (1856), 435 486; 16 (1857), 153–183. Thorough study of Vorstius's disposition for Socinianism.

Shriver, Frederick. "Orthodoxy and Diplomacy: James I and the Vorstius Affair." *The English Historical Review* 85 (July 1970), 449–474. The best source on detailing the varied political and theological motives of James I for his rejection of Vorstius.

"Vorstius, Conradus." In *Biografisch Lexicon voor de Geschiedenis van het Nederlandse Protestantisme,* vol. 1, pp. 407–410. Kampen, 1983.

Woude, Cornelius van der. *Sibrandus Lubbertus: Leven en Werken.* Kampen, Netherlands, 1963. Enlightening study of the correspondence Vorstius had with Lubbertus and others, with much primary source material here not to be found elsewhere; see especially pp. 198–258.

JOEL R. BEEKE

VOSMEER, Sasbout

VOSMEER, Sasbout (1548–1614), first apostolic vicar of the Holland Mission. Born on 3 March 1548, in Delft, Holland, the scion of a patrician family, Vosmeer matriculated in the theology faculty at Louvain in 1564 and received his ordination as a priest in 1572. Having obtained his licentiate in 1574, Vosmeer was appointed vicar-general of the archdiocese of Utrecht in 1583. In 1592 he became apostolic vicar of the Holland Mission with *potestas delegata,* when Ottavior Mirto Frangipani (1542? 1612), head of the recently established nunciature at Cologne, transferred to Vosmeer his powers over "the lands conquered by the heretics," including the supervision and authority over the regular and secular clergy in the rebellious provinces of the Netherlands. Vosmeer was consecrated archbishop of Philippi i.p.i. in 1602, and Frangipani's delegation of powers was confirmed by pope Clement VIII (r. 1592–1605), who added several other privileges, including the right to confer benefices, but exempted the Jesuits from Vosmeer's jurisdiction.

Vosmeer's position as *de facto* head of the Holland Mission was by no means unchallenged. His authority was questioned first by the canons of the Haarlem chapter, founded in 1571, and then by the Jesuit missionaries operating in the northern Netherlands since 1592. The Haarlem canons in particular disputed the legality of Vosmeer's nomination of Albert Eggius (1554–1610) as vicar-general of their diocese in 1599. After Eggius's death both parties reached a provisional settlement (1611), which was revised and finalized five years later under Vosmeer's successor, Philip Rovenius (1572–1651). The Jesuit missionaries viewed Vosmeer's uncompromising Bérullian stance vis à vis the Dutch authorities as unpractical and instead advocated a more conciliatory Salesian or Ignacian pragmatism. Moreover, whereas Rovenius and his Holland clergy viewed themselves as the rightful continuation of the old religious hierarchy, the Jesuits denied Vosmeer's claims to *potestas ordinaria* and considered the rebellious northern Netherlands as virgin mission territory in which they could freely exercise the *pastoralia*. Neither the unilaterally imposed *Decretium Nuntii* or *Forma* by Frangipani (1598) nor the mutually agreed upon *Articuli* of 1610 between Vosmeer and the Jesuit provincial Florence de Montmorency (1580–1659) could definitively settle the dispute. In addition to this Catholic infighting, Vosmeer's activities were viewed as subversive by the authorities of the nascent Dutch Republic, and in 1604 he was banished from the provinces of Holland, Zeeland, and Friesland on the accusation of *crimen laesae majestatis*. Having led an ambulant mission until then, Vosmeer was subsequently forced to spend the remainder of his life, with two brief exceptions, at Cologne, where he died on 3 May 1614.

Vosmeer was the founder of the Holland Mission. Apart from the establishment of the Brotherhood of Saint Willibrord and Boniface (1602) and his personal missionary activities in the vicinity of Delft, Vosmeer's greatest achievement was the creation of a seminary for Dutch priests at Cologne in 1602, the forerunner of the Collegium Alticollense. The limited geographic reach of the Holland Mission during Vosmeer's term of office would define the boundaries of the religious map of the northern Netherlands for the lifetime of the Dutch Republic and beyond. His indefatigable efforts could not solve the structural shortage of Catholic pastors nor stop the ongoing process of Protestantization in the northern Netherlands.

BIBLIOGRAPHY

Cornelissen, J. D. M., ed. *Romeinsche Bronnen voor den Kerkelijken Toestand der Nederlanden onder de Apostolische Vicarissen, 1592–1727.* Pt. 1, *1592–1651.* Rijks Geschiedkundige Publicatien, no. 77. The Hague, 1932. Collection of documents relating to the religious situation in the Netherlands under Vosmeer and Rovenius.

Gerlach, P. "Familie en Jeugdjaren van Sasbout Vosmeer, 1548–1563." *Archief voor de Geschiedenis van het Aartsbisdom Utrecht* 72 (1953), 1–52. Detailed discussion of the family background and early years of Vosmeer.

———. "De Studietijd van Sasbout Vosmeer te Leuven, 1563–1579." *Archief voor de Geschiedenis van het Aartsbisdom Utrecht* 72 (1953), 152–171. Deals with Vosmeer's study period at Leuven.

Janssen, J. A. M. M., and M. G. Spiertz. *Gids voor de Studie van Reformatie en Katholieke Herleving in Nederland, 1520–1650.* The Hague, 1982. Contains a list of the "Relationes" or reports by Vosmeer and Rovenius on the Holland mission from 1602 to 1648 as published in modern works and journals; see especially pp. 114–121.

Jong, J. de. "Het Utrechtsche Vicariaat en de Strijd over de hierarchische orde in de 17de Eeuw." *De Katholiek* 164 (1924), 73–103. Deals with the ambiguous legal position of the apostolic vicar in the church hierarchy.

Knuif, W. L. S., and R. G. R. Smeets. "Sasbout Vosmeer." *Archief voor de Geschiedenis van het Aartsbisdom Utrecht* 41 (1915), 321–407. A biographical sketch of Vosmeer's life until 1608.

———. "Sasbout Vosmeer." *Archief voor de Geschiedenis van het Aartsbisdom Utrecht* 43 (1917), 135–192. Second part of biographical sketch of Vosmeer's life, including his last years and his struggle with the Jesuits.

Rogier, L. J. *Geschiedenis van het katholicisme in Noord-Nederland in de 16e en 17e eeuw.* 2 vols. Amsterdam, 1947. Classic, somewhat biased general history of Catholicism in the northern Netherlands.

Tracy, James D. "With and Without the Counter-Reformation: The Catholic Church in the Spanish Netherlands and the Dutch Republic, 1580–1650." *Catholic Historical Review* 71 (1985), 547–575. Excellent overview of the histographical literature since World War II.

MARCUS P. M. VINK

VOSSIUS, Gerardus Joannes (1577–1649), Dutch scholar and humanist. Vossius was born in Heidelberg in March or April 1577; his father, a Protestant minister, was active in the Palatinate, Flanders, and Holland (Dordrecht). In September 1595, upon completing his studies at the Latin school in Dordrecht, Vossius enrolled as a grant holder of the Leiden Estates College for prospective ministers; he then studied philosophy and theology at Leiden University and was awarded the master of arts degree. He won appointments in 1600 as rector of the Latin school of Dordrecht and in 1615, through the help of his friend Hugo Grotius, as regent of the Leiden Estates College. In the conflict between Remonstrants and Contra-Remonstrants, Vossius took an intermediate position on the issue of predestination while defending the Remonstrants against the charge of heresy; this stance could have cost him his post in 1619 in the wake of the victory of the Contra-Remontstrants and their political partners. Three years later he obtained a post as professor of rhetoric and history at Leiden University. He opened the Athenaeum Illustre at Amsterdam in 1632, serving as the first rector and professor of history and politics. Vossius was married to Elisabeth van den Corput from 1602 to 1606 and to Elisabeth Junius from 1607 to 1649; he had two daughters and six sons, all of them gifted and all but one of whom died before their father. Vossius himself died on 17 March 1649. He left many disciples and was remembered for his publications in the fields of philology, rhetoric, poetics, historiography, and biblical and ecclesiastical history.

As a student at Leiden Vossius was influenced by the moderate theologian Franciscus Junius, author of *Le paisible chrestien* (1593). Vossius believed that the church of the first five centuries was nearest to Christian truth, and that all Christian churches belonged to the one church of Christ. He dwelled more on what bound Christians together than on what divided them, and stressed the value of a dignified human existence inspired by Christian ethics. Although in principle he accepted the sinfulness of man's nature, he gave credit to the power of human freedom of will as created by God. Attacked in his native country, Vossius found a spiritual homeland in England, where his publications won great recognition. He corresponded on friendly terms with William Laud and James Ussher, archbishops of Canterbury and Armagh, and in 1629 he received a canonry in the Canterbury cathedral chapter. His numerous publications on biblical and church history were influential, especially in paving the way for a more critical study of the textual sources of religious history. These works include the *Historia Pelagianismi* (1618), his *Theses theologicae* (1628), the pioneering study *Dissertationes tres de tribus symbolis* (1641), his essays on genealogy, the life and death of Christ (1643 and 1656), the series *De baptismo disputationes* (1648), and a chronology of the Bible (1659).

BIBLIOGRAPHY

Primary Sources

Vossius, Gerardus Joannes. *Opera in sex tomos divisa*. Amsterdam, 1695–1701. All of Vossius's works (except the handbooks he wrote for the Latin schools) are published in these six volumes.
————. *Gerardi Joannis Vossii et clarorum virorum ad eum epistolae collectore Paulo Colomesio Ecclesiae Anglicanae presbytero*. London, 1690; Augsburg, 1691; London, 1693. A thousand letters written by and to Vossius, 772 of which are also printed in vol. 4 of the *Opera*.

Secondary Sources

Lem, G. A. C. van der, and C. S. M. Rademaker. *Inventory of the Correspondence of Gerardus Joannes Vossius, 1577–1649*. Republica Literaria Neerlandica, no. 7. Assen, 1993. An inventory of nearly 3,400 letters written by and to Vossius and preserved in print and manuscript form. Includes a list of studies on Vossius from the period 1981–1992.
Rademaker, C. S. M. *Life and Work of Gerardus Joannes Vossius, 1577–1649*. Republica Literaria Neerlandica, no. 5. Assen, 1981. A biography with comprehensive bibliographies of Vossius's works, his preserved manuscripts, and studies and publications on Vossius up to 1981.
Wickenden, Nicholas. *G. J. Vossius and the Humanist Concept of History*. Republica Literaria Neerlandica, no. 8. Assen, 1993. The author provides a thorough description of Vossius's religious thinking.

CORNELIS S. M. RADEMAKER

VOWS AND OATHS.

Both vows and oaths involve solemn promises that create moral obligations between an individual and God. Moreover, courts may hold the person who makes a vow or takes an oath liable for performance of the promise and may impose penalties for default.

The person who takes an oath promises another human being that he or she will tell the truth or perform some other lawful act and calls upon God to warrant the sincerity of his or her intention; this, in effect, makes God a third party to the transaction, in addition to the two human actors. The oath taker assumes a solemn obligation to fulfill the promise, under penalty of divine punishment should he or she fail to do so.

A vow, by contrast, is a promise that involves only two parties: the promisor makes a commitment directly to God and thereby creates a binding obligation that he or she must discharge. The vow normally involves a promise to perform some act (or sometimes to refrain from an action), often in return for, and frequently contingent upon, some favor that God is asked to grant. Both vows and oaths have root deep in the human psyche and appear in most societies from remote antiquity. Medieval people depended to an unusual degree upon oaths and vows as methods of creating or formalizing obligations. During the early Middle Ages (roughly between 700 and 1200) oaths and vows knit together the entire social fabric.

Oaths constituted the preferred method for transacting many types of business. They were used in court to support legal claims; merchants used them to conclude contracts; soldiers took oaths to affirm allegiance to a king or feudal lord; townspeople subscribed to the obligations of membership in guilds and confraternities through oaths of admission. Oaths constituted the usual method of solemnizing nearly all important undertakings.

At the same time, however, people also regarded swearing an oath as a serious and potentially dangerous act, one that they generally preferred to avoid save for the most serious and formal occasions. Confessors, preachers, and theologians cautioned against the terrible consequences of perjury: a false oath, they warned, would call down God's vengeance upon the offender and condemn him or her not only to an eternity of unimaginable horrors in the afterlife, but quite possibly to awful retribution in this life as well.

From the beginning of the thirteenth century, however, the value of oaths seems to have depreciated. They gradually became at once more commonplace and less central to late medieval and early modern societies. Oaths continued, of course, to play a role in judicial proceedings, as they still do; but as courts came to place greater emphasis on the testimony of witnesses and the presentation of documentary evidence, reliance on judicial oaths as a form of proof correspondingly declined. Promissory oaths, such as oaths of office and oaths of allegiance (which modern societies also continue to use), likewise became more routine and less awesome than they had previously been.

At the same time churchmen were concerned that casual oaths were becoming altogether too common and condemned needless swearing as a moral failing. Handbooks for confessors and other pastoral guides written after 1200 accordingly expressed greater concern about unseemly swearing and profane invocation of God and the saints than their predecessors had done. Although late medieval moralists denounced unnecessary swearing as an affront to God, they enjoyed scant success in repressing the practice. Sixteenth-century Protestant reformers agreed with Catholic divines that casual swearing was an outrage that Christian societies should not tolerate. Protestant countries often treated casual swearing as tantamount to blasphemy and prosecuted both as crimes against public decency and order.

Like their pagan counterparts, Christians during the early centuries made vows to perform various kinds of works that they hoped would please God. From the third century onward this practice became institutionalized in monastic communities. Monks and nuns, then and now, customarily make three vows: they promise God that they will remain chaste, renounce all personal property, and obey their religious superiors. When aspiring monks or nuns first enter a community, they normally take temporary vows, binding only for a limited period—typically one, two, or three years. Candidates who successfully complete the probationary period may then became full-fledged religious; during the ceremony of profession, the new religious makes perpetual vows, binding for life.

Laypeople, too, often made vows, as many still do. Married persons vow lifelong fidelity to one another. Medieval widows, for example, frequently made vows of chastity as protection against efforts to marry them off. Penitents vowed to go on pilgrimage or to perform some other action to make amends for their sins. Those who were ill vowed good works of various kinds if God would free them from their sickness. Popes from Urban II (1088–1099) onward urged the faithful to vow to go on a Crusade, and untold hundreds of thousands did so; in return for their vows, they received an indulgence, a promise that their participation in the Crusade would erase the temporal punishment that their sins deserved.

Those who took a vow were not always subsequently able or willing to fulfill it. Medieval popes claimed that the "fullness of power" (*plenitudo potestatis*) that Christ bequeathed to Peter and his successors included the power to remedy this situation either by authorizing substitution of some easier task for the one originally promised (which is known as commutation of a vow) or even by dispensing from the obligation to fulfill the vow altogether (known as redemption of a vow). Persons who sought release from their vows needed to petition the pope to grant them a commutation or redemption. The petitioner had to pay a series of fees to the papal Curia for processing the application and in addition was usually required to make a further offering for some pious cause when the petition was approved. During the fourteenth and fifteenth centuries the routine granting of petitions for votive relief became an increasingly important

source of papal revenues. Luther and other sixteenth-century reformers recoiled from this practice. Their denunciations of the practice of raising money through the commutation and redemption of vows struck simultaneously at the theoretical underpinnings of papal power and at an important source of papal income. Thus release from vows emerged very early as a leading issue in the Reformation.

The oath assumed a special significance for the Anabaptist wing of the Reformation. The Anabaptists were much given to a literal reading of the Sermon on the Mount; accordingly, their reading of the Matthean passage (5:33–37) prompted them to conclude that it was wrong for Christians to swear oaths. While they observed that, in keeping with the dominical saying, their simple speech was every bit as reliable as formal oaths, the fact of the matter was that their refusal to swear oaths put them outside the bonds of society, the viability of which depended on common values and common principles.

This Anabaptist sentiment found expression as early as the Schleitheim Articles of February 1527 and is found in every Anabaptist-Mennonite confession of faith of the Reformation era. The numerous records of court proceedings against Anabaptists tell of Anabaptists unwilling to affirm their statements by the swearing of an oath, instead insisting that the dominical command elevated their simple speech to oathlike importance. An extensive discussion of the oath is found in Peter Riedemann's *Rechenschaft* of 1545. The Anabaptist argumentation simply clung to the dominical command and argued that the oath was not possible in worldly and secular matters.

BIBLIOGRAPHY

Brundage, James A. "The Votive Obligations of Crusaders: The Development of a Canonistic Doctrine." In *The Crusades, Holy War and Canon Law*, pp. 77–118. London, 1991. This chapter traces the development of legal doctrines concerning the enforcement of crusading vows.

Capelle, Germaine Catherine. *Le voeu d'obéissance dès origines au XIIe siècle: Étude juridique.* Bibliothèque d'histoire du droit et droit romain, vol. 2. Paris, 1959. Survey of juristic treatments of the monastic vow of obedience.

David, M. "Parjure et mensonge dans le Décret de Gratien." *Studia Gratiana* 3 (1955), 117–141. This article describes the treatment of perjury and its consequences in the basic medieval textbook of canon law.

Fraher, Richard M. "Conviction according to Conscience: The Medieval Jurists' Debate concerning Judicial Discretion and the Law of Proof." *Law and History Review* 7 (1989), 23–88. On judicial evaluation of purgatory oaths as evidence.

Guindon, Bernard. *Le serment: Son histoire, son caractère sacré.* Ottawa, 1957.

Helmholz, Richard H. "Crime, Compurgation and the Courts of the Medieval Church." *Law and History Review* 1 (1983), 1–26. Deals with the judicial use of oath-helpers in ecclesiastical courts.

Hinschius, Paul. *Das Kirchenrecht der Katholiken und Protestanten in Deutschland.* 6 vols. Berlin, 1869–1897. See vol. 5, pp. 337–350, for an examination of the role of oaths in early medieval judicial procedure and its adoption by canon law.

Kolmer, Lothar. *Promissorische Eide im Mittelalter.* Regensburger historische Forschungen, no. 12. Kallmünz, Germany, 1989. Catalogs and classifies numerous examples of the use of oaths to secure simple promises.

Korner, Theodor. *Iuramentum und frühe Friedensbewegung, 10.–12. Jahrhundert.* Münchener Universitätsschriften, Abhandlungen zur rechtswissenschaftlichen Grundlagenforschung, vol. 26. Berlin, 1977.

Turlan, Juliette. "L'obligation 'ex voto.'" *Revue historique de droit français et étranger* 4th ser., 44 (1955), 502–536. Sketches the ancient (especially Roman) roots of the legal enforcement of votive promises.

JAMES A. BRUNDAGE

WAGNER, Valentin (c.1510–1557), humanist teacher and rector, Lutheran pastor and reformer in Brasov (Kronstadt, Romania). Little is known about Wagner's early life except that he seems to have received humanist training in the local school. The first reliable information concerning Wagner dates from 1542, when he was commissioned by reform-minded individuals in Brasov to continue his education at the University of Wittenberg. Among the advocates of reform in Brasov at that time were Johannes Honter, a member of the inner council, the town magistrate Johann Fuchs, the city pastor Jeremias Jekel, and Bartolomaus Bogner, who in 1544 was called to Levoča in county Spiš (Slovakia) to assist in the introduction of the Reformation there.

Upon his return from Wittenburg, Wagner became a schoolteacher and gained recognition for his mastery of Greek. He prepared a grammar and a Greek catechism, which was sent to the patriarch of Constantinople, and a hymnbook in German as well as school poems and a commentary on Seneca. He may have contributed to the preparation of the *Formula reformationis Coronensis* (1542–1543)—and certainly was involved in its modification—and of the *Reformatio ecclesiarum Saxonicarum in Transylvania* (1547), which was intended to confirm the Wittenberg teachings and practices as the basis of the ecclesiastical life for the Transylvanian Saxons. After Honter became city pastor of Brasov in April 1545, Wagner became rector of the school; he would later succeed Honter as city pastor in 1549. He returned to Wittenberg in 1554, where he received his master's degree. Until his death in 1557, Wagner had to contend with the growing influence of Swiss theology, which was spreading among the Magyars and some Germans in Transylvania. He first assisted and then carried on the work of Honter and infused the Reformation in Brasov with the theological views of his Wittenberg mentor Melanchthon.

BIBLIOGRAPHY

Primary Sources

Wagner, Valentin. *Katechesis*. Coronae, 1550.
———. *Praecepta vitae Christianae Valent. Wagneri Coronen.* 1554.
———. *Prima rudimenta Christianae religionis. In usum pueritiae Coronensis.* 1554.
———. *Odium Calvinianorum.* Brasso, n.d.

Secondary Sources

Myss, Walter, ed. *Lexikon der siebenbürgischen Sachsen.* Thaur, 1993.
Reinerth, Karl. "Des kronstädter Magisters Valentin Wagners Wittenberger Studium." *Archiv für Reformationsgeschichte* 59 (1968), 25–41.
———. *Die Gründung der evangelischen Kirchen in Siebenbürgen.* Studia Transylvanica 5. Cologne, 1979.

DAVID P. DANIEL

WALES. Having lost what remained of its political independence in 1284, Wales was conquered but not completely integrated into the English realm. It kept its own language and a rich and vigorous native culture. It was divided between the shires of the Principality in the north and west and the autonomous lordships of the Marches in the south and east, most of which were in the possession of the Crown by the beginning of the sixteenth century. By then, also, the social and economic condition of Wales was more similar to that of England than in earlier centuries, and the time was ripe for an Act of Union (1536–1543) between the two countries. The late medieval church had already passed more closely under the control of the English monarchy, and its bishops and higher clergy were mainly royal nominees, Englishmen, and absentees. The houses of religion were small and decayed, the parish clergy mostly poor and ill educated, and the population, though loyal, was badly instructed and superstitious. The Welsh church was manifestly in need of reform, yet there was almost no evidence of criticism or opposition. Contemporary currents in the direction of improvement, like the *devotio moderna*, pietism, Renaissance inspiration, or heresies (old or new) made little impact under such unfavorable social conditions. As in some outlying parts of England, the upland nature of the terrain, a scattered pastoral farming population, small towns, the small size of prosperous merchant and artisan classes, few schools, and the absence of a court, capital, printing press, or university all made for an adherence to age-old custom. Wales was less qualified to welcome reform than to defend the traditional church.

Henry VIII's reforms were imposed from above, with little demand from below, on a Wales almost completely under his control. The enforcement of his royal supremacy met with virtually no opposition from the native clergy or people. The forty-seven monasteries and friaries, all of which were valued in *Valor Ecclesiasticus* at less than £200 a year, were dissolved without protest between 1536 and 1540 and their possessions acquired by local families of gentry sooner or later. The suppression of shrines and places of pilgrimage was distinctly more unpopular but encountered no overt protest. The gradual introduction of English service and a vernacular Bible had little effect on a population most of whom spoke only Welsh, except for the inhabitants of market towns and a few areas like south Pembrokeshire and the border districts. Efforts to introduce Protestant teaching, notably by Bishop William Barlow in Saint David's diocese, were impeded by the acute shortage of Welsh-language preachers and the absence of a printed literature in Welsh.

Yet Henry's reforms were accepted without rebellion, partly because he was regarded as belonging to a Welsh dynasty and partly because he was a masterful king who had imposed firmer rule. Moreover, the leading gentry families were anxious to remain on good terms with the Crown, which they regarded as a potential source of increased authority and possessions for themselves. Nor had laymen been given any lead in opposing royal policies by the clergy, monastic or non-monastic. One has also to remember that, however great were the constitutional implications of displacing the pope and establishing the royal supremacy, of dissolving the monasteries, or encouraging the use of the vernacular in religion, a large part of the old church order had been preserved intact. Loyal Welsh poets could therefore praise Henry for dealing firmly with enemies such as the pope and "false monks". Nonetheless, an undercurrent of resentment ran through Wales. The Welsh had disliked Henry's treatment of Catherine of Aragon and her daughter, the suppression of shrines and pilgrimages had been thoroughly unpopular, and few had understood or liked the English language, which had been used to promulgate reform by statute, book, and sermon.

If Henry's reformation had been mainly political, Edward VI's constituted a religious revolution. Pilgrimages, holy days, candles, incense, and other customary practices were done away with; images, pictures, and rood lofts were removed; and the clergy were allowed to marry. In 1549 the Protestant *Book of Common Prayer,* the use of which was enforced throughout the realm, substituted English services for Latin ones. Most of the people of Wales, knowing only Welsh, resented the new and incomprehensible rite. When in 1550 altars were replaced by Communion tables, this was another fundamental change bitterly disliked in most of Wales. Equally unpopular were the further confiscations of church property: the dissolution of the chantries, appropriation of the treasures of parish churches, and the seizure of episcopal and capitular estates.

Reactions to all these changes varied. A minority who understood English may have welcomed the new doctrine. A leading Welsh scholar, William Salesbury, made a brave effort to provide for his compatriots' needs by publishing a Welsh translation of the Epistles and Gospels contained in the prayer book. But the reactions of the majority seem to have been reflected in popular poetry, which severely criticized the English liturgy ("faith of Saxons"), the married clergy, the despoiling of parish churches, and the pillaging of ecclesiastical property. The Welsh, who had hitherto prided themselves on their proverbial loyalty to the church, regarded the Edwardian reformation as forcing them to swallow a detestable new-fangled and alien heresy. If the uprisings that were feared in Wales did not eventuate, this was not for want of acute dissatisfaction but because the key landowners remained loyal to the government.

The accession of Mary Tudor was warmly greeted on religious grounds but also because she was the legitimate heiress of the Tudors. Her restoration of the Roman faith was generally welcomed by clerics and laypeople, especially by the poets, though a number of priests were deprived of their livings, mainly because they had married. That Wales had only three martyrs—one of them being the bishop of Saint David's, Robert Ferrar—and fewer than a dozen religious exiles indicates not only the lack of Protestant sympathies but also the absence of persecuting bishops. Leading Catholics like Bishop Goldwell of Saint Asaph tried hard to raise the level of belief and worship, but met with little success. By the time of Mary's death in 1558 she had forfeited much of her popularity as a result of an unfortunate marriage, unsuccessful foreign policy, disastrous warfare, poor harvests, and widespread disease.

The Elizabethan Settlement, although similar to her brother's efforts, with its Protestant complexion and English prayer book, was widely accepted in Wales. Frequent religious changes since the 1530s had induced confusion, uncertainty, and apathy among the populace; there was a general willingness to accept a church "by law established" that offered some prospect of stability. But throughout Elizabeth's reign, bishops reported widespread ignorance, resistance to change, and adherence to old ways among the largely illiterate masses. The emergent factions of convinced Catholics and Protestants were both minorities who battled hard for mastery. Catholics pinned their faith on a handful of sympathetic landowners, seminary priests, Catholic literature in Welsh and English, and politico-military intrigue. They achieved relatively little success, except in Monmouthshire, Flint, and the borders. In 1603 they numbered only 808 avowed recusants as opposed to a conforming population of 212,450, though the diocese of Llandaff had a higher percentage of recusants than any other diocese in England or Wales.

Protestants depended heavily on the loyalty of most of the gentry to the queen and her regime, an allegiance reinforced by many years of hostility to the papacy and Spain and the association of Catholicism with subversion and treachery.

The church also owed much to the Elizabethan bishops, who, by contrast with their medieval predecessors, were mostly Welshmen, resident and conscientious reformers. They were gradually able to improve the quality of the higher clergy and parish priests, though much remained to be achieved, and preachers were in short supply. The most desperate need was a Welsh translation of the Bible and the order of service. An act of Parliament of 1563 required the episcopate to undertake the work, and in 1567 Bishop Richard Davies and William Salesbury published the New Testament and prayer book in Welsh. A much more successful translation appeared in 1588, when Bishop William Morgan published his Bible, and in 1599 his prayer book.

A trickle of other printed Protestant literature in Welsh also appeared and slowly grew in volume. In the long run, these works had an enormous impact by making Reformation doctrine intelligible and acceptable and by stimulating preaching and catechizing. They were equally influential in helping to keep the Welsh language, literature, and nationality alive and vigorous. This influence was also reinforced by the acceptance among intellectuals of a Protestant reinterpretation of Welsh history that sought to prove that the Reformation was not a neoteric English heresy but a return to the pristine Christianity first brought to the ancient Britons in their golden age in apostolic times. Nevertheless, allegiance to the Reformed church and, for that matter, to revived Catholicism as well, was confined largely to the better educated among the clergy and gentry. The majority would remain illiterate, badly instructed, and bound by age-old custom until the Reformation came of age in Wales after the spread of Puritanism in the seventeenth century and the religious revivals of the eighteenth.

BIBLIOGRAPHY

Ballinger, John. *The Bible in Wales*. London, 1906. Useful bibliographic survey, though somewhat dated.

Herbert, Trevor, and Gareth Elwgn Jones, eds. *Tudor Wales*. Cardiff, 1988. A helpful overview, with documents.

Jones, J. Gwynfor. *Wales and the Tudor State: Government, Religious Change and the Social Order, 1534–1603*. Cardiff, 1939. A valuable collection of documents.

Mathew, David. *The Celtic Peoples and Renaissance Europe*. Reprint, New York, 1974. Stimulating and attractively written.

Pierce, William. *John Penry: His Life, Times and Writings*. London, 1923. The best study of the only sixteenth-century Welsh Puritan of any significance. Good on Elizabeth's reign.

Thomas, J. D. Hugh. *A History of Wales, 1485–1660*. Cardiff, 1972. Good general summary.

Thomas, W. S. K. *Tudor Wales*. Llandysul, Wales, 1983. Useful outline survey.

Williams, Glanmor. *Welsh Reformation Essays*. Cardiff, 1967. Contains a number of useful essays.

———. *Recovery, Reorientation and Reformation: Wales, c.1415–1642*. Oxford, 1987. The only full modern study of sixteenth-century Wales.

———. *The Welsh and Their Religion*. Cardiff, 1991. Contains important studies of aspects of the Reformation.

Williams, Llewelyn. *The Making of Modern Wales*. London, 1919. Dated, but still valuable; attractively written.

GLANMOR WILLIAMS

WALTHER, Rudolf. *See* Gwalther, Rudolf.

WAR. *See* Counts' War; Pacifism; Peasants' Revolt; Wars of Religion.

WARHAM, William (c.1456–1532), English churchman and patron of humanism. Warham was the last archbishop of Canterbury before the breach of the English church with Rome. Though active in administration and diplomacy under Henry VII and in the early years of Henry VIII's reign, his political influence and ecclesiastical authority were eclipsed by Cardinal Thomas Wolsey. In 1515 he retired from politics to his diocese, though he appeared at state occasions such as the Field of the Cloth of Gold (1520). Warham sided with Henry VIII over the "divorce" from Catherine of Aragon; as a canon lawyer he had doubted the validity of the marriage from the beginning, and in 1527 told Wolsey that "howsoever displeasantly the Queen took this matter, yet the truth and judgment of the law must have place." Appointed one of Catherine's counselors, it is not surprising that he gave little advice beyond warning that "the wrath of the prince is death." The issue of royal supremacy, however, brought him out in opposition to Henry. He is generally credited with the limiting clause "as far as the law of Christ allows" in the clergy's acknowledgment of Henry's authority (1531). As John Fisher identified with John the Baptist in the marriage case, Warham saw himself in the role of Becket vis-à-vis royal supremacy. In February 1532 he registered a formal protest against all recent antipapal legislation. His death in August 1532 removed an obstacle to Henry's definitive breach with Rome.

A conservative churchman, active in the prosecution of heresy, Warham was also a friend to humanism. He is most notable as a major patron of Erasmus, to whom he gave generous gifts of money and a regular pension. Erasmus dedicated to him the *Dialogues of Lucian* (1514) and his great edition of Jerome (1516). Warham also received dedications from Richard Croke, Thomas Linacre, and John Longland. Erasmus frequently called Warham his "great Maecenas" and praised his piety, learning, liberality, and simplicity of life. His portrait was painted by Hans Holbein.

BIBLIOGRAPHY

Dowling, Maria. *Humanism in the Age of Henry VIII*. London, Sydney, and Dover, N.H., 1986.

Erasmus, Desiderius. *Pilgrimages to Saint Mary of Walsingham and Saint Thomas of Canterbury.* 2d ed., rev. and corr. Edited and translated by John Gough Nichols. London, 1875.

Gairdner, James. "William Warham." In *Dictionary of National Biography,* edited by Sidney Lee. Reprint, Oxford, 1921–1922.

Knighton, C. S. "William Warham." In *Contemporaries of Erasmus,* edited by Peter G. Bietenholz and Thomas B. Deutscher, vol. 3. Toronto, Buffalo, and London, 1986.

MARIA DOWLING

WARS OF RELIGION. The French religious wars occupied four decades of turmoil that constituted a crucial period for the future history of France. At the end of the sixteenth century a new society emerged, more rigorously hierarchial than it had been at midcentury, with a government that had cast aside many of the constitutional restraints that had operated in earlier times. In religious terms the challenge of a militant Calvinism had been replaced by a defensive minority, resented by a reformed yet chastened Catholicism and tolerated officially by an increasingly absolute ruler, who retained his traditional title of "the most Christian King." The declared civil wars and their concluding edicts of pacification were as follows: 1562–1563 (Amboise); 1567–1568 (Longjumeau); 1568–1570 (Saint-Germain); 1572–1573 (La Rochelle); 1574–1576 (Beaulieu); 1577 (Bergerac); 1580 (Fleix); and 1586–1598 (Vervins for peace with Spain and Nantes for the settlement with the Huguenots). In every province riots, massacres, and local revolts took place intermittently between the battles and devastation of the official wars. This was also the battlefield for the European contest of Reformation and Counter-Reformation ideals. Spanish, papal, Savoyard, and English forces intervened, and large mercenary German armies appeared regularly on French soil. Moreover, the Revolt of the Netherlands against Philip II of Spain was closely connected with affairs in France.

There has been much debate about the causes of the wars. To take two examples at opposite ends of the spectrum, Denis Crouzet (*Les Guerriers de Dieu,* 2 vols., Paris, 1990) has argued that the conflicts were based on religious passions ranging from Catholic apocalyptic panic to rationalized Protestant iconoclastic fury, whereas Henry Heller (*Iron and Blood,* Montreal, 1991) has found beneath the appearance of religious motivation social tensions amounting to class war. The most likely general explanation is the coincidence of rival religious enthusiasms with the contention of aristocratic factions at a time of governmental and economic instability.

The importance of secular concerns is evident from the fact that in the first half of the wars the Huguenots were in opposition to the Crown, whereas in the second half their principal enemies, the Catholic League, assumed this role and even adapted Huguenot political thinking to their own use. If any pattern is discernible in these long drawn-out conflicts, it can be seen in the secular theories with which the opposition parties justified their actions. The Huguenots and the Catholic League experienced the same evolution in their political ideas. At first it was maintained that the party was opposing not the Crown itself but rather evil counselors who had usurped royal authority. In the second phase it was contended that the Crown had so overstepped its constitutional powers that armed resistance was legitimate. Polemicists in this phase produced a plethora of historical precedents. In the third phase the earlier arguments were subordinate to radical and abstract theories of the sovereignty of the whole community over the ruler, expressed in terms of a contract of government. These theories owed much to Roman and canon law and to the conciliar writers who had tried to limit the powers of the pope in the fifteenth century. Acting through its representatives, the community might oppose, overthrow, and even kill a tyrant king.

Huguenot Resistance. The accidental death of Henry II in 1559 created a vacuum at the center of power. The king's widow, Catherine de Médicis, was left with four young sons, three of whom successively became kings of France as Francis II (r. 1559–1560), Charles IX (r. 1560–1574), and Henry III (r. 1574–1589), while the fourth, Francis, duke of Alençon and later Anjou, died childless in 1584. The government of Henry II had been riven by rival factions, among whom the most important were the houses of Guise and Montmorency. At his death the former were in the ascendancy through the marriage of Francis II to Mary Stuart, Queen of Scots, whose mother was Mary of Guise. The latter's two brothers—Francis, duke of Guise; and Charles, cardinal of Lorraine—became the virtual rulers of France. Both were strong enemies of heresy. The duke had won a heroic reputation in the recent war against Philip II, and the cardinal, one of the richest and most powerful prelates of the age, was to become a leader of the Counter-Reformation, soon to achieve its final form in the last session of the Council of Trent.

The head of the rival house was Anne de Montmorency, constable of France and friend and mentor to the late king. His sincere Catholic faith pulled him in one direction and his family interests in the other. His sister, Louise de Châtillon, favored Reformed opinions, and her three sons—Gaspard II de Coligny, admiral of France; Francis d'Andelot, colonel general of the infantry; and Odet de Coligny, despite being cardinal-bishop of Beauvais—became leaders of the Protestant cause. Two of the constable's sons—Marshal Francis, governor of Paris; and Henry de Damville, governor of Languedoc—were Catholics prepared to compromise with the Huguenots. The Bourbons constituted a fourth family of vast potential influence through their dynastic right to succeed to the throne should the Valois line fail. The principal representatives were three brothers—Antoine, who was king of Navarre through his marriage to Jeanne of Navarre; Louis I of Condé; and Charles, the staunchly Catholic cardinal of Bourbon. Antoine vacillated briefly toward the Protestant camp, while his strong-minded wife and his brother Condé played a directing part in the Huguenot party.

The factions of the great expanded through networks of clientage to encompass intermediate and lesser ranks of the nobility of the sword. For three generations they had served in foreign wars. Now employment in the royal army and pensions from the king were cut nearly to the vanishing point at a time when the factions of the princes were expanding. About one-third of the warrior nobility became members or supporters of the Reformed religion in the years 1559–1561. It may be that many rural seigneurs had become detached from the administration of their estates and were suffering from the inflation of prices as the real value of income from peasant dues decreased. Russell Major, however, has argued that the nobility could readily adapt to the price rise and that, if some noble houses suffered economically, it was their expenditures on the civil wars that was the cause ("Noble Income and Inflation and the Wars of Religion in France," *American Historical Review* 86 (1981), 21–48). If the issue of economic motives for noble involvement in the wars remains uncertain, the sincerity of many noble conversions to Calvinism does not. Nancy Roelker has shown the deep sincerity of many noblewomen in old families, such as the La Rochefoucauld and the Rohan, who converted before their husbands ("The Appeal of Calvinism to French Noblewomen in the Sixteenth Century," *Journal of Interdisciplinary History* 2 (1972), 391–418). Of course, there were also many instances of hypocrisy in which noble commanders switched sides for their own profit. Clearly, there were some who were moved by material advantage, others who loyally followed their patron regardless of religion, and others again who felt a true vocation to do God's will in the world. Hence, contemporary opinion distinguished between political and religious Huguenots. Something of the diversity of motives within the Protestant nobility can be seen in a conspiracy of lesser seigneurs to take charge of the royal court at Amboise and remove the royal family from the tutelage of the Guises. The plot failed with much bloodshed in March 1560, and Condé was later indicted as its secret promoter.

Calvinism had its greatest numerical strength in the towns, where the pastors and elders (usually bourgeois notables) often found it impossible to restrain the iconoclastic fury of the lower classes. Protestant riots and demonstrations were answered by the massacre of heretics by Catholic mobs, often instigated by the lower clergy and by expiatory processions. The anarchy grew under the Guisard administration, while Catherine de Médicis and the chancellor, Michel de L'Hôpital, began quietly to develop a policy of moderation. Francis II died suddenly in December 1560, and the queen mother became regent in the minority of

Charles IX, her supporters replacing the Guises on the royal council. Strong Protestant and anticlerical sentiment was manifest at the representative Estates-General meeting at this time in Orléans. To stem the incoming Protestant tide, three grandees—Francis of Guise, Constable Montmorency, and Marshal Saint-André—formed a triumvirate to pressure the government, while the regent proceeded to call a colloquy of clergy and pastors at Poissy in the hope of some kind of religious compromise. Its failure did not deter her from issuing an edict of toleration in January 1562, which met with strong opposition not only from the triumvirs but also from two groups who suffered few defections to Calvinism—the episcopacy and the magistrates of the high court of the Parlement of Paris. By this time the Huguenots had completed their military preparations, establishing a protector system whereby the nobles could mobilize the manpower of the congregations. The spark that ignited the first civil war in this inflammatory situation was the massacre by Francis of Guise and his followers of a Calvinist congregation found worshiping in the town of Wassy.

During this war the Huguenots made an alliance with the English, who occupied Le Havre. At Dreux, the one major battle of the war, the rival commanders, Condé and the constable, were captured, while Marshal Saint-André was killed. Antoine of Navarre died in the royal army outside Rouen, and Francis of Guise was assassinated during the siege of the Protestant stronghold of Orléans. After the Peace of Amboise, which made a point of granting degrees of freedom of worship according to social status, the royal court undertook a long tour of the provinces (1564–1566) to enforce the settlement, and the chancellor began a series of judicial and administrative reforms culminating in an assembly at Moulins. The reforms were aborted by the onset of the second war, which began with a Huguenot attempt to seize the court at Meaux in the misapprehension that the march of a Spanish army along the eastern frontier to repress the Revolt of the Netherlands was the start of a concerted campaign by the two monarchies to eradicate heresy. The constable was killed in the one major engagement of this war, the battle of Saint-Denis. A tenuous peace collapsed after six months, when the royal council ordered the arrest of the Huguenot leaders. This failed coup, promoted by the cardinal of Lorraine, was the event that persuaded the defenders of the Huguenot cause to shift the emphasis from the theory of evil counselors to the argument of constitutional resistance. The third war that followed saw campaigns on several fronts. Condé was killed at the battle of Jarnac, but Coligny, reinforced by a large German army, held the royal forces at bay.

The first three wars had eliminated most of the faction leaders, but Antoine of Navarre, Louis I of Condé, and Francis of Guise left sons, all named Henri, to take the place of the fathers. Catherine de Médicis returned to the policy of moderation. She persuaded Charles IX to resume the traditional hostility toward the Habsburgs and to move closer to England and the leaders of the Netherlands opposition to Philip II. This entailed reconciliation with the Huguenots and the negotiation with Jeanne of Navarre of a marriage between Henry of Navarre (from 1589 Henry IV of France) and the queen mother's daughter, Marguerite. Jeanne of Navarre died four months before the wedding, which occurred in Paris on 18 August 1572. Six days later the Saint Bartholomew's Day Massacre began, and most of the Protestant wedding guests, together with thousands of other victims, were slaughtered. Although the initiative in this atrocity was neither the king's nor his mother's, the Crown accepted responsibility and claimed that the killing had been necessary to anticipate a Protestant plot. Coligny was the principal martyr, and his policy of intervention in the Netherlands was temporarily set aside. The flood of Huguenot polemics that responded to this seeming act of treachery alleged long premeditation and extreme duplicity on the part of Catherine de Médicis and Charles IX. In the years that followed the most radical Huguenot ideas of resistance were enunciated. The best known of these works were the pseudonymous *Reveille-Matin*, (Alarm Bell; 1573–1574), François Hotman's *Francogallia* (1573, but the historical and constitutional parts composed earlier), Théodore de Bèze's *De Jure Magistratum* (Right of Magistrates; 1574), and the pseudonymous *Vindiciae contra tyrannos* (Defence of Liberty against Tyrants; 1579, probably written by Philippe Duplessis-Mornay).

Bereft of their leaders, the Huguenots defended the bastion of La Rochelle and in the south set up federal republics governed by elected assemblies. Within the royal army besieging La Rochelle, a group of disaffected moderate Catholics known as malcontents, or politiques, conspired against the government. They included the sons of the late constable and the young Bourbon princes, Henry of Navarre and Henry I of Condé, who had survived the massacre by forced conversion. Their figurehead was the king's youngest brother, Francis, duke of Alençon. In Languedoc Damville moved into alliance with the Huguenots. Although a peace had been negotiated outside La Rochelle, the south remained defiant and the plots of the politiques continued within the royal court. A few weeks before the death of Charles IX in May 1574, the plans of the conspirators leaked out, and there was a series of arrests. At the news of his brother's death, the new sovereign, Henry III, was in Poland, where he had been elected king a year earlier. When he returned to France, he found a new civil war about to commence. Alençon's coalition of politiques and Huguenots was supported by a large German army under Johann Casimir of the Palatinate. After nearly two years of warfare, Henry III granted the Huguenots the most favorable terms they had ever received under the so-called Peace of Monsieur, named after Francis, duke of Alençon, who received Anjou in appanage. The king also called a meeting of the Estates-General at Blois.

The first national Catholic League was formed under the guidance of the House of Guise to combat the indulgence shown to heretics in the Peace of Monsieur. It was the Catholic League's contention that the favorites Henry III had gathered round him, contemptuously named the *mignons*, had perverted royal authority and betrayed the Catholic church. Thus, the League recapitulated the evil counselors theme once advanced by the Huguenots. The Catholic League dominated the Estates-General and committed Henry III to yet another war against the Protestants. Such action was opposed by the jurist Jean Bodin, a member of Alençon's retinue and a deputy in the third estate. Bodin had just published his celebrated work defining the near-absolute sovereignty of the king, *Six livres de la République* (Six Books of the Commonwealth; 1576). When the indecisive war of 1577 was over, Alençon-Anjou intervened in the Netherlands against Spain, a policy condoned but not effectively supported by his brother. In 1579 the queen mother undertook a journey of pacification in the south and negotiated a new treaty with the Huguenots at Nérac, where Henry of Navarre had taken charge of the movement, though not without the jealous rivalry of his cousin, Henry I of Condé. Nevertheless, a new civil war was fought in 1580. The self-interest of the nobles seemed to deny any coherent political or religious theme. At Nancy, Henry of Guise's brother, Charles of Mayenne, conferred with Charles III, duke of Lorraine, and the Calvinist Casimir to concert efforts against Henry III. Meanwhile, the exploitation of the unprivileged by the seigneurs and the warbands provoked ferocious peasant and artisan revolts in Vivarais and Dauphiné. When not indulging in ostentatious religious pieties and the lurid extravagances of the *mignons*, the king busied himself with governmental reforms, ordaining sweeping changes after holding an assembly of notables at Saint-Germain in 1583. In 1584 the political scene was transformed by the death of Anjou. The reconverted Protestant Henry of Navarre was now heir presumptive to the Crown of France.

Catholic Resistance. Now that their leader was so close to the throne, the Huguenots supported theories of dynastic monarchy and abandoned their justification of resistance. Philippe Duplessis-Mornay wrote of kingship by divine right, François Hotman recast his *Francogallia*, and both appealed to Gallican Catholic tradition when they condemned the excommunication of Henry of Navarre and Henry I of Condé by Pope Sixtus V. The revivified Catholic League saw this as politique hypocrisy and began to argue in terms of an ancient constitution whereby the Catholicity of the most Christian king had priority over secular arrangements, such as the Salic law of succession. Such was the thesis of Louis D'orléans, whose *Advertissement des catholiques anglois* (Warning from English to French Catholics; 1586) suggested that French Catholics would suffer under a Protestant ruler in the way English Catholics had suffered under

Queen Elizabeth. Moreover, the Catholic League was now very different from its 1576 format. In Paris a revolutionary secret organization of fanatical Catholics known as "the Sixteen" was set up. A few members of the high magistracy were to be found in its ranks, but its strength was in lesser clergy, bourgeois merchants and officials, attorneys, artisans, and laborers. In many other towns that had experienced the threat or actuality of Protestant takeovers, Catholic notables formed leaguer councils and cooperated with noble clients of the Guisard faction.

Henry III hoped to create his own faction by advancing the fortunes of his two *archimignons*, Jean-Louis de Nogaret and Anne d'Arques, respectively dukes of Épernon and Joyeuse, but the former leaned toward Navarre while the latter had ties with the Catholic League. Having allied itself with Spain by the Treaty of Joinville, the League obliged the king to declare war on the Huguenots. This strange three-cornered contest has been called the "War of the Three Henries" (Henry III, Henry of Guise, and Henry of Navarre). Joyeuse was sent with a royal army against Navarre in the south. Guise commanded a force opposing a German army that had marched through Burgundy and was approaching Paris. Épernon was given control of a third army, which the king held in reserve in the hope that Guise would fail in his task and be discredited, and that Épernon would come forward at the vital moment to secure victory. Joyeuse, according to this plan, would have disposed of Navarre, leaving the king supreme. Events did not turn out this way. Navarre's veterans shattered the glittering ranks of the *mignons* and killed Joyeuse at Coutras, and Guise defeated the Germans, obliging the king to send Épernon to escort them to the frontier before Guise could further exploit his success. Meanwhile, in Paris the Sixteen were acting in increasing independence of the Guisard leadership and planned coups against the royal government. These plots were frustrated by a secret agent in their midst who was reporting the details to the chancellor, Philippe Hurault de Cheverny.

In May 1588 the Sixteen activated their revolutionary organization in all the sixteen districts of Paris (hence their sobriquet). Guise had entered the capital in open defiance of the king's command, and royal troops had been stationed at strategic points in the city to cow the populace. The troops soon found themselves blocked by the barricades erected by the militants. Henry III's nerve failed him, and he issued no orders to the soldiers, who were rescued by Guise. As the revolutionaries threatened to trap the king in the Louvre, he and his court fled ignominiously by an unguarded gate. A revolutionary commune was installed in the Hôtel de Ville, and the humiliated sovereign was obliged to recognize it and to surrender to the Catholic League by signing the Edict of Union in July. The defeat of the Spanish Armada by the English lifted his morale, and he began to plot his revenge. In September he replaced his chief ministers, partly to secure servants who would accept the coup

he had in mind and partly to use them as scapegoats during the inevitable criticism his regime would receive from another meeting of the Estates-General he had convened at Blois. Just before Christmas 1588 Henry III used the assembly as the forum for his masterstroke. He arrested the leading deputies of the league and had his guardsmen murder the duke of Guise and his brother, Louis, cardinal of Guise.

Leaguer reaction to the royal coup was like the Huguenot response to the Saint Bartholomew's Day Massacre. Indeed, in some respects it was even more radical. Tyrannicide was a minor theme in Huguenot polemic, but the Catholic League described Henry III as the biblical tyrant Holofernes and called for a new Judith to destroy him. At the end of July 1589, the friar Jacques Clément was to answer the call. In the meantime the Catholic League developed doctrines of popular sovereignty similar to those of the Huguenots but with the added edge that there was a greater measure of effective popular participation in leaguer affairs. Moreover, the League combined its secular theories with advocacy of the right of the church and of the pope especially to depose a ruler who endangered the spiritual welfare of his subjects. Such exhortations were preached in fiery sermons by the parish priests and codified, with additional personal invective, by Jean Boucher, associate of the Sixteen, curé of Saint-Benoît, and an influential member of the Sorbonne (the Faculty of Theology of Paris). His *De justa Henrici tertii abdicatione* (Just Deposition of Henry III; 1589) appeared in Latin after the regicide and included vilification of his would-be successor. After the Blois coup, when popular indignation was at its height, the Sorbonne deposed the last Valois, and its sentence was registered by the leaguer Parlement of Paris, which had been purged of politique members. The Council of Forty was created by the league to act as a national government in conjunction with Charles of Guise, duke of Mayenne and lieutenant general of the kingdom. Navarre's uncle, the cardinal of Bourbon, was declared king as Charles X, even though he remained in his nephew's custody. Nearly all the major cities supported the Catholic League. In desperation Henry III had turned to Navarre, who united his forces with the remains of the royal army in April 1589. The two were advancing on Paris when the assassin's knife ended the Valois dynasty.

Henry IV was nothing if not a pragmatist. The first Bourbon king had to balance the need to retain the loyalty of his Protestant followers against the necessity to win the support of moderate Catholics. At this stage he could not contemplate another religious conversion, but he readily declared Catholicism to be the official religion of state and offered his protection to all who would submit to him. While he could not win over some of the most powerful of the late king's courtiers, such as the self-serving Épernon, his attitude prevented the defection to the League of many Gallican bishops and won over many Catholic magistrates, who regarded themselves as the protectors of national independence for both church and state and abhorred the league's ultramontane alliances with the pope and Spain. Henry IV's immediate task was also to defeat Mayenne's armies in the field. He achieved substantial victories at Arques and Ivry and in the spring of 1590 laid siege to the capital.

The Sixteen ruled Paris with a reign of terror, beating and hanging suspected politiques. They replaced those curés not of their persuasion, but they failed to make any basic change in the structure of municipal government. Despite the committees they had established in each city district, they could not prevent men more moderate than themselves from winning places in elections to the Hôtel de Ville. The leaguer Parlement protested against Sixteen terrorism, and several notables who had been members of the Sixteen at the beginning withdrew from the group, whose leadership devolved upon lesser men of the law. The latter criticized Mayenne's conduct of affairs and even wrote independently to the pope and the king of Spain to request direct assistance. After enduring extreme hardships during the six-month siege of 1590, Paris was saved by a Spanish army from the Netherlands commanded by Alessandro Farnese, duke of Parma. Other leaguer towns showed an independence of Mayenne and at the same time experienced internal divisions. Some, such as Bayeux, Toulouse, and Marseille, endured the rule of popular demagogues, and many suffered from plague and famine. To add to the problems of the Catholic League, the cardinal of Bourbon died in 1590. The principle of electing a Catholic king was now widely accepted, but there were too many candidates among the princes of Guise, Lorraine, and even Savoy. Rival English and Spanish armies operated in Brittany and Normandy, and in both these provinces peasant revolts broke out. Charles Emmanuel I, duke of Savoy, invaded Provence, only to find himself opposed by a local faction of leaguer nobles. Amid all this disaffection there probably remained a majority of Catholics who preferred the Catholic League to a Protestant king.

As the magistracy and the Mayenniste faction began to regain authority in Paris, the Sixteen reverted to terrorism. In November 1591 they summarily executed three of the judges, including Barnabé Brisson, a distinguished jurist who was acting as the head of the leaguer Parlement. Mayenne marched into the capital with his own guards, occupied the Bastille, hanged four of the Sixteen, and drove the others into hiding. A year later, however, he was obliged once again to countenance the political activities of the radicals in order to counterbalance the spread of politique opinion. With an eye to the continuance of his own authority, he postponed the meeting of the leaguer Estates-General intended to elect a Catholic king. Meanwhile, the League's military situation continued to deteriorate. Rouen was saved from the English and royal armies besieging it only by another intervention on the part of the duke of Parma.

When Mayenne finally convoked the Estates-General in Paris at the beginning of 1593, the occasion marked the final turning point in the religious wars. The instructions with which the deputies had been provided called for the election of a French Catholic prince to the throne and sweeping constitutional changes, such as the strict control of taxation by an annual national assembly, the provision of local estates in every province, and the representation of the provinces on the royal council. A Spanish envoy at the Estates-General took the initiative in proposing as sovereign the Infanta, Isabella Clara Eugénie, the daughter of Elisabeth de Valois (sister to the last Valois kings) and Philip II. To this the leaguer Parlement responded with a declaration in favor of a male French sovereign as allegedly prescribed by constitutional law. The Spaniards shifted ground to suggest joint rule by the Infanta and a suitable prince to whom she would be married, but by this time a different initiative had appeared in another quarter. With masterly timing Henry IV declared his willingness to accept instruction in the Catholic faith. The Sixteen fulminated against this arch-hypocrisy, as they did against the military truce negotiated at the time. In due course Henry IV attended Mass, and the Estates-General, after voting to receive the decrees of the Council of Trent, faded away without accomplishing anything.

The ultramontane enthusiasm of leaguer extremists had now to contend not only with their opponents' appeal to national patriotism and the Gallican tradition but also with the cold douche of mockery. While the deputies of the Catholic League were meeting in Paris a group of politique writers and jurists secretly circulated the *Satire Ménippée*, a Rabelaisian account of the Estates-General and the family of Guise. It is true that in riposte Louis D'Orléans composed a satire on the lies and lusts of the Béarnais (Henry IV). A third dialogue, less fictitious in nature, was *Dialogue d'entre le Maheustre et le Manant* (Dialogue between the Courtier and the Laborer), also written in 1593 and probably by François Morin de Cromé, one of the most radical of the Sixteen. This piece defended the virtuous Sixteen and attacked the noble leadership of the Catholic League as severely as it did the partisans of Navarre. It was censored by Mayenne and reprinted, with a little doctoring, by royalist propagandists to show how the League was undermining the structure of society. In fact, all three of these satires suggested that the real victims of the conflicts were the common people and that the nobles were continuing the wars at their expense. The massive uprisings of the Croquants, which were about to occur in south-central France, gave some substance to these beliefs. The demands of the leaders of this peasant proletariat, who put differences of religion aside to oppose the nobles and their warbands, revealed the fissures that divided society horizontally.

While the Croquant revolts were gathering strength in Périgord and Limousin in the spring of 1594, Henry IV recovered Paris and Rouen. The son of Henry of Guise came to terms with the king and was rewarded with the governorship of Provence, from which office he expelled the defiant Épernon. In 1595 Mayenne submitted and the pope granted absolution to the king. Of all the leaguer grandees only Philippe-Émmanuel de Lorraine, duke of Mercoeur and the Guisard governor of Brittany, continued to offer opposition. Henry IV still faced many problems. Since his conversion the Huguenots regarded him with suspicion and cooperated grudgingly in the open war with Spain he was now conducting. Tax revenues were only slowly recovered from the towns and provinces that had recently submitted, and the costs of buying the allegiance of the leaguer grandees were exorbitant. Nor did he readily receive the aid he requested from an assembly of notables summoned to Rouen in 1596. Nevertheless, the king was able to impose peace in 1598 and to turn to the reconstruction of the country. Following a treaty with Mercoeur, the king's agents concluded long negotiations with the Huguenots to grant a new edict of toleration at Nantes and then signed a peace agreement with Spain.

The religious wars ended not only because of the exhaustion of the combatants but because of the fear of anarchy from below. The governing classes ultimately shelved their differences and looked in common to the Crown as the only force that could restore order. At the same time, the lower orders appealed to the king to end the wars and protect them from their superiors. In these circumstances Henry IV and his minister, Maximilien de Béthune (later duke of Sully), were able to lay the foundations of Bourbon absolutism. The failure of the Huguenot and leaguer revolts had implanted a distrust of the representative institutions to which they had appealed. Gallican, royalist, and politique doctrines became the new secular credo. They included the responsibility of the king to God alone, the vesting of legislative sovereignty in the Crown, and the dominance of the interest of state over private privilege and corporative right. As for religion, the Huguenots were to remain for a time a minority with legal rights and a measure of military independence, and the zeal of the Catholic League was to be transmuted into the seventeenth-century revival of Catholic spirituality.

[See also Amboise, Conspiracy of; Catherine de Médicis; Catholic League; Charles IX of France; Elizabeth I of England; Henry III of France; Henry IV of France; Johann Casimir; Lorraine-Guise, House of; Poissy, Colloquy of; Politiques; Saint Bartholomew's Day Massacre; Valois, House of; Wassy, Massacre of.]

BIBLIOGRAPHY

Barnavi, Elie. Le parti de Dieu: Étude sociale et politique des chefs de la Ligue parisienne, 1585–1594. Louvain, 1980. Treats the Sixteen as a revolutionary movement.
Baumgartner, Frederic J. Radical Reactionaries: The Political Thought of the French Catholic League. Geneva, 1976.
———. Change and Continuity in the French Episcopate: The Bishops and the Wars of Religion, 1547–1610. Durham, N.C., 1986. Useful for the political alignment of the bishops during the Catholic League.
Benedict, Philip. Rouen during the Wars of Religion. Cambridge, 1981. This book provides demographic details for Huguenots and Catholic Leaguers.
Bitton, Davis. The French Nobility in Crisis, 1560–1640. Stanford, Calif., 1969. Discusses the economic fortunes of the nobility in the Wars of Religion
Buisseret, David. Sully and the Growth of Centralized Government in France, 1598–1610. London, 1968. Shows the effects of the civil wars.
Davis, Natalie Zemon. Society and Culture in Early Modern France. Reprint, Cambridge, 1987. Analyzes popular culture and rationalizes religious iconoclasm and massacre.
Dewald, Jonathan. The Formation of a Provincial Nobility: The Magistrates of the Parlement of Rouen, 1499–1610. Princeton, 1980. Argues that the provincial nobility of sword and robe formed an integrated class.
Diefendorf, Barbara B. Beneath the Cross: Catholics and Huguenots in Sixteenth-Century Paris, New York, 1991.
Farr, James R. Hands of Honor: Artisans and Their World in Dijon, 1550–1640. Ithaca, N.Y., 1988.
Greengrass, Mark. France in the Age of Henri IV: The Struggle for Stability. London, 1984.
Hickey, Daniel. The Coming of French Absolutism: The Struggle for Tax Reform in the Province of Dauphiné, 1540–1640. Toronto, 1986. Examines the economic tension between the social orders and reactions to centralization.
Holt, Mack P. The Duke of Anjou and the Politique Struggle during the Wars of Religion. Cambridge, 1986.
Huppert, George. Les Bourgeois Gentilshommes: An Essay on the Definition of Elites in Renaissance France. Chicago, 1977. Examines cultural disparities between the orders.
Kelley, Donald R. The Beginning of Ideology: Consciousness and Society in the French Reformation. Cambridge, 1981. Discusses the genesis of ideas in their social and political context.
Kingdon, Robert M. Myths about the Saint Bartholomew's Day Massacres, 1572–1576. Cambridge, Mass., 1988. Discusses the nature and diffusion of Huguenot propaganda.
Lloyd, Howell A. The State, France, and the Sixteenth Century. London, 1983. Discusses the development of concepts of the state in the light of religious and economic problems and government policies.
Major, J. Russell. Representative Government in Early Modern France. New Haven, 1980. Especially strong on local institutions. Regards sixteenth-century French government as essentially decentralized.
Neuschel, Kristen B. Word of Honor: Interpreting Noble Culture in Sixteenth-Century France. Ithaca, N.Y., 1989. A study of noble patronage based on the clientèle of Louis I of Condé.
Roelker, Nancy Lyman. Queen of Navarre, Jeanne d'Albret. Cambridge, Mass., 1968.
Salmon, J. H. M. Society in Crisis: France in the Sixteenth Century. Rev. ed. London, 1979.
———. Renaissance and Revolt: Essays on the Intellectual and Social History of Early Modern France. Cambridge, 1987. Contains essays on peasant revolts, the Sixteen, and political thought.
Schalk, Ellery. From Valor to Pedigree: Ideas of Nobility in France in the Sixteenth and Seventeenth Centuries. Princeton, 1986. Suggests that the change in emphasis from virtue to lineage in defenses of the nobility of the sword resulted from criticism of noble behavior in the civil wars.
Sutherland, N. M. Princes, Politics and Religion, 1547–1589. London, 1984. Contains valuable essays on Catherine de Médicis and other leading personalities in the religious wars.
Yardeni, Myriam. La conscience nationale en France pendant les guerres de religion. Paris, 1971. Traces the growth of patriotic sentiment in reaction to the Catholic League.

J. H. M. SALMON

WASSY, MASSACRE OF. The small town of Wassy (spelled Vassy in the sixteenth century, when the population was about three thousand) lies in southeast Champagne, twelve miles west of Joinville. The massacre of French Protestants that occurred there on 1 March 1562 was one of many in the period, but it is particularly significant as a vital link in the chain of events leading to the outbreak of the first religious war in France. This is because, unlike most other such atrocities, it was personally directed by one of the great princes of France, François de Guise. With the constable of France, Anne de Montmorency, and Marshal Saint-André, Guise had formed a triumvirate to oppose the policy of the queen mother, Catherine de Médicis, who had tried to impose toleration by issuing the Edict of January six weeks before the massacre.

Joinville, a rival administrative center to Wassy, was the base of the Guise family. Within Wassy royal officials, conducting a feud with Protestant members of the town council, had for some time been importuning the Guises at Joinville to suppress the local Calvinist church. On 1 March François de Guise, accompanied by members of his family and an armed escort of 200 men, passed through Wassy when a Protestant service, attended by at least 500 people, was being lawfully conducted in a barn near the Catholic church. According to a speech later made by Guise to the Parlement of Paris, he had sent some gentlemen to remonstrate peacefully with the worshipers, who stoned and fired upon them. His soldiers then fired through the windows of the barn, and he and some of his men entered, killing and mutilating men, women, and children. Some were shot as they escaped through the roof, and others burst out and were cut down in the streets.

According to Protestant accounts, the massacre had been premeditated, and there had been no provocation. Contemporary Protestant estimates of casualties were some 50 dead and 250 wounded. A pro-Guise pamphlet suggests half that number. A Protestant version had it that the Wassy militia had prepared in advance to join Guise in the killing, but it also reported that Guise disciplined the militia captain for failing to act earlier against the Huguenots. Subsequent judicial inquiries tended to favor the Catholic interpretation. The massacre took place at a time of great political and religious tension. The declaration of Louis de Condé, the Protestant leader, which began the first war, was issued a month after its occurrence.

[See also Wars of Religion.]

BIBLIOGRAPHY

Cimber, L., and F. Danjou, eds. *Archives curieuses de l'histoire de France.* Paris, 1835. See vol. 4 (1st ser.) pp. 103–65, where four contemporary sources are reproduced; the first and third provide the Protestant interpretation, the second and fourth the Catholic.

J. H. M. SALMON

WATT, Joachim von. *See* Vadian, Joachim.

WEBER THESIS. Since the seventeenth century, commentators have posited a connection between Protestantism and economic development. Of all the interpretations advanced, the one propounded by the German sociologist Max Weber (1864–1920) has proved the most compelling and controversial.

Weber argued that capitalistic enterprise and entrepreneurs had long existed throughout the world. But in the post-Reformation Occident appeared a new form of capitalism, characterized by the rational organization of formally free labor and a distinctive ethos fusing systematic and relentless pursuit of profit through continuous, rational enterprise with severe restrictions on consumption. Espousing methodical capital accumulation and this-worldly asceticism, the capitalist spirit that now legitimated and directed economic activity differed radically from what Weber termed "traditionalism," the morality of customary levels of income for the many, ostentatious but guilt-ridden consumption for the few, and dutiful observance of inherited norms that animated other economic systems.

The new spirit was rooted in Protestant doctrines, Weber asserted. He did not claim that reformers, many of them hostile to economic change, deliberately promoted capitalism, but that over time certain of their teachings about justification and salvation were elaborated in ways that unintentionally fostered and sanctioned capitalist behavior. Calvinist notions of predestination and God's utter transcendence in particular induced profound anxiety among believers lacking ecclesiastical mediation or rituals for atonement. Puritan divines taught, however, that the faithful could attain some assurance of their own election while glorifying God by observing a code (the Protestant ethic) comprising assiduous practice of a vocation—a worldly occupation that fulfilled divinely stipulated tasks—and an ascetic lifestyle. Adherents of sects, even those rejecting a predestinarian creed, were likewise urged to prove their membership among the regenerate by conducting themselves according to the same code.

Embraced by the bourgeoisie, this ethos had momentous effects, Weber believed, even after the initial religious impulses receded. Continuous moneymaking, at first a means of honoring God, turned into an end in itself; systematic, rational planning and discipline, originally mandated to control sinful human nature, came to govern all relations; the drive to demonstrate election by ceaseless activity and self-scrutiny became the dynamic that impelled the unceasing competition and innovation intrinsic to capitalism.

Many sociologists value the Weber thesis for the methodological principles and concepts it embodies, as well as for shedding light on such general issues as the influence of belief systems on behavior, the demystification of Western life and thought, and the often paradoxical dynamics of the modernization process. For a variety of epistemological, conceptual, and empirical reasons, however, historians frequently question the validity of the thesis as an account of early modern European religious, social, and economic development. They argue that Weber relied on atypical texts, adopted an untenable idealist approach, proposed an inconsistent and indefinite theory that cannot be tested, ignored alternative explanations of his findings, oversimplified and misunderstood the phenomena he described, and failed to articulate clear and convincing causal relationships among them. Not all these criticisms carry equal weight, for Weber is repeatedly misread and his position misrepresented. Nevertheless, he often presented his ideas in ambiguous ways and cited insufficient evidence to sustain his thesis.

Yet if many scholars have rejected the Weber thesis, some have tried to reformulate it more persuasively. The best known attempt, R. H. Tawney's *Religion and the Rise of Capitalism* (London, 1926), agrees with Weber that Calvinism inadvertently produced an ideology justifying acquisitive, individualistic capitalism. But what to Weber represented the transformative secularization of essentially religious notions, Tawney regarded as the ascendancy of elements inherent in Calvinism. In his view, Calvin and his followers had always commended the economic virtues of the urban industrial and commercial classes to whom their message was primarily directed, seeking only to moralize economic endeavor. Before about 1650, collectivist and regulative elements of their tenets prevailed, pointing business activities toward the creation of a sanctified society. After that point, however, the unabashed expression of an expansive capitalist spirit triumphed as a result of economic and political change. Entrepreneurs now validated their behavior by invoking Calvinist precepts that harmonized with their individualistic mentality, while ignoring an equally Calvinist ethic of social obligation.

More recently, Gordon Marshall has defended a revised version of Weber's thesis by reference to Scotland, a case usually thought to refute it. Despite Weber's own caveats, the thesis has also been extended across subject, space, and time. Michael Walzer has portrayed Puritanism as a disciplining revolutionary ideology; other scholars have sought to employ Weber's insights in studies of topics as diverse as secularization in modern America and third world economic development.

On several occasions, the debate over the Weber thesis has been declared completed. But the continuing salience of issues it raises—from the impact of ideas on society, to interpretive approaches to knowledge, to the emergence of "economic man"—suggests that its contributions are not yet exhausted.

[*See also* Capitalism.]

BIBLIOGRAPHY

Green, Robert W., ed. *Protestantism, Capitalism, and Social Science: The Weber Thesis Controversy.* 2d ed. Lexington, Mass., 1973. Includes excerpts from Weber and several of the leading proponents and critics of his thesis.

Lehmann, Hartmut, and Günther Roth, eds. *Weber's Protestant Ethic: Origins, Evidence, Contexts.* Cambridge, 1993. Essays giving an overview of Weber's scholarship, its critics, and alternative interpretations.

Marshall, Gordon. *Presbyteries and Profits: Calvinism and the Development of Capitalism in Scotland, 1560–1707.* Oxford, 1980.

———. *In Search of the Spirit of Capitalism.* New York, 1982. The best recent explication of Weber's work and the controversies surrounding it. Includes a comprehensive bibliography and chronology of Weber's works in translation.

Poggi, Gianfranco. *Calvinism and the Capitalist Spirit.* Amherst, Mass., 1983. An exposition and extension of the argument in *The Protestant Ethic* in light of Weber's other works.

Schluchter, Wolfgang. *The Rise of Western Rationalism: Max Weber's Developmental History.* Berkeley, 1981. Originally published as *Die Entwicklung des okzidentalen Rationalismus*, Tübingen, 1979. Examines the process of rationalization depicted in *The Protestant Ethic* as well as in Weber's other contributions to the sociology of religion.

Walzer, Michael. *The Revolution of the Saints: A Study in the Origins of Radical Politics.* Cambridge, Mass., 1965.

Weber, Max. *General Economic History* (1923). New Brunswick, N.J., 1981. Compiled after Weber's death from lecture notes taken by his students, it contains a brief statement of the thesis within a multifaceted definition of capitalism and account of its emergence.

———. *The Protestant Ethic and the Spirit of Capitalism* (1904–1905). London, 1991. The original and fullest presentation of the Weber thesis.

Zawart, Anscar. "The History of Franciscan Preaching and of the Franciscan Preachers, 1209–1927." *Franciscan Studies* 7 (1928), 418–423. A useful brief survey with a full list of Wild's published writings.

ROBERT S. DUPLESSIS

WEDDINGS. In the Roman empire wedding ceremonies were secular affairs that did not involve the participation of any religious leaders. They centered on a procession of the bride and her attendants to the groom's house, followed by a celebratory meal. By the fifth and sixth centuries Christians were expected to include a nuptial blessing by a priest as part of their wedding ritual; in Italy this was usually bestowed at the church door and in France as the newly married couple lay in bed. This blessing never became an absolute requirement for a valid marriage in the Middle Ages, however, for church leaders continued to accept the Roman notion that the consent of the two parties was the key element in any marriage. The exchange of marriage vows came to be considered a sacrament, administered by the couple to each other; only after this was done did the priest bless the union.

Though in theory a couple's free exchange of consent was all that was required for Christian marriage before the Reformation, canon lawyers and other church officials increasingly held that in order to be completely legitimate, a wedding ceremony should involve an announcement of the couple's intention to marry prior to the wedding (this came to be termed "reading the wedding banns"), a public exchange of vows, a wedding ring, marriage gifts, and a priestly blessing. None of these was absolutely required, however, and despite numerous prohibitions of clandestine weddings at many medieval church councils, the church continued to regard those who married in secret as having a valid marriage. This created great confusion, for it could set the word of one spouse against the other as to whether there had actually been a freely given agreement to marry; agreements made in taverns, for example, were often disputed.

Most medieval weddings were not secret, however, but public occasions, with the priest gradually assuming a more prominent role, though this varied throughout Europe. In England and France weddings began to be celebrated inside the church in the fourteenth century, though in Germany they were still held at the church door and in Italy normally in private homes, with upper-class families only rarely asking for a priestly blessing as part of the ceremony. Medieval weddings often involved a procession from the bride's house to the church and from there to the groom's house—or, in Italy, directly from the bride's house to the groom's—accompanied by loud music, shouting, and the shooting off of guns, followed by feasting and dancing that could go on for several days. Because of the raucous nature of these celebrations, the church usually forbade weddings during Lent or other periods of fasting and penitence. Folk customs thought to encourage procreation, such as pouring grain on the bride's head, were also a significant part of weddings in many areas, and the whole ceremony was seen as an opportunity for lewd jokes, drinking bouts, and love songs.

During the late Middle Ages both church and civil authorities attempted to restrict the festivities that accompanied wedding ceremonies, the church primarily on moral grounds and city governments on both moral and financial grounds. City sumptuary laws set limits on the amount that could be spent on any wedding and the number of guests that could be invited, though upper-class citizens were permitted larger and more costly weddings than lower-class citizens.

Such restrictions on weddings increased in severity and scope in Protestant areas after the Reformation. Many Protestant church authorities adopted wedding liturgies that required that the ceremony take place within the church and mandated that the wedding banns be read three times before the wedding. Though there was disagreement, some Protestant writers thought that marriages made in secret should be declared completely invalid. Martin Luther and John Calvin both argued that parental consent should be required for a valid marriage, an idea that some Protestant areas wrote into law. Protestant secular authorities, such as princes and

city councils, attempted to limit wedding celebrations even more than had pre-Reformation authorities. They passed wedding ordinances that forbade those who had not attended the church service from attending the feast that followed, prohibited the reciting of obscene poetry, and forbade the guests to accompany the bride and groom to their marriage bed, a practice that had been the occasion of much drinking and joking. In an attempt to downplay the physical side of marriage, clergy were forbidden to bless the bridal chamber or to participate in any "superstitious" practices involving fertility, such as throwing grain or untying knots. (Tying knots was a common magical practice thought to create impotence in men.)

Judging by how frequently wedding ordinances were reissued, these prohibitions were not initially successful in transforming weddings into solemn occasions. Protestant clergy, recognizing that people would have to be convinced that the proper tone of a wedding was Christian reverence rather than exuberant celebration, began attempting to communicate this in wedding sermons and devotional literature. Collections of wedding sermons were published beginning in the late sixteenth century that were viewed as proper gifts, particularly for brides-to-be. These emphasized the solemnity of the occasion, recommending that joint prayer substitute for the friendly toasting and singing as the final activity of the spouses before entering the marriage bed for the first time. Wedding sermons frequently stressed the proper role of each spouse both in the ceremony and in the marriage to follow; the man was to be authoritative, though loving, and the woman obedient. All popular customs that hinted at the possibility of female dominance, such as the bride's placing her foot over the groom's during the ceremony, were to be avoided.

Catholic wedding practices changed as well after the Council of Trent. The church attempted to impose a uniform ceremony throughout Catholic Europe, substituting the words of the Roman ritual for what had been many local variants. The decree *Tametsi*, adopted by the Council of Trent in 1563, declared that the presence of witnesses and a parish priest were required for a marriage to be considered valid, though it was decades and sometimes centuries before this was fully accepted. Priests were encouraged to urge their parishioners to wait until after the actual wedding ceremony before beginning sexual relations instead of viewing betrothal as the acceptable starting point. They were also encouraged to transform the blessing of the marriage bed from a celebration of fertility into a solemn sermon about marital chastity and to refrain from participating in any noisy and disorderly public celebrations. In attempting to limit the festivities that accompanied weddings, Catholic authorities were both trying to make them more pious and moral and asserting that the approval of the priest, not the community at large, was the most important element.

Despite all attempts by authorities, weddings continued

to be a mixture of the sacred and profane. They included widely varying customs and traditions, some of whose meanings had no doubt long been forgotten by the participants. Perhaps in the long run both the Protestant and Catholic reformations were most successful in their demands that weddings be public matters, but this had been the case with most weddings already. Because the marital couple was the key economic, social, and, in many ways, political unit in European society, the ceremony that transformed two individuals into one couple could not help but have many aspects and many meanings.

[*See also* Family; Marriage; *and* Social Discipline.]

BIBLIOGRAPHY

Belmont, Nicole. "The Symbolic Function of the Wedding Procession in the Popular Rituals of Marriage." In *Ritual, Religion and the Sacred: Selections from the Annales*, edited by Robert Forster and Orest Ranum, pp. 1–7. Baltimore and London, 1982.

Brundage, James A. *Law, Sex and Christian Society in Medieval Europe.* Chicago, 1987. A masterful survey that considers weddings along with many other aspects of sexual and marital life.

Burguière, André. "The Marriage Ritual in France: Ecclesiastical Practices and Popular Practices, Sixteenth to Eighteenth Centuries." In *Ritual, Religion and the Sacred: Selections from the Annales*, edited by Robert Forster and Orest Ranum, pp. 8–23. Baltimore and London, 1982.

Klapisch-Zuber, Christiane. "Zacharias, or the Ousting of the Father: The Rites of Marriage in Tuscany from Giotto to the Council of Trent." In *Ritual, Religion and the Sacred: Selections from the Annales*, edited by Robert Forster and Orest Ranum, pp. 24–56. Baltimore and London, 1982.

Roper, Lyndal. "'Going to Church and Street': Weddings in Reformation Augsburg." *Past and Present* 106 (1985), 62–101.

MERRY E. WIESNER-HANKS

WEIGEL, Valentin (1533–1588), mystic Lutheran pastor in Zschopau (Saxony) whose spiritualist writings, published posthumously, influenced the pietism of Johann Arndt and the mysticism of Jakob Böhme. Born in Naundorf (Saxony), Weigel studied at Leipzig and Wittenberg before accepting a pastorate at Zschopau in 1567. Although his published writings denounced the institutional church and doctrinal theology, he was a popular preacher and was frequently commended by his superintendent for his charitable work among the poor. In 1572 Weigel wrote a tract defending his orthodoxy, *Ein Büchlein vom wahren seligmachenden Glauben* (A Booklet on True, Soulsaving Faith), and he signed the Formula of Concord (1576) without apparent hesitation. Throughout his life Weigel successfully concealed most of his radical ideas. But after his death, his published writings reveal the work of a radical spiritualist who sought to synthesize the late medieval mysticism of Thomas à Kempis, Johannes Tauler, Johannes (Meister) Eckehart, and the *Theologia Deutsch* with the thought of Sebastian Franck and Paracelsus.

Weigel's thought defies easy summary. His emphasis on the imminence of God in all creation has led many scholars to describe him as a pantheist and a gnostic theosophist. In his complex blend of philosophy and theology, Weigel challenged orthodox understandings of heaven and hell, allegorized the Bible almost completely into a cosmic philosophy, and redefined the historical Christ as a divine principle within all humanity. If properly nurtured, he argued, this divine spark in the human soul would eventually supplant scripture, grace, the organized church, theology, and all the historical elements of religion.

Apart from his acknowledged dependence on the writings of Franck, Weigel's relation to the broader radical Reformation is not clear. His strident renunciation of all lawsuits, interest on loans, oath swearing, and warfare echoes themes dominant among the Anabaptists, and some historians have noted parallels between Weigel's mystical thought and that of Thomas Müntzer. But there is little evidence of direct contact with any specific radicals, and his writings were not widely known until the first half of the seventeenth century. Denounced by orthodox Protestant theologians, "Weigelianism" enjoyed widespread popularity among a heterogeneous array of pietist groups, followers of Böhme, and Rosicrucians throughout the seventeenth and eighteenth centuries.

BIBLIOGRAPHY

Hochhuth, Karl W. H. "Mittheilungen aus der protestantischen Secten-Geschichte in der hessischen Kirche: Die Weigelianer und Rosenkreuzer." *Zeitschrift für die historische Theologie* (1862), 86–159; (1863), 169–253. Provides an overview of Weigel's intellectual legacy, particularly in its relation to the Rosicrucian movement.

Israel, August. *M. Valentin Weigels Leben und Schriften.* Zschopau, Germany, 1888. A careful bibliography of Weigel's manuscript and published works; includes summaries and excerpts from his writing.

Koyré, Alexandre. *Mystiques, spirituels, alchimistes du XVIe siècle allemand.* Paris, 1971. See the chapter on Valentin Weigel, pp. 131–184.

Maier, Hans. *Der Mystische Spiritualismus Valentin Weigels.* Gütersloh, 1926. An insightful summary of Weigel's thought and influence.

Stockum, Th. C. van. *Valentin Weigel, Doper en Paracelsist.* Amsterdam, 1948. As the title suggests, situates Weigel within the context of Anabaptist and Paracelsian thought.

Wehr, Gerhard. *Alle Weisheit ist von Gott: Gestalten und Wirkungen Christlicher Theosophe.* Gütersloh, 1980. Gives brief sketches of Weigel, J. V. Andreä, Böhem, Ötinger, and Michael Idahn, and the tradition of Christian theosophy.

Weigel, Valentin. *Sämtliche Schriften.* Edited by Will Erich Peuckert and Winfried Zeller. Stuttgart, 1966–1978.

JOHN D. ROTH

WEIGELIN, Sebastian. *See* Lotzer, Sebastian.

WELFARE. *See* Social Welfare.

WESTPHAL, Joachim (1510–1574), Gnesio-Lutheran controversialist pastor and church administrator in Hamburg. Westphal studied twice in Wittenberg and taught linguistics for a brief period. In 1541 he became pastor in Hamburg and a superintendent in 1571 (after 9 years of acting in that capacity). He participated in the Hamburg controversy over the descent of Christ into hell and in the polemics against the Interim of 1548. In the 1550s he was the leading Lutheran spokesman in the second controversy over the Lord's Supper. His anti-Interim "Over Aaron's Golden Calf" placed him in opposition to Melanchthon, who had been engaged in developing Elector Moritz of Saxony's response. Yet Westphal may have genuinely expected his preceptor's support in his battle against the doctrine of the spiritual presence of Christ in the Eucharist, for if Melanchthon was accused of giving in too much on the Interim, the Catholics too believed in the bodily presence.

The arrival in 1549 of Albert Hardenberg, former associate of Martin Bucer and friend of the Calvinist Jan Łaski, in Bremen and of Dutch refugees from England who sought exile in northern Germany worried Westphal. Łaski informed Calvin of Westphal's attack on their doctrine of the Eucharist, which Westphal equated also with that of "a certain Dutchman," by whom he meant Cornelis Hoen. When Calvin responded, the polemic was on.

Melanchthon sought to stay out of the fray, but, pressured to disavow Calvin—who had accepted Melanchthon's formula in the *Variata* (1541)—he chose to reject the doctrine of ubiquity which most Gnesio-Lutherans, including Westphal, used in defense of the bodily presence of Christ. Melanchthon wrote that this doctrine reopened the door to "papist" errors. The results of the polemics were that the Dutch refugees were not allowed to settle; Hardenberg was forced to leave; and the Lutherans reaffirmed the doctrine of the bodily presence.

BIBLIOGRAPHY

Pettegree, Andrew. "The London Exile Community and the Second Sacramentarian Controversy, 1553–1560." *Archiv für Reformationsgeschichte* 78 (1987), 223–252. Provides a welcome analysis of the controversy's issues and of Westphal's role. Bibliographical information in notes.

Schade, Herwarth von. *Joachim Westphal und Peter Braubach.* Hamburg, 1981. Westphal's correspondence on religious developments with his friend, a major publisher in Frankfurt. Useful discussion of context.

DERK VISSER

WEYER, Johann (also Weier; 1515–1588), prominent physician and early opponent of witch trials. Weyer was born the son of a merchant in Brabant. As a student of the humanist philosopher Cornelius Agrippa, who had won the acquittal of an accused witch in a much-publicized trial in 1519, Weyer acquired a lifelong interest in exploring the grounds and mitigating the frightful consequences of such accusations. He studied medicine at the universities of Paris and Orléans, where he graduated as a doctor of medicine in 1537. In 1550 he was named personal physician to Duke William of Jülich-Cleve.

Under the protection of this tolerant ruler, Weyer developed his theory attributing most witchcraft confessions to the melancholic delusions of mentally impaired older women. His conclusions were published as *De praestigiis daemonum* (On the Deception of Demons) in 1563 and repeated in a condensed version, *De lamiis* (On Witches), in 1577. Using medical, legal, and religious arguments, he sought to prove that the devil implanted in minds weakened by age, sickness, and hallucinogenic unguents fantasies associated with the practice of witchcraft—flying through the air, consorting with demons, causing bad weather and other malicious mischief, and, most important, the pact with the devil bestowing these miraculous powers. As hapless dupes of the devil, according to Weyer, the witches were essentially harmless and should not be tortured or punished. Torture itself, he pointed out, often extracted false confessions to win release from unbearable pain.

While not denying the reality of pacts with the devil, Weyer argued that, being contracts between unequal partners as between an adult and an infant, they were invalid in the case of witches, but not, however, in the case of magicians (*magi infames*) who knowingly sought the devil's connivance. Weyer's contention that a witch's crime was strictly spiritual and outside the competence of secular authority challenged the late medieval doctrine of equating witchcraft with the heresy of devil worship, a capital offense whether or not the alleged crime had harmed anyone. Weyer followed Erasmus in reasoning that heresy should be treated with Christian instruction rather than punishment.

Weyer's confessional allegiance has been disputed by historians because, although he gave no credence to Catholic rites and charms to counteract the power of the devil, his writings do not give a clear evidence of Protestant conversion. He appears to have been less concerned with doctrinal differences than with fostering a more humane approach to the problem of witchcraft on both sides of the religious divide. His view that those bewitched or afflicted by demonic powers should seek relief in prayer and the strength of their Christian faith indicates a Protestant bias. Weyer's treatise, which was placed on the Index of Prohibited Books, won few adherents and abundant criticism from contemporaries, most notably from Jean Bodin and Johannes Brenz. Scholars continue to debate his overall impact on the witch craze.

BIBLIOGRAPHY

Primary Source

Wieri, Johannes. *Opera Omnia.* Amsterdam, 1660.

Secondary Sources

Baxter, Christopher. "Johann Weyer's *De Praestigiis Daemonum*: Unsystematic Psychopathology." In *The Damned Art*, edited by Sydney Anglo. London, 1977. Challenges claims for Weyer's positive influence on witch hunting. Gives direct quotes from Weyer in French translation.

Binz, Carl. *Doktor Johann Weyer, ein rheinischer Artzt, der erste Bekämpfer des Hexenwahns*. Bonn, 1885. The standard biography.

———. "Weyer, Johann." In *Allgemeine Deutsche Biographie*, vol. 42, pp. 266–270. Berlin, 1897.

Diefenbach, Johann. "Dr. Johann Weyer." In *Der Hexenwahn vor und nach der Glaubensspaltung in Deutschland*, pp. 236–241. Mainz, 1866. A brief overview of Weyer's treatise and its importance.

Midelfort, H. C. Erik. "Johann Weyer and the Transformation of the Insanity Defense." In *The German People and the German Reformation*, edited by R. P. Hsia. Ithaca, N.Y., 1988. Authoritative analysis of Weyer's legal arguments against witch persecution.

Robbins, Rossel H. "Weyer, Johan." In *The Encyclopedia of Witchcraft and Demonology*, pp. 538–540. New York, 1959.

Schneider, U. F. "Das Werk 'De praestigiis daemonum' von Weyer und seine Auswirkungen auf die Bekämpfung des Hexenwahns." Unpublished diss., University of Bonn, 1951. Extensive bibliography.

Schottenloher, Karl, ed. *Bibliographie zur deutschen Geschichte im Zeitalter der Glaubensspaltung*. Stuttgart, 1957. See vol. 2, p. 383.

KARIN BRINKMANN BROWN

WHITAKER, William (1548–1595), English administrator and antipapal polemicist. His career epitomized the penetration of high Calvinist theology and moderate (conforming) Puritan priorities into the late Elizabethan establishment. Born in 1548, the son of well-to-do but determinedly papist Lancashire parents, he was raised as a Protestant by his uncle Alexander Nowell. A pupil at Saint Paul's School, London, and an undergraduate at Trinity College, Cambridge, he rose to become regius professor of divinity in 1580 and was elected master of Saint John's College in 1586.

Whitaker's career was founded on his activities as an antipapal polemicist. Under the patronage of William Cecil and John Whitgift, he wrote six major works refuting catholic writings by the likes of Nicholas Sanders, Edmund Campion, Roberto Bellarmino, Thomas Stapleton, and John Dury (Duraeus). His style of divinity was heavily Reformed, or Calvinist. Dedicated to the proposition that the pope was the Antichrist, Whitaker defended the true church in terms of its succession to the doctrine of the apostles, and he juxtaposed the authority of scripture to that of the church and human tradition in a brutally straightforward way. Whitaker's own position was uncompromisingly predestinarian, indeed, supralapsarian. He placed relatively slight emphasis on issues of ceremony or church government. For him the word *episcopus* primarily meant an ordinary minister of the word and only secondarily referred to a human authority raised in the church for the maintenance of order and control of heresy. Whitaker clearly assumed that his own doctrinal position was coterminous with that of the Church of England, an assumption encoded in the Lambeth Articles, which he helped draw up in 1595 as a means of stilling further predestinarian dispute at Cambridge.

Although there is no evidence that Whitaker himself was either a Nonconformist or a presbyterian, he was a known associate of Puritans and ran Saint John's in the interests of the Puritan grouping among the fellows. He faced considerable conformist opposition in the college, but by basing his case on the maintenance of order and of his own powers as master and by showing considerable skill in the manipulation of his links with leading courtiers, he prevailed until his sudden death in 1595 allowed something of a conformist backlash.

BIBLIOGRAPHY

Primary Source

Whitaker, William. *Opera Theologica*. 2 vols. Geneva, 1610.

Secondary Sources

Lake, Peter. *Moderate Puritans and the Elizabethan Church*. Cambridge, 1982.

Porter, Harry C. *Reformation and Reaction in Tudor Cambridge*. Cambridge, 1958.

PETER LAKE

WHITE MOUNTAIN, BATTLE OF. The decisive contest of the Protestant revolt in Bohemia was fought on 8 November 1620 across the "White Mountain" (Bílá Hora), a featureless plateau just west of the city of Prague. Hostilities had begun after the Defenestration of Prague, in 1618, and soon took on European dimensions. The estates of Bohemia raised an army and found support among their predominantly Lutheran neighbors in Silesia, Moravia, and Austria. By the end of 1619 they also secured important Calvinist backing, electing the elector palatine, Frederick V (son-in-law of James I of Great Britain), to the Bohemian throne in place of the Habsburg ruler and entering into alliance with the prince of Transylvania.

But Ferdinand II, the deposed Catholic king, was equally active and proved to have more resources at his disposal. He was able to call on troops provided by the Spanish branch of his dynasty and by the Catholic League in Germany, led by his brother-in-law, Maximilian of Bavaria. His undisputed election as Holy Roman Emperor in August 1619 helped to neutralize most of the Protestant German princes. The French and the Dutch were distracted by internal dissensions, while England sought only a mediatory role. Though it sent an army into Hungary, Transylvania proved an unreliable partner. Thus by 1620 the scales were weighted against victory for the Protestants in Bohemia.

Nevertheless, the scale and suddenness of their eclipse on White Mountain, after a skirmish lasting little more than an hour, took contemporaries by surprise. King Frederick and his entourage panicked and fled the country. Viewing the outcome as divine providence, Ferdinand hastened to expel first the Protestant clergy and then, by 1628, all those who refused to convert to Catholicism. Though their larger plans for the Counter-Reformation throughout the empire failed, the Habsburgs had eliminated, almost at a stroke, one of the most important Protestant communities in Europe.

[*See also* Bohemia *and* Defenestration of Prague.]

BIBLIOGRAPHY

Gindely, Anton. *Geschichte des Dreißgjährigen Kriegs.* 4 vols. Prague, 1869–1880.

Kavka, František. *Bílá Hora a české dějiny.* Prague, 1962. A study of the place of the Thirty Years' War in Bohemian history.

Polišenský, Josef V. *The Thirty Years' War.* London, 1971. Narrative and analysis, from the Bohemian perspective, of the entire conflict unleased by the Defenestration of Prague.

Sturmberger, Hans. *Der Aufstand in Böhmen: Der Beginn des Dreißigjährigen Kriegs.* Munich, 1959. A useful short account of the central European context.

Tapié, Victor-Lucien. *La politique étrangère de la France et le début de la guerre de trente ans, 1616–1621.* Paris, 1934. Major study of the European context of the Bohemian Revolt, which draws on Czech sources.

R. J. W. EVANS

WHITGIFT, John (c. 1530–1604), English prelate. Archbishop of Canterbury for twenty years, Whitgift was a dominating presence in the Elizabethan church. His was a career founded on the favor of the queen and his own strongly authoritarian opposition to Puritanism. The son of a Lincolnshire merchant, Whitgift was educated in Edwardian Cambridge at Queens' and then Pembroke Hall. He became a fellow of Peterhouse in 1555. A Protestant, he weathered Mary Tudor's reign in England and did not take holy orders until 1560. Thereafter, his rise was meteoric. In 1563 he became Lady Margaret professor of divinity, and in 1567 he became briefly master of Pembroke Hall before moving on to Trinity and the regius chair in the same year. All the while he was collecting other preferments—the rectory of Teversham in Lincolnshire in 1560, a prebendal stall at Ely and a royal chaplaincy in 1568, and the deanery of Lincoln in 1571.

By the late 1560s Whitgift's career had taken a definitively anti-Puritan turn. In 1565 he had signed a letter to William Cecil requesting lenience on the issue of the surplice, but thereafter he aligned himself against the godly cause. He was instrumental in drawing up new statutes for the university that greatly enhanced the powers of the Heads of Houses (Masters of the various colleges), and as vice-chancellor he used these new powers to remove Thomas Cartwright from the Lady Margaret chair of divinity. He subsequently deprived Cartwright of his fellowship at Trinity in 1571. The

following year he took up the cudgels against the presbyterian *Admonition to the Parliament* and thereafter became engaged in a long-running polemical exchange with Cartwright. In 1577 he was elevated to the see of Worcester. On the death in 1583 of the disgraced Edmund Grindal, Whitgift succeeded him as archbishop of Canterbury. Almost certainly the queen's personal choice, he now tried to put his anti-Puritan principles into practice by strictly enforcing clerical subscription to three articles endorsing the royal supremacy, the Thirty-nine Articles, and *The Book of Common Prayer.* Many Puritans could not accept this last condition, and a crisis broke out, with privy councillors, Parliament men, and local gentry lined up against the archbishop. Whitgift, in effect, backed down, and many ministers were allowed limited or modified subscription. Throughout the 1580s Whitgift continued to pursue the cause of unity and uniformity by using and strengthening the powers of High Commission and Star Chamber. Whitgift's relationship with the queen remained close, and in 1586 he became the first Elizabethan churchman to be made a privy councillor.

Hitherto his room for anti-Puritan maneuver had been cramped by the influence of such patrons of the godly as the earl of Leicester (Robert Dudley), Francis Walsingham, and Walter Mildway, but in the late 1580s many of these first-generation councillors began to die off. In alliance with Christopher Hatton, the new lord chancellor, Whitgift was able to seize the initiative and definitively crush the organized Puritan movement. The conformist cause was now in the ascendant, and apart from one nasty moment—when it looked briefly as though the new king, James I, might make significant concessions to the Puritans at the Hampton Court Conference—Whitgift was able to hand over the church, the episcopacy, and the prayer book to the safely conformist hands of his protégé Richard Bancroft, his successor as archbishop of Canterbury.

In many ways Whitgift was a conventional Protestant of his generation; he always believed that the pope was the Antichrist, and his commitment to a recognizably Calvinist position on predestination was enshrined in the Lambeth Articles of 1595. Perhaps the most cited text in his antipresbyterian works was John Calvin's assault on the Anabaptists. His defense of the church had always been organized around the twin pillars of the doctrines of adiaphora and of the royal supremacy. Where scripture was silent, the authority of the Christian prince began, and it was in terms of that divinely ordained authority—who applied the scriptural principles of order, decency, unity, and uniformity to the externals of church government and liturgy—that Whitgift defended the status quo. For Whitgift the material interests of the church and the status and wealth of the learned clergy were also at stake in the confrontation with the Puritans, whom he tended to see as an ambitious faction of clerical agitators acting as the cat's-paw for sinister lay interests. It was no accident that Whitgift himself kept a large household, displayed conspicuous hospitality, and was vehement in defense of the right of the clergy to hold high secular office.

As he was not a man of great intellectual flexibility, the polemical logic of his engagement with presbyterianism and his own commitment to the central tenets of the English Reformed tradition prevented Whitgift from developing a subtle or religiously or emotionally compelling rationale for the ecclesiastical status quo. A man with a short temper and an authoritarian cast of mind, he was a natural administrator who both ran and defended the institutions of the English church as he found them. His career was founded on a close bond with the queen (she playfully referred to him as her "little black husband"), and it was fitting that Elizabeth died with Whitgift holding her hand and that he died with the words *pro ecclesia dei* on his lips.

BIBLIOGRAPHY

Primary Source

Whitgift, John. *The Works of John Whitgift* (1851). 3 vols. Reprint, New York, 1968.

Secondary Sources

Collinson, Patrick. *The Elizabethan Puritan Movement.* Reprint, Oxford, 1990.

Dawley, Powel M. *John Whitgift and the Reformation.* London, 1954.

Horie, Hirofumi. "The Origin and Historical Context of Archbishop Whitgift's 'Orders' of 1586." *Archiv für Reformationsgeschichte* 83 (1992), 240–257.

Lake, Peter. *Moderate Puritans and the Elizabethan Church.* Cambridge, 1982.

———. *Anglicans and Puritans? Presbyterianism and English Conformist Thought from Whitgift to Hooker.* London, 1988.

McGinn, Donald J. *The Admonition Controversy.* New Brunswick, N.J., 1949.

Porter, Harry C. *Reformation and Reaction in Tudor Cambridge.* Cambridge, 1958.

Strype, John. *The Life and Acts of John Whitgift.* 3 vols. Oxford, 1822.

PETER LAKE

WIED, Hermann von (1477–1552), elector-archbishop of Cologne. Hermann von Wied was the fourth son of Count Frederick of Wied-Runkel and Agnes of Virneburg. In view of his parents' early death and with no prospect of succession, he was directed to an ecclesiastical career. Already in 1483 he received a benefice (*Domizellarpfründe*) from the Cologne cathedral chapter (which, for reasons of social standing and family politics, was dominated by the sons of the counts of Rhine-Wetterau), in 1490 he was made a full canon, and in 1493 he was admitted to the faculty of law in Cologne, without obtaining a degree. On 14 March 1515 he was elected archbishop. Yet he did not request ordination as bishop until 1518, and his ceremonial entry into Cologne was delayed until 15 July 1522 since the city wanted to have its independence recognized beforehand. In the imperial election of 1519, Hermann favored

Charles V from the beginning, whose coronation he celebrated in Aachen on 23 October 1520. After the Diet of Worms in 1521, he endeavored to enforce the edict against Luther in his territory by actively suppressing followers of the reform and later Anabaptists.

In the first two decades of his rule, Wied enacted mining and mint regulations, reformed law and police, and thus paved the way to the early modern period of government. Moreover, in the interest of their strengthening he pursued reforms of the church. In 1527, for example, in a long-standing dispute over the practice of curial benefits, he decided that he would fill unoccupied benefices in the future, even in the so-called papal months. Reforms in the duchies of Jülich-Cleve-Berg and the Anabaptist kingdom in Münster confirmed for Wied, who had become the administrator of the bishopric of Paderborn in 1532, that continued reforms were necessary.

The reform statutes, drafted by Johannes Gropper and adopted by a provincial synod in March 1536, signaled the transition from pre-Reformation church politics to Catholic reform. The statutes provided for the elimination of abuses, but also demanded the acknowledgement of the papal constitutions and the imperial laws. They were published in 1538, along with Gropper's theological compendium for the instruction of the clergy. The decisions remained on paper, however, which possibly may be traced to the growing influence of Protestant-minded councilors, the sympathies of several counts for the Reformation, and the skeptical reserve of the archbishop.

A new attempt—now more distinctly evangelical—was undertaken after Wied had met with Martin Bucer in Hagenau in 1540 and the Diet of Regensburg in 1541 had urged the Catholic imperial estates to carry out a "Christian order and reformation" in their territories. On 10 May 1542 the provincial estates of the electorate of Cologne demanded that the elector submit the outline of a Christian Reformation. In December Wied directed Bucer to do this. In view of deep theological differences, the collaboration with Gropper did not materialize. Bucer's reform order, on which Philipp Melanchthon collaborated for a while, was based on the Nuremberg-Brandenburg church order of 1533 and other orders. It declared the holy scripture as the only norm of belief. It was evangelical but took tradition into consideration. Although it is unclear to what extent the elector was able to comprehend theological differences, he personally scrutinized the *Einfältige Bedenken*. The order was approved by the provincial diet on 26 July 1543, while the cathedral chapter refused agreement.

Supporters and opponents—the latter had repeatedly demanded Bucer's recall—bolstered their views in pamphlets and also by appeals and protestations. Thus the forces polarized early: counts, knights, and cities as well as a minority of the cathedral chapter supported the elector, while the Cologne city council, the university, the majority of the cathedral chapter, and from 1544, the Jesuits opposed him. Promptly the pope and emperor demanded that Wied rescind the reforms. But the elector held firmly to his reform notions because of his evangelical conviction, despite the worsening political situation (which included the defeat of Jülich-Cleve in the Geldric conflict). The anticipated support of the Schmalkald League, meanwhile, failed to materialize. On 16 April 1546 Wied was excommunicated by Pope Paul II; on 24 January 1547, under imperial pressure, the provincial estates broke with him, so that abdication was the only course that remained for him. He moved to Wied, where he died on 15 August 1552.

A success of the Cologne reformation would have shifted the majority relations in the electoral council in favor of the Protestants and possibly opened the entire northwestern part of the empire to the Reformation. Thus an important bastion for the subsequent advance of the Counter-Reformation remained intact.

BIBLIOGRAPHY

Franzen, August. *Bischof und Reformation: Erzbischof Hermann von Wied in Köln vor der Entscheidung zwischen Reform und Reformation.* 2d ed. Münster, 1972.
Gerhards, H., and Wilhelm Borth, trans. and eds. *Einfältiges Bedenken: Reformationsentwurf für das Erzstift Köln von 1543.* Düsseldorf, 1972.
Jedin, Hubert. "Fragen um Hermann von Wied." *Historisches Jahrbuch* 74 (1955), 687–699.
Pfeilschifter, Georg, ed. *Acta reformationis Catholicae ecclesiam Germaniae concernentia saeculi XVI.* Regensburg, 1959–1974. See vol. 2, pp. 118–318.

GÜNTER VOGLER
Translated from German by Susan M. Sisler

WIENER, Paul (d. 1554), reformer in Slovenia and first superintendent of the Lutherans of Transylvania. He was probably born in Krainburg near Ljubljana (Laibach) in Krain (Slovenia) and studied at the University of Vienna. In 1520 he became a member of the cathedral chapter and also a member of the diet. During the 1530s he became an advocate of reform and assisted Primus Truber in fostering Reformation views among the Slovenes. However, after the battle at Mühlberg, he was arrested for having distributed Communion in both kinds, for having conducted an evangelical memorial service rather than a requiem mass at the funeral of Queen Anna, and for having remarried after the death of his first wife. He was examined by Bishop Urban Textor, taken to Vienna, and examined again on the basis of the confession of faith he had prepared, one that consciously followed the paradigm of the Augsburg Confession. After appealing to the monarch, he was allowed to accept banishment and emigrated to Transylvania.

In 1548 he arrived in Sibiu (Hermannstadt), whose evangelical city pastor, Matthias Ramser, had recently died. In 1549 he was listed as pastor, and in May 1552 he was elected as city pastor after the death of Bartolomäus Altenberger, Ramser's replacement. In February of the following year he was elected the first superintendent, or bishop, of the Lutherans in Transylvania and shortly thereafter ordained six new pastors. However, his term of service was brief. He died during an outbreak of the plague in Sibiu on 16 August 1554. Despite his brief career in Transylvania he helped to set the theological direction followed by his co-worker and successor as city pastor and bishop, Matthias Hebler.

BIBLIOGRAPHY

Elze, Theodor. "Paul Wiener: Mitreformator in Krain, Gebundener des Evangeliums in Wien, erster evangelischer Bischof in Siebenbürgen." *Jahrbuch der Gesellschaft für die Geschichte des Protestantismus in Österreich* 3 (1882), 1–52. This article includes correspondence.
Reinerth, Karl. "Das Glaubensbekenntnis Paul Wieners, des ersten evangelischen Bischofs der Siebenbürgen Sachsen." *Archiv für Reformationsgeschichte* 67 (1976), 203–231.
Teutsch, Georg Daniel. *Die Bischöfe der evangelischen Kirche A.B. in Siebenbürgen.* Pt. 1, *Die Bischöfe der Jahre 1553–1867* (1933). Reprint, Cologne, 1978. See pp. 11–22.

DAVID P. DANIEL

WIGAND, Johann (1523–1587), German Lutheran theologian and bishop. Wigand was born in Mansfeld into a self-consciously Lutheran family. He studied at Wittenberg (1538–1545, interrupting his studies to spend 1541–1544 teaching at Saint Lorenz's school in Nuremberg). Wigand played important roles in many of the mid-sixteenth-century theological controversies of German Lutheranism. His theological influence helped pave the way for the Formula of Concord and the rise of Lutheran orthodoxy later in the century.

During his first pastorate (1546–1553, in Mansfeld, where he taught dialectic and physics in the local school), Wigand showed his commitment to Lutheran doctrine and practice. He published two tracts in 1550 critical of the Mainz Catechism (1549) of Bishop Michael Helding of Sidon (1506–1561). In 1552 Wigand wrote supporting the position of Matthias Flacius Illyricus in the adiaphorist controversy and helped local clergy in their opposition to the appointment of Georg Major as ecclesiastical inspector. In 1553 Wigand published the theological basis for this action in two works against Major's understanding of the necessity of good works for salvation.

In 1553 Wigand moved to Magdeburg as pastor and superintendent of the local *ministerium*. He assumed primary responsibility for editing and writing a history of the church, the *Magdeburg Centuries*, published at Basel from 1559 to 1574. From this work grew Wigand's collaboration with Matthaeus Judex (1528–1564) on the *Syntagma*, analyses of scripture using Melanchthon's Aristotelian dialectical methodology.

In Magdeburg Wigand sought to define Lutheranism vis-à-vis Roman Catholicism: opposing periodic attempts to reintroduce Roman Catholicism and writing against Peter Canisius's larger catechism (1556). Here also he participated in the intra-Lutheran debates of the day; he consistently took Gnesio-Lutheran positions, signing an opinion against Osianderism (1555) and publishing works against sacramentarianism (1557) and adiaphorism (1559).

In April 1560 Wigand moved to the University of Jena, which was split between Gnesio-Lutherans (e.g., Flacius) and Philippists (e.g., Viktorin Strigel). Wigand joined the controversy—he served as recorder at the Weimar Disputation between Flacius and Strigel (August 1560). This disputation revealed a disagreement between Flacius and Wigand that eventually split the Gnesio-Lutheran wing of German Lutherans: Flacius asserted against Strigel that Original Sin is the substance of fallen humanity—a view that Wigand saw as Manichaean.

Wigand left Jena in November 1561, becoming superintendent of Wismar, Mecklenburg, in 1562. There he struggled against sacramentarians and Anabaptists. The University of Rostock awarded him the doctorate in 1563, and Wigand became an important ducal adviser.

After another stint at Jena (1568–1573) came a teaching appointment at Königsberg (1573–1575). Wigand was then elected Lutheran bishop of Pomerania (serving from 1573 to 1587), where he engaged in further theological controversy, questioning the Christology of his neighboring bishop and erstwhile friend, Tilemann Hesshus of Samland. Eventually Hesshus was deposed and Wigand assumed episcopal duties of Samland as well. Wigand was thus able to support the acceptance of the *Book of Concord* (1580) in these areas.

Wigand remained a determined advocate of confessional Lutheranism, both theologically and methodologically. His work spans the period between the deaths of Luther (1546) and Melanchthon (1560) and the rise of Lutheran orthodoxy.

BIBLIOGRAPHY

Bente, F. *Historical Introductions to the Book of Concord.* Reprint, Saint Louis, 1965. Interprets Wigand in relationship to the emerging sixteenth-century Lutheran confessional consensus.

Diener, Ronald. "Johann Wigand, 1523–1587." In *Shapers of Religious Tradition in Germany, Switzerland, and Poland, 1560–1600,* edited by Jill Raitt, pp. 19–38. New Haven and London, 1981. The most complete biographical sketch of Wigand in English.

Kolb, Robert. "The Advance of Dialectic in Lutheran Theology: The Role of Johannes Wigand, 1523–1587." In *Regnum, Religio et Ratio: Essays Presented to Robert M. Kingdon,* edited by Jerome Friedman, pp. 93–102. Sixteenth Century Essays and Studies, vol. 8. Kirksville, Mo., 1987. Explicates Wigand's theological method, with special reference to the *Syntagma.*

———. *Confessing the Faith: Reformers Define the Church, 1530–1580.*

Saint Louis, 1991. An analysis of Wigand's attitude toward the Augsburg Confession in the context of emerging Lutheran confessionalism.

WILLIAM R. RUSSELL

WILD, Johann (also Ferus; 1495–1554), German Franciscan renowned as an outstanding Catholic preacher. Little is known of Wild's early life except that he was born in Swabia and entered the order of observant Franciscans around 1515. In 1528 he was called to the Franciscan church in Mainz, where he gained a reputation as a highly effective preacher. Although devoted to his faith, Wild eschewed the personal invective and polemics widely indulged in by all sides of the Reformation conflict, even conceding that he had "dug some pearls" from the writings of the reformers. With his gentle presence, sincere conviction, and simple eloquence, he won a large following and has been credited with halting the advance of Lutheranism in Mainz.

In 1539 Wild was named to the cathedral pulpit in Mainz. In 1552 his courageous stance against the marauding troops of Albert of Brandenburg helped save the cathedral from destruction by fire.

Foremost a preacher concerned with interpreting scripture, explaining Catholic liturgy, and making dogma comprehensible to ordinary people, Wild was content to leave learned exegesis to scholars. The irenic spirit and often theologically imprecise formulations of his sermons drew criticism when these moved from the pulpit to the printed page, appearing unrevised and only with his reluctant consent as "commentaries." In 1550 Wild's sermons on the gospel of John were actually published without his foreknowledge and promptly placed on the Index of Prohibited Books by the Sorbonne, which considered them riddled with errors and heretical statements. In 1554 the Spanish Dominican Domingo de Soto found them to contain sixty-seven errors, and they were placed on the Index of the Spanish Inquisition.

Despite these objections, Wild's archbishop, Sebastian von Heusenstamm, insisted that he prepare all of his sermons for publication. By the time he died in 1554, many had appeared in first editions and translations; the remainder were published posthumously under the direction of Philip Agricola. Wild's works generally received high praise from Catholic clergymen, going through almost two hundred editions. They incurred no displeasure in Rome until 1590, when Sixtus V placed them on the Index "to be corrected." In 1596 they were condemned outright, remaining on the Roman Index until 1900.

BIBLIOGRAPHY

Paulus, Nikolaus. *Johann Wild: Ein Mainzer Domprediger des 16. Jahrhunderts.* Cologne, 1893.

Tüchle, Hermann. "Ferus (Wild), Johannes." In *Neue Deutsche Biographie,* vol. 5, pp. 101–102. Berlin, 1961.

Zawart, Anscar. "The History of Franciscan Preaching and of the Franciscan Preachers, 1209–1927." *Franciscan Studies* 7 (1928), 418–423. A useful brief survey with a full list of Wild's published writings.

KARIN BRINKMANN BROWN

WILDENAUER, Johann. *See* Egranus, Sylvius.

WILLEMSZ, Engel. *See* Merula, Angelus.

WILLIAM OF ORANGE ("the Silent"; 1533–1584), prince of Orange, count of Nassau, and leader of the Revolt of the Netherlands. William of Orange was born on 25 April 1533 at Dillenburg in Nassau. On the death of his cousin Reynier of Nassau-Breda (1544), he inherited the enormous possessions of the Netherlands branch of his family, including the principality of Orange. He lived thereafter in the Netherlands as a courtier of Charles V and, as he reached maturity, was given a series of diplomatic and military assignments. In 1555 Charles appointed him to the Netherlands council of state, and in 1559 Philip II named him stadtholder of Holland, Zeeland, and Utrecht.

William supported his fellow nobles against the political and ecclesiastical reforms of Philip II. His opposition was based upon support for the traditional rights and privileges of the Netherlands and on a principled aversion to Philip's religious policies. Raised as a Lutheran, William had converted to Catholicism when he moved to court, but he maintained contact with his Lutheran relatives and seems to have imbibed the latitudinarian ideas prevalent in his adopted country. In 1563 he and the count of Egmont forced the king to remove Cardinal Antoine Perrenot de Granvelle, Philip's chief minister in the Low Countries, but when rioting and iconoclasm broke out in August 1566, William worked successfully to restore order. When the prince learned that Philip had dispatched Fernando Álvarez de Toledo, the third duke of Alba, to wipe out all remaining traces of sedition, he withdrew to Dillenburg, an act that probably saved his life.

In 1568 William invaded the Netherlands with an army composed largely of German mercenaries. The population failed to rise on his behalf, and Alba's army forced him to retreat. The next few years were spent in negotiations with the French Huguenots and other potential supporters. In 1572 he attempted a second invasion, but the Huguenots were prevented from intervening by the Saint Bartholomew's Day Massacre. This time, however, most of the towns in the Netherlands rose on his behalf. Though Alba broke the siege of Mons, temporarily reduced much of the country to obedience, and once again drove William back to Dillenburg, true revolution was now a possibility. On 21 October 1572 William landed at Enkhuizen determined to free his country or to "make his sepulchre."

Alba was recalled in 1573, leaving the Spanish high command in disarray. After four years of hard fighting, William emerged as the leader of a "common fatherland" that included all seventeen provinces, but his triumph was short-lived. The fragile union was threatened from the start by the very forces that had brought it into being: religious strife and devotion to local privilege. The towns fought each other for commercial advantage and found it almost impossible to agree on taxation and on the distribution of other war-related burdens. Meanwhile, the Calvinists had gained control in Holland and Zeeland. Like their revolutionary counterparts in Brabant and Flanders, they sought to deny religious freedom to the Catholics, who were still a majority in most areas. William himself joined the Reformed church in 1573 but refused to abandon the principle of religious toleration. His efforts to restrain the zeal of his co-religionists did little to reassure the Catholics, while the Calvinists accused him of trimming. Fearing Calvinist domination of the Union of Utrecht (1579), he supported it only with great reluctance.

When the king appointed Alessandro Farnese, duke of Parma, as his captain-general in the Low Countries, these squabbles proved fatal. Equally skilled in war and diplomacy, Parma quickly regained the allegiance of Hainaut, Artois, and Walloon Flanders and began to move against the towns of the union, beginning with Maastricht. Hoping to bring on a war between France and Spain, William prevailed upon the States-General to offer the crown of the Netherlands to the duke of Anjou, brother of Henry III of France. The attempt ended in bloody fiasco, and the remainder of William's life was spent in trying to hold back Parma's inexorable reconquest of the south.

In 1580 the king outlawed William. The prince responded with an *Apologie* setting forth the justice of his cause, but he was shot to death on 10 July 1584 by an assassin hoping for the king's reward. In the following year Parma took Antwerp and regained control of the south. The seven northern provinces then formed the Dutch Republic. It was a development that William had hoped to avoid. He was as committed to Netherlandish unity as he was to religious toleration and believed that the t.vo were inextricably linked. Though a mediocre general, he was a political visionary, a leader of rare determination, and a gifted conciliator who is rightly regarded as the father of his country.

BIBLIOGRAPHY

Duke, Alastair. *Reformation and Revolt in the Netherlands*. London, 1990.
Geyl, P. *The Revolt of the Netherlands*. 2d. ed. Reprint, London, 1980.
Parker, Geoffrey. *The Dutch Revolt*. Rev. ed. London and New York, 1988.
Wedgewood, C. V. *William the Silent*. Reprint, London, 1989.

WILLIAM S. MALTBY

WIMPFELING, Jakob (1450–1528), German humanist and reformer of Alsace. On the eve of the Reformation, he represented late medieval reform efforts similar to those of two of his friends, Sebastian Brant (1457–1521), the author of *The Ship of Fools*, and Geiler von Kaisersberg (1445–1510), the great penitential preacher. Wimpfeling attacked moral abuses, especially of the clergy. Educated at Freiburg, Erfurt, and Heidelberg, he began his reform efforts at Schlettstadt (Sélestat) in Alsace. He became a professor of poetry and rhetoric at Heidelberg. As cathedral preacher in Speyer, he stood in an ambivalent relationship to Italian humanism. He admired classical form but hated pagan morals. When he was invited to join the Rhenish sodality of humanists promoted by Conradus Celtis, he responded with the shy demurrer that he would only be a crow among the nightingales or an owl among the falcons.

He published against his critics an *Expurgatio contra Detractores*, in which he outlined his life and pointed to the simplicity and regularity that placed him above the clergy of his time. His major work was *De Integritate*, along with his *Epitome Germanicarum rerum*, arguing that historical tradition and evidence established the fact that Alsace and Lorraine were German and belonged to the empire. He warned against the designs of the French king on Alsace, the pearl of the empire, and later history proved him to have been right.

BIBLIOGRAPHY

Herding, Otto. *Jakob Wimpfeling und Beatus Rhenanus: Das Leben des Johannes Geiler von Kaysersberg*. Munich, 1970. In the foreword, pp. 10–42, Herding provides a concise analysis of Wimpfeling and a comparison with Geiler; on pp. 42–50 he discusses the life of Geiler by Beatus Rhenanus.
Knepper, Joseph. *Jakob Wimpfeling, 1450–1528: Sein Leben und seine Werke* (1902). Reprint, Nieuwkoop, 1965. Remains the best biography, written from a conservative Catholic point of view, proper for Wimpfeling.
Overfield, James H. *Humanism and Scholasticism in Late Medieval Germany*. Princeton, 1984. Discusses Wimpfeling, pp. 81–86, *et passim*.
Spitz, Lewis W. *The Religious Renaissance of the German Humanists*. Cambridge, Mass., 1963. See pp. 41–60 and 301–306.

LEWIS W. SPITZ

WIMPINA, Konrad (also Koch; 1460–1531), German Catholic academic and theologian, opponent of Martin Luther, and adviser to Elector John I of Brandenburg. Born to a family named Koch in Buchen (Odenwald), Wimpina took his later name from the town of Wimpfen (Württemberg), where he held a canonry. He collected a variety of academic degrees, beginning with a baccalaureate in philosophy from the University of Leipzig in 1482 and ending with a doctorate in theology in 1503. He took orders in 1500.

In 1505 Wimpina was engaged by Elector John I of Brandenburg to play a major part in founding the University of Frankfurt an der Oder. During his twenty-five-year tenure there, he served intermittently as rector and dean of the theology faculty, setting the institution's conservative disposition in accord with his own scholarly predilections and the staunch Catholicism of the elector. A keen disputant in the scholastic mode and enamored of abstract metaphysical speculation, Wimpina exemplified the late-medieval approach and concerns that were fast becoming anathema in more advanced humanist circles. His devotion to scholastic theology and his recourse to classical mythology and philosophy in support of Christian truth drew particular ire from colleagues at Wittenberg, foreshadowing, in the early years of the sixteenth century, the religious and intellectual divide that would later separate them.

Although sensitive to clerical abuses, Wimpina stands out as an early and abiding critic of the Reformation and of the learned Catholics who failed to defend the old church. His anti-Lutheran writings were largely intended to furnish his fellow churchmen with reasoned arguments grounded in traditional Catholic theology, and to refute the heretical propositions of the reformers. Against Luther's theses on indulgences, Wimpina drafted his own theses, which Johann Tetzel defended in 1517 to gain his expeditious doctorate from Pope Leo X. Other works defended monastic vows, the priesthood, the Mass, and church teaching on justification through faith and good works.

In 1530 Wimpina attended the Diet of Augsburg as theological adviser to Elector John and worked on the *Confutatio*. His tone and behavior remained philosophical and scholarly, and his writings were devoid of the rude polemics so frequently indulged by combatants in the religious conflict.

BIBLIOGRAPHY

Primary Source

Wimpina, Konrad. *Tractatus de erroribus philosophorum in fide christiana*. Leipzig, 1983.

Secondary Sources

Albert, P. P. "Wimpina, Konrad." In *Lexicon für Theologie und Kirche*, vol. 10, p. 931. Freiburg, 1931.
Brecher, A. "Wimpina, Konrad." In *Allgemeine deutsche Biographie*, (1898), vol. 43, pp. 330–335. Berlin, 1971. A brief critical examination of Wimpina's character and career.
Michalski, A. "Wimpina, Konrad." In *Lexicon für Theologie und Kirche*, vol. 10, pp. 1174–1175. Freiburg, 1965.
Negwer, Joseph. *Konrad Wimpina: Ein katholischer Theologe aus der Reformationszeit*. Reprint, Nieuwkoop, 1967. The most thorough work on Wimpina.
Schottenloher, Karl, ed. *Bibliographie zur deutschen Geschichte im Zeitalter der Glaubensspaltung*. Stuttgart, 1957. See especially vol. 2, p. 393.

KARIN BRINKMANN BROWN

WISHART, George (c.1513–1546), Scottish reformer and martyr. After Patrick Hamilton, Wishart was the second great martyr of the Scottish Reformation, a notable hero of John Knox's *History of the Reformation* (written between 1559 and 1572). Much is therefore known about him, yet he remains a puzzle. Like Hamilton, he was educated at Louvain. He was back in Scotland by the mid-1530s, possibly teaching at Montrose, in Angus, and the Mearns, his native area and one already noted for Protestant sympathies. But in 1538 he fled to England, escaping the harsher climate of Scotland where the king, James V, and his greatest churchman, Cardinal David Beaton, were resolutely upholding the Catholic church. He preached and stirred up trouble in Bristol. In 1539 he went to Germany and Switzerland, returning in 1543 to England and then to Scotland. His approach, raising rather than answering questions, seems to have had something in common with Thomas Müntzer's; his theological position, certainly on the Eucharist, was Zwinglian rather than Lutheran.

Thus far there seem good reasons why the man who became the most dynamic and influential Protestant preacher in Scotland between 1544 and 1546 should have been seen as the greatest threat to the church; indeed, the puzzle is why he was not silenced earlier. He traveled widely, preaching throughout Angus and the Mearns; making a huge impact in Dundee; going to Ayrshire, heartland of reform in the west; and everywhere gaining support from local nobles and lairds. He was a man of immense courage and charisma. In December 1545 he took his greatest risk, preaching near Edinburgh, at Leith, and in January 1546 at Haddington. Then, despite the protection of local lairds, Beaton caught up with him; he was arrested at the house of the laird of Ormiston and taken to Saint Andrews, where in March he was tried by Beaton and burned.

The security that Knox describes Beaton enjoying after Wishart's death was illusory and short-lived. At the end of May, as a direct result of Wishart's execution, a group of Protestant lairds led by Norman Leslie, son of the earl of Rothes, broke into Beaton's stronghold at Saint Andrews and murdered him, contemptuously hanging his body on the castle wall. Yet the issue may not have been wholly religious. Wishart, the inspiration for the Protestant cause, may have been an agent for Henry VIII, whose determination to get rid of Beaton had already been seen in a plot in 1544 to kill him in which "a Scotsman named Wishart" acted as the go-between for the Scottish conspirators and the earl of Hertford. They failed in 1544, but they were to succeed in 1546. Wishart may, then, have represented not just the internal threat to the cardinal, violently trying to hold the line of Catholic orthodoxy in the uncertain years after the death of James V (1542), and pushed into persecution with the execution not only of Wishart but also of a group of Protestants in Perth (1544). Wishart may have represented also the murderous impulse of Henrician Catholicism for whom the Protestants of Scotland were preferable to the papists.

BIBLIOGRAPHY

Primary Source

Wishart, George. *Memoir of George Wishart*. London, 1876.

Secondary Sources

Cowan, Ian B. *The Scottish Reformation: Church and Society in Sixteenth-Century Scotland*. London and New York, 1982. Very good on the regional variations in the spread of reform.

Sanderson, Margaret H. B. *Cardinal of Scotland: David Beaton, c.1494–1546*. Edinburgh, 1986. An excellent study of the early Reformation, with sensitive analysis of its leading opponent.

JENNY WORMALD

WITCHCRAFT. Conceptually defined and punished long before the Reformation, witchcraft became a serious concern throughout Christendom primarily during the confessional century (1560–1660). Although belief in the efficacy of harmful sorcery has flourished in many human societies, only in Christian Europe did such fears ever engender massive numbers of trials and executions of suspected witches, the vast majority of whom were women.

The shaping of witchcraft doctrine was a long and complicated process. At its base lay the ancient notion of malevolent sorcery, or *maleficium*, which was feared and punished by Greek and Roman laws. Spells—manipulating occult and evil deities by both incantations and the skillful use of physical objects to perform the sorcerer's will—populate classical and medieval literature alike. A few enlightened pagans scoffed at sorcery, while the church fathers warned that such magic was necessarily diabolic, but most people never doubted that it worked. The Christian successor states to the Roman Empire continued to criminalize *maleficium* because it was directly harmful to people or property. Although such trials seem to have been extremely rare before 1300, it is known that later medieval Europeans, who left more abundant records, prosecuted hundreds of people for *maleficium*.

Before *maleficium* could become witchcraft, it had to be diabolized. The notion that inexplicable misfortunes somehow proceeded from the Devil was an old Christian idea, but the process by which *maleficium* resulted from a formal pact between the Devil and a sorcerer developed gradually in medieval Europe. The most important precondition for the eventual diabolization of *maleficium* was undoubtedly the diabolization of thirteenth-century heretics. In 1233, relying on information from a German inquisitor, Pope Gregory IX issued the bull *Vox in Rama*, which described both the obscene forms of homage offered by heretics and the promiscuous nocturnal orgies in which they engaged afterward. Bulls by later popes, such as that issued by John XXII in 1318, reinforced the notion that religious dissenters—generally Waldensians, who, in fact, led exemplarily plain and sober lives—were really Devil-worshipers who engaged in nocturnal orgies.

There was, however, no obvious link between heretics and sorcerers. Soon after 1300 a few prominent people, including two French bishops and a deceased pope, were accused of practicing ritual magic through invocations of devils. In 1324 a prominent Irish woman, Lady Alice Kyteler, and several associates were charged with harmful sorcery allegedly performed with diabolic aid. In this, the first occasion when a group of people were tried for diabolic *maleficia*, a few lesser defendants were eventually burned or otherwise punished, although Lady Alice escaped. When trials for sorcery performed through a diabolic pact resumed much later in the century, defendants were no longer prominent. Two such cases appear in the earliest surviving dossier of criminal cases tried by Europe's greatest secular tribunal, the Parlement of Paris. A sorceress and her client were tortured and burned for performing love magic through diabolic aid in 1390; a similar case a year later produced an identical result.

Even with *maleficium* partially diabolized by 1400, the concept of witchcraft still largely lacked the notion of nocturnal flights to diabolic assemblies. Apparently such beliefs were strongest in Italy. The earliest known trials involving night-flying took place before the inquisitors of Milan between 1384 and 1390, when two women were convicted and burned for attending the nocturnal "society" of a supernatural queen called *Signora Oriente*. Although the goddess instructed them in magical healing and in forms of divination for theft and sorcery, there is no trace of *maleficium* in either trial. In Italy in 1428, before a secular court in the Papal States, the first detailed confession occurred in which all the elements of diabolism, harmful sorcery, and nocturnal flight to witches' assemblies were finally—and lethally—combined.

The first treatise describing the witch cult, Johann Nider's *Formicarius*, was composed during the Council of Basel in the mid-1430s, reworking information about heresy trials provided by a secular judge from Bern and a Dominican inquisitor from Lausanne. Within a decade the private secretary of the antipope elected by this council produced the first literary portrait of witches in a long French poem mistitled *Le champion des dames Ladies*. (The margins of an early copy contain the first drawing of witches flying on broomsticks.) By 1440 full-fledged witch trials began to be recorded in regions loyal to the antipope elected at Basel—for example, in French Switzerland and such nearby Alpine districts as Savoy and Dauphiné. At about the same time, a German-Swiss chronicler described the first collective persecution of witches in southern Switzerland, backdating the event to 1428. He claimed that more than a hundred people had been burned by judges of the prince-bishop of Sion because they had flown on chairs to wild nocturnal assemblies, where the Devil appeared in bestial form and urged them to commit *maleficia*.

Three points should be noted about these fifteenth-century trials. First, as Richard Kieckhefer has shown, diabolism was usually interjected into sorcery cases by ecclesiastics: 54 percent of sorcery cases tried by church courts included diabolic elements, compared with only 11 percent of sorcery cases tried by secular courts (and only 6 percent of sorcery cases recorded in vernacular languages rather than Latin). Moreover, diabolism is entirely absent from extant testimony against accused witches though frequently present in witches' confessions obtained under torture. Finally, the doctrine of the witches' sabbath emerged primarily in mountainous districts between Dauphiné and northern Italy, replete with Waldensian heretics. In some of these regions the earliest vernacular term describing witches was derived from "heretic" or "Waldensian"; in such places, where the same inquisitors tried Waldensians in 1430 and witches a decade later, women made up a small minority of suspects.

More than thirty treatises dealing with witchcraft were composed during the fifteenth century by clerics, lawyers, and philosophers, reflecting a reciprocal interplay between trial evidence and theory in their descriptions and explanations of witchcraft doctrine. In 1486, however, the publication of the *Malleus Maleficarum* (The Hammer of [Female] Witches) provided a landmark in the spread of witch trials. Although it had little to say about diabolic pacts and never mentioned witches' assemblies or night-flying, the *Malleus* remained important for several reasons. It provided the first detailed guidebook for conducting a witch trial. Its popularity was unparalleled: it was printed fourteen times between 1487 and 1520. Although written by two inquisitors who had conducted many witch trials, it encouraged secular judges to pursue suspected witches. Last, but far from least, the *Malleus* (whose authors had not long before tried two men and forty-eight women for witchcraft in southern Germany) insisted by its title and emphasized in its text that virtually all witches were women.

No further editions of the *Malleus Maleficarum* appeared between 1520 and 1580, when a second cycle began. From the beginning of Martin Luther's revolt until the onset of confessionalization in Protestant and Catholic Europe around 1560, witchcraft trials rarely exceeded fifteenth-century levels. Officials of both church and state seemed far more preoccupied with prosecuting Anabaptists in the empire and "Lutherans" in western and southern Europe than in punishing sorcerers for diabolic pacts. Only the Devil himself settled accounts with a Renaissance *magus* like Doctor Faustus, who in real life wandered unhindered through Germany during the zenith of Reformation activity.

Once mainstream Protestantism and Tridentine Catholicism had begun to settle into confessional blocs, witch hunting resumed across Christendom. Luther applauded the execution of four witches at Wittenberg in 1541. John Calvin encouraged Geneva's magistrates to "extirpate the race of witches" from a rural district in 1545, resulting in eight trials and three deaths. The general resumption of witch hunting around 1560, however, took place on a totally unprecedented scale. After the final triumph of Calvin's political allies, Geneva tried about ninety witches within fifteen years (1556–1570), executing more than thirty of them. In southwestern Germany, where handfuls of incidents had resulted in the executions of only one or two witches at a time before 1560, a witch-hunting panic at Lutheran Weissenstieg in 1563 resulted in sixty-three executions. Witch trials reappeared during the 1560s in the records of Christendom's largest appellate court, the Parlement of Paris. Recorded witch trials began then in such places as the Channel Islands and parts of French Switzerland; in more remote European regions, such as Norway and Hungary, recorded trials and executions of witches began around 1570. Edicts criminalizing witchcraft were proclaimed for the first time in both newly confessionalized kingdoms of the British Isles, England and Scotland, in 1563.

By 1580, when the *Malleus Maleficarum* was finally reprinted and other demonologies by such well-known authors as Jean Bodin also appeared, witch hunting was enormously extensive and intensive across Europe. In three major Swedish towns witch trials became seven times more common after 1580 than before. Essex, England's most witch-ridden county, conducted more trials during the 1580s than in any other decade, as did the Parlement of Paris. Across the western edge of the Holy Roman Empire, in the great duchies of Luxembourg and Lorraine, recorded trials and executions of witches mushroomed spectacularly after 1580, as they did in Switzerland's most witch-ridden zone, the Pays de Vaud.

The heartland of witch hunting in confessional Europe, however, was the Germanic core of the Holy Roman Empire; anyone trying to grasp the true scale of this phenomenon between 1560 and 1660 must begin there. Oddly enough, the best available guide to the size of witch hunts in the old Reich (a source that remained unknown to western scholars until 1980) was assembled on orders from a leader of the Nazi Reich, Heinrich Himmler. A special branch of the SS (*Schutzstaffel*), with unparalleled access to archives throughout Nazi-ruled Europe, collected information on approximately thirty thousand witch trials, the vast majority of which occurred in Germanic lands during the sixteenth and seventeenth centuries. Although this mountain of Nazi-era documentation has yet to be fully explored, some provisional conclusions about the general pattern of witch hunting in Germany and the rest of Europe can be made. First, at least twenty thousand witches probably died in the Holy Roman Empire, which included modern Austria and Switzerland. Second, more witches were tried and executed in the empire than in the rest of Christendom combined, although some witches were killed almost everywhere from Iceland to Muscovy during the seventeenth century.

Both in Germany and elsewhere a large majority (usually around 80 percent) of executed witches were female. Witchcraft was by far the most common and widespread capital crime in Reformation Europe to be strongly skewed toward adult women. Sometimes—for example in the English county of Essex or the Belgian province of Namur—more than 90 percent of executed witches were women; the highest known ratio of men in any area where there were numerous accusations can be found in the Pays de Vaud of French Switzerland, where one-third of the thousand witches executed between 1580 and 1620 were male. Notions of female inferiority were the veriest commonplaces of sixteenth-century Europe; both the demonologists and their critics shared a misogynistic streak. Women's presumed weakness of body and intellect left them few means of empowerment other than relying on the Devil and his evil spells to strike back at their enemies—or so many people thought, fearing the *maleficia* usually wrought by old women.

Many accused German witches died during witch-hunting panics, which were produced by chain-reaction accusations of one's "accomplices" or fellow witches seen at sabbaths, nearly always made under torture. Erik Midelfort, in an exemplary investigation of such panics (defined as episodes resulting in twenty or more deaths in one place in one year), concluded that they were socially dysfunctional phenomena that usually occurred in the smaller independent territories of the empire, especially in ecclesiastical principalities. Although there were few measurable confessional differences in the severity of witch hunts during the sixteenth century, after 1600 Catholic districts tended to be significantly worse, averaging more than twice as many executions per trial as did Protestant regions (8.6 vs. 3.5). The worst of the known witch-hunting episodes anywhere in Europe occurred in the ecclesiastical principalities of Catholic Franconia, Würzburg, and Bamberg during an especially bleak, famine-ridden phase of the Thirty Years' War (1627–1632). Once such a panic got underway, the use of extensive torture to seek out further "accomplices" made it self-perpetuating until all plausible suspects had been eliminated. Arresting prominent women and men eventually provoked a crisis of confidence in the legal machinery of witch hunting and thus the abandonment of organized persecution, but by then hundreds of witches had already died. In southern Germany six places executed more than 250 witches each, and another ten places executed at least a hundred.

Various arguments have been advanced to explain differences between Protestant and Catholic styles of witch hunting. Midelfort, working with evidence showing far greater Catholic severity in southern Germany, suggested that the region's Lutherans adopted a "providentialist" explanation for such natural disasters as hailstorms, events that often provoked witch hunts. "Witchcraft in itself can do nothing," proclaimed Johannes Brenz, Württemburg's leading theologian, and evangelical Christians must accept God's chastisements in the spirit of Job. Catholic spokesmen, reacting against all Protestant positions during the seventeenth-century apogee of confessionalism, abandoned any providentialist emphasis. The only avenue of opposition still open to German Catholics after 1600 was criticism of witch-hunting methods. This could be eloquent and influential, however, as in the *Cautio Criminalis* printed anonymously at the height of episcopal panics (1631) but written by a Jesuit, Friedrich Spee.

Sometimes, as in French Switzerland, Protestant governments persecuted witches even more severely than Catholics did, and there were several solidly Protestant blocs of northern Europe where witch hunting was introduced only after the Reformation. Different circumstances require different explanations. The most influential argument comes from Keith Thomas, who suggested that post-Reformation England eliminated many traditional ecclesiastical remedies for dealing with the effects of sorcery and magic but put nothing new in their place. Pious Protestants fought witchcraft with prayer and fasting but despised exorcisms as superstitious magic. Consequently, Protestants were ritually defenseless against various forms of *maleficium* and easily provoked to accuse witches rather than face inexplicable misfortune with the Job-like stoicism their theologians recommended.

It is disturbing to realize that the two most powerful criticisms of the whole witch-hunting mentality (one by a Protestant, one by a Catholic) were published early in the confessional century, near the start of the age of witch panics and of the most intensive persecution. Johann Weyer's *De praestigiis daemonum*, printed in 1563, constitutes the most thorough challenge to orthodox witchcraft doctrine. It was also the bulkiest, virtually doubling in size from five books and 479 pages in its original edition to six books and 934 pages in its sixth and final version in 1583. Weyer, a court physician to Duke William V of Cleves in northwestern Germany, embraced a Protestant standpoint in attributing all the *maleficia* of witches to the "illusions and spells of demons" of his title; but his originality and significance rest largely on the medical explanations that he offered for the behavior and confessions of these accused women. What really afflicted witches, Weyer claimed, was not some imaginary Satanic pact but the real disease of melancholy. Instead of punishment, they needed treatment.

Weyer's diagnosis of witches' melancholia provoked him to extensive reconsideration of witchcraft's theological implications and legal consequences. His radicalism required him to invalidate the injunction of *Exodus* 22:18 against permitting witches to live on the grounds that the Hebrew text referred only to poisoners. He tried to explain how the delusions about witches' sabbaths were produced, including a discussion of hallucinogens (book 3, chapters 17–18). Weyer devoted two books to the victims of witches' supposed *maleficia* and how to treat them. His final section proposed legal reforms that would not only reduce or even eliminate the physical punishment of witches but also greatly increase the penalties against Faustian magicians. Weyer's tolerance of accused witches, however, was also informed by a misogyny reminiscent of the *Malleus Maleficarum*: women were "that sex which by reason of temperament is inconstant, credulous, wicked, uncontrolled in spirit, and (because of its feelings, which it governs only with difficulty) melancholic; [the Devil] especially seduces stupid, worn-out, unstable old women" (book 3, chapter 6).

Michel Eyquem de Montaigne's inconspicuous discussion of witches in his essay "On Lameness," first published in 1588, contrasts with Weyer's enormous length; but its criticism of the conventional wisdom about diabolic witchcraft is no less fundamental. This skeptical jurist (and typical Renaissance misogynist) asserted that people should not be believed about their supernatural activities. After thorough questioning of an old witch who had admitted her guilt, Montaigne boasted that his judgment was not "throttled much by preconceptions" but "in the end, and in all conscience, I would have prescribed medicine rather than execution."

Montaigne's dry voice was soon drowned out by a cacophony of new demonologies after 1580, coinciding with the reappearance of the *Malleus Maleficarum*. Weyer's bulky work appeared in six German translations and two French versions before Montaigne's essay of 1588, but none afterwards. The *Démonomanie des sorciers*, a detailed refutation of Weyer by the famous French jurist Jean Bodin, appeared in 1580; it enjoyed a moderate literary success, including translations, about equal to Weyer's. New demonologies appeared among Catholics, including those of the episcopal vicar of Trier, Peter Binsfeld (1589); the Lorraine privy councillor Nicholas Remy (1595); and the Belgian Jesuit Martin Del Rio (1599), whose work rivaled Weyer's in length and the *Malleus* in popularity. The most important Protestant demonology during this period was published by a monarch, James VI of Scotland, in 1597. Although Weyer was never decisively refuted, witch-hunting panics reached new peaks in many parts of Germany in the 1590s. Events eventually overtook both the German physician and the French skeptic.

Nowhere was the contrast between erudite demonology and witch-hunting practice more flagrant than in the flagship of the German Counter-Reformation, the duchy of Bavaria. Prolonged debates after a 1590 witch-hunting panic eventually resulted in the publication of Europe's most elaborate legislation against the crime of witchcraft, a forty-page edict promulgated in 1611, which remained in force for two centuries. Yet this ferocious-sounding law (for example, a year in jail on bread and water merely for consulting a fortune-teller) actually inaugurated a period of sharply reduced trials and executions in Bavaria. In 1612 a district judge who had convicted and executed nine witches was himself imprisoned, tortured, and ultimately beheaded at Munich in

1613 for employing illegal procedures in witch trials. Comparable scruples dominate the history of witchcraft cases tried before the premier Catholic court system, the Parlement of Paris (where Bodin failed to have witchcraft classified as an "exceptional" crime, for which confessions might be verified through torture), which after 1589 made repeated and generally successful efforts to restrain overzealous local prosecutors. The Bavarian case curiouslys parallels the Protestant example of James Stuart, witch interrogator and demonologist of the 1590s, who became acutely skeptical about witchcraft charges around 1610, seven years after becoming James I, king of England.

In Mediterranean Catholic lands witchcraft remained a "mixed" crime subject to either ecclesiastical or secular courts. Here three great Inquisitions—the Spanish (1478), Portuguese (1536), and Roman (1542)—claimed jurisdiction over witchcraft, with interesting results. All three were deeply concerned about any form of diabolism, especially the witches' pact with the Devil and the rituals of the sabbath, but cared little about the witches' *maleficia*. Consequently, relatively few suspects were denounced to these Inquisitions by frightened and angry victims of witches' spells, and extremely few witches were ever executed by any Holy Office during the age of the great hunts: none, so far as is known, by the Roman Inquisition; one by the Portuguese, in 1626; and about a dozen by the Spanish Inquisition, all between 1549 and 1610.

Most of these Spanish Inquisitorial trials were an aberration, provoked by a Pyrenean spillover from a French witch-hunting panic in 1609 and conducted without regard to the Inquisition's long-established guidelines on witchcraft. In 1538, for example, Spain's Holy Office warned its officials that they should not believe the *Malleus Maleficarum*, even if its author "writes about it as something he himself has seen and investigated, for . . . he may have been mistaken, as others have been." The 1609 panic was soon stopped through the efforts of a skeptical inquisitor, Alonso Salazar y Frias, who conducted empirical tests of witches' salves and ointments and even attempted individual on-site, minutely detailed verifications of the confessions of witches who claimed to have attended the same sabbath. (Two of Salazar's nine groups of four witches still agreed in all essential details.) No inquisitor, including Salazar, denied that witchcraft existed. The crucial question, which had split the Spanish Inquisition's policy committee in 1526, was whether witches attended the sabbath in reality or in imagination and thus whether their diabolic apostasy was imaginary. With a few exceptions inquisitors remained skeptical about witches' flights to sabbaths, because the soul could not leave the body, and the body could not fly. Thus, they tended to treat witchcraft as superstition rather than actual heresy and to punish it mildly. Henry Charles Lea, no apologist for the Holy Office, long ago praised the "wisdom and firmness of the Inquisition" for making witch hunting "comparatively harmless" in Spain.

Even if they did not execute witches, inquisitors were nonetheless tempted to diabolize folklore. One fascinating example is the transformation of the *benandanti* of Friuli, originally agrarian magicians, chosen by virtue of having been born with cauls, who claimed to engage in ritual battles against witches in order to protect the fertility of the next harvest. Around 1580 the Roman Inquisition began to investigate this superstition. By 1650 *benandante* had become a synonym for "witch." Without employing torture the Friuli inquisitors persuaded the boastful members of this fertility cult that they could not "go out" at night to confront witches without employing the same essentially diabolic techniques as the witches themselves used. The *benandanti*, however, admitted attending sabbaths only after the Roman Inquisition had adopted rigidly skeptical procedures toward investigating witches in an *Instructio* of 1623, so none of them ever risked a death sentence.

In their attitudes toward witchcraft, as in so much else, the Protestant states of northern Europe stood at the opposite extreme from the major Mediterranean Inquisitions. From Iceland to Estonia these northern lands continued to punish numerous cases of *maleficium*, but, except for Scotland, with its demonologist monarch, James VI, they paid relatively little attention to collective acts of diabolism. Historians trace the first appearance of elements of witches' sabbaths (always in incomplete forms) in England to 1612; in Sweden to 1596; and in Denmark not until 1632. In Finland, as the direct extension of a major witch-hunting panic in northern Sweden, the witches' sabbath seems to have reached the western coast (populated mostly by Swedes) around 1670. In the most remote northern areas, such as Estonia or Iceland, it never seems to have developed at all.

Most of Protestant northern Europe intensified its prosecutions of harmful sorcery slightly later than did central Europe. Denmark, where the future demonologist James VI (James I of Great Britain) first learned about diabolic witchcraft, did not define this crime until 1617, and its most important outbreak of trials immediately followed; Norway, a Danish dependency, held almost 85 percent of its 863 witch trials during the seventy years after 1617. Sweden, which punished harmful sorcery in its medieval national code, never revised these laws, and its most important witch hunt did not begin until 1668. Over 70 percent of Finland's 710 witch trials occurred in the second half of the seventeenth century. The kingdom of Scotland, whose witchcraft statute was passed in 1563 and whose first important witch panic dates from 1591, was relatively precocious and extraordinarily severe in hunting witches. Although only seventeen people were hanged in England's worst panic (Essex, 1645), almost 250 special commissions "for tryall and burning" were issued in one Scottish county in 1649—a panic resembling the very worst German cases.

Northern European court systems, rarely affected by Roman law and relying instead on accusatory procedure and jury systems, usually forbade the use of torture, thereby making German-style witch-hunting panics all but impossible. Jury convictions were not difficult to obtain, however, especially when plaintiffs alleged serious forms of *maleficium*. In Denmark, for example, more than two-thirds of 1,715 testimonies against accused witches involved causing illness of human begins (30 percent), deaths of human beings (16 percent), or the death and illness of cattle (22 percent). In Norway, 32 percent of about four hundred instances of *maleficia* concerned human illness or injury, while 22 percent involved human death, and, in a region more dependent on fishing than on dairying, more charges involved nautical misfortunes (sunken ships or sudden storms) than illness or death of livestock. In England, modern scholarship on witchcraft—concentrating on the social dynamics between accusers and accused rather than on the type of *maleficia*—has revealed that accused witches were usually less well-off than their accusers and had often cursed or bewitched people who had refused to give them food or lend them something. Personality also played a part: the essential witch trait, according to Christina Larner, was "a ready, sharp and angry tongue. The witch had the Scottish female quality of *smeddum*: spirit, a refusal to be put down, quarrelsomeness." Protestant Europe had problems digesting the lesson of Job.

In eastern Europe, where Catholicism eventually overcame serious challenges, witchcraft trials developed even later than in northern Europe. In the best-studied region, Hungary, trials multiplied only after the Turkish occupation ended; nearly two-thirds of its 472 known executions for witchcraft occurred between 1690 and 1760. The larger kingdom of Poland apparently followed a similar pattern: more than half of its known executions for witchcraft took place between 1676 and 1725, or after its mid-seventeenth-century devastations had ended. In both lands the spread of diabolism can be traced to areas populated by ethnic Germans or to those closest to the Germanic empire.

Moreover, both kingdoms lacked any central appellate jurisdiction to mitigate the severity of local courts; wherever such courts exercised effective control, witch hunting remained within relatively narrow limits. It is extremely instructive to compare the huge jurisdiction of the Parlement of Paris—which diminished the vast majority of more than 1,200 local court sentences in witchcraft cases it reviewed between 1565 and 1640—with the ineffective appellate court system of the Holy Roman Empire, the *Reichskammergericht*, which emitted equally lenient sentences to those who appealed their witchcraft convictions but lacked the authority to enforce its decisions. Many other European states, such as Scotland and Denmark, had appellate jurisdictions that ruled on only a fraction of their witch trials. It is extremely rare to find a parallel to the Parlement of Paris, which as early as 1602 required that all sentences in witchcraft cases be reviewed by them and quashed all but a handful of the death sentences imposed by lower courts.

Modern research on witch hunting in Reformation Europe has uncovered much about various popular beliefs that was interwoven with the synthesis of *maleficium* and diabolism. Many were essentially local concerns, ranging from the British belief in animals that were "witch's familiars" and the Hungarian belief in vampires, to the belief in "good" witches, such as the *benandanti* and related varieties of shamans extant in eastern and southern Europe. Such beliefs merged awkwardly with official demonology. Some widespread popular concerns, such as the belief in werewolves, were deemed irrevelant by both Protestant and Catholic demonology. Other popular practices helped to provoke witchcraft accusations, as, for example, the ubiquitous folk healers and diviners—the motley army of "cunning folk," *devins-guérisseurs*, and *wahrsagers* scattered across Christendom—who might also turn up among the accused if their diagnoses failed. A few elements of demonology, such as the Devil's mark, an anesthetic scar on the witch's body (stressed primarily in Protestant areas), gradually passed into local folklore.

The most important transconfessional phenomenon related to seventeenth-century European witch hunting, however, was the belief in diabolic possession. It proved particularly dangerous because it enabled the victim to identify the responsible witch even while displaying symptoms of bewitchment in public. Moreover, it could become a group condition, affecting children, adolescents, or communities of nuns, creating circumstances that could lead to multiple accusations and thereby to a witch-hunting panic. Some of the most famous and sinister episodes in the history of seventeenth-century witchcraft—from the accusations against the Jesuit Urbain Grandier by the Ursulines of Loudun (1632–34) to the outbreak at Puritan Salem in 1693—began in this manner. While Catholics possessed the spiritual weapon of exorcism and the supernatural power of a transubstantiated Host to expel demons, Protestants had no practical remedies for possession except prayer and fasting. Since exorcisms were not infallible, Catholics also resorted to prosecution in order to punish the witches responsible for causing such possessions.

The decline of witch hunting remains one of the most perplexing etiologic problems confronting contemporary scholarship on witchcraft. It seems obvious that no decisive new arguments were advanced during the seventeenth-century scientific revolution in order to discredit it. Protestant and Catholic authors continued to affirm its reality; John Wesley was not alone in claiming that "giving up witchcraft is, in effect, giving up the Bible." The only Protestant clergyman with sufficient temerity to do so, Balthasar Bekker of the Dutch Reformed church, was defrocked after publishing his skeptical history of the Devil and his powers, *De betoov-*

erde Wereld (The Enchanted World), in 1693. Nevertheless, the decriminalization of witchcraft proceeded apace in western Europe's leading monarchies, from Jean-Baptiste Colbert's statute of 1682 defining *maleficium* as either imposture or poisoning to the formal repeal of England's witchcraft statutes in 1736. Witch trials continued to be held, however, and not only in eastern Europe. In Bavaria and neighboring lands they occurred in fourteen different years between 1750 and 1775, when the last known German witch died at Kempten. The last known execution of a legally convicted witch occurred in the Swiss Protestant canton of Glarus in 1782. Elite lay culture finally ended witch hunting during the eighteenth century, an age replete with humorous portraits of lame and harmless devils and concluding with such masterful satires as Johann Wolfgang von Goethe's *Walpurgisnacht* (1808) and Francisco de Goya's *Los caprichos* (1796). What actually declined was the fear of the Devil and therefore of his *maleficia*, at least among the ruling classes of western Europe.

[*See also* Astrology; Magic; *and* Women.]

BIBLIOGRAPHY

Ankarloo, Bengt, and Gustav Henningsen, eds. *Early Modern European Witchcraft: Centres and Peripheries.* Oxford, 1990.
Behringer, Wolfgang. *Hexen und Hexenprozesse in Deutschland.* Munich, 1988.
———. *Mit dem Feuer vom Leben zum Tod: Hexenverfolgung in Bayern.* Munich, 1988.
Cohn, Norman. *Europe's Inner Demons.* London, 1975.
Ginzburg, Carlo. *The Night Battles.* Baltimore, 1983.
Henningsen, Gustav. *The Witches' Advocate.* Reno, 1980.
Kieckhefer, Richard. *European Witch-Trials, 1300–1500: Their Foundations in Popular and Learned Culture.* London, 1976.
Klaniczay, Gábor. *The Uses of Supernatural Power.* Princeton, 1990.
Labouvie, Eva. *Zauberei und Hexenwahn: Ländlicher Hexenglaube in der frühen Neuzeit.* Frankfurt, 1991.
Larner, Christina. *Enemies of God: The Witch-Hunt in Scotland.* Baltimore, 1981.
Levack, Brian P. *The Witch-Hunt in Early Modern Europe.* New York, 1987.
Midelfort, H. C. Erik. *Witch-Hunting in Southwestern Germany, 1562–1684.* Stanford, Calif., 1972.
Monter, E. William. *Witchcraft in France and Switzerland.* Ithaca, N.Y., 1976.
Muchembled, Robert. *La sorcière au village, XVe–XVIIIe siècle.* 2d ed. Paris, 1991.
Soman, Alfred. "The Parlement of Paris and the Great Witch-Hunt." *Sixteenth Century Journal* 9 (1978), 31–45.
Thomas, Keith. *Religion and the Decline of Magic.* London, 1971.
Weyer, Johann. *De praestigiis daemonum.* Binghamton, N.Y., 1991.

E. WILLIAM MONTER

WITTENBERG. The Ascanian Albert the Bear (r. 1123–1170) extended his dominion eastward and in 1159/60 called peasants and townsmen to the conquered territories. Some settled at the fortress on the northern shore of the Elbe river, which safeguarded the intersection of trade routes linking Magdeburg to the east and the Baltic Sea coast to the south. In 1260 Wittenberg became the capital of the dukedom of Saxony-Wittenberg, to which the Saxon electorship was linked in 1355.

Duchess Helen founded a Franciscan monastery after 1261 and members of the Ascanier family were interred there until 1423. Duke Rudolf I had a chapel built in the castle in 1330 and established the Chapter of All Saints with a provost and six chaplains to offer services and memorial masses for deceased members of the Ascanier family. In 1346 Clement VI (r. 1342–1352) placed the Chapter of All Saints under papal jurisdiction, thereby removing it from the jurisdiction of the bishop of Brandenburg. In 1400 Boniface IX (r. 1389–1404) incorporated the city church into the Chapter of All Saints. Nevertheless, the chapter became a center of medieval devotion. From 1342, more and more indulgences could be gained in the chapel.

In 1293 Wittenberg received its town charter. The townsmen began the reconstruction of their Chapel of the Madonna. The aisle (still extant) was finished around 1300. They erected the two towers on the west side around the middle of the fourteenth century, and the nave was consecrated in 1439.

After the Ascanians in Wittenberg died out in 1422, a member of the house of Wettin, Frederick I ("the Valiant"), margrave of Meissen, (r. 1381/1423–1428), received the dukedom of Saxony-Wittenberg, including the Saxon electorship as a fief of the empire. In 1485 the brothers Ernst (r. 1464–1486) and Albert (r. 1464–1500) divided the dominion of the Wettin family. Ernst received Wittenberg with its electorship, while Albert received Leipzig with its university. When Frederick II of Saxony (r. 1486–1525) succeeded his father, Ernst, in government, he decided to develop the town of Wittenberg.

In lieu of the old fortress he had a magnificent Renaissance castle constructed. In 1496/97–1509 the castle church was built. Not only was it equipped with a main altar and nineteen side altars by outstanding architects but, because of Elector Frederick's passion for collections, it became at the same time the storage site for a growing collection of relics. This development reached its peak during 1519, when, besides the hours, almost nine thousand masses were celebrated. In 1520 more than nineteen thousand relics were counted, and each relic allowed the purchase of indulgences for 100 years, 100 days, and 101 quadragenes (the forty days of Lent).

In 1502 Frederick founded a university. Given the name Wittenberg in its Greek translation, Leucorea, it lured many humanists. The co-founder, Johannes von Staupitz (c.1469–1524), transferred a course of study for Augustinian hermits to Wittenberg. Frederick also supported the construction of the Black monastery. In return the Augustinian hermits were obliged not only to hold memorial services for deceased members of the Wettin family but also to supply a lecturer of moral philosophy and a professor of biblical exegesis. A Franciscan had to provide an introduction to the work of John Duns Scotus. Other professors were awarded positions at the All Saints' monastery.

Frederick brought Lucas Cranach the Elder (1472–1553) to Wittenberg in 1505. Not only did Cranach build the town's largest, (and still extant) private house but, at the same time, he created a very productive workshop for painters. Later he used his art for the cause of the Reformation and taught Martin Luther to employ images in the service of the Reformation.

When Luther held the lectorship in moral philosophy in 1508–1509, Wittenberg had about two thousand inhabitants. In 1512 he was made professor of biblical studies; and soon after he accepted the office of municipal preacher (*Prädikant*), which was filled by the city government. Luther had learned from the humanists in Erfurt that the scriptures should be interpreted by consulting the texts in their original languages. This fact placed him in opposition to scholastic theology. Since no established traditions existed as yet at the Leucorea and because there were instead humanists among the learned and the learning, he met little resistance and great openness. Thus, Wittenberg provided favorable conditions for the development of Reformation theology, which, at the same time, created the basis for a reform of the university as such. It is through Luther's approach to biblical exegesis that humanist education became a necessary condition for the study of theology. Hence, the university created professorial chairs in both Hebrew and Greek. The latter was taken in August 1518 by Philipp Melanchthon, in whom humanistic education gained an outstanding teacher and the Reformation gained an influential theologian. The university in Wittenberg, shaped by humanism and reform, became a model for other universities.

Luther's reform message transformed Wittenberg fundamentally. Luther and Melanchthon attracted so many students that the Leucorea became the most highly attended German university. This not only stimulated the town's economy but also led to extensions of buildings and construction of new ones. While the founding of the Leucorea had already lured an initial group of printers to Wittenberg, a flourishing book trade developed as a result of Protestant pamphlets. Printers, publishers, bookbinders, and typefounders helped promote Wittenberg to a leading role within the German empire, not only because of their numbers but also because of their quality. For example, the 1545 Lutheran Bible of Wittenberg was regarded as the normative Bible for many decades. The written style of the German language developed by the printers of Wittenberg, which evolved through the cooperation of editors with Luther, plus the sheer number of Luther's texts propagated by them—including the translation of the Bible—had a strong influence on the evolution of a uniform style of written German.

As a result of the Reformation in Wittenberg the medieval institutions experienced substantial reorganization. On 6 January 1522 the general chapter of the German observant Augustinian hermits assembled in the Black monastery decided to allow individual members of the order to withdraw from it, resulting in the swift dissolution of monasteries. On 10 January 1522 Luther's fellow friar Gabriel Zwilling removed the images of saints from the Chapel of the Holy Spirit, the temporary place of worship for the Augustinian friars. This modest church deteriorated and was demolished in 1542. Soon Luther lived with only one other friar in the large monastic building, where he gave lectures and hosted refugees.

In 1525 Luther married Katharina von Bora. The former monastery became their home; it had room not only for Luther's family but also for relatives, students, refugees, and guests. Luther's home became the embodiment of hospitality among Protestant vicarages.

In 1526 Elector John the Constant began the construction of a large rampart around the town. In 1536 he built a new house for Melanchthon to replace his dilapidated cabin. This structure has survived and became a museum in 1954.

The abandoned Franciscan monastery became an almshouse, and its church became a granary. Following Luther's counsel the town purchased grain at low prices in order to sell it below excessively high prices in case of a price increase, thus protecting the townspeople from the greed of the nobles and the peasants.

Elector Frederick stopped collecting relics, which were put on display for the last time in 1523. During Christmas 1524 masses without community participation were discontinued in the castle church as well. After Frederick's death on 5 May 1525, Elector John dissolved the All Saints' monastery and had the valuable reliquaries melted down. Henceforth, the castle church served above all as church of the university and later became the burial place of the two princes of the Reformation, Frederick and John, as well as of the reformers Luther and Melanchthon.

In the Schmalkald War Wittenberg capitulated to Charles V on 19 May 1547, and Wittenberg, along with the Saxon electorship, devolved upon the Albertine member of the house of Wettin, Moritz of Saxony, who was able to win back the fugitive Melanchthon. Elector August (r. 1553–1586) transformed Luther's house into student housing, and adjacent to it he constructed a building for lectures, a library, and dormitories: the Augusteum. The Leucorea became a stronghold of orthodox Lutheranism and remained an outstanding university until the beginning of the Thirty Years' War (1618–1648). This war inflicted great damage upon the town and the university, from which both recovered only gradually. In the Seven Years' War (1756–1763) the Prussians conquered Wittenberg. Saxons and Austrians liberated the town in 1760, but in doing so they destroyed its northern half and the castle, including the castle church.

Under Napoleon (r.1804–1814/15) Wittenberg served as a fortress until it was liberated in January 1814. In 1815 Wittenberg devolved upon Prussia. In 1816 the Leucorea and the University of Halle were merged. Wittenberg obtained an evangelical seminary at the Augusteum, including a valuable part of the university library.

Thus, Wittenberg preserved its supraregional significance by nurturing the legacy of the Lutheran Reformation. Since 1617, when the Leucorea initiated a centennial celebration of the Reformation, anniversaries of key dates and events have repeatedly drawn visitors to Wittenberg.

In 1821 a statue of Luther was erected in the marketplace, and one of Melanchthon was unveiled in 1865. In 1885 a bust honoring Johannes Bugenhagen was put up on the north side of the town church. In 1830 an oak tree in Luther's honor was planted in the place where Luther had burned the compilations of canon law and the bull threatening him with excommunication.

In 1844 preservation and alteration work on Luther's house was begun. Dedicated in 1883 was the Luther hall, located within the house, which has come to be the most significant museum of the Lutheran Reformation and which was refurbished in time for the five-hundredth anniversary of Luther's birth in 1983. From 1885 to 1892 the house was converted into a monument of the German Reformation to commemorate the reformers, spiritual pioneers of the Reformation, princes, and councils, as well as towns supporting the Reformation and even the art of the Reformation period. In 1983 portraits of non-German Reformation leaders were installed in the windows. The castle church, which had been remodeled slightly after 1814, was designated to become an "honorary monument of the Reformation." In 1858 a bronze door bearing the text of Luther's Ninety-five Theses replaced the original door that had held the theses (it had burned in 1760).

Wittenberg has always been considered the uncontestable center of German Protestantism and has frequently served as the site for historic gatherings. Held here in 1848 was the first German *Kirchentag* (a regional deliberative congress of the Lutheran church), which led to the foundation in 1849 of the central commission for the home mission of the German Evangelical church. Also founded in Wittenberg were the Luther society in 1918 and the Deutsche Evangelische Kirchenbund in 1922. In 1933 the first German national synod convened here, and in 1937 the Wittenberg Alliance was formed, acting as a bastion of the "center" during the strife between church and state. The designation "Luther town"—in use since 1922—was introduced officially in 1938. The various memorials (the oak tree in Luther's honor, Luther's house, Melanchthon's house, the statues of Luther and Melanchthon, Cranach's house, and the castle church) continue to draw visitors from all over the world.

[*See also* Education; Luther, Martin; Melanchthon, Philipp; *and* Universities.]

BIBLIOGRAPHY

450 Jahre Martin-Luther-Universität Halle-Wittenberg: Wittenberg, 1502–1817. Vol. 1. Halle, 1952. For newer works, see *Lutherjahrbuch: Organ der internationalen Lutherforschung,* published annually.

Bellmann, Fritz, Marie-Luise Harksen, and Roland Werner. *Die Denkmale der Lutherstadt Wittenberg.* Weimar, 1979.

Bünger, Fritz, and Gottfried Wentz, eds. *Germania sacra. Abt. 1: Die Bistümer der Kirchenprovinz Magdeburg. Das Bistum Brandenburg.* Vol. 3, pt. 2. Reprint, Berlin, 1963.

Friedensburg, Walter. *Geschichte der Universität Wittenberg.* Halle, 1917.

Herricht, Hildegard, ed. *Bibliographie zur Geschichte der Universität Wittenberg.* Halle, 1980.

Junghans, Helmar. *Wittenberg als Lutherstadt.* 2d rev. ed. Berlin, 1982. New edition in preparation.

HELMAR JUNGHANS
Translated from German by Wolfgang Katenz

WITTENBERG, UNIVERSITY OF.

In 1485 the brothers Ernest and Albert divided the territory of the Wettins. Ernest received the duchy of Saxony-Wittenberg along with the electoral title, while Albert received Leipzig and its university. When Frederick III succeeded his father, Ernest, in 1486, he began to give greater prominence to the city of Wittenberg. This included the founding of a university, the Leucorea, which was above all intended to educate jurists for administrative service in the electorate.

With an imperial privilege of 6 July 1502, the university opened its doors on 18 October of the same year and gained papal approbation afterward. Corresponding to the late medieval order of rank, the theology faculty was first, followed by the faculties of law, medicine, and the arts. The curriculum of the faculty of theology offered the main scholastic schools of thought—Thomism, Scotism, and Ockhamism. At the same time, humanists were welcome. The *poetae laureati* were considered equal to liberal arts graduates, and humanist courses of study were planned. Even if several humanists who had been attracted to Wittenberg soon moved elsewhere, the encouragement of their interests was part and parcel of the university. The Erfurt humanist Nicholas Marschalk (c.1470–1525) brought his printing office to Wittenberg. In 1505 he published an introduction to Greek, which challenged the theologians to learn the original languages of the Bible.

Johannes von Staupitz, cofounder of the Leucorea, provided for the establishment of a monastery of Augustinian hermits in Wittenberg and combined it with a course of monastic study. The Augustinians were obligated to provide a professorship in moral philosophy and biblical exegesis, while the Franciscans were to provide for a professional chair in Scotism.

When the Augustinian hermit Martin Luther received his doctorate in theology on 19 October 1512 and subsequently became professor of biblical exegesis, a new epoch began. Luther increasingly made use of the biblical humanist methods of exegesis he had acquired in Erfurt. Developed in Wittenberg was an antischolastic theology based on scripture, the early church fathers, and German mysticism. Luther's close friendship with Georg Spalatin, a student of Marschalk's, who as secretary to the elector of Saxony was responsible for the university, furthered the influence of the new theology at the university and the acquisition of suitable books.

Before Luther, humanist studies had no significance for the three faculties of theology, law, and medicine. The theological method propounded by Luther presupposed a humanist training, which concentrated on languages and history, while the study of Aristotle and the Scholastics lessened in importance. This led to a reform of the university beginning in 1518, when Philipp Melanchthon assumed the newly created professorship in Greek. The humanist university reform movement experienced a breakthrough in Wittenberg, which subsequently led to educational reform. This reform of theology and education, together with its prominent representatives, attracted students, so that after 1520 Wittenberg came to be the largest German university.

Luther and his colleagues, not the jurists, shaped the Leucorea until his death in 1546. Melanchthon remained a member of the arts faculty, but he also gave lectures in theology and represented the new theology at religious debates. In 1521 the jurist Justus Jonas moved to the theology faculty, where he taught until 1541. Johannes Bugenhagen began his activities in 1521 with exegetical lectures and in 1533 became a member of the theology faculty. As minister of the city of Wittenberg and reformer of various territories, he helped shape the emerging Lutheran church. Caspar Cruciger took over a professorship in theology in 1528 and, together with Georg Rörer, set in motion the Wittenberg edition of Luther's works which were published beginning in 1539. The Luther Bible, completed in 1534, came about with the help of theologians and philologists of the university.

In 1535 Elector John Frederick entrusted to the faculty of theology the examination for all who sought ordination in the electorate of Saxony or for places outside Saxony as far away as Hungary. In 1539 the first consistory began its work in Wittenberg. It was comprised of theologians and jurists from the university.

In 1547, as a result of the Schmalkald War, Wittenberg became part of Albertine Saxony. The new elector, Moritz, urged Melanchthon to return to Wittenberg, which gave rise to the Leucorea's new prosperity. The Gnesio-Lutherans reproached Melanchthon and his students for having yielded too readily to the Augsburg Interim (prompting the adiaphoristic controversy in 1548–1552). Melanchthon's death in 1560 prompted his students to prefer his teachings to those of Luther.

Georg Major, professor of theology after 1544, made a lasting impact through his scriptural interpretation. When he asserted, like Luther, that good works, although not nec-

essary for salvation, are evidence of living faith, he incurred the vigorous criticism of Nikolaus von Amsdorf (beginning the Majorist controversy of 1552–1559).

After 1569 Christoph Pezel attempted to harmonize the theologies of Wittenberg and Geneva. As this was not expressed openly, the advocates of this way of thinking were called crypto-Calvinists. In 1574 Elector August had four crypto-Calvinists arrested, and he called to Saxony Jakob Andreae, who in 1577 brought about the Formula of Concord and in 1580 the *Book of Concord*.

In 1581 the Wittenberg professors had to decide whether they would sign the Formula of Concord or give up their positions. Two jurists, two physicians, and one mathematician chose to leave Wittenberg. The prestige of the Leucorea, which was loyal to the *Book of Concord*, grew again, for which the Wittenberg superintendent and theology professor Polykarp Leyser (1552–1610), appointed in 1577, was vitally instrumental.

Elector Christian I (r. 1586–1591) promoted and encouraged Calvinism. A shake-up followed, and as a result Leyser lost his position in 1587. After 1589 Urban Pierius (1546–1616) used his position as professor of theology and superintendent to drive away opponents. With the death of Christian I on 25 September 1591, this attempt at a "second reformation" lost its support. Duke Frederick William I of Saxony-Weimar (r. 1586–1602) and Elector John George of Brandenburg (r. 1571–1598) assumed the guardianship of Christian II (r. 1601–1611) and brought Lutheranism back to the Leucorea and to the electorate of Saxony. This led again to dismissals and new appointments. Aegidius Hunnius (1550–1603) came to Wittenberg in 1592 and became the cofounder of Lutheran orthodoxy. Grounded in the *Book of Concord*, he fought Samuel Huber's doctrine of predestination; as a consequence Huber (1547–1624) had to leave Wittenberg in 1594. In 1596 Leonhard Hutterus (1563–1616) began his teaching activity in Wittenberg. He represented the theology of the *Book of Concord*, with a particularly strong commitment to Luther. As a scriptural theologian, he developed the doctrine of inspiration. In 1609 he published his *Compendium locorum theologicorum ex scripturis sacris et libro Concordiae collectum*, which saw numerous editions. In 1619, with his *Loci communes theologici*, he established the comprehensive dogmatic theology of orthodox Lutheranism.

The number of students decreased under Christian II. It then rose during the era of Lutheran orthodoxy, making Wittenberg again the most heavily attended German university until the Thirty Years' War (1618–1648) caused its steep and permanent decline.

[*See also* Gnesio-Lutherans *and* Philippists.]

BIBLIOGRAPHY

Aland, Kurt. "Die Theologische Fakultät Wittenberg und ihre Stellung im Gesamtzusammenhang der Leucorea während des 16. Jahrhunderts." In *450 Jahre Martin-Luther-Universität Halle-Wittenberg*, vol. 1, pp. 155–237. Halle, Germany, 1952.

Friedensburg, Walter. *Geschichte der Universität Wittenberg*. Halle, Germany, 1917.

Friedensburg, Walter, ed. *Urkundenbuch der Universität Wittenberg*. Magdeburg, 1926. See vol. 1.

Großmann, Maria. *Humanism in Wittenberg, 1485–1517*. Nieuwkoop, 1975.

Junghans, Helmar. *Wittenberg als Lutherstadt.* 2d rev. ed. Berlin, 1982.

Rosin, Robert. "The Reformation, Humanism, and Education: The Wittenberg Model for Reform." *Concordia Journal* 16 (1990), 301–318.

HELMAR JUNGHANS
Translated from German by Susan M. Sisler

WITTENBERG CONCORD. This document was an agreement concerning the doctrine of the sacraments negotiated at Wittenberg in May 1536 by south German theologians and north German evangelical (i.e., Lutheran) theologians. The Wittenberg Concord was a product of the ongoing intra-Protestant attempts in the Reformation era to form a confessional consensus.

The sacramental debates among the magisterial reformers of the period focused on the Lord's Supper. Protestants agreed in their rejection of transubstantiation and its accompanying sacrificial understanding of the Mass, but they disagreed over how to interpret the Lord's Supper. The Wittenberg Concord was drafted with reference to this question.

The origins of the Wittenberg Concord can be seen in the meetings of Protestant theologians (and, occasionally, politicians), both before and after the 1530 Diet of Augsburg. The Marburg Colloquy of 1529 served mainly to highlight the differences between the parties, rather than to achieve agreement. Another meeting, in December (at Schmalkalden, Hesse), was likewise unable to bridge the differences, as was the last such attempt before the Diet of Augsburg in the spring of 1530 at Nuremberg. A common Protestant understanding of the Sacrament was not realized, and the various Protestant groups produced separate confessions for Augsburg (e.g., from south Germany came the Tetrapolitan Confession, from Switzerland came the *Ratio Fidei* of Huldrych Zwingli, and from Saxony came the Augsburg Confession).

In the course of these events, Martin Bucer took the lead in efforts to secure a standard Protestant interpretation of the Lord's Supper. Bucer's endeavors to promote Protestant unity, specifically on this sacramental question, were particularly important in the negotiation and reception of the Wittenberg Concord.

Bucer sought meetings with the Lutherans already at the Diet of Augsburg, but his offers were rejected. Immediately following the diet, he traveled north to confer with Martin Luther at Coburg, where Luther was sequestered. Bucer told Luther that his associates and he had always taught in accordance with the Lutheran position. Luther remained unconvinced, however, and did not sign the articles Bucer proposed.

When Bucer left Coburg, he passed through Nuremberg, and met with Luther's associates Philipp Melanchthon and Andreas Osiander, who were returning to Saxony from Augsburg. Later that year, Bucer approached the Swiss theologians Zwingli and Johannes Oecolampadius in an attempt to work out an acceptable sacramental formula. Zwingli even accepted, with qualifications, the formula, "The real body of Christ is truly offered." At Schweinfurt (1532) Bucer helped convince the southern Germans to subscribe to the Augsburg Confession, thus paving the way for their acceptance into the Schmalkald League. In 1534 Bucer participated in the Stuttgart conference that led to the influential south German theologian Ambrosius Blarer's acceptance of "real presence" language with respect to the Sacrament and the city of Augsburg's adoption of the Augsburg Confession. The final meeting of importance for the origins of the Wittenberg Concord was at Kassel, in December 1534, where Bucer formally declared acceptance of Luther's strongly worded Confession Concerning Christ's Supper (1528). In 1535 the Schmalkald League expanded to include a number of south German cities and principalities, and the meeting that was to yield the Wittenberg Concord was set for the spring of 1536.

This meeting was originally scheduled for early May in Eisenach, Saxony, but an illness of Luther caused a postponement. On 21 May Bucer led the delegation from south Germany into Wittenberg, Melanchthon was appointed recorder, and the Wittenberg Concord was signed on 29 May. At the conclusion of the conference, celebratory worship services were held and the Lord's Supper was celebrated.

The Wittenberg Concord has three parts. The first deals with the Lord's Supper and was signed by the twenty-one theologians in attendance. The second and third parts were "On Baptism" and "On Absolution." These sections testify to the value of infant baptism and of private confession and absolution. The Wittenberg Concord concludes with a commitment for "both sides to refer this matter to other preachers and superiors" and an affirmation of the Augsburg Confession and its apology.

The prefatory statement ("We have heard Dr. Bucer explaining his opinion and that of others who have been with him, concerning the sacrament of Christ's body and blood, in this way . . .") indicates the main purpose of the meeting: the south Germans were to demonstrate they taught in conformity with the Lutherans. Still, the concord reveals compromise on both sides. The south Germans did not insist on "memorial" language, and they accepted the *manducatio indignorum* (i.e., even the unworthy receive the real presence of Christ). For their part, the Lutherans did not insist on a precise definition of "unworthy" and accepted the qualification of the word "with" in the phrase "that with the bread and wine the body and blood are truly and substantially present, offered, and received." Nevertheless, the document has a strongly Lutheran character, particularly with respect to the "real presence" ("by the sacramental union, the bread is the body of Christ . . .") and the *manducatio indignorum*.

The reception and influence of the Wittenberg Concord varied from rejection in places such as Ulm and Constance to official recognition at Worms, Augsburg, and elsewhere. It helped ameliorate the confrontational and polemical climate that had characterized the confessional debates. In fact, Bucer sent one of his students, Johannes Marbach, to study under Luther at Wittenberg. When Marbach returned to Strasbourg, he assumed a leading role in events that moved the city to become Lutheran.

The Wittenberg Concord set an important early precedent for negotiations regarding Protestant unity, with its affirmation of the Augsburg Confession (and its apology) as the *sine qua non* of Lutheran confessionalism. In fact, the most salient sections of the Wittenberg Concord were incorporated virtually verbatim into the Formula of Concord (1577).

BIBLIOGRAPHY

Backus, Irena. "Polemic, Exegetical Tradition, and Ontology: Bucer's Interpretation of John 6:52, 53, and 64 before and after the Wittenberg Concord." In *The Bible in the Sixteenth Century*, edited by by David Steinmetz. Durham, N.C., 1990. Investigates Bucer's enduring presuppositions regarding the Lord's Supper.

Bente, F. *Historical Introductions to the Book of Concord.* Reprint, Saint Louis, 1965. Places the Wittenberg Concord in the context of the emerging sixteenth-century Lutheran confessional consensus.

Bizer, Ernst. *Studien zur Geschichte des Abendmahlsstreits im 16. Jahrhundert.* Darmstadt, 1962. Focuses on the compromising nature of the Wittenberg Concord.

Haile, H. G. *Luther: An Experiment in Biography.* Rev. ed. Princeton, 1983. Gives particular attention to the meeting at Wittenberg that produced the Wittenberg Concord.

Jacob, Henry E., ed. *The Book of Concord.* Vol. 2. Philadelphia, 1908. Contains English translations of important primary sources and a select bibliography of nineteenth-century research.

Kittelson, James, and Ken Schurb. "The Curious Histories of the Wittenberg Concord." *Concordia Theological Quarterly* 50.2, (April, 1986), 119–137. Investigates the influence of the Wittenberg Concord on Lutheranism's Formula of Concord, with reference to current research.

Köhler, Walther. *Zwingli und Luther: Ihr Streit über das Abendmahl nach seinen politischen und religiösen Beziehungen.* Vol. 2. Reprint, New York and London, 1971. Interprets the Wittenberg Concord as an ambiguous agreement that Luther later rejects.

Kolde, Theodor. "*Wittenberger Konkordie.*" In *Realencyclopädie für protestantische Theologie und Kirche*, edited by Albert Hauck, vol. 21, pp. 383–399. Leipzig, 1908. An abbreviated translation of this excellent investigation, with its thorough guide to the ample primary sources, appears in *The New Schaff-Herzog Encyclopedia of Religious Knowledge*, edited by Samuel M. Jackson, vol. 12, pp. 396–400, Grand Rapids, Mich., 1950.

Maurer, Wilhelm. "*Wittenberger Konkordie.*" In *Die Religion in Geschichte und Gegenwart*, edited by Hans von Campenhausen et al., vol. 6, pp. 1784–1785. Tübingen, 1962. A brief overview with a helpful bibliography.

Russell, William R. *Luther's Theological Testament: The Schmalkald Articles.* Minneapolis, 1994. Discusses the proceedings of the May 1536 meeting at Wittenberg and the content of the Wittenberg Concord in relation to the Schmalkald Articles.

WILLIAM R. RUSSELL

WITZEL, Georg (1501–1573), Catholic theologian. Born in the German village of Vacha, Witzel was an engaging and prolific author who strains conventional categories. A pupil of Martin Luther and an early convert to Lutheranism, he was also one of the first to reject Luther, returning to the church of Rome and devoting a long life to Rome's defense and church reunion. Though ordained a priest and loyal to Rome, he remained married as he worked tirelessly on tasks of ecumenism, ecclesiastical reform, and ecclesiastical concord, striving to heal the schism that opened around (and within) him in his youth. Convinced that the church of Rome was the true communion, he never dismissed a number of the more severe strictures advanced by Luther against the vices and greed of the papacy of that age but instead provoked anger and resentment among more than a few fellow Catholics as he pressed for fundamental reforms within the church. Pessimistic concerning the efficacy of controversial theology ("book merely begets book," he nonetheless wrote), he produced a corpus of more than 130 theological works. (Eck said of him that he brought forth writings "oftener than the rabbit her young.") His own life was punctuated by sudden flights and harassments provoked by his frank criticisms of Catholics and Protestants alike.

After entering the University of Erfurt in 1516 (earning distinction in classical studies) and joining the newly formed Erasmian Sodality, Witzel found himself powerfully attracted to the ideas of Luther. At the age of twenty he went to Wittenberg, where he pursued study of the scripture and the early Fathers. Upon his ordination as a priest the following year and his subsequent marriage to Elizabeth Kraus, he experienced the first of the losses and forced removals his views were to cost him. Losing his vicarage in Vacha because of his marriage, he journeyed with his wife to her birthplace, Eisenach, where he secured a new vicarage.

Upon appointment as consultant in religious matters to the court of Duke George of Saxony in 1538, Witzel assumed the task of assisting in the formulation of a reform program that would follow a middle path between papal and Lutheran extremes. In 1539 Witzel assumed the task of assisting in the composition of a reform program that would follow a middle path between papal and Lutheran extremes. In 1539, in collaboration with Martin Bucer at a religious colloquy at Leipzig, he worked out a reform program inspired by the old motto "Back to the simple apostolic Church!" Drawing on Justin's Apology (A.D. 150), the proposed program advocated simplicity and emphasized the communal nature of divine services. It was to abolish private Mass, place on equal footing the Latin and German languages, revise the canon of the Mass, and reduce the number of feast days.

The ideas in the program were later developed by Witzel and published in 1540 in a work titled *Typus Ecclesiae Catholicae*, which drew on quotations from the Fathers ranging from Clement to Bernard of Clairvaux, emphasized that faith was based upon the authority of divine law (which must be understood and interpreted according to the tradition of the church), and held up the church of antiquity as the ideal form for a renewed church.

Witzel's lifelong vision of a return to a simple, apostolic church seems to have been inspired by the church as it existed in the eighth century guided by the doctrines of the first four councils. The dream of healing a "wounded religion"—of working toward reforms so that at least "something might be improved and purified within the house of God"—was a constant inspiration for Witzel. Called a papist by Lutherans and a Lutheran by Catholics and denigrated as a vacillator even by some modern commentators, Witzel learned that an age of turmoil and bitter doctrinal struggle is rarely eager to reward moderate men capable of recognizing merit on both sides of a vast controversy. Those bent on tracing the great division that arose in Christianity in the age of the Reformation can study the great liturgist Georg Witzel with profit; throughout his life this priest occupied a perilous position precisely at that line of division.

BIBLIOGRAPHY

Primary Sources

Volz, Hans, ed. *Drei Schriften gegen Luthers Schmalkaldische Artikel von Cochlaeus, Witzel und Hofmeister (1538 und 1539)*. Münster, 1932.
Witzel, Georg. *Via regia sive de controversis religionis capitibus consiliandis sententia*. Helmstedt, 1983.

Secondary Sources

Dolan, John P. "The Influence of Erasmus, Witzel and Cassander in the Church Ordinances and Reform Proposals of the United Duchees of Cleve During the Middle Decades of the 16th Century." *Reformationgeschichtliche Studien und Texte* 83 (1957), 119. Though focused on three thinkers, this work devotes about as many pages to Witzel as to the other two combined. Its second chapter alone, "Witzel and the Continuity of Reform Policy," supplies nearly sixty pages of valuable information concerning Witzel's doctrinal, educational, and liturgical views. Further material concerning Witzel appears at other places in the treatise.
———. *History of the Reformation*. New York, 1965. Useful observations concerning Witzel are scattered throughout this volume; see esp. chap. 8 for an excellent introduction to his life and thought written from a sympathetic perspective.
Kathrein, Werner. "Ein Reformgutachten Georg Witzels (1501–1573) für Herzog Georg den Bärtigen von Sachsen aus dem Jahr 1538." *Archiv für mittelrheinische Kirchengeschichte* 44 (1992), 343–379.
Pralle, L. "Die Volksliturgischen Bestrebungen des Georg Witzel, 1501–1572." *Jahrbuch für das Bistum Mainz*, 1948.
Richter, Gregor. *Die Schriften George Witzels Bearbeitet: Bibliographisch nebst einigen bisher ungedruckten Reformationsgutachten und Briefen Witzels* (1913). Reprint, Nieuwkoop, 1963. A comprehensive bibliographic guide to Witzel's writings and correspondence, in addition, it contains the Latin and German texts of several of his reform tracts, a portrait of him, a photographic reproduction of a page of his handwriting, and several pages of his own written remarks concerning a 1553 catalog of his writings.

JOHN M. DOLAN

WOLSEY, Thomas (1472?–1530), cardinal archbishop of York, lord chancellor of England, and leading minister to Henry VIII. Wolsey's reputation as a churchman has never been high. By virtue of his position as leading royal minister (c.1513–1529) and papal *legate a latere* (1518–1529), he exercised unprecedented power over the English church, which, so his critics have maintained, he used merely to further his own private ends. Nor has it helped his reputation that he exercised this power on the eve of the English Reformation; those unsympathetic to the late medieval church have portrayed him as a typical representative of a Roman Catholic church in terminal decline, while Roman Catholics have sought to blame him for a catastrophe that should not have occurred. What has rarely taken place is any detailed assessment of what his aims and achievements as a churchman were.

There is nothing out of the ordinary about somebody of Wolsey's background—his father was a reasonably successful innkeeper and butcher of Ipswich—going to university (in his case New College, Oxford) and proceeding from there to a successful career in church and state. By 1508 he was in royal service, and with the accession of Henry VIII in 1509 his career began to take off. By 1515 he was archbishop of York, and in that same year he became both a cardinal and lord chancellor. But since Canterbury, which traditionally had primacy over York, was held by William Warham, it was not until 1518, when he became *legate a latere*, that he was legally master of the English church, and it was not until 1524 that his legatine commission was granted him for life.

His first task as legate was to establish his authority over what, from one point of view, can be seen as a mosaic of deeply entrenched vested interests. These included his fellow bishops, traditionally extremely protective of their own jurisdiction and financial rights, and the many religious orders, whose monastic houses were such a dominant feature of the late medieval landscape. Many of these, but especially the more wealthy and influential, were exempt from episcopal control, and it was the stated purpose of the legatine commissions to provide Wolsey with powers to reform all the religious orders; most especially he was given the right to conduct legatine visitations. In November 1519 Wolsey held a meeting of leading abbots and priors to discuss reform. There followed in 1520 legatine statutes for the Benedictines, and in 1521 for the Augustinians, these two orders being by far the most important in England.

Wolsey's powers over the secular clergy were initially not nearly so well defined, but he quickly declared his intentions by calling a meeting of bishops for March 1519 to consider reform and in the same year issued legatine constitutions for the English church. Full details of these have not survived. It is unlikely that they were radical, but they were a way of making clear that he had no intention of presiding over a church that was not functioning effectively.

Not surprisingly, some opposition arose to Wolsey's assertion of his novel authority—among the religious orders from the numerically small but influential Franciscan observants, from some ordinary clergy, and most dangerously from Wolsey's point of view, from the archbishop of Canterbury, William Warham, who in December 1518 had attempted to upstage Wolsey by calling his own reforming council. All this opposition, including Warham's, was remarkably halfhearted and ineffective for two reasons. First, Wolsey was a most skilled negotiator, always seeking to conciliate rather than to confront. Second, he had the support of the king, who was determined to be master of his own church.

By 1524 the legatine machinery was in place. The bishops, including Warham, had made their compositions with him, whereby they bought back their jurisdictional rights, but at the same time secured both legatine support in any conflict with the religious orders within their dioceses and some protection from the Crown lawyers, who in Henry VII's reign had attempted to challenge their jurisdiction. Wolsey's legatine powers undoubtedly brought him financial gain—from these episcopal compositions, from legatine visitation fees (procurations), from legatine testamentary jurisdiction, and the like. He also introduced the practice, common on the Continent, of holding more than one episcopal see; thus in 1518, despite the fact that he was already archbishop of York, he became bishop of Bath and Wells, exchanging this see for Durham in 1523, and Durham for Winchester in 1529. But his chief concern was with power rather than money, and the real question is for what ends he sought it.

One purpose has already been suggested: he was anxious to increase royal control, thereby making it easier for the Crown to obtain more money from the church and to increase royal ecclesiastical patronage. It is less easy to establish how beneficial for the church this increase was, since much of the evidence is missing and hard to interpret. But the fact that historians are increasingly of the view that in the 1520s the English church was in good shape suggests that a favorable verdict is in order. Moreover, many of his appointments appear to have been good ones, and those he sought to remove from office deserved to be so.

Most significantly, he responded immediately to the challenge posed by the Lutheran heresy: Lutheran works were prohibited; propaganda sermons such as those delivered by England's leading theologian, the bishop of Rochester, John Fisher, in 1521 and 1526 were organized; and those suspected of Lutheranism, such as Thomas Bilney, were tried before legatine courts. More creatively, in 1528 and 1529 Wolsey obtained papal authority to embark on major monastic and diocesan reform, the essence of his plan being to streamline the religious orders so that they would be a more effective force in the battle against Luther and to enable his bishops to exercise more effective control by creating many more, and smaller, dioceses. To provide the English with a better-educated clergy he founded a new college at Oxford, at which theological studies, using both old and new methods, that is, both Scholasticism and humanism, were to dominate.

Sadly for Wolsey, and for the fate of Roman Catholicism in England, in October 1529 Henry VIII dismissed him from office, and just over a year later he died. The reasons for Wolsey's downfall remain a matter of some debate. Was he brought down by faction, led by the dukes of Norfolk and Suffolk, resentful of his enormous political power, or was it Henry himself who decided to dispense with his services, and if so why? Wolsey's position was undoubtedly undermined by the failure in July 1529 of the Second Legatine Court sitting in London to grant Henry what he was determined above all else to obtain, a divorce from his first wife, Catherine of Aragon. A new strategy was required. By accusing his cardinal legate of praemunire for exercising his legatine powers to "provide" priests to benefices, Henry was sending a strong reminder to Clement VII that papal power in England survived only because the king allowed it. When by the following summer it became clear that Clement was not to be frightened in this way, and that, furthermore, important sections of the English church were unsympathetic to his demands for a divorce, Henry's answer was to arrest Wolsey on a charge of high treason as the clearest possible signal that he was determined to get his way. Wolsey died—at Leicester Abbey on 29 November—before he could be put on trial. Nevertheless, Wolsey deserves to be remembered as one of the first victims of the Henrician Reformation, for he was certainly politically destroyed by it.

BIBLIOGRAPHY

Gwyn, Peter. *The King's Cardinal: The Rise and Fall of Thomas Wolsey.* London, 1990. Contains the first detailed research on Wolsey's exercise of legatine powers; some people may think that it passes a far too favorable judgment.

Haigh, Christopher. "Anti-Clericalism and the English Reformation." *History* 68 (1983), 391–407. Useful for both a revisionist view of the late medieval church and, as regards Wolsey, a corrective to Gwyn.

Harper-Bill, C. "Archbishop John Morton and the Province of Canterbury, 1486–1500." *Journal of Ecclesiastical History* 29 (1978), 1–21. Provides a most useful comparison.

Kelly, M. J. "Canterbury Jurisdiction and Influence during the Episcopate of William Warham, 1503–1532." Ph.D. thesis, University of Cambridge, 1965. An unpublished thesis, but despite the title, an essential work for Wolsey.

Knowles, David. *The Religious Orders in England.* Vol. 3. Cambridge, 1961. Still the best work on the religious orders, though perhaps overcritical, and unsympathetic to Wolsey.

O'Day, Rosemary, and Felicity Heal. *Continuity and Change: Personnel and Administration of the Church of England, 1500–1642.* Leicester, 1976. Contains some important revisionist essays on the pre-Reformation English church.

Pollard, A. F. *Wolsey.* London, 1929. Highly critical of all aspects of Wolsey's activities, but especially of his churchmanship.

Schuster, L. A., R. C. Marius, J. P. Lusardi, and R. J. Schoek. *The Yale Edition of the Complete Works of Saint Thomas More.* Vol. 8, *The Confutation of Tyndale's Answer.* New Haven, 1973. Very useful on Wolsey's response to heresy, but see Gwyn.

Thompson, S. "The Pastoral Work of the English and Welsh Bishops, 1500–1558." D.Phil. thesis, University of Oxford, 1984. An unpublished thesis, but very important for episcopal activity in Wolsey's time.

PETER GWYN

WOMEN. Since the late 1960s, women's history has developed as a new field of historical inquiry as scholars have begun systematically to examine the experiences of the half of the human population that had been largely left out of traditional historical scholarship. This research has involved both the reinterpretation of well-known texts and images and the discovery of new sources that provide evidence of women's lives.

Both types of research are ongoing in Reformation scholarship. Theologians and intellectual historians are reexamining the writings of major and minor reformers to discover their ideas about women and other related subjects such as marriage, motherhood, sexuality, and the family. They are examining how these ideas were communicated through the use of plays, woodcuts, marriage and funeral sermons, pamphlets, letters, and popular stories. Art historians are analyzing the paintings, woodcuts, and engravings that were produced to support both the Protestant and Catholic Reformations to find positive and negative images of women, and to see how female characters and attributes were used symbolically, such as the pope being shown as the whore of Babylon in Protestant pamphlets.

By combing archives and private family documents, social historians are discovering that the institutional and political changes that accompanied the Reformation often affected women's lives at least as much as the changes in religious ideas. The closing of the convents, secularization and centralization of public welfare and charitable institutions, changes in marriage and baptismal ordinances, the possibility of divorce, clerical marriage, the closing of public brothels, and the hardships created by the religious wars all had a particular impact on women, and have been the focus of local and regional studies.

Historians of women have also begun to explore women's responses to the Reformation, responses of both words and actions. Women were not simply passive recipients of the Reformation message, but left convents, refused to leave convents; preached; prophesied; discussed religion with friends and family; converted their husbands, left their husbands; wrote religious poems, hymns, and polemics; and were martyred on all sides of the religious controversy. Official sources, such as tax lists, city council minutes, and court documents, reveal some of these actions, as do the published and unpublished writings of women. Finding such sources can be difficult, for fewer women than men recorded their thoughts, ideas, and reactions, and when they did, their writings were rarely saved, for they were not regarded as valuable. Many of Luther's letters to women, for instance, are still extant, though only a few of theirs to him are. None of his wife's numerous letters to him survive, though most of his to her do. Finding information about women in official sources poses special problems, for sources are arranged by male names, occupations, and places of residence, with women recorded only sporadically and then often only when widowed or single. Despite these difficulties, however, a picture of women's responses to the Reformation is slowly emerging, enabling one to compare these across class, regional, and confessional lines as well as to the more familiar responses of men.

The comparison of female and male experience first undertaken as part of women's history led in the 1980s to an interest in gender itself, that is, in how past and present societies determine what the consequences of biological sex differences are. Historians now recognize that not only were women's experiences shaped by the fact that they were women but men's by the fact that they were men, and a few Reformation historians are beginning to question, for example, what effects the Reformation had on notions of masculinity or ideas about real and symbolic fatherhood. For some, gender has become a standard category of historical analysis just like social class, so that their investigations of all aspects of the Reformation, even those that initially may not seem to have much to do with women, now question how these affected relations between the sexes or differed for women and men.

The Reformers' Ideas about Women. Much disagreement has arisen in the late twentieth century among scholars in their assessments of the religious reformers' ideas about women. One of the reasons for this is that many of the most important religious leaders of the period were not consistent, expressing strongly negative opinions of women at some points and very positive ones at others. For example, Martin Luther notes at one point, "There is nothing better on earth than a woman's love," and at another, "Women are created for no other purpose than to serve men and be their helpers. If women grow weary or even die while bearing children, that doesn't harm anything. Let them bear children to death; they are created for that" (*Sämmtliche Werke*, Erlangen and Frankfurt, 1826–1857, vol 61, p. 212; vol. 20, p. 84). A second is that other leaders, such as John Calvin, expressed their view of women only obliquely while considering other issues, so that their opinions must be extrapolated and require a high degree of interpretation. A third is that many contemporary scholars have strong personal or religious convictions regarding certain religious leaders or the denominations they founded, so that it is sometimes difficult for them to accept the opinions they find. Despite the contradictions and ambiguities in the writings of religious thinkers, and the differences of opinion among modern scholars, however, one can make some generalizations about the impact of religious change on ideas about women.

Though they broke with the institutional structure and denounced many of the theological ideas of the Catholic church, the Protestant reformers did not break sharply with the medieval scholastic theologians in their ideas about women. For Luther, Zwingli, Calvin, and the leaders of the English Puritans, women were created by God and could be saved through faith; in that respect women and men were spiritually equal. In every other respect, however, women were to be subordinate to men. Women's subjection was inherent in their very being and was present from creation—in this the reformers agreed with Aristotle and the classical tradition, though Luther in particular denounced the ideas of Aristotle on other matters and saw the scholastic attempt to reconcile Aristotle and the Bible as misguided. Most reformers accepted Eve's principal responsibility for the Fall and thought this had made women's original natural inferiority and subjection to male authority even more pronounced. Protestants generally supported Paul's teaching that women should be silent in church, though Calvin, alone among sixteenth-century leaders, noted that this teaching was determined by tradition and custom rather than divine commandment and so might be open to change; but he did not see this change happening in the near future or make any practical attempts to bring it about. A few small Anabaptist groups that emphasized the importance of divine revelation took the visions of their female members seriously, although not until the seventeenth-century Quakers did any group officially allow women to hold positions of religious authority.

The Protestants did break with official Catholic teachings on the relative merits of celibacy and marriage and wrote large numbers of tracts trying to convince men and women to marry and advising spouses (particularly husbands) how best to run their households and families. It is in this pro-marriage literature that one finds the most positive statements about women, for the writers recognized that many of their readers were former priests and monks who had been trained to regard marriage, sexuality, and women in general as destroyers of their spiritual well-being. The writers used the story of Eve being created out of Adam's rib as proof that God wanted women to stand by the side of men as their assistants and not be trampled on or trod underfoot (for then Eve would have been created out of Adam's foot);

these directives always mention as well, however, that women should never claim authority over men, for Eve had not been created out of Adam's head.

Protestant marriage manuals, household guides, and marriage sermons all stress the importance of husbandly authority and wifely obedience. For almost all Protestants, this obedience took precedence over women's spiritual equality; a woman's religious convictions were never grounds for leaving or even openly disagreeing with her husband, though she could pray for his conversion. The only exceptions to this generalization were some radical reformers who did allow women to leave their unbelieving spouses, but the women who did so were expected to remarry quickly and thus come under the authority of a male believer. Women were continually advised to be cheerful rather than grudging in their obedience, for in doing so they demonstrated their willingness to follow God's plan. Men were also given specific advice about how to enforce their authority, which often included physical coercion; in both Continental and English marriage manuals, the authors use the metaphor of breaking a horse for teaching a wife obedience. Though the opinions of women who read such works were not often recorded, one gets the impression from private letters that women knew they were expected to be obedient and silent, for they often excused their actions when they did not conform to the ideal. Such letters also indicate, however, that women's view of the ideal wife was one in which competence and companionship were as important as submissiveness.

The Protestant exhortation to marry was directed to both sexes, but particularly to women, for whom marriage and motherhood were a vocation as well as a living arrangement. Marriage was also regarded as a way for women to control their sexual urges, which in the sixteenth century were regarded as much stronger than men's. Unmarried women were thus suspect, both because they were fighting their natural sex drives and because they were upsetting the divinely imposed order, which made woman subject to man. It is important to recognize, then, that the Protestant elevation of marriage is not the same as, and may in fact directly contradict, an elevation of women *as women*.

The opinions of Protestant leaders about marriage and women were not contained simply in written works but were communicated to their congregations through marriage sermons and homilies; because people in many parts of Europe were required to attend church, there was no way they could escape hearing them. Their opinions were also reflected in woodcuts and engravings that illustrated religious pamphlets, an important tool in the spread of Protestant ideas. The ideal woman appears frequently in both sermons and illustrations: sitting with her children, listening to a sermon or reading the Bible, dressed soberly and with her hair modestly covered. Negative depictions also appear: the nun who quotes her psalter while her attention is elsewhere; the priest's concubine; prostitutes or women dressed extravagantly buying indulgences or expensive rosaries; disobedient wives being beaten by their husbands.

Catholic reformers responded to the Protestant elevation of marriage by reaffirming traditional doctrine and emphasizing that the most worthy type of Christian life was one both celibate and chaste. Spouses who took mutual vows of chastity within a marriage or left marriage to enter cloisters were praised. Catholic authors also realized, however, that despite exhortations to celibacy, most women in Europe would marry, and so wrote marriage manuals to counteract those written by Protestants. The ideal wife they described was exactly the same as that proposed by Protestant authors—obedient, silent, pious—and their words give clear indication that they still regarded women as totally inferior. Thus the opinions of learned Catholic authors about women, as well as about marriage, tended to reaffirm traditional negative ideas, though the harshest criticisms were generally reserved for specific women who challenged male authority in some way rather than simply being addressed to women in general in the style of Tertullian or Jerome. Catholic leaders from the late sixteenth century on often recognized that women were useful allies in the fight to reconvert or hold areas to the Catholic faith, so they did not openly express the type of harshly misogynist ideas that were common in pre-Reformation writers.

The Protestant Reformation. Just as scholars disagree about the reformers' ideas, they also debate the impact of these ideas, for the Protestant and Catholic Reformations both expanded and diminished women's opportunities. In terms of the Protestant Reformation, the period in which women were the most active was the decade or so immediately following an area's decision to break with the Catholic church or while this decision was being made. During this period, many groups and individuals tried to shape the new religious institutions. Sometimes this popular pressure took the form of religious riots, in which women frequently participated. In 1536 at Exeter in England, for example, a group of women armed with shovels and pikes attacked workers who had been hired by the government to dismantle a monastery. Sometimes this popular pressure took the form of writing, when women and men who did not have formal theological training took Luther's notion of the "priesthood of all believers" literally and preached or published polemical religious literature explaining their own ideas.

Women's preaching and publishing of religious material stood in direct opposition to the words ascribed to Paul (*1 Tim.* 2: 11–15) that ordered women not to teach or preach, so that all women who published felt it necessary to justify their actions. The boldest, such as Argula von Grumbach, a German noblewoman who published a defense of a teacher accused of Lutheran leanings, commented that the situation was so serious that Paul's words should simply be disregarded: "I am not unfamiliar with Paul's words that women should be silent in church, but when I see that no man will or can speak, I am driven by the word of God when he said, 'He who confesses me on earth, him will I confess and he who denies me, him will I deny' " (Ludwig Rabus, *Historien der heyligen Außerwolten Gottes Zeugen, Bekennern und Martyrern*, n.p., 1557, fol. 41). Ursula Weyda, a middle-class German woman who attacked the abbot of Pegau in a 1524 pamphlet, agreed, as did Marie Dentière, a former abbess who left her convent to help the cause of the Reformation in Geneva and published a letter to Marguerite d'Angoulême in 1539 defending some of the reformers exiled from that city. Katharina Zell, the wife of one of Strasbourg's reformers and a tireless worker for the Reformation, asked that her writings not be judged according to the standards of a woman but simply according to the standards of a divinely inspired Christian.

Zell's wish was never granted, and women's writings were always judged first on the basis of gender. Argula von Grumbach's husband was ordered to force her to stop writing, and Marie Dentière's pamphlets were confiscated by the very religious authorities she was defending. Once Protestant churches were institutionalized, polemical writings by women (and untrained men) largely stopped. Women continued to write hymns and devotional literature, but these were often published posthumously or were designed for private use.

Women's actions as well as their writings in the first years of the Reformation upset political and religious authorities. Many cities prohibited women from even getting together to discuss religious matters, and in 1543 an act of Parliament in England banned all women except those of the gentry and nobility from reading the Bible; upper-class women were also prohibited from reading the Bible aloud to others. Class as well as gender hierarchies were to be maintained at all costs, though women's diaries reveal that this restriction was rarely obeyed and that they frequently read the Bible to themselves and to others.

The ability of a woman to act out her religious convictions was largely dependent on class in reality as well as in theory. Though none of the reformers differentiated between noblewomen and commoners in their public advice or writings, in private they recognized that noblewomen had a great deal of power and made special attempts to win them over. Luther corresponded regularly with a number of prominent noblewomen, and Calvin was even more assiduous at trying to win noblewomen to his cause. Their efforts often succeeded, for in a number of cases female rulers converted their territories to Protestantism or influenced their male relatives to do so. In Germany, Elisabeth of Brunswick-Calenburg brought in Protestant preachers and established a new church structure; in France, Marguerite d'Angoulême and her daughter Jeanne of Navarre supported Calvinism through patronage and political influence; in Norway, Inger of Austraat, a powerful and wealthy noblewoman, led the opposition to the Norwegian archbishop, who remained loyal to Catholicism. The most dramatic example of the degree to which a woman's personal religious convictions could influence events occurred in England, when, after Mary Tudor attempted to wrench the country back to Catholicism, Elizabeth created a moderately Protestant church. In all of these cases political and dynastic concerns mixed with religious convictions, in the same way they did for male rulers and nobles.

Once the Reformation was established, most women expressed their religious convictions in a domestic rather than a public setting. They prayed and recited the catechism with children and servants, attended sermons, read the Bible or other devotional literature if they were literate, and served meals that no longer followed Catholic fast prescriptions. Women's domestic religion often took them beyond the household, however, for they gave charitable donations to the needy and often assisted in caring for the ill and indigent. As it had been before the Reformation, most women's charity was on a case-by-case basis, but there are also examples from Protestant areas of women who established and supported almshouses, schools, orphanages, funds for poor widows, and dowry funds for poor girls. The secularization of public welfare that accompanied the Reformation did give some women the opportunity to create permanent institutions to deal with social problems; evidence from wills indicates that women were, perhaps not surprisingly, more likely than men to make bequests that specifically benefited other women.

The women whose domestic religious activities were most closely scrutinized in the first generation of the Protestant Reformation were the wives of the reformers. During the first few years of the Reformation, they were still likened to priests' concubines in the public mind and had to create a respectable role for themselves, a task made even more difficult by the fact that many were, in fact, former nuns. They were often living demonstrations of their husbands' convictions and were expected to be models of wifely obedience and Christian charity. The women whose status was most tenuous were the wives of English bishops. Not only were many forced into exile or, worse yet, repudiated by their husbands during Mary's reign, but their marriages were not formally approved by Elizabeth, so that their children could always be declared bastards. Bishops were expected to live like wealthy noblemen and were accorded high rank at all ceremonial occasions, but their wives had no rank whatsoever. Long after Continental pastors' wives had succeeded in making theirs a respectable position, bishops' wives in England still had not achieved even legal recognition despite all their efforts at maintaining pious households.

No matter how much it was extolled in Protestant sermons and domestic conduct books, the vocation of mother and wife was not enough for some women, whose religious convictions led them to leave their husbands and continue to express their religious convictions publicly, even at the cost of their lives. One of the most famous of these was Ann Askew, an English woman who was tortured and then executed for her religious beliefs in 1546. Askew was one of the few women martyrs to come from a gentry or middleclass background. Of the people executed for religious reasons during the reign of Mary Tudor in England, one-fifth were women, and most of these were quite poor; wealthy people who opposed Mary fled to the Continent.

Most of the women executed for religious reasons in early modern Europe were Anabaptists. The interrogations of Anabaptists are one of the few sources we have for the religious ideas of people who were illiterate. From these records, it is clear that many women could argue complicated theological concepts and had memorized large parts of the Bible. Anabaptist women actively chose the path of martyrdom, often against the pressure of family members, and the records of their trials reveal a strong sense of determination. Their strength of purpose may now appear heroic, but to many of their contemporaries Anabaptist women seemed demonically inspired, and in some ways the interrogations of Anabaptists parallel later witchcraft interrogations. In both cases, young women were stripped naked before they were tortured and were asked not only to confess their beliefs but also to name accomplices; the beliefs they were accused of were viewed as so pernicious that normal rules of legal procedure did not apply; most of those accused were poor.

At the same time that it created new roles for women—religious polemicist, pastor's wife, domestic missionary, philanthropist, martyr—the Protestant Reformation also rejected many of the activities that had previously given women's lives religious meaning. Religious processions that had included both men and women, such as that of Corpus Christi, were prohibited, and laws restricted the celebration of baptisms, weddings, and funerals, all ceremonies in which women had played a major role. Lay female confraternities, which had provided emotional and economic assistance for their members and charity for the needy, were also forbidden, and no all-female groups replaced them. The new charitable funds founded by women for women often had men as their overseers, and in any case did not bring together women of different classes as comembers the way confraternities had, but made sharp distinctions between the bestower and recipient of charity. The reformers attempted to do away with the veneration of Mary and the saints, though women continued to pray to Mary and Saints Anne and Margaret, the patron saints of childbirth, for centuries. The Protestant martyrs replaced the saints to some degree as models worthy of emulation, but one was not to pray to them, and their names were not given to any days of the year, which stripped the calendar of celebrations honoring women.

The Protestant rejection of celibacy had the greatest impact on female religious, both cloistered nuns and women who lived in less formal religious communities. One of the first moves of an area rejecting Catholicism was to close the monasteries and convents, either confiscating the buildings and land immediately or forbidding new novices and allowing the current residents to live out their lives on a portion of the convent's old income. In England and Ireland, where all monasteries and convents were taken over by the Crown, most nuns got very small pensions and were expected to return to their families, though not all did. Many Irish nuns fled to religious communities on the Continent or continued to fulfill their religious vows in hiding while they waited for the chance to emigrate. In many cities of the Netherlands, the convents were closed, their assets liquidated, and the women given their dowries and a pension. Though some returned to their families, others continued to live together in small, informal domestic groups. Because Catholic ceremonies and organizations were banned, it is difficult to find information about the subsequent life of these women, termed *kloppen* or *geestelijke maagden* ("holy maidens"). Land-ownership records and family genealogies reveal that groups of them lived together or near one another long after areas became officially Protestant; these groups actually grew in number during the seventeenth century. Many were members of wealthy and prominent upper-class families who had only slowly accepted the Reformation, so they were supported by their families in their decisions to remain unmarried and devote themselves to religious activities. Even when prominent families did become Protestant, they sometimes continued to support convents because of long-standing traditions. For example, the convent at Vadstena in Sweden had long housed female members of the Swedish royal family, and when Swedish rulers became Protestant in the 1520s they thought it inappropriate simply to close it down. Instead they attempted to convince the nuns to accept Protestantism willingly, but the nuns resisted, stuffing wool and wax in their ears when they were forced to attend Lutheran services. The convent survived until the 1590s, when royal patience gave out; the nuns were then forcibly evicted and the convent's treasures and library confiscated.

This link between convents and prominent families was most pronounced in the Holy Roman Empire, where many convents had been established by regional ruling houses or by the wives and daughters of emperors. Many of them had been reformed in the fifteenth century, and long traditions of power, independence, and prestige combined with a reinvigorated spiritual life to make reformed convents the most vocal and resolute opponents of the Protestant Reformation. For the nuns who were were nobles, their determination had social and political as well as religious roots. They recognized that as women they could have no office in any Protestant church; the role of a pastor's wife was an unthinkable decrease in status for a woman of noble standing.

In some territories of central Germany, the nuns' firmness combined with other religious and political factors to allow many convents to survive for centuries as Catholic establishments within Protestant territories. In the bishoprics of Magdeburg and Halberstadt, which became Protestant, half of the female convents survived, but only one-fifth of the monasteries. One factor in this survival rate was certainly the women's zeal, but another was that religious and political authorities did not regard the women's institutions to be as great a threat as the men's. The marriage market for upper-class women also played a role. The cost of dowries was rising in early modern Germany, and wealthy families often could not afford to marry off all their daughters to appropriate partners; even Lutheran nobles opposed the closing of convents because they had no idea how they would otherwise support their female relatives.

Some convents also survived as religious institutions by accepting Lutheran theology except for its rejection of the monastic life. For example, Anna von Stolberg was the abbess of the free imperial abbey of Quedlinburg, and so governed a sizable territory, including nine churches and two male monasteries. When she became Protestant in the 1540s she made all priests swear to Luther's Augsburg Confession and turned her Franciscan monastery into an elementary school for both boys and girls, an interesting gender reversal of the usual pattern of male authorities transforming female convents into schools or using convent property to fund scholars (male, of course) at universities. She continued to receive both imperial and papal privileges, for Catholic authorities were unwilling to cut off support from what was, at any rate, still a *convent*. She was also not uniformly criticized by Lutheran leaders, however, who emphasized that she was, at any rate, *Lutheran*. Quedlinburg was not the only abbey in this situation. At least fourteen Lutheran convents in the relatively small territory of Braunschweig-Lüneburg survived into the nineteenth century, most of which have remained religious establishments for unmarried women to the twentieth century.

It is difficult to determine how many convents throughout the empire were able to survive as either Catholic or Protestant institutions, because their existence was in some ways an embarrassment to secular and religious authorities attempting to enforce a policy of religious uniformity. Many of the urban convents in south Germany, such as those in Strasbourg and Nuremberg, fought disbanding as long as they could, despite being forced to listen to daily sermons, being denied confessors and Catholic ceremonies, and even having residents forcibly dragged out by their families. (The few male monasteries that actually opposed the Reformation were simply ordered shut and their residents banished from the territory, an action that could not be used against convents, as their residents were usually the daughters of local families and would have nowhere outside the territory to go.) Finally urban authorities often gave up their direct attacks and simply forbade the taking in of new novices, so that the convents slowly died out. A few also followed the central German pattern of becoming Protestant; one convent in Ulm survived as a Protestant institution until the nineteenth century.

The distinction between Protestant and Catholic that is so important in understanding the religious and intellectual history of sixteenth-century Europe may have ultimately been less important to the women who lived in convents and other communal groups than the distinction between their pattern of life and that of the majority of laywomen. Evidence from convents in Braunschweig and Augsburg indicates that Protestant and Catholic women lived together quite peacefully for decades, protected by the walls of their convent from the religious conflicts surrounding them. Women in the Netherlands and England, denied the possibility of remaining in their convents, continued to live together, letting their formal religious affiliation remain a matter of speculation, both for contemporaries and for historians. The Protestant championing of marriage and family life, which some nuns accepted with great enthusiasm as a message of liberation from the convent, was viewed by others as a negation of the value of the life they had been living; they thus did all in their power to continue in their chosen path.

The Catholic Reformation. The response of the Catholic church to the Protestant Reformation is often described as two interrelated movements, a Counter-Reformation and a reform. Women were actively involved in both movements, but their actions were generally judged more acceptable when they were part of a reform drive; even more than the medieval Crusades, the fight against Protestants was to be a masculine affair.

The masculine nature of the Counter-Reformation was intimately related to one of the key aspects of church reform—an enforcement of cloistering for women. Reforms of the church beginning with the Gregorian in the eleventh century had all emphasized the importance of the control of female sexuality and the inappropriateness of women religious being in contact with lay society; claustration was a key part of the restrictions on Beguines in the fourteenth century and of the fifteenth-century reform of the convents. The problem became even more acute after the Protestant Reformation, for numerous women in Europe felt God had called them to oppose Protestants directly through missionary work or to carry out the type of active service to the world in schools and hospitals that the Franciscans, Dominicans, and the new orders such as the Jesuits were making increasingly popular with men. For example, Angela Merici founded the Company of Saint Ursula in Brescia, Italy. The company was a group of lay single women and widows dedicated to serving the poor, the ill, orphans, and war victims, earning their own living through teaching or weaving. Merici received papal approval in 1535, for the pope saw this as a counterpart to the large number of men's lay confraternities and societies that were springing up in Italy as part of the movement to reform the church.

Similar groups of laywomen dedicated to charitable service began to arise in other cities of Italy, Spain, and France, and in 1541 Isabel Roser decided to go one step further and ask for papal approval for an order of religious women with a similar mission. Roser had been an associate of Ignatius Loyola, the founder of the Jesuits, in Barcelona. She saw her group as a female order of Jesuits that, like the Jesuits, would not be cut off from the world but would devote itself to education, care of the sick, and assistance to the poor, and in so doing win converts back to Catholicism. But this vision was going too far. Ignatius was horrified at the thought of religious women in constant contact with laypeople, and Pope Paul III refused to grant his approval. Nevertheless, her group continued to grow in Rome and in the Netherlands, where they spread Ignatius's teaching through the use of the Jesuit catechism.

The Council of Trent reaffirmed the necessity of claustration for all women religious and called for an end to all uncloistered communities. Enforcement of this decree came slowly, however, for several reasons. First, women's communities themselves fought it or ignored it. For example, followers of Isabel Roser were still active into the seventeenth century, as is evident from Pope Urban VIII publishing a bull to suppress them (1630), and reporting that they were building convents and choosing abbesses and rectors. The residents of some of Roser's communities and other convents that fought strict claustration were often from wealthy urban families who could pressure church officials. Second, church officials themselves recognized the value of the services performed by such communities, particularly in the area of girls' education and care of the sick. Well after Trent, Carlo Borromeo, a reforming archbishop in Milan, invited in members of the Company of Saint Ursula, and transformed the group from one of laywomen into one of religious who lived communally, though they still were not cloistered. From Milan, the Ursulines spread throughout the rest of Italy and into France and started to focus completely on the education of girls. They became so popular that noble families began to send their daughters to Ursuline houses for an education, and girls from wealthy families became Ursulines themselves.

The very success of the Ursulines led to the enforcement of claustration, however, as well as other Tridentine decrees regulating women religious. Wealthy families were uncomfortable with the fact that because Ursulines did not take solemn vows, their daughters who had joined communities could theoretically leave at any time and make a claim on family inheritance. (Solemn vows bound one permanently to a religious establishment and made an individual legally dead in the secular world.) The Ursuline houses in France and Italy were gradually ordered to accept claustration, take solemn vows, and put themselves under the authority of their local bishop, thus preventing any movement or cooperation between houses. They were still allowed to teach girls, but now only within the confines of a convent. Some houses fought this order as long as they could, though others accepted claustration willingly, having fully internalized church teachings that the life of a cloistered nun was the most worthy in the eyes of God.

Thus the only active apostolate left open to religious women was the instruction of girls, and that only within the convent. No nuns were sent to the foreign missions for any public duties, though once colonies were established in the New World and Asia, cloistered convents quickly followed. The exclusion of women from what were judged the most exciting and important parts of the Catholic Reformation—countering Protestants and winning new converts—is reflected in the relative lack of women from the sixteenth century who were made saints. Only 18.1 percent of those individuals from the sixteenth century who were made saints were women, whereas 27.7 percent of those from the fifteenth century had been women. Sixteenth-century male saints tended to be missionaries or opponents of Protestantism, while female saints were generally mystics or the reformers of existing religious orders. The best known of these—indeed, the most famous religious woman of the sixteenth century—was Teresa of Ávila, a Carmelite nun who recorded her mystical visions in a spiritual autobiography and reformed her Carmelite order. Though Teresa did not advocate institutionalized roles for women outside the convent, she did chafe at the restrictions placed on her because of her sex, and thought of herself as a Counter-Reformation fighter, viewing the new religious houses she established during her reforming efforts as answers to the Protestant takeover of Catholic churches elsewhere in Europe.

It is easy to view Teresa as a complete anomaly, but in many ways she fits into a pattern of women's religious experience that was quite common in Spain, the Spanish colonies, and Italy. Other nuns also composed spiritual autobiographies and shared them with others, and acted as reformers and social critics, combining mysticism and activism. Many of these women acquired a reputation for special holiness, becoming, in the words of the time, "living saints." Early modern rulers in Spain and Italy established special relationships with such women, asking for their advice on political matters and for their intercession with God. Laywomen who felt a sense of religious vocation (*Beatas*) were also often taken seriously, helping to resolve local conflicts and being sought for advice on political and personal, as well as religious, issues. Though some women who gained reputations for holiness were later charged with inventing their visions and falsifying their miracles, others gained power over political leaders, who in turn used the approval of such women as an endorsement of their policies and an enhancement of their prestige.

But the respect accorded to Teresa and other "holy women" did not lead to any lessening of the call for the claustration of religious women. Their separation from the world lessened the ability of women's communities to solicit funds, and the post-Tridentine emphasis on the sacraments meant that most benefactors preferred to give donations to male houses whose residents could say Mass. Thus many female houses grew increasingly impoverished and more interested in the size of the dowry of a prospective entrant than in the depth of her religious vocation. By the later seventeenth century convents in many parts of Europe were both shrinking and becoming increasingly aristocratic. The long-range effects of claustration were not an increase but a decrease in spiritual vigor.

The effects of the Catholic Reformation on religious women were thus to a great degree restrictive. What about laywomen in Catholic Europe? Here the balance sheet is more mixed, in large part because of the ambivalent attitudes of church leadership about marriage noted earlier. Post-Tridentine leaders also criticized many aspects of popular religion as having no basis in church-approved tradition, including the intensive veneration of Saint Anne, Mary's mother, who had become particularly popular with women in the fifteenth century. Pamphlets detailing her life story were embellished with legends about three marriages and children other than Mary and often illustrated with a female trinity—Mary, Anne, and Anne's mother, Emerentia. Such pamphlets became less common by the late sixteenth century, and illustrations of Mary began to show her with both parents. Mary herself was also portrayed differently. Up to the early sixteenth century she was generally shown as an adult woman, capably caring for the infant Jesus while an older Joseph hovered in the background or was not shown at all. By the late sixteenth century she was depicted as an adolescent girl, clearly under the protection of a strong and vigorous Joseph, who was now a much more dominant figure. Joseph replaced Anne as the fully human individual most often held up for emulation, and his cult grew in popularity with the spread of the Catholic Reformation, although it was not as popular with women as Anne's had been.

In Italian cities Catholic reformers began to open institutional asylums for repentant prostitutes (*convertite*) and also asylums for women who were felt to be at risk of turning to prostitution or losing their honor, such as orphans, poor unmarried women and widows, and those whose marriages had failed (*malmaritate*). Women in these institutions were taught basic skills with which to support themselves, usually weaving, and given large doses of religious and moral instruction. The drive to cloister all women's communities affected them as well, though some were able to remain uncloistered, with the residents even allowed to keep any wages earned, because it was seen as important to prevent the women from landing back on the streets. In Catholic theory marriage was indissoluble, but in practice the *malmaritate* houses offered women who had been abandoned or victimized by their husbands a respectable place to live, an alternative that was unavailable in Protestant areas.

During this period the confessional box was used more widely, for the Counter-Reformation church saw private confession as a way to combat heresy. Catholic women married to Protestant men could find in the priest hearing their confession a man who could give them a source of authority to overrule or disobey their husbands. The husbands recognized this possibility, for court records in Venice indicate that men charged with heresy often beat their Catholic wives after they came home from confession. No Catholic author went so far as to recommend that Catholic wives leave Protestant husbands, but in practice Catholic authorities put fewer blocks in the path of a woman who did. Protestant city councils in Germany were suspicious of any woman who asked to be admitted to citizenship independently and questioned her intently about her marital status. Catholic cities such as Munich were more concerned about whether the woman who wanted to immigrate had always been a good Catholic than whether she was married, particularly if she wanted to enter a convent.

Catholic writers were also more open in their support of women working to convert their Protestant or indifferent husbands, and even of daughters attempting to convert or inspire their parents, than were Continental Protestant writers. England and Ireland provided the most dramatic example of the importance of Catholic women's domestic religious activities. In 1559 Queen Elizabeth ordered that everyone attend services in the Anglican church or be penalized with fines or imprisonment. Many English and Irish Catholics outwardly conformed, but others did not, becoming what were termed *recusants*. Among these were a large percentage of women, who posed a special problem for royal officials. A single woman or widow found guilty of recusancy could be fined, but a married woman, according to common law, controlled no property, and imprisoning her would disrupt her family life and harm her husband, who might not even share her religious convictions. The Crown tried a variety of tactics to solve the problem, but only the most adamant Protestant men were willing to back measures that would allow a wife to be legally responsible as an individual for her religious choices and put her husband's property at risk. Catholic husbands often outwardly conformed and attended services, leaving their wives to arrange for private masses held in the home, or even to shelter illegal Catholic missionaries. Because of this situation, while Continental Catholicism was becoming increasingly parish-oriented after the Council of Trent, Catholicism in England and Ireland grew increasingly domestic. As stories were collected about the persecution of Catholics, a new type of Catholic heroine emerged—capable, benevolent, intelligent, and in many ways crafty in her dealings with authorities—an ide-

alization, but one modeled on real recusant women, for judges and the Privy Council frequently complained about the influence such women had on their husbands, children, and servants. This new ideal took her place beside the cloistered nun and the obedient housewife as a model for Catholic women.

Gender and the Reformation. Along with studies that focus specifically on ideas about women, women's own actions and writings, and the direct effects of the Reformation on women, a few scholars have begun asking broader questions about the effects of the Reformation on what is generally termed the "social construction of gender." This area involves, first, an analysis of notions of masculinity, for the Protestant rejection of celibacy and championing of family life meant a new ideal for men as well as for women. Most Lutheran household manuals published in the sixteenth century were directed toward men (this body of literature is, in fact, termed the *Hausvaterliteratur*, the "housefather literature") but only in the 1990s have scholars begun to view these as part of men's, as well as women's, history. The strong religious sanctions they gave to husbandly authority and the transformation of the household into a religious unit they envisioned shaped ideas of proper behavior not only for females, but also for males. The suspicion of persons who were not married often extended to men, with bachelors criticized as being selfish or shiftless and in some areas excluded from high government positions.

Exploring the social construction of gender goes beyond simply adding "men's history" to women's history, however, and involves careful analysis of such factors as the language used by reformers. For example, Protestants often termed the church a "brotherhood" rather than the "Holy Mother Church," at a time when "brotherhood" was not usually used for organizations that included women; they also praised the beliefs and actions of the "common man," at a time when "common woman" meant prostitute. Women were thus linguistically excluded or marginalized, and though this exclusion may not have been conscious, contemporary scholars have demonstrated the power of the implicit use of language in shaping people's perceptions of themselves and their world. Attention to gender differences is also beginning to reveal nuances in previously accepted conclusions about class differences in the Reformation. For example, lower-class married women often participated in iconoclastic riots and heckled preachers while their husbands remained at home, so that class antagonisms alone do not explain these events. Gender differences also appear to have shaped relations between generations in ways that earlier analyses of the effects of the Reformation on family life did not recognize. For example, fathers appear to have been more willing to let their sons marry spouses of a different faith than their daughters (particularly if the bride brought a large dowry), which shaped both emotional relations within the family and marriage patterns, especially among the wealthy.

Using gender as a category of analysis to evaluate the Reformation is only beginning, and is possible only with the continued exploration of women's distinctive experiences and actions, for we still know much more about the lives of men in the sixteenth century than we do about women. Existing studies point out where one may find sources on women and provide a few models, but further research in other geographic areas, time periods, confessions, and social groups is needed before it will be possible to make the types of conclusions about women and the Reformation, or gender and the Reformation, that have to this point been made about "man" and the Reformation.

[*See also* Courts, *article on* Marriage Courts; Divorce; Family; Marriage; Sexuality; Social Discipline; *and* Witchcraft.]

BIBLIOGRAPHY

Arenal, Electa, and Stacey Schlau. *Untold Sisters: Hispanic Nuns in Their Own Works*. Albuquerque, 1989. Provides long selections in both Spanish and English from the works of many Spanish and New World nuns, as well as interpretations of their writings.

Bainton, Roland H. *Women of the Reformation*. 3 vols. Minneapolis, 1971, 1973, 1977. Three volumes of biographical sketches, arranged geographically.

Blaisdell, Charmarie. "Calvin's Letters to Women: The Courting of Ladies in High Places." *Sixteenth Century Journal* 13 (1982), 67–84. Discusses the ways in which reformers' relationships with women shaped their theology.

Chrisman, Miriam U. "Women of the Reformation in Strasbourg, 1490–1530." *Archives for Reformation History* 63 (1972), 143–167. An analytical early study in a special issue that still provides an important theoretical framework.

Davis, Natalie Zemon. "City Women and Religious Change." In *Society and Culture in Early Modern France*, edited by Natalie Zemon Davis, pp. 65–96. Stanford, 1975.

Douglass, Jane Dempsey. *Women, Freedom and Calvin*. Philadelphia, 1985. The best example of how the traditional methods and sources of intellectual historians and theologians can be used to gain dramatic new insights.

Dresen-Coenders, Lène, ed. *Saints and She-Devils: Images of Women in the Fifteenth and Sixteenth Centuries*. London, 1987.

Greaves, Richard L., ed. *Triumph Over Silence: Women in Protestant History*. Westport, Conn., 1985. Wide-ranging collection with several essays on the Reformation period.

Harrison, Wes. "The Role of Women in Anabaptist Thought and Practice: The Hutterite Experience of the Sixteenth and Seventeenth Centuries." *Sixteenth Century Journal* 23 (1992), 49–70.

Irwin, Joyce, ed. *Womanhood in Radical Protestantism*. New York, 1979. Provides extensive examples of (male) Anabaptist ideas.

Jacobsen, Grethe. "Women, Marriage and Magisterial Reformation: The Case of Malmø, Denmark." In *Pietas et Societas: New Trends in Reformation Social History*, edited by Kyle C. Sessions and Phillip N. Bebb, pp. 57–78. Kirksville, Mo., 1985.

Jenkins-Blaisdell, Charmarie. "Renée de France between Reform and Counter-Reform." *Archives for Reformation History* 63 (1972), 196–225. Still provides an important theoretical framework.

Karant-Nunn, Susan. "Continuity and Change: Some Effects of the Reformation on the Women of Zwickau." *Sixteenth Century Journal* 13.2 (1982), 17–42.

——. "*Kinder, Küche, Kirche*: Social Ideology in the Wedding Sermons of Johannes Mathesius." In *Germania Illustrata: Essays Presented to Gerald Strauss*, edited by Susan Karant-Nunn and Andrew C. Fix, pp. 121–140. Kirksville, Mo., 1991. Discusses the ideas of a typical early Lutheran pastor.

Roelker, Nancy. "The Role of Noblewomen in the French Reformation." *Archives for Reformation History* 63 (1972), 168–195. An early study that still provides an important theoretical framework.

Roper, Lyndal. " 'The Common Man,' 'The Common Good,' 'Common Women': Reflections on Gender and Meaning in the Reformation German Commune." *Social History* 12 (1987), 1–21. The best example of an analysis of the interplay between Reformation ideas and notions of gender.

——. *The Holy Household: Women and Morals in Reformation Augsburg*. Oxford, 1989. Investigates political, social, and economic change along with that brought by the Protestant Reformation; quite controversial.

Thompson, John Lee. *John Calvin and the Daughters of Sarah: Women in Regular and Exceptional Roles in the Exegesis of Calvin, His Predecessors and His Contemporaries*. Geneva, 1992.

Warnicke, Retha M. *Women of the English Renaissance and Reformation*. Westport, Conn., 1983.

Wiesner, Merry E. "Ideology Meets the Empire: Reformed Convents and the Reformation." In *Germania Illustrata: Essays Presented to Gerald Strauss*, edited by Susan Karant-Nunn and Andrew C. Fix, pp. 181–196. Kirksville, Mo., 1991. The only study in English of German convents.

——. "Studies of Women, the Family and Gender." In *Reformation Europe: A Guide to Research II*, edited by William S. Maltby, pp. 159–188. Saint Louis, 1992. A bibliography and bibliographic essay.

Wunder, Heide. *"Er ist die Sonn', sie ist die Mond": Frauen in der frühen Neuzeit*. Munich, 1992. Most extensive discussion of women in early modern Germany available. Vast bibliography of works in many languages, including English.

MERRY E. WIESNER-HANKS

WONDERYEAR. This term refers to a one-year period in the Netherlands between the springs of 1566 and 1567. In Brabant's old-style calendar, which began the year at Easter, the events traditionally seen as the opening and closing of the Wonderyear very nearly correspond to the year 1566 itself. During that time, which contemporary sources refer to more simply as "The Troubles," religious and political turmoil on a countrywide scale emerged, seeming by midyear to presage a thorough change in the religion of the Netherlands. By its end, when dissident forces had almost entirely been vanquished, Catholic hegemony and Spanish-Habsburg rule in the Netherlands were severely shaken. Over the next generation the chain of events begun in the Wonderyear would lead to the Revolt of the Netherlands and the formation of an independent, officially Calvinist, Dutch republic in the northern provinces.

The wonder that began the year was the presentation on 5 April of the Compromise of the Nobility, which pledged its signers' lives and fortunes to defend the realm against the introduction of the Inquisition. It culminated years of increasing friction between Philip II and his Netherlands subjects over the costs of government, international trade policy, local control of political patronage, and religious policy. While Philip pushed his government toward a thorough re-organization and reinvigoration of the traditional church, with emphasis on systematic enforcement of post-Tridentine Catholic orthodoxy, religious dissent spread widely and gathered strength through the heavily populated areas of the country. Rampant fears that the Spanish Inquisition would be introduced led local and regional authorities, regardless of their particular religious sympathies, to resist any encroachments on their traditional privileges which might lead to such an eventuality. Although the high nobility generally did not join the hundreds of lesser nobles who signed the Compromise, its most prominent members—William of Orange; Lamoraal, count of Egmont; and Filips van Montmorency, count of Hoorne—offered Philip's regent, Margaret of Parma, no support to resist the Compromise's demands for a moderation of Philip's edicts against heresy.

The result was a virtual collapse of central government authority through the spring. Popular support for the Beggars, as the signers of the Compromise and their followers were called after 5 April, was widespread. Increasingly large numbers of people flocked to "hedge preachings," which were held in the countryside near many cities. After late April the Calvinist consistories embraced the movement and began systematically to organize an overtly functioning Reformed church in the Netherlands. With the central government's attitude ambiguous and with large, if ill-defined, numbers of the nobility seeming to offer the new groups protection, local authorities did little to hinder their growth. The entire politics of the Netherlands was held in suspense while the regent Margaret awaited Philip's response to demands that he renounce his religious policy and summon the States General to bring about a general reconciliation of the country's tensions. There were incessant rumors and intimations that the king would not be gracious. The heady, almost apocalyptic mood of the country was tinged with constant anxiety and fear of retribution. By summer the seemingly spontaneous preachings had evolved into armed gatherings, often of enormous proportions. On Sundays around the beginning of July, contemporary observers estimated attendance at the various assemblies around Antwerp as high as thirty thousand, or nearly one in three inhabitants. Moreover, some preachers and their noble patrons had begun to assemble bands of irregular troops, always in the name of protection but often posing a threat to established authorities.

At the end of July the Beggars made a second request for a prompt gathering of the States General, this time adding a call for general religious toleration. When Margaret persuaded them to keep the peace and aid in the suspension of the preachings for twenty-four days, however, they were also powerless to control events, which appeared to take on a life of their own. Beginning at Steenvoorde in West Flanders on 10 August, a wave of iconoclasm spread through

Flanders and North Brabant, reaching Antwerp ten days later and continuing north to many areas of the northern provinces as late as October. The despoiling of religious sites happened in many places so suddenly and completely that many accounts echo George Gilpin's observation from Antwerp that "it doe make it rather miraculous then mans worcke."

The image-breaking changed everything. At first it seemed that the Calvinists had staged a successful coup and that religion in the Netherlands would be transformed. In Antwerp and several other cities the preachers moved inside the walls, declarations of toleration were made, and construction began on Protestant meeting houses. A consortium of businessmen came together in early September determined to offer Philip three million gold gulden—an enormous sum, even in terms of Philip's treasury—in exchange for toleration and protection. The threat was also clear that if the king demurred, the money would go into military preparations already in progress, and he would be forced to accept the Protestants in any case. This was not to be. Although the iconoclasm had been widespread, it was not universal. Many areas, including cities like Brugge, Brussels, Leuven, and Lille, did not experience it. In fact, the shock of the disturbances and the widespread fear of social upheaval that they aroused led many previously dissident elements—most notably Egmont—to rally behind the regent and the forces of order. With money from Spain, Margaret was able to raise enough troops to begin to garrison insecure towns and firm up the government's position. Through the fall her position was also strengthened by increasingly plausible reports from Spain of Philip's plans to send an army to put a definitive end to any revolt. Initially this also added impetus to Calvinist efforts to raise troops and strike a defiant attitude. By the end of December, though, the balance had clearly begun to shift in the regent's favor. Valenciennes, which had refused to accept a garrison, was besieged by government troops after 17 December. A relief attempt resulted in crushing defeats for the Beggars at Watrelos and Lannoy (26–28 December) and a general collapse of the military threat in the western regions. The situation remained unsettled until spring, when a Beggar force threatening Antwerp was wiped out at Oosterweel (13 March), and Valenciennes finally surrendered (24 March). Thereafter, resistance quickly became hopeless and collapsed. By May Margaret was firmly in control, while many of the surviving dissidents and rebels sought safety in the huge stream of religious and political refugees going into exile.

Traditionally, historians understood the Wonderyear chiefly in confessional and nationalist terms. In the 1940s, however, Erich Kuttner renamed it the "Hungeryear" and pronounced the events of 1566 a failed proletarian revolution, precipitated by high grain prices and widespread hunger following crop failures in 1565. The succeeding generation has produced a multitude of detailed local studies which make any ideologically inspired interpretation of the Wonderyear difficult. Social tensions did become acute as harvest time approached, and cultural hostility to the traditional church's use of devotional images was widespread, but the outbreaks of iconoclasm in August and September generally did not involve riotous explosions of popular rage—rather, they mostly show signs of careful planning and organization and possibly even systematic coordination. In places where determined local authorities clearly opposed and stood up to it, iconoclasm was minimal. Indeed, the social and political caution that characterized some Calvinist ministers led Phyllis Mack Crew to see the "troubles" emerging from a general crisis of authority on all levels, which left people unsure of what behavior was and was not officially sanctioned and protected. In 1566 the ministers "portray[ed] themselves and their doctrine as fundamentally ambiguous"; the systematic revolutionary ideology that characterized the Netherlands Calvinists in later years was more a result of the Wonderyear's repression than its cause. More recent research by Andrew Pettegree describes the rapid and intense evolution that the Wonderyear brought upon the Calvinist churches in the Netherlands as they made the sudden shifts first from underground and fugitive communities to leaders of a countrywide movement of reform and then back to exile to regroup and recover. The Calvinist reform's initial failure in the Wonderyear led it, in exile, to make important refinements of doctrine and polity and "to complete the identification of Calvinism with the cause of the revolt," which would soon transform the Netherlands forever after.

Indeed, the revolutions of fortune that the Wonderyear brought the Netherlands reform can be seen affecting virtually every important cause and person its events touched. Many of the previous era's greatest political figures, such as Egmont and Hoorne, came to ruin, along with a host of lesser lights. Even Margaret of Parma, her political reputation fatally damaged, would soon return to obscurity. Orange, the country's greatest magnate in 1566, the next year found himself a fugitive in exile, groping toward the identity and path that would later carry him to greatness as the leader of the revolt. Traditional Burgundian Catholicism, amorphous and inclusive, within which wide ranges of theological exploration and ambiguity could be tolerated, was finally discredited in favor of the post-Tridentine version, a fighting faith with a sectarian consciousness that in many ways resembled the new religion it sought to defeat. Other important modalities from the Netherlands reform's earlier years—Anabaptism, Lutheranism, and Sacramentarianism—did not disappear but found themselves increasingly marginalized in the Catholic/Calvinist polarity that dominated Netherlands religious discourse after 1567. The Wonderyear was also the final blow to Charles V's "composite" Habsburg imperial organization, in which the Spanish kingdoms and the Burgundian circle had arguably coequal status. Hereafter it was clearly a Castile-centered empire, in which the Netherlands were important but clearly played a subordinate role.

BIBLIOGRAPHY

Crew, Phyllis Mack. *Calvinist Preaching and Iconoclasm in the Netherlands, 1544–1569.* Cambridge, 1978.
Deyon, Solange, and Alain Lottin. *Les "casseurs" de l'été 1566: L'iconoclasme dans le nord de la France.* Reprint, Lille, 1986.
Duke, Alastair. *Reformation and Revolt in the Low Countries.* London and Ronceverte, W.Va., 1990. See particularly chap. 6, "The Time of Troubles in the Country of Holland," written in collaboration with D. H. A. Kolff.
Kuttner, Erich. *Het Hongerjaar, 1566.* Reprint, Amsterdam, 1964.
Marnef, Guido. *Antwerpen in Reformatietijd: Ondergronds Protestantisme in een Internationale Handelsmetropool, 1550–1577.* Louvain, 1991. Section on the Wonderyear gives most up-to-date bibliography on current research.
Parker, Geoffrey. *The Dutch Revolt.* Rev. ed. London and New York, 1990. Best recent overview of the period in any language.
Pettegree, Andrew. *Emden and the Dutch Revolt: Exile and the Development of Reformed Protestantism.* Oxford, 1992. Extremely good on evolution of Netherlands church in general, with extensive section on the Wonderyear.

GUY WELLS

WORMS, DIET OF. After his coronation in Aachen, Charles V announced on 1 November 1520 his first diet, to be convened in Worms on 6 January 1521. (The provision of the Golden Bull of 1356 that had designated Nuremberg as the site of the first meeting of the diet was ignored because Nuremberg had been hit by the plague.) Charles V arrived in Worms on 28 November, but the diet did not open until 27 January 1521; it was concluded on 25 May, having been one of the most significant assemblies in the history of the empire in the sixteenth century. On 26 May the emperor promulgated the recesses of the diet with laws on governmental administration, judicial procedures, public order, and an imperial taxing regulation for financing the emperor's formal journey to Rome as well as the support of governmental administration and the courts. (The new judicial procedures and the imperial taxing registration proved to be permanent institutions. Regulations pertaining to safety and order did not come into being because no agreement could be reached on central economic questions.) At the same time the Edict of Worms against Luther and his followers, dated 8 May, was signed by Charles V. This edict, which was not part of the recess, had been drafted by the papal legate Girolamo Aleandro but had been reworked by the imperial court in the direction of strengthening the authority of the emperor.

When the diet had been announced, the proposed agenda had been the maintenance of law and public peace, public and constitutional order, regulations for government in times of the emperor's absence, assistance for the emperor's journey to Rome, and the recovery of lost imperial territories. These topics reflected, on the part of the estates, the hope that power and responsibilities would be reallocated within the empire; the emperor, meanwhile, professed the monarchical character of his rule and endeavored to strengthen his authority and centralize power. The ensuing deliberations were affected by the growing conflict between Charles V and France, the tensions between the emperor and Pope Leo X, the renewal of the Turkish threat, the Comunero uprisings in Spain, general considerations regarding the governance of those territories bound to Charles through personal fealty, and, finally, by the "Luther affair." The diet brought an end to the movement for imperial reform and resulted in compromise settlements that were slightly in the emperor's favor. For example, the long-standing demand for a governance structure involving the estates was met only with respect to periods when the emperor was absent; this structure, moreover, was to be presided over by the emperor's representative, and its decisions on central matters were subject to the emperor's approval.

The *causa Lutheri*, which originally had not been a matter for consideration, was placed on the agenda—despite the bitter objections of Aleandro and the initial refusal of the emperor—at the insistence of the saxon elector Frederick III ("the Wise") with support from the estates. Another addition to the agenda was discussion of the grievances against Rome and the church, "the gravamina of the German nation," as advocated especially by Luther's enemy Duke George of Saxony. The estates had threatened to ignore the emperor's wishes. The approach of the emperor's advisers, headed by Chièvres and Gattinara, was determined mainly by foreign-policy concerns, while the estates were chiefly motivated by church political and legal considerations, but also by their concern over the possibility of a mass movement in support of the Wittenberg monk. On 19 February they refused to approve an imperial mandate against Luther. Luther was subsequently granted safe passage to Worms; his statement and refusal to recant during the hearing of 17–18 April proved to be the reason why the diet took on world-historical significance. The assembled delegates were scarcely aware that, with the official declaration of conscience of one individual, the course was set for the division of western Christendom into various confessions.

BIBLIOGRAPHY

Reuter, Fritz, ed. *Der Reichstag zu Worms von 1521: Reichspolitik und Luthersache.* 2d ed. Cologne, 1981. A symposium with important contributions by recognized experts on key personalities, relevant issues, and problems connected with the diet.

RAINER WOHLFEIL
Translated from German by Robert E. Shillenn

WORSHIP. *See* Liturgy; Piety; Popular Religion.

WTENBOGAERT, Johannes (also Uytenbogaert; 1557–1644), Dutch theologian and church leader. Born in Utrecht, he was sent by the local consistory of the Dutch Reformed church to Théodore de Bèze's school in Geneva for his education in theology. Here he met Jacobus Arminius, a student sponsored by the church of Amsterdam. They became friends for life. Wtenbogaert was to follow the ideas of Arminius and become the most important of his defenders. After returning to his country he became a minister in his native town (1584).

In 1591 he was called to the ministry in The Hague and also named chaplain at the court of Stadtholder Maurice of Nassau, prince of Orange. He became closely connected to Johan van Oldenbarnevelt, the advocate of Holland.

When at the University of Leiden the dispute arose between Arminius and Franciscus Gomarus on predestination (1604), Wtenbogaert interceded for Arminius and pleaded for toleration. He found Oldenbarnevelt at his side. Maurice inclined to the views of Gomarus. In 1609 Arminius died, and Wtenbogaert took over the leadership of his party. In 1610 he drew up a remonstrance to the States of Holland imploring religious freedom. It was signed by forty-four ministers of the Dutch Reformed church. It is from this remonstrance the followers of Arminius in the Netherlands are called "Remonstrants." The Remonstrants were a minority in the church but had powerful backing in the States of Holland until in 1618 Maurice carried out a coup d'état against Oldenbarnevelt, who was sentenced to death. Wtenbogaert fled to Antwerp and later to France. At the Synod of Dordrecht (1618–1619) Arminianism was condemned, and the Remonstrants (including Hugo Grotius) were exiled or imprisoned. The exiles went to Antwerp, where they founded under the leadership of Wtenbogaert "The Remonstrant Brotherhood," a church that still exists. (There are forty-five congregations in the Netherlands and one in Germany.)

In 1625 Maurice died, and gradually the Remonstrants came back to the Netherlands. In 1626 Wtenbogaert returned from exile. He gave the Remonstrants their church order and defended their rights in many books and pamphlets. He tried in vain to obtain permission for their readmission to the Reformed church. Until his death he remained militant. The dilemma of both Wtenbogaert and Oldenbarnevelt was that they tried to force upon the Reformed church and the United Netherlands toleration for a dissident movement within its ranks, and in this way they came up against the boundaries of tolerance.

His numerous works include *Tractaet van't Ampt ende Authoriteyt eener hoogher Christelicken Overheyt in Kerkelicke saeken* (Treatise on the Office and Authority of a Christian Government in Church Matters). Here he is close to Erastian views, but he attributes authority to the government only in matters of church order, not in religion. His main work, *De Kerkelicke historie* (Church History), was published after his death. Here he endeavored to prove that the views of Arminius have their roots in early Christianity.

BIBLIOGRAPHY

Brandt, G. *History of the Reformation.* Translated by T. Wood. 4 vols. London, 1720–1722. No publications on Wtenbogaert exist in English, although he is mentioned in this work.

Harrison, A. W. *The Beginnings of Arminianism to the Synod of Dort.* London, 1926. Contains a discussion of Wtenbogaert.

Hoenderdaal, G. J. "Wtenbogaert." In *Biografisch Lexicon voor de Geschiedenis van het Nederlandse Protestantisme,* vol. 2, pp. 464–468. Kampen, 1983.

Rogge, H. C. *Bibliotheek der Remonstrantsche Geschriften.* Amsterdam, 1863. See pp. 86–105.

———. *Brieven en onuitgegeven stukken van Johannes Wtenbogaert* (Letters and Unpublished Documents of Johannes Wtenbogaert). 3 vols. Amsterdam, 1868–1874.

———. *Johannes Wtenbogaert en zijn tijd.* 3 vols. Amsterdam, 1874–1876.

Wtenbogaert, Johannes. *Praestantium ac eruditorum virorum epistolae ecclessiasticae et theologicae.* Edited by van Limborch and Hartsoeker. Amsterdam, 1704. Contains Wtenbogaert's letters in Latin as well as letters of other theologians of the period.

GERRIT JAN HOENDERDAAL

WULLENWEVER, Jürgen (1488?–1537), merchant and mayor of Lübeck. Wullenwever was born in 1488 (or earlier) in Hamburg. A merchant like his father, he moved to Lübeck in 1525, where he married, attained citizenship, and entered the Novgorod Traveller Society. Even though he was not pious, he joined the Reformation movement, which brought him political success. He became the demagogic spokesman of the Committee of Sixty-four, which confronted the patrician council in 1530 for financial control and further progress of the Reformation and—together with an additional Committee of One Hundred—achieved great influence. In 1531 two Catholic mayors fled. The council was then complemented from the committees, and Wullenwever himself became a councillor in February 1533, and a short while later mayor. To strengthen Lübeck's Baltic Sea trade, he tried to suppress the Dutch with a blockade of the sound and a pirate war. After the death of Frederick I, he wanted to take advantage of the uncertainty of the Danish succession for Lübeck's profit, but he found little support. Only Henry VIII was ready to oppose the Dutch, as well as Copenhagen and Malmö and the peasants who opposed the Catholic nobility. In the spring of 1534 with the help of the community in Lübeck itself Wullenwever was able to defend himself against the growing criticism of the council and the burghers and, in the new elections, to get rid of the patrician element in the council.

His pact with the counts Christoph von Oldenburg and

Johann von Hoya gave the name to the Counts' War, which was directed against Holstein and Denmark, and in which Lübeck's prowess was no match for its ambitious goals. Therefore Wullenwever sought new allies in the northern kingdoms. In the neighboring Hanseatic cities he supported the citizens' opposition against the council authorities. But in November 1534 peace had to be concluded with Holstein, and, after burdensome defeats, with Denmark in 1536. At that time the old order had been restored in Lübeck—except for the Reformation—and Wullenwever himself, under the pressure of a mandate from the imperial court, of other Hanseatic cities, and of internal enemies in Lübeck, had left the council in August 1535. In November he was arrested by the Bremen archbishop Christoph, who turned him over to his strict Catholic brother, Duke Heinrich the Younger of Braunschweig-Wolfenbüttel. After several interrogations under torture with Danish and Lübeck participation Heinrich had Wullenwever executed on 24 September 1537 on the charge of breaking the public peace. There was also word of betrayal, church robbery, and Anabaptism. The trial was legally questionable, but it was a victory of the existing order against its political-social threats, a triumph of the territorial powers over the municipal will to self-assertion, and a demonstration against the Reformation.

BIBLIOGRAPHY

Korell, Gunter. *Jürgen Wullenwever: Sein sozialpolitisches Wirken in Lübeck und sein Kampf mit den erstarkenden Mächten Nordeuropas.* Abhandlungen zur Handels- und Sozialgeschichte 19. Weimar, 1980.

Postel, Rainer. "Heinrich der Jüngere und Jürgen Wullenwever." In *Reformation und Revolution; Beiträge zum politischen Wandel und den sozialen Kräften am Beginn der Neuzeit; Festschrift für Rainer Wohlfeil,* edited by Rainer Postel and Franklin Kopitzsch, pp. 48–67. Stuttgart, 1989.

Waitz, Georg. *Lübeck unter Jürgen Wullenwever und die europäische Politik.* 3 vols. Berlin, 1855–1856.

RAINER POSTEL
Translated from German by Walter D. Morris

WUNDER, Hans. *See* Bünderlin, Johann.

WÜRTTEMBERG. Although only about half the size of the later Napoleonic kingdom of the same name, the sixteenth-century duchy of Württemberg was the largest and most important territory in the southwestern corner of the Holy Roman Empire. The successful establishment of the Reformation in Württemberg, as a result of which many of the imperial cities and smaller principalities in the region were able to follow suit, was a great victory for the Protestant cause in the empire.

The first decade and a half of the Reformation in Germany coincided almost exactly with the period (1519–1534) during which the headstrong and violent Duke Ulrich, driven from Württemberg by the army of the Swabian League as punishment for a variety of offenses against his subjects and his neighbors, lived in exile while his duchy was incorporated into the lands of Archduke Ferdinand of Austria (later Emperor Ferdinand I). During his exile Ulrich himself adopted the Protestant faith (1523–1524) and soon thereafter found an ally in Landgrave Philipp of Hesse, whose eagerness to strike a blow for the Reformation, for the rights of territorial princes, and against the Habsburgs made the restoration of Ulrich to Württemberg a major goal of Hessian politics. In May 1534 Philipp, taking advantage both of the collapse of the Swabian League and of Archduke Ferdinand's preoccupation with the struggle against the Turks on the eastern frontiers of the Empire, reconquered Württemberg for Ulrich at the head of an army paid for mostly by anti-Habsburg France.

Now a more stable and less bellicose man than he had been in 1519 but still energetic and ruthless in the pursuit of his own interests, Ulrich was determined to introduce the Reformation into his duchy, an intention that appears to have enjoyed widespread support among his subjects. The Treaty of Kaaden (June 1534), by which Austria recognized Ulrich as reigning duke, permitted him to support the Augsburg Confession (i.e., Lutheranism) but forbade the toleration of Sacramentarians (i.e., Zwinglians). Ulrich, however, had personal ties to both Lutheran and Zwinglian reformers, was under pressure from both Lutherans and Zwinglians to favor their cause, and was a firm believer in Philipp of Hesse's policy of mediating between the two Protestant factions. So he initially entrusted the reformation of his duchy to two theologians, the mildly Zwinglian Ambrosius Blarer from Constance and the Lutheran Erhard Schnepf, who was called from his chair of theology at Marburg. After patching together a compromise formula on the contentious question of the real presence in the Sacrament (July 1534), Blarer and Schnepf set to work replacing those clergymen who would not conform to the new order with suitable Protestants.

Soon, however, the confessional balance began to tip in favor of Lutheranism. The need to provide the new territorial church with uniform ceremonies and institutions led Ulrich to turn for assistance to the Lutheran reformer of Schwäbisch-Hall, Johannes Brenz, whose reputation as an expert on ecclesiastical organization was already well established and who had friends and supporters among Ulrich's advisers. The addition of Brenz's catechism to the church order of 1536 and Brenz's reorganization of the University of Tübingen in 1537–1538 placed the Württemberg church on a firmly Lutheran doctrinal basis, even though Swiss-style simplicity of ceremonies and decor (as opposed to the high-church style favored by Wittenberg) remained a permanent feature of ecclesiastical life in the duchy. Ulrich's dependence for security on the Schmalkald League, which he joined in 1538, also helped to tip the scales toward Lu-

theranism. Finding himself overworked, outmaneuvered, and out of favor, Blarer left the duke's service in 1538, and Württemberg subsequently became an unequivocally Lutheran territory.

During the 1540s the duke and his advisers made considerable progress in providing the Württemberg territorial church with a stable system of ecclesiastical administration. Parish visitations, though apparently not held annually as Brenz had recommended in 1535, became more and more frequent, and by 1547 there was a central body of lay and clerical "visitation counselors" who had the responsibility for dealing with the problems uncovered by the visitations. At the same time, an embryonic structure of local ecclesiastical administration, centered in districts supervised by "deans," had been outlined. But in 1548 all this work was undone by the forcible reintroduction of Catholicism under the provisions of the Augsburg Interim. Although Ulrich, who had been on the losing side in the Schmalkald War and whose key fortresses were occupied by the emperor's Spanish troops, had no choice but to proclaim the Interim, he nevertheless offered refuge to Brenz and other clergymen whose opposition to the Interim had made them outlaws. Moreover, with encouragement and counsel from Brenz and with the support of the population, which remained stubbornly loyal to the new faith, the duke and his advisers proved adroit at defeating the spirit of the Interim while obeying its letter. For example, dismissed pastors were reemployed as preachers or catechists, which allowed them to minister to their flocks without interfering with the priests who said Mass as the Interim required.

By the time that Moritz of Saxony's successful uprising against Charles V in the spring of 1552 made it possible to abolish the Interim in Württemberg, Duke Ulrich had died (November 1550) and been succeeded by his son, Duke Christoph (1515–1568), a pious and theologically articulate Lutheran who, with Brenz as his chief theological adviser, devoted his best efforts as ruler to the reorganization and consolidation of the Lutheran church in his duchy. Rather than simply revive the institutions that had been established by Duke Ulrich, Christoph and Brenz began afresh and established a system of church government that was more centralized than Ulrich's had been, that made a clearer distinction between ecclesiastical and secular administration as well as between ecclesiastical and secular finances, and that devoted much more attention to the discipline of public morals. A central governing body, first called the *Visitationsrat* and then the *Kirchenrat* ("consistory"), was established in 1553, by which time superintendents responsible for the intermediate and local levels of ecclesiastical administration had been appointed and a central church treasury under ecclesiastical control had been established. A marriage court was set up in 1553 and by 1554 a system of moral discipline had been put into effect. Meanwhile, Brenz's Württemberg Confession (1551) had been adopted as an official confession of the Württemberg church, and the church order of 1553 had established uniform rites of worship. In 1556 Brenz's Cloister Ordinance turned fourteen of the duchy's major monasteries into "cloister schools" where deserving but needy teenage boys were prepared at public expense to study theology at the University of Tübingen. Three years later ordinances for the entire school system of the duchy, the essential features of which had been established in the reign of Duke Ulrich, were drafted. Finally, in 1559 all of these ordinances and some others, many of them revised and expanded, were incorporated into the so-called Great Church Order, the constitution of the Lutheran territorial church in Württemberg.

Both on paper and, to a large extent, in practice as well, the Württemberg consistorial system of church government was beautifully simple and effective. In each of about twenty-seven districts, the pastor designated as local superintendent supervised the work of the pastors and schoolteachers and conducted semiannual visitations of all the parishes, inquiring into the doctrine and the morals of all the pastors and teachers (as well as those of the ordinary parishioners) and noting any problems with respect to the state of churches, parsonages, and schools or the health and wellbeing of the pastors and teachers. He then forwarded a report to his immediate superior, one of the four general superintendents, who in turn periodically forwarded the accumulated visitation reports to the consistory in the ducal chancellery in Stuttgart. The consistory, a committee of theologians and secular officials, had responsibility for the management of church property and for the collection and disbursal of the income that flowed from that property into the church treasury. It also had the authority to appoint, dismiss, and exercise general supervision over all clergymen and schoolteachers. Twice a year the members of the consistory, augmented by the presence of the four general superintendents, met as the synod (synodus) to formulate and to recommend to the duke whatever new policies or regulations seemed necessary as a result of the visitations. The synod was also the apex of the order for the discipline of public morals and was the only body authorized either to impose or to lift the penalty of excommunication. Although

dear to the hearts of both Brenz and Duke Christoph, this system of moral discipline, in contrast to the other aspects of their ecclesiastical handiwork, was intensely unpopular and never worked well.

The clarity and simplicity of its essential features, its careful balancing of the authority of the prince's secular bureaucracy with the need of the church for its own administrative structures, and its observed effectiveness in practice caused the Württemberg consistorial system to be widely copied in the rest of Protestant Germany in the years and decades after 1559, a process encouraged by the dukes and their officials, including Brenz and his successor as supreme superintendent of the Württemberg church, Jakob Andreae. Wherever the word *Kirchenrat* appeared in the ecclesiastical legislation of Protestant territories, it was a sure sign that the Württemberg system was being copied or at least that it had had an important influence. The Rhine Palatinate (1564), Braunschweig-Wolfenbüttel (1569), Saxony (1580), Hesse (1610), and electoral Brandenburg (1614) are among the most important territories affected. This is further testimony to the general significance in the history of the Reformation and of German Protestantism of Württemberg's territorial reforms.

[*See also* Andreae, Jakob; Brenz, Johannes; Christoph of Württemberg; Formula of Concord; *and* Lutheranism, *overview article*.]

BIBLIOGRAPHY

Brecht, Martin, and Hermann Ehmer. *Südwestdeutsche Reformationsgeschichte: Zur Einführung der Reformation im Herzogtum Württemberg, 1534*. Stuttgart, 1984. An excellent modern survey, with ample listing of the available literature in German.

Estes, James Martin. *Christian Magistrate and State Church: The Reforming Career of Johannes Brenz*. Toronto, 1982. Chaps. 1, 4, and 5 deal in a summary way with the history of the Reformation in Württemberg, with special emphasis on the personal contribution of Brenz.

Press, Volker. "Die württembergische Restitution von 1534: Reichspolitische Voraussetzungen und Konsequenzen." *Blätter für württembergische Kirchengeschichte* 87 (1987), 44–71. A fine essay on the restoration of Duke Ulrich in 1534 and its consequences for the Reformation in Württemberg and the Empire.

JAMES M. ESTES

XYZ

XAVIER, Francis (Span., Francisco de Jassu y Javier; 1506–1552), Jesuit saint and missionary to Asia. Xavier was born at Xavier castle in Navarre, the fifth son of a minor nobleman. He entered the University of Paris in 1525, took a licentiate in 1531, and taught Aristotle. His roommates at the Collège de Sainte Barbe were Pierre Favre and Ignatius Loyola. Ignatius converted his roommates and four other students to his dream of missionary work in Palestine. Xavier studied theology at Paris (1533–1537), then joined his companions at Venice to sail for Palestine. When war prevented their sailing, the companions put themselves at the pope's disposal. The companions decided eventually to found the Society of Jesus, or Jesuits.

John III of Portugal wanted Jesuit missionaries for his Asian empire. Xavier sailed from Lisbon for India in 1542 as Jesuit superior and papal nuncio. He won many converts in India (1542–1545), then spent the next two years in various islands of Indonesia, especially the Moluccas. His time was spent partly with Portuguese traders and officials, partly with the native peoples. In 1547/48 he returned to India and reorganized Jesuit work there. In 1549 he sailed for Japan and laid the foundations of Christianity; the Jesuit mission in Japan enjoyed fifty years of remarkable expansion before persecution crushed it. Xavier recognized that mission success in China would increase the prestige of Christianity in Japan, but before trying to enter China he had to return to India briefly. In April 1552 he sailed for China, where Westerners were forbidden entry; after his initial effort to smuggle himself in failed, he fell sick and died 3 December 1552 on an island off the China coast. Xavier was canonized in 1622 and named patron of foreign missions by Pius XI in 1927.

BIBLIOGRAPHY

Primary Sources

Xavier, Francis. *Briefe, 1542–1552*. Munich, 1950.
———. *Le lettere e altri documenti*. Rome, 1991.
———. *The Letters and Instructions of Francis Xavier*. St. Louis, Mo., 1992.

Secondary Sources

Brodrick, James. *Saint Francis Xaiver, 1506–1552*. Reprint, Garden City, N.Y., 1957. A detailed but readable biography.
Maynard, Theodore. *The Odyssey of Francis Xavier*. Reprint, Westminster, Md., 1950. A good popularization.
Schurhammer, Georg. *Francis Xavier: His Life, His Times*. 4 vols.
Rome, 1973–1982. This massive work, more than 3000 pages, is exhaustive and exhausting.

JOHN PATRICK DONNELLY

XIMÉNEZ DE CISNEROS, Francisco. *See* Jiménez de Cisneros, Francisco.

YOUTH. *See* Education; Social Discipline.

ZACCARIA, Antonio Maria. *See* Barnabites.

ZANCHI, Girolamo (Lat., Hieronymus Zanchius; 1516–1590), Calvinist theologian, former Augustinian canon, and Italian refugee. Zanchi was born on 2 February 1516 in Alzano, near Bergamo, in northern Italy. At the age of fifteen, upon the death of his parents, he entered the Bergamo monastery of the Augustinian Order of Regular Canons, where he devoted the next ten years to the study of the classical languages, of Aristotle, and of the scholastics—particularly the works of Thomas Aquinas. In 1541 Zanchi was sent to Lucca, where under the guidance of the prior, Peter Martyr Vermigli, he not only studied the church fathers but also was introduced to the writings of the Swiss and German reformers, notably Philipp Melanchthon, Martin Bucer, John Calvin, and Martin Luther.

Zanchi fled Italy in 1552 to avoid arrest by the Inquisition. After a ten-month stay in Geneva, where he attended Calvin's lectures and listened to his sermons, he accepted a call to the academy of Strasbourg to teach theology and the philosophy of Aristotle. Zanchi's tenure in Strasbourg was marked by his long and bitter controversy with the Lutheran Johannes Marbach over the Lord's Supper and the doctrine of predestination. To end the controversy, which had dragged on for years, in the autumn of 1563 Zanchi finally resigned from his position and left Strasbourg.

After a four-year interim as pastor of a congregation of Italian refugees in Chiavenna, Zanchi received a call from the University of Heidelberg to become the successor of Zacharius Ursinus in the chair of theology. He arrived in Heidelberg in January 1568 to begin the most significant and productive period of his career. His profound scholarship soon earned him widespread fame and recognition, and his counsel and judgment in theological matters and controversies were sought throughout the Reformed world of continental Europe and even England.

Upon the expulsion of all Reformed professors from Heidelberg in 1576 by Ludwig VI, the Lutheran elector of the Palatinate, Zanchi accepted a position at the newly founded academy in Neustadt, where he chose to remain even after Heidelberg had been restored to the Reformed faith a few years later. Zanchi died on 9 November 1590 during a visit with friends in Heidelberg, where he was buried in the university church.

At his death Zanchi left an impressive corpus of writings; many of these had already appeared in print, while others were unpublished. Zanchi's sons immediately began to collect his works, including his correspondence, and in 1619 a complete edition, printed in Geneva by Samuel Crespin in three folio volumes divided into eight parts, appeared under the title *Zanchii Omnia Opera Theologica.*

The key to Zanchi's thought is the medieval scholastic tradition in which he had been reared and which provided him with the philosophical categories that influenced his thinking. Far from considering these categories inappropriate, Zanchi found them not only useful but even necessary for the proper understanding of biblical truth. It is not surprising, therefore, that in all his major theological treatises, on almost every point, Zanchi reveals a striking congruity between his own views and those of Thomas Aquinas. This is not simply a matter of form and method but of common ontological and epistemological presuppositions derived from the philosophy of Aristotle in its modified Thomistic form. As for Thomas, the unifying principle for Zanchi's theology is the principle of causality. It dominates his doctrine of God; it determines the relation between Creator and creature; it provides the analogy by which knowledge of God is possible; it characterizes the doctrine of providence and predestination and explains the entire order of salvation. Indeed, it would be possible to present Zanchi's teachings on scripture, God, creation, providence, and predestination without ever mentioning Christ, and they would suffer little or no distortion from doing so.

In the theology of Zanchi, at the very point of transition from Reformation to orthodoxy, one observes a clear shift from the Christocentric orientation of Calvin and Luther toward a metaphysics of causality that henceforth would characterize Reformed orthodoxy. In a real sense this makes Zanchi the father of Protestant Scholasticism.

BIBLIOGRAPHY

Primary Source

Zanchius, Jerome. *The Doctrine of Absolute Predestination Stated and Asserted.* Translated by A. M. Toplady. Reprint, Grand Rapids, Mich., 1977. A short early treatise submitted by Zanchi to the city council of Strasbourg in defense of his doctrine and the only one of Zanchi's writings available in English. Includes a biographical essay on Zanchi by the translator.

Secondary Sources

Donnelly, John Patrick. "Calvinist Thomism." *Viator* 7 (1976), 441–455. Demonstrates the major roles played by both Zanchi and Peter Martyr Vermigli in the emergence of Calvinist Scholasticism.
———. "Italian Influences on the Development of Calvinist Scholasticism." *Sixteenth Century Journal* 7 (April 1976), 81–101. Shows the importance of Zanchi and Peter Martyr Vermigli in the development of Calvinist Scholasticism.
Fatio, Olivier. *Méthode et théologie: Lambert Daneau et les débuts de la scolastique réformée.* Geneva, 1976. An excellent analysis of the influence of Zanchi on the development of Reformed Scholasticism and of Zanchi's theology in relation to Daneau.
Gründler, Otto. *Die Gotteslehre Girolamo Zanchis und ihre Bedeutung für seine Lehre von der Prädestination.* Neukirchen-Vluyn, Germany, 1965. An examination of Zanchi's theology in comparison with Thomas Aquinas and John Calvin. Demonstrates the influence of Aquinas on Zanchi's thought and identifies Zanchi as one of the earliest architects of Reformed Scholasticism.
Kittelson, James M. "Marbach vs. Zanchi: The Resolution of Controversy in Late Reformation Strasbourg." *Sixteenth Century Journal* 8 (October 1977), 31–44. One of the best articles on the bitter controversy between Zanchi and Marbach; elucidates the theological issues at stake in this prolonged debate.
Tylenda, Joseph N. "Girolamo Zanchi and John Calvin." *Calvin Theological Journal* 10 (1975), 101–141. A most informative article on Zanchi's relationship with Calvin, based on their correspondence.

OTTO GRÜNDLER

ZÁPOLYA, János,

ZÁPOLYA, János, (Hung., Szapolyai; 1487–1540), king of Hungary from 1526 to 1540. The patronage of Matthias I Corvinus, king of Hungary (r. 1458–1490), lifted the Zápolya family from obscure noble status to the highest levels of aristocratic honor and influence in the Hungarian kingdom. When Hungary's ruler, Lajos II, and many of the leading magnates and prelates died in the Battle of Mohács in 1526, Zápolya was already the largest landholder in the kingdom, the *voivode* ("governor") of Transylvania, and the recognized leader of a considerable faction among the lesser nobility. Within a few months Zápolya was elected and crowned king of Hungary, but this personal triumph proved to be short-lived. Ferdinand of Habsburg also made a determined bid for the Hungarian throne, and his invading army quickly routed Zápolya's forces. Ferdinand's Hungarian backers then proceeded to elect and crown him king in 1527.

In desperation Zápolya retaliated by seeking the support of the sultan Süleyman I, who was more than happy to exploit the divisions among his Christian enemies for his own advantage. In 1529 Süleyman came north and besieged Vienna. Although the Turks were unable to capture the city, their intervention saved the Hungarian throne for Zápolya. Thus Zápolya retained his crown, and Ferdinand I eventually had to seek an accommodation with his Hungarian rival. In 1538 the two kings agreed in the Treaty of Nagy-várad (Oradea) to allow Zápolya to remain in possession of Hungary until his death, after which Ferdinand I and his heirs would inherit the throne. The Turks refused to allow the agreement to be implemented and soon after Zápolya's death seized the central third of the kingdom for themselves.

Zápolya's reign coincided with the early spread of the Protestant Reformation in Hungary. Although the king remained formally a Catholic during his entire life, his relationship to the accumulating religious divisions of his time was highly convoluted and usually dominated by political considerations. Before the Battle of Mohács Zápolya and his followers were among the most fervent opponents of Luther in Hungary. They strongly supported the decision of the diet in 1523 that declared that those professing Lutheran doctrines should be punished with the loss of their property and burned at the stake as heretics. Nevertheless, the harsh stance of the Zápolya faction against Luther's followers derived less from Catholic zeal than from political motives. After he became king, Zápolya made some halting steps against Lutheranism among the German townspeople of Transylvania, but his attacks on Protestantism ceased as his political difficulties escalated. He became preoccupied with the retention of his crown and had little time to spend on arguments over Christian doctrine. His personal religious inclinations did not direct him toward Protestantism, but he did little to arrest its spread.

As part of seeking an accommodation with the Habsburgs, Clement VII excommunicated Zápolya in December 1529. The excommunication would stay in force for the remainder of Zápolya's life. He did his best to try to turn the fact of the excommunication to his own advantage. His representatives occasionally dropped broad hints directed at Rome that the pope's action hindered Zápolya's ability to deal with Protestantism in Hungary. Simultaneously his agents continued to reassure the pope that despite his lack of support by Rome Zápolya remained a loyal Catholic who desired to maintain the old religion in his kingdom. Zápolya shrewdly tried to use the specter of Protestantism to press the pope toward greater support for his rule. His policy toward Rome constituted a more subtle version of his blunt policy toward Vienna. By playing the Turkish card, he had forced Ferdinand I to come to an accommodation with him; and by hinting at a Protestant card, he hoped to compel greater support from the pope.

Rome responded by urging peace between the rival rulers. Invoking the danger of driving Zápolya and his followers completely into the arms of the Turks, both Clement VII and his successor, Paul III, continued to encourage Ferdinand I to come to an agreement with Zápolya. Both pontiffs also carefully kept Vienna well informed of their actions in regard to Hungary so that Rome would avoid any appearance of secretly backing Zápolya. After the Treaty of Nagy-várad Paul III resumed direct relations with Zápolya by sending a nuncio to his court and confirming some of Zápolya's ecclesiastical appointments.

Zápolya's personal attitude toward religion cannot be disentangled from the demands of his political situation. Certainly his alliance with the Turks revealed that he would not refuse even the most desperate measures to retain his kingdom. Perhaps if he had perceived a similar political advantage in Protestantism, he would have been more favorably inclined toward the new religious teachings. Near the end of his life Zápolya began to show some signs of increasing sympathy for Protestantism. In 1538 under the pressure of several prelates, who were eager to suppress Protestantism, he organized the first Reformation-era colloquy in Hungary. The dispute ended inconclusively, and Zápolya refused to allow the Catholic clergy to punish any of the Protestant participants. When he died on 22 July 1540, Zápolya left behind an increasingly ambiguous religious legacy: according to at least one observer, after receiving last rites, he took Communion in both kinds.

BIBLIOGRAPHY

Barta, Gábor. *Az erdélyi fejedelemség születése* (The Birth of the Transylvanian Principality). Budapest, 1979. Covers Zápolya's reign.

———. "Humanisták I. János király udvarában" (Humanists at the Court of János I). In *Magyar reneszánsz udvari kultúra* (Hungarian Renaissance Court Culture), edited by Ágnes Várkonyi and Júlia Székely. Budapest, 1987. Covers the attempt by Zápolya's court and chancellery to continue the previously established humanist traditions.

Bunyitay, Vince, Rajmund Rapaics, and János Karácsonyi, eds. *Monumenta Ecclesiastica tempora innovatae in Hungaria religionis illustrantia.* 5 vols. Budapest, 1902–1912. Extensive document collection covering the first half of the sixteenth century.

Fraknói, Vilmos. *Magyarország egyházi és politikai összeköttetései a római szent-székkel* (The Ecclesiastical and Political Connections of Hungary with the Roman Holy See). 4 vols. Budapest, 1901–1903. The first part of vol. 3 covers Zápolya's relations with Rome.

Hóman, Bálint, and Gyula Szekfú. *Magyar történet* (Hungarian History). 5 vols. Budapest, 1935. Vol. 3 still constitutes an indispensable interpretation of sixteenth-century Hungary.

Pach, Zsigmond Pál, and Ágnes Várkonyi, eds. *Magyarország története, 1526–1686* (The History of Hungary, 1526–1686). Budapest, 1985. Part of a recent synthesis of Hungarian history by the members of the Institute for Historical Studies.

Szerémi, György. *Magyarország romlásáról* (On the Ruin of Hungary). Edited by György Székely, translated by László Erdélyi. Budapest, 1979. A chronicle of Zápolya's reign by his Catholic chaplain.

Zoványi, Jenó. *A reformáczió Magyarországon 1565-ig* (The Reformation in Hungary to 1565). Budapest, 1922. Authoritative Protestant interpretation.

Zsilinszky, Mihály. *A magyar országgyűlések vallásügyi tárgyalásai a reformatiotól kezdve* (The Debates over Religion by the Hungarian Diets since the Time of the Reformation). 4 vols. Budapest, 1880–1897. Thoroughly documented Protestant interpretation.

PETER SCHIMERT

ZÁPOLYA, János Zsigmond (Hung., Szapolyai; 1540–1571), "elected" king of Hungary and ruler of Transylvania (r. 1559–1571). As the only child of János Zápolya, king of Hungary, and Izabella Jagiellon, daughter of Sigismund I of Poland, János Zsigmond's birth plunged Hungary into a political and military crisis. His father died a few days after János Zsigmond's birth, and some in Hungary sought to make János Zsigmond king. This decision would have deprived Ferdinand I, already elected and legally crowned king of Hungary, from assuming power. The Zápolya party desired to keep the royal authority for themselves and feared that Ferdinand I could not protect them from the Turks. The crisis forced Sultan Süleyman I's hand. He came to Hungary during the summer of 1541, defeated the Habsburg forces, occupied Buda, and recognized the rule of Zápolya over Transylvania. As a result Hungary was divided into three sections: the pro-Habsburg forces held western and northern Hungary, the Turks possessed the center, and a council of regency, acting in Zápolya's name, governed Transylvania and the several eastern Hungarian counties (the Partium). This solution satisfied almost no one in Hungary but admirably suited the interests of the Turks.

Despite the resistance of Queen Izabella, who wanted to preserve her son's truncated inheritance, some of Zápolya's supporters eventually came to terms with Ferdinand I. The Habsburg had never given up his claim to all of Hungary, although he lacked the means to take possession of the kingdom. Then in 1551 Izabella and her son were forced to leave Transylvania for Poland, and Ferdinand's agents took control of eastern Hungary. The Turks responded by attacking, and they expanded their holdings in central Hungary as this effort to unify Hungary under Ferdinand I and to drive out the Turks failed miserably. By 1556 Izabella and Zápolya had returned and resumed power in Transylvania and the Partium. Three years later the queen died, and Zápolya ruled in his own right.

His eleven-year reign was notable for two developments: one political and the other religious. First, the Habsburgs accepted temporarily the autonomy of Transylvania and the Partium. Second, Transylvania experienced a rapid expansion and radicalization of the Protestant Reformation. In no small measure Zápolya's personal religious sensibilities and policies accelerated these trends, even though Queen Izabella remained a staunch Catholic for her entire life and had raised her son in the old faith. But she could not defend Catholicism vigorously, or attack the Protestants, even if she had been so inclined, since political realities in Transylvania prevented such actions. The queen permitted the free practice of Lutheranism and accepted the extensive secularization of ecclesiastical lands. After his mother's death, Zápolya initially persisted in the Roman religion and tolerated Protestantism until 1563, when he abandoned Catholicism and openly adopted Protestantism. His conversion confirmed the dominance of the new religious doctrines in Transylvania and opened the way for rapid further radicalization of religious life. The collapse of the Catholic hierarchy, the ex-pulsion of many regular clergy, and the continuing uncertainties of the political situation all allowed the advancement of even more radical religious movements.

Zápolya's religious odyssey led from Catholicism, to Lutheranism, to Calvinism, and eventually to Unitarianism. His original abandonment of Roman Catholicism may have been motivated to some extent by political considerations. He ruled over a largely Protestant people, and his conversion increased his personal popularity. His subsequent religious development, however, can best be traced to his turbulent youth, his restless intellectual curiosity, and especially to the eclectic thinkers who surrounded him. His court preacher Francis Dávid, who often exercised a decisive influence in religious matters on the young ruler, underwent a similar journey from Catholicism to Unitarianism. Dávid's religious development anticipated the course that Zápolya would take. The court physician Giorgio Biandrata introduced both Dávid and Zápolya to antitrinitarian works and arguments. Biandrata played a decisive role in converting Zápolya to Unitarianism, while the persuasive sermons of Dávid helped to create a large Unitarian congregation in Transylvania. Zápolya took an active interest in questions of Christian doctrine, and he organized a number of disputations. Even during the last years of his life, when he had formally become a Unitarian, the ruler continued to practice toleration toward Lutherans, Calvinists, and Catholics. Zápolya also promoted education and planned to establish a university at Gyulafehérvár (Alba Iulia).

After Zápolya's sudden death in 1571 Unitarianism—never united in doctrine—lost its prominent position in Transylvania. Nevertheless Zápolya's brief reign secured the existence of Protestant movements and the tradition of religious toleration in Transylvania.

BIBLIOGRAPHY

Balázs, Mihály. *As erdélyi antitrinitarizmus az 1560-as évek végén* (Transylvanian Antitrinitarianism at the End of the 1560's). Budapest, 1988. Analysis of Unitarian doctrines at the height of the movement in Transylvania.

Bitskey, István. *Hitviták tüzében* (In the Fire of Religious Debate). Budapest, 1978. Provides an excellent discussion of the origins and growth of Unitarianism in Transylvania.

Hóman, Bálint, and Gyula Szekfú. *Magyar történet* (Hungarian History). 5 vols. Budapest, 1935. Vol. 3 still constitutes an indispensable interpretation of sixteenth-century Hungary.

Makkai, László, et al., eds. *Erdély története* (A History of Transylvania). 3 vols. Reprint, Budapest, 1987. Provides step-by-step analysis of the establishment of Transylvania's autonomy during the middle decades of the sixteenth century.

Pach, Zsigmond Pál, and Ágnes Várkonyi, eds. *Magyarország története, 1526–1686* (The History of Hungary, 1526–1686). Budapest, 1985. Katalin Péter wrote the thoughtful section on sixteenth-century religious life. She emphasized the role of political motives in János Zsigmond's successive conversions.

Zoványi, Jenó. *A reformáczió Magyarországon 1565-ig* (The Reformation in Hungary to 1565). 2 vols. Budapest, 1922 and 1977. Highly detailed on the debates between the Unitarians and the Calvinists.

Zsilinszky, Mihály. *A magyar országgyűlések vallásügyi tárgyalásai a reformatiotól kezdve* (The Debates over Religion by the Hungarian Diets since the Time of the Reformation). 4 vols. Budapest, 1880–1897. Thoroughly documented Protestant interpretation.

PETER SCHIMERT

ZELL, Katharina

ZELL, Katharina (1497/98–1562), activist and author in early Reformation Strasbourg. The daughter of a master carpenter, Katharina Schütz was born into a well-connected Strasbourg family. Her paternal uncle Hans sat on the city council; her sister Elizabeth married Michael Schwenker, another magistrate; her legal guardian and the coexecutor of her will, Jacob Meyer and Matthias Pfarrer, were among Strasbourg's most influential leaders. Family and friends encouraged her childhood fascination with religion, and along with a circle of women friends she was won over to the evangelical cause by reading Martin Luther's early works. She and Luther corresponded, and throughout her life she valued him as her deliverer from spiritual crisis.

In December 1523 she married Matthias Zell, a priest twenty years her senior who had launched the local reformation. Clerical marriage was a novelty, and its opponents hastened to accuse Matthias Zell of libertinism and assault against a burgher's daughter, charges Katharina Zell refuted in *Entschuldigung Katharine Schutzinn für M. Mathias Zellen iren eegemal* (Apology . . . for her Lawful Husband, 1524), an attack on obligatory priestly celibacy. Scripture allowed clerical marriage, and those who opposed it, such as the bishop of Strasbourg, had transparent financial motives: they wanted to collect the fines for clerical fornication and the fees levied on priests' bastards. Men needed the discipline of marriage, she wrote; she and Matthias had married to set an example. Theirs was a happy marriage, blighted only by the deaths in infancy of their two children. Katharina Zell took on all the duties of an early modern pastor's wife: keeping a household; acting as hostess to visiting dignitaries (including, in Zell's case, Johannes Oecolampadius and Huldrych Zwingli); and visiting the sick, the pregnant and newly delivered, and the imprisoned.

Zell simultaneously pursued a public career unusual for a sixteenth-century woman. Her defense of clerical marriage was followed by "Den Leydenden Christglaubigen Weybern der Gemain zu Kentzingen" (The Suffering Christian Wives of Kentzingen; 1524), a pamphlet written to console women whose husbands had fled to Strasbourg to escape persecution, and in which the heroines of the Old Testament were held up as models of behavior. Along with Lucas Hackfurt, superintendent of Strasbourg's welfare system, Zell organized the massive relief effort to care for the thousands of local victims of the Peasants' War who swamped the city for months in 1525, seeking food, shelter, and medical care. In the mid-1530s she edited a set of four hymn booklets. Later, in much-remarked-upon breaches of the convention that

women should be silent in church affairs, she conducted part of her husband's funeral in 1548, and in 1557 wrote a blistering *Ein Brieff an die gantze Burgerschafft der Statt Straszburg* (Open Letter to All the Citizens of Strasbourg), upbraiding his successors for their religious intolerance. Caring for a syphilitic nephew launched her on a successful campaign to improve conditions in Strasbourg's frightful pox hospital. Her last publication (1558) was a set of devotional meditations written for Felix Armbruster, a friend forced by leprosy to give up his political career.

Throughout her career, Katharina Zell defended the downtrodden and the dissident. She called for toleration of both Catholics and Anabaptists, and when the Marburg Colloquy of 1529 failed to heal the rift between Swiss and Saxon Protestants, she wrote Luther to urge him to let Christian love moderate his hostility. In the late twenties she, her husband, and another leading pastor, Wolfgang Capito, had befriended Kaspar von Schwenckfeld, a Silesian spiritualist who had taken refuge in Strasbourg. After Matthias's death, Katharina grew more openly involved with Schwenckfeld and with a group of prominent men and women who preferred his ideas to the Lutheranism of the mid-century clergy. Her last public acts were to conduct funerals for Felicitas Scher, wife of the city physician Johann Winther von Andernach, and his sister-in-law Elizabeth Heckler, both of whom had been refused clerical services because of their ties to Schwenckfeld.

Katharina Zell's courage, organizational skills, and sharp tongue provoked admiration and uneasiness among her contemporaries. She herself felt a dissonance between her understanding of her duties as a Christian and the deferential silence expected of her as a respectable woman. In her first book she claimed (perhaps disingenuously) that Matthias Zell did not know she had written and would not approve of her publishing his defense; she regarded her childlessness as a sign of divine displeasure and must have known her husband's colleagues thought him henpecked. In excusing her independence, she cited scripture, including assurances that God would enable women to prophesy (*Jl.* 2:28–29) and Mary Magdalene's role as annunciator of Christ's resurrection. Thus fortified, she counted herself a "mother of the church" in Strasbourg.

BIBLIOGRAPHY

Abray, Lorna Jane. *The People's Reformation: Magistrates, Clergy, and Commons in Strasbourg, 1500–1598.* Ithaca, N.Y., 1985. Provides a context for Zell's career from the 1530s on; for background on the early Reformation see Chrisman, *Strasbourg and the Reform.*

Bainton, Roland. "Katherine Zell." In *Women of the Reformation in Germany and Italy*, edited by Roland Bainton, pp. 55–76. Minneapolis, 1971. A detailed account of her whole life, emphasizing her charity and religious toleration. Illustrated.

Brady, Thomas A., Jr. *Ruling Class, Regime and Reformation at Strasbourg, 1520–1555.* Leiden, 1978. Useful for Zell's family connections and for the political context in which she worked.

Chrisman, Miriam Usher. *Strasbourg and the Reform*. New Haven, 1967. Describes the religious climate in which Zell began her career as a reformer; for the later decades, see Abray.

———. "Women and the Reformation in Strasbourg, 1490–1530." *Archiv für Reformationsgeschichte* 63 (1972), 143–168. Situates Zell among the handful of women active in the early Strasbourg reformation.

Russell, Paul A. *Lay Theology in the Reformation: Popular Pamphleteers in Southwestern Germany, 1521–1525*. Cambridge, 1986. Discusses Zell and other women pamphleteers, drawing comparisons with the laymen in his sample; summarizes the arguments of her 1524 defense of her marriage and open letter of solidarity with the women of Kentzingen.

LORNA JANE ABRAY

ZELL, Matthias (1477–1548), pioneer of the evangelical movement in Strasbourg. Son of an artisanal family in Kaysersberg, Alsace, Zell was educated (M.A., B.Theol.) in the nominalist tradition at the University of Freiburg, where he was rector in 1517–1518. Preferring a preaching and pastoral career to the academic life, he came to Strasbourg in 1518 to take up appointments as cathedral preacher, priest of the cathedral parish, and episcopal *poenitentiarius*; the latter office made him the bishop's designate for the absolution of particularly grave sins reserved for episcopal attention. Already uneasy with the failure of his fellow clergymen to respect canon law, troubled by what he regarded as too onerous burdens placed on the laity, Zell was soon attracted to Martin Luther's teachings, and in 1521 he began to preach as an evangelical, beginning a series of sermons on Paul's letter to the Romans.

Three preachers before Zell had been driven out for similar offenses, and now the bishop of Strasbourg, Wilhelm von Honstein, tried to secure the cooperation of the cathedral chapter to remove Zell from his post. The effort failed for three reasons. The cathedral officials divided among themselves over what they took to be episcopal interference in their jurisdiction. Zell's sermons were extremely popular, moving truculent burghers to threaten the clerical authorities with violence if they moved against Zell. When the canons locked him out of the cathedral's main pulpit, members of the carpenters' guild constructed a portable pulpit that they wheeled in and out of the building for Zell to use. Finally, the city council, unsure of who spoke for Christian truth when the priests quarreled among themselves, long suspicious of the bishop and the upper clergy, and frightened by the potential for popular violence, decided to extend a cautious protection to the popular "Master Matthias."

From 1521 until 1523 Zell was the sole clerical leader of the local reformation. In that year he recruited Wolfgang Capito, provost of the prestigious Saint Thomas chapter, for action on behalf of the rebels. Zell did not so much change Capito's theology as convince him that the conservatives, not the innovators, were responsible for the rising violence in the city. Thereafter Capito and Zell worked closely together and were soon joined by Martin Bucer, a former Dominican, already married, and recently arrived in Strasbourg fleeing persecution. Zell engineered Bucer's integration into the nascent Strasbourg church, providing him with a forum for his theological lectures, allowing him to preach in the cathedral, and supporting his irregular installation as pastor of Saint Aurelia.

Although Capito and Bucer eventually eclipsed him at the head of the local evangelical movement, Zell remained its pioneer. The first evangelical preacher to avoid dismissal and one of the first of the local clergy to marry, he formed a partnership in 1523 with the redoubtable Katharina Zell, a pioneer evangelical in her own right. Zell published the first local defense of the Reformation, a *Christliche verantwortung* (Christian Answer) to the bishop (1523), and joined Capito in a published rebuttal of the bishop's excommunication of the married clergy the following year. He was the first of the Strasbourg clergy to baptize in German, in 1524, and in 1525 published the city's first evangelical catechism.

Like Capito, Zell was slow to distance himself from the Anabaptists and was drawn to the ideas of the Silesian spiritualist Kaspar von Schwenckfeld. In common with his wife, he never accepted force as a legitimate tool of conversion. He did accommodate himself to his city's rapprochement with Saxon eucharistic theology in the Wittenberg Concord of 1536, even journeying with his wife to Wittenberg to meet Luther. Not a scholar like Capito, and not a theologian like Bucer, Zell's passion was for pastoral action. To him preaching was the essence of the Reformation, and he did it brilliantly. Forceful, plainspoken to the point of coarseness, Zell alarmed the city's rulers by his continued drive to improve the piety and morals of the Strasburghers, and by his insistence that charity and fidelity to the faith must take precedence over profit and political convenience. Strasbourg's defeat at the emperor's hands in the Schmalkald War of the 1540s and the subsequent threat of a Catholic restoration drove him to the brink of defiance of city rulers apparently prepared to sacrifice Protestantism to preserve the city's independence. His death in 1548, at the height of the crisis, brought thousands of mourners to his funeral, a measure of his own and his church's abiding hold on the townspeople's loyalties.

BIBLIOGRAPHY

Abray, Lorna Jane. *The People's Reformation: Magistrates, Clergy and Commons in Strasbourg, 1500–1598*. Ithaca, N.Y., 1985. Provides a context for Zell's career from the 1530s on; for the earlier decades, see Chrisman, *Strasbourg and the Reform*, and Stafford, *Domesticating the Clergy*.

Brady, Thomas A., Jr. *Ruling Class, Regime and Reformation at Strasbourg, 1520–1555*. Leiden, 1978. Analyzes the political context in which Zell worked and provides information on his connections with the governing class through his wife, Katharina Schütz.

Chrisman, Miriam Usher. *Strasbourg and the Reform.* New Haven, 1967. Describes the religious climate in which Zell began his reforming career; compare Stafford, *Domesticating the Clergy*, which focuses on his early ideas. For the later decades, see Abray and Brady.

———. *Bibliography of Strasbourg Imprints, 1480–1599.* New Haven, 1982. Lists Zell's publications.

Kittelson, James M. *Wolfgang Capito: From Humanist to Reformer.* Leiden, 1975. Explains Zell's role in winning over Capito; after 1523 the two worked closely together until Capito's death in 1541.

Stafford, William. *Domesticating the Clergy: The Inception of the Reformation in Strasbourg, 1522–1524.* Missoula, Mont., 1976. Chapter one analyzes Zell's *Christliche verantwortung* (Christian Answer) of 1523 in detail, arguing that Zell was more outraged by clerical misbehavior than by clerical power, and was developing a program for a church that would emphasize the preaching of the gospel and put fewer material and spiritual demands on the laity. See also Chrisman, *Strasbourg and the Reform*, and Abray, *The People's Reformation*, for the arguments over clerical power.

LORNA JANE ABRAY

ŽEROTÍN, Karl (Czech., Karel Senior; 1564–1636), Czech humanist, Moravian magnate and politician, and leading figure of the Moravian branch of the Unity of Brethren. Žerotín was educated at the Unity of Brethren school at Ivančice (Moravia), at the academy of Johannes Sturm in Strasbourg, and at the Calvinist universities in Geneva and Basel, where he was a pupil of Johann Jacob Grynaeus and Théodore de Bèze. He traveled through Germany, Italy, the Low Countries, England, and France as a soldier in the troops of Henry IV of France in 1591. Žerotín had an extensive knowledge of European culture and languages, was an excellent orator and letter writer, and had close contacts with Reformation intellectuals in Germany and Switzerland. His extensive correspondence (thousands of letters in Czech, Latin, German, French, and Italian) are among the most interesting Bohemian and Moravian sources for the intellectual history of the sixteenth and seventeenth centuries.

From 1594 Žerotín took part in the policies of the Moravian estates, originally in the land supreme justice court, later in the opposition of the estates against emperor Rudolf II. He was one of the leading figures of the Hungarian-Austrian-Moravian Confederation of Estates (1608), which supported archduke Matthias of Habsburg. He was the supreme captain—the president—of the provincial government of Moravia from 1608 to 1615. During the Bohemian uprising (1618–1620) he was loyal to the Habsburg dynasty, but after 1620 he hid persecuted Protestants, including the philosopher and pedagogue Jan Amos Komenský (Comenius) and other priests of the Unity of Brethren. As a result of the forced re-Catholicization of Moravia and Bohemia by the Habsburgs, he moved to Wrocław (Silesia). The university library there has preserved his important collection of books.

Žerotín was an extremely complicated personality. Influenced by Calvinist theology and political theory, he tried to find a harmony between his profound religious faith and political activities. He was a partisan of religious liberty and a defender of the provincial privileges of Moravia (*Apologia* of 1606 and other Czech writings). Thus he came in conflict with leading figures of the Unity of Brethren in Bohemia (such as Václav Budovec of Budov in 1608–1609 and 1618–1620). He was a high-principled legitimist and a skeptic in political affairs. The evaluation of Žerotín's evolution from an exemplary member of the Unity of Brethren to a traitor to the Protestants and his own country is still a problem of Czech historiography.

BIBLIOGRAPHY

Chlumecky, Peter. *Carl von Zierotin und seine Zeit, 1564–1615.* 2 vols. Brno, 1862–1879. The first, incomplete, political biography with a collection of select sources.

Fukala, Radek. "Politický program Karla staršího ze Žerotína v době českého stavovského povstáni." *Folia Historica Bohemica* 15 (1991), 465–477. Recent interpretation of Žerotín's political activities from 1618 through 1620.

Kopecký, Milan. "Karel starí ze Žerotína a jeho Apologie" (Karel Senior of Žerotín and his Apology). *Z kralické tvrze* 8 (1975–1976), 1–19. A study of Žerotín with an edition of his Czech Apology.

Odložilík, Otakar. *Karel starší ze Žerotína, 1564–1636.* Prague, 1936. A complete biography, written from the point of view of the Unity of Brethren.

Rejchrtová, Noemi, ed. *Karel starší ze Žerotína, Z korespondence* (Select Correspondence of Karel Senior of Žerotín). Prague, 1982. A select edition of Žerotín's letters, with a biographical study and a bibliography of other editions of his correspondence.

Válka, Josef. "Karel starí ze Žerotína." *Z kralické tvrze* 13 (1986), 1–7. Recent biographical study from the point of view of Moravian history.

JAROSLAV PÁNEK

ZURICH first appeared in history as a small Roman military and customs post known as "statio Turicensis." Shortly after 401 the Roman garrison was removed, and by the second half of the sixth century the Alemannic can be said to have dominated the scene. Zurich emerged in the early Middle Ages as a Christian city, if one can really call it a city at that time: Emperor Louis the German later referred to it as a *Fleck*, by which he meant a very tiny place.

The language in which Zwingli preached and the knowledge of their origins—about which Bullinger, Zwingli's successor at Zurich, was so proud—reveals that at the time of the Zwinglian Reformation a central part of the Alemannic heritage still dominated German Switzerland. There can be no doubt that this heritage influenced the nature and form of the Zwinglian Reformation and its spread.

The central institutions which developed at Zurich in the medieval period were very important for the Reformation. Louis the German, the grandson of Emperor Charlemagne, founded the nunnery of the Fraumünster in 853 for his daughter. It stood on the site at which it was believed that the martyrs Felix and Regula had been beheaded and provided a central focus for the city's identification with these powerful spiritual protectors. Long before the coming of the Reformation the Zurich city council had busied itself with achieving greater control over this vital urban foundation.

The two other major ecclesiastical foundations that played an important part in the city's history were the Großmünster and Saint Peter's Church. The origins of Saint Peter's go back to the early Middle Ages, when the church was established as a parish church for the city's population. The Großmünster was a collegiate church in which the canons obeyed the Benedictine rule; it is customary to associate its founding with Charlemagne, whose hunting lodge is said to have been nearby. The Großmünster was responsible for serving the large parishes on the right bank of the Limmat River, while the Fraumünster cared for those on the left. As in the case of the Fraumünster (the nuns' cloister), the town council struggled hard to bring the often-unruly canons under their control. Many were involved in hiring and selling soldiers for the Italian wars. Often the canons continued drinking and gambling afer the services of the Großmünster had begun.

Using a theory of corporate authority, the council asserted that the "citizens" had delegated their authority to them. In principle this conception of authority knew no limits and also fitted extremely well with the belief that the city was a Christian community ruled by secular and spiritual officers whose cooperation guaranteed civic harmony. One consequence of the Reformation was to clarify the function of both civil and ecclesiastical authority in a Christian civic commonwealth. According to Zwingli and his followers, the visible church coincided with the structures of the city itself, while the spiritual realm served in Zwingli's words as the "soul of the city" and was presided over by the clergy. The invisible church of the elect was known not by men but rather by God alone, though Zwingli added that the members of the Zurich community were to be called elect by "a human judgment." These ideas, which denied the spiritual realm any coercive power, may well have come from Marsilio da Padova's *Defensor Pacis*. Beatus Rhenanus, a friend of Zwingli, the Hebraist Ceporin, and probably Leo Jud were involved in the first two editions of this work, published by Johann Froben in 1522, of which there were at least three copies of in Zurich.

When the Reformation began, it was Zwingli's good luck that during the Middle Ages the Großmünster had developed a school that would become the first Reformed theology faculty in Europe and would serve to spread Zwinglian theology. When Zwingli became the people's priest at the Großmünster on 1 January 1519, the church became the center of the Reformation in Zurich.

Zurich became a member of the Swiss Confederation in 1351 (*Der ewiger Bund*) and, like the seven other regions of the original Confederation, was *Reichsunmittelbar* (directly under the authority of the emperor). Its position as an imperial city had been reconfirmed in 1262, and Zurich functioned as the *Vorposten* ("outpost") of the Confederation. Its guild constitution had been secured in 1336 by the revolt of the guilds led by the knight Rudolph Brunn. The *Constaffel* (the organization of the nobles, knights, and rich citizens) had to share power with the thirteen city guilds in the great and small councils, which acknowledged the principle of representation although they co-opted their own members.

At several points, it seemed as if Zurich's Reformation might be crushed by the majority of the Confederates. Even after the Second Kappel War, the victorious Catholics were satisfied, however, with stopping the spread of Zwinglianism and re-Catholicizing the jointly governed regions of the Confederation. The old Confederation was a weak union, for it had neither a constitution nor a legal code. Indeed it was not until the beginning of the fifteenth century that it had a name and not until the nineteenth century that it adopted an official seal. The oaths of fellowship which bound the thirteen regions together reflected the late medieval conception of freedom: each member was at liberty to pursue its own interests.

Modern Views of the Significance of the Urban Reformation in the Southwest German Imperial Cities. In the last three decades modern historians have begun to note carefully the function and structures of the southwest German imperial cities. Eberhard Naujoks was the first to observe closely the similarity of the guild constitutions and the corporate theories of participation and delegation in the governments of many of them. Bernd Moeller carried Naujoks's work much further. His examination of the development of Zwingli's and Bucer's theologies led him to conclude that they were "urban" theologians. Indeed, Moeller might just as well have said that their theology was a theology for urban oligarchs. He also added that the imperial cities were the centers of culture of the German empire, which probably explains the Erasmian cast that never left Zwingli's theology. Though Moeller did not mention it, when Zwingli talked about the "people," he meant the members of the guilds.

Moeller added a second important conclusion when he examined the significance of the first Zurich Disputation (29 January 1523). When the disputation ended and it had been proved that many of the beliefs and practices of the old church did not enjoy the support of scripture, the council asserted that it would now accept only the authority of scripture in matters of religion. In fact the council had made this decision before the disputation began. Moeller claims that this decision marked the founding of the first Protestant church in Europe. This development also made Zwingli the founding father of the Reformed churches. Similar reformations took place in the imperial cities of southwest Germany and enabled the town councils to gain full control over local churches. Thomas Brady's criticism of Moeller—

namely that the imperial cities were not isolated, but rather were part of the medieval landscape—is also of value.

Zwingli's Urban Reformation. Moeller and others have noted that Zwingli did not define his ecclesiology at the end of the first disputation because he believed that the visible church was coterminous with structures of the city-state. This conception was basic to his ecclesiology and to his idea of how the reform movement should be spread in the Confederation and especially in the cities—though Zwingli's reform was accepted by rural regions as well, as the Toggenburg, Glarus, Graubünden, and a good half of Appenzell all confirm. Zwingli's sense of politics and pragmatism are also obvious in each of the urban reform movements with which he was closely identified. His alliance with the town councils at Zurich, in particular the great council, which gained more power during the Reformation, was practical. Zwingli was also able to win the friendship and support of the Röist family, which was the wealthiest and most influential family in the city and provided both the mayor and the captain of the papal guard during the crucial early years of the Reformation at Zurich. Others, including members of the *Constaffel*, formed an influential segment of the small council that supported Zwingli. Even though the small council was the center of opposition to the Reformation, the minority favoring Zwingli was decisive. Among their number were influential members of the Saffron guild (spices) and the guild zur Meisen (cloth dealers, wine dealers, saddlers, and painters). Like Zwingli, Zurich's politicians had doubts about such matters as mercenary service and favored certain Erasmian-style reforms. Zwingli thus came to Zurich with ready-made allies.

The decision of the Zurich council to accept the authority of scripture solidified the alliance between the councils and Zwingli. Sure of support, Zwingli was able to cope with his own radical followers who first sought the establishment of a Christian council ready to speed the progress of reform. Frustrated by Zwingli's willingness to accept the council's delay in abolishing the Mass after the end of the second disputation (October 1523), they eventually founded a separate church (21 January 1525) which practiced adult baptism and rapidly found a following. The *Täufer*, or Anabaptists, as they are now called, also fished in the troubled waters of peasant social unrest. The council responded by enforcing infant baptism, which served as a symbol of membership in Zurich's Christian civic commonwealth. The former leader of the *Täufer*, Felix Manz, was drowned in Lake Zurich with a millstone tied round his neck, and thus became the first radical to be executed there. Zwingli and his allies emerged from the fight even closer than before.

Zwingli then turned to his enemies on the right and launched an attack from the pulpit upon the supporters of mercenary service abroad, whom he wrongly saw as an organized opposition. The result was the execution of the French pensioner councillor (*Ratsherr*) Jakob von Grebel in 1526. Grebel had been an important figure in the affairs of the city and was the father of Conrad Grebel, the leader of the *Täufer* movement in Zurich. The suspicion that Zwingli took vengeance upon the father because of the sins of the son is hard to avoid. The mercenary party was effectively smashed, but the confidence of Zurich's citizen militia in its officers was shaken, for the officers they trusted were removed or left the city.

The center of resistance to Zwingli's reform program was in the *Constaffel*, and in late June 1529 Zwingli's allies in the councils, urged on by his preaching, abolished the special place in the constitution that the *Constaffel* had enjoyed. It was reduced to the rank of a guild and its large representation in the councils reduced to that of a normal guild. This great victory for the reform movement also opened the way for the policies that led to the Second Kappel War. After Zurich's defeat the *Constaffel* was restored to its traditional position.

Finally, the cooperation between the magistrates and the theologians in the city was exemplified by the establishment of the *Ehegericht* ("marriage court"), which continued the work in Zurich of the bishop of Constance's marriage commission. By the time the council issued the Morality Ordinance in 1530, the activities of the court had been extended to the general supervision of morality. The councillors appointed to the court heard the advice of the theologians before they made their decisions in the interest of the community.

What did Zwingli believe was the key to his success? He certainly believed that it was due to the Holy Spirit that his biblical preaching influenced the community. However, it was his alliance with the council, which he termed the "highest authority among us," that was crucial. Writing to Ambrosius Blarer on 9 October 1523, Zwingli discussed how the council dealt with the problem of iconoclasm in the city and so made his own influence clear. He asserted, as he had done during the first disputation, that the gathering was a Christian assembly in which the visible church was represented by the council of two hundred. In his letter to Blarer of 4 May 1528, Zwingli clarified his conception of the visible church and dismissed Luther's assertion that Christ's kingdom was not of this world. Zwingli argued that the presbyters of the council of Jerusalem were not merely elders but also, like the Zurich councillors, men of affairs. He also asserted that the council had to decide secular matters. He developed his argument along lines laid down earlier by Marsilio da Padova and presented a case for the role of the Christian magistrate in the external affairs of the visible church.

The Application of Zwingli's Methods. How did Zwingli's alliance function? The decision to abolish the Mass and to replace it with the celebration of the Lord's Supper (*das evangelische Abendmahl*) was reached in the Zurich great council by a narrow margin. Those who voted in favor of abolishing the Mass acted upon the advice of the city's theologians: Zwingli, Jud, Heinrich Engelhardt, Caspar Megander, and Oswald Myconius. It is important to stress the fact that the great council voted on a matter that was both civil and spiritual; however, the councillors depended upon the advice of the theologians when voting against the Mass. Here was a crucial aspect of Zwingli's conception of how the spiritual and secular power should cooperate in the government of a Christian society. It was also clear that the Zwinglian model could be introduced with the aid of the corporate structures of a city-state. As Zwingli said, "When the gospel is preached and all, including the magistrates, heed it, the Christian man is nothing else than the faithful and good citizen; and the Christian city nothing other than the Christian church."

Zurich under Bishop Heinrich Bullinger. Zurich's defeat and Zwingli's death in the Second Kappel War (11 October 1531) threatened to shake the foundations of Zwingli's Reformation at Zurich. It was clear that Bern wished to expand westward and was unwilling to support a continuation of the war, especially after the disastrous battle on the Gubel (24 October 1531). The second territorial peace was agreed upon on 16 November and received the seal necessary to make it binding at Zug on 20 November. The Protestant Alliance, or *Christliche Burgrecht*, was ended and the way opened for the partial re-Catholicization of the jointly ruled territories of the Confederation. The peace treaty signaled the military as well as the religious ascendancy of the Catholic cantons, which lasted until the fourth territorial peace of 1712 (following the Second Villmerger War). They tolerated the religion of the Reformed, but only as an inferior faith, one which was unable to match their "true and undoubted faith."

As a result of the peace and the separate capitulation signed by Bremgarten, Heinrich Bullinger and his father, the former dean of the rural chapter of Bremgarten, became refugees and lost a good portion of their wealth. In both his theological writings and his ecclesiastical diplomacy, Bullinger was always compelled to consider the political situation in the Confederation in light of the power of the Catholic regions. This explains his taking care to avoid internal disagreement among the Reformed and his willingness to make concessions, where possible, to keep the peace. His successes outside of Zurich and Switzerland were in large part due to his skill in strengthening and restoring the Zurich church and then confirming its place of leadership among the Reformed in the Swiss Confederation, a situation that was maintained until the collapse of the old Confederation in 1798.

His first major problem arose before he became the city's bishop. On 9 December 1531 the Zurich council asked him to succeed Zwingli; on the same day, however, the council accepted the Meilener Articles. Framed by the region's inhabitants, these articles demonstrated the deep-seated popular dislike of politically motivated reformers. Zwingli and Jud, pastor of Saint Peter's church, were singled out for special criticism. The situation was so tense that for a short time a return to the old church was at least a possibility.

Bullinger had already signed the articles despite the content of articles two and four, which were directed against the political activities of the clergy. However, supported by the rest of Zurich's clergy (Erasmus Schmid, Hans Schmid, and Engelhardt of Fraumünster, Rudolf Thumysen and Jud, and Niclaus Zehnder, dean of the Zurich chapter), he refused to countenance any effort to prevent them from preaching the gospel freely as prophets of God's living word. Bullinger told the council on 13 December that the clergy would refrain from becoming involved in the affairs of state as long as they were free to preach the gospel. The council agreed and Bullinger became the *Antistes*, or bishop (i.e., the chief representative of the church), people's priest at the Großmünster, and, until 1537, superintendent of the schools. He was expected to supervise the Latin lower school at the Fraumünster and the Latin upper school at the Großmünster, as well as the exegetical Prophecy (*Prophezei*) as planned by Zwingli in 1523 and begun at the Großmünster in 1525. Its work had first resulted in a Swiss-German translation of the Old Testament, which was finished by 1529. Bullinger's interest in the German schools of the city came later.

Under Bullinger the curriculum of the Prophecy became more formalized and followed the educational program as presented in his *Studiorum ratio* of 1527, wherein a series of sermons was to be given on the particular biblical book under study. The sermons, held in the nave of the Großmünster, were given by one of the faculty members and discussed in Latin by the students and in German for interested laymen. Lay participation lessened when Bullinger began to hold some of the meetings of the students in the foundation house of the Großmünster, where among other things the use of German exegesis was carefully considered. Bullinger's *In omnes apostolicas epistolas commentarii*, first published by Christoph Froschauer in 1537, was a product of the Prophecy and outsold Calvin's later work on the same subject.

The faculty of the exegetical Prophecy and the Latin upper school were the only Reformed faculty in Europe until the founding of the Geneva Academy in 1559. The seminary was called the Carolinum, because it was believed that Charles the Great had founded the Großmünster. In keeping with the council's policy of using the lands of the old church to finance Reformation projects, the number of canons at the Großmünster was reduced so as to free enough prebends to finance the salaries of the professors. The faculty included the Hebraist Konrad Pellikan, the Latinist Jacob Ammann, the Hellenist Rudolf Collin, the theologian Theodor Bibliander, and the natural scientist and ethicist Conrad Gessner. Later, Peter Martyr Vermigli and Josias

Simmler became faculty members. The teaching and writing of these men clarified and defended the Zwinglian theology and in many ways continued the tradition of Christian humanism's sacred philology. In this work they were aided by the ablest of the clergy.

An unofficial advisory group soon grew up around Bullinger that discussed the internal and external problems they faced in propounding their teachings. For example, the mandate issued by Bullinger and Jud in 1532 relegated the catechetical training of the young men of the city to the clergy. Jud published a short catechism in 1534 which Bullinger prefaced. After the publication of Jud's longer catechism, a portion of the task of catechizing was handed over to the city's school teachers, who were in the process of coming under the authority of the synod. (Outside the city the rural clergy supervised catechetical training.) The humanist historian Johann Stumph, another member of Bullinger's circle, wrote an account of the conflict with Luther over the presence of Christ's body in the Lord's Supper, one that communicated the Zurich church's anger at Bucer's role in the affair and Bullinger's view of the matter. The Zurich clergy, led by Johannes Wolf and Bullinger, printed their final answer to Luther's criticism of their doctrine of the Lord's Supper in 1545. The *Wahrhafte Bekenntnis der Diener der Kirchen zu Zürich*, which represented an official statement, was the work of Bullinger's circle and, of course, had the approval of the city government. The same is true of the Consensus Tigurinus of 1549, the work of Calvin at Geneva and of Bullinger's circle at Zurich, which clarified the agreement between Geneva and Zurich regarding the question of the Lord's Supper. Yet another example is Rudolf Gwalther's letter to Bishop Richard Cox of Ely, dated 26 August 1573, in answer to Cox's questions about how to counter the arguments of the Presbyterians: in the name of the Zurich church Gwalther explained that the bishop's office was apostolic, an argument that Archbishop John Whitgift would soon take up. Finally, the two confessions of faith, the Helvetica Prior (1536) and especially the Helvetica Posterior (1566), which linked the German Swiss much more closely to Calvin's Geneva and which generally strengthened Protestantism in the Confederation, were also in part a joint effort by Bullinger and his informal circle. The confession began as Bullinger's personal confession, was given by Bullinger to Elector Frederick III of the Palatinate for the Augsburg Reichstag of 1566, and was then discussed with the Genevans and the Zurich theologians led by Bullinger. The central importance of Bullinger's circle was not reflected in the city's constitution, but it was crucial to the Swiss Reformation. The same can be said of Bullinger's *Zeitungen*, which served as a veritable intelligence service for his friends and allies.

Bullinger had been ordained at Zurich in 1528 and shortly after his appointment became a member of the guild zur Meisen. This was the most influential guild in the city after the *Constaffel*, and gave Bullinger both citizenship and a power base that he used with great skill to promote the interests of the territorial church and the international reform movement. A few months later Bullinger gained the privilege of appearing before the council at any time either alone or accompanied by representatives of the city's clergy or professors of the Carolinum. This right became the basis for the cooperation between Bullinger, the church, and the council. As time went on, Bullinger's *Fürträge* ("lectures" or "proposals") before the council became an important element in the council's policy decisions. From very early on he had the friendship of Hans Rudolf Lavater, soon to be one of the city's two mayors.

Bullinger knew that he could rely upon the city's pastors for support, but this did not prevent Jud from proposing in 1532 the establishment of morality courts for each congregation, to be selected by the congregation itself. Oecolampadius had made a similar proposal, and Bullinger was as opposed to Jud's proposal as he had been to Oecolampadius's. Bullinger, like Zwingli before him, envisioned a Christian state in which the supervision of morality lay in the hands of the council (i.e., the Christian magistrate). Indeed, in answering Jud he used the corporate idea of the delegation of authority by the people to the great council. According to one scholar's recent description, the church under Bullinger was "inclusive," rather than "exclusive," as in Calvin's Geneva.

Early in his career Bullinger was responsible for two developments that strengthened the Zurich church. After the Second Kappel War many influential members of the council considered confiscating and then selling the lands and wealth of the Großmünster to pay the city's war debts. Bullinger's appearance before the council on 17 February 1532 and his lucid arguments against such an action saved the cathedral's wealth for the educational services and other needs of the Reformed church. The Großmünster's wealth was hereafter administered by a special office called the *Obmannamt*.

Even more important was Bullinger's role in drafting the articles for the new synodical order, which he presented to the council on 22 October 1532. The new synodical order was established by the authority of the council to encourage "a godly Christian life." It placed the control of the visible church in the hands of magistracy and thus continued the tradition already accepted by Zwingli. The visible church and city were coterminous. All candidates for parish appointments had to swear an oath of loyalty to the council before they could be appointed. The semiannual meetings of the synod were presided over by eight members of the small council and one of the burgomasters who was not serving during the six-month period in which the synod was called. Bullinger as *Antistes* represented the church and reported to the presiding officers concerning the problems that the conduct of the clergy had caused. The order also provided for the training and examination of all candidates for the ministry. It made it clear that new candidates were not elected but rather were introduced to the parish by a representative of the council, who admonished the parish to obey the new pastor but also to report his misdeeds. The new pastor was also accompanied by the appropriate dean, though the dean had no authority to appoint him. Three years later Bullinger presented the council with exact proposals for the church's liturgy. The council accepted them, and thereby the structure of the restored Zurich church was complete. Throughout his career Bullinger admired and sought to follow Zwingli's prophetic preaching, and indeed no one understood it better than he did, as his *De Prophetae Officio* reveals. The council's decision to appoint the twenty-seven-year-old theologian from Bremgarten to the post of *Antistes* of the Zurich church made possible the recovery of the church and enabled Zurich to play a leading role both among the Protestant estates of the Confederation and in Protestant Europe, especially England.

[*See also* Bullinger, Heinrich; Consensus Tigurinus; Jud, Leo; Kappel, Peace of; *and* Zwingli, Huldrych.]

BIBLIOGRAPHY

Baker, J. Wayne. *Heinrich Bullinger and the Covenant: The Other Reformed Tradition.* Athens, Ohio, 1980.

Bonjour, E., H. S. Offler, and G. R. Potter, ed. *A Short History of Switzerland.* Reprint, Greenwood, Conn., 1985. The best history of Switzerland in English.

Farner, Oskar. *Huldrych Zwingli.* 4 vols. Zurich, 1946–1960. This is a detailed biography; very useful but hard to read.

Gäbler, Ulrich. *Huldrych Zwingli: His Life and Work.* Philadelphia, 1986. This book offers a very solid introduction to Zwingli's life and work.

Gäbler, Ulrich, and Erland Herkenrath, ed. *Heinrich Bullinger, 1504–1575: Gesammelte Aufsätze zum 400. Todestag.* 2 vols. Zurich, 1975. An excellent set of essays that shed new light on Bullinger's activities.

Gordon, Bruce. *Clerical Discipline and the Rural Reformation: The Synod in Zürich, 1532–1580.* Bern, 1992. A very interesting and useful study.

Haas, Martin. *Huldrych Zwingli und Seine Zeit: Leben und Werk des Zürcher Reformators.* 2d ed., rev. Zurich, 1976. This is the best political biography of Zwingli's life and work.

Heusler, Andreas. *Schweizerische Verfassungsgeschichte* (1920). Reprint, Aalen, 1968. This is a good constitutional history of Switzerland, but it is becoming outmoded.

Jacob, Walter. *Politische Führungeschichte und Reformation: Untersuchung zur Reformation in Zürich, 1519–1528.* Zurich, 1970. The role of the wealthy guildsmen and members of the *Constaffel* in the Zwinglian Reformation at Zurich is carefully documented.

Largiadier, Anton. *Geschichte von Stadt und Landschaft Zürich.* 2 vols. Erlenbach, 1945. This is the only modern book on the subject, but a three-volume study of the city's history will appear in the next few years.

Meyer, Helmut. *Der Zweite Kappeler Krieg: Die Krise der schweizerischen Reformation.* Zurich, 1976. This is a good book and carefully examines what happened during and after the Second Kappel War.

Moeller, Bernd. "Zwingli's Disputationen: Studien zu den Anfängen der Kirchenbildung und des Synodalwesens in Protestanismus." *Zeitschrift der Savigny-Stiftung für Rechtsgeschichte* 87, 91 (1970–1974). A very complex work; interesting, but not for beginners.

———. *Reichsstadt und Reformation: Bearbeitete Neuausgabe.* Berlin, 1986. This is the basic statement of Moeller's argument.

Morf, Hans. *Zunftverfassung und Obrigkeit in Zürich von Waldmann bis Zwingli.* Zurich, 1969. Together with Jacob's research, this book gives a clear picture of the function of the Zurich constitution and of the men who ruled through it.

Muralt, Leonhard von. "Renaissance und Reformation." In *Handbuch der schweizer Geschichte*, vol. 1. 2d ed. Zurich, 1980. An excellent long article by one of Switzerland's best historians.

Naujoks, Eberhard. *Obrigkeitsgedanke, Zunftverfassung und Reformation: Studien zur Verfassungsgeschichte von Ulm, Esslingen und Schwäbische-Gmünd.* Stuttgart, 1958.

Pestalozzi, Carl. *Heinrich Bullinger: Leben und ausgewählte Schriften.* Elberfeld, 1858. The standard work on Bullinger.

Pfister, Rudolf. *Kirchengeschichte der Schweiz.* Zurich, 1964. See vol. 2. A modern and useful church history of Switzerland.

Peyer, Hans Conrad. *Verfassungsgeschichte der alten Schweiz.* Zurich, 1978. This is the most modern constitutional history of Switzerland.

Potter, G. R. trans. *Church and State, 1528: A Letter from Zwingli to Ambrosius Blarer 4 May 1528.* Occasional Papers of the American Society for Reformation Research. Edited by Robert C. Walton. Detroit, 1977. A good translation.

———. *Zwingli.* Reprint, Cambridge, 1984. Certainly the best Zwingli biography in any language. Luckily it is in English.

Walton, Robert C. *Zwingli's Theocracy.* Toronto, 1967. This book began a discussion about Zwingli's conception of a Christian civic commonwealth.

———. "The Institutionalization of the Reformation at Zurich." *Zwingliana* 13.2 (1972), 497–515. This essay is still relevant.

ROBERT C. WALTON

ZURICH ACADEMY.

ZURICH ACADEMY. This institution owed its origins to the mandate of September 1523 for the reform of the Großmünster foundation, which included a provision to reform the Carolinum, the city's Latin school. Reform was postponed, however, until the canon responsible for the Latin school, Johann Niessli, who was hostile to the Reformation, died on 3 April 1525. When Huldrych Zwingli was named *Schulherr*, or director of education, he not only reformed the curriculum of the Carolinum but also introduced the study of Greek and Hebrew.

The study of the biblical languages made possible the introduction of biblical exegesis into the curriculum. The process of biblical exegesis was called *Prophezei*, or prophecy (*1 Cor.* 14:26–33), and it consisted of exegetical lectures during the senior year of the Latin school. The first lecture of the *Prophezei* was on 19 June 1525. Thereafter, every morning of the week, except Fridays and Sundays, senior students at the Latin school assembled in the choir of the Großmünster, along with foreign guest scholars and interested residents of Zurich. The city pastors were also required to attend for their reeducation. First, the Hebrew teacher gave an exegesis of the Hebrew text of a passage from the Old Testament; then, Zwingli interpreted the passage in Latin, by using the Greek text of the Septuagint; finally, a preacher, often Leo Jud, summarized in German the scholars' expositions. Thus the *Prophezei* was originally a Bible study that was added to the curriculum of the Carolinum.

In the beginning the Hebraist Jacob Ceporinus was the only professor, along with Zwingli. After Ceporinus's death in 1525 the school hired three faculty members: Konrad Pellikan, a Hebraist; Rudolf Collin, a Greek professor; and Jakob Ammann, a Latin professor. Collin and Ammann lectured at noon and at four in the afternoon. Oswald Myconius presented lectures on the New Testament at three in the afternoon in the choir of the Fraumünster. In 1531 Theodor Bibliander was appointed professor of Old Testament to replace Zwingli. Other distinguished early professors included Peter Martyr Vermigli, who became professor of Old Testament in 1556, and Hans Wolf, who was appointed professor of theology in 1563.

Heinrich Bullinger became *Antistes*, or head of the Zurich church, after Zwingli's death in 1531. He was also appointed *Schulherr*, and during his lifetime the *Prophezei* developed into a true academy, or theological college. There was no university at Zurich until 1833, and the academy was not a substitute for a university education. For senior students it held a spot between Latin school and university as sort of a preparatory course of study for the Reformed ministry. This informal distinction between the lower students at the Carolinum and the senior students preparing for pastoral duties was made official only in 1601, when the city council formally established the Collegium Humanitatis. Senior students could attend lectures in the sciences, mathematics, politics, and rhetoric, as well as advanced lectures in theology and the biblical languages. During the sixteenth century students often continued their education at universities abroad before being certified as pastors in the Zurich church. When, in 1537, the *Schulherr* became an office separate from the *Antistes*, Bullinger continued to participate as a professor.

The *Prophezei* and the academy had great impact both in Zurich and abroad. All of Zwingli's exegetical works had their origin in the *Prophezei*. The Zurich Bible, a translation into the local German dialect, was also a product of the *Prophezei*. Most likely Bullinger's *Decades* resulted from theological lectures given at the academy. The clergy in Zurich received their basic biblical and theological education at the academy. Institutions similar to the *Prophezei* came into existence in Strasbourg, Basel, the Netherlands, England, and Scotland.

BIBLIOGRAPHY

Biel, Pamela. *Doorkeepers at the House of Righteousness: Heinrich Bullinger and the Zurich Clergy, 1535–1575.* Bern, 1990. Includes a chapter on Bullinger and the Zurich clergy as educators, pp. 166–199.

Gäbler, Ulrich. *Huldrych Zwingli: His Life and Work.* Philadelphia, 1986. Includes a section on the *Prophezei* and on Zwingli's exegetical works and the Zurich Bible, pp. 99–103.

Gagliardi, Ernst, Hans Nabholz, and Jean Strohl. *Die Universität Zürich 1833–1933 und ihre Vorläufer.* Zurich, 1938. Part 1 traces the history of the academy and *Prophezei* through the sixteenth century.

Locher, Gottfried W. *Die Zwinglische Reformation im Rahmen der europäischen Kirchengeschichte.* Göttingen, 1979. Includes material on the *Prophezei* and their influence on the establishment of similar institutions elsewhere in Europe.

Wirz, Johann Jacob. *Historische Darstellung der urkundlichen Verordnung welche die Geschichte des Kirchen- und Schulwesens in Zürich betreffen.* Vol. 1. Zurich, 1793. Covers the growth of the academy in relation to the Carolinum and *Prophezei*.

Zürcher, Christoph. *Konrad Pellikans Wirken in Zürich, 1526–1556.* Zurich, 1975. Excellent study of Pellikan. Includes material on his participation in the *Prophezei*.

J. WAYNE BAKER

ZURICH AGREEMENT. *See* Consensus Tigurinus.

ZWICK, Johannes (c.1496–1542), Protestant reformer of Constance. He came from a patrician family that had moved from St. Gall to Constance. Already as a child he had been identified for an ecclesiastical career. In 1509, after first attending school in the imperial and episcopal city of Constance, he matriculated at the University of Freiburg to study law. Here he associated with Bruno and Basilius Amerbach, as well as with Ulrich Zasius (1461–1535). In 1518, the year he was ordained, Zwick went for three years with his brother Konrad to Italy to continue his studies. He became familiar with the "causa Lutheri" and received the degree of *Doctor iuris utriusque* in Siena in 1521. Next he taught at the university in Basel where he joined the local circle of humanists and became acquainted with Desiderius Erasmus (1467–1536).

In the fall of 1522 (and shortly after his secret marriage), he assumed the parish of Riedlingen on the Danube and continued the reform preaching of his predecessor. From 1523 he had contacts with important Swiss and South German reformers. In November 1523 he participated actively in the second Zurich Disputation. He opposed the Peasants' War (1524–1525). Nonetheless, the peasants named him one of the arbitrators in their negotiations with the Swabian League. In the fall of 1525 Zwick was removed from his pulpit. He returned to Constance and served in 1525/26 as preacher at Saint Stephen's, where he was appointed by the city council but unsalaried. Together with his relative and friend Ambrosius Blarer (1492–1564), he established and organized the reformation in Constance.

After Blarer's departure in 1531, the spiritual leadership in the city fell solely to Zwick. His fundamentally positive cooperation with the city council was notable. In 1529 Zwick endorsed the abolition of images. In the same year, as president of the synod of Frauenfeld, he represented the interests of the city in the reformation of Thurgau. With the support of the city council, Zwick served resolutely for the "unitas ecclesiae" in Constance and opposed everything and everyone that could endanger this unity, including Anabaptists and irenic Schwenckfelders. Even the Wittenberg Concord (1536) was rejected by Zwick for theological and political reasons. He strove for what has been called "sanctification as a whole" (Bernd Moeller) and defined the relationship between faith and works in keeping with the letter of James. All of his writings showed a decidedly pastoral and pedagogical preoccupation.

His prayer book for young people (*Gebätt für Jung lüt*, c.1540), which represents the best of contemporary Protestant devotional literature, was particularly important. As prominent was Zwick's contribution to the Constance hymnal (*Nüw gsangbüchle*, 1540), which contains seventeen of his own hymns and is counted among the best musical accomplishments of the Reformation. At the beginning of the book is a programmatic treatise written by Zwick. The city's school order, introduced in 1538 and finally established in 1541, was essentially Zwick's work and lasted beyond the end of the reformation in Constance (1548). In the summer of 1542 he received a call as a preacher to the city of Bischofszell in Thurgau. Here he died of the plague in the fall of that year. A number of his sermons, meditations, and songs were published posthumously by Blarer.

BIBLIOGRAPHY

Moeller, Bernd. *Johannes Zwick und die Reformation in Konstanz.* Gütersloh, 1961.

ULMAN WEISS
Translated from German by Susan M. Sisler

ZWICKAU. A Saxon city and wool-weaving center, Zwickau had a population around 7,500 in 1531. Here the city council inclined earliest to Martin Luther, seeking his references for clerical vacancies from 1519. It called Nikolaus Hausmann (1478/79–1538), a known Luther adherent, as pastor, who took up his post in May 1521. Prior to his arrival, the Catholic priest was in absentia, but other preachers practiced the cure of souls. The two most important for the Reformation were Sylvius Egranus and Thomas Müntzer, both initially attractive to the council as critics of the Catholic church. Egranus was an Erasmian who ultimately remained loyal to the Catholic church, accepting its view of justification and the sacraments. Beginning in the fall of 1520, Müntzer attacked him for these tendencies and for hobnobbing with councillors. From this time Müntzer championed the poorer weavers in Saint Katherine's congregation and developed a mystical theology. Duke Johann (elector from 1525), brother of Frederick III of Saxony, forced his dismissal in April 1521.

As the city council continued to erode earlier popular participation in government and as it imposed new taxes and regulations, the disaffection of many craftsmen grew. Radical religious tendencies found expression in the "Zwickau Prophets," especially the weaver Niclas Storch, who found an audience in the former Müntzerian circle during the fall of 1521. In December the prophets fled to avoid interrogation. The council and Hausmann labored throughout the 1520s to eliminate sympathy for their mystical, antiauthoritarian, and inconsistently antipedobaptist views.

During the 1520s the council steadily encroached upon the church and the sphere of religion as it expanded its secular purview. In March 1522 some councillors allegedly participated in vandalizing the city's Cistercian monastery. In an effort to calm and convert the people, the council invited Luther to preach in Zwickau the following month. It bought out the local Dominicans. Only during the emergency of the Peasants' War was it finally able to exclude the powerful Franciscans. The process of institutional reform was now complete, and indoctrination of the people continued. When on 24 March 1524 Communion was offered to the laity in both kinds, only twenty people accepted it. By 1530 the council had achieved almost full conformity with Lutheranism.

Ironically the council became estranged from Luther (and his close friend Hausmann) over the question of church governance. At issue was the selection and supervision of the clergy, such as Paul Lindenau, Conrad Cordatus, and Lorenz Soranus, all of whom severely criticized the councillors from the pulpit. Alienated, Hausmann left for Wittenberg in May 1531. Elector Johann called both sides to a hearing at Torgau in August. Councillor Hermann Mühlpfort called Luther "the German pope," and Luther condemned Zwickau. Johann's solution, in keeping with his and his heir Johann Friedrich's ecclesiastical policy for all their lands, was that the elector, not the council or the pastor, would govern the church in Zwickau. With this decision, the conciliar Reformation came to an end, and princely domination of religion began.

[*See also* Müntzer, Thomas; *and* Zwickau Prophets.]

BIBLIOGRAPHY

Bräuer, Helmut. *Zwickau und Martinus Luther: Die gesellschaftlichen Auseinandersetzungen um die städtische Kirchenpolitik in Zwickau, 1527–1531.* Karl-Marx-Stadt, 1983. An indispensable Marxist analysis by the German historian most informed on early modern Zwickau.
———. *Thomas Müntzer und die Zwickauer: Zum Wirken Thomas Müntzers in Zwickau, 1520–1521.* Karl-Marx-Stadt, 1989. Portrays the polarization of society during Müntzer's stay in Zwickau from a Marxist perspective, seeing the tensions largely in economic terms.
Karant-Nunn, Susan C. *Zwickau in Transition, 1500–1547: The Reformation as an Agent of Change.* Columbus, Ohio, 1987.
Scribner, R. W. "The Reformation as a Social Movement." In *The Urban Classes, the Nobility and the Reformation*, edited by Wolfgang J. Mommsen, pp. 49–79. Stuttgart, 1978. Reprinted in Scribner, R. W., *Popular Culture and Popular Movements in Reformation Germany*,

pp. 145–174, London, 1987. Shows that religious events in Wittenberg, Zwickau, and Leipzig were "significantly shaped by social factors."

SUSAN C. KARANT-NUNN

ZWICKAU PROPHETS. When Thomas Müntzer accepted the position of preacher in Zwickau's Saint Katherine church in August 1520, he became acquainted with the economic plight of the craftsmen, mainly wool weavers, of that quarter, including weaver Niclas Storch. Storch represented himself as a prophet, with whom the Holy Spirit communicated and even gave the gift of foretelling the future. Müntzer himself moved toward the belief that God revealed himself directly to the individual through the inner word, and he claimed to enjoy such revelation.

Modern scholarship on the relationship between Müntzer and Storch has suffered from an indiscriminate acceptance of accounts about Storch that originated much later and from a Lutheran point of view that sought to deepen Storch's culpability. Extant sources suggest that Müntzer rather than Storch wielded the greater influence. It also has not been proved, though often claimed, that Storch absorbed Taborite or Waldensian ideas while traveling in Bohemia.

With Müntzer's dismissal in April 1521, Storch found somewhat greater scope for his preaching than he had before. Later Müntzer confessed, albeit under torture, that himself had founded conventicles as such in Zwickau. In December 1521 the city council heard rumors of such a secret brotherhood, as well as stories of "heretical" teaching and of women preaching. In cooperation with the pastor Nikolaus Hausmann, they cited the reputed leaders for questioning, but the three who acquiesced in, even if they did not use, the title Zwickau Prophets fled to Wittenberg. Apart from Storch, the most articulate (and the only learned man among the three) was Marcus Thomae, called Stübner because his father owned a bathhouse in Elsterberg; he was neither a native nor a permanent resident of Zwickau. He had studied in Wittenberg and was acquainted with both Philipp Melanchthon and Müntzer. The third, Thomas Drechsel, was a blacksmith of respectable provenance but precarious economic existence. His role as a "prophet" was minor.

Luther being in the Wartburg, Melanchthon interviewed the men and was impressed with Stübner's learning. According to Melanchthon, Stübner was more insistent on adult baptism than Storch, but all three claimed to have intimate conversations with God and to prophesy; they believed that the end of the world was at hand. In this period of itenerant preachers and high individualism, Melanchthon, Nikolaus von Amsdorf, Frederick III of Saxony, Georg Spalatin, and others considered the trio's assertions.

When consulted by letter, Luther urged restraint; only the claim that infants should not be baptised gave him pause and moved him to defend pedobaptism more completely than he had. By March 1522, as unrest over Reformation changes spread in Wittenberg, Luther was no longer so moderate. In early April Stübner presented his views personally to Luther, who rejected them. Luther later met with Drechsel and with Storch, with similar results.

Stübner converted the Swabian teacher Martin Borrhaus, who has erroneously been identified as one of the Zwickau Prophets. Andreas Bodenstein Karlstadt developed his mystical and antipedobaptist convictions independently. The subsequent histories of the prophets are for the most part unknown. Storch wandered from village to village, weaving and telling of his visions. He was rumored to be in the vicinity of Zwickau in 1534 and 1536. There is no evidence that Storch left a variety of Anabaptism in his wake.

BIBLIOGRAPHY

Bender, Harold S. "The Zwickau Prophets, Thomas Müntzer and the Anabaptists." *Mennonite Quarterly Review* 27 (1953), 3–16.

Friesen, Abraham. *Thomas Muentzer, a Destroyer of the Godless: The Making of a Sixteenth-Century Religious Revolutionary.* Berkeley, 1990. All biographies of Thomas Müntzer contain some treatment of the prophets. Friesen agrees that Müntzer had greater influence on Storch than Storch had on Müntzer. See especially chapter 4, "Zwickau and the Prophets."

Karant-Nunn, Susan C. *Zwickau in Transition, 1500–1547: The Reformation as an Agent of Change.* Columbus, Ohio, 1987. Discusses the prophets' background, alleged teachings, and the identity of their followers.

Wappler, Paul. "Thomas Müntzer in Zwickau und die 'Zwickauer Propheten.'" In *Wissenschaftliche Beilage zu dem Jahresberichte des Realgymnasiums mit Realschule zu Zwickau.* Zwickau, 1908. Reprinted in *Schriften des Vereins für Reformationsgeschichte,* 71.182, Gütersloh, 1966. Despite many subsequent corrections of detail and interpretation by scholars, this remains the basic treatment, thorough in its use of sources.

SUSAN C. KARANT-NUNN

ZWILLING, Gabriel (Greek, Didymus ["twin"]; 1487–1558), Protestant reformer. He studied at the University of Prague and, from 1512, in Wittenberg. At this time Zwilling was already an Augustinian monk, like Martin Luther, on whose recommendation he continued his studies in Erfurt, beginning the winter semester of 1516. A year later, however, he returned to the University of Wittenberg, where, on 11 February 1518, he gained his M.A.

Exactly when Zwilling took up the Reformation cause is unclear. During Luther's time at Wartburg castle, he came under the influence of Andreas Bodenstein von Karlstadt, which led him on 6 and 13 October 1521 to preach against the adoration of the Sacrament and against private masses; he demanded the administration of Communion in both kinds and announced that he would no longer say Mass. Soon afterward he left the monastery at Wittenberg, together with other monks of his order. At Christmas during the same year in the small Saxon town of Eilenburg, he disseminated reform ideas from the pulpit—wearing secular clothes. At Wittenberg in 10 January 1522 he took a stand against the hanging of pictures in churches; on the following day, along with other former monks, he burned pictures, altars, and leftover holy oil from the monastery church.

Zwilling reconciled himself with Luther after the latter's return from Wartburg castle, and admitted having followed the wrong path in spreading the Reformation. On 17 April 1522 Luther, urging restraint, recommended him as preacher to the town of Altenburg. But this move provoked the resistance of the town's Augustinian canons, who had the right to fill the post, and the elector, Frederick III of Saxony, also expressed reservations. Zwilling thus went to Neustadt on the Orla river. At the end of 1523 he became preacher in Torgau, where, in May 1525, he also obtained a living and was married. His sermons may have led to the storming of the Franciscan monastery in Torgau on Ash Wednesday 1525. During the late 1520s he helped establish the church order there, as well as the town's school system. He became superintendent, but, because of his opposition to the Interim (1548–1552), he was removed from office. He was, however, able to remain in Torgau and to acquire the patronage of the duchess Katharina, the mother of the electors Moritz and August.

BIBLIOGRAPHY

Plitt. "Gabriel Didymus." In *Allgemeine Deutsche Biographie*, vol. 5. Leipzig, 1877.

SIEGFRIED HOYER

ZWINGLI, Huldrych (1484–1531), Protestant reformer and founder of Reformed tradition. Of the many designations that emerged from his life by which others sought to identify him, two in particular, Toggenbürger and pastor, pleased him. With the one he celebrated his place of birth, the high Alpine valley of Toggenburg; with the other he affirmed his calling, the role that was at the center of his adult life. The two suggest something of the commitments that would shape his theology, its specific orientations, its references, and its allusions.

Zwingli was born on 1 January 1484 to a prosperous peasant family who lived and farmed in the Toggenburg Valley (in the Swiss canton of St. Gall). As a Toggenbürger, Zwingli was heir to the political traditions of the Confederation of Swiss Cantons—who had sworn allegiance against the emperor, their legal lord, and had achieved in practice real autonomy—and, in particular, of the Swiss peasantry, renowned for its mastery of arms and its greater autonomy from its lords.

To be a Toggenbürger was also to be "of the land," both cultivated lands and forests. It was to belong, as his father did, to a peasant commune and to participate in its particular configuration of decision-making. Zwingli would draw upon his childhood in the metaphors of his preaching: he would warn Martin Luther of the futility of jays' struggles on lime-twigs; he would urge the unity of a gaggle of geese against eagles; and he would find in marmots' and squirrels' responses to danger analogies to explain the working of divine providence in human lives. His childhood in the Toggenburg Valley would bring to the "shepherd" a specificity and immediacy. When Zwingli preached about the duties of the pastor in "Der Hirt" in 1523 (published in 1524), he could cite how shepherds handled each sheep according to its temperament and strength and then explain, "so must God's shepherd deal with his flock in various ways, but always prompted by love."

Little is known about Zwingli's education. It was eclectic, guided by his father and his uncle: he studied Latin first in the household of his uncle (1489–1494), at the time priest and dean in Wesen, then at Basel (1494–1496). He later studied at Bern with Heinrich Wölflin (1496–1498), at the University of Vienna (1498–1502), and finally at the University of Basel, where he received a baccalaureate in 1504 and a master of liberal arts in 1506. During those years he studied in the *via antiqua*, as well as classical Greek and Roman literature and philosophy. Zwingli also came in contact with humanism, first as it was articulated in the work of Wölflin and later, in Basel, as it was discussed in learned circles and as it was printed in the houses of Johannes Amerbach (1443?–1513) and Johannes Froben (1460–1527).

At age twenty-two, Zwingli was ordained and placed as "parish priest of Glarus," one of the smallest cantons of the confederation. There he would remain until 1516, traveling with Glarus troops to the great battle in 1515 at Marignano (Melegnano), where he confirmed his opposition to mercenary service. At Glarus Zwingli began his pursuit of biblical humanism in earnest—studying the church fathers and the Bible and applying to them the principles of humanistic hermeneutics. As soon as it was published, he purchased Desiderius Erasmus's *Novum Instrumentum*, for which he learned Greek, and sometime during 1514–1516, he returned to Basel in order to talk with Erasmus, "the most learned of all scholars." By 1516 Zwingli had embraced Erasmus's principle that Christian belief and worship must be based upon the word of God itself. From there it was a short but pivotal step to the more radical "you must leave all [human learning] and learn the meaning of God purely from his own simple Word."

In 1516 Zwingli became people's priest at the Benedictine abbey at the great medieval pilgrimage site of Einsiedeln, where his care of souls extended to pilgrims. There he saw firsthand the practices and the commerce of pilgrimages. During this time Zwingli intensified his study of Greek, copying the Pauline epistles word for word from Erasmus's Greek New Testament and reading the Greek fathers, in particular the Froben edition of Chrysostom, which included his sermons on the gospel of Matthew. He would deepen and broaden his readings of the Latin fathers, sending for the works of Ambrose, Jerome, and Cyprian, among others.

Zwingli's preaching at Einsiedeln, described by the Strasbourg reformer Caspar Hedio as "elegant, learned, weighty, rich, penetrating, and evangelical, clearly such as to return us to the effect of the ancient theologians," brought him to the attention of Zurich. When the position of people's priest at the Grossmünster in Zurich fell vacant in 1518, Zwingli, who sought the position, was the leading choice. Support for Zwingli was not unanimous: his liaison with a local woman of humble status nearly cost him the appointment, and he was required to break off that relationship as part of the terms of his appointment. He first mounted the pulpit in the Grossmünster on 1 January 1519, his thirty-fifth birthday, and announced that he intended to break with traditional practice: he would preach not from appointed scriptural texts, as was directed by the lectionary, but right through the gospel of Matthew "from A to Z," beginning the next day with the first chapter. Thus, with his entrance into Zurich, he put into practice his conviction that Christian life must begin with the pure word of God.

Until Zwingli's death in 1531, Zurich would be his home. He was welcomed in 1519 by the canons of the Grossmünster, the councilors, and many of the townspeople. He brought to Zurich his love of the Swiss Confederation, the opposition to Swiss foreign involvements, his learning, and the power of his preaching. Zwingli's education, both formal and in the years following, would lead him to a particular vision of true Christianity, but that vision would be forged within the specific community of Zurich, with its social configuration, civic identity, traditions of worship, and relationship with its land. All of his reformist writings would be published there, most by his friend, the publisher Christoph Froschauer (d. 1564).

In his *Gebetslied in der Pest* (Plague Song) of 1519, written while he was recovering slowly from his nearly fatal encounter with the plague, Zwingli articulated the understanding of God and his own relation to him that would shape his work in Zurich: "do what you will, nothing surpasses me, I am your tool, to make whole or break." Throughout his life Zwingli held that God could effect whatever he willed and that Zwingli himself was God's tool, acting out God's will in the world. Zwingli did not divide divine omnipotence between *potentia ordinata* and *potentia absoluta* but held the potentiality of God's efficacy in the world as itself absolute. For Zwingli God was not merely omnipotent but also active in the world, working through human beings to effect his will.

In Zwingli's conception of human nature, intimated in the *Gebetslied in der Pest* but formulated most fully in 1524 in the first full explication of evangelical religion, *De vera et falsa religione* (Commentary on True and False Religion), the influence of Augustine was most explicit. Following Augustine's anthropology, Zwingli argued that man was by nature a sinner, and the nature of man's sin was self-love, the preference of self over God and neighbor. Zwingli contrasted divine and human natures: while God was absolutely good, man was imperfectly wicked, and while God was powerful and efficacious, man was fragile and dependent, an instrument of God's will.

By 1522 Zwingli was preaching against Roman practices—indulgences, the penitential system, pilgrimages, the cult of saints, the worship of Mary, the hypocrisy of clerical celibacy, and monastic asceticism—and calling for worship derived solely from the words of scripture. In January 1523 the Zurich town council convened what would be the First Disputation to discuss formally the content and effects of evangelical preaching. For it Zwingli published his 67 *Artikel*, which asserted the fundaments of his evangelicalism: Christ is the only savior for all humankind; the "catholic church" is defined as those who believe Christ is Lord; scripture is the sole authority in defining things Christian; works are only so good as they are Christ's; clerical celibacy, fasting, feast days, pilgrimages, special clothing, cords, signs, and orders or sects of the religious are false, the theft of Christian freedom; God alone absolves human sinning; the necessary function of secular authority is the restraining of human action; and scripture designates no purgatory and no separate priesthood. Perhaps Zwingli's biggest victory in this disputation was the town council's formal endorsement of the principle of *sola scriptura* and, along with it, Zwingli's evangelical preaching. Ten months later, in October 1523, the town council convened the Second Disputation to discuss the place of images in worship and the nature of the Mass. Although this disputation was less conclusive, it made evident the spreading circle of evangelical preachers, as Zwingli was only one of a number to present a range of evangelical visions of reform in the discussion. By October 1523 Zwingli's intellectual and personal leadership of the Christian community in Zurich was manifest.

For Zwingli God's speaking, the scriptures, had itself agency. In 1525, along with Leo Jud and Konrad Pellikan, he would found the *Prophezei*, a learned circle whose activity was the mastery of biblical languages (Hebrew, Greek, and Latin), and the study of the Bible, applying humanist principles of philology and classical literary theory. Meeting every week for the rest of Zwingli's life and beyond, the *Prophezei* provided an early model of evangelical education.

Whereas Zwingli's understanding of God was explicit from his earliest days there, his conception of Christ, stated cryptically in the 67 *Artikel*, was explicated only over time as he addressed specific debates in Zurich and beyond—on the nature of the Mass, the place of images in worship, the function of baptism, the Eucharist, the nature of human salvation, and the community of Christians. Beginning in 1523 Zwingli faced increasing pressure from his close associate Jud, various iconoclasts, and nascent Anabaptists to reform worship in Zurich, on the one hand, and ever sharper criticism from those loyal to Rome on the other. In a series of pamphlets published in response to such challenges during 1523–1525, he set forth his understanding of the meaning of Christ's life and death as it pertained to the Mass: Christ's life was a moment in human history when God took on human form, with its temporal finitude, out of love for humankind and made possible human salvation; his death was a one-time sacrifice that absolved all humankind throughout history of Original Sin. Christ's death was singular. It could not be reenacted in the Mass: no sacrifice reenacted by human beings could capture, even in metaphor, the scope and magnificence of the original sacrifice God made for humankind.

In April 1525 the town council of Zurich abolished the Mass and instituted Zwingli's reformed Communion service, or Last Supper. Christ's "presence" was defined there: "where two or three are gathered in my name, there shall I be." In Zwingli's Eucharist Christ was to be present not in body, not in the elements, but among the faithful, in spirit. There would be no transubstantiation (no priest would facilitate the transformation of the elements) nor consubstantiation (no body or blood would be present). The elements remained their simple substances, bread and wine. No priest would reenact in word or gesture the Crucifixion. Instead, Christians in Zurich were to gather to commemorate the Last Supper; to recall through faith and the simple elements of bread and wine, both administered to all those gathered, the historic moment when Christ lived among men; and to affirm his lasting spiritual presence.

Just as Zwingli was defining the reformed liturgy in Zurich, a group of his one-time followers began to baptize each other in their new faith, Anabaptism. In responding to them, during the years 1525–1527, Zwingli explicated the meaning of Christ's sacrifice for baptism. Since Christ's death had accomplished a cleansing for all humanity, both past and those to be born, baptism, for Zwingli, did not save: infants who died before baptism were not damned. Indeed, he would suggest that Socrates and other pre-Christian philosophers numbered among the saved. It was, rather, an initiation, bringing one into the community of Christians. There one could enact one's faith and equally important, strengthen through companionship that fragile faith. Baptism was not, therefore, a confirmation of faith but the ritual that signaled one's entrance into the Christian community. Baptism enabled one to live among those who would help in the pursuit of a life honoring God.

By 1527 Zwingli had defined the two sacraments of his understanding of the church—baptism and Communion. All others—penance, confirmation, marriage, extreme unc-

tion, and ordination—were no sacraments, according to scripture. Penance was a matter of private piety between each Christian and God. Confirmation was made unnecessary by Zwingli's understanding of baptism. Extreme unction belonged to the simple duties of each pastor. Ordination, like extreme unction, had been falsely elevated to a sacrament; in Zwingli's church, synods, not bishops, would supervise the pastorate, beginning with the first synod, which took place in 1528. Marriage, finally, belonged to the secular realm, which now enforced Christian morality. In May 1525, with Zwingli's full support, the Zurich town council instituted a marriage court to adjudicate marital conflicts, decide divorces, and ensure proper Christian behavior in each marriage in Zurich.

These debates also contributed to Zwingli's definition of the nature of the true church. The true church comprised all those who believed in the life and death of Christ as Zwingli had explicated them from scripture. He would not allow that the faithful might be discerned from the unfaithful by word or by act: rituals did not delimit its membership, nor did professions of faith or works. Though the membership of each congregation could be known, the true church's membership—those who believed in the meaning of its two rituals, baptism and Communion, who believed, in other words, in the reality of the community of Christians as those among whom Christ was "present"—was not necessarily visible. The effects of collective faith were visible, however. For Zwingli the true church was active. It sought to realize Christ's two commandments—to love God and one's neighbor. The first meant that its members worshiped God himself, not in images or music but through Communion and receiving God's word as it was preached, read aloud, and spoken. The second Zwingli would invoke in his discussion of specific practices within Zurich: in *Welche ursach gebind zů uffrůren* (Who is the Source of Sedition; December 1524), Zwingli would apply it to the obligations of lords to their tenants, the payment of tithes and the relations between peasants and their lords, and the Christian poor. Faith for Zwingli could not be separated from the Christian's life in his or her community. Faith did not, in other words, distinguish the individual Christian so much as lead to participation in the community of Christians.

The last years of Zwingli's life were dominated by the effort to build a Protestant alliance. The nature of that alliance was determined in October 1529 at the Marburg Colloquy, Zwingli's one meeting with Luther. There the differences among the evangelical theologians were reduced, but one, concerning the Eucharist, was discovered to be irreconcilable. To Marburg Zwingli brought techniques and categories of biblical exegesis learned from humanism, his intimate familiarity with Erasmus's Greek New Testament, and the resonances it had for him in Greek patristic authors. For Zwingli Christ's "spiritual" presence had reality, as it was understood in the Greek tradition. Luther's biblical understanding of "spirit" was distant from Zwingli's. Moreover, for Zwingli Christ's physical presence could only be understood as temporal. Following Neoplatonism, Zwingli argued that matter deteriorates and decomposes. As human, Christ was embodied; as body, Christ's person was temporally finite. Christ's presence, Zwingli asserted to Luther, could only be spiritual; spiritual, that presence was nonetheless "real."

Marburg represented the end of one kind of Protestant alliance among the leading theologians, but from 1525, when the Reformation was instituted in Zurich, to his death, Zwingli was also building another kind of international Protestant alliance. He worked to link first Swiss cantons, then south German imperial cities, and finally Protestant principalities in a common liturgy and ethic. Disputations were convened at Baden in 1526 and Bern in 1528, providing a forum for Zwingli's vision of the Reformation. He wrote to town councils and preachers encouraging, even admonishing, reform. Constance would join Zurich in 1527; Bern and St. Gall in 1528; Basel, Schaffhausen, Biel, and Mühlhausen in 1529; and Hesse briefly in 1530. With these alliances, founded in shared liturgies and ecclesiologies, the confederation became confessionally divided.

Zwingli's vision of a Protestant Europe followed the model of the confederation: politically autonomous and diverse states linked together through alliances and a shared vision of Christian life. These efforts also suggested something of the particular balance Zwingli envisioned between the universal and the local in each congregation: they would share the eradication of Roman practices, the institution of the central sacraments of baptism and Communion, and the ethic of brotherly love. As he wrote in the *Fidei ratio* of 1530, the church would comprise many congregations. They would retain the particularism of their own dialect, as well as all aspects of collective life outside the church—social and political arrangements, and economic practices that were not immoral by Christian standards.

Zwingli's efforts were cut short by his death at Kappel on 11 October 1531, to many the inevitable conclusion of a life spent in direct negotiation with the political powers of his day. Leadership of the church would pass to his successor in Zurich, Heinrich Bullinger (1504–1575), who would bring Zurich into an international Protestant community. It suggests something of the potency of Zwingli's influence that the Catholic troops on the field at Kappel believed it necessary not only to dismember his body but to cut up his heart so that it might not become a relic for all those who believed he was indeed God's instrument.

In the summer before his death, Zwingli wrote an explication of his faith, *Expositio fidei*, to the French king Francis I (r. 1515–1547). Zwingli's reconception of the relation between the church and public life was suspect to many of his contemporaries—his church seemed too "political." It would provide the foundation, however, for Cal-

vin's particular conceptualization of the church. So, too, Zwingli's understanding of the Eucharist, so abhorrent to Luther, though not taken up immediately, would come to permeate many Protestant liturgies; it is the direct source for the Anglican liturgy. Though there is no Zwinglian church today, Zwingli's theology shaped the Reformed tradition fundamentally—in its orientation to politics, its activist ethic, its understanding of the nature of Christ's "presence" in the world, and its sense of itself as working God's will in the world.

BIBLIOGRAPHY

Primary Sources

Zwingli, Huldrych. *Sämtliche Werke*. Zurich, 1982–.
———. *Selected Writings of Huldrych Zwingli*. 2 vols. Translated and edited by E. J. Furcha and H. Wayne Pipkin. Allison Park, Pa., 1984. Most recent and best translation of major works of Zwingli into English.

Secondary Sources

Farner, Oskar. *Zwingli the Reformer: His Life and Work*. Translated by D. G. Sear. Hamden, Conn., 1968. A brief and eloquent biography of the reformer; among the most sympathetic to Zwingli.
Furcha, E. J., and H. Wayne Pipkin, eds. *Prophet, Pastor, Protestant: The Work of Huldrych Zwingli after Five Hundred Years*. Allison Park, Pa., 1984. A collection of excellent articles, centering on Zwingli's theology, by leading Zwinglian scholars.
Gäbler, Ulrich. *Huldrych Zwingli: His Life and Work*. Translated by Ruth C. L. Gritsch. Philadelphia, 1986. Perhaps the least sympathetic biography of Zwingli in English.
Locher, Gottfried W. *Zwingli's Thought: New Perspectives*. Leiden, 1981. An important collection of essays by one of the most penetrating scholars of Zwingli.
Potter, G. R. *Zwingli*. Reprint, Cambridge, 1984. The fullest biography of Zwingli in English.
Stephens, W. P. *The Theology of Huldrych Zwingli*. Oxford, 1986. An explication of the major themes in Zwingli's theology.
———. *Zwingli: An Introduction to His Thought*. Oxford, 1992. An abbreviated version of the preceding.
Walton, Robert C. *Zwingli's Theocracy*. Toronto, 1967. Explores political dimensions of Zwingli's thought in relation to the Zurich magistracy.
Wandel, Lee Palmer. *Always Among Us: Images of the Poor in Reformation Zurich*. Cambridge, 1990. Explores Zwingli's theology as it pertains to social ethics.

LEE PALMER WANDEL

ZWINGLIANISM. The original Reformed Protestant tradition developed in three phases. Initially Zwinglianism defined itself largely by its differences from Lutheranism. It received its distinctive character during the Reformation in Zurich from Huldrych Zwingli and Heinrich Bullinger in the 1520s and 1530s. In the second phase, from the 1540s until the late sixteenth century, Zwinglianism not only exercised great influence among the Reformed churches of Europe but also faced a challenge from Calvinism, the second Reformed tradition. Finally, in the late sixteenth and the early seventeenth century, Zwinglianism was, to a large extent, subsumed under Calvinist orthodoxy within the Reformed tradition. Nevertheless, aspects of the tradition continued to have an influence.

Origins, Early Development, and Consolidation. By 1540 there was a distinctive Zwinglian tradition, which differed from both established Lutheranism and emerging Calvinism. Three issues in particular—the Eucharist, the Christian community, and the moral law—defined Zwinglianism in contrast to Lutheranism. The problem of the Eucharist (which became clear during the mid-1520s) turned on Zwingli's rejection of Luther's doctrine of the real presence; instead the bread and the wine signified the body and blood of Christ. Zwingli and Luther each published works against the other's position in 1527 and 1528. Finally they met personally at Marburg in 1529 to discuss it, but they failed to reach an agreement. Then, in 1536, the First Helvetic Confession, written largely by Bullinger, reaffirmed the Zwinglian view of the Eucharist. Later in 1536 Bullinger rejected the Wittenberg Concord, which was mostly the work of Martin Bucer. Though Bullinger held to a slightly different view of the Eucharist from Zwingli, he defended Zwingli's position throughout his career. He engaged in controversy with the Lutherans Johannes Brenz and Jakob Andreae as late as the 1570s.

The second area of disagreement with Lutheranism was the nature of the Christian community. Zwingli and Bullinger held to a single sphere rather than to Luther's doctrine of the two kingdoms. Zwingli argued that the elders of the New Testament were the equivalent of the magistrates of his day. The council of the Christian city thus rightfully ruled both the civil community and the church, which were virtually identical. He rejected the idea of a separate church court independent of the magistrate's courts, and he felt that excommunication, if used at all, should be directed only against flagrant sinners. Both Bullinger and Zwingli felt that excommunication in the hands of an ecclesiastical court smacked of papal discipline. In the end, their concept of the Christian community was the most distinctive and lasting aspect of the Zwinglian tradition.

Dispute about the nature of the Christian community was also at the root of the conflict between the Zwinglians and the Anabaptists. The Swiss Anabaptists advocated congregations of committed believers, independent of the civil magistracy, with the right to discipline their own members. Such a concept directly challenged the view of both Zwingli and Bullinger that the ecclesiastical and civil communities were identical and that both were under the direction and discipline of the magistracy. This Zwinglian view of the Christian community may well have been influenced by the theory of Marsilius of Padua, and it was undoubtedly also a product of the communal character of the Swiss urban setting. There was also, however, a theological basis. Zwingli's defense of infant baptism was connected with the Old Testament idea of the covenant that he began to develop during his conflict with the Anabaptists in the mid-1520s.

Bullinger's much fuller statement of covenant theology further instructed his concept of the Christian community. Since there was only one covenant in history, the pattern for the Christian community had been set in Old Testament times. Though the minister had the duty of advising the magistracy from the Bible concerning God's will, it was the Christian magistrate who, like the Old Testament kings, was fully in charge of the community. Therefore the magistrate's laws were the only basis for community discipline—there was no separate church discipline.

The third, and closely related, area of disagreement was the relationship between the moral law and the gospel. Zwingli included the moral law within the gospel rather than juxtaposing law and gospel within the two kingdoms as Luther did; Zwingli stated that the moral law was God's will for all people. Bullinger stated it even more clearly, directly in connection with the covenant. Moral law was part of the human obligation in the covenant. The two conditions of the covenant were faith in God and love of neighbor. These main obligations had been stated in the Decalogue, the summary of the moral law. Therefore the moral law was the source for the magistrate's law and the basis for Christian discipline.

During the later 1520s the Zwinglian reform spread from Zurich to southern Germany and to other parts of Switzerland. Several south German cities, notably Strasbourg and Constance, were attracted to Zwinglianism, and Zwinglianism also made inroads in the states of Hesse and Württemberg. But imperial politics assured that the influence of Zwinglianism waned during the 1530s and nearly ceased to exist in the 1540s. Within the Swiss Confederation, Schaffhausen, the city of St. Gall, and Appenzell, as well as much of the Graubünden (Grisons), accepted Zwinglianism by 1526. Bern became Zwinglian in 1528 under the leadership of Berchtold Haller. Basel was reformed under Johannes Oecolampadius in 1529. Though Oecolampadius fully agreed with Zwingli on the Eucharist, in 1530 he challenged Zwingli's concept of the Christian community and discipline as being solely in the hands of the magistrate. Basel's defection from Zwinglianism was later exacerbated under Simon Sulzer, a Lutheran.

The Period of Great Influence. Zwinglianism's period of great influence lasted from approximately 1540 until late into the sixteenth century. Though the influence of Zwingli and Bullinger can also be traced in France, Hungary, and Austria, the main areas where Zwinglianism had an impact were Switzerland itself, the Palatinate, the Netherlands, England, and Scotland.

In 1540 Zwinglianism was still the only expression of Reformed Protestantism in Switzerland. All the Protestant churches in the Swiss Confederation were Zwinglian in their theology, and all of them, even Basel, held to a Zwinglian type of discipline, with the civil magistrate in control of the community. John Calvin arrived on the scene in 1536, however, and soon the Calvinists began to challenge the Zwinglians. Three areas of dissent with Zwinglianism emerged—the Eucharist, predestination, and church discipline.

The first issue, the Eucharist, was the easiest to resolve. After lengthy negotiations, Bullinger and Calvin came to an agreement on the Eucharist in the Consensus Tigurinus of 1549. This agreement assured a modicum of friendship between the two men.

The second area of disagreement, predestination, was more difficult. While Calvin held to a double decree, Bullinger's view was a more moderate single predestinarianism with strong universalist undertones. Bullinger not only defended Zwingli's teaching and his own position in correspondence with Calvin but also severely criticized Calvin's doctrine during the Bolsec controversy. He consistently defended Theodor Bibliander, professor of Old Testament at Zurich, against Calvin's criticisms. Bibliander rejected personal election, holding instead to a doctrine of prevenient grace whereby God had adopted all humans as children until they forced him to reject them because of their unbelief. Even though Bibliander was forced to retire in 1560 after clashing with Peter Martyr Vermigli on predestination, Bullinger still supported Bibliander and praised him until his death in 1564. Predestination remained an issue between Zwinglians and Calvinists into the next century, with the Arminian controversy.

The issue of Christian discipline and the role of the civil magistrate in the church was the most acrimonious area of disagreement. Calvin followed Oecolampadius in insisting on an ecclesiastical court, or consistory, for church discipline and excommunication. Such a discipline, independent of the civil government, was necessary to ensure the purity of the church, to protect the good, and to bring the sinner to repentance. Ironically, Bullinger was instrumental in aiding Calvin to gain victory on the matter of discipline in Geneva. In 1553 Bullinger persuaded the Zurichers, in order to promote peace in Geneva and to assure concord between the churches at Geneva and Zurich, to agree that the Calvinist system of discipline was not contrary to scripture. Once Calvin established the independence of the consistory's discipline from the civil magistrate, his system of discipline began to compete with the Zwinglian system within the Reformed churches throughout Europe.

The first challenge came in the late 1550s in the Vaud. Bern had occupied the Vaud in 1536 and immediately pushed through a reform of the entire territory according to the Zwinglian system that prevailed at Bern. Pierre Viret and Théodore de Bèze, professors at the new academy at Lausanne, were Calvinists, as were many pastors in the Vaud. The first and perhaps most dramatic sign of trouble between the Zwinglians and Calvinists in the Vaud came in 1554 when several Zwinglian pastors objected that Calvin's teaching on predestination was unscriptural. In 1558 a controversy over discipline arose in which the Calvinists insisted on a church discipline independent of the council at Bern. The Bernese council, though willing to compromise, refused to allow an autonomous church court or consistory, and ordered all pastors either to accept the Bernese (Zwinglian) system or to resign. The action of the council was fully supported by Johannes Haller, the chief pastor in Bern, and by Wolfgang Musculus, the Zwinglian professor of theology at Bern. About thirty Calvinist pastors and professors left Lausanne for Geneva and France.

The next important clash over the issue came at Heidelberg, in the Palatinate, between Thomas Lüber (Erastus), a Zwinglian, and Kaspar Olevianus, a Calvinist. Lüber argued that excommunication should not be used at all in the church and that the Christian magistrate should be sovereign in the Christian community, fully in charge of all discipline. Bullinger himself became involved in 1568 when he wrote to Frederick III in support of Lüber. In the end, however, Lüber lost, when a compromise church order was adopted in the Palatinate in 1570. While the new presbytery did not have complete independence, it still operated with vigor. The first person to be excommunicated by the Calvinists in Heidelberg was Lüber.

The next clash came in the Netherlands in 1574, where the Calvinists attempted to take the initiative. Twenty-six delegates met in a synod at Dordrecht and drew up a Calvinist church order for the Reformed churches in the Netherlands, which included a discipline independent of the civil government. But the civil authorities, including William of Orange, rejected this Calvinist arrangement and instead established a Zwinglian system in which the civil authorities not only appointed the ministers but also dealt with discipline. Caspar Coolhaes of Leiden was the only minister who defended the Zwinglian system, citing Zwingli, Bullinger, Rudolf Gwalther, and Musculus. In 1582 Coolhaes was the first to be excommunicated by the Dutch Calvinists.

Some scholars have questioned the influence of Zwinglianism in the Netherlands. None of Zwingli's works was published there in the sixteenth century. Even though there were close to fifty Dutch editions of Bullinger's works, none of them deals specifically with the distinctively Zwinglian teachings on the Eucharist, on predestination, and on the Christian community. There is some evidence, however, of Zwinglian influence. Ioannes Anastasius Veluanus held a Zwinglian view of the Eucharist in the 1550s. Moreover, Veluanus, along with two other men, Gellius Snecanus in the 1580s and Cornelius Wiggertsz in the 1590s, held to a covenant idea close to Bullinger's. Furthermore, all three subscribed to weak predestinarian ideas—far from the Calvinist position—which extended from synergism to outright universalism. Though one might argue that an Erasmian influence was at work here, it is still true that the Remonstrants of the early seventeenth century cited Bullinger to defend their viewpoint. Nevertheless, Calvinism gradually took hold in the Netherlands, so that by the time of Synod of Dordrecht in 1618 both Calvinist discipline and theology had become ascendant.

In England Zwinglianism had a much greater influence than Calvinism during most of the sixteenth century. In the early 1530s William Tyndale's covenant idea was influenced by Zwinglian ideas. Miles Coverdale published his English translation of Bullinger's *Der alt gloub* (*The Olde Fayth*) in 1541. John Hooper lived with Bullinger in Zurich from 1547 to 1549. Archbishop Thomas Cranmer's theology was influenced by Zwinglianism. During the persecution under Queen Mary Tudor, twenty English scholars went into exile in Zurich, a group that would provide six bishops for the English church under Elizabeth I. In 1566 Bullinger was consulted during the Vestiarian Controversy. Bullinger wrote a reply to the papal bull against Elizabeth that was published in Latin in 1571 and in an English translation the next year. Bullinger's *Decades* (fifty sermons in five groups of ten) was made a required textbook for all ministers studying for ordination in the diocese of Lincoln in 1577 and in the province of Canterbury in 1586. Rudolf Gwalther, who became the leader of the Zurich church at Bullinger's death in 1575, also had close ties in England. Gwalther himself traveled to England in 1537; his son received a master of arts degree from Oxford in 1574; and he corresponded with many English churchmen.

The Zwinglian influence in England is particularly evident in the areas of covenant theology and the Christian community. Tyndale, Coverdale, and Hooper all developed a covenant theology in connection with their contacts with Zurich, and the covenant idea continued to hold a fascination for the English throughout the sixteenth and seventeenth centuries. The English conception of the Christian community and the role of the civil government in the church was also Zwinglian until the later sixteenth century, when it was confronted by English Calvinism. In the early 1570s, Walter Travers and Thomas Cartwright began to advocate the presbyterianism that they had learned in Geneva from Bèze. The publication of Lüber's *Explicatio* in 1589 aided those, like John Whitgift and Richard Hooker, who defended the Zwinglian arrangement against the Calvinists. Nevertheless, the Calvinist influence in England grew tremendously after 1600. During the sixteenth century nearly fifty editions of Bullinger's works were published in England in English translation; after 1600 only one was published, anonymously.

There was also a Zwinglian influence in Scotland. George Wishart, one of the earliest Scottish reformers, studied with Bullinger in the early 1540s, published an English translation of the First Helvetic Confession, and won John Knox to Reformed Protestantism. Knox stood within the Zwinglian tradition until he went to Geneva in 1554 and became a Calvinist. Both Knox and his successor as leader of the Scot-

tish Reformed church, Andrew Melville, were advocates of the Zwinglian covenant theology that had a strong impact on the Scottish church and politics. Under Melville, however, the Scottish Reformed church became Calvinist in matters of church polity and discipline.

The widespread Zwinglian influence in the later sixteenth century was partially a result of the Second Helvetic Confession of 1566. Written by Bullinger, it was well received by all the Reformed churches in Europe and translated into nine languages. One reason for its wide acceptance was that Bullinger did not emphasize the distinctive elements of Zwinglianism. In an early draft, Bullinger included two remarks critical of Calvin on predestination, but he deleted them after Bèze objected. In the matter of the Christian community, he barely mentioned the covenant. He also did not specify the Zwinglian type of discipline nor criticize the Calvinist system of discipline. These elements made it possible for the confession to be an affirmation of unity, but such would not always be the case.

Subsumption under Calvinism. There had been a dual tradition in Reformed Protestantism since the 1530s. Bullinger and Gwalther were champions of the Zwinglian first Reformed tradition for more than a half century. In the later sixteenth century, the Zwinglian tradition waned as the more militant and dogmatic Calvinist orthodoxy triumphed under Bèze. Despite the apparent strength and vigor of the Zwinglian tradition in Reformed Protestantism throughout most of the sixteenth century, it nearly ceased to exist as a separate entity by the early seventeenth century. Throughout Europe, even in Zurich itself, Zwinglian theology tended to be subsumed under Calvinist orthodoxy.

The one issue on which the Zwinglian tradition was able to withstand the pressures of Calvinism, at least in some areas of Europe, was the Christian community. In Zurich the system that was created by Zwingli and institutionalized by Bullinger survived until the collapse of the old confederacy in 1798. In the Netherlands the civil magistrates continued to direct the affairs of the Christian community despite the objections of the Calvinists. In England, except for a brief period in midcentury during the Civil War, the Zwinglian, or Erastian, approach to the relationship between the civil and ecclesiastical spheres remained the norm throughout the seventeenth century. Indeed, one could argue that the Zwinglian viewpoint on the Christian community fed into and helped to sustain the more modern concept of state sovereignty as articulated by latter-day Erastians, such as Thomas Hobbes.

On the matter of predestination, however, the new Calvinist orthodoxy swept everything before it, even in Switzerland. In Basel a student of Bèze's, Amandus Polanus (d. 1610), introduced the doctrine of double predestination with its increasingly attendant emphasis on the limited atonement. Bern also succumbed, after a struggle. Samuel Huber (d. 1624) advocated a universalist approach. In support of his position—that everyone is predestined to salvation and that a person is condemned only because of willful lack of faith—Huber appealed to Bullinger. Huber's opponent was Abraham Musculus, who defended the Calvinist position at a disputation in 1588. The council decided for Musculus, and Bern thus opted for Calvinist orthodoxy.

Nor did Zurich escape the new orthodoxy. After Gwalther's death, Johann Stucki (d. 1609) defended Bèze's point of view on predestination as a representative of Zurich at the Huber disputation at Bern. Markus Baumler, another Zurich theologian, also subscribed to the viewpoint of Calvinist orthodoxy. But Johann Jakob Breitinger (d. 1645), who became the leader of the Zurich church in 1613, was the most important advocate of the Calvinist position on predestination. The position of orthodox Calvinism was self-evident to Breitinger, and he read that point of view back into the early years of the Zurich Reformed church. At the Synod of Dordrecht, in 1618, he argued that Bullinger had fully agreed with Calvin, and thus he defended Bullinger's good name against the Remonstrants, who asserted that Bullinger had agreed with Jacobus Arminius.

The decisions of the Synod of Dordrecht on predestination became the dogma of the entire Reformed church. There was now, ostensibly, only one Reformed tradition. Despite this fact, the covenantal thrust of Zwinglian thought continued to exist within that tradition. In the seventeenth century the Zwinglian covenantal tradition was resurrected by such men as Moise Amyraut and Johannes Cocceius (Koch) as a corrective to the rigid predestinarian dogma of Calvinist orthodoxy.

[*See also* Bullinger, Heinrich; Jud, Leo; Oecolampadius, Johannes, *and* Zwingli, Huldrych.]

BIBLIOGRAPHY

Baker, J. Wayne. *Heinrich Bullinger and the Covenant: The Other Reformed Tradition.* Athens, Ohio, 1980. A study of Bullinger's theology of the covenant; how it flavored his other ideas, including predestination and the Christian community; and how it differentiated his theology from Calvin's. The appendixes deal with his influence in the Netherlands and England.
———. "Church Discipline or Civil Punishment: On the Origins of the Reformed Schism, 1528–1531." *Andrews University Seminary Studies* 23 (1985), 3–18. An essay dealing with the views of Zwingli, Oecolampadius, and Bullinger on Christian discipline.
———. "Christian Discipline and the Early Reformed Tradition: Bullinger and Calvin." In *Calviniana: Ideas and Influence of Jean Calvin,* edited by Robert V. Schnucker, pp. 107–119. Kirksville, Mo., 1988. An essay dealing with the differences between Calvin and Bullinger on Christian discipline, Calvin's struggle in Geneva over the issue in the 1540s and 1550s, and Bullinger's support of Calvin during the Berthelier affair.

Duke, Alastair. *Reformation and Revolt in the Low Countries.* London, 1990. Excellent study of the origins and development of Protestantism in the Netherlands from 1518 to 1618, including the decline of the Zwinglian influence and the rise of Calvinism.
Gäbler, Ulrich. "Zwingli the Loser." In *Huldrych Zwingli, 1484–1531: A Legacy of Radical Reform,* edited by E. J. Furcha, pp. 1–12. Montreal, 1985. An essay dealing with the reasons for the common perception that Zwingli was the loser among the reformers. Deals with the issue of church discipline.
Gäbler, Ulrich, and Erland Herkenrath, eds. *Heinrich Bullinger, 1504–1575: Gesammelte Aufsätze zum 400. Todestag.* Vol. 2, *Beziehungen und Wirkungen.* Zurich, 1975. Essays that deal with Bullinger's relationships with other reformers and his influence in other parts of Europe, including England, Hungary, and Austria.
Kressner, Helmut. *Schweizer Ursprünge des anglikanischen Staatskirchentums.* Schriften des Vereins für Reformationsgeschichte, no. 170. Gütersloh, 1953. Sees the teaching of Bullinger and Gwalther on the Christian community as the source of John Whitgift's justification of the Anglican state church.
Locher, Gottfried W. *Die Zwinglische Reformation im Rahmen der europäischen Kirchengeschichte.* Göttingen, 1979. An exhaustive study of the Zwinglian Reformation and the impact and influence of Zwinglianism throughout Europe.
———. *Zwingli's Thought: New Perspectives.* Studies in the History of Christian Thought, no. 25. Leiden, 1981. The final chapter, "Zwingli's Influence in England and Scotland," is especially provocative.
McNeill, John T. *The History and Character of Calvinism.* Reprint, Oxford, 1973. About one-fifth of the text is devoted to Zwinglianism. Although McNeill recognizes that the roots of the Reformed tradition were in Zwinglianism, in the end he treats Zwinglianism as part of Calvinism.
Moeller, Bernd. *Reichsstadt und Reformation.* Schriften des Vereins für Reformationsgeschichte, no. 180. Gütersloh, 1962. An insightful essay dealing with the reasons for the successes of Zwinglianism in the imperial cities of southern Germany in the 1520s and 1530s. (English translation in *Imperial Cities and the Reformation: Three Essays,* edited and translated by H. C. Erik Midelfort and Mark U. Edwards, Jr., reprint, Durham, N.C., 1982.)
Pollet, J. V. *Huldrych Zwingli et le Zwinglianisme: Essai de synthèse historique et théologique mis à jour d'après les recherches récentes.* Paris, 1988. A collection of essays on Zwingli and Zwinglianism, including Pollet's famous article "Zwinglianisme," originally published in 1951 in *Dictionnaire de théologie catholique.*
Rorem, Paul. *Calvin and Bullinger on the Lord's Supper.* Nottingham, 1989. Deals with the differences between Bullinger and Calvin on the Eucharist, their negotiations, and their eventual agreement in the *Consensus Tigurinus.*
Staedtke, Joachim, ed. *Glauben und Bekennen: Vierhundert Jahre Confessio Helvetica Posterior.* Zurich, 1966. Essays dealing with the theology and history of the Second Helvetic Confession, and its acceptance and influence in Switzerland, Germany, France, Austria, and Hungary.
Walton, Robert C. "The Institutionalization of the Reformation at Zurich." *Zwingliana* 13 (1972), 497–515. An excellent treatment of Zwingli and Bullinger on the sovereignty of the Christian magistrate over the church. Demonstrates that the system set up under Zwingli and Bullinger survived in Zurich until the collapse of the old confederacy in 1798.

J. WAYNE BAKER

APPENDIX: MAPS

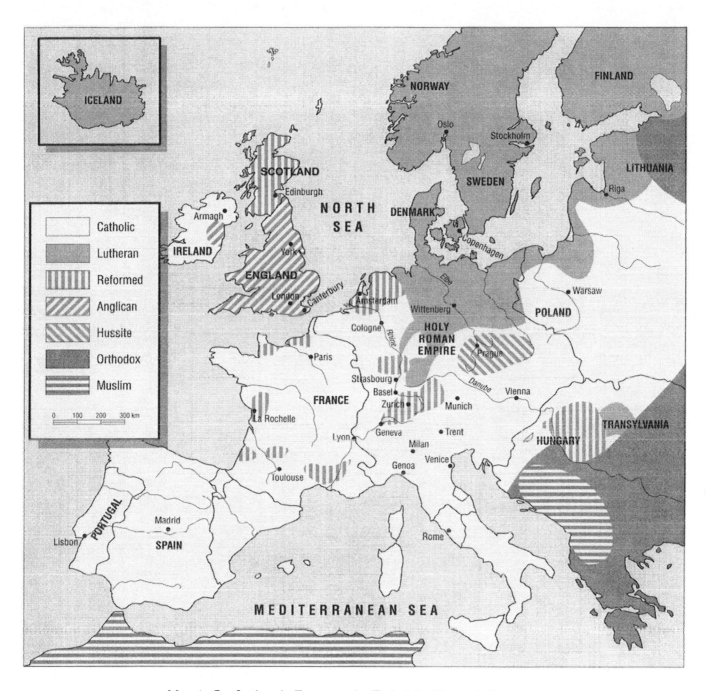

MAP 1: Confessions in Europe at the End of the Sixteenth Century.

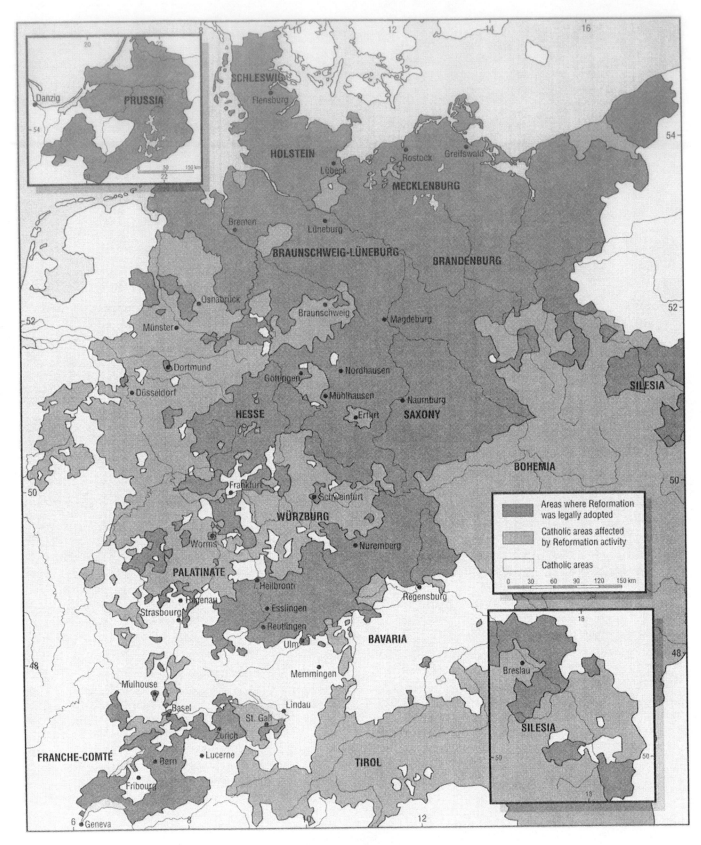

MAP 2: Expansion of Protestantism in Germany to 1570.

332

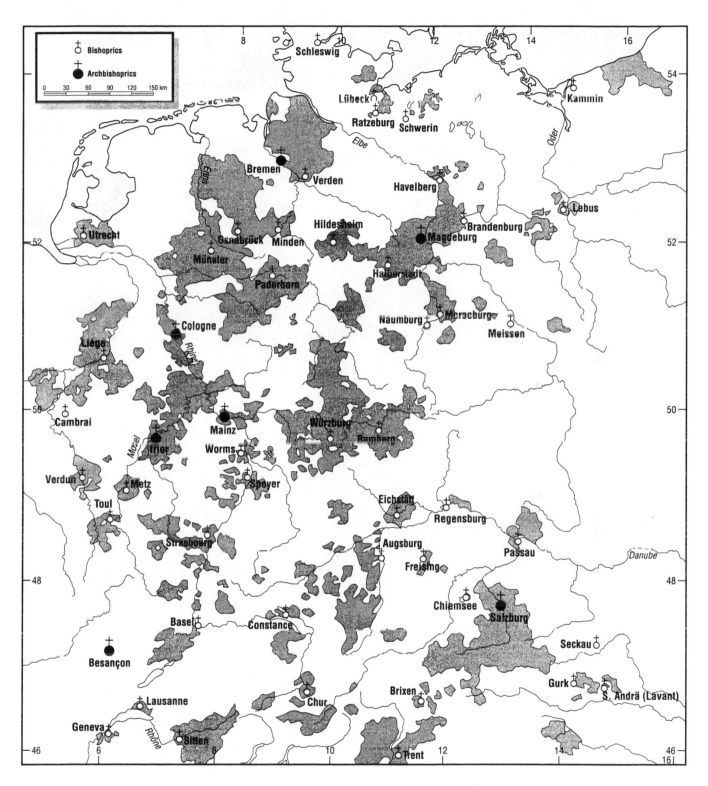

MAP 3: Ecclesiastical Territories in Central Europe (Holy Roman Empire) in the Sixteenth Century.
Most of the smaller, unidentified territories are abbacies.

333

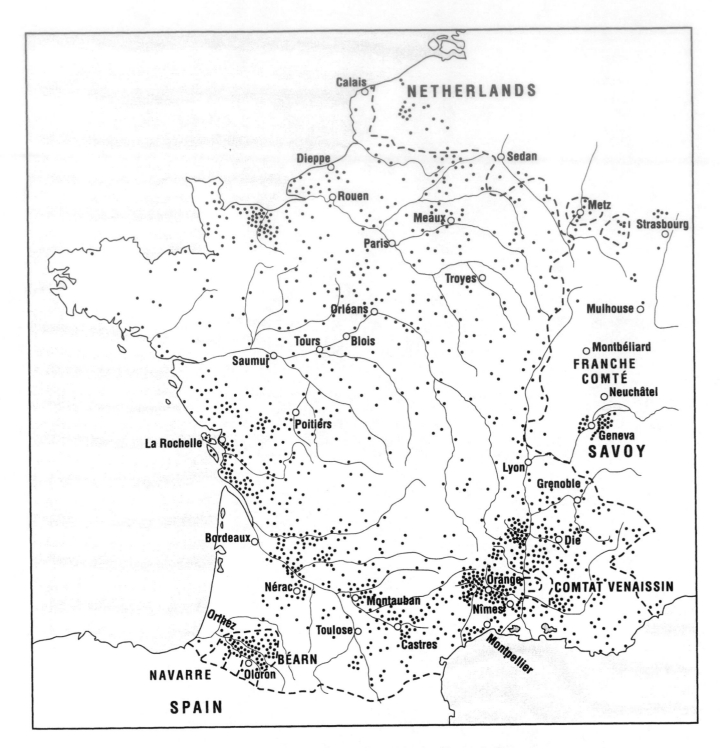

MAP 4: Reformed Churches in France in the Sixteenth Century.

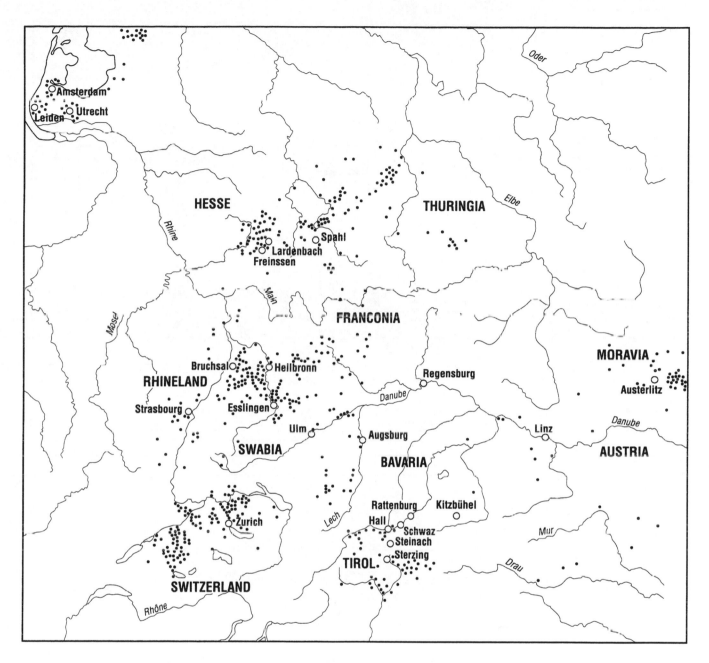

MAP 5: Anabaptism in Germany, Switzerland, Austria, and the Low Countries in the Mid-Sixteenth Century.

335

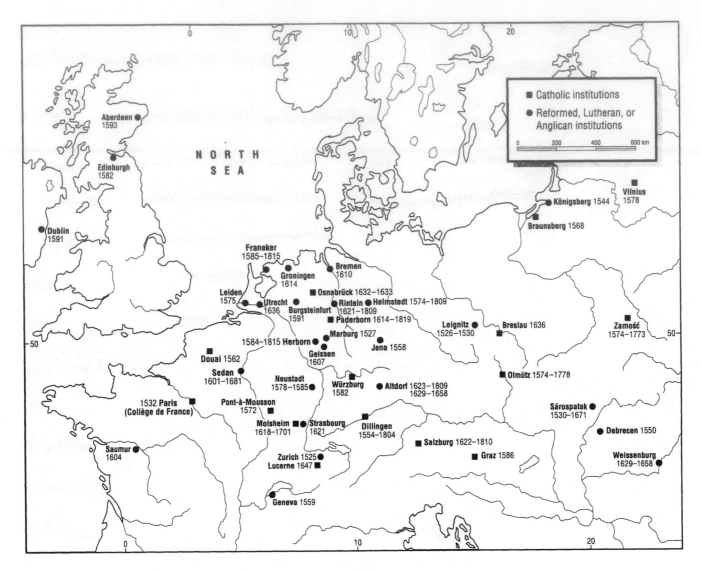

MAP 6: Protestant and Catholic Universities Founded from the Beginning of the Reformation until the Early Seventeenth Century.

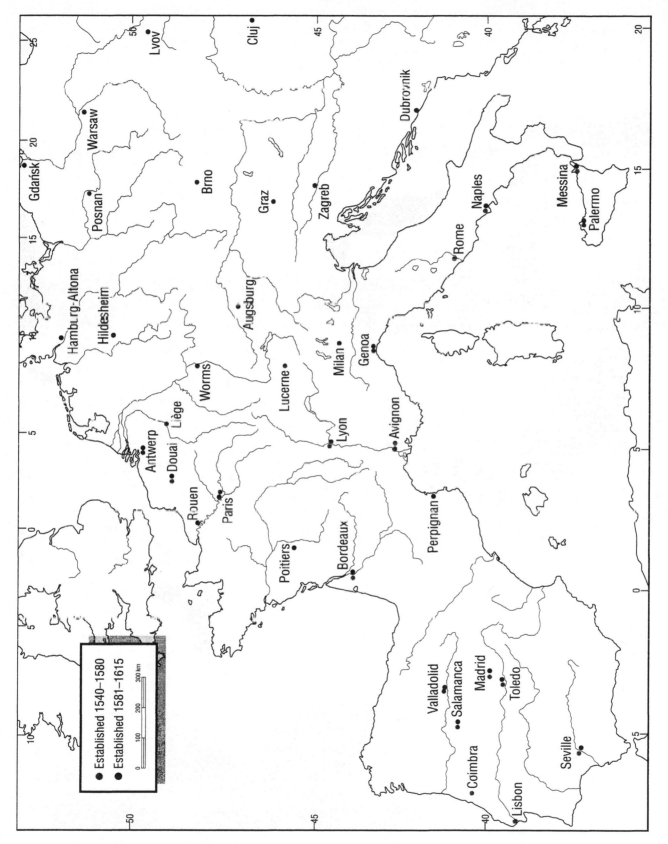

MAP 7: Sites of Jesuit Activities (Colleges, Residences, etc.) from the Mid-Sixteenth to the Early Seventeenth Century.

Established 1540–1580
Established 1581–1615

0   100   200   300 km

Gdańsk
Lvov
Warsaw
Cluj
Posnan
Brno
Graz
Zagreb
Dubrovnik
Hamburg-Altona
Hildesheim
Augsburg
Worms
Liège
Antwerp
Douai
Rouen
Paris
Lucerne
Milan
Genoa
Rome
Naples
Messina
Palermo
Lyon
Avignon
Poitiers
Bordeaux
Perpignan
Valladolid
Salamanca
Madrid
Toledo
Coimbra
Lisbon
Seville

337

MAP 8: The Catholic Church in Spanish America from the Early Sixteenth to the Early Seventeenth Century.
For archbishoprics the date of the establishment of the bishopric is in parentheses.

DIRECTORY OF CONTRIBUTORS

Lorna Jane Abray
Associate Professor of History, Scarborough College, University of Toronto
Brunfels, Otto; Laity; Zell, Katharina; Zell, Matthias

Giuseppe Alberigo
Professor of Church History, Università degli studi di Bologna
Seripando, Girolamo; Trent, Council of

Marvin W. Anderson
Professor of Church History, Southern Baptist Theological Seminary
Lismanino, Francisco; Vermigli, Peter Martyr

Christiane Andersson
Visiting Professor of Art History, Johann Wolfgang Goethe-Universität Frankfurt
Cranach, Lucas the Elder; Cranach, Lucas the Younger; Riemenschneider, Tilman

David Armitage
Assistant Professor of History, Columbia University
Discoveries in the New World

Rollin S. Armour, Sr.
Professor of Christianity, Mercer University
Hoffman, Melchior

Elizabeth Armstrong
Fellow, Emeritus, Somerville College, University of Oxford
Estienne, Robert I

Alan G. Arthur
Associate Professor of History, Brock University
Popular Religion, *article on* Popular Religion in France

Margaret Aston
Essex, United Kingdom
Lollardy

Cornelis Augustijn
Professor of Church History, Emeritus, Vrije Universiteit, Amsterdam
Classis; Corput, Hendrik van den; Dordrecht, Synod of; Helmichius, Werner; Lydius, Martinus; Triglandus, Jacobus

Jeff Bach
Assistant Professor of Brethren Studies and Director of Peace Studies, Bethany Theological Seminary, Richmond, Indiana
Tetzel, Johann

Irena Backus
Professor of the History of the Reformation, Université de Genève
Bible, *article on* Biblical Hermeneutics and Exegesis; Dentière, Marie; Patristics

P. Renée Baernstein
Assistant Professor of History, Miami University
Negri, Paola Antonia

J. Wayne Baker
Professor of History, University of Akron
Bibliander, Theodor; Bolsec, Jérome; Bullinger, Heinrich; Erastianism; Gwalther, Rudolf; Haller, Berchtold; Jud, Leo; Kappel, Peace of; Musculus, Wolfgang; Vadian, Joachim; Zurich Academy; Zwinglianism

Carl Bangs
Professor of Historical Theology, Emeritus, Saint Paul School of Theology, Kansas City, Missouri
Arminius, Jacobus; Episcopius, Simon; Hooft, Cornelis Pieterszoon; Remonstrance of 1610; Remonstrants; Veluanus, Ionnes Anastasius

Robin B. Barnes
Professor of History, Davidson College
Apocalypticism; Astrology; Millenarianism; Prodigies and Portents

Kenneth R. Bartlett
Professor of History and Renaissance Studies, Victoria College, University of Toronto
Marian Exiles

Remigius Bäumer
Professor of Church History, Albert-Ludwigs-Universität Freiburg
Pighius, Albertus

Frederic J. Baumgartner
Professor of History, Virginia Polytechnic Institute and State University
Catholic League; Henry II of France; Montmorency, Anne de; Placards, Affaire des; Tournon, François de; Valois, House of

Phillip N. Bebb
Associate Professor of History, Ohio University
Scheurl, Christoph; Spengler, Lazarus

Guy Bedouelle
Professor of Church History and Dean, Faculty of Theology, Université de Fribourg
Bible, *article on* Editions of the Bible; Dominicans; Lefèvre d'Étaples, Jacques

Joel R. Beeke
Professor of Church History and Systematic Theology, Puritan Reformed Theological School, Grand Rapids, Michigan
Acronius, Ruardus; Bastingius, Jeremias; Taffin, Jean; Venator, Adolphus Tectander; Vorstius, Conradus

F. E. Beemon
Associate Professor of History, Middle Tennessee State University
Marnix van Saint Aldegonde, Philip

Barrett L. Beer
Professor of History, Kent State University
Dudley, John; Ponet, John

Jerry H. Bentley
Professor of History, University of Hawaii
Naples

Wiebe Bergsma
Fryske Akademy, Leeuwarden, The Netherlands
Bogermannus, Johannes; Friesland; Lubbertus, Sibrandus; Snecanus, Gellius

Eckhard Bernstein
Professor of German, College of the Holy Cross
Hutten, Ulrich von

Jodi Bilinkoff
Associate Professor of History, University of North Carolina at Greensboro
John of the Cross; Popular Religon, *article on* Popular Religion in Spain; Teresa of Ávila

Christopher F. Black
Senior Lecturer in Modern History, University of Glasgow
Confraternities; Ormaneto, Niccolò

Charmarie J. Blaisdell
Associate Professor of History, Northeastern University
Renée of France; Ursulines

Karlheinz Blaschke
Professor of Saxon History, Technische Universität Dresden
George, Duke of Saxony; Miltitz, Karl von; Sylvanus, Johannes

Pierre Blet, S.J.
Pontificia Universitas Gregoriana
Gallicanism

Peter Blickle
Professor of Early Modern History and Chair, Department of Early Modern History, Universität Bern
Common Man; Peasants; Twelve Articles

Reinhard Bodenmann
Hoerdt, France
Hedio, Caspar

Mirjam Bohatcová
Prague, Czech Republic
Melantrich of Aventin, George

Andrea Bolland
Assistant Professor of Art History, University of Nebraska–Lincoln
Palladio, Andrea

John E. Booty
Professor of Anglican Studies, Emeritus, University of the South
Anglicanism; Book of Common Prayer

Frank L. Borchardt
Professor of German, Duke University
German Language

Agostino Borromeo
President, Istituto Italiano di studi Iberici, Rome
Augustinians; Emser, Hieronymous; Guerrero, Pedro; Patronato Real; Rome

Franz Bosbach
Professor of Early Modern History and Chair, Department of Early Modern History, Universität Bayreuth
Empire

William J. Bouwsma
Jane K. Sather Professor of History, Emeritus, University of California, Berkeley
Postel, Guillaume

Stephen B. Boyd
Associate Professor of Religion, Wake Forest University
Marpeck, Pilgram

Thomas A. Brady, Jr.
Professor of History, University of California, Berkeley
Knights' Revolt; Luther Renaissance; Schmalkald League; Sturm, Jakob; Swabian League

Siegfried Brauer
Evangelische Verlaganstalt, Berlin
Protestantism, *article on* Hitstory of the Term

Martin Brecht
Professor of Church History and Chair, Department of Church History, Westfälische Wilhelms-Universität Münster
Luther, Katharina; Luther, Martin

Susan Brigden
Tutor in Modern History and Fellow, Lincoln College, University of Oxford
Fish, Simon; Frith, John; London

Karin Brinkmann Brown
Adjunct Assistant Professor, Hunter College, City University of New York
Aepinus, Johannes; Agricola, Stephan; Altenstaig, Johannes; Alveldt, Augustin; Ayala, Felipe Guamán Poma de; Bacon, Francis; Bader, Johannes; Bajus, Michael; Christoph of Württemberg; Dietenberger, Johann; Gaismaier, Michael; Gerbelius, Nikolaus; Pelargus, Ambrosius; Salmerón, Alfonso; Sarpi, Paolo; Schatzgeyer, Kaspar; Schnepf, Erhard; Thamer, Theobald; Thomas, Illyricus; Trithemius, Johann; Ulrich of Württemberg; Vannius, Valentin; Weyer, Johann; Wild, Johann; Wimpina, Konrad

James A. Brundage
Ahmanson-Murphy Distinguished Professor of History, University of Kansas
Vows and Oaths

Ulrich Bubenheimer
Professor of Evangelical Theology and Religious Education, Pädagogische Hochschule Heidelberg
Bodenstein von Karlstadt, Andreas; Müntzer, Thomas

David Buisseret
Director, Hermon Dunlap Smith Center for the History of Cartography, Newberry Library, Chicago, Illinois
Béthune, Maximilien de; Henry IV of France

Melissa Meriam Bullard
William Smith Wells Professor of History, University of North Carolina at Chapel Hill
Medici, House of

Peter Burke
Professor of Cultural History, Emmanuel College, University of Cambridge
Carnival; Festivals; Latin Language; Popular Religion, *overview article*; Popular Religion, *article on* Popular Religion in Italy

Amy Nelson Burnett
Assistant Professor of History, University of Nebraska–Lincoln
Basel

Bartlett R. Butler
Professor of Music, Emeritus, Luther College
Hymns; Music; Nicolai, Philipp

Dino S. Cervigni
Professor of Italian, University of North Carolina at Chapel Hill
Cellini, Benvenuto

Mary Jane Chase
Mercy College
Cathedrals, *article on* The Continent; Monasteries, *article on* The Continent

Carl C. Christensen
Professor of History, University of Colorado at Boulder
Art; Baldung, Hans; Grünewald, Matthias; Manuel, Niklaus

Margaret Christian
Assistant Professor of English, Pennsylvania State University, Allentown Campus
Preaching and Sermons, *article on* England

Kenneth E. Christopherson
Professor of Religion, Emeritus, Pacific Lutheran University
Engelbrektsson, Olav; Kalmar Union; Thomissøn, Hans

Harry Clark
Professor of Library and Information Studies, Emeritus, University of Oklahoma
Oporinus, Johannes

Michel Cloet
Professor of Early Modern History, Katholieke Universiteit Leuven
Triest, Antoon

Ivan Cloulas
General Conservator, Archives de France, Paris
Catherine de Médicis; Charles IX of France

Richard Glenn Cole
Professor of History and Chair, Department of History, Luther College
Frosch, Johann; Froschauer, Christoph; Günzburg, Johann Eberlin von

Barry Collett
Senior Lecturer in History, University of Melbourne
Congregation of Santa Giustina of Padua; Monasticism

Patrick Collinson
Regius Professor of Modern History, University of Cambridge
Dering, Edward; Foxe, John; Grindal, Edmund; Jewel, John; Puritans; Vestiarian Controversy

John W. Cook
President, Henry Luce Foundation, New York, New York
El Greco

Allison P. Coudert
Lecturer, University Honors College, Arizona State University
Alchemy

Franz Courth
Professor of Dogmatics and the History of Dogma, Theologische Hochschule Vallendar
Mariology, *article on* Popular Piety; Saints, *article on* Sainthood

Alexander Cowan
Senior Lecturer in History, University of Northumbria at Newcastle
Concubinage

Peter Cunich
Lecturer in History, University of Hong Kong
Monasteries, *article on* The British Isles

Charles F. Daniel, Jr (deceased)
Assistant Professor of History, University of Rhode Island
Linck, Wenceslaus

David P. Daniel
Director, Slovenska Akademické Informacná Agentúra, Bratislava
Confessions in Eastern Europe; Dévay, Mátyás Bíro; Hebler, Matthias; Heltai, Caspar; Höe of Höenegg, Matthias; Honter, Johannes; Hungary; Lam, Sebastian; Láni, Elias; Liber Bursae Wittenbergae; Martinuzzi, George Utješenović; Melius, Péter Somogyi; Oláh, Nicholaus; Roggendorf, Hans Wilhelm; Šcultéty, Severín; Synods, *article on* Synods in Eastern Europe; Szenci Molnár, Albert; Třanovsky, George; Tschernembl, George Erasmus von; Wagner, Valentin; Wiener, Paul

Clifford S. L. Davies
Fellow and Tutor, Wadham College, and Lecturer in History, University of Oxford
Henry VIII of England

Johan Decavele
Archivist, Ghent City Archives
Cassander, Joris; Dathenus, Petrus; Ghent; Heyden, Gaspar van der; Titelmans, Pieter; Utenhove, Jan

Hans-Ulrich Delius
Professor of Church History, Ernst-Moritz-Arndt-Universität, Greifswald
Augustine

Ronald K. Delph
Assistant Professor of History, Eastern Michigan University
Steuco, Agostino

Richard L. DeMolen
St. Joseph's Seminary, Yonkers, New York
Barnabites

Philippe Denis
Senior Lecturer in the History of Christianity, University of Natal
Morély, Jean

Thomas Deutscher
Professor of History, St. Thomas More College, University of Saskatchewan
Farnese, House of

Harald Dickerhof
Professor of Medieval History, Katholische Universität Eichstätt
Seminaries

Barbara B. Diefendorf
Professor of History, Boston University
Bourg, Anne du; Chambre Ardente; Coligny, Gaspard II de; Coligny, Odet de; La Rivière; Paris; Parlement; Riots, Religious

John M. Dolan
Associate Professor of Philosophy and Co-chair, Program in Human Rights and Medicine, University of Minnesota
Witzel, Georg

L. S. Domonkos
Professor of History, Youngstown State University
Henckel, Johann

Gordon Donaldson (deceased)
Her Majesty's Historiographer in Scotland and Professor of Scottish History and Palaeography, University of Edinburgh
Scotland

John Patrick Donnelly
Professor of History, Marquette University
Acquaviva, Claudio; Bellarmino, Roberto; Bernardino de Loredo; Canisius, Peter Canisius's Catechism; Estella, Diego de; Faber, Johannes; Fabri, Johann; Gropper, Johannes; Laínez, Diego; Polanco, Juan Alonso de; Politi, Ambrogio Catarino; Possevino, Antonio; Religious Orders; Suárez, Francisco; Xavier, Francis

Heinz Dopsch
Professor of Comparative Regional History and Medieval History and Chair, Department of History, Universität Salzburg
Salzburg

Richard M. Douglas
Professor of History, retired, Massachusetts Institute of Technology
Sadoleto, Jacopo

Maria Dowling
Lecturer in History, St. Mary's University College, Strawberry Hill
Lilly, William; Linacre, Thomas; Warham, William

Daniel R. Doyle
University of Minnesota
Viglius, Joachim van Aytta van Zuychem

Eileen T. Dugan
Associate Professor of History, Creighton University
Billicanus, Theobald; Funerals; Kettenbach, Heinrich von; Ulm

Alastair C. Duke
Reader in History, University of Southampton
Doopsgezinden; Flanders; Merula, Angelus; Sartorius, Jan

Robert S. DuPlessis
Professor of History, Swarthmore College
Weber Thesis

Winfried Eberhard
Associate Professor of Medieval History, Forschungsschwerpunkt "Geschichte und Kultur Ostmitteleuropas," Berlin
Hussites; Utraquists

Mark U. Edwards, Jr.
President, Saint Olaf College
Reformation

Ilonka Egert
Humboldt-Universität zu Berlin
Bremen

Carlos M. N. Eire
Professor of History and Religious Studies, University of Virginia
Beatas; Cano, Melchior; Congregation of San Benito of Valladolid; Iconoclasm; John of Ávila; Peter of Alcántara; Ponce de la Fuente, Constantino; Quiñones, Francisco de los Angeles; Riots, Religious; Soto, Domingo de; Vergara, Juan de; Viruès, Alonso Ruiz de

Steven G. Ellis
Associate Professor of History, University College Galway, National University of Ireland
Ireland

Sir Geoffrey Elton
Regius Professor of Modern History, Emeritus, University of Cambridge
Cromwell, Thomas; England

James M. Estes
Professor of History, Victoria College, University of Toronto
Brenz, Johannes; Secular Magistrate, Office of; Württemberg

R. J. W. Evans
Professor of European History, University of Oxford
Bocskay, Stephen; Bohemia; Bohemian Brethren; Defenestration of Prague; Letter of Majesty; Opus Tripartitum; Vienna, Peace of; White Mountian, Battle of

Yael Even
Associate Professor of Art History, University of Missouri–St Louis
Iconography

James K. Farge, C.S.B.
Senior Fellow, Pontifical Institute of Mediaeval Studies, University of Toronto
Beda, Noël; Collège de France; Cop, Nicolas; Faculty of Theology of Paris; Vitoria, Francisco de

James R. Farr
Associate Professor of History, Purdue University
Illegitmacy; Sexuality

Olivier Fatio
Professor of Protestant Theology and Chair, Department of Church History, Université de Genève
Daneau, Lambert; La Faye, Antoine de; Orthodoxy

Dieter Fauth
Bayerische-Julius-Maximilians-Universität Würzburg
Alber, Matthäus; Kirchmeyer, Thomas

Paula Sutter Fichtner
Professor of History, Brooklyn College and Graduate Center, City University of New York
Austria; Ferdinand I; Habsburg, House of; Matthias; Maximilian I; Maximilian II; Rudolf II

Paula Findlen
Associate Professor of History, University of California, Davis
Science

Josef Finkenzeller
Professor, Ludwig-Maximilians-Universität München
Purgatory

Massimo Firpo
Professor of Modern History, Università degli studi di Torino
Morone, Giovanni

Stephen Fischer-Galati
S. Harrison Thomson Distinguished Professor of History, University of Colorado at Boulder
Ottoman Empire

Andrew C. Fix
Associate Professor of History, Lafayette College
Family of Love; Niclaes, Hendrik; Ries, Hans de

Manfred P. Fleischer
Professor of History, Emeritus, University of California, Davis
Hess, Johann; Moibanus, Ambrose; Silesia

Maureen Flynn
Associate Professor of History, Hobart and William Smith Colleges
Piety

Marc R. Forster
Assistant Professor of History, Connecticut College
Amandi, Johannes; Camerarius, Joachim; Homberg, Synod of; Truchsess, Georg von Waldburg

Julian H. Franklin
Professor of Political Science, Columbia University
Bodin, Jean

Josef Freitag
Privatdozent, Freiburg, Germany
Church Offices, *article on* Roman Catholic Offices

Jerome Friedman
Professor of History, Kent State University
Antisemitism; Cabbala, Christian; Christian Hebraica; Joselmann of Rosheim; Münster, Sebastian; Servetus, Michael

Abraham Friesen
Professor of History, University of California, Santa Barbara
Borrhaus, Martin; Hutter, Jacob; Mennonites; Philips, Dirk

Thomas A. Fudge
Assistant Professor of Religion, Warner Pacific College
Hus, Jan

Alexandre Ganoczy
Professor of Catholic Dogmatics and Ecumenical Theology, and Chair, Department of Catholic Dogmatics, Bayerische-Julius-Maximilians-Universität Würzburg
Calvin, John

Timothy George
Dean, Beeson Divinity School, Samford University
Baptism, *article on* Theological Views; Consensus Genevensis; Consubstantiation; Helvetic Confessions; Nicodemism; Schleitheim Articles; Transubstantiation

B. A. Gerrish
John Nuveen Professor of Historical Theology, Divinity School, University of Chicago
Eucharist

Elizabeth Geudeke
Research Fellow, Vrije Universiteit, Amsterdam
Amsterdam

Mary E. Giles
Professor of Humanities, California State University, Sacramento
Osuna, Francisco de

Jean-François Gilmont
Reader, Faculty of Philosophy and Letters, and Conservator, Université Catholique de Louvain
Books of Martyrs; Printing

Jónas Gíslason
Reykjavik, Iceland
Iceland

Elisabeth G. Gleason
Professor of History, University of San Francisco
Beneficio di Cristo; Capuchins; Consilium de Emendanda Ecclesia; Contarini, Gasparo; Evangelism; Flaminio, Marcantonio; Querini, Vincenzo; Theatines

John B. Gleason
Professor of English, Emeritus, University of San Francisco
Colet, John; Grocyn, William

John C. Godbey
Professor of Church History, Meadville/Lombard Theological School
Racovian Catechism; Sozzini, Fausto and Lelio

Hans-Jürgen Goertz
Professor of Social and Economic History, Universität Hamburg
Anticlericalism

Bruce Gordon
Lecturer in Modern History, University of St. Andrews
Megander, Caspar

Anthony Grafton
Dodge Professor of History, Princeton University
Casaubon, Isaac; Estienne, Henri II; Scaliger, Joseph Justus

W. Fred Graham
Professor of Christian History, Michigan State University
Presbyterianism

Richard L. Greaves
Robert O. Lawton Distinguished Professor of History, Courtesy Professor of Religion, and Chair, Department of History, Florida State University
Baptists; Congregationalism; Courts, *article on* Church Courts; Marprelate Tracts; Nonconformity; Separatists

Mark Greengrass
Senior Lecturer in History, University of Sheffield
Henry III of France

Ole Peter Grell
Carlsberg Senior Research Fellow, Wellcome Unit for the History of Medicine, University of Cambridge
Calvinism; Malmø

Paul F. Grendler
Professor of History, University of Toronto
Carioni, Battista; Index of Prohibited Books; Universities; Venice

Martin Greschat
University Professor of Church History and Contemporary Church Affairs, Justus-Liebig-Universität Gießen
Bucer, Martin

D. Jonathan Grieser
Assistant Professor of Religion, University of the South
Cratander, Andreas; Draconites, Johann

Gordon Griffiths
Professor of History, Emeritus, University of Washington
Estates-General

Egil Grislis
Professor of Religion, University of Manitoba
Latvia

Eric W. Gritsch
Professor of Church History, Emeritus, Gettysburg Lutheran Seminary, Pennsylvania
Asper, Hans; Vocation

S. Groenveld
Professor of Early Modern Dutch History, Rijksuniversiteit Leiden
Mandenmaker, Jan Arendszoon; Nassau, Maurits van; Oldenbarnevelt, Johan van

Leonard Gross
Executive Director, Historical Committee of the Mennonite Church and Director, Archives of the Mennonite Church, Goshen, Indiana
Hutterites; Riedemann, Peter

Otto Gründler
Director, The Medieval Institute, and Professor of Comparative Religion, Western Michigan University
Zanchi, Girolamo

Hans Rudolf Guggisberg
Professor of Modern History, Universität Basel
Castellion, Sébastien; Toleration

John F. Guilmartin, Jr.
Professor of History, Ohio State University
Schmalkald War

Charles D. Gunnoe, Jr.
University of Virginia
Crato von Krafftheim, Johannes; Palatinate

Peter Gwyn
Rieucazé, France
Wolsey, Thomas

James Haar
W. R. Kenan, Jr., Professor of Music, University of North Carolina at Chapel Hill
Lasso, Orlando di; Palestrina, Giovanni Pierluigi da

Mary Jane Haemig
Assistant Professor of Religion, Pacific Lutheran University
Amerbach, Bonifacius; Amerbach, Johannes; Constance

Andrej Hajduk
Pastor, Lutheran Church of Zvolen, Slovak Republic
Radašín, Michael; Stanšič Horváth de Gradecz, Gregor; Stöckel, Leonard

Michael A. Hakkenberg
Assistant Professor of History, Roanoke College
Belgic Confession; Gomarus, Franciscus; Hommius, Festus; Plancius, Petrus

Toivo Harjunpaa
Professor of Church History, Emeritus, Pacific Lutheran Theological Seminary, Berkeley, California
Juusten, Paavali

Craig Harline
Associate Professor of History, Brigham Young University
Boonen, Jacob; Hovius, Mathias; Riethoven, Maarten van; Van der Burch, Henri-François

Marilyn J Harran
Professor of Religion and History, Chapman University
Eber, Paul; Rörer, Georg

Hans-Peter Hasse
Universität Leipzig
Blarer, Ambrosius

Wolf-Dieter Hauschild
Professor, Westfälische Wilhelms-Universität Münster
Bugenhagen, Johannes; Lübeck

Patrick Hayden-Roy
Assistant Professor of History, Nebraska Wesleyan University
Brant, Sebastian; Denck, Hans; Franck, Sebastian; Frecht, Martin

John M. Headley
Distinguished University Professor, University of North Carolina at Chapel Hill
Gattinara, Mercurino Arborio di

Felicity Heal
Lecturer in Modern History and Fellow, Jesus College, University of Oxford
Chapters; Church Finances; Church Offices, *article on* Anglican Offices; Convocations; Cox, Richard; Parker, Matthew

Simo Heininen
Professor of Church History, Helsingin Yliopisto
Finland

Gernot Heiss
Associate Professor of History, Universität Wien
Mary of Hungary and Bohemia

Henry Heller
Professor of History, University of Manitoba
Dolet, Étienne; Meaux

J. A. Wayne Hellmann
Associate Professor of Historical Theology, St. Louis University
Carmelites

Scott H. Hendrix
Professor of Reformation and Modern Church History, Gettysburg Lutheran Seminary
Rhegius, Urbanus

Volker Henn
Senior Academic Adviser, Universität Trier
Hanseatic League

A. I. C. Heron
Professor of Systematic Theology and Chair, Department of Reformed Theology, Friedrich-Alexander-Universität Erlangen-Nürnberg
Calvinism

Arno Herzig
Professor of History, Universität Hamburg
Reuchlin, Johannes

Francis Higman
Professor and Director, Institute for Reformation History, Université de Genève
Caroli, Pierre; Farel, Guillaume; Lausanne; Marot, Clément; Olivétan, Pierre Robert; Roussel, Gérard

Hans J. Hillerbrand
Professor of History and Religion and Chair, Department of Religion, Duke University
Antichrist; Corpus Catholicorum; Corpus Doctrinae; Corpus Reformatorum; Johann Casimir; Matthijs, Jan; Pamphlets; Periodical Literature; Persecution; Philips, Obbe; Reference Works; Renato, Camillo

Paul Hiltpold
Lecturer, California Polytechnic State University
Valladolid

James A. Hinz
Proprietor, F. Thomas Heller Rare Books, Swarthmore, Pennsylvania
Bernhardi, Johannes; Schegk, Jakob

Dale Hoak
Professor of History, College of William and Mary in Virginia
Becon, Thomas; Edward VI of England; Seymour, Edward

R. Gerald Hobbs
Professor of Church History, Vancouver School of Theology
Bible, *article on* Translations of the Bible; Bible, *article on* Biblical Commentaries

Gerrit Jan Hoenderdaal
Professor of Protestant Theology, retired, Rijksuniversiteit Leiden
Wtenbogaert, Johannes

Philip T. Hoffman
Associate Professor of History and Social Science, California Institute of Technology
Lyon

Mack P. Holt
Associate Professor of History, George Mason University
Montmorency, House of; Valois, François de

Irmgard Höß
Professor (Extraordinaria) of Medieval and Modern History, retired, Friedrich-Alexander-Universität Erlangen-Nürnberg
Althamer, Andreas; Spalatin, Georg

R. A. Houston
Professor of Modern History, University of St. Andrews
Literacy; Population

Siegfried Hoyer
Professor of Early Modern History, Emeritus, Universität Leipzig
Glareanus, Heinricus; Zwilling, Gabriel

R. W. Hoyle
Senior Lecturer in Historical and Critical Studies, University of Central Lancashire
Aske, Robert; Pilgrimage of Grace

R. Po-chia Hsia
Professor of European History, New York University
Jews; Social Discipline

Kristina Hübener
Research Assistant, Universität Potsdam
Estates; Lusatia

William V. Hudon
Professor of History, Bloomsburg University
Clement VII; Gentile, Giovanni Valentino; Gregory XIII; Gribaldi, Matteo; Julius III; Marcellus II; Oratory of Divine Love; Paul III; Paul IV; Pio, Rodolfo; Pius V

Alvaro Huerga
Pontificia Università S. Tommaso d'Aquino
Alumbrados; Granada, Luis de; Luis de Leon

Hjalti Hugason
Assistant Professor of Church History, Háskóli Íslands
Thorláksson, Guðbrandur

Peter Humfrey
Reader, School of Art History, University of St. Andrews
Lotto, Lorenzo

Judith J. Hurwich
Chair, Department of History, Convent of the Sacred Heart, Greenwich, Connecticut
Godparentage

Herbert Immenkoetter
Associate Professor of Medieval and Modern Church History, Universität Augsburg
Augsburg; Augsburg, Peace of

Grethe Jacobsen
Head, Danish Department, Kongelige Bibliotek, Copenhagen, Denmark
Popular Religion, *article on* Popular Religion in Scandinavia

Carol Janson
Associate Professor of Art History, Western Washington University
Bruegel, Pieter the Elder

Gustaaf Janssens
Archivist, Archief van het Koninklijk Paleis, Brussels
Albert VII of Austria; Farnese, Alessandro; Hopperus, Joachim; Margaret of Parma

Denis R. Janz
Professor of the History of Christianity, Loyola University, New Orleans
Catechisms; Confirmation; Thomism

Jeffrey P. Jaynes
Assistant Professor of Church History, Methodist Theological School in Ohio, Delaware, Ohio
Church Ordinances; Corvinus, Antonius; Dietrich, Veit

Norman Jones
Professor of History, Utah State University
Acts of Supremacy; Acts of Uniformity; Capitalism; Elizabeth I of England; Elizabethan Settlement; Usury

Kenneth J. Jorgensen
Assistant Professor of History, Albertus Magnus College
Somaschi

Wayne James Jorgenson
Associate Professor of Church History, Sacred Heart Major Seminary, Detroit, Michigan
Eastern Orthodoxy

Helmar Junghans
Professor of Church History, Universität Leipzig
Augsburg Confession; Bernhardi, Bartholomeus von Feldkirchen; Hausmann, Nikolaus; Leipzig Disputation; Wittenberg; Wittenberg, University of

Frank Kaempfer
Professor of History and Chair, Department of East European History, Westfälische Wilhelms-Universität Münster
Russia

Robert J. Kalas
Associate Professor of History, Mount Saint Mary's College, Emmitsburg, Maryland
Nobility

Henry Kamen
Professor of Investigation, Consejo Superior de Investigaciones Científicas, Barcelona
Acontius, Jacobus; New Christians

Benjamin J. Kaplan
Assistant Professor of History, Brandeis University
Coolhaes, Caspar; Cooltuyn, Cornelis; Duifhuis, Hubert; Moded, Hermannus; Sybrandszoon, Taco; Taurinus, Jacobus; Utrecht

Susan C. Karant-Nunn
Professor of History, Portland State University
Churching; Grumbach, Argula von; Marriage, Defenses of; Zwickau; Zwickau Prophets

Thomas Kaufmann
Privatdozent for Church History, Georg-August-Universität Göttingen
Evangelical Movements

Benjamin Keen
Professor of History, Emeritus, Northern Illinois University
Las Casas, Bartolomé de

Ralph Keen
Assistant Professor of Religion, University of Iowa
Cochlaeus, Johannes

James F. Keenan, S.J.
Associate Professor of Moral Theology, Weston Jesuit School of Theology, Cambridge, Massachusetts
Casuistry

Donald R. Kelley
James Westfall Thompson Professor of History, Rutgers University
Hotman, François

Seong-Hak Kim
University of Minnesota
L'Hôpital, Michel de

A. Gordon Kinder
Honorary Lecturer, Department of Spanish and Portuguese, Manchester Metropolitan University
Corro, Antonio del; Diaz, Juan; Pérez de Pineda, Juan; Reina, Casiodoro de; Valdés, Juan de; Valera, Cipriano de

John N. King
Professor of English, Ohio State University, and Editor, Literature & History
Coverdale, Miles; Crowley, Robert; English Bible; Hooper, John

Robert M. Kingdon
Hilldale Professor of History, University of Wisconsin–Madison
Compagnie des Pasteurs; Consistory; Geneva; Goulart, Simon; Resistance Theory; Saint Bartholomew's Day Massacre

Philip L. Kintner
Rosenthal Professor of Humanities, Grinnell College
Refugees

Karl-Heinz Kirchhoff
Münster
Knipperdolling, Berndt; Münster; Rothmann, Bernhard

James Kirk
Reader in Scottish History, University of Glasgow
Melville, Andrew; Scottish Books of Discipline; Scottish Confession

Mary Em Kirn
Professor of Art History, Augustana College
Dürer, Albrecht; Stoss, Veit

James M. Kittelson
Professor of History, Ohio State University
Capito, Wolfgang; Marbach, Johannes; Pappus, Johann; Strasbourg; Tetrapolitan Confession

Jüri Kivimäe
Director, Tallinna Linnaarhiiv
Estonia

Steffen Kjeldgaard-Pedersen
Professor of Church History, Københavns Universitet
Agricola, Johann; Free Will

Walter Klaassen
Professor of History, Emeritus, Conrad Grebel College, University of Waterloo
Grebel, Conrad; Hätzer, Ludwig

Peter J. Klassen
Professor of History and Dean, School of Social Sciences, California State University, Fresno
Moravia

Wolfgang Klausnitzer
Professor of Fundamental and Ecumenical Theology, Otto-Friedrich-Universität Bamberg
Episcopacy; Ordination

Robert Jean Knecht
Professor of French History, Emeritus, and Honorary Senior Research Fellow in Modern History, University of Birmingham
Bologna, Concordat of; Francis I of France; Francis II of France

Paul W. Knoll
Professor of History, University of Southern California
Poland

Ernst Koch
Pastor, Evangelische-lutherische Kirche in Thüringen
Chytraeus, Nathan

Hans-Joachim Köhler
Bibliotheca academica Verlag, Tübingen
Pamphlets

Pavel Kolárovský (deceased)
Chair, Department of Church History, Univerzita Komenského Bratislava
Thurzo, George

Robert Kolb
Missions Professor of Systematic Theology, Concordia Seminary, St. Louis, Missouri
Amsdorf, Nikolaus von; Andreae, Jakob; Chemnitz, Martin; Formula of Concord; Kaiser, Leonhard; Lutheranism, *article on* Theology; Major, Georg; Maulbronn, Colloquy of; Musculus, Andreas; Selnecker, Nicholas; Spangenberg, Cyriakus

Joop W. Koopmans
Rijksuniversiteit Groningen
Mijle, Adriaan

Benedikt Kranemann
Outside Lecturer in Liturgical Studies, Deutsches Liturgisches Institut Bibliothek, Trier, Germany
Clerical Vestments

Ulrich Michael Kremer
Director, Studienseminar für das Lehramt an Gymnasium, Magdeburg
Ingolstadt; Mainz

Micheal Kwatera, O.S.B.
Assistant Professor of Theology, Saint John's University, Collegeville, Minnesota
Liturgy, *article on* Roman Catholic Liturgy

Peter Lake
Professor of History, Princeton University
Admonition Controversy; Cartwright, Thomas; Chaderton, Laurence; Whitaker, William; Whitgift, John

Jan Blahoslav Lášek
Chair, Department of Church History, Univerzita Karlova
Augusta, Jan; Israel, George; Luke of Prague

Adolf Laube

Professor of Church History, Martin Luther-Universität Halle-Wittenberg

Berlichingen, Götz von; Böheim, Hans; Fugger, Jakob; Lotzer, Sebastian; Schappeler, Christoph; Strauss, Jakob

Martin Schwarz Lausten

Associate Professor of Church History, Københavns Universitet

Christian II; Christian III; Denmark; Frederick I of Denmark and Norway; Laurentsen, Peder; Palladius, Niels; Pedersen, Christian; Sadolin, Jørgen Jensen; Tausen, Hans

Robin A. Leaver

Professor of Church Music, Westminster Choir College

Hymnals; Praetorius, Michael

Stanford E. Lehmberg

Professor of History, University of Minnesota

Byrd, William; Cathedrals, *article on* The British Isles; Chantries; Elyot, Thomas; Gibbons, Orlando; Parliament; Tallis, Thomas; Tudor, House of; Vicegerent in Spirituals

Harry Lenhammar

Professor of Church History and Chair, Department of Theology, Uppsala Universitet

Agricola, Michael; Vasa, Gustavus

Paul Douglas Leslie

Senior Pastor, Église Évangélique Baptiste de Québec, Neufchatel, Canada

Blarer, Thomas

Urs B. Leu

Historian and Scientific Librarian, Zentralbibliothek Zürich

Gessner, Conrad

Brian P. Levack

John Green Regents Professor in History, University of Texas at Austin

Possession and Exorcism

Daniel Liechty

Philadelphia, Pennsylvania

Fischer, Andreas; Glaidt, Oswald; Judaizers; Sabbatarianism; Sacramentarians

Carter Lindberg

Professor of Church History, Boston University

Sacraments

Mary Lindemann

Associate Professor of History, Carnegie Mellon University

Medicine and Healing

Robert D. Linder

Professor of History, Kansas State University

Viret, Pierre

Jennifer Loach

Fellow and Tutor, Somerville College, University of Oxford

Bonner, Edmund; Grey, Jane; Mary Tudor

David Loades

Professor of History, University College of North Wales, University of Wales

Latimer, Hugh; Ridley, Nicholas

Paul Douglas Lockhart

Assistant Professor of History and Assistant Chair, Department of History, Wright State University

Copenhagen, Diets of; Counts' War

Oliver Logan

Lecturer in History, University of East Anglia

Valier, Agostino

Sigrid Looß

Project Editor, Institut für historische Theologie, Martin Luther-Universität Halle-Wittenberg

Bünderlin, Johann; Clarenbach, Adolph; Froben, Johannes; Hergot, Hans; Ickelshamer, Valentin; Lüber, Thomas; Mörlin, Joachim; Rothenburg ob der Tauber; Ulhart, Philipp

David W. Lotz

Washburn Professor of Church History, Union Theological Seminary, New York, New York

Protestantism, *overview article*

Ronald S. Love

Canada Research Fellow, University of Saskatchewan

Navarre, House of

Ben Lowe

Assistant Professor of History, Florida Atlantic University

Caxton, William; Foxe, Edward; Reformatio legum ecclesiasticarum; Spanish Armada

Ingetraut Ludolphy

Professor, Friedrich-Alexander-Universität Erlangen-Nürnberg

Frederick III of Saxony

Ingė Lukšaitė

Senior Research Fellow, Institute of Lithuanian History, Lithuanian Academy of Sciences, Vilnius

Lithuania

Eric Lund

Associate Professor of Religion, Saint Olaf College

Speratus, Paul

Thorkild C. Lyby

Associate Professor of Church History, Faculty of Theology, Aarhus Universitet

Copenhagen, Confession of; Frederick II of Denmark and Norway; Vormordsen, Frans

John E. Lynch, C.S.P.

Professor of the History of Canon Law, Catholic University of America

Law, *article on* Canon Law

Guy Fitch Lytle III

Dean, School of Theology, University of the South

Articles of Religion; King's Book

Diarmaid MacCulloch
Lecturer in Church History, University of Bristol
Cranmer, Thomas

William S. Maltby
Professor of History, University of Missouri–St.Louis
Álvarez de Toledo, Fernando; Arias Montano, Benito; Azpilcueta, Martín de; Granvelle, Antoine Perrenot de; Guevara, Antonio de; Jiménez de Cisneros, Francisco; Mariana, Juan de; Quiroga, Gaspar de; Spain; William of Orange

W. Gordon Marigold
Professor of Languages, Emeritus, Union College, Barbourville, Kentucky
Cats, Jacob

Marie Juliette Marinus
Research Assistant, Nationaal Fonds voor Wetenschappelijk Onderzoek, Brussels
Lindanus, Wilhelmus; Malderus, Joannes; Torrentius, Laevinus

A. Lynn Martin
Reader in History, University of Adelaide
Auger, Émond; Maldonado, Juan; Ultramontanism

Dennis D. Martin
Assistant Professor of Theology, Loyola University, Chicago
Carthusians; Denis the Carthusian

Jean-Pierre Massaut
Professor of Modern History, Université de Liège
Clichtove, Josse van

Jan Materné
Algemeen Rijksarchief, Brussels
Antwerp; Plantijn,

Christoffel Constance J. Mathers
Associate Professor of History, Randolph-Macon College
Enzinas, Francisco de; Jiménez de Cisneros, Garcia; Sepúlveda, Juan Ginés de

Mickey L. Mattox
Durham, North Carolina
Cuspinian, Johannes

Gerhard May
Professor of Church History and Director, Institute for European History, Johannes Gutenberg-Universität Mainz
Marburg Confession

Thomas F. Mayer
Associate Professor of History, Augustana College, Rock Island, Illinois
Bale, John; Hooker, Richard; Howard, Thomas; Magistracy, *article on* The British Isles; Morison, Richard; Pole, Reginald; Starkey, Thomas; Tunstall, Cuthbert

William A. McComish
Église Nationale Protestante de Genève
Diodati, Jean

James McConica
Fellow, All Souls College, University of Oxford
Erasmus, Desiderius; Oxford, University of

Thomas M. McCoog, S.J.
Archivist, British Province of the Society of Jesus, London, and Member, Jesuit Historical Society, Rome
Allen, William; Campion, Edmund; Douai College; Parsons, Robert; Recusancy; Southwell, Robert

Adriana A. N. McCrea
Assistant Professor of History, Dalhousie University
Sidney, Philip

William McCuaig
Assistant Professor of History, Erindale College, University of Toronto
Della Casa, Giovanni

Bernard McGinn
Naomi Shenstone Donnelley Professor, Divinity School, University of Chicago
Mysticism

Frederick J. McGinness
Director and Lecturer, Complex Organizations Program, Mount Holyoke College
Martin, Gregory

James Edward McGoldrick
Professor of History, Cedarville College, Cedarville, Ohio
Balnaves, Henry; Barnes, Robert

Alister E. McGrath
Research Lecturer in Theology, University of Oxford, and Research Professor of Systematic Theology, Regent College, University of British Columbia
Justification; Sanctification; Scholasticism

Elsie Anne McKee
Archibald Alexander Professor of the History of Worship, Princeton Theological Seminary, New Jersey
Church Offices, *article on* Calvinist Offices

Donald K. McKim
Academic Dean and Professor of Theology, Memphis Theological Seminary, Tennessee
Ramus, Petrus

R. Emmet McLaughlin
Associate Professor of Religious Studies, Villanova University
Clergy; Schwenckfeld, Kaspar von; Spiritualism

Andrew M. McLean
Professor of English, University of Wisconsin–Parkside
Barlow, William; Death

Jo Ann McNamara
Professor of History, Hunter College, City University of New York
Nuns

David O. McNeil
Professor of History, San José State University
Budé, Guillaume

Raymond A. Mentzer, Jr.
Professor of History, Montana State University
Berquin, Louis de; Languedoc

Judith P. Meyer
Assistant Professor of History, University of Connecticut, Waterbury
La Rochelle

Nelson H. Minnich
Professor of History and Church History of the Renaissance and Reformation, Catholic University of America
Adrian VI; Aleandro, Girolamo; Campeggio, Lorenzo; Giustiniani, Tommaso; Lateran Council, Fifth; Leo X; Observantism; Pio, Alberto

Bernd Moeller
Professor of Church History, Georg-August-Universität Göttingen
Disputations

E. William Monter
Professor of History, Northwestern University
Flagellants; Inquisition; Magic; Rio, Martin del; Savoy; Witchcraft

Ingun Montgomery
Professor of Church History, Universitetet i Oslo
Andreae, Laurentius; Erik XIV of Sweden; Norway; Sture, Sten the Younger; Västerås, Diet of

Walter L. Moore
Professor of Religion, Florida State University
Eck, Johann

Gerard T. Moran
Director, Moran Information and Publishing Service, Amsterdam, The Netherlands
Time

Jo Ann Hoeppner Moran (Cruz)
Associate Professor of History, Georgetown University
Education

Gérard Moreau (deceased)
Herstal, Belgium
Ernest of Bavaria

Robert Muchembled
Professor of Modern History and Chair, Department of History, Université de Paris XIII (Paris-Nord)
Richardot, François

Janel Mueller
William Rainey Harper Professor in Humanities, University of Chicago
Parr, Katherine

Richard A. Muller
P. J. Zondervan Professor of Historical Theology, Calvin Theological Seminary, Grand Rapids, Michigan
Predestination; Scripture

Terence R. Murphy
Associate Professor of History, American University
Book of Homilies; Conduct Books

Sara T. Nalle
Associate Professor of History, William Paterson College of New Jersey
Cuenca

Charles G. Nauert, Jr.
Professor of History, University of Missouri–Columbia
Agricola, Georgius; Agrippa, Heinrich Cornelius; Crotus Rubeanus

Ulrich Nembach
Professor of Practical Theology, Georg-August-Universität Göttingen
Preaching and Sermons, *article on* Germany

James Arne Nestingen
Professor of Church History, Luther Seminary, St. Paul, Minnesota
Book of Concord; Gnesio-Lutherans; Luther's Catechisms

Kristen B. Neuschel
Associate Professor of History, Duke University
Condé, Henri I; Condé, Louis I

Henk van Nierop
Associate Professor of History, Universiteit van Amsterdam
Brederode, Hendrik van; Popular Religion, *article on* Popular Religion in the Low Countries

José C. Nieto
Mary S. Geiger Professor of Religion and History and Chair, Department of Religion, Juniata College, Huntingdon, Pennsylvania
Illuminism; Valdés, Alfonso de

Bodo Nischan
Professor of History, East Carolina University
Albert of Brandenburg; Brandenburg; Briessmann, Johann; Frederick III of the Palatinate; Osiander, Lucas II; Prussia

Byron J. Nordstrom
Professor of History and Scandinavian Studies, Gustavus Adolphus College
Charles IX of Sweden

Carlos G. Noreña
Professor of Philosophy, University of California, Santa Cruz
Vives, Juan Luis

Donald Nugent
Associate Professor of History, University of Kentucky
Poissy, Colloquy of

Paul L. Nyhus
Frank Andrew Munsey Professor of History, Bowdoin College
Grynaeus, Simon; Kessler, Johann

Francis Oakley
Edward Dorr Griffin Professor of the History of Ideas and President, Emeritus, Williams College
Conciliarism

Marvin R. O'Connell
Professor of History, University of Notre Dame
Louvain; Stapleton, Thomas

Jeannine E. Olson
Associate Professor of History, Rhode Island College
Bourbon, House of; Briçonnet, Guillaume; Crespin, Jean; Diaconate; Du Moulin, Charles; Geneva Academy; Jansenism; Languet, Hubert; LeClerc, Pierre; Libertines; Pacification of Ghent

Oliver K. Olson
Visiting Associate Professor of Theology, Marquette University
Flacius Illyricus, Matthias; Magdeburg

John W. O'Malley
Professor of Church History, Weston School of Theology
Giles of Viterbo; Ignatius Loyola; Jesuits

Eberhard H. Pältz
Professor of Protestant Theology and Chair, Department of Church History, Friedrich-Schiller-Universität Jena
Böhme, Jakob

Jaroslav Pánek
Associate Professor of History and Deputy Director, Institute of Czech History, Univerzita Karlova
Budovec of Budov, Václav; Mitmánek, Václav; Přáza, Paul; Rožmberk, Vilém and Petr Vok; Schlick of Passauni, Joachim Andreas; Strejc, Jiří; Žerotín, Karl

James A. Parente, Jr.
Professor of German and Dutch, University of Minnesota
Drama; Vondel, Joost van den

Charles H. Parker
Assistant Professor of History, St.Louis University
Corneliszoon, Arend; Donteclock, Reynier; Dordrecht

John B. Payne
Diefenderfer Chair in Mercersburg and Ecumenical Theology and Professor of Church History, Lancaster Theological Seminary, Pennsylvania
Philosophy of Christ

Katalin Péter
Scientific Adviser, Institute of History, Magyar Tudományos Akadémia, Budapest
Bethlen, Gabriel; Bornemisza, Péter; Dávid, Francis; Kálmáncsehi, Márton; Károlyi Gáspár; Sylvester, János; Szegedi Kis, István; Sztárai, Michael

Luther D. Peterson
Professor of History, State University of New York College at Oswego
Menius, Justus; Philippists; Synergist Controversy

Andrew Pettegree
Reader in Modern History and Director, St. Andrews Reformation Studies Institute, University of St. Andrews
Haemstede, Adriaan Corneliszoon van; Micron, Maarten; Saravia, Adrianus

Sabine Pettke
Lecturer in Church History, Universität Rostock
Oldendorp, Johannes

Vinzenz Pfnür
Professor, Westfälische Wilhelms-Universität Münster
Colloquies; Confutation; Excommunication

Peter O'M. Pierson
Lee and Seymour Graff Professor of History, Santa Clara University
Charles V; John of Austria; Lepanto, Battle of; Philip II of Spain; Portugal

H. Wayne Pipkin
Chaplain, Moscow Protestant Chaplaincy
Blaurock, George; Hofmeister, Sebastian; Rinck, Melchior

Miloslav Polívka
Historical Institute, Česká Akadamie Věd, Prague
Červenka, Matthias

Lorenzo Polizzotto
Associate Professor of History, University of Western Australia
Savonarola, Girolamo

Richard H. Popkin
Professor, Emeritus, Washington University, and Adjunct Professor of History and Philosophy, University of California, Los Angleles
Skepticism

Harry C. Porter
Lecturer in History, retired, University of Cambridge
Cambridge, University of

Allyson M. Poska
Assistant Professor of History, Mary Washington College
Popular Religion, *article on* Popular Religion in Portugal

Rainer Postel
Professor, Universität der Bundeswehr Hamburg
Hamburg; Schleswig-Holstein; Wullenwewer, Jürgen

Paolo Prodi
Professor of Modern History, Università degli studi di Bologna
Paleotti, Gabriele

Adriano Prosperi
Professor of Modern History, Università degli studi di Pisa
Catholic Reformation; Giberti, Gian Matteo; Italy; Siculo, Giorgio

Cyriac K. Pullapilly
Saint Mary's College, Notre Dame, Indiana
Baronio, Cesare; Neri, Filippo

Eddy F. Put
First Assistant, Algemeen Rijksarchief, Brussels
Boonen, Jacob; Hovius, Mathias

John E. Quam
Senior Pastor, First Evangelical Lutheran Church, Manchester, Iowa
Erikssøn, Jørgen; Lunge, Vincens

Sheila J. Rabin
Assistant Professor of History, Saint Peter's College, Jersey City, New Jersey
Brahe, Tycho; Copernicus, Nicolaus; Kepler, Johannes

Cornelis S. M. Rademaker
Zierikzee, The Netherlands
Vossius, Gerardus Joannes

Jill Raitt
Catherine Paine Middlebush Professor in the Humanities and Chair, Department of Religious Studies, University of Missouri–Columbia
Bèze, Théodore de; Harmony of Confessions; Montbéliard, Colloquy of; Protestant League; Salvard, Jean-François; Toussain, Daniel; Toussain, Pierre

Tarald Rasmussen
Faculty of Theology, Universitetet i Oslo
Tradition

Gerhard Rau
Professor of Theology, Ruprecht-Karls-Universität Heidelberg
Hyperius, Andreas

Glyn Redworth
Oxford, United Kingdom
Gardiner, Stephen; Six Articles

Virginia Reinburg
Associate Professor of History, Boston College
Devotional Practices; Liturgical Calendar; Missals

Gustav Reingrabner
Professor, Universität Wien
Horner Bund; Jörger Family; Khevenhüller Family; Vienna

Wolfgang Reinhard
Professor of Modern History, Albert-Ludwigs-Universität Freiburg
Curia Romana; Missions; Papacy; Papal Diplomatic Corps; Papal States; Sixtus V

Konrad Repgen
Professor of Medieval and Modern History, Emeritus, Rheinische Friedrich-Wilhelms-Universität Bonn
Reform

Richard Rex
Assistant Under-Librarian, Cambridge University Library
Fisher, John

Philip Lyndon Reynolds
Director, Aquinas Center of Theology, Emory University
Indulgences

Lawrence F. Rhu
Associate Professor of English, University of South Carolina
Spenser, Edmund

Louise Rice
Assistant Professor of Art History, Duke University
Michaelangelo Buonarroti; Veronese, Paolo

Nancy Lyman Roelker (deceased)
Professor of History, Emeritus, Boston University
Antoine of Navarre; Jeanne of Navarre

Saskia Rohde
Research Assistant, Universität Hamburg
Reuchlin, Johannes

Cl. Rooze-Stouthamer
Ellewoutsdijk, The Netherlands
Faukelius, Hermannus; Teellinck, Willem

David Rosand
Professor of Art History, Columbia University
Titian

Robert Rosin
Associate Professor of Historical Theology, Concordia Seminary, St. Louis, Missouri
Cordatus, Conrad; Cruciger, Caspar; Grynaeus, Simon; Hesshus, Tilemann; Jonas, Justus; Mathesius, Johannes; Myconius, Friedrich; Myconius, Oswald; Peucer, Caspar; Trotzendorf, Valentin

John D. Roth
Associate Professor of History, Goshen College, and Editor, The Mennonite Quarterly Review
Entfelder, Christian; Hottinger, Hans; Nikolsburg; Weigel, Valentin

George A. Rothrock (deceased)
Professor of History, University of Alberta
Cateau-Cambrésis, Treaty of; Chateaubriand, Edict of; Lorraine-Guise, House of; Navarre, House of

Bernard Roussel
Director of Studies, History and Theology of the Reformation, École Pratique des Hautes Études, Section des Sciences religieuses
Béarn; Gallic Confession; Pagnini, Sante

Steven Rowan
Professor of History, University of Missouri–St. Louis
Law, *article on* Roman Law

William R. Russell
Adjunct Professor of Religion and Lutheran Campus Pastor, North Dakota State University
Aurifaber, Johannes; Beurlin, Jacob; Hunnius, Aegidius; Naumburg, Declaration of; Schmalkald Articles; Schmalkalden; Strigel, Viktorin; Wigand, Johann; Wittenberg Concord

Lawrence V. Ryan
Joseph S. Atha Professor of Humanities, Emeritus, Stanford University
Ascham, Robert

Thomas Max Safley
Associate Professor of History, University of Pennsylvania
Courts, *article on* Marriage Courts; Divorce; Family; Marriage

Oskar Sakrausky
Bishop, Evangelische Kirche augsburgischen Bekenntnisses, Fresach, Austria
Truber, Primus; Ungnad, Hans von Sonnegg

J. H. M. Salmon
Marjorie Walter Goodhart Professor of History, Emeritus, Bryn Mawr College
Huguenots; Politiques; Wars of Religion; Wassy, Massacre of

Paul Robert Sanders
Director, Institut Biblique de Nogent, Nogent-sur-Marne, France
Consensus Tigurinus

Margaret H. B. Sanderson
Head of Publication and Education, retired, Scottish Record Office, Edinburgh
Beaton, David

Heinz Scheible
Director, Melanchthon-Forschungsstelle, Heidelberger Akademie der Wissenschaften
Melanchthon, Philipp

Peter Schimert
Assistant Professor of History, Miskolci Egyetem
Mohács, Battle of; Pázmány, Péter; Stephen Báthory; Transylvania; Zápolya, János; Zápolya, János Zsigmond

Alois Schmid
Professor of Bavarian and Frankish Regional History, Friedrich-Alexander-Universität Erlangen-Nürnberg
Hagenau, Colloquy of; Marburg, Colloquy of

Georg Schmidt
Professor of Early Modern History and Chair, Department of Early Modern History, Friedrich-Schiller-Universität Jena
Diet

Heinrich Richard Schmidt
Lecturer, Universität Bern
Bern

Luise Schorn-Schütte
Münster, Germany
Braunschweig; Church Offices, *article on* Lutheran Offices

Susan E. Schreiner
Associate Professor of the History of Christianity and of Theology, Divinity School, University of Chicago
Church; Faith; Pelagianism

Anne Jacobson Schutte
Professor of History, University of Virginia
Vergerio, Pier Paolo

Reinhard Schwarz
Professor of Church History, Ludwig-Maximilians-Universität München
Charity; Good Works

Robert W. Scribner
Reader in the Social History of Early Modern Europe, University of Cambridge
Cologne; Communalism; Peasants' War; Sacramentals; Saints, *article on* Cult of Saints

Gottfried Seebaß
Professor of Church History, Ruprecht-Karls-Universität Heidelberg
Heidelberg, University of; Hut, Hans; Osiander, Andreas

Patrica Seed
Professor of History, Rice University
America

André Séguenny
Researcher and Editor, Bibliotheca dissidentium, Centre National de la Recherche Scientifique, Strasbourg
Raków

Domenico Sella
Professor of History, University of Wisconsin–Madison
Milan

Frank C. Senn
Pastor, Immanuel Luthern Church, Evanston, Illinois
John III of Sweden; Liturgy, *article on* Protestant Liturgy; Sigismund III Vasa

Kyle C. Sessions
Professor of History, Illinois State University
Alber, Erasmus; Hassler, Hans Leo; Rhau, Georg

Douglas H. Shantz
Associate Professor of Religious Studies, Trinity Western University
Crautwald, Valentin

Christine Shaw
Senior Research Fellow, European Humanities Research Centre, University of Warwick
Alexander VI; Julius II

Paolo Simoncelli
Professor of Modern History, Università degli studi di Roma "La Sapienza"
Benedetto da Mantova; Biandrata, Giorgio; Carnesecchi, Pietro; Celsi, Mino; Curione, Celio Secondo; Ochino, Bernardino

Trygve R. Skarsten
Professor of Church History and President, Lutheran Bible Institute of Seattle
Aslaksen, Cort; Beyer, Absalon Pedersson; Friis, Peder Claussøn; Helie, Paul; Hemmingsen, Niels; Magnus, Olaus; Norvegus, Laurentius; Odense, Diets of; Palladius, Peder; Petri, Olaus and Laurentius; Stockholm Bloodbath; Sweden; Uppsala, Diet of

Donald Dean Smeeton
Professor of Religious Studies, ICI University, South Africa
Tyndale, William

Alan G. R. Smith
Professor of Modern History, University of Glasgow
Cecil, William

Hilary Dansey Smith
Callander, United Kingdom
Preaching and Sermons, *article on* Spain and Portugal

Jeffrey Chipps Smith
Professor of Art History, University of Texas at Austin
Architecture

Thurman L. Smith
Professor of History, Lincoln Land Community College, Springfield, Illinois
Coins

C. Arnold Snyder
Associate Professor of History, Conrad Grebel College, University of Waterloo
Sattler, Michael

Philip M. Soergel
Associate Professor of History, Arizona State University
Miracles

Paula Sommers
Professor of French, University of Missouri–Columbia
Marguerite d'Angoulême

Joke Spaans
Lecturer, Fryske Akademy
Coornhert, Dirk Volkertszoon; Herbertszoon, Hermannus

Mathieu Spiertz
Professor of the History of Dutch Catholicism, Katholieke Universiteit Nijmegen
Fontanus, Johannes

Lewis W. Spitz
William R. Kenan University Professor, Emeritus, and Professor of History, Emeritus, Stanford University
Celtis, Conradus; Lutheranism, *overview article*; Mutianus Rufus, Conrad; Peutinger, Conrad; Pirckheimer, Willibald and Caritas; Wimpfeling, Jakob

Bart Jan Spruyt
Et Houten, The Netherlands
Hoen, Cornelis Henricxzoen

James M. Stayer
Professor of History, Queen's University at Kingston
Anabaptists; Community of Goods; Hubmaier, Balthasar; John of Leiden; Mantz, Felix; Melchiorites; Polygamy

David C. Steinmetz
Amos Ragan Kearns Professor of the History of Christianity, Duke University
Staupitz, Johann von

Walter Stempel
Pastor and Archivist, Evangelische Kirchengemeinde Wesel, Germany
Jülich-Cleve

Gerald Strauss
Distinguished Professor of History, Emeritus, Indiana University
Aventinus, Johannes; Bavaria; Frankfurt am Main; Gravamina; Sachs, Hans; School Ordinances; Visitations

Glenn S. Sunshine
Assistant Professor of History, Central Connecticut State University
Chandieu, Antoine de la Roche; La Rochelle, Synod of; Nîmes, Synod of; Synods, *article on* Synods in Western Europe

N. M. Sutherland
Professor of Early Modern European History, Emeritus, University of London
Amboise, Conspiracy of

Edward A. Synan
Professor of the History of Mediaeval Philosophy, Emeritus, Pontifical Institute of Mediaeval Studies and University of Toronto
Biel, Gabriel; Nominalism; Ockhamism

Lech Szczucki
Professor of the History of Philosophy and Chair, Department of the History of Modern Philosophy, Institute of Philosophy and Sociology, Polish Academy of Sciences, Warsaw
Antitrinitarianism; Socinianism

Larissa Juliet Taylor
Assistant Professor of History, Colby College
Preaching and Sermons, *article on* France

J. Ignacio Tellechea Idígoras
Professor of Church History, Universidad Pontificia de Salamanca
Carranza, Bartolomé

Thomas Tentler
Professor of History, University of Michigan
Confession; Penance

Marcel Tetel
Professor of Romance Studies, Duke University
Montaigne, Michel Eyquem de; Rabelais, François

Barbara Sher Tinsley
Visiting Scholar, Stanford University
Baduel, Claude; Raemond, Florimond de; Sturm, Johann

Patricia Vettel Tom
Lecturer in Art History, Washington University
Iconography

John Tonkin
Professor of History, University of Western Australia
Marxism; Reformation Studies

James D. Tracy
Professor of History, University of Minnesota
Baerdes, Willem Dirkszoon; Brès, Guy de; Church and State; Emden; Emden, Synod of; Magistracy, *article on* Germany and the Low Countries; Netherlands

Mark D. Tranvik
Director of Admissions and Lecturer in Church History, Luther Seminary, St. Paul, Minnesota
Baptism, *article on* Popular Practices

J. B. Trapp
Professor of the History of the Classical Tradition, Emeritus, Warburg Institute, University of London
More, Thomas

Robert Trisco
Professor of Church History, Catholic University of America, and Editor, The Catholic Historical Review
Borromeo, Carlo; Pius IV

Pamela Tudor-Craig
Adjunct Professor of Art History, Grinnell College in London, and Professor of Art History, American Heritage Association, London
Holbein, Hans the Younger

Mario Turchetti
Professor of Modern History, Université de Fribourg
Aubigné, Théodore-Agrippa d'; Bellay, Jean and Guillaume du; Duplessis-Mornay, Philippe; Gallars, Nicolas des; La Noue, François de; La Renaudie, Jean du Barry; Magistracy, *article on* France; Nantes, Edict of; Olevianus, Kaspar

Maarten Ultee
Professor of History, University of Alabama
Saint-Germain, Colloquy of; Saint-Germain, Edicts of; Saint-Germain-des-Prés

Wacław Urban
Professor of History, Wyższa Szkoła Pedagogiczna, Kielce
Consensus Sendomiriensis; Łaski, Jan; Polish Brethren; Stancarus, Francis

John Van Engen
Professor of History and Director, Medieval Institute, University of Notre Dame
Brothers and Sisters of the Common Life

Marc Venard
Professor of Modern History, Emeritus, Université de Paris X (Paris-Nanterre)
Assembly of Clergy; France

Mary Black Verschuur
Lecturer in History, University of Nebraska at Omaha
Edinburgh

L. J. Andrew Villalon
Associate Professor of History, University of Cincinnati
Machiavelli, Niccolò

Marcus Vink
University of Minnesota
Barrefelt, Hendrik Jansen van; Grotius, Hugo; Lipsius, Justus; Rovenius, Philip; Vosmeer, Sasbout

Derk Visser
Professor of History and Chair, Department of History, Ursinus College
Covenant; Junius, Franciscus; Nadere Reformatie; Sarcerius, Erasmus; Ursinus, Zacharius; Westphal, Joachim

Ingeborg Berlin Vogelstein
Reformation Bibliographer, Ambrose Swasey Library, Saint Bernard's Institute, Colgate Rochester Divinity School, Rochester, New York
Sleidanus, Johannes

Bernard Vogler
Professor of Modern History, Université de Strasbourg II (Sciences Humaines)
Pflug, Julius; Popular Religion, *article on* Popular Religion in Germany

Günter Vogler
Professor of German History, Humboldt-Universität zu Berlin
George of Brandenburg-Ansbach; Geyer, Florian; Nuremberg; Nuremberg, Peace of; Wied, Hermann von

Jozef Vozár
Historical Institute, Slovenská Akadémia Vied, Bratislava
Miners' Revolt

Harry Vredeveld
Professor of German, Ohio State University
Egranus, Sylvius; Hessus, Eobanus

Gary K. Waite
Associate Professor of History, University of New Brunswick
Batenburg, Jan van; Joris, David; Menno Simons

Greg Walker
Lecturer in English, University of Leicester
Bilney, Thomas

Richard Ernest Walker
Associate Professor of German and Chair, Department of Germanic and Slavic Languages and Literatures, University of Maryland at College Park
Gengenbach, Pamphilius; Murner, Thomas; Nas, Johannes; Stifel, Michael

Peter G. Wallace
Associate Professor of History, Hartwick College
Cities

Robert C. Walton
Professor and Director, Seminar for Modern Church and Theological History, Westfälische Wilhelms-Universität Münster
Oecolampadius, Johannes; Switzerland; Zurich

Lee Palmer Wandel
Associate Professor of History and Religious Studies, Yale University
Begging; Church Discipline; Liturgical Calendar; Social Ethics; Social Welfare; Zwingli, Huldrych

Sara Warneke
La Trobe University College of Northern Victoria
Pilgrimages; Travel

Retha M. Warnicke
Professor of History and Chair, Department of History, Arizona State University
Anne of Cleves; Askew, Ann; Boleyn, Anne; Catherine of Aragon; Seymour, Jane

Ann K. Warren
Adjunct Associate Professor of History, Case Western Reserve University
Anchorites

Günther Wartenberg
Professor of Church History, Universität Leipzig
Alesius, Alexander; Brück, Gregor; Interims; Leipzig; Moritz of Saxony; Saxony

J. Denny Weaver
Professor of Religion and Chair, Department of Religion, History, and Political Science, Bluffton College
Pacifism

Édith Weber
Université de Paris IV (Paris-Sorbonne)
Goudimel, Claude

Horst Weigelt
Professor of Church History, Otto-Friedrich-Universität Bamberg
Campanus, Johannes

James Michael Weiss
Associate Professor of Church History and Director, Senior Capstone Seminars, Boston College
Beatas Rhenanus; Hosius, Stanislaus; Humanism; Renaissance

Ulman Weiss
Erfurt, Germany
Bader, Augustin; Erfurt; Lang, Johannes; Sickingen, Franz von; Usingen, Bartholomäus Arnoldi von; Zwick, Johannes

Guy Wells
Wellington, Ohio
Sonnius, Franciscus; Wonderyear

Timothy J. Wengert
Associate Professor of the History of Christianity, Lutheran Theological Seminary at Philadelphia
Adiaphora; Antinomianism

Benjamin Wood Westervelt
Assistant Professor of History, Lewis and Clark College
Roman Catholicism

Robert Whiting
Principal Lecturer in History, University College of Ripon and York St. John
Popular Religion, *article on* Popular Religion in England and Scotland

Ulrich Wickert
Professor of Church History, Emeritus, Humboldt-Universität zu Berlin
Mariology, *article on* Theology

Jared Wicks
Professor of Fundamental Theology and Dean, Faculty of Theology, Pontificia Universitas Gregoriana
Bañez, Domingo; Cajetan; Controversial Theologians; Molina, Luis de; Prierias, Sylvester Mazzolini

Merry E. Wiesner-Hanks
Professor of History and Director, Center for Women's Studies, University of Wisconsin–Milwaukee
Celibacy and Virginity; Prostitution; Weddings; Women

George H. Williams
Hollis Professor of Divinity, Emeritus, Harvard University
Radical Reformation

Gerhild Scholz Williams
Professor of German and Comparative Literature, Washinton University
Paracelsus

Glanmor Williams
Professor, Emeritus, University of Wales
Wales

Rainer Wohlfeil
Professor, Emeritus, Universität Hamburg
Worms, Diet of

Eike Wolgast
Professor of Modern History, Ruprecht-Karls-Universität Heidelberg
Speyer, Protestation of

Juliaan Woltjer
Professor of Dutch History, Emeritus, Rijksuniversiteit Leiden
Revolt of the Netherlands

Jenny Wormald
St. Hilda's College, University of Oxford
Buchanan, George; Hamilton, Patrick; Knox, John; Mary Stuart; Stuart, House of; Wishart, George

William J. Wright
Professor of History, University of Tennessee at Chattanooga
Hesse; Krafft, Adam; Lambert, François; Pack Affair; Philipp of Hesse

Andrzej Wyczański
Vice-President and Scientific Secretary, Polish Academy of Sciences, and Professor of Modern History, Uniwersytet Warszawski-Białystok
Sigismund I of Poland

David S. Yeago
Associate Professor of Systematic Theology, Lutheran Theological Southern Seminary, Columbia, South Carolina
Grace

T. C. Price Zimmermann
Charles A. Dana Professor of History, Davidson College
Colonna, Vittoria; Sack of Rome

Jonathan W. Zophy
Professor of History, University of Houston–Clear Lake
Electors; Holy Roman Empire

Karl-Heinz zur Mühlen
Rheinische Friedrich-Wilhelms-Universität Bonn
Christology; Law, *article on* Theological Understanding of Law; Sin; Two Kingdoms

Christoph Zürcher
Bellmund, Switzerland
Pellikan, Konrad

SYNOPTIC OUTLINE OF CONTENTS

The outline presented on the following pages is intended to provide a general view of the conceptual scheme of this encyclopedia. Entries are arranged in the ten major conceptual categories listed below.

Sites, Regions, Polities
Historical Events
Religious Groups and Movements
Ecclesiastical Institutions
Creeds, Confessions, Texts
Theology
Social History
Popular Religion
Biographies
Reformation Studies

Within each conceptual category, entries are listed in some or all of the following geographic regions, as applicable: Pan-Europe; Germany; Switzerland; France; British Isles; Italy, Spain, Portugal; Low Countries; Scandinavia; and East-Central Europe. Because the headings for these categories are not mutually exclusive, some entries in the encyclopedia are listed more than once.

SITES, REGIONS, POLITIES

Germany

Augsburg
Bavaria
Brandenburg
Braunschweig
Bremen
Cologne
Constance
Emden
Erfurt
Frankfurt am Main
Hamburg
Hesse
Holy Roman Empire
Ingolstadt
Jülich-Cleve
Leipzig
Lübeck
Magdeburg
Mainz
Münster
Nuremberg
Palatinate
Prussia
Rothenburg ob der Tauber
Saxony
Schleswig-Holstein
Schmalkalden
Ulm
Wittenberg
Württemberg
Zwickau

Switzerland

Basel
Bern
Geneva
Lausanne
Switzerland
Zurich

France

Béarn
France
La Rochelle
Languedoc
Louvain
Lyon
Meaux
Paris

Saint-Germain-des-Prés
Savoy
Strasbourg

British Isles

Edinburgh
England
Ireland
London
Scotland
Wales

Italy, Spain, Portugal

Cuenca
Italy
Milan
Naples
Papal States
Portugal
Rome
Spain
Valladolid
Venice

Low Countries

Amsterdam
Antwerp
Dordrecht
Flanders
Friesland
Ghent
Louvain
Netherlands
Utrecht

Scandinavia

Denmark
Finland
Iceland
Malmø
Norway
Sweden

East-Central Europe

Austria
Bohemia
Estonia
Hungary
Latvia
Lithuania
Lusatia
Moravia

Nikolsburg
Ottoman Empire
Poland
Raków
Russia
Salzburg
Silesia
Transylvania
Vienna

HISTORICAL EVENTS

Pan-Europe

Colloquies
Iconoclasm
Synods
    Synods in Western Europe
    Synods in Eastern Europe

Germany

Augsburg, Peace of
Counts' War
Emden, Synod of
Hagenau, Colloquy of
Homberg, Synod of
Interims
Knights' Revolt
Leipzig Disputation
Marburg, Colloquy of
Maulbronn, Colloquy of
Nuremberg, Peace of
Pack Affair
Peasants' War
Schmalkald War
Worms, Diet of

Switzerland

Peace of Kappel

France

Amboise, Conspiracy of
Bologna, Concordat of
Cateau-Cambrésis, Treaty of
La Rochelle, Synod of
Montbéliard, Colloquy of
Nîmes, Synod of
Placards, Affaire des
Poissy, Colloquy of
Saint Bartholomew's Day Massacre
Saint-Germain, Colloquy of
Wars of Religion
Wassy, Massacre of

Predestination
Purgatory
Reform
Resistance Theory
Sabbatarianism
Sacraments
Saints
    Sainthood
Sanctification
Scripture
Secular Magistrate, Office of
Sin
Social Discipline
Social Ethics
Socinianism
Synergist Controversy
Toleration
Tradition
Transubstantiation
Two Kingdoms
Ultramontanism
Vocation
Vows and Oaths
Zwinglianism

SOCIAL HISTORY

Pan-Europe

America
Antisemitism
Architecture
Art
Astrology
Begging
Capitalism
Carnival
Celibacy and Virginity
Church Finances
Churching
Cities
Clerical Vestments
Coins
Common Man
Concubinage
Courts
    Church Courts
    Marriage Courts
Death
Discoveries in the New World
Disputations
Divorce
Drama

Education
Empire
Estates
Family
Festivals
Flagellants
Godparentage
Humanism
Hymns
Iconoclasm
Iconography
Illegitimacy
Judaizers
Laity
Latin Language
Law
    Roman Law
Literacy
Magic
Marriage
Medicine and Healing
Music
Nobility
Pamphlets
Peasants
Persecution
Polygamy
Population
Printing
Prostitution
Refugees
Renaissance
Resistance Theory
Riots, Religious
School Ordinances
Science
Sexuality
Social Discipline
Social Ethics
Social Welfare
Toleration
Travel
Universities
Usury
Vows and Oaths
Weddings
Witchcraft
Women

Germany

Diet
Electors
German Language

Gravamina
Hanseatic League
Heidelberg, University of
Magistracy
    Germany and the Low Countries
Preaching and Sermons
    Germany
Schmalkald League
Swabian League
Wittenberg, University of

Switzerland

Geneva Academy
Zurich Academy

France

Chambre Ardente
Collège de France
Estates-General
Faculty of Theology of Paris
Magistracy
    France
Parlement
Politiques
Preaching and Sermons
    France

British Isles

Cambridge, University of
Douai College
Magistracy
    The British Isles
Marian Exiles
Oxford, University of
Parliament
Preaching and Sermons
    England

Italy, Spain, Portugal

America
Discoveries in the New World
Preaching and Sermons
    Spain and Portugal

The Low Countries

Magistracy
    Germany and the Low Countries

Scandinavia

Hanseatic League

East-Central Europe

Horner Bund

REFORMATION STUDIES

INDEX

N.B.: Volume numbers are printed in boldface type, followed by a colon and relevant page numbers. Page numbers printed in boldface indicate a major discussion.

and Helvetic Confessions, **2:**220
and John Hooper, **2:**254
and Hungary, **2:**274
and Leo Jud, **2:**356
on justification, **2:**365
and Jan Łaski, **2:**396
and Francisco Lismanino, **2:**428
and Thomas Lüber, **2:**457
and magistracy, **2:**488, 490
and Péter Somogyi Melius, **3:**48
on moral law, **4:**324
and Wolfgang Musculus, **3:**104
and Nonconformists, **3:**153
and Kaspar Olevianus, **3:**174
on predestination, **3:**334, **4:**325
and radical Reformation, **3:**376
on radical Reformation, **3:**376
and Petrus Ramus, **3:**387
as Reformation historian, **3:**399
and Camillo Renato, **3:**422
and Second Helvetic Confession, **4:**326
sermons of, **3:**324
and Gellius Snecanus, **4:**70
and Lelio Sozzini, **4:**90
and Synod of La Rochelle, **2:**394–395
synods under, **4:**135
and vestiarian controversy, **4:**326
in Zurich, **4:**314, 315
and Zurich Academy, **4:**317
Bünderlin, Johann, **1:**230–231, **2:**135, **3:**16, 101
and Augustin Bader, **1:**109
and Hans Denck, **1:**469, 470
and Christian Entfelder, **2:**50
Bunyan, John, **4:**190
Burch, Henri François van der. *See* Van der Burch, Henri François
Burck, Joachim, **3:**107, 145
Burckhardt, Georg. *See* Spalatin, Georg
Burckhardt, Jakob, **3:**420
Burdach, Konrad, **2:**168
Büren, Daniel von, **2:**237
Burgenland, **1:**102
Burghley, Lord. *See* Cecil, William
Burgo, Nicolas de, **2:**121
Burgonius, Anianus, **2:**396
Buridan, John, **3:**151
Burke, Peter, *as contributor,* **1:**264–265, **2:**103–106, 400–401, **3:**295–299, 307–309
Burkhardt, Franz, **2:**316
Burnet, Gilbert, **3:**402
Burnett, Amy Nelson, *as contributor,* **1:**125–127
Burreus, Dionysios, **2:**62
Burroughs, Jeremiah, **1:**410
Busaeus, Thomas, **2:**71
Busale, Girolamo, **1:**56
Busche, Hermann von dem, **1:**455, **2:**42, 501
Busleiden, Jerome, **3:**89
Butler, Bartlett R., *as contributor,* **2:**290–299, **3:**104–116, 145–146

Butler, Samuel, **3:**367
Butzer, Martin. *See* Bucer, Martin
Buyzere, Jacob de, **2:**115
Den Byencorf der Heilige Roomsche Kercke (Philip Marnix van Saint Aldegonde), **3:**14
Byrd, William, **1:**231, 281, **3:**108, **4:**144

Cabbala, **2:**340, 341, **3:**426
Christian, **1:233**
Andreas Osiander and, **3:**184
Guillaume Postel and, **3:**321
Cabbalistic studies, **1:**312
Cabide, Alvaro, **3:**332
Cabié, Robert, **2:**448
Cabrini, Francesco, **4:**203
La Caducée, ou l'Ange de la Paix (Théodore-Agrippa d'Aubigné), **1:**88
Caesarius of Heisterbach, **3:**10
Cahera, Gallus (Havel), **4:**207
Caius, John, **3:**40
Cajacob, Jörg. *See* Blaurock, Georg
Cajetan, Cardinal, **1:**169, 170, **233–234,** 290, 396, 422, **2:**51, **3:**129, 152, 414
biblical exegesis by, **1:**156
as Dominican, **1:**493
on faith, **2:**92
on Fifth Lateran Council, **2:**398
and Jakob Fugger, **2:**150
and Louvain, **2:**455
and Karl von Miltitz, **3:**63
and Ambrogio Catarino Politi, **3:**291
and Johann Tetzel, **4:**149
and Thomism, **4:**153
Calasanz, José, **3:**415
Calasanzio, Giuseppe, **2:**25
Calendar. *See* Liturgical calendar
Calenus, Hendrik, **1:**201
Calfhill, James, **2:**34
Caliari, Paolo. *See* Veronese, Paolo
Calignon, Soffrey de, **3:**127
Calistus III (pope), **3:**227
Calov, Abraham, **3:**181
Calvi, Francesco, **2:**83
Calvin, John, **1:**169, **234–240,** 348, 352, 359, 412, **2:**70, 127–128, 386, 403, **3:**71, 355, 356, **4:**69, 218
and Jakob Andreae, **1:**36
and antinomianism, **1:**51
and Antoine of Navarre, **1:**62
apocalypticism of, **1:**65
on artistic images, **1:**74–75
on astrology, **2:**482
and Augsburg Confession, **1:**377
and Augustine, **1:**99
and baptism, **1:**116, 117, 118, **2:**181
and Jeremias Bastingius, **1:**127–128
and Théodore de Bèze, **1:**149–151
and Giorgio Biandrata, **1:**151–152